The Blackwell Encyclopedia of
Modern Christian Thought

Edited by
Alister E. McGrath

Consulting Editors

Duncan Forrester ● Donald Hay ● David Jasper ●

Fergus Kerr ● Gordon E. Michaelson Jr ●

Oliver O'Donovan ● Wolfhart Pannenberg ●

Dewi Z. Philips ● Rowan D. Williams

Copyright © Blackwell Publishers Ltd, 1993

First published 1993
First published in USA 1993
First published in paperback 1995
Reprinted 1996, 1997 (twice), 1998, 1999

Blackwell Publishers Ltd
108 Cowley Road
Oxford OX4 1JF, UK

Blackwell Publishers Inc.
350 Main Street
Malden, Massachusetts 02148, USA

British Library Cataloguing in Publication Data
A CIP catalogue record for this book is available from the British Library

Library of Congress Cataloging in Publication Data
The Blackwell encyclopedia of modern Christian thought/edited by
Alister McGrath
700 pp., 246 x 171mm
Includes bibliographical references and index.
ISBN 0–631–16896–6 (hbk) — ISBN 0–631–19896–2 (pbk)
1. Theology – 18th century – Encyclopedias. 2. Theology – 19th
century – Encyclopedias. 3. Theology – 20th century – Encyclopedias.
4. Theologians – Biography – Encyclopedias. I. McGrath, Alister E., 1953–
BR95.B58   1993   93–12925
230'.09'03–dc20   CIP

Typeset in Ehrhardt 9.5 on 11pt
by TecSet Ltd, Wallington, Surrey
Printed and bound in Great Britain by MPG Books Ltd, Bodmin, Cornwall

This book is printed on acid-free paper

The Blackwell Encyclopedia of
Modern Christian Thought

Contents

List of Contributors

W.J. Abraham
Southern Methodist University

Ray S. Anderson
Fuller Theological Seminary

David J. Atkinson
Corpus Christi College, Oxford

Paul D.L. Avis
Exeter

John Barton
Oriel College, Oxford

Richard Bauckham
University of St Andrews

D.W. Bebbington
University of Stirling

Nigel Biggar
Oriel College, Oxford

David Brown
University of Durham

Delwin Brown
Iliff School of Theology, Denver

Bryan Burton
Presbyterian Church, New Jersey

Peter Byrne
King's College, London

Anne Carr
University of Chicago

Keith W. Clements
Bristol

E. David Cook
Green College, Oxford

Kenneth Cragg
Wycliffe Hall, Oxford

Ingolf Dalferth
University of Frankfurt

Sheila Greeve Davaney
Iliff School of Theology, Denver

Gavin D'Costa
University of Bristol

R. Detweiler
Emory University

Millard J. Erickson
Southwestern Baptist Theological Seminary

Samuel Escobar
Eastern Baptist Seminary, Philadelphia

Paul S. Fiddes
Regent's Park College, Oxford

David Ford
University of Cambridge

Gerhard O. Forde
Luther Northwestern Theological Seminary

Duncan Forrester
University of Edinburgh

Richard T. France
Wycliffe Hall, Oxford

Mark R. Francis
Catholic Theological Union, Chicago

Timothy J. Gorringe
St John's College, Oxford

Richard Harries
Oxford

LIST OF CONTRIBUTORS

Donald Hay
Jesus College, Oxford

Russell Hittinger
Catholic University of America

Leslie Houlden
University of London

David Jasper
University of Glasgow

Robert W. Jenson
St Olaf College, Northfield

J.T. Johnson
Rutgers University

Gareth Jones
University of Birmingham

L. Gregory Jones
Loyola College, Baltimore

Fergus Kerr
Blackfriars, Edinburgh

William Klempa
Presbyterian College, Montreal

Robin A. Leaver
Westminster Choir College, Princeton

Jung Young Lee
Drew University

Thomas G. Long
Princeton Theological Seminary

Andrew Louth
Goldsmiths College, London

James Wm McClendon, Jr
Fuller Theological Seminary

Alister E. McGrath
Wycliffe Hall, Oxford

David McLellan
University of Kent at Canterbury

John Macquarrie
Christ Church, Oxford

Bruce D. Marshall
St Olaf College, Northfield

Gilbert Meilaender
Oberlin College

Hugo A. Meynell
University of Calgary

Gordon E. Michalson, Jr
University of South Florida

Michael Moxter
University of Tübingen

Lesslie Newbigin
Selly Oak Colleges, Birmingham

Juliet Newport Kane
Oxford and London

Mark A. Noll
Wheaton College

Gerald O'Collins
Gregorian University, Rome

Oliver O'Donovan
Christ Church, Oxford

Clare Palmer
University of Glasgow

Stephen Pattison
The Open University

W.S.F. Pickering
Cambridge

John Polkinghorne
Queens' College, Cambridge

Ronald H. Preston
University of Manchester

John Punshon
Earlham School of Religion

Bernard M.G. Reardon
University of Newcastle upon Tyne

Richard H. Roberts
University of St Andrews

Geoffrey Rowell
Keble College, Oxford

Christopher Rowland
The Queen's College, Oxford

Colin A. Russell
The Open University

Leland Ryken
Wheaton College

Risto Saarinen
University of Helsinki

M. James Sawyer
Western Seminary, San Jose

Christoph Schwöbel
University of London

Charles Sherlock
Ridley College, Melbourne

Christopher Sugden
Oxford Centre for Mission Studies

Kenneth Surin
Duke University

Stewart Sutherland
University of London

Shunichi Takayanagi
Sophia University, Tokyo

Anthony C. Thiselton
University of Nottingham

John B. Thomson
St Paul's College, Grahamstown, Cape Province

Antonie Vos Jaczn
State University of Utrecht

Geoffrey Wainwright
Duke University

Gordon S. Wakefield
Westminster College, Oxford

Andrew Walker
University of London

Francis Watson
University of London

Fraser N. Watts
University of Cambridge

John B. Webster
Wycliffe College, Toronto

Frank Whaling
University of Edinburgh

Rowan Williams
University of Oxford

Robert R. Williams
Hiram College

Trevor Williams
Trinity College, Oxford

Edward J. Yarnold
Campion Hall, Oxford

Carver T. Yu
China Graduate School of Theology,
Hong Kong

Introduction

Christianity remains a major presence in the modern world. Although there has been an erosion of its power bases in western Europe, it continues to be of major significance in North and South America. The collapse of Marxism in eastern Europe has seen a resurgence of Christian activity in that region, with former university faculties of theology being re-established and new ones founded. The expansion of Christianity continues in sub-Saharan Africa and the countries of eastern Asia, such as Korea. There is thus an ongoing need for a reliable overview of its leading ideas and their impact upon the modern world.

The present volume is designed as an authoritative, readable and reliable reference source for all those who are interested in, or wish to learn about, the main features of modern Christian thought. It aims to inform, stimulate and correlate and to direct attention to other sources for further information. Modern Christian thought is massive and complex, with considerable regional and denominational variations; this volume aims to provide as comprehensive and reliable a guide as possible to the movement.

The term 'modern' is notoriously difficult to define; it is here taken to mean the period in western culture which began with the Enlightenment, dating from the opening of the eighteenth century. 'Christian thought' is here not taken in the narrow academic sense of 'Christian theology', but is understood to embrace the general economic, social, political, aesthetic and cultural outlooks of Christianity in the modern world. The work adopts a non-advocational stance, avoiding the precommitment to conservative or liberal attitudes which so seriously reduces the value of existing publications of this type. Every effort has been made to ensure a balanced appraisal of the situation, avoiding polemical or unbalanced presentations.

The complexity of surveying so vast an area of thought is reflected in the structure of this book. It is hoped that the following observations will allow readers to make more effective use of the work and understand its structure better.

The basic structure of the work is that of a collection of major essays on the central themes of Christian thought, surveying the developments which have taken place during the modern period. The basic requirements of individuals needing a convenient summary of such developments – such as college students or journalists – have been borne in mind in commissioning such entries. Both students and specialists will find themselves informed by this work. Each of these essays is conceived as a review of schools of thought, personalities, literature and debates, allowing the reader to gain an overview of the main developments associated with this theme over the period in question. Detailed suggestions for further reading are provided. For example, a substantial essay on ETHICS covers the entire field of modern Christian ethical debate, and allows the reader to develop this subject to whatever level seems appropriate by the judicious use of the bibliography and cross-references.

A second cluster of major articles deals with philosophical movements which have exercised considerable influence over the development of Christian thinking during this period. Examples of such articles include the ENLIGHTENMENT, EXISTENTIALISM, KANTIANISM, and MARXISM. A third set of articles deals with the relatively small number of Christian theologians who have exercised considerable individual influence during this period, such as KARL BARTH, JONATHAN EDWARDS, and JOHN HENRY NEWMAN. These are supplemented by biographical and bibliographical entries for a much larger number of individual writers who are agreed to be of significance in relation to the development of Christian thought during the modern period. Unless otherwise stated, all biographical entries were compiled by Juliet Newport Kane and Clare Palmer.

A number of themes are of such complexity that they have been dealt with in special ways.

Jesus Christ

The figure of Jesus Christ is of central importance to the Christian faith. It is quite impossible to survey each and every aspect of modern Christian thinking concerning his identity and significance. The reader is thus directed within the work to individual entries of direct importance, such as CHRISTOLOGY, HISTORICAL JESUS, QUEST OF, and SOTERIOLOGY. There is no individual survey article entitled 'Jesus Christ'.

The sciences

A major difficulty arises through the continuing achievement of the sciences. The success of the Newtonian theories in explaining the regularities of planetary orbits had already established the physical sciences as a serious intellectual force. The growing success of the sciences during the nineteenth and early twentieth centuries makes a detailed consideration of the relation between Christianity and the sciences of central importance to any survey of modern Christian thought. In the past, this relation has generally been surveyed in a single article, a single-authored 'omnium-gatherum' which explores the manner in which Christian theology and the sciences have interacted. This has caused serious difficulties, not least on account of the very different methodologies adopted by the different sciences. The present volume abandons this unsatisfactory approach and offers four substantial essays, each written by a leading expert in the field, exploring the relationship between Christianity and the four leading branches of the sciences: biological, physical, psychological and social. Together, these articles provide a substantial overview of the complex manner in which Christian thought has come to terms with the insights and methods of these major and influential academic disciplines.

Protestantism

The presentation of modern Protestantism has caused especial difficulty. Of all the Christian denominations, it is Protestantism which has been most deeply affected by the Enlightenment on the one hand, and by significant regional variations on the other. This observation has had a major impact on the structure of this work. Whereas it is possible to survey modern Roman Catholic and Eastern Orthodox thought in individual articles, regional and denominational differences within Protestantism are of such magnitude that a general survey article on 'Protestant theology' would be of little value. Protestant theology has thus been surveyed in three distinct, yet related, manners.

1   A group of articles on PROTESTANT THEOLOGY surveys general developments within the movement by region – for example, Britain, Germany, the USA, Australia and the Netherlands. Each article has been written by a leading authority on Protestant theology, located in the region being surveyed.

2   Significant denominational differences and emphases are noted in a series of articles, such as PRESBYTERIANISM, ANGLICANISM and BAPTIST THOUGHT, each written by a scholar operating within the denomination in question. This allows the reader to understand the issues and developments which have been of particular importance to individual components of Protestantism.

3   Major transdenominational movements which have had a significant influence on the shaping of modern Protestantism have been noted, such as FUNDAMENTALISM, EVANGELICALISM and LIBERALISM. Each article has been written by a scholar familiar with and sympathetic to the movement in question, yet willing to address its weaknesses. On occasion, major differences exist between the

British and North American embodiments of the movement (as in the case of evangelicalism and liberalism). In this case, the topic has been divided into two separate articles, each written by a leading scholar based in the region in question.

Asian Christian thought

For similar reasons, the traditional format of a general article on 'Asian Christian thought' has been abandoned, as insensitive to the specific features of the development of Christian thought in the various regions of that continent. In place of one general article, this work provides major single-authored essays on Christianity in China, India, Japan and Korea in an attempt to do justice to the considerable regional variations encountered.

God

Traditionally in works of this kind a distinction is made between 'the doctrine of God' and 'the doctrine of the Trinity'. In the modern period, these two doctrines have become so closely linked that their separation would be forced and artificial. For this reason, discussion of the Trinity is subsumed under a major discussion of the doctrine of GOD.

Finally, the assistance of all who contributed to the production of this ambitious work must be fully acknowledged. The editor also wishes to acknowledge the invaluable assistance of members of the Reference Department of Blackwell Publishers and the cooperation of an international team of contributors. Without them, this work could never have been produced.

Alister McGrath
Oxford

A

abortion See MEDICAL ETHICS; SEXUAL ETHICS.

aesthetic theory Aesthetic theory is an invention of the eighteenth century, the product essentially of loss of confidence in inherited ecclesiastical access to the divine together with new interest in the psychology of the human subject. There had of course been philosophical reflection on the nature and perception of beauty since Plato, and this flourished again in the Middle Ages and during the Renaissance. But, in an unprecedented flood of books after 1700, particularly in Britain and Germany, this new field of philosophical enquiry rapidly took the shape which it has retained until recent times. The domain of the beautiful was separated from that of the religious, the ethical and anything remotely practical, while the individualistic turn in epistemology led to emphasis on private experience. Aesthetics, as originally conceived by A.G. Baumgarten, who coined the word in 1735 in connection with his reflections on certain aspects of poetry (imagery, metre and so on), was intended to focus on perception by the senses (as the Greek *aisthesis* suggests) in contrast to conceptual thought, the traditional concern of logic – on sensibility, then, rather than on rationality. What promised to become a discovery of the sensuous and bodily aspects of human involvement with things in the world, artefacts as well as natural objects, failed to escape from the subject/object dualism which held the age captive.

According to David Hume, whose essay 'Of the Standard of Taste' of 1757 is the most succinct and accessible of the texts which founded the new discipline ('criticism', as British writers preferred to call it well into the nineteenth century), 'Beauty is no quality in things themselves; it exists merely in the mind which contemplates them.' Edmund Burke's *Philosophical Enquiry into the Origin of Our Ideas of the Sublime and Beautiful* of 1757, another fundamental text and equally readable, sought, by calling beauty a 'social quality', to defend the possibility of a universal science of taste; but his eloquent appreciation of the 'delightful horror' of 'the sublime' signalled the turn from the objects of traditional religious worship to situations which stimulate certain emotional reactions.

Immanuel Kant's *Critique of Judgement* of 1790, offered as a transcendental investigation of taste, created the language which has dominated aesthetic theory since. Kant insisted that the experience of beauty is, properly, an entirely *disinterested* satisfaction. He also made the decisive separation between the aesthetic and all other aspects of human concern, the religious and the ethical in particular: beauty has no purpose beyond itself, however it may appear ('purposiveness without purpose').

G.W.F. Hegel, whose massive lecture course on aesthetics appeared posthumously in 1835, confirmed the distinction between art, as a spiritual experience, and religion, as a spiritual experience (so Hegel thought) for relatively backward and uncivilized people. In contrast to Kant, he regarded the beauty of the fine arts (the phrase 'les beaux arts' appears about 1750) as superior to the beauty of the natural world, on the grounds that the fine arts are an embodiment of spirit (*Geist*). For Hegel this meant an embodiment of the spirit of a nation or an age, but his emphasis on the genius and

1

originality of the artist opened the way to the still prevalent idea that a work of art is essentially the expression of a ('private') psychological or emotional experience on the part of the artist, which he or she (usually) wants to share with the rest of us. Works of art thus become means by which people reveal their souls, or at least their finer feelings, to one another. This 'expression' theory of art has always been challenged by some variation of an 'art-for-art's-sake' theory, stemming from Kant's idea and to be found, for instance, in Clive Bell's highly influential text *Art* of 1914 – an insistence on aesthetic experience as disinterested contemplation of a work's form. Far from being mere occasions for the outpouring of otherwise secret emotions, works of art become impersonal structures to which listeners or observers must, with a certain self-detachment, learn simply to submit. Aesthetic theory thus remains trapped between subjectivism and formalism. Works of art, not surprisingly, turn out to be either 'expressionist' or 'abstract'.

More recently, however, there have been various attempts to put aesthetic theory on an entirely different footing. With LOGICAL POSITIVISM, of course, as in A.J. Ayer's *Language, Truth and Logic* of 1936, aesthetic terms were held (like ethical ones) 'simply to express certain feelings and evoke a certain response'. There was 'no possibility of arguing about questions of value in aesthetics, but only about questions of fact'. As Ludwig Wittgenstein's later work became better known, in the 1950s, some philosophers, following his advice to look for differences rather than presuppose definable essences, began to deny the very possibility of any general aesthetic theory. For example, what reason is there to believe that aesthetic experience is such an isolatable unitary phenomenon as traditional aesthetic theory has always supposed? Should we not discuss the 'fine arts' one by one – what does listening to music have in common with looking at buildings or going to the ballet? Such an anti-theoretical, pragmatic and piecemeal approach, while it may well deflate the pretensions of the philosophy of art, seems, on the other hand, to have no place for the passionate intensity in Wittgenstein's occasional remarks, particularly about music.

Wittgenstein's scattered remarks about music would not give legitimacy to aesthetic theory as so far understood nor constitute his own theory, but in them he rejects the idea that music must be either a sound-picture of something in the world or a self-contained 'playing' whose only content is itself. In effect, then, in aesthetics as elsewhere, Wittgenstein seems to leave us with the thought that, if only we could give up our need to theorize, we should have no difficulty in understanding art.

In 'The Origin of the Work of Art' of 1935-6, his famous essay on Van Gogh's picture of an old peasant's boots, Martin Heidegger seeks another way out of aesthetic theory by returning to the work of art itself. Far from being the expression of the artist's private experience, the work of art sets up a 'world', precisely by preserving the materiality of what Heidegger calls 'earth' – stone, wood, metal, colour, tone and so on. In a work of art, according to subsequent essays, one participates in a quartet of suprahuman forces – earth, sky, mortality and the sacred – which constitute the human world. It is thus the world to which we belong, prior to distinctions between matter and form, ethics and aesthetics, secular and sacred, and so on, that a work of art is held to reveal. In his own way, then, Heidegger seeks to reconnect the sensuous and bodily aspects of the human way of being in the world with a self-disclosure of the sublime.

A more satisfactory way out of aesthetic theory may have to await the dissolution of the subject/object dichotomy and the settling of the controversy between idealism and realism.

See also ROMANTICISM.

Bibliography

Beardsley, Monroe C. 1966: *Aesthetics from Classical Greece to the Present: A Short History*. New York: Macmillan.

Caygill, Howard 1989: *Art of Judgement*. Oxford: Blackwell.

Eagleton, Terry 1990: *The Ideology of the Aesthetic*. Oxford: Blackwell.

Tilghman, B.R. 1984: *But is it Art? The Value of Art and the Temptation of Theory*. Oxford: Blackwell.

FERGUS KERR

Africa, South See PROTESTANT THEOLOGY: SOUTH AFRICA.

African Christian thought See PROTESTANT THEOLOGY: SOUTH AFRICA.

agnosticism See ATHEISM.

America, United States of See BLACK THEOLOGY; EVANGELICALISM: USA; FUNDAMENTALISM; LIBERALISM: USA; PROTESTANT THEOLOGY: USA.

analogy, principle of See LANGUAGE, RELIGIOUS; PHILOSOPHY OF RELIGION.

Anglicanism 'Anglicanism' is the term usually employed to denote the distinctive features of the *ecclesia Anglicana* – the national church of England, as it emerged from the sixteenth-century Reformation. The worldwide expansion of English influence, initially through the annexation of Ireland and Scotland, and subsequently through the colonization of North America in the seventeenth century, the Indian subcontinent in the late eighteenth century and sub-Saharan Africa in the nineteenth, brought with it a significant enlargement of the sphere of influence of Anglicanism. The parody of Anglicanism as 'the British empire at prayer' contains at least an element of truth; Anglicanism has exercised relatively little influence outside those realms once subject to British presence or rule.

The Elizabethan Settlement (1559) brought at least a degree of stability to the English church in the aftermath of the fluctuations of the events under Henry VIII, Edward VI and Mary Tudor. At this point, the English church emerged as a *via media* between the Roman Catholic and Protestant (especially Calvinist) churches. The growing influence of Puritanism within the English church led to increasing political and religious instability during the reign of Charles I (1625–49), eventually leading to his deposition and subsequent execution under Oliver Cromwell. During the Commonwealth, a systematic attempt was made to redirect Anglicanism in a more reformed direction, as may be seen from the Westminster Confession (1646). The restoration of Charles II (1660) led to the re-establishment of Anglicanism, and its enforcement at every level through laws such as the Test Act (1673).

The ENLIGHTENMENT had its origins in England, and from its outset had a major impact upon Anglicanism. DEISM became widespread within English Anglicanism during the eighteenth century. At this point, Anglicanism appears to have lacked the theological and spiritual resources to deal with the challenges raised by the new emphasis upon reason: the defection of the Non-Jurors – nine bishops (including Archbishop Sancroft of Canterbury), some 400 priests and an indeterminate number of laity – in 1690 led to the Church of England being deprived of some of its most able minds. The result was that religious renewal and revival in the eighteenth century took place largely outside the established church, through individuals such as John Wesley and his brother Charles (see METHODISM) and the evangelical revivals of the period (see EVANGELICALISM: BRITAIN).

The emergence of Anglicanism as a major religious and theological force (as opposed to an official state religious ideology) is to be dated from the nineteenth century, and specifically from the rise of the Oxford movement (usually put at 1833) and the growing influence of John Henry Newman. This movement, initially linked with the University of Oxford, was concerned to restore the lost high church ideals of the seventeenth century; this vision, however, came to be linked with an increasing emphasis upon the importance of apostolic Christianity, and a renewed interest in the ceremonial and liturgical achievements of the hitherto neglected medieval period. A series of publications, most notably the *Library of the Fathers* (edited by Newman, E.B. Pusey and John Keble from 1836), gave new impetus to patristic studies, which increasingly became seen as an essential reference point for Anglican self-definition. Newman's emphasis upon the role of tradition, linked with a growing emphasis upon the role of the church as a historical institution, made Anglo-Catholicism (as the high church movement was known from 1838 onwards) the leading intellectual and religious force within Anglicanism until the eve of the First World War.

A major reorientation within Anglo-Catholicism was signalled by the publication of *Lux*

Mundi (1889). Concerned to 'put the Catholic faith into its right relation to modern intellectual and moral problems', this collection of essays marked the acceptance of critical methods within the movement. Although this fell short of MODERNISM, it occasioned considerable anxiety on the part of more conservative members, such as H.P. Liddon. More positively, the work consolidated an emphasis upon the importance of the INCARNATION within Anglicanism. For a period of perhaps fifty years (1889–1939), many observers concluded that Anglicanism was 'the religion of the Incarnation'. The incarnation came to serve as the theological foundation of Anglican social ethics, giving legitimacy to the social and political involvement of the church in the world, and fostering a new concern for the material order. This concern can be seen particularly in the writings of Brooke Foss Westcott (1825–1901) – especially his *Incarnation and the Common Life* (1893) – and Charles Gore (1853–1932).

A new concern also developed for theological method (see METHOD IN THEOLOGY). Anglicanism was increasingly portrayed as a form of Christianity which brought together Scripture, reason and tradition, where others – it was alleged – gave one element priority over the others. Although this is untenable, it came to be linked with the more justifiable, and distinctively Anglican, notion of 'dispersed authority', by which theological and religious authority was understood to be 'dispersed' among, for example, Scripture, tradition and the *consensus fidelium*. This idea has had significant impact upon Anglican ecumenical discussions, and continues to be of importance in shaping Anglican understandings of how authority is to be exercised within the church.

Anglo-Catholicism reached its zenith in the 1920s and 1930s, with the great Anglo-Catholic Congresses of 1920, 1923, 1927, 1930 and 1933 attracting considerable attention. Yet the movement was largely spent as a theological force. After the First World War, Anglicanism became increasingly influenced by modernism. The 'Churchmen's Union' (founded in 1898) was renamed the 'Modern Churchmen's Union' in 1928. The group of individuals linked with this movement were generally marked by a strong antipathy towards Anglo-Catholicism, and a

belief in accommodationist strategies as a means of enhancing the credibility of Christianity in the modern period. These trends are evident in the development of exemplarist approaches to the death of Christ (see SOTERIOLOGY) by writers such as Hastings Rashdall, and reductionist approaches to the divinity of Christ and the resurrection. These developments caused considerable concern within Anglicanism, and were addressed – only to be declared largely irresolvable – by the Archbishops' Commission report *Doctrine in the Church of England* (1938).

The Second World War (1939–45) offered a respite from theological debate, which continued through the 1950s. Preoccupied with such issues as the revision of canon law, the Church of England was virtually totally unprepared for the crises of the 1960s. The 'death of God' movement in the USA was paralleled by the 'Honest to God' debate in Britain, centring on the book of that name by Bishop John A.T. Robinson (see PROTESTANT THEOLOGY: BRITAIN). This work ushered in a period in which Anglican theology was virtually totally dominated by radical and liberal writers, such as Maurice F. Wiles, Geoffrey W.H. Lampe, Don Cupitt and Dennis Nineham. The English religious academy, which had been earlier dominated by Anglo-Catholic thinkers (such as N.P. Williams, Lionel Thorton and Arthur Michael Ramsey) now came to be seen as committed to liberal and radical attitudes. This development, which parallels related patterns in Europe and North America, is not specifically Anglican, in that it reflects a general loss of confidence in the western world in traditional approaches to Christianity and a growing distrust of institutionalized authority. During this period, many American and Canadian Anglican seminaries moved towards committed liberal stances.

By the middle of the 1980s the dominance of liberalism was over. English Anglicanism came to be increasingly influenced by Evangelicalism. This development may be traced to the National Evangelical Anglican Congress, held at Keele University in 1967, which committed evangelical Anglicans to work within the structures of the Church of England. This development was given practical guidance by J.R.W. Stott, and theological legitimation through J.I. Packer.

This development has not been paralleled elsewhere in western Anglicanism, where evangelicalism has generally flourished outside Anglican structures.

The increasing divergence within the Anglican church, which is so significant a feature of modern Anglicanism, may be explained on the basis of a number of developments.

1 Anglicanism originally found one of its central foci in the *Book of Common Prayer* (1662), which embodied the 'spirit of Anglicanism' in a fixed liturgical form. Anglican churches throughout the world had this in common, along with a common ecclesiastical structure. Yet the process of liturgical revision, which became of major importance in the 1970s, resulted in the Anglican churches in England, Canada, the USA and Australia adopting different liturgical forms, thus severely weakening the theological convergence of the movement.

2 The growing trend towards decentralization, linked with an increasing concern on the part of nations such as Australia and Canada to shake off their 'colonial' image, has led to a new concern to develop distinctively national or ethnic approaches to Anglican identity. In its traditional forms, Anglicanism has been perceived as too 'English' or 'colonial' to maintain its credibility in the post-colonial era. As a result, Anglicanism has become increasingly diverse, reflecting its local concerns and resources. This trend gives every indication of continuing in the years ahead.

The future of Anglicanism remains uncertain. With a severe reduction in numbers in North America, and a general stagnation in its growth throughout the western world, it is far from clear what its future role will be. The greatest growth in the movement is associated with southern Africa, where evangelism and spiritual formation are generally regarded as being of greater importance than theological reflection. Nevertheless, it seems safe to assume that Anglican theology and theologians will continue to make an impact on modern Christian theology for some time to come.

See also ECCLESIOLOGY; ETHICS; SPIRITUALITY, CHRISTIAN.

Bibliography
Borsch, F.A., ed. 1984: *Anglicanism and the Bible*. Wilton, CT: Morehouse-Barlow.
McAdoo, H.R. 1965: *The Spirit of Anglicanism*. London: Black.
Ramsay, A.M. 1960: *From Gore to Temple: The Development of Anglican Theology*. London: Longman.
Sykes, Stephen, and Booty, John, eds 1988: *The Study of Anglicanism*. London: SPCK.

ALISTER E. MCGRATH

Anglo-Catholicism See ANGLICANISM.

anonymous Christians See KARL RAHNER.

anthropology, Christian The doctrine that human beings are created in the image and likeness of God, subject to temptation and fallen into sin, redeemed through Jesus Christ and destined to share in God's eternal glory. The term 'anthropology' had its origin in the late sixteenth century in Protestant humanism and began to appear as one of the loci in systematic theology in the mid-nineteenth century (Farley, 1984, p. 57). A Christian doctrine of human being has its foundation in the Old Testament account of the creation of the first human beings out of the dust of the ground and their endowment by the Creator with the divine image and likeness.

In the biblical account of creation, humans have their origin on the sixth day of creation and are taken from the earth, as are the other creatures (Gen. 1: 24; 2: 7). The creation of the human out of the dust of the ground is simultaneously a formation of the human through a divine 'breathing' of the breath of life (Gen. 2: 7). The Bible does not inform us as to how or when this occurred, only that the human is uniquely formed as the creature bearing the divine image and oriented to God. Whether the formation of the human body took place through a process of evolution (see BIOLOGICAL SCIENCE AND CHRISTIANITY) or was directly created by God is a question not answered by Scripture. What we are told is that the destiny of the human is under divine determination, even as the origin of the human was through divine agency.

The Hebrew term *nephesh*, most often translated as 'soul', designates all that has life and breathes, and is applied both to human beings and to animals (Gen. 1: 12, 24; 9: 10, 12, 15, 16). As contrasted with the Greek view, the soul (*nephesh*) is the concrete life of the body and therefore intimately belongs to the body. Since *nephesh* is bodily life, the soul can 'long' and 'be satisfied', or 'hunger' and 'be filled' (Ps. 107: 9). The soul can be poured out in death, be devoured or be killed (Lam. 2: 12; Ezek. 22: 25). The soul (the life) of the flesh is in the blood (Lev. 17: 11); in fact, the soul of all flesh is the blood (Deut. 12: 23).

Nephesh is often coupled with other, more concrete words, especially with *basar* (flesh) and *lev*, *levav* (heart). The Hebrew has no distinct word for 'body' as does the Greek (*soma*). *Nephesh* is often used in parallel with *basar*, never in contrast. The terms are not used as a natural contrast such as 'body and soul', but are often virtually synonymous, being two ways of referring to the self in both its physical and nonphysical existence (Hill, 1984, p. 100; Anderson, 1982, pp. 209 ff.).

Ruach (spirit), unlike *basar*, is never used as a practical synonym for *nephesh*, but is frequently employed in contrast to the *nephesh*. Where *nephesh* means 'life', *ruach* means 'vigorous life', or an inspired life. God will often take away the spirit from a person and give another spirit, for better or for worse (1 Sam. 10: 6; 16: 13, 14). In particular, God will give his own Spirit to a chosen person and will even be asked to bestow it upon one who seeks it (Ps. 51: 10–12). Heart (*lev*) commonly signifies the seat of intelligence, cunning, good or wicked thoughts, pride, humility, joy, but never compassion, tenderness or intense feeling. The Israelites expressed feeling through terms relating to the bowels, or entrails, not the heart. Consequently, when Jesus rebukes his disciples for hardness of heart, it is their lack of insight or sheer stupidity he is referring to, not their callousness and lack of feeling.

New Testament anthropology depends upon the Hebrew construct of the human as a duality of the physical and nonphysical animated by the 'breath of life' and empowered by spirit. The Greek term *psyche* is used as a general equivalent of *nephesh* and is often translated as soul, or life. The apostle Paul's use of the terms body (*sarx*, *soma*), soul (*psyche*) and spirit (*pneuma*) presents difficulties in translating into English so as to remain faithful to Paul's essentially Hebrew concept of the unity of the self while, at the same time, respecting his psychological depiction of persons who are controlled by either spiritual or unspiritual desires and actions.

Those whom Paul describes as 'fleshly' (*sarkikos*) are also 'soulish' (*psychikos*). Paul never uses the body and the soul as contrasts for spiritual and unspiritual, or for mortal and immortal, as do the Greeks. Instead, he uses the terms to designate qualities of life expressed through both the physical and the nonphysical life. 'Spirit' and 'spiritual' signify a divine quality of life, received as a gift from God and having a share in God's Spirit. 'Flesh' and 'carnal' do not signify merely a natural or physical quality of life but a corrupt, self-centred and mortal kind of life. It is not human nature that is the enemy of the spirit, but distortion or corruption of that human nature that is the enemy (Hill, 1984, pp. 101–2).

The use of body, soul, and spirit as three distinct components of the human being is therefore questionable. Those who hold to this three-part division are called 'trichotomists', while those who view the human being as essentially 'body and soul' are called 'dichotomists'. The early church was confronted with these issues in the Christological debate with Apollinaris of Laodocea in the fourth century. Influenced by Platonic dualism, which posited a gulf between the worlds of body and spirit (*nous*), Apollinaris became convinced that the soul performed the function of mediating between these two poles. The soul was thus not understood as purely either physical or mental. This trichotomous view was condemned at the Fourth Council of Constantinople in AD 869-79. Despite this, many continue to hold to a three-fold division of the human self due to the New Testament use of these terms. Hebrews 4: 12, for example, speaks of a 'dividing of soul and spirit', and Paul prays for the preservation of 'spirit and soul and body' (1 Thess. 5: 23). In other passages, however, soul and spirit are used as synonyms of the self as a unity. Luke records Mary's song as expressing this when she says, 'My soul magnifies the Lord, and my spirit rejoices in God my Saviour' (Luke 1: 46–7). Here it is clear that there is a single subject which is expressed alike in the terms 'soul' and 'spirit'.

If Hebrew anthropology is determinative for a Christian view of the human self, then a strict dualism between body and soul as well as a trichotomy between body, soul and spirit must be rejected (Berkouwer, [1957] 1962, p. 209). What is distinctive about human beings is not that they have a 'soul' which animals do not possess, nor that they have a 'spirit' which other creatures do not possess, but that, as 'ensouled body' and 'embodied soul', the 'spirit' of that existence is opened towards God in a unique way as the source of life. The whole of human life, body and soul, is thus oriented towards a destiny beyond mortal or natural life. This endowment of life is experienced as the image and likeness of God. While the physical body itself is not held to be in the image of God, human beings as 'embodied souls' are in the image of God.

The consensus of modern theologians seems to be that the human spirit should not be viewed as a third aspect of the self, as distinguished from body and soul. Rather, the human spirit is the existence of the self as ensouled body and embodied soul as the particular moral and spiritual agent responsible for loving God with all one's heart, mind and soul, and one's neighbour as oneself (Matt. 22: 37–9). The 'life' which is constitutive of human being is at the same time a bodily life, a life of the soul, and a spiritual life. It would not be life of the spirit if it were not for the fact that body and soul in their interconnection constitute a living person. Because there is a precedence which the soul exercises with respect to the body, the soul becomes the primary orientation of the spirit in this life. This allows for a duality of human being without creating a dualism and opposition between body and soul. In the resurrection, there will be a 'spiritual body', suggesting that the concept of a disembodied soul is alien to a biblical anthropology even through the experience of death and resurrection (1 Cor. 15: 44; 2 Cor. 5: 1-10).

We look in vain for some indication in Scripture as to the process by which each newborn infant inherits the special endowment which constitutes the human soul as opposed to a merely creaturely soul. Medieval theologians alternated between two views on this question. 'Traducionists' held that the soul originates in the act of conception. A 'soul seed' (in contrast to a 'body seed') detached from the soul of the parents to become the independent soul of the child. 'Creationists', on the other hand, held that each person's 'soul' was implanted at the moment of conception by a divine act, an immediate creation *ex nihilo* (Anderson, 1982, pp. 42 f.). Through the sexual act, the parents create the proper physiological conditions for the existence of a human being, but they are only secondary agents in the process. Regarding this debate, Karl Barth has suggested that none of these theories leads us one step forward with regard to the origin of the human (Barth, [1948] 1960, p. 573). The most that we can say is that a human person begins as any other creature in a biological process which entails fertilization and cell division. However, even in that process, the resulting life form carries the form of the human, even in its prenatal stage.

A Christian anthropology holds that biological life is a necessary but insufficient condition to be human. The life of the human seems to be contingent upon more than biological life (*bios*) to have vital human life (*zoe*). In the New Testament, *zoe* refers to a person's life made abundantly full, and this life is inseparable from Jesus Christ as the source of life (John 10: 10; 1 Tim. 6: 11, 12, 19).

In the second creation account the divine image is not possessed by the single individual: 'it is not good that the man should be alone' (Gen. 2: 18). Only when the man and the woman exist as complementary forms of human being is there a sense of completeness: 'This at last is bone of my bones and flesh of my flesh' (Gen. 2: 23). From this passage, some contemporary theologians view this image and likeness more in relational terms than as a static attribute or rational/spiritual capacity. It is in relationship with other persons as well as with God that the divine image is expressed (Berkouwer, [1957] 1962, pp. 87 ff., 179, 197 f.; Barth, [1948] 1960, p. 196). This 'ecological' relation between the physical and the nonphysical aspects of the human self, and between one human and another, is positively determined by this divine endowment and is subject to disorder and destructiveness when humans fall out of God's grace through sin.

In the biblical account, the original humans are depicted as being in a state of innocence, under divine command and preservation, though subject to temptation. Sin emerged as an act of self-determination in disobedience to the divine command. As a result, they experienced shame, confusion, guilt, and a sense of alienation from God as well as distrust of each other (Gen. 3). The effect of sin produced disunity at the social, psychological, and spiritual core of human life such that the original unity of personal well-being as embodied soul and ensouled body became disrupted and subject to dissolution and death (see DEATH, THEOLOGY OF). The image of God as social, spiritual and moral health was corrupted and became the source of pride, jealousy, hatred and violence against others. The ecology of human life in terms of relationship with the earth, with other humans, and with God was thrown out of balance so that injustice, oppression, poverty and war permeated all of human society.

A Christian view of the human is rooted in this biblical portrayal of the origins and destiny of persons as bearing the divine image, as objects of divine love and grace and of infinite value, despite the inveterate tendencies towards evil and violence found in every culture. The solidarity of all persons as bound together in a common humanity despite differences of race, religion, sexual orientation and culture is a concept derived out of the New Testament construct of the Adam–Christ relation. The figure of Adam stands as the bond of all humanity in a common origin and a common fate for the apostle Paul. But this does not stand as some universal principle accessible to general knowledge. It is only through the person of Jesus Christ that Paul can say that 'even as one man's trespass led to condemnation for all men, so one man's act of righteousness leads to acquittal and life for all men' (Rom. 5: 18).

Paul attributes cosmic and anthropological significance to the INCARNATION of God in the person of Jesus, 'descended from David according to the flesh and designated Son of God in power according to the Spirit of holiness by his resurrection from the dead' (Rom. 1: 3). Paul's vision of humanity is first of all through Christ and then back to Adam. In the relation of Christ to Adam, all of humanity is bound into a solidarity of life under God's election and promise, and thus all is bound up in the solidarity of sin. Sin is not attributable to biological, racial or cultural forms of humanity.

Rather, sin is a disruption of the core social paradigm for humanity found in every race, culture and nation. Because the consequence of sin is death, it is death that is the basic human dilemma, not merely sin. Thus Paul says, 'If, because of one man's trespass, death reigned through that one man, much more will those who receive the abundance of grace and the free gift of righteousness reign in life through the one man Jesus Christ' (Rom. 5: 17). True humanity is now found in Christ who has conquered death, so that all humans who die due to Adam's sin can now find their humanity restored in being related to Christ.

In a Christian anthropology, human nature is not defined ultimately by tracing back humanity to its origins, nor by explaining humanity in terms of its existence under the conditions of sin. Rather, human nature is creaturely life experienced as personal, social, sexual and spiritual life under divine determination, judgement and promise. In a Christian anthropology, sin is understood as a failure to live humanly in every area of life as social, personal, sexual and spiritual. Therefore, salvation from sin is also to be experienced as the recovery of true humanity in each of these aspects of life. The tendency of some to view salvation as 'saving souls' without regard to the total life of the person as a physical, social and psychological being is more of a Greek concept than a Christian one. From the perspective of a Christian anthropology, salvation touches each area of a person's embodied life, though not with equal effect, short of the resurrection of the body.

Critical ethical issues relating to the conception of life as well as to the termination of life (see MEDICAL ETHICS; SEXUAL ETHICS) are first of all questions as to what constitutes human life. A Christian anthropology is the underlying moral basis of ethical rules for living and dying. We are to 'love our neighbours as ourselves' (Matt. 22: 39). The unborn, though not persons in the full sense, are 'neighbours' in the human sense and thus constitute a moral demand upon the living for the preservation of life within the limits of human possibility. Physical life has intrinsic and relative value as possibility, though it does not constitute an absolute value. The absolute value of human life is upheld by God through the frailties, torments, and trauma of life on this earth.

A Christian anthropology is the positive moral basis for the liberation of human sexuality from degradation, oppression and exploitation; in Christ, 'there is neither Jew nor Greek, slave nor free, male nor female', for in Christ all are one (Gal. 3: 28). Human personhood is male and female, male or female, equally and mutually human, a polarity and community of personal being manifest through biological sexual differentiation, but under the promise of freedom from such limitations through life beyond death.

Because our humanity is under divine determination, judgement and redemption – from Adam to Christ – a Christian vision of the human is liberating, hopeful and therapeutic. In life beyond death through the new humanity of Jesus Christ, there will no longer be 'mourning, nor crying, nor pain' (Rev. 21: 4). The final vision of humanity is more human than human imagination or experience can picture.

See also PNEUMATOLOGY.

Bibliography

Anderson, Ray S. 1982: *On Being Human: Essays in Theological Anthropology*. Grand Rapids: Eerdmans.

Balthasar, Hans Urs von [1963] 1967: *A Theological Anthropology*, trans. New York: Sheed and Ward.

Barth, Karl [1945] 1959: *Church Dogmatics* III/1, trans. Edinburgh: T & T Clark.

Barth, Karl [1948] 1960: *Church Dogmatics* III/2, trans. Edinburgh: T & T Clark.

Berkouwer, G.C. [1957] 1962: *Man: The Image of God*, trans. Grand Rapids: Eerdmans.

Burns, J. Patout, ed. 1981: *Theological Anthropology: Sources of Early Christian Thought*. Philadelphia: Fortress Press.

Elmore, Vernon O. 1986: *Man as God's Creation*. Nashville: Broadman Press.

Farley, Edward 1984: Toward a contemporary theology of human being. In *Images of Man*, ed. J. William Angell and E. Pendleton Banks. Macon, GA: Mercer University Press.

Fichtner, Joseph 1978: *Man the Image of God: A Christian Anthropology*. New York: Alba House.

Hill, Edmund 1984: *Being Human: A Biblical Perspective*. London: Geoffrey Chapman.

Jewett, Paul K. 1975: *Man as Male and Female*. Grand Rapids: Eerdmans.

Laver, Eugene, and Mlecko, Joel, eds 1982: *A Christian Understanding of the Human Person:*

Basic Readings. New York: Paulist Press.

Macquarrie, J. 1983: *In Search of Humanity: A Theological and Philosophical Approach*. New York: Crossroad Publishing Company.

Moltmann, Jürgen [1971] 1974: *Man: Christian Anthropology in the Conflicts of the Present*, trans. John Sturdy. Philadelphia: Fortress Press.

Pannenberg, W. 1985: *Anthropology in Theological Perspective*. Philadelphia: Westminster.

Porteous, N.W. 1962: The nature of man in the Old Testament. In *The Interpreter's Dictionary of the Bible*, ed. George A. Buttrick, vol. 3. New York: Abingdon.

Thielicke, H. [1976] 1984: *Being Human – Becoming Human*, trans. G.W. Bromiley. New York: Doubleday.

Wolff, H.W. [1973] 1974: *Anthropology of the Old Testament*, trans. Margaret Kohl. Philadelphia: Fortress Press.

RAY S. ANDERSON

anti-Semitism See JUDAISM AND CHRISTIANITY.

apocalyptic See ESCHATOLOGY.

apologetics Apologetics has been defined as 'reasoned defence, especially of Christianity' (*Concise Oxford Dictionary*). Christianity, at least as understood by virtually all people everywhere, whether they have been believers or not, entails that there is a God, that humanity is somehow estranged from God through its own fault, and that God has acted to remedy this estrangement through the life, death, and resurrection of Jesus Christ. An apologetic defence of Christianity may thus be expected to include argument to the effect (1) that there is a God; (2) that human beings are radically estranged from God; (3) that the life and death of Jesus Christ would be such as to constitute a remedy for this estrangement; and (4) that this life and death occurred as a matter of historical fact.

1 Arguments for the existence of God, with respect to their soundness or unsoundness, and their significance for Christian belief, are dealt with elsewhere (see EXISTENCE OF GOD, PROOFS OF; FAITH AND REASON).

2 Of those who have depicted the human condition with an eye to the alleged need of humankind for Christianity, Augustine and

Blaise Pascal are perhaps the most notable; on their account, human beings are consumed by a restless desperation which cannot be assuaged short of the truth of the Christian revelation, and which otherwise will drive them at best to trivial distractions and at worst to destructive violence. Others, for example Jean-Paul Sartre, have envisaged the human plight with equal pessimism without drawing theistic or Christian conclusions.

3 The question of how the life and death of Jesus Christ can be a universally effective remedy for human sin has been answered by theories of the atonement (see SOTERIOLOGY). The view that Jesus saves us simply by setting us a moral example (Peter Abelard, Hastings Rashdall) has generally been regarded as inadequate by Christians; but what has seemed to many to be the only alternative, that Jesus satisfies the divine wrath by undergoing the suffering that the rest of humankind owed God by way of punishment, has not unreasonably been thought to presuppose an irrational or immoral view of God. Suppose A has been justly offended by the action of B, but stops being so as a result of taking it out on a wholly innocent party C; such a sequence of events is certainly quite possible in human interactions, but throws no good light on the intelligence or the moral character of A. An interesting modern approach to the problem is to suggest that in the life of Jesus 'myth became fact' (C.S. Lewis, J.R.R. Tolkien); hereby God influences the minds and hearts of human beings, without abrogating their freedom, rather in the same way that human beings have tried to influence one another through the profound and symbol-freighted fictions which are 'myths' properly speaking. At this rate to 'demythologize' Christianity (Rudolf Bultmann), to excise from it all the elements which are analogous to myth, would be to deprive it of those very features which have made it such an enormous force in human affairs. As is the case with many myths, the story of Jesus is about a divine human being or a human God; other myth-like features of the story are the mysterious birth of the hero, his rescue in the nick of time from deadly dangers immediately afterwards, his precocious development, his miraculous deeds, his tragic and early death, his symbolical manner of dying, and his return to life (C.G. Jung).

4 Some apologists (most recently W. Pannenberg and G. Habermas) have thrown a great deal of weight on the historical evidence for the RESURRECTION of Jesus, making the whole case for Christianity depend on this. The historical Jesus, it is argued, at least implicitly claimed divine authority in his proclamation and work; this claim was confirmed by God through his resurrection. Not that Jesus acquired a divine nature which was not previously his through that event; 'rather, from the perspective of the resurrection, Jesus is recognized as the one who he was previously' (Pannenberg, [1964] 1968, p. 137). The traditional 'argument from prophecy', which dilates on the manner in which what was anticipated in the Old Testament is fulfilled in the New, has been greatly compromised as a result of the tendency of modern biblical scholarship to interpret literal and detailed fulfilment of prophecies as due to the biblical writers' or editors' tailoring of the prophecies to fit the fulfilments, or of the fulfilments to fit the prophecies, or both. However, Jesus Christ may still be seen as that to which the whole of Scripture points in a manner more subtle than that, rather as a character or event may be seen as central to a great novel or poetic drama, or a figure to a picture of very complex composition (H.U. von Balthasar, N. Frye). A rather similar point may be made in relation to the traditional 'argument from miracles'. Whatever doubts may reasonably be maintained about the attribution of particular miracles to the historical Jesus, it may be argued that wholesale fiction (whether deliberate or in good faith) on the part of the evangelists is unlikely, given the structure and nature of the Gospels as they stand, the probable environment in which they were composed and the shortness of the period which elapsed between the life of Jesus and the time in which they reached their final form. For the contention that apologetics is at best a pointless and at worst a blasphemous enterprise, since God has revealed God's nature and will for humanity and this revelation can only be embraced in faith or rejected in sin (Karl Barth), see FAITH AND REASON.

The whole business of apologetics has been impugned, notably by Karl Barth, on the ground that it accommodates the Christian proclamation to what is acceptable within the horizon of sinful human beings, and therefore fatally compromises it. That apologists have sometimes been guilty of diluting the faith in order to commend it to their hearers must not be denied; but unless acceptance of Christianity can be shown to be in accordance with basic human capacities to apprehend facts and values, it is hard to see why it should be preferred to any cognitive absurdity or moral monstrosity whatever. Others will have it that to argue in favour of specifically Christian beliefs is unduly to devalue non-Christian religions. Now it is true that to argue *for* the existence of God or the divinity of Christ is to argue *against* the contradictories of these doctrines, and therefore to imply that those who maintain them are to that extent in error. But this is by no means to say that Christians do not stand to learn a great deal from those of other religions and of none – from Marxists about zeal for the realization of the reign of God on earth, from Jews about the patient endurance of affliction, from Muslims about the immediacy of the presence of God, from Buddhists about the vanity of self-indulgence, from Confucians about preservation of the traditional decencies of civilized life, from atheistic humanists about a proper concern for the affairs of the present world and so on and so on.

See also PHILOSOPHY OF RELIGION.

Bibliography

Aquinas, Thomas 1955–6: *On the Truth of the Catholic Faith. Summa Contra Gentes*, 2 vols. Garden City: Doubleday.
Carnell, E.J. 1956: *An Introduction to Christian Apologetics*. Grand Rapids: Eerdmans.
Chesterton, G.K. 1912: *Orthodoxy*. London: John Lane.
Habermas, G. 1980: *The Resurrection of Jesus*. Grand Rapids: Baker.
Lewis, C.S. 1952: *Mere Christianity*. London: Bles.
Lewis, C.S. 1960: *Miracles*. London: Collins.
Lonergan, B.J.F. 1970: *Insight: A Study of Human Understanding*, chapter 20. New York: Philosophical Library.
Meynell, H.A. 1987: Faith, objectivity, and historical falsifiability. In *Language, Meaning and God*, ed. B. Davies. London: Chapman.
Moreland, J.P., Nielsen, K., et al. 1990: *Does God Exist? The Great Debate*. Nashville: Thomas Nelson.
Newman, J.H. [1870] 1955: *A Grammar of Assent*. New York: Doubleday.
Pannenberg, W. [1964] 1968: *Jesus, God and Man*, trans. London: SCM Press.
Pascal, B. [1670] 1966: *Pensées*. Harmondsworth: Penguin.
Penelhum, T.M. 1985: *Butler*. London: Routledge and Kegan Paul.
Richardson, A. 1947: *Christian Apologetics*. London: SCM Press.
Tennant, F.R. 1937: *Philosophical Theology*. Cambridge: Cambridge University Press.

HUGO A. MEYNELL

Arab Christian thought Muslim tradition records a prayer of Muhammad on his return from a forlorn foray to Al-Ṭā'if in hope of a better response than that accorded him by the obdurate pagans of his native Mecca. At the nadir of his fortunes before the Hijrah he prayed: 'O Lord, to You I complain of my helplessness, my paucity of resources and my insignificance *vis-à-vis* other men. Most Merciful of the merciful, You are the Master of the helpless and You are my Lord, to whom will You abandon me?'

Islam has rarely been so vulnerable since, at least in its Sunni form. The sentiment, however, broadly fits the situation of Arab Christianity within *Dār al-Islām*, the realm of the final faith. The crucial factor is Christian minority status. Through all the Islamic Caliphates down to the demise of the last in 1924, Arab Christianity retained its devotional practices and its personal status law on the condition of total political submission and inferiorization. This status as *dhimmis* induced a close introspection and a certain stagnancy of spirit, under the variable threat of insecurity as local circumstances oscillated.

It follows that the salient fact concerning modern Arab Christian thought is the emergence of the Christian communities into the contrasting milieu of nation-state nationalism that followed the collapse of Ottomanism in the prelude to and the aftermath of the First World War. In the long debate about Ottomanism and Arab independence, Christian Arabs played a notable part, contributing significantly to the literary revival and the new sense of the *waṭaan*, or 'motherland', which displaced the old *Ummah*, or 'realm' (of Islam).

The new pattern was at once more hopeful and more precarious. It gave Christian Arabs participatory citizenship, but exposed them to the moods and movements of relations with Islam, in contrast to the old contractual subordination. It meant that Christian intellectual thinking was heavily politicized, the more so because theological awareness had long been interiorized within the separate Christian communities, with all too little motivation to engage in doctrinal debate with Islam. This isolation was accentuated by differences in the Arabic language as used by the two faiths and by the age-long Islamic instinct of hostility to the central elements of Christian doctrine and liturgy, to Christology, atonement and Eucharist.

This division between Islam and Christianity is complicated by two factors: (1) the differing circumstances obtaining in the several states and regimes within which Christian thought proceeded, with particular reference to Egypt and Lebanon, where the Christian dimension was most prominent; and (2) the issues besetting Arab Christians as a result of the rise of Zionism and the implanting and consolidating of the state of Israel within the region.

The ambition for and the actual emergence of the separate Arab states early in the twentieth century belong with an Arabism dominated by Islam. Muhammad is the supreme Arab of history: the Qur'an is the sacred eloquence of Arabic. A Christian Arabism must perforce share Arab aspirations and the Arab ethos; yet in part these are at odds with crucial Christian credos. Long traditions of thought have not often been conducive to the realization of how in some ways they are not at all at odds. Divine unity, creatorship in God and creaturehood in man, a sacramental tenancy of the good earth and a reverent empiricism that sees a laboratory also as a sanctuary – these are shared by mosque and church.

Undertaking these ambiguous negatives and positives of inter-theology was complicated by the Greek 'formation' of basic Christian theology, both Chalcedonian and Monophysite, from the time of the church Fathers – those dominant middle-easterners, as we would now have to call them. It was complicated also by the European connections of the Christian minorities, used – either willingly or unwillingly – as representatives of western interests. Moreover, those same western interests had deferred or thwarted Arab independence by the device of the 'mandate' system.

Some Christian instincts were for a prudent confessionalism in which Copts, for example, played safe within an Egyptianism inevitably dominated by Islam. Other Christians, however, strove to assert a vigorous role in the knowledge that the pharaonic dimension was more squarely theirs than it was Islam's. The point is in perennial dispute. Maronites in Lebanon were a special case because of their majority presence (as confirmed by the census), their romantic attachment to 'Phoenician' memories and their rugged sense of identity with its Francophile aegis. In its extreme form their Christian 'Arabism' ceased almost to be 'Arab' at all, and the will to identify Lebanon, however territorially expressed, with Maronitism finally plunged the country into chronic civil war.

Elsewhere, however, and in a minority in Lebanon too, there were Christian thinkers who advocated an alignment with Islam and Muslims in which Arabism became the dominant emotion for all. This advocacy stemmed, in part, from a certain anticlericalism and also from dismay over religious division. Shibly Shumayyil (1860–1917) argued for a 'secular' Arabism in which Christians would concede and approve Islam as its cultural dimension. Farah Antūn (1874–1922), a Syrian émigré in 'British Egypt', castigated Christian confessionalism and urged Muslims also to draw Islam away from *Ummah* and *Sharī'ah* oppressiveness into a simple religious personalism, so neutralizing religious division and enabling Arab unity. His long-lived contemporary, Khalīl Sakākīni (1878-1953) echoed his de-confessionalism and summoned Islam to end that 'badge of servitude' which *dhimmī* status had imposed. He himself finally acceded to Islam in the wake of a sharp personal crisis described in his diary (1955, trans. *Such, O World, Was I*).

These and other figures must be seen as precursors of those Christian Arabs who engendered the now notorious Ba'th regimes. Their ideologue was Michel Aflaq (1912–1989) of Damascus, taking some cues from the ill-fated Lebanese Antūn Sa'ādah (1904–1949). In close concert with the Muslim Samīr al-Bitār, via Damascus and the Sorbonne, Aflaq argued for a 'Syrian' ardour in which love of fatherland subdued religious dimensions in a common devotion to the flag. This 'greater Syria' concept, suborned later by politicians and brutality, meant to privatize religious dogmas and worships and channel their distracting energies and emotions into the service, and near-worship, of the state. The distinctive notes of Christian theology would be silenced and Islam, no less disconcertingly, would be assumed to persist as a cultural dimension recognized, indifferently, by all Arabs. As a protest against obscurantist religion and introverted confessionalism Ba'thism had its point. As a prescript for faith it was near treachery.

There were other publicists and journalists who called on Arab Christians to 'cherish Islam as their brother Muslims do', and so to turn the believer in them into the mere citizen – though, on this reckoning, 'mere' no longer. There were, of course, deep implications for secularism in these counsels but they came only at a tangent to the urge for Arab unity within the state. Few were ready for the massive problematics of outright secularism, given the long traditions of Islam. By the same token it is clear that these political preoccupations of the debate tended to displace authentic theological reckoning with beliefs as a clue to being or as a response to its mystery. None of these mentors were theologians, fewer still metaphysicians.

There was in Egypt, to be sure, continuing vitality in Coptic studies and in theology for internal awareness. The public face of things, however, was occupied with the bi-communal nature of Egyptianism. Relations were often strained between successive Coptic Patriarchs and their *Majlis Milli*, or Coptic Council, with the laity urging for what the hierarchy often distrusted in terms of modern thought and organization – a situation much improved in recent years. Muslim–Coptic relations suffer intellectually from the dominance of political factors, though the emergence of the Middle East Council of Churches in 1976 (when the Orthodox churches joined the Near East Christian Council) has helped to bring the problems into wider and cooperative focus and to address the spiritual demands imposed by the Lebanese civil war, the diaspora and plight of the Palestinians and the role of global politics in the chronic anxieties of the region.

The underlying trauma of personal existence in the twentieth-century middle east is well intimated in the extensive literary achievement of an Egyptian Muslim, Najīb Maḥfūẓ (born 1912), Nobel prizewinner and an able exponent of Egyptian identity and spiritual malaise in general. He is in some initial debt to a redoubtable Egyptian, the Copt Salāmah Mūsā (1887–1958), whose story mirrors the ferment involving both religions. Mūsā's lively curiosity led to his fascination by European figures like H.G. Wells, Bernard Shaw, Jean Jacques Rousseau and James Frazer (see his autobiography, *The Education of Salamah Musa*, trans. 1961). Tracing modern science to Egyptian pyramidal engineering and hieroglyphics, he coveted for modern Egyptians a discerning pharaohism in which Muslim and Christian would be compatibly Egyptian. For long he deplored what he saw as the archaic survivalism of his own Coptic heritage, though he came later to appreciate its role in the conservation of the past. His ideas of 'Egyptianizing' Arabic touched a raw nerve. For Arabic has always been at issue between the faiths that use it. For all his idiosyncrasies, Salāmah Mūsā is a useful window into the stresses of the Coptic mind as Egypt struggled towards the 'Abd al-Nāṣir years and the final exit of British power.

Theology, by nature, was less inclined to relate intensively to the westernism which fascinated such lay minds, while samplers like Salāmah Mūsā were not equipped to tackle theology. Thus vital issues of faith tended to go by default or be confined within the parameters of domestic ecclesiology, burdened as these were by political preoccupations. There were also inhibiting 'politics' between the churches, notably over the custody of 'holy places' or the rights of confessionalism within the state systems. The connections of (Chalcedonian) Orthodoxy with Greece have become fruitful and positive, especially in Lebanon, while the Uniate Churches, generated variously throughout the Ottoman period, have enjoyed the scholarly stimulus of their association with Rome, the various Roman Orders and the prowess of the Maronite College in Rome. These assets have in some way compensated for the long subordination of the local Arab clergy in these churches to a traditionally foreign hierarchy. Churches of western Reformed or Anglican hue have been stimulated by a sense of incorporation into the mind of current theology.

This has perhaps been most evident in the area for which it has been most urgent and painful, namely the response of Arab – and especially Palestinian – Christian thinking to the experience of Zionism. The depth of this predicament is seldom appreciated by those who do not live it. Arab Christians are committed, like the rest, to biblical loyalties. They stand in the New Testament tradition of a people of God, by grace not heredity, through faith not birth, who acknowledge a crucial ancestry of the spirit in the Judaic story in which Jesus and the disciples bequeathed the Christ-event which made them such. That Judaic story, for authentic reasons drawn from Europe, not the Arab east, has opted for an essentially political self-expression, repudiating as inauthentic its long diaspora and reconstituting a territorial statehood in what its own initiating document (in the sense that it gave political sanction to the Zionist dream), the Balfour Declaration of 1917, named Palestine. (Oddly, perhaps callously, the Declaration spoke of 'existing population' without naming the Palestinians.) That decision has occasioned a large displacement, a prolonged deprivation, a bitter oppression and a desperate anxiety that only statehood can allay. For such statehood, by every logic of the Zionism which opposes it, is the territorial, political *sine qua non* of secure identity.

Palestinian nationalism collides inevitably with the Christian association, through Jesus himself and the Hebrew Scriptures. For Christians it is the paradox of belonging with Israel in the Bible and Israel in Zionism. The one is benediction, the other malediction. The spiritual ancestor is the present adversary. So the Scriptures themselves become ambiguous. How does one 'bless the Lord God of Israel' when the Israel of today is that of Ben Gurion, Begin, and Shamir?

The temptation of some Islamic fundamentalism to respond to the mystique of 'God chose the Jews' with that of *Allāhu akbar* is strong, but also barren. Broadly the Palestinian Liberation movement has thus far striven to be 'secular'. Arab Christians, deeply committed to it, differentiate strongly between anti-Semitism and anti-Zionism, though many in Israel and beyond decry and deny the distinction. Palestinians, according to them, aim to finish off what Hitler meant.

Collaboration of 'peace Christians' with the peace movement in Israel is difficult as long as it implies, or is manoeuvred to imply, that all is well between victor and victim. Nevertheless, there are ventures of Palestinian Christian thinking which attempt to 'appreciate' what underlies the trauma of the Jewish soul and the Jewish logic for the state, while urging the claim of 'justice, only justice'. Na'īm Ateek, of the Anglican church in Jerusalem, seeks under that title (Deut. 16: 20) to outline what he calls 'a Palestinian theology of liberation'. Father Elias Chacour of the Greek Catholic church writes out of personal tragedy under the title *Blood Brothers* (1984), making an Arab Christian case for peace with righteousness between the Jewish and the Arab claim. These, like the founders of Nevi Shalom, or Waḥat al-Salām, 'oasis of peace', exemplify the struggle to relate positively to a legitimacy in Zion while resisting the injustices of Zionism. The whole situation has an indeterminate character. The Arab Christian response is realistic enough to know that the final determinants lie not with them but with the inner counsels Zionism has about its own probity, and also with the preponderant Islam, which – since the seventh century – has always been the arbiter of Arab Christian experience and the ruling circumstance of its mind.

See also ISLAM AND CHRISTIANITY.

Bibliography
Antonius, George 1938: *The Arab Awakening*. New York: Capricorn Books.
Ateek, Naim S. 1989: *Justice, and Only Justice: A Palestinian Theology of Liberation*. New York: Orbis.
Betts, Robert B. 1978: *Christians in the Arab East*. Atlanta: John Knox Press.
Chacour, Elias, and Hazard, David 1984: *Blood Brothers*. Old Tappan, NJ: Revell & Co.
Cragg, Kenneth 1991: *The Arab Christian: A History in the Middle East*. Louisville: Westminster Press.
Hourani, Albert 1983: *Arabic Thought in the Liberal Age, 1798–1939*. New York: Cambridge University Press.

KENNETH CRAGG

Arnold, Matthew (1822–1888) English poet and literary critic. Educated at Winchester, Rugby (where his father Thomas was headmaster) and Balliol College, Oxford, Arnold was a government inspector of schools, a fellow of Oriel College and, from 1857 to 1867, professor of poetry at Oxford. Best known for his poems, he was also a religious thinker who stressed Christianity as personal and ethical rather than philosophical in character and purpose. Adopting a literary-critical approach to the biblical text, he opposed literal interpretations of the Bible, which he saw as unscientific. His writings on religion include *St Paul and Protestantism* (1870), *Literature and Dogma* (1873), *God and the Bible* (1875) and *Last Essays on Church and Religion* (1877).

Bibliography
ApRoberts, R. 1983: *Arnold and God*. Berkeley, Ca.
Robbins, W. 1959: *The Ethical Idealism of Matthew Arnold*. London.
Trilling, L. 1949: *Matthew Arnold*. London.

Asian Christian thought By the dawn of the modern period Christianity had established a presence in many parts of Asia; and it has recently experienced spectacular growth, especially in South Korea. The complexity of the Asian Christian experience is such that the topic has been divided between key regions of Christian influence, with a separate article for each. See CHINESE CHRISTIAN THOUGHT; INDIAN CHRISTIAN THOUGHT; JAPANESE CHRISTIAN THOUGHT; KOREAN CHRISTIAN THOUGHT.

atheism The *Oxford English Dictionary* offers a suitably generous definition of the arena to which this article belongs: 'Disbelief in, or denial of, the existence of a God'. The entry adds, '*Also*, Disregard of duty to God, godlessness (*practical* atheism)'. The significance of this apparent duality of types of atheism is considerable, but, as I shall argue when I return to this point, not exhaustive.

There are, however, a number of other preliminary points of terminology which it is as well to deal with at the outset before beginning the substantive discussion. There is a now common usage of the term 'agnosticism' which would properly be subsumed under the first part of the OED definition of 'atheism': '*agnosticism*, which means literally "not-know-ism", is in this context the belief that we do not have sufficient reason to affirm or to deny God's existence' (Hick, 1963, p. 4). There is evidence presented in the OED that the use of the term 'agnostic' owes much to T.H. Huxley, who gave to it the rather stronger sense of one who does not believe that there *can be* knowledge of a God who transcends this world. Nonetheless, the use suggested by John Hick is now widespread, and unless otherwise specified in this essay will be the meaning intended by the term 'agnosticism' and its correlate, 'agnostic'. However, there is an important difference to be marked. In the OED version of Huxley's view, he was an agnostic, but not an atheist. On his account, we could no more know that God does not exist, than that God does exist. The quotation given from Hick (above) leaves open the rather different possibility that someone might conclude from the fact that they do not have sufficient reason to affirm the existence of God, that disbelief in God is the appropriate attitude. The pre-eminent role given to reason and having reasons in the definitions of 'atheism' and 'agnosticism' on this view will be the subject of further comment in due course.

There is one further set of distinctions which must be explored before engaging in the main discussion. If as a first general point it is accepted that atheism should be understood as a positive form of *disbelief*, then that immediately distinguishes it from agnosticism but leaves open the question of what, if anything, is the object of disbelief. The technical philosophical term which can be used is to ask whether atheism is 'intentional' in character. The issue here is one of whether in order to use the characterization of atheism as disbelief properly, we must always assume that disbelief is always disbelief *in* x or y, or disbelief *that* x or y is the case or *that* x or y exists.

Thus there are two separate questions here, each of which as we shall see raises different theological issues. The first is whether atheism is best or, even more strongly, inevitably understood as the rejection of a particular belief or range of beliefs, or whether atheism can be understood as the positive affirmation of a set of beliefs which explicitly or implicitly excludes belief in God. In the first case atheism would be seen as logically parasitic upon particular religious beliefs. In the second case atheism would be a rival set of beliefs to the various forms of religious belief, which excludes or rejects central or defining tenets of some or all of those forms of religious belief. I shall argue that a proper discussion of atheism embodies all of these possibilities.

This leads naturally to the second question: if atheism does in various forms, and in some of these forms does as a matter of definition, involve the rejection of particular religious beliefs, is there a clear account of *which* religious beliefs are sufficiently central to be part of the definition of the difference between atheism and belief? For example it may well be widely accepted that rejection of the belief in the immortality of the soul does not of itself imply atheism, but what about the belief that God exists? 'Elementary, dear philosopher', you may reply, 'for that surely is quite at the heart of the distinction.' The difficulty here is that there are one or two difficult examples which do not quite fit the simplicity of the definition. On the one hand there is the example of Fyodor Dostoevsky's Ivan Karamazov. Ivan is widely regarded as a classic literary portrayal of atheism, and yet he affirms to his brother Alyosha 'I accept God' (Dostoevsky, [1879-80] 1912). Or, another example, Paul Tillich, one of the giants of twentieth-century Protestant theology, affirmed, 'It is as atheistic to affirm the existence of God as it is to deny it' (Tillich, [1951] 1953, p. 263). Of course there is a tale to be told in each case in order to extrapolate the apparently convoluted logic; but the point of citing these two examples at this stage is to make the initial point that just as there may be complexities in specifying what certain forms of atheism are affirming, so equally there are inner circles to be discerned in the account of what atheism, or perhaps better, atheisms, may be denying.

One point of considerable significance is encapsulated in the question of whether atheism is better understood as the belief that there is no God, or as the belief that there is no personal God, or as the belief that there is no person who is God. Each of these possibilities rests upon a series of suppositions about what is distinctive and definitive of theism, which is normally taken to be the opposite of atheism. My general point at this stage can be put in the following way: there are at least as many forms of atheism as there are forms of theism.

Forms of atheism

We must now review, in the light of this first general thesis, some of the range of types of atheism. The first problem is one of the principle of classification to be used. I have already suggested at least two different principles: the first is to look for a classification which is formal and which seeks for a categorization which is essentially logical; the second is to seek a classification which is based upon the substance or content of the types of atheism in question. This latter is in the end theological, and seeks to differentiate types of atheism according to the particular theological beliefs which are rejected. In this section of the article I shall consider the formal or logical range of types of atheism, and shall consider the theological implications in the next section.

Atheism and evidence One classic form of atheism, of which there are many and varied examples, is based upon the argument that the evidence for belief is so inadequate and indeed is counterweighted by evidence against belief in God in such a fashion that the correct evaluation of that evidence points to atheism as the conclusion. One very crude version of this was to be found in the anti-God museum, dedicated to the cause of atheism and fostered in the post-sputnik euphoria of the former Soviet Union. The claim was that since Russian space capsules had now scanned the heavens and had found no evidence of God, then the inadequacy of religious belief had been demonstrated.

Of course, there are many more sophisticated versions of atheism based upon a review of evidence than this poor specimen, but at least it serves as a means of clarifying the logical character of this first type of atheism. The central feature is to make the difference between atheism and belief a matter of evidence. The latter is to be understood as empirical evidence, and the form of argument appropriate to settling the issue is akin to the form appropriate to other examples of empirical enquiry. The most important recent example of such an enquiry is to be found in Richard Swinburne's *The Existence of God* (1980). His conclusion is that, 'On our total evidence theism is more probable than not.' A form of atheism which is of the same logical type and sophistication would conclude by substituting the word 'atheism' for the word 'theism' in this quotation. In the history of the debate earlier this century there is an excellent example of just such a disagreement. In his *Philosophical Theology* (1968), F.R. Tennant, the Cambridge theologian and scientist, developed what he called 'a cumulative argument' for the existence of God. There are similarities to Swinburne's enterprise, for both are concerned with the grand theme of the best supported hypothesis to explain the rich and variously experienced empirical world in which we live. Each is concerned to range over a wide variety of types of empirical evidence, and each is prepared to offer at best a well supported hypothesis as the conclusion. An atheistic response to Tennant was proposed by his friend and Cambridge colleague, C.D. Broad. Broad properly pointed out that just as Tennant had avoided some of the more naive mistakes of some types of Christian apologetics, and had therefore vanquished equally naive atheistic counter-arguments, so too in principle could a cumulative atheistic argument be constructed.

The fundamental point in the present context is that these examples characterize this first type of atheism very clearly indeed. On this view, atheism is to be defined as a particular reading of our experience of the empirical world: atheism is then committed to two basic claims, and also to a third. The first is that there is no direct evidence of the existence of God. The second is that our experience of the empirical world neither requires nor supports the hypothesis that there is a God. These two claims are compatible with the type of agnosticism defined above in the quotation from John Hick. The third claim which differentiates atheism from that form of agnosticism can take one of two forms. The first is that there is evidence against the belief in God, such as the existence of certain forms of undeserved or disproportionate suffering. The second is a claim that in the absence of evidence for the existence of God, and in the absence of any need for such a hypothesis since our empirical experience is quite well understood without it, then atheism is the correct inference to be drawn inductively from our experience of the world. Other variants on these will be examined below.

Atheism and the contradictions of belief For some, the case for atheism rests upon the claim that

theism requires belief in a God who is the bearer of contradictory properties. Thus, for example, there has been much discussion of whether God can be both timeless and also a Being who acts in history (see Pike, 1970; Swinburne, 1977). In relation to the question of the nature of atheism, this type is based upon the premise that any object of belief must be free of contradictions, if that belief is to be regarded as reasonable. The corollary is that if the belief in question, in this case theism, requires belief in the coexistence of contradictory properties, in this example belief in a God who is both 'outside' time and yet is an agent 'within' time, then that belief must be rejected.

This form of atheism generates profound and difficult questions, both about the nature of God, and about the nature of logic and rationality, which have been at the heart of theological and philosophical debate from the days of Augustine and earlier, through the work of Anselm and Thomas Aquinas, Immanuel Kant and Søren Kierkegaard, to Karl Barth and the response to him in our own century.

The problems in question have at their respective roots, the question of whether terms such as 'person' or 'identity' or 'acts' or even 'is' apply to God in such a way that the same rules of logic, of what constitutes a contradiction, apply as when they are used of human beings. Of course these issues have also been clothed in the language of theology and given theological substance through the classical debates of Christological and Trinitarian theology (see GOD). The central point of current relevance is that some forms of atheism derive their intellectual character from the charge that there are certain central tenets of theism which involve accepting (or ignoring) contradictions. These forms raise specific theological questions to which I shall return in the final section of this article.

Atheism and the meaningfulness of the language of theism There are at least three different forms which atheism of this type might take.

The first may be illustrated by reference to the German philosopher Immanuel Kant. In his most important philosophical work, *The Critique of Pure Reason* ([1781] 1961), he established to his own satisfaction what are the limits of intelligibility of thought and, by implication therefore, of language. Of particular interest were the limits of what could be properly thought in the context of the philosophical discussion of religious belief. It was certainly not his intention to substitute atheism for theism, for his stated intentions included showing the limits of reason in order to give adequate logical space for belief. However his strictures upon what it was possible to think and therefore to say were by the standards of theology very severe indeed, and there is a significant theological industry devoted to establishing that the influence of Kant and the ENLIGHTENMENT has been essentially corrosive of belief. To a significant extent I believe that this is a fair charge to lay. The caveat is that it all depends upon what is meant by 'belief'.

There is no doubt that certain subsequent forms of atheism have drawn very significantly upon Kant, and also that most statements of the creeds as traditionally understood do not survive an acceptance of Kantian principles. This can be seen most clearly with regard to both form and substance in Kant's *Religion Within the Limits of Reason Alone* ([1793] 1960). The form of Kant's rejection of traditional belief becomes absolutely plain. He retains much of the traditional language but translates that language into the language of morality. The substance of the rejection is that much traditional belief is rejected as anthropomorphic, and much religious practice is at best irrelevant as traditionally understood, or more probably a form of superstition. However, Kant did not by any stretch of the imagination give an endorsement to atheism, for he retained the language of theism, and *Religion Within the Limits* is full of references to God and the will of God. What is true, nonetheless, is that he established very clearly a route which many subsequent forms of atheism were to follow.

The second type of atheism to be considered under this heading follows very naturally from a consideration of Kant. In his widely influential *Language, Truth and Logic* ([1936] 1946), A.J. Ayer argued that the language of tradition is meaningless. His claim was based upon an exposition of the principles of the movement known as 'logical positivism', which was based on a very tight, indeed severe, definition of factual meaning. The central tenet is that the meaning of an apparently fact-claiming sentence is tied to its method of verification (later,

falsification). If, as he argued, there is no adequate specification of what counts as verifying/falsifying such a claim as 'God loves us', or even 'God exists', then the appearance which the relevant sentences have of making a factual claim is no more than appearance, and the sentences in question must be rejected as meaningless, or at best an expression of some emotion. In either case a very strong form of atheism is being adopted (see LOGICAL POSITIVISM).

There followed from this a veritable dust storm of responses, the first quarterly haze of proposed refutations of Ayer's position soon becoming a monographed cloud of careful analyses (see Flew and MacIntyre, 1955; Ferré, 1962). One positive outcome for theology was the implicit invitation, particularly to those from a Protestant context, to re-examine much of the detailed discussion of these issues in the work of, for example, Aquinas and T. Cajetan, on the Analogy of Being, and on the analogical use of language in theology.

The third form of atheism appropriately mentioned in this section is that of Ivan Karamazov (see Dostoevsky, [1879–80] 1912; Sutherland, 1977). It was to the lips of this classic embodiment of atheism that Dostoevsky gave the words 'I accept God.' The rejection of belief which Ivan expounded to his brother Alyosha, was, in Alyosha's words, 'Rebellion'. The rebellion had two roots. One was a very clear and devastating statement of the horrors of the suffering of the innocent – itemized in horrendous detail by Dostoevsky from newspaper reports of the time. The subtlety which followed this, however, was an attempt to undermine the argument which might still be thought to be appropriate about whether such suffering provided conclusive, or merely provisional, evidence against the claims of theism. Dostoevsky used all the genius of a great novelist to give Ivan the strongest possible case against belief. Ivan's rebellion was in the end against a god, the god of 'the Russian boys and their professors', who was at best trivial. His way of making this case was to show that on the premises which they adopted, the language of belief had been trivialized. The meaning of the statements of their theology at most could be cashed in terms of a clever intellectual game, but more appropriately confined to the kind of chatter which could be overheard 'while snatching a free moment in the pub'. This is very radical atheism indeed which mockingly leaves to the believer the shell of a religious language which is essentially trivial. The final rub is that the Russian boys and their professors do not see the irony.

Atheism and explanation The final type of atheism to which our attention should be directed is most succinctly introduced by P.S. Laplace's reported statement, referring to the claim that God is the ultimate explanation for everything: 'I have no need of that hypothesis.' Since the time of Laplace, however, the relevant forms of atheism have gone one stage further: they have not simply rejected the hypothesis of God, they have offered in its place fully elaborated explanations for phenomena regarded by believers as requiring 'that' hypothesis. Indeed the explanations which they offer even claim to explain the existence of belief and therefore of 'God'. The clearest recent examples of such explanatory theories are embodied in MARXISM and Freudianism. These theories offer not simply world views which exclude God as an item in the inventory of what there is, but they offer respectively alternatively different accounts of the origins of this mistaken belief. Thus Freud gives an account of belief in God as a form of illusion, that is, based upon subconscious wishes whose cause is to be found in complex psychological mechanisms. On the other hand Marx explains religion and religious belief, in his well-known characterization, as 'the opiate of the masses'. Belief in God is a product of and has its role to play in the dialectical struggle of class warfare.

Perhaps the most important solace which belief can draw from this is that both these theories cannot be correct, and indeed they are as incompatible with each other as they are with the belief in God which they reject. What they illustrate very well, however, is that atheism need not be regarded as simply a negative rejection of specific beliefs. Atheism, in certain forms, consists of what is regarded as a 'total' world view, which may well also seek to include by explaining it as a natural phenomenon, belief in God.

Here endeth the survey of different types of atheism! It remains now to examine some of the theological implications.

Theological implications
There are some general reflections prompted by consideration of the nature of atheism within an *Encyclopedia of Modern Christian Thought*.

The theological implications which can be drawn from the discussion of atheism depend upon the understanding which is held of the nature of theology. Thus if one takes the view that the nature of theology is essentially a matter of giving a rational or systematic statement of truths revealed in one form or another, then this exposition of the many forms which atheism can take will have little impact upon the practice of theology. At most some theological effort will be devoted to showing in theological terms why any particular form of atheism is misguided.

Alternatively if the conception of theology is based upon a foundation of natural theology, then significant intellectual effort will be devoted to countering the forms of atheism based upon assessment of the empirical evidence for or against theism. Equally, effort will be devoted to showing that any alleged contradictions within theistic belief are in fact apparent rather than real.

In each of these views of theology, the agenda is set predominantly by the context and nature of religious belief. Atheism in such a context is to some extent parasitic upon those forms of belief. However, there are alternative conceptions of theology, in which the possibility of the agenda being set elsewhere is not only countenanced, but is assumed to be part of the 'given' of theology. For example, Paul Tillich's characterization of all theology as 'answering' theology or 'apologetic' theology makes quite explicit the principle that the agenda of theology is in significant measure set by the questions posed for theology by the culture in which we live. The issue, however, is not that the agenda is set by the difficult questions which, for example, atheism sets for particular beliefs or theological formulations. Tillich's point is that it is the task of the theologian, to use a word less often heard these days, to answer the 'existential' questions formulated within and by contemporary culture.

My comment upon this has two elements. The first is that even if one does not accept the universality of Tillich's characterization as applying to all theology, nonetheless it is clear that theology which is 'answering' is in the best position to identify the key questions which are preoccupying any particular culture. This relates to the second element of my comment in the following ways. At one extreme, a theology which is 'answering' may appropriately help reformulate the questions, before answering them; at the other extreme, a theology which is not methodologically committed to listening to the world beyond theology may fail to notice that its affirmations are becoming increasingly ignored, because they are answers to questions which are no longer being asked. This was a fundamental failing of 'the Russian boys and their professors'. What they were discussing was no longer on the agenda of Ivan and, increasingly, his brother Alyosha. The tragedy of it was that they did not realize what was happening culturally around them.

In formulating his account of atheism in such subtle and profound terms through Ivan, Dostoevsky was choosing the path of regarding the essential role of theology as an answering role. The question set by Ivan about the very intelligibility of theism was to be set and answered in the fifth book of *The Brothers Karamazov*, titled *Pro and Contra*. In fact the serialized version of Book Five turned out to be mostly 'contra', and Dostoevsky planned the sixth book as the answer, as the direct opposite to the view of the world stated earlier (see Sutherland, 1977).

His worry quite properly was that it might not turn out to be a 'sufficient answer'. The reason for this is the devastating power which he had shown in the creation of Ivan. However, what is clear is that he anticipated many of the most searching questions which atheism would put to belief in the century which followed the publication of this portrayal of atheism as a challenge to the very meaning which the language of belief might possibly have.

See also EXISTENCE OF GOD, PROOFS OF; EXISTENTIALISM; FAITH AND REASON; PHILOSOPHY OF RELIGION.

Bibliography

Ayer, A.J. [1936] 1946: *Language, Truth and Logic*. London: Gollancz.
Berman, D. 1988: *A History of Atheism in Britain: From Hobbes to Russell*. London: Croom Helm.
Dostoevsky, F.M. [1879–80] 1912: *The Brothers Karamazov*, trans. Constance Garnett. London: Heinemann.
Ferré, F. 1962: *Language, Logic and God*. London: Eyre and Spottiswoode.
Flew, A., and MacIntyre, A., eds 1955: *New Essays in Philosophical Theology*. London: SCM Press.
Freud, S. [1927] 1962: *Future of an Illusion*, trans. W.D. Robson-Scott. London: The Hogarth Press.
Hastings, J., ed. 1908: *Encyclopaedia of Religion and Ethics*. Edinburgh: T & T Clark.
Hick, J. 1963: *The Philosophy of Religion*. Englewood Cliffs: Prentice-Hall.
Kant, I. [1781] 1961: *The Critique of Pure Reason*, trans. N.K. Smith. London: Macmillan.
Kant, I. [1793] 1960: *Religion Within the Limits of Reason Alone*, trans. T.M. Greene and H.M. Hudson. New York: Harper.
Pike, N. 1970: *God and Timelessness*. London: Routledge.
Sutherland, S.R. 1977: *Atheism and the Rejection of God*. Oxford: Blackwell.
Sutherland, S.R. 1984: *God, Jesus and Belief*. Oxford: Blackwell.
Swinburne, R. 1977: *The Coherence of Theism*. Oxford: Oxford University Press.
Swinburne, R. 1980: *The Existence of God*. Oxford: Oxford University Press.
Tennant, F.R. 1968: *Philosophical Theology*. Cambridge: Cambridge University Press.
Tillich, P. [1951] 1953: *Systematic Theology*, vol. 1. London: James Nisbet.

STEWART SUTHERLAND

atonement A term coined by the English Reformer William Tyndale in 1526 to translate the Latin term *reconciliatio*, and often used, especially in nineteenth-century works of theology, to refer to the salvific consequences of the death of Christ. The phrase 'theories of the atonement' is often used to refer to ways of understanding the manner in which the salvation of humanity is possible through the life, death and resurrection of Christ. See SOTERIOLOGY.

Auden, W[ystan] H[ugh] (1907–1973) English poet and literary critic. He was educated at Christ Church, Oxford, where he started writing poetry and became identified with a left-wing literary circle which included C. Day Lewis, Stephen Spender and Louis MacNeice. In 1939 he emigrated to the USA; and in 1956 he became professor of poetry at

Oxford, where he spent much of the last part of his life. His poetic works include *Poems* (1930), *The Orators* (1932), *Another Time* (1940), *The Age of Anxiety* (1947), *Nones* (1951) and *Homage to Clio* (1960), as well as works of prose and plays. The death of his devout Anglo-Catholic mother in 1941 confirmed his increasing interest in the religion of his childhood, and was a significant influence on his subsequent writing, starting with *New Year Letter* (1941, called *The Double Man* in the USA). His Christmas oratorio, *For The Time Being* (1944), was written for his friend Benjamin Britten to set to music; whilst the sequence *Horae Canonicae* (published in *The Shield of Achilles*, 1955) is an extended Good Friday meditation, hinting at the influence of T.S. Eliot.

Bibliography

Morgan, E.K. 1965: The analysis of guilt: poetry of W.H. Auden. In *Christian Themes in Contemporary Poets*. London.

Osborne, C. 1980: *W.H. Auden: The Life of a Poet*. London.

Simon, U. 1984: Horae canonicae. In *Images of Belief in Literature*, ed. D. Jasper. New York.

Aulén, Gustaf (1879–1977)   Swedish Lutheran theologian and Bishop of Strangas. A professor of systematic theology at the University of Lund, he was, with Anders Nygren, the leader of the motif-research school, which stresses man's incapacity to know God unaided and seeks to identify the true shape and nature of Christianity through the recurring motifs of its different traditions. For Aulén, the fundamental Christian motif is that of God's selfless, giving love, as expressed in Christ's atoning self-sacrifice on the cross. He promoted Lutheran studies, arguing that Luther recognized this fundamental motif, in contrast to the scholastics, who saw the death of Christ as a function of God's justice. His best-known work is *Christus Victor* of 1931, an exposition of the atonement which draws on the New Testament, the church Fathers (especially Irenaeus) and the Reformers, as well as on the insights of motif-research, to argue for a return to the 'classic' view of atonement, as the triumph of God and the vindication of Christ, rather than as primarily 'satisfaction' for a just God. Other works include a systematic theology, *The Faith of the Christian Church* (1932, trans. 1954), *Reformation and Catholicity* (1959) and *Jesus in Contemporary Historical Research* (1974).

Bibliography

Andren, C.-G. 1979: *Renewal: A Central Concept in Gustaf Aulén's Work*. Lund.

Weigel, G. 1954: *Survey of Protestant Theology in Our Day*.

Auschwitz   See EVIL, PROBLEM OF; JUDAISM AND CHRISTIANITY.

Australia   See PROTESTANT THEOLOGY: AUSTRALIA.

authority   The term 'authority' is complex, and carries with it a number of associations, including that of power. This point was noted in the report on this theme by the Anglican–Roman Catholic International Commission (ARCIC) and serves to identify the themes of the present article.

> Although the word sometimes implies the power to compel compliance, authority is normally distinguished from power. Most characteristically it stands for an invitation and a summons to men to exercise their freedom in ways indicated by the bearer of authority. Even God, from whom all authority is derived, seeks from men free obedience, not forced servitude. When, on the contrary, authority relies too much upon compulsion, it lapses into what is called authoritarianism.
>
> *(Yarnold and Chadwick, 1977, p. 8)*

Immanuel Kant insisted that the principle of moral authority must be internal (see KANTIANISM). For Kant, the moral will is autonomous, and gives itself the law which it obeys; the ultimate motive for moral action is duty for duty's sake, not obedience to the commands of God. Other writers have followed the same line of thought. J. Martineau in *The Seat of Authority in Religion* of 1890 saw reliance on authority as 'second-hand belief'; one must rely instead on conscience, which, as the work of the

Holy Spirit, is the 'communion of affection between God and man'. External criteria, whether provided by the church or the Bible, are '*un*moral rules for finding moral things'. A. Sabatier also criticized religions which are based upon external authorities, whether the Bible or the church; these are like 'schoolteachers, who help the child to discover the truth for himself' (*Les Religions d'autorité et la religion de l'esprit* of 1899). True religion involves receiving into oneself the spirit of Christ as a 'life principle, the permanent inspiration of his thoughts'. Even John Henry Newman, while defending the Catholic teaching on papal authority, held that conscience is the 'Divine Authority . . . on which in truth the Church herself is built' (Newman, [1875] 1910, p. 252). F.D.E. Schleiermacher, attaching as he did a supreme importance to religious feeling, grounded authority in the ability of those who have true God-consciousness to communicate this consciousness to others ([1821–2] 1928, pp. 611–3). Friedrich von Hügel saw authority as one of the three elements of religion, together with the rational and the mystical.

The Reformation *sola scriptura* has been developed in recent years by Karl Barth. While only Scripture as the Word of God has direct and absolute authority, the church is endowed with a mediate and relative authority; it consists in 'the voice of others in the Church reaching me in . . . common declarations and as such preceding my own faith' (Barth, [1938] 1956, p. 593). Just as the duty to honour our parents does not detract from our fundamental duty to God, so too the church's authority does not detract from the authority of Jesus Christ, but is both established and limited by it. All authority in the home and the state is an imitation of the church's authority (pp. 586–7). D.E. Nineham, on the other hand, against fundamentalist claims for the sufficiency of a literal interpretation of Scripture, argued that the church never finds in Scripture an 'external and objective norm' for solving its problems (1969, p. 198).

The Anglican–Roman Catholic International Commission (ARCIC), while professing that Scripture is the 'primary norm for Christian faith and life' (ARCIC, 1982, Auth. Eluc. 2), saw Scripture as 'a normative record of the authentic foundation of the faith' rather than as the normative foundation itself, for that is Christ;

and as the means through which 'the authority of the Word of God is conveyed', rather than as the authoritative word itself. It is not so much Scripture on its own as the 'common faith' of the community formed by Scripture which sets the criterion by which individuals test their belief (Auth. I.2). This conception of the 'common faith' of the community is often expressed by the term *sensus fidelium*. For Newman ([1859] 1961) the faithful may preserve the faith, though perhaps in unarticulated form, even though many bishops may abandon it; they therefore should be consulted by the hierarchy in matters of doctrine.

ARCIC usefully distinguished between various forms of authority found in the church. Apart from the authority of Scripture, there is the authority, springing from fidelity to the gospel, with which the whole Christian community and each of its members address the world. Second, within the church, there is the authority with which individual Christians bear responsibility for one another. This may be based on an inherent quality of wisdom or holiness; but it may also derive from an office, above all that of an ordained minister. Both inherent authority and the authority that comes from office are charisms or gifts of the Spirit; they are given not for the sake of the bearer of authority, but for the service of the whole church, 'for building up the body of Christ' (Eph. 4: 12) both by pastoral leadership and teaching. Authority exists for the *koinonia* (fellowship or communion) of the church (ARCIC, 1982, Auth. I.4–5).

Roman Catholic ecclesiology, while not overlooking the importance of inherent charisms, places great emphasis on the authority that comes from office, speaking of 'jurisdiction' (the power necessary for the exercise of office) and 'magisterium'. The latter term, by which Thomas Aquinas referred to the teaching function of both bishops and theologians, has in recent church pronouncements been restricted to the teaching office of bishops, or even to the bishops themselves who exercise the office (Congar, [1976] 1982, pp. 297–313). A distinction is drawn between the 'extraordinary magisterium' of bishops when they define doctrine in a general council, and the 'ordinary magisterium' of their day-by-day teaching. The difficulty in defining the relationship between theologians and the magisterium (in the modern restricted sense of the term) is the cause of considerable tension in the Roman Catholic church today (Sullivan, 1983, pp. 24–34, 174–218).

Characteristic of the Roman Catholic understanding of authority is the role attributed to the pope as bishop of Rome, which was formally defined at the First Vatican Council (Vatican I: 1870). The Council attributed to the pope within the whole church a primacy held in succession to the primacy which Christ conferred on St Peter (Matt. 16: 18; John 21: 15–17). There have been many attempts to define the nature of this primacy. Traditionally a distinction has been drawn between primacies of jurisdiction and honour – though the latter originally implied a primacy not of ceremony but of rank, and probably involved canonical powers. Cardinal R. Pole (d. 1555) suggested that the pope exercises a primacy of sacrifice (Ratzinger, [1987] 1988, p. 42); Paul VI (1964, p. 656) spoke of a primacy of 'service, ministration and love' ('famulatus, ministerii, amoris'). ARCIC (1982, Auth. II.19) envisaged the papacy not as 'an autocratic power over the Church but a service in and to the Church which is a communion in faith and charity of local churches'. The Second Vatican Council (Vatican II) balanced the doctrine of papal primacy with that of collegiality: together with the pope, who is the head of the college, the bishops are the 'subject of supreme and full power over the universal Church' (*Lumen Gentium* 22).

The primacy of the pope is said to include both supreme jurisdiction and infallible magisterium. Critics of the doctrine of papal infallibility often fail to observe the rigorous restrictions which Vatican I attached to its definition. According to the Council the pope's infallibility is not distinct from the general infallibility of the church, and is confined to occasions when he is expressly teaching the whole church on a matter of essential doctrine; it is not claimed as an inherent capacity for discerning truth, but as a divine protection against error only at the moments when such teaching is given. It was understood at the Council – though the point was not explicitly included in the definition – that the pope would be bound to consult the whole church before venturing on an infallible definition (Yarnold and Chadwick, 1977, pp. 26–9). Despite the wishes of the ultramontane party, who wished to magnify papal powers, the purpose of infallibility is not to obviate the need for thought, but to maintain the unity of the church.

It is claimed therefore that there are three organs of infallibility in the church: the church's general infallibility (the *sensus fidelium*), the infallibility of the bishops (including in their number the bishop of Rome) both in general councils and in their ordinary magisterium, and the infallibility of the pope without the bishops. The occasions when popes have had recourse to this infallible authority are rare; only two such occasions are claimed in recent centuries, namely the definitions of two dogmas concerning the Virgin Mary in 1854 and 1950.

The concept of infallibility has been criticized for implying a 'propositional' view of revelation. ARCIC however explains that the church in defining a dogma does not claim that the formulas used are 'the only possible, or even the most exact, way of expressing the faith'. But 'although the categories of thought and the mode of expression may be superseded, restatement always builds upon, and does not contradict, the truth intended by the original definition' (1982, Auth. I.15).

Even among Roman Catholics the doctrine of infallibility has been subjected to critical scrutiny in recent years. The condemnation of contraception by Paul VI has led to the re-examination of the claim of Vatican I that infallibility extends to matters of morals as well as faith (*de fide vel moribus*); the alleged infallibility of the ordinary magisterium has also been questioned (Ford and Grisez, 1978; Sullivan, 1983, pp. 136–52). Hans Küng not only rejected the doctrine of infallibility, but attributed teaching authority to theologians rather than bishops (Küng, [1970] 1971, pp. 181–97). B. Tierney argued that the doctrine was invented in the thirteenth and fourteenth centuries by Franciscan theologians in order to consolidate papal approval of their statutes on poverty. F. Oakley sought to rehabilitate the conciliarist position that the general council is over the pope.

Other churches, while generally accepting that the Holy Spirit guarantees the church's *indefectibility* or general continuance in fidelity to the gospel, do not accept the need for an infallible teaching authority. Recent Anglican thinking has defined authority in the Anglican Communion as 'dispersed'; according to S. Sykes, teaching authority is based on the reading and preaching of the Scriptures in the liturgy rather than on dogmatic pronouncements. A special authority is attributed to the 'Chicago–Lambeth Quadrilateral' of Scriptures, creeds, sacraments and historic episcopate (see ECUMENISM).

ARCIC came surprisingly close to expressing agreement between Roman Catholics and Anglicans on the doctrine of papal infallibility. One aspect of the doctrine which remained unresolved was *reception*, though even here there was some consensus. Anglicans believe that a definition cannot be accepted as binding in faith until the whole church has reflected on it and seen that it is in conformity with Scripture and tradition (1982, Auth. II.29). Though the Vatican I decree taught that an infallible act of teaching is not conditional on the consent of the church, Vatican II implied that reception is at least a guarantee that a definition does in fact fulfil the conditions of infallibility (*Lumen Gentium* 25). Newman had already put forward a similar view ([1875] 1910, pp. 303, 372). Y. Congar indicated that for Roman Catholics reception has a decisive importance, not as conferring juridical validity on a definition, but because otherwise a definition has no vital force (Congar, 1972, pp. 399–401). Among the Orthodox the doctrine of *sobornost* (conciliarity) put forward by A. Khomyakov maintained that the decrees of a council are not binding until they are accepted by the whole church (Khomyakov, 1895, pp. 94-5).

Reference has been made above to the *Final Report* of the Anglican–Roman Catholic International Commission. The same subject has been discussed in other ecumenical dialogues, most fully in that between Lutherans and Roman Catholics in the USA (see Lutherans and Catholics in Dialogue, 1980).

See also ECCLESIOLOGY; FUNDAMENTALISM; LIBERALISM (BRITAIN and USA); TRADITION.

Bibliography

ARCIC (Anglican–Roman Catholic International Commission) 1982: *The Final Report*. London: CTS/SPCK.

Barth, K. [1938] 1956: *Church Dogmatics* I/2: *The Doctrine of the Word of God*, trans. G.T. Thompson and H. Knight. Edinburgh: T & T Clark.

Congar, Y. M.-J. 1972: Reception as an ecclesiological reality, trans. J. Griffiths, *Concilium* 7, 8, pp. 43-68.

Congar, Y. M.-J. [1976] 1982: A semantic history of the term 'magisterium', and A brief history of the forms of the magisterium and its relations with scholars, trans. In *Readings in Moral Theology No. 3: The Magisterium and Morality*, ed. C.E. Curran and R.A. McCormick. New York: Paulist Press, pp. 297–331.

Ford, J.C., and Grisez, G. 1978: Contraception and the infallibility of the ordinary magisterium. *Theological Studies* 39, pp. 258–312.

Khomyakov, A. 1895: Fifth letter to Mr Palmer. In *Russia and the English Church during the Last Fifty Years*, ed. W.J. Birkbeck. London: Rivington Percival, pp. 91–8.

Küng, H. [1970] 1971: *Infallible? An Enquiry*, trans. E. Mosbacher. London: Collins.

Lutherans and Catholics in Dialogue. 1965: *I: The Status of the Nicene Creed as Dogma of the Church*; 1974: *V: Papal Primacy and the Universal Church*; 1980: *VI: Teaching Authority and Infallibility in the Church*. Minneapolis: Augsburg Publishing House.

Newman, J.H. [1859] 1961: *On Consulting the Faithful in Matters of Doctrine*. London: G. Chapman.

Newman, J.H. [1875] 1910: Letter to the Duke of Norfolk. In *Certain Difficulties felt by Anglicans in Catholic Teaching*, vol. 2. London and New York: Longmans Green.

Nineham, D.E. 1969: The use of the Bible in modern theology. *John Rylands Bulletin* 52, pp. 178–99.

Paul VI, 1964: Ecclesiam Suam. *Acta apostolicae sedis* 56, pp. 609–59.

Ratzinger, J. [1987] 1988: *Church, Ecumenism and Politics*, trans. R. Nowell. Slough: St Paul Publications.

Schleiermacher, F.D.E. [1821-2] 1928: *The Christian Faith*, trans. D.M. Baillie *et al.* Edinburgh: T & T Clark.

Sullivan, F.A. 1983: *Magisterium: Teaching Authority in the Catholic Church*. New York/Ramsey: Paulist Press.

Sykes, S. 1978: *The Integrity of Anglicanism*. London: Mowbray.

Wright, J.R., ed. 1988: *Quadrilateral at One Hundred: Essays on the Centenary of the Chicago–Lambeth Quadrilateral 1886/88–1986/88*. Cincinnati: Forward Movement Publications; London and Oxford: Mowbray.

Yarnold, E.J., and Chadwick, H. 1977: *Truth and Authority: a Commentary on the Agreed Statement of the Anglican–Roman Catholic International Commission, Venice 1976*. London: CTS/SPCK.

EDWARD J. YARNOLD

B

Balthasar, Hans Urs von (1905–1988) Swiss theologian. Born in Lucerne, Balthasar studied philosophy and German literature at the universities of Zurich, Vienna and Berlin. His doctoral thesis on German idealism was subsequently published as *Apokalypse der deutschen Seele* (three vols, 1937–9). In 1929 he joined the Society of Jesus where, in his philosophical studies, he came under the influence of Erich Przywara (1889–1972) whose understanding of *analogia entis* had a profound effect on him. For his theological studies he went to the Jesuit Scholasticate at Lyon-Fourvière and studied under Henri de Lubac, who inspired in him and his contemporaries there (such as Aloys Grillmeier and Jean Daniélou) a lasting love of the Fathers of the church, which came to fruition in his important studies of Origen (*Parole et mystère chez Origène*, 1957) and Gregory of Nyssa (*Présence et Pensée*, 1942), and his seminal work on Maximus the Confessor (*Kosmische Liturgie*, 1941; second edition, enlarged to include translations of important works by Maximus and two of Balthasar's articles, 1961). This period was also marked by a deepening love of French literature (especially twentieth-century French Catholic literature) and the beginning of his long commitment to the work of translation. This started with important selections from Origen (1938), Gregory of Nyssa (1939), and Augustine (1942) and continued with his translations of Paul Claudel and his mentor at Lyon-Fourvière, Henri de Lubac, amongst others. After Lyon, he was briefly editor of *Stimmen der Zeit* and then spent eight years as student chaplain at Basle, where he met Adrienne von Speyr, a medical doctor and the wife of Werner Kaegi,

later professor of history at Basle and author of a massive biography of Jacob Burckhardt, and received her into the Catholic church. Adrienne von Speyr was a visionary: Balthasar became her amanuensis and the publisher of her visions and meditations, which profoundly influenced his own theological development. Together they decided to found a secular institute, a kind of religious order whose members would continue to fulfil their normal avocation in the world. The Jesuit authorities deemed such a task incompatible with membership of the Society, and Balthasar reluctantly left the Society in 1950, though he remained deeply attracted to Ignatian spirituality. This led to a long period in the ecclesiastical wilderness: he was alone among major Catholic theologians in not being called to the Second Vatican Council as a *peritus*, something he resented. In the wake of Vatican II his restoration to favour began: in 1967 he was made a member of the Papal Theological Commission and soon gained a reputation as a 'conservative'. He certainly distanced himself from others such as Hans Küng and Karl Rahner, both of whom he attacked, the latter in his notorious *Cordula* (1966); and he set up a rival periodical to *Concilium* called *Communio*. He was widely regarded as the favourite theologian of Pope John Paul II, who named him a cardinal in 1988. Balthasar died a few days before the ceremony.

Balthasar's theology matured slowly during and after the Second World War. As he never held any academic post – from 1948 onwards he divided his time between running a publishing house (Johannes Verlag), writing, translating and editing, and being chaplain to his secular institute in Basle – his intellectual development pursued paths unusual in twentieth-century theology. Informing everything were his studies in German literature and philosophy and his thorough initiation in (especially Greek) patristic theology. The influence of Adrienne von Speyr is evident from the early 1940s: his *Heart of the World* ([1945] 1979), a meditation on the Sacred Heart in a bewitching kind of prose-poetry, is inconceivable without her. Adrienne's influence can perhaps be summed up in two words – Marian and Trinitarian: everything begins in the *response* of the creature to God's self-manifestation, a response of fruitful obedience that makes the incarnation of the Son of God possible. Through the incarnation, humanity is called to its vocation as the body and bride of Christ. The creature is thus caught up in the life of the Trinity, its obedience shadows the obedience of the Son to the Father, an obedience that leads the Son in love to show solidarity with the creature in the God-forsakenness of its rejection of God, and thereby to redeem it. The saving love of the Trinity is revealed in the Son of God's *descensus ad inferos*, his descent to the place of the damned, where God remains God and his power is manifest: here is redemption, here the 'magic of Holy Saturday'. Adrienne's imagery in all this, which Balthasar borrows, is very physical: the imagery of bridal union is that of physical consummation, not of the wedding, of blood, not lace.

But Basle provided another important influence for Balthasar's theology: the great Swiss Calvinist theologian Karl Barth. In his great work on Karl Barth ([1951] 1971), Balthasar traced the development of Barth's theology from his commentary on Romans, through to the early sections of the *Church Dogmatics*, paying attention particularly to the way in which Barth focused his anti-Catholic polemic on the rejection of *analogia entis*. Balthasar was warmly appreciative of and responsive to Barth's vision of biblical theology as God's own witness to his self-revelation, but argued that the doctrine of *analogia entis* (interpreted with Przywara in the light of the declaration of the fourth Lateran Council that any likeness between God and the creature discloses a still greater unlikeness) fulfilled such a vision rather than undermined it. Whereas Barth tends (more in theory than in practice) to isolate the Bible and its witness, Balthasar sees the witness of the Bible as the fulfilment of all human attempts to respond to the mystery of being.

The 1950s saw the exploration of further paths in Balthasar's theological development. There were studies of two young Carmelite saints, Thérèse of Lisieux ([1950] 1953) and Elisabeth of Dijon ([1952] 1956): if theology is rooted in the response of the creature, it is necessary to attend carefully to those whose response has been whole-hearted – the saints. There were studies, too, of two (Catholic) novelists, the Austrian Reinhold Schneider (1953) and the French Georges Bernanos ([1954] 1956): for novelists (particularly *these* novelists) explore the myriad variety of the wanderings of the creature. There were many other studies: an edition of the section of Thomas Aquinas's *Summa theologiae* that deals with special gifts of grace, especially prophecy, which Balthasar's commentary explores, conscious of the contemporary example of Adrienne von Speyr (1954); a short work on the Jewish philosopher Martin Buber (1958, trans. 1959); a work on contemplative prayer (1955, trans. 1961) which sought to overcome the dichotomy found in much Catholic teaching on prayer between meditation on Scripture and a (more exalted) contemplation.

All this led up to the consummation of Balthasar's theological achievement in his trilogy: *Herrlichkeit* (seven parts, 1961–9, trans. *The Glory of the Lord*, 1982–91), *Theodramatik* (five parts, 1973–83) and *Theologik* (two parts, 1985). The first part has the subtitle *A Theological Aesthetics*: this makes explicit an insight of Balthasar's that had long underlain his thought – that God reveals himself, not simply as truth or goodness, but as *beauty*. Consequently, Christianity, as the creature's response to God's self-revelation, is not simply a collection of true dogmas, or a way of life, but the response to a vision that inspires and deeply influences one's way of life and that we seek to discern more and more clearly, more and more truly. The first volume of *Herrlichkeit* is largely concerned with exploring the response of faith to the revelation of God's beauty, devoting space to the traditional theme of the spiritual senses and drawing attention to the variety and complementarity of responses that God's revelation calls forth. Then in a series of important studies of Christian figures from

Irenaeus, Denys the Areopagite and Anselm to Dante, Gerard Manley Hopkins and Péguy, Balthasar goes on to explore the variety of ways in which Christians have used aesthetic categories to interpret God's self-manifestation. He next places twentieth-century western theology in the context of its heritage by exploring how the west has used the category of the beautiful to save humanity from 'forgetfulness of being', from Homer to Martin Heidegger by way of almost anyone one can think of. This exploration forms an important and exciting cultural history of the west, revealing Balthasar's wide learning and searching insight. The two following volumes explore the revelation of the Glory of the Lord in the Old Testament and in the New Testament, centring on the revelation of the Glory of the Lord in his *descensus ad inferos*, a summary of his more extensive exposition of this theme in the *Theologie der drei Tage* (1969, trans. *Mysterium Paschale*, 1990). There was to be a final volume, *Ökumene*, showing how *gloria Dei* draws the various Christian traditions into convergence. But this final volume was never written, partly because Balthasar felt the work for the other parts of his trilogy more pressing (he was already sixty-five) and partly because he doubted whether the vision behind the final volume was yet accessible. The second part of the trilogy, *Theodramatik*, draws on Balthasar's wide understanding of drama in western culture, and uses insights drawn from this to present the engagement between God and humanity in revelation and redemption in a broader perspective that incorporates as authentic elements grace and human free will, Christology, the church and the sacraments, and eschatology. The final part, *Theologik* (thus entitled, a kind of tribute to G.W.F. Hegel), raises in this richer context the fundamental questions of truth and orthodoxy.

Henri de Lubac, in a famous comparison, contrasted with Hegel's 'speculative Good Friday' what he called Balthasar's 'contemplative Holy Saturday'. This draws attention to Balthasar's own characterization of his theology as a 'kneeling theology' and also to the paramount significance of the *descensus* motif. This is certainly the heart of Balthasar's theology, which unites the cosmic dimension of patristic theology and the affective mysticism

of the later west, as well as traditions of humane learning that reach back to the Renaissance (and are often felt to be ill-at-ease in the post-Tridentine Catholic church). De Lubac has also called Balthasar 'perhaps the most cultured man in Europe'. But alongside the central works of the Balthasarian canon, discussed above, there has been a constant stream of articles and pamphlets addressing matters of current concern. Some of the more notorious – *Cordula* (1966), *Die antirömische Affekt* (1974) – have fostered the idea of Balthasar as a conservative, dismayed by Vatican II. But his was one of the voices to which Vatican II responded (see his *Schleifung der Bastionen*, 1952); his more recent concern is for faithfulness to the tradition as declared at that council.

The importance of Balthasar's theology is manifold. It sets the work of theology in a much wider context than has been traditional, requiring it to draw on a broader range of human experience and reflection, to take genuine account of the cultural context in which theology is worked out (an insight that has wider implications than even Balthasar began to explore, as he himself acknowledged); it overcomes traditional dichotomies between theology and spirituality, not by subordinating one to the other, but by calling in question both cherished convictions of academic theology and traditional expectations as well as some current trends in spirituality. His reception in the modern church suffers from the sobriquet 'conservative' that attaches to him, as well as to others such as Daniélou and de Lubac, though it fits them all ill: his vision might be more appropriately characterized as radical, in the true sense of that word (which does not mean fashionable).

See also CHRISTOLOGY.

Bibliography

Writings

1937–9: *Apokalypse der deutschen Seele*, 3 vols. Salzburg.

[1941] 1961: *Kosmische Liturgie*, 2nd, enlarged edn. Einsiedeln: Johannes Verlag.

1942: *Présence et Pensée*. Paris: Beauchesne.

[1945] 1970: *Heart of the World*, trans. San Francisco: Ignatius Press.

[1950] 1953: *Thérèse of Lisieux*, trans. D. Nicholl. London: Sheed and Ward.

[1951] 1971: *The Theology of Karl Barth*, trans. New York: Holt, Rinehart and Winston.

[1952] 1956: *Elizabeth of Dijon*, trans. A.V. Littledale. London,: Harvill Press.

1953: *Reinhold Schneider*. Cologne and Olten: Jakob Hegner.

[1954] 1956: *Georges Bernanos*, French trans. M. de Gandillac. Paris: Le Seuil.

1957: *Parole et mystère chez Origène*. Paris: Le Cerf.

[1961] 1981: *First Glance at Adrienne von Speyr*, trans. San Francisco.

[1961–9] 1982–91: *The Glory of the Lord*, trans. J. Riches et al. Edinburgh: T & T Clark.

1966: *Cordula*, Einsiedeln: Johannes Verlag.

[1969] 1990: *Mysterium Paschale*, trans. A. Nichols. Edinburgh: T & T Clark.

1973–83: *Theodramatik*. Einsiedeln: Johannes Verlag.

1985: *Theologik*. Einsiedeln: Johannes Verlag.

Critical works

Riches, J., ed. 1986: *The Analogy of Beauty: The Theology of Hans Urs von Balthasar*. Edinburgh.

Riches, J., 1989: Hans Urs von Balthasar. In *The Modern Theologians*, ed. D. F. Ford, vol. 1. Oxford: Blackwell. pp. 237–54.

Saward, J., 1990: *The Mysteries of March*. London: Collins.

ANDREW LOUTH

baptism See SACRAMENTAL THEOLOGY.

Baptist thought The Baptists were those Christian groups arising in the seventeenth century who held, like the Congregationalists, that the church should consist of none but self-conscious believers, but who went further by asserting that baptism should be administered only to those making a personal profession of faith. The larger group, the Particular Baptists, accepted the Calvinist principles of the 1689 Confession drawn up in London. The smaller group, the General Baptists, professed the Arminian views set out in the Orthodox Confession of 1679. Since they desired to reproduce a pattern of churchmanship from the New Testament, both bodies were pre-occupied in the early eighteenth century with such issues as whether hymns should be sung in worship and whether hands should be laid on the newly baptized. At a meeting of Dissenting ministers at Salters' Hall in 1719, a majority of Particular Baptists were willing to renew their subscription to the doctrine of the Trinity, but a majority of General Baptists, preferring to use nothing but biblical language to expound the faith, declined to do so. Thereafter the rationalist temper of eighteenth-century thought encouraged most General Baptists to move towards a Socinian Christology and ultimately, in the following century, to converge with the Unitarians. The same temper induced a number of influential Particular Baptist ministers to adopt a higher form of Calvinism. Chief among them was John Gill, those treatise *The Cause of God and Truth* of 1735–8 defended the doctrine of election on rational grounds. Others, however, including those responsible for training ministers at Bristol Baptist Academy, professed a more moderate version of Calvinism. This tradition, powerfully reinforced in the later eighteenth century by the reception of the thought of Jonathan Edwards, culminated in Andrew Fuller's *The Gospel Worthy of all Acceptation* of 1785. Fuller's theology supplied the evangelistic impetus for the Baptist Missionary Society (1792) and remained the standard of denominational orthodoxy long into the nineteenth century.

In North America the Philadelphia Association of Particular, or Regular, Baptists adopted an amended version of the 1689 Confession in 1742. The Separate Baptists, who evolved from Congregational churches created by the Great Awakening of the early eighteenth century, were less concerned with precise doctrinal statements, but accepted the Philadelphia Confession when they gradually merged with the Regulars in the later eighteenth century. The cause of American liberty was championed by many English Baptists such as Robert Robinson, and in the early republic Baptist leaders such as Isaac Backus in Massachusetts and John Leland in Virginia insisted on the separation of church and state, an enduring characteristic of Baptist thought. In the rapid expansion of the Baptists in early nineteenth-century North America the imperative to spread the gospel took priority over theology. General, or Freewill, Baptists played their part, and in 1833 the New Hampshire Confession, which was to be widely adopted by Baptists in the Reformed tradition, was noncommittal on points of difference between Calvinists and Arminians. Nevertheless systematic divinity gradually returned to favour, leading, for example, to the publication of *A Manual of Theology* in 1857 by the southern theologian John L. Dagg. After considerable controversy the southern states formed their own Baptist Convention in 1845, perhaps less through objections to northern anti-slavery than through an insistence on using exclusively Baptist agencies for Christian mission. Groups of Anti-Mission Baptists went further by refusing to support any para-church agencies whatsoever. Baptist exclusivity reached its apogee in the Landmark movement, which from the 1850s would not recognize a believer's baptism unless it was performed by an officer of a properly organized Baptist church.

A different form of distinctive teaching marked the so-called Scotch Baptists, a body that adopted the principles set out by Archibald McLean of Edinburgh in *The Commission given by Jesus Christ to his Apostles Illustrated* of 1785. McLean held that true faith is simply rational assent and that churches must be led not by a single minister but by a plurality of elders. The influence of the Enlightenment is also evident in Robert Hall's *On Terms of Communion* of 1815, which argued that Baptists should show tolerance in admitting Christians not baptized as believers to the Lord's Supper. Those in England who did not agree with Hall and who maintained a higher Calvinism from the past gradually emerged as a separate denomination of Strict and Particular Baptists. A distinct testimony was also maintained between 1770 and 1891 by the New Connexion of General Baptists, whose Arminian theology was as evangelical as that of the Methodists.

As the nineteenth century wore on the differences that had formerly divided Calvinist from Arminian were increasingly forgotten in the Baptist mainstream. Partly under American influence, a tendency towards revivalism put theology at a premium. Victorian Baptists were also swayed by the American example to reject the union of church and state and, towards the end of the nineteenth century, to see in total abstinence from alcohol a solution to the social problem. Much Baptist thinking in the Victorian era was a reaction against the high churchmanship of the Oxford movement (see ANGLICANISM). Its sacramental teaching made Baptists turn from their traditional Calvinist view of the Lord's Supper as a distinctive means of grace towards a form of Zwinglian memorialism, and its priestly ethos persuaded many Baptists to repudiate the very notion of ordination to Christian ministry. The denomination exalted the minister as preacher. C.H. Spurgeon published weekly sermons in which a definite Calvinism was toned down by Victorian sentimentalism. In the Down Grade Controversy of 1887–8 Spurgeon denounced the liberal theological trends – a tendency to neglect the atonement, downplay hell and dismiss other biblical teachings – that he discerned among some of his younger brethren in the ministry. Partly through his influence, the denomination entered the twentieth century more theologically conservative than most other nonconformists.

In North America a number of mediating theologians – Augustus Hopkins Strong, William Newton Clarke and Edgar Young Mullins – attempted to express evangelical orthodoxy in modern thought forms. At the University of Chicago there were advanced liberals such as Shailer Mathews, and by the First World War biblical criticism was generally accepted at the northern seminaries. Walter Rauschenbusch proclaimed the social gospel in *Christianity and the Social Crisis* of 1907. Simultaneously, however, holiness teaching and premillennialism were drawing many Baptists in a conservative direction. The resulting polarization led to the postwar controversies between fundamentalists (see FUNDAMENTALISM), led by W.B. Riley in the north, J. Frank Norris in the south and T.T. Shields in Canada, and modernists (see MODERNISM), among whom H.E. Fosdick was prominent. There were parallel developments in England, where F.B. Meyer was a leading spokesman of Keswick holiness and premillennial teaching while John Clifford championed the social gospel. Yet in England debate was neither so fierce nor so sustained. Among the small but growing Baptist communities of Germany, Russia and elsewhere the fundamentalist controversy seemed largely irrelevant, though it did impinge on English-speaking missionaries in China and India.

The later twentieth century witnessed significant debate among Baptists about the ecumenical movement. England produced a notable champion in the historian E.A. Payne, but suspicions of liberal theology, left-wing politics, bureaucratic tendencies and Roman Catholic influences created powerful worldwide resistance and sometimes schism. In the academic sphere particular attention was paid by George Beasley-Murray to baptism and by H. Wheeler Robinson to the Old Testament. A mildly liberal commentary on Genesis of 1969 by the Oxford scholar G. Henton Davies was one of the factors behind the divisive debates in the Southern Baptist Convention between advocates and opponents of biblical inerrancy. Despite Baptists numbering in their ranks the American Harvey Cox, the author of the radical manifesto *The Secular City* of 1965, and the Englishman Michael Taylor, who in 1971 publicly doubted the divinity of Christ, most sections of their worldwide community have remained theologically conservative. The writings of the theologian Carl F.H. Henry and the evangelist Billy Graham equally illustrate Baptist loyalty to evangelical convictions.

See also EVANGELICALISM (BRITAIN and USA); PROTESTANT THEOLOGY (BRITAIN and USA).

Bibliography

Brackney, W.H. 1988: *The Baptists*. New York: Greenwood Press.

Brown, R. 1986: *The English Baptists of the Eighteenth Century*. London: Baptist Historical Society.

Clipsham, E.F. 1963–4: Andrew Fuller and Fullerism: a study in evangelical Calvinism. *The Baptist Quarterly* 20, pp. 99–114, 146–54, 214–25, 268–76.

George, T., and Dockery, D.S., eds 1990: *Baptist Theologians*. Nashville, Tenn.: Broadman Press.

Lumpkin, W.L. 1959: *Baptist Confessions of Faith*. Valley Forge, Pa: Judson Press.

McBeth, H.L. 1987: *The Baptist Heritage*. Nashville, Tenn.: Broadman Press.

Nettles, T.J. 1986: *By His Grace and for His Glory*. Grand Rapids, Mich.: Baker.

Tull, J.E. 1972: *Shapers of Baptist Thought*. Valley Forge, Pa: Judson Press.

Wacker, G. 1985: *Augustus H. Strong and the Dilemma of Historical Consciousness*. Macon, Ga: Mercer University Press.

Ward, W.R. 1973: The Baptists and the transformation of the church, 1780–1830, *The Baptist Quarterly* 25, pp. 167–84.

D.W. BEBBINGTON

Barth, Karl (1886–1968) Swiss Protestant theologian, one of the most influential of the twentieth century.

Life and early thought

Karl Barth was born in Basle, Switzerland. His university education in theology was in Bern, Berlin (where he studied under Adolf von Harnack and Hermann Gunkel), Tübingen and Marburg (where Wilhelm Herrmann was, he said, '*the* theological teacher of my student years' (Busch, 1976, p. 44).

From 1911 to 1921 he was a pastor in the Swiss industrial and agricultural village of Safenwil. Here, as he taught, preached, engaged in politics and trade union struggles and followed the course of the First World War, he went through a crisis in his German liberal Protestant theology. The support of the war by his former teachers in Germany was a special scandal. How had Christianity come to be so uncritically involved in western culture and society? His attempt to rethink his theology began with writing a commentary on Paul's epistle to the Romans; and the second, fully reworked 1922 edition of this became the book marking the beginning of distinctive twentieth-century Protestant theology. One label applied to it was 'theology of crisis', pointing both to its original meaning of 'judgement' and also to the crisis in western civilization and religion represented by the First World War. Another label was 'dialectical theology', meaning especially the denial of any continuity or natural point of contact between God and humanity or between the gospel and culture: the contact is utterly God's initiative, and it comes first through a massive 'no' focused in the crucifixion of Jesus Christ, after which the only way through is by the 'yes' of God in the resurrection. Typical liberal points of contact in the human moral sense or in feeling or consciousness or rationality or civilization were rejected, as were more Catholic tendencies to trust in the church or spirituality. Above all, religion was devastatingly criticized for being a human attempt to escape from, domesticate or distort God. With explosive vehemence and vivid rhetoric Barth evokes the Jesus Christ he finds through Romans: 'We stumble when we suppose that we can treat of Him, speak and hear of Him – *without being scandalized*' (Barth,

[1922] 1968, p. 280). What especially concerns Barth is to 'let God be God', which means recognizing God's otherness and the crisis for all humanity that this creates. Each moment of time confronts the judgement of God and only because of the 'impossible possibility' of faith in the gospel is there a way through.

The 1920s were spent by Barth rewriting his Romans commentary, taking a polemical part in the massive debate it initiated (not least with Harnack), settling into university chairs in Germany, first at Göttingen then at Münster, and trying to find a way forward for his theology. His first major attempt, the first volume of a *Christian Dogmatics* published in 1927, was judged by himself to be a false start and the project was left uncompleted. The main catalyst, leading to what he considered a breakthrough, was his study of Anselm of Canterbury, published in 1931. What he discovered in Anselm's 'faith seeking understanding' was that theology did not have to justify itself by some outside criterion; it has its own rationality and internal coherence in the form of witness to the event of Jesus Christ. His refusal to give priority to any framework, foundation or conceptuality in preference to the gospel, together with his confidence that this is a fully rational procedure, became the hallmark of the rest of his life's theology. The main conflict in the interpretation of this development in his thought determined the principal debate in European Protestant theology during the middle third of the twentieth century. On the one hand, his Anselm book and the *Church Dogmatics* ([1932–68] 1956–75) which followed it were seen as in discontinuity with his *Romans*, reneging on its radical critique and existential relevance in the interests of a renewed orthodoxy and a form of dogmatic theology that should be ruled out by the otherness of the God of *Romans*. Rudolf Bultmann held this and his theology became for many the main alternative to Barth's. On the other hand, Barth himself never agreed that there was such discontinuity. The new move could be seen as a massive development of the one point of contact allowed in *Romans*, Jesus Christ. The dialectic is embodied in the history of his life, death and resurrection; he is the bearer of the crisis, of judgement; and the otherness of God does not mean his distance or

unknowability but his presence in this form which can only be known through the witness of Scripture and the Holy Spirit. The primary task of theology is to describe this, to identify God through his self-revelation and to try to discern what corresponds to that revelation in life and thought.

Soon after beginning the *Church Dogmatics* Barth was involved in organizing church resistance in Germany to Hitler and National Socialism, supporters of which had become dominant in the mainstream German Protestant churches. He reaffirmed his rejection of natural or historical 'points of contact' and also his emphasis on 'God alone' and 'Jesus Christ alone' over against the association of Hitler and German national destiny, culture and race with the purposes and revelation of God. In 1935 he was deprived of his post and expelled from Germany. He became a professor in the University of Basle until his retirement. Through the Second World War he championed the Allied cause and opposed Swiss neutrality. In the postwar period he continued his political role and argued against Reinhold Niebuhr, who urged support for the cold war with the Soviet Union. A major critical biography of Barth has yet to appear and there are many questions about the relation of his life to his theology that deserve discussion.

The Church Dogmatics

The *Church Dogmatics* is in four 'volumes', each in fact comprising between two and four large tomes. Volume I is on the doctrine of the Word of God. Volume I/1 is about the three forms of the Word of God (preached, written and revealed); about how it is the criterion for dogmatics; and about its content, the triune God, Father, Son and Holy Spirit. Volume I/2 treats the three forms in more detail – the revealed form in the incarnation of the Word in Jesus Christ, the written form in Scripture and the preached form in church proclamation. So Barth's 'prolegomena' describe what might be called the 'grammar' of Christian faith as Trinitarian, and some commentators have found this a helpful key to his theology (see for example Jüngel, [1966] 1976).

Volume II is on the doctrine of God. Volume II/1 treats the knowledge of God, the main emphasis being on God's initiative in revealing himself, which yet does not do away with God's hiddenness or allow one to presume on the revelation – it must be constantly given afresh in life before God. Then Barth treats the reality of God. His main description of the being of God is as 'the one who loves in freedom', a transposing of the traditional language of being, substance, essence and transcendence into the 'actualist' concept of free loving, given biblical content. There is then an exposition of the 'perfections of the divine loving' (grace, holiness, mercy, righteousness, patience and wisdom) and the 'perfections of the divine freedom' (unity, omnipresence, constancy, omnipotence, eternity and glory). Volume II/2 is on the election of God (Barth's preferred term for predestination). Barth transforms the doctrine of his own Calvinist tradition about 'double predestination' (some to heaven, some to hell) by centring both rejection and election in Jesus Christ, who takes all rejection on himself and also both elects all and is himself elected. There is no symmetry between election and rejection – the 'yes' of Jesus Christ has the last word, and there is hope even for the one whom the Bible seems to consign most decisively to rejection, Judas Iscariot. The election of Jesus Christ leads to the election of the community of Israel and the church, and only in that context is it right to talk about the election or rejection of the individual. Barth here ties salvation, and a universal hope for all, into the being of God who determines himself from all eternity through Jesus Christ. This volume concludes with the grounding of ethics in the doctrine of God (each major doctrine includes an ethics) and the relation of ethics to God's claim, decision and judgement.

Volume III is on the doctrine of creation. Volume III/1 is on God's work of creation, its goodness and the relation of creation to God's covenant. Volume III/2 is on human being. Jesus Christ is the 'real' human being and the criterion for true humanity. The main features of humanity are to be created for God; to be defined as a covenant partner of God in history and called to live for others; to be soul and body related to God through spirit; and to be temporal, with death as the created limit of historical existence and Jesus the one who has died and risen as Lord of time. Volume III/3 is on 'The Creator and His Creature' and covers

providence (a comprehensive affirmation of God's preserving, accompanying and ruling all that goes on); evil understood as an 'impossible possibility' which has no future; and heaven, angels and demons. Volume III/4 is the ethical section of the doctrine of creation. Its main theme is that God as Creator gives the freedom to live in gratitude before God (free on the sabbath, in confession and in prayer), with other people (freedom between man and woman, parents and children, near and distant neighbours), in respect for life (human and other) and in limitation.

Volume IV, on the doctrine of reconciliation, is the longest, and interweaves themes traditionally treated as Christology, sin, soteriology, pneumatology, ecclesiology, justification, sanctification and vocation. The final part, IV/4, is the ethical section and was only partially completed before Barth's death. The other three parts are together probably the crowning achievement of Barth's mature theology. The pattern of the three is the same. Each begins with the person and work of Jesus Christ (IV/1 – the Lord as servant, the judge who is judged in our place and who empties himself; IV/2 – the servant as Lord, the royal man who is raised up by God; IV/3 – Jesus as the true witness, the victor over all that opposes him, and the light of life). Next comes the treatment of the specific aspect of sin which is exposed by each aspect of Jesus Christ – pride resists accepting what God become man does for us; sloth refuses to take an active part in the new life given by Christ; falsehood, in cruder and subtler forms, resists, distorts and creates alternatives to the witness of Christ. Then comes the way of human salvation – justification by faith through which the Christian community is gathered (IV/1); sanctification in love, through which the community is built up (IV/2); and vocation in hope, which sends the community out as witnesses in word and life. The structure of IV/1, 2 and 3 provides a dynamic integration of themes that are often separated and the overall pattern is Trinitarian. Everything is oriented on the person of Jesus Christ, with his life, death and resurrection as the unsurpassable truth of reality, in time and eternity. 'In Barth's interpretation of reality, the life-history of one human being has taken the place held in the

West's traditional metaphysics by . . . the Ground of Being' (Jenson, 1989, p. 41).

Barth did not live to write any of the projected final Volume V on eschatology.

Interpretation and assessment

There are some characteristic modes of thought found throughout the *Church Dogmatics*, helpfully identified and discussed by Hunsinger (1991). Barth's 'actualism' sees being in terms of event and act. He gives such radical priority to God's activity that some critics find human activity and freedom devalued – he, on the contrary, refuses any competition between truly human and divine freedom, seeing them perfectly united yet distinct in Jesus Christ. His 'particularism' critically redefines all general theological conceptions in relation to Jesus Christ, a move criticized by those who give more important roles to other frameworks or criteria. His 'objectivism' sees revelation and salvation as given by God and valid quite apart from the subjective responses of human beings. This is questioned as regards how far it takes account of the importance of human response to God and whether its view of the sovereignty of God is compatible with the vulnerability of God in Jesus Christ. Barth's 'personalism' acts as a corrective to misinterpretations of his objectivism: God deals in fully personal terms with human beings, through personal address and the invitation to mutual love and covenant. This is seen by some as too anthropomorphic, to which Barth responds that God chooses human form through which to speak. What Hunsinger calls Barth's 'realism' points to the crucial status of theological language. He takes a middle way between literalism (a one-to-one correspondence between our language and God) and pure symbolism or expressivism (no real reference at all). It is an analogical understanding which emphasizes above all the primacy of God in enabling literally inadequate language about himself to convey truth. Barth takes a similar position on the historicity of the Gospel narratives: they are not necessarily literal history, nor are they myth or fiction; rather, they are sufficiently reliable testimony to unique events through whose canonical form God still witnesses to himself and salvation. Because of the great twentieth-century interest in both language and epistemology, Barth's realism in the above sense has aroused great controversy. Finally, there is Barth's 'rationalism', in line with his study of Anselm, which sees theological discussion as rational and cognitive and needing to have appropriate criteria internal to faith for interpretation, for truth claims and for the development of doctrines. This too has provoked deep disagreement from those with different views of rationality or with less cognitive views of faith and theology.

Barth himself was suspicious of the value of too much concentration on discussing such modes of thought or on other second-order or methodological discourse in theology. He was eclectic among conceptualities and above all concerned to grapple with the content of the major questions and to portray Christian truth, however it might be justified in other terms. His major contributions are probably in the lively restatement and development of such vital topics as: the Trinity; the priority, freedom and love of God; Chalcedonian Christology in dynamic relation with sin, salvation, the Holy Spirit and church life and mission; ethics in relation to all the doctrines; the dignity of humanity seen through Jesus Christ; and the role of Scripture in Christian life and thought. Because of the scale of the issues and of Barth's treatment of them the critiques of his thought cannot be summarized briefly but must usually take the form of developing alternative accounts of the same matters, incorporating nuanced and often comprehensive critique of Barth (for instance the major works of Rudolf Bultmann, Paul Tillich, Hans Urs von Balthasar, Hans Küng, Jürgen Moltmann, Wolfhart Pannenberg, Eberhard Jüngel and many theologians from beyond continental Europe). The primary task of Christian self-description did also lead him into numerous discussions with other theologies, philosophies, world views and disciplines, as well as discussions of current events in church and society, but he avoids any systematic integration of such material, and in particular he resists marrying Christianity to any autonomous quest for ultimate meaning.

See also CHRISTOLOGY; GOD; PROTESTANT THEOLOGY: GERMANY.

Bibliography

Writings

[1922, revised edn] 1968: *The Epistle to the Romans*, trans. London and Oxford: Oxford University Press.

[1931] 1960: *Anselm: Fides quaerens intellectum*. London: SCM Press; Richmond, Va.: John Knox Press.

[1932–68] 1956–75: *Church Dogmatics*, trans. G. Bromiley *et al.* Edinburgh: T & T Clark.

[1952] 1972: *Protestant Theology in the Nineteenth Century*, trans. London: SCM Press; Valley Forge: Judson Press.

[1957] 1961: *The Humanity of God*, trans. London: Collins; Richmond, Va.: John Knox Press.

[1963] 1979: *Evangelical Theology*. London: Weidenfeld and Nicholson.

Critical works

Balthasar, Hans Urs von [1951] 1972: *The Theology of Karl Barth*, trans. New York: Doubleday-Anchor.

Berkouwer, G.C. [1954] 1956: *The Triumph of Grace in the Theology of Karl Barth*, trans. Grand Rapids: Eerdmans.

Busch, E. [1975] 1976: *Karl Barth. His Life from Letters and Autobiographical Texts*, trans. London: SCM Press; Philadelphia: Fortress.

Hunsinger, G. 1991: *How to Read Karl Barth. The Shape of his Theology*. New York and Oxford: Oxford University Press.

Jenson, R. 1989: Karl Barth. In *The Modern Theologians*, vol. 1, ed. David F. Ford. Oxford and New York: Blackwell, pp. 23–49.

Jüngel, E. [1966] 1976: *The Doctrine of the Trinity: God's Being is in Becoming*, trans. Grand Rapids: Eerdmans.

Jüngel, E. [1982] 1986: *Karl Barth, A Theological Legacy*, trans. Philadelphia: Westminster Press.

Sykes, S.W., ed. 1979: *Karl Barth: Studies of his Theological Method*. Oxford: Clarendon Press.

Torrance, T.F. 1962: *Karl Barth: An Introduction to his Early Theology, 1910–1931*. London: SCM Press.

DAVID FORD

Baur, Ferdinand Christian (1792–1860)

German Protestant theologian. For most of his life a professor of theology at Tübingen, he pioneered radical approaches to biblical criticism which anticipated later historical-critical methods, and he was the founder of the Tübingen school of New Testament criticism. He was influenced by the ideas of G.W.F. Hegel and F.D.E. Schleiermacher, and his students included Albrecht Ritschl and David Friedrich Strauss. In *Untersuchungen über die sogenannten Pastoralbriefe des Apostels Paulus* (1835), he applied Hegelian principles of thesis and antithesis (conflicting Gentile and Jewish parties within the early church) which produce a synthesis (the old Catholic church) in his interpretation of early church history. In *Paulus, der Apostel Jesu Christi* (1845, trans. 1873–5), he caused controversy by using his insights into early church conflicts to present the early church as radically divided, and to question the authorship of some epistles traditionally ascribed to Paul. He used similar historical and dialectical principles to explain the development of major Christian doctrines such as the Trinity and the atonement, and to trace the origins of the Gospel narratives. Among other works, he wrote a series of books on church history of the first three centuries.

Bibliography

Harris, H. 1975: *The Tübingen School*. Oxford.

Hodgson, P.C. 1966: *The Formation of Historical Theology: A Study of F.C. Baur*. New York.

Bengel, Johann Albrecht (1687–1752)

German Lutheran minister and theologian, best known for his critical edition of the New Testament (1734), which marked the beginning of modern textual criticism, and for his textual commentary on the New Testament, *Gnomon Novi Testamenti* (1742), which has been of lasting influence.

Bibliography

Burk, J.F.C. 1837: *A Memoir of the Life and Writings of Johann Albrecht Bengel*.

Krause, G., ed. 1977–: *Theologische Realenzyklopädie*, article on Bengel by M. Brecht. Berlin.

Berkhof, Hendrikus (b. 1914)

Dutch Reformed theologian and ecumenist; professor of systematic theology at the University of Leiden. His work in the area of dogmatics and the theology of history takes account of modernist philosophies and biblical-critical methods, whilst remaining rooted in traditional Reformed theology. His best-known work is his systematic theology, *Christian Faith* (trans. 1979); other works include *Christ the Meaning of History* (trans. 1966), and *The Doctrine of the Holy Spirit* (trans. 1964).

Berkhof, Louis (1873–1957) Dutch Reformed theologian. Born in the Netherlands, Berkhof went to the USA in 1882 and was ordained into the Christian Reformed church (originally Dutch speaking). His education included two years under B.B. Warfield and G. Vos at Princeton Seminary (1902–4). From 1906 to 1944 he taught systematic theology at Calvin Seminary in Grand Rapids, Michigan, where his robust and methodical Reformed theology influenced many future preachers. His best-known work is his *Systematic Theology* (1941), which remains an influential textbook; other works include *Principles of Biblical Interpretation* (1950).

Bibliography
Bratt, J.D. 1984: *Dutch Calvinism in Modern America*. Grand Rapids, Mi.
Wells, D.F., ed. 1985: *Reformed Theology in America*, article on Berkhof. Grand Rapids, Mi.

Berkouwer, Gerrit Cornelis (b. 1903) Dutch Reformed theologian; a professor of dogmatics in the Free University of Amsterdam. His theology is in the tradition of Abraham Kuyper and Herman Bavinck, and has as its primary concern the correlation between faith and revelation. He challenged the liberal tendency to prioritize the subjective – humanity's response of faith – over and above the objective – the divine initiative of self-revelation, which takes place primarily through the Spirit's interpretation to individual believers of the words of Scripture. Faith in itself is of no value: it is only significant in terms of its object, Jesus Christ; human knowledge is produced not merely by mental activity but by revelation. An authoritative and sympathetic critic of Karl Barth (in *Karl Barth*, 1936, and *The Triumph of Grace in the Theology of Karl Barth*, 1954, trans. 1956), he has also specialized in Roman Catholic dogma and was an observer at the Second Vatican Council; his works in this area include *Barthianisme en Katholicisme* (1940), *Conflict with Rome* (1948) and *The Second Vatican Council and the New Theology* (trans. 1965).

His major work is the eighteen-volume *Studies in Dogmatics* (trans. 1952–75).

Bibliography
Baker, A. 1964: *Berkouwer's Doctrine of Election*. Phillipsburg, NJ.
De Moore, J.C. 1980: *Towards a Biblically Theological Method: A Structural Analysis and a Further Elaboration of Dr G.C. Berkouwer's Hermeneutic-Dogmatic Method*. Kampen.
Hughes, P.E., ed. 1969: *Creative Minds in Contemporary Theology*, article on Berkouwer. Grand Rapids, Mi.

biblical criticism and interpretation 1: Old Testament

Biblical criticism

Biblical criticism is the application of rational methods of enquiry to the text of the Bible (Morgan, 1988). Virtually all of modern biblical study might reasonably be called critical, but it is customary to use the term 'biblical criticism' to refer to those rational procedures that are closest to the text itself, and to exclude Old Testament theology, biblical archaeology, and historical and sociological study of the world of the Old Testament. These disciplines draw on biblical criticism rather than forming part of it.

Biblical criticism proper comprises a number of procedures whose roots can be traced back to the Renaissance and Reformation. At the root of all modern biblical study lies *textual criticism*, pioneered by Erasmus (*c*. 1466–1536). Textual criticism (sometimes referred to as 'lower' criticism to distinguish it from the 'higher', that is, more speculative, types to be discussed later) is concerned with establishing the original form of the biblical text as it left the hands of its first scribes. It is perhaps the only form of rational study of the Bible that has almost never been controversial, and biblical scholars have practised it in a continuous line from the time of Erasmus to the present. More far-reaching issues were raised in the Old Testament commentaries of Martin Luther, who insisted on establishing the literal or natural sense of the text as against what medieval allegorization had made of it. This opened the way for noticing contradiction and unevennesses in the text, and modern criticism rightly claims Luther as its founder, even though it was not until the eighteenth century that such questions came again to the fore.

Other forms of criticism developed as part of the European ENLIGHTENMENT. In the sixteenth and seventeenth centuries rationalist and deist freethinkers, in Holland and especially in England (Reventlow, 1984), became interested in historical inconsistencies within the Bible, and in particular in details of the Pentateuch that pointed to someone other – and much later – than Moses as its author. By comparing the legislation in Deuteronomy with the account of the reformation instigated by King Josiah (2 Kgs 22–3), for example, Thomas Hobbes (1588–1679) was able to argue that Deuteronomy, not the whole Pentateuch, was the book found in the Temple in that king's reign; and also that it had been compiled only at that time, in the seventh century BC rather than in the time of Moses (perhaps thirteenth century). It is from this period that the association of criticism with scepticism derives, for such conclusions were felt by many to be irreverent, even blasphemous, even though the foundation on which they rested was purely rational and not in itself irreligious.

The prime task of criticism has continued to be to ask questions about origins: the origins of the biblical texts and of the materials from which they were formed. The task continues to be in principle religiously neutral, but attracts a hostile response from those who believe that the answers to such questions are part of the deposit of faith (for instance that God has revealed that Moses wrote the Pentateuch) and therefore that the quest for a solution by rational means betrays a religious scepticism. Sometimes this issues in proposals for a *post-critical* reading of the Bible, and we shall return to this under 'Biblical interpretation'.

Because of its concern for (historical) origins, 'biblical criticism' is now frequently replaced by the term 'the historical-critical method'. This writer considers the older term to be preferable, however, since criticism is a primarily literary rather than historical procedure, and it is not a method, but (at most) a group of methods or (better) a set of questions which critics put to the text. These questions have traditionally concerned three things: the literary development of texts; the pre-literary, oral developments that lie behind the texts; and the final process of editing or redaction by which the texts have reached their present form. Each type of question has been given one or more technical terms in the modern era (Barton, 1984). (For a defence of the term 'historical-critical method', see BIBLICAL CRITICISM AND INTERPRETATION 2: NEW TESTAMENT.)

Literary or source criticism This asks whether a given text forms a literary unity or is instead the product of several discrete 'sources' woven together. This is the oldest form of biblical criticism after textual criticism, and in the eighteenth and nineteenth centuries was often known as 'higher' criticism to differentiate it from the 'lower' criticism of the textual critics. Its earliest successes were in the analysis of the Pentateuch (Rogerson, 1984), culminating in the hypothesis put forward by Julius Wellhausen (1844–1918), according to which the Pentateuch had been compiled from four separate documents, J, E, D, and P. In modern times Wellhausen's hypothesis has been attacked from several sides. Some scholars have argued that it is wrong in detail: for example, that there were more source documents than Wellhausen supposed, or on the other hand that one or more of them never existed (the existence of E, the most fragmentary of the four, has often been questioned). Others have argued that source criticism is mistaken in principle. It has been said that ancient Israel was essentially an oral culture which did not work with paper and ink to the extent posited by Wellhausen, and that it is anachronistic to suppose a complex literary history for the Pentateuch. Others again have argued that the Pentateuch is essentially a unity though incorporating later additions (Whybray, 1987). While it cannot be said that the Wellhausen hypothesis has been dislodged, it clearly no longer occupies the unquestioned status it once had in Old Testament studies. In particular, many biblical scholars now share the view that it was wrongheaded in principle, not just mistaken in practice, and that source analysis is not a suitable tool for Old Testament study. It remains to be seen how far this conviction will prevail.

Form criticism One of the earliest forms of dissatisfaction with source criticism was felt by those who believed that – whether right or wrong on its own ground – it had deflected attention from another equally important aspect of the text: its pre-literary growth in the oral tradition of ancient Israel. Scholars such as Hermann Gunkel (1862–1932) argued that beneath the written text of the Bible oral genres could be discerned, and that by studying these we could discover a good deal about Israel in a time earlier than even the earliest of the Pentateuchal sources. His technique for enquiring into these pre-literate levels of the text came to be known as 'form history' (*Formgeschichte*) or 'form criticism' (Koch, 1969). Form criticism began as an approach to the legends underlying the stories in Genesis, and to the Psalms, but has since expanded to encompass every type of Old Testament literature.

One of the aims of form critics has been to identify the oral setting in which each genre was used (known in German as its *Sitz im Leben*). This has produced a great deal more information about the social life of ancient Israel than is available from a simple reading of the Old Testament. For example, a form-critical study of the Psalms suggests many conclusions about the worship of Israel, and may even make it possible to reconstruct festivals whose character is only dimly known from the historical books. Legal genres have also been studied, and the operation of the Israelite lawcourt reconstructed, at least in outline.

Closely related to form criticism is *traditio-historical criticism*, which may be called the form criticism of very large blocks of material. M. Noth and G. von Rad, its main exponents, sought to identify from the Pentateuch the earliest orally transmitted outlines of the history of Israel, and thereby to show what Israelites of the 'Judges' period believed about their own history. Von Rad did this by extracting a basic 'historical credo' from Deuteronomy 26, and arguing that it had formed the thread on which all the later, detailed stories had been strung (Rad, 1966). Noth thought more in terms of a number of 'blocks' of oral material, each centring on one particular incident or group of incidents: the promise to the patriarchs, the settlement in the land, etc. The (later) Pentateuch then represented the amalgamation of these originally separate and orally transmitted traditions into a continuous narrative work, presenting each tradition as though it were the common possession of all the tribes of Israel, when it had originally been the folk memory of only one small group (Noth, 1972). In recent years interest in traditio-historical criticism has waned, its theories being widely thought too speculative. But most scholars would continue to hold that there is indeed oral tradition underlying the Pentateuch, however difficult this is to reconstruct.

Redaction criticism If form and traditio-historical criticism deal with what underlies the present written text, redaction criticism is concerned with that text in its final form. Once it is conceded, with Wellhausen, that the Pentateuch is the result of weaving together originally discrete sources, it becomes reasonable to ask about the people who carried out the compilation. And the same is true, *mutatis mutandis*, of the compilers of the prophetic books, where again it is widely agreed that small units of material have been put together by a hand other than the prophet's own. Since it is to editors or 'redactors' that we owe the form the biblical books now have, one would expect criticism to be as concerned with their work as with their underlying sources. Redaction criticism accordingly asks what the redactor is saying by arranging his source material in this way rather than in some other. The term *composition criticism* is now sometimes used to describe the same set of questions; and when there is heavy emphasis on the redactor's use of sources to advocate a controversial message, *rhetorical criticism* may be the preferred term.

Like so many other methods, redaction criticism has been most successful in its application to the historical books. The observation that there is a common style throughout Joshua, Judges, Samuel and Kings wherever the editor is composing freely led to the hypothesis (developed especially by M. Noth (1981)) that these books constituted a 'Deuteronomistic history' of Israel. In this history the criteria by which kings and rulers were judged were taken from the Book of Deuteronomy. Studies of the J source in the Pentateuch have similarly shown that it is not a mere collection of miscellaneous material but represented, even before its incorporation into the finished Pentateuch, a sophisticated work. Its material has been carefully chosen to contribute to its overall presentation of the history of Israel as a history of divine mercy in the face of human sin.

Redaction criticism has a certain amount in common with newer 'literary' approaches to the Bible, in which there is little interest in either the underlying strata of the text or in questions of historicity, but an exclusive concentration on the literary technique of the biblical authors; but with this difference, that redaction critics continue to think of the text as composite and see the redactors' skill in the way they have woven pre-existing material together, not in producing an original work out of nothing. Redactors, that is to say, are not authors in the modern sense.

A 'critical' approach to the Bible, it should be noted, does not mean one that takes the findings of all or any of these 'criticisms' as self-evidently correct. They are merely the most significant examples of the directions in which scholars have been led by a concern to approach the text rationally. What makes them critical is their attention to the text itself rather than to traditional theories about it – from which it follows that it is equally possible to accept the findings of criticism itself in an 'uncritical' spirit. Asking critical questions about the text has in a sense to be done afresh in each generation, and in some measure by every reader for himself or herself. In so far as there are now 'traditions' of critical scholarship, these are to be seen on the analogy of traditions within the growth of science: corrigible theses on which there has arisen a consensus, not dogmas to which assent is required.

Biblical interpretation

Traditionally, biblical interpretation (sometimes also called 'exegesis') has been the attempt to find nourishment for the Christian life in the text of Scripture by applying appropriate techniques. In the Middle Ages this generally took the form of allegorizing the text so that it came to apply to aspects of the Christian's life, the doctrine of the church, and the progress of the individual soul. These types of interpretation settled eventually into the pattern of the 'fourfold sense' of Scripture – literal, moral, figurative, and anagogical (Smalley, 1941). The Reformers encouraged attention to the 'literal' sense, but this continued to mean the 'plain' sense of the text *for the Christian reader*, so that spiritual nourishment remained the first priority in exegesis.

A major shift in approaches to the interpretation of texts in general, and of the Bible in particular, came with the work of F.D.E. Schleiermacher (1768–1834). Schleiermacher argued that the interpretation of the Bible was only an example of the interpretation of texts in general, and that one should apply the same principles to one as to the other. In interpreting any text, he believed, there were three stages: understanding, exposition and application (Hirsch, 1976). To understand a text it is necessary to think oneself into the frame of mind of its author, and to think the author's thoughts after him or her. This means, above all, reading the text on its own terms and without reference to what one would like to be able to derive from it – in sharp contrast to the old medieval methods. The next step is to expound or explain the text for the benefit of others, paraphrasing it in one's own words and relating it to one's own categories of thought. Schleiermacher makes the wise and subtle observation that any exposition of a text becomes for others a text itself, and so is subject to the same need for sympathetic understanding and for restatement in *their* own terms. The task of exposition has to be done again and again, because the context of those who read biblical expositions is constantly changing. The third stage is application, in which the text is related to the concerns and interests of the modern reader. There are texts with which this third stage hardly arises – texts which are, as we say, of purely antiquarian interest; but for most literary texts and certainly for the Bible, the issue of their relevance to contemporary concerns will usually need to be addressed.

Whether consciously or unconsciously, most biblical scholars from the rise of biblical criticism till very recently embraced a theory of interpretation more or less like that of Schleiermacher. In biblical criticism, and especially in the three modes of it discussed above, there has been a clear determination to begin with the text on its own terms and to seek to understand it. Source criticism arises from the discovery that a given text cannot be understood because it is incoherent, and this results in the conclusion that it is composite – the amalgamation of several separately coherent texts to make one incoherent one. Form criticism argues that the text is more comprehensible if it is seen as in origin oral rather than written. Redaction criticism notes that certain details of the text make more sense if they are the work of an overall editor, whose intentions can be discerned by observing how he has changed the underlying text. In all three 'methods' the question of understanding is paramount. That which has been understood is then expounded to readers of articles and commentaries. Only after that does the question of the application of the text to modern life arise. This delay has been the cause of popular dissatisfaction with historical-critical method from its very beginning. Biblical scholars seldom succeed in applying the text to the circumstances of their own day, and when they do, their work is often judged to be inadequate. This may be part of the price for staying close to Schleiermacher's principles.

In recent years biblical interpretation has moved into what is sometimes called a 'postcritical' phase. In this the heritage of Schleiermacher is largely abandoned and there is a return to some features of 'pre-critical' exegesis. Correspondingly, the traditional methods of biblical criticism are also cast aside in favour of newer methods. The post-critical movement has a secular and a religious wing, but the two are in close contact.

During the 1980s there developed an influential school of secular *literary interpretation* of the Bible, whose main watchword is 'the final form'. Historical questions about the origin and growth of the Bible are consciously rejected, and attention is focused instead on the text exactly as it is. The meaning of the text, it is argued, is not the result of the intentions of the author or compilers, but is generated by the shape of the text itself in the form that now lies before us. This is the point of view adopted, for example, in the influential *Literary Guide to the Bible* (Alter and Kermode, 1987 and Alter, 1981; cf. Wright, 1988) and in other works by its contributors. One cannot call such 'holistic' readings of the Bible pre-critical, for they are certainly not unaware of the problems of the genesis of the biblical text, and their concern is not to nourish the Christian soul. On the contrary, they are normally accompanied by disclaimers of any religious intention or even interest in the exposition of Scripture. Never-

theless, the quest for literary unity and aesthetic satisfaction in the finished texts occupies to some extent the same place as the quest for edification in pre-critical methods. In Schleiermacher's terms, the order of interpretation is no longer understanding–exposition–application, but application–exposition–understanding. The text has first to be appropriated by the modern literary reader; only then can it be properly expounded; and only through its successful exposition is it properly comprehended.

This reversal can be seen still more clearly in various kinds of 'committed' exegesis which form part of the 'religious' wing of holistic exegesis. In *feminist* readings of the Old Testament (for instance Trible, 1984) (see FEMINIST THEOLOGY), and in those based on LIBERATION THEOLOGY, it is normal to deny quite explicitly that the kind of value-neutral, unprejudiced reading implied by Schleiermacher as the first stage in interpretation can ever occur. Everyone (and many 'literary' critics would agree with this) starts from some standpoint; the attempt to be neutral means only that one shuts one's eyes to the fact of one's own prejudices. Far better to become aware of one's own point of view and make sure that it is a correct one. Feminism and liberation theology, which are structurally very similar, hold that one can understand the Bible aright only if one begins from a position of self-identification with the oppressed (women and/or the poor) and interprets texts in the light of that commitment. By so doing one can be led to expound the text in a way which is encouraging to the oppressed and challenging to their oppressors; and in offering such expositions one will come truly to see what the text means. This again stands Schleiermacher on his head, and has a good claim to be thoroughly post-critical.

In the 1970s the ideas of *literary structuralism* (see Barton, 1984) were frequently applied to the study of the Old Testament (see POSTMODERNISM). This movement stressed that the meaning of a text is inherent in its internal structures, particularly in contrasts within in. It seemed in many ways specially well suited to the study of the Bible, so many of whose books are anonymous and multi-authored – especially the narrative portions which make up about half of the Old Testament. Books in biblical studies written in this phase of interpretation

39

generally stressed features such as chiasmus and inclusio as means by which the text has acquired its present shape. At present structuralism has given way to various varieties of *poststructuralism* (Culler, 1981). *Deconstruction* challenges the integrity of all texts and all authors by asking questions such as whose interests are served by a given text and how it comes to be perceived as convincing, moving, challenging, and so on. In *reader-response criticism* it is argued that meaning is not generated even by the text as such (let alone by the author) but by the interaction between text and reader. Both these successors to structuralism have claimed the interest of biblical scholars, being practised especially in the pages of the American journal *Semeia*. They often seem to be popular with biblical scholars whose stance on questions of biblical authority is somewhat conservative. This may be because, unlike conventional biblical criticism, they do not require the critic to fragment the text or get beneath its surface: on the contrary, they defend its precise existing form as that which generates the meaning the student should be looking for.

Indeed, there are holistic readings which derive from purely theological considerations – though in the nature of the case they are close to secular holistic study in practice and therefore often make common cause with it. The movement known as *canonical criticism* developed in two parallel strands during the 1970s and 1980s. One strand was historically orientated. J.A. Sanders argued (Sanders, 1972) that the subject matter for biblical study should not be the putative earlier stages in the biblical text, but the process by which these stages gradually developed into the finished form we now have. The authority of the biblical text lies in the tradition-process, not in textual fixity.

The other branch of the movement was put forward by B.S. Childs, who argued (Childs, 1979) on the contrary that it was the final form of the text which was the text 'canonized' by Jews and Christians, and that this, therefore, should be the stuff of Christian theological interpretation. Furthermore, each biblical book must be interpreted as part of the whole canon, not in isolation; for the church and the synagogue never intended that books should be taken out of their canonical context and interpreted so that they could seem at variance with each other. Neither branch of canonical criticism seems to have been widely accepted in its full form (cf. Barr, 1983), but they have helped to contribute to a post-critical climate in modern biblical studies. It is no longer unusual to find scholars defending the complete forms of biblical books as the basis for exegesis (for example, the whole book of Isaiah instead of only Proto-, Deutero- or Trito-Isaiah), or talking about the meaning of the whole Bible. In this biblical specialists are joining hands with secular literary critics who have long felt that conventional biblical criticism was too prone to ignore the form of the text as it lies before us, and to go off on flights of fancy in quest of the 'original'.

Post-critical interpretation can also be seen at work in some of those who have been pursuing NARRATIVE THEOLOGY. In this kind of theology a traditional theological concern for metaphysics is replaced with an interest in 'story': theological truth emerges not from philosophical analysis but from narration. Such a theology obviously has natural affinities with the Old Testament, half of which is narrative. Narrative theology has had a concern not to dig beneath human narratives to find out 'what really happened', but to stress that what matters is the story as believed in and recorded by generations of believers. It will be seen that applying this model to the Old Testament again produces an emphasis on the final form rather than on hypothetical underlying sources.

The future of biblical interpretation seems likely for some time to come to run on divergent tracks. In Anglo-American criticism holistic reading is in the ascendant, and this tends to produce post-critical interpretations which have some things in common with pre-critical approaches. In the German-speaking world, on the other hand, though holism is not without its advocates (for instance, R. Rendtorff, 1985), for the most part traditional criticism continues to be the norm. It will be interesting to see whether any way will now be found of recombining the two approaches, or whether the divergence turns into a complete divorce.

See also LIBERALISM: BRITAIN; LITERATURE AND THEOLOGY; METHOD IN THEOLOGY; PROTESTANT THEOLOGY (GERMANY and NETHERLANDS).

Bibliography
Alter, R. 1981: *The Art of Biblical Narrative*. London

and Sydney: George Allen and Unwin.

Alter, R., and Kermode, F., eds 1987: *The Literary Guide to the Bible*. London: Collins.

Barr, J. 1983: *Holy Scripture: Canon, Authority, Criticism*. Oxford: Oxford University Press.

Barton, J. 1984: *Reading the Old Testament: Method in Biblical Study*. London: Darton, Longman and Todd.

Childs, B.S. 1979: *Introduction to the Old Testament as Scripture*. Philadelphia: Fortress Press.

Culler, J. 1981: *The Pursuit of Signs: Semiotics, Literature, Deconstruction*. London: Routledge and Kegan Paul.

Hirsch, E.D. 1976: *The Aims of Interpretation*. Chicago and London: University of Chicago Press.

Koch, K. 1969: *The Growth of the Biblical Tradition*. London: A & C Black.

Morgan, R., with Barton, J. 1988: *Biblical Interpretation*. Oxford: Oxford University Press.

Noth, M. 1972: *A History of Pentateuchal Traditions*. Englewood Cliffs: Prentice-Hall.

Noth, M. 1981: *The Deuteronomistic History*. Sheffield: JSOT Press.

Rad, G. von 1966: The problem of the Hexateuch. In *The Problem of the Hexateuch and Other Essays*. London and Edinburgh: Oliver and Boyd.

Rendtorff, R. 1985: *The Old Testament: An Introduction*. London: SCM Press.

Reventlow, H. 1984: *The Authority of the Bible and the Rise of the Modern World*. London: SCM Press.

Rogerson, J.W. 1984: *Old Testament Criticism in the Nineteenth Century: England and Germany*. London: SPCK.

Sanders, J.A. 1972: *Torah and Canon*. Philadelphia: Fortress Press.

Smalley, B. 1941: *The Study of the Bible in the Middle Ages*. Oxford: Blackwell.

Trible, P. 1984: *Texts of Terror*. Philadelphia: Fortress Press.

Whybray, R.N. 1987: *The Making of the Pentateuch: A Methodological Study*. Sheffield: JSOT Press.

Wright, T. 1988: *Theology and Literature*. Oxford: Blackwell.

JOHN BARTON

biblical criticism and interpretation 2: New Testament 'Modern' New Testament interpretation is mainly associated with the interpretative paradigm known as the 'historical-critical method'. Biblical interpretation of a more traditional type has of course persisted in church contexts, and the increasingly interdisciplinary nature of contemporary biblical studies is leading many scholars to question the almost exclusively historical orientation of their discipline. Nevertheless, although it is possible to point to serious weaknesses in the way that the historical-critical approach has often been pursued, it is very unlikely that it will simply be abandoned in favour of more literary-critical or theological approaches. The case against it has so far not been strong enough to justify such a drastic solution, and, as a living and developing interpretative tradition, it has often shown that it is capable of responding to criticism and modifying its practice accordingly. (The article on BIBLICAL CRITICISM AND INTERPRETATION 1: OLD TESTAMENT gives a résumé of methods of criticism; in doing so, it also argues the case for an alternative term to 'historical-critical method'.)

Although the historical-critical method is not a monolithic entity susceptible to precise definition, the following recurrent characteristics can be identified.

1 The main emphasis falls upon reconstructing the sense of the text within its initial historical context. This involves procedures both internal and external to the text: by means of textual criticism, exegesis and historical reconstruction one attempts to recover the wording, the meaning, and the context of the original document, and by means of comparative study of other related texts (canonical and non-canonical) one tries to reassemble the horizons within which the text originally 'made sense'. The continuing prestige of the commentary, among the various genres of scholarly writing, is a sign of the importance still attached to the close study of individual canonical texts. This is one of a number of points of contact with 'pre-critical' approaches.

2 The New Testament texts can also be treated not as objects for study in their own right but as historical evidence for reconstructing the development of earliest Christianity. Here too, the canonical texts must be supplemented by non-canonical ones. It is perhaps at this point that biblical scholarship comes closest to secular historiography, which is likewise interested in reconstructing relatively unified, coherent historical processes out of the fragmentary surviving evidence. Yet the critical significance of Christian origins for Christian thought and reflection also influences the presentation here, as, for example, in the assumption that what is 'early' is of higher

value than what is 'late' by virtue of its greater proximity to the moment of origin. One of the problems with this type of work (and, to a lesser extent, with the exegetical work described above) is the fact that one is constantly forced into speculation by the shortage of satisfactory evidence; this is the fundamental reason for the competing hypotheses that accompany virtually every major issue in early Christian history. The scepticism that this engenders in the outsider should be balanced by the participant's conviction that, at least at certain points, genuine clarifications are being made and real progress achieved. In addition, willingness to suspend judgement in the face of uncertainty is a mark of any responsible historiography.

3   These interrelated exegetical and historical tasks constantly find themselves in conflict with tradition. Church tradition was by no means indifferent to many of the matters with which historical criticism occupied itself; it held clear views on matters such as authorship, historicity, the limits of dissent between different biblical writing, and the relation of text to doctrine. The historical-critical approach tends to distrust the pronouncements of tradition on such issues, and the advances it claims for itself have often occurred when inherited traditional presuppositions are questioned and more plausible alternative positions affirmed. It is this dissenting, often iconoclastic tendency within the discipline which has in some quarters given it a reputation for being 'destructive'. Thus attempts are constantly made to subvert its challenge by offering new arguments for 'conservative' views, or by claiming that it is based on presuppositions of its own which are at least as questionable as those it opposes. Within the standard theological curriculum, New Testament studies is the discipline in which the tension between tradition and modernity is most sharply felt (see LIBERALISM: BRITAIN).

4   This inescapable tension with traditional belief is one of the factors that lead many biblical scholars to seek a secular, humanistic basis for their discipline outside the spheres of church and Christian theology, and the fact that most biblical research is undertaken within the secular modern university provides institutional support for this move. Here, it is said, it is possible to carry out 'objective', 'purely

historical' research, free from the partisan pressures that a church setting may still impose. While the notion of an absolute, presuppositionless objectivity has been often and rightly criticized, the term 'objectivity' retains its value in designating an approach which has secured a measure of freedom from specific institutional pressures – that is, from certain forms of censorship. Without the social space represented by the claim to 'objectivity', it would be impossible for scholars and students of widely differing beliefs and commitments to engage in the interpretative debate.

5   Nevertheless, the secularity of modern New Testament studies should not be exaggerated. The demand that historical-critical results should be made 'relevant' to contemporary Christian preaching and practice is widely felt to be a legitimate one, and New Testament scholars with no sense of commitment to the church are a minority. Despite the alleged 'gap' between biblical studies and systematic theology, the relationship between the two disciplines has historically been a close and complex one. On the one hand, there are very few modern theologians who are not deeply indebted to the findings of historical criticism, even though their primary interests may lie elsewhere; on the other hand, theological interests have often provoked new ways of pursuing historical-critical enquiry. Where biblical scholars criticize theologically motivated 'distortions' of historical realities, their criticism is not normally directed against theology as such and may well complement the self-criticism internal to systematic theology. It is true, however, that the two disciplines are incommensurable in the sense that the one tends to bracket out and make private the scholar's beliefs and commitments in a way that is unacceptable within the other, with its greater sense of responsibility towards ongoing Christian tradition. It is this structural feature that can make dialogue between the disciplines difficult.

Following this rather formal depiction of modern New Testament scholarship within its institutional context, we turn next to a delineation of some of the specific issues that, for various reasons, have acquired particular significance and still constitute a claim to permanent, irreversible achievement.

The quest of the historical Jesus

In reaction against the CHRISTOLOGY inherited from the early church, the historical-critical approach has sought to rehabilitate the humanity of Jesus of Nazareth; not just the physical fact of his humanity, which is after all affirmed in every orthodox Christology, but its specific historical and cultural contours. Historically, an important influence on the QUEST OF THE HISTORICAL JESUS was the Christology of Socinianism, with its exemplarism and its rejection of the orthodox doctrines of the Trinity, the incarnation, and the atonement. A work such as John Locke's *The Reasonableness of Christianity* of 1695 indicates how easily such doctrines can simply be ignored, under Socinian influence, and Jesus presented as an ethical teacher whose role is to remind humanity of the natural morality it has forgotten, all in the context of an apologetic defence of the Christian faith. However, the somewhat narrow rationalism of such works does not fully explain the sense of theological excitement with which the quest was undertaken during its late-eighteenth- and nineteenth-century heyday, when it commanded far wider public interest than its modern counterpart. It was held that contemporary challenges to the credibility of Christian faith could be met if the Protestant differentiation of the authentic origin from inauthentic church tradition were to be more radically pursued, that is, relocated within the New Testament itself. From a very early date – and especially in Paul – we find the beginnings of the dogmatizing tendencies that eventually issued in the imposing but now problematic structures of orthodoxy. But 'from the beginning it was not so', and (at least for the Protestant Christian) it is precisely the beginning that really counts, establishing the criteria by means of which subsequent developments are to be judged. As J.G. Herder wrote in 1796, 'Whoever contributes to bringing back the religion of Jesus from a meretricious slavery and from a painfully pious Lord-Lording to that genuine gospel of friendship and brotherliness, of convinced, spontaneous, free, glad participation in the work and intent of Jesus as they are clearly set forth in the Gospels – he himself has taken part in Christ's work and has advanced it' (quoted in Kümmel, 1973, p. 83). Albert Schweitzer speaks in a well-known passage of the quest of the historical Jesus as 'loos[ing] the bands by which he had been riveted for centuries to the stony rocks of ecclesiastical doctrine, and rejoic[ing] to see life and movement coming into the figure once more' (Schweitzer, [1906] 1954, p. 397).

It is customary to regard Schweitzer and Rudolf Bultmann as responsible for bringing the 'quest' in its nineteenth-century form to an end, the one by pointing to the historical distortions created by modern theological concerns, the other by scepticism about the historical trustworthiness and the theological significance of the gospel material. The earlier project is then distinguished sharply from the 'new quest of the historical Jesus' undertaken by a group of German scholars in the 1950s and 1960s, less sceptical than Bultmann but still influenced by his existentialist hermeneutic. This widespread representation of scholarly history is, however, far too schematic, and the continuities between the modern study of the historical Jesus and its nineteenth-century precursors are at least as strong as the discontinuities. One should therefore speak of a single 'quest', and acknowledge its crucial influence on most types of modern Christology even where 'ecclesiastical doctrine' has not been perceived merely as 'stony rocks'. Within New Testament studies, the theological impulses that have always accompanied the historical questions are still present today when work on the historical Jesus is undertaken from within a perspective oriented towards liberation, feminism, or the reassessment of Christian–Jewish relations.

The Jesus Christ of church doctrine

The expression 'the historical Jesus' indicates a willingness to differentiate this figure where necessary from the Christ of the church's faith, even though the latter also has deep roots within the New Testament. The problem of 'the so-called historical Jesus and the historic, biblical Christ' (M. Kähler) was sharply posed by H.S. Reimarus in a posthumous essay on the intention of Jesus published by Lessing in 1778 (Reimarus, [1778] 1970). Reimarus argued that central Christian doctrines about Jesus – notably his atoning death and his resurrection – were invented by the disciples after the hopes expressed in Jesus' nationalistic and this-worldly eschatological preaching were abruptly shattered by his crucifixion. Although Reimarus's deistic presuppositions (see DEISM) would soon come to seem outdated, many of the problems that he raised could not be dismissed so quickly. How was it, for example, that 'the proclaimer became the proclaimed' (R. Bultmann)? Jesus preached that the kingdom of God was at hand (Mark 1: 15); the early church preached that Christ died for our sins and was raised on the third day, in accordance with the Scriptures (1 Cor. 15: 3–5). Did Jesus understand himself as 'the Messiah', whose death and resurrection were announced beforehand in Holy Scripture, or are these beliefs the product of the early church? Contemporary scholarship inclines towards the latter, more sceptical view, and finds confirmation for this position in the modern tendency to question whether Jesus used the phrase 'son of man' in a messianic sense.

The distinction between Jesus' preaching and early Christian belief is one of the New Testament scholar's most important hermeneutical instruments, and the theological assessment of the results attained by this means have been very varied: some have welcomed the new opportunities thus provided for the critical reassessment of TRADITION, whereas others have denied the theological legitimacy of an appeal to a 'so-called' historical Jesus other than the one Jesus Christ of Christian faith. Contemporary restatements of the latter position tend to stress the authority for the church of the Gospel texts in their final form (Frei, 1974), and to differentiate rather sharply between the tasks of the historian and of the theologian. The aim is to present the historian as a secular and somewhat marginal figure whose results must be relativized or even set aside within the context of Christian faith. Ultimately what is at stake here is the question of the nature of theology as a discipline: whether it is hermetically sealed from serious interaction with neighbouring disciplines, or whether interaction and dialogue are essential to its existence and development.

The kingdom of God

Turning now to the content of Jesus' preaching, it has proved something of an embarrassment that, although agreement about the centrality for Jesus of 'the kingdom of God' (see KINGDOM OF GOD: NEW TESTAMENT) is virtually universal, it has been difficult to determine exactly what this phrase meant for him. Over and against tendencies to find its referent in the ethical community founded by Jesus (Albrecht Ritschl) or in individual religious experience (W. Herrmann, Adolf von Harnack), Johannes Weiss asserted in 1892 'the completely apocalyptic and eschatological character of Jesus' idea of the kingdom' (Weiss, [1892] 1971, p. 56), in the belief that this creates an unbridgeable gap between the preaching of Jesus and responsible modern Christian preaching. (It is ironic that a discovery which was supposed to constitute such a severe problem for theology turned into one of the most productive of modern theological insights, occasioning the positive reinterpretations of ESCHATOLOGY associated with theological existentialism, the 'theology of hope', and liberation theology.) Yet although this suggestion marked a clear advance, it was unable to account satisfactorily for the sayings in which Jesus appears to speak of the kingdom as already present. As C.H. Dodd showed (1935), a great deal in Jesus' teaching becomes clear on the assumption that he spoke of the eschatological era proclaimed by the Old Testament prophets as already having arrived. Much of the subsequent discussion has therefore been devoted to attempts to reconcile the present and the future dimensions of the kingdom, and, while there is widespread agreement that Weiss and Dodd are both one-sided, clarity on this issue has not been attained.

One possibility, put forward by N. Perrin in *Jesus and the Language of the Kingdom*, is that 'the kingdom of God' is not a unitary concept but a symbol whose meaning 'is not exhausted by any one apprehension of the reality it represents' (Perrin, 1976, p. 43). The fact that much of Jesus' language about the kingdom occurs in the comparatively open-ended literary form of the parable may lend some support to this suggestion. Another possibility, exploited by a number of liberation theologians, would be to stress the this-worldly, millenarian character of the future hope. If both present and future sayings refer to the divine action on a single plane, so that we no longer have to distinguish the historical from the supra-historical realm, then a unitary understanding of 'the kingdom of God' may still be possible. The kingdom of God is realized wherever – as in the ministry of Jesus – injustice and the social barriers it creates are overcome, in anticipation of the eschatological goal of full, unbroken human community. Yet the enigma still remains of a Jesus who can teach his disciples to pray, 'Thy kingdom come', but can also state that 'the kingdom of God *has* come upon you' (Luke 11: 2, 20). This problem may be seen as symptomatic of a difficulty inherent in the whole enterprise of recovering the Jesus of history: again and again, the quest for the origin fails to attain what it seeks, an initial moment of clarity and transparency which can then be played off against subsequent ambiguities and distortions. However 'authentic' certain aspects of the synoptic tradition may be, the need for interpretation always remains.

Differences between the Gospel texts
The quest of the historical Jesus reached its reinterpretation of the figure to whom the Gospel texts point only by way of a new approach to the texts themselves. Emblematic of this new approach is the shift from the Harmony to the Synopsis as the indispensable tool for scholarly study of the Gospels, signalled by J.J. Griesbach's *Synopsis* of 1776. For the Harmony, the fourfoldness of the Gospels is a problem and the aim is to minimize differences to such an extent that the canonical collection approximates as closely as possible to a single text. The Synopsis shares this preoccupation with differences, but now assesses them positively rather than negatively, finding in them the path to historically and theologically relevant knowledge. Henceforth progress will occur by way of comparison rather than harmonization.

First, attention is focused on the agreements and disagreements between the first three Gospels and on the search for a genetic explanation of these phenomena. Griesbach's suggestion that Mark used not only Matthew (as in the traditional explanation) but also Luke ultimately proved unconvincing, but more significant than this failure is the fact that the whole issue of synoptic relationships was now regarded as of crucial significance. The initial period of experimentation with different hypotheses came to an end with the gradual victory of the classical 'two source' hypothesis

during the second half of the nineteenth century, and for most contemporary New Testament scholars this hypothesis, postulating the priority of Mark and 'Q', still makes more sense than its rivals of the problems that arise out of detailed exegesis. The contemporary desire to interpret each Gospel 'as a whole' raises the hermeneutical question of the possibility of an exegesis independent of source criticism, but it does not seriously challenge the propriety of source criticism as such.

Second, agreements and disagreements may be assessed not only for the information they provide about synoptic origins but also for the insights that they give into the theological concerns of the individual evangelists. If Matthew and Luke have used Mark, then comparison of the later with the earlier versions of stories or sayings will to some extent enable us to retrace the later evangelists' process of composition. Whereas in Mark the rich man addresses Jesus as 'Good teacher', eliciting the reply, 'Why do you call me good? No-one is good but God alone' (Mark 10: 17–18), Matthew replaces this with 'Teacher, what good deed . . . ?', to which the response is, 'Why do you ask me about what is good?' (Matt. 19: 16–17). Redaction criticism alerts one to the potential significance of this and hundreds of other apparently minor disagreements between the evangelists, and the overall effect is to sharpen one's sense of the individuality of each Gospel and of the irreducible fourfoldness of the canonical collection. There is also a reminder here that the tradition about Jesus reaches us by way of multiple interpretations, and not in pure, unmediated form.

Historicity
These reorientations make unavoidable the question of 'historicity'. Earlier discussion raised this question in connection with the RESURRECTION of Jesus. In the sixth of his *Discourses on the Miracles of our Saviour*, dating from 1729, Thomas Woolston argues that early Christian belief in Jesus' resurrection rests on the fraud to which Matthew 28: 11–15 inadvertently bears witness. Rebuttals such as Thomas Sherlock's *The Tryal of the Witnesses of the Resurrection of Jesus* of 1729 constructed 'evidence for the resurrection' so as to demonstrate the truth of that event and of the

Christian gospel as a whole. (This approach continues in popular apologetic, and even recurs, in slightly more sophisticated form, in Wolfhart Pannenberg's Christology.) Later deists such as Peter Annet and H.S. Reimarus pointed to the numerous discrepancies and contradictions in the resurrection narratives as evidence in favour of the fraud theory, in the process making a number of acute textual observations. It is important to note that, although general rationalist or empiricist theories about the impossibility of miracles undoubtedly played a major role in the increasingly sceptical climate, an equally important part was played by growing awareness of problems inherent in the texts.

D.F. Strauss's *Life of Jesus Critically Examined* ([1835] 1972) represents the single most important landmark in the process of critical questioning. Strauss dispenses entirely with all theories of fraud and deliberate deception, finding the origin of miracle stories in the beliefs and traditions of the culture that generated them. His demonstration of the legendary character of much of the Gospel material rests far less on the 'rationalist presuppositions' which conservative apologetic claims to identify than on painstaking exegetical enquiry. Subsequent historical-critical research into these stories has remained dependent on the methodology established by Strauss.

The problem of historicity affects not only narrative but also teaching material. It was again Strauss who pointed out the particular difficulty posed in this respect by the Gospel of John. If in early Christian preaching the proclaimer becomes the proclaimed, in the Gospel of John the proclaimer becomes the proclaimed *within his own proclamation*. The synoptic Jesus proclaims the kingdom of God as something other than himself, even if intimately related to himself; the Johannine Jesus proclaims himself as the bread of life, the light of the world, the good shepherd, the resurrection and the life, and the true vine. His disciples no longer follow him in the way (Mark 10: 32, 52), they must learn that he himself is the way (John 14: 6). While it is possible to overemphasize the difference between John and the synoptics, it remains impossible to avoid the conclusion that, if one is permitted to apply the criterion of historical reliability at all, John is considerably less

'reliable' than the synoptics. It is true that this apparently negative judgement does not do justice to the special character of the fourth Gospel, whose freedom stems from an understanding of the Spirit as leading the disciple into all the truth (John 16: 13); but it is also true that the Gospel's character as a free interpretation rather than factual report only becomes clear once the issue of historicity has been raised.

The same issue also affects modern discussion of the synoptic sayings tradition, which attempts to discriminate between material deriving from Jesus and from the early church, labelled 'authentic' and 'inauthentic' or 'secondary' respectively. (The terminology may perhaps be open to criticism, but the problem it designates still remains.) This discrimination has been practised quite successfully in some areas; in the case of the parables, for example, it is often possible to make provisional distinctions between later dogmatic developments and the original parable, although certainty in such matters is rarely possible. In other areas, however, consensus has proved hard to attain. Some would find the roots of this impasse in the still influential but perhaps excessive scepticism of Rudolf Bultmann, who in his *History of the Synoptic Tradition* ([1921] 1963) stressed the creative role of the early church. Others would claim that Bultmann was essentially correct and that the problem is inherent to the material.

New Testament authorship

The authorship of the various New Testament writings is an issue of some importance because of the close traditional connection between apostolicity and canonicity. The canon includes a few works which tradition does not ascribe to apostles (notably Mark and Luke/Acts), but even here a close relationship with individual apostles (Peter and Paul respectively) is postulated. Here as so often, the effect of the historical-critical approach has been to expose the fictions of tradition. The names 'Matthew', 'Mark', 'Luke' and 'John' all refer to historical individuals, but their links with the Gospels that bear their names are at best tenuous. Critical scholarship has also cast doubt on traditional views about the authorship of fourteen of the twenty-one New Testament letters, although in ten of these cases an individual author is explicitly named in the first verse. In the case of Revelation, the ascription to 'John' (1: 1, 4, 9 and so on) is generally accepted, but the identification with the apostle John, the traditional author of the Gospel and Epistles that bear his name, is rejected. Thus, only seven of the twenty-seven New Testament books retain the author assigned to them by tradition: that is, the seven certainly authentic letters of Paul – Romans, 1 and 2 Corinthians, Galatians, Philippians, 1 Thessalonians and Philemon. It is still possible to defend most of the traditional ascriptions of authorship, but those who do so are conscious of a minority status in the face of a widespread consensus.

This situation radically affects one's view of the New Testament canon. The origins of the canon are now found in the early church's deep desire for a body of texts deriving directly from authoritative apostolic origins at only one remove from Jesus Christ himself, resulting in the fiction that these texts do not proceed from the church's own midst but from a transcendent source. The effect of this is to place a critical question mark against every tendency to ascribe an undifferentiated and absolute authority to the New Testament canon.

The New Testament texts in historical context

The canon has the further effect of preserving texts that have become separated from the historical circumstances that originally brought them into being. It has been argued by Brevard Childs in his *The New Testament as Canon* (1984) that this separation is essential to their new canonical role. Nevertheless, the historical-critical tradition has assumed that the quest for the original meaning of the texts is worthwhile and that this will be furthered by critical reconstruction of their original historical setting. In the case of the Pauline letters, for example, we should understand these texts within the broader context of Paul's developing relationship with the various congregations. Each letter represents one side of a dialogue, and it is important to be able to deduce from incidental indications something of the nature of the situation Paul is addressing. (As recent work has shown, this applies even to Romans, apparently the most general of Paul's letters.) While it has always been recognized that Paul's letters are addressed to specific situations, it is

characteristic of the historical-critical method to seek to apply this insight as fully as possible to the exegesis of the text in question. In practice the results of this procedure are often speculative and open to criticism, but at best this type of critical reconstruction can restore a text to a plausible life setting within specific forms of human interaction.

It is often said that the effect of such reconstruction is to distance the canonical text from the present by binding it so firmly to its circumstances of origin; and the desire for an exegesis oriented towards contemporary actualization has been widely expressed, perhaps most notably in Karl Barth's commentary on Romans ([1922] 1933). Yet it may be that there are theological as well as historical reasons for rejecting Barth's claim that 'the differences between then and now, there and here . . . are, in fact, purely trivial' (p. 1). Paul himself sees authoritative written texts (*to gramma*, 2 Cor. 3: 6) as characteristic of the old covenant, whereas the new covenant is characterized by the presence of the Spirit. This relativization of all writing, including Paul's own, is safeguarded by a hermeneutic which insists on reading the texts through the filter of an original context that differs from our own.

The early Christians in historical context

Study of the broader social and cultural contexts within which early Christianity developed is also increasingly important for the historical-critical paradigm. It is no longer adequate to think in terms of the (Jewish or Hellenistic) 'background' to the New Testament, as though the early Christians' relationship to their own wider context was largely accidental and peripheral; the new challenge is to conceive of early Christianity as a movement *within* first-century Judaism and Hellenism in the light of ever increasing knowledge of this broader field. In the process, a number of well-known stereotypes have been subjected to severe criticism. Thus Martin Hengel's book *Judaism and Hellenism* (1974) challenged the assumption that 'Judaism' and 'Hellenism' designate two clear-cut and mutually exclusive entities, the one deriving largely from the Old Testament, the other from classical Greece. While the distinction is unavoidable, it passes too lightly over the fact that by the time of Jesus Palestine had been subjected to Hellenistic cultural influence for more than three centuries, an influence which even its opponents could not entirely escape.

E.P. Sanders, in his *Paul and Palestinian Judaism* (1977), rejects the biased and inaccurate view of Judaism that proceeds from an uncritical reading of the Pauline texts from within the Lutheran tradition. Neither the later rabbinic writings (which can in any case be used as evidence for first-century Judaism only with extreme caution) nor earlier texts such as the Dead Sea Scrolls and apocalyptic books fit the conventional view: that 'late Judaism' (*sic*) is a legalistic religion in which one attempts to earn salvation by obedience to a multiplicity of arbitrary regulations. On the contrary, early Judaism is best characterized by the phrase 'covenantal nomism', which points to the priority of God's covenant with the Jewish people for virtually every form of Jewish belief. A more accurate exegesis of the Pauline texts confirms these findings. In *Jesus and Judaism* (1985), Sanders extends his critique to the representation of Judaism as a mere 'background' intended to highlight the superiority of Jesus' teaching and practice, a contrast that issues in conflict and crucifixion. Historically, Jesus and the movement he founded must be located alongside other groups within first-century Judaism.

Another example of the contemporary quest for a more sophisticated grasp of context is Wayne Meeks's *The First Urban Christians* (1983), which argues that Pauline Christianity cannot be adequately understood apart from its social setting; significant topics include the shift from a rural to an urban context, the social level of Pauline Christians, existing models for the formation and structure of the *ekklesia*, and so on. Meeks criticizes the isolation of New Testament scholarship both from secular study of the Roman empire and from later church history, and ascribes this isolation to a 'retreat from critical history into theological positivism' (1983, p. 1). It would be a mistake, however, to conclude that studies such as this are theologically irrelevant and can be safely left to those who happen to be interested in history or sociology. On the contrary, they constitute a challenge to rethink theological positions in the light of new insights from related disciplines.

Narrative criticism

Another indication of the increasingly interdisciplinary nature of contemporary New Testament studies is to be seen in the development of a 'narrative criticism' (see NARRATIVE THEOLOGY) influenced by literary studies, and especially by the formalist analysis of texts in a purely intrinsic manner without reference to extrinsic matters such as their historical circumstances of origin. Yet narrative criticism is also a logical development out of redaction criticism, two of whose limitations it seeks to correct. First, redaction criticism directs its interest almost exclusively towards points of redactional intervention, and this prevents a proper grasp of a narrative text as a whole. Second, redaction criticism also undermines the integrity of the texts by subjecting them to the findings of source criticism. The Gospels are interpreted not on their own terms but in relation to their sources, and the texts are thereby bound to the (hypothetical) process by which they came into existence.

Thus Matthew 4: 18–22 shares with Mark 1: 16–20 the story of the call of the first disciples; the differences are only minor. In Mark, this story is the starting point of a highly problematic relationship. On the one hand, the disciples are appointed to be apostles (3: 14–19) and are given to know the secret of the kingdom of God (4: 11). On the other hand, their hearts are hardened and they neither see, hear, nor understand (6: 52; 8: 17–18). Even when Peter confesses Jesus as the Christ, his understanding is so flawed that he is immediately identified with Satan (8: 29–33). Mark does not even rule out the possibility that Peter's subsequent denial of Jesus and the flight of the other disciples is the end of the relationship, for 16: 8 makes it hard to see how the promise of reconciliation (14: 28; 16: 7) can be fulfilled. In Matthew, on the other hand, the pericope of the call of the disciples belongs within the context of a much more stable relationship. Jesus almost immediately begins the instruction of the disciples (5: 1–2), in preparation for their eventual role of teaching all nations to observe what he commanded (28: 19–20), and we find fewer and less harsh references to their failures. The same passage functions differently within different narrative wholes.

A second example of the kind of reorientation proposed by narrative criticism is taken from Mary Ann Tolbert's *Sowing the Gospel* (1989). It has long been customary to distinguish the 'authentic' parable of the sower (Mark 4: 3–9) from its 'secondary' interpretation (4: 14–20). If, however, we adopt a synchronic rather than a diachronic approach, the four types of ground in both parable and interpretation may be related to the different responses to Jesus narrated in the Gospel itself. The seeds sown along the path, which Satan snatches away, are to be identified with the scribes, Pharisees and Herodians who have already emerged as Jesus' most implacable opponents. Those who hear the word with joy but fall away in the face of persecution are the disciples. Herod (6: 14–29) and the rich man (10: 17–22) exemplify the seed choked by thorns – cares, riches, desires. Finally, the largely anonymous individuals who come to Jesus for help (including a number of women) represent the good soil which bears much fruit.

Narrative criticism is still at a fairly early stage in its development, but its synchronic approach is already bringing to light interpretative possibilities which the more traditional diachronic orientation has failed to notice.

Feminist criticism

Also at a comparatively undeveloped stage is feminist criticism and exegesis of the New Testament, a situation exacerbated by the very small number of women scholars working in New Testament studies. Nevertheless, the potential of this mode of criticism is indicated by a number of works, most notably Elisabeth Schüssler Fiorenza's *In Memory of Her* (1983). Unlike many feminist scholars in Old Testament studies, Schüssler Fiorenza still works mainly within the framework of historical criticism, although from an 'engaged' feminist perspective in which there is no pretence that the nature of one's results is a matter of indifference. Subtitled 'A Feminist Theological Reconstruction of Christian Origins', Schüssler Fiorenza's book presents the original Jesus movement as permitting and encouraging the equal discipleship of women, liberating them from patriarchal structures. This equality survived into the apostolic period, as is indicated by Galatians 3: 28 and other Pauline

evidence for women's full participation in the life of the church. However, the household code in Colossians, Ephesians, and 1 Peter points to the growing patriarchalization of the church, a tendency which reaches its climax in the pastoral epistles. Thus the Christian church abandoned and attempted to conceal its egalitarian origins, and it is the task of feminist exegesis to recover a heritage which was almost lost, and to offer an explanation and a critique of that act of forgetting, often perpetuated in modern male scholarship.

In the background of this discussion is the contemporary question whether the church and the Christian faith should be regarded as essentially and irredeemably patriarchal, or whether the authentic gospel offers a liberation from the structures of patriarchy. Over and against post-Christian feminists such as Mary Daly and Daphne Hampson, Christian feminist scholars claim that the latter is the case, without denying the magnitude of the problem posed not only by Christian tradition but also by the New Testament itself. Feminist sensitivity to issues of gender has implications for men as well as women, and it is possible that feminist exegesis might restore to New Testament studies a dimension of existential engagement that many complain is lacking at present. Such an exegesis would concern itself not only with the reconstruction of Christian origins, but also with the use of the New Testament texts in the past and the present both to justify and to criticize an overwhelmingly patriarchal church.

Although it can make effective use of historical-critical insights, feminist exegesis constitutes a challenge to the dominance of the historical-critical method in its insistence on the need for engagement, its concern with usage as well as original meaning, and its direct involvement with contemporary theological discussion. Along with literary modes of biblical interpretation, with which it can interact fruitfully, feminist exegesis is a welcome sign of a more pluralistic future for New Testament studies in which questions of origins are no longer the only proper scholarly pursuit. (See FEMINIST THEOLOGY.)

See also LITERATURE AND THEOLOGY; METHOD IN THEOLOGY; PROTESTANT THEOLOGY (GERMANY and NETHERLANDS).

Bibliography

Barth, K. [1922, 2nd, revised edition] 1933: *The Epistle to the Romans*, trans. E.C. Hoskyns. London: Oxford University Press.

Bultmann, R. [1921] 1963: *The History of the Synoptic Tradition*, trans. John Marsh. Oxford: Blackwell.

Childs, B.S. 1984: *The New Testament as Canon: An Introduction*. London: SCM Press.

Coggins, R.J., and Houlden, J.H., eds 1990: *A Dictionary of Biblical Interpretation*. London: SCM Press; Philadelphia: Trinity Press International.

Dodd, C.H. 1935: *The Parables of the Kingdom*. London: James Nisbet.

Drury, J., ed. 1989: *Critics of the Bible 1724–1873*. Cambridge: Cambridge University Press.

Frei, H.W. 1974: *The Eclipse of Biblical Narrative: A Study of Eighteenth and Nineteenth Century Hermeneutics*. New Haven and London: Yale University Press.

Hengel, M. 1974: *Judaism and Hellenism: Studies in their Encounter in Palestine during the Early Hellenistic Period*, 2 vols. London: SCM Press; Philadelphia: Fortress Press.

Kümmel, W.G. 1973: *The New Testament: The History of the Investigation of its Problems*. London: SCM Press.

Meeks, W.A. 1983: *The First Urban Christians: The Social World of the Apostle Paul*. New Haven and London: Yale University Press.

Moore, S.D. 1989: *Literary Criticism and the Gospels: The Theoretical Challenge*. New Haven and London: Yale University Press.

Morgan, R., with Barton, J. 1988: *Biblical Interpretation*. Oxford: Oxford University Press.

O'Neill, J.C. 1991: *The Bible's Authority: A Portrait Gallery of Thinkers from Lessing to Bultmann*. Edinburgh: T & T Clark.

Perrin, N. 1976: *Jesus and the Language of the Kingdom: Symbol and Metaphor in New Testament Interpretation*. Philadelphia: Fortress Press; London: SCM Press.

Räisänen, H. 1990: *Beyond New Testament Theology: A Story and a Programme*. London: SCM Press; Philadelphia: Trinity Press International.

Reimarus, H.S. [1778] 1970: *Fragments*, ed. C.H. Talbert. Philadelphia: Fortress Press; London: SCM Press.

Reventlow, H. von 1984: *The Authority of the Bible and the Rise of the Modern World*. London: SCM Press.

Sanders, E.P. 1977: *Paul and Palestinian Judaism: A Comparison of Patterns of Religion*. London: SCM Press.

Sanders, E.P. 1985: *Jesus and Judaism*. London: SCM Press.

Schüssler Fiorenza, E. 1983: *In Memory of Her: A Feminist Theological Reconstruction of Christian Origins*. London: SCM Press.

Schweitzer, A. [1906] 1954: *The Quest of the Historical Jesus: A Critical Study of its Progress from Reimarus to Wrede*. London: A & C Black.

Strauss, D.F. [1835] 1972: *The Life of Jesus Critically Examined*, ed. P.C. Hodgson. Philadelphia: Fortress Press; London, SCM Press.

Tannehill, R. 1986: *The Narrative Unity of Luke–Acts: A Literary Interpretation*. Vol 1, *The Gospel According to Luke*. Philadelphia: Fortress Press.

Tolbert, M.A. 1989: *Sowing the Gospel: Mark's World in Literary-Historical Perspective*. Minneapolis: University of Minnesota Press.

Weiss, J. [1892] 1971: *Jesus' Proclamation of the Kingdom of God*, ed. R.H. Hiers and D.L. Holland. Philadelphia: Fortress Press; London: SCM Press.

FRANCIS WATSON

biological science and Christian thought

Biological science has always had an intimate relation with theology. On design in nature, on analogous trends in biological and spiritual development, and above all on the nature of human life, each has had much to say to the other over a period of many centuries. These and other issues became invested with a new urgency and received a sharper focus in the nineteenth-century debates over evolution. Since then the Darwinian controversies have been extended in some circles to modern times, still colouring much twentieth-century thinking, but, taken on their original Victorian terms, they give a grotesquely distorted view of the total relationship between biology and theology. There is much more to this than merely questions of evolution versus Christianity.

The following account will summarize the issues in roughly the historical order of their appearance.

Natural theology

In NATURAL THEOLOGY living things were among the most obvious exemplars of the skill of the Creator. In 1691 John Ray's *The Wisdom of God manifested in the Works of Creation* considered (amongst other things) 'the admirable structure of the bodies of man, and other animals; as also in their generation, &c.', while William Derham's *Physico-Theology* of 1713 demonstrated 'the being and attributes of God' from the way the whole universe was constructed for the benefit of man (a common emphasis in classical natural theology). There was even a book entitled *Insecto-Theologia* (by F.C. Lesser, in 1738). Nor did such writing cease after Darwin, though natural theology had by then received a severe jolt. Biology furnished illustrations at a popular level, from E. C. Brewer's *Theology in Science* of 1860 to several chapters of *The Great Design* edited by Frances Mason (of 1932), and later variants. B. Boedder's *Natural Theology* of 1891 and F.H. Cleobury's *A Return to Natural Theology* of 1967 argue the case at a more philosophical level and tend to avoid specific examples; and with the possible exception of Pierre Teilhard de Chardin, natural theology has tended to move over the last century towards geological and (more recently) physical science. Finally, it may be noted that natural theology has been revived by the process theologians, as in C. Hartshorne's *A Natural Theology for our Time* of 1967 (see PROCESS THEOLOGY).

The challenge of evolution

When Charles Darwin published his *Origin of Species* in 1859 he unleashed upon the Victorian church a complex challenge at no less than five different levels. Because the arguments are still encountered today, and because the issues are of great theological importance, they will be briefly rehearsed here.

The authority of Scripture Biological evolution in all its forms requires millions of years and therefore an 'old earth'. Thanks to the geological work of Charles Lyell and many others the latter had become widely accepted in Darwin's era. Today the age of the earth is commonly given as around 4500 million years, and of life as around 3500 million years. Such data are totally at variance with a literal understanding of the six 'days' of the Genesis creation. For this reason, and on account of the question of the nature of man (see below), it was commonly assumed that biological science had undermined the whole authority of Scripture (S. Wilberforce, C. Perry and others). However it should be pointed out that:

1 The 'old earth' challenge came first from geological rather than biological science.
2 Objections to evolution on this basis were comparatively limited in the nineteenth century.

3 The issues of Scriptural exegesis raised by Darwin were precisely the same as those raised by Copernicus and Galileo and could be similarly settled by the concept of 'accommodation'.
4 Many evangelicals with their high view of biblical inspiration accepted a non-literal interpretation on exegetical grounds; thus several writers followed G.L.L. de Buffon in equating Genesis 'days' with immensely long periods of time, Thomas Chalmers proposed a gap between Genesis 1: 1 and 1: 2, and the geologist Hugh Miller suggested that they were days in which the writer received successive visions of creation (a view expanded recently (Wiseman, 1977)).
5 Concerted opposition to evolution on these grounds began with the 'fundamentalist' movement of the 1920s to 1930s (see FUNDAMENTALISM) and has been prolonged by its modern descendant, 'creationism'. Amongst evangelicals today evolution is accepted or tolerated more readily in Britain than the USA (in America the issues are further clouded by political considerations).

The nature of man The most obvious objections to evolution in Victorian times arose from a revulsion at the prospect of kinship with 'lower' animals. The question had been aired long before Darwin (by J.J. Rousseau, for example), though he gave it a new scientific focus. Much opposition arose from an innate sense of human dignity rather than for any specific theological reason (Lyell and many others). Also there was (and is) considerable discontinuity in the fossil record which disclosed numerous important 'missing links'. To retain something of the special character of mankind, A.R. Wallace in the nineteenth century denied that natural selection can account for man's higher faculties and invoked 'latent powers' in explanation. In the twentieth century Julian Huxley stressed human uniqueness and saw in evolution 'a trend towards sentience'. Many other non-theological attempts were made to modify evolutionary materialism to accommodate human self-valuation. Many years later Michael Polanyi was to declaim that 'it is the height of intellectual perversion to renounce, in the name of scientific objectivity, our position as the highest form of life on earth.'

In theological terms the doctrine of a special creation of humanity did seem clearly taught by Genesis, even though the language may have been mythological. The *Imago Dei* was retained as the fallacy of naive reductionism became clear ('man is *nothing but* an ape'), and the unity of body and soul was recovered from New Testament anthropology (see ANTHROPOLOGY, CHRISTIAN). As early as 1872 it could be stated that the application of Darwinism to 'man's physical structure' was 'a matter of supreme indifference to Christianity' (E.O. Haven), while Charles Kingsley warned against importing into Scripture 'our own human theories or prejudices' since in Genesis 'the means, the How of creation, is nowhere specified'.

Man in society Historically it was at this level that evolution appeared to be most dangerous for the Victorian church. Writing in the aftermath of Robert Chambers's anonymously published *Vestiges of the Natural History of Creation* of 1844 (a pre-Darwinian manifesto for evolution), the geologist Adam Sedgwick condemned the work as 'rank, unbending, and degrading materialism' because it has 'annulled all distinction between physical and moral' (1845). Were it to be true, 'religion is a lie; human law is a mass of folly, and a base injustice; morality is moonshine; our labours for the black peoples of Africa were works of madmen; and man and woman are only better beasts!' When his friend Darwin sent him a copy of the *Origin*, Sedgwick deplored any severance of links between the material and the moral through which 'humanity, in my mind, would suffer a damage that might brutalize it, and sink the human race into a lower grade of degradation than any into which it has fallen since its written records tell us of its history.'

Such sentiments were common in Victorian days, and not only among the orthodox like Sedgwick. They bespoke a deep alarm lest private and public morality might be undermined. Once again the theological and political are inextricably intertwined. Theologically a wholly materialist view of man would unquestionably erode traditional views of morality derived directly from Judaeo–Christian origins. Yet it may be argued that evolution *per se* did not and cannot contribute to such erosion. Only

in a completely reductionist sense could it add substance to the fears of a Sedgwick. Politically there was a real danger that the fragile structures of Victorian industrial society would collapse through unrest or even revolution, the workers possibly encouraged to imitate nature with its Darwinian law of the jungle. It was small wonder that Karl Marx wished to dedicate *Das Kapital* to Darwin or that many capitalists used religious arguments to discredit the whole Darwinian scheme.

On the other hand Victorian evolutionary theory led also to the opposite phenomenon of social Darwinism. It was said by Bernard Shaw that Darwin had the luck to please anyone with an axe to grind, and nowhere is that aphorism more true than in questions of human morality. At first social Darwinism provided encouragement for factory masters to imitate 'nature red in tooth and claw' and redouble oppression, knowing that only the fittest survived. By the same token the American millionaire J.D. Rockefeller counted Darwin on his side. However not everyone took that view. T.H. Huxley denied that ethical norms could be derived from evolution. Other writers sought to derive them from a genuine synthesis of evolution and Christianity, no one being more conspicuously successful than the scientist/ theologian Henry Drummond, whose *Natural Law in the Spiritual World* of 1883 and *The Ascent of Man* of 1894 achieved phenomenal circulations and related evolutionary progress to the conversions he had witnessed at Moody and Sankey missions in Edinburgh. Drummond saw in evolution the divinely ordained method for perfecting the human race.

Drummond owed much to Herbert Spencer, by whom Darwinism was transmuted into a doctrine of unlimited social progress, fuelled by a belief in the evolution of society itself. Such utopian hopes were challenged by proponents of the second law of thermodynamics (with its inevitable but slow 'running down' of the universe), amongst them physicists like Lord Kelvin and theologians like W.R. Inge. Blatantly at variance with traditional Christian eschatology, these euphoric fantasies were finally shattered by the onset of the First World War, after which the alternative scenario of cosmic hopelessness was adopted by German nihilism (Heim, 1962).

Since that time little was heard of morality based on evolution until the developments in ethology following the Second World War. Landmarks include K. Lorenz's *On Aggression* of 1963, E.O. Wilson's *Sociobiology* of 1975 and R. Dawkins's *The Selfish Gene* of 1976. Each of these attempts to derive moral values from biological science, conceived within an evolutionary framework. They suggest that behaviour patterns like aggression or altruism are genetically induced and, in their different ways, imply a kind of biological determinism. Extrapolation of sociobiological theory to behaviour problems for human beings involves much oversimplification and has been widely criticized, not least by Marxists, who rightly object to any pseudo-scientific justification for the social status quo, and by Christians, who, with equal right, stress the biblical doctrine of individual human responsibility.

Finally, it must be observed that Christians who oppose evolution have often found it a convenient explanation for all manner of social ills. Such was the case for R. Cock's *Evolution and War* of 1928 and C.L. Clarke's *Evolution and the Break-up of Christendom* of 1930, while more recent 'creationist' writers have associated evolution with a variety of scourges ranging from Hitler's anti-Semitism to the tolerance shown by some evangelical writers in questions of abortion.

Design and purpose in nature Charles Darwin was heir to a long English tradition in natural theology. Yet at the heart of his work lay the theory of natural selection; it is not a divine *fiat* that produces new species, but rather the inexorable processes of variation, procreation and survival. In other words, *nature* selects. At first sight this appears to undermine the whole foundation of the argument from design because it seems to eliminate purposive design itself. He wrote: 'There seems to be no more design in the variability of organic beings, and in the action of natural selection, than in the course the wind blows.' What we see instead is the *illusion* of design.

From this it might have been presumed that teleology was banished from science and blind chance was substituted. Yet the survival of natural theology (see above) shows that this was not the case, and the adoption of Darwinism by many of the orthodox indicates that the matter was nowhere near as clear-cut as might have been expected (or as certain opponents of the Victorian church tried to suggest). There are at least three reasons for this survival.

In the first place, there was, and often is, a powerful intuitive belief in design that yields only reluctantly to mere intellectual argument. The human *ego* shrinks from the nihilistic implications of blind chance. To illustrate this we need look no further than Darwin himself, who wrote: 'I am conscious that I am in an utterly hopeless muddle. I cannot think that the world, as we see it, is the result of chance; and yet I cannot look at each separate thing as the result of Design'; and of the sense of purposive design in orchid fertilization he remarked: 'that often comes over me with overwhelming force, but at other times it seems to go away.'

Secondly, in many respects Darwin's ideas demonstrate strong continuity with the traditions of natural theology. Many of the more percipient natural theologians eschewed an anthropocentric viewpoint, denying the universe to have been created simply for man. So did Darwin. Adaptation to changing environments, so essential to the case for natural selection, had also been stressed by William Paley and his fellow authors. Above all, perhaps, Darwin joined many of the natural theologians in espousing a linear view of history, in contrast to the cyclic views implicit in J.B. Lamarck. So integral is such a conception to both Old and New Testament understanding of the historical process that W. Cannon has remarked that the success of Darwinism was nothing less 'than the triumph of a Christian way of picturing the world over the other ways available to scientists'.

Thirdly, many Christian writers saw a larger scheme of design in the evolutionary process. The American botanist Asa Gray perceived that only thus could one account for the apparent waste in a nature marked by immense superfecundity and myriads of apparent dead ends. Charles Kingsley wrote of natural theology, 'That we should have to develop it I do not deny. That we should have to relinquish it I do', adding the memorable lines: 'We knew of old that God was so wise that he could make all things; but behold, he is so much wiser than even that, that *he can make all things make themselves*.'

Since those days a multitude of Christian writers on evolution have expressed similar views to those of Kingsley, from Henry Drummond to Teilhard de Chardin. Thus in 1895 J. Morris could publish *A New Natural Theology based upon the Doctrine of Evolution*. Today the debate between upholders of design and those who invoke only chance has moved away from the strictly biological field and has acquired cosmic dimensions. Most notably J. Monod has stressed the deterministic character of natural processes ('necessity') following certain happenings that may be attributed to 'chance'. Amongst the latter he includes mutations in organisms leading to new species. However, as A.R. Peacocke observes, there seems to be no reason to raise such randomness 'to the level of a metaphysical principle in interpreting the universe' (Peacocke, 1979).

During the nineteenth century agonized questions prompted by Darwinism over chance or design led to a resolution of yet another problem, one generated by its most profound challenge to the Christian church: the role of God in history.

The role of God in history The question may be starkly put: in the process of evolution of species *does nature select, or God?* If the former, what is the role of the latter? Responses to the question are as varied now as they were in Victorian England, and the positions adopted in no case were new even then. Nor have they always been adopted solely under challenge from Darwinism. But it may be helpful to enumerate them briefly as responses to biological evolution.

1 *Atheism*. A Jesuit priest, Joseph Bayma, expressed a common reaction in the immediate aftermath of *The Origin of Species*: Darwin was 'the mouthpiece or chief trumpeter of that infidel clique whose well-known object is to do away with all idea of God'. Similar sentiments abound in popular anti-evolutionary literature up to our own day. Setting aside the question of motivation, we are confronted with the implication that, as Charles Hodge put it, 'this is atheism to all intents and purposes.' The empirical evidence is fairly clear. Neither in Darwin nor in any of his most prominent followers was atheism an issue. Agnosticism was professed by leading scientific naturalists, certainly, but few went further than that. Strict atheism existed chiefly in the rhetoric of Darwin's opponents.

2 *Pantheism*. Again, a strictly pantheistic reaction to Darwinism is hard to document, though hints of it may be discerned in T.H. Huxley's references to 'Dame Nature' and in his whole strategy of sacralizing nature as part of his programme for secularizing society (Russell, 1989). Perhaps the nearest approximation to pure pantheism is to be found in the *Creative Evolution* of Henri Bergson (of 1907), where 'God' was more or less to be identified as an immanent *élan vital*. Bergson's essay in speculative philosophy is chiefly interesting today as an early reaction against the strictly mechanistic views he attributed to Darwin.

3 *Deism*. A limitation of the role of God in history to the First Cause alone was quite common among those who denied any incarnational theology yet shrank from openly adopting an atheistic position. A common enough creed in the eighteenth century, and probably adopted by Darwin's grandfather Erasmus and his predecessors Lamarck and Chambers, DEISM occasionally appears as a response to Darwinism itself. For long associated with the traditional argument from design, it does not seem to have commended itself to the new Darwinians (except as a rhetorical substitute for atheism). Perhaps it may be discerned in R. Dawkins's *The Blind Watchmaker* of 1986, whose title shrewdly harks back to the favourite image of God in eighteenth-century natural theology. Far more popular from the eighteenth century onwards has been an important variant of deism: semi-deism (a term apparently devised by R. Hooykaas).

4 *Semi-deism*. On this view God created the universe and occasionally intervenes in its affairs, in both human and natural history. It was a view influentially held by men of science from Isaac Newton onwards, and in Darwin's day was espoused by Lyell and other geologists and was effectively the creed of many ordinary Christians, despite its vulnerability to the charge of being merely a God-in-the-gaps philosophy. Perhaps the most profoundly important effect of Darwinism on theology is that it made such a position inherently untenable, though it still appears to undergird much thinking of the modern 'creationist' school.

5 *Radical theism*. The position was well put

by Kingsley. Writing to F.D. Maurice in 1863, he observed of people's reactions: 'Now they have got rid of an interfering God – a master-magician, as I call it – they have to choose between the absolute empire of accident, and a living, immanent, ever-working God.' For Kingsley and a great many after him Darwinism had exposed the fallacy of a God occasionally interfering (as in the creation of a new species) and had polarized the choice into blind chance on one hand or the ever-working, sustaining God of New Testament theology on the other. This radical theism was adopted by many who, like Aubrey Moore, recognized that Darwinism 'under the disguise of a foe, did the work of a friend'. It was no longer possible to see God as 'an occasional visitor' to his own universe.

This last viewpoint is a view shared today by many who write on evolution, whether from an evangelical perspective or otherwise. Its main rival is process theology which, however, is much more loosely connected with problems generated by evolution.

The nature and origins of life
A common description of a living organism, however simple, is that it has the functions of self-conservation (by acquiring materials and energy from its environment), self-regulation (it is at least to a degree autonomous), and self-reproduction (so forming a species). The Darwinian controversies brought into sharp focus the age-old question: what is life? It became the ultimate candidate for reductionism: can all biology be explained in terms of physics and chemistry? From Jacques Loeb to Francis Crick the answer has been in the affirmative, but, as Peacocke has pointed out, this has involved a certain ambiguity. At the level of *explanation* for the laws governing molecular processes its means one thing, at the level of *ontology* quite another. Few scientists would demur at the former meaning. But physics and chemistry alone seem unable to account for all biological phenomena (in which Peter Medawar includes heredity, infection, sexuality, and so on), for which something like a systems approach is more promising than one dependent on physico-chemical categories (Peacocke, 1979).

Closely allied to ideas of the nature of life are problems concerning its origins. At a purely chemical level the vitalistic notion that certain 'organic' *substances* required life for their production had been eliminated at about this time. But whether living *organisms* could be produced from non-living matter (abiogenesis) was a different question. Certain evidence (now known to be spurious) suggested that perhaps they might, and this gave support to those who wished to banish all theological categories from science. Thus Ernst Haeckel complained that Darwin had failed to go far enough in allowing a divine creation of the first living creatures: he was 'inconsistent and not sincere'. Others (such as T.H. Huxley and John Tyndall) remained sceptical about present-day abiogenesis but did not deny it in the remote past.

From vague Victorian ideas about the 'protoplasm', recognition of living cells and the laws of Mendelian genetics, credible theories as to the origin of life had to wait some considerable time. Given that the fundamental building bricks of all living matter were amino acids, C.E. Guye in 1919 computed that the odds against their forming even a simple protein by chance were 10^{161} to 1. As for the synthesis of amino acids themselves, A.I. Oparin (1924 and 1937) and J.B.S. Haldane (1929) invoked processes of photosynthesis in a primordial ocean ('primeval soup'). Both of these writers were committed to the dialectical materialism of Marxist thought, an association that did not facilitate the immediate adoption of their views in the west. However in 1953 S. Miller performed secret experiments which demonstrated that simple precursors of amino acids (such as CH_2O and HCN) could be obtained by electrical discharges through mixtures of methane, ammonia, hydrogen and water. From these life could be credibly said to have begun. The fact that even simple molecules of amino acids have a specific geometrical asymmetry known as chirality (or 'handedness') has recently been connected with a fundamental asymmetry in the universe ('electro-weak interactions') resulting in the formation of what are known as L-amino-acids and D-sugars (Mason, 1991). Since 1971 M. Eigen and others have studied mathematically the kinetics of a system capable of replicating information-bearing molecules, such as DNA, stressing both the indeterminacy and the inevitability of such a process.

Theological reactions to the possibility of abiogenesis have varied widely. As early as 1910 the *Catholic Encyclopedia* saw 'no insuperable difficulty' in such a phenomenon. More recently both Jehovah's Witness and 'creationist' writers have rejected it, ostensibly on the grounds of inherent probabilities. However Peacocke has seen the 'creative role of chance' enshrined in the work of I. Prigonine and Eigen as expressing 'God's gratuitousness and joy in creation as a whole, and not in man alone'. But perhaps the last word should come from J. de Rosnay (Montenat *et al.*, 1985):

> I believe that if we are to respect the many implications of the origin of life and to avoid reducing it to one particular area – whether science, philosophy or religion – we must consider it simultaneously from a scientific, a philosophical and a religious perspective.

See also CREATION, DOCTRINE OF; LIBERALISM (BRITAIN and USA); PHYSICAL SCIENCE/PSYCHOLOGICAL SCIENCE/SOCIAL SCIENCE AND CHRISTIAN THOUGHT.

Bibliography

Barbour, I.G. 1966: *Issues in Science and Religion*. London: SCM Press.

Berry, R.J. 1988: *God and Evolution*. London: Hodder and Stoughton.

Brooke, John Hedley 1991: *Science and Religion: Some Historical Perspectives*. Cambridge: Cambridge University Press.

Burke, Derek, ed. 1985: *Creation and Evolution*. Leicester: Inter-Varsity Press.

Dillenberger, John 1961: *Protestant Thought and Natural Science*. London: Collins.

Greenwood, William O. 1938: *Biology and Christian Belief*. London: SCM Press.

Heim, Karl 1962: *The World: Its Creation and Consummation*. Edinburgh and London: Oliver and Boyd.

Jaki, Stanley L. 1983: *Angels, Apes, and Men*. La Salle, Ill.: Sherwood Sugden.

Lindberg, David C., and Numbers, Ronald L., eds 1986: *God and Nature: Historical Essays on the Encounter Between Christianity and Science*. Berkeley: University of California Press.

Livingstone, David N. 1987: *Darwin's Forgotten Defenders: The Encounter between Evangelical Theology and Evolutionary Thought*. Grand Rapids: Eerdmans.

McDougall, William 1934: *Religion and the Sciences of Life*. London: Methuen.

Mason, Stephen F. 1991: *Chemical Evolution: Origins of the Elements, Molecules and Living Systems*. Oxford: Clarendon Press.

Montenat, Christian, Plateaux, Luc, and Roux, Pascal 1985: *How to Read the World: Creation in Evolution*. London: SCM Press.

Moore, James R. 1979: *Post-Darwinian Controversies: A Study of the Protestant Struggle to Come to Terms with Darwin in Great Britain and America 1870–1900*. Cambridge: Cambridge University Press.

Oldroyd, David R. 1980: *Darwinian Impacts: An Introduction to the Darwinian Revolution*. Milton Keynes: Open University Press.

Peacocke, A.R. 1979: *Creation and the World of Science*. Oxford: Oxford University Press.

Russell, Colin A. 1985: *Cross-Currents: Interactions Between Science and Faith*. Leicester: Inter-Varsity Press.

Russell, Colin A. 1989: The conflict metaphor and its social origins, *Science and Christian Belief* 1, pp. 3–26.

Wiseman, P.J. 1977: *Clues to Creation in Genesis*. London: Marshall, Morgan and Scott.

COLIN A. RUSSELL

black theology A movement, especially significant in the USA during the 1960s and 1970s, concerned with ensuring that the realities of black experience were represented at the theological level. The first major evidence of the move towards theological emancipation within the American black community dates from 1964, with the publication of Joseph Washington's *Black Religion*, a powerful affirmation of the distinctiveness of black religion within the North American context. Washington emphasized the need for the integration and assimilation of black theological insights within mainstream Protestantism; however, this approach was largely swept to one side with the appearance of Albert Cleage's *Black Messiah* (1969). Cleage, pastor of the Shrine of the Black Madonna in Detroit, urged black people to liberate themselves from white theological oppression. Arguing that Scripture was written by black Jews, Cleage claimed that the gospel of a black Messiah had been perverted by Paul in his attempt to make it acceptable to Europeans. Despite the considerable overstatements within the work, *Black Messiah* came to be a rallying point for black Christians determined to discover and assert their distinctive identity.

The movement made several decisive affirmations of its theological distinctiveness during 1969. The 'Black Manifesto' issued at the Interreligious Foundation for Community Organization, meeting at Detroit, Michigan, placed the issue of the black experience firmly on the theological agenda. The statement by the National Committee of Black Churchmen emphasized the theme of liberation as a central motif of black theology:

> Black Theology is a theology of black liberation. It seeks to plumb the black condition in the light of God's revelation in Jesus Christ, so that the black community can see that the gospel is commensurate with the achievement of black humanity. Black Theology is a theology of 'blackness'. It is the affirmation of black humanity that emancipates black people from white racism, thus providing authentic freedom for both white and black people.

Although there are evident affinities between this statement and the aims and emphases of Latin American LIBERATION THEOLOGY, it must be stressed that, at this stage, there was no formal interaction between the two movements. Liberation theology arose primarily within the Roman Catholic church in South America, whereas black theology tended to arise within black Protestant communities in North America.

The origins of the movement can be traced to the rise in black consciousness which was so distinctive a feature of American history in the 1960s. In their survey of the development of the movement, G.S. Wilmore and J.H. Cone distinguish three stages:

1 1966–70. During this developmental phase, black theology emerged as a significant aspect of the civil rights struggle in general, and as a reaction against the dominance of whites in both seminaries and churches. At this stage, black theology was developed within the black-led churches, and was not particularly academic in its outlook. The issues of primary importance centred on the use of violence to achieve justice, and the nature of Christian love.

2 1970–77. In this period of consolidation, the movement appears to have moved away from the churches to the seminaries, as the movement became increasingly accepted within theological circles. The focus of the movement shifted from issues of practical concern to more explicitly theological issues, such as the nature of liberation and the significance of suffering.

3 1977 onwards. A new awareness of the development of liberation movements in other parts of the world, especially in Latin America, became of importance within black theology. Alongside this new sense of perspective came a new commitment to serving black-led churches, and the fostering of fellowship and collaboration between those churches.

The most significant writer within the movement is generally agreed to be James H. Cone, whose *Black Theology of Liberation* (1970) appealed to the central notion of a God who is concerned for the black struggle for liberation. Noting the strong preference of Jesus for the oppressed, Cone argued that 'God was Black' – that is, identified with the oppressed. However, Cone's use of Barthian categories was criticized: why, it was asked, should a black theologian use the categories of a white theology in articulating the black experience? Why had he not made fuller use of black history and culture? In later works, Cone responded to such criticisms by making a more pervasive appeal to 'the Black experience' as a central resource in black theology. Nevertheless, Cone has continued to maintain a Barthian emphasis upon the centrality of Christ as the self-revelation of God (while identifying him as 'the Black Messiah'), and the authority of Scripture in interpreting human experience in general.

Since the 1970s, an interest in black theology and a new concern to understand the 'black experience' has become widespread in Afro-Caribbean communities worldwide. The original base of the movement has been considerably broadened, to include black communities in Britain as well as the original centre of the movement in the USA.

See also PROTESTANT THEOLOGY: SOUTH AFRICA.

Bibliography
Cleage, A.B. 1969: *The Black Messiah*. New York:

Sheed and Ward.

Cone, James H. 1970: *A Black Theology of Liberation.* Philadelphia: Lippincott.

Cone, James H. 1986: *For My People.* Maryknoll, NY: Orbis.

Salley, C., and Behm, R. 1970: *Your God is too White.* Downers Grove, IL: InterVarsity Press.

Washington, J.R. 1964: *Black Religion.* Boston: Beacon Press.

Washington, J.R. 1967: *The Politics of God: The Future of the Black Churches.* Boston: Beacon Press.

Wilmore, G.S., and Cone, J.H., eds 1979: *Black Theology: A Documentary History 1966–79.* Maryknoll, NY: Orbis.

ALISTER E. MCGRATH

Boff, Leonardo (b. 1938) Brazilian Roman Catholic liberation theologian (see LIBERATION THEOLOGY). A Franciscan priest, he was educated in Brazil, Oxford, Louvain, Würzburg and Munich, where he received his doctorate. He is a professor of systematic theology at the Institute for Philosophy and Theology in Petrópolis, Brazil. His brother Clodovis is also a leading liberation theologian. Founded in his own experience of the oppression of the poor in South America, his theology highlights the material poverty of the man Jesus and the relative power and wealth of those who opposed him, presenting Christ as liberator, not only from personal sin, but from the material oppression caused by structural, corporate sin; his Christology is developed in *Jesus Christ Liberator* of 1972. His new models for the church, based on his experience of the 'base community', highlight the early church experience of community, cooperation and charism: his books on the subject include *Church: Charism and Power* (1981, trans. 1985) and *Ecclesiogenesis: The Base Communities Reinvent the Church* (1986). His work, with its emphasis on the doctrine of man rather than that of the church, has brought him into conflict with church authorities: a colloquy in 1984 imposed on him a year's silence, during which he wrote *Trinity and Society* (1986), in which he offers the fruitful communion of the three divine persons as a model for a human society based on collaboration and equality.

Bibliography

Boff, L., and Boff, C. 1986: *Liberation Theology: From Confrontation to Dialogue.* New York.

Boff, L., and Boff, C. 1987: *Introducing Liberation Theology.* Tunbridge Wells.

Ferm, D.W. 1986: *Third World Liberation Theologies: An Introductory Survey.* New York.

Bonhoeffer, Dietrich (1906–1945) German Lutheran pastor, theologian and ecumenist. He studied at Berlin, Tübingen and Rome and after ordination worked in Barcelona, New York and London. He was a lecturer and pastor at the University of Berlin with an increasing interest in ecumenism when Hitler rose to power in 1933; he joined the Confessing Church, signing its Barmen declaration in 1934. On a lecture tour in the USA when war was declared in 1939, he chose to return to Germany, where he became involved in a plot on Hitler's life. Arrested in 1943, he was executed by the Gestapo in Flossenbürg in April 1945. Early theological works influenced by Karl Barth were followed by spiritual writings such as *The Cost of Discipleship* (1937, trans. 1948). His *Ethics* (1949, trans. 1955) was uncompleted at the time of his arrest; *Letters and Papers from Prison* (1951, trans. 1953), based on fragments smuggled from Tegel prison, argues for 'religionless Christianity': the church exists 'for others', and if it is to be relevant in a world 'come of age', it must discard traditional religious expressions which have become meaningless in an age of increasing secularization. His thinking has been influential in modern theological development; other works include *Act and Being* (1931, trans. 1962).

Bibliography

Bethge, E. 1970: *Dietrich Bonhoeffer.* London.

Dudzus, O., ed. 1986: *Bonhoeffer for a New Generation.* London.

Dumas, A. 1972: *Dietrich Bonhoeffer, Theologian of Reality.* London.

Gruchy, J. de 1987: *The Making of Modern Theology.* London.

Bossuet, Jacques Bénigne (1627–1704) French preacher and Bishop of Meaux (1681–1704). A leading churchman of his time, he was a noted preacher and a tireless opponent of Protestantism in France. Increasingly involved in court and ecclesiastical affairs, he defended the autonomy of the French Catholic church against papal claims. Whilst tutor to the

Dauphin (1670–81) he wrote a classic statement of divine sovereignty over universal history, *Discours sur l'histoire universelle* (1681) and *Politique tirée de l'écriture sainte* (1679), an early attempt at a philosophy of history, which notes the duties as well as the divine right of kings. Other works include *Traité de la connaissance de Dieu et de soi-même* (1722), a discourse on the nature of God and man, as well as several devotional books.

Bibliography

Chadwick, O. 1987: *From Bossuet to Newman*. Cambridge.

Löwith, K. 1957: *Meaning in History*. Chicago, Ill.

Britain   See ANGLICANISM; EVANGELICALISM: BRITAIN; LIBERALISM: BRITAIN; PROTESTANT THEOLOGY: BRITAIN.

Brunner, Emil (1889–1966)   Swiss Reformed dialectical theologian. For most of his career a professor of theology at Zurich, he was influenced by, *inter alia*, Søren Kierkegaard and Martin Buber, and is often associated with Karl Barth and neo-orthodoxy. He responded to F.D.E. Schleiermacher and liberal Protestantism by reasserting the importance of the Scriptures: although he questioned their historical character and held that they are not verbally inspired, he saw them as the primary instrument, with the Spirit, by which we may know God. God is uniquely revealed in Jesus Christ, whom he affirmed in *The Mediator* (1927, trans. 1934) as both human and divine. He differed from Barth on the issue of natural theology, maintaining that man could obtain limited apprehension of God through general revelation in creation, history and conscience. His major work of dogmatics was published in three volumes (1946–60, trans. 1946–62). He was also concerned with what he saw as the essential corollary of Christian doctrine: ethics and social issues; two books in this field were banned by the Nazis, *The Divine Imperative* (1932, trans. 1937) and *Man in Revolt* (1937, trans. 1939).

Bibliography

Hughes, P.E., ed. 1969: *Creative Minds in Contemporary Theology*, article on Brunner. Grand Rapids, Mi.

Kegley, C.W., ed. 1962: *The Theology of Emil Brunner*. New York.

Ramsey, P. 1983: *Nine Modern Moralists*. Lanham, MD.

Buber, Martin (1878–1965)   Jewish theologian and philosopher. Born in Austria, he taught from 1938 to 1953 at the Hebrew University in Jerusalem after leaving Nazi Germany, where he had been teaching at Frankfurt. A preacher of Zionism and Hasidic mysticism, he studied the role of the Jewish faith in relation to the human race and its main religions, and his thought influenced later developments in inter-faith dialogue. His theology was accessible to, and influential upon, Christian theologians such as Karl Barth, Dietrich Bonhoeffer, Emil Brunner and Friedrich Gogarten. His best-known work, *Ich und Du* (1923, trans. *I and Thou*, 1937), shows the influence of existentialism on his thought. It distinguishes between the I–Thou and the I–It relationships: the former involves the whole person in a relationship of acceptance (typified by man's relationship with God), whilst the latter represents a partial, conditional relationship such as that of confrontational proselytization. Other works include *Vom Geist des Judentum* (1916), *Das Königtum Gottes* (1932, trans. 1967) and his translation of the Hebrew Scriptures into German, which remains in use.

Bibliography

Balthasar, H. von 1961: *Martin Buber and Christianity*. Harvill Press.

Friedman, M.S. 1976: *Martin Buber: The Life of Dialogue*. Chicago, Ill.

Friedman, M.S. 1981–4: *Martin Buber's Life and Work*. New York.

Bultmann, Rudolf (1884–1976)   German theologian, one of the most influential New Testament scholars and theologians of this century. Born in Wiefelstede in Germany, the son of an Evangelical-Lutheran pastor, Bultmann taught in Breslau (1916–20) and Giessen (1920–1) before moving to Marburg in 1921, where he remained until his retirement in 1951. A member of the Confessing Church in Germany opposed to Nazism from its foundation in 1934, and himself an Evangelical-Lutheran pastor, Bultmann continued living and writing in Marburg after his retirement, until his death in 1976.

Bultmann's principal writings, *The History of the Synoptic Tradition* ([1921] 1963), *The Gospel of John: A Commentary* ([1941] 1971), *New Testament and Mythology* ([1941] 1953), *Theology of the New Testament* ([1953] 1955), *Glauben und Verstehen I–IV (Faith and Understanding* ([1933] 1987) and *Theologische Enzyklopädie* (1984), indicate the range and depth of his exegetical, theological, and philosophical abilities. Moreover, Bultmann's wholly admirable refusal to bow to the pressure of National Socialism during the years 1933–45, as both churchman and academic, earned him lasting respect from such different figures as Karl Barth and Hannah Arendt.

Since his death in 1976, however, Bultmann's significance for contemporary research and theology has gradually been eroded. Today, Bultmann's exegetical findings are almost universally challenged; his theology is attacked as too reductive; and he is criticized for too narrow a dependence upon the philosophy of Martin Heidegger, now condemned for his participation in National Socialism. In the three significant areas of his work, therefore, Bultmann appears to have been superseded.

This tendency to consign Bultmann to theology's past, however, has been ill-conceived; granted that certain themes in his work appear inherently linked to the perspectives of the middle of this century, still much remains to be developed in Bultmann's thought. Specifically, this potential can be considered via three central issues, which preoccupied Bultmann himself and which remain signal today: the question of the historical Jesus; theology's relationship with philosophy; and the task of a theological hermeneutics.

The central task of Christian theology is to say things of universal significance about a particular person, Jesus of Nazareth, who lived and died nearly two thousand years ago (see CHRISTOLOGY). This issue lies at the heart of the New Testament, and in turn dominates Bultmann's exegesis. Influenced by his teachers in the HISTORY OF RELIGIONS SCHOOL, Bultmann addresses in particular the tension between the factual life of Jesus and the narrated accounts of his being the Christ. It is this basic distinction between 'Jesus' and 'Christ' which

dominates Bultmann's approach to the question of the historical Jesus (see HISTORICAL JESUS, QUEST OF).

Terminologically, this distinction is between the *Historie* or 'historicity' of Jesus' life, about which one learns by critical exegesis of the New Testament; and the *Geschichte* or 'historicality' of Christ's significance, which one encounters in Christian witness, proclamation, and, ultimately, the power of the Holy Spirit. The dichotomy of *Historie* and *Geschichte* is found in the work of Martin Kähler, and before Kähler in that of David Friedrich Strauss; but Bultmann's own insights developed these ideas considerably.

Conventional wisdom suggests that Bultmann reduces the *Historie* of Jesus to the simple fact of his existence; that is, merely that Jesus lived and died. Thus, for Bultmann Jesus' existence becomes solely the precursor of the genuine subject matter of theology, the *Geschichte* or proclamation of Christ as salvation for all peoples. These two poles of Christology, though greatly unbalanced, are related by Bultmann's understanding of ESCHATOLOGY, which he regards as the presence and expression of God's eternal will within time. In this way, the consistency of Bultmann's answer to the question of the historical Jesus appears to be secured by his desire to emphasize primarily Christ's contemporary significance for the individual.

Bultmann's introduction of eschatology, however, as the theological basis of both *Historie* and *Geschichte*, undermines this interpretation precisely because it addresses the futurity both of God's will and of human existence; that is, the openness of the encounter between God and the individual. Bultmann's Christology appears to present a closed system, in which the name 'Christ', proclaimed on the basis of the fact of Jesus' life, reveals the authentic nature of life turned towards God. In fact this is not the case; rather, the goal of Bultmann's theology is the individual's encounter with the risen Lord, which occurs in the power of the Spirit. Far from being a form of Christomonism, therefore, Bultmann's Christology is conditioned by his spirituality or pietism.

This has significant implications for any understanding of the Christological basis of Bultmann's theology. Instead of a crude distinction between brute fact and existential narrative, one finds a desire to address the authentic meaning of Jesus Christ's life, death, and resurrection; its willed origin in God; and its eternal relevance for the life of the individual. Implicitly, therefore, Bultmann's is a Trinitarian theology: the goal of the incarnation as revelation is not the discovery of particular details concerning God's being, but rather the direct encounter of the individual with divine glory; an encounter which is of eternal significance. The task of theology, for Bultmann, is thus to articulate a definite understanding of the kerygmatic Christ, the Christ one narrates becoming the necessary mediation between the historical Jesus, whom research reveals to have been a particular individual, and the risen Lord, of whom theology makes universal truth claims. Hence, and employing traditional terminology, one can say that Bultmann's treatment of the question of the historical Jesus demonstrates the *fides quae creditur* in this theology; that is, the 'faith which is believed', Bultmann's doctrine of Christ.

This implies that Bultmann's theology is more sophisticated and traditional than recent commentary has supposed. The full extent of this sophistication, however, is only revealed as one considers the philosophical foundations of Bultmann's position. Again, this can be expressed in orthodox terminology: if Bultmann's doctrine of Christ constitutes the *fides quae creditur*, the 'faith which is believed', what for Bultmann is the *fides qua creditur*, the 'faith by which one believes'? This question establishes Bultmann's understanding of the relationship between theology and philosophy, which inevitably raises his intellectual relationship with Martin Heidegger.

Bultmann's debt to Heidegger is often expressed in terms of the former simply borrowing from the latter the terminology of EXISTENTIALISM, thereby giving to it an explicitly theological sense. In this way, Heidegger's relevance is reduced, because his work does not impinge upon Bultmann's fundamental, theological concerns. Such commentary, however, is erroneous. The existential drift in Bultmann's language is nothing more than the general terminology of his religious tradition: with little imagination one may, in this

sense, speak of Martin Luther's existentialism, or Saint Augustine's, in so far as these writers addressed the particular circumstances of the individual as he or she is encountered by God in Christ.

In fact, Heidegger's influence upon Bultmann is quite specific, identifiable in a definite understanding of revelation. Already in *Sein und Zeit* of 1927 Heidegger was developing a particular idea of the relationship between beings and Being; that is, existence and that which transcends it. In the years following 1927, Heidegger referred to this relationship as the 'ontological difference': simply, the dynamic which establishes the relationship between existence and transcendence. This relationship is necessary because of the meaning of revelation as it occurs between beings and Being: what is revealed is not factual evidence, but rather the intentionality of revelation itself. Revelation occurs: as such, it reveals nothing more nor less than the mutual dependence of beings and Being.

Heidegger derived this understanding of the event of revelation from his analysis of the conditions of possibility of human existence, and in turn he sought to apply it to a wide range of situations and themes: the initial analyses of instrumental being in *Sein und Zeit* gave way in the 1930s to interpretations of revelation in works of art and, after the Second World War, to the 'irruption' of such events of revelation into poetic texts. Bultmann, by contrast, is concerned solely with one event of revelation; but that event is the eschatological event itself, the encounter between the risen Lord and the individual. Heidegger's understanding at this point is the key to Bultmann's own interpretation of this event as one of meaningful revelation.

For Bultmann, the question of the nature or essence of the individual is of no interest: the individual exists only in encounter; this is where his or her being before God is revealed. Bultmann requires, consequently, a concept of revelation which reveals nothing objectively, but everything in terms of a necessary encounter between transcendence and immanence. What Bultmann finds in Heidegger is precisely such an understanding: effectively, Bultmann's theological appropriation of Heidegger's concept becomes a specific example of the event of the ontological difference as a relational category.

In terms of the language of *fides qua creditur*, the 'faith by which one believes', this understanding of revelation functions to explain both what occurs in the act of narrating Christ and, simultaneously, the encounter with the risen Lord. Philosophically, therefore, this concept of revelation gives meaning to Bultmann's understanding of eschatology. Christ's being cannot, for Bultmann, be encountered or expressed objectively; still less should it, theologically, be encountered or expressed subjectively (that way lies absolute relativism). The alternative, as elaborated by Bultmann, is to understand the Christ event as the ontological difference, *in person*. This, inherently Chalcedonian, understanding of the doctrine of Christ, continues Bultmann's answer to the question of the historical Jesus, whilst simultaneously developing that Christology into a genuine *theology*. On Bultmann's analysis Christ, as the Revealer, becomes the pivot around which all questions of being – human or divine – turn. Without this eventful understanding of revelation, one risks reducing Christianity to a faith of crude eschatological realism; with it, one ensures the necessity of a continuous process of representation and interpretation in both Christology and theology. This necessity, and its implications, are Bultmann's legacy to contemporary thought.

The development from Bultmann's early, exegetical writings to his later, overtly theological position, was mediated in 1941 by the publication of his essay *Neues Testament und Mythologie* ([1941] 1953). This essay is often regarded negatively; that is, as constituting Bultmann's attempt to rid the New Testament texts of objectifying language. In terms of Bultmann's understanding of the event of revelation, however, one can regard it in a different light. Thus, it becomes an attempt to condition the reader to understand the message of the New Testament purely eschatologically, in Bultmann's developed sense of this word. In fact, Bultmann argues, this is not simply how the New Testament can be fruitfully interpreted; it is how it should be interpreted. It is this element of moralizing exegesis in Bultmann's thought which is questioned today.

The advantage of Bultmann's event theory of revelation is that it provides a basically theological framework in which to interpret not only the encounter with Jesus Christ, but also the stories told about him. In other words, and on the basis of a sophisticated philosophy of encounter and revelation, Bultmann's theology provides a flexibility which, in its best sense, can sustain a wide variety of different images of Jesus. Hence, the differing Christologies of Edward Schillebeeckx, Jon Sobrino and Jürgen Moltmann all benefit from Bultmann's emphasis upon a relational understanding of eschatology. Regarded, therefore, in terms of a theological hermeneutics, Bultmann's thought addresses the question of how to present the Christ story as being new today.

Bultmann's failing, however, is that he is still wedded to the notion that there can be one, definitive, image of Jesus Christ: this conviction pervades his entire thought. In an age which accepts pluralism in theological hermeneutics (a position implied by Bultmann's philosophical framework), as argued by David Tracy in *The Analogical Imagination* of 1981, Bultmann's refusal to consider alternatives to his own partial image of Jesus Christ is problematic. Any theology does of course need to be contextual; yet Bultmann's attains its context by seeking a constituency within the world of the New Testament itself. Contemporary theological hermeneutics deems this impermissible: there is no single 'message' of the New Testament in the sense Bultmann sought. Here one detects the underlying liberal Protestantism of Bultmann's theology.

Despite this criticism, Bultmann's theology remains a powerful if often misunderstood interpretation of the Christ event. Together with Karl Rahner's, Bultmann's stands as the most successful attempt to philosophize about the foundations of theology in the twentieth century. If his exegesis is contradicted today, and his own particular theological conclusions persistently challenged, still Bultmann's understanding of the engagement of theology and philosophy remains a valid attempt to address the universal significance of Jesus of Nazareth. (See PHILOSOPHICAL THEOLOGY.)

Bibliography

Writings

[1921] 1963: *The History of the Synoptic Tradition,*

trans. J. Marsh. Oxford: Blackwell.

[1933] 1987: *Faith and Understanding*, trans. L.P. Smith. Philadelphia: Fortress Press.

[1941] 1971: *The Gospel of John: A Commentary*, trans. G.R. Beasley-Murray, R.W.N. Hoare and J.K. Riches. Oxford: Blackwell.

[1941] 1953: New Testament and mythology. In *Kerygma and Myth: A Theological Debate*, vol. 1, ed. H.W. Bartsch, trans. R.H. Fuller. London: SPCK.

[1953] 1955: *Theology of the New Testament*, 2 vols, trans. K. Grobel. London: SCM Press.

1957: *History and Eschatology: The Presence of Eternity*. New York: Harper and Row.

1961: *Existence and Faith: Shorter Writings of Rudolf Bultmann*, selected, trans. and introduced by S.M. Ogden. London: Hodder and Stoughton.

1984: *Theologische Enzyklopädie*, ed. E. Jüngel and K.W. Müller. Tübingen: J.C.B. Mohr.

Critical works

Johnson, R.A., ed. 1987: *Rudolf Bultmann: Interpreting Faith for the Modern Era*. London: Collins.

Jones, G. 1991: *Bultmann: Towards a Critical Theology*. Cambridge: Polity Press.

Painter, J. 1987: *Theology as Hermeneutics: Rudolf Bultmann's Interpretation of the History of Jesus*. Sheffield: Almond Press.

GARETH JONES

Bushnell, Horace (1802–1876) North American Congregationalist minister and theologian. He studied at Yale and worked as a journalist before returning to Yale to teach, where he was converted to traditional American Protestantism and became a Congregational minister. He was attracted by the religious writings of S.T. Coleridge and German idealism, which he combined with strands of Puritan thought in an approach which anticipated later American liberal theology and the social gospel movement, and which brought him into controversy with conservative churchmen. In *God in Christ* (1849) he challenged the adequacy of traditional religious language to describe, for instance, the Trinity, examining the significance of image and analogy; his rejection here of the idea of the crucifixion as propitiation or substitution – its

significance was primarily moral – was further developed in *The Vicarious Sacrifice* (1866). In *Christian Nurture* (1847) he argued against the prevailing revivalism for conversion as a gradual and educative rather than a sudden experience.

Bibliography

Cross, B.M. 1958: *Horace Bushnell: Minister to a Changing America*. Chicago.

Smith, D.L. 1981: *Symbolism and Growth: The Religious Thought of Horace Bushnell*. Chico, Ca.

business ethics See ETHICS.

Butler, Joseph (1692–1752) English bishop, theologian and moral philosopher. He read law and divinity at Oriel College, Oxford, and was Bishop of Bristol (1738–50) and Bishop of Durham (1750–2). His only systematic work, *Analogy of Religion* (1736), is a major exposition of Christian revelation. Written in opposition to the deists of his day, it argued for the rational probability of the Christian revelation by presenting an analogy with 'the constitution and course of nature'. He distinguished between 'natural' and 'revealed' religion, arguing that the similarities between the two also pointed to the probability of the truth of Christianity. His moral philosophy, found mainly in *Fifteen Sermons* (1726), stresses 'conscience', 'self-love' and 'benevolence' as the essential characteristics of human nature: humans have the innate ability to recognize what is 'right', and human morality is ultimately produced by people living according to their 'true' natures. He was an opponent of John Wesley and George Whitefield, but his methods of argumentation influenced many subsequent thinkers, including David Hume and John Henry Newman.

Bibliography

Duncan-Jones, A. 1952: *Butler's Moral Philosophy*. Harmondsworth.

Mossner, E.C. 1936: *Bishop Butler and the Age of Reason*. New York.

Penelhum, T. 1985: *Butler*. London

C

Calvinism See PRESBYTERIANISM.

Campbell, John McLeod (1800–1872) Scottish minister and theologian. Educated at Glasgow and Edinburgh, and ordained into the Church of Scotland, he was removed from his ministerial post in 1831 by the General Assembly for departing from orthodoxy, and he became pastor to an independent congregation in Glasgow (1833–59). In opposition to the Westminster Confession of Faith and some interpreters of Calvin, he held that Christ's death was not only for the elect but for the whole world (though he was not a universalist); that 'assurance of faith' was a condition of salvation; and that Christ's death was not a penal substitution averting the wrath of God, but an atonement for sin effected through Christ's perfect confession and repentance of sin. He also held that the incarnation, not the atonement, is the chief event of salvation. His ideas are set out in *The Nature of the Atonement* (1856), and they influenced Karl Barth, Thomas F. Torrance and J.B. Torrance, among others.

Bibliography

R.S. Wright, ed. 1960: *Fathers of the Kirk,* article on Campbell.
Tuttle, G.M. 1986: *So Rich a Soil: John McLeod Campbell on Christian Atonement.* Edinburgh.

Canada See PROTESTANT THEOLOGY: CANADA.

capitalism Capitalism is a form of economic organization, a set of institutions in which the resources available to a society, including all human resources, are organized to produce goods and services for that society. Four features of capitalist organization serve to distinguish it from other methods of organizing an economy. The first is the institution of private property. Private property requires that social conventions or law prevent others from taking property by force, and that the property owner has complete freedom of action in respect of the use and disposition of that property. In particular, the government and other authorities may not interfere in any way with private decisions. Their role is to protect the rights of property holders. The doctrine of unconditional and exclusive use of property is based on the natural rights concept of Roman law.

The second feature of capitalism is a reliance on markets for the exchange of goods and services. Money acts as a medium of exchange (and a store of value) so that economic agents are delivered from the constraints of barter, where an agent's wants have to be coincident with another's supplies and vice versa. In a market system, an agent can sell a wide range of services (including labour services) and goods to one group, and then with the proceeds make purchases from a quite different group. A market system provides both incentives and information, via the role of prices. The incentive aspect is related to the concept of private property rights. The owner has to evaluate the returns to a particular resource in a variety of different uses, before making a decision. The existence of market prices makes that evaluation straightforward. The expectation is that a rational owner will divert resources from sectors where returns are low to sectors where returns are higher. The information aspect of market prices is that the supplier of a good does not have to know precisely who is in the market with demands for the good. Without a price system, he would need this information in detail, before making supply decisions. It should be obvious that markets, like the institution of private property, need the support of social mores and/or legal structures if they are to function effectively. At the least, it is necessary that transactions should have some mutual trust, whether supplied by convention or by legally enforceable contracts, for trading to take place. There is an important role for government and the judicial system.

The third essential feature of capitalism is the organization of production in firms or corporations, which are owned and directed by the suppliers of capital, who then employ the labour force. The reasons for this form of organization are quite complex, but in essence have to do with monitoring the effort of the labour force. Without monitoring, and with a given wage, a worker has no incentive to apply himself to the fullest extent. Within a large operation a hierarchy of monitoring emerges, with higher-level workers monitoring the efforts of lower-level groups. The issue then is who is to monitor the top executive. The problem is avoided if that person is also the owner of the capital, who receives the residual income. He has every incentive to be energetic and prudent in his work, since the return to his capital depends on his efforts. There are, however, two drawbacks. One is that the size of the firm is effectively limited to the size of organization that the capitalist–owner can control and monitor. The other is that he takes all the risks attached to the residual income, given that the workers are paid first from the revenues of the operations. These two drawbacks to the owner-managed firm have given rise to the most enduring institution of capitalism – the joint-stock company. First given legal recognition in 1856 in Britain, it allows the ownership of a corporation to be held by shareholders, whose financial commitment is limited to the capital subscribed to purchase the shares. This solves the problem of the limitation of size imposed by the capital resources of a single owner. It also spreads the risks: in particular, shareholders can hold a few shares in a number of companies (a portfolio of shares), and thereby spread the risks of holding their wealth. The problem of

monitoring the activities of the firm is solved, in part at least, by the device of having a board of directors, elected by the shareholders at an annual meeting, with responsibility for the appointment and supervision of the management.

The fourth feature of capitalism is the development of financial markets, the role of which is to channel the savings of private individuals to productive investment. As soon as a firm requires more financial capital than is available from its founders, then it must find alternative sources. Modern banking had its origins in deposits which the owners did not wish to use immediately for consumption, which were then lent by money lenders and banks to traders and productive firms which needed to finance their operations. So long as the depositors did not all require their money at the same time, the banks could afford to pay interest on deposits, while earning a return on the loans. In addition to borrowing from banks, firms could raise external finance by selling bills of exchange, fixed-interest bonds, and shares direct to the public. The issue of these financial instruments was often organized by the banks, and secondary markets for them were organized in the form of stock markets and bond markets, so the lender could usually realize his loan without affecting the original borrower.

Capitalist economies appear to have three empirical characteristics. The first is that they have provided an environment within which economic growth takes place and general living standards increase. The second is inequality of both wealth and income. Low income can be due to a number of causes affecting the ability of a household to earn income. Ill health or old age may prevent a person from working. Lack of employment opportunities in the locality where a person lives may lead to prolonged unemployment. Poor skills or education may mean that only low-paying jobs are open to a worker. At the other extreme, a well qualified worker with a scarce skill can expect to be employed with a high income. To this may be added inequalities in the ownership of capital and hence inequality in incomes from capital. Capital can be accumulated by a process of saving and by entrepreneurship. But concentrations of wealth often arise by inheritance. The third empirical characteristic is the emergence of major

65

concentrations of economic power in large industrial and financial companies. The growth of major firms and financial institutions presumably follows a logic of economies from large-scale organization, both in producing goods and services and in dominating the relevant markets.

The origins of capitalism have been the subject of a wide-ranging debate since Max Weber ([1905] 1930) advanced his thesis that capitalism prospered in the Protestant ethic (see WORK AND LEISURE) that emerged from Calvinism in both Britain and continental Europe in the sixteenth and seventeenth centuries. This thesis was given a critical exposition by R.H. Tawney ([1926] 1938), and has generated a large historical and sociological literature (see Samuelsson, 1961). The conclusion seems to be that while certain features of the Protestant ethic were indeed conducive to capitalist development, there was also an awareness, at least in seventeenth-century Calvinism, of the dangers of the accumulation of wealth for its own sake, and of the responsibilities that wealth implied.

The Christian evaluation of capitalism needs to be seen in the context both of secular discussions of capitalism since the development of economic analysis in the late eighteenth century and of the development of theological ethics relevant to economics (see ECONOMIC ANALYSIS AND ETHICS). The interaction of these two elements may be summarized by setting out two contrasting positions.

The procapitalist position emphasizes a number of advantages of the capitalist system, which are then shown to be consonant with Christian ethics. The key advantage of the capitalist system is seen to be its ability to deliver the goods: capitalist economies have proved to be highly effective at both generating economic growth and raising living standards. This is consistent with the biblical emphasis on the human race as stewards of God's creation, with the injunction to be fruitful and multiply and with dominion over the created order. The second advantage is that it stresses personal responsibility. The market system is seen as a mechanism for rewarding those who live careful and productive lives, and for punishing the lazy and careless. In early nineteenth-century writings the market system was described as the

setting for the working out of God's providence. Against the criticism that the capitalist system merely encourages selfishness and self-seeking, the argument is advanced that self-seeking behaviour is actually conducive to the common good, along the lines of an argument first adumbrated by Adam Smith. In seeking personal gain, the supplier is forced to address the needs of customers; in so doing, his self-seeking is harnessed to a useful social purpose. Furthermore, self-seeking behaviour is to be expected of fallen mankind. The capitalist system is realistic in its understanding of human motivation. Finally, a capitalist system is praised for the scope that it gives for the exercise of personal freedom. The theological argument is that the creation of humankind in the image of God requires that we have a very high regard for the rights of the individual. In so far as a capitalist market system permits an individual to pursue his or her own goals in life, without let or hindrance, it is respecting those rights.

The anticapitalist position focuses on a number of detrimental features of capitalism. First, the capitalist market system produces inequality of incomes: the income of a person is determined by the resources that he can contribute to the market – labour, physical resources and financial capital. Those who have little to contribute will have low incomes: indeed they may be marginalized. The Christian concern for the poor and disadvantaged is adjudged to take precedence over the workings of the market. While personal charity and concern for the poor are to be encouraged, the claims of economic justice require that action be taken by governments to ensure that no one is left in poverty. Second, the emphasis on competition in markets is criticized for its neglect of the communal and cooperative aspects of human life. Scepticism is expressed about the Smithian notion that the pursuit of personal gain is consonant with the public good. In any case, selfishness is contrary to the Christian virtues. Third, it is argued that freedom in a capitalist society usually implies much greater freedom for those with resources than for the poor. In any case, freedom needs to be balanced by a sense of obligation to and responsibility for one's fellow human beings. Fourth, the organization of production is criticized for the powers that are given to the owners of capital, who may have no involvement in the actual task of production, and for the conflicts between capital and labour that are created by a structure within which their interests are opposed.

The debate for and against market capitalism generates its sharpest disagreements over the role of the political authorities in the allocation of resources. Procapitalists would wish to assign them a very limited role in providing a framework of law within which private market transactions can be effected without intervention. Anticapitalists see so many defects in the capitalist system that they argue for a prominent role for the political authorities in allocating resources and regulating market activity. Procapitalists would respond that the authorities lack the competence to undertake these tasks, so that their interventions are usually counterproductive, and that the authorities (at least in a democracy) are also in the 'market place' for votes, so that their interventions are not likely to be disinterested.

See also CHRISTIAN SOCIALISM; ETHICS; MARXISM; SOCIAL QUESTIONS.

Bibliography

Demant, V.A. 1952: *Religion and the Decline of Capitalism*. London: Faber and Faber.

Friedman, M. 1962: *Capitalism and Freedom*. Chicago: University of Chicago Press.

Griffiths, B. 1984: *The Creation of Wealth*. London: Hodder and Stoughton.

Hay, D.A. 1989: *Economics Today: A Christian Critique*. Leicester: Apollos; Grand Rapids: Eerdmans.

Hayek, F.A. von 1944: *The Road to Serfdom*. London: Routledge.

Munby, D.L. 1961: *God and the Rich Society*. Oxford: Oxford University Press.

Novak, M. 1982: *The Spirit of Democratic Capitalism*. New York: Simon and Schuster, American Enterprise Institute.

Preston, R.H. 1979: *Religion and the Persistence of Capitalism*. London: SCM Press.

Samuelsson, K. 1961: *Religion and Economic Action*. London: Heinemann; New York: Basic Books.

Smith, A. [1776] 1970: *The Wealth of Nations*. Harmondsworth: Penguin.

Tawney, R.H. [1926] 1938: *Religion and the Rise of Capitalism*. Harmondsworth: Penguin.

Weber, M. [1905] 1930: *The Protestant Ethic and the Spirit of Capitalism*, trans. Talcott Parsons, ed. R.H. Tawney. London: Allen and Unwin.

DONALD HAY

Cartesianism Cartesianism is the fresh orientation towards the thinking subject introduced by the philosophy of René Descartes (1596–1650). Originating in systematic 'doubt' and dependent upon an assumed link between truth and certainty, Cartesianism culminates in powerful dichotomies between subject and object and between mind and body. Largely in the form of background assumptions, the resulting conceptuality has profoundly shaped the terms within which much modern – especially Protestant – theology has come to expression. Specifically, the Cartesian framework often dictates the form of modern accounts of God, revelation, and faith and, more broadly, of theological conceptions of the relationship between faith and knowledge and between Christianity and culture. Its continuing influence can be observed in the numerous efforts by contemporary thinkers to criticize or otherwise supplant Cartesianism.

Arising out of Descartes's efforts to overcome doubt and uncertainty in the grounding of knowledge, the Cartesian starting point finds expression in the famous dictum, *cogito ergo sum* ('I think therefore I am'): in his search for 'clear and distinct ideas', Descartes managed to doubt everything except that he was thinking. The moment of sheer reflexive consciousness thus grounds the Cartesian project. The chief threat to certainty in philosophy is thereby subdued by an inflation of the importance of individual consciousness; simultaneously, epistemology is subtly given pride of place in philosophical method.

The *cogito* would subsequently become the compressed symbol for several developments decisive for modern Christian thought. The powerful role played by scepticism – by Descartes's elevation to the level of a 'method' the insistence on doubting everything he could bring to consciousness except for consciousness itself – seriously undermines the epistemological importance of every sort of received authority, including the authority of revelation, Scripture, and tradition. The moment of self-awareness conveyed by the *cogito* becomes the antecedent to all other cognitive claims, religious or otherwise. Received authority is displaced by self-reference. Cartesianism thus effectively establishes all certainty on the basis of a prior self-certainty, a result that both makes an element of reflexivity fundamental to the Cartesian outlook and provides considerable momentum to emerging modern notions of intellectual and personal autonomy.

Consequently, instead of the 'self' depending for its identity upon the stability imposed by a fixed moral and religious order that is external to it, the 'self' turns out to be the fixed point that, in turn, provides stability and order to an external world that is otherwise in doubt. Cartesianism both puts in question the relationship between the believer and the external world and makes individual subjectivity pre-eminent in the adjudication of this relationship. The importance of individual consciousness as the locus of certainty and, thereby, the source of truth is radically elevated. Often referred to as the 'turn to the subject', this shift in reference from what is 'outside' to what is 'inside' the thinker or believer is fundamental to the emergence of modernity, eventually gaining further definition through Immanuel Kant's transcendental philosophy (see KANTIANISM).

The specific results for theology of this foundationalist and dualistic epistemology are both profound and pervasive. Of particular consequence for theology is the obvious fact that Cartesianism charts a path to objective knowledge that passes through a prior subjectivity, or appeal to the thinking subject. Any claim to 'objective truth' – including theological truth – is thereby mediated by some level of subjective truth or meaningfulness, with Cartesian theologians staking out their distinctive positions according to where, within human consciousness or culture, they find this zone of meaningfulness. Language about anything external to the believer, including language about God, gains its very intelligibility only by virtue of a preceding appeal to some general, presumably universal, feature of human consciousness.

Cartesianism thus implicitly helps to underwrite a vast array of apologetic theological strategies, based on the disclosure of a presumed latent commensurability between the Christian message and the specified feature of human consciousness. Prominent examples of this commensurability – or of typical 'corridors' between faith and human nature – would include F.D.E. Schleiermacher's notion of 'absolute dependence' and Paul Tillich's concept of 'ultimate concern'. For such thinkers, Christian faith turns out to be a latent feature of human consciousness as such – a fortuitous result, given the priority of the reflexive subject in the knowing process and, moreover, the increasing difficulty of grounding faith in something 'external' to the believer, such as natural scientific or historical enquiry. A religious content once conceived of as being 'outside' the believer turns out to be 'inside'. The long-term effect for theology is to guarantee that, within a Cartesian framework, all reflection or language about God must be self-referential or self-involving in some way: Cartesianism forges an inescapable conceptual link between anthropology and theology, making the former a virtual 'vestibule' through which the latter must pass before it assumes intelligibility and epistemological integrity (Thielicke, [1968] 1974, pp. 44–5). When Kant subsequently claims that 'I must not even say, "*it is* morally certain that there is a God" but "*I am* morally certain"' (Kant, [1781] 1965, p. 650), or when Rudolf Bultmann claims that in order to speak of God we must first speak of ourselves (Bultmann, [1948] 1961), they are exhibiting this larger Cartesian theological result. Cartesianism thus provides the implicit conceptual framework for 'liberal' theology's many-faced project of establishing areas of overlap between Christian faith and secular insight.

In addition to promoting a commingling of language about human consciousness and language about God, Cartesianism has underwritten the modern theological preoccupation with the idea that God is best thought of as a pure 'subject', and never as an 'object'. Since any thought or language about God appears, by Cartesian terms, to 'objectify' God, post-Cartesian thinkers have endeavoured in numerous creative ways to get beyond the subject–object dichotomy in connection with God-language. Indeed, the powerful German Protestant tradition running from the idealism of Kant and G.W.F. Hegel (see HEGELIANISM) and the romanticism of Schleiermacher, up through the dialectical theology of the first half of the twentieth century associated with Karl Barth, Emil Brunner, Bultmann, Tillich and others, can be viewed as the sustained search for 'non-objectifying' language about God. The same is true of the efforts of Jewish thinker Martin Buber to conceive of God as the 'Eternal Thou' who can never be an 'It'. Cartesian dualism, enhanced by Kantian transcendentalism, provides the conceptual terms within which much of this debate over non-objectifying God-language develops.

A powerful challenge to the Cartesian shape of this debate occurs around 1930, when Karl Barth outgrows his own heavily Cartesian, dialectical/existentialist hermeneutic and assumes a more 'dogmatic' hermeneutic through fear of an 'anthropological captivity' for theology. For the mature Barth, the self-referential Cartesian vestibule for theology leads directly to the reductionism represented by Ludwig Feuerbach, who formulated the famous dictum, 'the secret of theology is anthropology.' For Barth, if language about God begins with language about the self, we invariably end in empty language about ourselves. This Barthian challenge to implicitly Cartesian assumptions helps to set the terms for a considerable amount of theological debate during the middle third of the twentieth century, appearing, for example, in the debate over the relevance of existentialism to theology, in the polemics associated with a putative 'point of contact' between humanity and God, in numerous hermeneutical debates, and in the question of whether Christian faith is a general and universal possibility for humankind. Debates originally associated with early Lutheran and Calvinist confessions are thus recycled, now with fresh conceptual formulas provided by the Cartesian turn to the subject and by the general framework offered by the subject–object dichotomy.

While the Barthian challenge can be thought of as a Cartesian crisis from 'within', there have been other forms of resistance to Cartesianism from other quarters. Where Roman Catholic theology has been heavily Thomistic and Aristotelian in philosophical orientation, Cartesianism has not only had little impact but has come in for serious criticism on both philosophical and theological grounds. An important exception to this general rule would be the conflation of Thomistic and transcendental philosophical interests in the theology of Karl Rahner. Likewise, theologians working under the influence of Alfred North Whitehead's bipolar philosophical vision explicitly and forthrightly reject Cartesianism as posing a misleading view of consciousness, an untenable mind–body dualism, and an utterly inadequate metaphysics (see PROCESS THEOLOGY). The contemporary scene abounds in sophisticated assaults on Cartesianism, as both philosophers and theologians feel their way towards a genuinely post-Cartesian standpoint necessitated by profound political and social, as well as conceptual, changes. The Cartesian tradition itself has generated its own self-criticism through the phenomenology of Edmund Husserl, Martin Heidegger and those influenced by them (see EXISTENTIALISM). For Heidegger and post-Heideggerians especially, the Cartesian subject needs to be 'de-centred' in the name of a more general ontology not so closely tied to a misleading preoccupation with personal consciousness and philosophical anthropology. In its more recent, radical forms, associated particularly with the work of Jacques Derrida, this post-Heideggerian position 'deconstructs' the very notion of a 'subject' and utterly subverts the Cartesian motif of 'representation', producing revolutionary results for theological hermeneutics. With neither a 'subject' behind it, nor the capacity to 'represent' truths or meanings, the biblical text can have no 'message' in the traditional sense. The very idea of the text existing in relation to a reality external to it is placed in jeopardy.

Powerful challenges to Cartesianism have also emerged from the influence of the philosophy of Ludwig Wittgenstein. His later philosophy generates an ironic stance towards the very possibility of the systematic doubt with which Cartesianism begins, discloses the philosophical impotence of Cartesianism's mentalistic vocabulary, and undermines the subject–object dichotomy itself. By emphasizing the ways in which language and culture precede and determine our very capacity to attribute 'inner' episodes to ourselves, Wittgenstein's philosophy reorients us in fresh ways towards the 'outside', away from Cartesian subjectivity and towards shared linguistic and social practices. The general effect for theology is to direct attention away from individualistic and privatistic conceptions of faith and to underscore the ways in which being a Christian involves sharing in those linguistic and social practices distinctive of the Christian community. On this view, there is no pre-linguistic route, by way of a reflexive Cartesian consciousness or anthropological 'given', to Christian faith. Consequently, there is no point to the traditional liberal strategy of seeking correlations between Christian faith and natural modes of human insight or consciousness.

A broad spectrum of political and liberation theologies has likewise protested against the Cartesian terms in which modern theology has developed. Often with the aid of neo-Marxist and post-structuralist modes of analysis, radical feminist, African American, and third world thinkers have all criticized the elements of control, manipulation, and representation that they associate with Cartesian thinking (see FEMINIST THEOLOGY; LIBERATION THEOLOGY). The *cogito* is castigated as the conceptual expression of privatistic, imperialistic, and exploitative attitudes, and of the denigration of the body as well. Likewise, the foundation of Cartesian epistemology – the idea of an incorrigible 'ground' for knowledge – is decoded as the latent justification of the dominant power relations within the social setting. Cartesian dualism, in particular, is criticized as the hidden yet (for that very reason) powerful cultural vehicle for the rationalization and perpetuation of various forms of oppression: everything that falls outside the normative (that is, white, male, western European/North American) subjective consciousness or 'gaze' is relegated to the inferior status of that which is 'represented', 'objectified', and, thereby, controlled. On this view, Cartesian dualism is the condition of the possibility of the depiction of 'otherness' and, consequently, of the maintenance of forms of domination; sophisticated philosophy and theology implicitly codify and perpetuate in abstract terms the harsh realities of a world of racism, sexism, and economic and political exploitation. The dismantling of those harsh realities will, in turn, entail the dismantling of Cartesian modes of thought and cultural conceptualization. Serious theology thus cannot thrive apart from social and political transformation.

Ironically, then, Cartesianism maintains a high profile within modern theology precisely by virtue of the array of serious challenges to its authority and influence. Perhaps pre-eminent among the several strictly theological issues at stake in these ongoing debates is the question of an intelligible conception of transcendence, or divine 'otherness'. The overriding question concerns the very viability of depicting God as 'other' than ourselves and the world, if the subject–object dichotomy can no longer be relied upon as an adequate or acceptable framing device.

See also EPISTEMOLOGY, RELIGIOUS.

Bibliography
Barth, Karl [1932–68] 1956–75: *Church Dogmatics*, vols I–IV, trans. G. Bromiley *et al.* Edinburgh: T & T Clark.
Brown, James 1955: *Subject and Object in Modern Theology*. London: SCM Press.
Bultmann, Rudolf [1948] 1961: *Kerygma and Myth*, ed. Hans Werner Bartsch, trans. Reginald H. Fuller. New York: Harper and Row.
Cushman, Robert 1956: Barth's attack upon Cartesianism and the future in theology, *Journal of Religion* 36, pp. 207–23.
Daly, Mary 1973: *Beyond God the Father*. Boston: Beacon Press.
Descartes, René 1967: *Philosophical Works of Descartes*, 2 vols, trans. Elizabeth S. Haldane and G.R.T. Ross. Cambridge: Cambridge University Press.
Dews, Peter 1987: *Logics of Disintegration: Post-Structuralist Thought and the Claims of Critical Theory*. London and New York: Verso.
Frei, Hans 1957: Niebuhr's theological background. In *Faith and Ethics*, ed. Paul Ramsey. New York: Harper and Row, pp. 9–64.
Kant, Immanuel [1781] 1965: *Critique of Pure Reason*, trans. Norman Kemp Smith. New York: St Martin's Press.
Michalson, Gordon E., Jr 1985: *Lessing's 'Ugly Ditch': A Study of Theology and History*. University Park and London: Pennsylvania State University Press.
Rorty, Richard 1979: *Philosophy and the Mirror of Nature*. Princeton: Princeton University Press.
Stout, Jeffrey 1981: *The Flight from Authority*. Notre Dame: University of Notre Dame Press.
Thielicke, Helmut [1968] 1974: *The Evangelical Faith*, vol. 1, *Prolegomena: The Relation of Theology to Modern Thought-Forms*, trans. Geoffrey Bromiley. Grand Rapids: Eerdmans.
West, Cornel 1982: *Prophesy Deliverance! An Afro-American Revolutionary Christianity*. Philadelphia:

Westminster Press.

Wittgenstein, Ludwig [1953] 1958: *Philosophical Investigations*, trans. G.E.M. Anscombe. New York: Macmillan.

GORDON E. MICHALSON, JR

Cassirer, Ernst (1874–1945) German humanistic philosopher. He was educated at Berlin, Leipzig, Heidelberg and Marburg. With the rise of Nazism, he left a chair of philosophy at Hamburg to teach for two years at Oxford before becoming a professor at Oxford and at Göteborg in Sweden in 1935; in 1941 he moved to the USA to teach at Yale and Columbia. In *The Philosophy of Symbolic Forms* (1923–9, trans. 1953–7) Cassirer describes religion as one among several modes of human self-definition (including art, language and science) which use symbols to form experience. Whereas mystical systems make no distinction between the symbol employed and objective reality, religion, like linguistic symbols, uses symbols to point to an infinite realm beyond the finite. In *An Essay on Man* (1944) he further explores the relationship between myth and religion, which he sees as inextricable: they both originate in the 'feeling of the indestructible unity of life' and in the fear of death as a threat to that unity.

Bibliography

Klibansky, R., and Paton, H.J., eds 1936: *Philosophy and History: Essays Presented to Ernst Cassirer*. Oxford.

Schilpp, P.A., ed. 1949: *The Philosophy of Ernst Cassirer*. La Salle, Ill.

Strenski, I. 1987: *Four Theories of Myth in Twentieth Century History*. Basingstoke.

casuistry See ETHICS.

Catholic theology See ROMAN CATHOLIC THEOLOGY.

charismatic movement See PENTECOSTALISM AND CHARISMATIC CHRISTIANITY.

Chinese Christian thought Chinese theologians in the last several decades have been compelled by historical situations to engage in the task of contextualization, long before the term came to be used. Modern China has gone through a tortuous history of political turmoil, of intense searching for directions of cultural reconstruction, of rapid sociocultural transformation, and of continual intellectual reorientation in the quest for modernization. Chinese theologians thus found themselves in fertile soil for theological exploration on the one hand, yet overwhelmed by challenges from all directions on the other. They have also had to face the stark reality of communist rule since 1949. The year 1949 was in fact the watershed for the Chinese church, and one has to see the development of modern Chinese Christian thought in two phases – one before 1949 and one from 1949 onwards.

Christian thought from 1917 to 1949

Politically, modern China began in 1911 with the founding of the Republic of China. Socioculturally, however, the advent of the May-Fourth Movement (the New Culture Movement) in 1917 marked the beginning of the modern era. 1917 to 1949 was perhaps the most creative period for theological thinking, and in fact we see some of the best theological minds emerging to face the challenge of the times. There were several urgent issues to be addressed. There was the question of the relevance of religion in modern society. As science was regarded as the key to modernization, scientism, and together with it an anti-religious sentiment, was prevalent. There was the issue of China's cultural past: there was a strong iconoclastic mood, and as a result there was also a strong sense of cultural identity crisis. Thus there was a quest for cultural-historical continuity. There was also the issue of socio-economic order, in the face of rampant exploitation and abject poverty, with the communist totalitarian revolution looming on the horizon.

In response to some of the issues, leading Christian thinkers such as Tzu-chen Chao, Timothy T. Lew, Lei-ch'uan Wu, David Z.T. Yui and Pao-ch'ien Hsu came together to form the Apologetic Group in 1920 in Beijing. They stated their objective clearly in a declaration:

> Christianity is our greatest need in connection with the regeneration of

Chinese society, and spreading Christianity is our greatest obligation . . . We must make use of conceptions of modern science and philosophy to clear up religious misunderstandings and doubts . . . and to prove the truth of the claims of Christ.

(Chinese Recorder, 1920, p. 636.)

Together they published a journal called *The Life*, which had considerable impact both within and beyond the Christian circle.

T.C. Chao (1888–1979) can be regarded as representative of the group. Chao, Dean of the School of Religion at Yenching and one of the six copresidents in the founding of the World Council of Churches in 1948, believed that Christianity was the answer to China's national crisis. However, Christianity had to be radically reinterpreted, with the essence of the gospel uncovered from under the rubble of dogmas and traditions of the church.

Starting from the personality of Jesus Christ and his teaching of the kingdom of God, and using conceptual tools from Bowne, Bergson and Whitehead (Chao, 1925), Chao developed what may be called the 'Christo-centric personalism'. According to him, 'Christianity is Christ . . . a Christ life or Christ consciousness' (Chao, 1918, p. 287–8). Christ leads us to the very depths of our humanity and to the heart of the cosmos, to discover God's personality there. In this sense, 'Christianity is a personalism in which the Absolute is a person that comes into relation with His creatures' (ibid. p. 371).

God creates the world out of his own personhood; his own self is the 'substance' of creation (1955, pp. 139–43). The world is the continual outflowing and unfolding of God's personality, which is characterized by immediate self-consciousness, self-transcendence and self-direction in constant creation (1925, pp. 128–35, 181–8). The world, with God's personality as its ground and moving force, comes to the fullness of its being in its consciousness of itself as constantly moving forward with God in his creativity. As God creates and continues to create, his personality is being unfolded as love. Love points to God's self-limitation, without which his creatures would become sheer manifestations of his

continual activity (1955, p. 140). Because of love, not only do humankind and the cosmos have distinct personalities of their own, it also means that God constantly brings them back to himself for communion and partnership in continual creation. However, humanity enjoys the fruit of love from God but forgets to fulfill it in itself. This leads to the disintegration of human existence.

Jesus Christ is the revelation of God's love. Through his perfect personality he unveils the personality of God at the heart of both the cosmic and the personal world. He is therefore both divine and human personality manifested at their most concrete. In line with the liberal tradition, Chao understood Jesus as a man who became the Son of God through his radical consciousness of his unity with God, of the personality of God in the depths of his being and of the outflowing love from him. In acting out such consciousness, Jesus Christ became the concrete reality of God's personality. When 'the perfection of love' finds its complete fulfilment in the sacrifice of Jesus, God's revelation in Jesus is full, complete, and absolute. Following Jesus Christ, the human individual will rediscover the spark of divine personality in himself or herself, and come back to his or her true nature as the manifestation of God's personality. And with this, the human personality is able to be reintegrated. Thus Jesus Christ may be called 'the Saviour of our personality' (1923, p. 13). The kingdom of God is nothing but the universal consciousness and attainment of this reality, leading to a universal community of love.

As for the relevance of Christianity to China, Chao was convinced that 'the heart of the problem of reconstruction is the creation of a new spirit in man' (1922, p. 315). Only when a large number of individuals are regenerated is there hope for a radical change of social order. From his emphasis on moral consciousness and personality, we can see quite clearly that the Confucian humanistic tradition had left an indelible mark on Chao's thought.

It is quite interesting to note that Chao's theology underwent some significant changes, due mainly to his prison experience under the Japanese and the influence of Karl Barth, leading to his intense study of the Pauline epistles. The change was evident in *The Life of*

St Paul (1948b), in which he confessed that his earlier work *The Life of Christ* drew largely on his own imagination (p. 12), and in *Four Talks on Theology* (1948a), where he emphasized the transcendence of God, the pre-existence and the divinity of Christ, the reality of the spoken Word of God, and theology as faith seeking understanding. He even criticized the liberal interpretation of Christian faith as futile human effort and complete misunderstanding (p. 2).

While many of the Apologetic Group would basically agree with Chao's interpretation of Christianity, some, like Lei-ch'uan Wu and later Yao-tsung Wu, would take a more radical approach.

Lei-ch'uan Wu (1870–1944), professor and then president of Yenching University from 1929, agreed with Chao that the personality of Jesus Christ was the heart of Christianity. Yet Jesus himself was a revolutionary, whose aim was the establishment of a radically new social order. To achieve that Jesus was prepared to resort to political revolution. This was quite clear when Jesus identified himself as the Messiah, as the term in the Jewish context had clear political implications (1939, p. 82ff). In an essay written in 1939, he set forth Jesus' social, economic and political concerns, indicating that Jesus stood with the poor and called for the abolition of private property, for equal rights and equal sharing of all goods (1948, pp. 151–4). Such radical interpretation drew sharp criticism from Chao and others, but found strong support from Yao-tsung Wu, a Young Men's Christian Association secretary who was to have a great impact on the church in China for his leading role in founding the Three Self Patriotic Movement.

Yao-tsung Wu (1893–1979) embraced Christianity in 1918 through reading the Sermons on the Mount, deeply moved by the personality of Jesus and his teaching of love. Jesus' concept of love, however, goes beyond the personal realm for him; it means 'the uplifting of the masses, and the fulfilment of all necessary conditions that will make the uplifting possible' (1934a, p. 10). Influenced by Harry Ward and Reinhold Niebuhr while at Union Theological Seminary and Columbia University in the USA, he emphasized the inseparability of personal morality and the social condition. Salvation for him is therefore always social in nature even

when all the aspects of individual life are taken into account (1937, pp. 21–4). Thus 'the gospel of Jesus is a social gospel' (1934b, p. 146). Social analysis is therefore an integral part of proclamation. And in his analysis, China's problem was having a social order based on individualism and *laissez-faire*, giving rise to widespread exploitation, oppression and injustice. It had to be replaced by 'a social order based on the principle of communal labour, communal appropriation, and communal ownership' (1936, pp. 211). Christianity, Wu believed, could provide the spiritual impetus for such a transformation.

'There is in the universe,' Wu argued, 'a Force which penetrates and sustains all existence and all forms of life . . . It reveals itself in the world of nature as laws and in human society as love' (1936, p. 208). We call this Force 'God' or 'Father' to symbolize its intimacy to us, as we experience the force of love everywhere in our social relation. And Jesus is the unique revealer of the Force through his life of sacrificial love. The cross is the ultimate revelation and fulfilment of love. Yet this love is a severe love, which 'expresses itself as reproof and revolt against the oppressor' (p. 211). Certainly Jesus' gospel is a gospel of peace, yet 'real peace can only be built on justice', and Jesus is uncompromising towards anything that obstructs justice (p. 213). To follow Christ requires one to follow him even as 'he would attack relentlessly any individual, group or institution which would suppress and destroy life' (p. 211).

Wu was one of the earliest to reflect on the problem of violence in revolution and the theological implications of communism. In regard to violence, Jesus' love is ultimate and his reverence for personality is absolute, so the means for justice has to be in harmony with the way of love. One has to overcome evil with good, and should never resort to violence. Wu would criticize the communists for their tactics of violence. He identified himself as a pacifist who could not possibly join the communist party (p. 213). Yet at the same time he sought to integrate Christian faith and communist faith. The Marxist, according to Wu, has discovered the inevitability in the historical process through grasping the law of nature. Yet the Marxist revolution is only the first step towards the total liberation of humankind The law of love has to take over after the first step for a continual revolution, through which true personality and social communion may be achieved (cf. 1943). Thus Christianity has a definite role to play even after the communist revolution. With this integration, Wu saw it possible to work with the communists for national reconstruction. And Wu was on the way to becoming the most controversial person in modern Chinese church history.

There were other Christian thinkers who were more concerned with the problem of indigenization. They attempted to find conceptual tools congenial to the Chinese mind. Fu-ya Zia (1892–1991), Professor of Philosophy at Lingnan University who studied under Whitehead at Harvard, felt that Chinese Christian thinkers should not take concepts and categories developed in the west for granted as if they were something absolute. They should develop their own. For several decades he attempted to use indigenous concepts like Xin (nature), Dao (logos), Li (logos), Dung (dynamis), Qing (stillness), Ti (inner reality) and Tien-Jen-He-Yi (the oneness of God and Man) for theological construction.

There were more conservative thinkers who had much wider influence among the general public of the Chinese church. Yue-ming Chia (1880–1964) was professor of systematic theology at Nanking Theological Seminary. Theology, according to him, is a science. However, science, to be truly scientific, has to be bound and guided by the subject matter of its enquiry. Thus theology as science has to be guided by the objective reality of God as God in his revelation (1921, vol. 1, part 1, pp. 2–6). As in all sciences, reason can be misused, which will lead to misunderstanding. So in theology it has to be constantly guided and corrected by revelation (pp. 34–5). Only then can natural theology have its place in systematic theology (part 2, pp. 1–28). At the same time, theology is not merely a way to knowledge, it is a form of spirituality aiming first at sanctification, then proclamation (vol. 1, part 1, pp. 13–23).

Perhaps a more ardent defender of the conservative interpretation of Christian faith is Ming-tao Wang (1900–1991). Wang was a truly indigenous churchman and evangelist who insisted on complete independence from western denominations. He was well-known for his refusal to join the Three Self Patriotic Movement in the 1950s and for his long imprisonment, ending in 1979. In almost the same vein as David Friedrich Strauss's criticism of the rationalist reconstruction of the historical Jesus, Wang challenged the liberals on their basis for choosing to believe the biblical witness to Jesus' perfect personality while rejecting other parts of the Bible that had to do with Jesus' divinity (1978, vol. 7, p. 49). If the liberals chose not to believe in miracles they would make Jesus a liar, because in Matthew 11: 4–6 Jesus clearly referred to miracles, including resurrection, as indications of his identity (vol. 6, p. 156). At the same time his disciples, on whose witness liberal theologians depended for reconstructing Jesus' personality, should be regarded as the greatest liars, as they testified to the resurrection of Jesus. A liar's personality is not much worth imitating, and liars' testimony is not to be trusted. Christianity thus stands or falls with the reality or falsehood of Christ's resurrection and miracles.

Wang also relentlessly attacked the idea of building an ideal society on earth. All the social evils, according to him, stem from the corruption of human nature. People have to be transformed from within, and cannot attain this by their own efforts. They can only be regenerated through dying and being resurrected with Jesus Christ, and this is the heart of the gospel. Wang believed that only through personal salvation can there be hope for relief from social evils, but even then the relief is only temporary and never complete. The ultimate relief comes in Christ's second coming.

Wang's theology continues to have deep and widespread influence, both in China and the Chinese Christian communities overseas. One may even say that a significant portion of the Chinese church is shaped by Wang's theology. Thus Wang's thought has to be taken seriously if one is to understand the Chinese church.

Christian thought since 1949
Mainland China The impact of communist rule on the church in China can hardly be overestimated. The church underwent a process of reorientation in many aspects of its life, including theological reflection, amidst a deluge of movements in the 1950s leading

subsequently to the Cultural Revolution, which brought intense suffering upon the people.

According to Yi-feng Shen, pastor of Shanghai Community Church, 'the theological question which Christians in New China first encountered was that of the relationship between creation and redemption' (1988, p. 24). Or stated in another way, it was the question of the relationship between the sacred and the profane (p. 27). In more concrete terms, in what way should Christians view the communist revolution and how should they relate to it, if they were not to reject it out of hand? This was also a question of the relationship between revelation and history. Shen suggested that if God's creation was to have meaning at all, then redemption could not possibly be meant to negate creation but to fulfill it. At the same time, the incarnation and Jesus' participation in earthly life 'sanctified earthly existence . . . all profane things that are done to the glory of God can become "sacred"' (ibid.).

In response to the question, K.H. Ting, President of the China Christian Council, developed a more comprehensive theological framework. According to him God is immanent and ever working in the continual evolution of his creation, 'the end purpose of which is the emergence of a universe of a truly free humanity in the image of God' (England, 1982, p. 68). The evolutionary process is an educative process in which Christ is 'an exemplification of the fullness with which he reveals the nature and potentiality of the world'. And 'to say that man has fallen is really to say that he is not at present in his proper state, the state to which he ought to belong' (pp. 69–70). Thus the progress in which man moves from what he is to what he ought to be coincides with the continual working of God in his continual creation. And we 'discover the immanence of the transcendent God in history, in nature, in the people's movements and in the collectivities in which we find ourselves' (p. 70).

However, the questions of how the reality of evil in history should be regarded and in what way Christians should respond to social evils in New China still remain. The questions are raised because they have been highly relevant to Christian thinkers in Taiwan, and have to a large extent shaped their thinking.

Taiwan Taiwan has been under tight martial law for more than four decades, and a theology expressing the suffering and aspiration of the Taiwanese has gradually emerged. The Presbyterian church, in response to the sociopolitical crisis sparked off by Taiwan's ousting from the United Nations in 1971 and the USA's recognition of China in 1977, issued three consecutive declarations calling for self-determination for the people of Taiwan and demanding fundamental human rights. In these declarations a theological framework took shape. It is referred to as the 'theology of homeland and people'. The promise, possession and finally dispossession of the land is taken to be the dominant theme in the Old Testament. The land gives life, identity and hope to a people. The story of Israel is the story of God's involvement with a people in their struggle for freedom from domination and for self-determination in their own land. The Taiwanese are dispossessed of their land, in so far as they have not been treated as a people in their own land but as pawns to be sacrificed for the cause of reclaiming mainland China by the Guomindang, and their rights and needs have been consistently neglected. The Old Testament gives them the inspiration to struggle for self-determination in their own land (see Wang, 1988).

C.S. Song (b. 1929), deeply involved in the theological construction in Taiwan in the early years, attempts to provide a broader theoretical framework, not only for Taiwan, but for Asia as a whole. The key to the Asian framework is the concept of transposition. Transposition, according to Song, is incarnation. If the gospel is to emanate its power in different cultures, it has to be woven into the fundamental fabrics of those cultures. In so doing it can no longer stand as a distinct entity of its own: 'The gospel, when transposed from its biblical world to other cultural worlds, undergoes change itself as well as causing other worlds to change' (1982, p. 11). The interweaving, however, is an interweaving of experiences of peoples which cause God utter pain and prompt him into action, identifying with them, standing with them in their struggles (1979, pp. 35–98). Thus Song, in working out theological themes, weaves biblical stories together with stories of different times and cultures, so that the biblical stories are not only seen as relevant but are also seen in a very different light. Those stories are fundamentally stories of peoples, of their suffering, struggle and hope. In them one begins to see Jesus in a different light. 'Jesus who had shown the world . . . that God wanted justice for the poor and oppressed . . . was marked out by the religious and political powers to be broken, to be destroyed' (1990, p. 212). Jesus thus means crucified people.

Lien-hwa Chow (b. 1920), one of the most influential churchmen and theologians in Taiwan, is committed to a more traditional interpretation of Christian faith, though recognizing the need to shed the metaphysical cast of systematic theology in the west. He thus attempts to 'transpose' biblical theology into the Chinese world of thought, drawing intellectual resources from ancient Chinese texts. At the same time, while stressing the prophetic aspect of Christ, Chow reminds us that his priesthood and servanthood are equally important. Thus a foundation should be sought for working with the government without compromising the prophetic role of the church. And in fact, a theology of reconciliation is emerging as the most recent trend in Taiwan.

Hong Kong Theologians in Hong Kong have always considered themselves as part of the Chinese tradition, sharing a common historical destiny with the people of China. Again, relating Christian faith to the unique social, political and historical situation of Hong Kong has been the major concern. Out of his experiences of working with the labouring class in helping to build a labour movement in the 1970s, Raymond Fung developed the concept of man not only as sinner but also as 'the sinned against' (Elwood, 1980, p. 201). The concept has taken root in Christian consciousness in Hong Kong, as shown in Christians' response to sociopolitical issues. However, the approach of 1997 has become a powerful theological catalyst. From 1984 to 1991 three documents – *A Declaration of Convictions* in 1984, *A Christian Manifesto on Religious Freedom* in 1985, and *The Mission of the Church in the Nineties* in 1991 – were issued. And in the process of writing these documents, a theological framework also gradually emerged. They show a deep awareness of being at a unique historical juncture, and their dominant theme is the meaning of Christian

participation in history. The theme of God as the Lord and people as the subject of history is integrated with the theme of incarnation to provide a framework within which the church can participate actively in shaping the future not only of Hong Kong but also of China beyond the year 1997.

See also JAPANESE CHRISTIAN THOUGHT; KOREAN CHRISTIAN THOUGHT; OTHER FAITHS AND CHRISTIANITY.

Bibliography

Chao, T.C. 1918: The appeal of Christianity to the Chinese Mind, *Chinese Recorder* 49, pp. 287–96, 371–80.

Chao, T.C. 1922: The basis of social reconstruction, *Chinese Recorder* 53, pp. 312–18.

Chao, T.C. 1923: My religious experience, *Life* (Sheng-ming) 4, 3, pp. 1–16.

Chao, T.C. 1925: *Christian Philosophy* (in Chinese). Shanghai: Chinese Christian Literary Association.

Chao, T.C. 1948a: *Four Talks on Theology* (in Chinese). Shanghai: Association Press.

Chao, T.C. 1948b: *Life of St Paul* (in Chinese). Shanghai: Association Press.

Chao, T.C. 1955: *Interpretation of Christianity* (in Chinese). Hong Kong: Council on Christian Literature for Overseas Chinese.

Chia, Yue-ming 1921: *Systematic Theology*. Nanking: Nanking Theological Seminary.

Chu, T., and Lind, C., eds 1981: *A New Beginning*. Montreal: Canadian Council of Churches.

Elwood, D.J., ed. 1980: *Asian Christian Theology: Emerging Themes*. Philadelphia: Westminster Press.

England, J.C., ed. 1982: *Living Theology in Asia*. New York: Orbis.

Lam Wing-hung 1983: *Chinese Theology in Construction*. Pasadena: William Carey Library.

Shen, Yi-feng 1988: Theological reflections in the Chinese church, *Chinese Theological Review*.

Song, C.S. 1979: *Third-Eye Theology*. Maryknoll, NY: Orbis.

Song, C.S. 1982: *The Compassionate God*. New York: Orbis.

Song, C.S. 1990: *Jesus, The Crucified People*. New York: Orbis.

Wang, Hsien-chi, ed. 1988: *Collected Essays on Homeland Theology* (in Chinese). Tainan: Tainan Theological Seminary.

Wang, Ming-tao 1977: *The Meaning of Regeneration* (in Chinese). Hong Kong: Christian Alliance Press.

Wang, Ming-tao 1978: *Collected Works* (in Chinese), 7 vols. Taipei: Baptist Press.

Wu, Lei-ch'uan 1936: *Christianity and Chinese Culture* (in Chinese). Shanghai: Association Press.

Wu, Lei-ch'uan 1948: Christian faith and social

reform. In *Christianity and New China*, ed. Yao-tsung Wu. Shanghai: Association Press.

Wu, Yao-tsung 1934a: Make Christianity socially dynamic, *Chinese Recorder* 65, pp. 7–11.

Wu, Yao-tsung 1934b: *Social Gospel*. Shanghai: Association Press.

Wu, Yao-tsung 1936: Christianity and China's reconstruction, *Chinese Recorder* 67, pp. 208–14.

Wu, Yao-tsung 1937: Should Christianity concern itself in social reconstruction?, *Chinese Recorder* 68, pp. 21–4.

Wu, Yao-tsung 1943: *No Man Has Seen God* (in Chinese). Shanghai: Association Press.

CARVER T. YU

Christ, Jesus A central task of Christian thought has been the clarification of the identity and significance of Christ for the church and the world. The most important debates centring upon Jesus Christ to be dealt with in this volume may be found under the following headings.

1 BIBLICAL CRITICISM AND INTERPRETATION 2: NEW TESTAMENT. This includes a survey of scholarly opinion relating to the status and proper interpretation of the New Testament documents, especially the synoptic Gospels, which form the basis of theological reflection relating to the person and work of Christ.

2 CHRISTOLOGY. The theological exploration of the identity of Jesus Christ and the most appropriate ways of articulating his relationship to humanity and God.

3 FAITH AND HISTORY. The debate over how a historical event (the history of Jesus Christ) can be the foundation for a universally valid system of belief.

4 FEMINIST THEOLOGY. This entry deals with the question of whether the maleness of Christ is of decisive significance in relation to his perceived relevance in modern western culture.

5 GOD. An issue of recurring importance in relation to the Christian doctrine of God concerns the manner in which the historical figure of Jesus Christ is constitutive or determinative of God. This is developed classically in Trinitarian terms, with a direct relationship being established between the second person of the Trinity and the historical being of Jesus Christ; this

approach has been creatively explored and developed during the twentieth century.

6 HISTORICAL JESUS, QUEST OF. The attempt to reconstruct an accurate and neutral historical portrait of Jesus Christ, on the basis of the evidence available in the New Testament and scholarly investigation of first-century Palestinian culture and Jewish religious beliefs and expectations.

7 INCARNATION. The doctrine which articulates the significance of Jesus Christ in terms of the 'Word becoming flesh' – that is, of the second person of the Trinity assuming human nature and living out a historical existence on earth.

8 KINGDOM OF GOD: NEW TESTAMENT. The scholarly analysis of what is often regarded as the central feature of the preaching of Jesus.

9 RESURRECTION. The debate over the historical nature and theological implications of the resurrection of Christ.

10 SOTERIOLOGY. The exploration of the meaning of the death and resurrection of Christ for the transformation of the human situation, dealing with the nature of salvation itself and the manner in which this is related to the history of Jesus Christ.

Christian Socialism Christian Socialism, interpreted narrowly, refers to the activity of a small group of which F.D. Maurice was the intellectual leader in the years 1848–54; others were Tom Hughes, J.M. Ludlow, Charles Kingsley and E.V. Neale. After a break certain Christian groups from 1877 onwards have used the term and have related themselves in a general way to the impetus given by Maurice. So have a number of Christian social, though not socialist, groups; indeed the meaning of the term 'socialist' has itself varied.

The significance of the original Christian Socialist venture has to be understood against a broad historical background. Down the centuries the church developed a social theology in some detail, which survived the Reformation and the Renaissance, and was continued in England by Anglicans and Puritans alike until the end of the seventeenth century (see Tawney, 1926). By then it had to meet the challenge of a new society, capitalism, first in its merchant and later in its industrial form. It failed and disappeared. In the vacuum some clergy tried to deal with mercantilist economic theories, which flourished in the eighteenth century, and also made a contribution to the development of the new discipline of economics, which challenged mercantilism. In doing this they started afresh theologically; traditional social theology had vanished. At the end of the century they got a shock with the publication in 1798 of T.R. Malthus's *Essay on the Principle of Population*. The new dynamic economic order was entailing social change at a hitherto unprecedented rate; there were many gainers and many losers, and much social distress. Malthus sought to demonstrate that these social ills were unavoidable because of the inevitable pressure of population on the means of subsistence. He ended with a theodicy (which he subsequently withdrew) which maintained that this was necessary in order for God to achieve the full development of humanity which he intended. In the next thirty years a number of Christian theologians, faced with what they thought was a 'scientific' fact, developed an apologetic to justify it (briefly treated in Preston, 1983). The upshot was a defence of the new *laissez-faire* theory of the market and the 'laws' of competition and supply and demand as immutable laws of God's universe, as those of physics were held to be. This was the dominant view in Christian circles in 1848.

In the previous decades there had been the widespread and inchoate Chartist movement. In Scotland there had been Robert Owen's cooperative experiment at New Lanark. In France there had been various socialist utopian thinkers and movements. At this time 'socialism' had an atheist overtone, because of Owen and the French theorists, whilst 'communism' had a religious overtone.

By 1848 Maurice's theology had been clear for a decade. A man of wide and deep sympathy, he was moved by the social dislocations which lay behind Chartism. Ludlow had lived in Paris and was present at the events of February that year when Louis Philippe was overthrown. Kingsley was a Tory of a Burkeian type who was appalled by the squalor of early Victorian industrialism. Neale was attracted to the new cooperative movement, which in its consumer form began in 1844 with the Rochdale Pioneers.

In the next four years the Christian Socialist group produced a manifesto, several tracts and pamphlets, and set up a series of producers' cooperatives in London for builders, tailors, bakers and shoemakers, largely financed by Neale. They all failed within a few years through quarrels, dishonesty and the individualism of the workers. Maurice, who in any case was not a man of practical action, withdrew his support and the others went their different ways. Ludlow later became the Chief Registrar of Friendly Societies, and Neale became the secretary of the Cooperative Union and produced with Hughes the first textbook on the cooperative system.

The ideas of the Christian Socialists were ill assorted and unformed, but they had one basic conviction of lasting importance. Whereas the Christian apologists for *laissez-faire* were giving it a divine sanction, they saw that competition as an overall philosophy of how humans should relate to one another is, in Maurice's term, 'a lie'. But his organic view of society was far from what would be thought of as socialist. It was a hierarchical social paternalism which did not envisage any fundamental change in the structure of society, regarded the monarchy and aristocracy as the designated rulers and guides of society, and thought of the cooperative workshops as a means of eliminating class hostility. Maurice took the view, as many middle- and upper-class people have done, that workers need educating before they can take responsibility; he founded the Working Men's College in Camden Town.

Self-confidence and economic growth characterized the middle years of the century, and it was not until 1877 that the Christian Socialist movement restarted, with the founding by Stewart Headlam of the Guild of St Matthew. Its theological foundations were (1) a stress on the incarnation, as against the evangelical stress on the atonement; (2) the social significance of the Eucharist (see SACRAMENTAL THEOLOGY), as against the pietism of the early years of the Oxford movement; (3) building the kingdom of God on earth, in tune with the evolutionary optimism of many at the time (see KINGDOM OF GOD: POLITICAL AND SOCIAL THEOLOGY). In social strategy Headlam was very different from Maurice. The Fabian Society had been founded, and he was a member. The state rather than cooperatives was to be the prime mover in social reform. The Guild was to be like other subsequent groups in taking up uncritically a secular panacea, in this case Henry George's single (land) tax; and like many of them it was clerical in tone and elitist in its attitude to the working class.

The Guild of St Matthew was the precursor of several more such groups. The big Liberal victory in the 1906 General Election sparked off the Church Socialist League, based more on the industrial north of England and using 'socialism' in a statist sense. It took up guild socialism, a scheme for organizing production which would do away with the wage system, which was popular in the years immediately before and after the 1914–18 war. In 1916 came the Catholic Crusade based on the fatherhood of God and the brotherhood of man, an ironic echo of Liberal Protestantism, and the 'sacramental principle'. It hailed the Russian revolution of 1917 and later split between those who supported Joseph Stalin and those who supported Leon Trotsky. Anglo-Catholics who disliked both the ecclesiastical and political tone of existing groups formed what became known as the Christendom movement, running for many years a summer school of sociology and publishing a quarterly journal *Christendom* from 1931 to 1950. V.A. Demant was the leading thinker and Maurice Reckitt the chronicler and financial backer. It adopted the social credit economic analysis of the engineer Major C.H. Douglas. It was not part of the Christian Socialist movement, but it is hard to think of it apart from that context.

There were many more small groups, some short-lived, and several free church ones as against the Anglican ones (see Mayor, 1967). A diagram of the more recent ones is given in Ormrod (1987, p. 436). In 1960 the various surviving groups amalgamated to form the Christian Socialist movement, which has about 1200 members and in 1985 produced a glossy booklet, *Facing the Future as Christians and Socialists* (see Preston, 1988). In the penumbra of Christian Socialism there must be mentioned (as in the case of the Christendom movement) the Christian Social Union, founded in 1889 and continuing until 1920, when the Industrial Christian Fellowship, still in existence, grew out of it. The Christian Social Union was somewhat akin to the American social gospel movement. At one time it had about 6000 members, more than any other group, with some notable clerical leaders like Bishops B.F. Westcott, Charles Gore and William Temple, and Canon Scott Holland.

All these groups had an indirect influence on the labour movement, which has had a very different ethos from socialist parties on the continent. It grew out of the cooperative movement, the trade unions and the Independent Labour Party and was suffused with an ethical idealism with Christian undertones, so that a former general secretary of the Labour Party could say it owed more to Methodism than to Marx. This was not so much because of the various Christian Socialist groups, which were clerical and middle class, but because many working-class leaders learned to read, write and speak in Primitive Methodist (not United or Wesleyan) and Baptist congregations. Also in the years 1891–1918 there were up to fifty Labour Churches in existence, mainly in Lancashire and the West Riding of Yorkshire, which combined political commitment with aspects of Christian worship, often diluted.

These Christian Socialist groups were curiously untouched by Marxist theories until the 1930s, when a Christian Left group arose among intellectuals who took Marxism seriously (see Ormrod, 1987). There was a similar Roman Catholic Slant group in the 1960s after the opening to take Marxism seriously in Pope John XXIII's encyclical *Pacem in Terris* (1963). Roman Catholics have taken little part in Christian Socialist activity, chiefly because of papal condemnations of socialism from *Rerum Novarum* (1891) onwards. The first two social encyclicals of John Paul II, *Laborem Exercens* (1981) and *Sollicitudo Rei Socialis* (1988), have marked a change in stressing the primacy of labour. (See ROMAN CATHOLIC THEOLOGY.)

The Christian Socialist groups (and many of those on the penumbra of them) have had economic, sociological and theological weaknesses. Economically they have failed to distinguish competitive individualism, which they have been right to criticize as a false philosophy, from the market as a useful human device for dealing with a range of basic economic problems which every society has to solve, connected with how to allocate relatively scarce resources which have alternative uses. In this context the market is useful, provided it is contained within a firm social setting; and no adequate alternative has so far been offered. Christian Socialists have objected to competition as such; have talked of production for use and not for profit, treating profit also as an objectionable concept; they have held that service not self should be the motivation in human society, not unpacking the concept of self-interest precisely enough; and they have talked of 'common ownership' as if it were a panacea, oblivious of the empirical evidence of the political problems it can raise. Sociologically they have had little contact with working-class life, but they have had a useful function in querying the too easy acceptance of either traditional hierarchical assumptions or individualist *laissez-faire* assumptions in church circles. Theologically they have often combined sectarianism with a somewhat perfectionist understanding of human nature and society; they have been what are often called 'soft utopians', in the sense of setting out to build an ideal social order or kingdom of God, as against the 'hard utopians' of the Marxist kind who see it arriving only after conflict and struggle. However, on one basic point they have put a serious question to capitalism as by itself a sufficient ordering of society. If the three basic factors of production, land, capital and labour, are treated alike, and the market is not set in a firm social framework, it means that labour (persons) are treated as land and capital (things). It is hard to see how this can be justified by Christian theology.

See also CAPITALISM; ECONOMIC ANALYSIS AND ETHICS; MARXISM; SOCIAL QUESTIONS.

Bibliography

Backstrom, P.N. 1974: *Christian Socialism and Co-operation in Victorian England: Edward Vansittart Neale and the Co-operative Movement*. London: Croom Helm.

Binyou, G.C. 1931: *The Christian Socialist Movement in England*. London: SPCK.

Christensen, T. 1962: *The Origin and History of Christian Socialism*. Aarhus: Aarhus Universitetsforlaget.

Jones, P. d'A. 1968: *The Christian Socialist Revival 1877–1914: Religion, Class and Social Conscience in late Victorian England*. Princeton: Princeton University Press.

Mayor, S. 1967: *The Churches and the Labour Movement*. London: Independent Press.

Murray, A.D., ed. 1981: *John Ludlow: the Autobiography of a Christian Socialist*. London: Frank Cass.

Norman, E.R. 1987: *The Victorian Christian Socialists*. Cambridge: Cambridge University Press.

Ormrod, D. 1987: The Christian Left and the beginning of the Christian–Marxist dialogue. In *Disciplines of Faith: Studies in Religion, Politics and Patriarchy*, ed. Jim Obelkevich, Lyndal Roper and Raphael Samuel. London: Routledge, Kegan & Paul.

Preston, R.H. 1983: *Church and Society in the Late Twentieth Century: The Economic and Political Task*. London: SCM Press.

Preston, R.H. 1988: Christian Socialism becalmed, *Theology*, January.

Raven, C.E. 1920: *Christian Socialism 1848–1854*. London: John Murray.

Reckitt, M.B. 1947: *Maurice to Temple: A Century of the Social Movement in the Church of England*. London: Faber and Faber.

Tawney, R.H. 1926: *Religion and the Rise of Capitalism*. London: John Murray.

Waterman, A.M.C. 1991: *Revolution, Economics and Religion: Christian Political Economy 1798–1833*. Cambridge: Cambridge University Press.

RONALD H. PRESTON

Christology The aim of Christology is to give an account of the identity and significance of Jesus Christ, of who he is and why he is important. Modern Christian theology in the west, especially Protestant theology, has largely regarded the belief that Jesus Christ is the unique historical redeemer as the hallmark of a distinctively Christian view of the world; it has been the central conviction with which other beliefs must harmonize, and which – however dramatically it may be revised through engagement with modernity – cannot be given up without abandoning Christian theology altogether. More than any other classical theological topic, Christology has been the central preoccupation of distinctively modern Christian theology.

Modern Christologies have been concerned, in one sense, with traditional issues. In the manner of Christian theology from its earliest beginnings, they have attempted to develop adequate and justifiable descriptions of the person on whose identity the narrative in the Gospels turns, and suitable and compelling ways to conceive his saving significance (accounts, as modern theologians often put it, of 'the person' and 'the work' of Christ). But reflection on these traditional issues since the eighteenth century has been deeply structured by attention to several interrelated problems which, while they all have precedents in earlier theological discussion, take on new forms during and after the ENLIGHTENMENT and jointly constitute the primary axes on which modern Christology turns.

Particular identity and universal significance The social and intellectual forces of modernity have combined to support the idea that matters of ultimate meaning, value, and truth must in at least some form be available to all; access to that which is ultimately significant, however described, cannot be limited decisively by a person's historical, communal, and social location. But to believe in Jesus Christ as the unique historical redeemer is to ascribe ultimate and (at least in principle) universal significance to a particular person, the knowledge of whom is a contingent historical matter and requires contact of some kind with a particular historical community. Modern theologians have consistently sought Christological strategies which would enable them, as much as possible, to be both modern and Christian: to honour modernity's claim about equal access to ultimate matters while holding to the central Christian conviction that ultimate significance is to be ascribed uniquely to Jesus of Nazareth.

The divinity and humanity of Christ Classic Christian theology had been deeply shaped by the conviction that the whole human life of Jesus, from his birth in Bethlehem to the cross of Golgotha and his resurrection and exaltation by the Father, was itself the life of God: 'The Word was God . . . and the Word became flesh and dwelt among us' (John 1: 1, 14). This belief in INCARNATION was traditionally conceptualized theologically in the categories employed by the Council of Chalcedon (AD 451): Jesus Christ is one 'person' (the eternal Logos of the Father) in two 'natures' (divine and human). Modern theologians have been much concerned about what to make of the conviction that Jesus is God incarnate and how to handle its technical theological conceptualization, usually striving to uphold some version of the claim that the personal existence of Jesus as a whole has some kind of unique status and value.

The Christ of faith and the Jesus of history The development of modern methods of historical investigation has given rise to a persistent Christological question. What connection can there be, or need there be, between two different descriptions of 'Jesus': (1) Jesus the divine Christ who redeems humanity through his crucifixion and resurrection in human flesh, and is identified and described by reading the canonical Gospels as a unified narrative explicated in the New Testament as a whole; (2) Jesus the first-century Palestinian Jewish preacher of the kingdom of God who was crucified under Roman authority as a political criminal, and is identified and described by using generally applicable historical methods to read the documents of the New Testament as sources for the critical reconstruction of past events (see HISTORICAL JESUS, QUEST OF). Modern Christologies have repeatedly tried to show that while the two methods and descriptions differ, they refer to one and the same individual, and that the historical reconstruction of Jesus' identity is at least consistent with both the ascription of ultimate redemptive significance to him (however conceived), and the historicity of whatever aspects of the New Testament description of Jesus' life and destiny the theologian takes to constitute support for that ascription.

Enlightenment and the origins of mediating Christology in England
The basic orientation of much modern Christology first took shape in response to the emergence of DEISM as an established (if never widespread) outlook in English educated culture in the late seventeenth century. The deists articulated a moral and providential theism which found itself able to do without the belief that Jesus is the unique historical redeemer and decisive revealer of God. Whatever we need to know about God and human destiny can be discerned by anyone through sufficient attention to his natural environment; Christianity, and specifically Jesus, can at best repeat and reinforce this generally available knowledge.

In *The Reasonableness of Christianity* ([1695] 1958) John Locke aims to develop an account of redemption through Jesus Christ which mediates between the perceived extremes of Puritanism and deism. In established theological fashion, the Puritans explicated belief in redemption through Jesus Christ by specifying the location of both Jesus and themselves in the unique narrative plot of the Bible: themselves as fallen children of Adam who acquire sin, guilt, and death from their rebellious ancestor, and Jesus as the one who in fulfilment of God's narrated promises (behind which lies God's doubly predestinating decree), delivers the children of Adam from their lost condition. For Locke the deists are right to reject such a scheme, in which the need for redemption is universal but can be perceived only by some, and is made to depend on an arbitrary divine decision to consign all humanity to an evil fate because of one person's ancient misdeed. Redemption through Jesus Christ cannot be meaningful or intelligible on these grounds. But the deists are wrong to conclude that 'there was no redemption necessary, and consequently that there was none', thereby making Jesus Christ 'nothing but the restorer and preacher of pure natural religion' (p. 25).

At bottom, Locke's mediating strategy is to argue that belief in redemption and a redeemer is meaningful because generally available knowledge and experience testify to the need for them. Most of *The Reasonableness of Christianity* is taken up with a latitudinarian reading of the biblical story, according to which God has established as conditions for salvation belief that Jesus is the Messiah (as attested by his miracles and fulfilment of prophecy – a claim which became the focus of much subsequent debate) and a life of repentant moral effort. But it is not necessary to appeal to the biblical narrative in order to see the point of belief in redemption and a redeemer; on this matter God has displayed 'to common apprehensions . . . wherewithal to satisfy the curious and inquisitive, who will not take a blessing, unless they be instructed what need they had of it' (pp. 56–7). It is the 'common apprehension' of all reasonable people that they need a clear knowledge of God, of their moral duty, and encouragement and assistance to do their duty, but also that these universal human needs could only be attained with great difficulty by a few, and perhaps not at all, unless they were bestowed upon us by God. It is just these benefits which Jesus in fact brings, and this is his revelatory and redemptive work.

The importance of Locke's view lies not primarily in its content, but in its logic. The need for redemption is accessible on general grounds, and so belief in redemption and a redeemer is compatible with the requirements of the emerging Enlightenment for meaningful and reasonable convictions about ultimate matters. The belief that redemption has actually occurred, and occurred specifically in Jesus Christ, is a very different kind of judgement; it requires knowledge of a particular historical person, for which some kind of acquaintance with the biblical narrative is indispensable. The reality of redemption and the particular identity of the redeemer are matters of contingent historical and textually mediated fact, but the need for redemption is a matter of general, though perhaps only implicit, human awareness. Here appears in its infancy a distinctively modern kind of Christological strategy, which strives to maintain the belief that Jesus is the unique historical redeemer against the perceived alternatives of rejecting it as meaningless and unnecessary (like the deists) and upholding it only by appeal to sheer Scriptural or church authority (like the Puritans).

Where it is engaged with the Enlightenment, Christology in England in the eighteenth century takes this mediating logical pattern for granted. (A notable exception to this generalization in the wider world of English-speaking theology is the American Calvinist Jonathan Edwards, who makes many of the technical philosophical innovations of the British Enlightenment his own, but puts them in the service of an often highly original theology which declines to follow the mediating strategy, and includes robust accounts of divine election, incarnation, and original sin.) Even a theologian like John Wesley, who conceives Jesus' redemptive significance in a much richer and more biblically resonant way than a latitudinarian like Locke, and is of an utterly different religious sensibility, tends to think Christologically in the mediating pattern. Belief in Jesus as redeemer, while true because revealed by God, gets its meaningfulness and significance from being included in the biography of the individual through a distinctive conversion experience, an assurance of salvation which meets the struggling religious seeker's need for inner peace. Here, as in a quite different way for

Locke, believers do not so much find the meaning of their existence by tracing its inclusion in Jesus' life and destiny, as find Jesus' story significant because it fills a needed place in their own, relatively independent, biography or world view.

Enlightenment and Protestant mediating Christology in Germany

The leading figures of the German Enlightenment and their idealist and romantic (see ROMANTICISM) successors on the whole rejected the traditional belief that Jesus is the unique historical redeemer. But rather than simply discarding as false this belief and the biblical narrative from which it arises (as was typically the case in Enlightenment England and France), they radically reinterpreted them, seeking a usable truth beneath their no longer acceptable manifest meaning.

For Gotthold Ephraim Lessing none of the historical monotheisms may claim ultimate truth, though all have a role to play in the process, at once natural and divinely sustained, of humanity's ongoing enlightenment. In *The Education of the Human Race* of 1780 he suggests that even such seemingly obscure and irrational Christian teachings as the Trinity and 'the Son's satisfaction' may have a usable, if yet undiscovered, rational meaning – though if they do it will not depend on or be linked necessarily to the historical person Jesus of Nazareth. For, as Lessing proposed in a famous epigram, 'accidental truths of history can never become the proof of necessary truths of reason' (Lessing, 1972, pp. 94–5; 53).

Developing this train of thought considerably, Immanuel Kant argues that in the process of human moral self-reformation the *idea* of a redeemer is indispensable; we find ineluctably within our moral reason 'the idea of a person' who is utterly obedient to moral duty 'in the face of the fiercest onslaughts' (Kant, [1793] 1960, p. 55). Moral conversion in the face of radical evil can thus be construed as 'a practical faith in this Son of God', that is, as the effort to conform oneself to this idea, and so to see it as what Kant calls the 'archetype' (*Urbild*) of human moral perfection (ibid.). But this 'practical faith' obviates the traditional Christian belief in incarnation. If there were such a thing, Kant suggests, it would be something like the full instantiation of the *Urbild* in time. In some contexts Kant argues that this is impossible, but in any case it would be irrelevant: we need no 'empirical example' in order to pattern our own lives after the moral archetype; even if such an example were available 'in the appearance of the God-Man' (as many of Kant's theological contemporaries maintained), it would still be true that 'it is not that in him which strikes the senses and can be known through experience, but rather the archetype (*Urbild*), lying in our reason, that we attribute to him . . . which is really the object of saving faith' (pp. 56, 110). Thus Kant probes the universally valid 'rational meaning' embodied in the particulars of the gospel narrative, the true subject matter of which is not the person Jesus, but human moral transformation (p. 78). The name of Jesus never has to be mentioned, and as a historical individual he is simply dispensable.

In German idealism the key to a radical reinterpretation of the gospel narrative is provided by speculative metaphysics rather than moral philosophy. G.W.F. Hegel argues that in Christianity – especially in the central doctrines of Trinity, incarnation and the universal reconciling power of Christ's death and resurrection – there is first realized explicitly the ultimate truth at which all being and knowing aims, namely the comprehensive unity of the infinite and the finite, which is accomplished as 'absolute Spirit' completely identifies and so reconciles itself with its own finite and alienated self-objectification in nature and history. Christianity thus embodies the same truth of divine–human unity as philosophy, but does so in the medium of imagination and representation (*Vorstellung*, in Hegel's term), which is inadequate to this truth content. Interpreted in the only adequate form or medium, namely 'the concept' (*Begriff*), the Christian 'representations' disclose a profound tendency to negate themselves for the sake of their philosophically articulated content. So Hegel reads the crucifixion as the decisive negation of everything finite in the Christian *Vorstellung*: of Jesus himself as the particular person in whom God is uniquely incarnate, of human finitude as such, and so of the God who is abidingly transcendent and other to humans. Similarly, the philosophical meaning of the resurrection becomes the emergence of a human community which realizes in thought its own corporate oneness with God, a community where the world and God are reconciled in such a way that 'each cognizes itself in the other, finds itself in its essence' in the other (Hegel, [1827] 1985, p. 172). Thus the subject matter of the gospel narrative and Christological dogma is finally not Jesus, but the necessary process by which absolute Spirit overcomes its alienation from itself through the conquest of finitude, although the narrative and dogma remain uniquely suitable *Vorstellungen* for this process.

The Christological aim of Friedrich Schleiermacher is to give a robust account of belief in Jesus as the unique historical redeemer, which is at the same time congruent with modern *Wissenschaft*, that is, with the philosophical, historical, and natural scientific procedures and results stemming from the Enlightenment. A Christology which meets this aim will have to reconceive and reconstruct belief in redemption through Jesus Christ, but must maintain the ascription of ultimate significance uniquely to Jesus, without emptying it of any distinctive content (as some of Schleiermacher's rationalist theological contemporaries seemed to do) and without succumbing to the objections that such ascription is irrelevant or impossible (as with Kant) or at best irreducibly ambiguous (as with Hegel).

For Schleiermacher the Christological task, as implied by his overall conception of theology, is to describe systematically the Christian consciousness of redemption through Christ. The experience or consciousness of redemption necessarily presupposes and contains in it a general, unalterable consciousness of God as the '*whence* of our receptive and active existence', present to us in a 'feeling of absolute dependence' (Schleiermacher, [1821–2] 1928, §4: 4; cf. §§29: 1, 3; 32: 1). At the same time, this general God-consciousness never exists by itself, but only in combination with the awareness of a world with which we interact in thought and volition, or what Schleiermacher calls 'the sensible self-consciousness' (§5). When God-consciousness and self-consciousness combine in a unitary moment of experience only minimally and with difficulty, the 'religious emotions' which inform the experience as a whole have the basic character of pain (*Unlust*)

and deprivation; when the God-consciousness easily dominates the moment the experience has the basic tone of pleasure (*Lust*) and fulfilment. This 'antithesis' between the painful suppression and pleasurable dominance of the God-consciousness is 'the general form of self-consciousness', that is, of our experience of self and world (§62, proposition).

In Christianity this religious deprivation is experienced as our own doing, and so as 'sin', while release from this deprivation is experienced as wholly the act of another, and so as 'grace' and 'redemption' (§§63; 86; this same movement from suppression to dominance of God-consciousness by the act of another can be characterized theologically with equal justice as the completion of creation (§89)). Christianity is distinguished from other forms of religious consciousness not only by the centrality the axis of sin and redemption has in it, but because in it Jesus 'is distinguished from all others as redeemer alone and for all', and so the consciousness of redemption is 'essentially interconnected' with the ascription of ultimate redemptive significance uniquely to him (§11: 4, 3).

That Jesus is in fact the redeemer, and that this supreme status or 'dignity' (*Würde*) belongs to him alone, is for Schleiermacher simply a 'given' of Christian consciousness for which no proof can be offered, although how this distinctive conviction comes about can and must be explained (§13: postscript; §88: 2–3). But the intelligibility or meaningfulness of belief in Jesus as the redeemer depends on universal features of human experience: a basic God-consciousness and the misery of its suppression. These together constitute 'a consciousness of the need for redemption' (*Erlösungsbedürftigkeit*) which belongs to developed human experience generally, apart from the experience of redemption (§13: 2). Talk about a longing for redemption is a distinctively Christian way of expressing this basic fact of religious consciousness (§83: 2), and the fact may, along with the Christian consciousness of sin, emerge with full clarity only in connection with the experience of redemption (§§88: 2; 14: 2). But the fact itself is available to anyone with adequate self-knowledge (§14: 1), and it is this generally available awareness of the need for redemption which constitutes the necessary 'living receptivity' for the historically particular experience of Jesus as the redeemer (§§89: 1; 91). Thus Schleiermacher articulates a powerful version of the mediating logical pattern for specifying the relationship between Jesus' particular identity and the ultimate significance to be attributed to him.

Jesus' redemptive significance lies in an absolutely effective, unimpeded God-consciousness completely dominating every moment of his experience, the influence of which, mediated through church and Scripture, overcomes the suppression of God-consciousness in others (§§94; 88: 2; 100). To conceive Jesus' redemptive significance in this way is to regard him as the full historical realization of an ideal of perfection implied in the basic structure of human religious consciousness; as a real historical individual Jesus is not simply an example to be imitated (*Vorbild*), but a unique and irreplaceable embodiment of the human ideal or archetype (*Urbild*) upon whom redemption will always depend (§93: 2 – here Kant's term is used to assert what Kant denied). Regarding Jesus as the historical embodiment of an ideal of perfection implied in the human condition becomes for Schleiermacher, as for much subsequent Christology (however variously the ideal is conceived), the way to ascribe unique and ultimate significance to the person of Jesus, and so becomes the functional equivalent of the traditional doctrine of incarnation. It also provides the key to criticism and reinterpretation of the traditional doctrine, since it allows one to say that there is a genuine and unsurpassable existence of God in Jesus, without having to say that Jesus *is* God, and thereby undertake what Schleiermacher and many after him regarded as the impossible and religiously irrelevant conceptual tangles of the doctrine that in Christ unabridged divine and human natures are united in one person (§96: 3).

Schleiermacher quite consistently interprets Jesus' significance in terms of his distinctive consciousness, and correlatively finds in the specific events of Jesus' death and resurrection no special redemptive value beyond that which is exhibited by Jesus' whole life (§§99; 101: 4; 104: 4). Indeed, he suggests that the reading of the Gospels' climactic passion–resurrection sequence at once most historically probable and theologically satisfying is one in which the

'second life' of Jesus in his resurrection is 'wholly natural' and continuous with the first, so that the intervening 'death' was finally, if somewhat inexplicably, apparent rather than real (Schleiermacher, [1864] 1975, pp. 415f., 444–5, 479f.).

In the generation after his death, criticism of Schleiermacher's Christology focused primarily on his pivotal claim that Jesus is both a fully natural, historical person and the complete realization of archetypal humanity. Ferdinand Christian Baur and, more radically, David Friedrich Strauss subject this claim to sustained criticism on historical grounds of both a conceptual and an evidential kind. It is impossible, they argue, for Jesus to be a genuinely historically conditioned individual and at the same time the subject of a perfect God-consciousness which as such can be neither affected by nor the result of his natural and (sinful) social environment; moreover, the reality or actuality of such an individual cannot simply be read off the Christian consciousness of redemption, but must be established by an independent historical judgement. In his *Life of Jesus* of 1835–6 Strauss pushes the argument a step further: unprejudiced historical investigation of Jesus' life will support no ascription of unique redemptive significance to him, whether of a traditional or a more recent, mediating kind. Mediating Christology fails on historical grounds; it is an abortive compromise, satisfying neither to traditional faith in the incarnate divine redeemer nor to the demands of modern historical *Wissenschaft*. The best such effort is that of Schleiermacher, and precisely his Christology 'is the chain which still blocks the harbour of Christian theology against the open sea of rational science' (Strauss, [1865] 1977, p. 5).

Strauss's judgement was universally rejected in the theological mainstream of nineteenth-century German Protestantism, which accepted the compatibility, while maintaining the heterogeneity, of religious judgements about Jesus' ultimate significance with historical judgements about the course of his life and destiny, and also generally followed the mediating logical pattern for relating a meaningful notion of redemption to Jesus as a particular person (the type of issue Strauss pressed was, however, revived by Ernst Troeltsch at the turn of the century). Agreement on these principles proved compatible with considerable Christological diversity. For example, Albrecht Ritschl vigorously rejects metaphysics in theology and criticizes Schleiermacher for a one-sidedly 'religious', affective conception of redemption and the Christian life, which needs to be complemented by a moral orientation to the kingdom of God. At the same time, the meaningfulness of belief in redemption (or, to use Ritschl's preferred concepts, forgiveness and reconciliation) is established against the background of a generally perceived disparity between our actual condition and our spiritual calling to rise religiously and morally above the limitations of nature; this disparity is overcome through the life and work of Jesus, whose status as founder of the kingdom of God is grasped in a religio-ethical 'value judgement' harmonious with, though not reducible to, the results of critical historical investigation (Ritschl, [1874] 1900).

See also PROTESTANT THEOLOGY: GERMANY.

Christology in twentieth-century Protestant theology

The theological movement inaugurated by the publication in 1922 of the second edition of Karl Barth's *The Epistle to the Romans* ended up generating two quite different kinds of Christology.

By the mid-1930s and the inception of his *Church Dogmatics*, Karl Barth had reached the conviction that a theology which wants to be both coherent and distinctively Christian must, especially in the modern world, consistently govern everything it wishes to say about God, the world and humanity primarily by the criterion of 'Jesus Christ as he is attested for us in holy Scripture' (in the phrase, regularly invoked by Barth, of the Barmen Declaration's first thesis). 'The Christian message at its heart does not declare a concept and an idea', rather it recounts a history and 'declares a *name*', in such a way that 'all the concepts and ideas used in this account . . . can receive their meaning only from the bearer of this name and his history, not the reverse' (Barth, [1932–68], 1956–75, IV/1, pp. 16–17). This applies above all to the concept of God. The particular person Jesus of Nazareth, identified in the Scriptural narratives of the specific actions, sufferings, events, and circumstances which lead from Bethlehem to

Golgotha, is manifested in his resurrection and exaltation by the God of Israel as this God's own primal self-determination (*Selbstbestimmung*), as the one whom, in all his human particularity, God has from all eternity himself decided freely but irrevocably to be. Since God has fully bound his own being to this particular human history, he can be known only through a grasp of Jesus' narrated identity. And, having elected to be Jesus of Nazareth, God 'does everything general for the sake of this particular', and so 'the general (the world and humanity) exists for the sake of this particular. In this particular the general has its meaning and fulfilment' (II/2, pp. 53, 8).

This implies that our concepts and knowledge of ourselves as well as of God must be corrected and reshaped to conform to the narrative which identifies Jesus. For example, 'the Christian concept of sin is not to be won somewhere or another in empty space, without reference to Christ'; we can grasp our own pride, lassitude, and mendacity as evil supremely rejected by God, and so grasp them fully and properly, only by contrast with the obedience, active love, and veracity of Jesus Christ, as the 'bizarre antitype' of what we see in him (IV/3, p. 369). Any beliefs we may have about ourselves, including any sense we may have of what is or would be ultimately significant, must be tested by the gospel narrative – perhaps to be corrected, perhaps finally discarded. Belief in redemption through Jesus Christ cannot be meaningful because it fulfils a human need for redemption and a redeemer grasped, if only partially, without reference to him; the narrative which identifies Jesus as a particular person defines what is ultimately significant, and so serves as the decisive criterion for assessing and interpreting whatever expectations of ultimate meaning we may have (IV/1, p. 228; cf. pp. 223f., 123–8). If this relationship is reversed in the manner of modern mediating Christology, and Jesus only becomes significant as we experience the fulfilment of our expectations of ultimacy, then, having no significance inherent to himself, Jesus as a particular person will inevitably tend to vanish or dissipate into the experience itself, to which inherent significance truly belongs – a problem Barth thought strikingly, though not at all uniquely, illustrated by the Christology of his contemporary Rudolf Bultmann.

As a specific dogmatic topic, Barth locates Christology at the centre of 'the doctrine of reconciliation'. He there develops, as the counterpart to a radically Christological (and therefore Trinitarian) doctrine of God, a radically incarnational Christology: the particular human history which unfolds from Bethlehem to Golgotha is God's own; 'God himself' lives in Jesus' history 'as this one human being . . . as the free subject of his human decisions, resolves, and actions . . . but also in the terror, suffering, rejection and death' which come to pass here (IV/3, p. 42; cf. IV/1, pp. 176–7; 193–5). It is especially at this point, Barth argues, that we must allow our concept of God to be guided by the peculiar logic of the gospel narrative. This narrative depicts Jesus as at once 'true God', a God who has gone into the 'far country', identifying himself with all that opposes him for the sake of humanity (IV/1, §59), and (in consequence of this divine self-abasement) 'the true human being', exalted to share fully in the life of God (IV/2, §64); both are involved in saying that 'the Word became flesh'. Contrary to what an unrevised concept of God might lead us to expect, God does not lose himself or forfeit his divinity by becoming flesh in this way (or, more broadly, by 'the history of [the] relationships' between the Father, Jesus, and the Spirit, a history in which God's own being is fully engaged); God's divinity as enacted in this narrative shows itself to consist in the utterly self-actuated freedom of his love, and so in the capacity to transcend any opposition between himself and what is other than himself (IV/1, pp. 186–7; II/1, pp. 297–321). The Chalcedonian language of divine and human 'natures' or essences united in one 'person' or subject is for Barth a normative and useful means for articulating theologically God's enactment in Jesus' history of his capacity to become flesh, but it needs to be guarded against misunderstandings, especially by being interpreted as the conceptual rendering of an event graspable only in its narrated movement, rather than of a static state of affairs (IV/2, pp. 105–16).

Barth's steady ascription of ontological and epistemic primacy to Jesus' narrated particularity also guides his use of historical-critical analysis of the New Testament. This is clearest in his treatment of Jesus' resurrection. The gospel narrative and the broader New Testament witness to the resurrection cannot plausibly be read, Barth argues, except as attributing 'resurrection' to Jesus as its subject; the one to whom 'resurrection' happens and who is, as risen, present to his disciples is the very same one who was crucified and died in a definite place and time. This means that to hold the resurrection narrative true involves believing in the occurrence of a historical event – one which happens in space and time – of which the crucified Jesus is the subject. This is not, however, to deny that the resurrection narratives have the character of 'legend' or 'saga' for which we should not expect to find factual support by historical-critical means, however scrupulously employed (III/2, p. 446). The fragmentary, unharmonizable character of the narratives is indeed appropriate to their logically odd subject matter, namely a temporally real, divinely enacted transition across the fathomless abyss of death for which there is no analogue and no adequate conceptuality, and which therefore 'cannot be reached by a general polemic against the concept of a miracle which embraces nature, and certainly not by a general apologetic in support of this concept' (III/2, p. 451).

At mid-century the main alternative to Barth in Protestant Christology was represented in one way by Rudolf Bultmann and in another way by Paul Tillich. For Bultmann human existence is marked by an insistent question about what shall constitute authentic existence in the face of anxiety and insecurity. It is an engagement (even if only an implicit one) with this question of existence which constitutes the 'pre-understanding' necessary for grasping the message of Scripture and Christian proclamation in the present. 'It is a mistake to think we can understand a word of the New Testament without such a prior understanding . . . if it is to be understood as the Word of God' and so 'as a word with existential relevance' (Bultmann, 1955, p. 258; [1948] 1961, p. 194). The message of Jesus' cross and resurrection, when heard in faith as the event of God's address to us about the meaning of our existence, frees us (as neither philosophical understanding nor autonomous decision can do) from anxiety and for a life without the illusions of 'self-contrived security', in other words, for authentic existence (p. 19).

But the saving message of Jesus' death and resurrection is couched in mythological terms, that is, in 'objectifying imagery' which misleadingly presents the always invisible, uncontrollable reality and action of God as a series of visible, datable, events in space and time – events, moreover, of a sort which modern people, with their scientific approach to what purports to happen in space and time, cannot accept (Bultmann, [1948] 1961, p. 11; cf. pp. 197, 210). In order to address modern people in their search for authentic existence, the Christian proclamation must be stripped of this objectifying manner of presentation so as to expose the saving understanding of human existence which lies at its heart; it must be 'demythologized', yet not in such a way that the present event and experience of salvation ceases to be tied irrevocably to Jesus of Nazareth. Here, as often in modern Christology, talk of Jesus' cross and talk of his resurrection are viewed as radically diverse in logical type yet inseparably connected. Jesus' crucifixion is an event of past history, his resurrection is not (p. 34); the resurrection therefore needs to be demythologized in a way the cross does not. But their linkage in the New Testament is not to be undone; talk of the resurrection remains indispensable since, when demythologized, 'faith in the resurrection is nothing other than faith in the cross as the event of salvation' (p. 41). The historical event of Jesus' cross is disclosed to faith in the proclamation of his crucifixion and resurrection – but only in this nexus of faith and proclamation – as imbued with a significance which objective historical knowledge, entirely legitimate in its own sphere, could never discern: it is God's ever-present offer of salvation, of the possibility of authentic existence.

Tillich also argues that belief in redemption through Jesus Christ can only be intelligible when placed in the context of, or 'correlated' with, questions generated by putatively universal human experiences of anxiety and estrangement, from which we cannot help desiring a relief which we find ourselves unable to provide. Jesus' redemptive significance lies in the healing impact he has at once on our self-understanding and our very being; he can have this impact because he embodies that unity of ideal or essential humanity with actual human existence for which we all, in our estrangement, long. Our experience of redemption (or 'New Being', in Tillich's terminology) is mediated through the New Testament picture of Jesus crucified and risen, but that experience, and with it the legitimate affirmation that a bringer of New Being has actually existed in space and time, does not depend on the truth of any historical assertions about Jesus of Nazareth, which must be left 'to the incertitudes of our historical knowledge' (Tillich, 1951–64, vol. 2, p. 107).

In striving to display the meaningfulness of redemption through Jesus Christ by exhibiting it as the uniquely fitting solution to a generally perceptible human problem, Bultmann and Tillich continue a Christological pattern well established in modernity. Unlike Barth, they differ from typical nineteenth-century Protestant Christologies not in their basic strategic decision, but in their descriptions of the human condition and, correlatively, of Jesus' redemptive significance. And while they are much more sceptical than most nineteenth-century theologians about attaining either much historical knowledge regarding Jesus or much overlap between whatever knowledge is attained and Christological accounts of Jesus' redemptive import, they agree with many of their predecessors about the need to establish a relationship of non-competing autonomy between critical history and dogmatic Christology. A basic distinction must be made between two spheres of reality which may neither be separated nor synthesized in thought: objective events and human subjectivity. Each of these has a mode of access or knowledge uniquely appropriate to it: science (including historical criticism) and existential experience (Bultmann in particular is critical of Barth for offering a Christology, and especially a theology of the resurrection, which fails to honour these distinctions and relations; see Bultmann, 1955, pp. 259–61). Because it ties a transforming experience in the depths of the human subject to an objective event in the past, belief in Jesus as the eschatological redeemer poses a delicate conceptual problem, even a paradox (Bultmann, [1948] 1961, p. 209). So these theologians devote considerable energy to showing that the event and the experience are mutually necessary, and that the event–experience relation can be articulated while neither being made dependent upon, nor entailing, claims in the sphere of historical knowledge, and so without violating intellectual commitments which they take to be incumbent upon modern people.

Christology in twentieth-century Roman Catholic theology

Roman Catholic Christology has had its own complex history since the seventeenth century, but it is primarily in the twentieth century that Catholic Christology has become preoccupied with distinctively modern questions. Especially after the Second Vatican Council, the Christologies of Karl Rahner and Hans Urs von Balthasar have emerged as particularly far-reaching accomplishments.

Rahner aims to fashion a Christology which is at once faithful to the full range of the church's traditional Christological doctrine and thoroughly modern in its conceptual idiom. This requires the development of a 'transcendental Christology'. Human experience and knowledge for Rahner have two distinct but inextricably related dimensions: ordinary, 'categorial', interaction with particular objects and relations in space and time, and 'transcendental' structures of consciousness which make the apprehension of this whole categorial field possible, and therefore constitute a different level, abiding but 'pre-thematic', of our self-awareness (Rahner, [1976] 1978, p. 20). Our transcendental experience includes a hope and expectation that there will appear in history (that is, in the field of our categorial experience) an 'absolute saviour' (pp. 208–12; [1954–84] 1961– , vol. 11, pp. 93–4). In the pre-thematic, pre-linguistic depths of their transcendental experience, all human beings are the recipients of God's free but unreserved offer of himself as the fulfilment of their deepest longings. Since we can have even our deepest experiences only as mediated by an encounter with categorial realities outside ourselves, we will naturally seek definitive confirmation in space and time that the divine self-offer we experience is final and irrevocable. This could only come, Rahner argues, in the form of a historical person who (1) wholly accepts God's self-offer at the decisive juncture,

namely death, in a way which is manifest to others as definitive and accepted by God (in a way, that is, which implies something like 'resurrection'), and at the same time (2) does not simply point beyond him or herself to God's self-offer but *is* that offer unsurpassably embodied. Such a person, if there is one, would be 'an absolute mediator of salvation' ([1954–84] 1961–, vol. 11, p. 96). It is this transcendental *Ausschau* ('lookout') for an absolute saviour which makes belief in Jesus as the unique historical redeemer possible (that is, intelligible and meaningful), and keeps it from seeming to be merely 'a mythological overlay on historical events' ([1976] 1978, p. 207).

While a transcendental Christology can establish a universal *a priori* human orientation to an absolute saviour, Rahner insists that it cannot and need not demonstrate that Jesus of Nazareth, and only he, actually is the anticipated saviour; this must be presupposed ([1954–84] 1961–, vol. 5, p. 187). Whether there actually is a saviour and (if so) who the saviour is depend upon God's free decision, and so cannot be 'deduced' or derived from the transcendentally necessary idea of an absolute saviour, but must be discovered historically through an encounter with Jesus of Nazareth, mediated by Scripture and church (vol. 4, p. 143). Only two claims about Jesus need be historically credible in order to provide an adequate basis for believing in him as the historical realization of the idea of an absolute saviour: (1) that Jesus 'understood himself as the *eschatological* prophet, as the absolute and definitive saviour'; (2) 'the resurrection of Jesus' ([1976] 1978, p. 246). For Rahner, to show that these claims are 'credible' does not require demonstrating that they are true, but only that they are not subject to definitive refutation, and he thinks both claims can be interpreted in ways which clearly avoid such refutation. For example, Jesus' self-understanding as the definitive saviour, and indeed the traditional doctrine of his constant possession of the beatific vision, can be ascribed to his transcendental experience, exhibited but not expressly articulated in his words and deeds, and thereby rendered consistent with the modern exegetical commonplace that Jesus did not explicitly claim to be the Messiah ([1954–84] 1961–, vol. 5, pp. 193–215). Thus a transcendental orientation to an absolute saviour and a historical encounter with Jesus which focuses on his death and resurrection are mutually necessary: without the encounter the orientation would remain empty and unfulfilled; without the orientation the encounter would be irrelevant and unintelligible.

Rahner's notion of an absolute saviour also lends itself to development in terms of an evolutionary view of the world. The climax towards which the world's evolutionary development strives is the self-transcendence of worldly reality into the life of God, a process always grounded in God's free giving of himself to the world. To affirm that this process reaches a point where the graciously supported self-transcendence of material reality perfectly coincides with God's absolute gift of himself in and to that reality is to offer an evolutionary interpretation of what Christian faith has traditionally claimed about Jesus of Nazareth, namely that he is the incarnation of God ([1954–84] 1961–, vol. 5, pp. 157–92). But since an 'ascending', evolutionary Christology which finds in Jesus the fulfilment of transcendental hope for an absolute saviour properly ends up affirming the perfect unity of the divine and the human in him, it is consistent with a traditional 'descending, metaphysical' Christology, for which belief that 'God became man', interpreted in terms of the hypostatic union of divine and human natures, is not the conclusion but the 'primary axiom' (vol. 13, p. 218). More than that: the two types of Christology, while not reducible to one another, may be regarded as materially (and not only functionally) equivalent, although especially in the modern context the 'ascending' type should be treated as more basic. So, Rahner argues, it is possible to be theologically committed both to the doctrine of Chalcedon and to Christology in a modern conceptual idiom, without having to choose between the two.

Against Rahner's transcendental Christology, Hans Urs von Balthasar argues that the decisive events of the gospel drama have a specific shape and logic, unique to them, which precludes even a minimally adequate anticipation of their redemptive significance. What comes to pass on Jesus' cross is not simply an act of complete self-surrender to God in death, which might then serve as the indispensable 'productive pattern' (*Vorbild*) which frees us to repeat this act in our own death (Rahner, [1954–84] 1961–, vol. 18, p. 167), but, beyond that, 'an entirely unique bearing of the total guilt of the world by the entirely unique Son of the Father' (Balthasar, [1969] 1990, pp. 137–8). Especially when the passion narrative is read as the climax and fulfilment of the Old Testament, it becomes clear that in freely surrendering himself to God in death, Jesus 'must expose himself to the wrath of God' against all that is 'flesh' and 'sin', and must thereby accept (in what is also an inner-Trinitarian event) the 'second death' of complete God-forsakenness (Balthasar, [1969] 1990, p. 138, cf. pp 168–72). Jesus' crucifixion is therefore not just metaphorically but literally the end of even the most noble human hope and expectation, and this precisely in virtue of those features which make it an event for which there can be no analogy and which in the nature of the case cannot be repeated; therefore 'an idea of "transcendental hope for resurrection", before the depth of the world's guilt borne on the cross has been fathomed, is irresponsibly rash' (1985–7, vol. 2, p. 221, my translation).

Jesus' crucifixion, however, not only enacts fully God's judgement against our flesh and its expectations, but is also Jesus' complete embrace of our flesh in love for the Father and for us; he is our *Stellvertreter* (at once 'substitute', 'representative', and 'advocate'), not only in death but in obedience. Moreover, in the resurrection Jesus' total mission reveals itself as internal to God's own life, as that particular human life in which, with perfect adequacy, 'God portrays himself' (Balthasar, [1961–9] 1982, vol. 1, p. 432). The gospel drama is therefore God's own free but unreserved embrace of our sinful flesh, in the person of the Logos who himself responds in love and obedience to the Father who sends him into the flesh, even to the point of death and descent into hell. The cross of Jesus is ultimately 'the slaying of the Logos', who is not thereby lost in death, but conquers it in his resurrection through the freedom of the Spirit, as Balthasar argues in development of the doctrine of the Second Council of Constantinople (AD 553): 'Jesus Christ who was crucified in the flesh is true God, and one of the Holy Trinity' (Balthasar, [1973–83] 1988–, vol. 3, pp. 399–468, my translation; vol. 4, p. 11). Grasped in its proper Trinitarian depth, the gospel narrative not only breaks down all human perceptions of beauty, goodness, and truth, but reorients these broken perceptions around the centre to which it bears witness, and in this way reconstitutes and perfects them. Jesus' cross and resurrection are like a magnetic point around which history and culture take on a shape which could not be anticipated from any perspective they themselves provide, and which they could not otherwise have assumed. 'This single "point" of fact', Balthasar argues, 'contains a meaning that surpasses, consummates, and embraces every other projected meaning' (Balthasar, [1973–83], 1988–, vol. 2, pp. 115–16).

See also ROMAN CATHOLIC THEOLOGY.

Christology at the end of the twentieth century
Characteristically modern questions have continued to guide much of the Christological debate in western theology, with diverse results.

Wolfhart Pannenberg maintains that 'the task of Christology is to establish (*begründen*) on the basis of Jesus' history the true knowledge of his significance' (Pannenberg, [1964] 1977, p. 30). This means, on the one hand, that ascriptions of ultimate or redemptive significance to Jesus must be justified by a historically rigorous reconstruction of his life and destiny, for which the Gospels provide the primary source material. On the other hand, the meaningfulness and relevance of the redemptive significance ascribed to Jesus for historical reasons must be established on independent grounds, by showing that human beings in general have an interest in such things (p. 38; for an example, see pp. 264 9). A reconstruction of Jesus' words and deeds against their apocalyptic religious background shows that Jesus claimed authority as the decisive anticipation in history of God's complete self-revelation at the end of history. Jesus' claim is definitively vindicated by his resurrection, but belief in the resurrection can reasonably be maintained, Pannenberg argues, only if this event can be shown by ordinary historical means to have occurred, and he proposes that it is in fact the best explanation of the relevant historical data. Since Jesus' resurrection maximally anticipates in history God's eschatological self-revelation, it also makes him the incarnation of God; the resurrection does not simply disclose this to our knowledge, but retroactively establishes

Jesus' whole earthly life to be one of unity with God. Only in this way, Pannenberg maintains, can the full humanity of the historically reconstructed Jesus be held together with the claim that he is God's incarnation.

A similar structural pattern is apparent in the Christological writings of Edward Schillebeeckx and Hans Küng. Though more reserved than Pannenberg about the extent to which historical study can provide grounds for believing in Jesus' resurrection and for ascribing redemptive significance to him, they argue that Jesus as he is known through historical reconstruction must be the primary criterion for a Christological account of his significance. At the same time, a 'critical correlation' of the historically reconstructed Jesus with an independent analysis of contemporary human quests for ultimate meaning is necessary to display the relevance of the redemptive claims attributed to him in the reconstruction (of, for example, his *abba* experience of God and liberating praxis, which in Schillebeeckx's view are most central). Thus on the relation between Jesus' particular identity and his ultimate or redemptive significance these theologians are markedly closer to Rahner than Balthasar. Most recent Catholic theologies (for example, Catholic liberation and feminist theologies) tend to side with Rahner on this issue, whatever their agreement or disagreement with him on other Christological and theological matters.

Jürgen Moltmann develops a Christology in which Jesus' resurrection is interpreted in thoroughly eschatological terms, as at once God's radical 'no' both to death and to an evil social and political status quo and God's definitive promise of a future transformation of all creation. The significance of the resurrection, however, depends upon the cross, where the triune God loves the world by himself suffering complete, God-forsaken abandonment and death in solidarity with both the sinfully guilty and the suffering innocent, the Son by undergoing this death, the Father by giving him up to it: what happens on the cross is 'the unconditioned and therefore boundless love which proceeds from the grief of the Father and the dying of the Son and reaches forsaken men in order to create in them the possibility and the force of new life' (Moltmann, [1973]

1974, p. 245). At the same time, the relevance of what happens in Jesus' cross and resurrection is to be established by showing how it fulfils the yearnings of modern people, especially those who have suffered massive injustice, for a new world.

Eberhard Jüngel also shares the commitment, stemming from Barth, maximally to unify Christology and the doctrine of God: God defines himself as God precisely in the dead Jesus, and this divine self-definition reveals itself to us as such in Jesus' resurrection. The death of God thus lies at the heart of God's own being, and requires of theology the effort to think of God in a way which gets beyond the stalemate between traditional theism's notion of God as abstract immutable transcendence and atheism's denial of this God. The way to do this is not to assert God's capacity to suffer by simply denying his transcendence, but to think of God as 'the one who in his being can and does bear, can and does suffer, the annihilating power of nothingness, and thus the negation which is death, without thereby being annihilated' (Jüngel, [1977] 1983, p. 219). In seeking to establish the intelligibility and relevance of its radically Christological talk of God, Christian theology should move consistently 'from the inside out', seeking to attain from this Christological centre 'a concept of God which lays claim to universal validity' (p. viii).

Across a marked diversity in conceptuality and approach, the basic preoccupations of modern western (especially Protestant) Christology have proved strikingly durable. The future of Christology is likely to depend in large measure on whether this continues to be the case, or whether – as some modern Christologies themselves suggest – the importance of these issues may be relativized, though not neglected, and Christology oriented in other directions.

See also BIBLICAL CRITICISM AND INTERPRETATION: NEW TESTAMENT; ESCHATOLOGY; FEMINIST THEOLOGY; GOD; KINGDOM OF GOD: NEW TESTAMENT; RESURRECTION; SOTERIOLOGY.

Bibliography

Balthasar, H.U. von [1961–9] 1982–: *The Glory of the Lord*, 7 vols, trans. and ed. J. Riches *et al.* San Francisco: Ignatius Press.

Balthasar, H.U. von [1969] 1990: *Mysterium Paschale: The Mystery of Easter*, trans. Aidan Nichols, O.P. Edinburgh: T & T Clark.

Balthasar, H.U. von [1973–83] 1988–: *Theo-Drama*, 5 vols, trans. Graham Harrison. San Francisco: Ignatius Press.

Balthasar, H.U. von 1985–7: *Theologik*, 3 vols. Einsiedeln: Johannes Verlag.

Barth, K. [1932–68] 1956–75: *Church Dogmatics* I–IV (4 vols in 12 parts), trans. G. Bromiley *et al.* Edinburgh: T & T Clark.

Bultmann, R. [1948] 1961: New Testament and mythology, and Bultmann replies to his critics. In *Kerygma and Myth*, vol. 1, ed. H.W. Bartsch, trans. R.H. Fuller. New York: Harper and Row, pp. 1–44, 191–211.

Bultmann, R. 1955: *Essays Philosophical and Theological*, trans. J.C.G. Grieg. London: SCM Press.

Hegel, G.W.F. [1827] 1984–6: *Lectures on the Philosophy of Religion*, 3 vols. Vol. 3, *The Consummate Religion*, ed. P.C. Hodgson, trans. R.F. Brown, P.C. Hodgson and J.M. Stewart. Berkeley: University of California Press.

Jüngel, E. [1977, 2nd edn] 1983: *God as the Mystery of the World*, trans. D.L. Guder. Grand Rapids: Eerdmans.

Kant, I. [1793] 1960: *Religion Within the Limits of Reason Alone*, trans. T.M. Greene and H.H. Hudson. New York: Harper.

Lessing, G. 1972: *Lessing's Theological Writings*, ed. and trans. Henry Chadwick. Stanford: Stanford University Press.

Locke, J. [1695] 1958: *The Reasonableness of Christianity*, ed. I.T. Ramsey. Stanford: Stanford University Press.

Moltmann, J. [1973] 1974: *The Crucified God*, trans. R.A. Wilson and J. Bowden. New York: Harper and Row.

Pannenberg, W. [1964] 1977: *Jesus – God and Man*, trans. L.L. Wilkens and D.A. Priebe (with Afterword from 5th German edn). Philadelphia: Westminster Press.

Rahner, K. [1954–84] 1961–: *Theological Investigations*, 22 vols, trans. C. Ernst *et al.* New York: Crossroads.

Rahner, K. [1976] 1978: *Foundations of Christian Faith*, trans. W.V. Dych. New York: Seabury.

Ritschl, A. [1874] 1900: *The Christian Doctrine of Justification and Reconciliation*, 3 vols. Vol. 3, *The Positive Development of the Doctrine*, trans. of 1889 edn H.R. Mackintosh and A.B. Macaulay. Edinburgh: T & T Clark.

Schleiermacher, F. [1821–2] 1928: *The Christian Faith*, trans. of 1830 edn H.R. Mackintosh and J.S. Stewart. Edinburgh: T & T Clark.

Schleiermacher, F. [1864] 1975: *The Life of Jesus*, ed. J.C. Verheyden, trans. S.M. Gilmour. Philadelphia: Fortress.

Strauss, D.F. [1835–6] 1972: *The Life of Jesus, Critically Examined*, trans. G. Eliot, ed. P.C. Hodgson. Philadelphia: Fortress.

Strauss, D.F. [1865] 1977: *The Christ of Faith and the Jesus of History: A Critique of Schleiermacher's 'Life of Jesus'*, trans. and ed. L.E. Keck. Philadelphia: Fortress.

Tillich, P. 1951–64: *Systematic Theology*, 3 vols. Vol. 2, *Existence and the Christ*. Chicago: University of Chicago Press.

BRUCE D. MARSHALL

church, doctrines of   See ECCLESIOLOGY.

Cobb, John B. Jr (b. 1925)   North American theologian. He studied at the universities of Michigan and Chicago and at Chicago's Divinity School, and is professor of theology at the School of Theology at Claremont, California, and Director of the Centre for Process Studies at Claremont. Influenced by the thought of A.N. Whitehead, he is a leading exponent of PROCESS THEOLOGY, a method based on the philosophical presupposition that reality is not static, but in the process of 'becoming'. Central to his thought is the idea of the 'creative transformation', whereby all of human experience has the potential to be transformed by the divine Logos, as incarnate in Christ. He has been an early figure in the development of a theology of ecology and in the move away from the idea of God as 'male', as well as in the exploration of the relationship between Christianity and other religions, especially Buddhism (*Beyond Dialogue*, 1982). Other works include *Process Theology as Political Theology* (1982), *Christ in a Pluralistic Age* (1975) and *A Christian Natural Theology* (1965).

Bibliography

Brown, D., James, R.E., and Reeves, G., eds 1971: *Process Philosophy and Christian Thought*. Indianapolis.

Cobb, J.B., and Griffin, D.R. 1977: *Process Theology: An Introductory Exposition*. Belfast.

Coleridge, Samuel Taylor (1772–1834)   English romantic poet and thinker. A friend of Wordsworth, Coleridge published with him the *Lyrical Ballads* in 1798, inaugurating the romantic era in English literature.

Early influences on his religious thought include unitarianism, encountered whilst studying at Jesus College, Cambridge, and the revived pantheism of some strands of German literature. Although he subscribed to a largely Trinitarian theology, especially from about 1810 onwards, his ideas remained innovative and unconventional, and his innate mysticism was in contrast to the rationalist tendencies of much contemporary Protestantism. His subjective approach to revelation ('All revelation is *ab intra* [from within]') was coloured by his psychedelic experiences as an opium addict. He stressed the spiritual dimension of life, but held that no proof of religious truth could be established other than that of its benefits to human life, and he emphasized Christianity as a universal ethical principle. His religious works include *Lay Sermons* (1816), *On the Constitution of Church and State* (1830), *Aids to Reflection* (1825) and the posthumous *Confessions of an Enquiring Spirit* (1840); his influence can be traced to such nineteenth-century theologians and writers as Thomas Carlyle, John Henry Newman, T. Arnold, F. D. Maurice, and Ralph Waldo Emerson.

Bibliography

Barth, J.R. 1987: *Coleridge and Christian Doctrine*. New York.

Jasper, D. 1985: *Coleridge as Poet and Religious Thinker*. London.

Prickett, S. 1976: *Romanticism and Religion: The Tradition of Coleridge and Wordsworth in the Victorian Church*. Cambridge.

commercial ethics   See ETHICS.

Communion, Holy   See SACRAMENTAL THEOLOGY.

Comte, August (1798–1857)   French philosopher. He studied at the Ecole Polytechnique, where he later taught and held a post as examiner in mathematics (1837–44); later his work was financed by patrons. In *Cours de philosophie positive* (1830–42), he conceived of humanity as moving from eras in which man understood himself in theological and metaphysical terms, to a new era of 'positivism' in which deity is replaced by humanity and worship is directed towards man, the 'great being'. Religion *per se* was not to be rejected: he held that it should continue its function of regulating and unifying individuals, and he borrowed elements of Catholic ritual to develop an elaborate form of worship which revered scientists and scholars rather than traditional saints. His was an optimistic 'religion of humanity' which believed in man's perfectibility; in *Système de politique positive* (1822) he applied his utilitarian ethical principles to the social and political arena. He was a forerunner of the modern science of sociology.

Bibliography
Gouhier, H.G. 1987: *La philosophie d'August Comte*. Paris.
Lonchampt, J. 1889: *Précis de la vie et des écrits d'August Comte*. Paris.
Wright, T.R. 1986: *The Religion of Humanity*. Cambridge.

Cone, James Hal (b. 1938) North American black theologian. Educated at Garrett Theological Seminary and Northwestern University, he is professor of theology at Union Theological Seminary, New York. Influenced by the liberation theologies of South America in the 1960s and 1970s, he was impelled towards the development of a specifically black theology by the black insurrection in Detroit in 1967. Since then he has been a significant influence on the development of BLACK THEOLOGY, although some later exponents have modified his radical stance. In his earlier work (*Black Theology and Black Power*, 1969, and *A Black Theology of Liberation*, 1970) he was preoccupied with the secular issue of black power, seeing black theology as its religious counterpart: for him, black power was 'not only *consistent* with the Gospel of Jesus Christ, but . . . *is* the Gospel of Jesus Christ.' In later books such as *God of the Oppressed* (1975) he has focused on the experience of black Christianity at both a personal and a community level, exploring the experience of racism and the interpretation of Scripture and expounding the rediscovery of a black religious heritage. His most recent book, *For My People* (1984), offers a comprehensive overview of his thought.

Bibliography
Gayraud, G.S, and Cone, J.H., eds 1979: *Black Theology: A Documentary History 1966–79*. Maryknoll, NY.
West, C. 1982: *Prophesy Deliverance! An Afro-American Revolutionary Christianity*. Philadelphia.

Congar, Yves (b. 1904) French Dominican ecclesiologist. Ordained in 1930, he was director of the Dominican monastery at Strasburg and served as a member of the Theological Commission at the Second Vatican Council. His interest in ecumenism is based on a reassessment of basic traditions and doctrines, and his concern for the modernization of the church, including developing the role of lay people, is inspired by the thinking of Thomas Aquinas. His works include *Divided Christendom* (1937), *Lay People in the Church* (1952, revised 1965), *Ecumenism and the Future of the Church* (1967) and *Diversity and Communion* (1982).

Bibliography
Schilling, S.P. 1966: *Contemporary Continental Theologians*. London.

conscience See ETHICS.

creation, doctrine of In its doctrine of creation, classical Christian theology asserted that the world was made out of nothing by the agency of God. The creation was conceived of as contingent, having been brought into being and sustained by the Creator, and as moving towards its *telos* in the purpose of God. In its developed forms in Augustinian and later medieval thought, such a doctrine of creation was foundational for western cosmology until the seventeenth century. However, its coherence and intelligibility are now widely considered to have dissolved; accordingly, the doctrine of creation focuses some of the most enduring problems for Christian theology in the modern world.

The doctrine of *creatio ex nihilo* (creation out of nothing) asserts that the divine act of origination, unlike all creaturely acts of production, is accomplished without any pre-existent matter and is thus qualified by nothing external to God's freedom. That which originates from this divine act is an ordered reality. The creation as a whole, and each entity within the creation, is teleologically ordered, all things having their end within a structure of purposive relations ordained by the Creator. Within itself, moreover, the creation is hierarchically ordered, certain created realities serving others. Under God, the human creature is given dominion over the rest of creation; from this follows the firmly anthropocentric character of classical doctrines of creation. The order of creation is given by God and is not subject to change; understanding the creation is thus a matter of discovering its given order rather than imposing order upon creation through the projective activity of the mind. Existing in this order, the creation is, despite its fallenness due to human sin, 'good'; its goodness is its existence as a structured system ordered to divinely intended ends.

Creation is contingent and finite, and stands in a continuing relation to God. Whilst the creation has been given its own being (and therefore does not depend upon continuing acts of creation for its maintenance), it cannot be thought of in isolation from immediate dependence upon the sustaining activity of the Creator. The divine act of origination is thus inseparable from God's continuing providential activity, preserving and governing that which has been made. Moreover, the history of creation is not the outworking of a line of progress immanent to the creation itself, but rather the ruling of creaturely occurrence by the divine will. Accordingly, the Creator is to be conceived not simply as a supra-worldly cause, but as a personal being whose act of creation is the first act of relating to creation (and supremely the human creature) in the election, redemption and glorification of the people of God in Jesus Christ. In classical form, then, the doctrine of creation asserts as part of the Christian credo (1) that a reality distinct from God exists and (2) that this reality is not axiomatic (ontologically or epistemologically), but rather is by virtue of the antecedent reality of God.

The history of the doctrine in the modern era is largely that of the breakdown of this framework. Like its corollary, the doctrine of providence, the doctrine of creation has proved vulnerable because it works in territory where the rights of Christian theology to operate have been subject to sustained challenge, first by natural philosophy and more recently by natural science. Though the beginning of the breakdown is usually identified with the Enlightenment, it was to some extent prepared by certain developments in theology in the pre-Enlightenment centuries, especially in those theologies in which foundations for Christian faith were sought in natural philosophy, emancipated from particular religious claims. Some (for instance Buckley, 1987) suggest that this apologetic surrendering of theological foundations to non-theological disciplines prepared the way for the minimally theistic or non-theistic metaphysics of the post-Enlightenment era. In effect, the apologetic move undermined the axiomatic status of knowledge of the Creator by making knowledge of God consequent upon knowledge of the creature arrived at by a different route. This independence of knowledge of the creation was further reinforced by the elimination of the categories of transcendent purpose or order from natural scientific explanation. Espousing a mode of enquiry which sought to abstract elements from their interconnections, scientific method excluded the interpretative context which a doctrine of creation had offered in accounting for the natural order, and so gave rise to positivism or naturalism.

Nineteenth-century debates about the theory of evolution provided sharp illustrations of the point. Darwin's notion of natural selection posed problems for the classical doctrine of creation in two ways. First, its emphasis upon the randomness of the evolutionary process appeared to undermine the purposive character of creation. Second, its stress that the natural order is best explained not by teleological categories but by the advantages given to certain species by particular biological developments appeared to promote a crudely competitive understanding of the natural order. However much these ideas are qualified in more sophisticated evolutionary theory, as a whole the theory does not require notions of a divine Creator, and does not necessarily support either an ordered conception of the universe or affirmations of the unique dignity and status of the human creature.

In the hands of some (such as Isaac Newton), purely immanent explanations of the creation could be combined with a deistic understanding of God (see DEISM), in which the divine mind produces a regulated natural order functioning according to its own laws. However, such an account of God relegates divine activity to that of providing the initial impulse for the phenomena properly understood not through theology but through mechanics; a continuing divine relation to the created order is excluded, God is defined as 'Author', and the doctrine of creation is associated exclusively and minimalistically with *origins*. Despite severe attacks from David Hume's scepticism, deism proved deeply influential upon the rise of modern science, and versions of it still resurface in certain styles of Christian apologetic. Other developments which served to undermine the Christian doctrine of creation include the development of metaphysical pantheism (most significantly by Benedict Spinoza), which envisages no substantial difference between God and nature. In this way, pantheism dispenses with essential aspects of the classical theological consensus: an absolute act of origination, and the distinction between God and the creation. In more historically oriented versions (J.G. Herder and, on some readings, G.W.F. Hegel, for example), the impulse towards monism is expressed as a unity of nature and spirit. Some process philosophers (see PROCESS THEOLOGY) have continued this emphasis on the coinherence of divine action and worldly cause.

Some theologians in the modern era (notably F.D.E. Schleiermacher) have sought to lay emphasis on the notion of human contingency as a way of reasserting the Christian doctrine of creation (though in anthropological rather than cosmological form). However, part of the critique of the doctrine of creation since the Enlightenment has been concerned with the apparently negative evaluation of the freedom and dignity of human persons which it supports. Language of dependence has been interpreted as irreconcilable with full moral responsibility on the part of human agents, and as inevitably robbing human persons of their proper freedom. In the Enlightenment tradition, for which self-origination and self-determination became fundamental for the definition of the human person (the earlier philosophy of J.G. Fichte is the sharpest example here), these critiques have had particular cogency, and have

been continued in Marxist and existentialist philosophy, as well as in certain forms of social anthropology. Behind the criticism lies a further criticism of the notion of divine agency towards the creation. This criticism suggests that the notion of divine action is inherently repressive, and that divine creativity and human liberty are inversely proportional. To some degree this criticism trades upon the failure of post-Reformation Christian theology to specify a morally adequate account of divine action, and especially of the concurrence of divine and creaturely action, in such a way that the doctrine of creation could be seen as supportive of the creature's dignity.

A final, more recent, critique of the doctrine of creation has concerned its relation to the ecological crisis. Many now argue that abuse of the natural order can be rooted in the Judaeo-Christian tradition according to which the human creature is granted the role of subduing the earth. The mandate to subdue the earth, it is suggested, has been interpreted as giving licence to an exploitative attitude to the rest of creation. More especially, it can be argued that the Christian tradition, given its anthropocentric focus in the doctrine of creation, paved the way for modern technological understandings of the nonhuman creation as an objectified nonspiritual 'nature', having no inherent ends but only those which it is given by human users. It is, however, by no means clear whether modern technology owes more to the Christian doctrine of creation or to the instrumentalism of the post-Cartesian philosophical and scientific tradition. Some argue, for example, that one of the functions of the doctrine of creation is to prevent precisely such developments. Classically, the doctrine insists that the natural order does have an inherent teleology, which is given by the Creator and which prevents the human creature from regarding nature merely as raw material for human projects. Moreover, human dominion over nature is always exercised in a responsible relation to God, and is therefore more properly construed as stewardship rather than conquest.

Where the doctrine of creation formerly articulated a set of religious and cultural givens about the human person and the natural order, then, it does so no longer. Contemporary Christian theologies have developed a number of strategies for the restatement of the doctrine in a changed intellectual context. Theologians in the revisionist tradition take the Enlightenment and post-Enlightenment critiques with full seriousness, and seek to restate the Christian faith accordingly. For such thinkers, doctrinal construction takes place through the correlation of the symbols of faith with wider cultural developments. Thus Christian language concerning creation may begin with analysis of the phenomena of dependence or contingency, moving towards statements about God as ultimate ground. A closely related procedure involves elaborating the doctrine of creation as a foundational platform upon which to build subsequent Christian assertions; here the doctrine furnishes pre-theological grounds for belief and its doctrinal formulation. Very occasionally this is done in dialogue with natural science (as in Peacocke, 1979), but more usually it is undertaken in relation to human sciences and philosophy, continuing the focus on the human person which marks most Christian accounts of creation. In explicit rejection of these models (which are variants of the blend of natural philosophy and NATURAL THEOLOGY developed in the liberal tradition as a response to the Enlightenment), other theologians attempt a restatement of the classical scheme, looking very often to the work of Karl Barth as an example of theology holding to its own territory without concessions. Those who seek to follow this path (such as Tanner, 1988) propose that the root difficulty for theology lies in its alienation from its own proper grounds and modes of enquiry. By devolving responsibility for formulating the grounds for theology to non-theological disciplines, theology allowed the doctrine of creation to be absorbed by natural philosophy or natural science. The recovery of the doctrine, and the effectiveness of theological response to its critics, will depend upon a recovery of the internal logic of Christian theology at this point. Most of all, this will mean elaborating the doctrine of creation as part of the credo, rather than using it as a bridge to the wider scientific and philosophical culture. Furthermore, some (such as Torrance, 1981) argue that so construed, the Christian doctrine of creation lies at the heart of properly rational scientific activity.

See also BIOLOGICAL SCIENCE AND CHRISTIANITY; PHYSICAL SCIENCE AND CHRISTIANITY.

Bibliography
Anderson, B.W. 1967: *Creation versus Chaos*. New York: Association Press.
Barth, K. [1945] 1958: *Church Dogmatics* III/1. Edinburgh: T & T Clark.
Buckley, M.J. 1987: *At the Origins of Modern Atheism*. New Haven: Yale University Press.
Gilkey, L. 1959: *Maker of Heaven and Earth*. New York: Doubleday.
Hartt, J.N. 1985: Creation and providence. In *Christian Theology: An Introduction to Its Traditions and Tasks*, ed. P. Hodgson and R. King. Philadelphia: Fortress Press.
Moltmann, J. 1985: *God in Creation: A New Theology of Creation and the Spirit of God*. New York: Harper and Row.
Peacocke, A.R. 1979: *Creation and the World of Science*. Oxford: Clarendon Press.
Tanner, K. 1988: *God and Creation in Christian Theology: Tyranny or Empowerment*. Oxford: Blackwell.
Torrance, T.F. 1981: *Divine and Contingent Order*. Oxford: Oxford University Press.
Westermann, C. 1974: *Creation*. Philadelphia: Fortress Press.

JOHN B. WEBSTER

criticism, biblical See BIBLICAL CRITICISM AND INTERPRETATION (1: OLD TESTAMENT and 2: NEW TESTAMENT).

Croce, Benedetto (1866–1952) Italian idealist philosopher. He studied law and philosophy at Rome and Naples. Influenced by the thought of G.W.F. Hegel, his phenomenology of the mind, set out in *Filosofia dello spirito* (1902–17), classifies all human activity in four areas: art, philosophy, political economy and ethics. Behind this activity is a unifying creative Spirit operating in four broad forms: intuition, concept, individuality and universality. Theology is a function of concept, whilst religion belongs to the sphere of intuition; both are however temporary categories which point to the enduring greater Spirit. He opposed what he saw as the oppositional character of Hegelian dialectic; his aesthetic theory was integrative, seeing all forms of human activity as complementary.

Bibliography

Antoni, C., and Mattioli, R., eds 1950: *Cinquant' anni di vita intellettuale italiana, 1896–1946: Scritti in honore di Benedetto Croce*. Naples.

Bramstead, E.K., and Melhuish, K.J. 1978: *Western Liberalism: A History in Documents from Locke to Croce*. London.

Capanna, F. 1964: *La religione in Benedetto Croce*. Bari.

cross, interpretations of See SOTERIOLOGY.

culture and theology The concept of culture as posing a problem for theology has its roots in the romantic reaction to the rationalism of the eighteenth century; the contemporary form of the question arises from the missionary experience of the western churches.

Culture is the cultivation of those capabilities which constitute human excellence. The earliest use of the word in this sense occurs in 1867 in the phrase 'devoid of the grace of culture'. In the perspective of the Age of Reason, human excellence was widely defined as 'civilization', a word not used in the plural. There was only one ladder on which the human race could ascend towards excellence; peoples were on lower or higher rungs of the ladder. 'Primitive peoples' were not seen as peoples with distinct forms of excellence but as 'backward'. This was the perspective of the pioneer of cultural anthropology, E.B. Tylor, who was the first to give a formal definition of culture in the modern sociological sense: 'that complex whole which includes knowledge, belief, art, law, morals, customs and any other capabilities and habits acquired by man as a member of society' (Tylor, 1889). Tylor never used the word 'culture' in the plural, and his preferred word in any case was 'civilization'. The first use of the plural in English occurs in a rhetorical context in 1891: 'all races, all nations, all cultures'.

The romantic movement affirmed the unique value of the cultures of different peoples as evidence of human creativity. Its most powerful expression was in German, where the word *Kultur* was in use twenty years before its English equivalent. It affirmed that the cultures of different peoples were not to be judged by criteria drawn from the principles of the Enlightenment, but valued as distinct forms of excellence. But the nineteenth century also saw the birth of the new sciences of sociology and anthropology, which undertook to explain the phenomena of culture in rational terms analogous to those employed in the natural sciences. With these scientific tools, the different items in Tylor's 'complex' could be understood in terms of the functions which they performed in securing the stability and coherence of the society. Religion, as part of culture, could be accounted for in these terms.

The debate between the rationalist and the romantic elements in European thought depended for its data largely on the reports of foreign missionaries. The seventy-three volumes of the Jesuit *Relationes* (1610–1791) were the only source of knowledge about the native cultures of the 'mission fields', and stimulated great interest in Europe, especially in the evidently superior civilization of China. And the huge expansion of Protestant missions in the nineteenth and twentieth centuries made available knowledge of cultures of which little was otherwise known in Europe. This provided the data for the pioneers of the new science of cultural anthropology.

There was conflict of interest between the missionaries and the anthropologists. The former, living for long periods among the people concerned, were aware of the forces, both internal and external, which were bringing about change in the culture. The latter, staying only for short periods and relying for their information mainly on the acknowledged leaders of the society, its 'successful' members, tended to have a still rather than a moving picture of the culture. Moreover, the dominance of functionalist theory in their discipline led them to see each culture as a single, stable and coherent entity.

Missionaries, along with merchants and colonial governments, were agents of cultural change. A small minority among them, mainly German, strongly affirmed the native cultures and fought to protect them against the ravages of 'civilization'. The majority, mainly Anglo-Saxon, shared the reigning 'progressive' view of civilization, saw themselves as its representatives, and judged the societies they met by its standards. Their judgements were accepted by some, rejected by others. There were in every society some eager for change and some anxious to preserve the existing order. Missionaries often received their warmest welcome from among the disadvantaged sectors of society. Through programmes of education they brought into being a Christian elite fully at home in, and with impressive mastery of, the culture of the missionaries.

Protestant missionary leaders in the mid-nineteenth century had striven for the development of 'indigenous' churches in accordance with the famous 'Three Self' principle, but it was not until well into the twentieth century that movements began among the educated elite of these churches to recover elements of the traditional culture which had been discarded under the influence of missionaries. This did not, however, usually lead to the development of 'indigenous theologies' until the last quarter of the century when, in the work of the Theological Education Fund of the World Council of Churches, the word 'contextualization' was coined (1972). This called for a new style of theology which would not so much look back (as 'indigenization' did), but address the actual present context as the starting point for doing theology. This has led to the rapid development of 'third world theologies', which are the work of persons who have completely mastered western culture and write in the languages of Europe. They are generally (and understandably) marked by an element of antiwestern polemic.

Meanwhile, in the twentieth century a new wave of evangelical missions was launched, mainly from North America, many of whose representatives were eager to embrace the findings of cultural anthropology. They tended, as a result, to emphasize the singularity of each culture and to insist that the gospel must be communicated to each society in ways that would minimize cultural dislocation. The widely influential 'church growth' school of missiology adopted (early in the 1960s) the 'homogeneous unit principle', according to which Christianity must take a distinct and separate form in each human culture. But the findings of cultural anthropology were seen as tools for church growth rather than as opening up new insights into the meaning of the gospel. Consequently these new churches have not so far produced their own distinctive theologies.

Common to all Protestant missions has been the translation of the Bible into the languages of the peoples. In innumerable cases this has been the first written text in the language. The development of literacy immediately opens up a society to a multitude of external influences. The impact of this on culture has been chronicled by Lamin Sanneh (1989). Moreover, the availability of the Bible in the mother tongue has led, especially in Africa, to the rapid growth of independent churches which can claim to have a better understanding of the Bible than the missionaries. Theirs is also a form of third world theology, but it is mainly oral and it is directed to the evangelization of their own peoples, not to the removal of western cultural influence. Many western elements are cherished, but the language is that of the culture.

Roman Catholic missions have, until recently, followed a different course. The Bible was not generally made available in the mother tongue. Latin was the language of worship. A policy of 'adaptation' was recommended: the one universally valid form of Christianity was to be adapted to local cultures. The Second Vatican Council (1962–5) initiated revolutionary changes. The dignity of local cultures was to be affirmed. Worship was to be in the mother tongue. The new concept of *inculturation* was vigorously developed from 1970 onwards. The theological authorization for this was in the incarnation itself, where the eternal Word took flesh as a man of a particular culture. In an analagous manner the local church is to be encouraged to take the cultural form of its society. A large literature of inculturation is now being produced, and there is a welcome for the new insights which the various cultures can bring for the enrichment of the church's patrimony.

The terms 'contextualization' and 'inculturation' have come into western theology from missiology – a discipline which theology has generally ignored. In so far as culture has been a topic in western theology (even where the word was not used) the discussion has not taken account of crosscultural experience but has been concerned with the relation of human creativity to divine grace, of reason to revelation. H. Richard Niebuhr's classic *Christ and Culture* (1951), with its five-fold typology, has not had a successor. The long synthesis between Christianity and western culture has ended. Little has so far been done to bring the insights of missiology to bear on the inculturation of the gospel in a now largely pagan Europe.

Both 'contextualization' and 'inculturation' pose the problem of relativism. Are there any supracultural ethical norms? More seriously, are all claims to knowledge (including knowledge of God) so culturally determined that there is no criterion of truth? The rationalism of the Enlightenment saw the human race as a unity in which all claims to knowledge are to be judged at the bar of 'reason'. The romantic reaction extolled the creativity of the various human cultures. Cultural anthropology has tended to make culture absolute. The conflict between the rational and the romantic elements in European thought cannot be settled on the terms of either. Theology has its own critique of both. Certainly theologians have become more aware of the cultural conditioning of all claims to speak truthfully about God. There is no 'culture-neutral' theology. This salutary recognition has, however, been allied with the tendency towards scepticism about the possibility of knowing reality 'as it is' which is characteristic of European thought since Kant. Cultural relativism has invaded theology (see RELATIVISM, CULTURAL). But culture is not to be absolutized. The story which the church tells can, as missionary and ecumenical experience show, offer a focus for human unity other than that proposed by the Enlightenment. But this story, with its centre in the cross and resurrection of the eternal Word, will always provide both a critique of every culture and also the resources of divine grace to sustain the human enterprise of culture. The full meaning of that Word which was 'incultured' in Jesus Christ will only be known at the end when he has been recognized and acknowledged in the language and the praise of every culture.

See also MISSION, THEOLOGY OF; OTHER FAITHS AND CHRISTIANITY; POSTLIBERALISM; SOCIAL SCIENCE AND CHRISTIAN THOUGHT.

Bibliography

Conn, Harvie M. 1984: *Eternal Word and Changing World*. Grand Rapids: Zondervan Publishing House.

Donovan, Vincent J. 1983: *Christianity Rediscovered: An Epistle from the Masai*. Maryknoll: Orbis Books.

Kraft, Charles H. 1979: *Christianity in Culture*. Maryknoll: Orbis Books.

McGavran, Donald A. 1980: *Understanding Church Growth*, revised edn. Grand Rapids: Eerdmans.

Niebuhr, H. Richard 1951: *Christ and Culture*. New York: Harper Colphon Books.

Sanneh, Lamin 1989: *Translating the Message: The Missionary Impact on Culture*. Maryknoll: Orbis Books.

Schreitter, Robert J. 1984: *Constructing Local Theologies*. Maryknoll: Orbis Books.

Shorter, Alward 1988: *Towards a Theology of Inculturation*. Maryknoll: Orbis Books.

Stackhouse, Max 1988: *Apologia: Contextualization, Globalization and Mission in Theological Education*. Grand Rapids: Eerdmans.

Taber, Charles R. 1991: *The World is Too Much With Us: 'Culture' in Modern Protestant Missions*. Macon GA: Mercer University Press.

Tillich, Paul 1959: *Theology of Culture*. New York: Oxford University Press.

Tylor, Edward B. 1889: *Primitive Culture*, 2 vols. New York: Henry Holt and Co.

LESSLIE NEWBIGIN

D

death, theology of While the Bible takes death seriously, it does not develop a theology of death. The Hebrews understood death as the loss of life, the attenuation of the life force that integrates soul and body. Death is the weakest form of life, a scattering of one's vital powers, a pouring out of the soul (Isa. 53: 12; Job 30: 16). One who dies is like water spilled on the ground, not to be gathered up again (2 Sam. 14: 14). In the underworld, in Sheol, there is no real life, even though persons continue to 'exist' as shadows of the real self. The unity of the body and the soul is broken and the person cut off from the 'land of the living' (Isa. 38: 11).

Whatever the situation of those who have died may be, and that in Hebrew terms is quite ambiguous, they are now excluded from the community of those who praise Jahweh (Ps. 6: 5; 30: 9; 88: 10–12; Isa. 38: 18ff.). Death is therefore a part of life viewed as existence before God. This leads to an apparent ambivalence with regard to death and the individual in the Old Testament. The power of death has its limits, for it is God who kills and brings to life (1 Sam. 2: 6). It is he who returns humans to the dust (Ps. 90: 3). At the same time, there is a reticence towards death which is rooted in Israel's religion. Israel's God is the God of the living, not the dead. The dead are cut off from his hand (Ps. 88: 6). The bodies of the dead are unclean and must be removed from the sphere of that which is consecrated to God (Lev. 21: 1; Num. 19: 16).

On the one hand, death is human and natural, for it is part of God's determination for human nature and not merely a fate which has a power of its own over the human. To die at a ripe old age was not seen as something unnatural, but was something that one could take for granted

(Job 5: 26; Gen. 27: 2; 46: 30). This leads to the concept of a 'good death' which occurs in the natural course of human life. On the other hand, death could appear as a threat to life, as unnatural or as a sign of judgement, and even a curse, though this curse is that which humans originally caused to come upon themselves (Gen. 2: 17; 3: 19). Death, as a result of sin, came to be viewed as an end to the spiritual life of fellowship with God, and not merely a natural physical event.

Though there are various views as to the mortality or immortality of the human body as God created it, some hold that the human body originally possessed a kind of 'conditional immortality'. In this view, death only became a possibility for humanity through sin and the fall. Others suggest that the original human body was mortal, taken from the dust along with all creatures, so that 'dying' as a possibility of human flesh was natural to humanity. Death, as a specific result of sin, consequently entered into the mortal situation of the human as a judgement from God (Anderson, 1986, pp. 54ff.). This latter view seems to fit the biblical data better and allows for the experience of dying to be viewed as part of our created human nature while, at the same time, treating death as an enemy and a judgement of God upon sin.

The belief that humans possess an immortal soul placed in a mortal body is alien to a Hebrew anthropology which defines the soul and body bound together as the form of life; as such, both are subject to death (see ANTHROPOLOGY, CHRISTIAN). There is no concept of an immortal soul in the Old Testament, nor does the New Testament ever call the human soul immortal. Christian theology holds on the basis of a biblical anthropology that humans are in no way created to be or to become immortal by their nature. Rather, persons created in the image and likeness of God live within the limits of human nature bounded by mortality and are dependent upon God for the gift of immortal life through resurrection from the dead.

In the New Testament the basic orientation towards death is in continuity with that of the Old. In view of the RESURRECTION of Jesus from the dead, the New Tetament can even be said to have a 'contempt for death' (Thielicke, [1980] 1983, p. 32). On the basis of Christ's death for sinners, the apostle Paul can argue that death, which spread to all people through the sin of Adam, has now been overcome through the death and resurrection of one man, Jesus Christ (Rom. 5: 12; 15–16). The 'sting of death' is removed through the resurrection of Christ, asserts Paul (1 Cor. 15: 56). Though Christians continue to die, death no longer has power over those who belong to Jesus Christ. These are the 'dead in Christ', who will be raised when Christ returns to meet those who 'are alive at his coming' (1 Thess. 4: 13–18).

The status of those who die 'in Christ' during the so-called 'intermediate state' between death and resurrection is not clear from the biblical record. Some hold that the departed soul of the dead lives in a self-conscious disembodied existence awaiting the resurrection of the body. Others use the metaphor of 'soul sleep' to explain the interval between death and resurrection, rejecting the concept of elapsed time and preferring instead a 'timeless' continuing of personal identity, with resurrection, perhaps, to be experienced instantaneously following death (Thielicke, [1980] 1983, pp. 176–7). The disposal of the body following death in the Judaeo-Christian tradition has traditionally been through burial in the earth, and occasionally in water. Disposal by fire (cremation) has been rejected at various times by both Jews and Christians on theological grounds (Phipps, 1987, pp. 123ff.). In Christian theology, with the body having been formed 'from the dust' to 'return to the dust' (Gen. 2: 7; 3: 19), there seems no reason to reject any method of disposal that does not violate human sensibilities. The resurrection of the body does not seem to require literal recomposition of the same physical elements of which our earthly body consists (1 Cor. 15: 42–50).

While the Old Testament does not have a clearly developed theology of punishment after death, the relation between sin, death and punishment after death is an important theme in the New Testament. Death is the 'wages of sin', says Paul, and a punishment which has fallen on the entire human race (Rom. 5: 12–15; 6: 23). In the inter-testamental period a theory of rewards and punishments following death is depicted. The dead are no longer shadows which exist in Sheol without form or personality. They are spoken of as souls or spirits and survive as individual conscious beings. Moral obligations appear in Sheol. There the good and the bad receive compensation for their deeds done on earth. In 1 Enoch 22: 10–11, in the Apocrypha, Sheol is a place of torment, though the actual word 'Gehenna' is not used. These concepts underlie the warnings uttered by Jesus to avoid being 'cast into hell' where there is torment for the unrepentant (Matt. 5: 29–30; 18: 9; 22: 13; Luke 16: 24). Jesus spoke of existence after death where the righteous will be rewarded and the wicked punished (see the parables of Jesus near the end of his life, Matt. 24–5; also Jas. 5: 1–12; 2 Pet. 2: 4–10). Some hold that hell will be a literal place of punishment for those who die without repentance and faith in Jesus Christ (Morey, 1984, pp. 103, 250). Others view this punishment already to have been assumed by Christ so that 'judgement after death' is through the Christ who took this judgement upon himself (Anderson, 1986, pp. 71–80).

More recent concerns with death and dying have to do with the 'stages of dying', with persons experiencing successively denial, anger, bargaining, depression and finally acceptance (Kübler-Ross, 1975). The phenomenon of 'near-death' experiences, in which persons are apparently clinically dead but after recovery recount experiences of 'disembodied' consciousness, are viewed by some as evidence of life after death (Moody, 1978; Phipps, 1987, pp. 16–20). Others argue that these are actually 'near-death' experiences and not 'after-death' experiences, as a person cannot really be said to have died while living to tell about the experience. By definition, a dead person is one who cannot be resuscitated because his or her condition is irreversible (Phipps, 1987, p. 19).

In Christian theology, death is viewed as a passageway to life eternal with God, with the assurance of continued personal identity through resurrection of the body. Death is the 'last enemy to be destroyed in Christ' (1 Cor. 15: 26).

See also ESCHATOLOGY; MEDICAL ETHICS.

Bibliography

Anderson, Ray S. 1986: *Theology, Death and Dying*. Oxford: Blackwell.

Doss, Richard 1974: *The Last Enemy*. New York: Harper and Row.

Hick, John 1976: *Death and Eternal Life*. San Francisco: Harper and Row.

Jüngel, Eberhard [1971] 1974: *Death: The Riddle and the Mystery*, trans. I. and U. Nicol. Philadelphia: Westminster Press.

Kübler-Ross, Elizabeth 1975: *Death, the Final Stage of Growth*. New York: Macmillan.

Moody, Raymond 1978: *Reflections on Life After Death*. New York: Bantam Books.

Morey, Robert 1984: *Death and the Afterlife*. Minneapolis: Bethany House.

Phipps, William E. 1987: *Death: Confronting the Reality*. Atlanta: John Knox Press.

Rahner, Karl [1959] 1969: *On the Theology of Death*, trans. New York: Herder and Herder.

Thielicke, Helmut [1980] 1983: *Living With Death*, trans. G.W. Bromiley. Grand Rapids: Eerdmans.

RAY S. ANDERSON

deism 'Deism' is a label used in two distinct ways in theology and the philosophy of religion. Its most common reference in contemporary thought is to any view which holds that, while God created the world, he is no longer immanent in it. Deism in this sense is one option arising out of the PROBLEM OF EVIL – that which tempers either God's omnipotence or benevolence (or both) with the result that a continuing divine providence in creation is denied. It matters little if deism so defined has historical exemplifications, though it can be found articulated in some nineteenth-century treatments of the problem of evil (Mill, [1874] 1957, pp. 44–5, has something like it). Its importance is that of a theoretically possible option in the discussion of God and evil.

When used to denote a historical movement, 'deism' refers to a group of English writers active from the very late seventeenth century into the eighteenth, and to continental and American authors whom they influenced. This movement is *not* to be defined as denying the immanence of God in the world, but may be identified by reference to a group of related characteristics, which include the following:

1 attacks on the justice, rational basis and historical foundations of Christian revelation;

2 a rationalist approach to the foundations of religious faith – most commonly derived from the epistemology of John Locke;

3 the elevation of natural religion as the essence of religious truth.

Deism so defined is at the centre of the approach to religion of the ENLIGHTENMENT and the claims of Christianity during that period, and is of enormous historical importance in the development of such things as biblical interpretation and of liberal theology. The identification of deism is admittedly problematic. In eighteenth-century defences of theological orthodoxy 'diesm' was used as a label of abuse to group together all manner of writers who chose to be critical of the Christian creeds. Thus J. Leland's *View of the Principal Deistic Writers* (1757) cites Thomas Hobbes, David Hume and Lord Herbert of Cherbury as deists, alongside those normally classed as such by twentieth-century historians. No positive theology unites Leland's group, only scepticism of Christian ideas. Further difficulty arises because the style of liberal, latitudinarian theology of orthodox English divines tended to share characteristics 2 and 3 and was in effect sceptical of much traditional theology. Identification of the deists is compounded by the tendency (ironic or not) of theological radicals to present subversive ideas under the guise of saving 'true Christianity' from its medieval or Catholic corruptions.

Nothing other than a family resemblance definition of deism can stand in the face of these difficulties. A paradigmatic exemplification of deism can be found in Matthew Tindal's *Christianity as Old as the Creation or the Gospel a Republication of the Religion of Nature* of 1730. This teaches that natural religion (see NATURAL THEOLOGY) constitutes a sufficient means of human salvation. Christ's incarnation is thus not necessary, Jesus' mission being merely to republish the claims of natural religion. These positive views are supported on a variety of grounds, including an account of divine perfection and of human nature as unfallen and uniform. Epistemology in the form of Locke's account of faith and reason supports these to produce an argument for saying that saving faith must be: uniformly accessible to reason; independent of history; and simple. A Christian insistence on a miraculous, prophetic history culminating in the equally miraculous, unique, atoning incarnation is rejected along the way. It is false to a picture of God dealing impartially with a uniform human race and is without independent rational support outside the biased accounts of tradition. Other writers can be classed as deists in so far as they share features of this paradigm. The family extends in one direction towards those Enlightenment critics of deism who approached atheism (such as Anthony Collins) and in another towards those radical theologians who retained a greater use for Scripture and Jesus than Tindal (such as Thomas Woolston).

Natural religion in Tindal is a set of simple truths about God and his moral requirements for humanity that claims a number of advantages over traditional religion. It is unchanging and universal, open to all men at all times and places. It is completely transparent to human reason: nothing can be a truth of natural religion if it is mysterious or not demonstrable. It has no essential dependence on historical or Scriptural revelation. It is fit to stand as the common truth (and perhaps common origin) behind all religions. It matches the key principle that a just God should have given all men an equal chance of salvation, a principle which reliance on historical or Scriptural revelation can only violate for Tindal. It makes no impossible demands on humanity: where people fail to live up to all the requirements of the natural moral law God will take the intention for the deed and accept a sincere repentance as sufficient for reconciliation. An atoning saviour is not necessary. The God of natural religion is emphatically *not* departed or removed from his creation. His will is immanent, as the naturally grounded moral law, in every facet of creation. He continues to exercise a moral government over creation and the life of man. It is the perfection of this government, and not its absence, that makes miracles and special revelation irrelevant.

The origins of deism are manifold. Two sources are selected here: response to religious uncertainty and response to religious diversity. Both can be illustrated with reference to the Protestant/Catholic schism and to the writings of John Locke and Lord Herbert of Cherbury. Once the division in western Christianity assumed permanence in the seventeenth century it became apparent that Christianity had no single rule of faith to settle doctrinal disputes (neither appeal to tradition nor to Scripture worked). Locke, like a number of writers, searched for a common language in which doctrinal disputes might be adjudicated and discussed. A rule of faith independent of Protestant and Catholic models suggested itself: human reason, understood as common-sense reflection on contemporary facts and on such historical evidences as could be independently vouched for. As Locke in *An Essay concerning Human Understanding* ([1690] 1975, Book IV, chapter 15 ff.) and *The Reasonableness of Christianity* ([1695] 1958, *passim*) abundantly illustrates, this leaves little room for doctrines that cannot be demonstrated by the individual believer. His writings, and especially *The Reasonableness of Christianity*, also show how this same reliance on reason solves the problem of diversity. In the light of the divisions between national religious settlements, which form of faith a man can acquire seems determined by the accidents of his birth. Finding a creed that common sense can vouch for that is independent of the contingencies of politics and culture leads to a simplified form of religion which leaves out much that was thought to be essential to saving truth. It is but a short step to making this religious essence independent of *all* references to Christ and Scripture, a move that had already been taken by Lord Herbert of Cherbury. His religion of the 'common notions' consists of belief in a supreme God, the necessity of worshipping him, a reminder of fundamental human duties, the need for repentance, and the doctrine of an afterlife (see Byrne, 1989, p. 26). Being completely free of Christianity, these provide an answer to how classical philosophers and the newly discovered Confucian sages could be offered terms of salvation by a just and merciful God. (However, it is misleading to class Herbert as a deist owing to idiosyncrasies which make him unlike typical Enlightenment thinkers; see Byrne, 1989, pp. 31ff.)

Deism had continental versions which increased its influence on subsequent religious thought. Notable in this connection is Voltaire, whose *Philosophical Letters* of 1734 conveyed the essence of Locke's thought to a continental audience. A number of the important English works were translated into German. Reason and natural religion became the standard categories with which liberal German theologians of the late eighteenth century approached religious questions. The writings of G.E. Lessing and Immanuel Kant exhibit the same problems which the English deists wrestled with, notably those of how to reconcile the uniqueness, uncertainty and obscurity of Christian revelation with the universality, certainty and clarity of any true religion. Their solutions exhibit a similar pattern of response, namely a stress upon locating the truth of Christ and Christianity in a moral message substantially independent of history and mystery (see KANTIANISM).

Deism thus became part of the general legacy of the Enlightenment. Its contributions to later thought can be seen first in its opening up of the debate about the origins of Christianity, the status of Scripture in history and the nature of the historical Jesus. Deism has an interest in denying that Christianity and its Scriptures were unique in history and in distinguishing between the historical Jesus and the miraculous, atoning Christ of faith. It spawned a debate on the historicity of miracles (particularly the RESURRECTION) in which the issues and techniques of historical Gospel criticism were developed (see Burns, 1981, *passim*, and Byrne, 1989, pp. 88–110). It also raised in the clearest form the issues surrounding religious diversity and divine justice which still preoccupy theology and the philosophy of religion. Above all, its questions and solutions remain alive in all those versions of liberal Christianity and theism, popular and academic, in which the morality of religion is placed higher than doctrine and history, and a lowest common denominator of religion is sought in some form of natural law.

See also GOD; PHILOSOPHY OF RELIGION; PROTESTANT THEOLOGY: BRITAIN.

Bibliography

Bedford, R.D. 1979: *The Defence of Truth*. Manchester: Manchester University Press.

Burns, R.M. 1981: *The Great Debate on Miracles*. London: Associated University Presses of America.

Byrne, P.A. 1989: *Natural Religion and the Nature of Religion*. London: Routledge.

Craig, W.L. 1985: *The Historical Argument for the Resurrection of Jesus During the Deist Controversy*. Lewiston, NY: Edwin Mellen.

Gay, P. 1968: *Deism*. Princeton, NJ: Van Nostrand.

Hudson, L. 1977: Deism: the minimal religion of social utility, *Dialog* 16, pp. 205–210.

Leland, J. 1757: *A View of the Principal Deistic Writers*. London.

Locke, J. [1690] 1975: *An Essay concerning Human Understanding*. Oxford: Clarendon Press.

Locke, J. [1695] 1958: *The Reasonableness of Christianity*. Stanford: Stanford University Press.

Mill, J.S. [1874] 1957: *Theism*. Indianapolis: Bobbs-Merrill.

O'Higgins, J. 1971: Hume and the deists, *Journal of Theological Studies* NS 22, pp. 479–501.

O'Higgins, J. 1973: Archbishop Tillotson and the religion of nature, *Journal of Theological Studies* NS 24, pp. 123–42.

Pailin, D.A. 1971: Some eighteenth century attitudes to other religions, *Religion* 1, pp. 83–108.

Pailin, D.A. 1983: Herbert of Cherbury and the deists, *Expository Times* 94, pp. 196–200.

Stephen, L. 1881: *A History of English Thought in the Eighteenth Century*. London: Smith and Elder.

Sullivan, R.E. 1982: *John Toland and the Deist Controversy*. Cambridge, Mass.: Harvard University Press.

Torrey, N. 1930: *Voltaire and the English Deists*. New Haven, CT: Yale University Press.

PETER BYRNE

Denmark See PROTESTANT THEOLOGY: SCANDINAVIA.

Denney, James (1856–1917) Scottish Free Church theologian. Educated at the university and then at the Free Church College in Glasgow, he taught systematic and pastoral theology at Glasgow Divinity College from 1897 until his death. Moving away from liberalism towards evangelicalism in the course of his career, he remained sympathetic to modern biblical criticism. His emphasis was on theology that could be preached, and, in preaching, on the atonement, which he held to be purely substitutionary in character: his writings in defence of this position, such as *The Death of Christ* (1902) represent his major contribution. Other works include *Jesus and the Gospel* (1908), *The Christian Doctrine of Reconciliation* (1917), and commentaries on 1 and 2 Thessalonians (1892), 2 Corinthians (1894) and Romans (1900).

Bibliography

Hughes, P.E., ed. 1969: *Creative Minds in Contemporary Theology*, article on Denney. Grand Rapids, Mi.
Taylor, J.R. 1962: *God Loved Like That! The Theology of James Denney*. London.

Derrida, Jacques (b. 1930) French philosopher of language. Born in Algiers in 1930, Derrida inaugurated a new movement in critical theory, known as *deconstruction*, with his paper 'Structure, Sign and Play in the Discourse of Human Sciences' given in the USA in 1966. This paper and subsequent publications led him to international fame. He currently teaches at Yale University. Among his publications are: *De la grammatologie* (1967), *L'Ecriture et la différence* (1967), *La Carte postale* (1987) and *De l'esprit* (1987).

Derrida's philosophy of language – as all poststructuralist thought – resists final definition. His initial work was derived from the linguistic theories of Ferdinand de Saussure, who argued that language was a 'self-enclosed system'. Derrida began with Saussure's argument that the meaning of a word is the result of convention, and not of some ontological link between the word and what it signifies. From this, he argued that the final meaning of a word can never be determined, and that language is ultimately unable to convey truth. Every utterance is flawed.

The impact of this philosophy has been considerable. In literary theory, the idea that language always avoids final meaning has been fruitful. Deconstruction has emphasized, in its own critical writing, the instability of language by extensive use of puns and statements open to several meanings.

Bibliography

Culler, J. 1982: *On Deconstruction: Theory and Criticism after Structuralism*. London.
Norris, C. 1988: *Deconstruction*. London.
Sturrock, J. 1979: *Structuralism and Since*. Oxford.

dialectical theology See KARL BARTH; PROTESTANT THEOLOGY: GERMANY.

Dilthey, Wilhelm (1833–1911) German philosopher of history. He taught philosophy at Basle, Kiel, Breslau and Berlin, applying a relativistic methodology to his studies of philosophy, psychology and sociology. He pioneered the distinction between the methods used in studying natural science and those used in the human sciences in *Einleitung in die Geisteswissenschaften* (1883, unfinished). He rejected the supernatural, maintaining that knowledge may be obtained from understanding human psychology and culture-conditioned world views. Dilthey's historical methodology is radically secular, denying a divine role in history and viewing Christianity as a cultural phenomenon, and it forms the basis of modern philosophies of history. He wrote a biography of F.D.E. Schleiermacher (1870), and his influence may be traced on theologians such as Ernst Troeltsch and Martin Heidegger.

Bibliography

Bulhof, I.N. 1980: *Wilhelm Dilthey*. The Hague.
Hodges, H.A. 1952: *The Philosophy of Wilhelm Dilthey*. London.
Rickman, H.P. 1979: *Wilhelm Dilthey*. London.

dispensationalism Dispensationalism is a theological movement within EVANGELICALISM stressing an apocalyptic understanding of history. Its peculiarities arise from an interpretation of the history of redemption which sees the Old and New Testaments united eschatologically in a way that is consistent with a historical-grammatical (sometimes referred to as 'literal') interpretation of Old and New Testaments, and consistent with the fulfilment of the Old Testament promises to national Israel of an earthly kingdom ruled personally by the Messiah, Jesus Christ. It is a philosophy of history, adherence to which encompasses diverse theologies in the evangelical tradition, including the Calvinistic, Arminian, Pentecostal and charismatic.

Terminology

1 *Dispensation* (from the Greek *oikonomia*: management of a household): a distinguishable administration in the fulfilment of the divine purpose of creation, operative within history, during which God administers the world in a particular manner. The dispensations correspond historically to the successive stages of progressive revelation.

2 *Imminence*: the doctrine that Jesus Christ can return at any moment. No prophetic event must intervene before that return.

3 *The rapture* (Latin *rapio*: snatch, catch away): the church's expectation of being 'caught up in the clouds' to meet Christ at his return (1 Thess. 4: 15–17). The rapture is most commonly believed to be imminent (pre-tribulational), although some theologians argue that imminence need not necessarily imply a pre-tribulational rapture. Of these, some would place its timing at the middle of the tribulation, and a small but growing number see the rapture as post-tribulational.

4 *The tribulation*: a seven-year apocalyptic period of divine judgement upon the earth, delineated in the Books of Daniel and Revelation (interpreted futuristically). This period is also referred to as the seventieth week of Daniel. (This is based upon the prophecy of the seventy heptads ('weeks' in the Authorized Version) of Daniel 9: 24–7. The first sixty-nine heptads (interpreting each 'day' as signifying a literal year) are understood as having been completed at the first advent of Jesus Christ; the final heptad is viewed as being in the future, beginning when the Antichrist (the Beast of Revelation) signs a protective covenant with the nation of Israel, and culminating with the battle of Armageddon and the personal return of Jesus Christ).

5 *Premillennialism*: the teaching that Jesus Christ will return before the millennium and establish and reign over an earthly kingdom which will endure for one thousand years (Rev. 20: 1–6) in fulfilment of Old Testament prophecies, after which will occur the resurrection of the wicked and the final judgement of the present order, followed by the eternal state.

6 *The church as a 'parenthesis' (or 'inter-calation')* in God's prophetic programme*: earlier dispensationalists viewed the church as a complete *mystery*, that is, not revealed in any way in the Old Testament. The prophetic material of the Old Testament dealing with national Israel is yet to be literally fulfilled. As taught historically, Israel's rejection of the Messiah caused God to put his 'prophetic clock' on hold until the end of the church age at the rapture, at which time his programme for Israel will again start 'ticking'. This teaching implied that the church age was unrelated to God's primary design for history. Although holding to a sense of newness in the mystery character of the church, most contemporary dispensational scholars see the church age as the next step forward in the working out of the divine plan rather than understand it as an interruption in the divine plan for human history, unrelated to the rest of the historical process.

7 *Israel*: Israel is understood as always having reference biblically to national Israel, ethnic Jews, never to the church or Gentiles.

8 *Church*: the church is seen as the spiritual body of Christ consisting of all those who since Pentecost have been regenerated by the Holy Spirit. Stress is placed upon the overarching unity of the body of Christ, while the practical manifestation is seen in ways which do not conflict with the concept of the local church.

Origins and development

John Nelson Darby (1800–1882), a former priest in the Irish church, abandoned its ranks due to the apostasy he perceived therein. Forsaking the established church, Darby joined the movement later known as the Plymouth Brethren, where he developed a distinctive ecclesiology. He believed that the church was not to be identified with any institution but was a spiritual fellowship. Darby's ecclesiology became the catalyst for dispensationalism as a system. He posited radical discontinuity between the church and Israel, asserting that God had two separate peoples and two separate programmes which he was working out in history. This discontinuity made it incumbent to 'rightly divide the Word of truth' discerning which passages were addressed to Israel and which to the church. These features, coupled with a futurist view of biblical prophecy and the doctrine of the pre-tribulational rapture of the church, gave coherence to incipient dispensationalism.

The views and ideas of the Brethren movement spread to North America. Darby and Brethren expositors and evangelists gained a wide hearing, particularly among Presbyterians and Baptists, significant numbers of which adopted the dispensational historiography although few left their established denominational affiliations. In 1876 a group of prominent Presbyterian and Baptist preachers and educators organized the annual Niagara Bible Conferences for prophetic study, which continued for a quarter of a century.

The Bible Conference movement, following the pattern of the Niagara Conferences, spread dispensationalism widely. Working out of this context, C.I. Scofield in 1909 published the *Scofield Reference Bible*, which became the largest single force in spreading dispensational teaching.

In the wake of the fundamentalist–modernist controversy of the early twentieth century (see FUNDAMENTALISM), fundamentalists (most of whom were dispensationalists) found that they had lost control of their denominations and seminaries. In response, a plethora of new theological institutions dedicated to preserving orthodoxy arose. The dispensational perspective of the *Scofield Reference Bible* became the traditional framework of instruction in many of these institutions.

In succeeding decades the movement retained its apocalyptic perspective but a historicism, reminiscent of nineteenth-century adventism, modified the strict futurism of early dispensationalism in certain sections of the movement. Although strictly this historicist emphasis is not to be identified with dispensationalism, in the minds of many it has been, due to best-selling popular works. The historicist emphasis has had its greatest impact in Pentecostal and charismatic circles, which from their inceptions have been characterized by vivid apocalyptic expectations.

Major representatives
Apart from John Nelson Darby (see above), the leading figures in the movement have been the following.

1   C.I. Scofield (1843–1921): his *Rightly Dividing the Word of Truth* set the agenda for much of American fundamentalism. Scofield's *The Comprehensive Bible Correspondence Course*, first issued in 1896, became the foundational curriculum for churches and Bible institutes. His most important work, *The Scofield Reference Bible* (1909), put dispensational teaching in the hands of the layman. Over two million copies of the *Scofield Bible* have been sold. A revised edition, *The New Scofield Reference Bible*, was published in 1967.

2   Lewis Sperry Chafer (1872–1952): Chafer was the first president of Dallas Theological Seminary. His eight-volume *Systematic Theology* of 1947 became the standard theology of the 'Scofieldian' period of dispensationalism.

3   Alva J. McClain (1888–1968): president of Grace Theological Seminary, he contributed *The Greatness of the Kingdom* of 1959, a major dispensational study of the kingdom of God.

4   John F. Walvoord (b. 1910): as second president of Dallas Seminary and author of numerous works, including *The Millennial Kingdom* of 1959, *The Blessed Hope and the Tribulation* of 1976, *Israel in Prophecy* of 1962, *Daniel* of 1971 and *The Revelation* of 1966, Walvoord has been a leading spokesman for dispensational eschatology.

5   J. Dwight Pentecost (b. 1915): professor at Dallas Seminary, he penned *Things to Come* of 1958, a massive study of dispensational eschatology from the 'Scofieldian' perspective.

6   Charles C. Ryrie (b. 1925): a prolific writer, his major contributions to dispensational thought are *Dispensationalism Today* (1965), which traced significant refinements in dispensational thinking since the publication of the *Scofield Reference Bible*, and the *Ryrie Study Bible* of 1978, which has replaced *The Scofield* and *The New Scofield* Bibles as the study Bible of choice among many dispensationalists. Ryrie's work marked the beginning of the attempt to define the essence of dispensational teaching, and also set the direction for dispensational self-definition over the last decades of the twentieth century.

Major institutions
1   Moody Bible Institute (independent): founded in 1886 before the fundamentalist–modernist controversies, it was led from the first

by dispensational leaders and publishes the *Scofield Bible Correspondence Course*.

2   Biola University/Talbot School of Theology (independent): founded in 1907 as the Bible Institute of Los Angeles, it published until the 1970s the periodical *The King's Business*, the successor to *The Fundamentals*.

3   Dallas Theological Seminary (independent): founded in 1924, Dallas Seminary became synonymous with dispensationalism since its presidents and numerous faculty members published widely read volumes which championed dispensational themes. Its faculty have been major contributors to the development of dispensationalism from the older 'Scofieldian' perspective into the contemporary era of 'progressive dispensationalism'. Additionally, *Bibliotheca Sacra*, the oldest continuous theological journal in the USA, was acquired by Dallas Seminary in the 1930s and has functioned as the scholarly organ for the movement.

4   Grace Theological Seminary (Grace Brethren): founded in 1937, it publishes *Grace Theological Journal*, which has recently begun publishing the annual dispensational papers presented in conjunction with the Evangelical Theological Society, making available to the scholarly world current dispensational discussions.

5   Mission organizations: numerous mission organizations have arisen from the dispensational tradition, including: Campus Crusade for Christ, Jews for Jesus, Friends of Israel, SIM (Sudan Interior Mission), CAM Int'l (formerly Central American Mission), AIM Int'l (formerly Africa Inland Mission), Africa Evangelical Fellowship, Baptist Mid-Missions.

Issues and tensions
Hermeneutics Earlier dispensationalists insisted upon a consistent *literal* interpretation of prophecy. This insistence upon a *literal* interpretation did not imply a denial of figurative language or symbols. Rather, the term 'literal' has been employed to insist that all Scripture is to be interpreted in accordance with received linguistic conventions. In particular, the term is used in opposition to (1) older Covenant theologians' denial of a literal future fulfilment of the Old Testament prophecies concerning national Israel and the messianic kingdom; (2) the spiritual appropriation of those

prophecies/promises by the church; and (3) the theologians' fusion of Israel and the church into one virtually indistinguishable entity.

Founded upon the epistemological presuppositions of Scottish common sense and employing Baconian inductivism as a method, late nineteenth- and early twentieth-century dispensationalists approached the Bible as scientists, arranging the 'facts' in a literal fashion. Operating upon the assumption that the Bible *teaches* a single system, dispensationalism claimed to present the Bible's own view of itself.

A naive literalism seen in such slogans as 'if the plain sense makes sense seek no other sense' often characterized the earlier movement, particularly on the popular level. Such literalism often led early dispensational writers to see sharp distinctions between concepts such as the 'kingdom of God' and the 'kingdom of heaven', distinctions which contemporary dispensational scholars disavow. Early spokesman R.A. Torrey insisted, 'in ninety-nine out of one hundred cases the meaning the plain man gets out of the Bible is the correct one.' This insistence arose from the conviction that the Bible was God's message to the common man rather than to the scholar. Insistence on the 'literal' meaning of the text and upon common-sense interpretation opened the door for viewing the text apart from its historical context. In recent decades the Scottish common-sense epistemology has been supplanted by a critical realism, while the plain literal interpretation of earlier generations has been progressively supplanted by thoroughgoing historical-grammatical interpretation and coupled with increasing critical interaction and sensitivity to contemporary hermeneutical concerns, including the historical limitations of the interpreter.

Historiography Prior to the nineteenth century, Covenant theology had in practice denied the concepts of *development* and *progressive revelation* in Scripture. These issues of development and change in the Scriptures which gave birth to dispensationalism were the same issues which engaged higher criticism in the nineteenth century. In many respects dispensationalism represents the mirror opposite of higher criticism, confronting the same issues but solving them on totally different bases. Whereas modernism was optimistic concerning the improvement of the human condition through the development of culture, dispensationalism was thoroughly pessimistic. Both focused upon an understanding of the relation of the Bible to history. But while modernism viewed biblical history through the evolutionary lens of universal history, with naturalistic forces at work in the development of religion, dispensationalism contemplated human history exclusively through the lens of the Bible and answered the problem of change by appealing to divine intervention in human affairs.

Dispensational historiography views the world as a stage upon which the drama of cosmic redemption is fought between the divine forces and those of Satan. Each dispensation functions as an act in that drama. Development in the modern sense of the term may take place within dispensations, but not between. Hope for improvement of the human plight is Christological, posited in the return of Christ, rather than anthropological, in progressive human development in history. The unifying principle of history is eschatological, with God revealing his character and glory in successive dispensations.

While there is no universally agreed scheme of dispensations, the most commonly recognized scheme is that of C.I. Scofield: (1) innocence (encompassing humanity's pre-fall condition); (2) conscience (to the flood); (3) human government (until the call of Abraham); (4) promise (until Moses); (5) law (until the death of Christ); (6) church (the present post-Pentecost age); (7) the millennium. Each of these dispensations is inaugurated by God establishing a covenant with humanity which creates a relationship of responsibility between the covenanting parties. Normally the covenants are unconditional, based upon grace, whereby God binds himself to accomplish certain purposes despite any failure on the part of covenanted humanity. The significant exception is the conditional, bilateral Mosaic covenant which is replaced by the New Covenant.

The dispensational periodization of history has frequently been misunderstood as teaching different bases of salvation in different ages. This charge is vehemently denied. Salvation is always by grace and founded upon the atonement of Christ. The content of the revelation to be trusted by the individual in the various ages is what changes, not the means or basis of salvation.

Dispensational historiography has proved to have practical political implications. Dispensationalists have had a political bias towards the nation of Israel based upon God's promise to Abraham (Gen. 12: 3). A creeping historicism has led many dispensationalists to identify the founding of the nation of Israel in 1948 as a fulfilment of prophecy. This, in turn, has led to an often uncritical support for Israel, lest one be found working against the purposes of God.

Sine qua non Many regard the essence of dispensationalism as the periodization of history. There have however been many throughout the centuries who have recognized such a need, but who cannot be considered dispensationalists. Ryrie (1965) argued that the *sine qua non* of dispensationalism was its distinction between the church and Israel. As originally taught, dispensationalism posited a radical distinction between the church and Israel as two separate peoples with two radically separate destinies. The church was God's heavenly people; Israel, God's earthly people. The hope of the church was heaven; the hope of Israel, an eternal kingdom on the renewed earth. The radical distinction between Israel and the church has in recent decades been repudiated as most contemporary dispensational scholars argue for one eternal people of God but two distinct institutional organizations in history. Most contemporary dispensational scholars find Ryrie's *sine qua non* inadequate. While maintaining a distinction between the church and Israel, contemporary dispensationalists see so much continuity between Israel and the church that one critic has charged that on this issue dispensationalism and contemporary Covenant theology have become virtually indistinguishable.

Cessation of the charismata? There is widespread confusion as to *the* dispensational position with reference to the charismatic renewal. Classical Pentecostalism is thoroughly dispensational, while representatives of non-Pentecostal dispensationalism have argued against the continuation of the charismata. This opposition to the charismata however is not endemic to the dispensational system, but rather reflects an affinity of non-Pentecostal dispensationalists to the Calvinistic attitudes exemplified in B.B.

Warfield's *Counterfeit Miracles* of 1918.

Contributions of dispensationalism

Historically, in the USA it was a coalition of dispensational preachers, teachers and laymen that actively fought the modernistic attacks upon historic orthodoxy by (1) publishing works such as *The Fundamentals*, a twelve-volume paperback series of 1910–15 mailed to every pastor, missionary, theological professor, Bible teacher, Bible College and seminary student in the English-speaking world (over three million copies were distributed); (2) founding Bible institutes, colleges and seminaries out of which has arisen contemporary American evangelicalism.

Theologically, in the USA dispensational ecclesiology de-institutionalized grace by its emphasis upon the church as the spiritual body of Christ. This attitude played a major role in fostering an evangelical ecumenism which spread far beyond cooperation in the revivals of nineteenth-century American evangelicalism. This recognition of spiritual brotherhood de-emphasized denominational loyalties and gave cohesion to the evangelical world view. It has been suggested that the striking success of parachurch movements in the USA is due in measure to this de-institutionalization of grace which has characterized dispensationalism.

Another major contribution of the movement lies in its insistence upon an apocalyptic perspective, not only in understanding the Scriptures but also in accomplishing the present theological task. Ernst Käsemann has noted, 'Apocalyptic . . . was the mother of all Christian theology.' But institutional Anglo-American theology prior to the late nineteenth century was decidedly anti-apocalyptic in its perspective. George Ladd admitted, 'We must recognize our debt to dispensationalism . . . to all intents and purposes it revived the doctrine of the second advent of Christ and made it meaningful in the churches.'

Biblically, with its emphasis upon progressive revelation and the discontinuity of the church and Israel, dispensationalism anticipated the conclusions of contemporary scholarship with reference to Paul and the law, recognizing a significant discontinuity between the Old and New Testaments regarding the Christ event. On this issue, dispensational scholarship is closer to contemporary critical conclusions than to the conclusions of Covenant theology.

Practically, from the earlier advocacy of a 'literal hermeneutic' to the contemporary insistence upon historical-grammatical interpretation, dispensationalism has asserted the primacy of the Scriptures and the ability of the layman to interpret and understand them. Its common-sense hermeneutic opened the Scriptures for the layman and fostered comprehensive knowledge of and love for the Bible.

Due to apocalyptic expectations, a large number of early dispensationalists urged withdrawal from worldly occupations, politics and institutions, emphasizing instead evangelism and missions with the hope of saving as many as possible before the rapture. Thus, dispensationalism provided an impetus to the explosion of missionary activity of the twentieth century. At the same time it largely abandoned the public forum to secularism, viewing such involvement as 'polishing brass on a sinking ship'. Many contemporary dispensational theologians have rejected the narrow interpretation of salvation/redemption implicit in this mentality and its accompanying pessimism concerning the world, encouraging instead creative engagement with the social and political structures of society.

A tradition in transition

Since the 1970s a new era of development in dispensational thought has been underway. In recent decades its scholars have moved from the defensive posture of earlier years. Dispensational exegesis has moved beyond the naive literalism of earlier years to a more consistent application of the historical-grammatical method of interpretation. Contemporary dispensational scholars are critically re-evaluating the system and significant development is occurring. Eschatologically, a significant and growing number are comfortable with an *inaugurated eschatology* as opposed to the strict futurism of previous generations, seeing the kingdom of God as having been *already* inaugurated at Pentecost *but not yet* fully manifested. Since the *Scofield Bible* has lost the confessional status it enjoyed earlier in the century, it is more accurate to speak of contemporary dispensationalism as a tradition bound together by shared presuppositions (futurist premillennialism, a temporal distinction between the church and Israel with an accompanying national future for Israel in fulfilment of Old Testament prophecy, and historical-grammatical interpretation) rather than a system.

See also ESCHATOLOGY; KINGDOM OF GOD: NEW TESTAMENT; PENTECOSTALISM AND CHARISMATIC CHRISTIANITY; PROTESTANT THEOLOGY: USA.

Bibliography

Bass, Clarence [1960] 1977: *Backgrounds to Dispensationalism*. Grand Rapids: Baker reprint.

Blaising, Craig A., and Bock, Darrell, eds 1992: *Israel and the Church*. Grand Rapids: Zondervan.

Breshears, Gerry 1991: Dispensationalism bibliography, 1965–1990. Portland, Or.: Western Conservative Baptist Seminary.

Ehlert, Arnold D. 1965: *A Bibliographic History of Dispensationalism*. Grand Rapids: Baker Book House.

Fuller, Daniel P. 1980: *Gospel and Law*. Grand Rapids: Eerdmans.

Johnson, Elliot E. 1990: *Expository Hermeneutics: An Introduction*. Grand Rapids: Zondervan.

Kraus, C. Norman 1958: *Dispensationalism in America*. Richmond: John Knox Press.

McClain, Alva J. [1959] 1968: *The Greatness of the Kingdom*. Chicago: Moody Press.

Marsden, George M. 1980: *Fundamentalism and American Culture*. Oxford: Oxford University Press.

Poythress, Vern 1987: *Understanding Dispensationalists*. Grand Rapids: Zondervan.

Radmacher, Earl D. 1972: *The Nature of the Church*. Chicago: Moody Press.

Ryrie, Charles C. 1965: *Dispensationalism Today*. Chicago: Moody Press.

Sandeen, Ernest R. [1970] 1978: *The Roots of Fundamentalism: British and American Millenarianism, 1800–1930*. Grand Rapids: Baker reprint.

Weber, Timothy P. 1983: *Living in the Shadow of the Second Coming: American Premillennialism 1875–1982*, enlarged edition. Grand Rapids: Zondervan.

M. JAMES SAWYER

divorce and marriage See ETHICS; SEXUAL ETHICS.

doctrinal criticism See DOCTRINE AND DOGMA.

doctrine and dogma The terms 'doctrine' and 'dogma' have come to possess developed meanings, which distinguishes them from the broader notion of 'theology' *tout simple*. There has been a perceived need to make a distinction between corporate belief on the one hand and individual viewpoints on the other. Theology may be taken to refer to the views of any individual thinker on the nature of God. The term does not imply any commitment to a Christian denomination. 'Theology' is an individual's 'talk about God', which is not subject to the limiting conditions and insights of a tradition or community.

The use of the word 'doctrine' implies reference to a tradition and a community, where 'theology' more properly designates the views of individuals, not necessarily within this community or tradition, who seek to explore ideas without any necessary commitment to them. Doctrine defines communities of discourse, possessing a representative character, attempting to describe or prescribe the beliefs of a community. Doctrine entails a sense of commitment to a community, and a sense of obligation to speak on its behalf, where the corporate mind of the community exercises a restraint over the individual's perception of truth. Doctrine is an *activity*, a process of transmission of the collective wisdom of a community, rather than a passive set of deliverances. The views of theologians are thus doctrinally significant, in so far as they have won acceptance within the community.

The concept of 'reception' (by which a church accepts the views of individuals as representative of its ethos and outlook) is thus of central importance to the concept of doctrine, in that a community is involved in the assessment of whether a decision, judgement or theological opinion is consonant with its corporate understanding of the Christian faith, as perceived within that community. Doctrine may thus be provisionally defined as communally authoritative teachings regarded as essential to the identity of the Christian community. Christian doctrine may be regarded as the present outcome of that long growth of TRADITION in which the Christian community has struggled to arrive at an interpretation of its foundational traditions, embodied in the New Testament, which both does justice to its own present place in tradition and attempts to eliminate those doctrinal prejudgements which are to be judged as inadequate.

For historical reasons, the term 'dogma' has come to possess negative overtones. The mental transition between 'dogma' and 'dogmatic' has become too easy for comfort, apparently aligning the notion of 'dogma' with unacceptable forms of authoritarianism. Yet the idea remains significant, especially within contemporary Roman Catholic and Lutheran theology, even if the term used to express it has become partly discredited by historical developments. 'Dogma' designates doctrines which are defined as essential to Christian faith by universal assent. They are the non-negotiable elements of the Christian faith. As such, there are arguably only two dogmas: the Christological and Trinitarian dogmas, as defined by the ecumenical councils. It is no accident that these two areas of theology were singled out for especial criticism at the time of the ENLIGHTENMENT; not only were they especially vulnerable to the new insights and methods of the Enlightenment; to discredit such dogmas was, in effect, to discredit the AUTHORITY of the church. For an age in which inherited authority was regarded as an oppressive anachronism, the criticism of dogma became an intellectual weapon with which to combat the inherited authority of the past.

The criticism of dogma

The sixteenth-century Reformation initiated a sustained critique of the doctrine of the Christian church. The criteria employed by the Reformers (such as Martin Luther and John Calvin) for this purpose centred on the notion of fidelity to Scripture. If a doctrine could be demonstrated to be clearly stated within the Old or New Testaments, or clearly implied by those sources, then that doctrine was to be accepted within the Christian community. In practice, the magisterial Reformation tended to be fairly conservative doctrinally; the more radical suggestions for doctrinal criticism generally came from within the movement known as Anabaptism, or 'the Radical Reformation'. Nevertheless, the principle of doctrinal criticism had been firmly established. The doctrines of the church were, in principle, open to criticism and restatement in the light of agreed criteria.

Given the strength of the Lutheran and Reformed theological traditions in Germany, the German Enlightenment was obliged to engage substantially with the phenomenon of Christian doctrine, where the writers of the English or French Enlightenments were largely able to dispense with this obligation. From about 1750 onwards, writers of the *Aufklärung* mounted a sustained re-evaluation of the received doctrinal tradition of the Christian church. Where the Reformation employed fidelity to Scripture as the normative doctrinal criterion, the Enlightenment made a direct appeal to reason, regarded as a universal human category which transcended the historical particularity of Scripture.

Accompanying this significant development was a reconfiguration of the received understanding of the nature of the Reformation itself. G.E. Lessing, anxious to portray the Enlightenment as the natural heir to the theological programme of the Reformers, argued that Luther's primary concern was with the individual's right to private judgement. Lessing suggested that the modern appeal to reason was entirely consonant with Luther's concerns, thus allowing the programme of rational doctrinal criticism to be seen as a natural and necessary extension of the Reformation. In order to understand the background to the Enlightenment criticism of the received doctrinal tradition of the Christian churches on the basis of reason, it is necessary to explore the developing understanding of the relation between faith and reason. Three stages may be discerned in this development.

First stage Theology is a rational discipline (*scientia*). This position, associated with writers such as Thomas Aquinas, works on the assumption that the Christian faith is fundamentally rational, and can thus be both supported and explored by reason. Thomas Aquinas's Five Ways (see NATURAL THEOLOGY) illustrate his belief that reason is capable of lending support to the ideas of faith.

But Aquinas, and the Christian tradition which he represented, did not believe that Christianity was limited to what could be ascertained by reason. Faith goes beyond reason, having access to truths and insights of revelation, which reason could not hope to fathom or discover unaided. Reason has the role

113

of building upon what is known by revelation, exploring what its implications might be. In this sense, theology is *scientia* – a rational discipline, using rational methods to build upon and extend what is known by revelation.

The noted historian of medieval Christian thought, Etienne Gilson, made a now famous comparison between the great theological systems of the Middle Ages and the cathedrals which sprang up throughout Christian Europe at this time: they were, he remarked, 'cathedrals of the mind'. Christianity, according to Aquinas, is like a cathedral which rests upon the bedrock of human reason, but whose superstructure rises beyond the realms accessible to pure reason. It rests upon rational foundations; but the building erected on that foundation goes far beyond what reason could uncover.

Second stage Theology is the republication of the insights of reason. By the middle of the seventeenth century, especially in England and Germany, a new attitude began to develop. Christianity, it was argued, was reasonable. But where Thomas Aquinas understood this to mean that faith rested securely upon rational foundations, the new school of thought had different ideas. If faith is rational, they argued, it must be capable of being deduced in its entirety by reason. Every aspect of faith, every item of Christian belief, must be shown to derive from human reason.

An excellent example of this approach is to be found in the writings of Lord Herbert of Cherbury, especially *De veritatis religionis*, 'On the truth of religion', which argued for a rational Christianity based upon the innate sense of God and human moral obligation. This had two major consequences. First, Christianity was in effect reduced to those ideas which could be proved by reason. If Christianity was rational, then any parts of its system which could not be proved by reason could not be counted as 'rational'. They would have to be discarded. And second, reason was understood to take priority over revelation.

Reason is thus regarded as being capable of establishing what is right without needing any assistance from revelation; Christianity has to follow, being accepted where it endorses what reason has to say, and being disregarded where it goes its own way. So why bother with the idea of revelation, when reason could tell us all we could possibly wish to know about God, the world, and ourselves? This absolutely settled conviction in the total competence of human reason underlies the rationalist depreciation of the Christian doctrine of revelation in Jesus Christ and through Scripture.

Third stage Theology is redundant; reason reigns supreme. Finally, this potentially rationalist position was pushed to its logical outcome. As a matter of fact, it was argued, Christianity does include a series of major beliefs which are inconsistent with reason. Reason has the right to judge religion, in that it stands above it. This approach is usually termed 'Enlightenment rationalism', and is our concern in this discussion. Reason, regarded as a universal human category, was judged superior to both Scripture and tradition as a theological resource. The latter, it was argued, were tainted by the 'scandal of particularity', whereas reason was a universally accessible and valid resource. If a given matter of Christian doctrine could not be justified or established on the basis of pure reason, it was to be rejected as inauthentic and irrational. (See also FAITH AND REASON.)

Four areas of Christian theology may be singled out as being especially vulnerable to this form of criticism. It is significant that all four doctrines are, to a greater or lesser extent, grounded Christologically.

1 The physical resurrection of Christ. For the Enlightenment, the RESURRECTION was something of a nonevent. In that no contemporary analogy could be adduced for the event, it was argued (for instance by David Hume and Denis Diderot) that no historical event of that nature could have occurred. Present-day experience was to be regarded as normative in establishing past patterns of events; the traditional account of the resurrection of Christ, which has no equivalent in present-day experience, must therefore be rejected as unhistorical. A number of central doctrines, mostly Christological and eschatological, rested upon a traditional understanding of the resurrection, and were thus called into question.

2 The person of Christ. CHRISTOLOGY is generally regarded as one area of Christian doctrine to be especially vulnerable to rational criticism. The Enlightenment argued that the authority of Christ was essentially derivative, being grounded in the conformity of his

teachings and lifestyle to those established as acceptable and benevolent by the moral criteria of pure reason. Traditional doctrines, such as the two natures of Christ, were rejected as irrational and unnecessary. Christ could be regarded as a 'teacher of common sense' (Jaroslav Pelikan), who endorsed and was endorsed by human reason.

3 The work of Christ. SOTERIOLOGY was also vulnerable to this criticism. Doctrines such as original sin were rejected, both on rational and historical grounds. The human predicament was defined educationally, as a lack of proper understanding of God. The work of Christ was to educate humanity in the principles of the religion of reason, to which he was a prophet. Doctrines such as substitutionary atonement or the liberation of humanity from forces of evil were treated as premodern.

4 The Trinity. The Enlightenment adopted a simple doctrine of GOD, embodying all those qualities which reason declared to be virtues (John Locke). The doctrine of the Trinity was regarded as an irrational and unnecessary complication of an essentially simple picture, in which the simple God of pure reason (often conceived monadically) was contrasted with the mathematical impossibility of traditional Christian theology (Thomas Jefferson).

The 'history of dogma' movement
The rational criticism of dogma, noted above, came increasingly to be supplemented, and gradually to be replaced, by the science of the 'history of dogma', usually known in its German form *Dogmengeschichte*. The basic assumption of this movement was that the doctrinal formulations of the church, especially during the patristic period, were heavily conditioned by the social and cultural conditions of the era. This conditioning, which could be uncovered and subjected to critical scrutiny and evaluation by historical methods, made such doctrinal formulations inappropriate for the modern church, which was obliged to develop restatements of these doctrines appropriate to the modern period.

This programme can be seen at work in G.S. Steinbart's *Glückseligkeitslehre* (1778), in which the Augustinian doctrine of original sin – foundational to traditional understandings of baptism and the work of Christ – was argued to

represent a hangover from Augustine's Manichaean period. It represented the intrusion of pagan ideas into Christianity, and had no place in a proper Christian theology. Steinbart's analysis, which extended to include Anselm of Canterbury's doctrine of the satisfaction of Christ, represents a classic instance of the criticism of dogma by a critical study of its origins.

This programme, extended by writers such as F.C. Baur and A.B. Ritschl, reached its climax in the work of Adolf von Harnack. In his *History of Dogma* (which occupies seven volumes in English translation), Harnack argued that dogma was not itself a Christian notion. Rather, it arose through the expansion of Christianity from its original Palestinian context to a Hellenistic milieu. As a result, Christian writers absorbed the Hellenistic tendency to conceptualize, and to use a metaphysical framework to articulate the gospel. Harnack saw the doctrine of the INCARNATION as perhaps the most obvious instance of the influence of Hellenism upon Christianity, and argued that historical analysis opened the way for its elimination. For Harnack, the gospel was about Jesus himself and the impact which he had upon people. The shift from soteriology to the abstract metaphysical speculation of Christology is, for Harnack, an insidious yet reversible theological development. Harnack singled out Martin Luther as one who attempted to eliminate metaphysics from theology, and commended him as an example to posterity.

Although Harnack's emphasis upon the 'Hellenization' of the gospel is now regarded as overstated, the general principles which he developed are still regarded as valid. The historian of dogma can still discern areas of Christian theology in which a number of central conditioning assumptions appear to derive from Greek metaphysics. The modern debate about whether God can suffer (see SUFFERING, DIVINE) has drawn attention to the manner in which the classical notion of the *apatheia* of God appears to rest upon the theistic assumptions of Greek metaphysics, rather than the Old and New Testament witness to the acts of God in history.

George Lindbeck on the nature of doctrine
In his volume *The Nature of Doctrine* (1984), the

distinguished Yale theologian George Lindbeck provides an important analysis of the nature of Christian doctrine. One of the many merits of this book is the debate which it has initiated over this unjustly neglected aspect of Christian theology, which has assumed new importance recently on account of the impact of the ecumenical movement (see ECUMENISM). It is therefore only proper that this article should include a discussion of Lindbeck's influential analysis.

Lindbeck suggests that theories of doctrine may be divided into three general types. The *cognitive-propositionalist* theory lays stress upon the cognitive aspects of religion, emphasizing the manner in which doctrines function as truth claims or informative propositions. The *experiential-expressive* theory interprets doctrines as non-cognitive symbols of inner human feelings or attitudes. A third possibility, which Lindbeck himself favours, is the *cultural-linguistic* approach to religion. Lindbeck associates this model with a 'rule' or 'regulative' theory of doctrine. We shall consider each of these approaches briefly, making some critical comments in doing so.

The cognitive-propositional theory The first view of doctrine, which Lindbeck designates 'propositionalist' or 'cognitive', treats doctrines as 'informative propositions or truth claims about objective realities'. Lindbeck argues that it is to be rejected as voluntarist, intellectualist and literalist.

Lindbeck's criticism of 'cognitive' theories of doctrine has considerable force when directed against neo-scholastic understandings of revelation. For example, the view of the neo-scholastic writer Hermann Dieckmann, to the effect that supernatural revelation transmits conceptual knowledge by means of propositions, is clearly open to serious criticism along the lines suggested by Lindbeck. In this respect, Lindbeck has provided a valuable corrective to deficient cognitive models of doctrine.

Nevertheless, not all cognitive theories of doctrine are vulnerable in this respect. It is necessary to make a clear distinction between the view that an exhaustive and unambiguous account of God is transmitted conceptually by propositions on the one hand, and the view that there is a genuinely cognitive element to doctrinal statements on the other. Doctrinal

statements need not be treated as *purely* cognitive statements.

For example, many theologians of the medieval period understood dogma as a dynamic concept, a 'perception of divine truth, tending towards this truth (*perceptio divinae veritatis tendens in ipsam*)'. For such theologians, doctrines are reliable, yet incomplete, descriptions of reality. Their power lies in what they represent, rather than what they are in themselves. The point at which criticism is appropriate concerns whether such doctrines are adequate (to the strictly limited degree that this is possible) representations of the independent reality to which they allegedly relate. Given that they cannot hope to re-present it in its totality, and given the inevitable limitations attending any attempt to express in words something which ultimately lies beyond them, is the particular form of words employed the most reliable conceivable?

Underlying such attempts to achieve clarity of concepts and modes of discourse is the recognition that doctrinal affirmations are to be recognized as perceptions, not total descriptions, pointing beyond themselves towards the greater mystery of God himself. The Nicene controversy is an obvious example of a struggle to articulate insights in this manner. If an experience is to be articulated in words, in order to communicate or to attempt a communal envisioning of this experience, some form of a 'cognitive-propositionalist' dimension is inevitable. Yet this is not to reduce the experience to words, but simply to attempt to convey it through words.

The experiential-expressivist theory This approach, as defined by Lindbeck, 'interprets doctrines as noninformative and nondiscursive symbols of inner feelings, attitudes or existential orientations.' The Chicago theologian David Tracy argues for the need to bridge the gap between 'common human experience' and the 'central motifs of the Christian tradition', so that religious language 're-presents' and reaffirms this common experience at the level of self-conscious belief.

According to this approach, religions, including Christianity, are public, culturally conditioned manifestations and affirmations of prelinguistic forms of consciousness, attitudes and feelings. As Lindbeck argues, the attraction of this approach to doctrine is grounded in a number of features of late twentieth-century western thought. For example, the contemporary preoccupation with inter-religious dialogue is considerably assisted by the suggestion that the various religions are diverse expressions of a common core experience, such as an 'isolable core of encounter' or an 'unmediated awareness of the transcendent'.

The principal objection to this theory, thus stated, is its obvious inaccuracy. As Lindbeck points out, the possibility of religious experience is shaped by religious expectation, so that 'religious experience' becomes a hopelessly vague idea. 'It is difficult or impossible to specify its distinctive features, and yet unless this is done, the assertion of commonality becomes logically and empirically vacuous.'

The assertion that 'the various religions are diverse symbolizations of one and the same core experience of the Ultimate' is ultimately an unverifiable hypothesis, not least on account of the difficulty of locating and describing the 'core experience' concerned. As Lindbeck rightly points out, this would appear to suggest that there is 'at least the logical possibility that a Buddhist and a Christian might have basically the same faith, although expressed very differently.' The theory can only be credible if it is possible to isolate a common core experience from religious language and behaviour, and demonstrate that the latter two are articulations of or responses to the former.

Yet Lindbeck's critique of 'experiential-expressive' theories of doctrine fails to discriminate between two quite different 'experiential' approaches to doctrine. F.D.E. Schleiermacher – who Lindbeck appears to treat as the intellectual forebear of the 'experiential-expressive' approach – is not an exponent of an 'experiential-expressive' theory of doctrine, in Lindbeck's sense of the term. Indeed, Schleiermacher is arguably closer to Lindbeck's notion of a 'cultural-linguistic' approach to doctrine, on account of his emphasis upon the role of the community of faith. Christian doctrine, according to Schleiermacher, does not concern some 'prereflective experience' common to all religions but concerns the distinctively Christian experience of Jesus of Nazareth.

Schleiermacher draws a clear distinction between human religious consciousness in general, and the specifically Christian consciousness. It is this specifically Christian 'feeling' or 'apprehension of an immediate existential relationship', deriving from Jesus of Nazareth, that Schleiermacher identifies as the referent of Christian doctrine. This crucial distinction is lacking in the 'experiential-expressive' approach, expounded and criticized by Lindbeck, suggesting that it may be impossible to draw such a distinction within their parameters and on the basis of their presuppositions.

Furthermore, Schleiermacher insists that the experience to which doctrine relates is not *private*, but *corporate*. 'Christian piety never arises independently and of itself in an individual, but only out of the communion and in the communion.' The communal takes priority over the individual in Schleiermacher's account of the genesis and doctrinal articulation of religious experience. According to Schleiermacher, doctrines express an experience which has been constituted by the language of the Christian community (not some amorphous global prereflective experience) – a position which Lindbeck himself appears to endorse.

The cultural-linguistic theory Drawing on the writings of the cultural anthropologist Clifford Geertz, Lindbeck develops a theory of doctrine which he suggests may undergird a postliberal age in theology. Indeed, the recognition that human beings are dependent upon and shaped by their historical and cultural contexts may be argued to be fundamental to POSTLIBERALISM. Religion, Lindbeck suggests (and the parallel with Ludwig Wittgenstein will be obvious), may be compared to languages, with religious doctrines functioning as grammatical rules. Religions are cultural frameworks or mediums which give rise to a vocabulary and precede inner experience.

A religion can be viewed as a kind of cultural and/or linguistic framework or medium that shapes the entirety of life and thought . . . Like a culture or language, it is a communal phenomenon that shapes the subjectivities of individuals rather than being primarily a manifestation of those subjectivities. It comprises a vocabulary of discursive and nondiscursive symbols together with a distinctive logic or grammar in terms of which this vocabulary can be meaningfully deployed.

Just as a language is correlated with a form of life (as Wittgenstein pointed out in relation to 'language games'), so a religious tradition is correlated with the form of life it engenders, articulates and reflects. Lindbeck also suggests – tentatively, I think – that language is capable of shaping areas of human existence and action that are pre-experiential, thus providing an important qualification to, and extension of, the experiential-expressive theory.

A fundamental element in this understanding of doctrine and its attending theory of truth is the concept of *intrasystemic consistency*. In part, this understanding concerns rational coherence of systems: doctrines regulate religions, in much the way grammar regulates language.

Doctrine, then, describes the regulatory language of the Christian idiom. But how did this language come into being, and to what, if anything, does it refer? Lindbeck appears to suggest that the cultural-linguistic approach to doctrine may dispense with the question of whether the Christian idiom has any external referent. Doctrine is concerned with the internal regulation of the Christian idiom, ensuring its consistency. The question of how that idiom relates to the external world is considered to be improper.

For Lindbeck, doctrine is the language of the Christian community, a self-perpetuating idiolect. Indeed, at points he seems to suggest that conceiving theology as the grammar of the Christian language entails the abandonment of any talk about God as an independent reality and any suggestion that it is possible to make truth claims (in an ontological, rather than intrasystemic, sense) concerning him. 'Truth' is firmly equated with – virtually to the point of being reduced to – internal consistency.

Thus while illustrating his understanding of the regulative function of doctrines within theology, Lindbeck suggests that the Nicene creed 'does not make first-order truth claims'. In other words, the *homoousion* makes no ontological reference, but merely regulates language concerning both Christ and God.

Lindbeck suggests that Athanasius understands the term *homoousios* to mean 'whatever is said of the Father is said of the Son, except that the Son is not the Father.' In other words, Athanasius 'thought of it, not as a first-order proposition with ontological reference, but as a second-order rule of speech'. Only in the medieval period, Lindbeck suggests, were metaphysical concepts read into this essentially grammatical approach to the *homoousion*. In the patristic period, he argues, the term was understood as a rule of discourse, quite independent of any reference to extra-linguistic reality.

A more historically oriented approach to doctrine, such as that developed in A.E. McGrath's 1990 Bampton Lectures (published as *The Genesis of Doctrine*), draws attention to the manner in which doctrine defines communities of belief. This approach allows the varying historical weight placed upon the notion of doctrine to be understood, while giving some theoretical justification to the neutralization of doctrinal divisiveness in ecumenical dialogues.

See also LITURGY AND DOCTRINE.

Bibliography

Andresen, C., ed. 1980–4: *Handbuch der Dogmen- und Theologiegeschichte*, 3 vols. Göttingen: Vandenhoeck & Ruprecht.

Chadwick, O. 1957: *From Bossuet to Newman: The Idea of Doctrinal Development*. Cambridge: Cambridge University Press.

Deneffe, A. 1931: Dogma: Wort und Begriff, *Scholastik* 6, pp. 381–400, 505–38.

Lash, N. 1973: *Change in Focus: A Study of Doctrinal Change and Continuity*. London: Sheed and Ward.

Lindbeck, G. 1984: *The Nature of Doctrine: Religion and Theology in a Post-Liberal Age*. Philadelphia: Fortress Press.

Lonergan, B.J.F. 1967: The dehellenization of dogma, *Theological Studies* 28, pp. 336–51.

McGrath, A.E. 1990: *The Genesis of Doctrine*. Oxford: Blackwell.

Ommen, T.B. 1975: *The Hermeneutic of Dogma*. Missoula, Mont.: Scholars Press.

Pelikan, J. 1969: *Development of Christian Doctrine: Some Historical Prolegomena*. New Haven and London: Yale University Press.

Pelikan, J. 1971: *Historical Theology: Change and Continuity in Christian Doctrine*. New Haven and London: Yale University Press.

Sykes, S.W. 1984: *The Identity of Christianity*. London: SPCK.

Wiles, M.F. 1974: *The Remaking of Christian Doctrine*. London: SCM Press.

ALISTER E. MCGRATH

Dooyeweerd, Herman (1894–1977) Dutch Reformed philosopher. Born into a family that supported the ideas of Dutch theologian and statesman Abraham Kuyper, he was a civil servant and assistant director of the Kuyper Institute, where he studied the philosophical foundations of his own professional sphere of jurisprudence, finding them to be essentially religious. From 1926 he was a professor at the Free University of Amsterdam. He was a founder of the Christian philosophical system based on the 'Cosmonomic Idea', modelled on a complex of interrelating philosophical spheres. He maintained that basic religious presuppositions underlie all of philosophy and science, and he sought to assert the Christ-centred character of knowledge: without recognition of this, scientific and philosophical enquiry is incomplete. Although not widely accepted, Dooyeweerd's philosophy and in particular his Christian critique of philosophical theory influenced evangelical thinkers, including Hans Rookmaaker, Cornelius van Til and Francis Schaeffer. His works include *Philosophy of the Law Idea* (or Cosmonomic Idea) (1935–6) and *A New Critique of Theoretical Thought* (1953–8).

Bibliography

McIntire, C.T., ed. 1985: *The Legacy of Herman Dooyeweerd: Reflection on Critical Philosophy in the Christian Tradition*. Lanham, Md, and Toronto.

Dostoevsky, Fyodor (1821–1881) Russian novelist. Brought up in Moscow in the Russian Orthodox faith, his work was shaped by early traumas, which included a near-death experience when in 1849 his sentence of death for revolutionary activities was commuted to penal exile in Siberia minutes before being carried out. After completing his sentence as a private in the army, he began to make a precarious living as a journalist in St Petersburg defending his Slavophile and democratic views, hampered by gambling debts and censorship. He returned to the church in later life, seeing in Christianity Russia's hope and destiny. His novels were first published in serial form; they include *Crime and Punishment* (1865–6), *The Idiot* (1869), *The Possessed* (1871) and *The Brothers Karamazov* (1880). They do not reveal an abstract or systematic philosophy or theology, but are rather profound and penetrating studies of good and evil, of human beings in all their physical, spiritual, social and moral diversity. Dostoevsky comes closest to offering a formal exposition of religious and moral ideas in the 'Legend of the Grand Inquisitor' in *The Brothers Karamazov*, where he powerfully portrays the bankruptcy of an attitude or system which attempts to replace God with man.

Bibliography

Gibson, A.B. 1973: *The Religion of Dostoevsky*. London.

Jones, T. 1983: *Dostoevsky*. Oxford.

Peace, R. 1971: *Dostoevsky: An Examination of the Major Novels*. Cambridge.

Durkheim, Emile (1858–1917) French sociologist. He taught at Bordeaux and then at the Sorbonne, where he was responsible for teacher training and contributed to the secularization of education in France. A pioneer (with Max Weber) of modern sociological theory, his study of religion is contained in, among other works, *The Elementary Forms of the Religious Life* (1912, trans. 1915), in which he demonstrated the social and cultural origins of religion. Rather than expressing a transcendent reality, religion is a function of man's awareness of himself in relation to society: the 'beliefs, myths, dogmas and legends' of religion arise from collective human experience. Inspired by contemporary English and American ethnographic surveys of the Australian Aborigines and North American Indians, he was the first to classify religion in terms of its sociological functions (in *Primitive Classification*, 1903).

See also SOCIAL SCIENCE AND CHRISTIAN THOUGHT.

Bibliography

Lukes, S. 1987: *Emile Durkheim, His Life and Work*. Harmondsworth.

Pickering, W.S.F. 1975: *Durkheim on Religion: A Selection of Readings with Bibliographies*. London.

Pickering, W.S.F. 1984: *Durkheim's Sociology of Religion*. London.

E

Eastern Orthodox theology Both Russian and Greek Orthodox traditions have continued to flourish in the twentieth century, although Russian Orthodox theology has developed outside Russia for much of the century.

Russia and the Russian emigration
It has been, for the most part, Russian writers who have set the agenda for Orthodox theology in the twentieth century. Several reasons may be adduced for this: of all the historically Orthodox territories, Russia and Georgia alone enjoyed political independence after the seventeenth century, so that intellectual life had some chance of flourishing; war and social upheaval in the nineteenth century had generated fierce debate about Russia's relationship with its past, including its religious traditions, and the thought of G.W.F. Hegel and Friedrich von Schelling found an enthusiastic reception in this debate; nineteenth-century artists and writers were increasingly drawn into these issues, especially their religious dimension; and the bitter disillusionment of many political radicals at the turn of the century led a good many former Marxists back to the church, where they continued to produce critical and speculative work in great quantities. In the first decade of the twentieth century, this cautious *rapprochement* between church and intelligentsia sowed the seeds of many later theological developments, and for a while held out the prospect of an Orthodox theology capable of digesting the challenges of the western Enlightenment.

The metaphysical tradition Most of the major writers of this generation were heavily influenced by two nineteenth-century figures in particular, A.S. Khomyakov (1804–1860) and Vladimir Soloviev (1853–1900). Khomyakov argued, in a number of essays and pamphlets originally published in France, that Orthodoxy knew nothing of 'external' systems of authority: its decisions were the direct issue of the consent of the faithful, coming from the depths of their common life. For this common life, Khomyakov used the term *sobornost'* (a coinage from the Old Slavonic adjective used in the Nicene Creed for 'catholic'). And, as a supporter of the conservative cultural programme of the Slavophile movement, he ascribed the same kind of mystical communality to Russian peasant life, as a sort of natural base for ecclesial communion. Soloviev shares Khomyakov's interest in this idea of a 'base' for the life of the church in the natural order, but is less concerned with the special character of Slavonic community. He turns instead to the elaboration of a theory of cosmic unity and interdependence (*vseedinstvo*), centred on the image of divine wisdom, Sophia. Sophia is the ground of cosmic harmony, the divine agency working towards ever greater integration in the universe: the incarnation and the church are the culmination of the work of Sophia, and the church is thus above all the place where the divine and the created unite, where the lives of individuals are transformed into a state of organic relatedness. Soloviev, influenced by both Jewish-Gnostic speculation and the German mysticism of the seventeenth and eighteenth centuries, regularly spoke of Sophia as a personified 'Eternal Feminine'.

Both writers show traces of the influence of Hegel and Schelling, but both are also quintessentially Russian. Fascination with the possibility of overcoming the barriers of individuality characterized a wide range of nineteenth-century Russian intellectuals, anarchists and Marxists no less than Christians. The

120

two notions of *sobornost'* and Sophia became the common coin of religious thinkers in the generation after Soloviev, offering, in the eyes of many, a way of holding on to some of the commitments of social radicalism without the tyranny of a materialist metaphysic. Probably the greatest thinker of this generation was Sergii Bulgakov (1871–1944), who had been a precociously famous Marxist theoretician before returning first to a Hegelian theism with Slavophile overtones, then to the Orthodox church, in which he was ordained in 1917. Subsequently exiled from Russia, he was instrumental in establishing the Russian seminary in Paris, the Institut Saint-Serge, of which he was the first dean. His early essays on religious topics still make lively reading: he developed a Christian Socialist critique of both Marxism and liberal capitalism, and continued up to his final years to defend this reading of the political implications of Christian anthropology. He also wrote extensively on cultural and aesthetic matters: there is a significant essay on the early work of Picasso, detecting in the latter's work a contempt for the feminine and the material.

His most substantial achievement, though, was to elaborate Soloviev's 'sophiology' into a comprehensive theological and metaphysical scheme. Beginning with a large volume on religious metaphysics entitled *The Unfading Light* in 1911, he explored the implications of the doctrine of Sophia for our understanding of the human position in the world. The divine wisdom impels human beings, both in art and in economic work, to realize the fullest possible state of interdependent harmony in things: the sacraments of the church represent the summit of this cooperation between divine and human agency ('theandric' activity). At this period, Bulgakov was heavily influenced by Fr Pavel Florensky, another disciple of Soloviev, who brought to the latter's system an added interest in the history of aesthetics, folklore, linguistics and scientific theory. Something of this eclectic flavour is evident in *The Unfading Light*, and Bulgakov tends to follow Florensky in writing of Sophia as a kind of 'fourth hypostasis' alongside the persons of the Trinity. By the late 1920s this has changed: Sophia is now more clearly delineated as the divine *nature* itself, emptying itself out in perfect love and communion.

Sophia is thus the ground or rationale of the Trinitarian life of God, the motive force of creation, incarnation and the gift of the Spirit, and the principle by which redeemed humanity lives. At every level, the divine kenosis repeats itself. Thus Khomyakov's vision of the church's *sobornost'* is rooted in an account of the nature of God: the church is 'Sophia in process of becoming', the goal to which all creation moves. In Christ, the uncreated wisdom of God and the wisdom that is coming-to-be in creation, the *eros* of creation towards harmony, are inseparably united, so that the body of Christ, the church, represents and embodies in its sacramental life the same union of divine and created Sophia.

This system is worked through in three massive works of the 1920s and 1930s, *The Lamb of God*, *The Paraclete* and *The Bride of the Lamb*. The first of these in particular aroused much controversy among the Russian émigré community, and Bulgakov was condemned for heresy by the Muscovite hierarchy in 1935. His own bishop, however, defended him loyally, and he continued to hold a very important place in the life of the Russian community in exile, and in the early days of the ecumenical movement. His writings never had quite the same popularity outside the Orthodox world as those of his colleague and friend, Nikolai Berdyaev (1874–1948). They are both technical and diffuse, but represent one of the most serious attempts by any Orthodox theologian to produce a systematic theology integrating Scripture, tradition and idealist metaphysics.

Berdyaev's own work is less marked by specifically Russian and Orthodox themes, though it has often been taken to be typical of eastern Christianity. Khomyakov and Fyodor Dostoevsky are clearly influential, Soloviev less so; but it is Immanuel Kant and Friedrich Nietzsche who are often most in evidence in a vision deeply preoccupied with radical freedom and the creativity of will. Sophia and *vseedinstvo* are not congenial ideas for Berdyaev, and there is in his work a strong element of near-Manichaean tragic sensibility: he is intrigued by the notion of a primordial ground of non-being, sheer potentiality over against God – a notion shaped by the speculations of radical Protestant mystics like Jakob Böhme.

Both Bulgakov and Berdyaev had been involved in the production of a symposium in 1909 entitled *Vekhi* ('Signposts'), fiercely critical of the radical secularism of the Russian intelligentsia of the day. Among the other contributors, one in particular, Semën Frank (1877–1950) went on to acquire something of a comparable reputation to Bulgakov's, though on a smaller scale. More sympathetic to Soloviev, he was, however, critical of any sort of totalizing metaphysics – though he is also less of a voluntarist than Berdyaev. He shares with Bulgakov and the tradition behind him a conviction that true knowledge is only possible on the assumption of some kind of ontological communion preceding conceptual formulation; this communion is rooted in, but is not exhaustively definitive of, the life of God (the 'unfathomable', *nepostizhimoe*). The moral and spiritual task is to develop a collective consciousness, that is, a consciousness that can intelligibly and truthfully say 'we', in place of an aggregate of 'I's, and this requires the kenosis Bulgakov writes about. Less organic and less mythological in his idiom and imagery than most of his circle (and rather more attuned to the post-Kantian problematic in philosophy), he stands as something of a mediating figure between the tradition of Khomyakov and Soloviev and a less metaphysically ambitious approach.

The ecclesial tradition The Russian metaphysical tradition was in fact subjected to a severe critique from a slightly younger generation of émigrés, impatient with the cloudy rhetoric of 'religious philosophy' and eager to construct a synthesis more clearly grounded in specifically ecclesial tradition, especially in patristic theology. Georges Florovsky (1893–1979) was briefly a colleague of Bulgakov's in Paris, but left for the USA after publishing a magisterial history of Russian theology in 1937, in which he mercilessly castigated the sub-Hegelian sentimentality (as he saw it) of the whole Khomyakov–Soloviev idiom and demanded a return to the lucid objectivity of Hellenic categories of thought, as evolved in the patristic and early Byzantine periods (he had already published three weighty volumes on the history of theology up to the time of the Seventh Council). His project shows some parallels with Karl Barth's rejection of the heritage of religious philosophy; and indeed, Florovsky, who met Barth in 1931, was obviously touched by the same passion. Some of what he writes in the 1930s about revelation is strongly Barthian in tone. However, the centrality of a eucharistic ecclesiology in his work redresses the balance; and, despite his hostility to the cult of *sobornost'*, he writes in a very similar vein to Bulgakov on many matters. The church is the image of Trinitarian communion, in which isolated individuality is transcended. But his commitment to an unequivocally voluntarist, indeed indeterminist, metaphysic guarantees that this transcending of individuality remains a communion of distinct historical agents.

Vladimir Lossky (1903–1958), perhaps the best known of the twentieth-century Russian writers after Berdyaev, followed a similar path to Florovsky's though his contacts outside the Orthodox world were more with Anglicans and French Catholics. He was one of the distinguished group (including Daniélou and Massignon) who founded the review *Dieu Vivant* in Paris at the end of the Second World War; this was an important voice in the attempt to articulate a traditional but flexible and humanistic theology, equally open to the Fathers, to contemporary literary and philosophical culture and to (cautious) inter-faith dialogue, especially with Judaism and Islam. Lossky's most significant work was a relatively short book, *The Mystical Theology of the Eastern Church* ([1944] 1957), universally recognized as a brilliant synthesis of patristic theology, which also managed to be an original and constructive essay in doctrine. We find here an uncompromising insistence on the priority of 'negative' theology, not simply as a corrective, but as a moral and spiritual matter, a kenosis of the spirit in response to the free act of God; and this is connected to a conviction that the image of God is constituted in us by the *personal* – that which is unrepeatable, irreducible to the categories of 'nature' (the generic, the non-particular). We fulfil our personal potential in the risk, the *ekstasis*, of faith, leaving behind the self-defences of natural individuality (our species-being, as a Hegelian might say) and becoming that unique reflection of God's revelation in Jesus Christ which we are capable of becoming, *in* our distinctness, our personal uniqueness. Jesus, the Word incarnate, transforms the conditions of human nature so that the Spirit may produce a unique form of Christian holiness in each person. This Word–Spirit polarity, understood in terms of redeemed nature and redeemed persons, enables Lossky to balance 'institutional' and 'charismatic' elements in the doctrine of the church, and to construct an exceptionally rich doctrine of tradition as the entire process of the Spirit's personalizing work in the historical community (elaborated in some of his later essays). The miracle of the church is that it is a community of unique subjects whose uniqueness is not a matter of mutual rivalry but of the mutual nurture offered by the utterly diverse gifts and graces embodied in each member. And, as a community in which each is constituted in relation to all, the church is an image of the Trinity. As in Florovsky, the themes of the Russian metaphysical tradition surface again, chastened and clothed in more Scriptural and traditional garments. Despite his ecumenical friendships, Lossky was candid in his criticism of much in western theology, especially the credal *filioque*, which he regarded as destructive of the proper symmetry of Trinitarian doctrine, and so as pernicious in the life and spirituality of the church. Some slight mellowing appears in his late manuscripts, on this subject and in relation to the work of Bulgakov, whom he had attacked in the 1930s. His work won him some unexpected admirers, not least Albert Camus.

Other theologians Two other figures of the emigration should be briefly mentioned. Pavel Evdokimov (1901–1970) wrote prolifically on the art and spirituality of the eastern church. His theology is close to Lossky's, though he is far more at ease with the legacy of Bulgakov and the 'religious philosophers', and is also fond of using M. Eliade and C.G. Jung to reinforce points about the nature of religious symbolism. He insists on the distance between 'reason' and 'intellect' in the patristic sense, and – in an almost Kierkegaardian way – on the impotence of reason and the truth of subjectivity (though not the unredeemed *individual* subjectivity). His work is full of memorable images and turns of phrase, though sometimes infuriatingly impressionistic and unstructured. He is at his best on liturgy and iconography. Nikolai Afanasiev (1893–1966), in contrast, produced some detailed historical researches on canon law,

especially in its relation to councils of the church, and went on to elaborate a highly distinctive ecclesiology, owing something to Khomyakov, in which the entire presence of the church catholic in each particular eucharistic community is the leading idea. For Afanasiev, as for Evdokimov, western notions of an ontological distinction between clergy and laity were uncongenial, and Afanasiev puzzled many of his fellow-Orthodox by apparently providing no rationale for the threefold ministry in the church. He remains an unusual and original figure, whose ideas have had much indirect influence on the ecumenical movement through their development and (substantial) modification by Zizioulas (see below).

Nearly all the émigré theologians made use of the ideas of the medieval Byzantine theologian Gregory Palamas in elaborating their theories of the knowledge of God. Palamas had argued for a distinction in the divine life between the unknowable 'essence' of God and God's self-communication in 'energies' or 'operations' – that is, we may speak of what God *does*, but never of what God (ultimately) *is*. However, the theory guarantees that, since the 'energies' genuinely communicate the life of God, knowing God in the divine operations is true knowledge and transforming knowledge, as it entails new life, the transfiguration of spirit and body alike. Although Bulgakov was familiar with his writings, it was not until the 1930s that he became really significant as a point of reference. The Russian Athonite monk, Vasili Krivoshein (later Archbishop Basil of Brussels), published a number of articles in the early 1930s which, translated into French and English, marked the beginning of a 'Palamite' revival, and the Romanian scholar, Dumitru Staniloae, published a monograph on Palamas in 1938 (Staniloae went on to become the major creative theologian of the Romanian church, publishing several substantial works, including a three-volume dogmatics; his themes have much in common with Lossky's, but he has a more fully developed theology of creation, worked out in engagement with the writings of Maximus the Confessor). Among others writing on Palamas, John Meyendorff's work should be particularly noted: his monograph of 1959 was the first genuinely critical and comprehensive account and remains a classic. Along with the late Fr Alexander Schmemann, Meyendorff built up Orthodox theological education in the USA, and wrote numerous theological essays in addition to his historical and textual work. Schmemann's writings on liturgical theology and the sacraments have won wide acclaim beyond the boundaries of the Orthodox churches. A final name to mention here is that of Olivier Clément, who has written on the Fathers and on contemporary themes. A convert from atheism, his Christian understanding was decisively shaped by long study and collaboration with Lossky. His works have something of Evdokimov in their style, but are a good deal tougher intellectually. He has emerged as a profound and skilful apologist for the Christian faith in France, articulating an Orthodoxy that has nothing of the tribal or ethnic about it, and is fully in touch with the intellectual and emotional agonies of the twentieth century.

Greece

Before 1950 Before the liberation of Greece from the Ottoman empire in the 1820s, theological activity was mostly restricted to the researches of a few antiquarians and writings on the ascetical and spiritual life: by far the most important example of the latter is the work of Nicodemus of Mount Athos ('the Hagiorite', i.e. 'from the Holy Mountain'), who, in addition to producing treatises of his own, was largely responsible for collecting the classical anthology of earlier eastern writings on the life of the spirit known as the *Philokalia* (published 1782). This collection was hugely influential in the Balkans and Russia throughout the nineteenth century, serving to keep the Orthodox world in touch with its patristic roots at a time when its theology was generally in thrall to western models.

The influence of Protestant pietism upon Greek writers goes back to the eighteenth century, but it was in some ways reinforced by the foundation of the theological faculty at Athens in 1837, which was modelled on German prototypes. Dogmatics was separated from ethics and divorced from spirituality, and came to be seen as an exercise in elucidating propositions distilled from the Fathers and in defining a position over against specific Catholic and Protestant doctrines. The result was that

Greek theology from 1850 to 1950 was largely 'reactive', allowing its shape and agenda to be dictated by western handbooks and western controversies (over nature and grace, for instance, or details of sacramental theology). The ethos can be called 'pietist' in the sense that individual devotion and morality were seen as virtually unrelated to the structure of doctrine (any other conclusion would have jeopardized the idea of a 'proper' university discipline on the German pattern of the day). Doctrine was something to be believed and defended as true, but not as part of an organic understanding of corporate life and prayer. Thus the activity of the theologian and the traditional locus of theology in the community at prayer (especially the monastic community) grew further and further apart.

The popularity of pietist rigorism and a rather individualistic moralism, crystallized in the Zoe movement (founded in 1911), is intelligible as a reaction against widespread ignorance and apathy in the Greek church at all levels (though Zoe's energies were concentrated in and on the laity); but it is undeniable that this spirit led to a kind of 'colonial' domination of Greek Christianity by western European assumptions, in spiritual as in academic life. Standard works of systematics, above all C. Androutsos's very influential handbook of dogmatics (first published in 1907 and many times reprinted), followed the order of western texts, even when defending conclusions drawn from patristic and Byzantine sources. Occasionally, as in the work of Z. Rhōssis or Rhōsse (the first volume of his dogmatics was published in 1903), there are hints of an appropriation of distinctively Byzantine ideas in a more independent way (Rhossis insists that the name 'God' is a name for the agency, the *energeia*, rather than the essence of the divine, and he explores the idea that the unity of the Trinity is not abstract but actively constituted by the *perichōresis*, the mutual moving towards and indwelling in each other of the divine persons); but this stands side by side with a philosophical apologetic for Trinitarianism cast entirely in the language of a (poorly digested) late nineteenth-century idealism. The *Dogmatics* of P.N. Trembelas (published 1959–61) remains firmly in the mould of Androutsos, apparently innocent of developments in the wider Orthodox world.

The 1960s The 1960s witnessed a remarkable shift in theological life in Greece. Although much academic teaching of systematic theology remained very much as it had been, several writers began to produce work more consciously aligned with patristic methods and styles – emphasizing the location of theology within the corporate sacramental life of the church and criticizing the detached conceptualism of western and academic idioms in the name of a recovery of classical apophaticism, especially in its Palamite form. Clear connections between the life of the church and the Trinitarian structure of the divine life were explored, partly in response to the widespread use of this idea by Russian writers. There is a notable essay on this by Nikos Nissiotis (d. 1986), a senior and influential presence in the World Council of Churches, published in 1964: here, as in his longer works, there is to be found a stress on the communion of persons as the foundation of religious knowledge. The unknowability of God means that there is no static way of characterizing the divine life, no single concept for it: the life of God is active only as a pattern of divine gift and relation and is known only when God freely draws us into this pattern through the *koinōnia* of the church, established in Christ and constantly renewed and actualized in the Spirit. Western theology is seen as prone to overemphasize either Christ or the Spirit, and thus as failing to produce a proper doctrine of the church as image of the dynamic complementarity of God's life. There are obvious links here to Lossky and Florovsky, and Nissiotis is also enthusiastic about Palamas. It is worth noting that the Patristic Institute of Moni Vlatadon (Thessaloniki) began during these years in the 1960s the publication of a critical edition of Palamas, under the direction of Panayiotis Christou; the Institute also initiated (in 1968) a review of patristic studies (*Klēronomia*), which rapidly developed into an important international scholarly organ.

John Zizioulas Nissiotis's vision of the church is echoed in the work of John Zizioulas (also a prominent figure in the ecumenical movement and now Metropolitan of Pergamum), whose 1965 thesis has become one of the theological classics of modern Orthodox theology – and,

arguably, modern European theology *tout court*. This work on *The Unity of the Church in the Eucharist and the Bishop during the First Three Centuries* builds on, but significantly corrects, the work of earlier Russian writers, especially Lossky and Afanasiev, as well as incorporating wide-ranging historical scholarship into an original and brilliantly suggestive schema. Zizioulas's fundamental argument is that the early church conceived its unity as lying in the fact of being assembled around the eschatological Christ, as an anticipation of the perfect unity-in-plurality which is God's ultimate will for creation. This unity is made concrete in the Eucharist, celebrated originally by the bishop, who embodies the calling of Christ which effects universal communion and the final sovereign presence of Christ as the One upon whom all human futures converge. The bishop's ministry is authorized *by* the wider church *for* the local church: his task is to make visible the catholic church in a particular place, presiding over the worshipping assembly of those he has baptized and presenting their common prayer in Christ to the Father – a prayer which assumes (and finally makes explicit) the descent of the Holy Spirit on the assembly's self-offering. All this is centred upon the uttering of the thanksgiving prayer and the breaking and sharing of the 'one bread' of the Eucharist.

This closely argued ecclesiology, which has considerable implications for the practice of the contemporary church, is supplemented in Zizioulas's later writings by a broader theory of knowledge and reality. We must overcome the long heritage of division between being and relation, going back as it does to pre-Christian metaphysics; such a division implicitly privileges unity over plurality, the primordial solitariness of the source over the interaction of mutually constitutive lives. The Christian revelation of the Trinity tells us that being and relation are eternally 'contemporary' in the life of God, so that the work of God is always manifest in the realizing of unity in and only in an interactive manifold. It would thus be nonsense to think that we could know God's truth independently of communion with God and each other; and this carries with it an account of the relational character of human personality and a critique of both religious and secular myths of the autonomous individual.

Themes from Greek patristic thought, Russian theology and twentieth-century philosophical criticisms of 'logocentrism' and its erosion of difference (Levinas is cited in this connection) are woven together with real subtlety and freshness.

Christos Yannaras The development of Zizioulas's thought has evidently been marked by his engagement with the theology of another rebel against westernized academic dogmatics, Christos Yannaras, whose dissertation of 1970 was concerned precisely with the ontology of the person. Yannaras, who studied in western Europe in the 1960s, has developed a theological anthropology much influenced by Martin Heidegger: the idiom of the later Heidegger is blended with ideas from Maximus the Confessor and Gregory Palamas as well as some modern Russians (Berdyaev and Lossky in particular) to produce a complex and most original vision, now elaborated in a major treatise on *Person and Eros* (of 1974–5). He lays great stress upon the relational element implicit in the Greek word *prosōpon*: human reality exists only face to face with, towards (*pros*), the human reality of an other or the reality of the world itself. But this means in turn that human reality and the world's reality in general are actual and concrete only in relation to persons – only as *parousia*, presence, never simply as *ousia*, abstract essence. Knowledge thus has to do with presence, with the desire for relation; it depends on *ekstasis*, the transcending of the myth of a private individuality. Full or mature knowledge of our world is a moral and spiritual affair, a complete openness to universal presence. The condition of fallen humanity is one in which we have chosen individuality, separation from each other, a world of essences concealed from one another, with God as the primary being-in-itself, a First Cause to which we argue by abstracting from the realm of interlinked but ultimately fixed and separate 'atoms' of being. In this sense, western post-Enlightenment philosophical theology is a vast rationalization of the state of fallenness – a consistent theme in Yannaras from his earliest work in the sixties to his recent *Elements of Faith* (trans. 1991).

The issue of this is an integration of the philosophy of personal presence with the metaphysics of Palamas. The Palamite scheme of the divine *ousia* being actual for us only in the divine *energeiai* is translated into the affirmation that the divine *ousia* is itself only as personal *parousia*. But this means that, unless we fall into the fatal error of thinking of God as personal only in respect of us and our world, God's being must eternally exist in personal communion, as a life of mutual *ekstasis*. With the incarnation of the divine Word, the perfect personal being of God enters creation and sets up a network of relation in which human beings are finally liberated from the illusory world of self-subsisting essences into unrestricted communion – with God the Holy Trinity and with each other. Thus in the church human nature becomes properly personal: the impersonal, instinctual level of the will to self-preservation is overcome by the new life established in Christ's divine act of *ekstasis*, his refusal to live for himself. He empties himself of the power of divinity, reveals himself in need and suffering, not in manifest glory, and finally accepts death itself, all as part of a single action by which he opens for us a way to share the Trinitarian life. *Ekstasis* and kenosis coincide: Christ is present for us entirely as welcoming, unresisting, self-giving. His otherness to us is no obstacle to perfect communion. This communion enables us to live with each other in the same mode, not menaced by the absolute and unique otherness of other persons, but discovering a new 'mode of existence' (*tropos huparxeōs*, a venerable technical term in theology to define what is meant by *hupostasis* in the life of God) in loving and being loved. The Eucharist is the way in which such a life is concretely shared with us and implanted in us, and it is supremely the action of the Holy Spirit, who, as in Lossky's theology, transforms our individual life into true personhood.

Doctrinal truth can only be apprehended in the *event* of communion – meeting the incarnate Word in the community's sacramental life. The same holds true for ethics, which is not a science of differentiating good from evil, but a proclamation of the choice between life (communion) and death (isolation). Yannaras had begun to discuss the problem of humanity's self-isolation from the material environment and its death-dealing results long before ecological issues became fashionable in western theology, and he inherits much of Heidegger's passionate hatred of technocracy. Although this leads at times to a certain romanticism about traditional Greek peasant life ('Hellenic Slavophilism', in the words of one slightly sceptical reviewer), it has formed part of a consistent and courageous political witness in Greece. Yannaras has written extensively in the Greek religious and secular press on issues of the day – totalitarianism, pollution, nuclear policy – in a vein of pungent radicalism. He has done more than any other Greek theologian to keep alive a critical Christian voice in the public discourse of his nation, where Christian comment is all too often associated with unintelligent and self-serving conservatism.

Conclusion

Orthodox theology continues to show much vitality, not only in North America and western Europe, but in Asia, where figures like Georges Khodre in the Middle East and Paulos Gregorios (Paul Verghese) in India have echoed Yannaras and Clément in applying the insights of the Greek Fathers on the nature of the human person and human community before God to the political and ethical crises of our century. Paulos Gregorios in particular has written a good deal about the right use of science and technology, and has had much influence on the World Council of Churches. Recent developments in eastern Europe mean that the Romanian and Slavonic churches are now free to develop their intellectual life as never before, and there are already signs in Russia of a second 'religious renaissance', in the sense of a new fusion of Orthodox tradition with the main currents of European political and intellectual life. The work of the Higher School of Religions and Philosophy in St Petersburg is particularly important here. On the ecumenical scene, Orthodox theologies of the church, especially Zizioulas's model, have been crucial in moving western confessional debates on to a new level. There is still a very great deal to hope for from the Orthodox world in the renewal of both church and society in the west.

See also ECUMENISM; ETHICS; SACRAMENTAL THEOLOGY.

Bibliography

Copleston, F.C. 1988: *Russian Religious Philosophy. Selected Aspects*. Tunbridge Wells: Search.

Florovsky, G.V. 1972–29: *Collected Works*. Belmont, Mass.

Gavin, Frank 1923: *Some Aspects of Contemporary Greek Orthodox Thought*. Milwaukee and London.

Lossky, Vladimir [1944] 1957: *The Mystical Theology of the Eastern Church*, trans. London.

Nichols, Aidan 1989: *Theology in the Russian Diaspora*. Cambridge: Cambridge University Press.

Yannaras, Christos 1972: Theology in present-day Greece, *St Vladimir's Theological Quarterly* 16, 4, pp. 1–20.

Yannaras, Christos 1991: *Elements of Faith*, trans. Edinburgh: T&T Clark.

Zernov, Nicolas 1963: *The Russian Religious Renaissance of the Twentieth Century*. London: Darton, Longman and Todd.

Zizioulas, John 1985: *Being as Communion: Studies in Personhood and the Church*. New York: St Vladimir's Seminary Press.

ROWAN WILLIAMS

ecclesiology 'Ecclesiology' is a term that has changed its meaning in recent theology. Formerly the science of the building and decoration of churches, promoted by the Cambridge Camden Society, the Ecclesiological Society and the journal *The Ecclesiologist*, ecclesiology now stands for the study of the nature of the Christian church. H. Küng defines it as 'the theological expression of the church's image'.

Etymologically, 'ecclesiology' is derived from the Greek. Just as 'theology' is made up of the Greek *theos*, God, and *logos*, discourse (so, discourse about God), so 'ecclesiology' is composed of the Greek *ekklesia*, assembly, and *logos*, discourse. *Ekklesia* is a secular term for an assembly of persons and is derived from the verb 'to call'. It was employed by the translators of the Greek Old Testament (LXX) to render the Hebrew *qahal*, assembly, which in turn derives from the Hebrew for voice (*qol*). (The LXX also used *synagoge* to translate *qahal*.) In both Hebrew and Greek, then, the church is the assembly of those who are called out (of the world) or called together (to worship). The English 'church' comes from a different source: the Greek *kyriake*, belonging to the Lord (*kyrios*).

The transition from 'assembly' to 'church' in the theological sense is made in the New Testament. *Ekklesia* is found in only one of the Gospels – Matthew – where it occurs three times. On two occasions it means 'assembly' (Matt. 18: 17) but the third instance has the broader sense: 'on this rock I will build my church' (Matt. 16: 18). In the Epistles, *ekklesia* occurs frequently and three usages can be discerned. First, *ekklesia* refers to the local Christian assembly: 'all the churches of Christ greet you' (Rom. 16: 16). Second, *ekklesia* refers to the whole or universal church: 'I persecuted the church of God' (Gal. 1: 13). Third, *ekklesia* refers in the later, probably pseudo-Pauline Epistles, to what we might call the mystical church which is the body of Christ (Eph. 1: 22f.; Col. 1: 18).

As reasoned and informed reflection on the nature of the Christian church, ecclesiology has a number of departments: the sacraments and the ministry; authority in the church; worship; pastoralia; ecumenism. However, to avoid overlapping with other topics in the present volume, ecclesiology will here be taken in the narrower sense of *the critical study of the governing paradigms of the church's self-understanding*.

Ecclesiology assumes great urgency at times of conflict or renewal in the Christian church. Reformation, Enlightenment and revolution put Roman Catholic ecclesiology on the defensive until the Second Vatican Council (Vatican II) (1962–5). Protestant ecclesiology was reinvigorated through the influence of the religious revivals of the eighteenth century – in the theology of F.D.E. Schleiermacher in Germany and in the renewal of Anglican ecclesiology by the Tractarians in England. The ecumenical movement (see ECUMENISM) of the twentieth century took its impulse from the missionary expansion of the western churches (and thus ultimately from the eighteenth- and nineteenth-century revivals), but this original missionary motive soon became transposed into a renewal of ecclesiology in the Faith and Order component of the ecumenical movement and subsequently of the World Council of Churches. Through bilateral and multilateral dialogues, all traditions of the church have been compelled to reassess their self-understanding and their evaluation of other churches. The ecumenical encounter has generated a quest for Anglican identity in the Anglican Communion. Protestant churches have begun to reassess their view of the historic episcopate. Even the Orthodox, longstanding participants in the ecumenical process, are conducting an internal debate on the validity of their traditionally exclusive ecclesiology. But the most remarkable renewal of ecclesiology has taken place in the Roman Catholic church, culminating in the decrees on the church and on ecumenism of Vatican II. Intense theological ferment on the church, its ministry and its ecumenical relations has taken place in the Roman Catholic church since Vatican II, but during the pontificate of John Paul II a strong central authority has prevented this ferment from developing into policy and programmes for a fully ecumenical ecclesiology.

Jesus and the church

A question that fundamental ecclesiology (that is, the study of the presuppositions and principles of ecclesiology) has to face at an early stage, is whether Jesus Christ founded the church. Can it be claimed that Jesus Christ intended the church in any form remotely resembling the present? Modern ecclesiologists are acutely conscious of the eschatological horizon for the ministry of Jesus, as established by J. Weiss and A. Schweitzer at the end of the nineteenth and the beginning of the twentieth centuries. Surely the eschatological crisis anticipated by Jesus precluded any intention to found an ongoing institutional structure for his community?

This consideration certainly undermines the cruder forms of ultramontane Roman Catholic apologetic which traced the monarchical papacy and its centralized apparatus of church government back to dominical institution. It would also appear to rule out appeal to divine right for other mechanisms for securing the historical continuity of the church, such as the doctrine of the apostolic succession. However, other justifications, falling short of *ius divinum*, for the Roman primacy and the historic episcopate, are not necessarily affected. And an intensive, rather than extensive, ecclesiology, such as that of the Protestant Reformers, the Russian Orthodox theologians in exile, and the Roman Catholic ecclesiologists of the Vatican II era, especially H. de Lubac, who in one way or another see word and sacrament as constituting the church in every particular eucharistic community, is not vulnerable to the eschatological veto.

Indeed, the eschatological horizon of the New Testament, far from inhibiting all ecclesiology, actually demands a particular form of it. For biblical eschatology (taking the inter-testamental literature into account also) included a doctrine of the church as the messianic community of the last days, the gathered elect. The one dominical reference to the church as more than a local assembly ('on this rock I will build my church': Matt. 16: 18) should not be taken to mean 'that the church will stand unharmed while age after age of secular history is unrolled, but that the eschatological community will weather the storms of the last days, the last desperate attacks of evil before the End' (C.K. Barrett).

Modern ecclesiology tends to assume the truth of A. Loisy's celebrated dictum: 'Jesus foretold the kingdom and it was the church that came.' While Jesus looked for the reign of God in a new heaven and earth, where human beings would be as the angels in heaven, loosed from carnal earthly ties, the movement that emerged after his death consisted of a miscellaneous collection of men and women, mortal, sinful, implicated in the ways and means of the world, whose common life was largely determined by sociological factors and developed in a variety of ways. As we have noted, this conclusion is incompatible with any appeal to a God-given pattern for the church and its structures, whether papal, presbyterian or episcopalian. How do modern ecclesiologists respond to this dilemma?

Anglo-Catholics still generally insist on the validation of orders by the transmission of apostolic authority through the historic episcopate as a condition of eucharistic communion. Many have resisted the admission of women to the full ministry of the church on the grounds that if Jesus had intended this he would not have chosen only male apostles. The Anglican–Roman Catholic International Commission (ARCIC I) abandoned any appeal to *ius divinum* for the office of universal primate, acknowledging that this could not be supported from the New Testament or apostolic Christianity. In its place it proposed an appeal to God's providential government of the church which had seen fit to allow the role of the bishop of Rome to develop into that of universal pastor.

K. Rahner insists that we must be able to claim that the church was founded by Jesus and is not merely self-validating. In the light of the eschatological horizon of the New Testament Rahner is unable to assert that the structures of Catholicism – the episcopate and the Petrine office – can be traced back to the words or deeds of the historical Jesus. His tactics then are twofold. First, he argues that there is a genetic connection between the historical structures of Catholicism and the decisions and developments of the apostolic period. Second, he sets out the sort of a priori argument at which he excelled to show that the salvation announced by Jesus entailed a corporate dimension ('the full and historically actualized Christianity of God's self-communication is an ecclesial Christianity') and therefore cannot be based on mere subjective interiority but must confront us with objective authority. Thus Rahner is able to claim that the hierarchical church with an authoritative (and under certain conditions, infallible) teaching office (magisterium) 'springs from the very essence of Christianity'.

E. Schillebeeckx, on the other hand, abandons even Rahner's subtle and elusive appeal to *ius divinum*. Schillebeeckx points out that it is clear historically that Jesus did not intend to found a new religious community. He addressed the whole of Israel (symbolized by the twelve apostles) and the earliest Christians were conscious of being simply a community within the fold of the Jewish faith. It is 'historically untenable' and 'a sign of ideological fundamentalism' to claim, as many Christians still do, that the historical forms of the church go back to Jesus himself, and that the historical and contingent growth of the church represents a necessary development willed by God. However, Jesus certainly did intend that there should be faith in his message that led to communal discipleship. So Schillebeeckx rather cryptically asserts that 'the historical phenomenon which calls itself the church of Christ is a divine foundation by Jesus for humankind.' In other words, if we cannot claim that the church was founded *by* Jesus, we must insist that the church is founded *on* Jesus.

Main traditions of ecclesiology
Roman Catholic Roman Catholic ecclesiology in the modern period was defined in the face of

various threats to the medieval imperial conception of the church. The pre-Reformation conciliar movement had failed to curb the power of the pope in order to reform the church. The Reformation itself can be interpreted as a consequence of that failure and as a distorted and fragmented form of conciliarism, partially secularized by placing councils under the authority of princes and denying them infallibility. Gallicanism was an assertion of regional independence and Jansenism an attempt to assert Augustinian doctrines of grace (so formative for the Reformers) within the Roman Communion. The Enlightenment, a resurgence of confidence in the power of unaided human reason to regulate human affairs and to devise adequate forms of belief and worship, was naturally hostile to all forms of ecclesiastical authority based on tradition and privilege. The revolutionary era after 1789 reduced the Roman Catholic church to its lowest ebb since the Reformation.

Rome's response to these threats was largely defensive. The Council of Trent reformed abuses without regenerating theology. With its reiterated anathemas, Trent set the tone for Roman policy towards movements of incipient diversity of practice or theology – Gallicanism and Jansenism being condemned by Rome. The French Revolution and its aftermath curbed the power of the church: the pope was exiled, religious orders and seminaries were closed down and missionary work suspended. But the Roman church emerged from this period of humiliation with its claims undiminished and soon to be enhanced.

In early nineteenth-century Tübingen J.A. Möhler (1796–1838) and others provided a doctrine of the church as a Spirit-bearing body, living and dynamic, to complement the standard backward-looking appeal to the church's historical foundation and tradition. The ultramontanist thinkers of France, notably J. de Maistre (1753–1821), linked an imperial concept of the church to a repristinization of the values of the *ancien régime*. J.H. Newman's theory of development (1845) made it possible to embrace the discrepancies between the apostolic community and the regime of Pius IX with a good conscience. The First Vatican Council (1869–70), the culmination of decades of siege mentality in the Vatican under Pius IX,

magnified the office of the pope and defined papal infallibility. That infallible defining authority was exercised in the promulgation of the Marian dogmas (the immaculate conception in 1854; the bodily assumption in 1950). Pius X moved against the Roman Catholic modernists (see MODERNISM), who attempted to bring biblical criticism and a dynamic concept of development to bear on traditional ecclesiology, in 1907 and 1910, and the repression of theological dissent was repeated by Pius XII in *Humani Generis* (1950). Pius himself had promulgated the last official statement of high Roman ecclesiology in *Mystici Corporis* (1943) which identified the mystical Body of Christ with the empirical Roman Catholic church. The Second Vatican Council redressed the balance of Roman Catholic ecclesiology by asserting the prerogatives of the episcopal college while retracting nothing of the papal claims of Vatican I. Other ecclesiological themes of Vatican II – the 'people of God' and 'communion' images of the church – had the potential to revolutionize the policy and practice of Rome in the ecumenical context.

The Roman Catholic ecclesiology of the late twentieth century, thwarted in the approved ecclesiastical forum, has tended to become radical and subversive. Rahner held that pluralism in theology called in question the possibility of authoritative dogma. Küng embraced an ecclesiology close to Luther's, with an emphasis on the universal priesthood and an outright challenge to the infallibility of church or pope. His ecumenical theology now operates in the context of world religions. Schillebeeckx, though curbed by the Vatican, has abandoned the teaching *extra ecclesiam nulla salus* (no salvation outside the church) and developed a universal theology of salvation, with the slogan 'No salvation outside the world'. J.B. Metz's political theology is subversive of all oppressive, hierarchical systems: its starting point is the dangerous memory of the crucified Messiah brought into bifocal vision with the narrative of an oppressed people. Like Metz, the Latin American liberation theologians, such as G. Gutiérrez and L. Boff, have developed an ecclesiology oriented to egalitarian base communities (see LIBERATION THEOLOGY). However, John Paul II and J. Ratzinger have perpetuated the traditional ecclesiology of the *societas perfecta* – a hierarchical system mediating authoritative dogma, binding moral laws and salvific sacramental grace from the top downwards. (See also ROMAN CATHOLIC THEOLOGY.)

Protestant Protestant ecclesiology in the period after 1700 was the heir to a theologically sterile century, marked by a complacent acceptance of divisions in the church (between Rome and the churches of the Reformation, and between Lutheran and Reformed churches); by a confessionalism that treated the Augsburg Confession or the Formula of Concord, the Heidelberg Catechism or the articles of the Synod of Dort like holy writ; by a scholasticism in theological method that promoted logical analysis and systematic coherence and comprehensiveness; and by an exaggerated emphasis on doctrinal precision. In the late seventeenth and early eighteenth centuries the movement of spiritual vitality known as pietism reacted against the dead orthodoxy, as its leaders P.J. Spener and A.H. Franke regarded it, of the German Lutheran church. Whether in the form of spiritual rigour or of fervent devotion, it prepared the ground for a renewal of ecclesiology.

That renewal came in the work of F.D.E. Schleiermacher (1768–1834) who – to put it crudely – transposed Christian doctrines in his *Glaubenslehre* (trans. *The Christian Faith*, [1821–2] 1928) from an ontological to an existential mode. Schleiermacher drew on his education among the pietists (Moravians) and reacted against prevailing scholasticism, when he asserted that the church's *raison d'être* lay not in the realm of knowledge or of action but of feeling ('piety'), which is a consciousness of God mediated by the redeeming work of Jesus Christ. The particular Christian form of being dependent on God is conducive to fellowship or communion in which believers communicate their self-consciousness by means of speech and so edify one another – all distinction of priesthood and laity being incompatible with the Christian understanding of redemption in which Christ assumes all believers into the power of his God-consciousness and the fellowship of his unclouded blessedness. The sense of vital unity possessed by this fellowship is the presence of the Holy Spirit, and this impulse to unity will eventually prevail in the church (Schleiermacher was writing a dogmatics for a politically united Lutheran and Reformed church). The inner essence of the church, expressed in word and sacrament, never varies; the outward form of the church is subject to variation, but this is a matter of indifference. In effecting this return to the unchanging centre or essence of the church's existence, Schleiermacher could be regarded as picking up again the dominant concern of the Reformers who insisted that Christ is present in the church through word and sacrament and that these are sufficient to guarantee the authentic existence of the church.

If Schleiermacher played down the institutional aspect of ecclesiology, the church as a concrete society, this tendency was accentuated further by the man who saw his work as the antidote to Schleiermacher's, K. Barth (1886–1968). Barth's treatise on the church in *Church Dogmatics* ([1932–68] 1956–75) IV/1: 62, pp. 642–725), is a landmark in Protestant ecclesiology and superior to the other extensive tracts of the *Church Dogmatics* devoted to ecclesiology. Here Barth developed the impulse of his early theology of divine grace as intersecting vertically from above and as qualitatively different from all human aspirations or preparations, into what might be called an ecclesiological actualism. The positive substance of this is that the church is Christ's 'earthly-historical form of existence' (Barth is here developing D. Bonhoeffer's insight in his youthful work of 1930, *Sanctorum Communio*, that 'Christ exists as the church'). But as such the church in its true nature remains transcendent. The church exists only as a definite history takes place, its act is its being, its essence its existence. The church is not a human, social and historical institution – a divine but earthly society that spans the centuries – it exists only when it takes place. Therefore no concrete form of the community can as such be the object of faith. Barth was highly critical of the virtual identification that he detected in the more triumphalist forms of Roman Catholic theology between the mystery of the church as the body of Christ and the empirical church with its history, law and organization. However, having asserted the priority of the mystical church, Barth then goes on to insist on the imperative of concrete visible unity which could only be attained by traditions taking their historical identity ser-

131

iously and not trading it in for ecumenical goodwill. Barth develops an impressive exposition of the credal notes of the church: in doing so he comes remarkably close to Schleiermacher by asserting that the catholicity of the church is the persistence of its true identity and essence through all outward changes of form. (See also PROTESTANT THEOLOGY: GERMANY.)

Anglican At the Reformation, the English church had retained the structures of medieval catholicism (the parochial system, the historic episcopate, infant baptism, common prayer, canon law) but had abolished a number of medieval developments (celibacy of the clergy, penance, communion in one kind, the propitiatory sacrifice of the mass for the living and the dead, the cult of the saints). It had given the educated laity a voice by providing Bible and liturgy in the vernacular, retaining lay patronage, giving parliament authority in doctrine and worship and, above all, replacing the authority of the pope by the sacred lay figure of the sovereign. Richard Hooker (1554–1600) had moved beyond the first Reformers' doctrine of a church constituted by word and sacrament, to a concept of a visible divine society identified by its outward profession of faith, divided into several branches, and enjoying a real participation in the life of God through the sacraments (which were not, however, dependent for their efficacy on hierarchically validated and transmitted sacramental grace).

The Civil War had resulted in the abolition of the episcopate and the liturgy and the execution of the sacred figurehead. At the Restoration in 1660 the hierarchy was re-established along with the monarchy and a more emphatically episcopalian form of Anglicanism emerged. As successive sovereigns failed in their duty as nursing fathers of the church (by being Roman Catholics, Calvinists or Lutherans) the role of the bishop became accentuated. Meanwhile, the Methodist movement generated a spiritual fervour and seriousness that could doubtfully be contained within the established church. In the Oxford movement, launched in 1833 with the *Tracts for the Times*, this emotional religiosity, now tinged with romanticism, joined forces temporarily with the old high church tradition until the alliance was broken by the hostility of the church establishment and

Newman and his closest disciples moved to Rome.

The Oxford movement effectively challenged the consensus that had prevailed since the sixteenth century that the Church of England was a Protestant church. While the Tractarians held an unhistorical and jaundiced view of the Reformation, their fears were confirmed by the tendency of evangelicals to move to the lower end of the spectrum of churchmanship. Evangelical high churchmen, such as W.F. Hook, who combined justification by faith with a worship and mission centred on the sacraments, came to seem anomalous. The most impressive work of ecclesiology of this period is William Palmer's *A Treatise on the Church of Christ* (1838) which combined a positive verdict on the Reformation with an insistence on the apostolic succession.

An outspoken critic of the Oxford movement, F.D. Maurice (1805–1872) developed an alternative ecclesiology to which the concept of the divine order was central: the kingdom of Christ transcended the various empirical manifestations of the church. In his notable work *The Kingdom of Christ* ([1838] 1958) he identified the authentic signs of a spiritual society (baptism, creeds, forms of worship, the Eucharist, a ministry, Scripture) and argued that while Rome and dissent had distorted certain elements into a system, Anglicanism had preserved them more or less in balance. The key to Maurice's ecclesiology was the prevenient grace of God, manifested in the incarnation and the atonement, witnessed to in infant baptism, and responded to in justification by faith.

Late nineteenth-century Anglican ecclesiology, notably in C. Gore and R.C. Moberly, redressed the antipathy of the Tractarians to lay privileges and, while not compromising on the apostolic succession, emphasized the priesthood of all Christians and advocated a concept of ministerial priesthood which was a difference of function in the body of Christ. In the twentieth century Anglican ecclesiology suffered neglect in favour of a dominantly historical–critical study of Scripture and patristics, but two essays in biblical theology stand out: L. Thornton's ecclesiology of communion, *The Common Life in the Body of Christ* (1950), which was ahead of its time, and A.M. Ramsey's attempted synthesis between Tractarian and

Reformation principles in *The Gospel and the Catholic Church* (1936). (See also ANGLICANISM.)

Images of the church

Divine society The image of the church as a *societas perfecta* has been dominant in Roman Catholic ecclesiology until recent times, though it is not confined to that tradition: any ecclesiology that identifies the kingdom of God with the rule of some humans over others (theocracy) belongs to this model of the church. It understands the visible church to be endowed by divine authority with the power to formulate and enforce laws and teachings and identifies those with divine revelation. Its structure is that of a pyramid, its ethos is juridical. J.A. Möhler wrote: 'God created the hierarchy and in this way provided amply for everything that was required until the end of time.' The Dogmatic Constitution on the church prepared for Vatican I states:

> The church has all the marks of a true society. Christ did not leave this society undefined and without a set form. Rather, he himself gave it its existence . . . and gave it its constitution . . . It is so perfect in itself that it is distinct from all human societies and stands far above them.

These sentiments were reiterated in *Mystici Corporis* (1943) and in the draft schema for Vatican II which was rejected by the council fathers, who turned their face against a clerical, juridical and triumphalist concept of the church. *People of God* Vatican II brought this biblical term, with its obvious egalitarian implications which had all but disappeared from preconciliar Roman Catholic ecclesiology, to the forefront. It enabled the council to promote the doctrine of the universal priesthood of believers, founded on baptism (though without integrating this with the ordained priesthood). The image adds an eschatological perspective to ecclesiology: the people of God make their pilgrimage through this world; they are at the same time holy and in constant need of repentance. Vatican II did not shed all traces of triumphalism at this point, asserting that the church's vision of divine truth becomes ever clearer as it journeys on. H. Küng and K. Rahner exploited the council's admission of the sinfulness of the pilgrim church in an epistemological sense: the people of God may wander far from the truth and human traditions become mingled with the sacred deposit of faith. *Sacrament* Vatican II's image of the church as the universal sacrament of salvation has been subsequently developed by K. Rahner. As sacrament the church is a mystery (*sacramentum* being the received Latin translation of the Greek *mysterion*): its true nature and secret life are hidden. As sacrament the church is an effective symbol that communicates what it symbolizes and is taken up into the divine salvific self-communication. As sacrament it is an emblematic manifestation of 'the liturgy of the world' in which divine grace is already at work. As sacrament it is brought into conjunction with Christology and pneumatology, though W. Kasper demurs at applying Rahner's title 'primal sacrament' to the church as that should be reserved for Christ, pointing out that Vatican II stopped short of this identification by denoting the church 'as it were' (*veluti*) a sacrament. The unifying concept of sacrament enables the sacraments of the church to be integrated with the life of the whole body, not just with the ministry of the hierarchy.

Communion The image of the church as a communion (*koinonia* in the New Testament) is genuinely ecumenical. It was 'one of the guiding ideas – perhaps *the* guiding idea' of Vatican II (Kasper), though it was counterbalanced (some would say checkmated) by the residual image of the church as *societas perfecta hierarchica*. Luther had a remarkable concept of communion with Christ and all the saints through baptism. Hooker stressed the real participation in the life of God through the church's means of grace. The Lambeth Conferences of the Anglican Communion have consistently recognized that Christians are brought into communion with the body of Christ by baptism. The Orthodox notion of *synaxis* (in Latin, *communio*) celebrates the presence of the Holy Spirit in every (Orthodox) eucharistic communion. The theology of communion presupposes mutual recognition of the sacrament of baptism and draws out the implications of this for the imperative of eucharistic communion. The promise of this approach to ecclesiology is that it is Trinitarian (reflecting the communion of Father, Son and Holy Spirit), practical (capable of including degrees of communion – though not for the

Orthodox), realistic (embracing diversity in belief and practice) and eschatological (its final consummation is in heaven). Above all it is personalist and relational – the antithesis of juridical and hierarchical images of the church. The concept of communion has been developed by J. Zizioulas (Orthodox), J.-M.R. Tillard (Roman Catholic) and P. Avis (Anglican). It was the theme of the second report of ARCIC II, an exploration of the spirit and forms of communion that fall short of one Eucharist. Communion is central to the ecumenical quest since baptism into the body of Christ is the only basis for the mutual unconditional acceptance that leads to deeper mutual understanding and demands visible expression in a common Eucharist.

See also AUTHORITY; EASTERN ORTHODOX THEOLOGY; SACRAMENTAL THEOLOGY; TRADITION.

Bibliography

Abbot, W.M., ed. 1966: *The Documents of Vatican II*. London: Geoffrey Chapman.

Avis, P. 1989: *Anglicanism and the Christian Church*. Edinburgh: T & T Clark; Minneapolis: Augsburg/Fortress.

Avis, P. 1990: *Christians in Communion*. London: Mowbray; Collegeville: Liturgical.

Barth, K. [1932–68] 1956–75: *Church Dogmatics*, trans. G. Bromiley *et al*. Edinburgh: T & T Clark.

Bonhoeffer, D. [1930] 1963: *Sanctorum Communio*, trans. London: Collins.

Gore, C. 1889: *The Church and the Ministry*. London: Longmans.

Küng, H. 1971: *The Church*. London: Search.

Maurice, F.D. [1838] 1958: *The Kingdom of Christ*. London: SCM Press.

Moberly, R.C. 1910: *Ministerial Priesthood*, 2nd edn. London: SPCK, reprinted 1969.

Newman, J.H. [1845] 1974: *An Essay on the Development of Christian Doctrine*. Harmondsworth: Penguin.

Palmer, W. 1838: *A Treatise on the Church of Christ*. London.

Rahner, K. [1954–84] 1961– : *Theological Investigations*, 22 vols, trans. London: Darton, Longman and Todd.

Rahner, K. [1976] 1978: *Foundations of Christian Faith*, trans. New York: Seabury; London: Darton, Longman and Todd.

Ramsey, A.M. 1936: *The Gospel and the Catholic Church*. London: Longmans.

Schillebeeckx, E. [1989] 1990: *Church: The Human Story of God*, trans. J. Bowden. New York: Crossroad; London: SCM.

Schleiermacher, F.D.E. [1821–2] 1928: *The Christian Faith*. Edinburgh: T & T Clark.

Thornton, L. 1950: *The Common Life in the Body of Christ*. London: Dacre.

Tillard, J.-M.R. 1987: *Eglise d'églises*. Paris: Editions du Cerf.

Zizioulas, J. 1985: *Being as Communion*. New York: St Vladimir's Seminary Press.

PAUL D.L. AVIS

economic analysis and ethics There are three major strands in modern economic analysis: economic theory, normative economics (or 'welfare' economics) and econometrics. The intellectual roots of the first two strands can be traced back to the formative period of economics as a discipline in the late eighteenth and early nineteenth centuries mainly, though not exclusively, in Britain. Econometrics, the application of statistical methods to economic analysis, is distinctively a twentieth-century development. Christian thought has played little part in the formation of the discipline, despite periods when the church has had an active interest in social and economic matters. The church has generally accepted economic analysis as an objective study of the economy, just as it has accepted the findings of the physical sciences. Its contribution to debate has been in the areas of social ethics and public policy.

Two key features of economic theory, 'theoretical realism' and the deductive method, were first stated succinctly by J.S. Mill in his *Essay on the Definition of Political Economy* of 1836. Theoretical realism seeks explanations for economic behaviour in an understanding of how people take decisions and act. Introspection (how would *I* act in the circumstances?) becomes a source of hypotheses. In particular, Mill introduced the concept of 'economic man', whose economic behaviour is determined by a few basic propositions. From these propositions, by a process of deductive logic, conclusions are reached about 'tendency laws' in economics, which may or may not hold in practice depending on other factors that the analyst has not taken into account. Mill's views were stated with increasing refinement by economists throughout the nineteenth century, and were given classic expression by L. Robbins (1935).

Obviously, in this tradition the correctness of a theory depends on the choice of the initial propositions about human nature, and on the accuracy with which the deductive reasoning has been applied. The latter is mainly a question of appropriate techniques of analysis, and the search for accuracy can explain the high mathematical content of modern economic analysis. The choice of a model of human nature is more controversial. The consensus model is that of 'rational economic man', who can express preferences over the set of consequences of all his possible actions. The content of these preferences is not defined, though they have to fulfil technical conditions as to rationality. This model is the final stage in the development of a concept with its roots in utilitarianism; in making choices the individual is motivated by self-interest. In the cruder utilitarian versions, he or she maximizes utility by seeking pleasure and avoiding pain; in more recent formulations, the individual maximizes 'satisfaction'. This narrow conception of human motivation has come in for some criticism from economic theorists, but the attempt to broaden the model of man has not been successful. In part, this is because the simple model has proved particularly amenable to mathematical analysis. But another reason is the claim that economic behaviour which is not self-seeking and rational will not survive in a competitive market place against behaviour which is. The 'rational economic man' model is therefore the established paradigm in economic analysis, and is used to explain a wide range of economic behaviour of both consumers and producers.

For the originators of this method of analysis, the question of consistency with the real world of economic life was not an important issue. The model is self-evidently true: the presuppositions are based on introspection, and the logic is purely deductive. This view continued to be held by some into the twentieth century, notably L. Robbins, L. von Mises (1949) and F. von Hayek. However, the mainstream of economic thought in the twentieth century absorbed positivist empiricism via the writings of Karl Popper. The idea in physical sciences is that hypotheses are built up from universal physical laws to which are added initial or boundary conditions relevant to the issue under consideration, and from which, by deductive

logic, one arrives at a statement about an event for which an explanation is being sought. Popper ([1963] 1972) makes the point that while empirical observations consistent with a hypothesis cannot prove it, one inconsistent observation may be sufficient to falsify it. 'Falsifiability' thus becomes the criterion for describing an explanation as a scientific hypothesis. Unfortunately, the application of this criterion is not straightforward. First, the hypothesis itself dictates which facts from the real world are relevant to its evaluation: other facts may be overlooked or ignored. Second, the empirical failure of a hypothesis seldom persuades its originator to give it up: he or she will look for reasons to explain the failure, and seek to reformulate the theory to make it 'fit' better. Indeed I. Lakatos (1978) suggests that the 'hard core' hypotheses of a research programme cannot be addressed directly with empirical testing. They may however be eventually abandoned by the scientific community in favour of a set of hypotheses that are more fruitful in terms of explanation.

The positivist methodology was introduced to economics by T.W. Hutchinson (1938), who argued that economics should concern itself with empirically testable propositions. It was to this issue that the nascent subject of econometrics was addressed, though the initial concern was to calibrate economic models for quantitative economic policy rather than to test hypotheses. The econometricians took developments in mathematical statistics and applied them to economic models. Thus a hypothesis might be that the level of savings in an economy is a function of a number of variables including, for example, people's income, existing stocks of wealth, interest rates, price changes and so on. Statistical analysis then determines how much of the variation in saving can be accounted for by variations in each of these variables. However a precise 'fit' is not expected: we may have measured the quantities inaccurately, we may have missed out some other important determinant of saving and we cannot control for other disturbances in the system as would be possible with a controlled experiment. The significance of each variable on its own, and of the whole set of explanatory variables, is therefore tested statistically. Conventionally, effects revealed by the analysis are only admitted as significant if

135

the possibility that they occurred by chance is less than one in twenty (or more stringently, one in one hundred). Despite its sophistication, the relation of econometric analysis to the evaluation of hypotheses drawn from economic theory is unclear. 'Poor' results are seldom sufficiently conclusive to 'falsify' a theory in the Popperian sense. At best they may generate modification or development of the theory, but the core hypotheses remain untouched. Thus major debates about the effects of monetary policy between 'Keynesians' and 'monetarists' in the 1980s were in no way resolved by appeals to the evidence.

The third strand in economic analysis is normative or 'welfare' economics. The economists of the nineteenth century adopted the utilitarian theory of J. Bentham. All experiences give an individual pain or pleasure. Individuals want to increase those experiences that give pleasure and diminish those that give pain. Bentham proposed that the pain–pleasure calculus could be adequately summarized in a single cardinal measure of utility. Individuals are motivated by the objective of maximizing utility, and all human effort should be directed towards that end. The welfare of society as a whole is a 'sum' of the utilities of the individuals that make up the society, and public policy should seek to maximize the sum. The difficulty with this approach is that cardinal utility is not an operational concept when it comes to measurement.

The Pareto criterion is an alternative principle, still within the utilitarian framework, which appears to offer a solution to the problem. It states that social welfare is increased if at least one individual is made better off without any individual being worse off. So we only need to rank outcomes rather than assign utility values. The Pareto principle proves to be very powerful in generating conclusions about the best allocation of resources in an economy. These conclusions are summarized in the 'marginal equivalences'. For example, if the rate at which the economy can produce additional goods J by reducing the output of good K (and hence releasing resources for the production of J) is not equal to the rate at which consumers are willing to trade good K for good J then a rearrangement of production can yield higher satisfaction for at least one consumer, while leaving all the other consumers at the same level of satisfaction as before. The Pareto criteria include three such marginal equivalences. Their intellectual fascination for economists is enhanced by the fact that it can be shown that a competitive economy satisfies the criteria, with the implication that such an economy is Pareto-efficient.

Paretian welfare economics has been criticized on a number of grounds. It presumes that each individual is the best judge of his or her own welfare. It fails to take into account anything other than the welfare of individuals; it does not, for example, consider the degree of freedom that people enjoy. It is practically very conservative, since it is hard to find examples of economic change that will satisfy the criteria. In practice, we need a standard for social welfare that will enable decisions to be taken where some will gain and some will lose. Ideally, too, that standard should be able to dispense with cardinal utility, and work only with preferences across social states expressed by rational economic man. Unfortunately, technical analysis has shown that these preferences are not sufficient, by themselves, to generate a unique social ordering or 'social welfare function'. So in practice, prescriptive economics has reverted to the position that utility can be measured, using market prices as a proxy where available, and that in the absence of any guidance about the desired distribution of welfare the gains and losses of different individuals should be simply summed as in the Benthamite analysis.

As previously noted, Christian thought has been at best peripheral to the development of economic analysis in the last two hundred years, so that economics is almost exclusively an Enlightenment discipline. It is not however the case that the church has been uninterested in economic and social issues. On the contrary, there has been continuous commentary and criticism. Five streams can be identified. The first is associated with the ascendancy of evangelicalism in Britain in the first half of the nineteenth century. A second had its origins in the incarnational theology of F.D. Maurice, which was taken up by the Christian Socialists in the latter half of the nineteenth century, and by Charles Gore and William Temple in the first part of the twentieth century. A third stream is from the Roman Catholic church, beginning with the encyclical *Rerum Novarum* in 1891. A fourth stream is the work associated with the World Council of Churches since the 1960s. A fifth stream is the re-emergence of evangelical social thought in the past twenty-five years.

The reason why Christian theology had no impact on the development of economic thought at its formative stages in the late eighteenth and early nineteenth centuries has been provided by J.A. Schumpeter (1954). He shows that the Thomist concept of the economy as governed by natural law was never challenged. Society has an order that possesses an inherent logical consistency. The origin of that consistency, which is taken to be divine, does not affect in any way the methods by which we seek to study it. And because it has its own ordering, then normative analysis is concerned with laws and procedures that are conducive to that ordering. So if the function of the economy is discerned to be the provision of goods to meet human needs, then the public good is satisfied by the distinctly utilitarian objective of meeting those needs more comprehensively. This approach was adopted by Richard Whateley, not an evangelical, who sought to extend William Paley's natural theology to society. He believed, following Paley, that man's understanding of right and wrong depends on the pleasure or pain of particular actions; that the basis of economic life is exchange and that the benefits of exchange identified by Adam Smith are a 'natural' proof that God has endowed man with a social instinct; that a utilitarian approach to the creation of wealth did not exclude superior ethical standards once wealth was created; and that it was right to be optimistic about progress in human society.

Evangelicals relied on a doctrine of providence to support a similar approach. 'Moderate' evangelicals, the Clapham Sect and their successors, believed that providence operates for the most part through cause and effect. The natural order of the economy functions to reward the good and punish the bad, and to make people responsible for their actions. So they supported self-help, *laissez-faire* and free trade: but also noted the need for a moral basis which would enable people to live honest economic lives and to be generous to those in need. Virtuous action had to be spontaneous:

there is no ethical value in doing good by state command. The more extreme evangelicals responded to the economic and political crises, and natural disasters like outbreaks of cholera, by seeing the direct intervention of God in judgement. They enthusiastically adopted the Malthusian economic perspective with its emphasis on natural checks to overpopulation, which was seen as an incentive to sexual abstinence and economic self-improvement. To intervene in the economy was to counter the workings of providence.

The second stream was radically different from the evangelical approach of the early nineteenth century. Starting from the incarnational theology of F.D. Maurice, a group of Anglican academic theologians began to espouse the emerging doctrines of socialism, though they were at pains to emphasize the Christian ethical basis of their approach. Prominent early leaders were B.F. Westcott, Charles Gore and H. Scott Holland, who were involved in the Christian Social Union, founded in 1889 (see CHRISTIAN SOCIALISM). Their work took the form of a critique of the capitalist system based on four principles: brotherhood or cooperation in contrast to the competition of capitalism; labour as a responsibility and privilege for all; justice, which was defined to include the opportunity for everyone to lead a full and happy life; and the responsibility of government for maintaining the economic and social order. Above all, they rejected the concept of the economic system as a natural order of cause and effect uncontrolled by any moral responsibility. This group had a decisive effect on Anglican thinking on the economy for the next fifty years and beyond. A particular fruit of their work was the report of the Archbishops' Fifth Committee of Enquiry, *Christianity and Industrial Problems* of 1918, which claimed that Christian moral teaching applies as much to society, industry and economics as to the individual, and should therefore be judiciously applied to economic problems, despite the obvious difficulties with such a programme. The report calls for a living wage, action to deal with unemployment and casual labour schemes, cooperation between employers and workers, extension of municipal services, restrictions on profits and a housing programme. But it does not spell out how these might be achieved.

Many of these ideas were taken up and expanded by the Conference on Christian Politics, Economics and Citizenship (COPEC) which sponsored the work of twelve commissions to work on particular social issues in the period 1920–4. Their work was presented and discussed at the Conference in Birmingham in 1924. The conference was chaired by William Temple, who went on to write and speak on its themes over the next twenty years, including the period when he was an archbishop, culminating in his seminal work, *Christianity and Social Order* (1942). This work coincided with the emergence of Keynesian ideas in the late 1930s, which provided the intellectual justification and the policy tools to achieve many of the things that Anglican thinking had advocated in the previous thirty or forty years, without espousing socialism of the Marxist-Leninist variety. Keynes perceived defects in the capitalist system, notably in the tendency to unemployment, which required action by government to correct. Many of these ideas were incorporated in the report of the Beveridge Committee, *Full Employment in a Free Society* (1944), which became the framework for post-war economic policy in Britain.

The third stream of commentary on economic life has come from the Roman Catholic church, in a series of pronouncements beginning with *Rerum Novarum* (On the Condition of Labour) in 1891. With the exception of *Quadragesimo Anno* (On Reconstructing the Social Order) in 1931, there was little further development until the Second Vatican Council, since when there has been a steady stream of material, drawing both on biblical perspectives and traditional Roman Catholic themes, culminating in *Centesimus Annus* in 1991. The whole has developed into a coherent set of principles for economic life, identifying the responsibilities of all groups in the economy, including government. The principles include justice and participation, and human (economic) rights. Justice is defined to include not only justice in exchange (commutative justice) and in distribution, but also social justice defined as a right and obligation to be active and productive participants in the life of society. Hence economic rights include the meeting of basic needs, the right to earn a living, security in old age and sickness, and provision for the needs of families.

How these principles can be applied in practice in an advanced capitalist economy is explored in the US Bishops' Pastoral Message and Letter (1986). This emphasizes four priorities: fulfilling the basic needs of the poor; increasing the active participation of those marginalized or excluded; investment (both physical and human) to be directed to benefit the poor or economically insecure; and economic policies to be evaluated in terms of their impact on family life. Intervention in the economy is justified on the grounds that the economy is not a mechanism with inexorable laws in which people are objects tossed about by economic forces. But the level for intervention is to be determined by the principle of *subsidiarity*: a higher ordering in society should not take over what can effectively be achieved by a lower ordering. In particular, government should enable and encourage groups in society to take responsibility not only for themselves but also for their neighbours. Collectivist solutions, with great power over economic affairs being exercised by central government, are specifically excluded. The right to private property is upheld, but not as an absolute right, since it brings responsibilities to others as well. Business is seen as a trustee of resources, accountable not only for its personal ethics and profits, but also for its impact on the wider society.

When it comes to *application*, the nature of the Roman Catholic contribution is seen to parallel that of Anglican commentary. The autonomy of the discipline of economics, as a social *science*, is not challenged. The specific Christian contribution is to provide an ethical critique, and to urge the adoption of certain policy objectives by governments and legislatures. The Thomist conception of the economy as a natural order, functioning according to its own laws, is accepted as far as positive economic analysis is concerned, but there is no acceptance of its inherent ethical values, which need correction from the outside.

The fourth stream is linked to the emergence of ecumenical social ethics under the auspices of the World Council of Churches since 1948. Initially, the basis for this work was the concept of the 'responsible society': the freedom of the individual is to be constrained by a commitment to public justice and order, and the power of those with political authority or economic power is to be constrained by responsibility both to God and to those whose welfare is affected by the exercise of that power. In time this concept was found to be lacking: it was too obviously the product of western thought, and it was insufficiently comprehensive to deal with problems of international justice and the limits to growth. By 1975 the WCC had adopted the concept of 'the just, participatory and sustainable society', where society was consciously intended to be global and not merely national. In practice, the work of the WCC has tended to be driven by issues rather than theological principles: the North–South economic divide; the role of multinationals; the impact of science and technology; the needs of the poor; the impact of economic growth on the environment; and natural resource use. The general tone is radical, both in its criticism of western capitalism and in the economic policies that are advocated.

In recent years, a fifth stream of commentary on economic and social affairs has emerged among Reformed Protestants and evangelicals, both in Europe and in North America. The Reformed tradition has evolved from the Dooyeweerdian philosophical perspective, and has developed both a critique of the theory and practice of western capitalism as a product of Enlightenment thought (Goudzwaard, 1978), and as a methodological proposal for reconstructing economic analysis (Tiemstra, 1990) around the concept of stewardship, with a particular emphasis on economic institutions such as the family, the firm and the trade union. What is particularly significant about this work is that it refuses to accept the autonomy of 'economic science' as an intellectual discipline, and thereby distinguishes its critique from virtually every other Christian critique for the past two hundred years. The evangelical contribution is a more confused affair. There is an appeal to Scripture to provide an ethical framework within which economic policies and institutions may be evaluated. There is however little agreement on how the exegetical task is to be accomplished, or on conclusions to be drawn. Particularly in North America, the method has been used extensively by apologists for free market economics (such as North, 1974; Griffiths, 1982).

Economic analysis, in its present form, is an Enlightenment discipline, with a claim to intellectual autonomy in parallel with natural sciences. In practice, it operates with a particular doctrine of humankind, and with a utilitarian prescriptive basis. The contribution of Christian theology to the development of economic analysis in the past two hundred years has been minimal. Instead Christian commentators have developed critiques of economic institutions and policies, which have usually included (at least in western thought) a critical appraisal of capitalism. It is impossible to know whether these critiques have had any impact on either the theory or practice of economics.

See also CAPITALISM; ETHICS; MARXISM; SOCIAL QUESTIONS.

Bibliography

Blaug, M. 1980: *The Methodology of Economics or How Economists Explain.* Cambridge: Cambridge University Press.

Goudzwaard, B. 1978: *Capitalism and Progress.* Toronto: Wedge.

Griffiths, B. 1982: *Morality and the Market Place.* London: Hodder and Stoughton.

Hay, D.A. 1989: *Economics Today. A Christian Critique.* Leicester: IVP; Grand Rapids: Eerdmans.

Hilton, B. 1988: *The Age of Atonement: The Influence of Evangelicalism on Social and Economic Thought, 1795–1865.* Oxford: Clarendon Press.

Hutchinson, T.W. 1938: *The Significance and Basic Postulates of Economic Theory.* New York: Augustus M. Kelly.

Lakatos, I. 1978: *The Methodology of Scientific Research Programmes.* Cambridge: Cambridge University Press.

Mises, L. von 1949: *Human Action. A Treatise on Economics.* London: William Hodge.

Munby, D.L. 1956: *Christianity and Economic Problems.* London: Macmillan.

North, G. 1974: *An Introduction to Christian Economics.* Nutley, NJ: Craig Press.

Oliver, J. 1968: *The Church and Social Order.* London: Mowbray.

Popper, K.R. [1963] 1972: *Conjectures and Refutations.* London: Routledge and Kegan Paul.

Preston, R.H. 1979: *Religion and the Persistence of Capitalism.* London: SCM Press.

Preston, R.H. 1983: *Church and Society in the Late Twentieth Century: The Economic and Political Task.* London: SCM Press.

Robbins, L. 1935: *An Essay on the Nature and*

Significance of Economic Science. London: Macmillan.

Schumpeter, J.A. 1954: *History of Economic Analysis*. New York: Oxford University Press.

Temple, W. 1942: *Christianity and Social Order*. Reissued 1976 with Introduction by R.H. Preston. London: SPCK/Seabury Press.

Tiemstra, J.P., ed. 1990: *Reforming Economics: Calvinist Studies on Methods and Institutions*. Lewiston, NY: Edwin Miller Press.

US Bishops' Pastoral Message and Letter 1986: *Economic Justice for All: Catholic Social Teaching and the US Economy*. Washington DC: *Origins* 16, 24, November 27.

DONALD HAY

ecumenism Ecumenism can be defined as the movement which seeks the unity of Christians not so much by individual conversions as by the reconciliation of churches, and which emphasizes the mutual resolution of differences rather than the attempt to induce other churches to renounce their position and accept one's own.

In the period covered by this encyclopedia the reconciliation of divided churches was sought long before it was given the name of ecumenism. Among the German pietists (see LUTHERANISM), who sought unity for the sake of mission, N.L. von Zinzendorf (1700–1760) believed unity should not entail uniformity, since the churches had something to learn from one another; where formulations were incompatible, the differences were 'tropes' which God in his patience allowed to exist and used as means of edification until the churches could be united. Another branch of pietism, the separatists, on the other hand, commonly regarded the existence of distinct churches as a 'Babylon'.

Another German Protestant thinker who transcended church divisions was G.W. Leibniz (1646–1716), who advocated a cultural and political, as well as a religious, unity of Europe, in which, as in the medieval Holy Roman Empire, a leading role would be played by the emperor, now in the person of Tsar Peter the Great. In the eighteenth century Leibniz's principle of 'variety brought together in unity' inspired the Swiss movement known as 'reasonable orthodoxy', which wished the Protestant churches, while each retaining its identity, to be reconciled on the basis of unambiguous fundamental articles derived from the Bible.

Danish Lutheranism was another nineteenth-century breeding ground for early ecumenical thought. N. Grundtvig (1783–1872) believed that a single church already existed, born of the Spirit in baptism and based not on the infallibility of the Bible, but on the common baptismal creed. For S. Kierkegaard (1813–1855) with his existential understanding of the gospel, the churches were to serve the fundamental Christianity of the individual dedicated to God in faith. Such faith should combine the spirit of Catholicism with that of Protestantism: Lutheranism was a corrective, not a norm.

In England as early as the seventeenth century the theory of the *via media* formed the background of the development of ecumenism: the Church of England was seen as the middle way between the Reformation and Catholicism. Archbishop of Canterbury W. Wake (1657–1737), like his Prussian contemporary D.E. Jablonski (1660–1741), sought agreement on fundamentals; he saw the creeds of the first four General Councils as the best formulation of these fundamentals. His contacts with Catholicism were largely through the French Gallican church; he urged Catholics to limit papal primacy to one of 'place and honour'. One of his French correspondents, P.F. le Courayer (1681–1776), defended the validity of Anglican orders. Wake recommended the continental Protestants to accept episcopacy, but recognized the validity of ministers without episcopal ordination. He sought to persuade the churches to adopt a common worship and confession of faith. In Ireland Archbishop J. Bramhall (1594–1663) had thought it necessary to confer a form of conditional ordination on Presbyterian ministers who wanted to become Anglican priests.

The Orthodox church too was involved with the incipient ecumenism of this period, though the papacy continued to be viewed as a threat and the existence of Uniate churches in communion with Rome was deeply resented. Tsar Peter the Great (1672–1725) held conversations both with the Gallican doctors of the Sorbonne and Archbishop of Canterbury Thomas Tenison. At the same time a 'Lutheranized Orthodoxy' flourished in Russia. In the following century the Metropolitan of

Moscow, Philaret (1782–1867), explored re-union at a greater theological depth: although the Orthodox church alone was the true church, the less pure churches were not totally outside; providence fulfilled its mysterious purposes even through schisms.

Links between Anglicans and Orthodox were frequent. The Non-Jurors sought an association with the Russian and other Orthodox churches, and sent them copies of their new Communion Office. The Lambeth Conference of 1888 passed a resolution expressing hopes for eventual reunion with the Orthodox. Arch-bishop of Canterbury E.W. Benson (1829–1896) advocated a 'more or less formal acceptance of each other's position with toleration for any points of difference', and the authorization of intercommunion as a preliminary to reunion.

Immigrants to the USA brought some of their European attitudes with them; thus the Prussian union of Lutherans and Reformed (see below) found its counterpart among the immigrants from Germany. On the other hand the pastoral needs of an expanding country could inspire a new freedom in relations between the churches. Members of different churches were accustomed to sharing buildings and ministers; it was not until 1783 that an Anglican bishop was appointed. Anglican comprehensiveness led some to see the Episco-pal church in the USA as the comprehensive church in which all could be united; W. Huntington (1838–1918) proposed the four key elements of Anglicanism as a basis on which all Christians, even Roman Catholics, could unite. Huntington's four principles, adopted by the House of Bishops of the Episcopal church at Chicago in 1886 and by the Lambeth Conference of 1888, came to be known as the 'Chicago–Lambeth Quadrilateral' (1886–8).

Nineteenth-century Europe saw a number of attempts to reunite the churches. In 1817 King Frederick William III of Prussia established by law the 'Prussian Evangelical Church' which merged the Lutheran and Reformed churches. In 1841 his successor took part in the controversial establishment of a bishopric in Jerusalem to be filled alternately by the Prussian and English churches.

Most of the initiative for uniting the churches was taken by individuals or voluntary organiza-tions. In England F.D. Maurice proposed a theological rationale for ecumenism based on Christ's headship of the whole human race. E.B. Pusey's *Eirenicon* typifies the priority which the Tractarian movement gave to reunion between Canterbury and Rome; relations with the Orthodox, however, were not neglected, as is proved by the work of J.M. Neale in the founding of the Eastern Church Association in 1863. A.T. Mowbray's Home Reunion Society attached equal importance to free church involvement.

Among other voluntary movements in Britain which transcended denominational boundaries one can mention the Church of England's Society for Promoting Christian Knowledge (founded 1698), which enrolled a number of continental Protestants as 'corresponding mem-bers' and employed them in its missions, as did the Church Mission Society (founded 1799) – a practice which ceased later in the nineteenth century when episcopal ordination came to be considered indispensable. By the end of the century the Student Christian Movement (in which J.R. Mott was a pioneer) was beginning to bring together young people from all denominations.

One of the most powerful instruments in the ecumenical movement has been prayer for Christian unity. In 1835 an Italian priest, V. Pallotti, established the Octave of the Epiphany as a period of prayer for the universality of the faith and the unity of the church. By the middle of the century the Evangelical Alliance had organized an annual week of prayer for unity beginning on the first Sunday of the year. A similar Octave of Prayer running from 18 to 25 January was inaugurated by the Anglican (later Roman Catholic) P.J. Wattson (1863–1940), who founded an order, the Friars of the Atonement, dedicated to ecumenism; on the Roman Catholic side it was developed by the great French ecumenist Abbé Paul Couturier (1881–1953). In 1950 these dates became widely accepted, and each year's programme for prayer has since been agreed among the churches. Another sign of the power of prayer to unite separated Christians is provided by the Taizé community, which was founded by R. Schutz in 1940 as a Protestant religious community, but has promoted an ecumenical spirituality which has a great appeal, especially to the young.

A few individuals believed themselves called to promote unity by transferring their allegiance from one church to another while retaining some links with the church of their origin. Two examples of this lonely vocation are V. Soloviev (d. 1900), who passed from Orthodoxy to Roman Catholicism (there are however indications that by the end of his life he thought of himself as a member of both churches), and L. Gillet (d. 1980), who moved in the opposite direction.

In the twentieth century ecumenism became the concern not just of individuals and voluntary organizations but of the churches themselves. A key moment was the holding of the Edinburgh World Missionary Conference of 1910, under the presidency of Mott with J.H. Oldham as secretary. The conference numbered Orthodox as well as Anglicans and Protestants among its participants; the Roman Catholic church felt unable to accept an invitation to take part. The meeting declared that the aim of all missionary activity was 'to plant in each non-Christian nation one undivided Church of Christ'. It was agreed that the attempt to resolve doctrinal differences between the churches should be kept separate from collaboration in such missionary endeavour as that of United Bible Societies. 'Doctrine divides but service unites' became a common slogan. Several independent organizations emerged from Edinburgh to deal with different aspects of the ecumenical movement. Besides the International Missionary Council, Life and Work was set up to bring Christian influence to bear on matters of social justice and international peace. A third organization called Faith and Order was established to deal with doctrinal matters, and held its first world conference at Lausanne in 1927. Faith and Order has published a number of important reports, for instance on *The Doctrine of Grace* (1932), and *Baptism, Eucharist and Ministry* (1982). The work of these three organizations was coordinated when the World Council of Churches (WCC) was founded at Amsterdam in 1948. The International Missionary Council and Life and Work were absorbed into the WCC; Faith and Order has continued to exist as a committee of the Council. Among those whose vision led to the establishment of the WCC, mention should be made of William Temple of Canterbury (1881–1944), George Bell of Chichester (1881–1958) and N. Söderblom (1866–1931).

The WCC has found it easier to state what it is not than what it is. The 1950 'Toronto Statement' of the WCC's central committee affirmed that the Council is neither a super-church nor a body for conducting unity negotiations; membership of the Council did not even imply that member churches necessarily recognized one another as churches in the full sense. The Council's more modest aim was 'to bring the churches in living contact with each other'. The third Faith and Order conference at Lund in 1952 affirmed the need for 'the one Church' to 'find visible expression on earth', and recommended that the churches should 'act together in all matters except those in which deep differences of conviction compel them to act separately'. After years of discussion the New Delhi meeting of the WCC (1961) formulated the Basis of the Council so as to require faith in the divinity of Christ and in the Trinity, and placed emphasis on local unity: a visible and committed fellowship of 'all in each place', united by a common baptism and eucharist, joining in common prayer, possessing members and ministers accepted by all, reaching out together in witness and service, and united with Christians of all places and ages. This last aim however is in tension with the desire to preserve the existing links of such 'world confessional families' as the Anglican Communion and the Lutheran World Federation.

The Orthodox church, while believing no less strongly than the Roman Catholic church in its own privileged position as the one true church, became associated with the ecumenical movement much earlier than Rome. While many Orthodox theologians denied the validity of the orders and even the baptism of other churches, all could be put right by the principle of economy if these churches were united with Orthodoxy on the basis of the acceptance of Orthodox teaching. The Russian church especially showed interest in unity between the Anglicans and the Orthodox, an interest which was reciprocated at the Lambeth Conferences of 1888 and 1908. In 1920 the Patriarchate of Constantinople addressed a letter to all churches of Christ inviting them to form a league for mutual assistance. The Orthodox have participated in the WCC since its inception in 1948, while repeatedly protesting against proselytizing Protestant missions. With the Roman Catholic church, however, Orthodox relations have been clouded by a number of factors, prominent among them being the existence of the Uniate, or Eastern-rite, Catholic churches in communion with Rome. This problem has resurfaced in the 1990s with the recovery of religious freedom in eastern Europe.

The Roman Catholic church came late to the ecumenical movement. In 1864 the Holy Office forbade participation in the Association for the Promotion of Christian Unity; the only true church was that rooted in the Roman see. This affirmation, constantly repeated for the next century, was the theoretical basis for Rome's refusal to participate in the WCC; church unity was sought and prayed for in terms of individual 'conversions' or of 'return' to the Roman church. Thus Leo XIII (pope 1878–1903), who because of his repeated call for unity and his acknowledgement of the positive qualities of other Christian bodies has been given the credit for 'laying the bases of modern Catholic ecumenism', could still write of the 'unhappy state' of Christians separated from Rome. According to Pius XII in 1943, one cannot 'adhere to Christ as Head of the Church without loyal allegiance to his Vicar on earth' (*Mystici Corporis*).

In the years before the Second Vatican Council (Vatican II) two brave but abortive efforts were made to re-establish unity between Rome and Canterbury. In the 1890s the French Abbé Fernand Portal together with the Anglo-Catholic Lord Halifax appealed to Rome for the recognition of Anglican Orders; the result however did not fulfil their hopes, for the verdict of Leo XIII's bull *Apostolicae Curae* (1896) was that ordinations in the Anglican Communion are 'absolutely null and utterly void' (*irritas prorsus . . . omninoque nullas*) on grounds of deficient form and intention leading to the breach of the apostolic succession. The Archbishops of Canterbury and York rebutted the Pope's arguments in their *Responsio* of 1897. (The Lambeth Conference of 1920 nevertheless offered to submit Anglican clergy to 'a form of commission or recognition' 'if the authorities of other Communions should so desire', while asking the same of ministers who had not been episcopally ordained.) Halifax made a second attempt at reunion with Rome when in the 1920s he collaborated with Cardinal D.J. Mercier in setting up the Malines Conversations; they were cut short by Mercier's death in 1926.

The Roman Catholic ecumenical endeavour ceased to be the work of a few pioneers like M.J. Metzger (1887–1944, the founder of the *Una Sancta* movement) and the Dominican Yves Congar, and became part of official policy when in 1960 Pope John XXIII set up the Secretariat (later the Council) for Christian Unity under Fr (later Cardinal) A. Bea. The movement received its full impetus and theological basis in 1964 with the promulgation of the Vatican II Constitution on the Church (*Lumen Gentium* – LG) and Decree on Ecumenism (*Unitatis Redintegratio* – UR). The unity of Christians is to be sought for the sake of mission, so that a united church may be the 'visible sacrament' of the 'saving unity' to which God calls the whole human race (LG 9; UR 1). Christ's church is no longer said to be identical with the Roman Catholic church, but is said to 'subsist' in it (LG 8). Therefore divisions cause a defect of catholicity but not of unity, for unity is an inalienable characteristic of the Roman Catholic church (UR 4). Since religious bodies contain 'many elements of sanctification and truth', and have 'significance and importance in the mystery of salvation', their members are in an 'imperfect' communion with the Roman Catholic church, based on faith and baptism (LG 8; UR 3). Ecumenism involves conversion and renewal (UR 7); the share of Roman Catholics in the culpability for Christian divisions is acknowledged (UR 3). Ecumenical dialogue should be conducted on the principle that there is a 'hierarchy' of truths, in so far as they 'vary in their connection with the foundation of the Christian faith' (UR 11). Since 1968 Roman Catholic representatives have been full members of Faith and Order.

Many pairs of churches are currently conducting bilateral dialogues. A Faith and Order publication collected agreements reached in twelve sets of international bilateral dialogues up to 1981 (Meyer and Vischer, 1984); a Roman bibliography lists results of well over a hundred bilateral dialogues at international and more local levels up to 1984 (Puglisi and Voicu, 1984). Special mention should be made of the documents produced by the Anglican–Roman Catholic International Commission (ARCIC), namely the *Final Report* (1982) (comprising agreed statements on Eucharist, ministry and authority), *Salvation and the Church* (1987), and *The Church as Communion* (1991).

Conversations among churches have also been pursued at the national level, and have yielded significant results. One can point especially to the Catholic–Lutheran conversations in the USA, which since their inauguration in 1965 have produced an important series of agreements backed up by careful historical and doctrinal studies on such themes as the Eucharist and the doctrine of justification by faith. Valuable documents have also been published by the unofficial French Dombes group, which P. Couturier founded in 1937 for dialogue between Catholics and Protestants.

A notable degree of convergence is evident in all these bilateral dialogues, both as to method (the search for a language which avoids terms traditionally associated with polemics; the composition of 'agreed statements' rather than the comparison of the participating churches' views) and content (for example, Eucharist explained in terms of memorial rather than sacrifice or transubstantiation; the church explained in terms of 'communion').

Dialogue has in several cases resulted in the union of two or more churches, as in the formation of the United Reformed church in 1972 from the Congregational church of England and Wales and the Presbyterian church of England; and of the Uniting church in 1977 from the Australian Congregational Union, Methodist church and Presbyterian church. Two of the most comprehensive unions have taken place in India: in 1947 the Church of South India was formed out of the Anglican, Methodist, Presbyterian, Congregational, Lutheran and Reformed churches, and in 1970 the Church of North India brought together the Anglican, Congregational, Presbyterian, Methodist and Baptist communities with the Disciples of Christ. Different solutions were adopted in the two cases to the problem of the recognition and commissioning of ministries. For the Church of South India existing orders were left unaffected, but ordinations after the union were conferred episcopally; the Church of North India at once subjected all the clergy to a laying on of hands to supply whatever was lacking in God's eyes. Other plans, like the Church of England–Methodist scheme proposed in 1963 were unsuccessful, not least because it was not possible to devise a generally acceptable means of recognizing ministries.

In many countries Councils of Churches have been established to help the churches involved to co-ordinate their efforts and to make a common response to matters of shared concern. While in some of these Councils, for example in the USA, Roman Catholics have participated fully, in others they have felt unable to become full members for similar reasons which prevented them from becoming part of the WCC. In Britain the British Council of Churches was replaced in 1990 by the Council of Churches for Britain and Ireland with new objectives which enable the Roman Catholic church to accept membership.

The unity which is the aim of ecumenism has been expressed in various terms (though not everyone uses any one of them in the same sense), for example 'visible unity', 'organic unity', 'full communion', 'intercommunion', 'complete communion of faith and sacramental life'. Those who insist that a united church can and should admit of pluriformity of doctrinal formulation as well as liturgy, spirituality and canon law sometimes speak of 'reconciled diversity'. The Roman Catholic church believes in the need for a universal primacy endowed with ultimate teaching and jurisdictional authority; others, while accepting that unity requires a 'petrine ministry' to serve the unity of the universal church, do not believe it needs to be located in a single person.

See also ETHICS; LITURGY AND DOCTRINE.

Bibliography

ARCIC, 1982: *The Final Report*. London: SPCK and CTS.

ARCIC, 1987: *Salvation and the Church*. London: Church House Publishing/CTS.

ARCIC, 1991: *The Church as Communion*. London: Church House Publishing/CTS.

Bell, G.K.A., ed. 1920–57: *Documents on Christian Unity*, 4 vols. London: Oxford University Press.

Cullmann, O. [1986] 1988: *Unity through Diversity*, trans. M.E. Boring. Philadelphia: Fortress Press.

Faith and Order Paper No. 111 1982: *Baptism,*

Eucharist and Ministry. Geneva: World Council of Churches.

Faith and Order Paper No. 149 1990: *Baptism, Eucharist and Ministry 1982–1990: Report on the Process and Responses.* Geneva: World Council of Churches.

Fey, H.A., ed. 1970: *The Ecumenical Advance: A History of the Ecumenical Movement, vol. 2. 1948–1968.* London: SPCK.

Flannery, A., ed. 1975: *Vatican Council II: The Conciliar and Post Conciliar Documents.* Dublin: Dominican Publications.

Lutherans and Catholics in Dialogue 1965: *i. The Status of the Nicene Creed as Dogma of the Church.* 1966: *ii. One Baptism for the Remission of Sins.* 1967: *iii. The Eucharist as Sacrifice.* 1970: *iv. Eucharist and Ministry.* 1974: *v. Papal Primacy and the Universal Church.* 1980: *vi. Teaching Authority and Infallibility in the Church.* 1985: *vii. Justification by Faith.* Minneapolis: Augsburg Publishing House.

Meyer, H., and Vischer, L., ed. 1984: *Growth in Agreement: Reports and Agreed Statements of Ecumenical Conversations on a World Level.* Ramsey, NJ: Paulist Press; Geneva: World Council of Churches.

Puglisi, J.F., and Voicu, S.J. 1984: *A Bibliography of Interchurch and Interconfessional Dialogues.* Rome: Centro Pro Unione.

Rouse, R., and Neill, S.C., eds 1967: *A History of the Ecumenical Movement 1517–1948*, 2nd edn. London: SPCK.

Tavard, G.H. 1960: *Two Centuries of Ecumenism.* Notre Dame, Ind.: Fides; London: Burns and Oates.

EDWARD YARNOLD

Edwards, Jonathan (1703–1758) North American theologian. A Congregational minister in Massachusetts and for a brief period the president of the College of New Jersey at Princeton, Jonathan Edwards was a theologian with unusual philosophical acumen as well as the most formidable defender of Calvinism in the history of North America.

During his lifetime and for several generations thereafter, Edwards's reputation rested on his advocacy of religious revivals. But the recovery in the twentieth century of the full range of his works has also revealed his considerable power in metaphysics, ethics, and psychology. Although Edwards exerted considerable influence in Scotland (especially among evangelicals like John Erskine, Thomas Chalmers and James Orr, as well as indirectly on John McLeod Campbell), England (especially the Northamptonshire Baptist Association), Wales and the Netherlands, his work is best known and has been most thoroughly studied in the USA.

Edwards graduated from Yale College at sixteen and then studied theology privately for several years. During that period, he underwent a conversion in which, as he later put it, 'there came into my soul, and was diffused through it, a sense of the glory of the Divine Being' (Edwards, 1974, vol. 1, p. xiii). To communicate this divine glory became the burden of his life as pastor and theologian. Edwards served briefly as the minister of a Presbyterian church in New York City (1722–3) and a tutor at Yale College (1724–6), before in 1726 beginning his long association with the Congregationalist church in Northampton, Massachusetts. In July 1727 Edwards married Sarah Pierrepont of New Haven. Later he wrote that his wife attained intuitively the deeper sense of God for which he was forced to labour. Under Edwards's preaching, Northampton experienced waves of revivals in 1734–5 and again in 1740–2. Edwards's commitment to revival led him to publish the diary of David Brainerd, a family friend who as missionary to native American Indians exemplified what Edwards considered an ideal form of revitalized spirituality. This work has never been out of print since it appeared in 1749.

In 1750 Edwards was dismissed from his pulpit in Northampton when he offended prominent members of the community by insisting that their children make a creditable testimony of saving faith before being admitted as full members. Thereafter he lived with his large family in frontier Stockbridge, Massachusetts, where he preached to native Americans and pastored a small English congregation while also writing many of the treatises for which he won theological renown. Edwards died from an inoculation against smallpox on 22 March 1758, only weeks after beginning his service as the president of Princeton College.

Edwards's theology was constructed out of a lifelong and intimate study of the Scriptures. It also took shape in self-conscious dialogue with many of the most notable intellectual figures of his day, including John Locke, Isaac Newton, the Cambridge Platonist Henry More, and proponents of the eighteenth century's new affective ethics like the Third Earl of Shaftesbury and Francis Hutcheson. Although Edwards claimed not to study Calvin or other classic Protestants of the Reformation era, he was familiar with the major arguments from that period as well.

The unifying centre of Edwards's theology was the glory of God depicted as an active, harmonious, ever unfolding source of absolutely perfect Being marked by supernal beauty and love. The dynamic activity of the Godhead, especially as manifest in the Trinity, was ever in the forefront of his work. Against the melioristic trends of the eighteenth century, Edwards defended Augustinian convictions about the lostness of humanity and the need for divine grace to initiate the process of redemption. Yet with the spirit of his age, Edwards also promoted an affectional view of reality in which 'the sense of the heart' (one of his favourite phrases) was foundational for thought and action alike. The cast of Edwards's mind was relentlessly intellectual – 'many theorems, that appeared hard and barren to others, were to him pleasant and fruitful fields, where his mind would expatiate with peculiar ease, profit and entertainment', was the way his friend and student, Samuel Hopkins, put it (Edwards, 1957– , vol. 8, *Ethical Writings*, p. 401). As a result, his theological convictions were worked out in abstruse metaphysical questions as well as in response to more ordinary theological challenges. As a revivalist, Edwards shared the burden of George Whitefield for the conversion of the lost. As a promoter of holiness, Edwards shared (despite radical philosophical and major theological differences) points of contact with John Wesley (who edited some of Edwards's writings for publication in Britain). But as a Christian thinker, Edwards most resembled the Catholic, Nicole Malebranche, and the Anglican, George Berkeley, who also developed forms of theistic idealism in response to what they perceived as the materialist drift of their age.

Edwards's career as a publishing theologian began with his *Narrative of Surprising Conversions*, a work first written as a letter in 1736 to explain the course of revival in Northampton. Soon the rather breathless tone of this work gave way to more discriminating analyses in *Some Thoughts Concerning the Present Revival of Religion in New England* of 1743 and *A Treatise on the Religious Affections* of 1746. These works drew upon Edwards's experience in the revival to argue that true religion was a matter of the affections, or what might today be called habitual inclinations at the core of a person's being. *Religious Affections* detailed at length the kinds of religious emotions that were largely irrelevant to a determination of true spirituality (such as those manifesting a particular intensity). Rather, true spirituality could be shown by twelve 'marks' of affectional attachment to God, of which the last and most definite was consistent Christian practice.

The soteriology that lay beyond Edwards's analysis of revival was consistently Calvinistic. He held that the root of human sinfulness was antagonism towards God. Living faith involved much more than facts about God, but rather a new 'taste' of divine beauty, holiness, and truth. The fullest treatment of this soteriology came in 1754 when he published *A Careful and Strict Inquiry into the Modern Prevailing Notions of that Freedom of Will, Which is Supposed to be Essential to Moral Agency, Virtue and Vice, Reward and Punishment, Praise and Blame*. Here Edwards argued that the 'will' was not an independent faculty but only a way of talking about a person's choices. To 'will' something was to act consistently with one's character and in accord with the strongest motives acting on a person. Edwards laboured to show that eighteenth-century arguments for the indeterminacy of the will could be reduced either to a nonsensical infinite regression (since no action could be uncaused) or to amoral randomness (since a 'free will' in the sense defined by Edwards's opponents would have no connection with the moral character of the one who willed). The minute care with which Edwards attacked the notion of distinct human faculties and with which he linked volition to character made this work a landmark for theologians in America and Scotland for over a century.

A treatise published posthumously in 1758, *Original Sin*, expanded on the view of human nature present in *Freedom of the Will*. By suggesting that all humanity took part seminally in Adam's fall, Edwards hoped to show that individuals were both responsible for their own sinfulness and bound by a fallen nature until converted by God's sovereign grace. The questions raised by this work established the terms for discussing fallen human nature with which American Calvinists – both New Divinity Congregationalists like Edwards Amasa Park and Princeton Presbyterians like Charles Hodge – struggled until the mid-nineteenth century.

While he was busy with pastoral duties and publications on conventional theological topics, Edwards also continued to read widely in the era's scientific and philosophical literature and to record extensive private notations in his journals. With the transcription of these materials and their (still incomplete) publication in the twentieth century, students of Edwards can chart an impressive metaphysic that represented a speculative counterpart to the theocentricism of his other work.

Edwards was fascinated by the discoveries of Newton and his successors. Yet, fearing the drift of such ideas into materialism, he argued that the laws of science were not self-subsisting. Rather, they were products of God's self-conscious intellectual activity. Edwards was not threatened by the discoveries of science because he felt they revealed the regularity, harmony, and beauty of the Divine Being. A division between the spiritual and the material was as uncongenial to the pattern of Edwards's thought as it was commonplace in the Enlightenment more generally. To Edwards, progress in science showed more about the character of God than it did about the character of the physical universe since, as he wrote in extensive notes on the mind, 'that which truly is the substance of all bodies is the infinitely exact and precise and perfectly stable idea in God's mind, together with his stable will that the same shall gradually be communicated to us, and to other minds, according to certain fixed and exact established methods and laws' (1957– , vol. 6, *Scientific and Philosophical Writings*, p. 344).

Edwards's ethics showed the same concern for establishing God as the foundation. Behaviour that was moral in the strictest sense of the term arose, in his view, only from a heart regenerated by God's mercy. This case was made fully in *The Nature of True Virtue*, which was published posthumously in 1765, but it was also a persistent theme in many sermons and several other treatises. Edwards agreed with contemporary moralists like Shaftesbury and Hutcheson that humans possessed a natural capacity for recognizing morality and following the internal 'moral sense'. But he also contended that this kind of morality was inevitably prudential, pragmatic and ultimately an expression of self-love. Such socially useful behaviour fell far short of true virtue, since "tis evident that true virtue must chiefly consist in love to God, the Being of beings, infinitely the greatest and best of beings' (1957– , vol. 8, *Ethical Writings*, p. 550).

Edwards's thought was never without criticism or opposition. The respected Boston minister, Charles Chauncey, scoured the New England countryside to collect accounts of enthusiasm run amok during the Great Awakening. Edwards's younger contemporary, James Dana, thoughtfully challenged the model of human nature in his *Freedom of the Will*. Even the theologians who succeeded Edwards in New England, like his grandson Timothy Dwight and Dwight's famous pupil Nathaniel William Taylor, first professor of theology at Yale, felt that contemporary expressions of liberty (like those defined in America's War of Independence) made it necessary to modify Edwards's Augustinian accounts of depravity and regeneration. In the generations following his death, Edwards was more bypassed than refuted, but his thought nonetheless continued to win admirers (like H. Richard Niebuhr in the twentieth century), even in periods when American culture was preoccupied with material progress or secular liberation.

The contemporary revival of interest in Edwards, where the number of doctoral dissertations and academic essays has more than doubled every decade for the last half-century, may be dated from the publication of an intellectual biography in 1949 by Perry Miller, a Harvard professor of English who was America's most penetrating cultural historian at mid-century. This revival has been fuelled by a diverse combination of influences, including philosophers intrigued by Edwards's ethical arguments, dedicated proponents of Calvinism like Martin Lloyd-Jones in Britain and John Gerstner in America, the learned editors of the Yale edition and a full complement of academics, both secular (like Miller himself) and Christian, for whom the breadth of Edwards's vision, no less than the depth of individual themes in his work, remain a bracing rebuke to the material- and human-centred preoccupations of the late twentieth century.

See also FUNDAMENTALISM; PROTESTANT THEOLOGY: USA.

Bibliography

Writings

1957- : *The Works of Jonathan Edwards*, 9 vols to date. New Haven, CT: Yale University Press (definitive texts with editorial commentaries that are now the best introductions to Edwards's thought):
vol. 1, 1957: *Freedom of the Will*, ed. Paul Ramsey [1754];
vol. 2, 1959: *Religious Affections*, ed. John E. Smith [1746];
vol. 3, 1970: *Original Sin*, ed. Clyde A. Holbrook [1758];
vol. 4, 1972: *The Great Awakening*, ed. C.C. Goen [1736–42];
vol. 5, 1977: *Apocalyptic Writings*, ed. Stephen J. Stein [1747];
vol. 6, 1980: *Scientific and Philosophical Writings*, ed. Wallace E. Anderson [unpublished earlier];
vol. 7, 1985: *The Life of David Brainerd*, ed. Norman Pettit [1749];
vol. 8, 1989: *Ethical Writings*, ed. Paul Ramsey [1765, 1852];
vol. 9, 1989: *A History of the Work of Redemption*, ed. John F. Wilson [sermons].
1962: *Jonathan Edwards: Selections*, revised edn, ed. Clarence H. Faust and Thomas H. Johnson. New York: Hill and Wang (the best one-volume anthology).
1974: *The Works of Jonathan Edwards*, 2 vols. Edinburgh: Banner of Truth (a handy small-print edition reprinting the 1834 London edition and including a useful memoir by Sereno E. Dwight from 1829).

Critical works

Fiering, Norman 1981: *Jonathan Edwards's Moral Thought and Its British Context*. Chapel Hill, NC: University of North Carolina Press.
Hatch, Nathan O., and Stout, Harry S., eds 1988: *Jonathan Edwards and the American Experience*. New York: Oxford University Press.
Miller, Perry 1949: *Jonathan Edwards*. New York: W. Sloane Associates.
Simonson, Harold P. 1974: *Jonathan Edwards: Theology of the Heart*. Grand Rapids: Eerdmans.

MARK A. NOLL

Einstein, Albert (1879–1955) German-American scientist and philosopher. Born of a Jewish family in Germany, he studied in Zurich. Five revolutionary papers published in the *Annalen der Physik* transformed the course of an otherwise seemingly average career and marked him out as a scientific genius. In them he outlined, among other discoveries, his new theory of relativity, which defined the precise relationship between a particle's energy and its mass and overturned previous Newtonian 'certainties'. He held a succession of academic posts in Zurich, Prague and Berlin, before emigrating to the USA in 1935 and accepting a post at the Institute for Advanced Study at Princeton, where he worked intermittently for the rest of his life. The remainder of his life was spent attempting to construct an alternative theory to the principle of indeterminacy: 'What I'm really interested in is whether God could have made the world in a different way; that is, whether the necessity of logical simplicity leaves any freedom at all.' Although not formally religious, he did not accept a theory that would 'compel God to throw dice'. For him, the universe was essentially rational. However, the principle of indeterminacy is now widely accepted. His views on religion are outlined in the essay 'Science and Religion', now contained in his books *Out of my Later Years* (1950) and *Ideas and Opinions* (1954).

See also PHYSICAL SCIENCE AND CHRISTIAN THOUGHT.

Bibliography

Clark, R.W. 1973: *Einstein: His Life and Times*. London.
Pais, A. 1982: '*Subtle is the Lord . . .*': *The Science and the Life of Albert Einstein*. Oxford.
Paul, I. 1982: *Science, Theology and Einstein*. New York and Belfast.

Eliot, George (Mary Ann, later Marian, Evans) (1819–1880)   English novelist. As a girl she was converted in the evangelical tradition; under the influence of religious humanism and the ideas of liberal freethinkers she gradually relinquished her early faith. Largely self-taught and increasingly a major figure on the London literary scene, she published her first book in 1846. This was a translation of D.F. Strauss's *Life of Jesus* of 1835–6, a critical biography which found the character of the Gospel accounts to be mythological rather than historical. In 1854 she published a translation of Ludwig Feuerbach's *The Essence of Christianity* of 1841, which concluded that God is not a transcendental reality but a projection of man's aspiration to perfection – a view which Eliot shared. However, her fiction retained a strong interest in traditional religious and moral themes and she used Christian language and imagery as vehicles for exploring humanistic philosophical ideas. Christianity is sympathetically portrayed in, for instance, *Scenes of Clerical Life* (1858) and in *Adam Bede* (1859), whose heroine is a Methodist woman preacher. Other novels include *The Mill on the Floss* (1860), *Silas Marner* (1861) and *Middlemarch* (1871–2), and their success established her reputation as a novelist in her own lifetime.

Bibliography

Haight, G.S. 1968: *George Eliot: A Biography*. Oxford and New York.

Loades, A. 1984: Middlemarch as a religious novel. In *Images of Belief in Literature*, ed. D. Jasper. New York.

Paris, B.J. 1970: George Eliot's religion of humanity. In *George Eliot: A Collection of Critical Essays*, ed. G.R. Creeger. Englewood Cliffs, NJ.

Eliot, T[homas] S[tearns] (1888–1965) Anglo-American poet, playwright and critic. Born in St Louis, Missouri, he emigrated to England in 1914 and was naturalized in 1927. His education at Harvard, the Sorbonne and Merton College, Oxford, was followed by stints as a schoolteacher and with Lloyds Bank before his literary career developed, first as a critic and editor, and, increasingly, as a poet and playwright. Early works such as *Prufrock* (1917), *Poems* (1919) and *The Waste Land* (1922) reflect his period of agnosticism, when he was preoccupied with the alienation, fragmentation and rootlessness of modern society. His innovative style embodied his meaning through the use of fragment, rhythmic suggestion and allusion. From 1925 he moved towards Anglo-Catholicism, and his religious poems, principally *Ash Wednesday* (1930) and *Four Quartets* (1944), counterpoise modern style and concerns with a strong sense of tradition that includes the Christian mystics, Dante, the metaphysical poets and French symbolism. His plays, including *Murder in the Cathedral* (1935) and *The Cocktail Party* (1950), explore the relationship of the spiritual and the social/historical; his religious and social reflections are contained in *The Idea of a Christian Society* (1939) and *Notes Towards the Definition of Culture* (1948).

Bibliography

Braybrooke, N., ed. 1958: *T.S. Eliot: A Symposium for his 70th birthday*. London.

Bush, R. 1984: *T.S. Eliot: A Study in Character and Style*. Oxford and New York.

Smidt, K. 1961: *Poetry and Belief in the Work of T.S. Eliot*. London.

Ellul, Jacques (b.1912) French social scientist and Reformed lay theologian. For many years professor at the Institute of Political Studies in the University of Bordeaux, he has written on history, sociology, social criticism, biblical studies and ethics. Ellul challenged optimistic presuppositions about scientific progress and developing secularization. He saw mankind as increasingly dominated by the principle of the technical and championed personal freedom over and against complex modern authority structures which are in danger of controlling mankind collectively and depriving the individual of contact with God. In *The Meaning of Christ in the City* (trans. 1970) he presents the city as a paradigm of modern civilization, creating security and defence systems as a replacement for the divine, and he looks forward to the establishment of a new city ruled by God, the New Jerusalem. His works, which show the influence of Karl Barth, include commentaries on Jonah, 2 Kings and the apocalypse. They include *The Technological Society* (trans. 1964), *The Politics of God and the Politics of Man* (trans. 1972) and *The Ethics of Freedom* (trans. 1976).

Bibliography

Christians, C.G., and Hook, J.M. van 1981: *Jacques Ellul, Interpretation Essays*. Champaigne, Ill.

Hanks, J.M., with Asal, R. 1984: *Jacques Ellul: A Comprehensive Bibliography*. London.

Emerson, Ralph Waldo (1803–1882) North American thinker and poet. A Unitarian minister, he resigned from his Boston church in 1832 because of his unorthodox theological views and devoted his life to writing and lecturing. In 1833 he met S.T. Coleridge and W. Wordsworth and became a close friend of Thomas Carlyle; other influences include E. Swedenborg and, through Coleridge, I. Kant and the German romantics. He was a major figure in the development of modern American literature; his works include *Nature* (1838), two series of *Essays* (1841 and 1844) and *Representative Man* (1850). His teaching, although unsystematic, combined rationalism and mysticism and had popular appeal. He was a transcendentalist (although he did not use the term) in holding that 'the highest revelation of God is in every man'; to imitate Christ is to share 'a faith like Christ's in the infinitude of man'. Redemption is not dependent on the events of traditional historical Christianity; rather each human carries within himself the capacity for his own redemption. His was an essentially optimistic doctrine of self-reliance, stressing ethical religion and calling for a break with cultural and religious tradition: 'Imitation is suicide.'

Bibliography
Allen, G.W. 1981: *Waldo Emerson: A Biography.*
Carpenter, F.I. ed. 1934: *R.W. Emerson: Representative Selections.* New York.
Emerson Whicher, S. 1971: *Freedom and Fate: An Inner Life of R.W. Emerson.* Philadelphia.

Enlightenment   The term 'Enlightenment', which passed into general circulation only in the closing decades of the nineteenth century, remains resistant to precise definition. Any number of such definitions of the movement can be offered; these have all proved unsatisfactory, on account of their reductionist tendencies. It is a loose term, defying precise definition, embracing a cluster of ideas and attitudes characteristic of the period 1720–80, such as the free and constructive use of reason in an attempt to demolish old myths which were seen to have bound individuals and societies to the oppression of the past. If there is any common element underlying the movement, it perhaps lies more in *how* those who were sympathetic to its outlook thought than in *what* they thought.

The term 'Age of Reason', often used as a synonym for the Enlightenment, is seductively misleading, in that it implies that reason had been hitherto ignored or marginalized. In one sense, the Middle Ages was just as much an 'Age of Reason' as the Enlightenment; the crucial difference lay in the manner in which reason was used, and the limits which were understood to be imposed upon it. Nor was the eighteenth century consistently rational in every aspect. In fact, the Enlightenment is now recognized to be intellectually heterogeneous, including a remarkable variety of anti-rational movements such as Mesmerism or Masonic rituals. Nevertheless, an emphasis upon the ability of human reason to penetrate the mysteries of the world is rightly regarded as a defining characteristic of 'Enlightenment'.

The term 'rationalism' should also be used with caution when referring to the Enlightenment. In the first place, it should be noted that the term is often used in an uncritical and inaccurate way, designating the general atmosphere of optimism, grounded in a belief in scientific and social progress, which pervades much of the writing of the period. This use of the term is confusing, and should be avoided. Rationalism, in its proper sense, is perhaps best defined as the doctrine that the external world can be known by reason, and reason alone. This doctrine, which is characteristic of earlier writers such as R. Descartes, G.W. von Leibniz, B. Spinoza and C. Wolff, was subjected to intense criticism during the later eighteenth century, as the influence of John Locke's empiricist epistemology became widespread. Immanuel Kant, often protrayed as an exponent of the sufficiency of pure reason, is aware of its limitations. The epistemology developed in the *Critique of Pure Reason* of 1781 may be regarded as an attempt to synthesize the insights of rationalism and empiricism. This work may be regarded as bringing the early period of rationalism to a close. Despite according a particularly significant role to reason in his thought (as seen in *Religion within the Limits of Reason Alone*), Kant showed a keen appreciation of the implications of the empiricist emphasis upon sense experience. Nevertheless, rationalist attitudes persisted well into the nineteenth century, and constitute an important element of the general Enlightenment critique of Christianity.

The Enlightenment ushered in a period of considerable uncertainty for Christianity in western Europe and North America. The trauma of the Reformation and the resulting Wars of Religion had barely subsided on the continent of Europe, before a new and more radical challenge to Christianity arose. If the sixteenth-century Reformation challenged the church to rethink its external forms and the manner in which it expressed its beliefs, the Enlightenment saw the intellectual credentials of Christianity itself (rather than any one of its specific forms) facing a major threat on a number of fronts. The origins of this challenge may be traced back to the seventeenth century, with the rise of CARTESIANISM on the continent of Europe, and the growing influence of DEISM in England. The growing emphasis upon the need to uncover the rational roots of religion had considerable negative implications for Christianity, as subsequent events were to prove (see ATHEISM; EPISTEMOLOGY, RELIGIOUS).

The Enlightenment and Protestantism
It was Protestant, rather than Roman Catholic or Eastern Orthodox, theology which was especially open to influence from the new currents of thought which arose from the Enlightenment and its aftermath. Four main factors have been noted which may explain this observation, at least in part.

1 The relative weakness of Protestant ecclesiastical institutions. The absence of an authoritarian centralized structure, such as the papacy, meant that national or regional Protestant churches were able to respond to local circumstances, intellectual and political, with a far greater freedom than Roman Catholicism. Similarly, until quite recently individual Protestant thinkers experienced a degree of academic freedom denied to their Roman Catholic colleagues; the spirit of creative freedom which characterized Protestantism from its outset thus expressed itself in theological creativity and originality quite impossible for others.

2 The nature of Protestantism itself. While the 'essence of Protestantism' remains disputed, there is agreement that a spirit of protest is part of the birthright of the movement. The Protestant predisposition to challenge religious authority, and the commitment to the principle *ecclesia reformata, ecclesia semper reformanda* ('the reformed church must always be the church which is reforming itself'), encouraged a spirit of critical enquiry concerning Christian dogma. This attitude resonated with the ideals of the Enlightenment, leading to an alignment of many Protestant writers with the movement, and a willingness to absorb its methods and outlooks.

3 The relation of Protestantism and the universities. From its inception, Protestantism recognized the importance of higher education in the training of its ministers. The foundation of the Genevan Academy and Harvard College are obvious illustrations of this point. During the late sixteenth and early seventeenth centuries, the Lutheran and Reformed churches in Germany established university faculties of theology as a means of ensuring a constant supply of well educated clergy. During the eighteenth century, political protest was stifled in Germany; the only means by which radicalism could express itself was intellectual. The German universities thus become centres of revolt against the Old Regime. As a result, German university theologians (who were virtually entirely Protestant) aligned themselves with the Enlightenment, where the more conservative church leadership tended to side with the Old Regime. Radicalism was thus able to express itself theologically, at the level of ideas. Although apparently unable to achieve any significant social, political or ecclesiastical change, radicalism was able to mount a significant challenge to the ideas which undergirded the churches. Protestant theology was thus significantly affected by the methods of the Enlightenment, where Roman Catholic theology was not.

4 The varying local impact of the Enlightenment. It must be stressed that the Enlightenment was not a chronologically uniform movement. Although well established in western central Europe by the eighteenth century, the Enlightenment cannot really be said to have taken hold in Russia or the countries of southern Europe (such as Spain, Italy or Greece) until the late nineteenth or early twentieth century. Such countries were the strongholds of Roman Catholicism or Eastern Orthodoxy. In consequence, theologians of these churches did not feel under pressure to respond to the intellectual forces which were of

such major significance in regions historically associated with Protestantism.

The Enlightenment critique of Christianity: general overview

The Enlightenment criticism of traditional Christianity was based upon the principle of the omnicompetence of human reason. A number of stages in the development of this belief may be discerned. First, it was argued that the beliefs of Christianity were rational, and thus capable of standing up to critical examination. This type of approach may be found in John Locke's *Reasonableness of Christianity* of 1695, and within the early Wolffian school in Germany. Christianity was a reasonable supplement to natural religion. The notion of divine revelation (see REVELATION, CONCEPT OF) was thus maintained.

Second, it was argued that the basic ideas of Christianity, being rational, could be derived from reason itself. There was no need to invoke the idea of divine revelation. As this idea was developed by John Toland in his *Christianity not Mysterious* of 1696 and Matthew Tindal's *Christianity as Old as Creation* of 1730, Christianity was essentially the republication of the religion of nature. It did not transcend natural religion, but was merely an example of it. All so-called 'revealed religion' is actually nothing other than the reconfirmation of what can be known through rational reflection on nature. In Germany, this view found support among *Neologen* such as J.A. Ernesti, J.D. Michaelis, J.S. Semler and J.J. Spalding; 'Revelation' was simply a rational reaffirmation of moral truths already available to enlightened reason.

Third, the ability of reason to judge revelation was affirmed. As critical reason was omnicompetent, it was argued that it was supremely qualified to judge Christian beliefs and practices, with a view to eliminating any irrational or superstitious elements. This view, associated with H.S. Reimarus in Germany and the *philosophes* in France, placed reason firmly above revelation, and may be seen as symbolized in the enthronement of the Goddess of Reason in Notre Dame de Paris in 1793.

The Enlightenment was a European and American phenomenon, and thus took place in cultures in which the most numerically sig-

nificant form of religion was Christianity. This historical observation is of importance: the Enlightenment critique of religion in general was often particularized as a criticism of Christianity. It was Christian doctrines which were subjected to a critical assessment of a vigour without any precedent. It was Christian sacred writings which were subjected to an unprecedented critical scrutiny, both literary and historical, the Bible being treated 'as if it were any other book' (Benjamin Jowett). It was the history of Jesus of Nazareth which was subjected to critical reconstruction.

While every generalization is dangerous, there are excellent reasons for suggesting that the Enlightenment witnessed growing sympathy for the notion of 'natural' or 'rational' religion. This approach is illustrated in the title of Matthew Tindal's highly influential work, *Christianity as Old as Creation, or, The Gospel a Republication of the Religion of Nature* of 1730. On the basis of the foundational Enlightenment assumption of the rationality of reality, and the ability of human beings to uncover and apprehend this rationality, it was argued that whatever lay behind the various world religions was ultimately rational in character, and thus capable of being uncovered, described and analysed by human reason.

The idea of a universal rational religion was, however, at odds with the diversity of the world religions. As European knowledge of these religions deepened, through the growth of the genre of 'voyager literature', and the increasing availability of Chinese, Indian, Persian and Vedic religious writings, it became increasingly clear that the notion of a universal religion of reason faced difficulties when confronted with the evidence of the astonishing variety of human religious beliefs and practices. Many Enlightenment writers, perhaps more concerned with championing reason than with wrestling with the empirical evidence, developed a theory of religion which accounted for this diversity, at least in part.

In his *True Intellectual System of the Universe* of 1678, Ralph Cudworth argued that all religions were ultimately based upon a common ethical monotheism – a simple religion of nature, basically ethical in character, and devoid of all the arbitrary doctrines and religious rites of Christianity or Judaism. The primordial rational religion of nature had become corrupted through its early interpreters. One theory which gained an especially wide hearing was that the religions were essentially the inventions of cultic leaders or priests, whose main motivation was the preservation of their own interests. The Roman historian Tacitus had suggested (*Histories*, Book 5) that Moses invented the Jewish religious rites as a means of ensuring religious cohesion after the expulsion from Egypt; many writers of the early Enlightenment developed this notion, arguing that the variety of human religious rites and practices were simply human inventions in response to specific historical situations, now firmly in the past. The way was open to the recovery of the universal primordial religion of nature, which would put an end to the religious squabbles of humanity.

The Enlightenment also witnessed the development of a rudimentary psychology of religion, as seen in a developed form in David Hume's *Natural History of Religion* of 1757. (Although the term 'psychology' was introduced in the sixteenth century by Goclenius, it failed to achieve general acceptance until the eighteenth.) In his *Natural History of Superstition* of 1709, John Trenchard developed the idea of the inherent credulity of humanity, which permitted natural monotheism to degenerate into the various religious traditions of humanity. The enthusiasm with which this idea was received can be judged from the comments of the *Independent Whig* (31 December 1720), to the effect that 'the peculiar Foible of Mankind is Superstition, or an intrinsick and pannick Fear of invisible and unknown Beings.' For Trenchard, the religions represented the triumph of superstition over reason. By eliminating such superstitious beliefs and rites, a return to the universal and simple religion of nature could be achieved. A similar idea was developed during the French Enlightenment by Paul Henri Thiry, Baron d'Holbach, who argued (for example, in his *La contagion sacrée, ou, Histoire naturelle de la superstition* of 1768) that religion was a form of pathological disorder.

The Enlightenment attitude to religion was subject to regional variation, reflecting a number of local factors peculiar to different situations. One of the most important such factors is the movement generally known as pietism, perhaps best known in its English form of METHODISM. This movement placed considerable emphasis upon the experiential aspects of religion (for example, see John Wesley's notion of 'experiential religion'). This concern for religious experience served to make Christianity relevant and accessible to the experiential situation of the masses, contrasting sharply with the intellectualism of, for example, Lutheran orthodoxy, which was perceived to be an irrelevance. Pietism forged a strong link between Christian faith and experience, thus making Christianity a matter of the heart, as well as of the mind.

Pietism was well established in Germany by the end of the seventeenth century, whereas the movement only developed in England during the eighteenth century, and in France not at all. The Enlightenment thus preceded the rise of pietism in England, with the result that the great evangelical revivals of the eighteenth century significantly blunted the influence of rationalism upon religion. In Germany, however, the Enlightenment followed after the rise of pietism, and thus developed in a situation which had been significantly shaped by religious faith, even if it would pose a serious challenge to its received forms and ideas. (Interestingly, English deism began to become influential in Germany at roughly the same time as German pietism began to exert influence in England.) The most significant intellectual forces in the German Enlightenment were thus directed towards the reshaping (rather than the rejection or demolition) of the Christian faith. In France, however, Christianity was widely perceived as both oppressive and irrelevant, with the result that the *philosophes* were able to advocate the total rejection of Christianity as an archaic and discredited belief system. In his *Traité de la tolérance*, Diderot argued that English deism had compromised itself, permitting religion to survive where it ought to have been eradicated totally.

The Enlightenment critique of Christianity: specific areas of theology

Having outlined the general principles of the Enlightenment challenge to traditional Christian thought, it is now appropriate to explore how these impacted on specific matters of doctrine. The rational religion of the Enlightenment found itself in conflict with six major areas of traditional Christian theology.

Miracles Much traditional Christian apologetic concerning the identity and significance of Jesus Christ was based upon the 'miraculous evidences' of the New Testament, culminating in the resurrection. The new emphasis upon the mechanical regularity and orderliness of the universe, perhaps the most significant intellectual legacy of Newtonianism, raised doubts concerning the New Testament accounts of miraculous happenings. Hume's *Essay on Miracles* of 1748 was widely regarded as demonstrating the evidential impossibility of miracles. Hume emphasized that there were no contemporary analogues of New Testament miracles, such as the resurrection, thus forcing the New Testament reader to rely totally upon human testimony to such miracles. For Hume, it was axiomatic that no human testimony was adequate to establish the occurrence of a miracle, in the absence of a present-day analogue. Reimarus and G.E. Lessing denied that human testimony to a past event (such as the resurrection) was sufficient to make it credible if it appeared to be contradicted by present-day direct experience, no matter how well documented the original event may have been.

Similarly, Diderot declared that if the entire population of Paris were to assure him that a dead man had just been raised from the dead, he would not believe a word of it. This growing scepticism concerning the 'miraculous evidences' of the New Testament forced traditional Christianity to defend the doctrine of the divinity of Christ on grounds other than miracles – which, at the time, it proved singularly incapable of doing. Of course, it must be noted that other religions claiming miraculous evidences were subjected to equally great sceptical criticism by the Enlightenment: Christianity happened to be singled out for particular comment on account of its religious domination of the cultural milieu in which the Enlightenment developed.

Revelation The concept of revelation was of central importance to traditional Christian theology. While many Christian theologians (such as Thomas Aquinas and John Calvin) recognized the possibility of a natural knowledge of God, they insisted that this required supplementation by supernatural divine revelation, such as that witnessed to in Scripture. The Enlightenment witnessed the development of an increasingly critical attitude to the very idea of supernatural revelation, a trend which culminated in works such as J.G. Fichte's *Versuch einer Kritik aller Offenbarung* of 1792. In part, this new critical attitude was also due to the Enlightenment depreciation of history. For Lessing, there was an 'ugly great ditch' between history and reason. Revelation took place in history – but of what value were the contingent truths of history in comparison with the necessary truths of reason? The *philosophes* in particular asserted that history could at best confirm the truths of reason, but was incapable of establishing those truths in the first place. Truths about God were timeless, open to investigation by human reason but not capable of being disclosed in 'events' such as the history of Jesus of Nazareth (see FAITH AND HISTORY).

Original sin The idea that human nature is in some sense flawed or corrupted, expressed in the orthodox doctrine of original sin, was vigorously opposed by the Enlightenment (see SOTERIOLOGY). Voltaire and Jean-Jacques Rousseau criticized the doctrine as encouraging pessimism in regard to human abilities, thus impeding human social and political development and encouraging *laissez-faire* attitudes. German Enlightenment thinkers tended to criticize the doctrine on account of its historical origins in the thought of Augustine of Hippo (354–430), which they regarded as invalidating its permanent validity and relevance. The rejection of original sin was of considerable importance, as the Christian doctrine of redemption rested upon the assumption that humanity required to be liberated from bondage to original sin. For the Enlightenment, it was the *idea* of original sin itself which was oppressive, and from which humanity required liberation. This intellectual liberation was provided by the Enlightenment critique of the doctrine.

The problem of evil The Enlightenment witnessed a fundamental change in attitude towards the existence of evil in the world. For the medieval period, the existence of evil was not regarded as posing a threat to the coherence of Christianity. The contradictions between a benevolent divine omnipotence and the existence of evil were not regarded as an obstacle to belief, but simply as an academic theological problem. The Enlightenment saw this situation changing radically: the existence of evil metamorphosed into a challenge to the credibility and coherence of Christian faith itself. Voltaire's *Candide* was one of many works to highlight the difficulties caused for the Christian world view by the existence of natural evil (such as the famous Lisbon earthquake). The term 'theodicy', coined by G.W. von Leibniz, derives from this period, reflecting a growing recognition that the existence of evil was assuming a new significance within the Enlightenment critique of religion (see EVIL, PROBLEM OF).

The status and interpretation of Scripture Within orthodox Christianity, whether Protestant or Roman Catholic, the Bible was still widely regarded as a divinely inspired source of doctrine and morals, to be differentiated from other types of literature. The Enlightenment saw this assumption called into question, with the rise of the critical approach to Scripture. Developing ideas already current within deism, the theologians of the German Enlightenment developed the thesis that the Bible was the work of many hands, at times demonstrating internal contradiction, and that it was open to precisely the same method of textual analysis and interpretation as any other type of literature. These ideas may be seen in developed forms in works such as J.A. Ernesti's *Anweisung für den Ausleger des Neuen Testaments* of 1761 and J.J. Semler's *Abhandlung von der freien Untersuchung des Kanons* of 1771. The effect of these developments was to weaken still further the concept of 'supernatural revelation' and call into question the permanent significance of these foundational documents of the Christian faith (see BIBLICAL CRITICISM AND INTERPRETATION 1: OLD TESTAMENT and 2: NEW TESTAMENT).

The identity and significance of Jesus Christ A final area in which the Enlightenment made a significant challenge to orthodox Christian belief concerns the person of Jesus of Nazareth. Two particularly important developments may be noted: the origins of the 'quest of the historical Jesus', and the rise of the 'moral theory of the atonement' (see HISTORICAL JESUS, QUEST OF and SOTERIOLOGY).

Both deism and the German Enlightenment developed the thesis that there was a serious discrepancy between the real Jesus of history and the New Testament interpretation of his significance. Underlying the New Testament portrait of the supernatural redeemer of humanity lurked a simple human figure, a glorified teacher of common sense. While a supernatural redeemer was unacceptable to Enlightenment rationalism, the idea of an enlightened moral teacher was not. This idea, developed with particular rigour by Reimarus, suggested that it was possible to go behind the New Testament accounts of Jesus and uncover a simpler, more human Jesus, who would be acceptable to the new spirit of the age. And so the quest for the real and more credible 'Jesus of history' began. Although this quest would ultimately end in failure, the later Enlightenment regarded this 'quest' as holding the key to the credibility of Jesus within the context of a rational natural religion. Jesus' moral authority resided in the quality of his teaching and religious personality, rather than in the unacceptable orthodox suggestion that he was God incarnate (see INCARNATION).

The second area in which the ideas of orthodoxy concerning Jesus were challenged concerned the significance of his death. For orthodoxy, Jesus' death on the cross was interpreted from the standpoint of the resurrection (which the Enlightenment was not prepared to accept as a historical event) as a way in which God was able to forgive the sins of humanity. The Enlightenment saw this 'theory of the atonement' being subjected to increasing criticism, as involving arbitrary and unacceptable hypotheses such as original sin. Jesus' death on the cross was reinterpreted in terms of a supreme moral example of self-giving and dedication, intended to inspire similar dedication and self-giving on the part of his followers. Where orthodox Christianity tended to treat Jesus' death (and resurrection) as possessing greater inherent importance than his religious teaching, the Enlightenment marginalized his death and denied his resurrection, in order to emphasize the quality of his moral teaching.

It will thus be clear that the dawn of the Enlightenment represented a major new challenge to Christian theology, obliging it to engage with questions which hitherto had not featured prominently, if at all, on its agenda. The Enlightenment set the parameters for future Christian discussion, not just of the *nature* but also of the *plausibility* of its theological heritage. Although the credibility of the Enlightenment world view, especially its emphasis upon the total adequacy of human reason, has been severely challenged through the recognition of the non-universal character of human rationality and the social mediation of traditions of discourse and reasoning, the Enlightenment continues to remain a fundamental reference point for modern Christian thought.

See also CHRISTOLOGY; DOCTRINE AND DOGMA; GOD; MODERNISM.

Bibliography

Cragg, G.R. 1964: *Reason and Authority in the Eighteenth Century*. Cambridge: Cambridge University Press.

Dyson, A.O. 1982: Theological legacies of the Enlightenment: England and Germany. In *England and Germany: Studies in Theological Diplomacy*, ed. S.W. Sykes. Frankfurt and Berne: Verlag Peter Lang, pp. 45–62.

Flew, A. 1961: *Hume's Philosophy of Belief: A Study of His First Inquiry*. New York: Humanities Press.

Frei, Hans 1977: *The Eclipse of Biblical Narrative: A Study in Eighteenth and Nineteenth Century Biblical Hermeneutics*. New Haven and London: Yale University Press.

Gay, Peter 1973: *The Enlightenment, an Interpretation*, 2 vols. London: Wildwood House.

McGrath, Alister E. 1986: The Enlightenment. In *The History of Christian Theology I: The Science of Theology*, ed. Paul Avis. Grand Rapids: Eerdmans, pp. 206–29.

Michalson, Gordon E. 1985: *Lessing's Ugly Ditch: A Study of Theology and History*. University Park: Pennsylvania State University Press.

Pelikan, Jaroslav 1985: *Jesus through the Centuries: His Place in the History of Culture*. New York: Harper and Row, pp. 182–93.

Schweitzer, Albert [1906] 1981: *The Quest of the Historical Jesus: A Critical Study of Its Progress from Reimarus to Wrede*, trans. London: SCM Press, pp. 1–47.

Trevor-Roper, H.R. 1967: The religious origins of the Enlightenment. In *Religion, The Reformation and Social Change*. London: Macmillan, pp. 193–236.

ALISTER E. MCGRATH

environmental issues   See ETHICS.

epistemology, religious   The epistemological turn heralded in the rise of modern philosophy has proved to be an enduring crisis for Christian theologians and philosophers. Ironically, it was deep disputes in western Christianity which in part precipitated the quest for rational foundations not just for theological proposals but for any claim to truth. René Descartes (1596–1650) was deeply troubled by the conflicting theological claims which erupted in the Reformation. He correctly saw that they could not be resolved by appeal to the standard canons deployed by the disputants of the Reformation. Scripture and tradition themselves had been called into question as ultimate authorities, so deeper foundations had to be laid. This canonical crisis was exacerbated by the rediscovery of ancient sceptical material and by the revolutionary developments in thinking represented by the rise of the natural sciences. What began as a noisy conversation about the adequacy of ecclesial canons was quietly transformed into a deep discussion about the identity and interrelation of epistemic norms.

Descartes set the terms of the debate by delineating reason and experience as the two possible sources of all claims to truth. The seeds for such a move go far back into history. Deep echoes of the appeal to reason and experience can be found in Augustine's original formulation of the *cogito ergo sum* and in Aquinas's use of a natural theology which could in theory stand free of any appeal to special revelation. What is radically different is the status attributed to these in the Cartesian revolution. They are no longer appealed to in a rhetorical or fragmentary fashion; they become the foundations upon which the whole of Christian theology has to be erected methodically. The challenge this represents should not be located in the Cartesian turn inwards, as if this leads somehow inevitably into an abyss of subjectivism. The inward turn is merely the psychological dress of a deep impulse to establish all claims to truth in terms of objective arguments which can be formulated either a priori and deductively (the appeal to reason) or a posteriori and inductively (the appeal to experience). (See CARTESIANISM.)

In John Locke (1632–1704) we see how a deeply pious Christian and philosopher works out a rational case for Christianity. The cosmological and teleological arguments prove the existence of God; so the truth of theism is according to reason. Beyond that, there are truths above reason which are secured by divine REVELATION. The resurrection of the dead, for example, is believed because of the credit of the proposer; this in turn is secured by appropriate credentials like miracles and prophesy. In this scheme one is not limited to reason, for revelation functions as a quasi-epistemic concept, but reason must be judge and guide in everything. Moreover, truths contrary to reason cannot be countenanced at all. Tritheism, for example, is not a live option for a rational person. Such epistemic caution makes Locke wary of any appeal to direct experience of God; he is positively and correctly opposed to an appeal to private revelation.

David Hume (1711–1776) completely undercut the whole Lockean enterprise. On the one hand, he demolished the classical cosmological and teleological arguments for the existence of God by showing that the premises did not secure the conclusions. The various phenomena appealed to by Locke and by a host of those who followed him could be explained by any number of rival religious hypotheses. Moreover, the existence of widespread natural and moral evil counts against the theistic hypothesis. On the other hand, he called into question the status of miracles as credentials of revelation by arguing that the kind of evidence needed to secure supposed testimonies to miracles could not in the nature of the case be obtained. Even if the most unimpeachable witnesses claimed that someone came back from the dead, Hume would not allow this to overthrow the general law founded on universal experience that dead persons stay dead. Doubts about Hume's intentions and good faith did nothing to undermine the fundamental cogency of his proposals. Given the empiricist epistemology embraced by Locke, there was a heavy price to be paid within and without religion. Hume identified the price very cogently and precisely.

The aftermath belonged to Hume. Immanuel Kant (1724–1804) confirmed Hume's judgements about the collapse of natural theology (see KANTIANISM). At best philosophy could make room for faith; it could not provide rational foundations for it. Religious belief was acceptable in so far as it stayed within the bounds of reason. The rise of biblical criticism confirmed that Hume was fundamentally correct about the unavailability of good evidence for miracles. Indeed Hume's methodological strictures about the nature of evidence, which made it impossible to have good evidence for miracles, became a basic assumption of the logic of historical investigation. Moreover, the application of the methods of the human sciences, which Hume himself had done so much to launch, only served to explain in thoroughly naturalistic terms the rise and persistence of religion. The case for Christianity so carefully and passionately worked out by those committed to the epistemological turn in modern philosophy had collapsed. The Enlightenment offspring of the Reformation had devoured the parents (see ENLIGHTENMENT). The ensuing assimilation has been so complete that any attempt at resurrection has constantly appeared futile.

The great father of modern Protestant theology, Friedrich Schleiermacher (1768–1834), ingeniously attempted to rescue the faith by resigning all claims that belong to science or morality. Religion does not explain the world or extraordinary phenomena within it; nor does it depend on an outdated theory of divine intervention in revelation. Religion has its own a priori domain; religion is an expression of the feeling of absolute dependence on God which is the core of faith. Believers are directly aware of God and need no external support. Theology brings to self-conscious expression experience of God, and the theologian has the creative task of re-expressing this in appropriate terms across the changing generations. Thus the Trinity, while originally the very name of God in the Christian tradition, is relegated to the appendix of systematic theology. Having outlived its usefulness, it no longer serves to express the religious experience of Christian believers in the modern world. Intellectually the nineteenth century belongs to Schleiermacher. In the twentieth century his legacy has been given a new lease of life as theologians have grappled with the deepening awareness of the manifold phenomena of other religious traditions.

A radically different way to address the crisis of modernity was adopted by Søren Kierkegaard (1813–1855). Rather than stress emotion or feeling, Kierkegaard insisted that Christianity was really a matter of the will. To rely on reason is to avoid risk and faith; religion, on the contrary, is a matter of faith. The greater the improbability, the greater the faith. On standard canons of rationality, Christianity is improbable and impossible; it is paradoxical in the extreme. Christian commitment is a matter of grace and will; it neither needs nor depends on rational arguments. Hume and his friends are to be thanked for exposing the true basis of religion in faith and grace.

Kierkegaard remained in obscurity until the twentieth century. His genius initially came to light in his influence on the early Karl Barth (1886–1968), whose antipathy to any kind of natural theology was so marked that he advised a policy of extreme disengagement. One refused even to explain why one rejected natural theology. Barth returned to the theology of the Reformers and developed a doctrine of the Word of God which became the exclusive test of the church's language and witness. In spirit and form this is a profoundly Cartesian project. All that is said about God, creation, sin, and the like, has to be tested against a single foundational norm, although this norm is mediated in a threefold way in Christ, in the apostolic witness, and in the preaching of the church. The material canon of the Reformation, in this case Christ or the revelation in Christ, is treated as the sole epistemic norm of theology. Other possible norms like reason or experience are rejected as religiously incoherent. God is known fully and exclusively through Jesus Christ. To turn to other norms is to deny the reality of grace and to seek to justify oneself through one's works. What is deeply original here is that theological proposals about ecclesial canons, divine revelation in Christ and salvation are now construed as being in the same conceptual field as epistemic disputes about the foundations of knowing. Barth's position was modified over time, and it was developed in very different directions by disciples. Barth, however, does not extricate himself from the epistemological crisis of modernity. He is still smitten with Cartesian

anxiety. He attempts to relieve himself of this anxiety by converting specific theological claims into epistemic proposals which undercut the whole programme of the Enlightenment at its conceptual foundations. Friends saw this unique move as the work of genius; critics interpreted it as an outbreak of unbridled irrationalism.

None of these options proved satisfactory to the heirs of the Humean critique of theology. Logical positivists like A.J. Ayer transposed Hume's attack into a linguistic key by linking meaning, truth, and verifiability, and then insisting that strictly speaking all theological discourse was meaningless (see LOGICAL POSITIVISM). Clearly this kind of move could only be countered by philosophical proposals about language. It could not, therefore, be rebutted by appeal to faith, the will, religious experience or revelation, for these involved deploying the very concepts which the radically revised Humean criticism refused to countenance. If one was to argue for the truth of any theological assertion, one now had to engage in a preliminary stage of showing that in principle one could have theological assertions at all. This had the effect of postponing further work in religious epistemology for a full generation.

The fundamental work of a lost generation was not without its relevance. Various attempts were made to construe religion along non-cognitive lines with concomitant proposals about the grammar of religious discourse. These greatly enriched the understanding of the diversity of speech acts which can be performed in using religious discourse. They brought to light extremely important insights about the nature of RELIGIOUS LANGUAGE. They failed, however, to dislodge the deep conviction that in religion one could use language to make very important claims about the nature of the universe which were lodged in the very core of the Christian heritage. Once this was accepted, philosophers were free to return to questions about the justification of religious belief and to explore afresh how to respond to the Humean challenge.

Not everyone accepted this conclusion. An important exception inspired by the writings of the later Wittgenstein can be found in the work of D.Z. Phillips (see Phillips, 1976). Phillips insists that the solution to the positivist's challenge is to recognize the different uses to which language can be put. It is not the function of religious language to describe or explain the world. Religion has its own claims and their truth and meaning can be assessed only by criteria within religion itself. Religion does not make statements of fact. This is philosophically illegitimate, for religious claims do not satisfy the relevant conventional standards, and it is religiously inadequate, for religious commitment does not rest on how things go in the world. Religious discourse has its own logic within an organized religious community where it perfectly adequately guides and expresses basic attitudes to suffering, the future and the like.

Phillips's position has become something of a minority report in the debate about the epistemology of religious belief which has developed after the demise of positivism. Most of the current options involve concerted efforts either to draw the sting of the Humean challenge or to meet it head-on.

One way to draw the sting has been developed by a group of Reformed epistemologists led by Alvin Plantinga and Nicholas Wolterstorff (see Plantinga and Wolterstorff, 1983). Their initial strategy is to argue that most challenges to the rationality of religious belief rest on an unfounded commitment to foundationalism. Foundationalism is the view that for a belief to be rational it must either be a properly basic belief or be appropriately grounded on a properly basic belief. However, attempts to work out the criteria of proper basicality have so far proved inadequate. Those proposed to date, like self-evidence, being evident to the senses, incorrigibility, and the like, are subject to objection from compelling counter-examples. In the absence of such criteria there is nothing to prevent theists from including belief in God in the foundations of their noetic structure. From this perspective, it is entirely rational to believe in God without evidence, putting belief in God on a par with belief in other minds or belief in the existence of the past. Such a posture captures entirely naturally the depth of commitment characteristic of religious belief. In fact, discerning theists will feel free to offer their own analysis of knowledge, say, in terms of the proper functioning of the intellectual capacities given and designed by God. This in turn will provide a much better account of knowledge than those theories which are expressed in terms of coherence, reliability and the like.

One way to meet the challenge of Hume head-on is to call into question the conception of reason, evidence and argument adopted. This was precisely the strategy adopted by John Henry Newman (1801–1890) when he suggested that critics of Christianity too readily assumed, first, that all arguments must be codified in either a deductive or inductive form, thus ignoring the role of cumulative case arguments, and, second, that reliance on personal judgement be ruled out of court as subjective, thus ignoring the inadequacy of purely formal conceptions of rationality. Newman was convinced that the conventional epistemological wisdom was unduly restrictive and impoverished in its principles. Arguments can legitimately be expressed in a cumulative fashion; evidence for a claim can be tacit and may not be fully capturable in a formal calculus; and such arguments and evidence can legitimately lead one to certainty. In his day this network of suggestions fell on deaf ears. As the inadequacy of Enlightenment epistemologies becomes more apparent, it now constitutes an attractive alternative to those who want to steer a middle course between a natural theology which repeats the classical proofs of the past and a fideism which eschews reliance on reason in favour of faith.

Basil Mitchell (1973) and Richard Swinburne (1979) have plotted important versions of this tradition. They construe Christian theism as a largescale, integrative explanation which is to be accepted on the grounds that it provides the best explanation of various features of the world. The cosmological and teleological arguments are reworked, together with other arguments, into a cumulative case for the rationality of religious belief. Swinburne has attempted to codify the main segment of the argument in terms of probability. Mitchell is content to rely more fully on personal judgement in the evaluation of the relevant evidence. In a recent twist to the argument, advocated by Robert Prevost (1990), the ontological argument has been stated in such a way as to be also incorporated into the overall case for Christian theism. Within this schema, it is entirely appropriate to construe faith as unconditional. In that faith is a matter of trust in God, such trust should hold no matter what difficulties and dangers confront the believer. Indeed, the believer needs a certain tenacity both to withstand temptations to abandon faith and also to persevere sufficiently for relevant confirmation of his or her faith to be experienced. However, this does not entail that one believe in God no matter what the evidence. It is possible in principle for the case for Christian theism to be undermined and, were this to happen, talk of trust would no longer make sense.

An important ingredient in this form of revised natural theology is the appeal to religious experience as a crucial element in the overall case for Christian theism or as a single, independent argument for theism. Swinburne has proposed that the subjects' description of their religious experience should be accepted unless we have good evidence to believe otherwise. In following this strategy we are applying a common principle of perception he identifies as the principle of credulity. Broadly speaking, this states that perceptual claims should be construed as veridical, unless we have evidence to the contrary. The only alternative to the adoption of this principle is to embrace a radical scepticism about all our perceptual beliefs. A different move which would also permit us to accept the evidence of religious experience has been worked out by William Alston (see Alston, 1991). He works with a doctrine of perceptual practices which is meant to work for perception generally and is then applied with appropriate modifications to religious experience. In their own way these arguments seek to turn the flank of standard objections which have been levelled against the evidential value of religious experience either from conflicting reports of such experience or from reductionist, naturalistic explanations which would eliminate the need to refer to divine causality in order to make sense of them. In a way this trajectory of argument clearly echoes the legacy of Schleiermacher. Yet it seeks to provide an epistemological account of the value of religious experience which is lacking in Schleiermacher, and it abandons the suggestion that the whole of theology be grounded somehow on religious experience alone.

Given that those committed to a cumulative argument for theism tend to construe theism as an explanatory system, it is not surprising that they should look for analogies between religious systems of belief and scientific systems of belief. This opens up yet another way to vindicate the rationality of religious belief. Granting that science furnishes a paradigm case of knowledge, one develops an account of the logic of science and then attempts to show that the logic of religious belief is identical to that of scientific belief. In very general terms this is the position adopted by Thomas Torrance (see Torrance, 1969). Scientists arrive at their conclusions by allowing the object of their investigation to determine what should or should not be said about it. Equally, the task of the theologian is to allow the object of their enquiries, the Word of God, to determine the form and content of theological discourse. Each discipline will have its own particular way of attending to its object, but the common commitment to let the object of thought determine the content of thought calls for a critically realist account of science and theology.

Nancey Murphy (1990) has provided an especially interesting version of this approach to the epistemology of religious belief. After drawing on and defending Imre Lakatos's account of science as a series of competing research programmes, she attempts to show that it is feasible to construe various theological proposals as possessing all the features of scientific research programmes, such as a hard core of belief and an expanding belt of auxiliary hypotheses, data and the like. From this it is a very short step to the recommendation that theology deliberately adopt Lakatos's methodology for adjudicating between competing research programmes in science. Her proposal is partly descriptive and partly prescriptive. Religious systems of belief are sufficiently like scientific systems of belief to warrant the adopting in the case of religion Lakatos's methodology for deciding the rationality, which works in the case of science. Necessarily, the proof of the methodology will depend on its fruitful application in the field of faith; only time and appropriate evaluation can settle this.

In this particular strategy Hume has been turned on his head. One accepts that religious belief is to be grounded in a species of probabilistic reasoning. Moreover, given the resources and options open to him in his day, Hume was right to reject religion as irrational. However, over the last two centuries epistemology has advanced far beyond where it was in Hume's time. New developments in the history and philosophy of science have overturned Hume's simplistic analysis of probabilistic reasoning. When we identify the new insights which have emerged about the rationality of science and examine doctrinal traditions and controversies in the light of them, we have to reverse Hume's negative assessment of the rationality of religious belief. The exploration of religious belief in this fashion is, moreover, religiously illuminating. It insists that much more attention be paid to the actual beliefs of religious believers, rather than, say, some thinned down version of theism derived from natural religion or natural theology; and it suggests that theists identify and evaluate the kind of epistemic practices which are recommended by participant religious believers. Hence it not only allows but positively incorporates material which has traditionally been separated off into the fields of revelation and religious experience. In this way one makes a virtue of faith in the quest for positive epistemic evaluation.

Taken together, these developments represent a radical reversal of the consensus which has been common in philosophical and theological circles in the modern period. With the exception of developments in process theology, most theologians have abandoned any attempt to rebut or circumvent the objections lodged in the traditions of epistemology inspired by Hume and Kant. Process theologians like Schubert Ogden have kept alive a conception of philosophical theology which draws on the metaphysical suggestions of Whitehead and Hartshorne. Within this they have sought to wrestle with the cognitive challenges presented by critics of Christianity. Most theologians, however, have tended to construe theology as having its own cognitive resources in faith, Scripture, revelation, tradition and the like, and have tended to turn to philosophy for heuristic or hermeneutical purposes. The current situation is one of rapid change. Christian theologians now have epistemological options which were unheard of at the beginnings of the

modern period. These options in turn create significant space for fresh renderings of the Christian faith at the dawn of a new millennium.

See also NATURAL THEOLOGY; PHILOSOPHY OF RELIGION.

Bibliography

Alston, William 1991: *Perceiving God: The Epistemology of Religious Experience*. London: Cornell University Press.

Davis, Caroline Franks 1989: *The Evidential Force of Religious Experience*. Oxford: Clarendon Press.

Mitchell, Basil 1973: *The Justification of Religious Belief*. Oxford: Oxford University Press.

Murphy, Nancey 1990: *Theology in the Age of Scientific Reasoning*. London: Cornell University Press.

Phillips, D.Z. 1976: *Religion Without Explanation*. Oxford: Blackwell.

Plantinga, Alvin, and Wolterstorff, Nicholas, eds, 1983: *Faith and Rationality*. Notre Dame: University of Notre Dame.

Popkin, Richard 1979: *The History of Skepticism from Erasmus to Descartes*. London: University of California Press.

Prevost, Robert 1990: *Probability and Theistic Explanation*. Oxford: Clarendon Press.

Proudfoot, Wayne 1985: *Religious Experience*. London: University of California Press.

Swinburne, Richard 1979: *The Existence of God*. Oxford: Clarendon Press.

Torrance, Thomas F. 1969: *Theological Science*. Oxford: Oxford University Press.

W.P. ABRAHAM

eschatology Eschatology is discourse about endings, whether of an individual's life or the world, and about the events which traditionally attend these moments (judgement, heaven and hell). It achieved prominence in modern theology because exegetes of the New Testament became convinced that the best way to understand key concepts was in the light of the future hopes of Judaism. These looked forward to an ending of the present evil age, with a cataclysmic transition (the messianic woes) leading to the establishment of an age of righteousness when the deeds of humanity would be judged and the whole of creation be subject to the divine will. So, from being something of an afterthought in Christian theology, eschatology began to be placed by nineteenth-century New Testament scholarship at the centre of its own interests and those of theology generally.

The discovery of the Ethiopic Apocalypse of Enoch (part of the canon of Scripture of the Ethiopic church), with its central section's similarity to New Testament ideas about the heavenly son of man, helped contribute to a picture of Judaism in which there was an expectation of an imminent irruption of God into the old order and the establishment of a new creation. This type of hope was described as *apocalyptic eschatology* (to distinguish it from the more mundane hopes of rabbinic Judaism). This approach, which stressed divine agency in the coming of the eschatological kingdom, ran counter to the theology of those like Albrecht Ritschl who stressed its moral character and the human contribution to its coming. The decisive impact on that kind of assessment came in the work of Ritschl's son-in-law, Johannes Weiss. His work on the kingdom drove a wedge between exegesis and theology. On the basis of his exegesis, Weiss concluded that the coming of the kingdom was a future, cataclysmic affair in which humanity had little or no part to play. He recognized that such a view, which was rooted in the reconstruction of first-century eschatological beliefs, was unpalatable to the theological humanism of his day. Nevertheless, Weiss, and Albert Schweitzer after him, placed eschatology at the centre of the New Testament message. In the work of both Jesus was portrayed as a proclaimer of the imminence of God's transcendent kingdom. They suggested that this fervent belief dominated the outlook of the first Christians too. Schweitzer argued that the central thrust of eschatology conditioned the emergence of the distinctive features of Paul's Christ mysticism, which was a reaction to the delayed kingdom. The theory of the delay of the parousia was a further refinement of this consistently eschatological approach, so that the emergence of church order and doctrine were seen as attempts to come to terms with disappointed eschatological hopes. So the whole of early Christianity was thought of as a movement propagating, and then having to come to terms with, an imminent expectation of the end of the world.

To a significant degree the story of New Testament theology in the twentieth century has involved attempts to come to terms with these theories. Reactions to it have been various. There have been those like Karl Barth and Rudolf Bultmann who have accepted the eschatological interpretation but placed a greater emphasis on the critical final character of the Christ event borne witness to in the proclamation of the gospel. Eschatology ceases to have a temporal significance and is understood existentially. For Barth eschatology becomes a component of Christology, as the determinative revelatory moment by which the totality of existence should be judged is focused on Christ. Bultmann reduces the strictly eschatological component by seeking to extract the essence of what the mythology of eschatological discourse seeks to convey. The result is a message about the demand for authentic existence in the face of God's crisis. In this the cosmic, social and historical referents of eschatology are in effect reduced to a disposable alien mythological shell. The approach is largely continued in the emphasis on 'speech-event' in the work of E. Fuchs and G. Ebeling.

The individualist reduction of eschatology has been challenged by Bultmann's successors. Exegetically, Ernst Käsemann stressed the central role of the future hope and demanded that the key Pauline term of the righteousness of God be understood in terms of Jewish eschatology. Oscar Cullmann has consistently refused to allow that salvation history is some late development, but maintains that it is integral to the New Testament message. In systematic theology the central component of eschatology and its historical dimension has been stressed by J. Moltmann and W. Pannenberg. The RESURRECTION of Jesus becomes a key to understanding history, turning attention to the future of the world in God's purposes of which that event is a foretaste.

The central importance of eschatology for theology owes much to the influence of Ernst Bloch. The latter's utopianism represents an extreme form of Hegelian Marxism. Bloch's kaleidoscopic *The Principle of Hope* ([1959] 1986) indicates the importance attached to Christianity's chiliastic tradition as a countervailing force to an other-worldly messianism which has characterized much Christian eschatology. The utopian spirit is evident in the work of several thinkers outside the confines of Christian theology. The centrality of hope tinged with messianism is typical of the later work of Walter Benjamin, himself the close friend of Gershom Scholem, the pioneer of the revival of interest in the Jewish messianic and kabbalistic tradition. Even in the negative dialectics of Theodor Adorno (closely involved with both Scholem and Benjamin) the messianic component exercises a critical counterbalance to the rather pessimistic and complex analysis of the human plight.

In British New Testament scholarship there was always a reluctance to accept the Weiss/Schweitzer solution. C.H. Dodd, for example, dealt with the eschatological question by denying the centrality of futurist eschatology and stressing the arrival of the kingdom in Jesus' life. Dodd's solution is to characterize the kingdom as eternal and present. Its definitive appearance was realized in the Christ-event, and there is no further coming to look forward to. Anything further lies beyond history. In this his Platonism is everywhere apparent. It was an important component of his work to stress the way in which Paul left his Jewish sectarian and apocalyptic moorings and espoused a universalist gospel. In the hand of his successors like John Robinson there was a continuation of the task of rehabilitating the distinctive eschatology of the Gospel of John as reflecting the mind of Jesus. The parousia expectation then becomes a distortion of Jesus' hope of the vindication of himself and his work. An approach more sensitive to the resources of eschatological imagery for human understanding and flourishing is more evident in the work of the North American scholar Amos Wilder.

In the discussion of eschatology two strands call for attention. There is in German biblical scholarship a suspicion of apocalyptic, epitomized by the traditional Lutheran denigration of revelation. There has been a widespread view that there was a dichotomy in ancient Judaism between a Torah-centred Jusaism and a more historically and eschatologically oriented Judaism evident in the apocalypses. That dichotomy is said to be reflected in the clash between pharisaism and Christianity. Second, the preoccupation with eschatology has gone hand in hand with a belief that the dominance of eschatology precludes an interest in politics. In some of the major writings of the New Testament the stress on imminence is seen as being antithetical to practical political involvement. This is either because the focus was on another world soon to come or because the emphasis was placed on the divine initiative rather than human agency. In contrast to this, recent political theology has refused to allow a sharp division between history and eschatology. Together with its appeal to the utopian tradition influenced by Bloch, exponents of LIBERATION THEOLOGY, for example, have argued for the importance of human agency in seeking to create the future history of God's purposes. In so doing it has challenged a mainstream eschatology which rejected a this-worldly hope. This had incorporated the apocalyptic dualism into an account of God's purposes so that the future kingdom was utterly transcendent.

The founding father of liberation theology in Latin America, Gustavo Gutiérrez, has argued against the separation of secular from sacred history. Human history is seen as the arena of the fulfilment of God's saving purposes. Even if they consistently refuse to identify totally liberation of a political and economic kind with the totality of God's salvation, liberation theologians like Gutiérrez refuse to allow the latter to be regarded as a separate sphere of human experience. That has led them to a preparedness to 'read the signs of the times' and to seek to distinguish between human projects in the light of God's eschatological justice. Signs of God's presence are not, therefore, wholly ambiguous. Nor are they confined to the tested sacramental demonstrations in the confines of ecclesiastical activity. Although their account of eschatology has not been entirely influenced by Marxist Hegelianism, the contemporary disillusionment with the Marxist tradition in all its aspects might appear to have tainted their critique. It seems more likely that the point which they are seeking to make should be conceived as part of a theological challenge to a consensus on the relationship of history and eschatology. Following the evangelical behest they have argued that the eschatological judgement is now taking place in the willingness to respond to the needy in the world: the future judge is masked in the present order in the midst of the deprived, impoverished and oppressed (Matt. 25: 31ff.). An eschatological faith means attending to the forgotten of humanity in the midst of history.

See also DISPENSATIONALISM; KINGDOM OF GOD: NEW TESTAMENT; KINGDOM OF GOD: POLITICAL AND SOCIAL THEOLOGY.

Bibliography

Bauckham, R. 1987: *Jürgen Moltmann: Messianic Theology in the Making*. Basingstoke: Marshall Pickering.

Biale, D. 1982: *Gershom Scholem: Kabbalah and Counter-Culture*. Cambridge, Mass.: Harvard University Press.

Bloch, E. [1959] 1986: *The Principle of Hope*, trans. Oxford: Blackwell.

Bultmann, R. [1941] 1953: The New Testament and mythology. In *Kerygma and Myth: A Theological Debate*, vol. 1, ed. H.W. Bartsch, trans. R.H. Fuller. London: SPCK.

Bultmann, R. 1957: *History and Eschatology. The Presence of Eternity*. New York: Harper and Row.

Cullmann, O. 1967: *Salvation in History*. London: SCM Press.

Dodd, C.H. 1935: *The Parables of the Kingdom*. London: James Nisbet.

Gutiérrez, G. [1971] 1988: *A Theology of Liberation*, 2nd, revised, edition, trans. Sister C. Inda and J. Eagleson. Maryknoll: Orbis.

Held, D. 1980: *Introduction to Critical Theory*. Cambridge: Polity Press.

Hudson, W. 1982: *The Marxist Philosophy of Ernst Bloch*. London.

Moltmann, J. [1964] 1967 *Theology of Hope*, trans. J.W. Leitch. London: SCM Press.

Ploger, O. 1968: *Theocracy and Eschatology*. Blackwell: Oxford.

Robinson, J.A.T. 1957: *Jesus and his Coming*. London: SCM Press.

Schweitzer, A. [1906] 1910: *The Quest of the Historical Jesus*, trans. W. Montgomery. London: A & C Black.

Schweitzer, A. 1931: *The Mysticism of Paul the Apostle*, trans. London: A&C Black.

Weiss, J. 1971: *Jesus' Proclamation of the Kingdom of God*. London: SCM Press.

CHRISTOPHER ROWLAND

ethics Christian ethics comprises reflection upon moral matters within the context of Christian convictions about the nature of reality – divine and created, human and non-human. Usually this has meant that Christian ethics is distinct from philosophical ethics, which operates apart from theological presuppositions. Sometimes, however, Christian ethi-cists have supposed that theological tenets have no significant ethical contribution of their own to make, and in these cases the distinction has virtually disappeared. But even in other cases where it has remained, Christian ethical reflection has nevertheless been influenced by philosophical concepts and insights. Distinction here does not amount to separation.

Roman Catholic ethics
The Counter-Reformation and penitential discipline Of the several objections that the Roman Catholic church levelled at the Protestant doctrine of justification by grace through faith, one was that it ensues in moral laxity. In its reaction against Protestantism, therefore, the Council of Trent (1545–63) sought to tighten moral discipline in the Roman church by reasserting the sacrament of penance as the means whereby the state of justification is restored after post-baptismal sin. Thus the Counter-Reformation created a need to educate priests in the making of moral judgements, so as to enable them to impose a penance appropriate to the number, species, and circumstances of the sins confessed. Clerical preparation for the confessional became the dominant preoccupation of subsequent Catholic thinking about moral matters, and it led to the development for the first time of a separate science of moral theology.

This moral theology was characterized by its abstraction both from consideration of the spiritual grounds and end of moral life and from the more positive task of the cultivation of the virtues. Distinguished and distanced from dogmatic and spiritual (or ascetic) theology and approximated to canon law, its focus lay on the transgression of specific moral laws rather than on the spiritual state of rebellion against God. Its concern was with *sins* rather than *sin*.

Nature and grace This, however, was not the only respect in which modern moral theology bore the marks of the Counter-Reformation. For its emphasis lay, not only upon the role of *law* in moral life, but also upon the role of NATURAL LAW. Over and against the Protestant tendency to stress 'divine' law – that is, the moral law revealed by God in the Scriptures and, above all, in Jesus Christ – Roman Catholic moral theologians dealt primarily in terms of the moral law supposedly evident in the nature of things, especially in human nature. In so doing they relied heavily on the natural law theory of Thomas Aquinas (1225–1274) as mediated and developed by the great Spanish theologians, Francisco de Vitoria (c. 1485–1546), Francisco de Suarez (1548–1617) and Gabriel Vazquez (1549–1604), as well as by the Italian Roberto Bellarmine (1542–1621).

The promotion of natural law to centre stage, and the demotion of divine law to the status of understudy, signalled differences with Protestants over where to look first for the moral order, and over the capacity of human reason to discover it without the guidance of special revelation. On both points, Catholic moral theology gave nature the higher estimation.

However, this tendency to cede 'nature' a considerable measure of independence from 'supernature' did not go uncontested within Catholic circles. Indeed, the Jansenist controversy, which ran through the second half of the seventeenth century and most of the eighteenth century and has been described as 'the greatest storm ever to rock moral theology' (John Mahoney), had its centre in this issue. The Jansenists, taking their cue from the interpretation of Augustine offered by Cornelius Jansen (1585–1638) in his posthumously published *Augustinus*, argued that conduct according to natural law as grasped by natural reason is nevertheless sinful unless ordered by *caritas*, or love for God, which is a supernatural gift of grace. The church authorities, however, maintained the less pessimistic line of Trent, according to which fallen humans do have the natural resources to do good, albeit only intermittently; and before the end of the eighteenth century they had successfully quelled Jansenist resistance.

The permissibility of dissent from the moral law The Jansenist controversy, however, was not entirely about the relationship between 'nature' and 'supernature'. It was also about moral stringency. By the middle of the seventeenth century the theory of 'probabilism', invented by Bartolomeo de Medina (1527–1580), was widely disseminated in the Catholic church. According to this theory, a course of action which deviates from the law but for which a good moral case can be argued (that is, one which is 'probable') is morally permissible, even if a stronger case can be made for another course of action; and the probability of a case can either be 'intrinsic', consisting in the force of the argument itself, or 'extrinsic', consisting in the prestige of the authority who can be counted in its favour. The Jansenists were aghast at probabilism, which could and did lend itself to the justification of some outrageously lax (that is, permissive) conduct, sometimes on the sole ground of its being approved by a single authority. In its stead, the Jansenists advocated a rigorist form of 'tutiorism'. Tutiorism holds that in situations of doubt the safer (Latin: *tutior*) course should be followed; and in its rigorist form the safer course is always considered to be that of conformity to the law. On three occasions during the latter half of the seventeenth century – 1665, 1666, and 1679 – the church authorities condemned laxist conclusions at which some probabilist arguments arrived, and by the turn of the century laxism had virtually disappeared. But in 1690 Rome also censured extreme tutiorism. The continuing controversy over more moderate forms of probabilism and tutiorism was effectively resolved by Alphonsus Liguori (1696–1787), who developed the theory of 'equiprobabilism'. According to this, it is permissible to follow a probable opinion instead of the law, but only in cases where opinions for and against it are equally balanced.

The centralization of moral authority The prolonged debate provoked by probabilism reveals the continuing preoccupation of moral theology with law – and in particular the conditions under which it may be disobeyed. But it also displays the importance attached to the extrinsic authority of the church – in this case, as represented by the writings of prestigious moral theologians. Against Protestantism, with its doctrine of the priesthood of all believers and its advocacy of the principle of private judgement, the Counter-Reformation had reasserted the authority of the upper, clerical echelons of the ecclesiastical hierarchy. And, under subsequent pressure from the internal strife kindled by Jansenism and from the external threats posed by the Enlightenment, the French Revolution, and Napoleon, the teaching authority (or 'magisterium') of the church became increasingly concentrated in episcopal and papal hands. This tendency reached its culmination in 1870 when the First

Vatican Council asserted the infallibility of the pope in his moral teaching. Thereafter, extrinsic authority became virtually limited to officially approved authors. Pre-eminent among these were Liguori, declared a Doctor of the Church in 1871, and Aquinas, whose study was enjoined on all theological students in 1879 by Leo XIII in his bull, *Aeterni Patris*.

Up until the Second World War, Roman Catholic moral theology tended to run along the lines established during the Counter-Reformation, and it found typical expression in casuistic manuals whose basic pattern had been established by John Azor, SJ (1536–1603) in his *Institutiones morales* of 1600–11. The most influential of these manuals was the *Theologia moralis* of 1748 by Liguori, whose persistent pre-eminence was marked in 1950 by his designation as patron saint of confessors and moral theologians.

The Tübingen school and the renewal of moral theology It would be a mistake, however, simply to identify nineteenth- and twentieth-century Catholic moral theology with the manualist tradition. In the early nineteenth century the Tübingen theologians Johann Michael Sailer (1750–1832) and Johann Baptist Hirscher (1788–1865), influenced by the revival of biblical studies in Germany and by developments in Protestant theology, reacted against the legalistic preoccupations and the authoritarian stance typical of Counter-Reformation thinking. In his *Handbuch der christlichen Moral* of 1817, addressed not only to the clergy but to 'all educated Christians', Sailer presented the moral life as growth towards perfection by way of Christian discipleship as explicated in terms of the Sermon on the Mount. Hirscher described it in terms of the realization of the kingdom of God. Both based their moral theology directly on biblical teaching and concepts and described it in relation to spiritual life. Although their contemporary influence was limited to Germany, Sailer and Hirscher may be seen as the pioneers of an alternative tradition of Catholic moral theology, which can be traced through such figures as Francis Xavier Linsenmann (1835–1898), Theodore Steinbüchel (1888–1949), and Fritz Tillmann (d. 1953) to Bernard Häring.

The publication of Häring's *The Law of Christ* in 1954, and its subsequent popularity, was one of the main signals of widespread dissatisfaction with the dominant manualist tradition. In this seminal work, now translated into more than fifteen modern languages, Häring echoed the Tübingen school, albeit in terms shaped by the biblical theology movement, theological personalism, and existentialism; and he also heralded the new lines along which much Catholic moral theology was about to move. Addressing both laity and clergy, he depicts the moral life basically as a series of responses to the grace of God that takes the form of the imitation of Christ. The themes of conversion and the growth of virtue are given prominence. Unlike the Tübingen school, however, Häring's emphasis on moral and spiritual development is not such as to eclipse the traditional manualists' concern with judging the morality of particular acts.

Although the Second Vatican Council (Vatican II: 1962–5) said little directly about moral theology, it did establish a theological climate within the church that was more sympathetic to the lines of thinking represented by Häring. In its Decree on Priestly Formation (*Optatam Totius*) it affirmed that moral theology should derive more thorough nourishment from the teaching of the Scriptures. And in its Pastoral Constitution on the Church in the Modern World (*Gaudium et Spes*) it made a significant departure from traditional authoritarianism when, tacitly blurring the theological division made since the eighteenth century between the *Ecclesia docens* (the teaching church) and the *Ecclesia discens* (the learning church), it asserted that the making of concrete moral judgements is the responsibility of the whole of God's people, the laity as well as the clergy, even if the generation of moral principles remains the responsibility of the magisterium (the bishops and the pope in respect of their teaching authority). Further, both in *Gaudium et Spes* and in the Decree on Ecumenism (*Unitatis Redintegratio*) the Council implicitly sanctioned greater openness to potential sources of moral wisdom outside the Catholic church, whether in other Christian traditions or in the secular sciences.

In the years following Vatican II the movement away from the Counter-Reformation tradition has continued and developed. The 'transcendental' Thomism of Karl Rahner

(1904–1984), who has been described as 'the most prolific and greatest theologian of the century' (R.A. McCormick), has been influential in at least two ways. First, his anthropology has been introduced into moral theology by Joseph Fuchs, SJ, resulting in an emphasis on the depth of the moral act at the level of the 'fundamental option' for or against the call of God – an emphasis which relocates conventional moral concerns more immediately and dynamically in a spiritual context. Second, Rahner has challenged the traditional conception of (human) 'nature' as ontologically independent of 'supernature' or redeeming divine grace. Against this, he has asserted that 'nature' is an abstraction and that, in fact, it always exists in a supernatural order and is permanently enfolded by grace. As a consequence of this, Rahner has been able to argue that the virtue of the 'unbeliever' is not merely apparent (Augustine) nor necessarily precarious and intermittent (Trent), but implicitly motivated by *caritas*.

Natural law reconsidered In addition to exhibiting tendencies to reintegrate the moral with the spiritual, and the natural with the supernatural, some recent Catholic moral theology has set about reconceiving natural law. One prevailing trend has been to incorporate acknowledgement of the historicity of moral norms. So, for example, Bruno Schüller, SJ, an eminent continental moralist, has argued that as human nature develops in some respects, so too must specifications of the natural law. Another important revision of the traditional understanding of natural law has been to exchange 'physicalist' terms for 'personalist' ones (Bernard Häring). In general the argument here has been that human nature should not be understood in terms of what human and nonhuman animals share in common – that is, the biological – but rather in terms of what is distinctively human – that is, the personal. This reconception of natural law has had some very important ramifications, especially in sexual ethics. For whereas traditional moral theology holds the natural end of sexual relations to be the procreation of offspring, some personalist thinking takes it to be the mutual expression of responsible love – which, without further qualification, has the effect of removing the premise of the traditional objections to contra-

ception and homosexual practice.

The identification, made by some personalist thinkers, of the essentially personal with the human capacity for creative, rational transcendence, indicates another tendency in recent moral theology to alter the balance between reason and law in favour of the former. Whether under the influence of personalism, Kantianism, or existentialism, many contemporary moral theologians have ceased to view moral law as something simply given, which it is the task of conscience to apply in a logically deductive fashion. Rather, and sometimes claiming the authority of Aquinas himself, they emphasize the creative role of conscience in interpreting the meaning of a law for a unique person in a particular set of circumstances (for instance Mahoney, 1987). Some have exalted the importance of one species of circumstance, consequences, for determining the moral quality of acts (for instance R.A. McCormick).

In one school of thought, this exaltation of reason has come into conflict with the recent promotion of Scripture in moral theology. This is because some moral theologians (such as Franz Böckle in *Fundamentalmoral*, 1977), affirming what they believe to be the deep theological roots of Kantian 'autonomy', identify the Christian ethic with that at which 'theonomous' reason arrives, and so reject the project of trying to build a distinctively Christian 'ethic of faith' (of the kind advocated by Bernhard Stoeckle in *Grenzen der autonomen Moral*, 1974, trans. 'The Limits of Autonomous Morality').

Moral debate and dissent in the church It is not the case that these new departures in Catholic moral theology have established themselves as the basis of a new consensus within the church. For example, the more traditional concept of natural law as the given, ontological foundation of basic goods and duties has powerful and sophisticated contemporary advocates (such as John Finnis in *Natural Law and Natural Rights*, 1980). And Pope Paul VI's encyclical *Humanae Vitae* (1968) not only reaffirmed the traditional objection to contraception on traditional grounds, but did so in a manner that implicitly contradicted Vatican II's doctrine of episcopal collegiality.

Consequently, this encyclical has stimulated continuing debate about the nature of ethical authority in the church and the possibility of dissent, and about the relation of moral theologians to the magisterium (see Charles Curran and R.A. McCormick, eds, *The Magisterium and Morality*, 1982). This latter issue has been brought to the fore recently during the papacy of John Paul II, when the ecclesiastical authorities have taken steps to reassert more traditional teaching in Catholic institutions – most famously in the celebrated case of Charles Curran, whose canonical mission to teach on the pontifical faculty at the Catholic University of America was removed in 1986 (see Charles Curran and R.A. McCormick, eds, *Dissent in the Church* of 1988).

Social ethics Although traditional moral theologians tended to explicate the moral life in terms of the duties and sins of the individual, this does not mean that they entirely neglected its social dimension. For, whether under the rubric of the virtue of charity or that of the sixth commandment, they did treat war; and whether under the rubric of the virtue of justice or that of the seventh and tenth commandments, they did treat property rights. In addition, some moralists, most notably in the sixteenth and seventeenth centuries, devoted themselves to the study of justice in warfare (such as Vitoria and Suarez) and in economics, including prices and wages (such as Louis Molina, 1545–1600; Leonard Lessius, 1554–1623; and John de Lugo, 1583–1660).

In the late nineteenth century the social problems produced by industrial capitalism and the questions raised by the rise of socialism provoked Catholic moral theology to broaden its social horizon to include consideration of 'social justice' – that is, the justice of the distribution of benefits and burdens among individual and collective members of a society, and of the reciprocal relations between the rights of the individual and the claims of the community. In 1891 Pope Leo XIII addressed 'the social problem' in *Rerum Novarum*, an encyclical letter addressed to the whole church. In so doing he began what was to become a long and continuing tradition of papal statements on political, social, and economic justice, and which include, to date: *Quadragesimo Anno* (1931), *Mater et Magistra* (1961), *Pacem in Terris* (1963), *Populorum Progressio* (1967), *Octogesima Adveniens* (1971), *Laborem Exercens* (1981), *Sollicitudo Rei Socialis* (1987), and *Centesimus Annus* (1991).

These documents do comprise a tradition in that they are consistent on a number of basic points. They all argue for the securing of human rights, derived from the dignity of human nature, against infringement by the economically powerful or by the state. On the one hand, they affirm the worker's right to a just – that is, 'living' – wage and assert that it is the duty of the state to intervene in the market to defend this, as any other, right. But, on the other hand, state intervention for the sake of the common good must respect natural rights, especially the right to private property, which is deemed necessary for the due exercise of creative and responsible freedom, and the right to associate (as in labour unions). Further, state intervention should be subject to the principle of 'subsidiarity', which first received explicit mention in *Quadragesimo Anno*. According to this principle, interventions by the state should properly be 'enabling'; that is, they should offer help (Latin: *subsidium*) to individuals and to more primary forms of natural community (such as the family), so that these can exercise as much responsibility as possible. This papal tradition of social commentary espouses a Thomistic rather than Augustinian view of the state; namely, as a natural institution whose *raison d'être* is not merely to maintain law and order against the incursions of the wicked, but also to promote the common good, and that at a moral and spiritual as well as a material level.

However, if these papal statements comprise a tradition, they comprise a developing tradition. Whereas *Rerum Novarum* sought to solve the social problem by enabling workers to acquire private property, later encyclicals (such as *Quadragesimo Anno*, *Mater et Magistra*, and *Laborem Exercens*) seek it rather in participation by workers in the ownership or management or profits of the productive enterprise. And whereas *Rerum Novarum* rejected socialism indiscriminately, an increasing willingness to distinguish between different kinds of socialism and even to appreciate elements of socialist thought and practice can be traced through *Quadragesimo Anno*, *Pacem in Terris*, and *Octogesima Adveniens*; and both *Mater et Magistra* and *Laborem Exercens* concede that public ownership of the means of production may be right in certain circumstances. At a much more general level, the scope of this tradition can be seen to expand beyond the national context to international relations (especially in *Populorum Progressio* and *Sollicitudo Rei Socialis*) and even to the nonhuman environment (in *Centesimus Annus*).

Although these papal statements have been a major – even, arguably, the dominant – expression of recent Catholic moral thinking on political, social, and economic matters, they have certainly not been the only expression. There have also been Vatican II's *Gaudium et Spes* (1965), the International Synod of Bishops' *Justice in the World* (1971) and important utterances by national episcopates – such as the two Pastoral Letters of the US Bishops on nuclear weapons (*The Challenge of Peace*, 1983) and on the US economy (*Economic Justice for All*, 1986). And, of course, individuals have done important work in this field, most notably Jacques Maritain (1882–1973) on human rights, the state and democracy (*The Rights of Man and Natural Law*, 1943; *Man and the State*, 1951), and John Courtney Murray, SJ (1904–1967) on the right to freedom of religion (*The Problem of Religious Freedom*, 1965). (See also ROMAN CATHOLIC THEOLOGY.)

Anglican ethics

Natural law and natural reason In Book I of his *Treatise of the Laws of Ecclesiastical Polity* Richard Hooker (*c.* 1554–1600) established Anglican moral theology on foundations that owe much more to Thomas Aquinas than to Martin Luther. As a consequence, like Roman Catholic moral theology it has sought moral understanding primarily by reference to the natural law; and it has tended to esteem more highly than its Lutheran, Reformed, or Anabaptist counterparts the power of natural reason to discern what is good and right, without the aid of the grace of special revelation. Accordingly, it has also been more ready to accredit sources of moral wisdom other than Scripture – in particular, reason, experience, and empirical science. This is evident, for example, in the confidence that Joseph Butler (1692–1752) placed in common moral sense, and in the moral *philosophical* character of his influential writings (such as *Fifteen Sermons*, 1726; *Dissertation on the Nature of Virtue*, 1736). It is

also evidenced by the respect with which William Temple (1881–1944) regarded the contributions to ethical debate of experts in the social and human sciences, and by the Church of England's post-war proclivity – applauded by Ian Ramsey (1915–1972) – for multidisciplinary working parties on ethical issues.

Casuistry and conscience Anglicanism has inherited from Thomist moral theology a comparatively high regard for *natural* reason. It has also inherited a similar regard for moral *reasoning*. This has found expression in an Anglican tradition of casuistry, which flourished in the seventeenth century in the hands of divines such as William Perkins (1558–1602), Robert Sanderson (1587–1663), Joseph Hall (1574–1656) and Jeremy Taylor (1613–1667), and which Kenneth Kirk (1886–1954) sought to revive in the 1920s. In spite of the fact that its genesis was inspired by admiration for the intellectual sophistication and rigour of Roman Catholic moral theology, Anglican casuistry has differed from its traditional Roman counterpart in two respects. First, it has been set loose from the confessional. This means that its aim has not been to reach a retrospective judgement about the gravity of sins confessed, so that an appropriate penance might be imposed; but rather to aid the formation of prospective judgements about the right course of action to be taken. Second, out of a high regard for the liberty of individual conscience it has sought to aid the layperson directly, and not mediately through the priest. For this reason Anglican casuists have usually written in the vernacular rather than Latin. On occasion in the history of Anglican moral theology the high value placed upon liberty of conscience has combined with the high esteem of natural reason to erode belief in the need for moral reasoning. As examples of this take the confidence of Joseph Butler in the sufficiency of the intuitions of common moral sense, and of Joseph Fletcher in the sufficiency of love's insight (*Situation Ethics*, 1966).

The dogmatic and spiritual setting of ethics A more fundamental point at which the Anglican ethical tradition has diverged from its Roman counterpart after the Council of Trent is in its location of moral considerations within the larger context of theological and spiritual ones: Anglican moral theology stands firmly in the context of dogmatic and spiritual theology. Recent evidence of this may be found in R.C. Mortimer's *Elements of Moral Theology* of 1947, which, unlike its Roman equivalents, begins by treating 'the last end of man' before proceeding to discuss the internal and external rules of conduct, conscience and law. Also significant in this respect is O.M.T. O'Donovan's *Resurrection and Moral Order* of 1986, which, as its title suggests, treats moral life in the context of the Christian doctrines of creation and redemption. By taking as its aim the pursuit of holiness in grateful response to the justifying grace of God, and not merely the avoidance of sin, Anglican moral theology has avoided degeneration into a legalistic preoccupation with the observance of rules, and it has acquired a positive orientation towards the cure of souls. This Anglican connection between the moral, the spiritual, and the pastoral is well illustrated in the case of Kenneth Kirk, arguably the pre-eminent Anglican moralist of the twentieth century, whose most famous work is entitled *The Vision of God* (1931) and for whom the Regius Chair of Pastoral Theology at Oxford was renamed the Regius Chair of *Moral and* Pastoral Theology in 1932.

Social ethics Because the political context of the Church of England in the second half of the nineteenth century was – unlike that of the Roman Catholic church on the European continent – not such as to confront it with a militantly atheistic socialism, it was able to include among its responses to the 'social question' an Anglican variety of largely non-Marxist socialisms. The leading exponent of the earliest of these, CHRISTIAN SOCIALISM, was F.D. Maurice (1805–1872). Against the *laissez-faire* individualism of liberalism and its principle of competition, Maurice espoused a corporate vision of society in which the cooperation of different social classes is the norm. In his most famous work, *The Kingdom of Christ* of 1838, this social ideal is set in the theological context of a high, triumphalist Christology (not unlike those of Karl Barth and Karl Rahner), according to which the Christ who has redeemed all people in and for community already exercises universal lordship. Many Christian Socialists held the producer cooperative to be the major engine of social reform, but the Guild of St Matthew, which was founded by Stewart

Headlam in 1877, betrayed a certain Hegelian influence in reserving that role for the state.

The defence of private property has featured much less strongly in the Anglican response to the 'social question' than in its Roman counterpart. In his introduction to the symposium published as *Property: Its Duties and its Rights* in 1913, Charles Gore (1853–1932) acknowledges that property is necessary for the free expression of personality, but claims that the state has a duty to regulate it for the common good; and in one of the essays, Henry Scott Holland (1841–1918) welcomes the prospect of collective ownership. Further, in 1941 the Malvern conference on 'The Life of the Church and the Order of Society' passed a resolution making qualified criticism of the private ownership of industrial resources.

The Malvern conference had been called by William Temple, who has good claim to be the most eminent of Anglican social thinkers. With Maritain and the neo-Thomist school, Temple believed that the individual has a dignity anterior to society, but nevertheless needs to live in society and finds his or her fulfilment in serving the common good; and that the state is a natural institution designed to serve the common good by defending human rights and respecting the principle of subsidiarity. In the late 1930s, however, political experience and the influence of Reinhold Niebuhr combined to make Temple more appreciative of the entrenched reality of class interest and collective egoism, less sanguine about the possibility of giving social expression to Christian love, and therefore more critical of Hegelian optimism about the realization of social harmony and of Thomist optimism about natural morality. His most influential work in the field of social ethics is *Christianity and the Social Order* of 1942.

Since the Second World War, the leading representative of the Anglican tradition of social thought has been R.H. Preston, who shares its criticism of the principle of competition and its advocacy of the corporate nature of society and the essential sociality of the human individual. Nevertheless, Preston is severely critical of much of the tradition's failure to pay adequate attention to empirical data and the resultant vagueness of its ethics; of the rural utopianism of the 'Christian Sociology' of V.A. Demant (1893–1983); and of the failure of Anglican socialism to recognize the incomparable value of the market as a device for allocating scarce resources.

A constant feature of Anglican socialism that distinguishes it from its liberal Protestant counterpart is its interest in spiritual formation, especially through the eucharistic liturgy, as necessary to sustain *Christian* social and political commitment. This appears as early as Headlam and as recently as Kenneth Leech (*The Social God*, 1981).

Eastern Orthodox ethics
Until the publication of Misael Apostolides's *Tes Kata Christon Zoes Pragmateia* ('A Treatise on Life according to Christ') in 1847, there were no attempts in the Eastern Orthodox church to treat Christian ethics systematically. One reason for this is that the apophatic or mystical tradition of the Eastern church produced a strong suspicion of theological systematization as comprising an illegitimate human attempt to master divine reality – a suspicion that displays itself, for example, in the thought of Vladimir Lossky (1903–1958), one of Orthodoxy's most eminent twentieth-century theologians.

Apostolides's systematic ethics, and the handful of others that appeared during the following half-century, were slight and pastorally oriented. They were heavily dependent on western models; and, betraying the influence of Kant and scholastic manuals, their emphasis tended to fall strongly on the moral law.

The first major systematic work in Orthodox Christian ethics, the *Systema Ethikes* (of 1925) of Christos Androutsos (1869–1935), reflected the substance of this early tradition. Androutsos, the pre-eminent Greek Orthodox theologian of the early twentieth century, followed Kant and Schleiermacher in basing ethics on reason and denying any significant and proper discrepancy between its Christian and philosophical forms. His *Systema* contains few references either to the Bible or to the Fathers. Androutsos's work comprises the foundation of what has been labelled the 'Athenian' school of ethics.

In stark contrast to this is the specifically theological bent of the 'Constantinopolitan' school, whose leading representative was Vasilios (Basil) Antoniades (1851–1932). In his *Enchiridion Kata Christon Ethikes* of 1927 ('Handbook of Ethics according to Christ'), Antoniades draws on the Bible, the Fathers (especially Augustine), and Aquinas, to expound Christian ethics in terms of the form of life appropriate to the state of being in Christ.

Only recently have Eastern theologians sought to develop systematic ethics in specifically Orthodox terms. The 'Thessalonian' school of theology, which draws heavily on the Byzantine and post-Byzantine mystical tradition, found its first major ethical expression – albeit one that still depends heavily on the categories of western existentialism and personalism – in Christos Yannaras's (Greek: Giannaras) *The Freedom of Morality* of 1970. Ethical expressions of this tradition that are more purely Orthodox are the *Christianike Ethike Kata Tas Panepistemiakias Paradoseis* of 1971 ('Christian Ethics, University Lectures') of Georgias Mantzarides, and Stanley S. Harakas's *Toward Transfigured Life: The 'Theoria' of Eastern Orthodox Ethics* (Harakas, 1983). Harakas, writing in the alien, pluralist environment of America, stresses the prophetic importance of maintaining the integrity of the church, and so seeks to lodge ethics firmly in the context of Orthodox theology.

The spiritual and ecclesial context of moral life Indeed, it is one of the most important features of specifically Orthodox ethics that it is so tightly integrated into dogmatic and spiritual theology. The Christian life is conceived as 'theiosis' or deification, a process of spiritual growth whose end is the restoration in human being of the divine image and likeness.

Since God is triune, a community of three Persons united in love, the realization of divine similitude involves the individual's overcoming of sinful self-sufficiency and his becoming a person-in-community. Christian life, then, is necessarily life in *koinonia* or fellowship; and since it is by means of the sacraments, especially the Eucharist, that the regenerating grace of God is mediated, Christian life is specifically life in the fellowship of the church.

Ethos and the subordination of law Because of its emphasis on the presence of God's redeeming power – 'the law of the Spirit of life' – and its focus upon spiritual vitality and growth, Orthodox theology is more inclined to concern for the development of ethos than for the elaboration of a body of moral law. Indeed, it is characteristically wary of legalism – for one expression of this, take Yannaras's critique of proposals to codify Orthodox canon law in *The Freedom of Morality*. Nevertheless, Orthodoxy acknowledges that external regulation has an important role to play in Christian life, provided that it is remembered that the point of such regulation is to indicate the forms of conduct that are expressive of love and so conducive to spiritual perfection. In cases where the application of a moral rule is deemed likely to frustrate the expression of love or the promotion of theiosis, *economia* should be exercised and the rule suspended. In so far as the exercise of economy is the prerogative of an ecclesiastical authority – usually a bishop, a synod, or a spiritual father – this doctrine does not quite amount to a version of situation ethics.

Orthodoxy's traditional attention to the formation of ethos complements the recent revival of interest among Protestant moralists in the formation of virtue and character. But in its emphasis on participation in liturgy and the sacraments as means of such formation, it also provides a salutary supplement to the predictable Protestant tendency to be preoccupied with the morally formative use of (biblical) 'story'.

Social ethics In imperial Russia the Orthodox church was able to sustain the Byzantine vision of a *symphonia* or synthesis of church and state, in which the church's social calling was basically one of consecrating the political status quo. However, in the Ottoman and Soviet empires, where it was repressed, and in the pluralist west, where it has the status of a marginal minority, it has had to rethink its understanding of its social role. Vigen Guroian, writing in the USA, proposes a new Orthodox *via media* between accommodationism and sectarianism. The bases of this are, on the one hand, an ecclesiology that sees the church as a community whose *raison d'être* is simply to be an 'icon of perfection'; and, on the other hand, the doctrine of the incarnation, which establishes that the world is the 'matter' of the kingdom of God, and so implies that it is the task of the church to address it (Guroian, 1987). (See also EASTERN ORTHODOX THEOLOGY.)

Protestant ethics

Ethics, theological or philosophical? The influence of Philip Melanchthon (1497–1560) upon Protestant ethics in the sixteenth and seventeenth centuries was predominant and ambiguous. On the one hand, in his *Loci communes rerum theologicarum* of 1521 Melanchthon expounded right conduct in a section ('De Lege') which lies in the midst of a list of dogmatic topics running from God and creation to damnation and blessedness. Thus he encouraged his successors to make their ethics theological. But on the other hand, in his *Epitome philosophiae moralis* of 1541, where he identified the moral law basically with the law of nature, distinguished sharply between the moral law and the gospel of grace and assigned the exposition of natural law to philosophy, Melanchthon set an egregious precedent for separating ethics from Christian dogmatics. One who followed him in this direction was Bartholomaeus Keckermann (1571–1609), whose *Systema ethicae* of 1607 consists entirely of an Aristotelian philosophy of virtue. Others, however, followed Melanchthon in the opposite direction. For example, Johann Gerhard (1582–1637), the greatest theologian of Lutheran orthodoxy, not only treats ethics as part of a dogmatic system in his *Loci communes theologici* of 1610–22, but expounds the moral law in terms of the Decalogue. Likewise, J.A. Osiander (1622–1697) locates his casuistry firmly in a dogmatic context. Although, like Roman moralists, he begins his *Theologia casualis* of 1680 with chapters on conscience and law, these are actually only the 'premises' of the system which follows. That begins, in Book I, with chapters on the divinity of holy Scripture, God, and creation; and it ends, in Book VI, with chapters on death, resurrection, final judgement, the consummation of the age, hell, and heaven. The casuistry itself occurs in Books II–V.

The demise of casuistry By 1700 Protestant casuistry had effectively died. One of the reasons for its sudden (and permanent) demise is evident in the *Institutiones theologiae moralis* (1711) of J.F. Buddeus (1667–1729), who has been described as 'the greatest Protestant theologian and scholar of his age' (Kenneth Kirk). In the *Institutiones* Buddeus complains that Protestant casuists were unable as a matter of principle to deal with 'the inner cultivation of the spirit', and he devotes much of the first of three Books to a consideration of the pursuit of holiness, spiritual growth and the means by which these can be accomplished. Here Buddeus betrays the influence of pietism and its reaction against the theological (and ethical) rationalism of Protestant orthodoxy in favour of devotional and spiritual concerns.

But pietism was not the only cause of the disappearance of Protestant casuistry. Another was the emergence of a certain complacency about moral decision making resulting from a new-found confidence in the self-sufficiency of the individual's moral sense or reason or conscience. Evidence of this may be found in Buddeus, John Locke (1632–1704), Joseph Butler, Adam Smith (1723–1790), Jean Jacques Rousseau (1712–1778), and Immanuel Kant (1724–1804).

A third cause of the demise of Protestant casuistry was that the minds of late seventeenth- and eighteenth-century moralists were preoccupied with meta-ethical controversies about the nature and foundations of morality and moral epistemology. The names of Richard Cumberland (1631–1718), Joseph Butler, Francis Hutcheson (1694–1746), David Hume (1711–1776), Adam Smith, Richard Price (1723–1791), and William Paley (1743–1805) are usually associated with theories of natural law, conscience, moral sense and sentiments and utility, seldom with normative ethical analysis.

Reason as the measure of morals However, not all eighteenth-century moralists were uninterested in the specification of right conduct. Both Hutcheson and Paley, for example, treat the ethics of property rights, contracts, truth-telling, oaths, commerce, marriage and the family, political authority and war. But they do so largely as moral philosophers; that is, in abstraction from soteriology, and with primary reference to moral principles discerned in nature by reason rather than to those presented in specifically Christian sources. In this they are representative of the ethics of their age. Whether rationalist and deductive or empirical and inductive, reason – not revelation – was taken to be the measure of morality – as was made famously clear by Kant in his *Religion within the Limits of Reason Alone* of 1793. And even Kant, who acknowledged the problem of the reality of radical moral evil, declined to place ethics in a soteriological framework.

One outstanding exception to the increasing eighteenth-century trend to treat ethics without reference to the revelation and redeeming activity of God, is to be found in the thought of Jonathan Edwards (1703–1758). Edwards, a Calvinist theologian and philosopher in New England, clothed moral sense theory in Augustinian theology to argue that virtue consists essentially in affection, that true virtue consists chiefly in love for God, that apart from such love other virtues are less than true, and that human beings are incapable of it apart from the aid of regenerating grace.

Reason as Spirit in history In Germany the early nineteenth century saw a reaction against both the abstract rationalism of Kant's ethics, and its lack of a soteriological context. Influenced somewhat by pietism, Friedrich Schleiermacher (1768–1834) denied that morality is essentially about obedience to authoritative commands, arguing instead that it is a 'life-process' in which reason as an active and immanent power progressively organizes nature. The effect of this organization is to promote community and liberty simultaneously by engendering communities whose members respect each other's individuality – whether at the level of the family, the people or the state; and its progress is assured because reason and nature are united in the absolute ground of life, God. As reflection upon morality, then, ethics is not normative moral doctrine, but phenomenology of the activity of moral reason in history; and since Schleiermacher did not think that recourse to the Christian theological tradition is necessary in order to discern this dynamic natural law, ethics itself is philosophical, even if some of its metaphysical presuppositions are theological – such as the original unity of reason and nature and the 'redeeming' activity of reason. Nevertheless, Schleiermacher did have a conception of Christian ethics, although quite how he conceived its relationship with philosophical ethics is not clear. Certainly, they share the same content; for there is only one universal reason. Beyond that, it may be that Schleiermacher was inclined to understand their relation in what are, in effect, classic Thomist terms: Christian ethics presents natural ethics in sharper focus. For since the incarnation of God in Jesus Christ represents the perfect redeeming unification of reason with nature, Christian life and ethos might be expected to instantiate reason, and Christian ethics describe it, in an exemplary fashion.

On this point G.W.F. Hegel (1770–1831) was somewhat less equivocal. He was inclined to suggest that, although Christian theology has made important contributions to the development of human self-consciousness – and therefore to ethics – it has been sublimated into philosophy. Nevertheless, Hegel's ethics shares two important features with that of Schleiermacher: a soteriological presupposition, and an ideal reciprocity between the social matrix of morality and individual freedom. The soteriological presupposition is that absolute Spirit or Mind (*Geist*) is in the perfective process of progressively realizing itself in the world. The self-realization of Spirit manifests itself in the historical development of the human consciousness of human freedom – a development in which Christianity and the Reformation have been decisive moments: Christianity in its affirmation of human being as the vehicle of Spirit's self-realization, and the Reformation in its advocacy of the freedom of the individual conscience from (ecclesiastical and dogmatic) heteronomy. So far Hegel concurs with Kant. Where he differs (in Part 2 of *The Philosophy of Right* of 1821) is in denying that this freedom should be understood as freedom from all kinds of desire, and for obedience to the dictates of pure practical reason – in particular, its categorical imperative that one should act only in accordance with a maxim that can be willed as a universal law. Such a conception of freedom, Hegel complained, is entirely formal and has nothing to say about the values that do comprise the material premises with which practical reason works. These, according to Hegel, are mediated to individuals by certain natural kinds of community – family, civil society, and the state – to whose benefit they conduce. Because the individual's values are social in origin and intent, he naturally desires to serve his community (pre-eminently, the state) and is fulfilled in so doing. Nevertheless, he desires to serve the community freely and therefore rationally, and this requires that its social institutions be organized according to rational principles – in particular, in such a way as to respect the autonomy of individuals.

Against the inclination of Hegelian metaphysics to divinize nineteenth-century European culture by equating its development

with the work of God, Søren Kierkegaard (1813–1855) reasserted the classic Lutheran themes of the intractability of sin as voluntary rebellion (as distinct from ontic imperfection), and the opposition between God and 'reason'. The latter point he made notoriously in his interpretation of the story of Abraham and Isaac. Whereas Kant had used it to argue that putative divine commands should be subject to the judgement of reason, Kierkegaard used it to illustrate how God may legitimately command something that is usually regarded as immoral – how commitment to a religious *telos* may require the suspension of the ethical (*Fear and Trembling*, 1843). The seriousness with which Kierkegaard took God's 'otherness' in relation to human culture led him to emphasize the heavy 'inward' responsibility of the individual to differentiate himself from 'the public', by choosing himself in response to a divine calling (*Either/Or*, 1843). It also led him to set the radical demands of Christian discipleship at odds with the common moral sense of his time (*Works of Love*, 1847; *Training in Christianity*, 1850). At the time, however, Kierkegaard's prophecy against the spirit of the age went largely unheeded; and it had to wait for vindication until 1914.

The socialist realization of the kingdom of God Albrecht Ritschl (1822–1889) also reacted against Hegel, but in a neo-Kantian direction. For him, the significance of the dogma of the incarnation was not metaphysical (as it was for Hegel) but ethical. In calling Jesus 'divine', he argued, we make no claim about his metaphysical status; rather, we assign him absolute moral worth, especially as initiator of the kingdom of God – that is, the community where consciousness of God as Father issues in fraternal love for fellow humans (see KINGDOM OF GOD: POLITICAL AND SOCIAL THEOLOGY).

This conception of the kingdom of God, which Ritschl adopted from Schleiermacher, became central to much turn-of-the-century Protestant theology on both sides of the Atlantic as it sought to respond to 'the social question'. It featured prominently in the thought of Adolf Harnack (1881–1930), the leading representative of liberal Protestantism in Europe; and in the USA it became basic to the self-understanding of the social gospel movement. Walter Rauschenbusch (1861–1918), the foremost exponent of the social gospel, had, like Schleiermacher and Hegel, a strong conviction of the immanence of God in history, progressively working his purposes out. He took seriously the social transmission of sin and the corporate expression of evil. But he was confident of the historical possibility of bringing 'composite personalities' into God's kingdom and under the law of Christ. This law he held to comprise (self-sacrificial) love for the neighbour, the principles of cooperation and democracy, and the harmony of community and individual liberty (*A Theology for the Social Gospel*, 1918).

The rediscovery of sin and the critical transcendence of God In Europe liberal optimism about progress in the development of human culture was shattered by the apocalypse of the First World War, and by the conspicuous failure of international socialism to prevent it. Consequent disillusionment moved Karl Barth (1886–1968) to reach for Kierkegaardian themes such as the critical transcendence of God's command in relation to human 'ethics', which is expressive of 'the infinite qualitative distinction' between God and humankind; and the existential responsibility of the individual to choose himself in obedient response to it. In Barth's mature work (*Church Dogmatics*, 1932–68), the unintelligibility of God's command is much tamed by the Trinitarian analysis of his being and activity as Creator, Reconciler, and Redeemer, and by the decisive definition of his will in Jesus Christ. Nevertheless, Barth never relaxed his realist and personalist conviction that God is an active reality who is distinct from human agents but who freely engages them in personal relationship. As a consequence of this, he maintained an eschatological limitation upon all human endeavours and reasserted acts of prayer and worship as the basis of Christian morality (*pace* Kant).

Emil Brunner (1889–1966) and Dietrich Bonhoeffer (1906–1945) also based their ethical epistemology on the hearing of a divine command rather than on the casuistical interpretation of principle and rules. But they both made more overt, specific, and traditional use than Barth of concepts of natural or created 'orders' – in Brunner's case, the family, the economic process, the state, the community of culture, and the church (*The Divine Imperative*, 1932; *Justice and the Social Order*, 1943); and in Bonhoeffer's, labour, marriage, government, and the church (*Ethics*, 1949).

It fell to Reinhold Niebuhr (1893–1971) to play the role in North America that Barth had played in Europe. Disillusioned with the liberal optimism of the social gospel, not by war but by his experience of industrial strife, Niebuhr acquired a heightened appreciation of the recalcitrance of sin and a penchant for more sober readings of the human condition by the likes of Kierkegaard. In *Moral Man and Immoral Society* of 1932 he presented a version of Luther's doctrine of the two kingdoms, arguing that scope for the transcendence of self-interest by self-sacrificial love at a social level is extremely limited; and that the securing of justice may well require – and warrant – the 'rational' use of violent coercion. Thus he abandoned the pacifism of the social gospel for what he called 'Christian realism'.

Love and justice Niebuhr did not, however, regard the spheres of love and justice as absolutely separate. Distancing himself from Luther and approximating Augustine, he believed that love can qualify the pursuit of justice. Indeed, he argued that justice needs to aspire to the 'impossible ideal' of love, lest it degenerate into something less than itself (*An Interpretation of Christian Ethics*, 1935). Here he differs on the one hand from Brunner, for whom the distinction between (intimate) love and (institutional) justice is sharper (*Justice and the Social Order*); and on the other hand from Joseph Fletcher, for whom justice is simply the form that love takes when it sets about allocating itself among more than one neighbour (*Situation Ethics*, 1966).

The ongoing debate about the relationship between love and justice depends crucially on the concept of love that is brought into play. In his major analysis of the nature of Christian love (*Agape and Eros*, 1930), Anders Nygren (1890–1978) contraposed Christian *agape*, conceived as entirely lacking in self-interest, with Hellenistic *eros*, conceived as acquisitive desire. Such a concept of Christian love is bound to be in conflict with the common concept of justice as comprising the maintenance of rights; and other (less Protestant) moralists have sought to reconcile them by arguing, partly by appeal to the doctrine of creation, for a legitimate form of self-love (for instance John Burnaby in *Amor Dei*, 1938). (See also LOVE, CHRISTIAN.)

Rules, situations, and the making of moral judgements A debate that has been running in Protestant ethics since the Second World War has been about the relative roles of rules and circumstances in the making of moral decisions. It was brought to the surface by the publication of Fletcher's *Situation Ethics* in 1966. In this influential book, Fletcher argued that love is the only Christian norm; that, although moral rules are useful guides to the kinds of action that usually express love, in the end love must discern in each situation what is the most loving thing to do; and that there will be some occasions when love will require the suspension of pre-fabricated rules. In its radical relativization of rules, Fletcher's situation ethics resembles the ethics of 'responsibility' espoused by H. Richard Niebuhr (1894–1962), Reinhold's younger brother, and the contextual ethics of Paul Lehmann. Unlike Fletcher, however, Niebuhr did not maintain that right action is determined by calculating what is the most loving thing to do. Rather, somewhat approximating Barth without being dependent upon him, he preferred to describe right action in terms of a response to the creating, governing, and redeeming activity of the triune God (*The Responsible Self*, 1963). Likewise, Lehmann has described it in terms of correspondence to what God is doing to 'humanize' the world (*Ethics in a Christian Context*, 1963). One of the most notable critics of such depreciation of the role of rules has been Paul Ramsey (1913–1988), who upheld the need for more specific and reliable indications of right conduct, and contended for a casuistry that is able to learn from morally novel situations (see *Deeds and Rules in Christian Ethics*, 1968). Although James M. Gustafson acknowledges the part that rules have to play, he prefers to speak of the making of a moral decision as an act of 'discernment' that is the product of a whole range of factors, including the history of the moral agent (*Ethics in a Theocentric Perspective*, vol. 1, 1981). For Gustafson, the making of moral judgements is far more the function of an *esprit de finesse* than of an *esprit de géométrie*.

In the field of social ethics, the debate about rules and circumstances appears in the form of an ecumenical debate about 'middle axioms'.

First coined by J.H. Oldham (1874–1969), and then developed by John C. Bennett, the concept has recently been championed by R.H. Preston. As Preston puts it, 'middle axioms' are 'directions' for social practice that stand midway between universal principles of social ethics and particular policies, and that embody both moral principles and informed empirical judgements (*Church and Society in the late 20th Century*, Appendix 2, 1983). In asserting the need for 'middle axioms', their advocates have sought to correct the tendency of much recent social ethics – both in Protestant circles and in the World Council of Churches – to move directly from very general principles to policy prescriptions without troubling to reach a considered judgement about the nature of the political, social, and economic facts. However, although it is true that Protestant moralists have often been negligent in their attention to empirical analysis and theory (for instance Barth), some (such as H. Richard Niebuhr and Gustafson) have strongly affirmed the need for Christian ethics to refer to the human and social sciences.

The formation of character and the ethos of the church More recently there has been a reaction against what is perceived to be a preoccupation with the morality of acts in favour of the consideration of the formation of virtues and character (see NARRATIVE THEOLOGY). Without doubt the most influential advocate of this shift of attention has been Stanley Hauerwas, who has emphasized the morally formative function of the (Christian) community and, in particular, of the (biblical) story from which the community takes its identity. These emphases have led him to contend for the distinctiveness of Christian ethics in a manner that is heavily dependent on the thought of John Howard Yoder, the outstanding contemporary representative of the Mennonite tradition. Like Yoder (*The Politics of Jesus*, 1972; *The Priestly Kingdom*, 1986), Hauerwas brings ecclesiology to the centre of social ethics, arguing that the Christian church exercises its social responsibility by bearing prophetic witness to God's kingdom through its own peculiar ethos, one characterized above all by the renunciation of violence (*The Peaceable Kingdom*, 1983). The similarity of this line of thought with that of Vigen Guroian, the Eastern Orthodox theologian (see above), is marked – as it is also with that of Wolf Krötke. Krötke, responding to the marginalization of the church in the former East Germany, has argued that Christian political involvement should be grounded in the Christian community; and that this community should function as the nursery of a distinctive ethos, based upon worship and marked by the rejection of force, the sharing of power, dialogue, and responsibility for humankind (*Bekennen–Verkündigen–Leben: Barmer theologische Erklärung und Gemeinden-praxis*, 1986, trans. 'Confession, Proclamation, Life: The Barmen Theological Declaration and the Practice of Community').

The Bible: window onto reality or nova lex? Hauerwas's assertion of the ethical role of 'story', especially the biblical story of God's redeeming activity that finds its epitome in the life, death, and resurrection of Jesus, has raised again the perennial question of how the Bible should be allowed to contribute to Christian ethics. Protestant ethics in the twentieth century has tended to look to the Bible, not for moral rules, but rather for a theological vision of reality in which to set the consideration of human conduct. Hauerwas is of this bent, although – in good Mennonite fashion – he does take what he perceives to be the pattern of Jesus' life to be a kind of *nova lex*. Thomas Ogletree differs in letting the Bible furnish 'constitutive structures of the life-world' – a kind of set of natural laws – that are more specific and morally normative than a theological framework, but much less specific than moral rules (*The Use of the Bible in Christian Ethics*, 1983). However, although the fashion is against them, not all contemporary Protestant moralists have ceased to regard the provision of rules as *one* of the ethical contributions that the Bible can make (for example, James Childress).

Contemporary movements and Christian ethics
Ecumenism During the first two centuries of the period under consideration, there has been commerce between the different traditions of Christian ethics. In the seventeenth century, for example, Protestant casuistry came into being partly out of envy at the sophistication of Roman Catholic moral theology; in the early nineteenth century the Tübingen school of Catholic moralists were influenced by develop-

ments in Protestant theology; and in the second half of the nineteenth century early Orthodox attempts at systematic ethics were shaped in part by scholastic manuals. Nevertheless for the most part, whether because of theological principle, historical prejudice, or geographical isolation, the various traditions have tended to develop with a large measure of independence from each other.

In the twentieth century, however, the level of interaction has increased enormously, largely due to the development of ecumenical instruments. Most notable of these was the Universal Christian Conference on Life and Work, with its conferences at Stockholm (1925) and Oxford (1937). This was eventually absorbed into the World Council of Churches (WCC) under whose auspices the third World Conference on Church and Society was held in Geneva in 1966. The Geneva conference was especially remarkable because it was the first occasion when Eastern Orthodox members played a full part, and it led to a period of direct cooperation between the WCC and the Vatican in a programme on Society, Development, and Peace (SODEPAX). For this, of course, Vatican II deserves much of the credit.

However, although this ecumenical era has seen Roman Catholic moralists pay more than traditional attention to dogmatic themes and biblical ethics, and some Protestant ethicists endorse just-war theory and espouse casuistry, it is still generally the case that Catholics (and Anglicans) base their moral reasoning on some concept of natural law, while Protestants base theirs more directly on Christian dogmas or on some construction of the ethical import of the Bible.

Political and liberation theology Since 1970, when the WCC established its Commission on the Church's Participation in Development and its Programme to Combat Racism, the ethics of the ecumenical movement have been heavily shaped by both political theology and LIBERA-TION THEOLOGY. Appearing in the 1960s in different parts of the world (Europe and Latin America, respectively) and with different theological orientations (political theology was dogmatic where liberation theology was biblical), these two movements nevertheless share important features in common. Among the most important of these is the conviction that

Christian theology and ethics should be done in the context of *praxis* – that is, active political commitment to the cause of the poor and oppressed – with its implication that political, social, and economic injustice are the forms of immorality most deserving of attention.

Despite their widespread and continuing influence, political and liberation theology have been subject to criticism. Their insistence on the priority of praxis over theory has been widely charged with making their (Marxist) understanding of the problem and its solution immune from theological criticism. They have also been chided for tending to move directly from theology to politics, and therefore lacking the precision that ethical concepts could provide (Gustafson, *Ethics in a Theocentric Perspective*, vol. 1); and for tending to reduce the religious concepts of sin and salvation to the purely secular ones of political injustice and liberation (for example, Sacred Congregation for the Doctrine of the Faith, *Liberatio Conscientiae*, 1986).

Feminism Since the late 1970s feminism in its various forms has impressed itself to a certain extent on many of the traditions of Christian ethics, and it has led to the development of Christian feminist ethics (see FEMINIST THEOLOGY). Although this body of ethics is almost as variegated as feminism itself, it nevertheless has certain characteristic features. In respect of its methodology, it is a species of liberation theology, taking its ethical cue from praxis; but in its case praxis comprises, specifically and primarily, attention to the experience, and action on behalf, of women as a historically oppressed and marginalized social group. Much of Christian feminist ethics, therefore, is occupied with criticizing manifestations of patriarchy – and, more broadly, hierarchy – in Christian thought, practice, and institutions in the name of equality. Although one of the elements of this equality is invariably autonomy, another is often mutuality. This second element is expressive of some anthropological insights yielded by the lived experience of women, which are of fundamental ethical significance: that human being is essentially 'connected' rather than atomistic and competitive, and that the human person always exists in a web of relationships, many of the most important of which are not chosen but

given. These anthropological tenets have produced criticism of two features of modern ethics: the ideal of detached and impartial moral judgement – and therefore of Lawrence Kohlberg's theory of moral development (Carol Gilligan, *In a Different Voice: Psychological Theory and Women's Development*, 1982); and the notion that rights and duties attach only to individual persons, and not also to kinds of relationship (Beverley Wildung Harrison, *Making the Connections: Essays in Feminist Social Ethics*, 1985). It has also ensued in criticism of features of prevalent concepts of Christian love: detachment, impartiality, self-sacrifice, and indifference to the value of the beloved.

Although salutary, the insight of human connectedness is not in itself original. Thomism has long affirmed (in principle) the essential sociality of human being and the rights of natural communities. However, when the principle of connectedness is supplemented and qualified by another feminist insight – the essential embodiment of human existence – then it begins to say something unusual. It illuminates the concreteness of human connectedness; understands love as that which begins with the *proximus* – the neighbour; and raises the status of the workaday business of building community at the level of personal relationships in relation to the grand, public work of building it by political and military action.

Particular moral issues

Marriage and divorce All major Christian traditions have always affirmed heterosexual marriage, permanent (either intentionally or ontologically) and exclusive, as the natural end of sexual relations. Although polygamy has been tolerated by the church in some cultures, monogamy has always been the norm. There has been a consensus about most of the purposes of marriage: the provision of the proper context for genital relations; the procreation and nurture of children; and the mutual completion and perfection of the married couple. There is variation, however, over the relative weight to be attached to these 'ends' of marriage, and there is disagreement over whether it has an additional, sacramental purpose.

Traditionally, the Roman Catholic church has esteemed celibacy more highly than marriage, to a large extent because of an Augustinian tendency to regard sexual desire and pleasure after the fall as invariably tainted by concupiscence and therefore sinful. Partly for the same reason, the Catholic (and, until recently, the Anglican) traditions have taken the procreation and nurture of children as the primary good of marriage, which, at least, justifies sex and, at most, orders it (see, for example, Pius XI, *Casti Connubii* of 1930). Nevertheless, in spite of the traditionally pejorative regard for the (narrowly) sexual dimension of marriage, the Catholic tradition has emphasized its positive, sacramental function. Here, marriage is supposed to be a special means of sanctifying grace, in that the love between husband and wife reflects that between Christ and his church (Eph. 5: 32).

The distinctive lines of the Protestant position were established by Luther when he asserted the moral superiority of marriage over celibacy, affirmed sexual relations less grudgingly and denied marriage the status of a sacrament. Among the reasons for this denial were the lack of dominical institution and the implicit depreciation of marriage outside the Christian church (see Helmut Thielicke, *The Ethics of Sex*, 1964). Still, Luther did attribute to marriage undertaken in Christian faith a sacramental role – in a weak sense – in his strong affirmation of its function as a school for the spiritual and moral education of both parents and children. This was a dimension that Schleiermacher was later to emphasize and expound.

Since the Second World War, Roman Catholic thinking has moved away from the traditional tendency to view the goods of marriage as comprising a justifying excuse for sex, and towards the classic Protestant position. Vatican II's *Gaudium et Spes* (1965), for example, asserts that the mutual love of husband and wife is the norm and meaning of marriage, although it adds the qualification that this is nonetheless ordained to serve the child that is its fruit. Meanwhile, some Protestant thinking has come to find the meaning of sex primarily in its promotion of the communion of the persons involved. This separation of the 'unitive' and 'procreative' functions of sex is partly ascribable to the new and widespread availability of means of artificial contraception – the traditional objection to the use of

which it subverts. It also subverts the main traditional objection to homosexual practice, and so makes more conceivable the notion of homosexual marriage.

On the subject of divorce the main Christian traditions are not agreed. Ever since the thirteenth century the Catholic church has held the scholastic view that, since marriage as a sacrament mirrors the love of Christ for the church, the marital bond between husband and wife is an objective, ontological reality that cannot be dissolved. This 'indissolubilist' position holds divorce to be not merely wrong, but impossible. All that is possible is the separation of the married couple, or the annulment of a marriage on the grounds of certain 'impediments' that have prevented it from becoming genuine.

Commonly, Protestants do not regard the marital bond as comprising a reality that is independent of the trust that obtains between the married couple and which remains when that trust has broken down irretrievably. They regard it as moral rather than ontological, and as consisting in fidelity. Since the claims of fidelity, like the love of God in Christ for his people, are without term, the marital bond *should* not be broken; but, because of the persistent power of sin in fallen humanity, it *can* be. In effect, then, Protestants tend to recognize the possibility of what the Eastern Orthodox call the 'moral death' of a marriage.

Not all Protestants, however, agree with the Orthodox in permitting divorce and remarriage. Opinion on this varies according to the interpretation of Jesus' teaching in the synoptic Gospels. Some hold that Jesus forbade divorce altogether; others that he conceded it as a permissible evil in cases of grave sexual sin – such as adultery, as sanctioned by the 'Matthaean exception' (Matt. 19: 9). Further, not all who regard divorce as permissible permit remarriage as well. The Church of England, for example, currently allows one but not the other, in an attempt to combine pastoral realism and compassion with witness to the call and judgement of permanent, Christ-like fidelity. (See also SEXUAL ETHICS.)

The modern business corporation Since the 1970s moral philosophers, especially in the USA, have turned their attention to business ethics and have produced a considerable body of literature on the subject. However, whereas Christian moralists have long engaged in the moral assessment of CAPITALISM and socialism as economic and social systems, and have given extended consideration to the rights of workers, the just wage (for example, John A. Ryan, *A Living Wage*, 1906; M. Fogarty, *The Just Wage*, 1961) and the just strike (for example, R.H. Preston, ed., *Perspective on Strikes*, 1975), only very recently have they begun to attend to other ethical issues that are peculiar to the modern business corporation. These include the responsibilities of professional managers beyond that of maximizing the shareholders' return, and the accountability of transnational corporations. Nevertheless, although Christian ethical reflection on these matters is generally slight as yet, some notable work has been done. George Goyder, for example, has drawn on the natural law tradition to argue for the wider social responsibility of the company and, more specifically, the social audit; and he has drawn on Leviticus 15, the medieval doctrine of usury, Emil Brunner and William Temple to argue against the perpetual share and for the regular and compulsory amortization of capital loans (*The Responsible Company*, 1961; *The Responsible Worker*, 1975; *The Just Enterprise*, 1987). While Michael Novak's work in this field does not reach Goyder's level of moral analysis, he has employed theological resources to mount an apology for the business corporation against traditional Christian suspicion. Although he acknowledges its sinfulness and fallibility, he argues that the corporation is basic to democratic capitalism, mediating between the isolated individual and the state, and that it displays seven 'signs of grace': creativity, liberty, birth and mortality, a social motive, a social character, innovative insight, and the acceptance of the risk of liberty and election (*Toward a Theology of the Corporation*, 1990). (See also ECONOMIC ANALYSIS AND ETHICS.)

War and peace With regard to war, the mainstream traditions of Christian ethics in the modern period have tended to endorse the theory of just war. Although it has been espoused more consistently in Roman Catholic moral theology, this theory has found powerful advocates among Protestants – most notably, in recent times, Paul Ramsey.

Originating with Augustine, just war theory was developed by Aquinas in the thirteenth century and then in the sixteenth and seventeenth centuries by the Jesuit moralists, Vitoria and Suarez. It stipulates six criteria of the justice of engaging in war (*ius ad bellum*) and two criteria of the justice of making war (*ius in bello*). The criteria of *ius ad bellum* are that war should be engaged upon only: (1) by the right authority; (2) with just cause; (3) with right intention; (4) as a last resort; (5) if the damage likely to be caused is proportionate to the evil to be remedied; and (6) with reasonable prospects of success. The two criteria of *ius in bello* are that the means of war should be: (1) discriminate in their infliction of harm; and (2) proportionate in the damage they cause.

Of these criteria, some have been controversial and have consequently undergone elaboration. Aquinas's identification of legitimate authority with the *princeps* or ruler, for example, becomes untenable as soon as the notion of just rebellion against a tyrant is entertained. It raises the question of who has the authority to command the waging of war against the *de facto* ruler – 'lesser magistrates' (Calvin and, eventually, Luther) or the 'people' (John Knox)? And, in the case of the 'people', who should be taken to represent their will?

Originally, just cause was restricted to injury suffered directly at the hands of an aggressor. Recently, it has been questioned whether that restriction should not be relaxed, so as to make it conceivable that injury suffered by subjects at the hands of their own rulers should provide a third (foreign) party with just cause for belligerent intervention on their behalf. Further, the concept of 'systemic' or 'structural' violence has challenged the assumption that the infliction of injury need be overt in order to comprise just cause for armed rebellion.

The principle of discrimination has always raised the question of which class(es) of people should be immune from (directly intended) assault. Augustine had identified these as those morally innocent of the original, 'criminal' act of aggression. However, given the difficulty of apportioning blame and of rendering any of the enemy's populace immune from attack if one holds to a notion of collective guilt, subsequent moralists made the class of 'innocents' codeterminate with those who threaten no harm (that is, who are literally *in-nocens*). So, by the modern period, the principle of noncombatant immunity had been established. It remains a moot point, however, whether immunity should be extended to civilian members of a government responsible for commanding the perpetration of the original injury; and – in the modern age of mass warfare – whether it should be enjoyed by groups of civilian workers directly engaged in the 'war effort'.

Since the Second World War, just war theory has been most exercised in arguments over whether there could be just use of atomic and nuclear weaponry, either in the waging of war or in deterring an enemy from launching one. The political context assumed in almost all of this discussion has been that of the confrontation between NATO and the Warsaw Pact. Some, like Paul Ramsey (*War and the Christian Conscience*, 1961; *The Just War*, 1968), have argued that within a 'counter-force' (rather than 'counter-population') strategy the military use of nuclear weaponry could be discriminate, proportionate, and therefore just. Others, like the US Roman Catholic bishops in their Pastoral Letter, *The Challenge of Peace* of 1983, have argued that the probability of escalation to full nuclear exchange, and therefore of consequent global devastation, is so high as to make any military use of nuclear weapons immoral. However, whereas the American bishops held that the purely deterrent use of such weapons is permissible as part of a policy of moving towards progressive multilateral disarmament, the report of a Church of England working party, *The Church and the Bomb* of 1982, and the outstanding book by John Finnis, Germain Grisez, and Joseph Boyle, *Nuclear Deterrence, Morality and Realism* of 1987, both concluded that the very intention to use them is itself immoral, and that the pretence of such an intention (the nuclear 'bluff') is both immoral and impracticable.

Given the end of the cold war, debate about nuclear weapons henceforth is likely to focus upon their proliferation and upon the morality of pre-emptive (nuclear?) strikes to prevent more countries acquiring a nuclear capability.

Although just war theory has been the dominant stance of the major Christian traditions, pacifism has been more or less present in all of them. It has been found in the Roman Catholic church – in, for example, the Catholic Worker Movement – but it received conditional recognition as a legitimate Christian option for the first time only in Vatican II's *Gaudium et Spes* (1965). It has been much more consistently present in Protestantism, not only in the historic 'peace churches' – the Mennonites, the Quakers, and the Brethren – but also in liberal Protestantism and the social gospel movement. This undoubtedly reflects the much stronger tendency among Protestants to take their ethical cue directly from a construal of Jesus' ethic.

Among contemporary Christian moralists by far the most impressive and influential advocate of pacifism is John Howard Yoder. Yoder's ethic takes the Mennonite form of the *imitatio Christi*, basing itself on a reading of Jesus' ethic as involving at its heart the principled repudiation of violence (*The Politics of Jesus*). He denies that pacifism amounts to an abnegation of social responsibility, arguing that the Christian church fulfils its responsibility by bearing witness to God's kingdom through its nonviolent ethos, and not by striving in god-like fashion to make history turn out right. With regard to his reading of the content of Christian ethics, Stanley Hauerwas is much beholden to Yoder. (See also JUST WAR; WAR AND PEACE.)

Conduct towards the nonhuman world Since the 1970s there has been a marked increase in the attention paid by Christian theologians and moralists to the question of human regard for and treatment of the nonhuman world. To some extent, this has been part of a general rise in awareness of, and concern about, the damage being inflicted upon the human environment. But it has also been provoked by the accusation, first made by the American historian, Lynn White, that (western) Christianity has been responsible for encouraging the rapacious exploitation of the natural world. It has done this, according to White, through its unparalleled anthropomorphism and its desacralization of nature (see, for example, 'Continuing the Conversation', in *Western Man and Environmental Ethics*, ed. I.G. Barbour, 1973).

In the responses made by Christian apologists two major thrusts may be discerned. First, there is the confession of Latin Christianity's tendencies to depreciate matter – and here (again) the blame is often laid at Augustine's feet – and to treat the nonhuman world as simply ordained to the service of humans. But, second, there is the recovery of neglected elements in the Christian tradition that espouse a more respectful and responsible regard for the natural world. Among traditonal sources that have proved particularly fruitful in this regard are the Bible, the Fathers (especially Irenaeus), western mystics such as Hildegarde of Bingen and Meister Eckhart, the Franciscan tradition, and Eastern Orthodoxy. And among the most important modern sources are Albert Schweitzer with his principle of 'reverence for life' (*Civilization and Ethics*, 1923); Teilhard de Chardin, SJ, with his cosmic Christology and his concept of the sacramentality of matter (*The Divine Milieu*, 1960) – features that his thought shares with Eastern Orthodoxy; and process theology, which understands God to be (entirely?) immanent in the dynamic, creative, organic process that is nature.

Much of the most important recent Christian rethinking about the nonhuman world has taken place at a theological rather than a strictly ethical level. Grace Jantzen (*God's World, God's Body*, 1984) and Sallie McFague (*Models of God: Theology for an Ecological, Nuclear Age*, 1987), for example, have both drawn from Hegel and process theologies to argue against the dominant, monarchical model of God, which sets him at a disparaging distance from the world, and in favour of seeing him as so immanent in the universe that it is fair to speak of it as God's 'body'. In similar fashion, Jürgen Moltmann has reacted against the emphasis on God's transcendence over nature that was bequeathed to Protestant theology in Germany by the debate over natural theology between the Confessing Church and the German Christians in the 1930s. Instead, in *God in Creation: an Ecological Doctrine of Creation* of 1985, he develops the cosmic dimension of Christology in pneumatological terms to argue for the indwelling of God, the Holy Spirit, in the created world.

In addition to these theological endeavours, significant work of an ethical kind has been done. At a fundamental level, there is James Gustafson's bid to replace anthropocentricity with theocentricity in Christian ethics (*Ethics in a Theocentric Perspective*, 2 vols, 1981–4). And at a more specific, normative level, there is Charles Birch and John Cobb's proposal that all natural entities should be understood as having some

intrinsic, as well as instrumental, value; that an entity's relative value can be assessed in terms of its 'richness of experience', which is deemed to be correlative to the presence of a nervous system and to its complexity; and that, according to this criterion, the intrinsic value of animals (but not of plants) is such that they have rights in relation to humans (*The Liberation of Life: From Cell to Community*, 1981). Andrew Linzey also argues for animal rights, though in more directly theological terms; and whereas Birch and Cobb would permit scientific experiments upon some animals for worthy purposes and as a very last resort, he forbids it absolutely (*Christianity and the Rights of Animals*, 1987).

See also JUSTICE; MEDICAL ETHICS; SOCIAL QUESTIONS; WORK AND LEISURE.

Bibliography

Biggar, Nigel 1989: A case for casuistry in the church, *Modern Theology* 6, 1, pp. 29–51.

Calvez, J.Y. 1961: *The Church and Social Justice: The Social Teaching of the Popes from Leo XIII to Pius XII, 1878-1958.* London: Burns and Oates.

Curran, Charles, and McCormick, R.A., eds 1986: *Official Roman Catholic Social Teaching.* New York: Paulist Press.

Frey, Christofer 1989: *Die Ethik des Protestantismus von der Reformation bis zur Gegenwart.* Gütersloh: Gerd Mohn.

Guroian, Vigen 1987: *Incarnate Love: Essays in Orthodox Ethics.* Notre Dame: University of Notre Dame Press.

Gustafson, J.M. 1978: *Protestant and Roman Catholic Ethics: Prospects for Rapprochement.* Chicago: University of Chicago Press.

Hall, Thomas C. 1910: *History of Ethics within Organized Christianity.* London: T. Fisher Unwin.

Harakas, Stanley S. 1973: Greek Orthodox ethics and western ethics, *Journal of Ecumenical Studies* 10, 4, pp. 728–51.

Harakas, Stanley S. 1983: *Toward Transfigured Life: The 'Theoria' of Eastern Orthodox Ethics.* Minneapolis: Light and Life Publishing Co.

Jonsen, A.R., and Toulmin, S. 1988: *The Abuse of Casuistry: A History of Moral Reasoning.* Berkeley: University of California Press.

McAdoo, H.R. 1949: *The Structure of Caroline Moral Theology.* London: Longmans.

McCormick, R.A. 1989: Moral theology 1940–89: an overview, *Theological Studies* 50, 1, pp. 3–24.

Mahoney, John, SJ 1987: *The Making of Moral Theology.* Oxford: Clarendon Press.

Niebuhr, H. Richard 1951: *Christ and Culture.* New

York: Harper and Row.

Oliver, John 1968: *The Church and Social Order: Social Thought in the Church of England, 1918–39.* London: Mowbray.

Troeltsch, E. [1911] 1976: *The Social Teaching of the Christian Churches.* Chicago: University of Chicago Press.

Wood, Thomas 1952: *English Casuistical Divinity.* London: SPCK.

NIGEL BIGGAR

Eucharist   See SACRAMENTAL THEOLOGY.

evangelicalism   The term 'evangelical' dates from the sixteenth century, and was used to refer to Catholic writers wishing to revert to more biblical beliefs and practices than those associated with the late medieval church. It was used especially in the 1520s, when the terms *évangelique* and *evangelisch* come to feature prominently in polemical writings of the early Reformation. In the 1530s the term 'Protestant' became more significant. However, this term was imposed upon evangelicals by their opponents, and was not one of their own choosing. 'Evangelical' is the term now used by evangelicals to refer to themselves.

Evangelicalism had tended to centre upon a cluster of four assumptions:

1   the authority and sufficiency of Scripture;
2   the uniqueness of redemption through the death of Christ upon the cross, often linked with a specifically substitutionary theory of atonement (see SOTERIOLOGY);
3   the need for personal conversion;
4   the necessity, propriety and urgency of evangelism.

All other matters have tended to be regarded as 'matters of indifference', in relation to which a substantial degree of pluralism may be accepted.

On account of the numerical strength and theological diversity of the movement, it is difficult to generalize concerning its characteristics. However, the following general features appear to be characteristic of the movement in its modern forms.

1   Evangelicalism is *transdenominational*. It is not confined to any one denomination, nor is it a denomination in its own right. There is no inconsistency involved in speaking of 'Anglican evangelicals', 'Presbyterian evangelicals', 'Methodist evangelicals', or even 'Roman Catholic evangelicals'.

2   Evangelicalism is not a denomination in itself, possessed of a distinctive ecclesiology, but has now become a *trend within the mainstream denominations*.

3   Evangelicalism itself represents an *ecumenical* movement. There is a natural affinity amongst evangelicals, irrespective of their denominational associations, which arises from a common commitment to a set of shared beliefs and outlooks. The characteristic evangelical refusal to allow any specific ecclesiology to be seen as normative, while honouring those which are clearly grounded in the New Testament and Christian tradition, means that the potentially divisive matters of church ordering and government are treated as of secondary importance.

4   Evangelicalism is a predominantly *English-language* movement, reflecting the major roles played in its development and consolidation by writers in Britain and the USA.

Underlying the first three points may be discerned an important point: historically, evangelicalism is not committed to any particular theory of the church, regarding the New Testament as being open to a number of interpretations in this respect, and treating denominational distinctives as of secondary importance to the gospel itself. This does not mean that evangelicals lack commitment to the church, as the body of Christ; rather, it means that evangelicals are not committed to any one *theory* of the church. A corporate conception of the Christian life is not understood to be specifically linked with any one denominational understanding of the nature of the church. In one sense, this is a 'minimalist' ecclesiology; in another, it represents an admission that the New Testament itself does not stipulate with precision any single form of church government which can be made binding upon all Christians.

In view of the importance of evangelicalism to modern Christianity in the USA and Great Britain, its development in each of these situations will be explored in separate surveys (EVANGELICALISM: BRITAIN and USA).

See also: BAPTIST THOUGHT; MISSION, THEOLOGY OF; PENTECOSTALISM AND CHARISMATIC CHRISTIANITY; and the various articles on PROTESTANT THEOLOGY.

evangelicalism: Britain Evangelical Christianity is a form of Protestantism that has been particularly marked by an expectation of conversions, a devotion to the Bible, and an emphasis on the atonement. It has also nurtured an activism that at times has inhibited thought. The movement began in the 1730s as a revival of the doctrine of justification by faith and its greatest shaping influence was the legacy of Puritanism. Nevertheless the early evangelicals in the Reformed tradition, often swayed by the American theologian Jonathan Edwards, upheld a stronger doctrine of assurance than the Puritans. They were inclined to trust the evidence of experience that they were numbered among the saved. The evangelical revival was also indebted to high Anglican and Roman Catholic writers, especially for teaching about holiness, and to continental Protestants, particularly the Moravians. John Wesley, the founder of Methodism, was remarkably eclectic in his theology. Wesley and his followers hammered out an Arminian scheme, holding that Christ died for all and that salvation might be lost, and added the conviction that entire sanctification is possible before death. John Fletcher, Wesley's intended successor as leader of his religious societies, defended Methodist belief from assault by champions of the Reformed tradition in the Calvinistic controversy of the 1770s. Only the New Connexion of General Baptists, formed in 1770, and a handful of others joined the Methodists in professing an evangelical Arminianism.

The majority of eighteenth-century evangelicals were Calvinists, but not assertively so. They showed little trace of fatalism, for they upheld the principle that a person is responsible for his own perdition if he does not heed the gospel, or of antinomianism, for they insisted on the obligation of good works following faith. They believed, in fact, that faith itself is a duty. Their Calvinism has been characterized as moderate: it has more affinities with sixteenth-

century Protestant teaching than with the scholastic theology of the seventeenth century. Such views were professed by George Whitefield and the societies of Calvinistic Methodists he brought into being. In Wales they were taught at Trevecca College, which was superintended by Howel Harris, and memorably expressed in the Welsh writings of William Williams of Pantycelyn. In Scotland the new revival-orientated version of Calvinism was championed in the established church by a growing school of ministers led by John Erskine, by the 'New Lichts' of the Secession Churches and by the Relief Church formed in 1761. A small but growing band of clergy in the Church of England felt their way to similar convictions, as classically recorded in Thomas Scott's *The Force of Truth* of 1779. William Romaine preached them from London pulpits, James Hervey gave them literary expression and Henry Venn embodied them in *The Complete Duty of Man* (1763). Other leading eighteenth-century exponents were John Newton and Richard Cecil. Evangelical Calvinism was most fully crystallized in English Dissent by the Baptist Andrew Fuller and the Independent Edward Williams.

Although evangelicals criticized the latitudinarian theology of the age for its unorthodoxy, they were deeply influenced by the Enlightenment modes of thinking that underlay it. Wesley taught that religion and reason go hand in hand. Evangelicals habitually appealed to the authority of John Locke and used his method of testing opinions by experience. They held the inductive science of Isaac Newton in high regard, treating theology as a discipline where Newtonian technique was appropriate. Several of their leaders, Wesley among them, dabbled in scientific investigation. Like their contemporaries, evangelicals dwelt on the argument for the existence of God based on evidences of design in the natural world. They saw the universe as orderly and law-governed. Providence watched over its welfare, directing the course of history and intervening from time to time in displays of judgement or mercy. A combination of the human quest for knowledge and the divine purpose for the world guaranteed a brighter future. As they witnessed the steady progress of the gospel, many evangelicals saw grounds for expecting the arrival of the millennium of truth, peace and justice. Technically they were postmillennialists, believing that the second coming of Christ would not take place until after the millennium. Their optimism about the trend of events inclined them, at least before the French Revolution, to favour political reform. They upheld religious toleration and, sharing the values of benevolence, happiness and liberty with their educated contemporaries, rallied to William Wilberforce's campaign against the slave trade. Although they rarely questioned a ranked social order, evangelicals such as Wilberforce did insist on the obligations of social superiors and advocated the extension of education among the poor. Charles Simeon trained several generations of Anglican ordinands at Cambridge between 1783 and 1836 in the whole range of enlightened opinion as well as in preaching technique. Thomas Chalmers transmitted to an even larger public a blend of theology and social policy founded on Scottish common-sense philosophy. Early evangelicalism was closely bound up with the Enlightenment.

This frame of mind was challenged from the 1820s by new views shaped by romanticism. Edward Irving, a Church of Scotland minister in London and a friend of S.T. Coleridge, led the way by questioning accepted techniques of mission. Instead of pragmatic methods based on business models, he advocated unplanned dependence on God. Irving's principle was to become the foundation of faith missions such as Hudson Taylor's China Inland Mission later in the century. Irving was also the central figure in the rise of premillennialism, the doctrine that a personal second coming will take place before the millennium. Premillennial teaching, championed in the Church of England by Edward Bickersteth and in the Free Church of Scotland by Horatius Bonar, produced a much gloomier world view wherever it was adopted. J.N. Darby propagated its dispensational form (see DIS-PENSATIONALISM) through and beyond the Brethren movement while, together with the legitimacy of glossolalia, Irving's version was taken up by his Catholic Apostolic Church. It was among premillennialists that there arose an insistence that Scripture must be interpreted literally. Alongside this conviction there grew up the belief that every part of the Bible must be equally inspired since all of it is the Word of God. Originally associated with Louis Gaussen,

a Swiss theologian who in 1841 expounded it in *Theopneustia*, this view made most headway in the Church of England, yet remained a minority view among evangelical clergy there as late as 1861. Following the constitutional revolution of 1828–32, Anglican evangelicals became stout defenders of their church as established. They did not share the fears of the Oxford movement that the state was interfering in the life of the established church, but instead denounced the movement for Romanizing. William Goode powerfully criticized its appeal to tradition in *The Divine Rule of Faith and Practice* of 1842.

Notwithstanding the rise of the Anglo-Catholics, evangelicalism exercised a pervasive influence over the Victorian era. High and broad churchmen alike used its terminology, public speakers took over its pulpit rhetoric and its scholars were far from negligible. T.H. Horne's *Introduction to the Critical Study and Knowledge of the Holy Scriptures* of 1818 was frequently reissued. Able Anglican theologians included E.A. Litton, the author of an *Introduction to Dogmatic Theology* of 1882–92, Nathaniel Dimock, a prolific writer on doctrinal themes, and, at a more popular level, Bishop J.C. Ryle. The greatest nonconformist equivalents were R.W. Dale, the author of a classic study of the atonement (1875), and P.T. Forsyth, a theologian whose numerous works centred on the doctrine of the cross. Scottish Presbyterians included in their ranks a large number – James Orr was a typical representative – who blended a breadth of humane learning with a depth of Christian conviction. Such men faced a number of challenges as the nineteenth century wore on. Darwinian evolution tended to undermine the argument from design for the existence of God, and was consequently denounced by a few evangelical leaders such as T.R. Birks. A greater number, however, took the new scientific understanding in their stride and the Scottish Free Church evangelist Henry Drummond turned it into a vehicle for apologetic. The assimilation of techniques of biblical criticism posed greater problems, leading, for example, to the censure of William Robertson Smith by the Free Church of Scotland in 1880–1. Nevertheless over the next two decades evangelicals generally came to accept that higher criticism was not inherently flawed and might yield spiritual benefits. Most serious as a threat to received orthodoxy was the moral critique of doctrine arising from the humanitarianism of the times. The idea of eternal punishment seemed particularly difficult to harmonize with the love of God. Against all such liberalizing tendencies the doughty Baptist C.H. Spurgeon took his stand in the Down Grade Controversy of 1887–8, but few evangelicals remained untouched by the milder spirit of the age (see LIBERALISM: BRITAIN).

A new factor that further blurred the sharp edges of dogma, and yet paradoxically stiffened the disposition to theological conservatism, was the holiness movement arising in the late nineteenth century. Its primary inspiration was the early Methodist doctrine of entire sanctification, but in the 1870s the legacy was presented in revamped form by the American Robert Pearsall Smith. Adapted so as to assuage Calvinist suspicions, sanctification by faith became the teaching of the Keswick Convention. By the early years of the twentieth century, as expounded by Bishop H.C.G. Moule and others, it had become the standard view of sanctification among Anglican evangelicals and widespread elsewhere. Holiness teaching in an Arminian form was also taken up by the Salvation Army, the Cliff College tradition in Methodism and a number of small churches. Combined with premillennialism, Keswick reinforced the resistance to broadening theological attitudes in the early twentieth century. Dean Henry Wace and W.H. Griffith Thomas criticized exaggerated claims for the findings of modern biblical scholarship and evangelical voices were heard suggesting that evolution should be rejected in the name of loyalty to the Bible. The First World War crystallized fears of German intellectual influences behind higher criticism and FUNDAMENTALISM emerged. At its strongest among certain Anglicans, the Brethren and the sectarian fringe, British fundamentalism was much feebler than its American counterpart. It lacked any intellectual rationale of the standing of the Princeton theology. Leading evangelicals with fundamentalist sympathies, such as the Baptist F.B. Meyer, president of the Advent Testimony movement, were swayed by Keswick teaching to exercise self-restraint. There was no total repudiation of liberal trends.

The most assertive statement of liberalism in the early twentieth century was probably the Congregationalist R.J. Campbell's work *The New Theology* of 1907. It was generally agreed that its virtual pantheism put it beyond the bounds of evangelical belief. It was also denounced because the novel views were presented as the underpinning of an advanced form of the social gospel. Nevertheless, at least in nonconformity, the social gospel was more usually depicted as an outgrowth of evangelical convictions. The Wesleyan Hugh Price Hughes and the Baptist John Clifford, the two leading exponents in Britain, insisted that the social gospel was complementary to the gospel for the individual rather than a substitute for it. Interest in social questions, though not precise political prescriptions, continued to be widespread among the more liberal evangelicals of the inter-war years. In the Church of England the label 'liberal evangelical' was at first adopted by those who were willing to experiment with higher forms of liturgy than had been normal, but the publication in 1923 of *Liberal Evangelicalism* by the Anglican Evangelical Group movement associated the term with a theologically progressive stance. The touchstone of division from the more conservative was a rejection of the element of substitution in the atonement. Yet liberal and conservative attitudes coexisted in evangelical Anglicanism as in the other historic British denominations of the inter-war years. Many, especially at leadership level, deplored the tendencies to polarization. Such centrists, among whom Canon Max Warren was the most prominent, steered evangelicals away from internecine debate during the 1930s and 1940s. It was Warren who, in 1942, established the Evangelical Fellowship for Theological Scholarship, a training ground for scholars, and shaped the team statement of the evangelical Anglican position, *The Fullness of Christ* of 1950. Likewise the Student Christian Movement, drawing on all the major Protestant denominations, narrowed the gaps between different kinds of evangelicalism as well as between the different confessions.

Conservative evangelicals, who often looked askance at such cooperative ventures, felt themselves to be an intellectually despised minority in the interwar years. Only a few scholars such as Donald Lamont, professor of practical theology at Edinburgh, cared to identify with the Inter-Varsity Fellowship (IVF) that linked the conservative Christian Unions in the universities. From 1945, however, the IVF sponsored a Tyndale Fellowship for Biblical Research, masterminded by F.F. Bruce, that aimed to promote conservative biblical scholarship. The leading theologian of the IVF, Martyn Lloyd-Jones, chaired from the 1950s an annual Puritan Conference for the study of Reformed divinity. The co-organizer of the conference, J.I. Packer, was to take a prominent part in the subsequent moulding of evangelical theology. His *Fundamentalism and the Word of God* (1958), strongly influenced by the American B.B. Warfield, provided an intellectual defence of a conservative view of Scripture. The only thinker of equivalent stature among evangelicals was John Stott, whose biblical expositions set fresh standards for other preachers. From the 1960s evangelicals also turned to liturgical scholarship and, in larger numbers, to social responsibility. The Shaftesbury Project, founded in 1969, was a seedbed for thinking about many social issues that verged on the political sphere. Fears of ecumenical cooperation were increasingly laid to rest, but evangelicals still generally preferred joint action, locally, nationally and internationally, with like-minded Christians. Charismatic renewal, though initially unsympathetic to scholarly endeavour, fostered fresh popular perspectives on most questions it affected. It eroded, for instance, lingering suspicions of Roman Catholicism. By the early 1990s its adherents, particularly in the so-called 'house churches', were becoming more systematic in their theological reflection and tended to align themselves as either Calvinist or Arminian, though some preferred an Anabaptist label. Charismatic vitality helped ensure that a reinvigorated evangelical movement would have a greater intellectual impact, at least on the British churches, in the twenty-first century than in the twentieth.

See also EVANGELICALISM; EVANGELICALISM: USA; PENTECOSTAL AND CHARISMATIC CHRISTIANITY; PROTESTANT THEOLOGY: BRITAIN.

Bibliography

Barabas, S. 1952: *So Great Salvation: The History and Message of the Keswick Convention*. London: Marshall, Morgan and Scott.

Bebbington, D.W. 1989: *Evangelicalism in Modern Britain: A History from the 1730s to the 1980s*. London: Unwin Hyman.

Gordon, J.M. 1991: *Evangelical Spirituality*. London: SPCK.

Jay, E. 1979: *The Religion of the Heart: Anglican Evangelicalism and the Nineteenth-Century Novel*. Oxford: Clarendon Press.

Morgan, D.L. 1988: *The Great Awakening in Wales*. London: Epworth Press.

Pratt, J.E., ed. 1978: *The Thought of the Evangelical Leaders: Notes of the Discussions of The Eclectic Society, London, during the Years 1798–1814*. Edinburgh: Banner of Truth Trust.

Rosman, D. 1984: *Evangelicals and Culture*. London: Croom Helm.

Sell, A.P.F. 1987: *Defending and Declaring the Faith*. Exeter: Paternoster Press.

Smyth, C. 1940: *Simeon and Church Order: A Study of the Origins of the Evangelical Revival in Cambridge in the Eighteenth Century*. Cambridge: Cambridge University Press.

Thompson, D.M. 1990: The emergence of the Nonconformist social gospel in England. In *Protestant Evangelicalism: Britain, Ireland, Germany and America, c. 1750–c.1950: Essays in Honour of W.R. Ward*, ed. K. Robbins. Oxford: Blackwell, pp. 255–80.

Toon, P. 1979: *Evangelical Theology, 1833–1856: A Response to Tractarianism*. London: Marshall, Morgan and Scott.

Walsh, J. 1966: Origins of the Evangelical Revival. In *Essays in Modern English Church History in Memory of Norman Sykes*, ed. G.V. Bennett and J.D. Walsh. London: Adam and Charles Black, pp. 132–62.

D.W. BEBBINGTON

evangelicalism: USA Evangelicalism has been of major importance in the USA, and has come to denote both a theological position and a historical movement. It derives its name from the Greek word $\varepsilon\upsilon\alpha\gamma\gamma\varepsilon\lambda\iota o\nu$, which is the essential message about Jesus Christ and the relationship to him. The English word 'gospel' is a rendition of the word 'Godspell', which is essentially the story of God. It is a movement spanning many centuries of time and with wide geographical extent.

Theologically, evangelicalism is an emphasis upon the gospel, which is understood as the good news of individual regeneration through a personal relationship to Jesus Christ. Evangelicals then are those who believe in and declare the necessity of conversion. There are several aspects to this concept and a number of subsidiary doctrines.

Evangelicalism stresses personal experience, or inward faith, rather than sacramentalism, or formal outward connection to the church or any other ecclesiastical organization. It also believes in the need for human transformation. Something is seriously wrong with the human, which cannot be rectified by resolution or education. There is a radical belief in grace, as the unmerited favour of God, received directly from God by the individual, accepted solely by faith, without the mediation of any human institution. Evangelicalism draws its understanding of the nature of salvation and of the Christian life, indeed of all spiritual truth, from the Bible, rather than tradition, any human institution, experience or reason. It thus can be rightly distinguished by a dependence upon the Bible as fully and uniquely authoritative. It also insists that the doctrines which it holds must be related to the issues of practical or ethical living, resulting in an emphasis upon personal holiness and concern for societal justice. Further, it emphasizes the urgency of evangelism, which is extended on a worldwide basis to become missions. Each of these doctrines is either a presupposition of, or an implication of, the basic commitment to the gospel.

Evangelicalism is closely related to, but distinguishable from, three other terms: orthodoxy, conservatism and pietism. It is generally orthodox in its theology, in the sense of holding to the theology of the great historic creeds of the church, but it subscribes to these doctrines not because the creeds teach them but rather because the Bible teaches them. It insists that merely subscribing to the doctrines or being orthodox in belief is insufficient for salvation. The belief must be accompanied by a personal experience of Jesus Christ.

Evangelicalism is also conservative in its theology, maintaining that there has been a once-for-all or normative revelation by God in his Word, and that the teachings of the Bible must therefore be preserved from any erosion of modern thinking. It is not, however, necessarily conservative in the sense of being closed-minded. At its best, it is not defensive and cranky; it is aggressive and optimistic, with confidence in the power of God and the ultimate triumph of Christ's kingdom. It is critical of the desire to preserve traditions, and is often critical of the social and political status quo as well. While it is sometimes associated with a conservative stance on political issues, this is not necessarily the case.

Pietism, a movement arising in the seventeenth and eighteenth centuries, emphasizes strongly the dimensions of personal experience and of inwardness. It insists that mere correct doctrinal belief is insufficient. At times, however, pietism has emphasized warmth of personal experience to the neglect of orthodox belief. Thus, it may lack the doctrinal commitments which are essential parts of evangelicalism.

Evangelicalism comes in many varieties. One significant issue is the denominational connection. Some evangelicals are found within 'mainline' denominations – older, more officially liberal groups. Many are found within separate denominations which are distinguished by a clearly evangelical bent. Yet others are independent evangelicals, either members of independent churches or unaffiliated to any local congregation. Another distinction is between charismatic or even Pentecostal evangelicals and non-charismatic evangelicals. The difference between these two groups is significant enough for them sometimes to be treated as separate or alternative groups, but for our purposes we will regard them as two varieties of evangelicals.

Evangelicalism is found worldwide. In the eastern European countries, it has been virtually the only form of Christianity, other than Roman Catholicism in countries like Poland and Eastern Orthodoxy in countries like those of the former Soviet Union, to survive and show vitality. Under oppression, it has been especially inhibited because of its emphasis upon evangelism, which is quite frequently restricted by totalitarian governments. Yet it has shown strength and retained the loyalty of its adherents, who find in its teachings and practice great encouragement in the face of severe opposition. In the former Soviet Union and a number of other eastern European nations, it is virtually equivalent to the Baptist denomination. Indeed, the Baptist Convention in the former Soviet Union is known as the Union of Evangelical Churches.

In Britain, the evangelical movement has led a twofold existence. It has demonstrated real strength within the Church of England, which in general has always had a stronger evangelical wing than have the state churches of continental European countries. In North America and especially in the USA, evangelicalism has been a numerically strong and in recent years even a politically powerful force, and has displayed many varieties. This has been, in the twentieth century, the place of residence of the largest segment of evangelicalism. In recent years, with the fading of the strength of American mainline denominations and the retraction of their foreign mission endeavours, evangelicalism as a worldwide force has grown in strength on a comparative basis. Thus Christianity's surge of growth in the third world is primarily an expansion of evangelicalism, particularly when this term is made inclusive enough to include Pentecostal and charismatic Christianity.

Evangelicals see their heritage as going back to the New Testament church, as depicted in the Book of Acts. There the kerygma was declared, and the life of the church was based upon the revelation from God as understood by the first believers. With the passing of time, however, a more liturgical and sacramental approach began to prevail, so that the medieval Catholic church increasingly deviated from what has traditionally been termed evangelicalism. There were during this period significant individuals and movements which displayed the basic evangelical motifs. Among these were Bernard of Clairvaux, Peter Waldo, the Brethren of the Common Life, and forerunners of the Reformation, such as John Wycliffe, Jan Hus, and Girolamo Savonarola. The term 'evangelical' was applied at the Reformation to Luther's emphasis upon salvation by grace. With the growth of Lutheran scholasticism and the effects of the state church, however, Lutheranism became characterized more by orthodoxy than by evangelicalism, a development which was paralleled in the Reformed church as well. The term 'evangelical' came to be virtually synonymous with 'Protestant'.

The history of evangelicalism in the USA is usually reckoned to begin with the occurrence of a number of evangelical awakenings during the eighteenth century in the North American colonies, in which large numbers came to faith in Christ. The strangely warmed heart of John Wesley ignited the great Wesleyan revival, both in England and in the colonies. The nineteenth century, with the expansion of the American frontier westwards, was characterized by powerful evangelical ministry. The frontier provided unique challenges to the church. With the uncertainty of life on the frontier, and the lack of permanent church ministries, revivalism became prominent. This involved a stereotypical form of preaching, in which the essentials of the message of salvation were presented and the hearers were called upon to make an immediate decision to 'accept Christ'. The church was active in evangelical ministries in urban areas as well. Charles Finney and Dwight L. Moody were leaders in this latter aspect of evangelicalism. The church played a significant role in sustaining black persons in their situation, both under slavery and in freedom. Its message was basically evangelical in content and tone.

Towards the end of the nineteenth century, North American evangelicalism began to undergo certain changes. Tension was arising between evangelical doctrine and modern learning, especially in such areas as biological evolution. The Bible conference movement brought together similar-minded believers from various denominations for Bible teaching and fellowship. Some of these groups, realizing that what they had in common was greater than their differences, began to draw up lists of 'fundamentals', basic, indispensable beliefs upon which fellowship rested. This gave rise to the name 'fundamentalists' for these believers (see FUNDAMENTALISM). Many of them saw their main task as opposing theological liberalism, which was spreading through the churches (see LIBERALISM: USA). In so doing, the movement became considerably narrowed. Whereas many of the original leaders of the movement were careful scholars, the momentum shifted towards zealous but sometimes poorly informed persons. As modernism progressively emphasized the 'social gospel', fundamentalists increasingly neglected the aspect of the evangelical heritage that had extended the implications of the Christian faith to issues of social problems. As liberals united in ecumenical councils, and in some cases even engaged in the merging of denominations, evangelicals withdrew fellowship from those of somewhat different theological conviction.

Fundamentalists sought to stem the growth of heterodoxy through two means. They succeeded in passing state laws forbidding the teaching of evolution in the public schools and the manufacture, sale or consumption of alcoholic beverages (although the prohibitionist movement was broader than merely fundamentalism). They also sought to exercise control of denominations, their foreign mission programmes and theological seminaries. In both areas, however, fundamentalism found itself fighting a losing battle. The famous Scopes trial over the evolution law in Dayton, Tennessee, in 1925 served to bring scorn and ridicule upon fundamentalism. In a denomination such as the northern Presbyterian church, the strength of the conservatives waned to the point where they were unable to elect their candidate, Clarence Macartney, moderator. In 1927 a reorganization of Princeton Theological Seminary led to the withdrawal of J. Gresham Machen, Robert Dick Wilson, O.T. Allis and others to form a new seminary in Philadelphia, Westminster Theological Seminary. Whereas in 1891 the fundamentalists had been successful in their insistence that Union Theological Seminary in New York City must either dismiss Charles Briggs or leave the denomination (it chose the latter course of action), now it was the conservatives rather than the liberals who were being forced from their posts.

The aftermath of this was that fundamentalists and their congregations began withdrawing in large numbers from the more liberal denominations of which they had been a part. They formed new, conservative denominations or remained independent congregations. Fundamentalism became a word of derogation, associated with poorly educated, isolationist, mean-spirited, dogmatic Christianity. It appeared that it would become irrelevant to the larger culture.

Beginning during and immediately after the Second World War, however, new vigour began to appear in American evangelicalism. The National Association of Evangelicals was organized in 1942 to provide a channel for evangelicals to work cooperatively. Fuller Theological Seminary was founded in 1947 to provide an evangelical alternative to Princeton Seminary. It was to be a school built upon the highest quality of theological scholarship, but thoroughly committed to the evangelical understanding of Christianity. Numerous young evangelical scholars were pursuing graduate study in first-class universities, acquiring impeccable academic credentials. Billy Graham came to prominence in 1949 with a brand of evangelism that sought to base its citywide campaigns upon cooperation among persons and churches of all theological varieties. The launching of the fortnightly magazine, *Christianity Today*, marked the effort of evangelicals to have a publishing voice parallel to *The Christian Century*, whose circulation it soon outstripped. This series of developments highlighted the rise of what came to be known as the 'new evangelicalism'. This new variety of evangelicalism emphasized the presentation of an intellectually respectable defence of the Christian faith and the application of that theology to the social issues of contemporary society.

Evangelicalism has shown a marked rise in popularity in the USA. A number of American politicians have acknowledged being 'born-again' believers, the most prominent instance being President Jimmy Carter. Noting that approximately thirty-five million Americans identified themselves as born again, George Gallup proclaimed 1976 the year of the evangelical. Numerous entertainers and professional athletes also accept that identity. Even the Association of Theological Schools in the USA and Canada, the accrediting association for seminaries, acknowledged in an official statement in 1990 the 'preponderance of evangelical schools' in the association, and the average enrolment of the evangelical seminaries is considerably larger than their more liberal counterparts.

A number of problems plague American evangelicalism in this period of great success, however. Ethical lapses by some of its most prominent public leaders, the televangelists, have tended to bring a bad name to the entire movement, these people being distortions and caricatures of evangelicalism.

There have also been doctrinal controversies within the movement. One of the first pertained to the inerrancy of the Bible. Conflict over this doctrine rent the faculty of one of the first major institutions of the new evangelicalism, Fuller Seminary. The debate broke out in the Evangelical Theological Society over the views of Robert Gundry, who subsequently resigned his membership of the society. The contention has spread to other doctrines as well. Dispute over whether the deity of Jesus should be thought of in metaphysical or merely functional categories has been a topic of considerable debate. Some have also modified the traditionally exclusive view of salvation. Clark Pinnock has suggested that all will have an explicit opportunity to believe in Jesus, so that those who have not had such an opportunity during life will have a chance to do so after death. There has also been an increased openness to varieties of annihilationism, with Pinnock, Philip E. Hughes, John Stott and others endorsing such a view.

A more recent disagreement has been over the nature of conversion and saving faith. One group, identified with Zane Hodges, insists that salvation is by pure faith, which does not require repentance of sin or acceptance of the lordship of Christ. These are necessary for discipleship but not for salvation. The opposing group, headed by John McArthur, contends that true faith must require repentance and commitment to Christ as lord, but not the performance of good works.

A more inclusive dispute is that between charismatic and non-charismatic evangelicals. These two basic groups have been present within evangelicalism throughout this century, beginning with old-line Pentecostalism and continuing through the neo-Pentecostal or charismatic phase (see PENTECOSTALISM AND CHARISMATIC CHRISTIANITY). In more recent years, however, the dispute has become more internal, with the rise of the 'third wave' associated with John Wimber and also known by such names as 'the vineyard', 'signs and wonders' and 'power evangelism'. These persons have advocated direct divine healing and believe that the lack of such in many evangelical circles results from the adoption of a twentieth-century western world view, in which miracles are deemed impossible.

Yet another topic of disagreement is almost more practical than doctrinal. It involves the so-called gospel of 'health, wealth and happiness'. This view, propounded by some of the evangelists who fell into public disgrace, holds that the sign of God's blessing upon individuals and groups is that he prospers them in the ways mentioned. It has some definite points of overlap with some of the other movements, particularly the third wave.

There has also been increasing difference of opinion over the role of women, both within the family and the church. The Council on Biblical Equality has argued for egalitarian roles for men and women within marriage and for full access for women to all offices and functions of ministry, while the Council on Biblical Manhood and Womanhood has contended that the husband is to be the head of the family and women ought not to teach or exercise authority in the church.

One other issue concerns the nature and role of the church. Large churches with more than 2000 persons in attendance at Sunday services have come to be labelled 'megachurches'. Generally functioning as self-sufficient entities, they have provided full-service ministries, from nursery schools to bowling alleys and exercise classes. They have geared themselves strongly to meeting felt needs and have emphasized the marketing of their services. To some, both inside and outside the church, this appears to be a transformation of church from ministry to business.

Style of worship has also been a source of tension within local congregations, often dividing over generational lines. Older Christians tend to prefer more formal worship, with congregational hymn singing, organ accompaniment, robed choirs singing anthems, and sermons. Younger Christians in evangelical churches in general lean towards praise choruses with guitar accompaniment, and the sharing with one another of spiritual concerns, insights and blessings.

The future of evangelicalism presents a paradox. On the one hand it has greater numerical strength and greater public influence than at any time in the modern era. It has managed to recapture some of its lost heritage, such as the emphasis upon social concern, without losing its distinctive thrust for evangelism. At the same time, however, there are signs that it may be in danger of decaying from within. A study of students in evangelical colleges and seminaries indicated a significant shift in attitudes and practices from those of their counterparts of an earlier generation, suggesting that the ethical distinction between them and the world has eroded. There are also some indications that the theological convictions of evangelicalism are less crucial for the coming generation of evangelicals than they have been for their parents and ancestors. Declining financial contributions also endanger local church, denominational and interdenominational ministries. The resolution of the paradox will determine the future of the movement.

See also DISPENSATIONALISM; EVANGELICALISM; EVANGELICALISM: BRITAIN; PROTESTANT THEOLOGY: USA.

Bibliography

Bloesch, Donald G. 1973: *The Evangelical Renaissance*. Grand Rapids: Eerdmans.

Dayton, Donald W., and Johnston, Robert K., eds 1991: *The Variety of American Evangelicalism*. Knoxville: University of Tennessee Press.

Hunter, James Davison 1983: *American Evangelicalism: Conservative Religion and the Quandary of Modernity*. New Brunswick, NJ: Rutgers University Press.

Hunter, James Davison 1987: *Evangelicalism: The Coming Generation*. Chicago: University of Chicago Press.

Magnuson, Norris 1977: *Salvation in the Slums: Evangelical Social Work, 1865–1920*. Metuchen, NJ: Scarecrow.

Marsden, George 1980: *Fundamentalism and American Culture: The Shaping of Twentieth-Century Evangelicalism, 1870–1925*. New York: Oxford University Press.

Noll, Mark A. 1986: *Between Faith and Criticism: Evangelicals, Criticism, and the Bible in America*. San Francisco: Harper and Row.

Quebedeaux, Richard 1978: *The Worldly Evangelicals*. New York: Harper and Row.

Ramm, Bernard L. 1981: *The Evangelical Heritage: A Study in Historical Theology*. Grand Rapids: Baker.

Shelley, Bruce Leon 1967: *Evangelicalism in America*. Grand Rapids: Eerdmans.

Wells, David F., and Woodbridge, John D. eds. 1975: *The Evangelicals: What They Believe, Who They Are, Where They Are Changing*. Nashville: Abingdon.

MILLARD J. ERICKSON

evangelism See EVANGELICALISM; MISSION, THEOLOGY OF.

evil, problem of Theodicy, in what is usually taken to be its classical or canonical form, is a philosophical and/or theological exercise involving a justification of the righteousness of God. (The term 'theodicy' is derived from the Greek *theos* (God) and *dikē* (justice); hence 'demonstrating that God is just'.) This demonstration requires the theodicist to reconcile the existence of an omnipotent, omniscient and morally perfect divinity with the existence and the considerable scale of evil. However, as the long and involuted history of theodicy shows, this project has never been a unitary and homogeneous undertaking. For this history reveals that theodicy is better seen as a designation which covers a number of diverse and even incompatible undertakings. Thus, for example, some theodicists (Richard Swinburne and John Hick come readily to mind) take the question of the *existence* of God to constitute the heart of theodicy, while others (such as the exponents of 'process' theodicy) consider theodicy's main problem to be that of determining whether (an *already* existing) divinity can justifiably be said to be responsible for the existence and the sheerly destructive nature and magnitude of evil. It would not therefore be misleading to say that theodicists do not even have a consensus on the question of the kind of primary *agenda* which confronts them.

The so-called 'problem of evil' is deemed by its proponents to have a venerable ancestry, and was apparently first formulated by Epicurus (341–270 BCE) in the form of a dilemma which perhaps receives its most succinct formulation in the words of David Hume: 'Is he willing to prevent evil, but not able? then he is impotent. Is he able, but not willing? then he is malevolent. Is he both able and willing? whence then is evil?' (Hume, [1779] 1948, p. 66). The prevailing consensus among those who operate within theodicy's canonical tradition holds that a long strand in the history of theology – stemming from St Augustine via St Thomas Aquinas and the Reformers to Schleiermacher and modern times – has addressed itself to the task of reconciling God's omnipotence, omniscience and benevolence with the existence and the considerable scale of evil. This received view declares, or covertly assumes, that all these philosophers and theologians were addressing themselves to essentially the same unchanging set of problems – problems invariably believed to cluster round the dilemma enunciated by Hume. This view is problematic, in so far as it implies that there is a single and unitary objective for theodicy to attain. To the extent that they do this, theodicists appear to conflate various theoretical and practical aspects of the problem of evil (or perhaps more appropriately, the *problems* of evil) which had best be kept separate. But, just as significantly, they overlook how theodicy is very much a creature of Enlightenment and post-Enlightenment thought, and how questionable therefore is the suggestion that, for example, St Augustine was dealing with essentially the 'same' problem as Richard Swinburne. Thus even a cursory reading of Augustine's texts indicates that he viewed the 'problem(s) of evil' in the context of the saving transformation of the human soul by God, in which case it would be implausible to maintain that (for him) these problems are concerned, necessarily, with the existence or the goodness of God (as they are for the contemporary theodicist): to be the author of our salvation, God has to be God, that is, divinity has constitutively to *be* and to be supremely good. The modern theodicy-problem, as the problem of the existence and/or the benevolence of deity, simply could not have posed itself to Augustine.

Where the distinction between 'theoretical' and 'practical' theodicies is concerned, it can be said that in its *theoretical* aspect theodicy appears to be concerned with two primary questions:

1 Can *moral evil* in itself be rendered intelligible?

2 Is *theism* intelligible in the face of the fact of evil?

In addition, there is a *practical* aspect to theodicy which can be expressed in terms of the following questions:

3 What does *God* do to overcome the evil and suffering that exist in God's creation?

4 What do *we* (*qua* creatures of God) do to overcome evil and suffering?

These two kinds of question concerning evil and suffering pave the way for distinguishing between 'theoretical' and 'practical' theodicies.

Theodicies with a 'theoretical' emphasis

Michael Peterson (1983) has helpfully suggested that there are four main approaches to theodicy (that is, what is depicted here as 'theoretical' theodicy): the free will defence (as formulated by Alvin Plantinga); the so-called natural law theodicy (Richard Swinburne); process theodicy (A.N. Whitehead and Charles Hartshorne); and the 'soul-making' theodicy of John Hick.

The free will defence is thought to have a long ancestry, and is sometimes alleged to extend as far back as St Augustine. But it is widely agreed that Alvin Plantinga is the most redoubtable of its modern advocates. Plantinga (1974) maintains that the free will defence aims to show that the following two propositions are not inconsistent:

1 God is omnipotent, omniscient and perfectly good.

2 Evil exists.

The way to do this, says Plantinga, is to find a third proposition which, together with (1), will entail (2). The third proposition is:

3 Evil exists because of the actions of free, rational and fallible human beings.

It is important to strees that Plantinga employs the notion of free will solely in order to construct a *defence*, that is, to show that the assertion that God exists is not logically inconsistent despite the presence and the profusion of evil in the world. He therefore makes no attempt to prove: (a) that (3) is true; or (b) that (3) is prima facie plausible; or (c) that we have good grounds for asserting (3). All that is required in order to demonstrate that (1) is not logically inconsistent with (2) is for (3) to be shown to be *logically possible*. For this reason he prefers not to call his argument a 'theodicy': to be a theodicy it will be necessary for the free will defender not only to show that (3) is logically possible, but also that one or more of (a)–(c) above is in fact the case. (For more on the distinction between a 'defence' and a 'theodicy', see Tilley, 1991.)

To show that (3) is logically possible, Plantinga employs a very formidable logical semantics. But his central insight underpinning this logical legerdemain is the conviction that it is logically impossible for an agent to create

193

another being such that it is necessarily the case that this being freely performs only those actions which are good or beneficial. Hence, as a corollary, it is always logically possible for there to be evil in a universe created by an all-powerful, all-knowing and benevolent deity.

Richard Swinburne has also used a version of the free will defence as an explanation of the existence of human evil. But he reinforces this defence with the claim that human agents can make 'genuine choices' (the precondition of the adequacy of the free will defence for Swinburne) only if they have knowledge of how to perform, or to abstain from, evil actions; and the existence of 'many natural evils' is believed by Swinburne to be a necessary condition of the possibility of this knowledge:

> the fewer natural evils a God provides, the less opportunity he provides for man to exercise responsibility. For the less natural evil, the less knowledge he gives to man of how to produce or avoid suffering and disaster, the less opportunity for his exercise of the higher virtues, and the less experience of the harsh possibilities of existence; and the less he allows to men the opportunity to bring about large scale horrors, the less the freedom and responsibility which he gives to them. (1979, p. 219)

For Swinburne a natural order containing evil evidently constitutes a schooling process necessary for the attainment of goodness, and the existence of evil can in all propriety therefore be reconciled with the existence of an omnipotent and good God.

Process theism is a philosophical theology based on the metaphysical system adumbrated by A.N. Whitehead (1862–1947) (see PROCESS THEOLOGY). But the process theodicy was really formulated by Charles Hartshorne (b. 1897). The core of process theism is supplied by the principle that God, while being absolute and unsurpassable, is also personal, social and temporal. God is bipolar, that is, God is infinite and so on, but also depends upon creatures to affect the course or shape of divine experience. Hartshorne denies that the existence of God can be disconfirmed by the presence of evil in the world. A renowned defender of the ontological argument for the existence of God,

he believes that the assertion 'God exists' is an a priori or necessary truth, and so cannot be negated by the empirical or contingent truth 'evil exists'. Either God's existence is logically impossible or it is logically necessary, in which case empirical evidence, such as that furnished by the existence of evil, has no bearing in principle on the question of the existence of God. Hartshorne therefore concludes that '[the problem of evil] is a mistake, a pseudo problem' (1966, p. 202). But why do apparently intelligent persons not realize that the very attempt to do theodicy is premised on an egregious failure to understand the true logic of theism? Hartshorne's answer is that theodicists have an inadequate doctrine of God, and it is precisely because they err in this respect that they are tempted to think that God must somehow be absolved of any responsibility for the existence of evil in the created realm. The need for theodicy will vanish once the 'self-contradictory' concept of God in 'classical theism' is replaced by the bipolar deity of process theology. Hartshorne is therefore an advocate of the dissolution, as opposed to the solution or resolution, of the 'problem(s) of evil'. The same strategy of dissolution is adopted by other notable process theologians. In the words of John Cobb and David Griffin:

> God seeks to persuade each occasion towards that possibility for its own existence which would be best for it; but God cannot control the finite occasion's self-actualization. Accordingly, the divine creative activity involves risk. The obvious point is that, since God is not in complete control of the events of the world, the occurrence of genuine evil is not incompatible with God's beneficence towards all his creatures. (1977, p. 53)

The 'problem of evil', Cobb and Griffin suggest, is to be dismantled by denying the concept of omnipotence it presupposes: the God of process theism cannot control finite beings but can only set them goals which this God then has to persuade them to actualize. The attenuation of divine omnipotence that is merely latent in, say, Plantinga's version of the free will defence, thus receives explicit endorsement in process theology.

The 'soul-making' theodicy is associated above all with John Hick. Central to any understanding of this theodicy is Hick's distinction between two basic kinds of 'answer' to the problem of evil. One 'answer ' – which Hick calls 'the Augustinian' – excludes the idea that a God who endows creatures with freedom and a modicum of power will intervene on the scale needed to prevent evil from occurring. Another 'answer' – which he terms 'the Irenaean' – sees evil as an integral feature of an environment in which souls are shaped by a God who desires all creatures to grow into an ultimately perfect relationship with their Creator. Hick's theodicy professes to stand within the latter tradition.

Like Plantinga, Hick employs a version of the free will defence. But he differs from Plantinga in emphasizing that it is necessary to go beyond the mere affirmation that the fact of human freedom is sufficient to show that God's existence is logically compatible with the existence of evil. Hick therefore incorporates his version of the free will defence into a theistic teleology, the central tenet of which is the conviction that God creates us as free beings for a purpose, that is, to enable us to fulfil our nature in relation to divinity by exercising our freedom in a world that both veils and reveals God. Like Swinburne, Hick provides an instrumental account of the existence of evil. Evil and suffering, on this view, are constitutive of the 'soul-making' process. But unlike Swinburne, Hick sees the need to posit a final state, beyond our earthly existence, in which this pedagogy of human salvation could be continued and completed. The process of 'soul-making' will reach its climax when all human beings enjoy a perfect relationship with their Maker, having finally been formed in God's likeness. For Hick, therefore, all forms of suffering are ultimately constructive because they somehow advance God's purposes in creating the world.

Theodicies with a 'practical' emphasis
The following passage from Elie Wiesel's book *Night* [1958] 1972 is something of a *locus classicus* for theologians who could be said to be exponents of theodicies with a 'practical' emphasis:

> The SS hung two Jewish men and a boy before the assembled inhabitants of the camp. The men died quickly but the death struggle of the boy lasted half an hour. 'Where is God? Where is he?' a man behind me asked. As the boy, after a long time, was still in agony on the rope, I heard the man cry again, 'Where is God now?' And I heard a voice within me answer, 'Here he is – he is hanging here on this gallows.'

The mode of argument espoused by proponents of 'practical' theodicies in response to such narratives is not ratiocinative. Unlike those who can be said to follow the 'theoretical' approach to theodicy, 'practical' theodicists such as Dorothee Soelle and Jürgen Moltmann do not set out to formulate a linear argument consisting of premises from which certain logically compelling conclusions have to be deduced. Their positions are shaped by an explicitly theological agenda which is headed by the following characteristic questions:

1 *What* are the different kinds and stages of suffering?
2 Who are the actual and typical *victims*?
3 Who are their actual and typical *oppressors*?
4 What social and historical *structures* enable the oppressors to afflict their victims?
5 How is suffering to be *overcome* by human beings?
6 What does *God* do when creatures suffer?

'Practical' theodicists decline to provide what they regard as abstract or merely theoretical 'answers' to such questions, and invariably deal with them by adverting to specific and concrete fictional or nonfictional episodes like the one supplied by Wiesel. Also important for the 'practical' theodicist is the phenomenon of 'protest' atheism, that is, the fundamentally moral 'rebellion' against God displayed most typically by Dostoevsky's character Ivan Karamazov, who repudiates any suggestion that innocent suffering can be redeemed or expiated by a divinely bestowed bliss in a post-mortem existence.

This 'praxis-oriented' approach is motivated by the belief that 'answers' to the above questions are to be sought by invoking the concept of a God who does not disengage from the evil that afflicts the creation and who 'shares' the sufferings of creatures. Thus for Soelle and Moltmann the only religiously appropriate answer that could be given to the Jew at the time of the executions depicted in Wiesel's harrowing story is the one given by its narrator: 'Here he is – he is hanging here on this gallows.' To quote Moltmann:

> With the Christian message of the Cross of Christ, something new and strange has entered the metaphysical world. For this faith must understand the deity of God from the event of the suffering and death of the Son of God and thus bring about a fundamental change in the orders of being of metaphysical thought . . . It must think of the suffering of Christ as God's potentiality . . . God suffered in the suffering of Jesus, God died on the cross of Christ, says Christian faith. ([1973] 1974, pp. 215–16)

Hence the only theodicy that can hope to make itself available to the inmates of places like Auschwitz is one that resolves itself into a theophany (a temporary self-revelation of God), in this case a suffering theophany. The position of the victim is regarded as paramount by the 'practical' theodicist, who consequently implies that the crucial question for the victim is not 'Is theism unintelligible because I am in torment?' but (as Moltmann implies in the above quoted passage) 'Is this God a God of salvation – is this God a God who can help?'. It is not maintained by this theodicist that such a question will necessarily be answered in the affirmative by the victim, rather the claim is that it is this question (or its cognates) which lie at the forefront of the intellectual horizon of the person who is afflicted, and not the question of the intelligibility of 'theism'.

An approach to the 'problem(s) of evil' from the standpoint of the victims of evil will therefore lead to SOTERIOLOGY, or more precisely (given the framework of the Christian mythos), to the Christian doctrine of the atonement. This is precisely the option proposed by the much neglected Scots theologian Peter Taylor Forsyth (1848–1921):

> The final theodicy is in no discovered system, no revealed plan, but in an effected redemption . . . It is not in the grasp of ideas, nor in the adjustment of events, but in the destruction of guilt and the taking away of the sin of the world. (1948, p. 211 and p. 220)

The axiom of divine immutability and impassibility is normally discarded by such theodicists in order to accommodate the notion of a suffering God (see SUFFERING, DIVINE). This notion is always given a Christological gloss: the God who suffers is the self-same God who suffers in the person of Jesus from Nazareth. Theodicy (if we can continue to call it that for someone like Moltmann) is thus effectively decomposed into Christology, or, more specifically, a theology of the cross. Indeed there is no real need for theodicy in the canonical sense of the term where this approach is concerned: in the face of God's self-justification on the cross of Christ, the attempt of the human thinker to justify God vis-à-vis the fact of evil (which of course is what theodicy essentially is) becomes superfluous. The Christian who takes atonement seriously has no real need for theodicy (or so the 'practical' theodicist contends).

The distinction between 'theoretical' and 'practical' theodicies is not meant to be absolute. Its value is essentially heuristic, in that it enables us to identify the respective strengths and weaknesses of the two approaches. It is easy to see that the merits of the one tend to be the demerits of the other, and vice versa.

It is often overlooked, especially by proponents of the 'theoretical' approach to theodicy, that their treatments of the 'problem(s) of evil' constitute a signifying practice, and that as theodicists they are producers of systems of signification. As such, the formulation of a response to the 'problem(s) of evil' (and suffering) is always 'interest-relative', relative in this case to a certain logical 'space' occupied by particular explanations and formulations. Thus, where the 'theoretical' theodicist is concerned, the object of explanation and its surrounding alternatives are:

Evil exists because
$$\left\{ \begin{array}{l} \text{the world is a} \\ \text{'vale of soul-making'.} \\ \text{we are free beings.} \\ \text{good is impossible} \\ \text{without the possibility} \\ \text{of evil.} \end{array} \right\}$$

whereas for the victim of such evil (and hence for the 'practice-oriented' theodicist) the object of explanation and its surrounding spaces are more likely to be:

Evil exists because
$$\begin{cases} I \text{ am imprisoned } here. \\ We \text{ are being tortured} \\ now. \\ You \text{ are indifferent to} \\ our \text{ hunger.} \\ God \text{ is an indifferent} \\ \text{spectator.} \end{cases}$$

The question of the relative merits of the two approaches to the 'problem(s) of evil' can therefore be broached in terms of the question of the adequacy or appropriateness of their respective 'spaces' of explanation or formulation. This of course presumes, perhaps without any real justification, that some kind of comparison can be made regarding the characters of these two spaces.

The strongest claim that can be advanced on behalf of the 'theoretical' approach is that even the most devastated victims have a need to come to intellectual terms with the putative causes, reasons and so on for their pain and suffering. Victims, it is argued, need to undertake some kind of intellectual reckoning with their plight, to have some means of justifying or not justifying, 'theoretically', their situation in relation to God (assuming of course that the question of God is a significant one for them).

Against this, the exponent of the 'practice-oriented' approach will be disposed to argue that the realities of evil and suffering can be so mind-stopping, so disruptive of speech, that any such purely theoretical exercise puts the theodicist in the position of Job's comforters, whose all too rational explanations of his plight only added to his torment. Moreover, it could be said that such ease of speech in the face of intractable evil and suffering constitutes a blasphemy against the One who is the fellow-sufferer alongside all victims.

It is virtually impossible to make a definitive adjudication of such claims and counter-claims. The predilection of the writer of this article is to favour the position of the 'practice-oriented' theodicist, if only for two reasons. First, this kind of theodicist appears in principle to be more attentive to the surd realities of evil and suffering; 'theoretical' theodicists are somewhat prone to traffic in propositions about evil as a principle or datum, rather than to attend, theologically or otherwise, to its causes and the possible means of overcoming or ameliorating it. Second, the 'practical' approach, taking as it does the form of theology of the cross or a doctrine of the atonement, lends itself more easily to formulation from within the circle of Christian faith. It sometimes appears that a mere metaphysical curiosity (which of course is not in itself necessarily a bad thing) is sufficient to pose the kinds of questions that claim the attention of the 'theoretical' theodicist. Again the principle of the interest-relativity of explanation and formulation has a force which demands to be acknowledged, and the emphatically Christian theologian, *qua* this particular kind of theologian, may want to align herself or himself with Forsyth, Moltmann, Soelle and others in approaching the problem of evil fully and unreservedly in terms of a doctrine of the atonement or a theology of the cross. She or he may even want to go as far as Moltmann and convict this metaphysical curiosity in the name of 'the Christian message of the Cross of Christ'.

A morality of theological knowledge

A putative response to the 'problem(s) of evil' that invokes so directly 'the Christian message of the Cross of Christ' will create problems inasmuch as it is, necessarily, an 'answer' circumscribed by an incarnational faith. Such an 'answer' will be acceptable only to the person who is not prepared to dismiss the suggestion that the 'grammar' of God incorporates a 'rule' to the effect that, as a consequence of the life, death and resurrection of Jesus of Nazareth, speech about creaturely suffering is in some sense speech about God's very own history. The only real alternative to not incorporating this 'rule' into the Christian 'grammar' of God is silence (in this case a silence that bespeaks the absolute absence, as opposed to the hiddenness, of divinity). Indeed, it could be claimed, as Soelle does, that it is very often the case that silence – a silence that is 'neutral' as regards the 'absolute absence' or 'hiddenness' of divinity – is the only morally appropriate response to occurrences of extreme and gratuitous suffering. 'Practical' theodicists are disposed to say that these two alternatives, speech about divinity, and a profoundly moral reticence about God's 'ways' with sufferers (which, provided they are expressed in separate levels of language, are not necessarily mutually exclusive) are the only plausible responses to be made to the 'protest atheistic' objections of the Ivan Karamazovs of this world.

It has to be declared at the outset that the principle of the theology of the cross is not one that can be vindicated by a philosophical or systematic theology. That redemption should be bestowed to humankind in and through a Nazarene who died on a cross at Golgotha nearly two thousand years ago is a truth that in the end can only be spoken by resorting to a theology of revelation open to the Word of God as 'given' in Holy Scripture. In this case, then, theodicy is a form of speech that must be moved away from philosophical theology (where in current practice it takes the form of the articulation or defence of an Enlightenment or post-Enlightenment 'theism') into the realm of dogmatics (which understands theological truth as precisely that which gives voice to the history of the crucified Nazarene). But here there is a real danger that we may try to say too much about 'godness', and that in so doing we may cease to be sufficiently dialectical, give insufficient emphasis to the notions of paradox and mystery, these being notions which must lie at the heart of any theology of the cross that hopes to be taken seriously. A 'morality of knowledge', heedful of Theodor Adorno's injunction that 'intelligence is a moral category', places the 'practical' theodicist under an obligation to the victims of evil not to overlook the sheerly intractable features of the 'problem(s) of evil'. Theodicy is inherently flawed: it requires us to be articulate, rational and reasonable in the face of that which is so often unspeakable. Theodicy, it could be said, is always doomed to be at variance with the profound truth that the 'problem(s) of evil' will cease to be such only when evil and suffering no longer exist on this earth. Until that time there is much substance in the charge that the theodicist's presumption (that words can somehow express the reality of the unspeakable) only trivializes the pain and suffering of those who are victims. It is therefore necessary to stress that we are not likely to bring much comfort to the victims of suffering with a theodicy, even when it is one

that is subsumed under a soteriology. Evil, in its root and essence, is a mystery. How God grapples with it and overcomes it is a mystery too (here Christ's descent into hell becomes a powerful and indispensable theological category). Holy Saturday, which is what is being adverted to here, is a mystery that the theologian must ponder over in the grasp of God's infinite love. Christians have the assurance of the victory of this love, but the theologian cannot use this assurance (nor the truth that evil is a mystery) either as an excuse for indifference or to provide a too hasty consolation for those who suffer.

The Christian crucified hope on behalf of those who suffer – a 'hope against hope' – is constrained by at least two imperatives:

1 that Christians must allow the beliefs and practices which underpin this hope, and the language in which it is expressed, to be 'interrupted' by the realities of pain and dereliction, especially as these are visited upon those who are innocent.

2 that the prayer and confessions which are constitutive elements of the process of sanctification cannot be pursued in isolation from the practice of messianic solidarity with all who are dehumanized (as J.-B. Metz points out). This solidarity will of course be one which strives to combat all manifestations of evil and suffering.

The theologian who reflects on the 'problem(s) of evil' must begin from a sense of failure, an awareness of the poverty and brokenness of her or his linguistic resources. She or he must, above all, sustain this sense of failure as she or he proceeds to reflect on these 'problems'. Then, and only then, will the theologian's reflections begin to approximate to the form of understanding demanded by a truly Christian response to the 'problem(s) of evil', that is, an understanding which, at least where the 'practical' theodicist is concerned, forsakes the attempt to seek a (merely 'theoretical') justification of God in order to engage in a historically conditioned articulation of what is involved in the divine justification of sinners. Because of what 'godness' is, the speech in which God justifies Godself by justifying sinners is necessarily one that is not transparent to itself.

But there is something else: any speech which allows itself to be interrupted by the narratives of what happened in Auschwitz or the Warsaw Ghetto, say, would perforce be one that was not transparent to itself.

See also PHILOSOPHY OF RELIGION.

Bibliography

Cobb, John B., and Griffin, David R. 1977: *Process Theology: An Introductory Exposition*. Belfast: Christian Journals.

Fiddes, Paul S. 1990: *The Creative Suffering of God*. Oxford: Oxford University Press.

Forsyth, Peter Taylor 1948: *The Justification of God*. London: Latimer House.

Hartshorne, Charles 1966: A new look at the problem of evil. In *Current Philosophical Issues: Essays in Honor of C.J. Ducasse*, ed. F.C. Dommeyer. Springfield, Ill.: Thomas, pp. 201–12.

Hick, John 1968: *Evil and the God of Love*. London: Fontana/Collins.

Hume, David [1779] 1948: *Dialogues Concerning Natural Religion*. New York: Harper.

McCabe, Herbert 1981: God: Evil, *New Blackfriars* 62, pp. 4–17.

McCabe, Herbert 1985: The involvement of God, *New Blackfriars* 66, pp. 462–76.

MacKinnon, Donald 1974: *The Problem of Metaphysics*. Cambridge: Cambridge University Press.

Metz, Johann-Baptist [1980] 1981: *The Emergent Church: The Future of Christianity in a Postbourgeois World*, trans. Peter Mann. London: SCM Press.

Moltmann, Jürgen [1973] 1974: *The Crucified God*, trans. R.A. Wilson and John Bowden. London: SCM Press.

Moore, Sebastian 1977: *The Crucified is No Stranger*. London: Darton, Longman and Todd.

Peterson, Michael L. 1983: Recent work on the problem of evil, *American Philosophical Quarterly* 20, pp. 321–39.

Plantinga, Alvin 1974: *God, Freedom and Evil*. London: Allen and Unwin.

Soelle, Dorothee [1973] 1975: *Suffering*, trans. E. Kalin. London: Darton, Longman and Todd.

Surin, Kenneth 1986: *Theology and the Problem of Evil*. Oxford: Blackwell.

Swinburne, Richard 1979: *The Existence of God*. Oxford: Clarendon Press.

Tilley, Terrence W. 1991: *The Evils of Theodicy*. Washington, DC: Georgetown University Press.

Wiesel, Elie [1958] 1972: *Night*, trans. Stella Rodway. London: Fontana/Collins.

KENNETH SURIN

existence of God, proofs of The principal types of argument for God's existence are as follows: the cosmological; the experiential (or 'argument from experience'); the moral; the ontological; the teleological (or argument from design). These have taken a wide variety of different forms. The titles are in most cases self-explanatory, with the possible exception of the cosmological and ontological. The former argues from the existence of the cosmos to the need for a First Cause; the latter, that the definition of God as containing all perfection must include his existence.

Though formal proofs of God's existence are at least as old as Plato and Aristotle and had sometimes been given a conspicuous place in earlier theological discussion, as with Thomas Aquinas's Five Ways (see NATURAL THEOLOGY), it was only really with the increasing prominence given to reason that came to be characterized as the Enlightenment that discussion of the issue in philosophical treatments of theology assumed centre stage. The founder of modern philosophy, René Descartes (1596–1650), defended versions of both the cosmological and ontological arguments. However, in the eighteenth century the argument which enjoyed most popularity was the teleological. This was particularly true among deists. Voltaire, for instance, despite his contemptuous dismissal of the Bible and of Samuel Clarke's defence of the cosmological argument, remained a convinced believer in God for precisely this reason. Another indication of the popularity of the argument from design in the eighteenth century is the fact that David Hume in his critique of the traditional proofs in his *Dialogues concerning Natural Religion* (published posthumously in 1779) devotes almost all his attention to refuting this argument. The force of this and the cosmological argument was still further weakened by the attacks of Immanuel Kant (1724–1804) (see KANTIANISM) and by the publication of Darwin's *Origin of Species* in 1859.

In marked contrast to the general trend of the nineteenth century, G.W.F. Hegel attempted to revive the ontological argument. But the distrust of purely intellectual forms of reason which is to be found in the romantic movement meant that justifications of religious belief also came to assume an experiential form, most influentially in F.D.E. Schleiermacher (1768–

1834). However, he had already been anticipated by Kant's practical justification of belief in God (his so-called moral argument), that, though we cannot prove God's existence, none the less we must hope for it if our moral life is not to end in an unresolved contradiction, with goodness and happiness bearing no relation to one another. John Henry Newman in the nineteenth century was to give a much more straightforward version of this argument, that our experience of the dictates of conscience compels belief in God.

But also present in Newman is an appeal to the cumulation of probabilities: that, instead of thinking of formal, deductive proofs, we should acknowledge that justification of belief in God may legitimately follow the normal pattern of human reasoning, with a number of different factors, individually weak, but cumulatively strong, building up a powerful case for theism. The image he offers is of a cord whose individual fibres are weak but which none the less, because they overlap, can be as strong as steel. It is this pattern of justification which has been followed in recent British philosophy, particularly in the writings of Basil Mitchell and Richard Swinburne. In Swinburne's case the argument from religious experience is seen as decisive, though he imposes upon it a degree of scientific rigour which Mitchell believes to be impossible.

Among theologians who accept the need for some form of rational justification it is the approach of Schleiermacher which continues to enjoy the most popularity. Paul Tillich may be seen in this light, as also may Karl Rahner, though inevitably many other influences are also present (existentialism in both cases; Friedrich von Schelling in the case of Tillich; and the transcendental Thomism of Joseph Maréchal in the case of Rahner).

Not all philosophers would accept the necessity for such proofs even in their modern inductive form (see PHILOSOPHY OF RELIGION). Karl Barth and Eberhard Jüngel would be two twentieth-century examples of theologians who totally reject the need for such an approach. Jüngel holds the search for such proofs responsible for the rise of modern atheism, a view which has also been endorsed by some historians of thought.

See also ATHEISM; EPISTEMOLOGY, RELIGIOUS; FAITH AND REASON; GOD.

Bibliography
Buckley, M.J. 1987: *At the Origins of Modern Atheism*. New Haven: Yale University Press.
Burrill, D.R., ed. 1967: *The Cosmological Arguments*. New York: Doubleday. (on cosmological and teleological arguments)
Hick, J., and McGill, A.C., eds 1968: *The Many Faced Argument*. London: Macmillan. (on ontological argument)
Mackie, J.L. 1982: *The Miracle of Theism*. Oxford: Clarendon Press.
Mitchell, B. 1973: *The Justification of Religious Belief*. London: Macmillan.
Swinburne, R. 1979: *The Existence of God*. Oxford: Clarendon Press.

DAVID BROWN

existentialism Existentialism is a form of philosophical enquiry which attaches primary importance to the immediate, lived experience of the individual. Unlike idealism, therefore, which concentrates upon ideas and how we know or understand them, and realism, which considers the world as a realm of objects, existentialism examines the ways in which the subject encounters other beings and events in a world dominated by the sense of its own finitude.

Developing this preliminary definition, existentialism can be considered either as an *attitude*, to be identified in a wide range of texts, and over a large timespan; or as a *movement*, limited to a more specific period. To understand existentialism more fully, it is necessary to consider both possible definitions.

Existentialism as attitude
Existentialism is an attitude towards human existence concerned with the life of the individual in the mirror of death. In other words, existentialism regards the individual not as a biological fact, or an object, but as a subject, a discrete being which is unique in the world because it recognizes that its life is destined to end in nothingness. Thus, using the language of popular psychology, existentialists speak of the individual's anguish when confronted by the reality of death, and of the pressures upon the subject's psyche which occur when the indivi-

dual regards his or her life as essentially contingent and accidental. Fundamentally, existentialism throws individuals back upon themselves; in seeking to analyse their predicament on the basis of psychological criteria, existentialism denies individuals recourse to any form of external support. Alone, the subject must understand his or her life in terms of an inevitable journey towards death.

The austerity of this attitude means that existentialism, rigorously applied, is incompatible with a religious or theological understanding of humanity (but see below, under 'Existentialism today'). The focus of attention in existentialism is the individual, not God; the categories and criteria it employs are drawn not from theology and religion, but from psychology and philosophy, as can be seen in the atheistic novels and drama of such writers as Albert Camus and Jean-Paul Sartre, Samuel Beckett and Harold Pinter. The goal of such writers, and of existentialism in general, is to thrust the individual out into what they regard as the real world; one in which each individual stands, irrevocably, alone. In this sense, the world is itself fractured and damaged: it can offer no solutions to the individual, being essentially constituted in isolation and otherness.

What is existentialism's appeal? Principally, it draws people away from intellectual or social institutions. That is, existentialism, in attempting to narrate the story of each individual in terms of his or her own fate, life experiences and drama, wants to elevate the subject to autonomy. Existentialist literature is, as a consequence, overwhelmingly biographical; in analysing in depth the story and psyche of one particular individual, existentialism establishes the importance of that person over against intellectual, religious and bureaucratic systems.

It is not difficult to see why this should have become so attractive in the postwar period. In a society growing ever more complex, existentialism seeks to banish the individual's anonymity, replacing it with self-knowledge. All that it asks in return is sincerity: one must recognize and accept the isolation and fate which existentialism reveals. One might say, therefore, that the ultimate goal of existentialism is to secure the integrity of the subject when confronted by the bureaucratic indifference of the modern world.

In this respect, existentialism is uniquely modern in its reflection upon the human condition; indeed, the expression 'reflection upon the human condition', is precisely the kind of existentialist cliché which has only become truly common over the last fifty years. Attempts, therefore, to speak of, for example, St Paul's existentialism, or St Augustine's, or Plato's, or Shakespeare's, are misguided if understandable: fundamentally, and as a response to bureaucratic indifference, the genesis of existentialism is a recent event.

Existentialism as movement
Existentialism as an attitude informs its historical development as a movement. Broadly speaking, and as a comparatively recent phenomenon, existentialism originated in the thought of Søren Kierkegaard; is recognized in the work of Friedrich Nietzsche; reached its zenith in the phenomenology of Martin Heidegger and the writings of Jean-Paul Sartre; and was effectively crushed, intellectually, by Maurice Merleau-Ponty and T.W. Adorno and, socially, by the political uprisings of the late 1960s. From then on, existentialism as a movement declined dramatically.

It would be wrong, however, to imply that existentialism as a movement sprang fully formed from the mind of Søren Kierkegaard and then inspired, in succeeding generations, Nietzsche, Heidegger and Sartre. This is not what is meant by the use here of the word 'movement'. Rather, by referring to existentialism as a movement, attention focuses upon its *development*. Existentialism as a movement is something which developed, from Kierkegaard to Sartre, over a period of approximately a hundred years. It stuttered into life, and it stumbled, albeit more rapidly, to its death; but in those hundred years its character was formed in the tension between society and the intellect.

The seeds of this tense relationship, and of existentialism, were sown by Immanuel Kant (see KANTIANISM). Kant's turn to the subject as the basis of philosophy, in response to Descartes's *cogito ergo sum* (see CARTESIANISM), stimulated philosophy's turn away from the cognition of the appearance of objects towards the lived experience of humanity. Despite the attempts by G.W.F. Hegel to establish this interest in reason and history and Karl Marx's attempts to establish the Hegelian dialectic in economic materialism, the nineteenth century saw the gradual development of an interest in the education of humanity via an appeal to the individual. Both Kierkegaard and Nietzsche are exemplars of this trend, which continued into the work of Heidegger and Sartre.

In the following section the principal themes of the work of specific existentialists will be examined and explained. Although they are taken individually, the reader is advised to give attention to the continuity between these thinkers, as it is this which gives to existentialism its special character as a movement. Although, therefore, these four idiosyncratic figures are the focus of attention, the reader must be aware that the whole time covering their periods of activity, that is, the years from 1840 to 1968, are years in which the developing influence of existentialism can be identified in culture and society, in music, literature and drama, as well as in philosophy. By concentrating upon Kierkegaard, Nietzsche, Heidegger and Sartre, the aim here is not to identify these four as the only thinkers who can be called existentialists, but to delineate existentialism's major themes and features as a movement.

Individual existentialists

Søren Kierkegaard Kierkegaard (1813–1855) is commonly regarded as the 'father' of existentialism. His works, twenty-four major texts produced in fourteen intensive years, 1841–55, include the *Philosophical Fragments* ([1844] 1985) and the *Concluding Unscientific Postscript* ([1846] 1968). In these texts, Kierkegaard was reacting against what he regarded as three major threats to the Christian religion in his day: the moribund nature of the Lutheran church in Denmark; the deadening effects of orthodoxy upon the individual believer; and the atheistic tendencies of Hegel's absolute idealism. In tackling these dangers, Kierkegaard developed a distinctive methodology which established his own existential insights into the human condition.

Kierkegaard's philosophical method is essentially *dialectical*. Unlike Hegel's dialectic, however, which was directed towards the ascension of consciousness to the level of absolute spirit,

Kierkegaard's dialectic concerned the development of the subject through various stages, towards what Kierkegaard regarded as humanity's final goal, Christian belief. Dialectics, consequently, is a method which examines and overturns previous definitions, events, possibilities, and interpretations.

Kierkegaard's pseudonymous writings of the 1840s, in which his identity was subsumed within that of the protagonist of the text in question, centred upon his theory that human existence develops through three basic stages: the aesthetic; the ethical; and the religious. Far from seeing these stages in any kind of causal progression, however, Kierkegaard regarded them as the different possibilities of human existence. As an existentialist, Kierkegaard was concerned with realizing the best, Christian possibility of the individual subject.

In this way, Kierkegaard sought to oppose Hegel's absolutist theory of historical development with his own vision of the subject's personal relationship with God. Kierkegaard's anthropological contemplation, therefore, was directed ultimately towards his understanding of God and God's action in the world. This meant that once he had completed his elaboration of the stages on life's way, Kierkegaard had then to turn and consider the means by which God encounters the individual. This, for Kierkegaard, is Jesus Christ.

Kierkegaard's understanding of human existence leads him to regard the subject as experiencing God in the present moment. But that experience of God is personalized for the believer in his or her relationship with Jesus Christ. This leads automatically to Kierkegaard's most substantial contribution to modern theology, his theory of the paradox of faith in which, in the present moment of encountering Jesus Christ, the subject experiences eternity. Against a background of temporality and a historical understanding of the individual, consequently, Kierkegaard was able to concentrate philosophy's concerns upon the subject in his or her present experience and encounter with eternal questions. In so doing, Kierkegaard was the first existentialist.

Friedrich Nietzsche Almost certainly, Friedrich Nietzsche (1844–1900) did not know of Kierkegaard throughout his own period of literary activity. Moreover, given Nietzsche's atheism, it is unlikely that he would have been greatly impressed by Kierkegaard's own explicit, Christian belief. Nevertheless, in Kierkegaard's concentration upon the subject and his or her fate before eternity, there is an intellectual precedent for Nietzsche's own subjectivism.

The point should be made here that Nietzsche, again like Kierkegaard, was not a professional philosopher. Rather, it is more accurate to describe Nietzsche simply as a writer, as is evident in the aphoristic literary style of his major works, such as *Beyond Good and Evil* ([1886] 1973), this work being the most complete statement of his philosophy. Nietzsche's aphoristic, almost autobiographical, style reflects the intense subjectivism of his central philosophical concern: the *Übermensch*, or 'Overman'.

Characterized by the slogan 'God is dead', Nietzsche's theory of the individual saw it rising above the constraints of academic philosophy, morality, common sense, bourgeois concerns and above all religion and Christianity, to exercise the absolute freedom and will which was its natural birthright. Nietzsche's self-appointed task, therefore, was pedagogic: by means of his episodic texts, Nietzsche sought to educate the human race towards realizing the Overman, that is, the modern subject free of all social and ideological constraint, in every individual life. Unlike Kierkegaard and later existentialists such as Sartre, however, Nietzsche's descriptive categories are not psychological. Rather, they are clearly derived from Schopenhauer's understanding of freedom and the human will.

Nietzsche's work was hardly read during his own lifetime, although the Swiss theologian, Franz Overbeck, who was to influence Karl Barth, was himself greatly indebted to Nietzsche. In terms of the development of existentialism, however, Nietzsche's contribution was twofold: he pushed the notion of subjectivism to its logical though precarious extreme; and he attached it to a thoroughgoing atheism. Both themes are explicit in the work of later existentialists.

Martin Heidegger Martin Heidegger (1888–1976) was himself greatly influenced by Nietzsche; but it was not in terms of the latter's subjectivism or atheism. On the contra-

ry, Heidegger's phenomenology sought to go beyond the subject–object dichotomy and to ignore the question of the existence of God. In so doing, Heidegger secured for himself a unique place in the existentialist movement.

It is important to refer specifically to phenomenology at this point, rather than simply to philosophy or even to existentialism, because Martin Heidegger's thought has been consistently misrepresented ever since he came to prominence in 1927 with the publication of his first major work, *Being and Time*. Heidegger himself repudiated the suggestion that he was an existentialist, going so far as to reject the way in which existentialists in general, and Sartre in particular, were appropriating his work. Heidegger, rather, regarded himself as a phenomenologist, and as such was concerned with the ontological question of how beings appear to be. Existentialism, in all of its subjectivism and use of psychological categories, Heidegger rejected.

How then is it that Heidegger seems so firmly lodged in the popular understanding as one of the greatest of all existentialists, the equal of Sartre in every respect? There are two important aspects to a full answer to this question. First, as was intimated above, Heidegger was heavily influenced by both Kierkegaard and Nietzsche, themselves existentialists. This influence resulted after Heidegger had separated from his teacher, Edmund Husserl, in the period 1916–19, over the question of which course phenomenology should pursue. Husserl, maintaining his earlier position, insisted upon pure consciousness as the subject matter of transcendental phenomenology. Heidegger, partly under the influence of Kierkegaard and Nietzsche but also because of his study of earliest Christianity (specifically, the Pauline Epistles), argued that phenomenology should be concerned with historical questions. This concern resulted in Heidegger's *Being and Time*.

Second, Heidegger made a specific term, *Dasein*, or 'existence', central to his 1927 text. The point of *Being and Time* was to arrive at an understanding of the conditions of possibility of *Dasein*. What in fact resulted, as Heidegger quickly realized, was a reification of what was in fact only half of the real question of how beings appear to be. This stimulated Heidegger's famous 'turn' away from phenomenology, which began as early as 1929. From then on, Heidegger was eager to explore what he called the ontological difference or relationship between Being and being, *Sein* and *Dasein*, as the way or path to understanding how things appear to be, that is, how revelation occurs. *Being and Time* was only preparatory to this larger question.

Bluntly stated, those who regard Heidegger as a part of existentialism concentrate solely upon *Being and Time*, ignoring the crucial work undertaken in Heidegger's many later texts. And indeed, considered only on the basis of his *Being and Time*, as Sartre certainly considered him, Heidegger *does* appear to be an existentialist: *Being and Time* can be construed, albeit tendentiously, as being overwhelmingly concerned with the subject.

After his 'turn', Heidegger's attention was devoted more and more to the interpretation of specific literary texts: here, his essays and lectures on Georg Trakl, Friedrich Hölderlin, and Heraclitus are pre-eminent. His fundamental premise is that the truth of how things appear to be must be understood as an event of revelation, an event or irruption of meaning which occurs in the act of interpretation. Heidegger's fullest position, consequently, is hermeneutic: as one who encounters events, he engages individually with the event. In this sense, arguably, Heidegger can still be regarded as an existentialist, though his apparent subjectivism seeks to be absorbed into Being itself.

A final word should be said here about Heidegger's politics. His membership of the National Socialist party in Germany during the years 1933–45 is now well documented, but has never been fully explained. Nor has his participation in Nazi propaganda; perhaps the simplest explanation is that Heidegger was, indeed, a Nazi. Whatever, it is the case that Heidegger is regarded popularly as the philosopher of *Dasein*, his earlier work which was compromised by his political actions in the 1930s. Anyone, therefore, who seeks to speak of Heidegger the existentialist must address the question of Heidegger's Nazi past.

Jean-Paul Sartre This question of political suspicion also came to haunt the existentialism of Jean-Paul Sartre (1905–1980), though in a very different fashion. Sartre was unable to reconcile himself to the failure of his early philosophy to address the social predicament of the proletariat in the period after the Second World War. Hence, Sartre repudiated his earlier existentialism in favour of Marxism, because of the very qualities which made it existentialist: its subjectivism and its analysis of the *individual's* mode of living in the world. It is ironic, but not insignificant, that the two greatest 'existentialists', Heidegger and Sartre, both rejected their existentialism in later years, though for very different reasons.

Sartre's primary existentialist texts were the novel *Nausea* ([1938] 1986) and the philosophical work *Being and Nothingness* ([1943] 1969), for which Sartre is perhaps most famous. With these can be included Sartre's lecture *Existentialism and Humanism* ([1946] 1989), which is the most accessible form of Sartre's basic ideas. This lecture is equally important for the extraordinary exchange it provoked with M. Naville, a Marxist theoretician, in which one recognizes a sign of Sartre's repudiation of his own earlier work. Effectively, from 1949 Sartre was a Marxist theoretician and not an existentialist.

Sartre is unique because he was as great a novelist and playwright as he was a philosopher and essayist; indeed, it would be fair to say that it was the very breadth of his own output which stimulated the explosion of interest in existentialism in the 1940s and 1950s in the theatre and in literature. When one considers the major themes of Sartre's existentialism, therefore, one examines ideas which are often most clearly expressed in fictional constructions; Sartre writes of the human condition and predicament as he saw it in the streets of Paris, from his window, rather than in the studies and lecture halls of a university. In other words, the most striking feature of Sartre's existentialism (and in this sense he is reminiscent of Nietzsche) is its immediacy: Sartre is writing the biography of a distinct, though anonymous, individual.

The vast wealth of detail that Sartre includes in his work reinforces this sense of the anonymous individual. Sartre is writing about someone anxious, living in a disjointed, fractured world; an individual obsessed with his or her own perspective, own encounters with other people and events, own death; an individual confronted, day and night, with the problem of being sincere to his or her subjectivism, of living in good faith. Sincerity and good faith, therefore, or its antithesis, bad faith: these are the cornerstones of Sartre's world. Existentialism for Sartre, despite the occasional opacity of his analysis, is about people discovering who they are in a world where only the subject is real, and where the ultimate reality of being a subject is that one will die. Confronted in this manner, all that can be achieved, freely, is to live life in good faith, with sincerity. This obsessive desire, which pushes the subject to extremes of behaviour, is a crucial element of Sartre's existentialism. The elaborate analysis of *Being and Nothingness* arrives at this simple conclusion quite early, then repeats it *ad nauseam*.

More than many of his followers, Sartre realized that the potential of this form of existentialism was limited; and for Sartre the realization that existentialism had to be replaced by Marxism came in the late 1940s, more specifically with the arrest of the communist leader Jacques Duclos, which Sartre likened to a conversion experience. Henceforth his work towards an explicitly ethical position, which had been hampered by his almost solipsistic emphasis upon the subject, was realized in political theory and practice. In this development, Sartre was heavily influenced by Maurice Merleau-Ponty. Although Merleau-Ponty eventually separated from Sartre over what he regarded as the latter's 'ultra bolshevism', Sartre later paid tribute to his one-time friend's significance after Merleau-Ponty's untimely death in 1961.

Existentialism and theology

After Sartre, existentialism as a movement in philosophy effectively ended. If the question of an 'existentialist' theology still persists, however, it is because theology is slow to take up society's lead. Consequently, and because of its historical significance, the relationship between existentialism and theology requires consideration.

Although Kierkegaard was clearly a Christian religious thinker, and Heidegger was always influenced by his strong Roman Catholic roots, both Nietzsche and Sartre were explicitly hostile towards any talk of God: Nietzsche with his claim that 'God is dead'; Sartre with his atheism. Moreover, existentialism's extreme subjectivism is, in general, incompatible with theology. The question of the relationship between existentialism and theology, therefore, of the relationship between a philosophy so obviously centred upon the subject and a science charged with speaking of a transcendent Being, is a difficult one. And yet, in the twentieth century it has often been reduced to the thought of one man: Rudolf Bultmann (1884–1976).

Bultmann's own biography is essentially straightforward. Trained in the liberal Protestant school, Bultmann broke with his teachers in the early 1920s under the influence of Karl Barth and dialectical or *Krisis* theology. This meant for Bultmann a move away from any attempt to relate the Christian religion to this-worldly culture so as to regard humanity in the image of God, towards Barth's axiom of the 'infinite qualitative distinction' between this world and God, with Jesus Christ as the only mediator between the two. Thus, the only way to speak of God for Bultmann was to speak of Jesus Christ as God's sole address to humanity.

The definitive shaping of Bultmann's understanding of this question took place in the 1920s, when in Marburg he came under the influence of Martin Heidegger. As was stated above, Heidegger's own phenomenology, ultimately, was concerned less with an existential analysis of the human predicament, on the level of *Dasein*, than with understanding the ontological difference or relationship between Being and beings, in which, via events of revelation, the philosopher could think through and interpret the dark (for Heidegger) meaning of life. At the deepest level, Bultmann's theology is a simplification of Heidegger's event theory of revelation, so as to concentrate solely upon one such event: the Christ event. Nevertheless, with the publication in 1927 of *Being and Time*, Heidegger supplied a vocabulary for describing and analysing human existence which Bultmann made use of from 1927 onwards. It is at this juncture that the question of Bultmann's existentialism is focused.

Throughout the late 1940s, 1950s, and into the 1960s, Bultmann was attacked for aligning theology with an essentially atheist philosophy, existentialism. Bultmann's rebuttal of this argument is informative. He claimed that

Heidegger's existentialist vocabulary, in which human being, *Dasein*, is analysed in terms of its temporality and historicity, is simply a secular codification of what the New Testament, and in particular the apostle St Paul and the evangelist St John, revealed to be the nature of human life in the light of God's revelation in Jesus Christ. Arguing this way, Bultmann was able to write extensively of the eschatological basis of human existence as understood in the New Testament, in such a way that, regarded objectively, the similarities with Heidegger's work are great. This can be seen most clearly in Bultmann's greatest work, *The Gospel of John: A Commentary* ([1941] 1971).

The so-called 'Bultmannian' school of biblical interpretation, principally Ernst Fuchs and Gerhard Ebeling (but surviving in certain attenuated cases in Britain and the USA even today), thrived during the first parts of the 1960s, but was quickly swept away by the waves of political consciousness which overcame society and theology from 1968 onwards. Wolfhart Pannenberg's half-serious remark, that 'Bultmann was a luxury we could no longer afford', neatly expresses the view of many theologians since 1970. Today the relationship between existentialism and theology is not a burning question.

Existentialism today
The political upheavals of the late 1960s heralded the death of existentialism as a popular philosophy, although intellectually it had been dealt hammerblows with its repudiation by Jean-Paul Sartre, its discrediting at the hands of Maurice Merleau-Ponty, and its condemnation by T.W. Adorno, most clearly in the latter's *Jargon of Authenticity* ([1964] 1973). Overwhelmingly, since 1968 existentialism has been identified with the petty-bourgeois, materialistic obsessions of the industrialized west. As such, its demise can be traced informatively in the public's relative loss of interest in such writers as Hermann Hesse, Albert Camus and Henry Miller, and the domestication of such playwrights as John Osborne, Samuel Beckett and Harold Pinter. The concerns of existentialist writers have not been those of society in general since 1970.

In theology, this reaction has been mediated by such people as Dorothee Soelle and Jürgen Moltmann in Germany, David Tracy in the USA, Edward Schillebeeckx in Holland, and more recently Albert Nolan in South Africa and Leonardo Boff in Brazil. Theologies today which concern themselves with the predicament of individuals and communities do so for the most part by employing social, political, and economic categories of description and analysis. In this way, one can see from a general survey of theology, amongst other cultural forms of communication, that existentialism was a movement which, from origins in the nineteenth century, reached its peak during the years 1938–68. Its decline since then has been dramatic.

Today it is possible to argue that in such developments as hermeneutic and postmodernist theology one can recognize remnants of existentialism. For example, the underlying philosophical assumptions of a hermeneutic theology like that of David Tracy, or a postmodernist theology like that of Mark C. Taylor, indebted as they are to Heidegger's thought, betray certain signs of a residual existentialism. But this would be a superficial conclusion. The move towards pluralism in theology in the 1980s has undermined any real possibility that existentialism might linger on into the work of contemporary figures; for the general acceptance of pluralism is antithetical to the reified and absolutist nature of existentialism. On the contrary, one must conclude that, for the foreseeable future at least, the reader interested in existentialism will be motivated by a desire to find out more about past figures and a past movement.

See also PHILOSOPHICAL THEOLOGY.

Bibliography
Adorno, T.W. [1964] 1973: *Jargon of Authenticity*. London: Routledge and Kegan Paul.
Bultmann, R. [1941] 1971: *The Gospel of John: A Commentary*. Oxford: Blackwell.
Caws, P. 1979: *Sartre*. London: Routledge and Kegan Paul.
Cooper, D.E. 1990: *Existentialism: A Reconstruction*. Oxford: Blackwell.
Cumming, R.D. 1979: *Starting Point: An Introduction to the Dialectic of Existence*. Chicago: University of Chicago Press.
Dobrez, L.A.C. 1986: *The Existential and its Exits: Literary and Philosophical Perspectives on the Works of Beckett, Ionesco, Genet, and Pinter*. London: Athlone Press.

Heidegger, M. [1927] 1962: *Being and Time*. Oxford: Blackwell.

Jones, G. 1991: *Bultmann: Towards a Critical Theology*. Cambridge: Polity Press.

Kierkegaard, S. [1844] 1985: *Philosophical Fragments*. Princeton: Princeton University Press.

Kierkegaard, S. [1846] 1968: *Concluding Unscientific Postscript*. Princeton: Princeton University Press.

Malantschuk, G. 1971: *Kierkegaard's Thought*. Princeton: Princeton University Press.

Nehemas, A. 1985: *Nietzsche: Life as Literature*. Cambridge, Mass.: Harvard University Press.

Nietzsche, F. [1886] 1973: *Beyond Good and Evil*. Harmondsworth: Penguin.

Pöggeler, O. 1987: *Martin Heidegger's Path of Thinking*. Atlantic Highlands, NJ: Humanities Press International.

Poster, M. 1975: *Existential Marxism in Postwar France: From Sartre to Althusser*. Princeton: Princeton University Press.

Sartre, J-P. [1938] 1986: *Nausea*. Harmondsworth: Penguin.

Sartre, J-P. [1943] 1969: *Being and Nothingness*. London: Routledge.

Sartre, J-P. [1946] 1989: *Existentialism and Humanism*. London: Methuen.

Theunissen, M. 1984: *The Other: Studies in the Social Ontology of Husserl, Heidegger, Sartre, and Buber*. Cambridge, Mass.: MIT Press.

Whiteside, K.H. 1988: *Merleau-Ponty and the Foundation of an Existential Politics*. Princeton: Princeton University Press.

GARETH JONES

F

faith The term 'faith' – like the parallel term 'experience' – defies simple definition. Partly this is because it is used to refer both to the transcendent objects of faith (*fides quae*) and to the range of human activities through which that object is apprehended and in which response is undertaken (*fides qua*). Moreover, 'faith' is used in association with or distinction from other terms (such as revelation, Spirit, knowledge or belief), terms which are themselves complex. Because it is thus porous, 'faith' is inherently polyvalent, designating aggregates of argument and conviction rather than a simple reality. A very generalized definition of faith as human response to the presence and activity of the transcendent needs expanding by identifying historically specific contexts and patterns of usage and contrast.

In the modern era, the context for discussion of faith has generally been shaped by two factors: widespread loss of confidence in the coherence of claims about divine agency and a corresponding concern to relate faith to the dynamics of human subjectivity. Though the more immediate background to these discussions is the Enlightenment critique of faith's cognitive capacity and its reliance on external authority, the roots go back at least as far as the Reformation critique of developed scholastic accounts of faith. Amongst the Reformers, Luther laid especial emphasis on faith as trustful confidence in the gospel. This recovery of the 'affective' character of faith was sharply distinguished from the apparent intellectualism and impersonalism of scholastic definitions in which faith was primarily understood as the mind's assent to divine truth (as an interpretation of Aquinas, this leaves much to be desired). Luther, moreover, rejected the scholastic notion of *fides formata* ('formed faith', active in good works), which he considered a privileging of meritorious human activity. Over and against this, he expounded faith as a divine gift to sinners, generated by the self-communication of God in Word and Spirit and wholly oriented to its object, Jesus Christ and his justifying work (hence the twin affirmation of 'faith alone' and 'Christ alone'). Calvin gives particular cognitive edge to such affirmations by defining faith as 'a steady and certain knowledge of the divine benevolence towards us, which, being founded on the truth of the gratuitous promises in Christ, is both revealed to our minds and confirmed in our hearts by the Holy Spirit' (Calvin, [1559] 1960, III. 2. vii). For the Reformers, then, 'faith' is correlative to a series of prior affirmations about God's saving relation to humanity, and humanity's contingent status as recipient of grace. The Catholic response at the Council of Trent (notably in the *Decree on Justification*) was to reject an exclusive construal of faith as confidence, to reaffirm the notion of *fides formata*, and to emphasize assent to revealed truth as taught authoritatively by the church. Though different understandings of faith evidently constituted a major disagreement in the early modern period, Protestant and Catholic theologians shared a framework for discussing faith: the priority of divine self-communication (however mediated) and the derivative character of human reponse (however construed) (see REVELATION, CONCEPT OF).

The collapse of this framework at the Enlightenment was in some measure prepared by developments in post-Reformation Protestant orthodoxy. It is certainly possible to overemphasize the rationalism of Protestant scholasticism, by ignoring its rejection of *fides historica* (mere acceptance of revealed data) and its nuanced discussions of saving faith and *assensus fiducialis* (faithful, trusting assent). However, orthodox thinkers did reintroduce a heavily intellectualist element into the notion of faith (against the radical personalism of Luther and the careful correlation of cognition and assent in Calvin). More importantly still, their discussions often take on a decidedly anthropological character by focusing on the dispositions of the believing subject. On some readings, the formalization of revelation and grace, their relative isolation from substantial Trinitarian and Christological doctrine, and the quasi-independent treatment of the act of faith already moves beyond the classical shape of the Reformation concept of faith.

The increasing prestige of rationalist natural philosophy from the seventeenth century onwards further undermined the capacity of Christian theology to offer a persuasive account of its inherited understandings. Most particularly, rationalist aversion to the notions of revelation (construed as a denial of the sufficiency of human reason) and of faith (construed as little better than untested opinion) eroded the chief building blocks of a positive theological description of faith. This critique gained especial force from the anti-authoritarian drive of rationalism, which is clearly at odds with notions of faith as submission to God as revealer or to the church as the repository of divine truth. By contrast, rationalist thinkers from Lord Herbert of Cherbury onwards rooted the Christian religion in certain innate principles or natural capacities of the human person. 'Faith' thereby shares the fate of many other central Christian concepts: it loses much of its cogency under pressure from an impersonal definition of the divine, an affirmation of the sole competence of human reason and an anthropology ill at ease with notions of human creatureliness.

Most accounts of faith since the latter part of the eighteenth century have been preoccupied with a search for an effective response to these developments. Protestant thought responded much earlier – official Catholic thought generally reaffirmed the Tridentine statements (as in the treatment of faith in the dogmatic constitution *Dei Filius* at the First Vatican Council). The post-Enlightenment Christian tradition has developed two major strategies by way of response. One is concerned to offer an account of faith as a general human possibility; another makes its account of faith strictly contingent upon positive exposition of the content of the Christian religion.

Major Protestant thinkers in the nineteenth century attempted to identify a sphere of human nature within which faith could be located and validated without appeal to the apparatus of transcendental theological claims which the Enlightenment had dismantled. By locating faith in the affective religious consciousness (Schleiermacher) or the moral sense (Ritschl), this move beyond rationalism tended to reinforce the subjectivity of faith. Protestant (and later Catholic) thinkers influenced by the existentialism of Kierkegaard and Heidegger produced prestigious accounts of faith as human reality. Tillich's celebrated definition of faith as 'a total and centred act of the personal self, the act of unconditional, infinite and ultimate concern' (1957, p. 8) exemplifies the generality of such accounts as 'universally valid' (ibid., p. 131). More closely tied to the personalism of the Lutheran tradition, Bultmann and later Ebeling construe faith as renunciation of self-wrought security in the face of the invading presence of the Word. Whilst anthropologically rich, their accounts are again hesitant in description of the objective referents of faith. With considerable philosophical sophistication, Rahner articulates an account of faith out of a metaphysics of human restlessness in the face of finitude, which is interpreted as a natural orientation of humanity to God. 'Faith' here becomes largely coterminous with the dynamics of human self-transcendence. Though demanding explicit expression in Christian confession, faith is an utterly primary aspect of the self's actualization of its existence.

This anthropological orientation has considerable resources for inter-religious dialogue, enabling different traditions to discover common ground in faith as a universal human reality behind explicit divergences in truth-claims. Sometimes expressed as a strong distinction between faith and belief (see Cantwell Smith, 1979), this represents a reassertion of the primacy of *fides qua*. A parallel movement in religious psychology analyses faith as the central dynamic within the structures of human growth, identifying stages through which persons pass in the process of maturing (see Fowler, 1981). The non-dialectical structuralism of such analyses has evoked criticism from those uneasy with a naturalist orientation.

Anthropologically grounded accounts of faith are characteristically revisionist and apologetic. Their concern is to establish the possibility of explicit Christian faith on prior grounds derived from analysis of the human subject; and they frequently issue in a resolution of the symbolic or positive aspects of faith traditions into expressions of some more general human capacity (whether metaphysical or experiential or ethical). A quite different approach mounts a vigorous critique of faith as human possibility, expounding faith in an objective theological framework in which central place is accorded to God's gracious action in revelation and reconciliation. Such an approach is most evident in Barth's massive redescription of classical Christian language in the *Church Dogmatics*, but can also be found in the work of Balthasar. For Barth, faith is to be understood as a miraculous consequence of revelation, a determination of the person only by the free action of God. More concretely, faith is wholly oriented to Jesus Christ as the one in whom we exist. An account of faith is thereby primarily an account of divine action, and only secondarily an account of the believing subject. Recent 'postliberal' discussions develop this refusal of general accounts of human capacity for faith by linking faith to the determinate realities (such as language and corporate practices) of the Christian tradition. In this way, they suggest that a persuasive theology of faith depends not on the demonstration of its anthropological possibility but on the promotion of a social ambience within which it can flourish, thereby linking faith to common life and worship, rather than to argument or experience.

Contemporary Christian thought displays widely divergent convictions about faith in relation both to the nature of humanity and the character of divine action, a divergence which is itself rooted in fundamental disagreements about how to continue Christian theology after the collapse of the intellectual culture in which its classical statements took their place.

See also FAITH AND HISTORY; FAITH AND REASON; METHOD IN THEOLOGY.

Bibliography
Barth, K. [1953] 1956: *Church Dogmatics* IV/1. Edinburgh: T & T Clark, pp. 610–42.
Bultmann, R., and Weiser, A. [1959] 1961: *Faith*. London: A & C Black.
Calvin, J. [1559] 1960: *Institutes of the Christian Religion*, 2 vols. London: SCM Press.
Cantwell Smith, W. 1979: *Faith and Belief*. Princeton: Princeton University Press.
Clements, K.W. 1981: *Faith*. London: SCM Press.
Ebeling, G. [1959] 1961: *The Nature of Faith*. London: Collins.
Fowler, J.W. 1981: *Stages of Faith*. San Francisco: Harper and Row.
Gössmann, E., *et al.* 1984: Glaube. In *Theologische Realenzyklopädie*, vol. 13. Berlin: de Gruyter, pp. 225–365.
Niebuhr, H.R. 1989: *Faith on Earth*. New Haven: Yale University Press.
Surtis, P., ed. 1972: *Faith: Its Nature and Meaning*. Dublin: Gill and Macmillan.
Swinburne, R. 1981: *Faith and Reason*. Oxford: Clarendon Press.
Tillich, P. 1957: *Dynamics of Faith*. New York: Harper and Row.

JOHN B. WEBSTER

faith and history The expression 'faith and history' refers to a cluster of problems generated by the apparently straightforward fact that Christian faith relies for its meaning and truth upon reference to the past. In the premodern period, issues connected with the problem of faith and history were typically subsumed under the wider rubric of the relationship between reason and revelation; the original problem assumed concentrated form in Tertullian's famous question, 'what does Athens have to do with Jerusalem?' Not surprisingly, the problem reaches its apex in Christology, since, from the very beginnings of Christian theology, efforts have been made to reconcile what is eternal and pre-existent in Christ with what is unique and unrepeatable in the historical figure of Jesus of Nazareth. The relationship between a present-day faith and a past 'event' that is itself conceptually unstable represents the heart of the faith and history problem.

With the rise of historical criticism of the Bible in the eighteenth century – and with the emergence of historical consciousness generally – the problem of faith and history assumed a fresh and increasingly urgent form. Powerful new notions of evidence, probability, and plausibility undermined traditional views of the accuracy of Scripture, resulting in numerous creative efforts to reconcile faith's relationship, not only to historical events, but to historical knowledge as well. Increasingly, the 'problem' of faith and history came to be associated with the apparently precarious dependence of Christian faith upon dubious or otherwise corrigible claims about the past. The inherited problems, as well as the newer, more modern difficulties, were both graphically conveyed by G.E. Lessing's famous image of the 'ugly ditch' between the 'accidental truths of history' and the 'necessary truths of reason', which has become a shorthand symbol of the faith–history problem. Lessing's image reveals that at least three discrete though related issues are at stake in the modern version of the problem of faith and history. First, there is the basically epistemological problem associated with temporal distance from soteriologically significant events. How can I be sure that the events reported in Scripture actually occurred, especially if those events contain a miraculous element? How much confidence can I place in a historical report that has been handed down through so many generations and is so far removed from eyewitness experience? How can I base my present-day experience of salvation on something so open to doubt? This aspect of the faith–history problem places the emphasis on the purely factual question of whether or not certain historical events of a presumably revelatory significance actually occurred.

However, a second difficulty conveyed by Lessing's image of the 'ugly ditch' supersedes merely factual considerations and introduces problems of a profoundly metaphysical sort. The issue at stake is the potential incommensurability between two classes of truths, the historical and the religious: we have the impasse here between particular historical truths on the one hand, and religious truths of a presumably universal significance on the other. This aspect of the faith–history problem has often been characterized as the 'scandal of particularity', since it entails the conceptually peculiar notion that 'saving truth' appeared in historical form at a specific time and place – as though 'saving truth' is not available prior to, or apart from, the occurrence of the relevant events. Significantly,

this metaphysical problem remains intact even if the strictly factual issue presented by temporal distance is satisfactorily resolved. As Lessing himself puts it, how can we be expected to 'jump with a historical truth to a quite different class of truths' and demand of ourselves that we should form all of our 'metaphysical and moral ideas accordingly?' 'If on historical grounds I have no objection to the statement that this Christ himself rose from the dead, must I therefore accept it as true that this risen Christ was the Son of God?' (Lessing, 1956, p. 54). In short, how can 'events' produce 'truths?' How can dogmatics be generated by history?

Yet a third layer of difficulties associated with Lessing's image of the 'ugly ditch' concerns the fundamentally existential problem of the gap or hiatus between myself (including my natural store of self-knowledge) and a basically alien religious message that is perhaps intellectually offensive and that even presumes to explain me to myself. While involving aspects of the purely epistemological problem associated with the issue of temporal distance, this existential gap goes beyond mere matters of intellectual assent to more complex matters of sensibility and autonomy. Modern, post-Cartesian notions of intellectual autonomy, buttressed especially by the Kantian emphasis on freedom of thought, create tremendous pressure to ground all certainty in *self*-certainty. Yet faith's reference to the past undermines the autonomy of the modern believer by orienting the search for salvation towards remote events occurring in the backwaters of the ancient Mediterranean world. In this form, the faith–history problem becomes the problem of religious 'appropriation'. In view of the existential gap between a modern, autonomous, secular believer and a religious message rooted in the past, this issue of appropriation concerns the process by which the distance between believer and message is mediated or offset. In a more than merely metaphorical sense, this existential gap, compounded by the associated difficulty of religious appropriation, has been capsulized for the modern period by Albert Schweitzer's conclusion to his survey of the nineteenth-century 'quest of the historical Jesus': namely, his claim that Jesus himself is a 'stranger' to us (Schweitzer, [1906] 1964).

The career of the faith and history problem in modern theology is basically the story of these three issues commingling in often confusing ways. Especially within the German Protestant tradition, the problem of relating Christian faith to historical knowledge assumed tremendous proportions, due to the powerful role played by the historical-critical method within the German universities. Kantian epistemology played a significant role in the nineteenth and early twentieth centuries in providing theological escape routes from the potentially destructive implications of historical criticism of faith's Scriptural basis by securing noumenal compartments beyond the reach of history. Thus, for example, theologians such as Albrecht Ritschl, Martin Kähler, and Wilhelm Herrmann could secure for faith a *sturmfreies Gebiet*, or zone of safety, immune to the ravages of historical criticism, because of an implicit commitment to a basically ahistorical philosophical principle informing their conceptions of faith. Typically, however, considerable instability attended these positions, as genuinely historical judgements often remained covertly attached to Christological claims, leaving these positions implicitly vulnerable to the theologically mischievous effects of historical criticism.

The pressures internal to the collective effort to reconcile faith and historical knowledge became most explicit in the career of Ernst Troeltsch. Troeltsch grasped that the real problem for faith was not a matter of the *results* of historical enquiry, but a product of the inevitable clash between faith and the very *presuppositions* of historical research (Harvey, 1966, pp. 5ff.). That is, the very operating procedures of the historian rule out in advance the special claims to truth that Christian faith traditionally makes. In particular, Troeltsch underscored the importance of the historiographical 'principle of correlation', which stipulates that all historical events must be located in their surrounding historical context and understood in terms of causal antecedents. As Troeltsch correctly saw, this commonplace historiographical principle – so deeply ingrained among historians that it goes largely unspoken – has the devastating effect of outlawing *in advance* any claim to absolute or final truth in ethical and religious matters: like political developments or social customs, ethical and religious truths are viewed as the product of time and place rather than as something 'dropped down' from above with their absoluteness intact. Moreover, the principle erodes the presumed uniqueness of Christianity by placing it in relation to outside cultural and religious influences. Finally, when applied to Scripture itself, the principle of correlation effectively eliminates the normal ways of avowing the *authority* of Scripture by suggesting that the Bible itself is relative to a world view and cultural environment no longer our own (Troeltsch, 1914).

Much of the debate over faith and history in the twentieth century can be viewed as an ongoing response to the problems disclosed by Troeltsch. In their several variations, the theological motifs of the 'Word of God' and the 'kerygma' at the centre of dialectical theology in the 1920s and 1930s signalled fresh efforts to make an explicit historical referent the heart of Christian faith while simultaneously claiming that faith's referent was inaccessible to historical research. As a reaction against certain liberal theological efforts to represent faith as continuous with 'general' (for instance, moral) truths accessible to the culture, the dialectical or neo-orthodox position represented a retrieval of the standpoint of Søren Kierkegaard. Especially in his Johannes Climacus writings, Kierkegaard had charted out a position designed both to overcome the Hegelian fusing of the rational and the historical (by orienting faith exclusively towards God's free and contingent act in Christ) and to seal off faith from the pernicious effects of historical enquiry (by making God's presence in history visible only to the 'eyes of faith'). The influence of this position no doubt came to its fullest expression in the career of Rudolf Bultmann, whose 'demythologizing' project can be taken as symptomatic of sophisticated efforts to domesticate the several difficulties that history and historical enquiry pose for faith. By appropriating the philosophy of Martin Heidegger to claim that the real content of faith is a certain existential 'understanding of existence' rather than propositions about the world, Bultmann effectively made Christian faith logically independent of any particular historical claim. Accordingly, faith could not then be reliant on any single datum of historical knowledge and was thereby made secure from any negative results of historical enquiry. Bultmann's position relied heavily on a distinction between the 'Jesus of history' (who held no theological significance) and the 'Christ of faith' (who was theologically decisive), a basically Kantian distinction mediated to Bultmann by both Kierkegaard and Kähler.

Ironically, dialectical theology's success in insulating faith from historical criticism implicitly put in question faith's connection to a specific historical event. This result became clear in the course of various responses to Bultmann, such as the so-called 'new quest' of the historical Jesus and the left-wing Bultmannianism of Schubert Ogden, both of which emphasized Bultmann's Heideggerian idea of a new 'understanding of existence' as the heart of faith. Likewise, both argued that such an understanding of existence must be a *general* possibility for humanity as such, and not tied only to the historical figure of Jesus: Jesus may embody this understanding of existence most authoritatively, but faith understood in this way does not *become* a possibility only with his historical appearance. Consequently, debates originating as discussions of the relation between faith and historical knowledge (Lessing's 'temporal' problem) subtly turn into debates concerning the relation between historical events and dogmatic truths (Lessing's 'metaphysical' problem), a distinction that is not always clearly observed. Similarly, debates about faith and historical knowledge may in fact, upon close inspection, turn out to be debates about the possibility of natural theology, as is the case with the disagreement between Bultmann and Ogden.

A quite different, explicitly anti-Bultmannian position has been charted out by Wolfhart Pannenberg, whose theology can be viewed as an explicit effort to dislodge the dualistic, Kantian–Kierkegaardian strategy of locating faith in some sort of noumenal zone that immunizes it against the effects of historical research. Pannenberg builds on a conception of faith understood as a genuine form of 'knowledge', rather than as a 'risk', a 'leap' or a contentless 'self-understanding'. In addition, he boldly offers a historical proof for the resurrection of Jesus, as part of his general strategy of depicting the robust cognitive content of faith, a content that entitles Christian theology to

maintain a position alongside other university disciplines or 'sciences'. Pannenberg underwrites his repudiation of the distinction between the 'eyes of faith' and the 'eyes of history' by eliminating the very distinction between 'history' and 'revelation' in a manner that is intentionally reminiscent of Hegel.

Since about 1970 the traditional debate over faith's relation to history and historical knowledge has been largely superseded by increasingly technical discussions of hermeneutics, by the quite different orientation towards history produced by liberation and political theologies (see LIBERATION THEOLOGY; MARXISM) and by the growing interest in 'narrative' as it relates to both Scripture and to theology generally (see NARRATIVE THEOLOGY). While certain features of these more recent discussions no doubt represent an authentic new stage in the debate over faith and history, there is a real sense in which problems inherited from the previous century remain present and unresolved. Chief among these, perhaps, is the precise relation between the meaning and truth of Christian faith and the occurrence of particular historical events.

See also BIBLICAL CRITICISM AND INTERPRETATION 2· NEW TESTAMENT; HISTORICAL JESUS, QUEST OF.

Bibliography

Bultmann, Rudolf [1948] 1961: *Kerygma and Myth*, ed. Hans Werner Bartsch, trans. Reginald H. Fuller. New York: Harper and Row.

Frei, Hans 1974: *The Eclipse of Biblical Narrative*. New Haven: Yale University Press.

Harvey, Van A. 1966: *The Historian and the Believer*. New York: Macmillan.

Kähler, Martin [1892] 1964: *The So-called Historical Jesus and the Historic Biblical Christ*, ed. and trans. Carl E. Braaten. Philadelphia: Fortress Press.

Kierkegaard, Søren [1844] 1985: *Philosophical Fragments*, trans. Howard V. Hong and Edna H. Hong. Princeton: Princeton University Press.

Kierkegaard, Søren [1846] 1968: *Concluding Unscientific Postscript*, trans. David W. Swenson and Walter Lowrie. Princeton: Princeton University Press.

Lessing, Gotthold Ephraim 1956: *Lessing's Theological Writings*, trans. Henry Chadwick. Stanford: Stanford University Press.

McGrath, Alister 1986: *The Making of Modern German Christology*. Oxford: Blackwell.

Michalson, Gordon E., Jr 1985: *Lessing's 'Ugly Ditch':*

A Study of Theology and History. University Park and London: Pennsylvania State University Press.

Morgan, Robert 1976: Ernst Troeltsch and the dialectical theology. In *Ernst Troeltsch and the Future of Theology*, ed. John Powell Clayton. Cambridge: Cambridge University Press, pp. 33–77.

Ogden, Schubert 1961: *Christ without Myth*. New York: Harper and Row.

Pannenberg, Wolfhart [1964] 1968: *Jesus: God and Man*, trans. Lewis L. Wilkens and Duane Priebe. Philadelphia: Fortress Press.

Robinson, James M. 1959: *A New Quest of the Historical Jesus*. London: SCM Press.

Schweitzer, Albert [1906] 1964: *Quest of the Historical Jesus*, trans. W. Montgomery. New York: Macmillan.

Troeltsch, Ernst 1914: Historiography. In *Encyclopedia of Religion and Ethics*, vol. 6, ed. James Hastings. New York: Charles Scribner's Sons, pp. 716–23.

GORDON E. MICHALSON, JR

faith and reason   A number of positions on the relation between faith and reason have been maintained by Christians and their opponents:

1   Faith and reason conflict; so much the worse for reason.
2   Faith and reason conflict: so much the worse for faith.
3   Faith and reason (or rather reason based on premises independent of faith) neither confirm one another nor conflict, when the nature and implications of both are properly understood.
4   Faith leads to reason and ultimately tends to be replaced by it.
5   Faith and reason confirm and enhance one another.

(It will be taken for granted here that what applies to Christianity and Christians applies *mutatis mutandis* to other religions and their adherents.)

1   The first position is represented classically by Tertullian's remark, 'Credo quia absurdum' (I believe because it is absurd); and by Luther's designation of reason as a whore. Its attractiveness is due to the fact that the believer's relation to God is evidently a great deal more than one to a conclusion reached by rational argument. The opponents of this position are apt to protest that the believer's relationship of love and adoration to the God specially (according to Christians) revealed in Christ presupposes that there is a God, and that that God is in fact specially revealed in Christ; and that unless these propositions can be shown to be reasonable, or at least not repugnant to reason, it is no more appropriate to believe them than to believe any other absurdity. To believe in a person is certainly other than merely to believe that something is the case; but the former kind of belief does seem necessarily to include the latter, at least in the circumstances of ordinary life. To believe in your doctor or bank manager is to believe that they will not respectively poison or ruin you. Similarly, to believe in God would seem to entail that God is able and willing to save those that put their trust in God; and it would be strange at once to hold such a belief and to admit that reason told entirely against it. It is difficult, at least at first sight, to see why beliefs which are contrary to reason are any more appropriate in religion than in science or in the ordinary affairs of life.

Faith based on reason is sometimes contrasted with faith based on experience. This contrast seems to be misleading. It may well be suggested (as it was by A.N. Whitehead) that religious experience provides grounds for belief in religious doctrines rather in the same way as sense-experience provides grounds for belief in scientific doctrines. But this is to imply rather that religious experience makes religious belief reasonable than that it constitutes a basis for it which is somehow independent of reason.

2   The second position is characteristic of the ATHEISM which has been especially prevalent since the Enlightenment. It is convenient to distinguish between two types of atheism, the existential and the theoretical; both types oppose faith to reason, but in ways which differ somewhat from one another. The existential atheist (typified by Friedrich Nietzsche and Karl Marx) lays emphasis upon the manner in which religious faith tends to frustrate the possibilities of authentic development and self-realization in human beings, both individually and socially. The more thoroughly reason is applied to religion and to the conditions of human well-being, according to this point of view, the more clearly will there stand out the fundamental conflict between them. Defenders of faith on this issue have not

usually had the effrontery to argue that religious faith has never constituted a pretext for increasing human suffering and frustration; but they have urged that this is not the whole story, and that such developments are abuses of religious faith rather than its essence. The theoretical atheist stresses rather the lack of good reasons for believing in God or in Christ, and the availability of good reasons for not believing in them. Theoretical atheists may again be divided into two kinds – those who concede that the supposition that there is a God makes sense; and those who deny that such a supposition is even coherent in the last analysis. The first type is perhaps represented by most traditional atheists, and has found a recent distinguished champion in J.L. Mackie. God is supposed to be an almighty, all-knowing and utterly benevolent person, on whom the cosmos depends for its existence. But all the standard arguments that such a being exists are unsound. 'Ontological' arguments invalidly argue from some divine attribute, like perfection or unsurpassable greatness, to divine existence. But, as Kant said, 'existence is not a predicate'; and given any collection of properties whatever, it may still be coherently supposed that the bearer of these properties does not exist. There is no need of any 'first cause' or 'sufficient reason' for the universe as a whole; since (among other objections) the series of causes might well be infinite, and we simply do not know how far the principle that all states of affairs must have 'sufficient reason' is applicable to the universe in general. And if the universe requires sufficient reason outside itself for its existence, why should not the same apply to whatever is invoked to explain it? Furthermore, even if it is granted that there is some entity on which all else depends, why should not this be something in the nature of 'matter', rather than the conscious moral agent which is what everyone means by God? The order in the universe and the apparent adaptation of means to ends that it displays, which at one time provided some prima facie grounds for belief that the universe is the work of a designer, has since the time of Charles Darwin been susceptible to another and more satisfactory explanation; very elementary organisms coming into existence by chance within a favourable environment over a long period of time, and more complicated organisms gradually evolving from them by a process of mutation and natural selection. Not only are there no sound arguments which demonstrate, or even make likely, the existence of God; but there is at least one conclusive argument against it. The existence of God as traditionally conceived is incompatible with the existence of evil, or at least with the existence of the quantity of evil which in fact infests the universe. It is of the essence of a good agent that he or she removes evil as far as possible from within his or her sphere of influence; the divine goodness is supposed to be infinite, the divine power and sphere of influence unlimited, and yet there is an enormous amount of evil.

The other and in some ways more radical type of theoretical atheism is associated with LOGICAL POSITIVISM, though it is defended by some thinkers who are not logical positivists (A.G.N. Flew, K. Nielsen). The crude form of theism whereby God is conceived as literally a person acting on a cosmic scale has been shown to be false about as conclusively as any doctrine can be, and is generally rejected by sophisticated believers. They on their part retain their beliefs, it is alleged, only by qualifying them to such an extent as to divest them of all meaningful content. A non-embodied person turns out in the final analysis to be no person at all; a 'creation' compatible with evolution, and with a universe developing by natural means into an elaborate form from primitive beginnings, is not 'creation' in anything like the traditional sense.

3   Our third position is approximated to by Immanuel Kant, and maintained in its pristine form by Karl Barth. It is associated with Protestantism of the 'classical' as opposed to the 'liberal' type. Kant said that he was destroying the pretensions of knowledge in order to make room for faith. He claimed to have shown that all attempts to establish the existence of God on the basis of theoretical reason (as necessarily existing as a consequence of the divine nature; as 'first cause' or 'sufficient reason' for the universe; or as accounting for the order within the universe) were inevitably doomed to failure. The same applied to the doctrines of the immortality of the soul and the freedom of the will. On the other hand, he thought that these three doctrines ought to be affirmed as a matter of 'practical reason', as

moral postulates. The critique of theoretical reason revealed that it had a bearing only on the realm of appearances, and not on that of things in themselves. While this principle removed the basis for traditional forms of argument for the existence of God, it was not without usefulness for religion, as arguments *against* divine existence were similarly invalidated. Furthermore, the scientific determinism which seemed to apply ineluctably to the human organism as part of the realm of appearances need not affect the freedom of the human moral agent in himself or herself; which freedom we must believe in if we are to act as moral beings. Also, it is morally appropriate for us to believe that virtue will ultimately be rewarded with happiness (not, as Kant strongly insists, that we ought to make the prospect of such happiness for ourselves a condition of acting virtuously); and for this to take place, since it palpably does not happen automatically or when this life only is taken into account, it is necessary that human beings should have the prospect of a life beyond this one, and that an almighty and just Being should exist to ensure that happiness will be apportioned to virtue in that life.

Karl Barth agrees with Kant's aspersions on theoretical arguments supposed to support theism and Christianity which do not themselves presuppose their truth; but objects to his attempts to replace these with moral arguments. (Barth's one-time associate, Emil Brunner, maintained a position close to Kant's on the question.) For the mature Barth, all forms of 'natural theology', all attempts to argue for theism or Christianity on a 'rational' or 'moral' basis which does not itself presuppose them, are to be repudiated. God is revealed in Jesus Christ; the human being can only submit to this revelation in faith, or reject it in sin. Belief cannot argue with unbelief, as though there were relevant premises accepted by both; it can only preach to it. Any supposed 'God' reached as a result of such argument would be an idol rather than the true God. This position has been objected to on grounds similar to those which we mentioned in relation to the first one discussed. There are many claims as to what has been divinely revealed, propounded by non-Christians as well as by Christians. Why should any one such claim, given that it can be only asserted as opposed to justified by argument, be counted as more acceptable than any other?

A position closely related to Barth's has recently been defended by Alvin Plantinga. Most of our beliefs are justified by other beliefs; and the question thus arises of whether some of our beliefs must not be 'basic', in that they are beliefs by which other beliefs must be justified, without themselves requiring such justification. It has been characteristic of the empiricism which reached its extreme form in the 'logical positivism' of the early twentieth century, that it confines such 'basic beliefs' to principles of logic on the one hand, and registers of items of direct experience on the other. Religious beliefs were dismissed by members of this school as being neither themselves basic nor derivable from such basic beliefs. Subsequent philosophers have generally agreed that the logical positivist account of basic beliefs is unsatisfactory; the beliefs which the logical positivists proposed as basic seemed neither justifiable in themselves, nor such that the edifice of beliefs which ordinary persons and scientists would normally take to be justified can be built on them. Yet there does seem to be a need for basic beliefs in the theory of knowledge; since unless there is some *basis* on which beliefs liable to be true can be distinguished from those liable to be false, the absurd conclusion appears to follow that no belief is in the last analysis any more liable to be true than its contradictory. Plantinga proposes that, for the religious believer, any religious belief which cannot be derived from other properly basic beliefs may itself be regarded as properly basic. Thus, 'There is a God', or 'God is uniquely revealed to humankind in Jesus Christ', may or may not be able to be shown to be reasonable by appeal to other beliefs; but if it cannot be thus supported, this need not worry the believer, since he or she may simply place that belief in the category of those beliefs which, while providing grounds for the rationality of other beliefs, do not themselves have or require such grounds. The main objection to Plantinga's contention is much the same as that previously mentioned against Barth's; if the privilege of being properly basic is allowed to the beliefs characteristic of Christian theists, why should it not be allowed to any belief which anyone wants to maintain, however intellectually absurd or morally frightful that belief is generally held to be?

As to the Kantian position, it might be granted that Kant has shown the *moral appropriateness* of beliefs central to Christianity, without any concession that such beliefs are liable to be *true*. Thus the belief that the mourners will be comforted, and the meek inherit the earth, may well hearten persons in the performance of their moral duty; but this provides no adequate ground for the belief that the mourners actually *will* be comforted or the meek inherit the earth. A rather similar point may be made in relation to an argument advanced by C.S. Lewis. According to Lewis, if we are to be truly moral, we have to believe that basic moral principles have some kind of objective existence as opposed to being merely dependent on human convention; otherwise it would make no sense to oppose on moral grounds conventions sufficiently firmly established, as plainly it does do. Furthermore, the existence of such principles may be supposed to make more sense if we presuppose the existence of a Being both entitled and likely to promulgate them, than if we do not. But it may be objected that even if human beings, given that they are to be at once morally virtuous and consistent, must *believe* that moral principles are not merely dependent on human convention, that by no means entails that they *are* not so dependent. It cannot be excluded a priori that, at least so far as the majority of human beings are concerned, moral behaviour is only possible if the agent assumes what is as a matter of fact false.

4   The fourth position is characteristic of philosophical idealism, as represented most impressively in the work of G.W.F. Hegel. As Hegel sees it, reason is everywhere active in the world, but at first unconsciously. For a while it appears as something other than and alien to human reason, when God is conceived as transcendent and apart from humanity. But when God becomes man with the advent of Christianity, it is revealed that the reason active in nature is none other than what comes to itself in human reason. Christianity proclaims this truth in a dramatic and pictorial manner, in the form of historical events; it remains for idealist philosophy to present it as it really is. It is perhaps not very surprising that while some who claimed to follow Hegel regarded his system as the vindication of religion in general and Christianity in particular, others, the 'left-wing Hegelians', thought of it as rather tending to their repudiation and supersession. For philosophical idealism is on the most conservative showing not merely *identical* with Christianity as preached and believed from the first, or it would be superfluous; and it might be asked what is the effective difference between treating idealism as the true essence of Christianity which until the advent of idealism had been incompletely or improperly understood, and envisaging idealism as a metaphysical truth of which Christianity had been an interesting but in many ways primitive anticipation?

5   A distinction has to be made between the Hegelian 'sublation' of Christian doctrine, and the medieval scholastic recasting of it, culminating in the system of Thomas Aquinas, which in some ways resembles it. Thomism has in common with Hegelianism that it aspires to an expression of what is supposed to be Christian truth in such a way as to display both its self-consistency, and its acceptability to a reason which does not presuppose its truth. But Thomism unequivocally preserves, as Hegelianism does not, the particular contingent claims as to matter of fact which have been central to traditional Christianity – that a particular human individual who lived on earth in the past, and about whom the Gospels inform us, was really and truly divine; that all human beings for weal or woe have to expect some kind of life after death; and so on. Furthermore, though Thomism seeks to display the Christian faith as a whole as reasonable, the reasonableness is of different kinds as applied to different doctrines; whereas the existence of God and the immortality of the soul, as Thomas claimed, may be shown on the basis of general rational principles alone, such doctrines as those of the Trinity and the incarnation have to be accepted on divine authority, for all that their mutual consistency, their compatibility with what is otherwise known and their vital relevance to human destiny may be displayed by the theologian.

How far is such a scheme, whereby faith and reason enhance one another, available for our own time? The positivism which has been the intellectual basis of so much contemporary atheism may be said to founder on the fact that its principles, once fully clarified and consistently implemented, appear to self-destruct; since there is no course of sense-experience by which one can verify or falsify the presumably meaningful non-analytic proposition, that all meaningful non-analytic propositions must be verifiable or falsifiable by sense-experience. Since the general downfall of positivism, philosophers have been inclined to urge that knowledge has no foundations at all – a scarcely tolerable position, since it seems to follow ineluctably from it not only that theism and atheism are no better founded than one another, but that science is no better founded than superstition, history than legend, astronomy than alchemy. More satisfactory than positivist foundations for knowledge, or the conviction which has arisen due to their apparent collapse that knowledge has and needs no foundations, is the view that belief is well-founded, and so tends to be true and therefore to amount to knowledge, so far as it is attentively, intelligently, and reasonably arrived at; that is to say, so far as it is based on attention to the relevant evidence in sensation or consciousness, envisagement of the full range of possibilities which might explain this evidence, and judgement that that explanation is most liable to be true which the evidence best confirms (Lonergan, 1970). If the real world is indeed none other than what is to be envisaged by intelligence and affirmed by reason on the basis of experience, it is an intelligible world. Hegel's conception of the world as rational, and of its rationality as indicative of a rational principle at the base of it, has already been alluded to. According to some more recent thinkers, the amenability of the world to human enquiry which is most conspicuously exemplified in science is best explained if it is due to something analogous to intelligent will, which is roughly equivalent to what everyone knows as God; divine intelligence accounting for the fact that it is intelligible, divine will for the fact that it has the particular kind of intelligibility that it has (in terms of oxygen rather than phlogiston, of special relativity rather than a luminiferous ether and so on). Religious experience and moral conscience may be regarded as signs of the existence and concern for humanity of the Being thus rationally affirmed to exist, even if taken by themselves they can be explained

without reference to it. As to evil, it is to be explained as due partly to the impairment of individual creatures due to the activity of other creatures and the operation of the laws of the world as a whole, partly to abuse by rational creatures of their freedom of will. (The PROBLEM OF EVIL might then be expressed as follows: *in what sense*, if any, can the intelligent will supposed to underlie the universe be said to be good, given the quantity of evil that exists, but also granted, as is stated by most of the great religious traditions, that there is to come about a consummation of the world in which those who have striven for virtue may hope to share?) The specifically Christian position may be commended both as amounting to what God might have done to remedy the plight of creatures who had surrendered to moral evil, and as tending to be corroborated by unprejudiced examination of the relevant historical evidence (see APOLOGETICS).

Whatever the merits or otherwise of the specifically Marxist account of the relation between reason and religious faith (see MARXISM), it has been quite influential, and so deserves some treatment by way of conclusion to this article. As Marx sees it, human beings used to be confronted by a hostile nature and society, and so were compelled to believe in gods and an afterlife in order to make life in this world endurable. Now the physical environment has been more or less mastered by technology; the religious illusion persists because society remains such that individuals and groups are pitted against one another rather than cooperating freely and harmoniously, as they will do when the classless society has come into existence as a result of the socialist revolution and the ensuing dictatorship of the proletariat. The condition of class conflict has reached an extreme form in early industrial society; however, as technology advances, and the social relations dependent upon it change accordingly, such conflict will in the long run inevitably disappear, and religion will disappear along with it. However, as things are in bourgeois societies, and indeed in socialist societies before the ultimate withering away of the state, religion is a reactionary force; progressive persons must therefore be engaged in a struggle against it.

Marxists believe that the theoretical case against religion is now complete; their opponents might well concede that, *if* this were the case, there would merely remain the practical problem of bringing about the political and social arrangements which would make pointless the illusory comforts which it provides. But it may be questioned whether the theoretical case against religion really *is* as complete as Marxists suppose. Marx's doctrine of 'historical materialism' distinguishes between the real bases of the actions of human beings in their economic and social circumstances, and the ideological forms in which they represent these to themselves – such as morality, law and religion. There is a nice question where science fits into this scheme. Marxists are in general scientific realists; that is to say, they are convinced that human ideas arrived at by means of the scientific method represent the truth about things, or at least tend to do so. But if the ideas of science are privileged in this respect, for what reason are they so? It is not easy to frame a pragmatic criterion which will unequivocally justify the ideas of science while definitely excluding those of religion. To say that ideas have warrant so far as they picture observable realities, as Marx was at one time inclined to do, is to disqualify most of science. But if it is allowed that ideas with no direct warrant in observation may all the same represent what is real, it is not immediately excluded that, for example, the idea of an unobservable God may do so. If it is protested that the theoretical entities postulated by scientists, even if not directly observable, are required adequately to *explain* what is so, it might be argued, on the lines set out earlier in this article, that a God is equally needed in the last analysis to provide an explanation for the observable and intelligible world as a whole.

See also EPISTEMOLOGY, RELIGIOUS; EXISTENCE OF GOD, PROOFS OF; FAITH; PHILOSOPHY OF RELIGION.

Bibliography

Anselm 1974: *Anselm of Canterbury*, vol 1, ed. Jasper Hopkins and Herbert Richardson. London: SCM Press.

Aquinas 1951: *Philosophical Texts*, ed. T. Gilby. London: Oxford University Press.

Brown, S.C., ed. 1977: *Reason and Religion*. Ithaca and London: Cornell University Press.

Copleston, F.C. 1955: *Aquinas*. Harmondsworth: Penguin.

Hume, D. 1955: Dialogues concerning natural religion. In *Hume Selections*, ed. C.W. Hendel, Jr. New York: Scribner.

Jaki, S.L. 1978: *The Road of Science and the Ways to God*. Chicago: University of Chicago Press.

Kant, I. [1793] 1960: *Religion Within the Limits of Reason Alone*. New York: Harper.

Kenny, A. 1983: *Faith and Reason*. New York: Columbia University Press.

Kierkegaard, S. [1846] 1962: *Philosophical Fragments*. Princeton: Princeton University Press.

Leslie, J. 1979: *Value and Existence*. Oxford: Blackwell.

Flew, A.G.N. 1966: *God and Philosophy*. London: Hutchinson.

Lonergan, B.J.F. 1970: *Insight. A Study of Human Understanding*, chapter 19. New York: Philosophical Library.

Mackie, J.L. 1982: *The Miracle of Theism*. Oxford: Clarendon Press.

Meynell, H.A. 1982: *The Intelligible Universe*. London: Macmillan.

Mitchell, B. 1974: *The Justification of Religious Belief*. New York: Seabury.

Mitchell, B., ed. 1971: *The Philosophy of Religion*. Oxford: Oxford University Press.

Nielsen, K. 1975: *Philosophy and Atheism*. Buffalo: Prometheus Books.

Penelhum, T.M. 1971: *Problems of Religious Knowledge*. London: Macmillan.

Swinburne, R. 1979: *The Existence of God*. Oxford: Clarendon Press.

Swinburne, R. 1981: *Faith and Reason*. Oxford: Clarendon Press.

HUGO A. MEYNELL

Farrer, Austin Marsden (1904–1968) British theologian and philosopher. A student and chaplain at Oxford and a contemporary of C.S. Lewis, he was Warden of Keble College from 1960 until his death. An Anglo-Catholic who emphasized logic and the interdependency of faith and reason, he wrote in the areas of philosophical theology (*Finite and the Infinite*, 1943; *The Freedom of the Will*, 1957; and *Faith and Speculation*, 1964), other theology, especially New Testament exegesis, and the theory of language.

Bibliography

Curtis, P. 1985: *A Hawk among Sparrows: A Biography of Austin Farrer*. London.

219

Eaton, J.C. 1983: *The Logic of Theism: An Analysis of the Thought of Austin Farrer*. Lanham, Md.

Eaton, J.C., and Loades, A., eds 1983: *For God and Clarity: New Essays in Honor of Austin Farrer*. Pittsburgh, Pa.

feminist theology Feminist theologies comprise a relatively new form of theological reflection that derives from the global movements for the emancipation of women in society and in the churches. Feminism names these diverse and collective movements which, in the nineteenth century and again in the twentieth, emerged in Europe and North America and then across the world. These movements recognize the historical and contemporary denigration, subordination and exclusion of women in culture, society and its institutions, including the family and the churches, and actively strive to promote the freedom, participation, and well-being of women in all these contexts. Feminist criticism, historical analysis, and theory building have contributed to these movements, as scholars, both women and men, seek to deepen understanding of the past and present situations of women and thereby to make activity for the freedom and equality of women more effective. In the churches the most obvious and practical expressions of the women's movements have been in the struggles for inclusive language, in reference both to God and to human persons, and for the admission of women to the ministry and to priestly ordination.

In this activity, feminist scholars have turned to exploring the relationships between various religious systems and their views of women in a broad arena that is now often called women's studies in religion. And feminist theology, at least in the west, may be seen as that area of study that is specifically concerned with historical and contemporary understanding of women in the religious texts, rituals and practices of Judaism, Christianity and Islam. As a form of reflection that has emerged from the struggles of women for equality, mutuality and reciprocity within the religious communities, feminist theology is usually understood as a form of critical LIBERATION THEOLOGY.

Within the Christian context, feminist theology examines the views about women and the activities, roles and practices of women found in the Scriptures, in the texts of the tradition, and in the theologies of the churches. In this work, scholars have brought to light the historical sources of the negative views about women in the Bible and in historical and more recent Christian thought, as well as the exclusionary practices of the churches with regard to women. As feminist theology developed, a threefold ideology about women was discerned in Christian thought and practice. In the Bible, the church Fathers and the writings of later theologians, women are seen as property, objects or tools; women are viewed as polluting, dangerously sexual or carnal; and women are romantically idealized as morally and spiritually superior to men but childlike and in need of protection in the private realm (Radford Ruether, 1975). This ideology led to views that connected women especially with sin and evil, asserted women's inability fully to image God or Christ, and excluded women from leadership, that is, from preaching, teaching, ministry or ordination in the churches. It thus entailed the exclusion of women from participation in major decision making in Christian life and practice.

At the same time, feminist scholars have also shown that women have been agents as well as victims within Christian history. Despite the massive exclusion and denigration of women found in the Christian traditions and despite the crippling ideologies that severely limited their autonomy and participation, women exercised significant leadership in virtually all the Christian traditions and historic periods (Radford Ruether and McLaughlin, 1979). The active involvement and creativity of women has always been integral to Christian life and thought. Women have held an important place in a tradition and a theology that has systematically named them as inferior, subjected and subordinate. Some scholars hold that Christianity, with its male symbols for God, its male saviour figure and its history of male leaders, thinkers and reformers is intrinsically patriarchal (under the rule of men), sexist (biased against women) and harmful to the well-being of women, and urge women to leave its oppressive environment (Daly, 1973; Hampson, 1990). Others claim that women are best served in retrievals of ancient or new forms of goddess religion that affirm the bodies and sexuality of women, the power and will of women, and the bonds of women with one another (Christ, 1987; Christ and Plaskow, 1979; Goldenberg, 1979).

Yet many feminist women remain in the churches and find the Christian symbols of God, Christ, the Spirit, the Christian understandings of the Trinity, Jesus, grace and the redemptive community both life-giving and capable of reform. This is the position of Christian feminist women who quarrel with the Fathers of the theological and ecclesiastical traditions and who urge that the experience of women be taken into account in studies of the Bible and Christian history, in theology, and in the ethics and practice of Christian life. These Christian feminist women, and the scholars who have developed the various Christian feminist theologies, hold that the patterns of thought and practice recorded in the sermons, commentaries, textbooks and histories of traditional Christian understanding are inadequate because they recount only the theories and deeds of men and ignore the thought and activities of women. Their record fails to acknowledge either the oppressive character of biblical and traditional Christian thought and practice or the leadership and activities of women in Christian history and theology (Carr, 1988; Radford Ruether and McLaughlin, 1979; Schüssler Fiorenza, 1983; Harrison, 1985).

As Christian feminist theology developed in the twentieth century, three tasks emerged which describe its character today. These include protest and critique, historical revision and theological construction. In addition, there is discussion and writing about feminist spirituality, an area of practice that includes the development of ritual, poetry, song, symbol and community formation specific to the concerns of women.

Protest and critique
The first moment of feminist theology, both logically and chronologically, is an analysis of the historical and contemporary images, symbols, concepts and practices of Christianity with regard to women. Feminist scholars have criticized patterns in the Bible and Christian tradition that are not only androcentric (male-centred and male-normed) but positively damaging to women. For example, centuries of interpretation of Eve, in the garden story of

Genesis 2–3, have named her, and thereby all women, as the source of sin and evil. The Fathers of the church continued and deepened this denigration of women, describing all women as sinful Eve, in contrast with the holiness and virginity of Mary, the mother of Jesus. The patristic Eve–Mary symbolic contrast has been used even in recent times (*Lumen Gentium*, Second Vatican Council).

Feminists who object to ancient and medieval views of women's subordination, in Augustine and Aquinas particularly, point out that these thinkers believed woman's inferiority was natural and thereby justified her state of subjection in the family, church and society (Børreson, [1968] 1981). Feminist scholarship has shown that St Thomas Aquinas, for example, who described woman as a misbegotten man, based his theological understanding of women on the political philosophy and outmoded biology of Aristotle, a dualistic framework of thought that similarly legitimated the 'natural' contrast between slaves and freemen. And the theology of Aquinas is still used in the Roman Catholic argument against the ordination of women.

A third example of protest and critique in feminist theology is directed towards recent theological perspectives which derive from subordinationist interpretation of the Bible. A notorious example is the theologian Karl Barth, who discusses the Christian view of women in his *Church Dogmatics* (III/1; III/4). While insisting on the equality of women with men, Barth nevertheless argues that women are related to men as 'B' is related to 'A' in the revealed Word of God, a view which has implications about the nature of God and about the essential character of women and of sexuality in Christian life. Feminist theologians dispute the revelatory status of the biblical view that Barth promoted in his assertion of women's derived, secondary status and of women's essential roles of helpmate and auxiliary to men (Arnold Romero in Radford Ruether, 1974).

The work of protest and critique is embodied in a number of collections of historical and modern texts (such as Clark and Richardson, 1977; Radford Ruether and McLaughlin, 1979) that emphasize the problematic character of the Bible and the Christian tradition with regard to women. Feminist theologians argue that in serious ways the texts and the practices of Christianity are contradictory to its affirmation of the full personhood of women, witnessed in their baptism. Christian feminist theology, in its critique of ideology, thus exposes the systematic distortion of women in Christian life and thought. In its protest, it claims that in so far as Christianity envisions God as a male in heaven it makes the male superior to women on earth (Daly, 1973). And it argues that Christian theology has similarly legitimated dualistic patterns of domination in the relations between God and humankind, Christ and church, adults and children, clergy and laity, rich nations and poor, whites and people of colour, men and nature (Radford Ruether, 1975). 'God as dominator', extended into human relationships, is from the perspectives of Christian feminist thought a distortion of the gospel, a distortion often found in the historical and modern expressions of Christian theology.

In this extension of feminist reflection to the other dominations of historical and contemporary Christianity, Christian feminist thought strives to be internally self-critical and to avoid reversal of dominative patterns. There are other issues which it addresses, as it examines the interstructuring of racism, classism, elitism and clericalism with sexism. Yet feminist thought focuses on the question of women, who are not just one group among many struggling for liberation but who are evenly distributed in *all* subordinated groups and in *all* races and classes. Women are a unique group. Neither a caste nor a minority, women are the majority of the human race. And some feminist thinkers hold that the domination of women is the original oppression that gives rise to the other oppressions of history. Thus feminist thought protests against sexism as a bias of the male–female relationship that results in the rape, torture, pain and exploitation of women and that fails to respect the full personhood of women. And feminist theology exposes the texts, traditions and practices of Christianity that denigrate women as the source of sin and evil, as inferior or incomplete persons and as incapable of leadership (preaching, teaching, ministry, ordination) or decision making in the Christian churches.

Historical revision

The bias of patriarchy and sexism and its harmful effects on women is the major impetus for feminism's protest and critique. However, it is also the case that women have been agents as well as victims in their religious lives. In every Christian period, women have reached and expressed the most profound religious self-transcendence. And women have produced their own spiritual and theological perspectives. As some secular historians have observed, the recovery of women's lost, forgotten or suppressed history has resulted in the most recent redefinition of history itself. To view the past through the eyes of women and from the perspective of women's subordination or freedom changes the usual historical assessments and realigns historical periodization. The goal of the integration of women's history into 'history' itself – men's history – derives from the recognition that the historical record is pervaded by patriarchal values and androcentric concerns (kings and conquests, not child rearing). Feminist historians, both women and men, hold that only the development of women's history will lead to a fully universal human history (Lerner, 1986; Degler, 1980).

The implications of women's history for Christian history are vast, in their suggestion of a history of ministry and theology that would incorporate the activity and theological vision of women, in popular religion, spirituality, mysticism, preaching, teaching and the organization and reform of religious groups. For example historians of ancient near-eastern religions, the Hebrew Bible, the New Testament and early Christianity, have put forward views that challenge the androcentric record and are the focus of scholarly discussion and debate. One scholar suggests that gender is relatively unimportant in polytheistic cultures, whereas it is central in the monotheistic religions of the Bible (Ochshorn, 1981). Another scholar argues that 'counter-voices' in the Hebrew Bible judge its dominant patriarchal themes, show the equality of female and male in creation and in erotic and mundane relationships, and reveal the saturation of the Scriptures with female imagery (Trible, 1978).

Feminist biblical scholarship has shown that the ancient goddess was positively appropriated by Hebrew and Christian monotheism (Radford

Ruether, 1983) and that the Jesus movement began as a reform within Israel that embodied an inclusive vision of the reign of God, goddess language and mythology, and the equal discipleship of men and women (Schüssler Fiorenza). Feminist historians show that women exercised leadership as prophets and apostles in the earliest Christian communities, as scholars and leaders of religious organizations in patristic and medieval times, as socially active organizers in Catholic Reformation circles and as religious and social reformers in nineteenth-century Europe and America (Radford Ruether and McLaughlin, 1979). Studies of medieval mystics have brought new attention to theological symbols of 'Jesus as mother' and the 'motherhood of God' as well as to the importance of gender in the analysis of religious symbols (Bynum Walker, 1982; Bynum Walker, Harrell and Richman, 1986). Traditions of androgynous and Spirit Christology that are inclusive of women have been discovered throughout Christian history (Radford Ruether, 1983). These patterns of female leadership and symbolism represent an important undercurrent to the androcentric mainstream of ecclesiastical and theological history. And these precedents offer a provocative incentive for contemporary feminist theological construction.

Theological construction

Beyond protest, criticism and the revision of history, feminist theology has been engaged in reformulating the whole of Christian theology. The movements for inclusive language and for the admission of women to ministry and priestly ordination lead to the exploration and development of new understandings of the major themes of Christian thought. Feminist scholars argue that the explicit incorporation of the perspectives of women have consequences for Christian understandings of God, Christ, the church, theological anthropology, sin, salvation and grace.

For example, the fundamental feminist question about the maleness of God in the imagery, symbolism and concepts of traditional Christian thought and prayer leads to new reflection on the doctrine of God. In spite of theological denials of sexuality (or any materiality) in God, the persistent use of masculine pronouns for God and the reaction of many

Christians against reference to God as 'she' would appear to affirm the 'maleness' attributed to God. Yet it is also logical that 'she' is not only as appropriate as 'he', but is perhaps necessary to reorient Christian imagination from the idolatrous implications of exclusively masculine God-language and the dominant effects of the father image in the churches and Christian practice. A new theory of the thoroughly metaphorical character of religious language has emerged in the light of feminist discussion of the doctrine of God. This theory argues that traditional analogical understanding has tended to stress the similarity between human concepts and God's own selfhood, while a metaphorical theology would focus rather on the God–human relationship and on the unlikeness of all religious language in reference to God even as it affirms some similarity (McFague, 1982).

There have been proposals for referring to God as 'parent' or as 'father and mother' or for the balancing use of feminine language for the Spirit, since the Hebrew word for Spirit is grammatically feminine. On the other hand, some feminist scholars have urged the move away from parental images entirely, since these are suggestive of childish rather than adult religious dependence. While parental images express compassion, acceptance, guidance and discipline, they do not express the mutuality, maturity, cooperation, responsibility and reciprocity required by contemporary personal and political experience. One feminist theologian argues that there is no adequate name for God at present, given the overwhelming bias of traditional Christian thought about God, and suggests the designation 'God/ess' for the matrix and source of all life (Radford Ruether, 1983).

Some feminist theologians call for the use of multiple metaphors and models for God and for the divine–human relationship, since none alone is adequate. The Bible itself uses many different human and cosmic designations, while in fact one metaphor (father) has become the dominant model in Christian thought and practice. One suggestion is the metaphor of God as 'friend' (McFague, 1982, 1987). There is a biblical basis for this in Jesus' saying about laying down one's life for one's friends (John 15: 13) and his reference to the Son of Man as friend of tax collectors and sinners (Matt. 11: 19); Jesus *is* the parable of God's friendship with people. This friendship is shown in his parables of the lost sheep, the prodigal son, the good Samaritan, and the 'enacted parable' of Jesus' inclusive table fellowship. The Gospels describe Jesus as critical of views of familial ties that failed to recognize the inclusive significance of his new community. They depict his presence as transforming the lives of his friends. Friendship to the stranger, both as individual and as nation or culture, is a model 'on our increasingly small and beleaguered planet where, if people do not become friends, they will not survive' (McFague, 1982).

The metaphor of God as friend corresponds to the feminist ideal of 'communal personhood', an ideal that entails non-competitive relationships among persons and groups that are characterized by mutuality and reciprocity rather than dualism and hierarchy. It responds to feminist concerns for expressions of divine–human relation that overcome the images of religious self-denial that have shaped women's experience in patterns of low self-esteem, passivity and irresponsibility. It suggests the ideas of mutuality, self-creation in community, and the creation of ever wider communities with other persons and the world (Plaskow, 1980). The theme of God's friendship is intensified in the life and death of Jesus, who reveals a God who suffers for, with, and in people and invites them into a community of suffering with God and for others (Moltmann, [1980] 1981). The theme unites theology with feminist spirituality in its emphasis on women's friendship and interdependence as these are related to the reciprocal interdependence of the whole of creation. There are limitations to the metaphor of God as friend, as there are to any metaphor, and these limitations point to the importance of the use of many different metaphors to suggest the unfathomable character of the divine–human relationship.

Another example of Christian feminist theological reflection concerns discussion of the doctrine of sin. Feminist thinkers point out that the Christian emphasis on sin as pride, overriding self-esteem or ambition is the result of a male-derived set of experiences. And while this theology may adequately reflect the experience of dominant males, it does not correspond to the experience of women. The 'sin' of women would more likely be characterized as lack of pride, lack of self-esteem, lack of ambition or personal focus. The women's movement has encouraged women to develop precisely these characteristics to offset the triviality, lack of self-discipline and serious responsibility that have constituted the stereotypes of the female personality, stereotypes that have been internalized by women in their own self-understanding. When women do assume responsibility and call for patterns and practices of equality and mutuality, they are criticized for adopting male (sinful) styles, for being 'pushy' and power-hungry. Such judgements are delivered from a male-centred theological and ethical understanding and are inadequate for many women (Plaskow, 1980).

Feminist theologians argue that cultural, social and theological systems have often prevented women from developing strong self-images and that there are negative moral and religious implications in the limited, self-sacrificing and passive roles women have been conditioned to accept. They hold that if the religious and moral lives of human persons are capable of development in some direct proportion to the achieved degree of freedom and responsibility, then women must take hold of their lives as responsible selves. While self-sacrifice is central to the ideal of Christian love, there has to be a healthy and free self before genuine and responsible self-giving can occur. In this way servitude is distinguished in feminist thought from an authentic ideal of service.

Thus feminist thought has urged the moral and theological significance of human agency in encouraging women to value their own lives as active and responsible selves. It has shown how male theological perspectives have dominated in understandings of sin as pride and rebellion against God and have failed to attend to the sin of those who are powerless, who lack agency, selfhood and responsibility, and who have consequently suffered abuse and violence. While women can sin in the ways of masculine culture, especially in the new roles they have assumed in that culture, their own 'feminine' formation suggests sins of passive failure to develop a sense of self, a sense of agency and responsibility. Sin is understood, in a feminist perspective, as the breaking of relationship with God, with other persons, and with nature and life itself. This can take the form of weakness as well as pride, in its denial of responsibility in both the personal and political realms. Conversely, salvation would be reformulated as the healing of broken relationships and as mutuality and reciprocity in relation to God and others (Saiving in Christ and Plaskow, 1979; Plaskow, 1980; McFague, 1982).

A final example of feminist theological construction is in Christology, which feminist analysis has found to be the doctrine most used against women (Radford Ruether, 1983). This can be seen in two ways. First, while the maleness of Jesus in history is indisputable, it has been assumed throughout Christian history to reveal the maleness of God, or at least to indicate that only male images can be used in reference to God. While Jesus called God *Abba* and is presented in the Gospels as referring to God as the Father, this has been interpreted to mean that God should be imaged only in male terms or thought of in analogy only with male human beings. But feminist scholarship argues that the maleness of Jesus is simply a contingent part of his particularity, like his Jewishness, his language, his work as a carpenter. Second, the maleness of Jesus has been interpreted to mean that the norm of humanity is the male and that male human being is closer to the ideal than the female. Thus the embodiment of Jesus as a man is understood as an ontological necessity rather than a contingent dimension of his historical reality. Both traditional perspectives have had a negative impact for women in Christian life and thought (Johnson, 1990).

In developing new understandings of Christology, feminist theology finds important meaning in the preaching, death and resurrection of Jesus, and in the tradition of wisdom Christology. Jesus' preaching of justice and peace for all is radically inclusive, especially of those who are marginalized. Thus he includes women among his followers and friends, even sinful women, and women were among his first witnesses. His message breaks all patterns of domination and offers a new pattern of mutual relationship among all in the realm of God. Jesus' *Abba* is not a patriarchal God but a God of compassion and intimacy who creates a community of women and men. The women disciples stood by Jesus at the time of his death, a death understood by feminist interpreters as incurred because of his radically inclusive ministry; for them Jesus' death means the death of patriarchy. And in the resurrection, first witnessed by Jesus' women disciples, the Spirit of God is poured out on women and men alike, symbolized in the new, and gender-inclusive, rite of baptism adopted by the early Christians (Johnson, 1990).

Finally, feminist theologians find it significant that one of the first figures with whom Jesus is identified is *Sophia* or Wisdom, a female personification of God in the Hebrew Bible who creates and renews the world. In the New Testament, Paul calls Jesus the wisdom of God (1 Cor. 1: 24), and John's descriptions of Jesus, especially in his long discourses, recall the figure of Sophia. Thus wisdom Christology suggests a way that the significance of Jesus Christ might be affirmed and even his divinity confessed in a non-androcentric pattern of imagery and thought. In Sophia-Jesus or Jesus as the wisdom of God, feminist liberation Christology discovers in Jesus the liberator of women, who returns them to full personhood through participation in the reign of God and who delivers women from every form of subordination (Johnson, 1990; Schüssler Fiorenza, 1983).

It should be noted that the preceding analysis of feminist theology represents only one interpretation, from an educated, white, middle-class point of view, and presents just a few examples in the pluralism of thought that has characterized feminist theological discussion from its inception. For feminist theology is committed to plurality and diversity, to the importance of the inclusion of many voices and many perspectives, and it understands its various proposals as contributions to a wider discussion and debate. For as feminist theology has developed, its awareness of the interstructuring of racism and classism with sexism has become more pronounced. In its attempt to be self-critical about issues of class and race, feminist understanding of the experience of women has also deepened. It is now apparent to feminist theologians that there is no single, universal 'women's experience' but rather great diversity among women. In different geographical contexts, in which there are various economic, political and social structures and different historical and ethnic traditions involved, the women's movements around the globe are developing their own, culturally specific, feminist understandings. They are similar in their advocacy of women's full dignity and participation in the structures of society and in the churches, but distinctive according to their ethnic, racial and economic contexts. Thus there is not only a pluralism within western feminist theology but a pluralism that is global. The views of women of the third world, women of colour (the writings of black women are now distinguished as womanist theology), women of different cultures and classes in Africa, Asia and Latin America offer distinctive formulations in Christian feminist theology (Grant, 1989; Fabella and Oduyoye, 1988; Katoppo, 1980).

An important context for feminist theology in many areas is the movement called women-church. This is the fluid and spontaneous networking of women (and interested men) who gather in small groups for discussion and liturgical celebration centred around or relevant to women's concerns. These concerns include not only feminist issues but a whole cluster of topics relating to justice, peace, ecology and new forms of community, ritual, imagery and theological expression. Women-church embodies mutuality and reciprocity in its structures, decision making, social action and symbol making. It is not separatist in orientation but rather offers a context for feminist experimentation and for discoveries to be refined (Radford Ruether, 1986). It is often, as well, an important context for the Christian feminist spiritualities that are one of the sources of the development of feminist theology.

Feminist spiritualities are diverse, depending on the situations of the participants. While some are specifically Christian, seeking to develop Christian symbolic language and liturgy in women-oriented but inclusive ways (Wolski Conn, 1986), others find Christian imagery, symbolism and language intrinsically patriarchal and have formed separate communities, often around the figure of the goddess. Using ancient, medieval or modern symbols and images of goddesses or 'the goddess', these groups offer a contemporary expression of religious experience and worship that is explicitly centred on women and the validation of women's experience, women's sexuality and relations to one another

(Starhawk, 1979). Both Christian and goddess feminist spiritualities (sometimes distinguished as 'reformist' and 'revolutionary') are a source of feminist theology, or thealogy, as a form of thought and writing and have had a significant impact on each other. There is some argument that goddess worship can result in mere reversal of dominance and there is doubt about the historical veracity of a genuinely woman-centred goddess tradition. This view suggests rather the importance of remaining within the churches and effecting change within their practices and theologies (Radford Ruether, 1986).

Another issue of some debate within feminist theology today concerns the question of whether women and men represent one human nature or two. Some feminist theologians hold that, beyond biological differences (sex), women and men are essentially the same. It is culturally conditioned and humanly constructed meanings that are ascribed to sexual differences (gender) that account for the historical denigration and subjugation of women. These feminist scholars argue for the equality and essential sameness of women with men in Christian thought and the practice of the churches. The difference of women from men is a matter of historical conditioning and one in which women have preserved important values which need to be fully integrated within contemporary Christian life and thought. Other feminist theologians hold that women are essentially different from men and stress the importance of physical embodiment, the special connection of women with nature that the possibility of motherhood entails, as well as the psychological and sociological significance of child bearing and child rearing (attachment and relationship to the mother for girls, separation and distinction for boys). These thinkers emphasize women's difference and propose that women's physical embodiment affords special insight that has been overlooked and needs to be taken seriously in all religious thought and ethics (Ruddick, 1989; Noddings, 1989).

Only in recent times have women been admitted to theological study and, in many denominations, to the ministry and priesthood. Some churches, notably the Eastern Orthodox and the Roman Catholic, still do not accept women for ordination although the numbers of women pursuing advanced theological study has increased in all seminaries and universities. Such study has allowed for the development of feminist theology and although its legitimacy is still questioned in some quarters, its critique, historical revision and theological construction are now generally accepted. There are journals of feminist thought in religious studies and theology in several countries and women are accepted as scholars and teachers in increasing numbers of seminaries and universities.

Theological discussion of the experience of women in relation to Christian themes has begun to affect the whole of theology, both Protestant and Roman Catholic, whether it is done by women or men. Few treatments of God, Christ, or the church and its ministry, sin, salvation or theological anthropology today fail to address the impact of the feminist critique or to take account of feminist historical and constructive work. Feminist and womanist theologies, derived from the women's struggle and from feminist spirituality, now comprise a diverse, pluralistic and vigorous intellectual movement within Christian life and thought.

See also BIBLICAL CRITICISM AND INTERPRETATION 2: NEW TESTAMENT; ETHICS.

Bibliography

Børreson, Kari Elisabeth [1968] 1981: *Subordination and Equivalence: The Nature and Role of Women in Augustine and Thomas Aquinas*, trans. Charles H. Talbot. Washington, DC: University Press of America.

Bynum Walker, Caroline 1982: *Jesus as Mother: Studies in the Spirituality of the High Middle Ages*. Berkeley: University of California Press.

Bynum Walker, Caroline, Harrell, Stephen, and Richman, Paula, eds 1986: *Gender and Religion: On the Complexity of Symbols*. Boston: Beacon Press.

Carr, Anne E. 1988: *Transforming Grace: Christian Tradition and the Experience of Women*. San Francisco: Harper and Row.

Christ, Carol P. 1987: *Laughter of Aphrodite: Reflections on a Journey to the Goddess*. San Francisco: Harper and Row.

Christ, Carol P., and Plaskow, Judith, eds 1979: *Womanspirit Rising*. New York: Harper and Row.

Clark, Elizabeth A., and Richardson, Herbert, eds 1977: *Women and Religion: A Feminist Sourcebook of Christian Thought*. New York: Harper and Row.

Daly, Mary 1973: *Beyond God the Father: Toward a Philosophy of Women's Liberation*. Boston: Beacon Press.

Degler, Carl 1980: *At Odds: Women and Family in America from the Revolution to the Present*. New York: Oxford University Press.

Fabella, Virginia and Oduyoye, Mercy Amba, eds 1988: *With Passion and Compassion: Third World Women Doing Theology*. Maryknoll: Orbis Press.

Goldenberg, Naomi Ruth 1979: *Changing of the Gods: Feminism and the End of Traditional Religions*. Boston: Beacon Press.

Grant, Jacquelyn 1989: *White Women's Christ and Black Women's Jesus: Feminist Christology and Womanist Response*. Atlanta: Scholars Press.

Hampson, Daphne 1990: *Theology and Feminism*. Oxford: Blackwell.

Harrison, Beverly Wildung 1985: *Making the Connections: Essays in Feminist Social Ethics*, ed. Carol S. Robb. Boston: Beacon Press.

Johnson, Elizabeth A. 1990: *Consider Jesus: Waves of Renewal in Christology*. New York: Crossroad Publishing Co.

Katoppo, Marianne 1980: *Compassionate and Free: An Asian Woman's Theology*. Maryknoll: Orbis Press.

Lerner, Gerda 1986: *The Creation of Patriarchy*. New York: Oxford University Press.

McFague, Sallie 1982: *Metaphorical Theology: Models of God in Religious Language*. Philadelphia: Fortress Press.

McFague, Sallie 1987: *Models of God: Theology for an Ecological, Nuclear Age*. Philadelphia: Fortress Press.

Moltmann, Jürgen [1980] 1981: *The Trinity and the Kingdom*, trans. Margaret Kohl. San Francisco: Harper and Row.

Moltmann-Wendel, Elisabeth, and Moltmann, Jürgen 1983: *Humanity in God*. New York: Pilgrim Press.

Noddings, Nel 1989: *Women and Evil*. Berkeley: University of California Press.

Ochshorn, Judith 1981: *The Female Experience and the Nature of the Divine*. Bloomington: Indiana University Press.

Plaskow, Judith 1980: *Sex, Sin and Grace: Women's Experience and the Theologies of Reinhold Niebuhr and Paul Tillich*. Washington, DC: University Press of America.

Radford Ruether, Rosemary, ed. 1974: *Religion and Sexism: Images of Women in Jewish and Christian Traditions*. New York: Simon and Schuster.

Radford Ruether, Rosemary 1975: *New Woman, New Earth: Sexist Ideologies and Human Liberation*. New York: Seabury Press.

Radford Ruether, Rosemary 1983: *Sexism and God-Talk: Toward a Feminist Theology*. Boston: Beacon Press.

Radford Ruether, Rosemary 1986: *Women-Church: Theology and Practice of Feminist Liturgical Com-*

munities. San Francisco: Harper and Row.

Radford Ruether, Rosemary, and McLaughlin, Eleanor, eds 1979: *Women of Spirit: Female Leadership in the Jewish and Christian Traditions*. New York: Simon and Schuster.

Ruddick, Sara 1989: *Maternal Thinking: Toward a Politics of Peace*. Boston: Beacon Press.

Schüssler Fiorenza, Elisabeth 1983: *In Memory of Her: A Feminist Reconstruction of Christian Origins*. New York: Crossroad Publishing Co.

Starhawk (Miriam Simos) 1979: *The Spiral Dance: The Rebirth of the Ancient Religion of the Great Goddess*. San Francisco: Harper and Row.

Trible, Phyllis 1978: *God and the Rhetoric of Sexuality*. Philadelphia: Fortress Press.

Wolski Conn, Joann, ed. 1986: *Women's Spirituality: Resources for Christian Development*. New York: Paulist Press.

ANNE CARR

Feuerbach, Ludwig (1804–1872) German philosopher of religion. After studying theology at Heidelberg, he went to Berlin, where he studied with G.W.F. Hegel. He first accepted and then rejected Hegel's ideas, holding that the Christian concept of a transcendent God has no objective reality: the divine being is rather the product of projected human aspirations. The optimistic atheism of his writings, with the material not the spiritual as the central principle of reality, influenced Friedrich Nietzsche and the materialist philosophy of Karl Marx and Friedrich Engels, especially his *Das Wesen des Christentums* (1841, translated by George Eliot as *The Essence of Christianity*, 1854). Other works include *Grundsätze der Philosophie der Zukunft* (1843), *Das Wesen der Religion* (1845), *Theogonie* (1857) and *Gottheit, Freiheit und Unsterblichkeit* (1866).

Bibliography
Kamenka, E. 1970: *The Philosophy of Ludwig Feuerbach*. London.

Wartofsky, M. 1977: *Feuerbach*. Cambridge.

Fichte, Johann Gottlieb (1762–1814) German idealist philosopher. After studying Protestant theology at the universities of Jena and Leipzig, Fichte encountered the work of Immanuel Kant in 1790, resulting in his *Versuch einer Kritik aller Offenbarung* of 1792. Here he argued that the arbiter of revelation must be moral law, which is the concern of human reason. In 1794 he was appointed to a chair of philosophy in Jena, and in the same year published his own idealist system, *Grundlage der gesamten Wissenschaftslehre*, which developed Kantian thought, positing a transcendental Ego (das Ich) from which all knowledge is derived, and which is 'the living operative moral order'. God is the absolute Ego, but is not personal; religion consists in 'joyously doing right'. In this work Fichte anticipates the later absolute idealism of Friedrich von Schelling and G.W.F. Hegel, and contributes to new currents of romantic thought. In 1799 he was dismissed from Jena for teaching 'atheism'; 1802 saw the publication of *Glauben und Wissen*; and in 1805 he wrote his major contribution to the philosophy of religion, *Anweisung zum seligen Leben*. In 1807–8 his *Reden an die deutsche Nation* fed the rise of German national consciousness. From 1809 until his death he was professor at Berlin.

Bibliography
Copleston, F. 1963: *A History of Philosophy*, vol. 7, *Fichte to Nietzsche*. Tunbridge Wells.

Simpson, D., ed. 1984: *German Aesthetic and Literary Criticism: Kant, Fichte, Schelling, Schopenhauer and Hegel*. Cambridge.

Finland See PROTESTANT THEOLOGY: SCANDINAVIA.

Forsyth, Peter Taylor (1848–1921) Scottish Congregationalist theologian. Born in Scotland, he studied at Aberdeen University and under Albrecht Ritschl at Göttingen before entering the Congregationalist ministry. He was principal of their seminary (Hackney College, London) from 1901 to 1921. Initially liberal in his theology, Taylor underwent a conversion to evangelicalism in his thirties, without relinquishing his commitment to methods of modern biblical criticism; he maintained that the biblical texts were inspired but not infallible. His chief contribution was in his study of the atonement, especially its ethical significance (God drawing humanity by the love evidenced in his self-sacrifice). In contrast to some more liberal contemporaries, he emphasized sin as deliberate human rebellion towards God, the holiness of God, and man's corresponding obligation to a life of holiness. His many works include *The Cruciality of the Cross* of 1909, *The Person and Place of Jesus Christ* of 1909 and *The Work of Christ* of 1910; reprinted in the 1950s, they were discovered to echo, independently, many of the concerns of Karl Barth.

Bibliography
Bradley, W.L. 1952: *P.T. Forsyth, The Man and His Work*. London.
Brown, R.M. 1952: *P.T. Forsyth: Prophet for Today*. Philadelphia.
Rodgers, J.H. 1965: *The Theology of P.T. Forsyth*. London.

Frei, Hans (1922–1988). North American theologian. Professor of religious studies at Yale, he was associated with NARRATIVE THEOLOGY and with postliberal styles of biblical studies. Viewing Scripture 'canonically', his method focused on the overall composition of the texts rather than on the significance of their documentary sources, and emphasized their purpose as story as a key to interpretation. In *The Eclipse of Biblical Narrative* of 1974 he argues that 'story' is not to be confused with 'fiction'; but the theologian must confine himself or herself to describing the world of the Bible as a world, with its own internal coherence, language and context, rather than attempting to systematize it into apologetic or dogma. That world, nevertheless, is unique in being a world in which all ages have lived. His other major work is *The Identity of Jesus Christ* of 1975.

Bibliography
Green, G., ed. 1987: *Scriptural Authority and Narrative Interpretation: Essays on the Occasion of the 65th Birthday of H.W. Frei*. Philadelphia.

Freud, Sigmund (1856–1939) Austrian psychiatrist. Brought up in a poor Jewish family in Vienna, he enrolled as a medical student in 1873. After graduating, he became increasingly interested in the mind and in the treatment of hysteria by hypnosis. His method, known as psychoanalysis, became increasingly popular, attracting students such as Alfred Adler and C.G. Jung, although by 1915 both of them had broken away from Freud's influence. In later life, while still a controversial figure, Freud became an international celebrity. This did not prevent his persecution by the Nazis, and he died in exile in London. Among his publications are: *The Interpretation of Dreams* (1900), *Totem and Taboo* (1913–14), *Civilization and its Discontents* (1930) and *An Outline of Psycho-Analysis* (1938).

Freud's psychoanalysis was primarily concerned with explaining symptoms such as hysteria, phobias (an expression which he invented) or obsessive neuroses by a consideration of the unconscious mind. This included examining dreams and associations with dreams, which brought to consciousness things hitherto concealed in the unconscious mind. At the basis of Freud's psychoanalysis was his assertion (rejected by Jung) that repressed infantile sexuality lay behind neurotic behaviour. He also argued that religion is built on the repression of childhood sexuality and the projection of these feelings onto a God figure.

See also PSYCHOLOGICAL SCIENCE AND CHRISTIAN THOUGHT.

Bibliography
Freud, S. 1953–74: *Standard Edition of the Complete Psychological Works*, trans. and ed. James Strachey. London: Hogarth Press.
Freud, S. 1960: *Letters (1873-1939)*, ed. Ernst Freud. Frankfurt am Main.
Gay, V.P. 1983: *Reading Freud: Psychology, Neurosis and Religion*. Chic, Calif.
Jones, E. 1953-7: *Sigmund Freud, Life and Work*, 3 vols. London.

fundamentalism A movement originating in the USA, which takes its name from the publication of a series of pamphlets during the early part of the twentieth century (1910–15) called *The Fundamentals: A Testimony to the Truth* (Torrey, [1917] 1980). The movement took on a more organized form with the convening of the World Conference on Christian Fundamentals in Philadelphia in May 1919.

In reaction to what was perceived as a 'modernist' trend in theology by the more liberally inclined theologians (see LIBERALISM; MODERNISM), the authors of *The Fundamentals* sought to restate the basic tenets of orthodox theology in the form of several 'fundamentals of the faith'. Among these were: an inspired and inerrant Bible; the deity of Christ and his atoning death for sin on the cross; his bodily resurrection and ascension; and his return to judge the world, consign the Devil and unrepentant sinners to hell and resurrect those who belonged to Christ to live eternally in heaven with God (Ellingsen, 1988, pp. 49–72). These fundamental doctrines were used as a touchstone to identify denominational leaders and theologians who were suspected of 'modernist' tendencies. Fundamentalism as a movement has both spiritual and theological antecedents in the evangelical revivals in Britain as well as in the USA.

In Britain the eighteenth-century revival led by John Wesley (1703–1791) led to an evangelical awakening which stressed a vital Christian experience as over and against what was perceived as formalism and spiritual deadness in the institutional church. In seeking to recover authentic Christian faith and life, Wesley emphasized Christian perfection, or 'perfect love', which became the spiritual and theological foundation for the nineteenth-century Holiness movement largely among North American Methodists. The Evangelical Alliance was formed in London in 1846 with almost 800 participants. The 'nonconformist' Scot, Thomas Chalmers (1780–1847), brought theological inspiration to the movement and led to the acceptance of nine doctrinal affirmations as a platform for the evangelical movement: the inspiration of the Bible; the Trinity; the depravity of man; the mediation of the divine Christ; justification by faith; conversion and sanctification by the Holy Spirit; the return of Christ and judgement; the ministry of the Word; and the sacraments of baptism and the Lord's Supper.

In North America, following the New England evangelical awakening which began in 1734, the theological Calvinism of Jonathan Edwards, which emphasized the hopeless condition of humanity and the sovereignty of God's saving grace, led to the establishment of theological schools committed to what became known as 'Old School' orthodox theology, centred at Princeton Seminary. This Old School theology was grounded in the Protestant orthodoxy of the seventeenth century, holding to an Augustinian view of human

nature as totally depraved, and to Calvin's view of the sovereignty of divine grace as the only basis for salvation. The doctrine of the atonement was based on the older Anselmic view of divine satisfaction made by the objective merits of Christ's substitutionary death for sinners, appropriated by grace through faith. Central to this orthodox theology was a view of the Bible as inerrant and the only source of divine revelation deductively discerned as objective truth from the factual statements of Scripture. Benjamin Warfield's prolegomena to Scripture as inspired revelation, along with Charles Hodge's Calvinist Systematic Theology, served as the foundation for this 'Princeton Orthodoxy'.

In the 1820s, under the influence of Nathaniel Taylor at Yale Divinity School, a 'New Haven theology' emerged which emphasized the positive side of human nature and a God more friendly than the 'angry God' of Edwards's day. Taylor considered himself to be orthodox, Calvinistic, and evangelical. The Princeton theologians, however, claiming to be the standard bearers of nineteenth-century evangelical orthodoxy, held a different view of him. His positive view of human nature placed him on the side of Pelagius, and not Augustine, in their opinion. According to this reckoning, one could not claim to be Calvinistic in theology, nor even orthodox. Into this scene burst Charles Finney, one of the most popular and successful revivalists of the first half of the nineteenth century. Ordained a Presbyterian, he made a break with that denomination and the Old School orthodoxy in favour of a gospel which appealed to the free moral agency of sinners. Finney's 'New School' theology spread rapidly, though it was fiercely opposed by the Princeton theologians, such as B.B. Warfield and Charles Hodge. Despite this opposition, the grassroots surge of evangelical experience found its way into the mainstream of American life. This vital and motivating force of revivalism spawned a proliferation of Bible Colleges and evangelistic campaigns.

Two quite separate movements thus converged to produce the impetus of the fundamentalist movement. The revivalist movement which began in Britain and spread to North America produced a movement centred on vital Christian experience, leading to a flood of new converts into the churches as well as renewed spirituality on the part of many former members. This movement, however, lacked a clearly defined theology, for the enemy was not so much theological heresy as spiritual deadness and ecclesiastical formalism. The other movement grew out of the theological struggle between defenders of orthodoxy, and the inroads of 'modernism' with its synthesis between the criteria of higher biblical criticism, scientific theories of human origins (evolution) and the basic tenets of Christian faith.

Of particular importance in this struggle was the nature of the authority of Scripture. The influence of German higher critical views of Scripture in the traditional centres of theological education in North America was seen as a devastating and even fatal undermining of divine revelation as the source of all truth. Those who embraced these new views on Scripture accepted the Bible's human origins and flawed historical sources. The fundamentalists countered by affirming the Bible's inerrancy in history and science as well as in faith and doctrine.

The theological concerns of the fundamentalists were popularized by the famous Scopes Trial of 1925 over the issue of evolution (see BIOLOGICAL SCIENCE AND CHRISTIANITY). William Jennings Bryan, a brilliant orator, debated against Clarence Darrow, who defended successfully the right of John Scopes to teach evolution to school-children. While the fundamentalists lost the battle in the eyes of the public, they regrouped to fight the war by separating from so-called 'liberal' schools and denominations. The departure of J. Gresham Machen from Princeton Theological Seminary in 1929 over the issue of theological liberalism in the faculty led to the founding of Westminster Theological Seminary as an attempt to establish a new centre of orthodox theology.

At this point, the theological concerns of the fundamentalists were clearly defined, but they had lost the battle for control of the theological and denominational centres, including Princeton, with the departure of Machen along with others who followed him. Fundamentalism now found its strongest ally in the revivalist movement, where it received popular support in the grassroots evangelicalism that

revivalism produced. Operating outside denominational boundaries, the movement had already established its distinctive identity on the platform of antimodernism. Dispensational theology (see DISPENSATIONALISM), imported from the Plymouth Brethren movement in England through the teaching of John Darby, found a ready soil in the American revivalist movement, where the literal interpretation of Scripture with a strong emphasis on eschatology prevailed. Dispensational theology, with its inherent pessimism regarding established religion, could be seen as predicting the rise of modernism, secularism and apostate religious structures. The alternative was to form biblically instructed communities of faith and independent churches. With the Bible as the only textbook for interpreting the events of history and as a manual for developing true faith and doctrine, dispensational theology quite naturally held to an inerrant and infallible view of Scripture (Poythress, 1987).

Fundamentalism had found in dispensational theology a systematic theology which could be taught in the local churches, could be used as an evangelistic tool and which could stand independently of all other theological traditions. Most important of all, to its adherents it appeared to offer a theological bulwark against the modernism which had contaminated the older denominational and theological centres. The chief expressions of fundamental antimodernism were already established through the evangelistic efforts of persons like Dwight L. Moody. Moody Bible Institute, founded in Chicago in 1886, was the first of several building their curriculum on evangelism, missions and dispensational Bible study. Dallas Theological Seminary, with Lewis Sperry Chafer at the helm, became the theological stronghold for dispensational theology. The Schofield Reference Bible, with its voluminous dispensational-oriented notes, became the standard Bible for the fundamentalist churches.

Charles E. Fuller, a radio evangelist based in Pasadena, California, had learned dispensational theology at the Bible Institute of Los Angeles directly from one of the earliest fundamentalist Bible teachers, Reuben A. Torrey. Later, Fuller was to join Harold John Ockenga from Park Street Church in Boston to found Fuller Theological Seminary in Pasadena,

California. Apart from Lutheran orthodoxy, which carried on its own struggles against modernism as an internal conflict (Rudnick, 1966), and the Pentecostal/Holiness movement, where evangelical piety and spirituality flourished, fundamentalism with its dispensational theology appeared to have become the primary shaper of American evangelical theology. But fundamentalism as a movement lacked sufficient internal theological cohesion and connection with traditional orthodoxy to sustain its momentum.

The period beginning in the 1940s in North America saw a split between those who held tenaciously to the battle for the fundamentals of the faith and those who manifested a growing concern for a conservative theological stance which combined a social conscience and ecumenical posture with more traditional formulations of orthodoxy, particularly as represented by the Reformed tradition. Those who claimed title to the word 'fundamentalist' as opposed to 'liberal' continued to draw the battle lines as the point of separation from 'apostate' liberal schools and churches, as well as separation from 'worldly' culture and society. A Christian personal ethic by negation marked the fundamentalist off from the rest of the world. Orthodox doctrine was not enough – a Christian lifestyle defined true faith in matters of dress, cosmetics, entertainment, and social life (Ammermann, 1987). A gospel of personal salvation took theological and ethical priority over meeting human social needs. The 'social gospel' was attacked as subversive to the 'spiritual gospel' through which human souls were saved from hell and granted eternal life.

The practical effect of this movement was to abandon the established theological centres to liberal theology in favour of setting up alternative schools committed to the 'fundamentals of the faith'. The theological vitality which fuelled many of these schools was dispensational theology. Many of the graduates of these schools, however, became disillusioned with the negative and separatist stance of the fundamentalists, and began to take the lead in formulating a new approach to defining the theological agenda. For these younger theologians, the term 'fundamentalist' no longer had any appeal. The old battle lines did not seem to be relevant to the critical issues facing a new generation of Christians. The negative and separatist stance taken towards culture, science and scholarly study by the fundamentalists was seen to be excessive and counterproductive.

Carl F.H. Henry, a product of fundamentalist revivalism, a graduate of a school founded by fundamentalists and a faculty member at Fuller Seminary, founded by a fundamentalist, opened the new agenda with his probing book *The Uneasy Conscience of Modern Fundamentalism* (Henry, 1947). Harold John Ockenga, the first President of Fuller Theological Seminary, coined the expression 'new evangelicalism' to distinguish this movement from fundamentalism (Marsden, 1987).

Those who continue to hold fundamentalist views distinguish themselves not only from liberalism, but from the so-called 'new evangelicals' by holding to a literal interpretation of the Bible as inerrant in all matters of which it speaks, including creation, historical events and human origins. Fundamentalists tend to view cultural factors as subversive of biblical faith and strongly reject secularism and humanism as antithetical to God's revealed truth in the Bible. While not known for involvement in issues concerning social justice, peace making and political reform, fundamentalists are often active in mounting campaigns against pornography, abortion and contemporary forces which break down and undermine the traditional family. Fundamentalism continues to be a vigorous force for evangelism, world mission and biblical instruction through a wide network of smaller denominations and independent churches.

See also EVANGELICALISM: USA; PROTESTANT THEOLOGY: USA.

Bibliography

Ammermann, Nancy Tatom 1987: *Fundamentalists in the Modern World*. New Brunswick, NJ: Rutgers University Press.

Barr, James 1977: *Fundamentalism*. London: SCM Press.

Cole, Steward G. [1931] 1963: *The History of Fundamentalism*, 2nd edn. Hamden, CT: Archon Books.

Dollar, George W. 1973: *A History of Fundamentalism in America*. Greenville, SC: Bob Jones University.

Ellingsen, Mark 1988: *The Evangelical Movement*. Minneapolis, MN: Augsburg Publishing Company.

Furniss, Norman F. 1954: *The Fundamentalist*

Controversy. Hamden, CT: Archon Books.

Gasper, Louis 1963: *The Fundamentalist Movement*. The Hague: Mouton.

Henry, Carl F.H. 1947: *The Uneasy Conscience of Modern Fundamentalism*. Grand Rapids: Eerdmans.

Marsden, George 1980: *Fundamentalism and American Culture – The Shaping of Twentieth Century Evangelicalism: 1870–1925*. New York and Oxford: Oxford University Press.

Marsden, George 1987: *Reforming Fundamentalism: Fuller Seminary and the New Evangelicalism*. Grand Rapids: Eerdmans.

Poythress, Vern S. 1987: *Understanding Dispensation-alism*. Grand Rapids: Zondervan Publishing Company.

Rudnick, Milton L. 1966: *Fundamentalism and the Missouri Synod*. St Louis: Concordia Publishing House.

Sandeen, Ernest R. 1970: *The Roots of Fundamentalism: British and American Millenarianism: 1800–1930*. Chicago: University of Chicago Press.

Torrey, Reuben A., ed. [1917] 1980: *The Fundamentals: A Testimony to the Truth*, 2nd edn, 4 vols. Grand Rapids: Baker Book House.

RAY S. ANDERSON

G

Gadamer, Hans-Georg (b. 1900) German philosopher. He studied at Munich and Marburg, and was professor of philosophy at Marburg, Leipzig, Frankfurt and Heidelberg. A lifelong friend and interpreter of Martin Heidegger, he has been most concerned with the philosophy of hermeneutics. Rather than focusing on the methodological questions underlying hermeneutics, as had been done since F.D.E. Schleiermacher's time, Gadamer's interest is in the ontological questions concerning the value and experience arising out of the hermeneutical process, which transcend scientific theory and defy complete critical interpretation. The view that 'meaning can be experienced even where it is not intended' is foundational to his thought. In his critique of aesthetic theories and theories of historicity, he argues for the impossibility of a prejudice-free critical standpoint in both, but goes further to challenge the prejudice against prejudice. Prejudice does not inevitably distort the truth – rather, it may constitute a continuity of tradition. He rejects the possibility of absolute reason: 'understanding' takes place not within the traditional 'subject–object' framework, but as a 'fusion of horizons'. This is not a return to pure subjectivism: rather it is an 'event' involving an 'elevation to a higher universality which overcomes not only one's own particularity, but also that of the other person' (an idea which reflects the influence of Hegelian thought). In his philosophy of language, he argues that interpersonal communication is crucial to the real determination of meaning: language is not merely a system of dispensable signs of ideas 'behind' it. His major work is *Truth and Method* (1960, trans. 1975).

Bibliography
Bleicher, J. 1980: *Contemporary Hermeneutics*. London.
Thiselton, A.C. 1980: *The Two Horizons: New Testament Hermeneutics and Philosophical Description*. Exeter.
Weisenheimer, J.C. 1985: *Gadamer's Hermeneutics: A Reading of Truth and Method*. New Haven, Conn.

Germany See PROTESTANT THEOLOGY: GERMANY.

God Theological modernity began with the conflict over the knowledge and identity of God, integral to the eighteenth-century European and American ENLIGHTENMENT. The labour of later theological modernity has been to 'overcome the Enlightenment', not by repealing but by transcending it.

The Ground of Crisis
The crisis had long historical roots. In that the Christian gospel is a missionary message, Christian teaching about God is always the reinterpretation of some antecedent teaching; the meeting is each time at once polemical and appreciative. In the history leading to the Christianity of Europe and America the initially encountered antecedent interpretation was that of Greece's religious thinkers, as these had provided a common theology for the religions of Mediterranean antiquity. The ancient and medieval church's reinterpretation of this theology had two structural features fateful for modernity.

Mediterranean antiquity defined 'deity' by immunity to time, by 'impassibility'; offensively to this definition, the gospel identifies its God by temporal events, of exodus and resurrection. In the conflicts of the fourth century, the Mediterranean theology was indeed reinterpreted: the doctrine of Trinity articulates God *in himself* by the biblical narrative of temporal missions and passion. But in the subsequent history of especially Latin Christianity, impassible deity reasserted itself in a separate *locus* on the one God, in which the definition of God by mere timelessness persisted. Thus the western church's traditional doctrine of God was two disparate teachings imperfectly stitched together. The doctrine of God's one being evoked a temporally immune and ontologically simple deity that would have been familiar to Aristotle; the doctrine of Trinity evoked the temporally involved and therefore ontologically complex God of the gospel.

The considerable agreements possible between Greek theology and the gospel were explained by a concept itself drawn from the former: Socrates and believers can agree in so much because there is a knowledge of God that is 'natural' to all humanity. Those doctrines of Mediterranean antiquity affirmed by Christian theology were thereby classified as given with our being; conversely, Christian teaching not shared with the Greek thinkers, for example that God is triune or unilaterally forgiving, was specified as 'revealed' in the sense of *added*.

The theological event of the eighteenth century was that constitutive intellectual policies of the Enlightenment turned the one *locus* of churchly teaching about God against the other. The resultant theological struggle has been almost entirely Protestant, Roman Catholicism and Orthodoxy having for different reasons confronted modernity in this fashion only in the present generation. Most practising believers have continued in the traditional way, enduring great cognitive dissonance.

The Enlightenment critique
A first such intellectual policy was suspicion of religious particularity. The seventeenth century had demonstrated that disputing churches would probably persist, each claiming the revelation of God. These had moreover devastated Europe in wars waged to prevent this demonstration. The search for a common teaching seemed obligatory. But if human commonality is an epistemic commendation,

what is common to *all* must be most reliable. Thus the doctrine of God supposed natural to humanity – in hidden fact, the particular doctrine of Mediterranean antiquity – gradually ceased to be the gospel's interlocutor and became instead its schoolmaster.

The seventeenth century's other great lesson was in the power of the new science; the Enlightenment was the eighteenth century's hope of applying this power generally. A decisive and widely applicable component of the new method was the 'critique of appearances'. Thus it appears that the sun goes round the earth; the new science was given its archetype by pressing the question, 'but does it really?' That Christianity's discourse about God should become an object of this critical enterprise was occasioned by its European–American role as established opinion. It was millennially handed on wisdom which the new science had suddenly discredited as mere bondage to appearances; generalizing this pattern, the Enlightenment applied a hermeneutic of suspicion to all tradition. With the appearances about God, it might be difficult to find norms for such critique. But churchly theology itself seemed to provide them, in the first of its two doctrines of God: if there is a theology given with our creation, no opinion about God can contest it. This left 'revelation' to take the role of the appearances. The one *locus* of inherited doctrine was again set against the other, now in essentially distrustful fashion.

The Enlightenment's theological critique was begun in English-speaking nations and exported. Already Herbert of Cherbury (1581–1648), impelled in all the ways just described, came to classical results. Cherbury renounced 'revelation' both because it must be mediated through tradition and because its claims cannot be established inter-subjectively. 'Reason' establishes a faith whose tenets are the shared faith of humankind, once the narratives and rituals established by history are stripped away: there is a personal Supreme Being; virtue is his appropriate service; failure of virtue requires inward repentance; in this and a future life God will reward virtue and repentance.

We must next note that when the deity of Mediterranean antiquity thus emerged into renewed independence, it did not reassume its old visage unaltered. This deity is identified as

235

the eternal Ground of the cosmos's temporal process; the cosmos of Isaac Newton is not, however, the cosmos of Aristotle. For antiquity, the world made one cosmos in that it had one divine *Aim*. For modernity, the world makes a cosmos in that it is one system of efficient causation; if the world-deity is now to reassert itself, it will appear as the world's *Agent*. Hence modernity's tendency to mechanistic metaphysics. If the world as described by laws of 'mechanics' is provided with an Agent designed to fit, thus creating a general view of reality, the cosmos will appear as a universal machine and its agent as the Engineer.

A universal Engineer will need to 'intervene' in the continuing operation of the world only in so far as he designed badly in the first place; by mechanistic standards, the gospel's God of new beginnings is incompetently godly. More generally, mechanistic metaphysics so construes cosmic order as to banish the freedom and contingency constitutive of history to the realm of *dis*order; the Christian God's very deity is invested in historical contingencies.

The pioneers of mechanism were such followers of René Descartes as Nicole Malebranche (1638–1715). In England, the turn of the seventeenth and eighteenth centuries saw a 'physicotheology' that undertook to demonstrate the existence and nature of God from the maxims and results of the new science; some of these works became international bestsellers.

A very different precursor of the Enlightenment, whose great influence was delayed, was Benedict Spinoza (1632–1677), for whom no part of biblical religion had other than prudential meaning. In his theology, the cosmos-Ground of pagan antiquity re-emerges less altered than in the mainline Enlightenment by its history in Christendom or its correlation to the new science. Spinoza's God is the system of nature itself, in so far as that system is its own infinite ground and the possible object of our adoration.

The more immediate founder of Enlightenment theology was John Locke (1632–1704). For the Enlightened world Locke was the pioneer who first plausibly extended scientific interpretation to human consciousness: as a field analogous to the gravitational field, in which psychic masses, 'ideas', interact following ascertainable laws. In such a consciousness, the God-idea was exotic and required immediate attention.

Locke begins with 'rational' arguments and definitions. An eternal Cause must exist, to explain the existence of temporal beings. This must be a personal Agent, since among its effects are personal beings. But such reasoning, in Locke's estimation, will hardly by itself support actual religious life, and he turns to consider 'revelation'. *The Reasonableness of Christianity as Delivered in the Scriptures* ([1695] 1958) became itself a Scripture of the eighteenth century. The decisive Enlightenment logic appears immediately: only we ourselves, in the rationality natural to us, can judge whether a putative revelation is authentic. The rule of critique is therefore: no genuine revelation will propose anything incompatible with our 'reason'. The positive evidence for a revelation must be empirical like that for any factual claim presented to our judgement: this can only be certification of the putative revelation-bearer by miracles.

Locke found Jesus certified; this left much uncertified. In Locke's delineation of Jesus' God, the biblical narrative about God plays no role. The doctrine of Trinity is simply omitted. Jesus is Messiah and Son of God; that is, he is the miraculously warranted teacher about God and is like unfallen Adam immortal. The grace of God is that he mercifully grants similar immortality to those who recognize the Messiah and follow him morally.

Most subsequent English- or German-speaking theological Enlighteners could adopt Locke's catechism. They inherited also the logic of his position: 'revealed' faith must continually be trimmed once 'natural' theology is made arbiter of its rationality. Most followed Locke also in his mediating intention. Thus in New England the 'broad and catholic' party of the mid-eighteenth century supposed they merely moderated Calvinist and pietist 'extravagances'; even the 'unitarianism' in which this movement eventuated reproduced Locke's doctrine, only rejecting explicitly what he quietly omitted.

There were more radical spirits. Eighteenth-century English and American 'deists' (see DEISM) made coherence with 'reason' also the positive certification of putative revelation. Thereupon their doctrine of God reduced to the 'natural' features of Locke's. Matthew Tindal (1656–1733) drew the consequence: the Christian revelation is but a republication of the natural knowledge of God; the will of God thus revealed is identical with the laws of his creation. The French Enlightenment imported deist doctrine but omitted its claim to be Christian, and so drops out of our story.

Very different theological responses to the new science were possible and attempted, but failed to exert long-term influence. Thus in New England Jonathan Edwards (1703–1758) was inspired by Newton and Locke to create the eighteenth century's only theological system on the grand churchly and speculative format. It was of thoroughgoing Trinitarian pattern and content. By a revisionary use of Locke's epistemology, Edwards freed Newtonian physics from mechanistic interpretation. He thereupon found in it no hindrance to Trinitarian faith but instead a vision of cosmic eventful harmony exactly appropriate to the triune God, who *is* the harmony of perfect community among Father, Son and Spirit. God and creation are each beautiful, in the way that a fugue is beautiful. It is God's musical beauty that is his very deity, and the creation's corresponding beauty that is its value to God and therefore its being.

The Enlightenment arrived late in Germany; in the meantime, a particular intellectual atmosphere had developed to receive it. The influence of Gottfried Wilhelm Leibniz (1646–1716) and Christian Wolff (1679–1754), whose metaphysics gave ontological status to developmental phenomena, made the German Enlightenment friendlier to history and more hopeful for reconciliations. Nevertheless, even the German development did not escape the Lockean logic. The 'Neologians', who strove for harmony between 'reason and revelation', gradually thereby undid the latter. Gotthold Lessing (1729–1781) pressed the German Enlightenment to a deist conclusion, but affirmed the history of actual religions as the still necessary way to this goal.

Immanuel Kant (1724–1804) created a new situation with his *Critique of Pure Reason* ([1781] 1963) (see KANTIANISM). He excised the problem of mechanism and undid 'natural' theology of the old style by one stroke: a critique of metaphysics itself, that invalidated questions about what reality is 'really' like. It does indeed appear to us, for instance, that all events must have a cause and that this circumstance must itself have a Cause, but that is only because otherwise such things as 'events' would not at all appear to our subjectivity.

Kant undertook the critique of metaphysics in part to clear a new, a-metaphysical location for discourse about God. The idea of God is an inevitable postulate within *moral* subjectivity: if we think the purposes of our duties, within the transcendental unity of thinking, and do not despair of those duties, we merely thereby think God. Moral action itself is then the affirmation of this idea's adequacy to reality. On that basis Kant provided a purified and perfected version of Enlightenment theology. God is the Lawgiver who decrees at once the purpose of creation and the goal of human willing. Recognition of God is thus our subjective possibility of acting freely to obey moral law, within the determining laws of creation. The Son is the eternal idea of morally perfected humanity, that lives among us also in our imperfection; no other incarnation or atonement is conceivable.

In Britain, the more direct continuation of Lockean theological critique was the empiricist philosophical tradition itself. In the twentieth century, following empiricism's 'linguistic turn', this came to new life in the question whether discourse about God can be *meaningful*. 'Verifiable' scientific assertion is taken as the general paradigm of descriptively meaningful discourse. Responses to the challenge are divided between those that seek for 'God-talk' some sort of meaning other than description and those that, sometimes returning to specific characters of biblical discourse, meet it directly.

Neo-Protestantism

Friedrich Schleiermacher The chief founder of later modernity's effort to transcend the Enlightenment's limits while maintaining its truth was Friedrich Schleiermacher (1768–1834). He made possible the 'neo-Protestant' project with one book, *On Religion: Speeches to its Cultured Despisers* ([1799] 1958). That he was German and exploited specific tones of the German Enlightenment made Germany the theological capital of later modernity.

Schleiermacher accepted the position set by Kant: God is given only as a lived postulate within human existence. But Schleiermacher had a different vision of humanity, that had emerged in the German Enlightenment and been deepened by pioneers of romanticism. We achieve humanity as we through history at once unfold an unpredictable wealth of potentialities and creatively integrate them into new harmony. Human persons and communities are to be works of art self-realized over time.

Schleiermacher begins as did Locke, with a different interpretation of consciousness. The defining problem of German philosophy after Kant was consciousness's constitutive unity with a world around it. In accord with his romantic vision of humanity, Schleiermacher locates this unity in the aesthetic sense for harmonious wholeness, which he calls 'feeling'. Only in feeling for our unity with reality is that unity given; knowledge and will, as separating modes of consciousness, follow dependently. And in that sensibility is thus prior to knowledge and will yet enables both, it is also the transcendental unity of consciousness for itself.

The life of sensibility in which we are one with ourselves and all things, Schleiermacher calls 'religion'. There is, however, no actual universal religion, only historically particular religions, for we have no feeling for the whole except as we are moved by some known or willed particular. Each actual religion has therefore an experiential focus; at the centre of Christian experience is the fellowship of Christ.

In so far as in our feeling for ourselves in the whole we experience our utter dependence upon the sensed whole, we sense totality as 'God'. God never becomes our object. The apparent descriptivity of statements about God is deceptive: they are *expressions* of our feeling of dependence within the whole, in the various modes of that feeling. Even to evoke the Whence of our feeling as 'God' misleads in so far as it suggests an object indexed by that word. Theology would therefore be done most purely with no mention of 'God', as pure critical description of 'the Christian God-*consciousness*'.

These moves did 'overcome' the Enlightenment, and established a pattern on which specifically Christian theology would again be possible, for Schleiermacher and for many to follow. But the doctrine of God which

Schleiermacher in his later work does provide, as a concession to limited spiritual development, is very much that of Spinoza, who therewith re-enters theological history. Schleiermacher is faithful to the Enlightenment in holding that theological truth must be found by critical reflection. The partners of critique are familiar: the – in Schleiermacher's terminology – 'philosophical' interpretation of God and historically mediated Christian discourse. The critique is supposed to be mutual, but the resultant account of God is again wholly determined by the first partner. The biblical God-narratives appear only as problems; at every step 'anthropomorphism' is the great danger. God's 'acts' are not events; also on their creaturely side they occupy no time. God's eternity is mere timelessness, the 'before' and 'after' of narrative can have for or about him no meaning of any sort. Omnipresence is the equivalent meaninglessness of 'here' and 'there'. Omniscience is not so much that God knows all as that he experiences nothing. The doctrine of immanent Trinity is rejected.

Only a few of the many inspired by Schleiermacher adopted his system. It was his general procedure in which the nineteenth century found the possibility of theological new beginning. A neo-Protestant theology begins with some *analysis of human existence*, to locate a necessary experiential function that is the home of 'religion'. This consciousness-embraced specification of religion carries with it a meta-doctrine of God's *non-objectivity*. Most schools acknowledge *history* as somehow the arena of actual religious life and choice. The theology of a historically actual religion is done by showing how it specifically *fulfils* the initially identified general need. With Christianity, this demands a methodological *Christocentrism*. Through the nineteenth and twentieth centuries, the procedure enabled theological enterprises of otherwise great variety.

In English-speaking lands, Schleiermacher's influence was partly through the export of continental neo-Protestantism. Partly, however, it served to transmit and theologically sanction romantic idealism more generally, which then often took its own paths. Thus Samuel Taylor Coleridge (1772–1834) was an idiosyncratic Schleiermachean indeed. He saw with startling clarity that traditional theology had founded itself on 'Greek' 'paganism'. This is defined by the equation of God with 'Being', to which a mechanistic or Spinozistic interpretation of the world is the eventual inevitable correlate. If the world is to be seen as hospitable to personality and community, God must instead be understood in 'Hebrew' fashion as *act* or *will*. The doctrine of Trinity, if freed of interpretation as three 'beings' in one 'being', states just this true reality of God.

In America, Schleiermacher and Coleridge together enabled the again idiosyncratic thought of Horace Bushnell (1802–1876). Formally Bushnell seems to reproduce Schleiermacher. But then he points to the religious emptiness of sheer atemporality and aseity, and uses Schleiermacher's critique of 'metaphysical' Trinitarianism crosswise to Schleiermacher's intention, to leave the dramatic language of biblical Trinitarianism and Christology as the sole language about God. The God needed by actual religion is the *living* God, who freely embraces his creatures in his life; and that is how we see him in the 'last metaphor' he has provided, the personhood and fate of Christ, and how metaphysically unencumbered Trinitarian language tells of him.

Georg Hegel Counterpoint to Schleiermacher at the founding of post-Enlightenment theology was the philosopher Georg Wilhelm Friedrich Hegel (1770–1831) (see HEGELIANISM). He began with critique in Enlightened style, but attacked both traditional and Enlightened theology. They are alike alienating; both set consciousness and God apart as subject and object, whereas religion is to be their unity. Yet Hegel was too concerned for truth permanently to adopt Schleiermacher's way of escaping the subject–object division. How can one insist *both* that theology is not merely expression of our God-consciousness but is knowledge of God, *and* that the subject–object division does not apply to the relation between God and us? Within the situation defined by Kant, the only possible solution is that our consciousness of God both posits and sublates his otherness from us, and that both movements are God's own movements done through our consciousness, positing and sublating an other for himself. And that precisely will be the central position of Hegel's system. According to Hegel, philosophy thinks 'in concept' what religion experiences in

symbols; true philosophy thinks the Christian symbols.

Kant had shown that what human subjects take for metaphysical truths are merely the demands of subjectivity itself. Very well, said Hegel, but that proposition is itself metaphysical, and as the final result of critical reflection is necessarily true. *All there is* is the self-expression and so self-realization of subjectivity. Religion symbolizes universal Subjectivity as the Creator-God.

Mechanism made ultimate reality and historical contingency mutually exclusive, thereby banishing the biblical God from reality. Hegel countered directly, making historical eventfulness itself the model of truth. The *movement* of history, precisely in what the Enlightenment saw as its irrationality, its contradictions and new emergents, makes it own sort of sense; why should not this sort of sense be the Reason of things? The way, for example, in which the French monarchy provoked its antithesis in popular revolutionary government, and this opposition was then sublated in the Napoleonic synthesis of both, has its own logic, not the logic of abstract reasoning but the logic of narratively creative mind, of 'spirit'. The Truth is absolute Spirit, Mind that in every event of history and by the one total event of universal history posits its own other, in order to achieve itself by knowing itself in this object. Religion symbolizes absolute Spirit, with its triadic dynamic, as the triune God.

Thus Hegel claimed to have vindicated the specifically Christian doctrine of God, as conceptualized in the doctrine of Trinity. The very being of the one God is, according to Hegel, Subjectivity positing its own other in whom to know and will itself, and achieving its own free personal identity in the carrying out of that knowing and willing. In religious symbols, the one God is the life of Father, Son and Spirit.

Thereby the old split in western Christianity's doctrine of God was indeed subverted. Yet Hegel's posterity has had repeatedly to ask: What 'triunity' does this doctrine finally describe? The narrative distinction and unity of the biblical Father, Son and Spirit? Or the in themselves changeless inner dialectics of a Consciousness who may after all be a God much like Kant's? Which half of the old doctrine has here absorbed the other? The key question is about the actuality of the Son. According to Hegel, he is the Meaning the Father finds in all things, as he knows himself in them. This may be the Logos-doctrine of the Fathers. But is the Son with equal finality Jesus of Nazareth? Jesus, according to Hegel, is the Son in so far as the Son appears in actual, historical religion. So the question is identical with the crux of all Hegel-interpretation: when Spirit achieves itself by the total event of history, does it leave the events *in* history behind? When thought is achieved, do symbols vanish?

Hegel's students divided on the questions just posed. The theologians in both resultant wings were neo-Protestantism's irritant radicals. Such 'right-Hegelians' as Philipp Marheineke (1780–1846) found in Hegel the possibility of protesting neo-Protestantism's usual compromises on an other than biblicist basis. Two 'left-Hegelians' became fateful figures for subsequent modernity. Ludwig Feuerbach (1804–1872) and David Friedrich Strauss (1808–1874) pressed their teacher's ambiguities to derive a new critique.

Feuerbach said bluntly: if the subject–object difference does *not* apply to our relation to God, then God is really not other than us. Hegel's posit of 'thought' as other than religion's symbolizing, of 'Spirit' as other than the dynamism of human striving, is merely a last effort to evade religion's secret: God *is* humanity, in so far as humanity is itself the target of human self-transcendence. The latter occurs when the meeting of 'I' and 'thou' opens to me human goods that *I* do not yet exemplify but now see nevertheless belong to *us*.

Feuerbach intended to help religion to its truth: religion truly is what neo-Protestantism supposes it is, the necessary human drive to fulfil ourselves; and our projection onto eternity of what we thereby value in ourselves, our dream of 'God', need only be freed from the alienating supposition that it is bound to something out there. Strauss had discovered projection also in the Christological direction: the identity of deity and humanity is eternal truth and so cannot be actualized in any one temporal phenomenon; biblical and dogmatic pictures of Christ are therefore 'mythological'

projections of eternal ideals onto a historical figure.

Left-Hegelianism has been repristinated in every generation of modernity, as in English theology of the sort represented by John Hick and Don Cupitt, and in American 'metaphor-theology' and 'feminist' theologies dependent on it. These proposals vary only according to the values purported to be projected. Also repristinated by the clearsighted, as by Mary Daly, is Strauss's eventual recognition that this path leads out of Christianity.

Other neo-Protestants We must give some impression of the variety of views which neo-Protestantism could accommodate. The least mainline were sometimes the most creative.

Gottfried Thomasius (1802–1875) can represent 'kenotic' theology, in which conflict between antecedent definition of deity by 'omnipotence', 'omnipresence' and so on and the temporal involvement of the gospel's God broke out afresh within neo-Protestant synthesis. The 'Christian experience' is of personal fellowship with God, mediated through Christ in the Spirit. But how can an omnipotent and omniscient being be truly present as a human person, to enable such experience? Thomasius was led to drastic expedients. '*Omni*potence' and so on are redefined as relative to creatures; a new set of attributes, *unqualified* 'potency' and so on are made constitutive of deity. God can lay the former by; in order to have fellowship with creatures, God the Son is no longer omnipotent, omniscient or omnipresent. 'Kenotic' thinking was brought into Britain by Peter Forsyth (1848–1921) and Charles Gore (1853–1932). Their influence has remained in a fondness for 'incarnational thinking' and a willingness to bend traditional conceptions of deity to suit.

Isaak Dorner (1809–1884) confronted a problem which Johann Fichte (1762–1814) had laid at the foundation of neo-Protestantism, over the possibility of characterizing God as personal: consciousness is necessarily *of* something it is *not*, so that 'an infinite consciousness' is an oxymoron. Dorner argued that God nevertheless can be conceived as personal if we *begin* with the doctrine of his triunity. 'Absolute Personality' as a supposed transcendental unity of one divine Consciousness falls to Fichte's critique, but as the ontologically complex eternal 'result' of the mutual life of Father, Son and Spirit it is real. This life is itself described much in Hegel's fashion; but that the Absolute is not the presupposition of the triune life but its 'eternal outcome', breaks with Hegel in a way perhaps determined by Dorner's insight, rare in his time, into the eschatological character of the gospel.

Liberal theology Neo-Protestantism's last great school was the 'liberal' theology, so called as it fitted the civil and churchly aspirations of the bourgeoisie. Its dominant interpreter was Albrecht Ritschl (1822–1889). Before a renewed power of mechanistic world views, particularly in ideological Darwinism, and the seeming failure of Hegelianism and other idealist attempts, liberalism returned to Kant for an initiating analysis of human existence. In Ritschl's version, humanity's specificity is a calling to establish the 'kingdom of God', the realm of rationally dictated political and social love. This is the kingdom 'of *God*' in that we can act freely in spite of natural determinism only as we trust a Will who gives the law at once morally to our action and naturally to the world.

We must for this freedom be *able* to trust God, which is the point at which the specifically Christian enters. The same historical-critical study of Scripture which liberates us from the Bible's dogmatic projections uncovers the 'historical', and so real, Jesus. From his teaching and fate we learn that God is love, so that despite our consciousness of guilt we need not fear God. The liberal theology is defined by this specific version and combination of neo-Protestantism's Christocentrism and attention to history.

Meaningful statements about God are, in Kantian fashion, 'value-judgements' and not 'fact-judgements'. To know God is to know we are supremely loved. All propositions about a being of God in himself are empty metaphysics.

Liberalism was broken by liberal biblical critics' own discovery that precisely the historical Jesus preached a 'kingdom of God' very different from the realm of our political and social achievement, and by the experience of the First World War, which cast doubt on such achievement generally. Where the latter experience lacked impact, as in North America, liberalism has continued as the presumed theology of mainline churchliness.

The true theological outcome of the nineteenth century is perhaps none of its schools, but nihilism: atheism not as mere negation of God's existence, but as itself a religious event. Specifically Christian discourse about God had suffered two centuries of polemic; but when a Spinozistic or mechanistic or Kantian deity then stands alone, in a once-Christian context, its vacuity is revealed. Most dramatically, Friedrich Nietzsche (1844–1900) proclaimed as both fate and promise an absolute human freedom possible only by the expelling of God, in which humanity's ruin and apotheosis will alike occur.

The twentieth century

Dialectical theology The development that marked the break between neo-Protestantism with its continuations and the distinctive theology of the twentieth century was the short-lived 'dialectical' theology. Karl Barth (1886–1968), a promising liberal radicalized by the Bible, pastoral responsibility for an industrial parish, the war, and the subterranean lure of nihilism, triggered the movement with the second, revised edition of his commentary, *The Epistle to the Romans* ([1922] 1933). This book fulfilled the critique of religion by ending the exemption previously granted western religion's non-biblical component. Exactly as neo-Protestantism said, religion – all of it, Christianity included – is humanity's labour of self-transcendence; just so it is our deepest fall, according to a gospel that proclaims a righteousness not our own. The God of religion is the Aim of our religious self-transcendence; that is, it is an idol. There can be such a standpoint from which to conduct a critique of all religion because the gospel is a contingent message that *intrudes* on our religious enterprise.

In dialectical theology's discourse about God can be seen a direct inversion of the liberalism in which the 'dialectical' rebels had been educated. As in liberalism, God appears as a moral-religious posit in the meeting of our human quest with the message of Christ. But the content of this meeting had been affirmation of our striving; now it is critique thereof. Where harmony had been, there is 'dialectic'. God is the sheer Other beyond what on any occasion throws back our movement of self-achievement; he is the Failure of precisely our spiritual journey towards him. He is the Eternity known only on the 'line of death' that shuts us into the temporal. The mere inversion was not stable and the 'dialectical' group disintegrated after 1930. A repertoire of mid-century theology was created on the divergent ways then taken. Two besides Barth himself are important for our special matter.

Rudolf Bultmann Rudolf Bultmann (1884–1976) and his school remained closest to once-shared positions, stabilizing them on their still neo-Protestant implicit basis. Bultmann took his starting analysis of human existence from 'existential' reading of the New Testament. The dialectical break with liberalism is maintained in that such a reading is said to mirror the *eschatological* character of the 'kerygma'. I exist in the decisions posed by every temporal encounter. Thus it is each time myself that is at stake; conversely, since I exist in decision, what I finally choose if I choose myself is precisely *to choose*: to be free from the past and 'open' to the indeterminate future. Authentic human being is 'eschatological existence', the surrender of all security.

To exist eschatologically, to give myself up in order to be myself, is to receive my destiny from an other than myself, and that is to meet God. The move is Schleiermacher's except that utter dependence is directed to what is not yet, rather than to the totality of what is. Thus God is 'the Insecurity of the future', the Coming One whose deity is his constant futurity.

Only within the meeting with God, and as an act by which we carry out that meeting, can we know or speak of God. This is true with any person, but since God is never object, in meeting with God we have no object, and therefore find only ourselves addressed, as the other's object. That is, God is there only as a *word*, that calls me to abandon all security.

Such a word must so pose the issue between openness to the future and security in the past that I cannot incorporate this word and its challenge into the continuity of my self-securing existence. The word of the cross does this, in that it is a proclamation of forgiveness, addressing me as one freed from the past, and in that it is a message about an alleged historical event, and so is a contingently intruding piece of news. God *is* this 'word-event'. Bultmann's followers, perhaps most creatively Ernst Fuchs, made an entire theological ontology around the latter concept.

Paul Tillich Paul Tillich (1886–1965) turned to theological construction only in the USA. There he had great influence, perhaps because of the way in which he joined and mediated major streams of neo-Protestantism, chastened but not disrupted by the 'dialectical' turn. Theology is done in the 'correlation' of questions arising from the human situation and formulable by existential analysis, with answers proffered by revelatory experience, that is, by events in which the Mystery that antecedently moves the questions makes itself manifest as the one that has done so. 'God' is the religious symbol for this Ground of being and Ground of meaning, always present in our lives as the Power that maintains us against non-being and meaninglessness. The Ground is *not* personal; nevertheless it is Life, in the interplay of being and meaning. That we are indeed open to this living Ground, is the revelation effected by the symbol of 'Jesus as the Christ'.

Deity as such is not determined by the story of Israel or Christ. Tillich's 'Trinity' is the set of three chief symbols by which revelatory experience answers existential questioning: the symbol of God responds to finitude, the symbol of Christ to estrangement, the symbol of Spiritual Presence to ambiguity. That there are precisely three, and that their distinction has foundation in deity itself, result from the dialectic of the divine Life, moving from isolation through otherness to reunion; knowledge of this dialectic is *not* peculiar to Christianity.

Karl Barth Barth took a very different path. He pushed critique of traditional assumptions to its previously proscribed limit, by asking why the theology labelled 'natural' should be more cognitively respectable than another, to be conceptual resource and arbiter. The confession that responds to the gospel is coherent within *itself*, and is true in that – and only in that – God accepts the pattern of its coherence as conformed to himself.

The bondage of the Lockean logic thus broken, subversion of neo-Protestantism itself became possible. Barth inverted the founding Schleiermachean procedure: instead of asking what is the human story and then how Christ fits into it, we must ask first what is the story of God in Christ and then about our place therein. Nor need we hold to the Kantian dogma. Revelation means precisely that God, who is his own object, has made himself ours also. Bultmann has it backwards; it is the otherness of an encountered object that truly breaks my unauthentic project of self-securing. In Christ I encounter an object beyond my manipulating; as this object, I know God straightforwardly, but *what* I know is that my attempt to control is finished. By these moves, the dialectic of *The Epistle to the Romans* is maintained, but where the sheer line between time and eternity was, there is now the narrative reality of Jesus Christ. The religious quest is ended not by inner breakdown, but by the presence in our world of an object that is God, to block and obviate the quest.

Barth thereupon unrolls a relentlessly Christian doctrine of God. The *Church Dogmatics* of 1932–68 *begins* with an – in itself standard western – doctrine of Trinity. At this position in a modern system, the doctrine recovers its original functions, eclipsed for centuries by subordination to an alien doctrine of the one God. The doctrine of Trinity is to identify the God to whom subsequent discourse will refer, and to establish the primary repertoire of concepts and warrants with which systematic problems will be attacked. By the demonstration which the following *loci* then make of these functions, Barth inaugurated the Trinitarian renewal of the later twentieth century, to which we will return.

The doctrine of Trinity displays God's relatedness to us as Father and Son in the Spirit as belonging to what God is in himself. Thus its concretion is the doctrine of election. That there is anything but God is his free choice, and the primal content of that choice is that there be Jesus Christ, precisely as he lived, died for sinners and rose. With God, there can be no difference between the act of choosing and the reality of what is chosen, nor between the act of choosing and the actuality of one who chooses. Therefore the history of Jesus Christ is eternally actual as the self-determination of God. The final metaphysical truth is the story of Jesus in Israel; all creatures occur only in that we have roles in that drama.

If then we ask *what* God is, in analogy to the old doctrine of his one being but now in the second place, the question has become: What sort of reality can the triune God have? The answer is dictated by what is already before us. God's reality is that of an *event*. God is the event of what happens with Jesus, in that this event eternally occurs. There are no presuppositions for the fact *that* this event occurs or for *what* occurs. Thus God is the wholly *free* event. And that is, God is 'his own conscious, willed and accomplished *decision*.' Between the Father and the Son in the Spirit, it is decided that the Father is God for us in the Son. It might have been otherwise decided, but in fact it is so decided; and the making of this actual decision is the event that is God. Finally, the event of God has 'pure' *duration*. God is not eternal because he has no goal or beginning or ways, but because he knows no loss or contradiction between them, only harmony. Indeed, as Father, Son and Spirit God is *history*, concretely the history between Jesus and his Father in their Spirit.

Remarkable analogies between Hegel's and Barth's systems appear also in their ambiguities and historical aftermaths. On a 'left' wing of Barth's influence are those most drawn by the critique of religion, by the inherent critique of also political liberalism, and by the rhetoric of God as 'event'. In so far as 'liberation theology' at all develops a discourse about God, it is of this sort.

A number of very individual English and American thinkers follow Barth's radicalism. We may mention Thomas Altizer, known generally for proclamation of the 'death of God'. Altizer has sought the possibility of faith within the spiritual situation described by Nietzsche, with its twin seductions of mere inhuman unbelief and mysticism, of leaving God merely *unsaid* and return into a fullness of divine *silence*. His theology is 'atheistic' in that he interprets cultural rejection of the eternally distant God of religion as correlate to the historical 'embodiment' of faith's God in the event of speech. 'God' is the name to be spoken in the presence of Silence that is present as other than itself.

On a different wing are those inspired by Barth's denial of an external basis for the rationality of Christian discourse, some of whom also take example from his creation of an encompassing Christological-Trinitarian ontology. American 'non-foundationalism', which may be represented by George Lindbeck, offers not so much its own teaching about God as a way to appropriate traditional doctrine, overcoming the latter's internal division not by excising its 'natural' part but by interpreting the whole as discourse within a specific language of the Christian community. Allowed to function by its own grammar, this language has its paradigmatic discourse about God in Scriptural narrative (see NARRATIVE THEOLOGY).

A more speculative project is that of Eberhard Jüngel. The history of western metaphysics, in which God functions as guarantor of the world, and permanence and domination are the ontological values, has ended by making God unthinkable and unsayable. Just in this situation we are free to begin with the contingent fact that God has nevertheless spoken and been understood. We hear him define himself by the word of the cross, and *beginning* with this hearing, we will have no specification of God's being prior to 'God says this word'. For God to be therefore means self-offering and perishability; and possibility is the primary ontological category. The actuality of these mandates is the doctrine of Trinity, which traces the being of God by the path of Jesus, and whose most pregnant formulation is that God *interprets* himself, to us and therein to himself.

Wolfhart Pannenberg shares with Barth the insistence that theology must not bow to alien modes of cognition as appropriate to certain spheres of reality. But he rejects every temptation to achieve this by isolating theology in a sphere of its own. God must be the God of the *whole* of reality. Modern critical investigations on the part of history and the modern sciences are not in fact alien to theology; indeed it is the gospel's working in western history that established their conceptual possibility. It is thus unsurprising that Scripture and modern reflection agree: reality is whole only at its end. It therefore belongs to God's being that it is verified only at an end of history. And if he is revealed in history, this can only be by a 'prolepsis' of his reality at the end. A narrative-Trinitarian identification of God is therefore jointly demanded by Scripture and modern reflection.

Thomas Torrance finds in the Fathers the same virtue as in Barth: we need not antecedently determine what is rational; divine reality *shows* itself and its appropriate forms of theory. Nor does theology confront in the sciences a different situation; contemporary physics experiences the 'sovereign' character of reality, which reveals depth after depth of intelligibility and to whose patterns science's methods continuously reconform themselves. It is the relation of God to his world, described by the doctrines of Trinity and incarnation, that enables cognition of all sorts.

Process theology We end with two continuing constructive projects. Anglo-American PROCESS THEOLOGY, in some continuity with the earlier school of Henry Nelson Wieman (1884–1975), has taken a different approach to modernity from those so far traced. 'Process' theologians begin with a Barthian-sounding critique of inherited natural theology: the latter has imposed a static conception of God's eternity inappropriate both to the gospel and to twentieth-century conceptions of reality. But process theologians' remedy is to refound theology on a new natural theology, that will allow a 'bipolar' theism in which both stability and change receive their due. This they find in the metaphysics of Alfred North Whitehead (1861–1947). The philosopher Charles Hartshorne and the theologians Norman Pittinger and Schubert Ogden may represent the group.

Momentary events are ontologically ultimate. Enduring entities are internally defined sequential sets of events; the being of an enduring entity as such is therefore an *abstraction*. It is in God's 'abstract character' that he is immutable, omniscient, etc. In his *concrete* being, God changes as the world changes, for the events that are *his* process are all events. God thus has experience, and his goals change materially with time; but the loving character of his purposing and the embracing perfection of his experience are unchanging. God is enriched in the world-process, and conversely draws that process towards new value by posing to it the possibilities that open in his experience. It is the deity of God that he is the world's harmony of stability and change.

Attempts to develop a 'process' doctrine of Trinity have proved difficult, perhaps just because so much of the conceptuality that in a traditional doctrine of Trinity emerges from the interpretation of God by the biblical narrative – such as that God is constituted in relation, or has the being of event – seems here to appear before the biblical narrative is employed. Once more we note a Hegelian sort of ambiguity: How reliable is this seeming?

Trinitarian construction The last enterprise to be described is an attempt further to develop Trinitarian doctrine itself. The effort is inspired by: the example of Barth and Hegel, to make the specifically Christian identification of God foundational for all discourse about him; belief that Trinitarian construction can incorporate modernity's critique of inherited notions of deity, to the benefit of faith; a variously occasioned turn to narrative ways of stipulating God's reality; critique of inadequate western Trinitarianism by ecumenically resurgent Orthodoxy; and experience that active Trinitarian doctrine is not a puzzle to be solved, but is itself the armoury with which to attack theological puzzles, notably those obstructing ecumenical dialogue. We may note Colin Gunton, Robert Jenson, Jürgen Moltmann, and Wolfhart Pannenberg.

The proposed revisions of inherited doctrine are often summarized by a slogan from Karl Rahner (1904–1988), a Catholic who has appropriated much of the neo-Protestant development: the immanent Trinity *is* the economic Trinity and vice versa. What must finally be said without equivocation is that the one God *is* the life between Jesus and his Father in their Spirit.

The relation of time to eternity, and so the character of both, must be conceived as constituted in the active relations of the three 'persons' as told in Scripture; the unity of God as one self-identical reality is to be reconceived in the same way. Thus the incarnation and more alarmingly the crucifixion and resurrection are not *in spite of* God's eternal unity; they *constitute* it; God's eternity does not negate time and change but grounds and integrates them in itself. According to Moltmann it is precisely biblical proclamation of the *death* of Jesus as a 'God-event' that breaks merely theistic conceptions of God and compels the doctrine of Trinity. According to Jenson Trinitarian dialectics results as soon as eschatological promise is seen as having biblical narrative content.

Jesus and his Father and their Spirit are each God, and the same God, as in the biblical narrative each points from himself to the other as the one God. Pannenberg and Jenson make the inner-Trinitarian relations reciprocal, so that the deity of Father, Son or Spirit depends each on the historical mission of the other two, and the single reality of God on their narrative mutuality. God acts on his creation as one God not in undifferentiated unity but through the mutuality of irreducibly different roles.

To accommodate these demands systematically, Pannenberg newly analyses the concept of essence, showing its interior relationality, so that the God stipulated by divine attributes and the triune God whose reality is the liveliness of his inner relations, are seen, and not only asserted, to be the same. Jenson reconceives infinity itself, by which deity is other than us, as the way in which the particular love actual between Jesus and his Father in their Spirit will *inexhaustibly* interpret all history. For both, *love* is Hegel's postulated 'good infinity', that negates finitude only by including it.

In most new proposals, the three divine hypostases are grasped as 'persons' also in the modern sense. Can then the one triune God be conceived, in classical western fashion, as a personal being? Some hope to have it both ways. Pannenberg renounces the attempt and conceptualizes the divine unity as the spiritual *field* of lively fellowship between Father, Son and Spirit.

See also CHRISTOLOGY; EXISTENCE OF GOD, PROOFS OF; FEMINIST THEOLOGY; PHILOSOPHY OF RELIGION; PNEUMATOLOGY; SUFFERING, DIVINE.

Bibliography

Altizer, Thomas J.J. 1977: *The Self-Embodiment of God*. New York.

Barth, Karl [1922, 2nd revised edn] 1933: *The Epistle to the Romans*, trans. E.C. Hoskyns. London: Oxford University Press.

Barth, Karl [1940–8] 1957: *Church Dogmatics* II/1 and II/2, trans. G.W. Bromiley and T.F. Torrance. Edinburgh: T & T Clark.

Bultmann, Rudolf 1960: *Existence and Faith: Shorter*

Writings of Rudolf Bultmann, selected and trans. S.M. Ogden. Cleveland: Meridian Books; London: Hodder and Stoughton.

Bushnell, Horace [1849] 1972: *God in Christ*. New York: AMS Press.

Cherbury, Edward Lord Herbert of 1633: *De religione gentilium: errorumque apud eos causis*.

Dorner, Isaak August [1807 on] 1880–2: *A System of Christian Doctrine*, trans A. Care and J.S. Banks. Edinburgh: T & T Clark.

Feuerbach, Ludwig [1841] 1957: *The Essence of Christianity*, trans. George Eliot, ed. E.G. Waring and F.W. Strothman. New York: Frederick Unger.

Flew, Antony and MacIntyre, Alasdair, eds. 1955: *New Essays in Philosophical Theology*. London: SCM Press.

Gunton, Colin E. 1978: *Becoming and Being: The Doctrine of God in Charles Hartshorne and Karl Barth*. Oxford: Oxford University Press.

Hartshorne, Charles 1964: *Man's Vision of God and the Logic of Theism*. Hambden, Conn.: Archon Books.

Hegel, Georg Wilhelm Friedrich [1827] 1984–7 *Lectures on the Philosophy of Religion*, 3 vols, ed. P.C. Hodgson, trans. P.C. Hodgson and J.M. Stewart. Berkeley: University of California Press.

Hick, John, ed. 1977: *The Myth of God Incarnate*. London: SCM Press.

Hirsch, Emanuel 1949–54: *Geschichte der neuern evangelischen Theologie*, 5 vols. Gütersloh.

Jenson, Robert W. 1982: *The Triune Identity*. Philadelphia: Fortress Press.

Jüngel, Eberhard [1978, 2nd edn] 1983: *God as the Mystery of the World*, trans. D.L. Guder. Edinburgh: T & T Clark; Grand Rapids: Eerdmans.

Kant, Immanuel [1781] 1963: *Critique of Pure Reason*, trans. N.K. Smith. London: Macmillan.

Kant, Immanuel [1793] 1960: *Religion Within the Limits of Reason Alone*, trans. T.M. Greene and H.H. Hudson. New York: Harper and Row.

Locke, John [1695] 1958: *The Reasonableness of Christianity as Delivered in the Scriptures*, ed. I.T. Ramsey. Stanford: Stanford University Press; London: A & C Black.

Moltmann, Jürgen [1973] 1974: *The Crucified God: The Cross of Christ as the Foundation and Criticism of Christian Theology*, trans. R.A. Wilson and J. Bowden. London: SCM Press; New York: Harper and Row.

Ogden, Schubert M. 1963: *The Reality of God and Other Essays*. San Francisco: Harper and Row.

Pannenberg, Wolfhart [1988] 1991: *Systematic Theology*, vol. 1, trans. G.W. Bromiley. Edinburgh: T & T Clark; Grand Rapids: Eerdmans.

Rahner, Karl 1970: *The Trinity*, selected and trans. J. Donceel. London: Burns and Oates/Herder & Herder.

Ritschl, Albrecht [1870–4] 1900: *The Christian Doctrine of Justification and Reconciliation*, 3 vols, trans. J.S. Black, ed. H.R. Mackintosh and A.B. Macaulay. Edinburgh: T & T Clark.

Robinson, James M., ed. [1962 and 1963] 1968: *The Beginnings of Dialectical Theology*, trans. K.R. Crim and L. de Grazia, vol. 1. Richmond, Virginia: John Knox Press.

Schleiermacher, Friedrich [1799] 1958: *On Religion: Speeches to Its Cultured Despisers*, trans. J. Oman. New York: Harper and Row; London: Kegan Paul, Trench, Trubner and Co.

Schleiermacher, Friedrich [1821–2] 1960: *The Christian Faith*, trans. and ed. H.R. Mackintosh and J.S. Stewart. Edinburgh: T & T Clark.

Spinoza, Benedict [1670] 1951: *A Theologico-Political Treatise and a Political Treatise*, trans. R.H.M. Elwes. New York: Dover Publications.

Strauss, David Friedrich [1835–6] 1972: *The Life of Jesus, Critically Examined*, trans. George Eliot, ed. P.C. Hodgson. Philadelphia: Fortress Press.

Thomasius, Gottfried 1886: *Christi Person und Werk*, 3rd edn, 2 vols.

Tillich, Paul 1951: *Systematic Theology*, vol. 1. Evanston: University of Chicago Press (reissued 1967, New York: Harper and Row).

Tindal, Matthew 1730: *Christianity as Old as the Creation: or, The gospel, a republication of the religion of nature*.

Torrance, Thomas F. 1982: *Reality and Evangelical Theology*. Philadelphia: Westminster Press.

Weischedel, Wilhelm 1972: *Der Gott der Philosophen*, 2 vols. Darmstadt.

ROBERT W. JENSON

Gogarten, Friedrich (1887–1967) German dialectical theologian. A Lutheran pastor and later a professor of systematic theology at Breslau (1931–5) and Göttingen (1935–53), he was a pioneer with Rudolf Bultmann, Karl Barth and Emil Brunner of dialectical theology. They developed their ideas in the journal *Zwischen den Zeiten* ('Between the Times') which was founded in 1922; but by its demise in 1933 it was clear that Gogarten's theology had diverged from that of Barth and Brunner. He emphasized justification by faith over and against the role of works in Christian discipleship, and held that biblical history is significant not as objective event but as subjective experience, accessed by faith; man's understanding of history, rather than any divine role, is the key. His works include *Entmythologisier-*

ung und die Kirche (1953, trans. *Demythologising and History*, 1955).

Bibliography
Bauer, A.V. 1967: *Freiheit zur Welt: Zum Weltver-ständnis und Weltverhältnis der Christen nach der Theologie F. Gogartens.* Paderborn.
Heron, A.I.C. 1980: *A Century of Protestant Theology.* Guildford.

Gore, Charles (1853–1932) English bishop and theologian. Educated at Harrow and Balliol College, Oxford, and Bishop of Worcester (1902–5) and of Birmingham (1905–11), he had a long and influential association with the Oxford movement and Oxford, where he was vice-principal of Cuddesdon (1880–3), first principal of Pusey House (1884–93) and Bishop (1911–19). Some of his writings reinforced traditional Anglo-Catholic dogma: *Ministry of the Christian Church* (1888, new edition 1919) upheld Catholic views of episcopal authority. He was also, however, ready to oppose orthodoxy, arguing against too Catholic a view of the sacraments in *The Body of Christ* (1901), and seeking to introduce Tractarianism to new developments in biblical criticism in works such as *Lux Mundi: A Series of Studies in the Incarnation* (1889), of which he was editor. In his Bampton Lectures, *The Incarnation of the Son of God* (1891), he argued that in 'emptying' himself to become a man, Christ relinquished divine omniscience and omnipotence. Often embroiled in theological controversy, Gore was also deeply committed to social action as integral to Anglo-Catholic Christianity, and he was actively associated with the Oxford Mission to Calcutta and the Christian Socialist Union.

Bibliography
Carpenter, J. 1960: *Gore: A Study in Liberal Catholic Thought.* London.
Prestige, G.L. 1935: *The Life of C. Gore: A Great Englishman.* London.
Reardon, B.M. 1971: *From Coleridge to Gore: A Century of Religious Thought in Britain.* Harlow.

Greek Orthodox theology   See EASTERN ORTHODOX THEOLOGY.

Greene, Graham (1904–91) English Catho-lic novelist. Educated at Balliol College, Oxford, he joined the Roman Catholic church in 1926 and worked on *The Times* from 1926–30, continuing to work intermittently as a journal-ist thereafter as his novel-writing career developed. His first success, *Stamboul Train* (1932), was followed by a succession of over twenty novels, many of them thrillers, often set in seedy or exotic locations inspired by his own extensive travels. Greene once quoted from a poem by Browning to describe his preoccupa-tion as a novelist: 'Our interest's on the dangerous edge of things./The honest thief, the tender murderer,/The superstitious athe-ist . . .'. The moral seriousness of his work is complemented by an instinct for topical political and social themes, and an outstanding ability to create memorable characters and atmospheres. Especially in a middle phase of his work starting with *Brighton Rock* (1938), Greene is explicitly Catholic in his themes, exploring moral and religious dilemmas, the tension between faith and doubt and good and evil, and 'the appalling strangeness of the mercy of God'. Other works in this period include *The Power and the Glory* (1940), *The Heart of the Matter* (1948), *The End of the Affair* (1951) and *The Quiet American* (1955). Greene also wrote plays and travel books, and two volumes of autobiography.

Bibliography
1960: Graham Greene: the religious affair. In *The Picaresque Saint*, R.W. Lewis. London.
Sharrock, R. 1984: *Saints, Sinners and Comedians: The Novels of Graham Greene.* Tunbridge Wells.
Stratford, P. 1964: *Faith and Fiction: Creative Processes in Greene and Mauriac.* Notre Dame, Ind.

Gutiérrez, Gustavo (b. 1928). Peruvian Roman Catholic theologian, a leading exponent of LIBERATION THEOLOGY. He was born and educated in Lima, and studied later at Louvain, Lyons and Rome. Ordained in 1959, he moved to Rimac, a slum area of Lima, where he continues to reside whilst working as a professor of theology at the Catholic University in Lima. During the 1960s he became increasingly aware of the gap between the theoretical nature of his training and the experience of violence, poverty and oppression of those among whom he lived. This situation became his starting point for the development of a theology emphasizing political and social as well as spiritual liberation: for him theology must be a response to the human condition, not a precondition of faith. In his earlier thought (as in the seminal *A Theology of Liberation*, 1971, trans. 1973) he evolved a philosophical/historical analysis of poverty, emphasizing Christ as liberator from oppressive conditions. Whereas in this phase the emphasis is on Exodus, his later thought (as in *We Drink from our Own Wells*, 1983, trans. 1984) shifts to the experience of captivity, and the unmerited and abundant grace of God who chooses to be present in suffering. Other works include *The Power of the Poor in History* (1979, trans. 1983) and *On Job* (trans. 1987).

Bibliography
Brown, R.M. 1980: *Gustavo Gutiérrez*. John Knox.
Brown, R.M. 1990: *Gustavo Gutiérrez: An Introduction to Liberation Theology*. Maryknoll, NY.
Maduro, O. 1989: *The Future of Liberation Theology: Essays in Honor of G. Gutiérrez*. Maryknoll, NY.

H

Harnack, Adolf von (1851–1930) German church historian and theologian. The son of an eminent Lutheran theologian, he taught at the universities of Leipzig (1874–9), Giessen (1879–86), Marburg (1886–9) and Berlin (1889–1921). A liberal Protestant of the school of Albrecht Ritschl, he specialized in patristics and early church history. In *Lehrbuch der Dogmengeschichte* (1886–9, trans. *History of Dogma*, 1894–9), he maintained that the dogma developed by Paul and later Catholicism originated in alien Hellenistic metaphysical thought; this 'husk' should be discarded in order to rediscover the true 'kernel' of Jesus' teaching, which in a popular theological book, *Das Wesen des Christentums* (1900, trans. *What is Christianity?*, 1901), he identified as the message of 'the kingdom of God'. He emphasized the ethical rather than the supernatural aspect of Christianity: the brotherhood of man, the fatherhood of God, the commandment of love and the infinite value of the human soul. A specialist in New Testament criticism, he dated the synoptic gospels surprisingly early in *Beiträge zur Einleitung in das Neue Testament* (1906–11, trans. under different titles, such as *Luke the Physician*, 1907, *The Date of the Acts and of the Synoptic Gospels*, 1911).

Bibliography
Glick, G.W. 1967: *The Reality of Christianity: A Study of Adolf von Harnack as Historian and Theologian*. New York.
Pauck, W. 1968: *Harnack and Troeltsch*. Oxford.
Rumscheidt, M. ed. 1989: *Adolf von Harnack*. London.

Hartshorne, Charles (b. 1897). North American process theologian. A teacher of philosophy at Chicago, Emery and Texas, he developed the metaphysical and philosophical thought of A.N. Whitehead into a full PROCESS THEOLOGY, focusing especially on God's nature and activity. In *The Divine Relativity* of 1948, he argues that a belief that the divine existence is both defined by and dependent on human reality is not incompatible with a belief in divine perfection. In *Anselm's Discovery: A Re-examination of the Ontological Proof for God's Existence* of 1965 and *The Logic of Perfection* of 1962 he argues for the a priori truth of the existence of God. For him, God's nature is not immutable, rather endlessly adaptable and changeable. His omniscience does not imply foreknowledge of events, for the future consists not of fixed actualities but of possibilities. Even the laws of nature are not fixed, but dependent on divine decisions. Change, not permanence, is the underlying principle of reality. 'God' is not necessarily a single entity, but a series of actual 'occasions' in which the divine takes concrete existence.

Bibliography
Gunton, C.E. 1978: *Becoming and Being: The Doctrine of God in Charles Hartshorne and Karl Barth*. Oxford and New York.
James, R.E. 1967: *The Concrete God: A New Beginning for Theology: The Thought of Charles Hartshorne*. Indianapolis.
Viney, D.W. 1985: *Charles Hartshorne and the Existence of God*. Albany, NY.

Hauerwas, Stanley (b. 1940) North American Protestant ethicist and theologian. Educated at Southwestern University and Yale, he was professor of Christian ethics at the University of Notre Dame, Indiana, before taking up his

249

current post as professor of theological ethics at Duke University, North Carolina. In *A Community of Character* of 1981 he challenges the assumption of contemporary Christian ethics that there is a special relationship between Christianity and western democratic liberalism. Christian ethics issue, rather, in a challenge to the insistence on human autonomy inherent in liberal theories of moral development. For him the idea of the Christian community as the locus of morality is crucial. Moral development is a dynamic of personal and social transformation which takes place in community, and is expressed not so much in a set of principles as in a series of stories. Stories are an expression of life and character rather than merely propositional, and as such they are a truer guide to ethical living than rationalistic moral principles arising out of the supposition that there is a universal moral law.

The Peaceable Kingdom of 1983 reflects his increasing emphasis on nonviolence as the hallmark of Christian community, challenging the church to offer 'a political alternative to every nation, witnessing to the kind of social life possible for those that have been formed by the story of Christ'. Other works include a study of medical ethics, *Suffering Presence* of 1986.

Bibliography
Christian, A.W. 1987: *Doctrines of Religious Communities*. New Haven, Conn.

Hegel, Georg Wilhelm Friedrich (1770–1831) German idealist philosopher. Born in Stuttgart, Hegel became professor of philosophy in Heidelberg and later in Berlin. Developing the critical idealism of Kant, he became the most influential philosopher of his generation in Germany. Among his publications are *The Phenomenology of Mind* (1807), *The Science of Logic* (1812), *The Philosophy of Right* (1821) and *The Philosophy of History* (1832).

Central to Hegel's thought is the principle of Becoming, rather than Being, with a related emphasis on history and change. He suggested that history developed by what he called a 'dialectical process'. One idea, or thesis, was contradicted by another idea, or antithesis; and eventually these two concepts resolved themselves into a higher harmony, or synthesis, which may in turn become a new thesis, beginning the process again. This historical process embodies *Geist* – Mind or Spirit – which realizes itself in history, although not identical with it. Everything is one with this Mind or Spirit, and failure to perceive this is alienation: the alienation of *Geist* from itself. The realization of Oneness – that everything is mental, and part of the evolving process of Mind – is the aim of the 'dialectical process'.

Hegel's influence has been vast in many different fields of thought. His emphasis on history influenced the development of biblical criticism; he provided the basis for a school of ethics; and most famously, he inspired, if by contradiction, the work of Ludwig Feuerbach and Karl Marx.

See also HEGELIANISM.

Bibliography
Findlay, J.A. 1958: *Hegel: A Re-Examination*. London.
Friedrich, C. ed. 1954: *The Philosophy of Hegel*. New York.
Inwood, M., ed. and trans. 1989: *Hegel* (selections). London.
Singer, P. 1983: *Hegel*. Oxford.

Hegelianism Hegel's relation to theology has always been controversial, because the complexity of Hegel's project is bound to stimulate controversy. Moreover, although his thought is famous, it is rarely studied in depth. In a pluralistic age many critics fail to see the need to respond to a now discredited Enlightenment rationalism, much less appreciate Hegel's project of responding to the Enlightenment's sceptical critique of theology as metaphysics that culminates with Immanuel Kant. Hegel's philosophy, like Friedrich von Schelling's, is a post-Enlightenment attempt to restore theology to its pride of place among the philosophical disciplines. In the first paragraph of his *Enzyklopädie* ([1830a] 1971) Hegel asserts that philosophy and religion have the same object and concern, namely truth, and that God and only God is the truth.

Yet Hegel does not simply return to precritical modes of thought, according to which theology is a special metaphysical science of a supersensible highest being. Hegel does not bypass the critique of metaphysics, but accepts it. Accordingly, his project involves both a critique of traditional theology and a reconstruction of theology. This double focus has given rise to the suspicion that Hegel's thought may be atheistic and subversive of theology. Such views are held by those who tend to regard the tradition as an ahistorical preserve of truth that, unproblematic and intact, merely needs restatement. On the other hand, Hegel's transformation and reconstruction of theology may disappoint those who maintain that theology is essentially a precritical mode of thought that is incompatible with modernity. Hegel believes that the antimodern traditionalists and the antitraditional modernists are both wrong. The theological tradition is not simply an error, but contains truth that has yet to receive adequate formulation. This truth must be distinguished from its traditional formulations, and reconstructed.

Hegel was among the first to assert that philosophical thinking arises within a prephilosophical historical situation or context, born in a crisis of alienation, estrangement and disunion, and that philosophy is its own time comprehended in thought. With the recognition of the historical shaping and influencing of thought, not only does the history of philosophy assume importance as a philosophical discipline, Being itself is discovered to be historical. Hegel's distinction of three attitudes of thought towards objectivity is a phenomenological 'history of Being' that acknowledges the historical nature of thought and reflection, and the need to move beyond the one-sided exclusiveness of traditional thought.

Since theology in the metaphysical sense arose in and along with the philosophical tradition and its understanding of Being, theology is necessarily caught up in debates about the meaning of Being. The question is whether theology is necessarily tied to precritical metaphysics, or whether it can be part of the modern or postmodern situation. Although Hegel is not a theologian but a philosopher of religion, he denies that theology is essentially precritical and holds that it can and should be distinguished from its precritical forms. Hegel's critique of the tradition shows that he denies that the tradition is immutable and cannot be changed. He believes that theological deconstruction is necessary (owing to the self-subversion of the tradition) and that theological reconstruction is possible. But he denies that the tradition is an error that cannot be retrieved or corrected because there is nothing salvageable. The tradition can and must be corrected, for it has been influenced by metaphysics and has become oblivious to its own insights.

In what follows I shall outline Hegel's discussion 'Three Attitudes of Thought Towards Objectivity' (in [1830a] 1971, §§19–83) and explore its implications for philosophical theology. Instead of positing God and human being in separation or in alienation and then trying to bring them into relation – as do both the theological tradition and its Enlightenment critics – Hegel focuses on their unity as given in the history of religion. This reflects Hegel's concern about the alienation and disunity of his own day, and points in the direction of a Christological theology. In addition, I shall draw upon Paul Ricoeur's contention that the theological tradition tends to suppress the tragic dimension of evil and suffering acknowledged by the Adamic myth. My thesis is that Hegel recovers the suppressed tragic elements and incorporates them in his treatment of the death of God. This incorporation of the tragic involves a reconstruction and critical corrective to the tradition.

The first orientation of thought towards objectivity: metaphysics

Hegel identifies three attitudes of thought towards objectivity, three construals of genuine being or the real. Reconstruction is evident in that what the tradition regarded as given, is now regarded as in part a subjective accomplishment, a transcendental attitude (*Stellung*) towards objectivity. These three attitudes are (1) the natural attitude and the world of everyday life (Edmund Husserl), that gives rise to metaphysics and ontotheology; (2) its inversion in the modern transcendental attitude, that reduces theology to anthropology; and (3) Hegel's postmodern, holistic alternative, in which every category of the logic is a determination of the absolute, or a metaphysical definition of God ([1830a] 1971, §85). The first attitude construes Being as substance, the second construes Being as subject. Both of these are foundational, but differ sharply as to whether the foundation is a transcendent highest being (ontotheology) or immanent, as anthropology. Although the first two attitudes can be correlated with epochs in the history of philosophy, they are not simply identifiable as particular philosophical systems. As underlying attitudes and/or construals, they pervade epistemologies and ontologies, influencing the way in which the ontological and epistemological task is construed and understood. The third attitude builds on the collapse of the first two owing to their one-sidedness, and construes Being as process. Being is neither a foundational substance nor a foundational subject, but rather is a social process in which opposites coincide while remaining distinct.

The first attitude is naively realistic. It lives immersed in the surrounding world and so has a mundanizing orientation. It lives in the unquestioning belief that thought presents things as they are in themselves. Without entertaining any doubts on this point, thought proceeds straightforwardly to the things themselves. Hegel observes that philosophy in its early stages and all the sciences, as well as everyday action and ordinary consciousness, live in this belief ([1830a] 1971, §26).

While this attitude is naive, it is by no means philosophically neutral. It generates what Hegel calls the epoch of metaphysics. The direct presencing of things serves as the model for construing all being, including Being itself. However, since mundane entities are involved in flux, evanescence and perishing, they are not ideally stable and fixed. They need a ground or foundation. There is a passage beyond the realm of becoming towards eternal, pure presence. There occurs an inversion of the real in favour of the ideal that is a flight from and concealment of primordial temporality and historicity. But the transcendent beyond or pure presence is in turn reified. Everything, including the self, world, and God, is interpreted as if it were a thing, a mundane entity already complete, that is, something that already is what it is, and present as a given. The ontotheological concept of metaphysics construes being as *a* being, albeit the highest, and is ahistorical.

Theological implications of the first attitude Hegel's critique of the tradition identifies issues which have by now become standard in process philosophy. It is directed chiefly at the categories of the understanding, not at the theological substance coming to expression in such categories. Hegel thinks that traditional theology is formulated in terms that are an expression of the block universe (William James). The metaphysical tradition conceived self, world and God as super or large entities, that exist in separation or isolation from everything else. It tended to draw a sharp distinction between God and world, and conceived God as the Beyond. Hegel observes that to push this distinction hard is to end up subverting the very point that is supposed to be made, for an infinite being that is opposed to the finite is restricted by that very opposition and is itself finite. Ontotheology demands an ontic foundation for ontology, and is part and parcel of the so-called metaphysics of presence. Hegel believes that, after Kant (see KANTIANISM), theology is no longer possible as a special metaphysics of a supersensible large entity. Rather it becomes a philosophical theology of spirit that culminates in the philosophy of religion.

The ontotheological conception underlies the royal or monarchical metaphor of classical theism. According to this metaphor, God creates and rules the world as an absolute monarch. God is the absolute master, and the religious believer is the slave. Although the slave can rebel, such rebellion is not capable of threatening, much less thwarting, divine rule. In this view there is a final teleology or salvation history which is anchored in the immutability of divine being. Thus the classical view issues in a divine comedy: whatever powers may try to oppose God are simply dispersed as impotent. Conflict is without seriousness or substance (*Natural Law*, [1802–3] 1975, 105f.). There is no recognition of the tragic depth of evil; rather tragedy is excluded.

The second attitude of thought towards objectivity: transcendental idealism
The construal of Being as a ready-made entity ignores and passes over the contribution of the mind to knowledge and truth. Kant's 'transcendental turn' amounts to a discovery of the mind's contribution to structuring knowledge. Hegel accepts the transcendental turn with qualifications, and contends that in classical philosophy there is insufficient acknowledgement of freedom and subjectivity. The recognition of freedom signals a break from the past,

which was dominated by the given. Instead things must correspond to thought and its conditions (Kant). This requirement signifies a tearing loose from traditions, foundations and moorings. If there is no exemplary past to appeal to, if there are no ready-made norms and criteria which can be accepted as givens, then these must be created.

The second attitude of thought towards objectivity is an inversion of the first. If, in the first attitude, thought is dominated by its object (or the past), the second attitude asserts the primacy of subjectivity and freedom. Being, formerly construed as already complete and given to subjectivity, is now grasped as relative to and shaped by subjectivity itself. Objectivity is an accomplishment of transcendental subjectivity. However, while transcendental idealism inverts metaphysics, it remains on the soil of metaphysics: it shifts the foundation from the world to subjectivity, from metaphysical theology to anthropocentric transcendentalism. Despite such a shift, Kant's transcendentalism retains a mundanizing, foundationalist orientation.

To absolutize subjectivity is to elevate non-identity into a first principle. When subjectivity is thus absolutized, it is sharply distinguished and separated from the world; conversely the world is denied intrinsic meaning and value and is reduced to a mere object of utility or natural resource. For Hegel, the Enlightenment culminates in a utilitarian outlook that has an instrumental conception of knowledge as power and mastery over nature, and whose fundamental criterion is relevance to subjectivity as determined by utility.

Theological implications This second attitude of thought towards objectivity may be hostile to theology. The traditional absolute is interpreted as an empty beyond, transcendent to reason and experience. Hegel observes that modernity creates a terrible dilemma for theology: either God (*ens realissimum*) is not an object at all and cannot be known, or God becomes a 'mere object', a block of wood or stone. Ontic transcendence is reduced to mundane presence, or, in Hegel's more poetic phrase, the sacred grove is reduced to mere timber. The sceptical side of the Enlightenment culminates in anthropocentrism that finds expression in utilitarianism, positivism and technism. But 'if

the Ideas [of pure reason: God, freedom, world] cannot be reduced to the block and stones of a wholly mundane reality, they are made into fictions (*Faith and Knowledge*, [1802] 1977, p. 58). Thus theology becomes a non-cognitive moral postulate (Kant) or yearning (J. Jacobi, J.G. Fichte). As a postulate, God has no being independent of the postulating moral consciousness.

Hegel does not accept the Enlightenment's elevation of subjectivity to the status of a first principle. He observes that 'It is the great advance of our time that subjectivity is now recognized as an absolute moment; this is an essential determination. However, everything depends on how subjectivity is interpreted' (*Lectures on the Philosophy of Religion*, [1827] 1984–6, vol. 3, p. 166). Modernity, or the Enlightenment, errs in identifying subjectivity as foundation: 'The Enlightenment, in its positive aspect, was a hubub of vanity without a firm core' ([1802] 1977, p. 56). In other words, the Enlightenment's principle of finite human subjectivity is insufficient to regenerate the unifying power, the normative content of philosophy, religion and politics. The Enlightenment's formal individualistic rationalism is itself a source of alienation, and is unable to overcome it.

Hegel's proposals
The first attitude of thought towards objectivity grasped thought and being together in an immediate unity and identity. Thereby it absolutized substance and failed to give difference, that is, subjectivity and subjective freedom, its due. Being is conceived as substance, an abstract identity that excludes not only difference, but relation. Thus the absolute is posited as a Beyond. The second attitude asserts the rights of subjectivity and freedom against the first. Against abstract identity it asserts difference. In Hegel's view, it replaces abstract identity with an equally abstract absolute difference, and abstract substance with an equally abstract solipsist subjectivity. Such finite solipsist subjectivity is insufficient to ground and unify culture. Thus the first and second attitudes of thought towards objectivity express alienation between the divine and the human. From his earliest publications Hegel recognized alienation as constituting the

need of speculative philosophy and sought to overcome such alienation.

This entailed nothing short of a rehabilitation of theology against Kant's criticisms. Hegel does not return to precritical modes of thought, but seeks to incorporate and respond to Enlightenment criticism. Philosophy of religion in Hegel's sense acknowledges the subjective turn of modern thought. But it is more than an anthropological account of religion. At the same time it is a philosophical theology that begins not by positing the divine and the human in abstract separation or alienation, but is conversant with the Protestant Reformation's understanding of faith as centred in divine–human reconciliation and Christology. Hegel's renewal of philosophical theology begins with the assumption that finite and infinite, human and divine, are not utterly severed, separated or estranged, but form a divine–human unity. This assumption reflects Hegel's concept of spirit (*Geist*) as originating in intersubjective recognition, and Hegel's positive assessment of Christianity as a source of reconciliation that helps to overcome alienation.

Hegel explores a Christological theology that seeks to articulate divine–human unity and community. He does this not by simply returning to or merely restating the classical doctrine of the person of Christ. Hegel rejects the two-natures doctrine on conceptual grounds, insisting that the divine and the human are not other. He reconstructs incarnation as a form of self-recognition in other. Religion is a mutual divine–human self-recognition in other, which has several levels that culminate in Christology. Although Hegel's reconstructed Christology is not free from ambiguity and problems, it points to and requires a reconstruction of Trinity as the social principle of freedom and community. The concept of God is reconstructed as Spirit (*Geist*) dwelling in its community. Several important implications must be noted.

First, we must examine Hegel's view of the relation of philosophy and religion. We have already observed Hegel's declaration that philosophy and religion both deal with truth in the sense that God and God alone is the truth. The issue is whether this makes Hegel's speculative philosophy dependent on Christianity. His declaration that religion can exist without philosophy, but philosophy cannot exist without religion, appears to mean that philosophy requires and depends on historical facts and experience, and that it assumes the Christian fact as a given (Yerkes, 1983). But this view is incorrect, for, according to Hegel, philosophy cannot be justified by experience or facts, but rather justifies (that is, provides conditions of possibility for and clarification of) experience. Moreover, Hegel agrees with G.E. Lessing that it is impossible to provide a historical foundation for eternal truths. Hegel believes that Christianity is not susceptible to a historical proof or justification. If Christianity is to be justified it will have to be justified by reason and philosophy; philosophy must show the rational element in religion and thus justify religion. However, philosophy for Hegel must be autonomous and self-justifying. Only because it is autonomous can philosophy provide justification for Christianity by generating it out of the concept.

The claim that Christian faith can be generated out of the concept gives rise to a question that was fiercely debated in the Hegelian school, namely, whether it is possible to deduce a specific historical fact from the speculative idea. Hegel does not actually claim to do so. Speculative philosophy can demonstrate the possibility of reconciliation and even that it must appear in time and be bound up with some particular individual, but it cannot decide which individual accomplishes and actualizes reconciliation. In this respect speculative philosophy of religion is related to and dependent on the faith of the Christian community.

However, when speculative philosophy reconstructs Christianity, it transforms Christian fact into a universal ontology. The incarnation is no longer simply a unique and unrepeatable historical fact, but rather becomes an ontological principle of divine–human relation that finds further actualization in God as Spirit in community. This transformation raises two issues. (1) With what justification does speculative philosophy transform the faith-claims of a particular historical religious community into a universal ontological structure? It is one thing for theology to find and develop the ontological implications of its basic fact, and quite another for an independent speculative philosophy to translate the particular claim of faith into a universal ontological structure. Hegel's reply would be that both philosophy and theology are concerned with truth, and that philosophy merely puts the truth of faith in its appropriate universal form. This response calls forth Søren Kierkegaard's protest, and insistence that faith is not knowledge but radical passion involving risk. (2) If historical fact is thus translated into universal ontological structures, is its historicity not undermined? Hegel's response would be that the goal of a philosophical theology of history is to overcome the rigid distinction between contingent truths of history and eternal truths of reason. The overcoming of history by history is for Hegel the philosophical import of the incarnation, the eternal in time.

Further, a philosophy that reconstructs and justifies the reconciliation of the divine and the human must necessarily carry out a critique of metaphysics and metaphysical theology. As early as his *Phenomenology of Spirit* ([1807] 1952) Hegel was clear about the criticism of abstract substance metaphysics. He tells us that in his view, which only the full execution of the system itself can justify, the true must be conceived and expressed not merely as substance, but equally as subject. This implies that the abstract substantial absolute is not yet a doctrine of God. The latter involves a grasping of the absolute as spirit, as subject to and a result of development. If substance must become subject, this implies that the absolute becomes, that is, is subject to a process of becoming, and that becoming, not being, is the fundamental category. Only such an absolute is capable of incarnation and of being not-other than the human.

The above formulation of substance become subject implies a revision of the monopolar conception of classical theism. Hegel's formulations exhibit a bipolar conception of the absolute. The bipolar concept of the absolute finds expression in the idea of God's other, or God's son. The latter expressions point to duality and difference in the absolute. This conception is crucial for showing how God can be positively related to the world and history, while nevertheless remaining the same. Further, the bipolar conception develops into an explicitly triadic conception of the absolute, that Hegel makes fundamental in his later

Lectures on the Philosophy of Religion ([1827] 1984–6). Christology and incarnation are central to Hegel's theological reconstruction, even though Hegel by no means simply takes over, but reconstructs and transforms the classical doctrines into social conceptions.

Such revisions of classical theism abound in Hegel's writings both early and late. The *Phenomenology of Spirit* portrays the collapse of metaphysical theology in the modern period as the self-emptying of abstract substance. Christianity contributes to this collapse in its central symbols of incarnation, crucifixion and death. Incarnation implies that the absolute is not simply substance, but has the structure of self-consciousness. God's self-knowledge involves self-recognition in other, and is the result of mediation by others. In incarnation the absolute is 'at home with itself' in an other. In short, incarnation is the mode of divine presence in the world, showing the latter to be an ethical (*sittliche*) presence. The reconciliation between the divine and the human manifests divine love.

Hegel's incorporation of tragic motifs: the death of God Hegel's orientation towards a Christological speculative theology allows him to articulate death and suffering as theological themes. In his early *Faith and Knowledge* he asserts that infinite grief must be incorporated as a moment of the supreme Idea. 'Good Friday must be speculatively re-established in the whole truth and harshness of its God-forsakenness' ([1802] 1977, p. 191). In the *Phenomenology of Spirit* Hegel treats the death of the mediator as a critique of abstract substance metaphysics. This is a theological criticism of substance metaphysics and classical metaphysical theology, specifically the classical conceptions of abstract eternity and transcendence. What dies is not the divine being *per se*, but its abstraction, that is, abstract transcendence, the infinite that, since it is opposed to the finite, is itself finite.

> The death of this representation contains at the same time the death of the abstraction of the divine being, that is not posited as self. It is the painful feeling of the unhappy consciousness, that God himself is dead. This hard word is the expression of the innermost simple self-knowledge, the return of consciousness

into the depths of the night of the I = I, which distinguishes and knows nothing besides itself . . . This knowing therefore is the inspiration through which substance has become subject, its abstraction and lifelessness perishes, and it becomes actual, simple and universal self-consciousness. ([1807] 1952, p. 546, my translation)

In this passage the death of God signifies a theological and not an atheistic critique of traditional theology. Hegel speaks here of the death, the nullity of abstract substance. He criticizes classical theism's monarchical metaphor for conceiving God as actual apart from relation, as absolute non-reciprocal Master. Such abstract immediacy must be qualified if God is to enter into relation, as the central Christian doctrine of incarnation presupposes and requires. The absolute must undergo a process of mediation with other, that is, become subject. This entry into mediation implies that conflict and tragedy are now theological possibilities as well. Hegel sides with those who affirm that if God enters into relation with what is other, this involves the possibility of suffering and passibility.

Hegel goes further and asserts that there is tragic suffering in God. He observes that Dante's *Divine Comedy* is without fate or a genuine struggle, because the absolute exists in it as sheer presence without opposition. By introducing and emphasizing the death of God as a theological theme, Hegel criticizes the tradition and recovers the tragic aspect of evil and suffering that it suppressed. The death of God means that there is suffering, pain and negation in God; there is suffering and tragedy in the divine itself (see SUFFERING, DIVINE). This point is made explicitly in several texts from Hegel's earliest writings to his latest. In *Faith and Knowledge* ([1802] 1977), Hegel insists that infinite grief must be incorporated as an *essential moment* in the absolute or divine Idea. In the 1827 *Lectures on the Philosophy of Religion* Hegel writes:

'God himself is dead', it says in a Lutheran hymn, expressing an awareness that the human, the finite, the weak, the negative, are themselves a moment of the divine, that they are within God himself, that finitude, negativity, otherness are not outside of God and do not, as otherness, hinder unity with God. Otherness, the negative, is known to be a moment of the divine nature itself. This involves *the highest idea of spirit*. ([1827] 1984–6, vol. 3, p. 326)

The theme of tragic suffering and negation in God is clear and consistent. Stephen Crites observes that 'The horrendous notion that God himself has died on the cross, which has been obscured by harmless conventional renderings of the story, is here restored not merely as an historical event but as a supreme speculative insight restored in all its original force and pitiless severity . . .' (1982, p. 51).

Hegel's view, while Christian, diverges significantly from classical orthodoxy by emphasizing divine suffering. This departure from orthodoxy is a retrieval of the tragic dimension of evil that the traditional metaphysical doctrines suppressed. Given his Christological orientation, it is necessary for Hegel to incorporate infinite grief into the divine Idea. This belies any reduction of the divine triad to a sheer undifferentiated unity or light, or to sheer self-sameness. Further, any divine 'sweetness and light' is broken and darkened by historical conflict between the divine and human: 'In its development this process is the going forth of the divine idea into the uttermost cleavage [*Entzweiung*] even to the opposite pole of the anguish of death, which is itself the absolute reversal, the highest love, containing the negation of the negative within itself [and being in this way] the absolute reconciliation' ([1827] 1984–6, vol. 3, p. 132). Reconciling love arises out of anguish at separation and death: 'Love as originating in infinite anguish is precisely the concept of spirit itself' (p. 140). Love cannot be conceived apart from infinite anguish. For this reason love has a tragic aspect. For Hegel any 'divine comedy' is found in and therefore is *inseparable from* the infinite anguish of Good Friday. The metaphysical tradition, under the domination of abstract impassible identity, separated the divine from the human, the comic from the tragic. Classical Christology not only failed to express adequately its deepest intentions, it condemned these as patripassianism.

Critical issues

Hegel's philosophy of religion rests upon two fundamental principles: (1) philosophy and religion both have a common object, namely truth in the sense that God alone is the truth; (2) philosophy and religion are nevertheless *not identical* in the way they each respectively grasp and hold the truth. Religion grasps the truth in the form of representation (*Vorstellung*), images and symbols. Representation corresponds to the level of consciousness, and this implies that its apprehension of truth is qualified by estrangement, alienation and otherness. In contrast, philosophy grasps the truth in the form of the concept (*Begriff*, Idea). The latter is truth in the form of truth. Since it falls to philosophy and not to religion to deal with the proper form of truth, philosophy is the final arbiter of truth in Hegel's system.

Hegel's proposals for theological reconstruction all rest upon his claim to generate the basic position of Christianity – save for the historicity and individuality of the redeemer figure – out of the concept. This reflects Hegel's judgement that the truth of Christianity cannot be established historically; if it is to be established and defended at all, it must be generated out of the concept, that is, it must be a conceptual defence and articulation. This means that Christianity must be reconstructed on the basis of Hegel's categorial ontology.

Classical Christian doctrines are not purely conceptual constructions, but are elaborations of the central images, metaphors and so on, of faith. The result is that classical doctrines are an uncritical mixture of faith and metaphysics. In contrast, Hegel contends that the task of speculative philosophy is to transform representations (*Vorstellungen*) into concepts (*Begriffe*). This transformation at the same time is supposed to accomplish a conceptual clarification of faith that preserves its content while altering its form. Indeed Hegel even maintains that speculative philosophy is more concerned to preserve the truth of orthodox Christianity than are contemporary theologians. All classical doctrines are in need of correction, as far as Hegel is concerned, especially the doctrines of

the two-nature Christology, Trinity, the concept of God as spirit, and eschatology.

Hegel's proposed transformations of *Vorstellungen* into *Begriffe* have been controversial. For given the non-identity in form between *Vorstellung* and *Begriff*, Hegel's transformed Christianity often appears not so much a preservation of the truth of Christianity as its betrayal. It is not reassuring to be told that this judgement itself is made from the subordinate standpoint of *Vorstellung* and reflects its limited consciousness of truth. Consider Hegel's repudiation of classical eschatological dualism and two-nature Christology. Consider also his philosophical treatment of the incarnation that transforms it from a particular historical individual into a doctrine of divine–human community.

The nub of the controversy is Hegel's claimed transformation of representation (*Vorstellung*) into concept (*Begriff*). Representation corresponds to the level of ordinary consciousness. At this level, the object of consciousness is regarded as given. Representation therefore corresponds to the position outlined above in the first attitude of thought towards objectivity, that is, to precritical metaphysics. Being is the beyond, and God is construed as a large entity (highest being, most real being and so on). In contrast to representation, concept (*Begriff*) is not empirical but transcendental. The concept reflects the transcendental turn (Kant) sketched in the second attitude of thought towards objectivity. The transcendental turn signifies that being is relative to subjectivity, and that the subject has primacy with reference to being. This means that what appears at the level of representation to be *given*, is, at the transcendental level, a *posit* of transcendental subjectivity. The problem of transforming *Vorstellungen* into *Begriffe* is the transcendental turn. The transcendental move seems to invert ordinary consciousness: what initially appears to be given turns out to be something posited.

The question is, can theology survive a transformation of representation into concept? It would seem that theology, in so far as it rests upon a given and asserts a transcendent highest being, belongs essentially to the first orientation of thought towards objectivity. This is equivalent to asserting that theology is essentially a precritical orientation and mode of thought.

Thus when theology is reformulated in transcendental terms at the level of concept, its object is grasped as relative to and in some sense dependent on transcendental subjectivity. Feuerbach drew the conclusion that the transcendental turn implies that theology is reducible to anthropology.

Hegel rejects this line of argument. The alternatives are not a discredited precritical metaphysics or a reduction of theology to anthropology. Moreover, although Hegel accepts the modern turn to the subject, he also qualifies such acceptance by noting that everything depends on how such subject relativity is interpreted. To begin with, Hegel does not interpret the transcendental in a foundationalist sense. Instead of constituting the object, Hegel's transcendental is a medium of access to the object and of reconstructing its meaning and truth. Moreover, Hegel observes that relativity to consciousness does not deprive the object of its independence. There is no conflict between non-foundationalist positing and the object possessing 'in itself' a reality independent of such positing, as Hegel observes in his *Lectures on the Philosophy of Religion*: 'The concept to be sure produces the truth – for such is subjective freedom – but at the same time it recognizes this truth not as something produced, but as the true existing in and for itself' (vol. 3, p. 345).

The other is not eliminated by the conceptual transformation of *Vorstellung* into *Begriff*. The transformation removes not the other or the object, but only its alien appearance. To eliminate what is alien is not necessarily to eliminate the other as such or to reduce it to the same. It is to enter into an intimate non-dominating relation with the other. Hegel thus breaks with foundationalist transcendental philosophy. In Hegel's qualified transcendentalism, the transcendental subject has renounced foundationalist ambitions; the other is not eliminated, but allowed to be.

The *Philosophy of Religion* lectures are important for understanding the culmination of the Hegelian system. Religion is the self-consciousness of absolute spirit. This phrase denotes both a human consciousness of God and God's self-consciousness mediated by humans. The *Philosophy of Religion* therefore culminates in a philosophical theology that articulates God as the spirit of the religious community. The doctrine of God is not to be identified simply with the logic – although Hegel insists that every category is a metaphysical definition of the absolute – but finds concrete expression in the *Philosophy of Religion* as the culmination of Hegel's philosophy of Spirit and ethical life (*Sittlichkeit*). It is only from the vantage point of the *Philosophy of Religion* that the absolute is grasped not merely as substance, but also as subject, and that the logic is seen to be not merely a theory of categories, but also a speculative philosophical theology.

See also CHRISTOLOGY; GOD; PHILOSOPHICAL THEOLOGY.

Bibliography

Writings

[1801] 1977: *The Difference between Fichte's and Schelling's System of Philosophy*, trans. H.S. Harris and W. Cerf. Albany: SUNY Press.
[1802] 1977: *Faith and Knowledge*, trans. W. Cerf and H.S. Harris. New York: SUNY Press.
[1802–3] 1975: *Natural Law*, trans. T.M. Knox. University of Pennsylvania Press.
[1803] 1979: *First Philosophy of Spirit*, trans. H.S. Harris, in Hegel, G.W.F., *System of Ethical Life (1802–3) and First Philosophy of Spirit (1803)*. Albany: SUNY Press.
[1807] 1952: *Phänomenologie des Geistes*, ed. Hoffmeister. Hamburg: Felix Meiner Verlag. English translations: *Phenomenology of Mind* (trans. J.B. Baillie, New York: Macmillan, 1910) and *Phenomenology of Spirit* (trans. A.V. Miller, Oxford: Oxford University Press, 1977).
[1812] 1969: *Wissenschaft der Logik*, trans. *Hegel's Science of Logic*, by A.V. Miller. New York: Humanities Press.
[1822] 1974: Foreword to H.F.W. Hinrichs' *Die Religion im inneren Verhältnisse zur Wissenschaft*, A.V. Miller in *Beyond Epistemology: New Studies in the Philosophy of Hegel*, ed. F. Weiss. The Hague: Martinus Nijhoff.
[1827] 1984–6: *Lectures on the Philosophy of Religion*, Vol. 1 *The Concept of Religion*, Vol. 2 *Determinate Religion*, Vol. 3 *The Consummate Religion*, ed. Peter C. Hodgson, trans. R. Brown, P. Hodgson and J. Stewart, with the assistance of H.S. Harris. Berkeley: University of California Press.
[1829] 1930, 1973: *Vorlesungen über die Beweise vom Dasein Gottes*, ed. G. Lasson. Hamburg: Meiner Verlag.
[1830a] 1971: *Enzyklopädie*, trans. *Hegel's Logic, Hegel's Philosophy of Nature, Hegel's Philosophy of*

Mind, by W. Wallace, together with the *Zusätze* in Boumann's text (1845) trans. A.V. Miller. Oxford: Clarendon Press.

[1830b] 1975: *Lectures on the Philosophy of World History*, trans. H.B. Nisbet. Cambridge: Cambridge University Press.

1948: *On Christianity: Early Theological Writings*, trans. T.M. Knox and Richard Kroner. New York: Harper Torchbooks.

Critical works

Crites, Stephen 1982: The Golgotha of absolute Spirit. In *Method and Speculation in Hegel's Phenomenology*, ed. M. Westphal. New Jersey: Humanities Press.

Fackenheim, Emil 1967: *The Religious Dimension in Hegel's Thought*. Chicago: University of Chicago Press.

Feuerbach, Ludwig [1839] 1972: Towards a critique of Hegel's philosophy. In *The Fiery Brook: Selected Writings of Ludwig Feuerbach*, trans. Zawar Hanfi. New York: Doubleday Anchor.

Hodgson, Peter C. 1989: *God In History: Shapes of Freedom*. Nashville, Tenn.: Abingdon Press.

Jaeschke, Walter 1990: *Reason in Religion: The Foundations of Hegel's Philosophy of Religion*, trans. J. Michael Stewart and Peter C. Hodgson. Berkeley: University of California Press.

Pannenberg, Wolfhart 1974: Die Bedeutung des Christentums in der Philosophie Hegels. In *Stuttgarter Hegel-Tage 1970*. Hegel Studien, Beiheft 11. Bonn: Bouvier Verlag, pp. 175–202.

Schlitt, Dale M. 1984: *Hegel's Trinitarian Claim: A Critical Reflection*. Leiden: E.J. Brill.

Williams, Robert R. 1992: *Recognition: Fichte and Hegel On The Other*. Albany, NY: SUNY Press.

Yerkes, James 1983: *The Christology of Hegel*, 2nd edn. Albany, NY: SUNY Press.

ROBERT R. WILLIAMS

Heidegger, Martin (1889–1976) German existentialist philosopher. From a peasant background, he studied for a period at a Jesuit seminary before going to Freiburg. There he went on to teach, and came under the influence of Edmund Husserl, whom he later succeeded (in 1929), after a period as associate professor at Marburg. He resigned his post at Freiburg in 1951. His major work, *Being and Time* (1927, trans. 1962) was an innovative attempt to apply hermeneutic phenomenology to a study of the nature of Being. He rejects the subjectivism of Husserl's transcendental phenomenology, which he sees as 'worldliness', evolving instead the philosophical concept of the essence of man

as Being-in-the-world, the formulation of which is a necessary preparation in the understanding of Being (*Dasein*, literally, 'thereness') itself. A leading exponent of EXISTENTIALISM and a major figure in twentieth-century philosophy, he influenced the work of Sartre and many theologians, especially R. Bultmann, P. Tillich – with whom he taught at Marburg – K. Barth and J. Macquarrie. They adopt as well as take issue with many of his existential categories, emphasizing the existential 'moment' when man responds to God by choosing 'authentic' existence.

Bibliography
Grene, M. 1957: *Martin Heidegger*. London and New Haven, Conn.

King, M. 1964: *Heidegger's Philosophy: A Guide to his Basic Thought*. Oxford.

Macquarrie, J. 1973: *An Existential Theology: A Comparison of Heidegger and Bultmann*. Harmondsworth.

Henry, Carl (b. 1913) North American Protestant evangelical theologian. Born in New York and converted to Christianity in 1933, he studied at Wheaton College, Northern Baptist Seminary and Boston University. He returned to Northern Baptist to teach theology (1940–7), and went on to Fuller Theological Seminary (1947–56) before becoming founding editor of the evangelical journal, *Christianity Today* (1956–68). He has been at the forefront of evangelical initiatives in evangelism and theology. His concern to develop an authoritative theological undergirding for evangelicalism is most fully expressed in his six-volume work, *God, Revelation and Authority* of 1976–82, in which he establishes a firmly propositional approach, emphasizing the superiority of the rational, objective mind in understanding Christian revelation, and upholding the inerrancy of Scripture. He is the author of over twenty books; *The Uneasy Conscience of Modern Fundamentalism* of 1948 was influential in discouraging conservative evangelical separatism, and his concern for the secular world has given impetus to the evangelical commitment to evangelism.

Bibliography
Fackre, G. 1984: Carl F.H. Henry. In *A Handbook of*

Christian Theologians, ed. D.G. Peerman and M.E. Marty. Nashville, Tenn.
Patterson, B.E. 1983: *Carl Henry*. Waco, Tex.

Herder, Johann Gottfried (1744–1803) German poet and critic. A writer and collector of poetry, folk songs and legends, and an early student of comparative literature, he was a significant influence on J.W. Goethe and, with G.E. Lessing, was influential in the literary movements of the German Enlightenment. For most of his life a Lutheran preacher at Weimar, he combined rationalist views and traditional religious belief. Although he applied critical methods to biblical interpretation, his conclusions were surprisingly conservative. In *Vom Geist der hebräischen Poesie* of 1782–3 he analysed the Psalms as literature (stressing, for example, the primacy of the poetry's setting) whilst holding that the Psalter represented the greatest poetry given to man by God; whilst in *Die älteste Urkunde des Menschengeschlechts* (1774–6) he argued for an allegorical interpretation of Genesis 3, but then went on to attach historical truth to the story of the fall and original sin. His study of human history as a natural science, *Ideen zur Philosophie der Geschichte der Menschheit* (1784–91, trans. 1800) anticipates later evolutionary theories and prefigures developments in the social sciences.

Bibliography

Clark, R.T. 1969: *Herder, His Life and Thought*. Berkeley, Ca.
Dietze, W. 1980: *J.G. Herder*. Berlin.
Koepke, W., ed. 1982: *J.G. Herder, Innovator Through the Ages*. Bonn.

Hick, John Harwood (b. 1922) British philosopher of religion and theologian. Best known for *The Myth of God Incarnate* of 1977, of which he was editor, he was educated at Edinburgh, Oxford and Cambridge, was a minister in the Presbyterian church in England, and has taught at Cornell, Princeton Theological Seminary, Cambridge and, currently, at Claremont Graduate School in California. His major contribution is in the comparative study of religions. He rejected Christian orthodoxy to argue against the uniqueness of Christ, and for a theistic rather than Christocentric theology that would enable adherents of different religions – which are equally valid in their methods and goals, and which will eventually unify – peacefully to coexist. In often polemical writings, he characterizes religion as a subjective experience of encounter, in which human freedom – not subscription to a set of 'givens' – is the guiding principle. In *Death and Eternal Life* of 1976 he argues for universal salvation; other works include *Faith and Knowledge* (1957), *Philosophy of Religion* (1963), *Evil and the God of Love* (1979) and *God Has Many Names* (1980).

See also OTHER FAITHS AND CHRISTIANITY.

Bibliography

D'Costa, G. 1987: *John Hick's Theology of Religions*. Lanham, Md.
Gillis, C. 1989: *A Question of Final Belief*. Basingstoke.
Mathis, T.R. 1985: *Against John Hick: An Examination of his Philosophy and Religion*. Lanham, Md.

historical Jesus, quest of Precritical study of the Gospels assumed that they presented a straightforwardly 'historical' account of the life and teaching of Jesus. With the rise of critical study of the New Testament in the eighteenth century, this assumption was challenged. The resultant historical-critical approach to the Gospel records has come to be known as the 'Quest of the Historical Jesus', the phrase used as the title of the English translation of Albert Schweitzer's classic account of the earlier phase of this movement ([1906] 1910).

The 'first quest'
Since Schweitzer's study (which was almost exclusively restricted to German scholarship) it has been usual to trace the beginnings of 'the quest' to a work originally published anonymously (and posthumously) under the auspices of G.E. Lessing in 1778 as the last of seven *Fragmente eines Ungenannten*, generally known as the 'Wolfenbüttel Fragments'; the work was entitled 'On the Purpose of Jesus and his Disciples' and was later revealed to have been the work of Hermann Samuel Reimarus, a teacher of oriental languages at Hamburg, who had devoted much of his life to promoting a 'rational religion' largely based on English deism

(see Reimarus, [1778] 1971). For Reimarus Jesus was a Jewish messianic leader whose ambition was nationalistic rather than religious, and who had no thought of starting a new religion. Christianity derived not from Jesus but from the determination of his disciples to maintain their influence by promoting Jesus as a spiritual redeemer, an aim which they forwarded by stealing his body and proclaiming his resurrection. The Gospels therefore present not the historical Jesus but a tendentious reconstruction by his self-interested disciples.

Similarly rationalistic accounts soon followed, varying in their specific approach, but all aiming to recover a Jesus different from the traditional object of Christian piety. In particular, the miraculous element in the Gospels' account of Jesus' ministry was typically played down or simply rejected, and the more theological elements of Christian faith traced to the creativity of Jesus' followers rather than to the reality of his historical life and teaching.

The most influential of these 'lives' was that of David Friedrich Strauss ([1835–6] 1973), notable for its sustained development of the category of 'myth' to explain the nature of the Gospel accounts. The translation of this work by George Eliot brought what had hitherto been a predominantly German development to the notice (and in many cases the wrath) of the British public. Other notable German examples were by J.G. Herder in 1796, Bruno Bauer in 1841–2, and F.D.E. Schleiermacher in 1864. One of the finest literary products of this movement (and almost the only non-German work noticed by Schweitzer) was the famous *Vie de Jésus* of Ernest Renan of 1863; while most of those mentioned by Schweitzer were German liberal Protestants, Renan was a French Catholic.

In British scholarship the move towards rationalism was less dramatic, but critical study of the Gospels nonetheless produced a new interest in attempting to write biographies of Jesus. J.R. Seeley's *Ecce Homo* of 1865 was widely read and discussed; while far from the radical approach of Strauss or Bauer, it was regarded by many as a significant move away from a theological to a more human, historical portrayal of Jesus. Other Victorian 'lives' (and there were many) tended to be less unsettling for traditional belief, the most influential being the very substantial *Life of Christ* by F.W. Farrar of 1874, in which critical scholarship was combined with piety and a high regard for the historical worth of the Gospels. Rather different, and also widely influential, was *The Life and Times of Jesus the Messiah* of 1883 by Alfred Edersheim, a convert from Judaism, in which great learning on matters of Jewish religion and history was brought to bear on the Gospel stories (which were themselves treated as thoroughly historical).

The products of the 'first quest' period varied from the extreme scepticism of Reimarus and Bauer to the confident piety of some of the Victorians. What unites them is the conviction that by the appropriate application of critical methods it is possible to reconstruct a genuinely 'historical' account of Jesus' life and teaching. But the understanding of what the appropriate methods are varies widely, and so therefore do the resultant portrayals of Jesus. With reference to Harnack's liberal Jesus (*Das Wesen des Christentums* of 1900), George Tyrrell made in 1909 a much-quoted comment that could, *mutatis mutandis*, be applied to most of the 'lives' of this period: 'The Christ that Harnack sees, looking back through nineteen centuries of Catholic darkness, is only the reflection of a liberal Protestant face, seen at the bottom of a deep well.'

The quest abandoned

The last two works considered in Schweitzer's survey were his own *Das Messianitäts- und Leidensgeheimnis: eine Skizze des Lebens Jesu* and William Wrede's *Das Messiasgeheimnis in den Evangelien*, both published in 1901, and together constituting, in Schweitzer's view, the final refutation of the quest of the historical Jesus. The chapter is headed 'Thoroughgoing Scepticism and Thoroughgoing Eschatology'; the scepticism is Wrede's contribution, the eschatology Schweitzer's.

Wrede's contribution was to put in question what had hitherto been a widely agreed starting point in studying the life of Jesus, the historical character of Mark's Gospel. For Wrede Mark was a dogmatic theologian, whose narrative was designed not so much to give an account of real events as to defend a belief in Jesus as Messiah, a belief Jesus himself never shared. The repeated emphasis on secrecy in Mark's Gospel therefore represents not a historical desire on the part of Jesus to restrain inappropriate messianic enthusiasm, but rather Mark's own invention to explain the embarrassing lack of material in the Jesus tradition supporting the church's (historically unfounded) belief that Jesus both was and claimed to be the Messiah.

Schweitzer's contribution (following and developing the work of Johannes Weiss, *Die Predigt Jesu vom Reiche Gottes* of 1892) was to challenge the liberal Protestant view of Jesus as primarily an ethical teacher, a view which could be sustained only by treating as unhistorical the pronounced eschatological dimension in the Gospels' account of his ministry. Jesus was not, he claimed, an inoffensive modern liberal, but a man of his own times, a fanatically eschatological prophet, expecting and promoting the immediate coming of the kingdom of God. The failure of this mission led to Jesus' own ultimate disillusionment, and left the church with a monumental task of theological reconstruction.

The effect of these studies was not only to call in question the specific accounts of Jesus which had emerged from the 'quest', but also to place an apparently unbridgeable gulf between the historical Jesus and the portrait offered by the evangelists. An important work by Martin Kähler (not noticed by Schweitzer) had already in 1892 proposed a distinction between *Der sogenannte historische Jesus und der geschichtliche, biblische Christus* (the latter being, in Kähler's view, the 'real' Christ, the former a false trail of no value), and German scholarship was soon to accept this terminology as axiomatic. The whole enterprise of searching for the historical Jesus was thus shown to be suspect in principle as well as harzardous in practice, and Schweitzer felt justified in pronouncing it dead.

A further blow to the quest soon came from a different perspective, with the rise of form criticism, which offered new literary grounds for questioning the historical basis of the Gospel traditions. In the hands of its most prominent practitioners, K.L. Schmidt, M. Dibelius and R. Bultmann, New Testament form criticism postulated an extended period of oral tradition during which the traditions which began from the historical Jesus were subject to unlimited modification and accretion to fit the developing life and thought of the early Christian commu-

nities. Allied with an existentialist philosophy, particularly in the thought of Bultmann, this literary approach left little prospect of ever getting behind the 'Christ of faith', since it was assumed that the early Christians, like good existentialists, were concerned not with bare facts, but with what was significant about the past as understood in terms of the current faith of the church. Following Kähler's terminology mentioned above, a distinction came to be taken for granted between *Historie* (bare factuality) and *Geschichte* (significant history); since the latter was taken to be the concern of early Christianity, there was little future in expecting the Gospels to offer us the former. (For a careful critique of this existentialist view of early Christian attitudes to the historical life and character of Jesus, see Stanton, 1974.)

Bultmann's position is summed up in his *Jesus* ([1926] 1934), which is deliberately a study of Jesus' *teaching* rather than his life. The introduction to this book includes the well-known sentence: 'I do indeed think that we can now know almost nothing concerning the life and personality of Jesus, since the early Christian sources show no interest in either, are moreover fragmentary and often legendary; and other sources about Jesus do not exist' (p. 8). On this basis the study of Jesus' life and personality in the preceding 150 years is dismissed as 'fantastic and romantic'.

From the 1920s on Bultmann dominated New Testament scholarship in Germany, and indeed in the world as a whole. It is then hardly surprising that, at least in Germany, the writing of 'lives of Jesus' virtually came to a halt among those who made any pretension to academic respectability.

The 'new quest'
This title derives from that of a book by J.M. Robinson (1959), which chronicles and supports the early stages of a 'revolt' within the school of Bultmann. The launching of this new approach is normally credited to Ernst Käsemann ([1954] 1964), though others within the Bultmannian group were also developing similar ideas, notably Ernst Fuchs (especially an essay of 1956, published in Fuchs's *Studies of the Historical Jesus*, trans. 1964). The proposal was not to abandon the insights of Bultmannian form criticism, but to recognize that, while the

fragmentary nature of the oral tradition might not allow a historical reconstruction of the *outline* of Jesus' ministry, sufficient of its key themes, both in his teaching and lifestyle, emerge in the tradition to allow a responsible portrait to be presented.

The first full-scale 'life' of Jesus to result from this methodological rethinking was that of G. Bornkamm ([1956] 1960). Here is none of the confident reconstruction of historical detail which marked at least some of the practitioners of the 'old quest', but a painstaking attempt, with due critical rigour, to 'compile the main historically indisputable traits, and to present the rough outlines of Jesus' person and history' (p. 53). The book is thus more an anthology of themes and characteristics of Jesus' teaching and activity than a 'story' as such. Another significant representative of this new thinking was the article 'Jesus Christus' by Hans Conzelmann in *Religion in Geschichte und Gegenwart* of 1959 (published as *Jesus*, trans. J.R. Lord, 1973).

These studies by leading followers of Bultmann marked the end of the 'no-go' period in the study of the historical Jesus in mainstream German scholarship, and the movement has continued, even though the simultaneous rise of redaction criticism has to some extent diverted attention from the subject matter of the evangelists to their own theological interests.

But, dominant as Bultmann was, his views did not control the whole of New Testament scholarship. The first half of the twentieth century did not see the same proliferation of lives of Jesus as before Schweitzer, but the quest had not been totally abandoned. An important and quite individual study was by Joseph Klausner, *Jesus of Nazareth*, published in Hebrew in 1922 and in English in 1925. In many ways Klausner foreshadows several more recent studies of Jesus from the Jewish perspective, setting him within his own cultural context and arguing that it is subsequent theological development which has turned a Jewish teacher into the Son of God of Christian orthodoxy. Other 'lives' continued essentially in the liberal tradition condemned by Schweitzer, such as S.J. Case's *Jesus: a New Biography* of 1927 and Maurice Goguel's *La Vie de Jésus* of 1932.

British scholarship, while not uninfluenced by the work of Bultmann and his followers, adopted a characteristically more conservative approach. One of the foremost British advocates of form criticism was Vincent Taylor, but his acceptance of the literary methods of the German scholars did not carry with it an acquiescence in their historical scepticism. Along with a series of studies in New Testament Christology, Taylor issued in 1954 a full-scale account of *The Life and Ministry of Jesus*, in which he takes issue with the prevailing scepticism on the possibility of writing a life of Jesus. He takes the outline of Mark's Gospel as his framework, and offers a more detailed chronological reconstruction of the development of Jesus' ministry than had been attempted for a long time (or indeed since).

Other British scholars, while not offering full-scale 'lives', represented a similar resistance to the radical scepticism of German scholarship, among them T.W. Manson, William Manson, A.M. Hunter and C.H. Dodd. Dodd especially continued to work at the area of history and the Gospels, and in particular attempted in *Historical Tradition in the Fourth Gospel* of 1963 to defend the use of John as a source of historical data about the life of Jesus. Earlier scholarship had virtually taken it for granted that John was a late and theologically motivated Gospel, and that therefore such historical data as might be available should be sought in the synoptic Gospels, but Dodd argued for an independent and valuable historical tradition used by John as well. (This line of reasoning was later to be taken further in J.A.T. Robinson's *The Priority of John* of 1985, arguing that John is not only *a* source of historical data, but the *primary* source, and constructing on that basis an account of Jesus' life which, while different in shape from that of Vincent Taylor, almost rivals it in confident reconstruction of the chronological development.) Dodd's life's work culminated in a deceptively simple account of the life and teaching of Jesus (Dodd, 1970), which represents the quintessence of the 'British alternative' to Bultmannian historical scepticism.

Even in Germany, however, there were alternative approaches which were not dependent on the Bultmannian 'new quest'. In 1957 Ethelbert Stauffer published *Jesu: Gestalt und*

Geschichte (trans. 1960, *Jesus and His Story*), not so much a life of Jesus as the prolegomena to one. Stauffer professes to eschew 'interpretation', and to offer only historical fact. His method is to call on a wide range of extra-biblical sources, primarily Jewish, to illuminate the Gospel stories, and the result is a much more optimistic assessment of the historical worth of the latter, and of the possibility of providing not only a portrait of Jesus but an impressive array of factual data to support it.

Joachim Jeremias has been more influential. Drawing on his impressive knowledge both of Aramaic language and of the history and culture of first-century Judaism, he wrote numerous studies of aspects of Jesus' life and teaching, aiming always to get behind the Gospel accounts as nearly as possible to the actual words of Jesus. His work culminated in *Die Verkündigung Jesu* of 1971, the first volume of a planned New Testament theology, the rest of which was never written (trans. 1971, *New Testament Theology, Part One: The Proclamation of Jesus*). An introductory section sets out Jeremias's approach to the Aramaic reconstruction of Jesus' sayings, and concludes that 'in the Synoptic Tradition it is the inauthenticity, and not the authenticity, of the sayings of Jesus that must be demonstrated.' The rest of the book offers a detailed reconstruction of the themes of Jesus' teaching in the light of their cultural setting, one of the most important such studies written this century, and one which exudes confidence in our ability to know the mind of the historical Jesus.

More recent developments

Jeremias's work points the way to the most fruitful aspect of continuing studies of the historical Jesus, the increasing readiness to set him firmly in the context of the Jewish world of his time, combined with a growing acquaintance among New Testament scholars with the historical data outside the New Testament which make this possible.

N.T. Wright (Neill and Wright, 1988, p. 379) has dubbed this new phase of scholarship the 'third quest'. The title has not caught on very widely, and Wright would be the first to admit that the scholars he treats together under this head represent a wide variety of starting points and conclusions. But his terminology does help

to emphasize that in contrast with the extreme historical caution of the Bultmannian scholars who launched the 'new quest', more recent Jesus studies (since roughly the early 1970s) have been markedly more optimistic about the possibility of a truly historical account of Jesus, and markedly more successful in utilizing a wide range of non-biblical historical data in producing it.

On the fringes of this development have been those accounts of Jesus (often written at a semi-popular level) which have located him, in deliberate defiance of the Gospel accounts, in the mainstream of Jewish nationalistic liberation movements. Best known of these was the work of S.G.F. Brandon, *Jesus and the Zealots* of 1967; others included H.J. Schonfield's and J. Carmichael's accounts. But Martin Hengel, one of the leading authorities on the Zealot movement, has decisively rejected such reconstructions in a series of studies, and a magisterial collection of essays edited by E. Bammel and C.F.D. Moule (*Jesus and the Politics of his Day* of 1984) has further undermined this approach.

Other 'alternative Jesuses' continue to be offered in recent writing, generally more at the level of journalism than of scholarship. An exception, however, is the work of Morton Smith (*Jesus the Magician* of 1978), who grounds his view of Jesus on various data derived from second-century and later writings, mainly gnostic, on the express basis that the New Testament Gospels represent a ruthless and successful cover-up by Christian 'orthodoxy' of a historical Jesus whose teachings and behaviour they found embarrassing.

The application of recent Jewish studies to the question of the historical Jesus was given an important impetus by Geza Vermes (1973). His attempt to locate Jesus in the real world of first-century Judaism (as a Galilean holy man, or 'charismatic', rather than in the context of the rabbinic establishment) was welcomed, even by those who could not accept his reduction of the Christological titles of the New Testament to meanings consistent with Jewish orthodoxy. This was one of a series of Jewish studies which have attempted to reclaim Jesus for Judaism (and therefore to dismiss Christianity as the invention of his followers).

A more sophisticated study by Ben Meyer (1979) also chides traditional New Testament scholarship for failing to appreciate the Jewish context and focus of Jesus' ministry, but offers a clearly Jewish Jesus whose challenge to the existing character of Israel inevitably (and deliberately) gave rise to a new movement distinct from the Judaism which rejected him. Meyer begins with a long methodological discussion, in which he takes issue with Bultmannian historical scepticism, and his discussion gives unusual historical weight to some of the more 'theological' pronouncements credited to Jesus in the Gospel tradition.

Anthony Harvey (1982) writes in full awareness of the results of critical study of the Gospels, and with no desire to belittle their significance, but still believes that the mood in New Testament scholarship, partly as a result of the application of advancing archaeological and other historical knowledge, has moved significantly towards recognizing 'the basic historical reliability of the gospels'. His study of the 'constraints' (political, legal, cultural and theological) imposed on Jesus' ministry by his historical setting has the effect of 'earthing' that ministry in a real period of history, and so increasing its historical credibility. The issue of how it was possible for Jesus to present a challenge to existing views and practices while necessarily operating within the cultural and intellectual context of those very norms, is one which is basic to any study of the historical Jesus, and which has been helpfully analysed in much recent work in this area (see, for example, J. Riches, *Jesus and the Transformation of Judaism* of 1980).

E.P. Sanders's earlier work, *Paul and Palestinian Judaism*, had successfully challenged the traditional Christian (and especially Lutheran) view of Pharisaic Judaism and of Christianity's relation to it. In *Jesus and Judaism* (1985) he attempted to explain how Jesus, whom he saw as an orthodox and law-abiding Jew in the Pharisaic tradition, contrived so to antagonize the majority of his own people as to be executed. The study is presented as a resolutely *historical* investigation, with no theological presuppositions, and is based on the assumption that the tradition of Jesus' *sayings* can hardly ever be treated as historically grounded. It is in the accounts of Jesus' activity that he seeks the explanation, and finds it in Jesus' mission as prophet of a new kingdom of God which was to include 'sinners' without requiring their repentance, and which would require a new temple. It was above all his cavalier attitude to the temple, the focus of Jewish national and religious identity and pride, which alienated Jews of all persuasions, and led to his death. Sanders's book represents a far more historically 'sceptical' approach than those just considered, but is at the same time in direct opposition to earlier existentialist thought in giving priority to historical fact, however hard it may be to obtain.

One of the more remarkable recent contributions is a 'historical novel' by Gerd Theissen, *Der Schatten des Galiläers* of 1986 (trans. 1987, *The Shadow of the Galilean*). Writing with a light touch, but drawing on an encyclopedic knowledge of the history of the period, Theissen aims to bring the historical Jesus to life by recreating for the reader the tensions of life for a Jew under Roman occupation and the various currents in contemporary Judaism. It is an outstandingly successful experiment, resulting in a realistic awareness of the world in which Jesus carried out his mission, and of the ways in which he would have been perceived by his contemporaries.

These quite varied books are merely a few representatives of a growing trend to search for the 'real' Jesus by using external data to control our understanding of the Gospel accounts. In the last decade of the twentieth century this trend is firmly established, and its literary products, even if far from agreeing with each other on the nature of the reconstruction offered, represent a consensus that the quest of the historical Jesus is a legitimate and potentially fruitful exercise.

See also BIBLICAL CRITICISM AND INTERPRETATION 2: NEW TESTAMENT; CHRISTOLOGY; FAITH AND HISTORY; RESURRECTION.

Bibliography

Bornkamm, G. [1956] 1960: *Jesus of Nazareth*, trans. I. and F. McLuskey. London: Hodder and Stoughton.

Bultmann, R. [1926] 1934: *Jesus and the Word*, trans. L.P. Smith and E. Huntress. New York: Scribner.

Dodd, C.H. 1970: *The Founder of Christianity*. London: Collins.

Harvey, A.E. 1982: *Jesus and the Constraints of History*. London: Duckworth.

Käsemann, E. [1954] 1964: The problem of the historical Jesus. In *Essays on New Testament Themes*, trans. W.J. Montague. London: SCM Press, pp. 15–47.

Keck, L.E. 1971: *A Future for the Historical Jesus*. Nashville: Abingdon.

Kissinger, W.S. 1985: *The Lives of Jesus: A History and Bibliography*. New York: Garland.

McArthur, H.K., ed. 1969: *In Search of the Historical Jesus*. New York: Scribner.

Marshall, I.H. 1977: *I Believe in the Historical Jesus*. London: Hodder and Stoughton.

Meyer, B.F. 1979: *The Aims of Jesus*. London: SCM Press.

Neill, S., and Wright, N.T. 1988: *The Interpretation of the New Testament 1861–1986*. Oxford: Oxford University Press.

Reimarus, H.S. [1778] 1971: *Reimarus: Fragments*, trans. R.S. Fraser, ed. C.H. Talbert. London: SCM Press.

Robinson, J.M. 1959: *A New Quest of the Historical Jesus*. London: SCM Press.

Sanders, E.P. 1985: *Jesus and Judaism*. London: SCM Press.

Schweitzer, A. [1906] 1910: *The Quest of the Historical Jesus*, trans. W. Montgomery. London: A & C Black.

Stanton, G.N. 1974: *Jesus of Nazareth in New Testament Preaching*. Cambridge: Cambridge University Press.

Strauss, D.F. [1835–6] 1973: *The Life of Jesus Critically Examined*, trans. George Eliot, ed. P.C. Hodgson. London: SCM Press.

Tatum, W.B. 1982: *In Quest of Jesus: A Guidebook*. Atlanta: John Knox.

Taylor, V. 1954: *The Life and Ministry of Jesus*. London: Macmillan.

Vermes, G. 1973: *Jesus the Jew*. London: Collins.

RICHARD FRANCE

history and faith See FAITH AND HISTORY.

history of dogma See DOCTRINE AND DOGMA.

history of religions school The 'history of religions school' (to use the traditional English translation of the German term *Religionsgeschichtliche Schule*) was founded in 1890, and was originally known as the 'little Göttingen faculty'. The school was destined to exercise considerable influence over biblical scholarship and Christological speculation in the first third of the twentieth century. In its early stages, the school was characterized primarily by little more

than its hostility towards the leading representative of liberal Protestant theology, Albrecht Ritschl. Particular criticism was directed against his methods of biblical interpretation, which appeared to be insensitive to the historical background of Christianity in Judaism.

However, other characteristics soon began to emerge. From its outset, the school proved itself to be of major importance in relation to both Old and New Testament studies, on account of its insistence that the religious developments of both Old and New Testaments, as well as those of the early church, had to be seen in the context of other religions. Biblical religion was not something distinct in its own right; its origins could be understood in terms of general developments in religious thinking at the time.

Hermann Gunkel's *Schöpfung und Chaos* of 1895 derived much of the Old Testament's themes of creation and chaos from Babylonian mythology. Gunkel argued that the basic elements of the Old Testament's notions of 'creation and chaos at the beginning and the end of time' were to be derived directly from Babylonian creation myths. The ideas in question were not distinctive to the Old Testament, but were derived from other religions with which Israel came into contact, especially during its periods of exile.

Wilhelm Bossuet's *Kyrios Christos* of 1913 considered the development of early Christian ideas in terms of their Hellenistic-Jewish context. Bossuet argued that the designation of Jesus as 'Lord (*kyrios*)' took place in a Gentile context, and related to the tendency of Gentile Christians to treat Jesus Christ as the central figure of a mystery cult, such as those which had achieved widespread influence in the Greco-Roman culture of the period. In a later work, *Hauptprobleme der Gnosis* of 1907, he explored the relation of Christianity to Gnosticism. Holding it as self-evident that Gnosticism antedated Christianity (an idea now regarded as highly problematic), Bossuet sought to derive a number of central Christian beliefs from their original Gnostic context. This development would have a significant impact upon Rudolf Bultmann and other New Testament scholars in the period after the First World War. Thus Richard Reitzenstein (1861–1931) argued in his *Die hellenistischen Mysterienreligionen* of 1910 that Paul was deeply indebted both to Gnosticism and to the Hellenistic mystery religions for much of his theology.

Other major personalities within the school included Johannes Weiss and William Wrede, noted for their contributions to New Testament eschatology and history, and Ernst Troeltsch, widely regarded as the systematic theologian within the movement.

See also BIBLICAL CRITICISM AND INTERPRETATION (1: OLD TESTAMENT and 2: NEW TESTAMENT).

Bibliography
Hahn, H.F. 1966: *The Old Testament in Modern Research*. London: SCM Press, pp. 83–118.
Kümmel, W.G. 1973: *The New Testament: The History of the Interpretation of its Problems*. London: SCM Press.
Morgan, R., 1990: History of religions school. In *A Dictionary of Biblical Interpretation*, ed. R.J. Coggins and J.L. Houlden. London: SCM Press, pp. 291–2.
Morgan, R., with Barton, J. 1988: *Biblical Interpretation*. Oxford: Oxford University Press.

ALISTER E. MCGRATH

Hodge, Charles (1797–1878) North American Reformed theologian. Ordained into the Presbyterian church in 1821 and professor of exegetical and didactic theology at Princeton for most of his career, he was a vigorous and influential champion of Calvinism and a chronicler of the political and ecclesiastical events of the Presbyterian church. He argued against religious experience at the expense of understanding, whether it were the mysticism of European romanticism or the revivalism associated with Charles Finney in the USA; and he opposed the moral optimism of contemporary romantic/idealist philosophies and Darwinism, using rational, propositional methods to stress the Calvinist doctrines of sin, biblical infallibility and the sovereignty of God in election. He wrote commentaries on Romans (1835), Ephesians (1856), 1 Corinthians (1857) and 2 Corinthians (1859); his major work, *Systematic Theology* of 1871–3, is still in use.

Bibliography
Hodge, A.A. 1880: *The Life of Charles Hodge*. New York.
Thorp, W., ed. 1946: *The Lives of Eighteen from Princeton*, article on Hodge by J.O. Nelson. Princeton, NJ.
Thorp, W., ed. 1985: *Reformed Theology in America*. Grand Rapids, Mi.

Holland See PROTESTANT THEOLOGY: NETHERLANDS.

Holocaust, Christian responses to See EVIL, PROBLEM OF; JUDAISM AND CHRISTIANITY.

Holy Spirit See GOD; PNEUMATOLOGY.

homosexuality See SEXUAL ETHICS.

Hopkins, Gerard Manley (1844–1889). English Catholic poet. Whilst at Balliol College, Oxford, he was influenced by E.B. Pusey and the Oxford movement, and he joined the Roman Catholic church in 1866, becoming a Jesuit priest in 1877. Having destroyed his early manuscripts in the belief that his poetry was incompatible with his religious vocation, he was encouraged by his superiors to take up writing again when a ship carrying Catholic exiles from Germany was shipwrecked. The result was his longest and most ambitious poem, 'The Wreck of the Deutschland'. After a period as a parish priest in Liverpool, he became professor of Greek at the Royal University, Dublin (1884–9). His poems, which include 'The Windhover: to Christ our Lord', are characterized by an intense feeling both for the essence of the object being viewed (which he termed 'inscape'), and for the subjective effect of viewing (which he termed 'instress'). Though not an original thinker, his highly original style, which poetically rendered the freedom of the spoken language, and his spiritual and artistic sensibility, mark him out as a major English poet.

Bibliography
Cotter, J.F. 1972: *Inscape: The Christology and Poetry of G.M. Hopkins*. Pittsburgh.
Kenny, A. 1988: *God and Two Poets: Clough and Hopkins*. London.
Kitchen, P. 1978: *G.M. Hopkins*. London.

human nature, doctrine of See ANTHROPOLOGY, CHRISTIAN.

Hume, David (1711–1776)   Scottish philosopher and historian, born in Edinburgh and frequently regarded as one of the key figures in the so-called Scottish Enlightenment, along with Adam Smith and James Boswell. He published *A Treatise of Human Nature* in 1739–40, and when this was not well received, rewrote it in two volumes: *An Enquiry Concerning Human Understanding* and *An Enquiry Concerning the Principles of Morals*. Still not receiving public recognition, he turned to history, and published a history of Great Britain in several volumes, for which he became widely known. He was also renowned during his life as a statesman, economist and army officer. His *Dialogues Concerning Natural Religion*, an attack on natural religion, was published after his death, in 1779.

Philosophically, Hume wanted to apply Newtonian scientific method to the study of humanity. He is most well-known for his work on causality. He argued that there is no logical link between cause and effect, only conclusions which we have drawn from repeated observation. Thus we can have no certainty that one event will follow from another; we can only assert a degree of probability. Hume also questioned ideas such as the existence of a personal identity which persists over time. His scepticism extends into metaphysics, with the contention that the existence of God cannot be demonstrated, but only seen as a probability.

Hume was – and still is – hugely influential, sometimes regarded as the greatest English-speaking philosopher. He was a crucial forerunner of modern empiricist philosophy.

Bibliography

Hume, D. 1874–5: *The Philosophical Works of David Hume*, 4 vols, ed. T. H. Green and T.H. Grose. London.

Mossner, E.C. [1954] 1980: *The Life of David Hume*, 2nd edn. Oxford.

Passmore, J. 1952: *Hume's Intentions*. Cambridge.

I

Iceland See PROTESTANT THEOLOGY: SCANDINAVIA.

idealism See HEGELIANISM; ROMANTICISM.

impassibility of God See SUFFERING, DIVINE.

incarnation Incarnation is a central Christian doctrine, according to which the Son or Word of God, the second Person of the divine Trinity, assumed a fleshly human body in Jesus Christ and lived a historical existence on this planet, subject to all the constraints and limitations of such an existence. As will be explained, this is a highly complex belief and its full elaboration is peculiar to Christianity. However, it should be noted that in other religions too there has been belief that divine beings have appeared on earth as human beings; for instance, in Hinduism Krishna is claimed to have been an *avatar* or descent of the high god Vishnu. The non-Christian parallels differ in various respects from what Christians understand by incarnation, but there is enough resemblance to make it clear that something like incarnation is a widespread and radical idea in the history of religion. This is not surprising, for if the goal of religion is some form of union between the human and the divine, then incarnation would seem to instantiate such a union in the most intimate way conceivable.

Because of the difficulties and complexities of the belief, it took a long time to formulate in a satisfactory manner. It was already taking shape in the New Testament, but it continued to be the subject of controversies and conciliar pronouncements for three or four centuries.

The solutions worked out during that period remained normative for the great majority of Christians for more than a thousand years, but from about 1750 onwards, following on the Enlightenment, the problem of incarnation has been re-opened and is still being debated among theologians today.

Clearly, one could entertain the thought of an incarnation only if one already had certain presuppositions. These would include the existence of God; more specifically, of a benevolent God who sufficiently cares for his creatures to be willing to accept the kind of involvement with them implied in incarnation. It is hard to see how a God who is 'wholly other' or utterly transcendent could become incarnate. On the other hand, it would seem to be also presupposed that a human being would have the capacity for receiving God, as required in an incarnation. Since it was the God of the Hebrew Scriptures who was presupposed by the early Christian theologians, we must ask whether the conception of God we find there would conduce to belief in an incarnation. The question cannot be answered by a straight affirmative. The Hebrew God was decidedly transcendent. Yet he was also deeply concerned with his people, and committed to them by a series of covenants. Again, while there was a strict prohibition of images because no creaturely image could truly represent the transcendent God, it was also claimed that the human being had been created in the 'image and likeness' of God (Gen. 1: 26).

It must be conceded that although the Hebrew conception of God and his relation to the world does not altogether rule out the idea of incarnation, it certainly does not make it easy, and this may explain why the New Testament writers, who were themselves steeped in the

269

Hebrew tradition, have obvious difficulty in moving in the direction of a belief in incarnation, and it is only in the very latest of the New Testament writings, especially John's Gospel, that we have what appears to be a definitely incarnational teaching.

Possibly the first followers of Jesus thought of him as an eschatological prophet (Schillebeeckx, [1974] 1979, p. 473), and though the term 'prophet' was a highly honorific one and susceptible of further development, it did not imply incarnation. The first detailed Christology is found in the letters of Paul, and although one must acknowledge that the question is not completely settled, it seems unlikely that Paul teaches an incarnational Christology. His basic teaching rests on a comparison of Christ with Adam. The latter had been created to manifest the 'image and likeness' of God but had failed. Jesus is the new creation, the new Adam or last Adam who, by succeeding, becomes the 'image of the invisible God' (Col. 1: 15). Some scholars, following the path of kenotic Christology, have read a fully incarnational teaching into the Christ-hymn used by Paul in Philippians 2: 5–11, which might be understood to speak of a pre-existent Christ who becomes incarnate to follow the way of the cross. But recent exegetes, such as J.A.T. Robinson and James Dunn, claim that there is no need to invoke such an interpretation. The language does in fact fit very well into Paul's main Christological teaching about the first and last Adams (Dunn, 1980, pp. 114–17).

Although passages indicative of an emerging incarnational teaching may be found in some books of the New Testament, for instance Matthew's Gospel and the Epistle to the Hebrews, a full-blown incarnational view comes only with John's Gospel, usually dated to near the end of the first century. John distinguishes without separating God and the Word or Logos. In paradoxical language, he says, 'The Word was with God, and the Word was God', or, in an alternative translation, 'The Word dwelt with God, and what God was, the Word was' (John 1: 1). The language is paradoxical because it simultaneously asserts both identity and difference. The same paradox appears later in the Gospel: 'I and the Father are one', balanced by the more complex 'I am in the Father and the Father in me' (10: 30; 14: 11). In 1: 14 incarnation is actually asserted: 'And the Word became flesh and dwelt among us, full of grace and truth.'

It is important to note this paradoxical character in John's assertions, for when it is said that the Word became flesh, such language would be nonsense if it were taken literally. In using the imagery of the 'Word' of God and in asserting that the Word is both identical to and distinct from God, John has indicated that he is using a theological style of language that calls for its own theological hermeneutic. He is also careful to leave an open space, as it were, for interpretation. 'The Word became flesh' is not spelled out. It cannot be a literal, descriptive assertion, and 'flesh' is as much a metaphor as 'Word'. To become flesh is to enter the world of the earthly and historical, but there is no attempt to say just how God or the Word could do this.

John's incarnational Christology became the pattern for future thinking on the subject, and increasingly attempts were made to convert his paradoxical and metaphorical language into a precise descriptive 'scientific' language. This was perhaps an inevitable consequence of the encounter between Christianity and Hellenistic culture, and especially the encounter with the philosophical ideas current among educated people of that time. For instance, John's understanding of the Word or Logos was drawn mainly from the Old Testament, but it soon became identified with the Greek notion of the Logos, the immanent rational principle of the universe. The church was soon embarked on a long series of controversies in which attempts were made to clarify and to render more precise this teaching.

The Arian controversy at the beginning of the fourth century was the best-known of these disputes. In John's Gospel, Jesus had declared that 'The Father is greater than I' (14: 29), but many Christians now believed that, as the eternal Word, Jesus must be declared fully equal to the Father. Arius was believed to have taught the subordination of Christ to the Father, and this teaching was condemned by the Council of Nicaea in 325 when the expression *homoousios* (of the same being) was adopted to indicate that the Father and the Son share eternally the same nature.

In saying that 'the Word was made flesh', the Gospel of John was ambiguous, for this could be understood as meaning either that the Word had assumed humanity in its completeness, or that the Logos simply animated a physical body. When in the fourth century the latter view was taught by Apollinarius, it was condemned by the Council of Constantinople (381) and it was asserted that the Word had assumed a complete humanity, a soul as well as a body.

It was now felt necessary to clarify further the relation of the divine and the human in Christ, especially since another alleged heretic of the time, Nestorius, was said (probably wrongly) to be teaching a dualistic doctrine of the person of Christ. This Nestorian view was condemned at the Council of Ephesus (431), but there was by now so much confusion that a further ecumenical council was summoned to meet at Chalcedon in 451 to try to clear up the issues. This Council produced the Chalcedonian definition. This may be regarded as the classic statement of orthodox Christian belief in the incarnation and even today it remains the norm for the great majority of Christians, though there have always been dissentients in the so-called 'monophysite' churches.

Chalcedon teaches that in the one person or hypostasis of Jesus Christ there concur two natures, a complete humanity and a complete divinity, and that they are united in his person 'without confusion, without change, without division, without separation'. No attempt is made to give a detailed explanation of this teaching, and it has been generally understood as setting the boundaries within which theological speculation would be permissible. Although there were in fact Christological controversies after Chalcedon, its influence, apart from the monophysites, continued to be paramount right through the Middle Ages and beyond. Even the Reformation did not overturn the Chalcedonian definition. It is true that Luther and Melanchthon criticized the abstract language of the classical Christology and called for a more definitely soteriological formulation, but that phase passed, and in the post-Reformation period the traditional beliefs about incarnation remained normative.

Only in the eighteenth century did there arise a serious challenge to the incarnational Christology. The Enlightenment had brought with it both the historical criticism of the biblical sources of Christology and the philosophical criticism of supernaturalism, along with the entire conceptuality which the church had inherited from the patristic age. Friedrich Schleiermacher, often called the father of modern theology, was a major influence in reshaping the church's understanding of Jesus Christ. On the negative side, he offered a searching analysis of the two natures teaching of Chalcedon, which he claimed to be incoherent. But his main purpose was affirmative, and in order to achieve it, he reversed the order of Christology. Instead of beginning with the eternal Word who in an act of condescension assumes a human existence, Schleiermacher began from the human Jesus, whom he interpreted as the completion of the creation of man, 'the one in whom the creation of human nature, which up to this point had existed only in a provisional state, was perfected' (Schleiermacher, [1821–2] 1928, p. 374). We can see in this view, which Schleiermacher did not hesitate to call a 'natural' Christology, an echo of that view of Jesus Christ as the new Adam taught by Paul and probably well-known in the earliest decades of the church. Schleiermacher, of course, gives it a more naturalistic and humanistic flavour.

The new style of thinking which Schleiermacher inaugurated has, with many variations, persisted down to the present. There has indeed been resistance, in the nineteenth century by Søren Kierkegaard and in the twentieth by Karl Barth and those who were influenced by him. The new approach has spread from Protestant to Catholic theologians, though some of the latter still defend the traditional conception of incarnation.

But those who embrace the post-Schleiermacher type of Christology – or, at least, many of them – would claim that they have not given up belief in incarnation. John A.T. Robinson, for instance, says that incarnation does not necessarily mean the pre-existence of a supernatural being who, at a certain moment of time, takes flesh:

> I believe that the word can just as truly and just as biblically (in fact, more truly and more biblically) be applied to another way of understanding it. This is: that one

who was totally and utterly a man – and had never been anything other than a man or more than a man – so completely embodied what was from the beginning the meaning and purpose of God's self-expression (whether conceived in terms of his Spirit, his Wisdom, his Word, or the intimately personal relation of Sonship) that it could be said and had to be said of that man, 'He was God's man' or 'God was in Christ' or even that he *was* God for us.

(Robinson, 1973, p. 179)

See also CHRISTOLOGY; DOCTRINE AND DOGMA; GOD; SOTERIOLOGY.

Bibliography
Adam, Karl 1957: *The Christ of Faith*. London: Burns and Oates.
Baillie, Donald 1948: *God Was in Christ*. London: Faber and Faber.
Barth, Karl [1953–5] 1956–8: *Church Dogmatics* IV/1 and 2, trans. Edinburgh: T & T Clark.
Cullmann, Oscar 1959: *The Christology of the New Testament*. London: SCM Press.
Dunn, J.D.G. 1980: *Christology in the Making*. London: SCM Press.
Fuller, R.H. 1965: *The Foundations of New Testament Christology*. New York: Scribners.
McGrath, A.E. 1986: *The Making of Modern German Christology*. Oxford: Blackwell.
Macquarrie, John 1990: *Jesus Christ in Modern Thought*. London: SCM Press.
Moltmann, J. [1989] 1990: *The Way of Jesus Christ*, trans. London: SCM Press.
Pannenberg, W. [1964] 1968: *Jesus, God and Man*, trans. London: SCM Press.
Robinson, J.A.T. 1973: *The Human Face of God*. London: SCM Press.
Schillebeeckx, Edward [1974] 1979: *Jesus, an Experiment in Christology*, trans. London: Collins.
Schleiermacher, F.D.E. [1821–2] 1928: *The Christian Faith*, trans. of 1831 edn. Edinburgh: T & T Clark.
Tillich, Paul 1957: *Systematic Theology*, vol. 2, Chicago: Chicago University Press.
Torrance, T.F. 1969: *Space, Time and Incarnation*. Oxford: Oxford University Press.

JOHN MACQUARRIE

Indian Christian thought Christianity became established in the Indian subcontinent at a relatively early stage. It seems likely that western merchants discovered the existence of the Pālghāt gap at an early stage, thus facilitating trade with southern India. Traditionally, it is believed that the apostle Thomas founded the Indian Mar Thoma church in the first century; even allowing for a degree of pious exaggeration here, there are excellent reasons for believing that Christianity was an indigenous element of the Indian religious scene by the fourth century. European travellers reaching India by land, prior to the opening of the ocean trading tour by the Portuguese navigator Vasco da Gama in May 1498, regularly report the presence of Christians in the region.

The arrival of the Portuguese may be taken to signal the opening of a significant new period in Indian Christianity, in which indigenous Christian traditions were supplemented by imported versions of the gospel, each reflecting aspects of its European context. The papal bull *Aeterna Regis Clementia* (21 June 1481) gave the Portuguese monarch the authority to trade with hitherto undiscovered lands, as well as investing him with 'spiritual power and authority from Capes Bojador and Nam as far as the Indies'. The bishopric of Goa was established as the potential base for a campaign of Portuguese evangelization of the interior.

The importance of this settlement was considerably enhanced through the arrival of Francis Xavier on 6 May 1542. A mere two years after having been formally recognized by the pope, the Society of Jesus was thus established in India. Xavier organized an extensive missionary enterprise, including the translation of Christian works into Tamil. As time went on, Dutch, English and French settlers moved into India, bringing their own versions of Christianity with them.

Initially, evangelization was seen as peripheral to the more serious business of trading. The first Anglican clergy in India, for example, were ships' chaplains, appointed by the English East India Company to provide pastoral care and spiritual support for the crews of their ships. However, a growing European presence in the region brought with it the tensions of the European religious situation of the seventeenth century, in which Protestantism and Roman Catholicism were viewed as mutually incompatible and radically divergent versions of Christianity. The establishment of Christianity in Europe inevitably meant that the political interests of Protestant and Roman Catholic nations, such as England and France, were seen as possessing strongly religious dimensions. Religion was one aspect of a broader struggle for political and economic supremacy. As a result, evangelization became increasingly imperative.

Humphrey Prideaux, dean of Norwich (1648–1724), may be regarded as indicative of this spirit of evangelistic adventurism. In his *Account of the English Settlements in the East Indies, together with some proposals for the propagation of Christianity in those parts of the world*, Prideaux pointed to the need to train people for the specific work of evangelism. Prideaux's idea was prophetic: a 'seminary' was to be established in England, with a view to prepare mission workers, until such time as the work could be handed over to agencies based in India itself. In this proposal may be seen the basis of the missionary movement, which was destined to exercise a significant impact over Indian Christianity.

Among the major contributions to European missionary work in India, the following may be singled out for special mention. The first major Protestant mission to India was based at Tranquebar on the Coromandel Coast, about 200 kilometres south of Madras. Among the German Lutheran missionaries of note were Bartholomäus Ziegenbalg (who directed the mission from its founding in 1706 to 1719) and Christian Frederick Schwartz (director from 1750 to 1787). However, the growing political power of Britain in the region inevitably favoured the activities of British missionaries, the first of which (the Baptist William Carey) began work in Bengal in 1793. This was assisted to no small extent by the decision of Clement XIV to suppress the Society of Jesus. The bull *Dominus ac Redemptor* (21 July 1773) abrogated 'all and every one of its functions and ministries'. The missionary activity of the Jesuits in India and elsewhere was thus terminated. Nevertheless, at least fifty Jesuits are known to have continued missionary work in India after the suppression of their order, despite the efforts of the Portuguese to repatriate them.

British missionary societies and individuals were thus able to operate in India without any major opposition from other European agencies.

Nevertheless, they received no support from the British authorities; the East India Company, for example, was opposed to their activities, on the grounds that they might create ill will amongst native Indians, and thus threaten the trade upon which it depended. However, the Charter Act (passed by parliament in London on 13 July 1813) revised the conditions under which the Company was permitted to operate: the new charter gave British missionaries protected status, and a limited degree of freedom to carry out evangelistic work on the Indian subcontinent. The result was inevitable: 'since 1813, Christian missions have never been wholly free from the stigma of undue dependence on government' (Stephen Charles Neill). The new charter also made provision for the establishment of an Anglican bishopric at Calcutta. Under Reginald Heber (1783–1826; Bishop of Calcutta 1823–6) missionary work was expanded considerably, and restricted to Anglicans (Lutheran missionaries being obliged to be re-ordained to allow them to continue operating in the region). Further revisions to the East India Company's charter in 1833 removed some of the restrictions imposed earlier upon missionary work.

It was inevitable that religious tensions would develop. In 1830, the Dharma Sabhā was formed, apparently as a reaction against intrusive forms of westernization in Bengal. The uprising of 1857 (generally referred to as 'the Indian Mutiny' by contemporary English writers) is often regarded as the outcome of this growing resentment at westernization.

It is therefore of considerable importance to explore the development of indigenous Indian approaches to Christianity, rather than note the expansion of theologies of essentially European provenance in the region. In its initial phases, such a theology tended to arise through Hindus assimilating Christianity to their own world view.

Rāmmohun Roy (1772–1833) was born of a Brāhman family in Bengal. His early contacts with Islam (and particularly the mystical tradition of the Sūfīs) led him to conclude that his Hindu religion was corrupted, and required to be reformed. In 1815 he founded the Ātmiya Sabhā, a movement dedicated to the reform of Hinduism which advocated the abolition of *sati* (often spelled '*suttee*': the practice of burning

Hindu widows alive on their husband's funeral pyre). His growing alienation from orthodox Hinduism (evident in his debate with Subramaniah Sāstri) led to an increasing interest in Christianity, which he came to regard as embodying a moral code which would be acceptable to right-thinking Hindus. This idea, which he promoted in his *Precepts of Jesus* of 1820, attracted considerable attention.

It also provoked considerable criticism from within European Christian circles, most notably from the Lutheran Deocar Schmidt. The essence of Schmidt's criticism was that the moral precepts of Christ could not be separated from the theological question of the identity of Christ and the subsequent implications of this for a Trinitarian concept of God. Rāmmohun Roy replied that it was impossible for a Hindu to accept a Trinitarian concept of God; nevertheless, a unitarian understanding of God, linked with an emphasis upon the gospel as a moral code, might well prove acceptable. It was possible for sins to be forgiven without the need for the atonement of Christ, an idea which he regarded as utterly alien to Hinduism (Brāhmo theism, for example, rejects both the ideas of revelation and atonement). In 1829 he founded the Brāhmo Samāj, a theistic society which drew upon ideas derived from both Hinduism and Christianity; among the ideas derived from the latter was the practice of regular congregational worship, then unknown in Hinduism. Under his successor Devendranāth Tagore, however, the Samāj moved in a more definitely Hindu direction. However, aspects of Rāmmohun Roy's critique of orthodox Christology were soon to come under criticism from other Hindus who had converted to Christianity: for example the Bengali writer Krishna Mohan Banerjee argued that there were close affinities between the Vedic idea of Purusha sacrifice and the Christian doctrine of atonement.

Keshub Chunder Sen (1838–1884) developed an approach to Christian theology which rested upon the assumption that Christ brought to fulfilment all that was best in Indian religion. This approach bears a direct resemblance to the western European idea, associated with writers as diverse as Thomas Aquinas and John Calvin, that Christianity brings to fulfilment the aspirations of classic antiquity, as expressed in the culture of ancient Greece and Rome. Unlike

Rāmmohun Roy, however, Keshub embraced the doctrine of the Trinity with enthusiasm. He argued that although *Brahman* was indivisible and indescribable, it could nevertheless be considered in terms of its inner relations of *Sat* ('being'), *Cit* ('reason') and *Ānanda* ('bliss'). These three relations were to be correlated with the Christian understanding of God the Father as 'Being', God the Son as 'Logos', and God the Holy Spirit as 'comforter' or 'bringer of joy and love':

> The New Testament commenced with the birth of the Son of God. The Logos was the beginning of creation and its perfection too was the Logos – the culmination of humanity in the divine son. We have arrived at the last link in the series of created organisms. The last expression of Divinity is Divine Humanity. Having exhibited itself in endless varieties of progressive existence, the primary creative force at last took the form of the Son in Jesus Christ.

This approach was developed by Nehemiah Goreh (1825–1895), who stressed the facility with which it was possible to move from a Hindu notion of God to that now offered by Christianity:

> May we, the sons of India, say that the unity with God, whom our fathers delighted to call 'Sat, Cit, Ananda Brahman', after which they ardently aspired, but in a wrong sense ... God has granted us, their children, to realize in the right sense? Was that aspiration and longing, though misunderstood by them, a presentiment of the future gift? I have often delighted to think so.

A related idea was developed more recently by Raimundo Panikkar in his *Unknown Christ of Hinduism*, in which he argued for the hidden presence of Christ in Hindu practice, especially in relation to matters of justice and compassion.

A similar approach was developed, but with considerably greater acumen, by Brahmabandhab Upadhyaya (1861–1907), based on an analysis of the relation of the Christian faith and its articulation in terms of non-Christian philosophical systems (as in Thomas Aquinas's use of Aristotelianism as a vehicle for his theological exposition). Why should Indian Christians not be at liberty to draw upon indigenous Indian philosophical systems, in undertaking a similar task? Why should not Vedanta be used in the expression of Christian theology, and the Vedas be regarded as the Indian Old Testament? Increasingly, the issue of an authentically Indian Christian theology came to be seen as linked with that of independence from Britain: theological and political self-determination came to be seen as inextricably linked.

There was growing emphasis within Indian thought in the first half of the twentieth century on growing into nationhood (eventually achieved in 1947). Among contributions to a Christian approach to independence, the following may be noted as having particular significance: C.F. Andrews's *The Ideal of Indian Nationality* of 1907, S.K. Datta's *Desire of India* of 1908, S.K. Rudra's *Christ and Modern India* of 1910, and K.T. Paul's *British Connection with India* of 1928.

The move towards independence resulted in Christianity finding itself in competition with rival ideologies: Gandhism and Marxism. A particularly important participant in this debate is Madathiparamil Mammen Thomas (b. 1916). From a Mar Thoma Christian background, M.M. Thomas has come to be regarded as a leading representative of an authentically Indian voice in modern theology. Thomas's critique of Gandhism is of especial interest. In the first place, Thomas was himself initially a Gandhian, only to become disillusioned with what he regarded as its inadequacies and fallacies. In the second, it represents an Indian Christian response to a distinctively Indian ideology. While appreciating its moral strengths, and particularly its protests against the dehumanizing tendencies of 'the machine age', Thomas argues that Gandhism elevated pragmatic strategies – such as *satyagraha* and *swadeshi* – into absolute moral principles, thus initiating a shift towards a form of pharisaic self-righteousness. Thomas argues that this ultimately represents an inadequate understanding of the human predicament, minimizing the effects of sin and masking the human need for redemption:

To attempt to 'spiritualize our politics' on the political plane, if seriously meant, is an expression of human self-righteousness and the doctrine of justification by works. And there may be a lot of difference from the political and ethical point of view between the 'holy war of the past' and 'a war for holiness', but from a religious perspective both equally arise out of man seeking a righteousness of the law in rebellion against the grace of God, and reveal the denial of one's own sinfulness and need of divine redemption.

Thomas regards Gandhi as having reduced Christianity to little more than a moral code or set of principles, and quotes with approval the letter to Gandhi from E. Stanley Jones: 'I think you have grasped certain principles of the Christian faith. You have grasped the principles but missed the person.' A similar criticism is directed against Indian Marxist writers, most notably E.M. Sankaran Namboodiripad, whose ideas Thomas declares to rest upon an inadequate anthropology.

Other issues have come to be of major importance within the Indian context in recent years, most notably the relation of the Christian gospel to the poor. Ideas which apparently owe their origins largely to Latin American LIBERA-TION THEOLOGY have made their appearance in such writings as John Desrochers's *Jesus the Liberator* of 1976 and Sebastian Kappen's *Jesus and Freedom* of 1978. It seems, however, that the continuing exploration of the relationship between Christianity and Hinduism is likely to remain a significant feature of Indian Christian theology for some time. For example, the relation between the Christian doctrine of incarnation and the Hindu notion of *avatar* has emerged as a significant debate within Indian theology (see Chakkarai, 1926). Christopher Sugden and Vinay Samuel summarize eight approaches to this question which may be discerned within contemporary Indian Christian thought:

1 the cosmic Christ includes all the various pluralities of religious experience;
2 Christianity takes shape within a pluralist environment, and so becomes a Christ-centred syncretism;

3 Christ is the unknown force for justice within Hinduism;

4 Christ is the goal of the religious quest of Hinduism;

5 Hinduism is related to Christianity as its Old Testament Scriptures;

6 Christianity is totally discontinuous with Hinduism;

7 the Hindu context gives rise to a specifically Indian form of Christianity;

8 Hinduism is to be addressed with the question of the poor and marginalized within society, a question which Jesus himself validated and addressed.

Finally, a major development within Indian Christianity has attracted considerable attention from theologians and church leaders. On 27 September 1947 the 'Church of South India' was inaugurated through the union of Anglican and Methodist churches in the region with the South India United Church (an amalgamation of Presbyterian and Congregationalist bodies). One of the fundamental principles of the union was the mutual recognition of the validity of Anglican, Methodist, Presbyterian and Congregationalist orders of ministry. Re-ordination was not required of any minister as a result of the union (see ECUMENISM). This development was hailed by many as a move towards church union. By its opponents, however, the union was seen as calling into question the role of the historic episcopate and undermining traditional (especially Anglican) understandings of episcopal ordination.

See also JAPANESE CHRISTIAN THOUGHT; MISSION, THEOLOGY OF; OTHER FAITHS AND CHRISTIANITY.

Bibliography

Boyd, Robin S.H. 1974: *Introduction to Indian Christian Theology*, 2nd edn. Madras: CLT.

Brown, L.W. 1981: *The Indian Christians of St Thomas*, 2nd edn. Cambridge: Cambridge University Press.

Chakkarai, V. 1926: *Jesus the Avatar*. Madras: CLS.

Chakkarai, V. 1932: *The Cross and Indian Thought*. Madras: CLS.

Chenchiah, P. 1938: *Rethinking Christianity in India*. Madras: Sudarisanam.

Gibbs, M.E. 1972: *The Anglican Church in India 1600–1970*. London: SPCK.

Laird, M.A. 1972: *Missionaries and Education in Bengal 1793–1837*. Oxford: Oxford University Press.

Neill, Stephen C. 1984–5: *A History of Christianity in India*, 2 vols. Cambridge: Cambridge University Press.

Panikkar, Raimundo 1981: *The Unknown Christ of Hinduism*. London: DLT.

Philip, T.M. 1986: *The Encounter between Theology and Ideology*. Madras: CLS.

Sugden, C.M.N., and Samuel, V.N. 1988: Indian Christian theology, in S.B. Ferguson and D.F. Wright, eds, *New Dictionary of Theology*. Leicester: Inter-Varsity Press, pp. 335–7.

Thomas, M.M. 1969: *The Acknowledged Christ of the Indian Renaissance*. London: SCM Press.

Ward, Marcus 1946: *Our Theological Task: An Introduction to the Study of Theology in India*. Madras: CLT.

ALISTER E. MCGRATH

interpretation, biblical See BIBLICAL CRITICISM AND INTERPRETATION (1: OLD TESTAMENT and 2: NEW TESTAMENT.

Islam and Christianity Until the mid-twentieth century confrontational, rather than mediating, patterns of thought characterized the Christian theological reckoning with Islam. The reasons were not far to seek. A certain anti-Christian animus is built into the fabric of the Qur'ān and is thereby given the sanction of inviolable truth. A measure of incrimination of Christian faith thus belongs, as Muslims see it, with divine revelation itself, disavowing the Christian understanding of Jesus as the Christ and, thus, of 'God in Christ'. This makes the Christian/Islamic scene quite distinctive from all other inter-faith issues. When Alice muses in Wonderland about emerging in 'the antipodes', a slip of the tongue produces 'the people of the antipathies'. The phrase fits much of the theology between these two monotheisms.

To be sure, antipathies are by no means the whole story. There are moods in which the Qur'ān itself is benign to Christian monks and Christian faithful at prayer, and there is much common territory to house what divides. Nevertheless, the contrarieties persist, have long dominated the mutual history and live in the psyche as well as in the mind. Thus the will to appreciate Islamic meanings, vital as it must be to Christian integrity, has to engage with that reluctance to look beyond domestic concerns which has so long attended Christian doctrine in both Christology and the cross.

Antipathies have to do with the criteria for God, the status of Jesus, the implications of prophethood, the form and authority of revelation, the relation of truth to text and the measure of divine response to the human situation. The Jesus who has been unwarrantably divinized has to be – as some recent Muslim writers have it – 're-Semiticized' into the prophet he truly was. Whereas medieval Christian thinkers saw Islam as 'a Christian heresy' they must correct, Islam insists that the 'heresy' is Christianity itself. Mutual 'hereticizing' does not take us very far.

Relations are further beset by debate about the cross. Was Jesus in fact 'vindicated' from the malice of would-be crucifiers by a rapture to heaven so that, in docetic terms, his demise was 'only apparent'? If so, the theology of redemptive love, and of a history which epitomizes the grace that is divine encountering the 'sin which is the world's', must be forbidden.

Modern Christian thought was heir to grooves of controversy from as far back as John of Damascus (c. 675–c. 749), which were painstakingly reproduced by, for example, the *Mizān al-Ḥaqq* of C.G. Pfander ([1829] 1910). His erudite labours were exemplary but tended to proceed from fixed premises of rival revelations, the one true and the other false. The fallibility of the credentials of Muhammad, moral and scriptural, was seen as crucial. Thomas Carlyle's *Heroes and Hero Worship* of 1840 – keenly savoured by Muslims to this day – served to lift the argument, but he still assigned the Qur'ān to well-meaning opacity.

The tireless translator Henry Martyn (1781–1812) was of different calibre. His theological yearning over Islam – for such it was – proved an anxious education into evangelical imponderables. He was convinced that once the New Testament was available to intelligent Muslims the Qur'ān would pass into limbo. In the interim, working with local *munshis*, or consultants, he met the intractables of vocabulary. 'I long to know what I seek after,' he wrote (Wilberforce, 1837, vol. 2, p. 250) and 'wondered what Paul would do in my condition' (p. 252). He had stumbled in his anguish on the ultimate travail of interpretation, though

his *Persian Tracts* of 1824 maintained much of the Pfander pattern. A century later his tradition of missionary scholarship was exemplified in Dutch-American mode by Samuel Zwemer (1867–1952), a pioneer Arabist in the Persian Gulf, founder of *The Muslim World Quarterly* (in 1911) and one of many to invoke hopefully the figure of the great Muslim theologian, Al-Ghazālī (1056–1111) as a pivotal mind relevant to both theisms.

Zwemer wrote in the wake of the demise of the Ottoman Caliphate, which he read as a sign of the disintegration of Islam. The post-imperial world of nation–states and rigorist resurgence is very different. His successor on *The Muslim World Quarterly*, Duncan Black Macdonald, and the French Islamicist, Louis Massignon, developed an appreciative theology of Islam, at once interpretative and mediatorial. It helped to temper the missionary impulse, which through numerous personalities saw the role of Christians towards Islam less in terms of polemic and more in terms of ministries of compassion, medicine and education (see MISSION, THEOLOGY OF). Guiding them, however, in the years between the world wars were mentors like Hendrik Kraemer, with his broadly Barthian stance, and the American philosopher William Ernest Hocking, author of the influential *Living Religions and a World Faith* of 1940.

A representative figure in that period was W.H. Temple Gairdner of Cairo, whose biographer, C.E. Padwick, proved herself a seminal writer in inter-faith theology by her study of the vocabulary of Muslim devotional life (Padwick, 1961), mediating skilfully between the *taqwa*, or God-awareness, of Muslims and Christian *confessio-imitatio Christi*.

In their wake, late twentieth-century literature reflects the changed climate of 'dialogue', chastened as it is by the image of Islam as obscurantist and resentful of the west in the context of the 'Islamic revolution' and the legacy of Ayatollah Khomeini. The tensions that are inseparable from the differing 'calendars' of culture are massive, just as debates about 'image' are subversive of real issues. A sober mutuality of theological meeting is the more urgent. What might it undertake?

Taken positively, Islam is a sustained consciousness of God, of divine unity and sovereignty. It is inadequately responsive to the issues of theodicy, of actual human secularity and to other liabilities of any and all theology. But it is profoundly served by the ritual discipline of *Salāt*, prayer, by the sanction of the *Ummah*, or community, and by a solidarity explicit in its institutions, especially the state, fasting and pilgrimage. As such, it institutionalizes Islam (capital) as the ultimate form of *islām* (lower case). (There is the same distinction between Muslim and muslim.) Arabic, of course, has no capital letters, so that the identity, or differentiation, of the two is implicit only. The difference is theologically significant. The historical, structural, dogmatic, institutional Islam is one thing, the inner, adjectival *islām* another.

The latter can in some sense be shared with Christianity. (Compare asking 'Is he Christian?' with asking 'Is he a Christian?'). It involves shared convictions about creation, divine lordship, law and prophethood. It means also common beliefs about humanity as entrusted with the natural order. It means a shared sense of the sacramental dimension in all physical experience, implicit in the Qur'ān's doctrine of the *āyāt*, or 'signs', of God, whereby science reads its clues and faith discerns its gratitude. Earlier polemic overlooked or concealed these common meanings between the two scriptures.

Prophethood, of course, belongs with them. Only in an entrusted universe is 'guidance' needed. Among puppets prophets are pointless. The Qur'ān is eloquent about human vocation and about the liability of the self for the self. From these common Semitic convictions both theologies proceed, the very controversies presupposing the agreements. How are we to reckon rightly with the divine liability for and to the human world, as creation and prophethood assume it? How far might it extend in the light of the human waywardness which Islam identifies for what it is? Broadly, Islamic theology sees that liability limited to revelation, law, exhortation and, finally, assessment and judgement. Christian theology sees it going further into the Christ-enterprise, into grace and suffering, into redeeming and remaking.

Clearly for both there was a risk about creation, a divine stake turning on the human will: *Islām* itself has to be willed, and may be withheld. Prophets are not inherently successful, neither by word only nor ultimately by any

power equation. What the Qur'ān calls *zulm* (evil flouting good), *shirk* (false worship), and *kufr* (giving the lie to truth) plainly happen. They entail suffering on any prophet who indicts them. The inter-theological question, therefore, is the place of God in the travail of the messengers, given the place of God in the sending of them. For the Christian understanding of the cross of Jesus is precisely there – 'God in Christ reconciling the world'.

Islam resists that reading, exempting divine transcendence from what is viewed unseemly. But what is divinely seemly? This is the core of the issue over Jesus, understood as an issue about God. Yet even in this point of impasse there are intriguing clues to 'incarnation'. All prophethood, certainly Muhammad's, becomes in some sense biographical. The 'Word' is not a handout giving information: it is a persona engaging with a hearing – or a hating. Revelation happens in situations. 'What is he saying?' soon becomes 'Who is he anyway?' Response to the situation makes or unmakes the case for what he preaches: 'the Word is made flesh.' There is truth through personality. Could it be that what God was saying lived a human life, so that 'bio-graphy' could be, in the Judaic phrase, 'the place of the Name'? If so, we will be on the way to what was always meant by the divine Sonship/servanthood of Jesus. Where Islam finds it necessary to speak of 'the divinity of the Book', the uncreated Qur'ān, Christian theology understands the divine 'Word made flesh'. At least the elucidation can be mutual.

Such considerations are areas of obligation if we bring together Islam/Christianity with that evasive conjunction 'and'. Mediation refrains from polemic and explores the positives in hope that they may enlarge and thus stretch the minds that think them, in hope, in turn, of the inter-growing of the communities around them. The business is urgent but is precariously proceeding.

See also ARAB CHRISTIAN THOUGHT; JUDAISM AND CHRISTIANITY; OTHER FAITHS AND CHRISTIANITY.

Bibliography

Borrmans, Maurice, 1981: *Orientations pour un dialogue entre chrétiens et musulmans*. Paris: Cerf.

Breiner, Bert, 1991: Christian/Muslim encounter, some current themes, *Islam and Christian Muslim*

Relations 2, 1, pp. 77–94.

Brown, Stuart, ed. 1989: *Meeting in Faith, 20 Years of Christian/Muslim Conversations.* Geneva: World Council of Churches.

Cantwell Smith, Wilfred 1959: Some similarities and some differences between Islam and Christianity. In *The World of Islam: Studies in Honour of Philip K. Hitti*, ed. James Kritzeck and R.B. Winder. London: Macmillan, pp. 47–59.

Cracknell, Kenneth, ed. 1984: *Christians and Muslims Talking Together*, London: British Council of Churches.

al-Faruqi, Isma'il 1989; Islamic Ethics. In *World Religions and Global Ethics*, ed. S.C. Crawford. New York: Paragon House, pp. 212–37.

Khoury, Paul 1975: *Islam et christianisme: dialogue religieux et defi de la modernité.* Beirut: Heidelberg Press.

Merad, Ali 1975: Dialogue islamo-chrétien: pour la recherche d'un langage commun, *Islamochristiano* 1, pp. 1–10.

Moubarac, Youakim 1972: *L'Islam et le dialogue, islamo-chrétien.* Beirut: Éditions du Cenacle Libanais.

Padwick, Constance 1961: *Muslim Devotions.* London: SPCK.

Pfander, C.G. [1829] 1910: *Mizān al-Ḥaqq*, trans. W.S. St Clair Tisdall. London: Religious Tract Society.

Rossano, Pietro 1982: Les grands documents de l'église catholique au sujet des musulmans, *Islamochristiano* 8, pp. 13–23.

Sanneh, Lamin 1989: Translatability in Islam and Christianity, with special reference to Africa, recapitulating the theme. In *Translating the Message: The Missionary Impact on Culture.* New York: Orbis Books, pp. 211–38.

Werff, Lyle L. van der 1977: *Christian Mission to Muslims: The Record, 1800–1938.* Monrovia, CA: William Carey Library.

Wilberforce, Samuel, ed. 1837: *Journals and Letters of Henry Martyn*, 2 vols. London.

Woodberry, J. Dudley, ed. 1989: *Muslims and Christians on the Emmaus Road.* Monrovia, CA: Marc Publications.

KENNETH CRAGG

J

James, William (1842–1910) North American philosopher and psychologist. The son of a Swedenborgian theologian and brother of the novelist Henry James, he studied at Harvard, where he began to teach anatomy and physiology, before becoming attracted by developments in the new science of psychology in Europe. He became professor of psychology (1887–97) and of philosophy (1897–1907). His major work on religion, *The Varieties of Religious Experience* of 1902, based on Gifford Lectures given in Edinburgh, presented a naturalistic and pragmatic view of religion, making an early distinction between 'personal' and 'institutional' religion, which he saw as very different in character. He made a scientific analysis of diverse and often dramatic religious conversion experiences, presenting conversion as a stage in human growth towards psychological integration. He upheld the validity of religion as a universal human phenomenon, and its potential value for psychological health and moral conduct, distinguishing between 'healthy-minded' and 'morbid-minded' religion, which were conditioned largely by temperament. Human beings had a 'right to believe', and if belief produced moral improvement (as it frequently appeared to do), then it should be embraced in the absence of prior scientific proof, which anyway was impossible to establish. The book continues to be influential in the study of the psychology of religion; other works include *Principles of Psychology* (1890), *The Will to Believe* (1897) and *Pragmatism* (1907). His interest extended to the study of psychic phenomena, and he helped found the American branch of the Society for Psychical Research.

See also PSYCHOLOGICAL SCIENCE AND CHRISTIAN THOUGHT.

Bibliography
Allen, G.W. 1967: *William James, A Biography*. New York.
Bixler, J.S. 1926: *Religion in the Philosophy of William James*. Boston.
Myers, G.E. 1986: *William James: His Life and Thought*. New Haven, Conn.

Japanese Christian thought Nestorian missionaries first gained a foothold in China during the seventh century, when they appear to have been mistaken for a Buddhist sect (Jing Jiao) but whether they reached Japan or not cannot now be verified. In the case of Japan, Christianity was first established through the activities of missionaries during the sixteenth century, especially after Francis Xavier landed at Kagoshima in 1549. The form of Christianity introduced to the country at this stage was the reinvigorated and reformed form of Catholicism arising from the Council of Trent and given new vitality through the spirituality of the newly founded Society of Jesus. The Kirisitan period, as this era in sixteenth-century Japanese history is known, saw the introduction of new ideas to Japan from the west, of which Christianity is perhaps the most important. The only theological book known to have been published during this period in Japan is the *Compendium catholicae veritatis*, a comprehensive textbook including a discussion of astronomy, a summary of Aristotle's *De anima*, and theology in the form of a summary of the *Catechismus Romanus*. This work was compiled and adapted for the Japanese situation by Pedro Gomes (1535–1600), and printed primarily for the use of seminarians. Although initially published in Latin, this textbook was adapted for the use of the laity in Japanese translation as *Dochirina Kirisitan*. The work placed a strong emphasis upon Christ's redemptive death on the cross.

The culture of the Kirisitan period indicates the considerable potential of Christianity for integrating with Japanese culture. This period of successful evangelization continued until the beginning of the seventeenth century, when the Tokugawa shogunate ended the spread of Christianity through prohibition decrees (forcing Christianity to go underground), and the systematic isolation of Japan from the west for two centuries. As a result, it was impossible for western missionaries to enter the country. Suppression and persecution set in, leading to the virtual eradication of Christianity from Japanese culture. Occasional exceptions may be noted. The shogunate policy-maker Arai Hakuseki (1657–1725), made favourable mention of Giovanni Sidotti's account of the Christian faith (1717), and Hirata Atsutane (1776–1843), an extreme national ideologue, appealed to hitherto forbidden Christian books published in Chinese when he criticized Buddhism and Confucianism. A central feature of the 'hidden Christianity' of the period was veneration of the Virgin Mary as intercessor, which allowed Christians to pass themselves off as Buddhists in the public eye.

In 1865, Japan re-opened its doors to the international community, ending its period of self-imposed isolation. At that time, there were some 60,000 Christian believers in the country, whose survival was widely acclaimed as a miracle of faith. However, only about half of those believers chose to associate with the newly recognized Catholic church; the remainder preferred to remain in cults which mingled Christianity with various forms of indigenous religion. The returnees to the church have until today constituted the core of a comparatively large section of the Catholic population around the city of Nagasaki, and provided the bulk of seminarians. However, in general, Catholic culture had no substantial impact on the development of Japan's modernization. An exception to this statement may be noted in the case of the new Meiji government, which was obliged to guarantee freedom of religion in response to the protest of the western ambassadors against religious prohibitions (1871). This freedom of religion was later incorporated into the Constitution promulgated by Emperor Meiji (1889).

Japan was forced to join the international community by Commodore Perry and his 'black ships' in the late-1880s. The weakened shogunate opened Japan's ports, an action which provoked vigorous internal protests and which eventually led to its downfall. The resulting restoration of imperial power led to the move of the capital away from the ancient seat of Kyoto to the eastern city of Tokyo and to the modernization of Japan along the lines of western European nations. During the preceding power struggle between the shogunate and the Satuma-Choshu faction, France had supported the shogunate, while Britain and the USA supported the Satuma-Choshu's demands for the restoration of the emperor. The resulting victory of the Satuma-Choshu group led to growing Anglo-American influence on the new Japan. Although Japan's Christian life was subject to Russian influences, especially in the north of the country, the Russo-Japanese war led to this becoming increasingly insignificant.

In the decades following the abolition of its prohibition, Christianity experienced a period of phenomenal growth, partly reflecting its novelty value, and partly on account of Japanese eagerness to assimilate western ideas and culture. An important factor in this context was the emergence of Protestantism as a significant presence in modern Japan, especially among intellectuals. This appears to have been due to the fact that the form of Protestantism which was introduced during this period by American missionaries was oriented towards ethics and social work, rather than doctrine, thus making an appeal to the ex-samurai's Confucian ethos. Many of these missionaries were also educationalists, such as William Elliot Griffis (1843–1928) and William Smith Clark (1926–1986), who positively influenced their students in a Christian manner through their strong personalities. For example, Clark was the first president of the Sapporo Agricultural College, founded for the development of Hokkaido; Nitobe Inazo (1862–1933), one of his students, belongs to the first generation of famous Meiji Christians.

Most of the now-famous Christian universities pride themselves in having such missionary-teachers as their founders during this period. Captain L.L. James (1837–1909) first taught in Kumamoto, and gathered round himself a group of young men, known as the Kumamoto Band, dedicated to Christianity. One of his disciples, Niijima Jo (1843–1890) founded the Doshisha English School, later to achieve the status of a university, thus becoming the first Japanese Christian founder of a private university. The emergence of such indigenous charismatic leaders bore witness to the increasing maturity of Japanese Christianity. Although initially reliant upon foreign missionaries, the Japanese churches gradually turned to indigenous Japanese for leaders.

Protestantism has had a considerable impact upon the process of Japanese modernization, and became a significant force in its cultural life. In a period when women were treated with scant regard, Christian missionaries took the initiative in their education, and produced Christian women leaders such as Tsuda Umeko (1864–1929). However, Japanese intellectuals came to realize that western nations were becoming secularized and that western churches were ceasing to be dominant and creative social forces. As a result, they turned to other world views, including forms of naturalism or Marxism. The considerable influence of Christianity upon literature in the Meiji period (1868–1912) gave way to a new interest in an indigenous 'natural supernaturalism', in which nature is regarded as divine, in the writings of famous novelists such as Shimazaki Toson (1872–1943) and Kitamura Tokoku (1868–1894).

Against this background, Christian charismatic leaders such as Uchimura Kanzo (1861–1930) and Uemura Masahisa (1858–1925) arose. Uchimura founded the Mukyokai (non-church) movement, partly in response to his disappointing experience of the condition of the churches in the USA, where he studied theology. Uchimura strongly asserted the identity of being Japanese and being Christian, but seemed to some to be theologically naive, tending to bracket together Jesus, Paul, Augustine, Luther and Calvin. Uemura was more theologically sophisticated, but was surpassed in this respect by Ebina Danjo (1856–1937), who is widely regarded as being the first original Japanese theologian, and is sometimes known as 'the Japanese Origen'.

With the coming of the Taisho period (1912–26), increasing alienation became evident between the government and the intellectuals. The latter, disturbed by mounting social unrest, turned increasingly to Marxism as the solution for Japan's ills. With the waning of the appeal of Christianity as a socially transforming agency, many Christian intellectuals turned to Marxism. This led to the development of forms of Christian Socialism, linked with writers such as Katayama Sen (1859–1933), Abe Isoo (1865–1949) and especially Kagawa Toyohiko (1888–1960). Such ideas became influential in the Social Party, and expressed themselves in Christian social and peace movements.

A number of significant developments can be detected in the period between the First and Second World Wars. Culturally, Japanese Christianity adjusted to the social and cultural diversification of the country, recognizing that it was one element among many in the religious marketplace. Intellectually, major developments took place within both Protestant and Catholic Japanese theology. The liberal theological agenda associated with Ebina Danjo gave way to a new interest in Barthianism. Takakura Tokutaro (1885–1934) is an example of this new wave in Japanese Protestantism: initially concerned to promote a biblical evangelical theology, Takakura later drew on the writings of Barth to provide a framework for his developing ideas. In Catholicism, a new interest in the scholastic period, especially the writings of Thomas Aquinas, developed, as was perhaps to be expected in the heyday of the New Scholasticism. Examples of writers to have adopted such an approach are Iwashita Soichi (1889–1940) and Yoshimitu Yoshihiko (1904–1945), converts from Uchimura's circle.

Although the First World War generated no anti-Christian feeling in Japan, the growing nationalist sentiment of the interwar period led to Christianity coming under increasing pressure. The United Church of Japan was formed in response to government pressure, and foreign missionaries faced increasing isolation and harassment. Some elements in Japanese Christianity tried to devise ways of bringing their faith into line with the conservative ideology of the emperor cult.

With the defeat of Japan, the churches regained their freedom, and experienced hitherto unparalleled opportunities for expansion. Foreign help poured into the country, and Christianity became increasingly prestigious. New Christian institutions of higher education were founded. However, with the fading of the memory of the wartime period, and with Japan experiencing increased economic prosperity, the Christian churches are experiencing something of an identity crisis.

In terms of theology, Japanese Christianity has now reached a level of professional competence on a par with the west in general. Major works of theology (including Barth's *Church Dogmatics*, Aquinas's *Summa Theologiae*, Bultmann's more significant works and many important patristic and mystical works) have now been translated, or are in the process of being translated. Examples of Japanese contributions to the world theological community can be instanced from the fields of systematic theology and biblical studies. The former is exemplified by Kitamori Kazo's *Theology of the Pain of God* ([1946] 1965) (which received considerable attention outside Christian circles), and the latter by Arai Sasagu's study of gnosticism in the Gospel of Thomas, or Tagawa Kenzo's study of Mark's Gospel. A longstanding Christological debate (1965–80) within Japanese theology between the Barthian writer Takizawa Katsumi and Yagi Seiichi concerns the significance of the historical figure of Jesus, particularly in relation to dialogue with Buddhism. Japanese Catholic theology has only emerged of late, in the period subsequent to the Second Vatican Council. Perhaps one factor which accounts for this later development is that Japanese Catholicism was more willing to adapt itself to Japanese culture, without confronting the theological issues thereby raised; whereas Protestant theology, especially under Barthian influence, was sensitive to the difficulties in relating Christianity to the non-Christian cultural situation. Since Vatican II, there has been an increase in ecumenical cooperation within Japan, especially evident in the recent new ecumenical translation of the Bible, which has become a bestseller in Japan and strength-ened the sense of unity among the churches. A Japanese Christian theology of religions is in the process of evolving. Perhaps most significantly, a new living and creative literary tradition has developed within Japanese Catholicism. One novel to emerge from this tradition – Endo Shusaku, *Silence* – has caught the imagination of many writers and theologians outside Japan. While Christian theology may not exercise a dominant influence in the pluralism of Japan's rapidly changing intellectual scene, it seems set to continue as a significant force.

See also CHINESE CHRISTIAN THOUGHT; KOREAN CHRISTIAN THOUGHT; OTHER FAITHS AND CHRISTIANITY.

Bibliography

Boxer, Charles Ralph 1951: *Christian Century in Japan, 1549–1650*. Berkeley: University of California Press.

Caldarola, Carlo 1978: *Christianity: The Japanese Way*. Leiden: Brill.

Cary, Otis 1976: *A History of Christianity in Japan: Roman Catholic, Greek Orthodox, and Protestant Missions*. Tokyo: Tuttle.

Drummond, Henry 1971: *A History of Christianity in Japan*. Grand Rapids: Eerdmans.

Fujita, Neil S. 1991: *Japan's Encounter with Christianity: The Catholic Mission in Pre-Modern Japan*. New York: Paulist Press.

German, H. 1965: *Protestant Theologies in Modern Japan*. Tokyo: International Institute for the Study of Religions.

Johnston, William 1968: *The Still Point: Reflections on Zen and Christian Mysticism*. New York: Fordham University Press.

Kadowaki, J.K. 1989: *Zen and the Bible*. London: Arkana.

Kitamori, K. [1946] 1965: *Theology of the Pain of God*. Richmond: John Knox.

Kumazawa, Yoshinobu, and Swain, David, eds 1991: *Christianity in Japan, 1971–90*. Tokyo: Kyo Bun Kwan.

Michalson, Carl 1960: *Japanese Contributions to Christian Theology*. Philadelphia: Westminster.

Ogawa, Keiji 1965: *Die Aufgabe der neueren evangelischen Theologie in Japan*. Basel: Reinhardt.

Powles, C.H. 1987: *Victorian Missionaries in Meiji Japan*. Toronto: Universities of Toronto and York Press.

Scheiner, Irwin 1970: *Converts and Social Protest in Meiji Japan*. Berkeley: University of California Press.

Spae, J.M. 1965: *Christian Corridors to Japan*. Tokyo: Oriens.

Takayanagi, S. 1975: Christology and postwar theologians in Japan. In *Postwar Trends in Japan*, ed. S. Takayanagi and K. Miwa. Tokyo: University of Tokyo Press, pp. 119–67.

Yagi, Seiichi, and Luz, Ulbrich, ed. 1973: *Gott in Japan*. München: Kaiser.

The Chesterton Review 1988: 14, 3 (August), containing articles on Christian writers of Japan.

The Japan Christian Yearbook, 1903–70. Tokyo: Kyo Bun Kwan.

SHUNICHI TAKAYANAGI

Jesus Christ See CHRIST, JESUS.

Judaism and Christianity Despite the Enlightenment, which allowed many distinguished Jews to integrate into European culture, the relationship between Judaism and Christianity in the modern era has remained tragic. Since the Second World War, however, serious attempts have been made to correct the prejudice of the past. The prime motive behind this reappraisal has been a sense of horror at the Holocaust and Christian complicity in it. Together with this has gone a growing awareness of 'the teaching of contempt' which prepared the ground for nineteenth- and twentieth-century anti-Semitism.

Although there were a few pioneering efforts before the Second World War, it was the Ten Points of Seelisburg in 1947 (from a meeting of the International Council of Christians and Jews at Seelisburg in Switzerland, mainly concerned with combating anti-Semitism) and the publication of *Nostra Aetate* by the Second Vatican Council in 1965 that marked the beginning of a revolution in Christian attitudes to Judaism. Affirming a common 'spiritual patrimony', the Vatican Council said that the passion of Christ 'cannot be charged against all the Jews' and the relationship with Judaism '*concerns the church as such*'. Also important for the new understanding has been a basic principle of dialogue, namely that other religions must be allowed to define themselves in their own terms. So Jews emphasize that Judaism is a living religion, to be respected in its own right. It is not identical with any one of the sects of first-century Palestine and certainly not with that of the plain text of the Hebrew Scriptures. Furthermore, Judaism has shown extraordinary spiritual and intellectual vitality throughout the medieval and modern periods, despite its history of being maligned and persecuted.

Post-Second World War developments were anticipated by a few remarkable pioneers. The Anglican scholar James Parkes was outstanding. Reinhold Niebuhr not only warned of anti-Semitism, but as early as the 1920s was calling for a new relationship in which Judaism was respected in its own right. From a Jewish point of view, however, more important than the work of individual theologians have been the official statements by church bodies. There have now been a good number of these, from all the main Christian denominations, and they are usefully collected together in a number of works mentioned in the bibliography, especially those edited by Helga Croner (1977 and 1985). Whilst many of the themes are repeated, they show an increasingly positive attitude towards Judaism. For example, whereas the World Council of Churches at its meeting in 1948 still insisted that Christians should try to convert Jews, this view is rejected in the later statements of the Rhineland and Protestant churches. Bishops of the Anglican Communion at the Lambeth Conference in 1988 produced a document strongly affirmative of Judaism, stressing the large area of common ground.

Basic to recent Christian theology on Judaism has been the attempt to get away from supersessionism, the notion that Christianity has simply replaced Judaism. It is recognized that this has been the root cause of so much of the damage. But is it possible to be free of supersessionism whilst at the same time remaining true to central Christian beliefs? Roy and Alice Eckhardt argue that a belief in the resurrection of Christ is inherently triumphalistic and anti-Judaic. They maintain that this belief must be given up as part of the price to be paid in affirming the validity of Judaism in its own right. An alternative approach suggests that through the resurrection of Jesus, God vindicated not only his person but his religion, which was Judaism. So the resurrection of Christ, far from undermining Judaism, could be seen as validating its central insights.

Christology has been a key area in recent debate. Paul van Buren maintains that Jesus is only a man, albeit a man through whom God has worked to bring faith to the Gentile world. This approach affirms Judaism but it sits uneasily with historic Christianity. Jan Pawlikowski, who is critical of van Buren's solution, stresses that Christianity is not simply a form of Judaism for Gentiles, but it offers a belief in the incarnation. However, his understanding of incarnation turns out to be God's closeness to us and his immanence. The problem of how the historic belief that the eternal Son of God has united humanity to himself in Jesus can be stated in a way which does not threaten Jewish self-understanding, remains. Yet the concept of God dwelling with and in his people is a strand within Judaism. There is a sense in which God incarnates himself in his people and its institutions, especially the Torah and those who allow their lives to be shaped by it. The incarnation of God in Jesus can be seen as both the culmination of this process and that which goes beyond it, so that a different analogy altogether is needed. The problem of speaking of the incarnation in relation to Judaism is the same as speaking of it at all. In order to speak, it is necessary to draw on continuity with other human experience. Yet if the incarnation is unique, all models, metaphors and analogies break down. It may be that if Judaism and Christianity are both to retain their own recognizable self-identity there are differences that have to be recognized rather than blurred. Genuine dialogue involves not only understanding and affirmation, but bringing in to the relationship what is distinct and different. Judaism brings to the relationship truth and insights from which Christians need to learn.

Closely linked with these fundamental theological themes has been a discussion of the covenant or covenants. All those who have tried to take a more positive view of Judaism emphasize that God's covenant with Judaism remains valid, with Romans 11: 28 and 29 being interpreted in a way that favours this. But is there one covenant in which Christians, through Christ, are able to share? Or are there two covenants, one for Judaism and one for Christianity? Van Buren has tended to favour the former approach, although his later thought suggests a plurality of covenants, one with every different cultural/religious grouping. Pawlikowski, building on the work of James Parkes, favoured two distinct ones. The one given at Sinai is essentially communal, concerned with the life of the people as a whole and their day-by-day living on this earth. The second, given through Christ, is essentially personal. People are called as individuals to a relationship with him which concerns not only this life but its fulfilment beyond space and time.

New Testament study has been important to the new relationship between Judaism and Christianity in various ways (see BIBLICAL CRITICISM AND INTERPRETATION 2: NEW TESTAMENT). First, there has been a rediscovery of the Jewishness of Jesus and his closeness to some of the religious groups of his time, particularly the Pharisees (See HISTORICAL JESUS, QUEST OF). From the Christian side E.P. Sanders and from the Jewish side Geza Vermes both firmly place Jesus within the context of first-century Judaism, attributing to him a much more favourable attitude to it than has been recognized in the past. Such work has been important in helping to dispel false stereotypes of Judaism, which are still widespread; for example, that Judaism is essentially legalistic and that the Pharisees were concerned only with the minutiae of the law and outward behaviour. The Pharisees are now regarded by many scholars as belonging to a creative religious movement to which Jesus was not essentially hostile, even though he criticizes some Pharisees and some Pharisaic attitudes. Secondly, there has been a growing awareness of the fact that much of the New Testament was written up after the split between the church and the synagogue, so that it reflects some of the hostility of that later quarrel. This poses a problem not only for the correct observance of Holy Week and the performance of passion plays, but every aspect of Christian teaching.

There is a huge gap between the insights of biblical scholars and what usually gets purveyed from Christian pulpits. The Vatican has tried to bridge the gap with its *Guidelines* of 1975 and its *Notes for Preaching and Catechesis* of 1985. SIDIC (*Service International Documentation Judeo-Chrétienne*) publishes regular teaching on how to avoid negative images of Judaism. In Britain institutes such as the Centre for the Study of Judaism and Jewish–Christian Relations at Selly Oak, Birmingham, and the Council for Christians and Jews are striving hard to re-educate priests and ordinands. This is a matter of profound importance for the Jewish community, whose prime concern is not theology for its own sake but for its effect in bringing about a more positive attitude to Judaism and therefore a securer life for Jews in the world.

From this point of view Christian attitudes towards the state of Israel are regarded as important by Jews. It is crucial to the new relationship between Judaism and Christianity that Christians understand Jews to be a people and not simply a religion. Furthermore, attachment to the land of Israel is for most Jews an essential aspect of their peoplehood. This raises theological questions about the promise of the land and the sense in which, if at all, that promise is still valid. There are then further questions about how far that promise can or should refer to the present state of Israel. Here theology and politics are inextricably mixed and in the absence of agreement, most churches prefer to treat the question in terms of international law.

From the Jewish point of view there have been some attempts to view Christianity in a positive light as being within the providence of God. These build on the views of Maimonides and, before him, of Halevi, who wrote, 'The nations merely serve to introduce and pave the way for the expected Messiah, who is the fruition, and they will all become his fruits.' The best-known modern work is Franz Rosenzweig's *Star of Redemption* (1971), in which Christianity is seen as God's covenant for the Gentile world.

Modern theological emphasis on the centrality of the concept of the kingdom of God in both the Hebrew Scriptures and in the teaching of Jesus has helped the relationship between Judaism and Christianity. For if it is the kingdom of God, rather than Christ or the church, that is the fundamental category, there is a basis upon which Jews and Christians stand together, whatever else might divide them. Through Christ Christians come to share the Jewish belief in God's kingdom. Similarly, through him they come to share the Jewish hope that God's kingdom will one day come in its fullness. This is dramatically illustrated by the 'Our Father', every petition of which is essentially Jewish.

See also ISLAM AND CHRISTIANITY; OTHER FAITHS AND CHRISTIANITY.

Bibliography

Braybrooke, Marcus 1990: *Time to Meet*. London: SCM Press; Philadelphia: Trinity Press International.

Brockway, Allan, Buren, Paul van, Rendtorff, Rolf, and Schoon, Simon 1988: *The Theology of the Churches and the Jewish People* (statements by the World Council of Churches and its member churches). Geneva: WCC publications.

Buren, Paul van 1980–3: *A Theology of the Jewish–Christian Reality*, 4 vols; *Discerning the Way* and *A Christian Theology of the People, Israel*. New York: Seabury Cross Road.

Croner, Helga, ed. 1977: *Stepping Stones to Further Jewish–Christian Relations* (an unabridged collection of Christian documents). New York: Paulist Press.

Croner, Helga, ed. 1985: *More Stepping Stones to Jewish–Christian Relations* (an unabridged collection of Christian documents 1975–83). New York: Paulist Press.

Ecclestone, Alan 1980: *The Night Sky of the Lord*. London: Darton, Longman and Todd.

Fisher, Eugene 1983: *Seminary Education and Christian–Jewish Relations*. Washington National Catholic Educational Association.

Küng, Hans 1992: *Judaism*, trans. J. Bowden. London: SCM Press.

Lambeth Conference 1988: Jews, Christians and Muslims, the way of dialogue. In *The Truth shall make you Free*, Appendix 6. London: Church House Publications.

Lapide, Pinchas 1984: *The Resurrection of Jesus*. London: SPCK.

Niebuhr, Reinhold 1986: The Relations of Christians and Jews in Western Civilization. In *The Essential Reinhold Niebuhr*, ed. Robert McAfee Brown, 1986. New Haven and London: Yale University Press.

Novak, David 1989: *Jewish–Christian Dialogue: A Jewish Justification*. Oxford and New York: Oxford University Press.

Parkes, James [1934] 1961: *The Conflict of the Church and the Synagogue*. New York: Meridian Books.

Parkes, James [1954] 1982: *End of an Exile*. Massachusetts: Mica Publications.

Pawlikowski, Jan 1982: *Christ in the Light of Jewish–Christian Dialogue*. New York: Paulist Press.

Rosenzweig, F. 1971: *The Star of Redemption*. London: Routledge and Kegan Paul.

Sanders, E.P. 1985: *Jesus and Judaism*. London: SCM Press.

Vermes, Geza [1973] 1983: *Jesus the Jew*. London: SCM Press.

Wigoder, Geoffrey 1988: *Jewish–Christian Relations since the Second World War*. Manchester and New York: Manchester University Press.

Common Ground, published four times a year by the

Council of Christians and Jews, 1 Dennington Park Road, London NW6 1AX; ed. the Revd Marcus Braybrooke.

RICHARD HARRIES

Jung, Carl Gustav (1875–1961) Swiss psychologist. He studied medicine at Basle and Zurich before working at the Burgholzi asylum in Zurich in 1900. Here he developed the expression 'complex' to describe reactions in word association tests which revealed things suppressed in the unconscious mind. These conclusions drew him to Sigmund Freud, with whom he worked from 1907 to 1912, until he broke away after disagreeing with Freud about his sexual interpretations of neuroses. He was made a professor of psychology in Zurich in 1933, and a professor of medical psychology in Basle in 1943. Among his important works are *Studies in Word Association* (1904–9); *The Psychology of the Unconscious* (1912) and the posthumous *Memories, Dreams, Reflections* (1963).

Jung is remembered as the founder of analytic psychology. He published important work on personality types – the introvert and the extrovert – and argued that the mind had four functions, thinking, feeling, sensation and intuition, one or more of which may predominate in an individual character (*Psychological Types*, 1921). He also introduced the distinction between a person's self and his or her assumed persona, or mask, which is used in social situations. He suggested the importance of the 'shadow side' of the personality, which, if not integrated into the self, can be projected onto others. Unlike Freud, Jung was positive about the function of religion. He argued that humanity has a 'collective unconscious' which expresses itself in universal human archetypes. Religions are ways of expressing this unconscious by means of myths and symbols.

See PSYCHOLOGICAL SCIENCE AND CHRISTIAN THOUGHT.

Bibliography
Fordham, F. 1966: *An Introduction to Jung's Psychology*, 3rd edn. Harmondsworth.
Jacobi, J. 1968: *The Psychology of C.G. Jung*. London.
Jung, C.G. 1953–79: *Collected Works 1875–1961*, 24 vols, trans. London.
Storr, A. 1973: *Jung*. London.

Jüngel, Eberhard (b. 1934) German Protestant theologian and philosopher of religion. He studied with Karl Barth, and began his career in East Berlin and Zurich, before moving to Tübingen in 1969, where he became professor of systematic theology and philosophy of religion, and director of the Hermeneutical Institute. Much of his work shows the influence of the great German thinkers, including G.W.F. Hegel, M. Luther, M. Heidegger and Barth, with whom he is in frequent dialogue; *The Doctrine of the Trinity* (1966, trans. 1976) is an interpretation and development of Barth's doctrine of God, and his *Karl Barth: A Theological Legacy* (trans. in part 1986) brings together his studies of Barth's thought. His scholarly interests are wide-ranging, and include hermeneutical issues, especially the theory of language (where he engages with Heidegger and H.-G. Gadamer); the Trinitarian nature of God and his relationship to the world; the ontological and theological implications of the incarnation and the cross; and the doctrine of justification by faith. The nature of God is supremely revealed in the humility he shows as he identifies with the suffering and death of Jesus on the cross; the nature of man, as understood through the doctrine of justification by faith, is essentially responsive and relational, rather than purely self-determining. Other works include *Death* (1971, trans. 1975) and *God as the Mystery of the World* (1977, trans. 1983).

Bibliography
Wainwright, G. 1981: Eberhard Jüngel, *Expository Times* 92.
Webster, J.B. 1986: *Eberhard Jüngel: An Introduction to his Theology*. Cambridge.

just war Christian moral reflection on just war constitutes one of several distinguishable but connected elements within a broader cultural tradition of just war that has developed over history in western society. This larger tradition also includes contributions by domestic and international law, political philosophy, the practical experience of statecraft and of war, and military ethics. At times the Christian component has dominated, while at other times other streams of thought have functioned as the principal carriers of the larger tradition. Though each of these elements can be differentiated from the others, the pattern of development of just war tradition as a whole has been one of interaction and cross-fertilization among them. Christian teaching on just war has not developed in isolation.

Early Christian moral reflection on war focused on whether Christians might justifiably participate in military activities. The historical origins of Christian just war tradition are thus to be found in the acceptance of military service by Christians, a development that began during the second century. The emergence of an authoritative theological rationale came later in the form of Augustine's *City of God* and other writings from the fourth and fifth centuries. Christian participation in war, for Augustine and his mentor Ambrose, was justified by the moral duty imposed by CHRISTIAN LOVE to protect an innocent neighbour from unjust attack. At the same time, however, CHRISTIAN LOVE for the attacker set limits on the violence that could be done to him. Augustine wedded this conception of the moral duty imposed by love to ideas on justified war drawn from the Old Testament and Roman culture, laying the groundwork for later systematic development of the just war idea during the medieval period and afterwards (see further Johnson, 1987, chapter 1).

In the Middle Ages just war tradition coalesced around two major categories, which in turn have provided the basis of Christian just war reflection in the modern period: the definition of a justified war (the *jus ad bellum*) and the definition of restraints to be observed in fighting justifiedly (the *jus in bello*). The former includes seven criteria: that there be a just cause (defence, recovering something wrongly taken, punishment of evil); a proper authority for the use of force (a secular ruler with no political superior); a right intention (to serve order, justice and peace, not to exercise hatred, lust for domination and such like); overall proportionality (preponderance of good over evil); reasonable hope of success; last resort; and the goal of producing peace. The *jus in bello* passed on to the modern period included two major requirements: that noncombatants be spared, so far as possible, the destruction of war and that in any case they not be directly and intentionally attacked (the principle of discrimination); and that just war be prosecuted without gratuitous or otherwise needless destruction (the principle of proportionality of means).

Early modern Christian just war theorists, most notably Francisco de Vitoria, Francisco Suarez, and the theologically trained jurist Hugo Grotius, emphasized the NATURAL LAW base of the inherited just war ideas, laying the groundwork for most subsequent development of just war tradition, Christian as well as secular. At the same time these theorists stressed the importance of the restraints to be observed in fighting, while allowing the question of justified resort to war to be increasingly formalized (see Johnson, 1981, chapter 6). The result of these two developments is seen most clearly in the development of international law, a major carrier of just war tradition in the modern period, almost wholly around the *jus in bello*.

Beginning with Paul Ramsey's work in the 1960s (see Ramsey, 1961 and 1968) focused chiefly on the debate over nuclear deterrence, Christian just war thinking has moved to recover the link Augustine forged between Christian love and what Ramsey called the 'twin-born' *permission* for Christians to engage in violence with *limitation* on that violence. His own concerns centred on the limits imposed by the principle of discrimination – the requirement of no direct, intentional attacks on noncombatants. This requirement, for Ramsey, derives immediately from Christian love and constitutes the uniquely Christian element in just war theory. Whatever nations may do on the basis of the political prudence counselled in the other just war criteria, Ramsey argued, Christians are permitted to engage in acts of war only if these acts satisfy the criterion of discrimination.

A direct implication of this line of argument is the immorality of 'strategic' counter-population attacks aimed at wearing down enemy morale, a form of warfare that became widespread during the Second World War and formed the original basis of nuclear targeting plans. Though Ramsey himself accepted the idea of counter-force nuclear attacks, other theorists used his argument to call into question the morality of any use of nuclear weapons, arguing that they are inherently indiscriminate as well as disproportionate (for example, National Conference of Catholic Bishops, 1983; Finnis, Boyle and Grisez, 1988). Still others extended just war reasoning to call in question all forms of contemporary war.

A weakness of this approach to Christian just war thinking was that it addressed the question of limitation without adequately addressing that of permission. This led in the 1980s to a recovery of Christian just war tradition on justifiable resort to war (see Johnson, 1981; National Conference of Catholic Bishops, 1983). The moral debate over the use of force against Iraq in the Persian Gulf crisis of 1990–1, in sharp contrast to the *jus in bello* focus of earlier debates centred on nuclear deterrence and on the Vietnam war, drew heavily on these *jus ad bello* ideas.

A particular feature of contemporary Christian just war thinking is the emergence of the idea that it, like Christian pacifism, begins with a presumption against violence (for example, National Conference of Catholic Bishops, 1983, p. 26). A better characterization of Christian just war tradition is that it begins with a presumption against injustice and an assumption that in the world as it is, there will be no way to combat injustice effectively save through resort to force. Yet that force must be employed within prescribed limits, else it will in turn be the source of new injustice. In this way Christian just war tradition aims to establish an endurable peace until God's purposes for the world are satisfied.

See also ETHICS; JUSTICE; SOCIAL QUESTIONS; WAR AND PEACE.

Bibliography

Finnis, John, Boyle, Joseph, and Grisez, Germain 1988: *Nuclear Deterrence, Morality and Realism*. New York: Oxford University Press.

Johnson, James Turner 1981: *Just War Tradition and the Restraint of War*. Princeton, NJ, and Guildford: Princeton University Press.

Johnson, James Turner 1987: *The Quest for Peace: Three Moral Traditions in Western Cultural History*. Princeton, NJ, and Guildford: Princeton University Press.

National Conference of Catholic Bishops 1983: *The Challenge of Peace*. Washington, DC: United States Catholic Conference.

Ramsey, Paul 1961: *War and the Christian Conscience: How Shall Modern War Be Conducted Justly?* Durham, NC: Duke University Press.

Ramsey, Paul 1968: *The Just War: Force and Political Responsibility*. New York: Charles Scribner's Sons.

J.T. JOHNSON

justice The idea of justice as giving to each his due, *suum cuique tradere*, has plural foci. Variously, it can denote: (1) an attribute of a legal act or product, in the ordinary sense of the adjudication of claims regarding deserts and entitlements according to law; (2) an attribute of an institution, which distributes in some fair way benefits and burdens, rights and opportunities, and powers and dependencies; (3) an attribute of individuals, regarding motivation or virtue. There are as many different conceptions of justice as there are ways of interrelating these legal, political and moral facets.

Since the eighteenth century, Christian reflection on justice has been galvanized by three distinct, but interrelated, problems. In the first place, the liberal rule of law, which gradually won the allegiance of most North Atlantic societies, formulates the terms of justice independent of theology. It is perhaps a measure of the success of liberalism, as both a theory and a set of practices and institutions, that virtually all of the Christian churches have re-evaluated their own traditions of justice in contrast to it. In the second place, the problems of social justice which emerged in the nineteenth century with industrialization, and then in the twentieth century with international wars and the growing disparity of economic resources along the north–south hemispheric axis, summoned social gospel and liberation theologies in many of the churches. Accordingly, there has been debate as to whether a theological conception of justice ought to (a) correct and fulfil the liberal, humanistic ideals, (b) stand in tension with them, or (c) provide a radical alternative to the strictly secular views. In the third place, there has been a persistent effort by theologians to distinguish between the demands of justice and the agapistic life unique to Christianity. In Protestant theology, this has represented a continuation of the traditional theological themes of law–gospel and justice–love, while in Catholic theology it has been the occasion for reflection upon the virtues of justice and charity according to the traditional distinction between nature and grace.

Contractarian, utilitarian, and de-ontological accounts of justice dominate academic discussion in the west, particularly that part of it that can be broadly described as liberal. Each of these has at least an indirect pedigree in Christian theology: contractarianism (Locke), in the biblical notion of covenant; utilitarianism (Mill), in the ideal of benevolence and practical charity; and de-ontology (Kant), in the biblical injunction concerning the golden rule. Although the prestige commanded by these theories was due in part to the fact that they satisfied certain religiously tutored intuitions about justice, there is wide agreement among modern theorists that the institutions of justice must stem from principles which command the assent of all rational agents, and that these principles are to be argued from religiously nonpartisan premises. Indeed, a salient feature of liberal theories of justice is the priority of the right over the good; which is to say that the moral criteria of a good life, and of virtue and vice, are sharply distinguished from, and systematically subordinated to, principles governing rights, obligations and sanctions. Procedural equality, due process and respect for individual rights take priority over substantive conceptions of what constitutes the end, or the perfection of, human action. Hence, justice takes as its principal theme the reciprocities of power and the balancing of freedom and equality.

The issues of balancing are the subject of extensive and complicated debates within liberal theory. In his *Theory of Justice*, for example, John Rawls develops a theory of certain primary goods which engender the claims and negotiations undertaken by autonomous agents. These goods, which include rights and liberties, powers and opportunities, income and wealth, and self-respect, are not to be viewed as ends, but rather as means which comprise the universal justice. Rawls's central expository device is the 'original position', in which, behind a 'veil of ignorance', the contractors construct a system of justice while prescinding from knowledge of what position they hold in society, what generation they are, or what their personal goals or lifeplans might be (Rawls, 1971, p. 12). Hence they can be expected, first,

to secure against unequal division of basic liberties, and, second, to endorse the 'difference principle', namely, that inequalities of wealth and authority are just only if they 'result in compensating benefits for everyone, and in particular the least advantaged members of society' (Rawls, 1971, pp. 302, 15). While Rawls's work represents the defensive of a welfare liberalism, Robert Nozick's *Anarchy, State, and Utopia* reflects a libertarian liberalism. Along with Rawls, Nozick takes the view that individuals are autonomous (according to the Kantian dictum that persons are ends in themselves). Nozick, however, traces out the parameters of justice on the basis of natural or fundamental rights which constitute inviolable limits, or 'moral side-constraints' (Nozick, 1974, p. 33) to state power. Rawls's difference principle, Nozick contends, violates these rights. The state, for Nozick, exists only to ensure protection of these rights and compensation for their violation.

Sharing the conviction that justice takes its bearings from individual autonomy, the priority of liberty, and the neutrality of public discourse as to substantive views of the good life, the Rawls–Nozick debate reflects an intramural controversy between the moderately left- and right-wings of liberalism. Some liberal critics have argued that the terms of this debate misrepresent the historical resources of liberalism (Gray, 1989); that it fails to recognize adequately the social nature of individuals (Sandel, 1982) or the full range of human goods which might become legitimate matters of public debate (Galston, 1980). Other contemporary critics question the liberal ideals of neutrality (MacIntyre, 1988), autonomy (Grant, 1985) and the strict distinction between the private and public (Unger, 1976).

Since the late nineteenth century, the churches have found themselves especially engaged in the problem of social justice – a problem that has tended to place them in either an ambivalent or a directly critical posture towards liberal theories and practices of justice. On the one hand, liberal cultures have proved remarkably successful not only in the development and distribution of the conditions for material well-being, but also in realizing the ideal of universal suffrage and democratic political participation. On the other hand, the heritage of colonialization and economic exploitation of the non-western world, international warfare, and the unequal distribution of power and wealth in market capitalism, have prompted the churches to articulate justice in a more substantive language of the common good than what is ordinarily allowed in liberal theories. In Walter Rauschenbusch's *A Theology of the Social Gospel* (1917), and in the body of doctrine which evolved from Pope Leo XIII's *Rerum Novarum* (1891), there emerged theologies of justice which, although embracing many of the elements of liberalism (such as dignity of the person, political equality and the existence of rights), nonetheless aspired to introduce theologically informed notions of solidarity and the common good.

Perhaps because of its international stature, the Roman Catholic Communion has been the bellwether for the social justice issues. Although Pius IX declared that it is 'an error to believe that the Roman pontiff can or should reconcile himself to, and agree with progress, liberalism and modern civilizations' (*Syllabus of Errors*, 1854, #69), the tradition of papal social thought beginning with Leo XIII's *Rerum Novarum* ('new things') gradually began to take modern social and economic institutions as problems to be corrected rather than as a set of unmitigated errors. Pius XI's *Quadragesimo Anno* (1931, #57–8) first introduced the term 'social justice' (*justitiae socialis lege*). *Divini Redemptoris* (1937), *Mater et Magistra* (1961), *Pacem in Terris* (1963), *Populorum Progressio* (1967) and a host of more recent magisterial encyclicals and documents have argued the point that social justice directs the external acts of all the other virtues to the common good, especially in matters pertaining to the distribution of wealth and property. Thus, the ideal of social justice is not limited to the formal and procedural facets of the rule of law in a minimal state, but is rather a result-oriented view of justice with regard to a superordinate common good.

There has been ongoing debate over (1) the origin of the expression 'social justice', and its relation to the traditional Thomistic idea of general or legal justice (Calvez, 1961, ch. 6), (2) the analytical usefulness of the term (Honore, 1968) and (3) its practical suitability for free-market societies. Friedrich A. Hayek has contended that 'the prevailing belief in "social justice" is at present probably the greatest threat to most other values of a free civilization' (Hayek, 1976, p. 66). Hayek's criticism was aimed particularly at the churches. According to Hayek, the primary question is whether 'there exists a moral duty to submit to a power which can coordinate the efforts of the members of a society with the aim of achieving a particular pattern of distribution regarded as just' (Hayek, p. 64). He argued that short of submitting to a totalitarian state, there are no principles of conduct which would allow individuals to arrange their affairs rationally so as to produce social justice. Notwithstanding the fact that magisterial teaching has gradually incorporated many elements of the liberal view of justice, Hayek's criticism is a reminder that the idea of social justice represents a conception of the common good that, while not completely antithetical to either classical or reformed liberalism, stands in an uneasy relationship to it.

The Catholic church has stood in a similarly uneasy position with regard to theories of justice developed in the third world. The Medellin Conference of Latin American Bishops in 1969 at Bogota, Columbia, and the publication of the Spanish edition of Gustavo Gutiérrez's *Teologia de la Liberacion* in 1971 marked the emergence of a wide-ranging set of theories which can be included under the rubric LIBERATION THEOLOGY. While there are some recent indications that liberation theologians have moved beyond reliance upon Marxism (Sigmund, 1990), the movement has been overtly dependent upon various strands of Marxist analysis. Gutiérrez, for example, rejected not only the distinction between political, legal and economic planes of justice, but also the liberal notion of the priority of individual rights and the ideal of justice as neutrality. Juan Luis Segundo, SJ, in *The Liberation of Theology* of 1976, has likewise argued for the subordination of rights to the task of the liberation and economic improvement of the poor. Vatican teachings, such as the encyclical *Octogesima Adveniens* (1971) and *Sollicitudo Rei Socialis* (1987), have endorsed the ideal of a 'preferential' option or love for the poor and oppressed. However, in *Instruction on Certain Aspects of the 'Theology of Liberation'* (1984), Cardinal Ratzinger has stiffly criticized heterodox aspects of the movement as well as any exclusive notion of the preferential option.

Liberation theology has put the church into the position of simultaneously engaging in two quite different, and not easily reconciled, discussions. The bulk of the encyclical tradition has tried both to accommodate and to correct liberal understandings of justice in the North Atlantic world. Indeed, the church has covered enormous ground in incorporating the ideal of individual rights and the usefulness of free-market economies (especially in *Centesimus Annus*, 1991). On the other flank, the liberation theologies have emphasized precisely those notions of human solidarity, the common good and practical charity which are also embedded in the encyclicals and which, without further qualification, would seem to be directly contrary to modern, liberal ideals of the rule of law. The pontificate of John Paul II has tried to negotiate these two conversations, even while retaining on each front a properly theological grammar of justice.

Protestant theologians have also engaged in the social justice issues, particularly during the period marked by the ascendancy of liberal Protestantism, from Albrecht Ritschl (b. 1822) until the First World War. The moral meliorism of the prewar era, however, gave way to more cautious approaches to the relation between theology and justice. Reinhold Niebuhr, for example, put the Christian ethic of self-sacrificial love and the ethic of justice in juxtapositional tension. In *Love and Justice*, he contended that: 'In so far as justice admits the claims of the self, it is something less than love' (Niebuhr, 1957, p. 28). Although justice without love is a justice that is less than justice, sin and its exploitations (even among the redeemed) guarantee that sacrificial love cannot be an adequate social ethic. Even the effort to codify and theorize justice is conditioned by the interests of the strong. The Niebuhrian project was to keep love and justice overlapping and in tension, without reducing one to the other and without viewing the conflict between the two as being normative. His work proved to be influential among both theologians and statesmen, among other reasons because it gave scope both to the modern idea of justice as a limited equilibrium of power, and to the traditional theology of agapistic self-sacrifice.

The polarity between love and justice was more sharply drawn by Anders Nygren. In *Agape and Eros*, Nygren held that the parable of the labourers in the vineyard (Matt. 20: 1–16) indicates that God's love is unmotivated by any reason extrinsic to itself, and hence that the parable 'is directed against the thought of worthiness and merit, against any attempt to regulate fellowship with God by the principle of justice' (Nygren, [1930] 1982, p. 86). Nygren's work, which can be regarded as 'the beginning of the modern treatment of the subject' (Outka, 1972, p. 1), set the terms of the discussion not only for those who wished to distinguish sharply between love and justice, but also for theologians like Joseph Fletcher and John A.T. Robinson, who collapsed the tension, if not the difference, between the two by regarding justice merely as either the distribution or the direction of love. Because charity and justice share an overlapping vocabulary of obligation and virtue, universality and equal regard for persons, there remains an ongoing theological discussion about how to distinguish between the two so that charity supplies something more than a merely motivational supplement to justice.

The problem has also surfaced in the debate over the morality and justice of warfare. Paul Ramsey, in particular, undertook a fresh re-examination of the JUST WAR tradition. Relying somewhat upon papal teachings that social charity is the soul or form of justice (*Quadragesimo Anno*, #89), Ramsey argued that the 'western theory of the just war originated, not primarily from considerations of abstract or "natural" justice, but from the interior of the ethics of Christian love . . .' (Ramsey, [1968] 1983, p. 142). Considered in its proper theological light, the legitimacy and limits of war are rooted in the regard, or preference, of charity for the innocent. While Stanley Hauerwas has agreed that justice is not the principal criterion of a Christian social strategy, he has taken a position quite different from Ramsey on the issue of war. The church, he says, 'does not have a social ethic; the church is a social ethic' (Hauerwas, 1983, p. 99). The virtues learned in the church may well lead to the pursuit of social justice, but not to any relative justice achieved by violence. Christian justice is subordinated to the ethic of service and witness to the kingdom, rather than to maintaining or supplementing the rule of law that obtains in the state. John

Howard Yoder, in a similar vein, has contended that the gospel concept of the cross is not a strategy for social justice, but rather an obediental love 'which puts one at the mercy of one's neighbour, [and] which abandons claims to justice for oneself and for one's own in an overriding concern for the reconciling of the adversary and the estranged' (Yoder, 1972, p. 243).

See also CAPITALISM; ETHICS; NATURAL LAW; SOCIAL QUESTIONS.

Bibliography

Calvez, Jean-Yves, SJ, and Perrin, Jacques, S.J. 1961: *The Church and Social Justice*, trans. J.R. Kirwan. London: Burns and Oates.

Galston, William A. 1980: *Justice and the Human Good*. Chicago: University of Chicago Press.

Grant, George Parkin 1985: *English-Speaking Justice*. Notre Dame: University of Notre Dame Press.

Gray, 1989. Social contract, community and ideology. In *Liberalisms*. New York: Routledge.

Gremillion, Joseph 1976: *The Gospel of Peace and Justice*. New York: Orbis Books.

Hauerwas, Stanley 1983: *The Peaceable Kingdom*. Notre Dame: University of Notre Dame Press.

Hayek, F.A. 1976: *Law, Legislation and Liberty*. Chicago: University of Chicago Press.

Honore, A.M. 1968: Social justice. In *Essays in Legal Philosophy*, ed. R.S. Summers. Berkeley: University of California Press, pp. 61–94.

MacIntyre, Alasdair 1988: *Whose Justice? Which Rationality?* Notre Dame: University of Notre Dame Press.

Niebuhr, Reinhold 1957: *Love and Justice*, ed. D.B. Robertson. Philadelphia: Westminster Press, 1957.

Nozick, Robert 1974: *Anarchy, State, and Utopia*. New York: Basic Books.

Nygren, Anders [1930–6] 1982: *Agape and Eros*, trans. Philip S. Watson. Chicago: University of Chicago Press.

Outka, Gene 1972: *Agape*. New Haven: Yale University Press.

Ramsey, Paul [1968] 1983: *The Just War*. Lanham: University Press of America reprint.

Rawls, John 1971: *A Theory of Justice*. Cambridge, Mass.: Harvard University Press.

Sandel, Michael 1982: *Liberalism and the Limits of Justice*. Cambridge: Cambridge University Press.

Sigmund, Paul F. 1990: *Liberation Theology at the Crossroads*. Oxford: Oxford University Press.

Unger, Roberto M. 1976: *Law in Modern Society*. New York: Free Press.

Yoder, John Howard 1972: *The Politics of Jesus*. Grand Rapids: Eerdmans.

RUSSELL HITTINGER

K

Kähler, Martin (1835–1912) German Protestant theologian. He studied law at Königsburg and theology at Heidelberg, Tübingen and Halle. For most of his career a professor at Halle, he criticized the liberal attempt to identify 'the historical Jesus' for driving a wedge between the Jesus of history and the Jesus of faith. He maintained that liberal methods of scholarship misunderstood the character and purpose of the biblical text, which was not a merely historical narrative; by so doing, they undermined ordinary people's access to Jesus, who is found primarily in the Bible and in the preached message of the church. His arguments, which in some respects anticipate the work of R. Bultmann and A. Schweitzer, are the subject of recent renewed study. His works include *Der sogenannte historische Jesus und der geschichtliche, biblische Christus* (1892, trans. *The So-Called Historical Jesus and the Historic, Biblical Christ*, 1964), and a major volume of dogmatics, *Die Wissenschaft der christlichen Lehre* (1883–7).

Bibliography

Braaten, C.E., and Harrisville, R.A., eds 1964: *The Historical Jesus and the Kerygmatic Christ*, article on Martin Kähler. Harrisville. Nashville, Tn.
Braaten, C.E., and Harrisville, R.A. eds 1962: *Kerygma and History*. New York.

Kant, Immanuel (1724–1804) German philosopher. He was born and lived his entire life in Königsberg in Prussia, where he became professor of logic. He published extensively from the 1750s onwards in cosmology and philosophy, but his mature philosophy is known through a series of writings produced in and after the 'critical decade' of the 1780s. Chief among these are: the *Critique of Pure Reason* of 1781 (and the second edition of 1787), *Prolegomena to any Future Metaphysics* of 1783, *Foundations of the Metaphysics of Morals* of 1785 (also translated as *The Fundamental Principles of the Metaphysics of Ethics*), the *Critique of Practical Reason* of 1788, the *Critique of Judgement* of 1790, *Religion within the Limits of Reason Alone* of 1793 and the *Metaphysics of Morals* of 1797.

Kant endeavoured to produce a complete picture of human knowledge. He argued that we can never know things in themselves, but only our experience of them. Following from this, he had to admit that we cannot know about the existence of God – God, he concluded, is not a matter of knowledge but of faith. Kant also produced significant work on morals, contending that morality springs from reason, and is a priori.

Kant has been a hugely influential figure in both theology and philosophy, and is often regarded as the greatest philosopher since Plato and Aristotle.

See also KANTIANISM.

Bibliography

Kant, I. 1922–3: *Immanuel Kant's Werke*, 11 vols, ed. E. Cassirer. Berlin.
Körner, S. 1955: *Kant*. Harmondsworth.
Lindsay, A.D. 1934: *Kant*. London.
Reardon, B. 1988: *Kant as Philosophical Theologian*. Basingstoke.
Scruton, R. 1982: *Kant*. Oxford.

Kantianism Immanuel Kant stood outside orthodox, practising Christianity, but his entire philosophy has important implications for religious belief, being a self-conscious attempt to harmonize apparently contradictory facets of the world view of the ENLIGHTENMENT. These facets bear particularly on the perceived clash between the claims of science and religion. Crucial here are, on the one hand, the naturally opposing commitments to the success of science in giving natural and deterministic explanations connecting all phenomena and, on the other, the belief that human beings are capable of rational self-direction and have a moral destiny in the universe which it is their duty to fulfil.

Both of these conflicting beliefs are metaphysical: they make claims about the structure of reality that go beyond what can be vouched for in experience. Experience can tell us only that so far as we have discovered events are explicable, intelligible and interconnected. Experience cannot assure us that the universe is such as to allow human beings to be free and to realize ultimate good. Kant accordingly took as one of his major preoccupations the settling of the due limits and scope of metaphysical knowledge. In outline, he sets about the reconciliation of the items in the Enlightenment world view by limiting the pretensions of its competing scientific and religious metaphysics and thereby producing an outcome in which each metaphysic can be true. This central preoccupation with metaphysics allows Kant to pursue another task of reconciliation – that presented by the conflict between rationalist and empiricist theories of knowledge, as they had developed from their common roots in Descartes.

René Descartes had set a standard for certainty which located it in such knowledge as was demonstrable from intuitive starting points (see CARTESIANISM). Both rationalists, like G.W. Leibniz, and empiricists, like David Hume, agreed that such knowledge was not available from the world disclosed by our senses. Rationalists then took this as showing that the true object of knowledge was an intelligible, rational world behind that of the senses. Empiricists, denying that pure reason alone could yield us knowledge of matters of fact, confined our knowledge to the observable world but lowered its certainty and reliability in the light of the Cartesian ideal.

Kant's solution to this dilemma in the *Critique of Pure Reason* ([1781] 1933) depended on the common assumption that there have to be elements of universality and necessity in the guiding principles of human knowledge, or as he would have it, there have to be a priori contributions to our knowledge of reality. But he made these a priori principles not descriptions of an intelligible, rational realm beyond the senses, but outlines of the *form* to which the matter of our experience of the ordinary world had to conform. The principles of general metaphysics become statements a priori of the form any intelligible experience of the world has to take. Because we can be assured a priori that, for example, any experience we can make sense of must be of a world in which all events are causally interconnected, so it is that our knowledge of the world of experience can be guaranteed to have the certainty that comes with its obeying, necessarily, rational principles of order.

The general metaphysical principles of rationalism turn out to be true when relativized into statements about the form and structure of empirical knowledge. This structure is dictated by two sources of any empirical knowledge we can make sense of: sensibility and understanding. Knowledge is of things, their properties, relations, actions etc. It requires that something be given to experience (via sensibility or intuition) and that experience of that given be ordered, comprehended through concepts supplied by understanding. Sensibility has an a priori structure – the mode in which things are given to human beings is as objects in space and time. Something similar is true of understanding, which turns out to have just twelve 'categories' (or higher-order concepts) to which *all* concepts applicable to experience can be traced. More convincing than this list of categories is Kant's argument, through sections of the *Critique of Pure Reason* entitled 'Transcendental Deduction', 'Refutation of Idealism' and 'Analogies of Experience', that *any* conceivable form of human experience must be such as to allow concepts of an objective world to apply to it (concepts within such categories as those of cause and substance). The argument turns around the necessity of experience having the richness capable of giving rise to self-consciousness, a richness which turns out to involve a rule-governed structure of the sort which allows the subject to be aware of a causal and temporal order – in other words of an objective world. Kant thus lays to rest the problem which arose out of the Cartesian ideal of certainty and the fear that only in the contents of my own private experience could that certainty be found.

From the a priori forms of intuition and understanding Kant is able to demonstrate a range of necessary truths about reality which can serve as the basis of certain knowledge. But the cost of establishing these truths of general metaphysics is a certain relativizing of their validity. The demonstration, say, that every event in the world must have a cause depends on the premise that the world is an object of possible experience: any world about which we can make judgements must be causally ordered. The principles of metaphysics cannot on this ground be applied to items beyond human experience. Concerning aspects of reality that lie beyond human experience we can know nothing, either a priori or a posteriori. Kant's thought here involves two things: the 'Copernican revolution' in philosophy and the distinction between appearances and things in themselves.

Prior to Copernicus astronomers took the apparent daily motion of the sun and stars to be real. After Copernicus we know these motions to have been nothing other than the motions of the earth projected onto these heavenly bodies. Prior to Kant metaphysicians took it that they had to discover the objective, necessary features of independent metaphysical reality which could then furnish the first principles of philosophy. After Kant we realize that such features are nothing other than the a priori necessities of human cognition which we falsely assume to be reading off metaphysical reality. Contrary to the empiricists we need to be able to anticipate reality for sure knowledge of it to be possible at all. But we can only anticipate it if it must conform to conditions of intelligibility that the human subject in effect lays down for itself.

Kant's way of expressing the subjective turn he gives to metaphysics is through the distinction between appearances and things in themselves. What is known of reality is only that which our faculties of cognition allow us to discover. Considered as it is in itself, we can

know nothing of the world, and specifically we cannot say that the necessary truths of experience apply to it. 'We can know nothing of the world in itself' is a tautology, asserting that we can only know the world as we can know it. But it is a significant tautology, reminding us that there may be aspects of reality that quite escape beings with our cognitive powers, and thus it allows us to avoid dogmatic statements of an absolute kind about the nature or limits of reality. This is to interpret the appearance/thing in itself distinction critically or negatively. But sometimes Kant allows himself to use his 'transcendental idealism' positively. In such uses 'things in themselves' figure as the mysterious ground of appearances; about them much of a positive sort is hazarded, especially in the interests of morality.

We can see in a preliminary way how Kant can reconcile the elements in the Enlightenment world view with the resources of the critical philosophy. The truths of general metaphysics – such as the causal principle – are allowed to be true only relatively. This is sufficient to guarantee the successful application of science to all aspects of experience. However, a claim of special metaphysics, such as that men have free will, will be allowed to be thinkable and this will be sufficient to ground practical allegiance to a humanist religious-cum-moral outlook. As part of this reconciliation Kant cannot allow any metaphysical proofs of such claims as that there is a God, or that men have an immortal soul or free will to withstand critical scrutiny. A large division of the *Critique of Pure Reason* (the 'Transcendental Dialectic') is devoted to exposing metaphysical proofs of these and other propositions of special metaphysics. His refutations remain profoundly influential today, none more so than his discussion of the proofs of God's existence (see EXISTENCE OF GOD, PROOFS OF).

Kant must show that God cannot be an object of metaphysical knowledge. With characteristic neatness he declares that there are three and only three possible proofs of the existence of God: the ontological, the cosmological and the physico-theological (design). The first, he argues, commits the cardinal error of arguing for a substantial conclusion about existence on the basis of truths of reason and definition alone. He repeats a criticism first made in his

'The Only Possible Ground of the Proof of the Existence of God' of 1763, which shows (for him) the inevitable futility of arguing that since existence is a perfection, a God with all perfections must exist in reality as well as in the understanding. In 1763 he wrote:

> But in these cases existence, whilst it commonly occurs in ordinary usage as a predicate, is not so much a predicate of the thing itself, but much more of the thought that one has of that thing. For example, 'Existence belongs to the sea-unicorn [*Narwahl*] but not to the land-unicorn.' This is to say no more than: the representation of the sea-unicorn is the concept of something to be found in experience [*ein Erfahrungsbegriff*], that is, it is the concept of an existing thing.
>
> *(Kant, 1900–56, vol. 2, p. 72, my translation)*

If it is at least reasonable to interpret existence-statements as directly about the relations between concepts and reality (rather than as ascribing properties to objects) then the force of the ontological proof can always be escaped. Kant thinks that the other two proofs depend on the ontological and its key idea of an absolutely perfect being which at the same time must be necessarily existent, but he has other objections to them. He cites as a key point that no univocal notion of cause will take us from the truth of experience that all events must have causes to the transcendent claim that everything (including the entire world of contingent things) must have a cause. All inferences of NATURAL THEOLOGY are thereby declared invalid. The design argument, though mentioned with respect, is said to prove at most that the *form* of the world requires a cause but not that its matter does.

In the *Critique of Pure Reason* God is given the status of a regulative idea (along with the soul and freedom). Its reality can neither be proved nor disproved. But certain practical interests to do with reason's endeavours to organize knowledge into theory lead us to postulate God's existence. This postulation achieves its full significance, however, only when the interests of morality are taken into account.

Kant's critical thoughts about the nature of morality are set out at greatest length in the *Critique of Practical Reason* ([1788] 1956). As in his writings on theoretical reason, Kant assumes that the deliberations of ethics will have a form as well as a content. It is this form he endeavours to set out. Some have naively assumed that he therefore thinks ethics lacks a content, as if for example we could deduce the concrete duties of humankind without paying attention to the actual conditions of human goals and circumstances. Nothing could be farther from his intentions. Another connection with his treatment of theoretical philosophy is his self-conscious attempt to sum up and reconcile elements in the philosophical tradition. He is particularly concerned to uncover what is correct and incorrect in the classical idea that morality gets its shape from a substantive end – happiness – which is the goal of all striving and the source of duty. Kant agrees that there must be a final goal achievable by moral striving (otherwise his humanistic vision would fail) but denies that morality can be deduced from any prior, determinate end. There is too much variety in human conceptions of happiness to make this possible. The nature of a happiness fit for rational beings to strive for can only be worked out after such conceptions have been filtered through the requirements of rational, moral law.

Kant's ethics cannot be straightforwardly teleological. He posits some basic notions of right which are the means of working out which ends are to be pursued. These come from the formal defining features of morality, which are: universality, rationality and impartiality. A moral principle is one which embodies these features and has a categorical, that is unconditional, force in consequence. Morality wears the aspect of a body of legislation which binds the human will. It can be binding as universal legislation without destroying (rather: it fulfils) human freedom because it is self-legislation, law which embodies the choice of reason itself. A moral principle is binding for Kant if it embodies universal, impartial, rational legislation. It then has the form of the 'Categorical Imperative': 'Act only on that maxim [principle] which you can at the same time will to be a universal law.' The bindingness of a moral principle comes from its having this form. Its content is worked out by considering what impartial, rational, universal legislation for creatures such as us might be. Consider: we wish to know if it should be a general duty on us to render assistance to those in need. We have to think if the appropriate maxim could be recommended to all rational beings as one that binds their conduct. We consider the generic interests of humanity and general facts, such as that all human beings, no matter what their particular ends, will require aid from others from time to time. A contrary maxim ('let me receive aid from others but not render it to them') would in contrast stand no chance of gaining universal acceptance as rational legislation. In this way the basic features of right dictated by the form of practical reason (morality) act as a filter through which facts about human nature and circumstances can be passed to yield determinate duties.

Impartial moral legislation will in general promote the existence of us all as rational beings without detriment to one another's unique projects. This flowering of rational nature is the goal of Kantian ethics. A possible conflict within it, however, gives scope for a more substantial argument for the postulate of God's existence. Out of morality flows the goal of the fulfilment of one's rational nature, indeed the principles of morality lay down conditions for promoting the pursuit of rational purposes by human beings through rules which harmonize each person's pursuit of the good with that of others. Fulfilling rational nature means attaining a state of virtue in which the maxims of one's action always embody respect for the demands of rational impartiality. But it also means attaining happiness, that is, the fulfilling of the particular rational plan of life that is uniquely one's own. If the world is not morally ordered then there is no guarantee that these two aspects of fulfilling rational personhood will not come into conflict. One will be able to obey the dictates of right only at the cost of frustration of the pursuit of personal goals (consider the just man who suffers for his virtue in a wicked community because he is just). We need the supposition, then, that despite appearances the world is under perfect moral government (that is: happiness is proportioned to virtue in the long run) to avoid the intolerable thought that two aspects of practical reason will be in fundamental conflict with one another. The concrete form that this thought about moral government takes is that of a God who dispenses happiness in accordance with desert, in the next life if not in this. In the special case of there being complete silence from theoretical reason on the existence or non-existence of God and of there being a rational (as opposed to personal) need for his postulation, practical interests can sway our belief. A practical, rational faith in God thus arises which is at the same time not the basis for metaphysical speculation. The postulate of God has just sufficient content to support the idea that the Enlightenment goal of happiness through the perfection of the rational life is not a chimera.

Kant has corresponding arguments in the *Critique of Practical Reason* for the immortality of the soul and the freedom of the will. Morality leads ineluctably to religion, but it might appear that it is a very thin form of religion until we take account of the arguments of *Religion within the Limits of Reason Alone* ([1793] 1960). This work does two things of note. First it enriches the terms of the philosophical religion that practical reason requires to be true in order to make sense of morality. Second it shows how a Kantian rational, practical faith nonetheless has need of the outward, historical forms of religious faith and institutions if its ends are to be achieved. The first task is attempted by analysis of the nature of evil in the human will. So radical is this that a use is required for notions of grace, atonement and other items from the Christian scheme of salvation. Each is given an appropriate ethical 'translation' and freed from any essential reliance on historical revelation in so doing. (This is one place in Kant's critical philosophy where many a positive thing is said about what must be true of things in themselves.) The second task is performed by stressing the social aspect of the ethical goal reason sets for humanity. It is nothing less than to achieve an ethical commonwealth on earth. In order to do so reason must make use, at least provisionally, of the contingent, changing external forms of traditional religion (particularly Christianity). These are helpful means of uniting good men to work for Kant's ethical version of the kingdom of God on earth.

Thus are the claims of science and religion reconciled in Kant. The metaphysical underpinnings of natural science are relativized to a degree. The claims of religion are narrowed in their essential content and made to rest on an autonomous practical reason which only needs the dogmatic pretensions of naturalistic, scientistic metaphysics to be limited in order to be secure in its essential beliefs about human nature and destiny.

As the most important philosopher of the Enlightenment, in whose work religious concerns were central, Kant's influence on subsequent religious thought was immense. Three forms of the Kantian legacy may be discerned. One outcome of Kant was the paradoxical rebirth of idealist metaphysics (illustrated by J.G. Fichte and G.W.F. Hegel) through concentration on Kant's theme of the role of the human subject in the constitution of its world. Such metaphysics gave ample opportunity in the early nineteenth century for philosophies which rivalled or reconstructed Christian doctrine in a radical way. A second response may be called the circumvention of Kant in those writers who found his confining of religion to practical reason too limiting, yet accepted much of his teaching about the nature of knowledge. In F.D.E. Schleiermacher and others (such as F. Max Mueller and Rudolph Otto) the approach adopted was to accept the Kantian account of the sources and limits of theoretical and practical reason, while seeking an a priori foundation of religion in a third form of human consciousness: that is, feeling, experience. A third response showing a direct following of Kant on the nature of religious thought is to be found in the neo-Kantian inspired liberal Protestantism of Albrecht Ritschl, who derived his epistemology from the reworking of Kant in writers such as R.H. Lotze. Ritschl's liberal Protestantism, of great importance in the shaping of nineteenth- and twentieth-century theology, shows Kantian influence in the form of: the thesis that religion grows out of the tension between man as spirit and as part of nature; the assertion that religious dogmas are judgements of value; the locating of religious destiny in living an ethically self-conscious life; and in the placing of Christianity's central concern in the realization of an ethically grounded community of the kingdom of God on earth. Liberal Protestantism found the essence of religion in practical, ethical consciousness for essentially the same reasons

as Kant: to establish a sure place for religion in an age of science.

See also EPISTEMOLOGY, RELIGIOUS.

Bibliography

Writings

[1781] 1933: *Critique of Pure Reason*, trans. N.K. Smith. London: Macmillan.

[1783] 1953: *Prolegomena to Any Future Metaphysics*, trans. P.G. Lucas. Manchester: Manchester University Press.

[1785] 1959: *Foundations of the Metaphysics of Morals*, trans. L.W. Beck. Indianapolis: Bobbs Merrill.

[1788] 1956: *Critique of Practical Reason*, trans. L.W. Beck. Indianapolis: Bobbs Merrill.

[1790] 1952: *Critique of Judgement*, trans. J.C. Meredith. Oxford: Oxford University Press.

[1793] 1960: *Religion within the Limits of Reason Alone*, trans. T.M. Greene and H.H. Hudson. New York: Harper and Row.

[1797] 1965: *The Metaphysical Elements of Justice* (Part 1 of *The Metaphysics of Morals*, trans. J. Ladd. Indianapolis: Bobbs Merrill.

[1797] 1964: *The Doctrine of Virtue* (Part 2 of *The Metaphysics of Morals*), trans. M.J. Gregor. New York: Harper and Row.

1900–56: *Gesammelte Schriften*, 23 vols. Berlin: Preussische Akademie der Wissenschaften.

Critical works

Byrne, P. 1979: Kant's moral proof of the existence of God, *Scottish Journal of Theology* 32, pp. 333–43.

Byrne, P. 1989: *Natural Religion and the Nature of Religion*. London: Routledge.

Cassirer, E. 1981: *Kant's Life and Thought*, trans. J. Hoden. New Haven: Yale University Press.

Collins, J. 1967: *The Emergence of the Philosophy of Religion*. New Haven: Yale University Press.

Despland, M. 1973: *Kant on History and Religion*. Montreal: McGill/Queen's University Press.

Fackenheim, E.L. 1956: Kant's concept of history, *Kantstudien* 48, pp. 381–98.

Gold, A. 1984: Kant's rejection of devilishness, *Idealist Studies* 14, pp. 36–8.

Green, R.M. 1978: *Religious Reason*. New York: Oxford University Press.

Körner, S. 1955: *Kant*. Harmondsworth: Penguin.

Loades, A. 1985: *Kant and Job's Comforters*. Newcastle-upon-Tyne: Avero.

Michaelson, G.M. 1989: Moral regeneration and divine aid in Kant, *Religious Studies* 25, pp. 259–70.

Reardon, B.M.G. 1988: *Kant as Philosophical Theologian*. London: Macmillan.

Silber, J.R. 1959: Kant's conception of the highest good as immanent and transcendent, *Philosophical Review* 67, pp. 469–92.

Silber, J.R. 1963: The importance of the highest good in Kant's ethics, *Ethics* 73, pp. 179–97.

Silber, J.R. 1967: The Copernican revolution in ethics. In *Kant*, ed. R.P. Wolff. London: Macmillan, pp. 266–90.

Walsh, W.H. 1963: Kant's moral theology, *Proceedings of the British Academy* 49, pp. 263–89.

Walsh, W.H. 1975: *Kant's Criticism of Metaphysics*. Edinburgh: Edinburgh University Press.

Wood, A.W. 1970: *Kant's Moral Religion*. Ithaca: Cornell University Press.

Wood, A.W. 1978: *Kant's Rational Theology*. Ithaca: Cornell University Press.

Yovel, Y. 1972: The highest good and history in Kant's thought, *Archiv für Geschichte der Philosophie* 54, pp. 238–83.

PETER BYRNE

Käsemann, Ernst (b. 1906) German Protestant New Testament theologian. He was professor of New Testament studies at Mainz, Göttingen and Tübingen. Influenced by Bultmann, he has emphasized the necessity of 'demythologizing' the gospels, whilst upholding the importance of the historical basis of Christianity: he has called for a 'new quest for the historical Jesus' which would end the separation of the Jesus of history from the Jesus of faith. His major work is a commentary on Romans (1973, trans. 1980). In this and other works (including *Perspectives on Paul*, 1969, trans. 1971) he contends that Pauline theology is based on the idea of the justification of the ungodly, rather than on the unfolding of progressive stages of the salvation history; and that the 'righteousness of God' is not a divine characteristic imputed to believers, but rather the divine will and ability to save humanity. His study of the early church led him to highlight the importance of Jewish and apocalyptic thought; he also wrote in the areas of ecclesiology and the social and political implications of the gospel (see *Jesus Means Freedom*, 1968, trans. 1970). During the Nazi period he was associated with the German Confessing Church, and he was active in the World Council of Churches.

Bibliography

Friedrich, J. *et al.*, eds 1976: *Rechtfertigung, Festschrift für E. Käsemann zum 70 Geburtstag*. Mohr.

Morgan, R. 1973: *The Nature of New Testament Theology*. London.

Wright, N.T. 1982: A New Tübingen School? Ernst Käsemann and his Commentary on Romans, *Themelios* 7.

Keble, John (1792–1866) English churchman and a founder of the Tractarian movement. Educated at Corpus Christi College, Oxford, he became a fellow of Oriel College at the age of nineteen, and was ordained priest in 1816. He spent most of his life in the parish ministry, combining his parochial duties with a professorship of poetry at Oxford from 1831 to 1841, and exercising considerable influence in the church through his leadership of the Tractarian movement; he wrote nine of its *Tracts for the Times* (1833–41). Other literary work includes the publication of a major cycle of poetry, *The Christian Year* (1827), the editorship of Richard Hooker's *Works* (1836) and, with J.H. Newman and E.B. Pusey, of the *Library of the Fathers* (1838), to which he contributed his own translation of Irenaeus. After Newman joined the Roman Catholic church in 1845, Keble worked with Pusey to keep Anglo-Catholicism alive within the Church of England; a vigorous opponent of liberalism and Protestant reforming tendencies, he wrote numerous pamphlets, many of which provoked controversy. Keble College, Oxford, is named in his memory.

Bibliography

Battiscombe, G. 1963: *John Keble: A Study in Limitations*. London.

Church, R.W. 1900: *The Oxford Movement*. London.

Coleridge, J.T. 1869: *Memoir*. Oxford.

Kierkegaard, Søren (1813–1855) Danish theologian and philosopher. The son of a Lutheran, he spent his life in Copenhagen, where he studied theology before becoming a writer and thinker. He was a stringent critic of the Lutheran church in Denmark, which he saw as worldly, but he is best known for his critique of the dominant philosophical system of the day, Hegelianism. He opposed Hegel's dialectic with his own form of existential dialectic, first set out in *Either–Or* of 1843; he criticized Hegel for attempting to define reality by philosophical systems rather than addressing the imperative experience of existence. Tending towards individualism (as in his dictum, 'truth is subjectivity'), he stressed the importance of the personal experience of faith, and argued for commitment and obedience over against mere proposition as the condition of knowing God. He also emphasized the gulf between the divine and the human, time and eternity: man's sinfulness and God's holiness made of God 'the absolutely Unknown'; but in Jesus Christ the gulf has been bridged. Nevertheless, he regarded the historicity of the Gospel accounts of Jesus as of secondary importance in the acceptance of Christianity; what mattered was the believer's experience of God. Sometimes called the father of EXISTENTIALISM, Kierkegaard has exercised a considerable posthumous influence on modern secular and religious thought, including Barth's dialectical theology and Bultmann's and Heidegger's existential philosophy. His many works include *Philosophical Fragments* (1844), *Fear and Trembling* (1844), *Sickness Unto Death* (1849), *Christian Discourses* (1850) and *Training in Christianity* (1850).

Bibliography

Dupre, L. 1963: *Kierkegaard as Theologian*. London.
Elrod, J.W. 1981: *Kierkegaard and Christendom*. Princeton, NJ.
Pojman, L.P. 1984: *The Logic of Subjectivity: Kierkegaard's Philosophy of Religion*. Alabama.

kingdom of God: New Testament The phrase 'the kingdom of God' (Greek *he basileia tou theou*), or Matthew's more Jewish equivalent 'the kingdom of heaven', is one of the most prominent features of the teaching of Jesus as recorded in the synoptic Gospels. Scholars of all shades of opinion agree both that it must have been a distinctive feature of Jesus' teaching, and that it represents a central element in his message. What is not so clearly agreed is what it means!

The distribution of the phrase
'The kingdom of God/heaven', or a functional equivalent such as 'his kingdom', occurs some seventy times in the synoptic Gospels, without counting the parallels where the same saying occurs in more than one Gospel.

In sharp contrast, John's Gospel mentions 'the kingdom of God' only in 3: 3, 5. In Acts 'the kingdom of God' is mentioned six times,

and 'the kingdom' alone once, to designate the content of early Christian preaching. The Pauline letters use the phrase nine times, and in addition refer occasionally to the kingdom of Christ (or 'of Christ and of God', Eph. 5: 5). A handful of similar references in other books, usually not offering the actual phrase 'the kingdom of God', complete the New Testament usage.

It seems clear, then, that while language about the kingdom of God passed into general Christian use, it was not of such focal importance in the thought of apostolic writers as it had been in both the public and the private teaching of Jesus. The usage of Acts suggests that it had begun to function as a stereotyped formula for the gospel message rather than with the dynamic variety of reference we find in the synoptic Gospels.

The meaning of the phrase
The Greek noun *basileia* (like the Hebrew *malkut*, which lies behind its biblical use) refers primarily to the abstract concept of 'kingship' or 'rule', and only secondarily to the concrete entity of a place or group of people who are ruled, which is the primary meaning of 'kingdom' in modern English. In the sixteenth century, however, 'kingdom' was an appropriate translation, since the abstract meaning was still alive and even dominant (see the *Oxford English Dictionary*). The subsequent change in English usage has not been reflected in Bible translations, with the result that modern readers confronted by the phrase 'the kingdom of God' naturally think of a place, group or situation rather than of the essential biblical idea of 'God ruling'. The modern tendency to abbreviate the biblical phrase from 'the kingdom of God/heaven' to simply 'the kingdom' (an abbreviation of which Acts 20: 25 is the only New Testament example, apart from Matthew's occasional use of a phrase such as 'the gospel of the kingdom' where the context makes the reference to God's kingdom clear) further strengthens the impression that there is some 'thing' to which it refers, and thus results in the misunderstanding of New Testament passages where the phrase would have been better translated as 'the rule of God'.

Underlying the phrase is the fundamental Old Testament conviction that God, as Creator, is king of what he has created, of the world in general, and of his people Israel in particular. This kingship is celebrated as a present reality, but the prophets also look forward to a future more effective establishment of God's rule. In later Jewish literature, while the actual phrase 'the kingdom of God' seldom occurs, the idea remains a feature both of basic theology and of hope for the future. In a Jewish context this hope was inevitably understood primarily in nationalistic terms, of the restoration of Israel's supremacy as the people of God. The synagogue prayer, the Kaddish, which goes back to the time of Jesus, included the clause, 'May he let his kingdom rule in your lifetime, and in the lifetime of the whole house of Israel, speedily and soon.'

Matthew's equivalent phrase, 'the kingdom of heaven', is a typically Jewish reverential paraphrase, avoiding direct use of the name of God. The phrase is used regularly in parallel with 'the kingdom of God' in Mark and Luke, and there is no discernible difference in meaning.

Jesus' teaching about the kingdom of God

Jesus' public preaching, according to the synoptic Gospels, began with the announcement of the arrival of the kingdom of God. The assertion that it 'has come near', coupled with the statement that (literally) 'the time has been fulfilled' (Mark 1: 15) expresses more than a hope for the future, and Jesus' exorcisms are explained as a sign that 'the kingdom of God has come upon you' (Matt. 12: 28), while in response to those who asked when the kingdom of God would be coming, Jesus replied that it 'is among you' (Luke 17: 21; the translation 'within you' is less likely).

But he also spoke about a future time when some would see the kingdom of God 'having come with power' (Mark 9: 1), and at the Last Supper looked forward to drinking new wine 'in the kingdom of God' (Mark 14: 25). This tension between the now and the not yet is neatly expressed in the traditional form of the Lord's Prayer, in which Jesus teaches his followers to pray 'Your kingdom come' (Matt. 6: 10), and yet the concluding doxology includes the recognition that already 'Yours is the kingdom'.

As long as the kingdom of God is understood to refer to a particular event or situation this tension remains problematic. Once it is granted, however, that God's kingship is a less concrete concept, it is easier to see how it can be understood both as already implemented in Jesus' ministry and yet still to be more powerfully worked out in the future. Jesus' parable of the mustard seed (Mark 4: 30–2) describes the coming of the kingdom of God in terms of a progression from small beginnings to ultimate completion. There is thus an element of paradox, of hiddenness, in the coming of God's kingship, like that of a seed which grows secretly by its own dynamic (Mark 4: 26–9). It is not yet obvious to all, since it requires special discernment to recognize 'the secret of the kingdom of God' (Mark 4: 11).

While the language of kingship suggests a political agenda, Jesus went out of his way to distance himself from the political aspirations of the Zealots, notably in his famous directive to 'Give to Caesar what is Caesar's, and to God what is God's.' Many of his followers apparently expected him to act to lead a movement for the restoration of Israel's national fortunes, but it is a supreme irony that having refused to do so, he was eventually executed as the purported 'King of the Jews'.

In this and other ways paradox is never far from Jesus' use of the language of the kingdom of God. Because it is the kingdom *of God* it can never be reduced to a human agenda. Its values and principles constantly offend against human expectation (see especially Mark 10: 13–16, 23–7). To accept God as king (to 'enter the kingdom of God') is to commit oneself to an alternative society in which 'The last will be first, and the first last.' These are the people described in the Beatitudes: the poor in spirit, the mourning, the meek, those who are hungry and thirsty for righteousness, the merciful, the pure in heart, the peacemakers, those who are persecuted for righteousness; 'Theirs is the kingdom of heaven' (Matt. 5: 3–10).

It is clear that Jesus' use of the phrase (of which we have seen only a few samples) is far too rich and varied to allow a simple definition of the kingdom of God in terms of any one situation or event. Its reference is to the victorious implementation of God's kingly rule, and its breadth of application is as broad as the whole purpose of God, as it applies to the varied situations of human life and history.

The kingdom of God in modern New Testament scholarship

This is one of the few aspects of Jesus' teaching which is universally agreed to be authentic. It satisfies fully the form-critical 'criterion of dissimilarity', in that the phrase is rare in contemporary Jewish literature and it does not have the same prominence in the language of the New Testament writers (even that of the synoptic evangelists when they are not reporting the words of Jesus). It is thus distinctive of Jesus himself.

But there has been less agreement about where the focus of Jesus' teaching lay. Nineteenth-century liberalism understood Jesus' teaching of the kingdom of God primarily in terms of the advance of human society towards the ideal of love and brotherhood. In sharp contrast Johannes Weiss, followed by Albert Schweitzer, and subsequently by Rudolf Bultmann and his school, laid stress on the eschatological context and focus of Jesus' teaching. For them Jesus was an apocalyptic prophet, preaching the imminent coming of the kingdom of God as a dynamic inbreaking into history. On this view (which came to be known as 'consistent eschatology') the kingdom of God remains for Jesus a wholly future hope, which nonetheless has its ethical effect on the present as people are called to live in the light of the imminent consummation (Schweitzer's 'interim ethics').

This growing consensus was challenged by C.H. Dodd (1935), who argued that the parables about the kingdom of God present it as a challenge to decision not because it is soon to come but because it is already present in the ministry of Jesus. Dodd called this view 'realized eschatology'; what on Weiss's view was for Jesus a future hope was, Dodd claimed, a present reality, as indicated in Mark 1: 15 and Matthew 12: 28. Dodd therefore played down, or reinterpreted, those sayings which had been understood to point to a future 'coming' of the kingdom of God.

Dodd's view has not been widely followed in its extreme form; indeed Dodd's later work suggests a less radical position. But his challenge to 'consistent eschatology' has been widely welcomed, and the present aspect of the kingdom of God in Jesus' teaching has since then been generally admitted. Joachim Jeremias's study of the parables built on Dodd's work, but incorporated the future aspect into what Jeremias called 'eschatology in the process of realization' (sich realisierende Eschatologie). The same tension between fulfilment and future hope is now almost universally recognized, and phrases such as 'inaugurated eschatology' or 'fulfilment without consummation' (Ladd, 1964) are commonly used to express it.

While the earlier debate over the time of the coming of the kingdom of God has therefore subsided, recent discussion has focused more on the meaning and function of the phrase. New Testament scholars (unlike New Testament translations) generally agree that the word 'kingdom' can be misleading, and speak of God's 'kingship', 'reign' or 'rule', the focus being not on the 'activity' as such but on the God who rules. B.F. Meyer (1979, p. 137) goes so far as to say, '"The reign of God" signifies "God" and signifies God precisely as Jesus knows him.' B.D. Chilton (1987), noting the use of the phrase 'the kingdom of God' in the Isaiah Targum, offers the paraphrase 'God in strength'.

N. Perrin (1976) explains the breadth of use of the phrase 'the kingdom of God' in the Gospels by arguing that it is not a concept or idea, with a single identifiable referent, but a symbol, and more specifically a 'tensive symbol', which serves to evoke a wide range of ideas relating to the deeply rooted belief that God is king. This means that 'its meaning could never be exhausted, nor adequately expressed, by any one referent' (p. 31).

Such scholarly comments suggest that the popular tendency to use 'kingdom' language as if it had a single clear area of meaning should be treated with caution. Such language is currently applied variously to the ideal of socioeconomic justice, or political reform, to radical Christian discipleship, or to a distinctively charismatic spirituality, or to life after death, to mention only a few such competing uses. While any such restriction of the range of meaning of the New Testament phrase may communicate well enough within any group who have agreed to this particular convention, it must lead to distortion if imposed on the understanding of the New Testament texts.

See also BIBLICAL CRITICISM AND INTERPRETATION 2: NEW TESTAMENT; CHRISTOLOGY; DISPENSATIONALISM; ESCHATOLOGY; KINGDOM OF GOD: POLITICAL AND SOCIAL THEOLOGY.

Bibliography

Ambrozic, A.M. 1972: *The Hidden Kingdom: A Redaction-Critical Study of the References to the Kingdom of God in Mark's Gospel*. Washington, DC: Catholic Biblical Association of America.

Beasley-Murray, G.R. 1986: *Jesus and the Kingdom of God*. Exeter: Paternoster Press.

Chilton, B.D. 1987: *God in Strength: Jesus' Announcement of the Kingdom*. Sheffield: JSOT Press.

Chilton, B.D., and McDonald, J.I.H. 1987: *Jesus and the Ethics of the Kingdom*. London: SPCK.

Dodd, C.H. 1935: *The Parables of the Kingdom*. London: James Nisbet.

France, R.T. 1990: *Divine Government: God's Kingship in the Gospel of Mark*. London: SPCK.

Jeremias, J. 1971: *New Testament Theology, Part 1: The Proclamation of Jesus*. London: SCM Press.

Kelber, W.H. 1974: *The Kingdom in Mark*. Philadelphia: Fortress Press.

Ladd, G.E. 1964: *Jesus and the Kingdom*. New York: Harper and Row. (2nd edn 1974: *The Presence of the Future*. Grand Rapids: Eerdmans.)

Meyer, B.F. 1979: *The Aims of Jesus*. London: SCM Press.

Perrin, N. 1963: *The Kingdom of God in the Teaching of Jesus*. London: SCM Press.

Perrin, N. 1976: *Jesus and the Language of the Kingdom*. Philadelphia: Fortress Press.

Riches, J. 1980: *Jesus and the Transformation of Judaism*. London: Darton, Longman and Todd.

RICHARD T. FRANCE

kingdom of God: political and social theology The kingdom of God is central to the ministry of Jesus, at least according to the synoptic Gospels. Its meaning has been the subject of much fruitful New Testament study this century (see KINGDOM OF GOD: NEW TESTAMENT). This article assumes that it is not a territorial nor a churchly term but that it refers to Jesus' disclosure in his own ministry of the nature of Yahweh's rule as king over the world. The Old Testament belief in Yahweh as king (for example in Psalms such as 97) comes to its full disclosure in Jesus' ministry, in his teaching, especially the parables, and in his 'mighty works'. It is a highly paradoxical rule by any

standard of human expectation; for while there are elements in Jesus' teaching which correspond to a fairly widespread ethical insight (such as the golden rule), the most distinctive elements are far removed from the assumptions of even the most thoughtful everyday morality. One example is the exhortation to forgiveness 'seventy times seven', solely because that is the way God's rule shows itself in his treatment of his erring subjects. Another, very challenging to a social and political theology, is the passage in Mark 10: 43 (and parallels) where Jesus says, 'You know that among the Gentiles the recognized rulers lord it over their subjects, and the great make their authority felt. It shall not be so among you . . . ' The paradox is that Jesus' ministry ended in apparent disaster, and God's way of exercising his kingly rule actually permitted this. Yet New Testament belief is that it in fact heralds the final triumph of God's kingly rule (of which the resurrection gospel is a foretaste), when he triumphs over all that is opposed to it. Meanwhile the paradoxical powers of the kingdom are a leaven at work in the world. In a decisive sense the 'last things' have been disclosed in the ministry of Jesus; Christians look to their final triumph, often expressed in the language of the parousia, or return of Christ.

The earliest Christians had a very short time perspective with respect to this (see 1 Cor. 7: 29), but they soon had to make a major modification in it. In his later epistles Paul no longer expects the parousia before his death. The latest book to be written of those accepted into the canon of the New Testament, 2 Peter, has its own way of dealing with this delay (3: 3ff.). But earlier than this, St John's Gospel had reinterpreted the thought of the parousia into the presence of the Holy Spirit in the community of the church.

However, a permanent problem remains. What is the relation of the kingdom of God, past (in the ministry of Jesus), present (in human history with the church as the herald of it), and future, to the ongoing life of the world? In the Old Testament God's people and his kingdom were one. Israel was a theocracy. The earliest Christians lived in various areas of the sprawling Roman empire, but no one could imagine that the empire was the kingdom of God in the sense that Israel was, even though

Jesus had combined his strictures on earthly rulers with the teaching that there are some things due to Caesar (without specifying which). So Christians were living in two kingdoms, one closely related to (and some thought identical with) the church, and the other ruled over by the emperor. What was the relation between the two? In due course various questions arose, and still arise, which are inescapable. How far is the kingdom of God a present and how far a future reality? In so far as it is a present one, how far is it to be identified with the church? Is its full realization to be expected in history or beyond it? If beyond it, how does this future realm of glory relate to the present realm of grace? In so far as it is to be realized in history, how far is there a progress towards it, or is it to come by dramatic divine intervention? If it is beyond history, how far can we expect any progress in human history, or are we only engaged in a 'holding operation' down the centuries until human history ends? We thank God for our creation and preservation; do we stop there and move straight to the hope of glory (as in the General Thanksgiving in the 1662 Book of Common Prayer of the Church of England)? Or do we work and hope for transformations in human history?

The New Testament tension between the 'now' and the 'not yet' in respect of the kingdom of God has been reflected in every period of Christian history, with tendencies to lean more towards one or the other. No comprehensive account of the interpretations of the kingdom of God in Christian history has been made; it would be a vast undertaking involving historical, sociological, ethical and theological analysis. It spills over into Christian attitudes to the entire phenomenon of human culture. Richard Niebuhr has shown in his seminal study *Christ and Culture* (1951) that five different (but in part overlapping) attitudes have continually recurred in Christian history, *all based on the same biblical data*. His typology has not been bettered.

In spite of its radical nature it has proved possible for the kingdom of God to be interpreted (as is the case with all terms in Christian theology) in a sociopolitically conservative or radical way. Conservative approaches are either satisfied with the status quo (an implausible position), or think that

whatever defects it has, any likely alternative would be worse, or even disastrous. Radicals are disposed to criticize the status quo, by criteria drawn from the concept of the kingdom, to reform social and political structures in the direction of its promised future. In practice, in the course of Christian history Christians have had a strong tendency to support the current status quo as an adequate expression of God's will, and thus take the conservative route; but there have always been minorities which did not. The majority attitude was the more plausible because the pace of social change was so slow between one generation and another as almost to seem static. But this has changed with the development of industrialism. We now have a new type of civilization in the history of the world, which for the last two centuries has let loose rapid social change, becoming ever more rapid, and affecting ever more areas of the world. In this setting radical tendencies in Christian thought have become much stronger.

The conservative approach tends to stress the future coming of the kingdom of God, and to think of it as wholly in God's hands; the radical approach tends to stress more the present possession of the gift of the kingdom, and the need to make more effective use of it in transforming human life. But there are exceptions. It is, however, important to stress when studies are made of the role and impact of the kingdom of God in social and political theology and in human affairs that no a priori assumptions should be made as to whether or not theological factors are an independent variable. There is a 'Christian' type of historical interpretation which exaggerates theological influences (for example in the abolition of slavery); but more pervasive is a tendency in the social sciences so to stress the conditioning factors in life that different theological understandings (such as of the kingdom of God) are attributed so much to varying economic and social factors that the possibility of their being a significant independent variable is minimized or denied. This is allied to the view that religion is a purely human construction and in no sense a human response to a divine disclosure. In assessing the influence of conceptions of the kingdom of God in human affairs no such a priori assumption should be made either way. This is not to deny that we have become much more aware of conditioning (not determining) factors with the development of sociology, Karl Marx being one of the pioneers.

This article is concerned with the place of the kingdom of God in recent political and social theology, but it is necessary to consider the centuries between the New Testament period and today. Thought of the two ages in the New Testament is echoed in St Augustine's two cities. Later, a tendency to identify the kingdom of God with the church developed, and this led to conflicts between the papacy and the Holy Roman Emperor. Martin Luther made a sharp distinction between God's two kingdoms, one of mercy and fellowship in the church (that of his right hand), and one of order and discipline in the world (that of his left hand). He thought it was far on in the history of the world, and at best we could hope that God would sustain rulers in preventing it from disintegrating before the parousia. John Calvin thought of the kingdom of God as partly embodied in a society in which rulers acknowledged God's sovereignty, and in which the church should play an active part. This is a good example of an understanding which could be interpreted in a socially and politically conservative or radical way. There has been a dynamic element in it which enabled it to play a significant part in the development of 'western' democracy (Lindsay, 1929), notably in the USA (Richard Niebuhr, [1937] 1956), and in the entrepreneurial spirit of capitalism (Tawney, 1926). It is a good example of a theological concept both moulding culture and being moulded by it. The radical element in Calvinism stems from its sense of the gulf between God's sovereign rule and human achievements, but this was interpreted more as a spur to renewed effort, an attitude which until recently has not characterized Lutheranism. On the other hand Calvinism can interpret the kingdom of God as a static obedience to a code of divine laws inherited from the past and understood ahistorically. Both Lutheranism and Calvinism came to be interpreted individualistically in the pietist movement of the eighteenth century, and this strain has been powerful since then. In it the kingdom of God has been interpreted as the rule of Christ in the soul of each believer. Indeed much of the Protestant missionary movement of the last century was inspired by the thought that the parousia could

be hastened by increasing the number of souls in whose hearts Christ's kingdom reigned (cf. Matt. 24: 14). Lastly in this brief run through the centuries, there have been before and after the Reformation, and there are today, chiliastic groups who think either that they are actually embodying the kingdom of God in their common life and institutions, or are organized for its imminent arrival.

The opposite of the pietist understanding of the kingdom became powerful in the middle and later years of the last century and in the first quarter of this. It was seen as an ideal society towards which humanity must strive in the strength of the impetus towards it given by Jesus. A secularized version of it is found in the belief in progress in human history, which was widespread at the same time, often assumed even if not explicitly stated (Baillie, 1950). Usually this was thought of as a gradual, evolutionary progress, though in Marx it appears as brought about by the forceful, dialectical struggle of classes.

This understanding of the kingdom of God as the gradual arrival of an ideal society through increasingly widespread human cooperative effort characterized much Protestant theology in the early years of this century (though challenged by Johannes Weiss and Albert Schweitzer). It was possible for this type of liberal theology to assess the Christian gospel by what it called the 'rational, moral and spiritual consciousness of mankind'. It was this theology that Richard Niebuhr had in mind when he wrote, 'A God without wrath brought men without sin into a Kingdom without judgement through the ministrations of a Christ without a cross' ([1937] 1956, p. 193). The Christian Socialist (see CHRISTIAN SOCIALISM) and social gospel movements had much of this aura, but both had greater depth. Both emphasized social and not just personal sins, and both saw the coming kingdom as judgement as well as promise; neither thought of progress as automatic. Nevertheless the kingdom of God was seen as an ideal social order, a cooperative commonwealth, not based on competition or profit, in which the law of love of Jesus' teaching could be directly embodied. Many hoped that the war of 1914–18, as a war to end war, could clear the way towards this. Such an outlook could not survive the postwar stresses, the economic depression of 1929, the rise of Nazism, Fascism and Stalinism, and a second world war. But it is not quite dead. The article on the kingdom of God in the *Dictionary of the Ecumenical Movement* (Lassky *et al.*, 1991, p. 569) says (mistakenly, as the dictionary in other places shows) that 'it is generally agreed that the kingdom of God is an ideal society characterized by equality, justice and peace.' In fact the relation of justice to the love of the New Testament commandment is one of the central issues in relating it to the kingdom of God (see LOVE, CHRISTIAN).

Six tendencies in recent social and political theology may be mentioned, as they bear upon the place of the kingdom of God.

1 *Christian realism.* This is mainly, but by no means exclusively, associated with Reinhold Niebuhr. The kingdom of God is, in his deliberately paradoxical phrase, a challenge to human discipleship but also an 'impossible possibility'. It presents a radical challenge to the status quo, emphasizing the provisionality of all human attempts to embody it, but at the same time it is an inspiration to change the status quo in the light of gospel criteria. There are no fixed limits set by God to human achievements, but neither are there guarantees that humans will succeed in their aims, or that if they do the gains will be permanent. Each generation has to appropriate what it has inherited and win its own victories. It may fail. The collapse of civilized Germany into the synthetic barbarism of Nazism is an awful warning. There is no immanent force in history leading to an ideal society. Yet the challenge remains to exercise discernment in contemporary affairs, and to work to move human affairs forward in the light of the kingdom of God.

2 *An ethic of inspiration.* Much mid-century Protestant theology took the kingdom of God very seriously. But how to move from it to concrete decisions in the political and social realms? Rudolf Bultmann taught that the Christian will know in each moment of decision what the love ethic of the New Testament requires. Emil Brunner related the radical kingdom ethic to the doctrine of the orders of creation (and Karl Barth and Dietrich Bonhoeffer used similar terms for much the same concept, wanting a term more dynamic than what they thought of as the static doctrine of the orders). All three stressed the sovereignty of God, which yields a divine command to be known in each situation by the Christian as he decides in it for or against the kingdom. This raises many questions about what empirical evidence is needed even to understand the data of a decision, and how one acquires it.

3 *Roman Catholic political theology.* Recent Roman Catholic theology has become much more biblically oriented, and has kept close to modern New Testament studies in understanding the past, present and future aspects of the kingdom of God in relation to life in the world. One of the notable changes at the Second Vatican Council (1962–5) was the abandonment of the tendency to identify the church too easily with the kingdom of God (*Lumen Gentium*, paragraphs 3, 9, 35ff.; *Gaudium et Spes*, paragraphs 39, 72). For the rest, there has been a development of political theology in which the eschatological dimensions of the kingdom of God are brought to bear on present-day society with an emphasis on deepening faith by praxis, a term with Marxist associations (Metz, 1969). This is developed more radically in liberation theology (see below).

4 *Eschatological utopianism.* This has the same radical approach to the present order as Christian realism, but assesses what to do not in the light of what appear to be the best possibilities, judged by present evidence, but in the light of the radically new future promised by God in his future kingdom. The contrast is made between *futurum* and *avenir*, a calculated as against an unforeseen future. But whilst we can and should be ready for the new and allow for the unexpected, it is not easy to see how one decides in the present what to do on the basis of what is to be new and not foreseeable from current data. Truth, it is said, lies in the future, and proves itself by changing the present in the direction of the future. The kingdom of God is seen as a radically new future for this world, drawing it towards a kingdom of righteousness, freedom and humanity in God's promised future (Moltmann, [1964] 1967). This view has been much influenced by a felt need to give a Christian alternative to the Marxist utopia, and may become less potent with the disintegration of Marxism.

5 *Liberation theology.* Originating in Latin

America, and therefore mainly Roman Catholic, since about 1965 LIBERATION THEOLOGY has spread to Asia, to a lesser extent Africa, and then from the third world to the first. It stresses the radical powers of the kingdom of God, challenging existing power structures, but goes on to say that in order to know how to respond to it in practice we need a 'science'. That science is seen as some form of Marxism, or quasi-Marxism. Liberation theologians are quite clear that the necessary social changes, even if revolutionary, are not to be equated with the kingdom of God, whose final realization will be God's gift. However, they insist that practical commitment to the cause of the poor is a prior condition for understanding the gospel of the kingdom. Without this, theology becomes an ideology of oppression (Gutiérrez, [1971] 1973).

6 *Non-violence as the key kingdom issue.* There has always been a minority in the church which has taken the gospel witness to Jesus' ministry that God exercises his kingly rule over the world through a cross in what is in essence a 'one kingdom' theology, and maintains that this is the way both the church and the worldly authorities should follow. This is the interpretation of the Historic Peace Churches. The belief is that if the church is faithful to the kingdom of God as a community of peace, God will use its faithfulness to make his kingdom a reality (Hauerwas, 1983). However, although no one has stressed more than Bonhoeffer God's suffering rule from the cross ([1951] 1971), he did not draw pacifist conclusions from it as necessary for Christians, but rather saw political struggle as a divine vocation. An understanding of the two kingdoms doctrine lay deep in his formation.

The church has never been sure how to handle the concept of the kingdom of God, with the paradoxically radical ethical elements associated with it, elements which it is clearly impossible to embody directly in the structures of the church itself, let alone in the state. Various expedients for bowdlerizing it or siphoning it off to a select group (the religious in the technical sense) have been adopted. Confusion still reigns. There are sixty-three entries under kingdom of God in the *Dictionary of the Ecumenical Movement*, drawn from ecumenical documents and those of different confessional traditions. They show the most varied use of the term, ecclesiologically and sociopolitically. Often it serves as a synonym for the Christian faith itself, or the gospel. Sometimes it seems to be thrown in as a makeweight. Not one of the entries faces the content of the kingdom in the New Testament or the paradoxical nature of God's kingly rule and seriously tackles how it bears on the power structures of human society. Clearly a cogent theology of civil society has yet to be widely accepted, and even its necessity is often not realized.

See also ESCHATOLOGY; ETHICS; SOCIAL QUESTIONS.

Bibliography

Baillie, J. 1950: *The Belief in Progress*. London: Oxford University Press.

Barth, K. [1951] 1961: *Church Dogmatics* III/4, trans. Edinburgh: T & T Clark.

Bonhoeffer, D. [1949] 1955: *Ethics*. London: SCM Press.

Bonhoeffer, D. [1951] 1971 (enlarged edition), trans. *Letters and Papers from Prison*. London: SCM Press.

Brunner, E. [1932] 1937: *The Divine Imperative*, trans. London: Lutterworth.

Gutiérrez, G. [1971] 1973: *A Theology of Liberation*, trans. London: SCM Press.

Hauerwas, S. 1983: *The Peaceable Kingdom*. London: SCM Press.

Hertz, K.H., ed. 1976: *Two Kingdoms and One World*. Minneapolis: Augsburg.

Lassky, N., Bonino, J.M., Pobee, J., Stransky, T., Wainwright, W., and Webb, P., eds 1991: *Dictionary of the Ecumenical Movement*. London and Geneva: World Council of Churches and Council of Churches for Britain and Ireland.

Lindsay, A.D. 1929: *The Essentials of Democracy*. London: Oxford University Press.

Metz, J.-B. 1969: *Theology of the World*, trans. London: Burns and Oates.

Moltmann, J. [1964] 1967: *Theology of Hope*, trans. London: SCM Press.

Niebuhr, H. Richard [1937] 1956: *The Kingdom of God in America*. Hamden, Conn.: Shoestring Press.

Niebuhr, H. Richard 1951: *Christ and Culture*. London: Faber.

Niebuhr, Reinhold 1943: *The Nature and Destiny of Man*, vol. 2. London: Nisbet.

Oden, T.C. 1964: *Radical Obedience: The Ethics of Bultmann*. Philadelphia: Westminster Press.

Oldham, J.H., ed. 1937: *The Kingdom of God and History*. London: Allen and Unwin.

Preston, R.H. 1987: *The Future of Christian Ethics*.

London: SCM Press, chapters 10–12.
Rauschenbusch, W. 1918: *A Theology for the Social Gospel*. New York: Macmillan.
Tawney, R.H. 1926: *Religion and the Rise of Capitalism*. London: John Murray.

RONALD H. PRESTON

Korean Christian thought   Christianity has enjoyed spectacular growth in Korea, despite its relatively brief existence there. With more than ten million believers, Christianity is now a dominant religion in South Korea.

The history of Christianity in Korea
Christianity was introduced into Korea about two centuries ago by Yi Sung-hun, who went to China and became a Christian. In 1784 he returned to Korea with books, crucifixes, images and information about Catholic rituals. He and his friends founded a small Catholic lay congregation, the first Christian church in Korea. When the church began to grow, waves of persecution followed. By 1884, only 17,500 widely dispersed Catholics remained, and Catholicism had almost disappeared (Moffett, 1962, pp. 33–4).

The Protestant century began when the isolationist policies of the Korean government ended with the ratification of the American–Korean treaty in 1883. In 1884, the Presbyterian Board of Missions transferred Dr Horace Allen from China to Korea as a physician for American diplomats (Hunt, 1980, p. 16). His treatment of Prince Min Young Ik, wounded in the 1884 *émeute*, opened up a unique diplomatic channel for his missionary activities. Missionary work began formally in 1885 when Horace G. Underwood, a Presbyterian, and Henry G. Appenzeller, a Methodist, secured quasi-governmental status as educators (Harrington, 1944, p. 49). Both stressed evangelism and education for the poor and oppressed. Early missionary strategy focused on women and the labouring classes, stressed elementary education and healing, and promoted indigenous evangelism (Paik, [1929] 1973, p. 191).

The Bible was translated into *Onmun* or *Hanqul*, the Korean scripts, because most people had no formal education and were unable to read the Chinese scripts. A strong emphasis on Bible study was the key to the expansion of the church. Bible schools, which

trained native leaders, grew from 45,000 in 1909 to 112,000 in 1934 (Rhodes, 1934, p. 564). The Nevius principles of self-propagation, self-governance and self-support contributed greatly to the development of a national consciousness and independence (Lee, 1983, p. 395). The spirit of self-propagation was clearly evident in revival meetings, and especially the famous revival meeting of 1907 in Pyungyang, which George Paik likened to the Great Awakening, since it became the source of Korean spiritual life (Paik, [1929] 1973, p. 374). Christian evangelism climaxed during the revival campaign 'Million Souls for Christ', of 1909–11.

In 1910, Japan annexed Korea as a colony. At first missionaries, following the American policy, took a pro-Japanese attitude and encouraged Korean Christians to support the Japanese government. However, after the Conspiracy Case of 1912, when 105 Koreans were arrested and imprisoned for plotting to assassinate the governor-general, Terauch, Korean Christian activism evolved into Korean nationalism. Despite a Japanese attempt to suppress and intimidate Christian activities, it was impossible to stop the new spirit of Korean nationalism. The 1 March 1919 Independence Movement was a pivotal event for Koreans. Out of thirty-three signatories of the document, fifteen were Christians. After the 1 March movement the church suffered greatly, as another wave of Christian persecution arrived under the guise of mobilization of a national spirit. Japan demanded Shinto worship of all Koreans, including Christians. In 1938 the Presbyterian General Assembly was forced to pass a resolution to participate in Shinto ceremonies. Having learned from earlier experience with ancestor worship, the Vatican's Congregatio de Propaganda Fide declared that Catholics could worship Shinto gods as long as it was merely an expression of patriotic respect to the Japanese imperial family (Lee, 1984, p. 23).

With the end of the Second World War in 1945, Korea was liberated from Japan but occupied by the Soviet Union and the USA, which divided Korea between north and south. The tragic civil war in 1950–3 resulted in multitudes of North Korean refugees, most of whom were Christians. The 1950s was a period of both disorientation and renewal for the church. Liberated from missionary domination, revival meetings resurged and new sects were formed. The decade of the 1960s was marked with student political unrest. The Rhee's corrupt government was overthrown in 1960, followed by a military coup in 1961. The church became an important voice for human rights and justice issues. Many prominent Christians were imprisoned for their involvement in the issue of human rights in the early 1970s.

The main trends of theological thinking

Although most Christians are conservative, the process of indigenizing Christianity in Korea produced several distinctive forms of theological thinking. Korean theological thought can be divided into three categories: pietistic fundamentalism, progressive liberalism and indigenous contextualism.

Pietistic fundamentalism Most Korean Christians are pietistic fundamentalists. New England pietism brought by early missionaries underlies the theological thinking of Korean Christians. The systematization of Korean FUNDAMENTALISM must be understood as a continuation of that tradition.

The early missionaries Horace G. Underwood and Henry G. Appenzeller were products of American pietism, deeply involved in the nineteenth-century American revival movement. Although they advocated education for the Korean masses, their primary goal was conversion of Koreans from heathenism. Eradication of heathenism was considered the ultimate victory of missionary work. Missionaries, therefore, introduced their puritan morality as a part of pietism. Being Christian meant temperance and the work ethic. It also meant not smoking, dancing or gambling. A basic characteristic of pietism is dualism: the radical separation of the inner and the outer, the secular and the religious, the church and the state. Pietism encouraged personal salvation instead of social and political justice. Missionaries thus discouraged Koreans from participation in the struggle against the Japanese colonial policy. Because of pietistic influence, most Korean Christians today remain passive towards the dictatorship of the Korean government.

The pietistic spirit of the American missionaries grounds an ultra-conservative fundamentalist theology in Korean Christianity. The situation of Korean churches under the Japanese colonial policy further promoted a fundamentalist world view. Conservative fundamentalism meant that the essence of Christianity was the salvation of individual souls, and that truth was found only in Scripture. Sun-yoo Kil (1869–1935), the initiator of the fundamentalist movement, became a popular revivalist and introduced early morning prayers modelled after Buddhist and Taoist practices. His practice of interpreting the Bible through the Bible was called 'self-hermeneutics'. He stressed the inerrancy of Scripture and the second coming of Christ. However, it was Hyung-ryong Park (b. 1897) who ultimately systematized Korean fundamentalism. Park taught that Korean churches should preserve the pietistic and puritan teaching of the missionaries. Deeply influenced by Gresham Machen, a well-known fundamentalist, Park believed in the inerrancy and verbal inspiration of Scripture. He denied the validity of modern science, especially evolutionary theory, and rejected biblical criticism. For Park, disbelief in the virgin birth, physical resurrection, miracles or the second coming of Christ constituted heresy. 'The attitude of the religion of Jesus Christ', he said, 'is not cooperation but conflict and conquest' (Ryu, 1982, p. 196). Under his leadership, the International Council of Churches in Korea was formed as a conservative alternative to the Korean National Council of Churches, part of the World Council of Churches, which was considered a liberal organization.

Progressive liberalism There are two schools of theology in progressive liberalism: a theology of religions and a sociopolitical theology. The former attempts to reconcile Christianity with other religions in Korea, while the latter is interested in the implications of the gospel in Korean sociopolitical situations.

1 Despite the ultra-conservative fundamentalism which has dominated the history of Korean Christianity, a new theology has developed that attempts to reconcile Christianity and other Korean religions. Among the pioneers of a theology of religions was an outstanding Confucian scholar, Byung-hon Choi (1858–1927), who initiated an evangelistic dialogue with Confucianists, Taoists and Buddhists. He believed it imperative that

Korean Christianity be addressed to multi-religious situations. 'Everyone says that his or her religion is the true religion . . . How can anyone distinguish a male bird from a female bird?' (Ryu, 1982, p. 53). While Christianity is one of many religions, the truth of Jesus as witnessed in Scripture is alone absolute. Choi analogized the Christian gospel to superior food. No one would continue to eat ordinary food if he had tasted superior food (Choi, 1907, pp. 230ff.). 'If Confucius knew the truth of Christ, he followed it. If Buddha knew the fruit of self-sacrificial love, he did not waste six years of struggle' (Choi, 1922, p. 91). Thus, Choi developed the theory that Christ was the fulfilment of all other religions.

Sung-whan Pyun expanded upon the fulfilment theory. He approached the relationship between Christianity and other religions, especially Buddhism, from the perspective of *Missio Dei*. His pivotal message that 'there is salvation outside the church' aroused controversy. He sought not to convert Buddhists, but to engage in dialogue. Seeking the continuity between Christ and Buddha, Pyun found that self-giving love was the point where Christianity and Mahayana Buddhism meet. If self-giving love is a way of salvation, then in it everyone, whether Christian, Buddhist or Confucian, can meet the saviour.

2   The first Christian intellectual to advocate social and political action was Chi-ho Yoon (1864–1945). Returning to Korea in 1894 after his education in the USA, he saw the inevitability of Korea's fall under her powerful neighbours. For Yoon, *Missio Dei* meant saving his nation through political activism (Min, 1978, p. 172). He was a leader of the attempt to assassinate the Japanese governor-general of Korea. Yoon later composed the lyrics of the Korean national anthem, expressing his love of nation and his faith in God. Being a praxis-oriented Christian theologian, politics and theology naturally came together for him.

Jai-jun Kim (b. 1901), who systematized political theology in Korea, saw himself as a sojourner of faith on earth. Using a socio-political and historical analysis, he saw in Korea the phophetic vision of social justice and holiness of Israel's faith. Salvation must be historical, and history must be critically judged by the history of salvation, that is, the historical events of Christ's death and resurrection. He affirmed that the suffering of Christians and the cross of self-denial are necessary for spiritual and social reform and transformation. He criticized fundamentalists and the early missionaries who discouraged Korean Christians from participating in political activities. Because of his liberal and political interpretation of Scripture, he was condemned by and expelled from the Korean Presbyterian church. His followers formed a new denomination known as Kitokyo Presbyterian church.

Yoon's progressive political theory became a theoretical basis for the nationwide movement against the government's oppression and dehumanization. Various human rights movements and democratic politics produced a flow of theological documents, one of the most important of which was the Theological Declaration of Korean Christians, signed on 20 May 1973. This marked the emergence of minjung theology and other indigenous theologies in Korea.

Indigenous contextualism After many years of missionary work and church expansion, Christianity became a Korean religion. Various attempts were made to indigenize the Christian faith. Two examples illustrate the significant development of indigenous theologies in Korea: 'sung' theology and 'minjung' theology.

Since the word 'sung' is often translated as 'sincerity', sung theology is also known as the theology of sincerity. Sung theology was formulated by Sung-bum Yoon (1916–1980), who felt that Christianity would never become a Korean religion until it was indigenized. As a thoroughgoing Barthian, he attempted to bring Barth's theology into the Korean world view, which was the core of Korean cultural and spiritual tradition. He believed that the Korean world view was represented in the thought of Yul-gok Lee, a renowned neo-Confucian scholar who developed a metaphysics of non-dualism. In this synthesis, the concept of sung, or sincerity, became the essence of understanding Christianity and neo-Confucianism. Sung was a contact point with Christianity because its Chinese character consists of 'word' and 'fulfilment'. In other words, sung means the fulfilment of the word, analogous to the incarnation of the Word in Christianity. In sung theology, *Hyo* or filial piety, the basis of

Confucian virtues, becomes the norm of Christian ethics. Sung theology is a major attempt to construct a Korean theology. It, however, has at least two issues that are still disputed by Korean theologians. The first is how to identify Yul-gok's neo-Confucian philosophy with the Korean world view; the second is how to indigenize Barth's theology, which was already indigenized in Europe. This double indigenization creates a syncretic theology.

Minjung theology is internationally understood as a genuine Korean theology. As the word 'minjung' is unique to Koreans, it is untranslated. It is also undefinable because of its holistic, dynamic and changing reality (Lee, 1988, p. 3). However, the literal meaning of minjung is 'the masses' or simply 'the people' who are politically oppressed, economically exploited, socially alienated and kept uneducated in cultural and intellectual matters (Moon, 1985, p. 1). Reminiscent of liberation theology in Latin America and other third world countries, minjung theology was born out of the human rights movement and the oppression of the poor in the 1960s and 70s. What makes this theology different from other liberation theologies is the idea of minjung as the subject of history, endowed with a rich cultural tradition.

Sok-hon Ham (1901–1989), who was imprisoned several times by the Japanese before the Korean liberation in 1945, and again by the South Korean police thereafter, was the father of minjung theology. His concept of *sse-al* became the basis for understanding the essence of minjung. Sse-al is the seed of human being that does not belong to the dominating structure of human society. It is like grass roots which are trodden down but rise again. It describes the spirit of minjung and signifies the death and resurrection of Christ.

Another important person who paved the way for the development of minjung theology is Chi-ha Kim (b. 1941), whose writings echo the voices of minjung. He was often imprisoned and tortured after his student days at Seoul National University. Most of his writings came from jail. 'Five Bandits', 'Yellow Earth', 'Cry of the People', 'Rice', 'Chang Il-dam' and other writings were used by Nam-dong Suh to formulate minjung theology.

Nam-dong Suh, like other dissenting scholars, was dismissed from his teaching position and imprisoned. His experience of imprisonment gave him a sense of solidarity with minjung. Among the many important contributions he made to the development of minjung theology, Chi-ha Kim's ideas of *han* and *dan*, and Joachim of Floris's interpretation of the Holy Spirit, are especially noteworthy. Han, like minjung, is unique to Korean experience. It is a particular form of suffering, similar to the blues of the black experience (Cone, 1983, p. xi). It can be grudge or resentment over injustice. It is an inward feeling of anger experienced individually or collectively. The han of minjung can be nullified by dan, which means to cut off the vicious cycle of han. Dan has two dimensions: self-denial at a personal level, and a curtailing of a vicious circle of revenge on a social level. Dan works towards the transformation of the world. Another important idea that Suh contributed to minjung theology is the renewal of the Holy Spirit in Korea. Using the interpretation of Joachim of Floris, he reintroduced the idea of millennium in the age of the Holy Spirit, which surpasses the Son and the Father. According to him, the Son surpasses the Father, and the Spirit surpasses the Son. In minjung theology, it is not Christology but PNEUMATOLOGY that becomes the centre of theological concern.

Another important figure in minjung theology is Byung-mu Ahn, a New Testament scholar who collaborated with Suh. Ahn's contributions are directly related to biblical studies. Taking Mark as the Gospel of minjung, he interpreted the minjung as the *oklos*, or the crowd of people with whom Jesus identified himself. Jesus was a minjung, and minjung, therefore, is equal with Jesus. Because Jesus and minjung are one, God is on the side of minjung, the poor, weak and oppressed. God loves minjung alone. His love is partial, because he sides with minjung. Ahn's emphasis on partial love rather than preferential love distinguishes his position from other liberation theologians. He also emphasizes the events of Jesus in history. While traditional European theology is based on kerygma, minjung theology is based on Christ-events in history. What happened to Christ in history is more important than the kerygma of the early church. Particularly, Jesus' death on the cross and his resurrection, the essential events of Christ, still take place in Korea.

There are many other theologians who contributed to the development of minjung theology. Young-hak Hyon utilizes shamanic rituals and mask dance to overcome the han of minjung. He sees han and dan in a dialectical tension which can be overcome through so-called critical transcendence in the humour of the mask dance and the ecstasy of shamanic rituals. Yong-bok Kim makes a distinction between political messianism, based on the ideology of rulers, and messianic politics, based on the servanthood of minjung. Other important concepts are continuing the development of minjung theology.

Besides minjung theology, other Korean theologies are now emerging. A good example is Don-sik Ryu's new Pyung-ryu theology, which attempts to interpret the gospel on the basis of the essential Korean ethos. Christianity in Korea is confronted with the question of a multi-religious dialogue that inevitably deals with a theology of religions. With conservative fundamentalism in the majority, it will be a great challenge for the Korean church to provide a creative synthesis and delicate balance of the multi-religious concerns and the conservative fundamentalism to produce a viable and sustainable theology in the twenty-first century.

See also CHINESE CHRISTIAN THOUGHT; JAPANESE CHRISTIAN THOUGHT; OTHER FAITHS AND CHRISTIANITY.

Bibliography

Choi, Byung-hon 1907: Sungsan Yuramki, *Theology Monthly Report* (Seoul; in Korean).

Choi, Byung-hon 1922: *All Religions Are Fulfilled in One* (in Korean). Seoul: The Literature Society of the Korean Church.

Cone, James 1983: Preface. In *Minjung Theology: People as the Subjects of History*, ed. Commission on Theological Concerns of the Christian Conference of Asia. Maryknoll: Orbis Books.

Harrington, Fred Harvy 1944: *God, Mammon and the Japanese: Dr Horace N. Allen and Korea–American Relations, 1884–1905*. Madison: University of Wisconsin Press.

Hunt, Everett Nichols, Jr 1980: *Protestant Pioneers in Korea*. Maryknoll: Orbis Books.

Kim, Hyung-chan 1978: Yun Chi-ho in America: the training of a Korean patriot in the south, 1888–1893, *Korea Journal* 8.

Lee, Jung Young 1983: The American missionary movement in Korea, 1882–1945: its contributions and American diplomacy, *Missiology: An International Review* 11, 4.

Lee, Jung Young 1984: Christian syncretism with other religions in Korea. In *Essays on Korean Heritage and Christianity*, ed. Sang Hyun Lee. Princeton Junction, NJ: Association of Korean Christian Scholars in North America, Inc.

Lee, Jung Young 1988: *An Emerging Theology in World Perspective: Commentary on Korean Minjung Theology*. Mystic, Conn.: Twenty-third Publications.

Min, Kyung-bae 1978: The early life of Yoon Chi-ho and the progressive idea of the Christian faith. In *Writings of National Study 1*. Seoul: Yonsei University Press.

Moffet, Samuel H. 1962: *The Christians of Korea*. New York: Friendship Press.

Moon, Hee-suk 1985: *A Korean Minjung Theology: An Old Testament Perspective*. Maryknoll: Orbis Books.

Paik, George [1929] 1973: *The History of Protestant Mission in Korea, 1832–1910*. Seoul: Yonsei University Press.

Park, Hyung-ryong 1965: Choice and evangelism, *Shinhak Jinam* (Seoul; in Korean).

Rhodes, Harry A. 1934: *History of the Korean Mission: Presbyterian Church, USA, 1884–1934*. Seoul: YMCA Press.

Ryu, Dong-sik 1982: *The Vein of Korean Theology* (in Korean). Seoul: Jungmang-sa.

JUNG YOUNG LEE

Küng, Hans (b. 1928) Swiss Roman Catholic theologian. An ordained priest, he taught at the Roman Catholic faculty at Tübingen until his status as an approved teacher was withdrawn by church authorities in 1979 and he moved to the Institute for Ecumenical Research at Tübingen. The range of his work is unusually broad, and works such as *On Being a Christian* of 1971, in presenting Christianity as relevant to the concerns of modern, humanist contemporary culture, have attracted a popular as well as a scholarly readership. A champion of theological reform in the Roman Catholic church, he has argued for a return to Scripture and the historical Jesus, as opposed to ecclesiastical tradition and papal infallibility, as the final authority in matters of faith and doctrine; he has also called for greater openness to the insights of modern rationalism and critical methods. His catholicity and progressive views have made him a pioneer of the ecumenical movement. In *Council, Reform and Reunion* (1961), he argued for even more radical reforms than those introduced at the Second Vatican Council, at which he was present. In *Justification* (1957, trans. 1964), he sought to demonstrate that the church's position on this controversial doctrine was originally similar to that of the Protestant church. Other works include *Infallible?* (1970),

Does God Exist? (1978, trans. 1980) and *Structures of the Church* (1962).

Bibliography

Häring, H., and Kuschel, K.-J., eds 1979: *Hans Küng: His Work and his Way*. London.

Hebbelthwaite, P. 1980: *The New Inquisition*. London.

Nowell, R. 1981: *A Passion for Truth*. London.

L

language, religious Issues about the validity and effectiveness of religious language have turned traditionally on questions about the linguistic and logical status of analogy, symbol, metaphor, allegory or other forms of indirect discourse. This has been the case from the writings of Thomas Aquinas to the contemporary theory of Paul Ricoeur. Language which otherwise signifies objects, events or states of affairs in the physical world has to be stretched by such linguistic devices to signify realities which lie beyond the empirical world.

The era of the Enlightenment, however, raised questions stemming especially from Kant which exposed the problematic character of all language as a representation of reality. In the twentieth century some thinkers have pressed the implications of Marxist, psycho-analytical and semiotic theories to suggest that language projects disguised modes of self-interest. Language, it is argued, constitutes an endlessly self-referring system, of which anchorages in extra-linguistic reality are either illusory or radically context-relative. Thus whereas the heart of the problem of religious language has traditionally been perceived to lie in its distinctively 'religious' character, especially since around 1967 the deepest problems of religious language are perceived to lie in the opaqueness and deceptiveness which supposedly characterize all language. The following three periods have distinctive features.

From 1700 to 1913
Kant's critique of human thought implied parallel questions about the status and limits of language. F.D.E. Schleiermacher (1768–1834) was the first theologian to accept the challenge of asking transcendental philosophical questions about language, namely to enquire into the conditions for the possibility of language as communication. His system of hermeneutics was a brilliant attempt, in the context of his times, to establish a theoretical basis for operative language. It is not generally recognized that in effect he partially anticipated Saussure in drawing a foundational methodological distinction between language as a system of regularities and potentiality ('grammatical' hermeneutics), and acts, processes or events of interpersonal communication which presupposed these patterned generalities ('psychological' hermeneutics).

As in many other areas of modern theology, different approaches to religious language are represented seminally in the respective concerns of Schleiermacher and of Søren Kierkegaard (1813–1855). Schleiermacher saw the problem of religious language as part of the problem of the nature of language as such, within which it constituted a special subcategory. Kierkegaard stressed the distinctive role of indirect communication in the service of faith. Parable, puzzle, story, paradox and contradiction invited and provoked active engagement on the part of the human will, which was precipitated into decision by such language. Moreover, any other mode of language would by implication attempt to make God a mere object of human thought, and thereby transpose the transcendent Other into an idolatrous human projection.

Outside theology developments in the philosophy of language, in psychoanalysis, social theory and semiotics took place which would, like time bombs, explode at a later period. Wilhelm von Humboldt (1767–1835) insisted that the world itself is a construct of language: all reality is 'linguistic', that is, we cannot get outside language to check what it is that language portrays. Karl Marx (1818–1883) saw language, like human thought, as a disguised vehicle for imposing or sustaining dominating interests. The Bohemian philosopher F. Mauthner (1849–1923) offered a critique of language which effectively questioned its capacity to communicate truth outside language. Sigmund Freud (1856–1939) saw language as a multi-layered disguise which served the interests of the self and its inner conflicts self-protectively. Religious language in particular represented distorted projections of inner conflicts between the libido and the repressive super-ego. Dreams, for example, both reveal and disguise repressed wishes.

The most innocent time bomb was placed by Ferdinand de Saussure (1857–1913), the acknowledged founder of modern linguistics. His correct insight that language-uses or communicative acts (*parole*) presuppose various abstract systems of linguistic potentialities (*langue*) would later be reinterpreted in such a way as to view language as an endlessly self-referring system. In POSTMODERNISM this gives rise to issues in religious language about the respective priority of human agency (inter-subjectivity) in effecting given linguistic choices as against the priority of semiotic networks (intertextuality) in determining the limits of what can be said by shifting social conventions.

From 1914 to 1967
This period witnessed a splitting apart of agenda between Anglo-American philosophy of language and the domination of continental European theories of language by phenomenology, existentialism and finally structuralism. E. Husserl's phenomenology was developed in one direction by M. Merleau-Ponty in France, and differently but within the same broad frame by M. Heidegger in Germany. Heidegger stressed the inseparability of language and interpretation and exposed the limits of positivist theories of language. The implications for religious language received their most widely known form in the work of Rudolf Bultmann, whose classic essay on demythologizing appeared in 1941. Combining Heidegger's theory of interpretation with Kierkegaard's concerns, which we have described, Bultmann argued that the language of myth impedes a

gospel or 'kerygma' which calls for active decision and obedience by appearing to present it as pseudo-objective description of states of affairs which took place in another time. Myth thereby transposes kerygma into mere report rather than summons to decision. Hence Bultmann calls for a programme of demythologizing which will, in effect, de-objectify most of the descriptive language of the New Testament.

In the Anglo-American tradition during this period the focus of interest was the very reverse, except that in both cases the tradition concerned tended to work with an over-polarized contrast between descriptive and indirect or non-cognitive language. B. Russell, R. Carnap, the Vienna Circle, A.J. Ayer and R.B. Braithwaite urged that language which described the physical world constituted the primary operative paradigm for all language. The work of the early Ludwig Wittgenstein was thought to point in the same direction, but for Wittgenstein, as against his empiricist colleagues, what was most important in life was that which 'cannot be said'.

In his *Language, Truth, and Logic* of 1936, A.J. Ayer expounded what amounted to a positivist world view, but clothed in the dress of a theory of language. He argued that language must belong to one of three categories: (1) logically contingent propositions which describe the physical world, the meaning of which can be verified by empirical check; or (2) logically necessary propositions which turn out to be formal, analytical or tautologous; or (3) emotive utterances reflecting attitudes or values which are logically 'non-sense' propositions, since their meaning cannot be empirically verified (see LOGICAL POSITIVISM).

Ayer's book became an influential landmark, more because of its presentational clarity and cogency than because of any profundity. He failed to take account of the complexity and variety of language. At almost precisely the time when Ayer was writing, Wittgenstein had emerged from his middle period. Some time between 1936 and 1938 Wittgenstein looked back on his own earlier attempt to draw a sharp contrast between propositions which describe the world and other language which could not genuinely be 'said', and observed that this had rested not on observation but on 'a *pre-conceived idea*' which 'can only be removed by turning our whole examination round' (Wittgenstein,

[1953–8] 1967, section 108). In his later work Wittgenstein abandons such 'super-concepts' as 'the nature of a proposition' and calls attention to the multi-layered variety of language-uses which operate in actual or hypothetical situations in life.

In 1955 R.B. Braithwaite developed an empiricist approach to religious language broadly in Ayer's tradition, allowing that religious stories could express attitudes and commitments even if they failed to meet the criteria of true-or-false propositions. Meanwhile debates about verification shifted to issues about falsification. Antony Flew in 1955 ruthlessly pressed the principle of falsification: what evidence could be said to count *against* the claim that God is love in order to demonstrate its cash-value? If religious believers can say that God is love in the face of such counter-evidence as cancer deaths, does not religious language begin to die the death of a thousand qualifications?

In the face of an aggressive empiricist or positivist agenda, a number of theologians and philosophers responded in various ways. Together with Austin Farrer, Basil Mitchell and others, three counter-approaches were adopted by Eric Mascall, John Macquarrie and Ian Ramsey. Mascall (1957) drew explicitly on the Thomist-Aristotelian tradition and carefully and rigorously reappraised the status and function of analogy. Analogy resists the collapse of divine transcendence into anthropomorphism or self-projection, but sustains cognitive truth-claims as against merely personal value-utterances.

John Macquarrie (1967) consciously became one of the very few writers of this period to enter into dialogue with both the phenomenological and existential tradition of Heidegger and the empirical tradition, which he viewed as reductionist by comparison. Ian Ramsey insisted that 'religious discourse deals in a profusion of models' (Ramsey, 1965, p. 18). But each model needs to be qualified, either by some disclaimer about its trans-empirical scope or by its convergence with other models. Only a plurality of models, each of which cancels out unwanted meanings suggested by others, addresses the problem of the death of a thousand qualifications by virtue of their co-joint operation as a whole.

Between 1951 and 1964 Paul Tillich expounded a view of religious symbols which drew heavily on the theory of C.G. Jung. Symbols, he argued, not only offer bridges between the conscious and unconscious, but also transcend the subject–object disjunctions of conceptual thought. God can be apprehended only through symbol, which supposedly 'participates in' the reality to which it points. By contrast, cognitive concepts of God are supposedly reductive and potentially idolatrous. While he constructively explores the power of symbols, Tillich does not rigorously defend all the implications of his approach as a linguistic theory. It is arguable that more constructive work was produced in this period by thinkers who sought to apply insights of the later Wittgenstein and of J.L. Austin to religious language. These included respectively D.M. High (1967) and D.D. Evans (1963), among others.

Since 1967

Probably the most influential thinker on religious language in this period is Paul Ricoeur (b. 1913). With Ricoeur, the phenomenological tradition of Merleau-Ponty and Heidegger and the structuralism of the early Roland Barthes is reunited with an awareness of Anglo-American theories of language. Ricoeur draws on Heidegger's notion of 'possibility' for his theory of narrative, but also on Max Black's philosophy of language and Ian Ramsey's theory of models for his account of religious metaphor.

In his early book *The Symbolism of Evil* (1960, trans. 1967) Ricoeur notes the dependency of religious language on 'double meaning expressions' characteristic of symbol and metaphor. We speak of sin and guilt in terms of wandering, estrangement and burden. But multi-level or double-level language, he rightly urges, plunges us of necessity into hermeneutics. Hermeneutics, he writes, must operate with two principles: with a 'hermeneutic of suspicion' which asks tough critical questions about validity, self-interest, self-deception and idolatrous projections; and with a 'hermeneutic of retrieval' in which we seek to listen in 'post-critical' openness to what symbols and narratives say. Ricoeur explicitly engages with Freud's theories as a critical tool in the service of suspicion. But Freud does not have the last word. Ricoeur writes: 'Hermeneutics seems to me to be animated by this double motivation: willingness to suspect, willingness to listen; vow of rigor, vow of obedience . . . The contrary of suspicion, I will say bluntly, is faith . . . ; faith that has undergone criticism, postcritical faith' (Ricoeur, *Freud and Philosophy: An Essay on Interpretation*, 1970).

Ricoeur stresses the creative and suggestive roles of symbol and narrative in religious language. The effects which language generates 'in front of' religious texts constitute his prime concern.

Nevertheless he also underlines the multiform character of different modes of religious discourse. These include prophetic address to the hearer or reader, hymnic praise, the projection of narrative worlds, and the indirect communication which characterizes biblical wisdom literature and is essential if we are not to equate God with idolatrous projections of human thought.

An important development in 1969 was the publication of John Searle's *Speech-Acts*. This built on the earlier work of John L. Austin of 1961, and led to a number of subsequent studies by Searle from 1979 to 1985. Searle, following Austin, explored the logical, extra-linguistic, and linguistic conditions necessary for the performance of certain illocutionary acts, such as promising, authorizing, declaring or commanding. In religious language declarations of repentance, forgiveness, praise, blessing, acquittal or liberation function in certain contexts as acts rather than as reports of events or of mental states. Especially in liturgy and worship, but also in transforming readings of religious texts, language may serve to operate as *acts* of worship, *acts* of praise, or *acts* of promise or commitment (elaborated in Thiselton, 1992).

Since 1967 intense attention has also been paid to the status of language and especially of written texts as such. A major contributory factor has been the earlier writings of Jacques Derrida (such as *Writing and Difference* of 1967, trans. 1978; *Of Grammatology* of 1967, trans. 1976; and *Speech and Phenomena* of 1967, trans. 1973). Derrida was influenced by his reading of Freud, Husserl and Heidegger, and by his collaboration with Roland Barthes and other Paris literary theorists. Together with Barthes he sought to reinterpret Saussure's theory of signs as providing the foundation for a poststructuralist, postmodernist theory of texts and semiotics. Texts, he claimed, are endlessly self-referring, ever-shifting textures, which invite and necessitate endless reinterpretation or rereading. They do not project stable linguistic meaning, but operate as fluidly changing networks in conjunction with shifting intertextual relations with other texts, in ways which mirror shifting social conventions and disguises. Jacques Lacan and Julia Kristeva also combine a poststructuralist or deconstructionist approach with a heavy utilization of psychoanalytical and sociopolitical theory.

From the standpoint of religious language two quite different responses have been offered. Those who are sympathetic with postmodernism emphasize the iconoclastic nature of ever-shifting texts. They call into question (like the Book of Job) fixed dogmas or traditions. Others argue that semiotic theory does not demand the world view implied by Derrida, and that postmodernist accounts of meaning ignore the interactive and intersubjective nature of language in the public domain. This aspect of language has been underlined by the later Wittgenstein, and more explicitly by K. Apel and Jürgen Habermas. Some feminist writers utilize Derrida's approach to argue for the dependence of structures of language on hidden sociopolitical conventions and power interests. But a more firmly anchored socio-critical account of language, which also leaves positive implications for feminist, black, and other liberation theologies, can be found in the hermeneutical theory of Habermas ([1981] 1984–7, vol. 2) (see FEMINIST THEOLOGY). The growing edge of the current debate about the status and power of religious language has now moved firmly into the area of hermeneutical theory.

See also LITERATURE AND THEOLOGY; NARRATIVE THEOLOGY.

Bibliography

Barbour, I.G. 1974: *Myths, Models and Paradigms*. London: SCM Press.

Evans, D.D. 1963: *The Logic of Self-Involvement*. London: SCM Press.

Habermas, J. [1981] 1984–7: *The Theory of Communicative Action*, 2 vols. Cambridge: Polity Press.

High, D.M. 1967: *Language, Persons and Belief*. New

York: Oxford University Press.

Macquarrie, J. 1967: *God-Talk*. London: SCM Press.

Mascall, E.L. 1957: *Words and Images*. London: Longmans, Green.

Radford Ruether, R. 1983: *Sexism and God-Talk*. London: SCM Press.

Ramsey, I.T. 1965: *Chistian Discourse*. London: Oxford University Press.

Ricoeur, P. 1974: *The Conflict of Interpretations*. Evanston: Northwestern University Press.

Ricoeur, P. [1983–5] 1984–8: *Time and Narrative*, 3 vols. Chicago: University of Chicago Press.

Soskice, J.M. 1985: *Metaphor and Religious Language*. Oxford: Clarendon Press.

Thiselton, A.C. 1980: *The Two Horizons*. Exeter: Paternoster.

Thiselton, A.C. 1992: *New Horizons in Hermeneutics*. London: Harper Collins.

Tracy, D. 1981: *The Analogical Imagination*. London: SCM Press.

Wittgenstein, L. [1953–8] 1967: *Philosophical Investigations*, 3rd edn. Oxford: Blackwell.

ANTHONY C. THISELTON

Leibniz, Gottfried Wilhelm (1646–1716) German philosopher and mathematician. He studied law at Leipzig before developing his interest in philosophy and mathematics; in the late 1660s he made his famous discovery of the infinitesimal calculus. From a Protestant family, he was active in attempts to reconcile the Protestant and Roman Catholic churches, and corresponded with J.B. Bossuet on the subject. He formulated traditional proofs of the existence of God, and maintained that suffering is a necessary evil which shows up the greater divine good; he was the first to use the term 'theodicy' in a book of that name of 1710. This belief, that we live in 'the best of all possible worlds', was the subject of a famous satire by Voltaire, but its rationalistic optimism was later an influence on Enlightenment religious thought. In *Monadology* (1720, trans. 1898), he developed the idea that all things are composed of an infinite number of 'monads', simple units containing spiritual energy which exist on a scale of ascending complexity, the highest being God. It proved difficult to reconcile this model with the Christian doctrine of the transcendent God, and in later life Leibniz became associated increasingly with 'natural' religion.

Bibliography

Brown, S. 1984: *Leibniz*. Brighton.

Russell, B. 1937: *Critical Exposition of the Philosophy of Leibniz*, 2nd edn. London.

Saw, R. 1954: *Leibniz*. Harmondsworth.

Leo XIII (1810–1903) Pope of the Roman Catholic church. A native of Carpetino, he was educated in Rome in theology and law, and in 1837 was ordained and entered the papal civil service. In 1843 he was made a bishop, and after a period as papal nuncio in Belgium he became Archbishop of Perugia (1846–78). Here he founded the Academy of St Thomas to promote Catholic thinking in modern philosophy and science. In 1853 he became a cardinal and in 1877 papal camerlengo. On the death of Pius IX in 1878 he was made pope. Despite the suspicion of conservative elements within the church, in a series of encyclicals Leo XIII paved the way for the formulation of a Catholic response to issues facing the modern world, such as industrialization and the growth of democracy. In *Aeterni Patris* (1879), he advocated a revival of Thomism as a way of understanding the relationship of the church to the modern world; his interest in the sphere of work is reflected in *Rerum Novarum* (1891). He reconciled himself to the legitimacy of secular political power, so long as it did not seek to interfere in the church's sphere, and he encouraged the formation of Catholic political parties.

Bibliography

Gargan, E.T., ed. 1961: *Leo XIII and the Modern World*. New York.

Soderini, E. 1934–5: *The Pontificate of Leo XIII*, 2 vols. London.

Wallace, L.P. 1966: *Leo XIII and the Rise of Socialism*. Durham, NC.

Lessing, Gotthold Ephraim (1729–1781) German playwright and Enlightenment thinker. The son of a Lutheran pastor, and a prominent critic and historian, he was a forerunner both of modern German drama and of nineteenth-century Protestant liberalism in Germany. Whilst in charge of the Duke of Brunswick's library at Wolfenbüttel he published the *Wolfenbüttel Fragments* (seven parts,

1774–8) by the German orientalist H.S. Reimarus, which challenged the validity of the Bible texts as an accurate portrait of Jesus. The resulting controversy led to the imposition of censorship by the Duke of Brunswick in 1778; a year later, Lessing published his play, *Nathan der Weise*, whose protagonist embodies his vision of moral, rational and tolerant Enlightenment religion. For him, Christianity was a religion of reason, moral and humanitarian rather than historical and revealed: 'the accidental truths of history can never become the proof of necessary truths of reason'; to search for truth was more important than to attain it. Lessing's writings on religion include *Ernst und Falk* (1778–80), *Die Erziehung des Menschengeschlechts* (1780), and *Neue Hypothese über die Evangelisten als blosse menschliche Geschichtsschreiber betrachtet* (1788).

Bibliography

Allison, H. 1966: *Lessing and the Enlightenment*. Ann Arbor, Mi.
Barth, K. 1972: *Protestant Theology in the Nineteenth Century*. London.
Chadwick, H. 1956: Introduction to *Lessing's Theological Writings*, ed. H. Chadwick. London.
Wessell, L.P. 1977: *G.E. Lessing's Theology: A Reinterpretation*. The Hague.

Lewis, C[live] S[taples] (1898–1963) British scholar and novelist and Christian apologist. Born in Belfast, he was educated at University College, Oxford, and in 1925 became a fellow of English language and literature at Magdalen College; in 1954 he became professor of medieval and Renaissance literature at Magdalene College, Cambridge. His critical works include *The Allegory of Love* (1936) and *A Preface to Paradise Lost* (1942). Having lost his faith at school, he was converted to Christianity between 1929 and 1931, a story told in his spiritual autobiography *Surprised by Joy* (1955). There followed a series of popular and highly influential Christian books, including *The Problem of Pain* (1940), *The Screwtape Letters* (1942) and *The Four Loves* (1960); a trilogy of science fiction novels (1938–45); and a series of novels for children, starting with *The Lion, the Witch and the Wardrobe* (1950). He became well-known in Britain through a series of talks on BBC radio from 1941 to 1944, published later as *Mere Christianity* (1952). He was a member of The Inklings, a group of Oxford writers and scholars including J.R.R. Tolkien and Charles Williams. Although a believer in supernatural Christianity, his emphasis is on the rational grounds for Christian belief. His sometimes detached but readable style, his penetrating psychological insight and warmth as well as his fertile imagination, ensure him a large readership in and beyond the Anglican church.

Bibliography

Beversluis, J. 1984: *C.S. Lewis and the Search for Rational Religion*. Grand Rapids, Mi.
Green, R.L., and Hooper, W. 1974: *C.S. Lewis: A Biography*. London.
Lindskoog, K. 1981: *C.S. Lewis, Mere Christian*. Illinois.

liberal Protestantism A movement which became of particular significance in nineteenth-century Europe and North America, stressing the importance of the religious personality of Jesus, and committed to an optimistic view of human nature and an evolutionary understanding of the nature of cultural development.

See LIBERALISM (BRITAIN and USA); MODERNISM; PROTESTANT THEOLOGY (BRITAIN; GERMANY; and USA).

liberalism: Britain Other articles describe various aspects and persons involved in the liberal tradition in theology (see the cross references at the end of this article). The aim here is to characterize what might be called the liberal mentality, especially as it has manifested itself on the British theological scene. In the theological context, the term 'liberal' refers not so much to a single identifiable set of beliefs as to a cluster of related phenomena which differ according to the intellectual, ecclesiastical or national setting in which they are found. It is therefore not surprising that British theology of this kind has had its own particular flavour, some aspects of it derived from features of British theology in general. Thus, much of it has been Anglican, much of it centred on Oxford and Cambridge, and much of it has had (by comparison, for example, with possible German parallels) a distinctly amateur feel, almost as if its propagators were putting forward suggestions for discussion, even flying kites, rather than offering solidly based academic proposals. Whatever charges of irresponsibility may be levelled against it, it has nevertheless placed before the public ideas which have every right to be on the agenda in the modern world, which many have fumbled for but not quite known how (or dared) to express, and which have stimulated discussion across the wider theological spectrum.

Though not all have recognized it with the same degree of clarity, a single principle may be said to underlie all liberal theological effort: that the claims of truth are ultimately higher than those of revelation, whether known from Scripture or through the church (see AUTHORITY; TRADITION) – claims now felt to be in potential or actual conflict. This principle, derived from the age of reason and the Enlightenment in seventeenth- and eighteenth-century European thought, has been held together with different levels and styles of fidelity to Christian faith, but its emergence constituted in effect a major turning point for everybody. Even those devoted in the highest degree to the authority of divine revelation lived henceforth in a world where their convictions were one among a number of options and they were compelled to appear before the tribunal of reason, even if only to justify their denial of its jurisdiction. Contrariwise, those affected by the principle of the primacy of independent criteria of truth have seemed to cede the authority of religious truth to that of various kinds of secular thought.

It has, however, not been difficult for those in the liberal camp and remaining within the Christian sphere of life to advance the argument that all truth, from wherever it is derived, is of God and that no honour is done to the Creator by restricting truth to particular streams of thought such as certain interpretations of the Bible or certain deliverances of church councils or popes – which is what 'revelation', seemingly so firm and fixed, turns out to boil down to. Whatever the justification for this argument, the distinctive trends of liberal theology have always been part of much wider movements in European thought. Liberals have not often won much credit for their pains from the representatives of these movements, which have tended more and more to despise or be indifferent to religion. And the churches and individuals of more conservative theological outlook have felt that if the Christian cause is to survive with any strength of conviction it cannot be on a liberal diet: that will lead only to a feeble dissolution into enveloping secularism (see SECULARIZATION).

Though it has roots in the largely philosophical questionings of the previous period (see DEISM), the term 'liberal' usually refers to theological developments of the nineteenth and twentieth centuries, and indeed its use in this context dates from the earlier part of that period. In England at that stage, its sense ran over into the political sphere as it described the views of those who were prepared to countenance government action to reform church organization and finances. It provoked the opposition of J.H. Newman and the Tractarians, who appealed to an enduring theological and ecclesiastical tradition as against the rationally inspired ideas of the reformers.

However, its chief use has related to a series of attempts to accommodate traditional Christian belief to various aspects of 'modern knowledge', whether from the side of history, literary criticism, the natural sciences or, more recently, the human sciences. English church life in the past century and a half has been punctuated by a series of controversies, all essentially the same in structure, occasioned either by some publication or by the activities of some person which have been perceived as, to say the least, inimical to accepted standards of faithfulness to Christian truth. On each occasion, the controversy has tended to be followed, once the dust has settled, by the general absorption of at least some aspects of the innovative matter in question. Nevertheless, that absorption rarely receives recognition and certainly has not prevented the same procedure operating the next time, with its accompaniment of outrage and recrimination.

The earliest major (and classical) case was that which was occasioned by the publication in 1860 of *Essays and Reviews*, a collection of essays by seven authors including B. Jowett and F. Temple. It well illustrates some of the main points already made. Thus its contributors included C.W. Goodwin reflecting on the incompatibility of science with the creation narratives in Genesis, and Benjamin Jowett on the role of Scripture as both spiritually edifying and yet needing to be interpreted in the light of a modern understanding of its literary and historical character. Here, as in subsequent episodes, the traditional view of the Old Testament as Christian prophecy and of the demonstrative force of miracles was laid aside.

The same issues came up time and again – whether with regard to the interpretation of the Bible, as when Charles Gore (*Lux Mundi*, 1889) advocated the non-historical character of the pre-Abrahamic chapters of Genesis and the genuine limitations of Jesus' human knowledge; or with regard to miracles, especially the virginal conception and physical resurrection of Jesus, as when Hensley Henson, seen as defective on these matters, was nominated to be the Bishop of Hereford (1917–18); or with regard to formal doctrines, as when the authors of *The Myth of God Incarnate* (Hick, 1977) challenged traditional Christology, the very heart of orthodox faith.

The widespread horror at this book's very title (admittedly a red rag to conservative bulls) illustrates another perennial feature of the story of English liberal theology in particular: it has been beset by sensationalism and persistent ignorance of well-established linguistic usage and debate. The term 'myth', long familiar to refer to representational, story-like religious discourse, is one example. Another is the outcry which attended J.A.T. Robinson's *Honest to God* (1963), which in effect popularized the thought of well-established theologians like Paul Tillich and Dietrich Bonhoeffer and chiefly sought to revitalize, by way of striking imagery, the orthodox ideas of God's involvement with his creation and his identification with the human condition in Christ. Its aspiration somehow to embrace within religious vision the best concepts and aspirations of secular culture and of the scientific outlook were widely perceived as apostasy rather than as vital for realistic evangelism (though there was ample evidence of relief among the many who took the contrary view).

These examples illustrate some of the recurring features of liberal theology's story, at least in Britain. Time after time, attention has focused on two matters: the interpretation of the Bible and the integrity of Christian doctrine. In the matter of the Bible, it has seemed to many

that approaches that took seriously the original settings of the biblical writings and external evidence concerning the history in and behind them were subversive of Christian faith. Doubt was being cast not only on many episodes in the Old Testament, some of them, like the Exodus, highly significant in Christian thought, but also on matters concerning the career of Jesus and what exactly he is likely to have stood for. It seemed that one had to choose between on the one hand standing firm (but on precisely what ground?) and on the other accepting evidence (but would the next book refute or alter it?) at the expense of retaining adequate backing for faith. It is not surprising that while liberals have seen some of their once-outrageous ideas (for example on the Book of Genesis) turn into commonplaces, their relentless openness with regard to the Bible, from both historical and literary sides, has been widely seen as at worst unwelcome and at best perplexing (see BIBLICAL CRITICISM AND INTERPRETATION (1: OLD TESTAMENT and 2: NEW TESTAMENT).

In the matter of the integrity of doctrine, the effect of liberal thought has seemed to involve a gradual attenuation of the orthodox doctrinal 'package'. First one, then another element has been challenged and apparently abandoned: the inspiration and authority of Scripture, the magisterium of the church, the incarnation, the Trinity, hell, life after death. Even moral norms might be destroyed, as in H.A. Williams's contribution to *Soundings* (Vidler, 1962) and his *Objections to Christian Belief* of 1963, where he drew on psychological insights to show the inadequacy of much ethical and pastoral thought and the crudity of traditional ideas of sin.

This common perception of the gradual erosion of Christianity as hitherto understood has naturally not been accepted by the champions of liberalism. Rather they have seen their programme as the restatement or re-presentation of Christian belief in various new and unprecedented contexts, both intellectual and social. Far from seeking to water down Christian belief, they have reckoned to rid it of dross, in the shape of outworn (and perhaps always unfortunate) ideas, and to restore its cutting edge, making it credible to the educated public of the modern west. This was very much the explicit object of Rudolf Bultmann's demythologization programme, originally put forward in the German setting, and widely seen in England as reductionist in content.

Whether the claim to be restating rather than abandoning can be justified is a question that came to a head in Barth's powerful rejection of liberal theology at the time of the First World War (1914–18), especially in reaction to Adolf von Harnack's *Essence of Christianity* of 1900, whose title epitomized the issue at stake and which was widely seen as the high (or low!) water mark of liberal formulation.

English theology has seen no episode of comparable gladiatorial splendour, and often the issues have seemed blurred and controversy to be almost trivialized by the relatively low level of debate. Nevertheless, making allowance for national differences, the essential problems have not been dissimilar, whether in Britain, Germany or France, and the intellectual situation addressed from the start by liberalism has not gone away. There has however been a certain polarization: liberal Christianity, virtuously and laboriously restated, has not exactly commended itself to a public increasingly alienated from religious loyalties, and where strong Christian faith remains it tends to be of anything but a liberal kind.

In such a climate, liberalism in theology and religion has been much denigrated; but its leading ideas and features, listed below, are far from negligible. Many have already come before us in the course of this discussion. There is no suggestion that all the following characteristics are to be found in the make-up of all who could be called liberal in theology or religion.

1 Particularly in Britain (but also in Germany, since Kant and Schleiermacher) liberalism has been associated with the rejection or suspicion of dogma (see DOCTRINE AND DOGMA), both in its strict sense of received doctrine and in its loose sense of rigid formulations of belief. Liberalism, by contrast, seeks to be open to possible new developments in knowledge and insight, from wherever they might be derived. This anti-dogmatic stance has resulted partly from theology's place in Britain alongside other disciplines in the universities rather than being segregated within church institutions.

2 The strong historical bias of liberal (and indeed other) theology led, from the first half of the nineteenth century, to a shift of attention with regard to Jesus from abstract Christology to his historical role and characteristics (see HISTORICAL JESUS, QUEST OF). Inevitably, he then appeared less as the cosmic redeemer than the moral teacher. The human Jesus could scarcely bear the doctrinal claims traditionally made for him. Yet, paradoxically and almost perversely, this Jesus, despite the obscurity of his career which historical Jesus research demonstrated, became the centre of liberal religious attention. Here there seemed to be the possibility of pure faith, unsullied by dogma. Harnack, notably, stressed Jesus' preaching of the kingdom of God and his role as the way to the Father as the heart of Christianity, together with its corollary of human brotherhood. In England, it is the threat to the plain historicity of the Gospels which has tended to be felt as the constant bane of liberal tendencies. In that connection, it is ironic that Bultmann has often been thought of as prominent in the liberal demonology because of his scepticism about our capacity to recover the history of Jesus, whereas in a German context he was opposed to much traditional liberal theology in his espousal of the need for 'decision' and his sense of faith as crisis. English liberalism has often been too sober, too intellectual, and too imbued with assumptions about steady progress in insight and discovery to have much sympathy with any hints of the ecstatic.

3 From its Enlightenment roots and from its persistent inclination to be open to science, liberalism has also had a built-in antipathy to the miraculous. Notwithstanding that aspects of modern physics have cast strong doubt on such attachment to the regularity of the behaviour of matter, liberals have tended to be sceptical of the biblical miracles, seeing them and subsequent wonders as the perceptions of more credulous or superstitious cultures. In line here with much ordinary secular opinion, this scepticism has been seen as endangering not only prominent elements in the Scriptural record but also central items of faith, such as the virginal conception and physical resurrection of Jesus. It is no wonder that discussion of the credibility of miracles and of numerous proposals for their reinterpretation along supposedly more 'natural' lines has been a recurring feature of controversy. No wonder

either that attention has often focused on how far the key belief in the incarnation was bound up with these apparently historical miracles and how far any belief in incarnation involved a disruption of the order of nature.

4   Scepticism about special interventions by God in the regularity of natural phenomena, as if from outside, is partly accounted for and partly compensated by a frequent liberal conviction of the immanence of God in creation. This was particularly prominent in the 'New Theology' of R.J. Campbell at the beginning of the twentieth century, but it has contributed to both the thought and the religious disposition of liberal Christians, with its common this-worldly orientation.

5   If liberalism has been critical of traditional dogma and often of dogma in principle, its strength has often seemed to be in the ethical sphere and indeed in the espousal of a moral style of spirituality. It showed itself between the wars in attachment to the pacifist cause and, especially on the liberal catholic Anglican side, in campaigning for social reform. High-mindedness has often accompanied sitting loose to doctrine, especially perhaps among Anglicans, and is probably a more deep-seated phenomenon than the liberalism of modern times.

6   Though devoted to openness and tolerance, and always eager to widen horizons (for example, to seek common ground between Christianity and other world faiths and to find ways of embracing them in a total religious concept), liberals have often been confident, even dogmatic, in their beliefs – far from meriting the common epithet of 'soggy'! There has been a sense of moving towards an age when liberal values and concepts would receive general acceptance by all reasonable people: the role of philosophical idealism in the roots of liberal religion has been considerable. Only relatively recently (apart from important exceptions earlier, such as Ernst Troeltsch) have a sense of cultural difference and an acceptance of different 'packages' of belief as having their own validity, each in its own setting, come to the fore. This perception of difference rather than progress as the way to look at Christian history is itself to be seen as a more refined testimony to traditional liberal readiness to accept the fruits of historical investigation, but it brings new problems concerning the identity or essence of Christianity (see RELATIVISM, CULTURAL).

It was surely never to be expected that liberal theology would capture the imagination of the masses. It has been largely an option for the educated, though not without its echoes in popular opinion (for instance on miracles). Yet it is surprising that, apart from its achievements by osmosis already referred to (such as in the wider acceptance of a critical approach to the Bible), it has had so little positive effect.

Much responsibility may be laid at the door of liberals' frequent failure to demonstrate religious strength in their form of Christianity. It has often seemed arid or unspiritual – not helpful in a time of spiritual hunger. In its rigorous honesty of thought, it has seemed not to offer what people generally seek in religion – a sense of contact with God and of drawing upon his resources. The Modern Churchmen of the 1920s and 1930s and Bishop Barnes of Birmingham with his, as it seemed, tasteless attempts to eradicate 'superstitious' attachment to the sacrament of the Eucharist were seen to typify this quality.

However, on the English scene itself, liberal catholicism may fairly claim to have accomplished more in this regard than other styles of liberalism (such as those just referred to), with its stress on sacramental worship and seriousness about prayer and spiritual discipline. In figures like Charles Gore and Michael Ramsey, it has produced leaders of undoubted spiritual stature. Their liberalism, however, showed more in relation to Scripture than to doctrine, and even there was far from radical in its conclusions. Ramsey's dislike of some of the products of liberal theology (such as the work of Maurice Wiles and *The Myth of God Incarnate*) well illustrates the mistake of treating 'liberal' as a label for a strongly homogeneous point of view. Perhaps it is best seen as a certain style or disposition in approaching religious belief, marked by a civilized readiness to consider arguments and evidence, even if one does not end up shifting one's ground very far. In that sense it is poles apart from fundamentalisms of various kinds and from any invoking of naked authority as capable of delivering fixed and final truth about the things of God. English liberals include both Michael Ramsey and Don Cupitt, with many varied persons between the two.

With its diversity and its disregard of authorities, liberalism looks like the end result of a process which began at the Reformation. To the orthodox or the cautious, this is the chaos that ensues once the genie is released from the bottle. It is, moreover, the expression in the religious sphere, where it is seen as inappropriate, of the freedom which has developed over the centuries in the intellectual and political affairs of the west: not just liberal theology's particular conclusions but its very nature as a phenomenon spring from this source. But so unstable is the result of such accommodation that Christianity receives the appearance of a chameleon; and, as the dictum goes, marriage to the spirit of the age is a quick way to widowhood. On the other hand, refusal to go courting leads to eccentric solitude and inaccessibility. It is no wonder, however, that though liberalism has been resisted by most of the established churches at each new proposal or endeavour, the firmest clamp-downs have come from the Roman Catholic authorities, in their treatment of Catholic MODERNISM particularly in the early part of this century, but also of others since (such as Hans Küng and George Tyrrell). Doubtless, in some cases liberal principles, essentially free-ranging, have produced bizarre and barely recognizable versions of Christian belief and practice, particularly when taken into the sphere of religious experience, which has often been an important dimension.

See also LIBERALISM: USA; POSTLIBERALISM; PROTESTANT THEOLOGY (BRITAIN and GERMANY).

Bibliography

Barnes, J. 1979: *Ahead of his Age: Bishop Barnes of Birmingham*. London: Collins.

Chadwick, O. 1983: *Hensley Henson*. Oxford: Clarendon Press.

Clements, K.W. 1988: *Lovers of Discord: 20th Century Theological Controversies in England*. London: SPCK.

Cockshut, A.O.J. 1966: *Religious Controversies of the 19th Century: Selected Documents*. London: Methuen.

Dawes, H. 1990: Liberal theology in the parish, *Theology* 93, pp. 117–24.

DeWolf, L.H. 1959: *The Case for Theology in Liberal Perspective*.

Glazebrook, M.G. 1918: *The Faith of a Modern Churchman*. London: John Murray.

Glover, T.R. 1917: *The Jesus of History*. London: SCM Press.

Hick, J., ed. 1977: *The Myth of God Incarnate*. London: SCM Press.

Iremonger, F.W. 1948: *William Temple*. London: Oxford University Press.

Mascall, E.L. 1965: *The Secularization of Christianity*. London: Darton, Longman and Todd.

Miller, D.E. 1981: *The Case for Liberal Christianity*.

Stephenson, A.M.G. 1984: *The Rise and Decline of English Modernism*. London: SPCK.

Vidler, A.R., ed. 1962: *Soundings: Essays Concerning Christian Understanding*. Cambridge: Cambridge University Press.

LESLIE HOULDEN

liberalism: USA Liberal Christian theologies in North America have generally maintained that religious beliefs are fallible and are thus to be held tentatively, that reason and experience in some combination provide the fundamental tests of beliefs, that divine and human realities are continuous rather than oppositional, and that central to Christianity is its ethical dimension, social as well as personal. Perhaps their most consistent mark, however, is a methodological one: the supposition that theology should always interrelate the spirit of its own time and the Christian past in a manner that allows each to make an essential and substantive difference to the formulation of theological claims. These persistent themes and this method have received quite varied expressions. An adequate understanding of liberal theology in America, therefore, requires consideration of its roots and development.

Historically, liberal theologies are reconstructions of Christian thought undertaken in response to the ENLIGHTENMENT and in basic sympathy with it. The Enlightenment, epitomized in Kant's focus on reason, drew on Newton to argue that the world is orderly and can be fathomed by human enquiry, and on Locke to defend human liberty, including freedom of thought, and the political sovereignty of the people. Interpenetrating both claims was a confidence in the essential goodness of humankind. The effect of the Enlightenment, as it pertained to religion, was the destruction of the hegemony of tradition in any form (church, dogma, Scripture) and the grounding of religious claims in ways that

325

opened them to critical, public scrutiny. The most obvious alternative to tradition as a basis for religious claims was human reason, the weapon that had been turned upon the authority of the past in the first place (see AUTHORITY; TRADITION). But there were differences within Enlightenment reflection about the meaning of reason, the extent of its powers, and the degree of its interdependence with other factors, particularly individual and collective experience. Hence Enlightenment modernity has been less univocal in what it affirmed than in what it rejected.

Liberal Christian theology (see also MODERNISM), heir to the Enlightenment, has also been more uniform in what it denies than what it affirms. This was evident already in its early European expressions. Partly in reaction to Kantian rationalism and partly in response to the limits that Kant himself had placed upon reason as it pertains to religion, F.D.E. Schleiermacher sought to ground Christianity apart from reason in what he claimed to be a *sui generis* and universal religious self-consciousness – 'the feeling of absolute dependence'. Albrecht Ritschl, drawing on the ethical side of Kant's work, based his analysis in the human experience of moral freedom and what he took to be faith's corollary, a Christian 'value judgement' or interpretation of the world. Mention of these alternatives already suggests what historical studies demonstrate, namely, that liberal theology, though united in a rejection of authoritarianism, is a variety of views and that this variety arises in part from a process of transformative self-criticism inherent within liberalism itself. (See Rupp, 1977, Gerrish, 1977, and, for a survey of some of this literature, Parsons, 1983.)

Liberalism gained an effective foothold in North American theology only in the last third of the nineteenth century, but it was prepared for by nearly a century of unitarian and proto-unitarian reflection. (The best history of religious liberalism in America is Hutchison, 1976). From cultural figures like Thomas Jefferson and Thomas Paine and religious leaders like William Ellery Channing and Octavius Frothingham there developed a 'modernist' habit of mind that associated the workings of God with the 'interior spirit' of the age. By mid-century even a progressive conservative like Horace Bushnell was saying, albeit half-heartedly, that orthodox doctrines ought to be revised to conform to the truths of new times.

After 1850 the cause of theological revision – then known as the 'new theology', later more commonly as liberalism – grew primarily among preachers rather than academics, encouraged by Bushnell's work and the writings of two Englishmen, F.D. Maurice and F.W. Robertson. As the nineteenth century progressed, its chief proponents were men like Henry Ward Beecher, Theodore Munger, Washington Gladden, Newman Smyth, and Charles A. Briggs. Their emerging concern was the relationship of religion and science and their continuing conviction was the ethical character of Christianity, but their underlying method was forthright revisionism. Said Briggs: 'It is sufficient that the Bible gives us the *material* for all ages, and leaves to man the noble task of shaping the material so as to suit the wants of his own time.'

In 1874 David Swing, a popular Chicago preacher, was tried for heresy for preaching his version of the new theology. Swing had proclaimed that the meaning and truth of Christian beliefs can only be assessed in relation to their cultural contexts, that the function of beliefs is to negotiate the vicissitudes of particular settings, that beliefs must always be revised for new situations, and that the particular needs of nineteenth-century America demanded a faith accepting of science and dedicated to the social good. Although attacked by the full force of Calvinist conservatism, Swing was acquitted. From that point on liberal theology was part of mainline or 'evangelical' American Christianity. (In the nineteenth century, the term 'evangelical' was used quite generally – frequently in opposition, first, to 'unitarian' and later also to 'humanist' – to refer to those who, whether liberal or conservative, explicitly located themselves within, and worked positively to appropriate, the inheritance of Christianity. Even as late as the 1920s the opposition to liberalism was 'fundamentalism', hence liberal theologians in America could still comfortably refer to themselves as 'evangelicals'.)

By the last decade of the nineteenth century liberalism had become strong enough and thus free enough to begin self-conscious systematic theological reconstruction. The first significant efforts of this sort, those by William Newton Clarke and William Adams Brown, followed, though loosely, the lead of the Ritschlians in Germany. The Ritschlian approach appears to have been fitting for at least three reasons. For one thing, the distinctively Christian moral datum to which it appealed was less overtly universalistic than Schleiermacher's 'religious experience' and thus more consistent with the persisting pluralism of American liberal thought. Secondly, Ritschlianism's ethical cast conformed to the new theology's social/ethical interpretation of Christianity, eventually to give rise to the 'social gospel'.

The third reason for the influence of Ritschl was more circumstantial. In the latter part of the nineteenth century, when Americans began to study in German universities, the Ritschlians not only dominated that theological scene, they also entered vigorously the struggle against the severe social disintegration caused by urbanization and industrialization. Their role, thus, modelled the kind of theological undertaking required back in America. Like Germany, the USA was awash with social turmoil. Conservative Protestantism, before the civil war a powerful voice for social justice, had become a purely private pietism. The new theology sought to fill the void and to address America's urban crisis. For this the Ritschlians provided a precedent.

The liberal theological programme in the USA peaked from the 1890s to the end of the 1920s. During this time it had two major, largely overlapping emphases. One was 'social Christianity' or the 'social gospel', whose most influential exponent was Walter Rauschenbusch. Like other liberals, Rauschenbusch believed that Christian theology must constantly be revised – 'reverence' for ideas no longer functional, he said, 'is a kind of ancestor worship.' For his time, Rauschenbusch emphasized the historical Jesus and the moral community that Jesus had initiated, that is, the kingdom of God. The kingdom is the divine order on earth, social in character and inclusive of the whole of human life. Salvation is 'saving the social organism . . . not human atoms'. The obstacle to the progressive achievement of God's kingdom is the historical accumulation of selfishness as it manifests itself in social and economic injustice. Rauschenbusch did not think the realization of the kingdom to be inevitable; in fact, his call for commitment to the kingdom was rather apocalyptic in tone. During the preceding century, he said, humans had conquered nature but they had failed to control themselves. Now there must be a revival of the 'social religion' of Jesus; otherwise, Rauschenbusch warned, there will be a 'deluge'. Rauschenbusch's language of crisis notwithstanding, however, even he betrayed a spirit of hope that the call to progress would be heeded. His optimism, even less restrained in other proponents of the social gospel, was the spirit of the age.

The other major expression of liberal theology in this period was the 'early Chicago school' which flourished during the decades 1910–30. Its representatives – for example Shirley Jackson Case, Shailer Mathews and Gerald Birney Smith – were the most erudite scholars of religion of the day. But they were not simply scholars. Indeed, their influence was partly due to their combination of theoretical enquiry and practical involvement in church and society. Active in local politics or as labour movement officials, public lecturers, lay educators or weekend preachers, they devoted the full range of their abilities to propagating a blend of political progressivism, confidence in reason, science and democracy, and a reconstructed Christian faith. The key to their reconstruction was the 'socio-historical method'. Sceptical in varying degrees about abstract speculation, these theologians interpreted Christianity as a socio-historical movement the beliefs of which were to be understood and evaluated pragmatically. Mathews, for example, analysed doctrines of God and the atonement throughout history as hypotheses that enabled people to adjust more or less satisfactorily to the personality-producing forces of the universe. The task of the contemporary theologian was not to reproduce some imagined essence of Christianity, either in its timeless purity or in a form revised to be palatable for the times, but to reformulate doctrines anew in each age so as to accomplish the same redemptive purpose that had governed its formations and reformations in the past. When pressed to justify his interpretation of this redemptive purpose, however, Mathews vacillated. Sometimes he appealed to Jesus as moral exemplar, on other occasions to the direction of human progress as this was discerned by the physical and social sciences within the context of democracy.

By the mid-1920s American liberalism was faltering, both with respect to its method and its anthropology. Regarding the latter, liberal systematic theologies were never quite as optimistic as critics claimed. But the ebullience of the liberals' rhetoric betrayed an undergirding optimism of spirit that far exceeded the moderation of their systems. Thus, the First World War profoundly shocked liberal confidence in human nature and hope for progress in history. With the war there began a process of severe reassessment, motivated by honesty within the movement and criticism from without. Though no single way beyond naive optimism dominated the liberal reassessment, the common aim was somehow to recover a classical Christian realism about human evil without relapsing into Calvinism. Before the liberals' anthropology could be reconstructed, however, neo-orthodoxy swept America. It had been prepared for by liberal self-doubt, so to many former liberals neo-orthodoxy seemed a solution.

Liberalism in this period also faltered at the point of its most definitive characteristic, theological method. In his highly influential analysis of American liberalism, Kenneth Cauthen (1962) distinguishes two liberal methods, those of the 'evangelical liberals' and the 'modernist liberals'. Evangelical liberals, Cauthen claims, 'accepted as normative for their thinking what they understood to be the essence of historical Christianity.' Usually this essence was taken to be the message of Jesus, Jesus' personality, or the special role of Jesus in the mediation of the Christian experience of God. Modernistic liberals, according to Cauthen, 'believed that there were elements of permanent significance in the Christian tradition which ought to be retained', but their basic outlook was determined by the outlook of the twentieth century.

In his more historical study of much the same period and perspective, William R. Hutchison (1976) challenges Cauthen's division. Hutchison denies that those whom Cauthen calls evangelical liberals were less at home in the modern age

or that Cauthen's modernist liberals were less committed to Christ and Christian tradition. Hutchison is probably right; Cauthen's division is not neatly evident among early twentieth-century liberal theologians. But if Cauthen's distinction does not identify a division among the liberals, it does point to the unresolved struggle *within* most of them between faithfulness to the Christian past and fidelity to the modern world. These liberal theologians sought to be both 'evangelicals' (in the nineteenth-century sense of that term) and modernists; theirs was a dual allegiance, to Christianity and to the spirit of their time. They hoped beyond hope that the essence of each would turn out to be the same. Hence, for a while, they acted on that hope, constantly adjusting their view of what the one 'really' meant in the light of what seemed at the time to be the best in the other. By the end of the 1920s, however, the strategy seemed futile; a Christian view of the 'workings of God' and the 'interior spirit' of the age appeared hopelessly at odds. In particular, the scientific spirit that once promised support for a modernized Christianity was now increasingly hostile to all religion. A liberalism both evangelical and modernist seemed impossible.

During the late 1920s and the 1930s the liberals were challenged from opposite directions. On their left the humanists championed loyalty to modernity alone. On their right fundamentalists advocated faithfulness to Christianity alone (see FUNDAMENTALISM). Each sounded like a clearer alternative, but neither was a solution for liberals, however perplexed. Thus, many liberals welcomed neo-orthodoxy; its non-biblicist appeal to revelation, they thought, provided methodological clarity. For others – especially process theologians, such as Bernard Meland and Daniel Day Williams – neo-orthodoxy was not a solution, but its message became a useful foil for liberal reassessment.

The liberal theologies that emerged in the 1960s, after three decades of neo-orthodox domination, are more chastened and more complex. Though generally they profess hope for significant human and social transformation, human evil is now more sobering in their view and the prospect for progress more fragile. Their conceptions of God, Christ and other Christian categories are also more diverse than those of earlier liberalisms, and for that reason less easy to classify precisely in terms of some defining 'liberal' characteristic. To the extent that 'liberal' Christian theology has a positive meaning, that is, as something more than 'not conservative', that has to do with the continuing question of method – how can, and should, one both take seriously the inherited Christian past and participate fully in the present age?

A few 1960s liberals adopted strategies of identity, much like those of the 1920s. Some expressions of the so-called death of God and secular theologies, for example, appealed to the model of Jesus or the incarnation in order to authenticate assent to contemporary realities and contemporary norms. Other, more sophisticated, liberal strategies in the 1970s and 1980s (for example those of Langdon Gilkey, feminists like Rosemary Radford Ruether and some liberation theologians) employed versions of a method of correlation to show how modernity and Christian faith (or, better, some aspect of each) have different roles to play in theological construction. (See FEMINIST THEOLOGY; LIBERATION THEOLOGY.) For Gilkey, biblical faith addresses the questions raised in modern experiences of finitude, temporality and so on. For Radford Ruether, the prophetic/messianic tradition of the Bible addresses questions raised by experience in the struggles against sexism, racism, and classism.

A number of different revisionary theologies constitute a third methodological strategy in recent liberalism. In one form, represented variously by John Cobb, Francis Schüssler Fiorenza and the current work of David Tracy, the Christian past and contemporary experience live in continuous dialogue, each vulnerable to challenge and transformation through a critical encounter with the other. A related revisionist method is developed by Schubert Ogden. For Ogden, the earliest apostolic witness of faith constitutes the criterion of the 'Christianness' of theology while contemporary standards of adequacy, fallible and changing as they are, provide the norms in terms of which a theology's claims to truth are to be judged. Rebecca Chopp's method is similar to Ogden's in that she locates the norm of Christian theological reflection in the contemporary situation; for her, however, as for many liberation theologians, that contem-

porary norm, in terms of which both experience and tradition are to be judged, is the Christian's involvement in liberating praxis.

For some American theologians during the 1970s and 1980s the effort to involve inherited Christian symbols and categories substantively in theological construction has come to seem artificial if not perverse. For them, the Christian mythos is so outmoded, so tied to oppressive structures of race, class and gender, or so widely ignored, that reconstructive work on behalf of the human future would proceed better without any dependency on Christian tradition. Until very recently, these judgements have seemed to be on the ascendant. Theologians representing this alternative – for example, post-Christian feminists and deconstructionists/post-structuralists – may best be understood as analogues of the humanists of the 1920s and 1930s.

Theological construction that seeks to be both 'evangelical' (in the nineteenth-century sense) and 'modernist', however, is perhaps now on the rebound. If so, that is partly a response to the resurgence of conservative forms of Christianity, whether as neo-fundamentalism and its more flexible Wesleyan corollaries (to which, in the USA, the term 'evangelical' now commonly refers see EVANGELICALISM. USA), or as postliberal theology (see POSTLIBERALISM). But the resurgence of this kind of Christian theological construction may prove to be most vigorous among racial/ethic Christian theologians and second-generation feminists, for whom the hermeneutics of appreciation and construction is given equal status with the hermeneutics of suspicion and deconstruction. Whether, for them, the precedents of earlier liberalisms or the liberalisms of the current theological establishment have anything significant to offer remains to be seen.

See also LIBERALISM: BRITAIN; PROTESTANT THEOLOGY (GERMANY and USA).

Bibliography

Arnold, Charles Harvey 1966: *Near the Edge of Battle*. Chicago: Divinity School Association.

Brown, Delwin 1990: The fall of '26: Gerald Birney Smith and the collapse of socio-historical theology, *American Journal of Theology and Philosophy* 11, pp. 183–201.

Cauthen, Kenneth 1962: *The Impact of American Religious Liberalism*. Lanham, MD: University

Press of America.

Dean, William 1986: *American Religious Empiricism.* Albany, NY: State University of New York Press.

Gerrish, Brian A. 1977: *Tradition and the Modern World: Reformed Theology in the Nineteenth Century.* Chicago: University of Chicago Press.

Hutchison, William R., ed. 1968: *American Protestant Thought in the Liberal Era.* Lanham, MD: University Press of America.

Hutchison, William R. 1976: *The Modernist Impulse in American Protestantism.* Oxford: Oxford University Press.

Parsons, Gerald 1983: Reforming the tradition: a forgotten dimension of liberal Protestantism, *Religion* 13, pp. 257–71.

Rupp, George 1977: *Culture Protestantism: German Liberal Theology at the Turn of the Twentieth Century.* Atlanta: Scholars Press.

Tracy, David 1975: *Blessed Rage for Order: The New Pluralism in Theology.* New York: Seabury Press.

DELWIN BROWN AND SHEILA GREEVE DAVANEY

liberation theology A variety of Christian movements in different parts of the world have adopted theological positions described as 'liberation theology', so that any adequate description of this contemporary trend should refer to a plural family of theologies of liberation. Their key concepts and methodologies were developed originally in Latin America during the three decades following the Second World War. Their concept of 'liberation' had political and cultural connotations, reflecting the postwar movements against colonialism in Africa and Asia and the revolutionary attempts to change radically the social structures in Latin America. Placing the origin of the movement and its thrust in that particular historical setting, Peruvian priest Gustavo Gutiérrez says that 'the theology of liberation offers us not so much a new theme for reflection as a *new way* to do theology. Theology as critical reflection on historical praxis.' ([1971] 1988, p. 12). Every theology is to be understood as a product of historical circumstances, and today this perspective has been adopted by black, Hispanic and Amerindian theologies in the USA, and theologies in Africa, Asia and the South Pacific and feminist theologies, all of which are 'an expression of a far-reaching historical event: the irruption of the poor' (Gutiérrez, [1971] 1988, p. xx).

Historical context and sources

Iberian Catholicism with its medieval and crusading spirit was brought to Latin America through military conquest in the sixteenth century. The church became a key component of the colonial structure, and scholastic theology provided an ideological explanation for the role of Christians in that society. After the movement of emancipation from Spain (1810–24) the church remained as a conservative force. Scholastic theology was not questioned by Latin American Catholics but it became irrelevant to the cultural life of these societies and unable to stand the onslaught of positivism and Marxism. The religious monopoly of Roman Catholicism was challenged from the early nineteenth century by the presence of Protestantism, that saw itself as a transformative force in society, its theology being more akin to the ideas of liberalization, democracy and progress. However Latin American theologies of liberation have been predominantly a Roman Catholic phenomenon that emerged as an outcome of several transformative processes within that church: the change of missionary strategies by European and North American Catholic missionaries in Latin America, the change of political alignment of some Catholic elites, and the pastoral and biblical renewal which received its impetus from the Second Vatican Council (Vatican II, 1962–7) and the Medellín Conference of Bishops (CELAM II in 1968), which tried to apply the thinking of that Council to Latin America.

The new Catholic missionaries were concerned with the social conditions and the decline of the church, and though at first influenced by the anti-communist stance of the cold war, their encounter with the appalling conditions of the poor brought about a change of practice in two directions. Europeans applied social analysis to understanding church and society, and North Americans became activists in a variety of grassroots actions for the poor. Their approach coincided with the change of political outlook and alignment of Catholic lay leaders such as Brazilian Paulo Freire (b. 1921), under the influence of French lay theologians Jacques Maritain and Emmanuel Mounier (1905–1950), within the Catholic Action movement of workers and students. Active involvement in these processes was part of the formative experience of theologians such as Juan Luis Segundo and Gustavo Gutiérrez, whose ideas became influential at the time of the Medellín Conference of Bishops. Key concepts and vocabulary of these theologians were adopted by the hierarchy in the final documents they issued, and the church called her new position a 'preferential option for the poor'.

According to Gutiérrez, liberation theology came as reflection on that new practice, but it was to be done 'in light of God's Word'. The French Bible-centred pastoral renewal was influential through the work of many of the missionary priests from Europe, and the use of biblical scholarship and biblical categories also became a new source of theological reflection within Catholic circles as a result of Vatican II. Influential theologians like Marie-Dominique Chenu (1895–1990), Yves Congar, Johann Baptist Metz and Karl Rahner had pioneered the way, sanctioned later by Conciliar decrees, that made the Bible the chief source of theology and placed it at the centre of the curriculum for the training of priests. In the use of biblical material and motifs, theologians of liberation represent this new moment in the life of their church. Besides Gutiérrez and Segundo, others like Severino Croatto, Leonardo Boff, and Porfirio Miranda have provided hermeneutical foundations to their theological work.

There was also interaction between Catholic liberation theologians and some Latin American Protestants linked to the ecumenical movement such as Emilio Castro from Uruguay, José Míguez Bonino (b. 1924) from Argentina and Rubem Alves (b. 1933) from Brazil, all of whom adopted liberation perspectives. Alan Neely (1977) surveyed Protestant antecedents of liberation theologies. One of these was the study carried on within the ecumenical movement of churches in situations of rapid social change, which reached its peak in a conference organized by the World Council of Churches on 'Christians in the Technical and Social Revolutions of Our Time' (in Geneva in 1966). The theological contributions of Harvey Cox, Paul Lehmann (b. 1906) and Jürgen Moltmann were influential in this process. It was understood that unjust structures and oppression in society had a dehumanizing effect contrary to God's design, and that God's action in history was aimed at humanization, 'to make and to keep human life human'. Consequently Christians were called on to take part in the historical process of our century, in which revolution represented the cutting edge of humanization. This agenda was to be implemented by the movement Church and Society in Latin America (ISAL), which first publicized the writings of Rubem Alves, Paulo Freire and Richard Shaull. Alves's book *A Theology of Human Hope* (1969) represents a Latin American interpretation of theologians such as Karl Barth, Rudolf Bultmann, Cox, Lehmann and Jürgen Moltmann. It preceded by two years the original Spanish edition of the classic book by Gustavo Gutiérrez, *A Theology of Liberation* (1971, trans. 1973).

The method of liberation theologies

The classic systematic overviews by Míguez Bonino (1975) and Gutiérrez ([1971] 1988) emphasize the fact that the starting point is the committed action of Christian people. Liberation theology is not just a new academic fashion, but its novelty comes from its source in a new *praxis*, in a new way of living and understanding the Christian presence and action in the world. This theological itinerary is clear: first, Christians perceive God moving in history to bring liberation for the poor, and consequently throw in their lot with him in obedience; second, they go to Scripture or to Christian tradition in order to read and understand. Only from the ground of commitment does one have access to the reality of biblical truth, because as Míguez Bonino says 'there is no truth outside or beyond the concrete historical events in which men are involved as agents. There is, therefore, no knowledge except in action itself, in the process of transforming the world through participation in history' (1975, p. 88). Argentinian Severino Croatto argues that this corresponds to a pattern found in the Bible itself, in which 'the biblical message wells up from the salvific happening . . . [which] is the point of departure for theology' ([1973] 1981, p. v). This determines a method in which 'I do not first carry out an exegesis of the biblical passage and subsequently relate it to the facts of our world or our oppressed continent. Rather, the facts must be and are prior to my interpretation of the biblical Word' (p. 11).

For these theologians, in Latin America praxis meant involvement in the cause of social and political liberation as defined by a Marxist analysis of history and of social reality. According to Míguez Bonino 'the thought of these men is characterized by a strict scientific-ideological analysis, avowedly Marxist. This is clearly seen in their way of relating praxis and theory and in their insistence on the rationality, conflict and radicality of the political realm. It can also be seen in the recognition of class struggle' (1975, p. 71). Marxism offers a tool for social analysis and a view of history permeated by a messianic and eschatological bent. For Míguez Bonino, Marxist analysis is projective and anticipatory, and involves 'a certain discernment of the future' (p. 35). It takes class struggle as the key to understanding present social reality, and it also announces the coming of an end to that struggle in the classless society that revolution will bring. In theologians like Gutiérrez, Míguez Bonino and Hugo Assman (b. 1933) there is an explicit criticism of capitalism and a rejection of political options that could be described as 'developmentalism', 'reformism' or a third way between Marxist socialism and capitalism. This mixture of science and anticipation was the ideological context within which Gutiérrez stated that 'the goal is not only better living conditions, a radical change of structures, a social revolution; it is much more: the continuous creation, never ending, of a new way to be human, a permanent cultural revolution' ([1971] 1988, p. 21).

The epistemology that privileges praxis can be traced back to the preference for action over contemplation characteristic of philosophy after Hegel, Feuerbach and Marx. As Yugoslav theologian Miroslav Volf has pointed out, 'a new consciousness has developed: the truth opens itself up, not to beholding but to doing and to changing . . . true thinking as opposed to false consciousness is for Marx thinking which reveals its power to establish the truth of this world. Revolutionary practice is the criterion of truth' (1983, p. 13). Theologians such as René Padilla (b. 1932) accept that liberation theology is correct in criticizing the rationalistic tendency in theology, because from a biblical perspective God's Logos became a historical person. However he offers a warning against the pitfall of pragmatism, the kind of theologizing that uses the biblical text to justify a position that has been adopted on either pragmatic or ideological grounds, because 'if there is no norm for evaluating praxis outside of praxis itself, the sheer utility will provide the only grounds for its justification – the end will justify the means. Only if faith has a cognitive content outside praxis itself can it serve as a criterion to evaluate praxis' (Padilla, 1983, p. 15).

The use of MARXISM in liberation theology has been criticized by Catholics such as James V. Schall and Michael Novak, and by evangelicals such as Emilio Núñez and others (Schipani, 1989). This was also the main thrust of official criticism from the Vatican in the Instructions of the Sacred Congregation for the Doctrine of the Faith in 1984 and 1986, signed by Cardinal Joseph Ratzinger. In the debates of the 1980s between some liberation theologians and the Vatican, a central argument was the use of Marxism, and a process of clarification and refinement took place. In his responses to criticism from the Vatican, Gustavo Gutiérrez was explicit about the limits he has set to his own use of Marxism. He says that some Marxist elements were part of the social sciences used for analysis, and he points to the fact that the Conference of Roman Catholic Bishops in their assemblies of Medellín (1968) and Puebla (1979) also used them (Gutiérrez, [1986] 1990, p. 11). However, he adds, 'it goes without saying that the Marxist philosophy of the human person and of atheism has never played a part in liberation theology' (p. 37).

Liberation theologies outside Latin America have emphasized the common situation of oppression in their origins, but in some cases have dismissed the use of Marxism. Thus black American theologian J. Deotis Roberts (b. 1927) says that 'it is rather easy for black theologians to enter into dialogue with Latin American liberation theologians because both are tuned in on an oppressed human situation' (Roberts, 1974, pp. 205–6) (see BLACK THEOLOGY). But he also contrasts the Catholic milieu, the reaction against totalitarian governments and the influence of Marxism in Latin America with the context of black theology, which is mainly Protestant, comes from a pluralistic society and faces the specific question of race. Morever, 'black theologians are not bound by church dogmas; neither do they seek church approval for their reflection' (p. 207). Roberts also emphasizes the intense and lively spirituality of the black church within which black theology was born, and the North American experience of reconciliation to which it was related. Aloysius Pieris, a Jesuit from Sri Lanka, stresses the validity of the great religions and rejects the Marxist criticism of religion. For him 'this Afro-Asian critique of Marxist occidentalism is also an implicit judgement on the militant stream of Latin American theology, which maintains a methodological continuity with western Marxism and a cultural continuity with European theology' (Fabella and Torres, 1983, p. 119). (See also METHOD IN THEOLOGY.)

The threefold theological agenda of liberation theologies

There is no systematic theology written from a liberation perspective, and the only theologian from this line that has attempted to cover the wide range of Christian doctrine is Juan Luis Segundo, whose most ambitious works were previous to the more recent definitions of liberation theologies. From the development of the movement and its interaction at a global level, the predominant note is the effort to carry on the theological work starting from the perspective of the oppressed person; for instance, assuming the position of the poor in Latin America and Asia or of the oppressed minorities like women, blacks and Hispanics in North America or blacks under apartheid in South Africa. The themes and methods of liberation theologies can be understood through what we perceive as the threefold agenda that has guided their work: a new formulation of Christian praxis, a new reading of history, and a new reading of Scripture.

The new formulation of Christian praxis was derived from the use of the social sciences to read the social conditions of Latin America, and has also been adopted in other parts of the world. The question of the so-called 'option for the poor' taken by the Catholic church in Latin America is understood by liberation theologians as a pastoral and political alignment. They insist that the biblical categories cannot be applied to our contemporary situation without the mediation of the social sciences. 'The poor' is not a vague term to refer to underprivileged people in society, but it has a very well defined meaning which at its core is sociological and which points to the existence of social classes and social struggles. For Gutiérrez, 'poor and oppressed people are members of a social class which is overtly or covertly exploited by another social class. The proletariat is simply the most belligerent and clear-cut segment of this exploited social class' (Gibellini, [1975] 1979, p. 8). What is expected from Christians is to opt for the poor, and that means 'to opt for one social class over against another; to take cognizance of the fact of class confrontation and side with the oppressed . . . to unite in fellowship with its interests, concerns and struggles' (pp. 8–9). The poverty of the poor demands a new praxis which, rather than acts of generosity to alleviate their plight, must be 'a compelling obligation to fashion an entirely different social order' (p. 8).

Liberation theologies offer also a new way of understanding history. In its original Latin American version this new view derived its critical dynamism from the Marxist conception of history as summarized above. Application of class analysis and emphasis on the social role played by the institutional churches brought a rereading of their history that had a shocking effect, especially when used for a critical understanding of missionary action within the framework of European imperial expansion after the sixteenth century. From that perspective both Catholic and Protestant missionary work have been criticized, provoking what Míguez Bonino calls a crisis of conscience 'when Christians discover that their churches have become the ideological allies of foreign and national forces that keep the countries in dependence and the people in slavery and need' (1975, p. 17). Historians that have adopted the liberation perspective, such as Argentinian Enrique Dussel (b. 1934) and Brazilian Eduardo Hoornaert (b. 1930), have modified the Marxist view, turning it more into a new outlook 'from the perspective of the poor' (Dussel, [1967] 1981; Hoornaert, [1986] 1988).

Going also beyond the confines of a Marxist reading of history, some liberation theologians interpret the emergence of a theological perspective that incorporates the view of the poor and oppressed as part of what Gutiérrez calls 'a far reaching historical event, the irruption of the poor' ([1971] 1988, p. xx).

This irruption would be part of the general movement of history towards *liberation* in which he distinguishes three levels, 'liberation from social situations of oppression and marginalization', 'a personal transformation by which we live with profound inner freedom in the face of every kind of servitude', and 'liberation from sin which attacks the deepest root of all servitude' (p. xxxviii). In other theologians awareness about the irruption of the poor in history has become part of the agenda of a theology of the Christian mission that must interpret the significance of the growth and flourishing of the Christian faith in the southern hemisphere parallel to the decline of Christendom in Europe (Costas, 1989). It brings to the debate the eschatological question which for Gutiérrez has been expressed in his insistence upon the concept that there is no sacred history within a world history, but only *one history*: 'one human destiny, irreversibly assumed by Christ the Lord of history' ([1971] 1988, p. 86).

The new way of reading Scripture can be better perceived, for instance, in the Christological and ecclesiological proposals of liberation theologies. The Christology of Jon Sobrino, a Jesuit theologian from El Salvador, intentionally starts from the biblical text rather than from the dogmatic statements of the church, and seeks to focus on the historical Jesus in order to provide a basis for Christian action: 'the course that Jesus took is to be investigated scientifically, not just to aid in the quest for truth but also in the fight for truth that will make people free' (Sobrino [1976] 1978, p. 35). Reading the texts of the Gospels, with due attention to the social and political context, Sobrino emphasizes the political dimension of the death of Jesus as the historical outcome of the kind of life he lived, and his suffering for the cause of justice which becomes the central challenge for discipleship today. Accepting the validity of this approach, which provides a fresh understanding of the biblical text, Padilla has criticized it for overemphasizing the political significance of Jesus' death and not paying enough attention to the soteriological significance of it, which is also an important part of the text (Samuel and Sugden, 1983, p. 28).

An ecclesiology carrying the logic of liberation theologies has been explored especially by the Brazilian Leonardo Boff, a Franciscan priest

who has tried to articulate the experience of the Basic Christian communities, the grassroots small groups in which poor people started to revive their Catholic faith, relating it to their daily experience in Latin America. For Boff 'a true "ecclesiogenesis" is in progress throughout the world, a Church being born from the faith of the poor' ([1981] 1985, p. 9). The concept of the church as the people of God, that was emphasized in Vatican II, has been an incentive for new pastoral practices, but according to Boff 'true ecclesiology is not the result of textbook analysis or theoretical hypothesis; it comes about as a result of ecclesial practices within the institution' (p. 1). Boff has been very critical of hierarchical authoritarianism and clericalism, that he sees practised in the Catholic church, and proposes 'new ministries and a new style of religious life incarnated in the life of the people' (p. 10). Boff argues that the key elements in all these proposals that come from praxis are characteristics of the model of church life that we find in the New Testament, and on the basis of the biblical data he questions some dogmatic assumptions.

The more recent debates around liberation theologies within the Catholic church have demonstrated that in spite of the criticism of some aspects of those theologies, the official teaching of the church affirms some of their tenets, and incorporates them to its understanding of the Christian faith. Within Protestantism there are efforts to demonstrate that in spite of their Catholic origins liberation theologies incorporate some of the main tenets of the Protestant Reformation (Shaull, 1991), but there are also critical approaches coming especially from evangelicals, that point to important and unsurmountable differences (Schipani, 1989). The publication of a revised edition of the classic work of Gustavo Gutiérrez, fifteen years after the first, provided an occasion to look at the wide repercussion of this theology around the world (Ellis and Maduro, 1989) and the form in which it has been incorporated into a variety of church and missionary situations.

See also ETHICS; JUSTICE; ROMAN CATHOLIC THEOLOGY; SOCIAL QUESTIONS.

Bibliography
Alves, Rubem 1969: *A Theology of Human Hope*. St Meinrad: Abbey Press.

Boff, Leonardo [1981] 1985: *Church: Charism and Power: Liberation Theology and the Institutional Church*. New York: Crossroad.

Costas, Orlando E. 1989: *Liberating News. A Theology of Contextual Evangelization*. Grand Rapids: Eerdmans.

Croatto, J. Severino [1973] 1981: *Exodus: A Hermeneutics of Freedom*, trans. Salvator Attanasio. Maryknoll: Orbis.

Dussel, Enrique [1967] 1981: *A History of the Church in Latin America*, trans. Alan P. Neely. Grand Rapids: Eerdmans.

Ellis, Marc H., and Maduro, Otto, eds 1989: *The Future of Liberation Theology: Essays in Honor of Gustavo Gutiérrez*. Maryknoll: Orbis.

Fabella, Virginia, M.M., and Torres, Sergio, eds 1983: *Irruption of the Third World*. Maryknoll: Orbis.

Gibellini, Rosino, ed. [1975] 1979: *Frontiers of Theology in Latin America*, trans. John Drury. Maryknoll: Orbis.

Gutiérrez, Gustavo [1971] 1988: *A Theology of Liberation*, 2nd revised edition, trans. Sister Caridad Inda and John Eagleson. Maryknoll: Orbis.

Gutiérrez, Gustavo [1986] 1990: *The Truth Shall Make You Free*, trans. Matthew J. O'Connell. Maryknoll: Orbis.

Hoornaert, Eduardo [1986] 1988: *The Memory of the Christian People*. Maryknoll: Orbis.

Míguez Bonino, Jose 1975: *Doing Theology in a Revolutionary Situation*. Philadelphia: Fortress Press.

Neely, Alan Preston 1977: *Protestant Antecedents of the Latin American Theology of Liberation*. Ann Arbor: University Microfilms.

Padilla, C. René 1983: Liberation theology (II), *The Reformed Journal* July, pp. 14–18.

Roberts, J. Deotis 1974: *A Black Political Theology*. Philadelphia: Westminster Press.

Samuel, Vinay, and Sugden, Chris, eds 1983: *Sharing Jesus in the Two Thirds World*. Grand Rapids: Eerdmans.

Schipani, Daniel S., ed. 1989: *Freedom and Discipleship: Liberation Theology in Anabaptist Perspective*. Maryknoll: Orbis.

Shaull, Richard 1991: *The Reformation and Liberation Theology*. Louisville: Westminster/John Knox Press.

Sobrino, Jon [1976] 1978: *Christology at the Crossroads: A Latin American Approach*. Maryknoll: Orbis.

Volf, Miroslav 1983: Doing and interpreting: an examination of the relationship between theory and practice in Latin American liberation theology, *Themelios* 8, 3, pp. 11–19.

SAMUEL ESCOBAR

Liguori, Alphonsus, St (1696–1787)   Italian Roman Catholic moral theologian. The son of a Neapolitan nobleman, he studied then practised law in Naples, until a professional error in 1723 led him to renounce his career. In 1726 he became a priest and in 1732 he founded the Congregation of the Most Holy Redeemer, or 'Redemptorists', at Scala, near Amalfi. Bishop of Sant' Agata dei Croti from 1762 to 1777, he was canonized in 1839.

Alphonsus's first ideas on moral theology are outlined in his *Annotations* of 1748 to the work of the Jesuit casuist Hermann Busenbaum. These he later developed into his own system, contained in *Theologia moralis*, first published in 1753 and 1755, with an eighth, definitive edition appearing in 1779. The method he developed is known as 'equiprobabilism' and concerns the legitimacy of adopting a 'probable' opinion in moral matters, an approach accepted by the Roman Catholic church but bitterly opposed by some at the time. Often called 'the father of moral theology' and much read in the nineteenth century (by, *inter alia*, John Henry Newman), his spiritual writings were also popular; they emphasized devotion to the Sacred Heart and to Mary as co-redemptrix.

Bibliography

Berthe, A.C. [1900] 1905: *St Alphonsus de Liguori*, 2 vols, trans. H. Castle. Dublin.

Henze, C., *et al.* 1961: article in *Bibliotheca Sanctorum*. Rome, cols 837–59.

Miller, D.F., and Aubin, L.X. 1940: *Saint Alphonsus*. Brooklyn.

literature and theology   During the nineteenth and well into the twentieth century, literature and theology belonged in separate compartments. It had not always been so. The artificial barrier which was established between biblical studies and other literary concerns was certainly unknown to Bishop Robert Lowth, who in 1753 published (in Latin) his *Sacred Poetry of the Hebrews*, or to romantic poets like Blake, Coleridge or Wordsworth (see ROMANTICISM). In the 1815 *Essay Supplementary to the Preface* to *Lyrical Ballads* Wordsworth affirmed 'the affinities between religion and poetry; between religion – making up the deficiencies of reason by faith; and poetry – passionate for the instruction of reason'. Samuel Taylor

Coleridge, especially in the posthumously published *Confessions of an Inquiring Spirit* of 1840, drew upon German scholarship and in particular the biblical criticism of J.G. Herder, J.G. Eichhorn, G.E. Lessing and F.D.E. Schleiermacher, from Herder specifically drawing an understanding of *Verstehen*, that imaginative comprehension by which we re-create and re-enter the world of the Bible and make it our own.

But in the early nineteenth century, Coleridge and Bishop Connop Thirlwall of St David's stood almost alone in Britain in appreciating the hermeneutic problems of reading Scripture, in understanding German critical theology and the 'higher criticism' which profoundly affected such writers as F. Hölderlin (1770–1843) and later in England Robert Browning and George Eliot. Generally, however, theology and the doctrine of plenary inspiration of the Bible remained conservatively separate from literature and literary scholarship, each construed as a threat to the other, so that Bishop Van Mildert of Durham, in his Bampton Lectures of 1814, could describe the application of literary methods to the reading of Scripture as 'moral defectiveness, unsoundness of faith, and disloyalty to the Church'.

A Marxist critic, Terry Eagleton, has ascribed the rise of English studies in the later nineteenth century to 'the failure of religion' (Eagleton, 1983, p. 22). Eagleton surveys the demise of the Victorian churches as a form of ideological control, and quotes George Gordon, professor of English literature at Oxford, who early in the twentieth century remarked

> England is sick, and . . . English litera-
> ture must save it. The Churches (as I
> understand) having failed, and social
> remedies being slow, English literature
> has now a triple function: still, I suppose,
> to delight and instruct us, but also, and
> above all, to save our souls and heal the
> State.

In this respect, the key Victorian figure is Matthew Arnold, whose educative programme from the Bible to literature, with its implicit claim for the moral centrality of English literature, was explicitly continued in the literary criticism of F.R. Leavis.

The most important critical statement on the relationship between literature and religion in the earlier part of the twentieth century in England is undoubtedly T.S. Eliot's 1935 essay 'Religion and Literature'. Eliot's first suggestion is that literature and literary criticism require the supplement of theology and ethics for their completion. Yet, somewhat paradoxically, he affirms that if the 'greatness' of literature cannot be determined solely by literary standards, 'we must remember that whether it is literature or not can be determined only by literary standards' (Eliot, [1935] 1951, p. 388). What Eliot proposes is a paradoxical and uneasy relationship between the two substantive categories of religion and literature, each retaining their independence, yet each judging and requiring the other. This sense of creative unease has remained crucial in the study of the relationship between literature and theology.

Eliot wrote his essay as a Christian. Yet as poet and critic he was much favoured by American New Criticism in the 1930s and 1940s, whose sense of the autonomy of the literary work promoted a liberal humanism, politically and socially, and made a sealed, verbal icon of the text. It was certainly the case that early formal academic study of 'religion and literature', at Chicago and Drew Universities in the 1950s, was a deliberate theological reaction against the self-sufficiency of New Criticism as theologians set out to assert the 'theological meanings and dimensions' of poetry (Hesla, 1978, p. 181). Nevertheless, the formalist approaches of the New Critics and later of structuralism as, in various ways, reactions against the excesses of historical scholarship, have provided the starting point for the growing army of 'literary critics of the Bible', whose representative monument is *The Literary Guide to the Bible* (1987), edited by Robert Alter and Frank Kermode.

To distinguish itself from the historical-critical concerns of most biblical criticism, literary criticism of Scripture has tended to be self-consciously ahistorical, examining narrative literary form or genre, but tending towards the iconoclastic and reactive. Its frustration is well summed up in the words of Northrop Frye in his book *The Great Code*:

Nothing said here will be new to Biblical scholars, who are well aware that the Bible will only confuse and exasperate a historian who tries to treat it as history. One wonders why in that case their obsession with the Bible's historicity does not relax, so that other and more promising hypotheses could be examined. (Frye, 1982, p. 42)

Yet this antihistorical bias, with its defence of textual autonomy, has limited the theological vision of criticism which is concerned with literature embedded in the social and historical self-understanding of a people and a church.

However, the term 'textuality' must now be taken seriously, not least since Rudolf Bultmann's essay of 1941, 'The New Testament and Mythology', on demythologizing. 'In the word of preaching and there alone we meet the risen Lord', Bultmann wrote, emphasizing that the unique voice of a text, its textuality, cannot be abstracted from the text itself. The serious study of the nature of text has preoccupied literary critics and theorists in recent years, but has been notably absent from theological or biblical studies. Where methodological preoccupations have increasingly intersected, however, is in hermeneutics, or the theory of interpretation, originally a branch of theology and then brought into a secular tradition by Wilhelm Dilthey (1833–1911) and Friedrich Schleiermacher (1768–1834). Schleiermacher combined the hermeneutic traditions in Protestant theology with the rhetorical and philological traditions of classical scholarship and the philosophy of Immanuel Kant and J.G. Fichte, paving the way for a hermeneutical tradition which includes Bultmann, Paul Tillich, H.-G. Gadamer and Paul Ricoeur in our own time.

Ricoeur is perhaps the most important thinker in the current cross-disciplinary debate over the methods and theories of interpretation. With a fundamental concern for language, poetics and narrative, Ricoeur has given repeated attention to biblical and theological questions, particularly the problem of evil. Although open to the methods of structuralist literary critics, Ricoeur maintains a fundamentally referential and ontological view of discourse and language (Poland, 1985, pp. 162–9), as distinct from the more radical theory of

poststructuralist, postmodernist writers like Jacques Derrida, Immanuel Levinas, Paul de Man, J. Hillis Miller and Harold Bloom. Derrida, in *Of Grammatology* ([1967] 1976), an extended study of language and writing, proposes to disengage language from its subservience to ideas, external point of reference and, above all, truth, challenging the western tradition of 'logocentrism against the disruption of writing, against its aphoristic energy' (p. 18). Derrida and his fellow postmodernists (see POSTMODERNISM) have been likened, with some justification, to the traditions of mystical writing, and to the 'negative theology' of Dionysius the Areopagite, Meister Eckhart and others. Increasingly critics have become aware of their debt to Rabbinic interpretative practices, and their close association with Friedrich Nietzsche's rhetorical writings is pervasive.

The assertion of the 'death of God' in the writings of Jewish critics and poetry has deeply affected the enormous and growing literature associated with the experience of the Holocaust and the death camps of the Second World War. Novelists and poets like Elie Wiesel, Primo Levi and Paul Celan reflect the theological impasse of the Holocaust. A major critic of postmodernity, George Steiner, has argued against 'the arts of negation in modern poetic and aesthetic movements', particularly in his book *Real Presences* of 1989, which, drawing on the dramatic theological journey of Dante, asserts a presence of sense in poetry, painting and music which is, finally, theological.

In the past decade there has been a growing, and increasingly complex, discussion of the relationship between theology, literature and the arts which has developed in breadth and urgency from the essentially literary and apologetic work of Helen Gardner in England or Nathan Scott in the USA. The study of linguistics since Ferdinand de Saussure's *Course in General Linguistics* of 1916 has spread through the work of the Russian formalists, to structuralism in literary and anthropological research, culminating in books like Edmund Leach's *Genesis and Myth* of 1969, and (with D. Alan Aycock), *Structuralist Interpretations of Biblical Myth* of 1983. Semiotics, narrative theology, metaphorical theology, aesthetics and feminist theology have all played important roles in the rereading of Scripture, religious autobiography, liturgical texts and their inter-textual relationship with 'secular' literature. Perhaps most energetic in recent years has been the growth of studies in rhetoric across a wide field of the human sciences, and the exploration of the relationship between the writings of the Christian tradition and the debate in classical rhetoric between Plato and Aristotle.

In European thought, the secularized Jewish Marxism of Walter Benjamin, Theodor Adorno, Max Horkheimer (of the Frankfurt school) and Ernst Bloch in *The Principle of Hope* of 1954–9 have broadly linked the religious traditions of western thought and literature with a critique of contemporary culture and society, closely concerned with issues of freedom and hope, reflected also in the renewed 'theologia crucis' of the German theologian Jürgen Moltmann. Critics within the Judaeo-Christian tradition have, so far, been less prepared to relate reflections on literature and theology to the thought, sprituality and writings of other religious traditions, although the controversy surrounding Salman Rushdie's *The Satanic Verses* of 1988 has begun to generate serious critical debate on the issue of fundamentalism and the status of Scripture from an Islamic perspective.

Any survey of the work of novelists, playwrights and poets from a religious or theological point of view must inevitably be highly selective and beg many questions about the nature of 'religious literature' and the relationship of literature with religion. In 1913 D.H. Lawrence wrote, 'I always feel as if I stood naked for the fire of Almighty God to go through me – and it's rather an awful feeling. One has to be so terribly religious, to be an artist.' In 1952 Samuel Beckett's two tramps wait endlessly and in futile paralysis, in *Waiting for Godot*. Fyodor Dostoevsky (1821–1881) has probably had more influence on theological reflection than any other novelist in modern times, notably in *The Brothers Karamazov* of 1880. The parable of the Grand Inquisitor in that novel is a sombre reflection on the relationship between Christ and the church, deeply influencing, among others, the modern Russian critic Mikhail Bakhtin.

The tradition of 'Christian' fiction and poetry in England has been maintained variously by G.K. Chesterton, C.S. Lewis, Charles Williams and T.S. Eliot, whose *Four Quartets* of 1943 has been described by Helen Gardner as an 'austere and rigorously philosophic poem on time and time's losses and gains'. Perhaps the two most important contemporary English Roman Catholic novelists are Graham Greene and Muriel Spark, whose most interesting 'theological' novel to date is *The Only Problem* of 1984, an eccentric meditation on the Book of Job. In Ireland, James Joyce (1882–1941) reacted powerfully against the narrowness and bigotry of Irish Catholicism, reflected particularly in the largely autobiographical *Portrait of the Artist as a Young Man* of 1914–15.

In the USA, Flannery O'Connor (1925–64) wrote two Gothic novels and a number of short stories concerned with the religion of the Bible belt in the southern states, dealing with religious fanaticism and the unexpected action of divine grace. Her best fiction, *Wise Blood* of 1949, is, in O'Connor's own words, 'a comic novel about a Christian *malgré lui*, and as such, very serious'. More recently in the USA, John Updike has written novels and poems which are often preoccupied with the sacred and religion in daily life.

France has been well supplied with poets and dramatists, like Paul Claudel (1868–1955), and novelists, like Georges Bernanos (1888–1948), who have an intense, usually Catholic, religious vision of the world. More complex and ambiguous are the novels of François Mauriac (1885–1970) who was deeply influenced by Dostoevsky. He reacted powerfully against the restrictive conventions, not the least religious and theological, of the prosperous French bourgeois society in his own area of Bordeaux.

There is no doubt that political changes will release a flood of literature from eastern European countries, much profoundly concerned with the religious and theological issues so long repressed there. Perhaps the most significant voice at present is that of Milan Kundera, the exiled Czechoslovakian writer, for whom the European novel is an 'art born as the echo of God's laughter, the art that created the fascinating imaginative realm where no one owns the truth and everyone has the right to be understood'. Kundera's most important novel,

The Unbearable Lightness of Being of 1984, takes its beginning from Nietzsche's idea of eternal return, and the terrifying prospect that 'if every second of our lives recurs an infinite number of times, we are nailed to eternity as Jesus Christ was nailed to the cross.'

It is difficult to predict what direction the study of literature and theology will take. Certainly the theology of the Judaeo-Christian tradition must take seriously the deconstructive implications of postmodernism, and in this sense perhaps the most characteristic writer of our century is the self-consciously Jewish Franz Kafka (1883–1924), whose riddling parables can claim direct descent from the parables of the Old and New Testaments. Harold Bloom has framed the direct question, 'Why does Kafka have so unique a spiritual authority?' (Bloom, 1987, p. 179). In a time which has lost its certainty about the nature of time, its myths and narratives; whose criticism has celebrated the fallacies of intentionality and referentiality; which is suspicious of meaning in text – where does theology integrate with the fictions of Thomas Pynchon, like *Gravity's Rainbow* of 1973, or Margaret Atwood's sombre feminist vision in *The Handmaid's Tale* of 1985? When reading religiously is an exercise which can connect the aesthetic, the ethical and the religious with the irony and humour of an uncertain literature, then it may contribute to what Yves Bonnefoy has called 'that faith in the meaning of the world that ensures the survival of society'.

See also BIBLICAL CRITICISM AND INTERPRETATION (1: OLD TESTAMANT and 2: NEW TESTAMENT); LANGUAGE, RELIGIOUS; NARRATIVE THEOLOGY.

Bibliography

Alter, Robert, and Kermode, Frank eds, 1987: *The Literary Guide to the Bible.* London: Collins.

Bloom, Harold 1987: *Ruin the Sacred Truths: Poetry and Belief from the Bible to the Present.* Cambridge, Mass. and London: Harvard University Press.

Daiches, David 1984: *God and the Poets.* Oxford: Oxford University Press.

Derrida, Jacques [1967] 1976: *Of Grammatology,* trans. Gayatri Chakravorty Spivak. Baltimore and London: Johns Hopkins University Press.

Detweiler, Robert 1989: *Breaking the Fall: Religious Readings of Contemporary Fiction.* London: Macmillan.

Eagleton, Terry 1983: *Literary Theory: An Introduc-*

tion. Oxford: Blackwell.

Eliot, T.S. [1935] 1951: *Selected Essays,* third edn. London: Faber.

Frye, Northrop 1982: *The Great Code: The Bible and Literature.* London: Routledge and Kegan Paul.

Hesla, David 1978: Religion and literature: the second stage, *Journal of the American Academy of Religion* 46, pp. 181–92.

Jasper, David 1989: *The Study of Literature and Religion: An Introduction.* London: Macmillan.

Poland, Lynn M. 1985: *Literary Criticism and Biblical Hermeneutics: A Critique of Formalist Approaches.* Chico: Scholars Press.

Prickett, Stephen 1986: *Words and the Word. Language, Poetics and Biblical Interpretation.* Cambridge: Cambridge University Press.

Scott, Nathan A., Jr 1985: *The Poetics of Belief.* Chapel Hill: University of North Carolina Press.

Wright, T.R. 1988: *Theology and Literature.* Oxford: Blackwell.

DAVID JASPER

liturgy and doctrine Liturgy is the corporate worship of the Christian churches, and doctrine is the churches' officially formulated teachings. Liturgy takes place in the gathered congregation as a ritual dialogue, in word and gesture, between God and the assembly of believers; its characteristic verbal forms include the reading of the Scriptures, the preaching of a sermon, the saying of prayers (of adoration, praise, thanksgiving, repentance, petition, offering, intercession), and the confession of faith (as in the recitation of creeds or in more spontaneous testimonies). Doctrine consists of statements made by the recognized teaching authorities within the churches concerning the content of the Christian faith, such as definitions agreed by ecumenical councils (for instance on God and Christ in the fourth and fifth centuries) or confessions emerging from movements of reform and renewal (for instance in the western church of the sixteenth century). In doctrinal statements a positive central core may be surrounded by the setting of boundaries, so that the faith is affirmed while alternatives are rejected (as in the refutation of non-Christian views) or warded off (as in the exclusion of opinions that internal debate has shown to be heretical). Both liturgy and doctrine involve, each in various ways, theological reflection; and reflective theology has, as part of its service to the churches, the task of helping to ensure that liturgy and doctrine, in their respective functions, remain substantially correlated. The interplay among liturgy, doctrine and reflective theology is, in historical fact, complex and often controversial, inevitably raising questions of AUTHORITY.

At the threshold of the modern west, the Protestant and Catholic Reformations illustrate the kind of controversies that arise when liturgical practice and doctrinal authority are perceived to be theologically discordant. Thus the Protestant Reformers intended to correct a cluster of observances – crucially focused on 'the sacrifice of the Mass' but including also the use of relics, prayers for souls in purgatory and the invocation of saints for the merits they had achieved by works of supererogation – that were the outcrop of what the Reformers judged to be distorted views on God, man and salvation but which the existing pastoral magisterium of pope and bishops connived at or even endorsed. In seeking to exalt 'Christ alone', 'grace alone', and 'faith alone', the Protestant Reformers appealed to the canonical Scriptures, which – though they themselves were to a great extent liturgically composed, chosen and transmitted - nevertheless enjoyed a privileged status in the determination of doctrine and could be used critically in relation to post-apostolic traditions. On their side, the Protestant Reformers issued – wherever they could secure civil and ecclesiastical support – their own orders for public worship 'according to the Word of God'. In the case of Anglicanism, such a 'Book of Common Prayer' would itself acquire the status of a locus of doctrine; in those Protestant churches where the liturgical formularies were rather minimal and a dominant structural place fell to the sermon, the conduct of worship and the interpretation of doctrine tended to reside in the hands of the local pastor. On the Roman Catholic side, the Council of Trent in its magisterial authority defended some cultic practices against Protestant misinterpretation; appealed to the traditional liturgy in support of controverted Catholic doctrines (as when the Roman collect of the thirteenth Sunday after Pentecost was invoked in favour of a growth in justifying grace after the initial act of justification); but also brought a somewhat purified liturgy under the more central control of the Roman magisterium through commis-

sioning a Roman Breviary (1568), Missal (1570), Pontifical (1596) and Ritual (1614) and establishing the Congregation of Rites (1588).

The next stage of interest in the interplay between liturgy, doctrine and theology belongs, however, to the development in the seventeenth and eighteenth centuries of the modern sense of history and of historical scholarship. In that period the great Latin liturgiologists collected the texts of eastern rites for publication in the western world, and the doctrinal questions raised by the existence of these generally orthodox liturgies in the officially heterodox churches of the Monophysites and the Nestorians as well as among the Byzantines did not escape the attention of the discerning. The French Oratorian E. Renaudot prefaced his *Liturgiarum orientalium collectio* of 1716 with a theological essay in which he argued that eastern liturgies, not being simply the words of the one great doctor to whom they might be attributed but having apostolic roots and having received the unanimous and uninterrupted approval of entire churches, possessed a value equal to the Latin and second only to the Scriptures as witnesses to the tradition. The Maronite J.A. Assemani, compiler of the *Codex liturgicus ecclesiae universae* of 1749–66, followed Renaudot closely in insisting on the doctrinal authority attaching to liturgies 'in virtue of their use in the churches'. In his *Bibliotheca ritualis*, published in Rome in 1776, F.A. Zaccaria included a dissertation on 'the use of liturgical books in dogmatic matters', arguing that universal agreement among eastern and western liturgies constituted a most solid argument in favour of a dogma, since the universal church could not have fallen into error. The ecumenical implications of these discoveries of historical scholarship would have to await the twentieth century for development.

Rome, meanwhile, had other fish to fry. At least four episodes internal to the Roman Catholic church raised the issues of liturgy, doctrine and theology in a period which saw the alternate challenging of the Roman magisterium and its consolidation. First, there was the persistent tendency on the part of the Gallicans to make alterations to the Roman liturgy on the ground that it contained 'much that is idle, profane, and foreign to true religion'; that phrase is found in an episcopal letter accompanying the Meaux Missal of 1709, which itself did away with the silent recitation of the canon of the Mass and introduced people's responses into the canon, thus leading to later suspicions of the 'heresy' that the consecration was not effected by the priest alone but by him and the people together. At the time, those who defended the credit of the Roman liturgy advanced arguments from its longstanding use and its authorization by the magisterium.

The Roman magisterium affirmed itself strikingly in Pius IX's promulgation in 1854 of the dogma of Mary's immaculate conception and would do so again in 1950 in Pius XII's dogmatic definition of Mary's assumption. In the theological justification of these dogmas, appeal is made to the worship practice of the (Roman Catholic) church. It is not simply that Mary has been unreflectively called 'spotless' and 'queen of heaven' in devotion, nor even that spontaneous popular feasts have long celebrated her conception (8 December) and assumption (15 August); Pius IX set special store by the fact that his papal predecessors had elevated the former feast in rank, and Pius XII would in turn supply new liturgical texts for the latter.

In some ways, the leading role of worship in the production of Marian dogma curiously illustrates one of the very theses of modernism that attracted condemnation by Rome at the turn of the nineteenth century. Thus the modernist George Tyrrell (1861–1909) wrote that 'the "deposit" of faith is not merely a creed, but is a concrete religion left by Christ to his church; it is perhaps in some sense more directly a *lex orandi* than a *lex credendi*; the creed is involved in the prayer, and has to be disentangled from it'; but while this could be read in favour of the productive power of devotion over doctrine, it could also be used to support the 'fideist' and 'poetic' views of Christianity by which the modernists were felt to threaten the hard substance of the faith and the objective, external authority of the magisterium in interpreting it.

The final episode to be mentioned in connection with the Roman magisterium is the twentieth-century liturgical movement, which in its early phases in some ways challenged Rome, then received the blessing of the Second Vatican Council (Vatican II), and now harbours some of the liberal protest against 'authoritar-ianism'. The movement is conventionally dated from the address of the Belgian Benedictine Lambert Beauduin (1873–1960) to the Malines congress on pastoral work in 1909, in which the worship assembly was innocently enough asserted to be the primary place where people learned and grew in the faith. But consequent moves towards the use of the vernacular were experienced – as they had already been in the sixteenth century – as a threat to magisterial control exercised through the Latin liturgy. Moreover, one of the leading theologians of the nascent liturgical movement, the German Benedictine Odo Casel (1886–1948), came under suspicion for his sympathetic presentation of the Hellenistic mysteries as a preparation for the Christian sacraments. In his encyclical *Mediator Dei* (1947), however, Pius XII gave guarded approval to several aims of the liturgical movement, while insisting that the liturgy remains 'subject to the Church's supreme teaching authority'. At last, Vatican II in its first constitution, *Sacrosanctum Concilium* (1963), gave strong endorsement to the active and intelligent participation of all the faithful in the liturgical assembly, which it saw as 'the principal manifestation of the Church'. This set in motion the thorough revision of the normative service-books of the Roman Catholic church, most notably producing the Missal of Paul VI (1969–70) and the *Order for the Christian Initiation of Adults* of 1972, wherein were harvested the labours of such as Josef Andreas Jungmann (1889–1975) on the theological history of the liturgy, Jean Daniélou (1905–1974) on biblical and patristic typology, and Cipriano Vagaggini (b. 1909) on the theology of worship. More recently, in the Roman Catholic church as in other bodies, liturgy has become the chosen field of operation for many liberals to undertake, officially or otherwise, their linguistic and ritual reforms of clericalism and patriarchy.

In its heyday, the liturgical movement had crossed confessional boundaries in such a way as to affect the theology and practice of worship in most of the western churches. The most influential Anglican figure was probably the English Benedictine Gregory Dix (1901–1952), who in *The Shape of the Liturgy* (1945) displayed the Eucharist as the Lord's chosen means of making himself present in a 'four-action' rite that resumed his own acts at the Last Supper in taking the bread and wine, giving thanks over them, breaking the bread, and distributing them to his disciples for their consumption as communion with him. The German Peter Brunner (1900–1981) located 'the worship of the congregation gathered in the name of Jesus' within God's universal plan of salvation at the levels of creation, redemption and consummation, seeing the 'divine service' in a characteristically Lutheran way as first 'God's service to us' and only then 'our service to God' (Roman Catholic theologians tend rather to treat the liturgy in the sequence of 'adoration of God' and 'sanctification of humankind'). The Swiss Jean-Jacques von Allmen (1917–1992) also gave a firmly salvation-historical account of Christian worship, paying an attention unusual in the Reformed tradition to its phenomenology of time, space and gesture. The Taizé brother Max Thurian (b. 1921) explored the biblical category of cultic memorial, showing how rites might be divinely instituted in order to bring successive generations into touch with formative acts of God in history and the living God who performs them. While there is little evidence of reform of rites in the eastern churches, such Orthodox theologians as Nicholas Afanasiev (1893–1966) and John Zizioulas (b. 1931) have advocated a eucharistic ecclesiology, seeing the invocation (*epiklesis*) of the Holy Spirit on the liturgical assembly as the ever-new constitution of the church.

The remarkable convergences found among liturgical theologians and in the revised service-books of many churches in the three decades after the Second World War were both a sign and a stimulus of ECUMENISM. Theologians of ecumenism seized the opportunity to treat worship as both a means and an end to the restoration or achievement of Christian unity. In a seminal essay of 1957, the Lutheran Edmund Schlink (1903–1984) observed that a 'category shift' takes place when what is expressed in prayer and preaching is translated into the form of dogma. In worship and witness, we face God and our fellow human beings more directly. In dogmatic statements, however, we are *talking about* (the proper way to) worship and witness; we are *teaching about* God, his acts, and the human response. The risk is that the teacher withdraws to 'a neutral position from which the encounter between God and man may be observed, described and be cast into didactic formulas'. Problems arise when 'attention moves away from the experience of salvation which comes through the gospel and is concentrated instead on giving a theoretical definition of the relationship between the divine and human contributions in redemption'. Schlink held that the 'structural change' from doxology to doctrine is responsible for some of the most persistent dogmatic problems in Christendom, for it is at the second level that differences show up. Schlink was not so naive as to think that dogma is unnecessary, but he considered it secondary and subject to marked historical and anthropological conditioning. He proposed an ecumenical concentration upon the primary forms of worship and witness, where (he was persuaded) we should rediscover an already-existing unity and fullness which differences in doctrinal statements had obscured.

Meanwhile, the Roman Catholic theologian Hans Joachim Schulz (b. 1932) in 1976 devoted a substantial book to arguing that an adequate 'unity in faith' could be drawn from the ancient eucharistic tradition which the divided churches have retained or restored. The words, actions and celebration of the eucharistic rites, and particularly the great eucharistic prayer or anaphora, provided in Schulz's opinion sufficient expression of Trinitarian faith and of doctrine concerning church, sacraments and ministry.

The Faith and Order Commission of the World Council of Churches was already working along somewhat similar lines and across the widest ecumenical range, as the Lima text on *Baptism, Eucharist and Ministry* (1982) was to show. As the official Roman Catholic response to the Lima text appreciated, 'the sources employed for the interpretation of the meaning of the Eucharist and the form of celebration are Scripture and Tradition . . . The presentation of the mystery of the Eucharist follows the flow of classical eucharistic liturgies, with the eucharistic theology drawing heavily on the content of the traditional prayer and symbolic actions of these liturgies.' In the Roman judgement, agreement along the lines of the Lima text could, when set within a satisfactory dogmatic and ecclesiological context which Rome reserved the right to define, mark an important step towards full communion between the churches. The so-called Lima Liturgy, which was composed as a practical illustration of the doctrinal convergences registered in the main text, has met with a widespread favourable response at several levels in many churches, showing at least the desire and longing for an instrument to embody and develop the unity of Christians at the Lord's table.

The Lima process has exemplified in our time many of the issues involved in the relation between liturgy and doctrine and in the responsibility of pastoral and teaching authorities to make concrete adjudications in the area of the overlap between worship and the more detached formulation of faith. The theological discussion has often been formulated in terms of the *lex orandi* and the *lex credendi*. The origins of this formulation were laid bare by Karl Federer in his detailed examination (1950) of writings by a fifth-century monk, Prosper of Aquitaine. In a text long attributed to Pope Celestine I, Prosper includes the phrase, 'ut legem credendi lex statuat supplicandi'. A disciple of Augustine, Prosper was arguing against semi-Pelagianism that all true faith, even the beginnings of goodwill as well as growth and perseverence, is from start to finish a work of grace. In various writings he points out that, following 1 Timothy 2: 1-4, catholic churches everywhere, led by the Spirit of God, daily plead the cause of the human race, asking that all categories of unbelievers may be brought to salvation. In this context, the phrase in question means quite precisely that 'the apostolic *injunction to pray* [for all people, which the church obeys in its intercessions, that they may come to the faith] sets the *obligation to believe* [that even the first motions towards faith are themselves a gift of God]'. Federer shows, however, that the broader argumentative principle at work here was already employed by many Christian theologians in the early centuries: thus Irenaeus and Tertullian appealed to the use of bread, wine, water and oil in the sacraments in order to confute the Gnostics' disparagement of matter; and Athanasius took the church's worship of Christ as a decisive ground of the Nicene position on Christ's deity as opposed to Arianism (for otherwise the church would be worshipping a creature and thus, unthinkably, committing idolatry).

Among contemporary theologians the American Catholic Aidan Kavanagh (b. 1929) has been most insistent that worship, or the *theologia prima* (the angelic praises of God are indeed in the Greek liturgies called 'theology'), must be at the base of all 'secondary theology'; but he has correspondingly little to say about how the wild growths to which devotion is always susceptible may, with proper theological responsibility, be pruned and trimmed by the pastoral and teaching authorities of the church. In *Mediator Dei* Pius XII went so far as to state that the reverse of Prosper's principle is also necessary: 'the law of our faith must establish the law of our prayer.' It is historically clear that a differentiation of purposes and contexts may drive liturgy and doctrine apart and even induce a certain rivalry between them. Which, then, is to have the upper hand, the *lex orandi* or the *lex credendi*? How far are these 'laws' descriptive, how far prescriptive? Where resides the authority to moderate them?

Several contemporary theologians have used the verbless *lex orandi, lex credendi* tag simply as a rubric under which to explore the relations between liturgy, doctrine and reflective theology, with the question of authority always at least implicitly present. According to the Russian-American Orthodox Alexander Schmemann (1921–1983), 'it is in the liturgy that the sources of faith – the Bible and tradition – become a living reality'; as the inbreaking of God's kingdom, the liturgical tradition is 'the ontological condition of theology', the latter's task consisting in 'the elucidation of the rule of prayer as the rule of faith'; any 'theological critique of the liturgy' will address concrete practices on the basis of an authentic 'ordo' of worship historically discerned at the heart of the tradition. The Swiss Reformed Dietrich Ritschl (b. 1929) recognizes that the Christian 'story' is liturgically transmitted and provokes theological reflection that has both a critical function and a 'doxological edge'; worship is both a first word and yet in a sense also a 'last word', so that it should not become a starting point for further 'scholastic deductions'. The Anglo-American Methodist Geoffrey Wainwright (b. 1939) has argued that Christian worship includes an intellectual moment from the start, the *intellec-*

tus fidei (and so, historically, the recognition of Christ's mediation in creation, for instance, in the Christological hymns of the New Testament will have come by way of theological reflection on the present experience of his sovereignty in redemption); and there is, therefore, a connaturality about the efforts of reflective theology to assist the pastoral and teaching authorities in their permanent task of clarifying the church's vision of God as it is expressed in the liturgy.

Wainwright's *Doxology* (1980) seeks to hold together 'worship, doctrine and life'. The coinherence of the three marked the 'mystagogical catecheses' by which the bishops of the early church instructed the neophytes in terms of the rites of their initiation. Several prominent contemporary theologians have returned to the ancient baptismal creed as a structure for teaching the faith in a comprehensive yet concise form: thus Karl Barth's *Dogmatics in Outline* of 1947, Joseph Ratzinger's *Introduction to the Christian Faith* of 1968, Wolfhart Pannenberg's *The Apostles' Creed in the Light of Today's Questions* of 1972 and Jan Milic Lochman's *The Faith We Confess: An Ecumenical Dogmatics* of 1982. The most ambitious project yet of Faith and Order in the World Council of Churches takes the Nicene and Apostles' Creeds as the 'theological basis and methodological tool' for *Confessing the One Faith* (1991). Following the ancient practice of explicating entire rites, Alexander Schmemann followed in detail the ritual *ordo* of the Orthodox church in expounding baptism (*Of Water and the Spirit*, 1974) and the Lord's supper (*The Eucharist: Sacrament of the Kingdom*, trans. 1987). By way of concentration, the French Catholic bishops took simply the fourth eucharistic prayer of the Roman Missal as the basis for catechesis in the whole Christian faith (*Il est grand, le mystère de la foi*, 1978).

See also DOCTRINE AND DOGMA; LIBERALISM: BRITAIN; SACRAMENTAL THEOLOGY; TRADITION.

Bibliography

Allmen, J.-J. von 1965: *Worship: Its Theology and Practice*, trans. H. Knight and W.F. Fleet. London: Lutterworth; New York: Oxford University Press.

Bouyer, L. 1956: *Life and Liturgy*, trans. London: Sheed and Ward.

Brunner, P. [1952] 1968: *Worship in the Name of Jesus*, trans. St Louis: Concordia.

Daniélou, J. [1951] 1956: *The Bible and the Liturgy*, trans. Notre Dame: University of Notre Dame Press.

Dix, G. 1945: *The Shape of the Liturgy*. Westminster: Dacre.

Fagerberg, D. W. 1992: *What is Liturgical Theology? A Study in Methodology*. Collegeville: Liturgical Press.

Federer, K. 1950: *Liturgie und Glaube: eine theologiegeschichtliche Untersuchung*. Freiburg in der Schweiz: Paulus Verlag.

Jungmann, J.A. [1925] 1965: *The Place of Christ in Liturgical Prayer*, trans. New York: Alba; London: Chapman.

Kavanagh, A. 1984: *On Liturgical Theology*. New York: Pueblo.

Schaeffler, R. 1989: *Das Gebet und das Argument: zwei Weisen des Sprechens von Gott*. Düsseldorf: Patmos.

Schilson, A. 1982: *Theologie als Sakramententheologie: die Mysterienlehre Odo Casels*. Mainz: Matthias Grünewald Verlag.

Schlink, E. 1957: Die Struktur der dogmatischen Aussage als ökumenisches Problem, *Kerygma und Dogma* 3, pp. 251–306. Trans. 1967 in *The Coming Christ and the Coming Church*. Edinburgh: Oliver and Boyd, pp. 16–84.

Schmemann, A. [1960–1] 1966: *Introduction to Liturgical Theology*, trans. A.E. Moorhouse. Portland, Maine: American Orthodox Press.

Schulz H.J. 1976: *Ökumenische Glaubenseinheit aus eucharistischer Überlieferung*. Paderborn: Bonifacius Verlag.

Vagaggini, C. [1965] 1976: *Theological Dimensions of the Liturgy*, trans. Collegeville: Liturgical Press.

Wainwright, G. 1980: *Doxology: The Praise of God in Worship, Doctrine and Life*. London: Epworth; New York: Oxford University Press.

GEOFFREY WAINWRIGHT

Locke, John (1632–1704) English philosopher. Educated at Westminster School, Locke became an undergraduate and subsequently a don at Christ Church, Oxford. He qualified as a medical doctor as well as a philosopher. He became secretary to Lord Ashley, 1st Earl of Shaftesbury. As a supporter of William of Orange, he was forced into exile in Holland, returning at the accession of William and Mary in 1688. His most important works are the *Essay Concerning Human Understanding* (1690), *A Letter Concerning Toleration* (1689), *Two Treatises of Government* (1690) and *Some Thoughts Concerning Education* (1693).

Locke's philosophy moves in the tradition of Cartesian rationalism and Newtonian science, although he has some significant differences with R. Descartes. He understands, for example, the word 'idea' to be sensory, rather than intellectual like Descartes. Human minds, for Locke, have no 'innate ideas' but all ideas are formed by sensation or by rational reflection. He also introduced the philosophical distinction between primary qualities (those which an object has in itself) and secondary qualities (those which involve interaction with another). Locke's political philosophy is extremely influential: in particular, his theory of property, by which labour gives land value, and the labourer ownership rights over the land. He advocated religious and political tolerance, since the limitations of human understanding made it difficult for anyone to claim absolute truth.

Locke is regarded as the founder of empiricism, and exercised great influence on French thought – on Voltaire in particular. He was also a significant influence on Thomas Jefferson, and the drawing up of the American constitution.

See also CHRISTOLOGY; DEISM.

Bibliography
Castelmann, M.V. 1967: *John Locke*.
Cranston, M. [1957] 1985: *John Locke*. London.
Dewhurst, K. 1984: *John Locke (1632–1704)*.
Yolton, J. 1985: *John Locke*: A Reference Guide. Boston, Mass.

logical positivism In 1830 the French philosopher Auguste Comte proposed that all attempts to discover theological and metaphysical explanations for the existence and intelligibility of the world (natural and social) should be abandoned definitively in favour of considering observable phenomena and verifiable states of affairs in order to work out the laws (natural and sociological) by which they are evidently governed. Thus what Comte called 'positivism' was born. The assumption from the outset was that theology and metaphysics were superseded.

In 1895 a new chair in the philosophy of the inductive sciences at the University of Vienna was offered to the physicist Ernst Mach. His principal concern by this time was to root out the last remaining non-empirical (metaphysical) elements from the philosophy of science and indeed from the natural sciences themselves. The eradication of metaphysics was taking much longer than Comte ever envisaged. Mach sought to show that science is simply an account of sense-given facts – ultimately, an account of *sensations*. His views were attacked at some length by V.I. Lenin as a form of solipsistic idealism, in his *Materialism and Empiriocriticism* (1908). In effect, however, Mach had set the agenda for one of the most influential movements in modern philosophy. His emphasis on the ultimacy of sensations meant two things. In the first place, every statement about the world had to be brought to the test of sense-experience (thus giving rise to what would later be called 'verificationism'). Secondly, Mach was moving close to regarding natural objects as logical constructions out of sensations ('phenomenalism' as it would be called).

In 1922 Mach's chair in Vienna was inherited by Moritz Schlick, also a physicist by training. He soon became the focus of a discussion group, including scientists and mathematicians as well as philosophers. By 1928 they became known as 'the Vienna Circle', had published their 'programme' for the reduction of all science to physics, and taken over the periodical *Erkenntnis* as the principal channel of their ideas. To their general acceptance of Mach's positivism they added a new interest in the developments in mathematical logic since the work of Gottlob Frege. In 1931 the movement received the name 'logical positivism', coined probably by H. Feigl, one of the original members of the Circle. Schlick preferred the name 'consistent empiricism'.

Wittgenstein's *Tractatus Logico-Philosophicus*, published in 1921, played a significant part in the genesis of logical positivism. Indeed, at the Circle's regular meetings between 1924 and 1926 the book was read out and discussed sentence by sentence. It was treated as the classic statement of the new philosophy. It had appeared in *Annalen der Naturphilosophie* and, in the edition with an English translation which came out in 1922, it seemed perfectly at home in C.K. Ogden's International Library of Psychology, Philosophy and Scientific Method, especially with its introduction by Bertrand Russell. It appeared as if Wittgenstein was applying mathematical logic to show that 'the totality of true propositions' coincides with 'the totality of the natural sciences' (cf. *Tractatus* 4.11), whereas nothing with a claim to truth might be said in ethics or aesthetics (6.42f.), not to mention theology.

From 1927, for a few years, Schlick coaxed Wittgenstein (then back in Austria) into taking part in regular discussions with himself and Friedrich Waismann. It was Wittgenstein, apparently, who first formulated what was to be known as the Verification Principle, according to which 'the meaning of a statement is the method of its verification'. Where no agreed empirical means of verifying or falsifying a statement presented itself, that is to say, it might safely be assumed that the statement in question had no meaning. It might reasonably be concluded, then, that the famous last words of the *Tractatus* – 'Whereof one cannot speak, thereof one must be silent' – meant, for Wittgenstein, that nothing mattered beyond the totality of the true propositions of the natural sciences. In fact, however, he believed that the important matters were precisely the ones of which one could not speak. Discussing the *Tractatus* with members of the Vienna Circle showed him how it lay open to a logical positivist interpretation and this finally provoked him to return to Cambridge and rethink his philosophical position entirely.

Schlick was murdered by a demented student in 1936 but by that time the threat of Nazism had already begun to disperse the Vienna Circle. Most of the original members found homes in the USA. It was above all through the teaching of Rudolf Carnap, first at Chicago (1935–52) and then at the University of California at Los Angeles (until 1961), that logical positivism entered into the mainstream of American philosophy. The work of the eminent philosopher W.V.O. Quine, for example, with its emphasis on physics as the paradigm of knowledge, its constant use of symbolic logic, and its predilection for behaviourism in psychology, incarnates the spirit of the Vienna Circle. There is little interest in ethics, let alone theology.

Things turned out quite differently in England. Waismann settled in Oxford in 1939 and played an important part, in the years immediately following the war, in the rise of linguistic analysis which, while retaining the empiricism, gave up the obsession with formal logic. Perhaps one might say that linguistic analysis was the form that logical positivism took where philosophers had been trained in classics rather than in physics. Waismann was himself a poet (though unpublished) and a deeply metaphysical thinker: his essay 'How I see Philosophy', in *Contemporary British Philosophy* (1956) is the finest short introduction to philosophy written in English this century. 'Oxford philosophy', as linguistic analysis came to be known in the 1950s, attracted a good deal of attention from Christian theologians and generated something of a style, if not exactly a movement, in British philosophy of religion.

Before coming to that, however, we need to go back to the Vienna Circle: in 1933 the discussions were attended by a young philosopher from Oxford, A.J. Ayer, then aged twenty-three. *Language, Truth and Logic* appeared in 1936 and, at least as far as ethics and theology are concerned, twisted all discussion in a positivist direction for the next fifty years. It is hard to think of any single book, at least since the eighteenth century, which has had such an impoverishing and destructive effect on ethics and theology. While Ayer modified his thesis in later books, his dismissal of the truth-claims of religious statements remains in place in his last major work, *The Central Questions of Philosophy* of 1973 – the text, somewhat bizarrely, of Gifford Lectures at the University of St Andrews, intended by their founder to promote the study of 'natural theology'.

Ayer, following Hume, divides all propositions which may be counted as 'genuine' into two classes. Propositions which, in Hume's terminology, concern 'relations of ideas' are such as 'cannot be confuted in experience' because 'they do not make any assertion about the empirical world, but simply record our determination to use symbols in a certain fashion' – in effect, the a priori (analytic) propositions of logic and pure mathematics. Propositions concerning 'matters of fact', as Hume said, are, in Ayer's terminology, empirical hypotheses, which need not be conclusively verifiable but 'some possible sense-experience should be relevant to the determination of [their] truth or falsehood.' Any proposition which fails to fit one or other of these two categories is 'metaphysical' – 'neither true nor false but literally senseless'. This means, as indeed Hume too thought, that much of what ordinarily passes for philosophy, being neither analytic nor empirically testable, is simply lacking in cognitive significance – in particular, as Ayer says, 'it cannot be significantly asserted that there is a non-empirical world of values, or that men have immortal souls, or that there is a transcendent God.'

In the famous sixth chapter of *Language, Truth and Logic* Ayer rapidly sorts what have traditionally been regarded as propositions in moral philosophy into (1) definitions of terms, (2) descriptions of the phenomena of moral experience, (3) exhortations to good behaviour, and (4) actual ethical judgements. The first category, being analytic, counts as philosophy in Ayer's scheme of things. The second category belongs to psychology and sociology. Exhortations are not propositions of any kind but 'ejaculations or commands which are designed to provoke the reader [sic] to action of a certain sort'. Ethical judgements, finally, turn out to be 'mere expressions of feeling'. In every case in which one would once have been said to be making an ethical judgement the function of the relevant ethical word turns out to be purely 'emotive' – 'to express feelings about certain objects, but not to make any assertion about them'. Thus Ayer articulates what came to be known as the emotive theory of values ('emotivism') – the doctrine that value judgements in general, and ethical judgements in particular, express emotions but say nothing one way or the other about what is objectively the case. Such ideas, since the 1930s, have spread widely and deeply in Anglo-American society. Philosophically speaking, it is only in the 1980s that these ideas have been challenged by a return to 'moral realism'.

As regards belief in a transcendent God, or any other of the beliefs traditionally associated with the Christian religion, Ayer applies the same test and concludes that the assertions which religious people customarily make may well express their feelings but have no power to represent what is or might be the case. As he says, this conclusion sits comfortably with what some theologians have often said: the existence and nature of God lie beyond the power of our minds to discern or even discuss, anything that we believe depends on a Pascalian wager or a Kierkegaardian leap of faith, anything that we

say must lack cognitive significance. Ayer does not go so far as to name any theologians, but it is not difficult to see that, at least superficially, theism without cognitive significance might go well with some forms of mysticism, fideism and the rejection of natural theology.

Far from challenging the very idea of empirical verifiability as the criterion of meaning and truth, not to mention its devastating effects in moral philosophy and theology, many theologians in the 1950s and 1960s sought rather to reconstruct Christian theism in ways that would supposedly meet and survive the logical positivist critique. One of the most remarkable documents in this dossier is 'The Significance of Christianity' by David Cox (*Mind*, April 1950). The word 'God', so it is suggested, is rightly used only in phrases such as 'meeting God' or 'encountering God'. The thesis that 'God is loving', for example, may be restated as the rule that 'no experience of meeting a person who is not someone who loves you can be rightly called "an experience of meeting God".' The word 'God' thus apparently becomes useful only for describing certain purely human experiences. Again, the doctrine that 'God created the world from nothing', while certainly seeming a particularly non-significant statement, may be reinterpreted, according to Cox, to mean that 'everything which we call "material" can be used in such a way that it contributes to the well-being of men.' Christianity, with such reinterpretations, is preserved, so Cox says, 'from the limbo to which metaphysics is being exiled (rightly, as I believe) by the logical positivists'.

Somewhat later, in 1955, R.B. Braithwaite in his Eddington Memorial Lecture at Oxford expounded 'An Empiricist's View of the Nature of Religious Belief'. Insisting (rightly) on the intimate relation between religion and ethics, he argues that the Christian religion provides a fund of 'stories' which encourage people to behave decently. Essentially, for Braithwaite, religion is, as Matthew Arnold suggested in *Literature and Dogma* of 1873, morality with a tinge of poetry. Neither truth nor falsity comes into it.

Such efforts to make the language of Christianity conform to assertions which would pass logical positivist or empiricist tests of meaning no doubt had a beneficial side.

Theologians were too embarrassed to indulge in grandiose metaphysical speculation or to cultivate the exuberant paradoxes of existentialism. Theologians should perhaps never say more than they absolutely have to: fear of saying more than makes sense is a chastening discipline. In retrospect, however, it seems that the spirit of logical positivism had a deeply intimidating effect. Some philosophers of religion, notably H.D. Lewis, argued that logical empiricism was a mistake, with disastrous consequences in *any* domain, let alone ethics and theology. Others, such as most notably Ian T. Ramsey, worked hard, within the parameters of the essentially positivist assumptions of what by then was called 'linguistic analysis', to bring out the 'oddity' and 'the logical impropriety' of religious utterances. Even if they seem so in form, these utterances are not to be treated like ordinary factual statements. Their significance is to be found in what Ramsey called 'disclosure situations'. The ice breaks, the penny drops, the duck turns out to be a rabbit. Ramsey's careful and often entertaining portrayal of how a situation unexpectedly becomes an 'encounter' or an event a 'revelation', while it may look like what Ayer would call sociological description, is actually an original attempt to ground religious assertions in empirically verifiable data. Ramsey remains the best example of how a fundamentally orthodox Christian theologian who willingly accepted and clearly respected the canons of logical empiricism sought to clarify his beliefs.

The effects of logical positivism pervade our culture. It is generally assumed, for example, that only factual statements convey objective truths – every other kind of utterance being either subjective or ideologically slanted. (In post-Nietzschean varieties of positivism even factual statements are not objective either.) One of the greatest obstacles in the way of Christian belief for many people is the assumption that, if religious assertions are not factual, they must be purely 'symbolic', 'metaphorical', and the like, and thus lacking all purchase on the real world. It may be wondered also what effect the power of this dichotomy between language as information and language as ejaculation has had in recent translations of Scripture and in new liturgies.

One option which appeals to many people is to reconstruct Christianity on the assumption that logical positivism is right: religious assertions say nothing one way or the other about the world, they are purely emotive. Don Cupitt, in the 1980s, has been the most eloquent exponent of such non-cognitivist theology. Cupitt rejects all forms of what he calls theological realism: the theory that God is an objectively existing quasi-personal being independent of human experience whose nature may be described in propositions with truth-value. Religion, for Cupitt, is a great communal work of art, a profound expression of the human spirit, a spontaneous, unmotivated but unstoppable upsurge of creative faith – which 'cannot strictly be ascribed either to God or to the self, because it is prior to the arising of any distinction between them'. Thus, in one bound, Christianity escapes from the logical positivist straitjacket and becomes what Cupitt calls aesthetic expressivism.

For many years past, of course, no philosopher would admit to subscribing to logical positivism. By another name, however, the anti-realism associated with Michael Dummett (Ayer's successor at Oxford) keeps something akin to the verification principle on the go. On this account, meaning is to be found only in terms which we can effectively recognize as establishing truth or falsity. We have to free ourselves of the illusion that we can (in the jargon) have verification-transcendent truths. We need not be confined to verification in terms of what is empirically observable or testable, nor need we assume that this new version of the verification principle has to apply globally – in every field of meaning. On the whole, at least by default of attention, the impression generally is, in the literature of this debate, that neither in ethics nor in aesthetics let alone in theology is there room for truths obtaining independently of our power to verify them. More generally still, in academic philosophy as in so many other domains, empiricist verificationism prevails, with expressivism in aesthetics and emotivism in ethics in its wake.

See also EPISTEMOLOGY, RELIGIOUS; FAITH AND REASON; LANGUAGE, RELIGIOUS; PHILOSOPHY OF RELIGION.

Bibliography
Cupitt, Don 1986: *Life Lines*. London: SCM Press.
Flew, Antony, and MacIntyre, Alasdair, eds 1955: *New Essays in Philosophical Theology*. London: SCM Press.
Hanfling, Oswald 1981: *Logical Positivism*. Oxford: Blackwell.
Hanfling, Oswald, ed. 1981: *Essential Readings in Logical Positivism*. Oxford: Blackwell (with good bibliography).
Lewis, H.D. 1965: *Philosophy of Religion*. London: English Universities Press.
Passmore, John 1985: *Recent Philosophers*. London: Duckworth.
Ramsey, Ian T. 1957: *Religious Language: An Empirical Placing of Theological Phrases*. London: SCM Press.

FERGUS KERR

Loisy, Alfred Firmin (1857–1940) French Roman Catholic biblical scholar. Ordained in 1879, Loisy taught biblical exegesis at the Institut Catholique de Paris, where he had completed his seminary training. A pioneer of the modernist movement (see MODERNISM), he developed a historical-critical approach to the Bible, teaching the non-Mosaic authorship of the Pentateuch, and the unhistorical character of the Genesis texts. As a result, he was dismissed from his post as professor of New Testament in 1893, and taught at the Ecole Pratique des Hautes Etudes (1900–4), and at the Collège de France (1909–30). In 1900 Adolf von Harnack's *Das Wesen des Christentums* was published, a classic statement of German Protestant liberalism. Two years later, Loisy published his controversial response, *L'Evangile et l'Eglise*, which offered a yet more radical exposition of the nature of Scripture and of Christianity itself. For Harnack, only the 'kernel' of Jesus' teaching was authentic, whilst the 'husk' of dogma elaborated by Paul and later Catholicism was of secondary value; Loisy maintained in contrast that it was precisely the later elaborations of the church that formed the basis of true Christianity: the 'kernel' could not accurately be known. A sequel was banned by the church in 1903, along with others of his writings, and he was excommunicated in 1908.

Bibliography
Jones, A.H. 1983: *Independence and Exegesis: The Study of Early Christianity in the Work of Loisy, Guignebert and Goguel*. Tübingen.
Ratté, J. 1968: *Three Modernists*. London.
Vidler, A.R. 1934: *The Modernist Movement in the Roman Church*. Cambridge.

Lonergan, Bernard (1904–1985) Canadian Jesuit theologian. He taught for many years in Canada before moving to a professorial position at the Gregorian University in Rome in 1953, where he remained until his retirement in 1965. After retirement, he lived in the USA as a member of Regis College until his death. A research institute in his name was founded in Toronto. His works include *Insight* of 1957 and *Method in Theology* of 1972.

Lonergan's principal concern was intellectual enquiry, and in particular the study of theological method. In his early work, Lonergan concentrated on the 'transcendental' method of Thomas Aquinas and those who had built on Aquinas's work. He divided the structure of human knowledge into four stages: experience, understanding, judgement and decision which acted on knowledge thus gained. From this, he developed his four 'transcendental precepts': be attentive, be intelligent, be reasonable, be responsible. His most famous book, *Method in Theology*, augments this conception. Method is defined as a 'framework for collaborative creativity'. The four stages of knowledge and the four transcendental precepts form the basis of this theological framework, with research, interpretation, history and dialectic corresponding to experience, understanding, judgement and decision. He thus attempted to construct a unified basis for theological method – indeed, for all intellectual endeavour – on which future theological work could build.

Bibliography
Corcoran, P., ed. 1973: *Looking at Lonergan's Method*.
Tracy, D. 1970: *The Achievement of Bernard Lonergan*. New York.

Lossky, Vladimir Nikolaevich (1903–1958) Russian Orthodox theologian. Son of the philosopher Nicolas Lossky, he studied at St Petersburg and, after expulsion by the Soviets in 1922, at Prague and the Sorbonne. The rest of his life was spent in the USA and in France, where he was dean and professor at the Orthodox Institute of St Denis in Paris. A champion of the Western rite in Orthodoxy, he presented Orthodoxy to the western church and sought *rapprochement* between the two. He defended Orthodoxy against sophiologists such as S. Bulgakov; his works include *The Mystical Theology of the Eastern Church* (1944, trans. 1957), *In the Image and Likeness of God* (1967, trans. 1975) and *Orthodox Theology* (1964–5, trans. 1978).

See also EASTERN ORTHODOX THEOLOGY.

Bibliography

Clement, O. 1959: Vladimir Lossky, un théologien de la personne et du Saint-Esprit. In *Messager de l'exarchat du patriarche russe en Europe occidentale* 30–1, pp. 137–206.

love, Christian The virtue of love – while defined in various ways – has regularly been understood as integral to the Christian life. Jesus summarizes the law in terms of the twofold command to love God and the neighbour (Mark 12: 28–31). St Paul's statement, 'he who loves his neighbour has fulfilled the law' (Rom. 13: 8) is more compressed still. St Augustine, in chapter 15 of his *On the Morals of the Catholic Church*, defines the cardinal virtues (temperance, fortitude, justice and prudence) as forms of love. Nevertheless, only as 'Christian ethics' came to be understood as a separate discipline, to be distinguished from theology more generally, has it been thought necessary to find and systematically develop a central principle of the Christian life. In the search for such a principle, love has much to recommend it. At the very least, we can say that sustained attention to the meaning of love has compelled Christians in the last several centuries to consider some of the most fundamental problems for their way of life.

Perhaps the most important and sustained body of reflection on the meaning of Christian love was initiated with the publication in 1930 (with a portion translated into English in 1932) of Anders Nygren's *Agape and Eros*. Nygren depicts a sharp contrast between the Platonic (and Augustinian) conception of *eros* and the Christian conception of *agape*, seeing them as distinct religious and ethical motifs which,

fundamentally, have nothing in common. In agape the initiative always lies with God, and our agape for the neighbour is at best a faithful response to God's love for us. By contrast, eros is said to be a love born out of our neediness, an 'acquisitive' and 'egocentric' love through which we attempt to satisfy our desire for union with one whose inherent attractiveness draws us. Unlike eros, agape does not aim at self-fulfilment. It is not drawn by the beauty or goodness of the loved one. Rather, it creates or bestows value on the loved one; it does not discover such value. Agape is therefore 'spontaneous' and 'unmotivated'; it has no reason for loving other than its own dynamism, its steadfast will to affirm the well-being of the other person.

That such a conception of love was no invention of Nygren's is clear. A century earlier Kierkegaard's *Works of Love* ([1847] 1962) had given expression to an equally vigorous image of Christian love as opposed to the erotic and committed to the neighbour for reasons other than any attractiveness or goodness which the neighbour might possess. Nevertheless, Nygren's work and some of the responses to it (for instance Burnaby, 1938; D'Arcy, 1956; O'Donovan, 1980) have both offered extensive commentary on the Augustinian vision of love and succeeded in focusing attention on a number of systematic questions. Among the most important are these:

1 Is Christian love essentially self-giving (or even self-sacrificing), or is there a proper place for self-concern within agape?

2 Is Christian love sheer beneficence (affirmation of the being and well-being of the neighbour), or is there a place for mutuality and reciprocity within agape?

3 If we do not follow Nygren in separating agape entirely from our own affections and sentiments (our needs and desires), can our love hope to be as faithful as God's agape is?

4 If agape is not dependent on any beauty or goodness of the loved one and is therefore at least implicitly universal and open to any neighbour, can there be any place for preference permitted within such love?

5 If agape is spontaneous, can its substance and its guidance be captured in any rule or rules?

Jesus summarizes the second table of the law in the command: 'You shall love your neighbour as yourself.' What meaning to give the words 'as yourself' here is by no means clear. Gene Outka (1972, pp. 55ff.) has described four different assessments of self-love in modern Christian ethics. Self-love is regarded by some – such as Nygren – as 'wholly nefarious' and forbidden to Christians. By some others self-love is judged to be 'normal, reasonable, and prudent' – passing over sometimes into selfishness, but equally often simply an ordinary feature of life which can then be used as a standard for how we ought to love others. Still others may justify self-love 'derivatively'; that is, we must at times take heed of our own needs in order not to burden others or in order to make clear to others how they must treat their fellow human beings. Finally, self-love can be thought definitely to be required by agape; it may be viewed almost as a mean between excessive regard for self and loss of self in regard for others.

If we think of love simply as an ethical principle divorced from its setting within Christian theology, the last of these may have the most to be said for it. In principle it may be difficult to show why we should not love the self as much as (if no more than) others. If we see agape essentially as egalitarian other-regard, we are likely to be driven in this direction. Of course, this may also lead us to conclude that the meaning of agape cannot adequately be described in abstraction from other Christian beliefs. To believe that we have been pardoned by God is to believe that we are ultimately secure, that we need have no ultimate concern for our well-being, since God has seen to it. This does not mean that we abandon our own projects in the world, as if acceptance by God meant loss of self. But it may mean that the focus of attention is shifted – that *Christian* love is not simply equal regard for human beings (counting oneself as equal to all others), but is commitment to the well-being of neighbours.

Even such a qualified devaluation of self-love, which sees the meaning of agape in the agent's own self-giving or (if the focus should be more on the neighbour) in the agent's affirmation of the neighbour's well-being, will give rise to a second question. Can there be no place for the joys of reciprocity in Christian love, no concern that love be returned?

This question exists – as an unresolved one – within the Gospels themselves. In Matthew 5: 46–7 Jesus says: 'For if you love those who love you, what reward have you? Do not even the tax collectors do the same? And if you salute only your brethren, what more are you doing than others? Do not even the Gentiles do the same?' By contrast, in John's Gospel (15: 12) Jesus commands the disciples to 'love one another as I have loved you.' This emphasis upon a mutual, brotherly love may be viewed as either an enhancement or a weakening of agape. It gives to agape, as Nygren noted, 'a depth, warmth, and intimacy that are without parallel elsewhere'; at the same time, however, it 'loses something of its original all-embracing scope' ([1930–6] 1953, p. 154).

Many have felt that a love lacking depth, warmth and intimacy could not be at the heart of Christian life and that, therefore, agape must include not only affirmation of the neighbour but also reciprocity. Thus, Martin D'Arcy suggests that '[t]he perfection of love . . . is to be found in personal friendship, whether between a man and a woman, between man and man or between man and God' (1956, p. 31). One could, of course, regard this as simply adding a *desire* for union to an affirmation of the neighbour's well-being. Even that, however, is not strong enough to satisfy everyone. Margaret Farley contends that love simply does involve 'affective union'. 'My loving affirmation unites me with you' (1986, p. 31). This affirmation will also, no doubt, give rise to desire for still greater union, but, Farley argues, it is itself already a union. That may be too strong a claim, but the concern of thinkers such as Burnaby, D'Arcy and Farley can be met to some degree if we hold that a reciprocated love must be the hoped-for fulfilment of agape.

Once we begin to make a place for such reciprocated affection, however, we may more readily pay attention not only to the power of agape itself to affirm the neighbour's life, but also to the beauty and goodness in the neighbour by which we are drawn towards affective union. And this, in turn, may seem to make our agape more changeable and less faithful, since both the beauty and goodness of the neighbour are subject to alteration. This may be problematic, if agape is a love that responds to God's own love and aspires to emulate the faithfulness of divine love. An unswerving fidelity in agape has probably been depicted more powerfully by Kierkegaard than by any other modern Christian thinker. 'No change . . . can take your neighbour from you, for it is not your neighbour who holds you fast – it is your love which holds your neighbour fast' ([1847] 1962, p. 76).

So rigorous a depiction of agape may, however, run the risk of making it more than a response to and imitation of God's love by creatures who are not themselves gods. To be sure, the goal – indeed, the obligation – of faithful love is central to Christian belief. Such faithfulness is not an attempt by creatures to resist the force of time; rather, it is an attempt to embrace time by giving love a history that extends without limit into the future (Farley, 1986, p. 40). But having granted that, it is difficult to deny that we may sometimes be unable to sustain some of our loving commitments when both we and the neighbour have changed greatly.

Acknowledging any place at all for attention to the neighbour's beauty or goodness also forces us to face a tension between the implicit universality of agape and the preference that characterizes so many of our most intense loves. Such preference is based on particular traits which only some people will possess. We may hold, as Kierkegaard often seems to, that agape can allow no preference in love, that 'it is an impossibility to love according to both explanations simultaneously' ([1847] 1962, p. 63). Then an agapeic life is likely to be possible only for a few who feel themselves called to seek to love universally. Apart from such 'Franciscan' possibilities, Christian thinkers have used three different approaches when seeking to make place for preference within agape.

First, we may argue that loves grounded in preference – though not generated by agape – are not evil in themselves; indeed, they are the work of the Creator who has fashioned our nature such that particular bonds of love are integral to human fulfilment. This was, for example, the view of Joseph Butler, who argued that our nature is so constituted by God that we naturally approve of extending our benevolence preferentially to some rather than others (Meilaender, 1981, pp. 29–32). Such preference may, of course, become evil, and agape

must set 'the boundaries within which special relations come into their own' (Outka, 1972, p. 271). Agape sets limits upon what may be done to others as a means of fostering our preferential loves, but it does no more than that.

For other Christians a second position – which makes agape less a purely negative principle in the moral life – is preferable. On this view, we should conceive of agape in terms like those of Jonathan Edwards: as benevolence to being in general (Meilaender, 1981, pp. 22–9). From such general benevolence we may then 'build down', seeking to incorporate particular loves as specifications or applications of this more universal benevolence. Because we are finite beings and cannot love all people equally, special attachments must remain a necessary part of life. But they are understood simply as specifications of universal love – specifications necessitated by our finitude. Whether such specifications, if really grounded simply in the fact of finitude, would capture the urgencies of our 'preferential' loves is a difficult question. Kierkegaard's teleological suspension of the ethical – in which, having suspended the universal, one simply loves nonpreferentially each neighbour in his or her particularity – is an attempt to describe a love that would be particular without displaying any preference.

Finally, some – in particular, critics of Nygren such as Burnaby and D'Arcy – have been drawn towards a third view which 'builds up' from particular attachments to a more universal love. Rather than attempting to derive particular, preferential bonds from agape, we may discern in those attachments a training ground. Learning how to love a few, we gradually become able to love more generally. Thus, on this view, one can allow that agape is more than a negative boundary-setting principle, but one need not seek to derive from it a justification of the more preference-laden urgencies of romantic love or friendship.

We might risk the generalization that, in modern Christian thought, the first two of these approaches have been characteristically Protestant. The third – especially when combined with a recognition that some Christians may be called even now to live in a 'Franciscan' manner free of preference – has been more characteristically Catholic.

Finally, among the differences in understanding agape that arose in the Protestant Reformation was one which has taken on new permutations in the modern period. The Reformers, attempting to come to terms with what Nygren has called the 'spontaneity' of agape, debated whether the law could have a 'third use' (as a guide for Christian living, in addition to its acknowledged uses to convict the heart of sin and, in civil life, to restrain sinful deeds). In many respects this was an argument about what it might mean to say with St Paul that to love the neighbour is to have fulfilled the law. More recently somewhat similar arguments have centred on the question: Can love's requirements ever be stated in exceptionless rules? Or must love act spontaneously, with an improvization directed to the precise situation?

There are several angles from which one can mount a theological argument for the necessity of freedom from 'laws' or 'rules' in the Christian life. For example, Reinhold Niebuhr's characteristic understanding of human nature as both finite and free – as always and indefinitely transcending the limits of nature and history – might suggest that no rule could ever be without exception. For no rule could state in advance what the limits of free human self-transcendence are. From a rather different angle – focused more on God's nature than ours – Karl Barth's 'divine command' theory suggests that any attempt to specify exceptionless rules must be guilty of interposing something (namely, a rule) between human beings and the God who freely claims their obedience. What Barth called 'special ethics' can only provide a kind of instructional preparation for the ethical event itself, for hearing the command of God in the moment.

A somewhat different approach, which has also emphasized freedom from rules in the Christian life, was popularized in the language of 'situation ethics'. Such a view – espoused, for example, by Joseph Fletcher and J.A.T. Robinson – has often seemed to be a Christian version of act utilitarianism (with love, rather than happiness or utility, as the value to be maximized in all moral choices). 'Our task', Fletcher writes, 'is to act so that more good (i.e. loving-kindness) will occur than any possible alternative' (1966, p. 61). Love's decisions must be made in the moment, lest we worry more

about adhering to a rule than truly serving the needs of our neighbours. Such claims were rigorously criticized by Paul Ramsey, who argued both that agape might need to be expressed in 'principled' rather than 'situational' ways, and that no social morality could grow from the soil of agape unless such principles were in fact possible and permissible explications of the meaning of love. Christian ethics for Ramsey became the attempt to use human reason to probe cases, seeking to give love a shape by clarifying more precisely the kinds of actions that could or could not conform to agape.

None of the issues discussed here is new to the modern period; however, they have been given rigorous and sustained attention in that period as Christian ethics has become a separate discipline. In particular, this period has seen increased attention to the presumed universality of Christian love for neighbours. This universality has provided some impetus for egalitarian currents of thought while also being shaped – for both better and worse – by those same currents. In any case, because the love command is likely to continue to occupy a central place in the Christian vision of the moral life, such questions will surely continue to engage the attention of Christian thinkers.

See also ETHICS; KINGDOM OF GOD: POLITICAL AND SOCIAL THEOLOGY; SPIRITUALITY.

Bibliography

Barth, Karl [1951] 1961: *Church Dogmatics*, III/4, trans. T.F. Torrance *et al.* Edinburgh: T & T Clark.

Burnaby, John 1938: *Amor Dei*. London: Hodder and Stoughton.

D'Arcy, M.C. 1956: *The Mind and Heart of Love*. New York: Meridian Books.

Farley, Margaret A. 1986: *Personal Commitments*. San Francisco: Harper and Row.

Fletcher, Joseph 1966: *Situation Ethics*. Philadelphia: Westminster Press.

Gilleman, Gérard [1954] 1961: *The Primacy of Charity in Moral Theology*, trans. William F. Ryan and André Vachon. Westminster: Newman Press.

Kierkegaard, Søren [1847] 1962: *Works of Love*, trans. Howard and Edna Hong. New York: Harper and Brothers.

Lewis, C.S. 1960: *The Four Loves*. New York: Harcourt Brace Jovanovich.

Long, Edward Leroy, Jr 1968: Soteriological implications of norm and context. In *Norm and Context in Christian Ethics*, ed. Gene H. Outka and Paul Ramsey. New York: Charles Scribner's Sons, pp. 265–95.

Meilaender, Gilbert C. 1981: *Friendship*. Notre Dame: University of Notre Dame Press.

Niebuhr, Reinhold 1935: *An Interpretation of Christian Ethics*. New York and London: Harper and Brothers.

Nygren, Anders [1930–6] 1953: *Agape and Eros*, trans. Philip S. Watson. London: SPCK.

O'Donovan, Oliver 1980: *The Problem of Self-Love in St Augustine*. New Haven and London: Yale University Press.

Outka, Gene 1972: *Agape*. New Haven and London: Yale University Press.

Pieper, Josef [1972] 1974: *About Love*, trans. Richard and Clara Winston. Chicago: Franciscan Herald Press.

Ramsey, Paul 1967: *Deeds and Rules in Christian Ethics*. New York: Charles Scribner's Sons.

Thielicke, Helmut [1958–9] 1966: *Theological Ethics*, vol. 1, trans. William H. Lazareth. Philadelphia: Fortress Press.

GILBERT MEILAENDER

Lutheranism The distinguishing problematic of Lutheranism since 1700 derives from an inner contradiction: attempting to hold Luther's understanding of justification by faith alone together with an anthropology inspired more by philosophical and humanist concerns (such as 'free choice of the will'; 'the moral progress of a continuously existing subject') (Iwand, 1959, p. 17; McGrath, 1986, p. 22). Pietism, the most important post-Reformation movement in Lutheranism, first made the problem explicit. Influential initially from about 1690 to 1740 and renewed in several awakening movements in the nineteenth century, pietism's avowed purpose was to bring about a second Reformation. The first, it claimed, had issued only in the 'dead orthodoxy' of the seventeenth century (Schmidt, 1965, p. 1898). Lutheran orthodoxy quite properly insisted on forensic justification, but could not effectively combine it with the more Aristotelian anthropology that had reasserted itself. So the orthodox systems were blamed for an 'objectivism' that tended to lose contact with the life of the subject. Pietism is the most persistent and fecund critical voice. The inherent suspicion of – not to say polemic

against – forensic justification, was already apparent in the reputed father of pietism, Philip Jakob Spener (1635–1705) (Schmidt, [1951] 1977, p. 13), and runs like a common thread through virtually all theologies opposed to Lutheran orthodoxy – pietist, biblicist, moralist, liberal, even some strands of neo-orthodoxy – down to the present. Martin Luther's recognition that justification does indeed render the old subject 'dead' but nevertheless simultaneously gives life to the new proposes a quite different anthropology: radical discontinuity, but yet simultaneity (*simul iustus et peccator*). Lacking a firm hold on that anthropology, Lutheranism since 1700 has halted between the 'objectivity' of orthodoxism and the 'subjectivity' of pietism and its variegated offspring.

Spener outlined pietism's basic reform programme in his classic work, *Pia desideria* ([1675] 1964), calling for a deepening of Christian life through Bible study and mutual edification in small conventicles (*collegia pietatis*). This meant a turn towards the subjective side in theology and church life. Experience of conversion and rebirth became the ground of all certainty. Progress in sanctification was rigorously urged. This was particularly pronounced in Spener's principal disciple, August Hermann Francke (1663–1727), professor at Halle. Halle pietism enjoyed wide influence beyond Germany in Scandinavia and eventually in the USA through the pioneer leadership of Henry Melchior Muhlenberg (1711–1787). Though more radical pietists (such as Gottfried Arnold (1666–1714) and Konrad Dipple (1673–1734)) departed from traditional beliefs, the mainstream accepted orthodox Lutheran doctrine – at least formally – and has remained a persistent conservative influence in church life as well as an impulse towards service and mission. The turn towards the subject meant, however, a fateful turn from theology as doctrinal truth claim to theology as an account of faith's experience and its practical and ethical consequences. Fertile soil was thereby prepared for several modern movements: Neology, rationalism, Enlightenment, romanticism (Hagglund, [1966] 1968, pp. 329–30; Schmidt, 1965, pp. 1904–5).

The turn towards the subject became more explicit in the later eighteenth-century academic theologies often referred to as 'Neology' ('new theology') (as in the work of J.F.W. Jerusalem (d. 1789), J.J. Spaulding (d. 1804) and J.S. Semler (d. 1791). Stress on practicality encouraged the discarding of dogmas not immediately 'useful' (Trinity, Christology, original sin, vicarious satisfaction). The demand for progress in Christian life fostered a more optimistic outlook, not only for the individual but also for society. Out of chiliastic hope (pietists tended to be millennialists) grew the idea of historical progress. The idea of historical progress could in turn be used to relativize the authority of ancient dogma and even Scripture itself. Semler applied the historical-critical method to the development of dogma and so is generally considered the founder of the history of dogma as a discrete discipline.

The turn towards the subject drives eventually to the idea of autonomy: freedom from the heteronomy of historical revelation and dogma ('positive religion') altogether in a more completely 'natural' religion. G.E. Lessing (1729–1781) proposed understanding historical revelation as a primitive stage in the 'education of the human race' which he hoped would culminate in a 'new eternal gospel' fully amenable to human reason. The move towards a fully autonomous self reached its high point when Immanuel Kant attempted to construct a *Religion Within the Limits of Reason Alone* in 1793 (see KANTIANISM). The autonomy of the self is grounded internally in the voice of moral law, the 'categorical imperative', the virtual voice of God within. Though unable theoretically to exclude the possibility of a historical revelation, Kant nevertheless (rightly!) saw that faith in such revelation from without would be the end of autonomy for the 'old self'. He resolutely turned his back on that prospect and tried rather to encompass the truth of historical revelation within the limits of practical religion.

The theological world recoiled in dismay over this ironic end to the search for autonomy. Instead of arriving at freedom the self is caught in the grip of the categorical imperative. God, once more or less safely distant in the objective orthodox heaven, had now moved in upon the subject altogether. As G.W.F. Hegel was quick to note, Kant did not succeed in removing heteronomy, but only moved the *heteros nomos* within the self, where it was more odious.

Luther's warning, that one who seeks to escape law apart from the quite 'objective' and alien righteousness of Christ will simply end in captivity to law, is realized in Kantianism.

The Kantian impasse spawned, basically, three attempts to recapture and provide new legitimation for the lost substance of the faith. All had an impact on Lutheranism in the nineteenth century. The first, a conservative reaction variously called 'supranaturalism', 'biblicism', or sometimes 'repristinationism' (G.C. Storr, 1746–1805; E.W. Hengstenberg, 1802–1869), attempted to build on the gaps in Kant's critiques. On the one hand the stringent moralism demands a doctrine of atonement, while on the other an inerrant Scripture provides warrant for the reassertion of such traditional doctrinal claims. Such moves – though often popular in the church – were retrograde, however, because they could not locate the source of difficulty and so only revived the problem of heteronomy. F.D.E. Schleiermacher (1768–1834) and his disciples sought to escape the heteronomy both of Kant's moralism and of historical revelation, by locating religion not in practical reason but in the immediacy of intuition and 'feeling' – a pietism of a 'higher order'. Theology could then be seen not as doctrinal law but as the explication of pious 'states of mind'. Heteronomy was seemingly bypassed, but – many thought – at the expense of the normative role of doctrine. HEGELIANISM, the third attempted escape, sought to overcome heteronomy by expanding reason itself to encompass the idea of historical revelation. No longer the object of thought, God is to be conceived as thought itself: the Absolute Spirit thinking itself out in and through the subject, transcending and returning to itself in the dialectic of the history of Spirit. Hegel thought thereby to reclaim the fundamental doctrines (Trinity, incarnation, atonement) rejected by rationalism. But, as Søren Kierkegaard (1813–1855) was to point out, the danger was then that the offence of historical revelation would be swallowed up in an immanent, world-historical thought process. L. Feuerbach (1804–1872) completed the triumph of anthropology by inverting Hegel, declaring theology to be the projection of human rather than divine spirit. 'Mediating theology' (C. Ullmann, 1796–1865; C.I.

Nitzsch, 1787–1876; R. Rothe, 1799–1867 and others) attempted to adapt the tradition to current thought via speculative idealism, but remained largely an academic exercise without much influence on church life.

The three strands of reaction to Kant contributed to a reshaping of Lutheran theology in the nineteenth and twentieth centuries broadly referred to as 'neo-Lutheranism'. (Care should be exercised in using the term. Europeans tend to use it to denote generally the nineteenth-century return to confessionalism, whereas Americans apply it more to recent theologies accepting the historical-critical method.) Neo-Lutheranism's basic aim was renewal and defence of the Lutheran heritage against attacks from without (rationalism, socialist revolutions, materialism and so on) as well as from within (such as the forced union with the Reformed in Prussian lands). In varying combinations, neo-Lutheranism rests on three pillars: the experience of rebirth; the power of the revealing Word in Scripture; the Lutheran confessions understood as fulfilment of the patristic tradition. Born out of the awakening movements of the early nineteenth century, neo-Lutheranism shows its debt to pietism. Following Schleiermacher's lead, theology is the unfolding of the content of the experience of rebirth. The theological explication of experience is confirmed and normed by Scripture (showing the influence of biblicism) and confessional tradition – both now understood in more Hegelian terms: Scripture as a 'history of salvation' and confessional tradition as the outcome of the development of dogma (J.C.K. von Hofmann, 1810–1877, is a prime example of these theological moves; see Forde, 1969).

Neo-Lutheranism has remained the fundamental shaping influence of Lutheranism to the present. However, the relative status and interrelation of its three pillars has meant continued uncertainty and vacillation in Lutheranism's self-understanding. Thus, Scandinavian pietist movements (as represented, for example, by H.N. Hauge (1771–1824) in Norway and C.O. Rosenius (1816–1868) in Sweden) were suspicious of more orthodox state church Lutheranism and formed separate cells (prayer chapels in Norway, and sometimes overt separation in Sweden). N.F.S. Grundtvig in Denmark, meanwhile, found the real basis for

certainty in the 'living Word' preached in the church and preserved in the ancient creeds, and fostered a 'folk religion'. In Germany, neo-Lutheranism tended to separate into two camps. One (centred around the Erlangen theologians J.W.F. Hoefling (1802–1853), G.C.A. Harless (1806–1879), J.C.K. von Hofmann and G. Thomasius (1802–1875)) emphasized experience and Scripture, understanding the church primarily as a priesthood of believers; the other (represented by T. Kliefoth (1810–1895), W. Loehe (1808–1872), F.J. Stahl (1802–1861) and C. Vilmar (1800–1868)) emphasized the historical tradition, understanding the institutional church more as the incarnational organ for divine activity carried out through a divinely sanctioned office of ministry. The Erlangen school was more influential in Norway, whereas the group around Stahl found more sympathy in Sweden. The differences subsequently left their mark on respective immigrant churches in the USA and Canada and continue to be reflected in ecumenical dialogue about ministry today. Perhaps the most conservative manifestation of neo-Lutheranism in America has been that of the Lutheran church, Missouri Synod, which has emphasized particularly the biblicist as well as the anti-unionist and repristinationist facets of the movement.

The uncertain foundations of neo-Lutheranism made resistance to the acids of modernity difficult, especially in academic circles. The end of the nineteenth century and the beginning of the twentieth saw a return to Kantian moralism on the one hand and the continued application of the historical-critical method to both Scripture and dogma on the other. Weariness from the speculative constructions of idealism engendered a pronounced anti-metaphysical bent, especially evident in the work of Albrecht Ritschl and his heirs. Subsequent academic Lutheran theology was almost totally dominated by historical pursuits: historical-critical study of the Scriptures; history of dogma; church history; and the history of religions. The confluence of these pursuits fostered a theology generally dubbed 'liberalism' (see LIBERALISM (BRITAIN and USA)). There was an almost unbounded confidence that historical progress and the ability of historical science to liberate from the dogmatisms of the past would lead to the 'kingdom of God'. The search for the historical Jesus and the rigorous use of historical methods, it was hoped, would uncover the real 'essence of Christianity'. The massive work of Adolf von Harnack is the most consummate realization of this liberal agenda.

The liberal programme, however, carried within itself the seeds of its own dissolution. The belief in progress was shaken by the actual 'progress' of history (two world wars and so on); the search for the historical Jesus and the essence of Christianity led instead to the discovery of the radical apocalyptic and eschatological outlook of the Scriptures. Lutheran theology from the 1930s onwards has been heavily influenced, therefore, by the rediscovery of Kierkegaard and the reaction of dialectical theology and neo-orthodoxy to liberalism.

In Sweden Lundensian theology, represented by Gustaf Aulén and Anders Nygren, has followed the somewhat independent path of attempting to overcome the relativizing effect of the history of dogma by identifying motifs (rather than dogmas) fundamental to Christian thinking throughout history ('motif research').

The distinctive character of current Lutheranism, however, is largely the result of its continuing search for its own roots in the Reformation and Luther's thought itself. Beginning in about the 1840s, when J.C.K. von Hofmann appealed to Luther in the argument over atonement, Luther was for the first time set against Lutheran orthodoxy on a substantive doctrinal issue (Hirsch, 1954, vol. 5, p. 427) and the uniqueness of Luther's own thought began to emerge as a viable alternative. Subsequent Luther research, most notably that inspired by Karl Holl and his students as well as by Swedish scholars (Carlson, 1948), thereby becomes crucial for the development and understanding of contemporary Lutheranism. Luther's understanding of the living Word, the distinction between law and gospel (Forde, 1969) and the theology of the cross continue to emerge as decisive critical factors for Lutheranism and contemporary theology in general. The way is opened thereby for a reappropriation of the anthropology (*simul iustus et peccator*) originally posited by Luther's understanding of justification, as well as an eschatologically nuanced view of God's two-fold rule in creation (traditionally: the two kingdoms

doctrine; see Hertz, 1976) and the Christian's vocation in society and the world (Wingren, [1949] 1960). The work of Gustaf Wingren and Hans Joachim Iwand (see Iwand, 1962–74) is perhaps most successful in putting the various strands together into a coherent and characteristically Lutheran stance today.

See also PROTESTANT THEOLOGY (GERMANY and SCANDINAVIA).

Bibliography

Braaten, C. 1983: *Principles of Lutheran Theology*. Philadelphia: Fortress Press.

Braaten, C. 1990: *Justification*. Minneapolis: Fortress Press.

Braaten, C., and Jenson, R., eds 1984: *Christian Dogmatics*, 2 vols. Philadelphia: Fortress Press.

Burgess, J., ed. 1990: *Lutherans in Ecumenical Dialogue: A Reappraisal*. Minneapolis: Augsburg Publishing House.

Carlson, E.M. 1948: *The Reinterpretation of Luther*. Philadelphia: Westminster Press.

Fackenheim, E. 1967: *The Religious Dimension in Hegel's Thought*. Bloomington: Indiana University Press.

Forde, G.O. 1969: *The Law–Gospel Debate*. Minneapolis: Augsburg Publishing House.

Forde, G.O. 1982: *Justification by Faith: A Matter of Death and Life*. Philadelphia: Fortress Press.

Forell, G., and McCue, J. 1982: *Confessing One Faith: A Joint Commentary on the Augsburg Confession by Lutheran and Catholic Theologians*. Minneapolis: Augsburg Publishing House.

Greschat, M., ed. 1977: *Zur neueren Pietismusforschung*. Darmstadt: Wissenschaftliche Buchgesellschaft.

Gritsch, E., and Jenson, R. 1976: *Lutheranism: The Theological Movement and its Confessional Writings*. Philadelphia: Fortress Press.

Hagglund, B. [1966] 1968: *History of Theology*, trans. G.J. Lund. St Louis: Concordia Publishing House.

Hertz, K.H., ed. 1976: *Two Kingdoms and One World*. Minneapolis: Augsburg Publishing House.

Hirsch, E. 1954: *Geschichte der neueren evangelischen Theologie*, 5 vols. Gütersloh: C. Bertelsmann Verlag.

Iwand, H.J. 1959: Die grundlegende Bedeutung der Lehre vom unfreien Willen für den Glauben. In *Um den rechten Glauben*, ed. K.G. Steck. Munich: Chr. Kaiser Verlag.

Iwand, H.J. 1962–74: *Nachgelassene Werke*, ed. H. Gollwitzer, W. Kreck, K. Steck and E. Wolf. Munich: Chr. Kaiser Verlag.

Kantzenbach, F.W. 1966: *Orthodoxie und Pietismus*. Gütersloh. Gütersloher Verlagshaus Gerd Mohn.

McGrath, A.E. 1986: *Iustitia Dei*, 2 vols. Vol. 2, *From*

1500 to the Present Day. Cambridge: Cambridge University Press.

Schilling, S.P. 1966: *Contemporary Continental Theologians*. Nashville: Abingdon Press.

Schmidt, M. [1951] 1977: Speners Wiedergeburtslehre. In *Zur neueren Pietismusforschung*, ed. M. Greschat. Darmstadt: Wissenschaftliche Buchgesellschaft, pp. 9–33.

Schmidt, M. 1965: Pietism. In *The Encyclopedia of the Lutheran Church*, ed. J. Bodensieck, vol. 3. Minneapolis: Augsburg Publishing House, pp. 1898–1906.

Schultz, R. 1958: *Gesetz und Evangelium in der Lutherischen Theologie des 19. Jahrhunderts*. Berlin: Lutherisches Verlagshaus.

Spener, P.J. [1675] 1964: *Pia Desideria*, trans. and ed. T.G. Tappert. Philadelphia: Fortress Press.

Thielicke, H. [1983] 1990: *Modern Faith and Thought*, trans. G.W. Bromiley. Grand Rapids: Eerdmans.

Wingren, G. [1948] 1957: *The Christian's Calling*, trans. C.C. Rasmussen. Philadelphia: Muhlenburg Press; Edinburgh: Oliver and Boyd.

Wingren, G. [1949] 1960: *The Living Word*, trans. V.C. Pogue. Philadelphia: Muhlenburg Press; London: SCM Press.

Wingren, G. [1954] 1958: *Theology in Conflict*, trans. E.H. Wahlstrom. Philadelphia: Muhlenberg Press.

GERHARD O. FORDE.

M

MacIntyre, Alasdair Chalmers (b. 1929) British philosopher. He was professor of sociology at Essex University until 1970, when he moved to the USA. Since 1988 he has been professor of philosophy at the University of Notre Dame, Indiana.

His early philosophical work ranges from a study of *Marxism and Christianity* (1954) to a consideration of the history of moral thinking in *A Short History of Ethics* (1965). He is primarily renowned for his recent works *After Virtue* (1981), *Whose Justice? Which Rationality?* (1988) and *Three Rival Versions of Moral Inquiry* (1990).

MacIntyre's recent work is a critique of the Enlightenment in general, and of the approaches of modern Anglo-American analytical philosophy in particular. He contends that the teleological context of pre-Enlightenment moral philosophy has been lost, and that this loss has generated the problems which remain unsolved in modern philosophy. Both inside and outside academic philosophy, he argues, an emotivism without absolutes has become widely accepted. In response to this, MacIntyre insists that all ethical schemes must be contextual, reflecting the community in which they are born and the traditions which the community inherits. He dismisses the idea of an ethic which is eternally valid, arguing that we can only justify our own ethical decisions by examining our own and others' ethical traditions. MacIntyre himself examines the Aristotelian tradition in western philosophy and proposes his own post-Enlightenment moral philosophy, based on a revised Aristotelianism, involving a rejuvenation of the traditional concept of the virtues.

His assertion that 'the Enlightenment project' has been a failure, and his questioning of modernity and the predominant Anglo-American philosophical tradition, have made MacIntyre a controversial figure in modern moral and political philosophy.

man, doctrine of See ANTHROPOLOGY, CHRISTIAN.

Marcel, Gabriel (1889–1973) French existentialist philosopher and playwright. A convert to Catholicism, he was influenced in the development of his existentialist theories by his wartime experience as a Red Cross official. He was preoccupied with the phenomenon of existential malaise in modern society, and with the onward march of technology, which he saw as a threat to man's dignity in assigning him a purely functional role in the tableau of history. Unlike existentialists such as J.-P. Sartre, he argued that man is a transcendent being and his existence cannot be reduced to the merely abstract and impersonal. His theories found dramatic expression in his plays; his theoretical works include *The Philosophy of Existence* (1949), *Mystery of Being* (Gifford Lectures, 1949–50), *Homo Viator: Introduction to a Philosophy of Hope* (1951) and *The Existential Background of Human Dignity* (1963).

Bibliography
Pax, C. 1972: *An Existential Approach to God: A Study of Gabriel Marcel*. The Hague.
Schilpp, P.A., and Hahn, L.E. 1984: *The Philosophy of Gabriel Marcel*. La Salle, Ill.

Maritain, Jacques (1882–1973) French Roman Catholic moral philosopher. Born in Paris,

359

he studied at the Sorbonne, where he was influenced by Henri Bergson. Then in 1906 he converted to Catholicism and developed an interest in neo-Thomist philosophy. His first philosophical publication was a critique of his former mentor, Bergson (1914); later works include *Distinguer pour unir, ou Les Degrés du savoir* (1932, trans. 1959), *Humanisme intégral* (1936, trans. 1938), *La Philosophie morale* (1960, trans. 1964), and *Le Paysan de la Garonne* (1966, trans. 1968). He attempted to relate the writings of Aquinas to metaphysics and the theory of philosophy, as well as to moral, social and political philosophy. His interest also embraced the theory and practice of art (see *Art and Scholasticism*, 1920), and whilst a professor at the Institut Catholique in Paris (1914–33) he founded, with his wife, a group dedicated to the pursuit of spiritual, intellectual and artistic life on Thomist principles. He was professor at the Institute for Medieval Studies in Toronto (1933–45), and at Princeton (1948–52), before being appointed French Canadian ambassador to the Vatican. In 1961 he went to live with the Little Brothers of Jesus in Toulouse, and in 1970 he joined the community.

Bibliography

Evans, J.W., and Ward, L.R. 1956: *The Social and Political Philosophy of Jacques Maritain*. London.
Herberg, W. ed. 1958: *Four Existentialist Theologians*. Garden City, NY.

marriage and divorce See ETHICS; SEXUAL ETHICS.

Marx, Karl (1818–83) German social and economic theorist, founder of communism. He studied law at Bonn and Berlin but his developing interests were in the area of the philosophy of history, where he was influenced by L. Feuerbach's materialism and by Hegelianism – he was a member of a group of 'young Hegelians' which included religious thinkers such as D.F. Strauss. Working for *Die rheinische Zeitung* but under pressure from the Prussian authorities who opposed his revolutionary activities, he moved to Paris (1843); then to Brussels (1845 until March 1848); and after a short period participating in revolution in his homeland, he settled in London in 1849, where

he devoted his life to study and writing. Of Jewish parentage, Marx was baptized in 1824, but became an opponent of religion. He acknowledged religion as a consolation for the oppressed, but believed that such consolation was illusory: religion was 'the opium of the people'. He argued that if the economic conditions that produced poverty were overturned, religion would become obsolete. Oppression of the working class was the hallmark of a social and economic system designated 'capitalism', and the established church was guilty of helping to uphold the capitalist status quo. His major work, *Capital*, of 1867, analysed this system, under which those who control the 'means of production' exploit a powerless labour force, which, in his *Communist Manifesto* of 1848, he called on to unite in bringing about revolution.

See also MARXISM.

Bibliography

Dupré, L. 1966: *The Philosophical Foundation of Marxism*. New York.
Lyon, D. 1979: *Karl Marx: A Christian Appreciation of his Life and Thought*. Tring.
McLellan, D. 1973: *Karl Marx: His Life and Thought*. London.

Marxism Marxism is an intellectual and political movement originating in the ideas of Karl Marx. Although almost as polymorphous as the various religions of which it has, at times, been such a vigorous critic, the body of Marxist thought contains three main components: an analysis of human societies which takes the major determinant of these societies to be their divisive and exploitative economic structure; a (sketchy) picture of an alternative method of social organization based on cooperation rather than conflict; and various political recommendations for facilitating the emergence of this superior form of society.

Undoubtedly the central component of any Marxist approach consists in what Marx himself called the materialist conception of history. This is the idea that the essential element in any understanding of human history is the fundamental role of the productive activity of human beings. The fundamental activity of human beings, on this view, is the way in which they obtain their means of subsistence by interaction with the natural, material world that surrounds them – in short, their labour. As Marx puts it in *Capital*:

> Labour is a process in which both man and nature participate, and in which man of his own accord starts, regulates, and controls the material reactions between himself and nature . . . by thus acting on the external world and changing it, he at the same time changes his own nature. He develops his slumbering powers and compels them to act in obedience to his sway.

The most famous formulation of this doctrine, again by Marx, runs as follows:

> In the social production of their life, men enter into definite relations that are indispensable and independent of their will, relations of production which correspond to a definite state of development of their material productive forces. The sum total of these relations of production constitutes the economic structure of society, the real foundation, on which rises a legal and political superstructure and to which correspond definite forms of social consciousness. The mode of production of material life conditions the social, political, and intellectual life process in general. It is not the consciousness of men that determines their being, but, on the contrary, their social being that determines their consciousness.

It is worth emphasizing that, in most forms of Marxism, the materialism consists not in any metaphysical doctrine about the world's consisting only of matter, but in the idea that to understand human beings and their history it is essential to begin with their material conditions of production. This is not to deny the validity of philosophical, political, artistic, or even, at the limit, religious activities, but only to insist that these activities are moulded by, and only ultimately intelligible in terms of, the prevailing forms of material production.

Thus, in Marx's view, it was a mistake – and typical of most religious conceptions of the world – to start from human consciousness and to proceed from this to an investigation of material reality. The correct approach was the other way round. The origin of the problem was not mistaken ideas but the mistaken nature of social reality which generated mistaken ideas: 'consciousness can never be anything else than conscious existence, and the existence of men is their actual life process . . . Life is not determined by consciousness but consciousness by life.' The materialist conception of history held that it was the way in which human beings responded to their *material* needs that determined the rest of society. The basic social process was the satisfaction of the material needs for food, clothing and shelter. Human beings satisfied these material needs in the natural world that surrounded them, a world which they transformed for their own ends through the process of labour. It was this labouring process – which Marx sometimes called 'material practice' – that was the fundamental human activity, and it was the starting point for any valid social science. Marx summed this up as follows:

> The production of ideas, of conceptions, of consciousness, is at first directly interwoven with the material activity and the material intercourse of men, the language of real life. Conceiving, thinking, the mental intercourse of men, appear at this stage as the direct efflux of their material behaviour. The same applies to mental production as expressed in the language of politics, laws, morality, religion, metaphysics, etc., of a people . . . Men, developing their material production and their material intercourse, alter, along with this their actual world, also their thinking and the products of their thinking.

Thus ideology had to be explained from material practice. But not all ideas were ideology and Marx did not wish simply to produce a more dynamic version of A.L.C. Destutt de Tracey's science of ideas. What made ideas into ideology was their connection with the conflictual nature of social and economic relationships which characterized the labour process. These conflicts were due, at bottom, to two factors. The first was the division of labour, beginning with the division between mental and manual labour, which implied the unequal distribution – both qualitatively and quantitatively – of both labour and its products. This entailed, secondly, the existence of private property and a situation in which the interest of the individual no longer coincided with that of the community. 'Out of this very contradiction', Marx continued,

> between the interest of the individual and that of the community the latter takes an independent form as the State, divorced from the real interests of individual and community, and at the same time as an illusory communal life, always based, however, on the real ties.

The consequence of all this was that

> all struggles within the State, the struggle between democracy, aristocracy, and monarchy, the struggle for the franchise, etc. etc. are merely the illusory forms in which the real struggles of the different classes are fought out among one another.

It was their connection with this class struggle and its social and economic basis that gave certain ideas their ideological force.

The above account is descriptive: the second main component gives it a critical edge by claiming that the development of the productive forces now allows, even compels, the emergence of a society based on radically different principles. In all previous societies (apart, perhaps, from the very earliest) the most important elements in them – the productive forces – had been owned by a small minority of the population who had used this economic power to exploit the majority. Thus hitherto existing societies were divided along class lines (class being defined by a common relationship to the means of production) and were inherently conflictual. This conflict had conditioned all the cultural aspects of such societies which were ideological in the sense that they embodied beliefs and practices which served to maintain an asymmetrical distribution of economic and political power. For those who held economic, and therefore political, power also controlled intellectual production: the ruling ideas of each age were the ideas of the ruling class. With its

visionary *mélange* of the thought of G.W.F. Hegel and D. Ricardo, Marxism insists that this state of affairs is not inevitable and that the growth of productive power gives birth to a society in which the major economic resources pass into common ownership, and distribution is capable of being organized no longer according to power, or even right, but according to need.

The accounts to be found in Marx (and most of his followers) of the political and economic organization of such a society are, at best, skeletal. Marx declined to write what he called 'recipes for the cookshops of the future'. This was reasonable enough in his own terms: since he held that ideas were largely determined by existing social arrangements, any detailed account of future communist society would be open to the charge of speculative idealism – the elaboration of ideas that had no firm root in actually existing society, a charge with which he himself castigated the utopian socialists. But it was, nevertheless, a lacuna which left later Marxists with little guidance as to the form which a post-revolutionary society should take.

The third element in Marxism is an account of how to move from the present to the alternative emerging society. In some versions, this is presented as an almost automatic concomitant of the breakdown of CAPITALISM which, under the pressure of the development of the productive forces, will prove as transitory as all previous modes of production. In other versions, the majoritarian working class is given a greater role in bringing about the revolutionary transformation of society. But any theory of proletarian revolution had to confront the difficult question of the political organization of the working class. Marx himself had not had to deal with the problem of the relationship between leadership, party and masses. The only organizations in which Marx was active were the Communist League, which was a propaganda group only several hundred strong, and the First International, which was a loose federation of sects and trade unions. The era of the mass party came only after Marx's death. Although he had declared that the emancipation of the working class would be achieved by the workers themselves, it was clear that their leaders, beginning with Marx himself, would be almost exclusively of bourgeois origin. Thus anyone –

from a Leninist proposing a highly centralized 'vanguard' party to lead workers (who would otherwise have the most inadequate views about politics) to a libertarian socialist who believed that political power should be vested directly in workers' assemblies – could claim, without fear of refutation, that they were in the true Marxist tradition.

These three components are all to be found in the work of Marx himself whose influence, so small during his lifetime, expanded enormously after his death. This influence was at first evident in the growth of the Social Democratic Party in Germany, but reached worldwide dimensions following the success of the Bolsheviks in Russia in 1917. Paradoxically, although the main thrust of Marxist thought was to anticipate that a proletarian revolution would inaugurate the transition to socialism in advanced industrial countries, Marxism was most successful in developing or third world countries such as Russia or, particularly, China. This success was due in large part to the two additions that Lenin made to Marx's legacy: the idea of the vanguard party and that of imperialism. In Lenin's view, the agents of revolutionary transformation could never, if left to their own devices, attain to a sufficiently revolutionary political consciousness and would therefore need the leadership of a party of professional revolutionaries who alone could provide the overall vision and guidance that would be essential in such a complex and far-ranging undertaking. Secondly, the relatively recent expansion of capitalist enterprise into Africa and Asia meant that the conflict which Marx had tended to see inside nation-states was now reproduced on a world scale as imperialism and colonialism, bolstering an otherwise decadent capitalism. These two additional ideas both explained to the victims of western power why they found themselves in such a parlous state and also gave their indigenous modernizing elites a justification for their anti-colonial struggles.

In the west, by contrast, the Marxist movement has met with little practical success. After the crises following the First World War, the lack of revolutionary enthusiasm among the working class, coupled with the growing disillusion with the Soviet version of Marxism, has entailed the virtual eclipse of Marxism as a political movement. All the earlier Marxist intellectual leaders, from Marx and Engels themselves to the Bolshevik leaders and Antonio Gramsci, had all been active politicians. After the Second World War, however, the most prominent Marxist thinkers tended to be theoreticians divorced from practice. This is certainly true of the two main innovative schools of western Marxism which have flourished in the last few decades. The French-inspired structuralist version, whose leading exponent was Louis Althusser, produced extremely subtle accounts of Marxism which privileged structure over agency and inculcated political passivity. The Frankfurt school, on the other hand, while conserving part of the Hegelian ancestry of Marxism in such thinkers as H. Marcuse and J. Habermas, advocated a critical theory of society which, although at times brilliant in its cultural analyses, was consistently evasive in politics and economics.

The gradual realization that Marxism did not contain the solutions originally expected has led to a less hostile attitude to Christianity. Indeed, the history of western Marxism can be read as one long attempt to rehabilitate the impact of the ideological superstructure of society (including religion) as at least relatively independent of the economic base. Marx himself had little to say about religion. His later works were influenced by the progressive scientific *Zeitgeist* which treated religion as outmoded superstition. His earlier writings, however, with their powerful metaphors of religion as the opium of the people, the flowers on the chain, or the sigh of the oppressed creature, have provided considerable food for reflective Christian thought, particularly for those who have read these comments as containing a positive evaluation of religion as a vehicle of protest. While Marx did not think religion wholly false, he did, nevertheless, insist that 'religion has no content of its own and lives not from heaven but from earth, and falls of itself with the dissolution of the inverted reality whose theory it is.' Thus, for him, religion was metaphysically and sociologically misguided and its disappearance was a necessary precondition for any radical amelioration of social conditions.

Among Marx's followers, V.I. Lenin and the Bolsheviks, by contrast, reverted to a pre-Hegelian view of religion as quite simply false.

With the installation of a crude form of dialectical materialism at the heart of Soviet ideology, its attitude to religion remained rigidly negative. In the west, however, the rethinking of the role of the superstructure led to a more generous approach. This is particularly the case with Antonio Gramsci, whose discussions of religion are probably the most suggestive of any Marxist thinker. One of Gramsci's prime interests was the role of intellectuals and of cultural hegemony. What Gramsci sought to study above all was the historical role of the Catholic church. In the *Prison Notebooks* of 1948–65 he was concerned to analyse in detail the changing relationship between the church and its members as providing the traditional model for the relationship of intellectuals to the masses. Thus the history of the church provided him with examples of both traditional and organic intellectuals, the medieval Catholic world was a supreme example of the exercise of hegemony, and the Reformation was a model for the intellectual and moral reform movement that Gramsci wished to see spearheaded in his own time by the Communist Party. The Party, as the Modern Prince, the collective intellectual consciousness of the working class, should learn the lesson of intellectual hegemony from the church which it was due to replace. The Frankfurt school, too, had some interest in religion: Walter Benjamin wrote essays which contained brilliant flashes of a secularized Jewish messianism; Ernst Bloch's massive and maverick *Principle of Hope* drew heavily on biblical sources; and Lukács's pupil Lucien Goldmann in his study of Jansenism produced the most impressive piece of Marxist analysis of religion. Structuralist versions of Marxism, however, although formally less hostile to religion, to which they allotted a place in the social structure, tended to neglect religion once it had been pigeon-holed.

In common with most other intellectual disciplines, Christian theology has been considerably influenced by some aspects of Marxism. Marxism has been the major critical social theory of the twentieth century, and those Christian thinkers who have felt that their religious beliefs had to have some connection with a social and political reform programme inevitably turned to Marxism for some inspiration. Writers as different as Jacques Maritain and Reinhold Niebuhr both subjected the Marxism of the 1930s to searching and sometimes positive evaluation. In post-1945 western Europe the polycentrism of Marxism inaugurated by the Sino-Soviet split and the distancing of European communist parties from Moscow meant that there was an increasing opportunity for 'dialogue' between Christianity and Marxism – particularly a Marxism that had taken account of the recently published writings of the young Marx, with their interest in philosophy and humanism. Within the Christian churches, also, a similar process could be discerned. In the reformulations of Marxism, the crucial issue was the breakdown of the hard-and-fast distinction between base and superstructure and of the consistent emphasis of the former at the expense of the latter: in theology, too, the distinction between God and human beings, heaven and earth, had been radically reformulated. Under the impact of existentialism and humanism, theology underwent a substantial shift of focus. Indeed, during the ensuing dialogue some positions became rather blurred: a Christian theologian could write a book entitled *The Death of God* while a Marxist atheist was the author of *God is Not Yet Dead*. Whether you were a Christian or a Marxist seemed almost to take second place to the question of what *kind* of Christian or Marxist you were.

This dialogue remained rather intellectual and eventually petered out. But this was not the case in non-European parts of the world, particularly Central and South America, where the common ground found in the fight for liberation appeared at some times to obliterate all distinctions. In the early 1970s the idea of a theology incorporating the Marxist materialist conception of history was only tentatively advanced by a few. By the end of the decade, however, there were a growing number of Christians who not only professed themselves to be Marxists, but also considered their Marxism to be an indispensable part of their Christianity. From the point of view of the third world, much previous western theology of the 'death of God' variety, with its proclamation of a 'secular gospel' and its concentration on humanism and the individual, derived its inspiration from L. Feuerbach and thus seemed static and ultimately conservative compared to the practical, revolutionary emphasis of Marx. The liberation theologians (see LIBERATION THEOLOGY) are convinced that basic revolutionary change is necessary. In the words of one of their leading exponents, José Míguez Bonino, their presupposition is that 'the socio-analytical tools, the historical horizon of interpretation, the insight into the dynamics of the social process, and the revolutionary ethos and programme which Marxism has either received and appropriated or itself created are, however corrected or reinterpreted, indispensable for revolutionary change.' Under the impact of Marxist approaches, liberation theology wishes to relativize the concepts in which the Bible is expressed and accord them no more permanent authority than it does to biblical cosmology. It seeks to give a social and political dimension to traditional Christian concepts, which tend to have become 'privatized'. Returning to the Marxist tradition which saw early Christianity as the religion of the oppressed, 'poverty' is not something spiritual or individual, but implies solidarity with the poor and a practical protest *against* poverty. And salvation is viewed, at least in the first instance, as liberation from specific social and political oppression. What is clearly evident in all these changes of perspective is the influence of the Marxist criticism of any individual morality divorced from the social and economic framework.

The relative enthusiasm for Marxism in Latin America – at least for its social analyses – contrasts sharply with the hatred of Marxism in much of eastern Europe and the former Soviet Union as a symbol of anti-religious oppression. In the latter context many have described Marxism itself as some kind of ersatz religion. Such a view contrasts strongly with the general approach of Marx himself, who was much more in line with the views of Friedrich Nietzsche or Sigmund Freud, where religion was viewed as a symptom with meaning that needed deciphering through some kind of 'genealogy'. In such a Marxism the concepts of alienation and emancipation play a central role and the account of Marxism as a secularized form of the Judaeo-Christian tradition gains in plausibility. Marxism obviously contains the idea that history has a purpose that is being relentlessly worked out and contains a powerful vision of future harmony to contrast with present discord. Marx's thought has an eschatological dimension which has strong religious roots. But a conception of the world can have a religious origin without itself being religious. While it may be just about possible to count Feuerbach among the theologians, to put Marx there as well is to disregard his trenchant criticism of the whole Feuerbachian approach. Nor will it do to say that Marxism's anti-religious stance is merely a product of local circumstances and not of its essence. It is, of course, true that Marx's account of religious alienation is born out of the extreme Lutheranism of his time, that Engels's views bear the stamp of the grim pietism rife in the Wuppertal of his boyhood, and that even Lenin's vitriolic remarks are understandable in the context of the virtually total subordination to Tsarist autocracy of the contemporary Russian Orthodox church. But the Marxist critique of religion goes beyond mere historical contingency. It is possible to claim that Marxism inherits major themes from Christianity, but the type of inheritance implies, here as in most cases, the death of the testator. Marxism may, in some sense and in some aspects, be a secularized religion, but it remains secularized and it should be treated in its own categories and not translated back into religious ones.

On such a view, the Marxist account of religion contains a strongly critical edge and one that Christians neglect at their peril. At its best, the Marxist critique of religion has the same rather cynical but sympathetic attitude that an insightful child can have of its parents. Certainly the Marxist approach is more powerful than the anaemic dissections produced by variants of logical positive and linguistic analysis or by the reductionist and narcissistic discussions of some disciples of Freud or Nietzsche. From a sociological or descriptive point of view, Marxism has made an impressive contribution by stressing the strong connection between religious beliefs and social and economic interests. In its aspirational – not to say Promethean – aspects it is less impressive: a secular faith which cannot deliver secular goods. Contrary to Marx's own famous saying, his followers have proved better at interpreting the world than at changing it.

See also CHRISTIAN SOCIALISM; ECONOMIC ANALYSIS AND ETHICS; FAITH AND REASON; SOCIAL QUESTIONS; WORK AND LEISURE.

Bibliography

Writings
Marx, Karl 1975– : *Collected Works*, 50 vols. Moscow: Progress Publishers.

Critical works
Bentley, James 1982: *Between Marx and Christ*. London: Verso.
Goldmann, Lucien [1957] 1964: *The Hidden God*. London: Routledge.
Gramsci, Antonio 1976: *Selections from the Prison Notebooks*, ed. Q. Hoare and P. Nowell Smith. London: Lawrence and Wishart, especially part III.
Gutiérrez, Gustavo [1971] 1974: *A Theology of Liberation*. London: SCM Press.
Kee, Alastair 1990: *Marx and the Failure of Liberation Theology*. London: SCM Press.
Kolakowski, Leszek 1978: *Main Currents of Marxism*, 3 vols. Oxford: Oxford University Press.
Lash, Nicholas 1981: *A Matter of Hope: A Theologian's Reflections on the Thought of Karl Marx*. London: DLT.
McGovern, Arthur 1980: *Marxism: An American Christian Perspective*. New York: Orbis.
MacIntyre, Alasdair 1971: *Marxism and Christianity*. Harmondsworth: Penguin.
McKown, Denis 1975: *The Classical Marxist Critique of Religion: Marx, Engels, Lenin, Kautsky*. The Hague: Nijhoff.
McLellan, David 1980: *Marxism after Marx*. London: Macmillan.
McLellan, David 1987: *Marxism and Religion: A Description and Evaluation of the Marxist Critique of Christianity*. London: Macmillan.
Thrower, James 1983: *Marxist–Leninist 'Scientific Atheism' and the Study of Religion and Atheism in the USSR*. Amsterdam: Mouton.

DAVID MCLELLAN

medical ethics Medical ethics is concerned with the questions of right, wrong, duty, conscience, good and evil as they arise in medical practice.

From the time of Hippocrates (b. 460 BC), if not before, practising physicians have sought to regulate their attitudes and behaviour by moral criteria. Most contemporary medical codes reflect the work of the Unitarian physician Thomas Percival who published an early book on medical ethics in 1803. In 1948, the World Health Organization (WHO) adopted a modern version of the Hippocratic oath, in which the practitioner pledges himself to the service of humanity, and to 'maintain the utmost respect for human life from the time of conception'. He swears 'even under threat, I will not use my medical knowledge contrary to the laws of humanity' (*Declaration of Geneva*).

The Judaeo-Christian tradition provided similar moral criteria. The Old Testament health laws, the attitude of Jesus Christ towards the sick and the ministry of healing within the church affirmed the sacred humanity of the sick person. Christians stressed the motive and duty of compassion in the care of the sick. There has been a strong relationship between Judaeo-Christian faith and medical practice.

There have also been areas of conflict. Certain theologies of life, providence and suffering opposed certain medical practices on the grounds that they implied that issues of life and death were not in the hands of God. As western society moved away from its Christian roots, further areas of disagreement between religion and medicine emerged.

Currently, the field of medical ethics is one of some confusion. First, there is no consensus on the fundamental basis for ethical decisions. Much medical practice is still rooted in convictions which are consistent with Christian faith (for example, the sanctity of human life, the duty of the alleviation of suffering, the right to truth, the need for informed consent, the importance of confidentiality in the relationship of trust between doctor and patient). However, the Christian theological basis for these convictions is often only a memory (see SECULARIZATION), or has been abandoned in favour of a consequentialist ethic in which the goodness of actions is measured only or largely in terms of consequences, or of a moral relativism in which moral values are regarded as matters only of private judgement and not objective truth. A consequentialist ethic tends to find unacceptable the Christian belief that innocent human beings have an absolute right not to be deliberately killed, arguing instead for the concept of 'a life worth living' (see Glover, 1977), resulting in very different judgements about, for example, abortion, treatment of handicapped neonates and the care of the dying.

Second, the rapid technological advances of recent years, although bringing many benefits, also raise questions about the nature and destiny of human beings. 'Is there something about man that dare not be changed, something in his very nature that dare not be violated, if he is to remain human?' (Thielicke, [1968] 1970). If there is something 'given' about our humanity, as Christians have affirmed, to what extent may we manipulate one another by medical interventions? Surgery, transplantation, artificial insemination and in-vitro fertilization, changing DNA to intervene in human heredity, pharmacological mood control, all raise this question. If human beings have the moral freedom to take responsibility for their health, does this freedom extend to control over the issues of life and death for oneself or for others?

Some Christian ethicists have expressed considerable concern at the reductionistic and technological mind-set of contemporary culture (O'Donovan, 1984). The more we see ourselves as interveners in the system, as problem solvers who by mere application of technical expertise can deal with life's difficulties, the more our estimation of what we can do, rather than what we should do, becomes the touchstone of what we will do. This is particularly pertinent in discussions about reproductive technology.

A third aspect of current confusion arises from the tension between the imperative of research and development, coupled with the enormous cost of modern medicine, and necessarily finite financial and other resources. Who may benefit, when not all can? On what basis are medical resources to be allocated? Is this a question of medical decision, local management, or national budget? To what extent is the practice of medicine inevitably constrained by politics and cost–benefit calculations? Procedures for allocating resources are essential; some, such as QALY (quality adjusted life years), are controversial.

Roman Catholic moral theologians, and (fewer) Protestant ethicists have in recent years engaged with the rapidly changing medical field at the level both of fundamental presuppositions and of particular moral prescriptions. Encyclicals, reports and books have been published; societies for medical practitioners and theologians have been formed; medical ethics is taught in theological faculties, and less so, though increasingly, in some medical faculties.

Here are two examples of a theological approach. In *Medical Ethics* (1972), Bernard Häring, a Catholic, develops a systematic approach to questions relating to the life, death and health of human beings. Belief in God the Creator is a call to co-responsibility within the world of human relationships. The incarnation of Christ sets a new value on the human body. The concepts of sin and redemption underlie our understanding of health and human dignity. Love and justice are to characterize all our activities. Christ's passion, death and resurrection shed a unique light on bodily existence, and the meaning of illness, suffering and death. In *Patient as Person* (1970), and *Ethics at the Edges of Life* (1978), the Protestant Paul Ramsey argues that Christian morality is derived from the claims of covenant loyalty to God, and not just (as in some secular ethics) from the ends in view. There is an ethic of means as well as ends. The obligations of medical ethics flow from the covenant relationship between doctor and patient. Ramsey argues for the radical equality of all people before God, and for the sacredness of each person as someone to whom is owed the duty of neighbour love.

We clearly cannot explore particular issues in medical ethics in any depth here. Current Christian interest includes: abortion; contraception; sterilization; human embryo research; genetic engineering; euthanasia; care of the dying, the mentally ill and the handicapped; transplantation; reproductive technology; experimentation; truth-telling in diagnosis; patient's consent and issues of confidentiality; the meaning of health; and allocation of resources. We will isolate a few of these for brief comment.

Abortion has led to considerable debate around two fundamental questions. The first concerns the status of the human foetus – whether it is personal, potentially or actually, and if so, from what stage of development. Christians have differed, some taking a gradualist view of human beginnings, others arguing from the doctrines of the *Imago Dei* and of the virginal conception of Jesus that the foetus is a person with a right to life from conception. The second question concerns the resolution of conflict between the rights of the foetus and other moral values, such as the life, health or wishes of the mother, the rights of the father, the conscience of the medical staff, the cost to society. Some Christians believe that foetus and mother are to be accorded equal protection in law. Others argue that as the mother is a person already in a developed network of human relationships, her life, and possibly her health (including social, psychological and economic well-being) and her wishes, are to be accorded more weight than the rights of the foetus. In many societies, the law supports the latter view. The principle of *double effect*, which depends on the distinction between intention and foresight, has sometimes been invoked, arguing, for example, that pregnancy may be terminated for the sake of the mother's health, while knowing but not intending that the foetus will die.

Catholic and Protestant thinkers have tended to take different views on *contraception*. Pope Paul VI's encyclical *Humanae Vitae* gives a Christian significance to the act of sexual intercourse. Responsible parenthood and faithfulness to God's design will recognize that every 'marriage act must remain open to the transmission of life'. The unitive and procreative aspects of sexual intercourse belong inseparably together, and the contraceptive mentality which seeks to separate them goes against true humanity. Not all Catholic thinkers concur (McCormick, 1981), and Protestants have tended to place more weight on individual freedom of choice and conscience, on the stewardship of responsible parenthood in an age of overpopulation, and on the view that a sexual relationship is not merely a series of sexual acts. The unitive and procreative aspects of sexual intercourse can belong in principle together, without requiring that every sexual act is open to procreation. Certain techniques which do separate these aspects in principle, however, such as AID (artificial insemination by an anonymous donor – often equated with adultery) or the use of a surrogate womb, have caused Christians of all traditions moral concern.

Ethical issues at the end of life are no less problematic. The definition of death itself is not unambiguous, nor is the point at which treatment of the living should give way to caring for the dying. Modern intensive care procedures, with technological possibilities for prolonging life and for prolonging dying, have led to proposals for theological as well as medical criteria to discern the presence of protectable human life. J. Fletcher (1979) outlined a series of 'indicators of personhood', such as minimum intelligence, capacity for self-control, capacity to relate to others and so on, without which the dying human being is no longer thought to be a protectable person. Such an approach has been criticized on the grounds that personal life is an 'alien dignity' conferred by God, not dependent on personal capacities.

In the debates concerning the termination of life by choice, whether the assisted suicide of active euthanasia, or the passive decision to 'let nature take its course', moral distinctions between 'acts' and 'omissions' are often made. To administer pain-relieving medication which incidentally shortens life is one thing. To allow a dying person to die with dignity and without intrusive medical intervention is another. Actively to cause the death of a patient – whether at their request or that of someone else – is yet a third. The distinction (favoured by some Catholic moralists) between 'ordinary' means (normal and tried medical procedures with a good likelihood of benefit) and 'extraordinary' means (which involve excessive burden or risk and uncertain benefit) can be useful, though today's 'extraordinary' is often tomorrow's 'ordinary'. Voluntary euthanasia also raises questions of the autonomy of human choice, the right of a person to choose death, difficulties in deciding what 'voluntary' means, the appropriate expression of compassion, and changes in the perceptions of the doctor's role.

The *doctor–patient relationship* is being affected in many ways. The loss of traditional privacy through the socialization and centralization of modern medicine, with computer data banks, leads to less intimacy and to serious questions of confidentiality. The professionalization of medicine raises questions, not least the need for full and informed patient consent. Economic constraints affect medical priorities. Issues of self-regulation and the relation of medical ethics to the law concern many doctors.

The definition of *health* is open to dispute. This depends partly on whether health is viewed in relation to disease (a pathological state), illness (the patient's perception of being unwell), or sickness (a social view of abnormality), and partly on whether 'health' is approached maximally in terms of human well-being (as proposed by the World Health Organization) or minimally in terms of the allocation of limited resources for health care delivery. In Christian terms, health can be understood in relation to *shalom*, God's purpose for well-being at all levels of life and relationship, enjoyed in part in this life, and in fullness in the life to come. Medical practice may facilitate this purpose, though the difficulties of commending Christian values in a pluralist society are manifold. In Christian terms, medicine takes place within a fallen and transient but redeemable world, in which death and suffering are inevitable, but in which there is hope of change. It must avoid the mechanization of physical life, seeing it only as a means to some other end. It must also avoid the absolutizing of physical life into an end in itself, ignoring spiritual realities.

See also ETHICS; SEXUAL ETHICS; SOCIAL QUESTIONS.

Bibliography

Church Information Office 1965: *Abortion*. London.

Church Information Office 1975: *On Dying Well*. London.

Duncan, A.S., Dunstan, G.R., and Welbourn, R.B. 1977: *Dictionary of Medical Ethics*. London: Darton, Longman and Todd. Revised and enlarged edn 1981.

Fletcher, J. 1979: *Humanhood: Essays in Biomedical Ethics*. New York: Prometheus.

Glover, J. 1977: *Causing Death and Saving Lives*. Harmondsworth: Penguin.

Häring, B. 1972: *Medical Ethics*. Slough: St Paul Publications.

Häring, B. 1975: *Manipulation*. Slough: St Paul Publications.

Hauerwas, S. 1988: *Suffering Presence*. Edinburgh: T & T Clark.

Lammers, S.E., and Verhey, A. 1987: *On Moral Medicine: Theological Perspectives In Medical Ethics*. Grand Rapids: Eerdmans.

Linacre Centre 1984: *Euthanasia and Clinical Practice*. London: Linacre Centre.

McCormick, R.A. 1981: *How Brave a New World?* London: SCM Press.

Mahoney, J. 1984: *Bioethics and Belief*. London: Sheed and Ward.

Noonan, J.T., Jr, ed. 1970: *The Morality of Abortion: Legal and Historical Perspectives*. Cambridge, Mass.: Harvard University Press.

O'Donovan, O.M.T. 1984: *Begotten or Made?* Oxford: Clarendon Press.

Ramsey, P. 1970: *The Patient as Person: Explorations in Medical Ethics*. New Haven: Yale University Press.

Ramsey, P. 1978: *Ethics at the Edges of Life*. New Haven and London: Yale University Press.

Thielicke, H. 1964: *Theological Ethics*, vol. 3, trans. London: James Clarke.

Thielicke, H. [1968] 1970: *The Doctor as Judge of Who Shall Live and Who Shall Die*, trans. E.A. Cooperrider. Philadelphia: Fortress Press.

DAVID J. ATKINSON

metaphor See LANGUAGE, RELIGIOUS.

method in theology Theological method exhibits and subserves, in the first place, the nature and character of the theology in question. Patristic and medieval usage can make of theology a word from God, a story about God, a testimony concerning God, a prayer to God. In modern usage, however, theology characteristically means the reflective enterprise that both feeds on and intends to serve those primary manifestations and deliverances of Christian faith that occur as revelation, narration, proclamation and worship. Reflective theology seeks to understand, clarify and explain the FAITH. As an activity of individual thinking believers, it usually takes guidance from the dogma or official doctrine of the faith community to which the theologian belongs (see DOCTRINE AND DOGMA). It may enrich both faith and doctrine; it may also criticize particular instances of faith and doctrine in the name of a more authentic faith and doctrine.

That last-claimed function brings to the fore the question of criteria for faith, doctrine and theology. In older usage, the question was put as that of 'authorities'; modern usage tends rather to speak of 'sources'. These are often grouped under four heads: Scripture, tradition, reason and experience. Since each of these is a different kind of thing and may exercise appropriately different functions, they may operate in various harmonious combinations. In practice, however, they sometimes assume competitive roles, especially when controversial issues in the life of the faith community need to be decided in a theologically responsible way. Certainly it is possible also to make a rough characterization of

369

a reflective theologian's method according to the relative prominence and respective functions occupied by Scripture, tradition, reason and experience in his or her work or system.

At the threshold of the modern period, the Protestant Reformers asserted the primacy of Scripture as the standard and source for criticism and renewal of a church that they perceived to have departed in its preaching and practice from primitive Christianity. Correspondingly, much of Martin Luther's and John Calvin's theology was done in the form of commentary upon Scripture, whether from the pulpit, the podium or the study. Yet they also made use of post-Scriptural tradition in so far as it had faithfully interpreted and channelled the biblical message. Thus Lutheran and Reformed confessions appropriate the ancient creeds and the dogmatic decisions of the great councils of the early church. While Luther formulated no theological system as such, Calvin's systematic exposition of Christian faith in the mature *Institutes* is basically creedal in structure and cites such favoured Fathers as Augustine and Chrysostom. Both Luther and Calvin held that human reasoning capacities had, in matters of salvation, been gravely impaired by the fall: the thinking of believers should be captive to Christ. For both Luther and Calvin, the experience of faith was the gift and product of the gospel, a fruit not a source.

In the Reformation controversies, Roman Catholic Christianity set great store by the continuity it claimed with the church of the apostles. The Council of Trent pronounced that 'the gospel' as both 'saving truth and moral discipline' is 'contained in written books and in unwritten traditions which, having been received by the apostles either from the lips of Christ himself or at the dictation of the Holy Spirit, have been handed down until they reached us'. There was and remains debate as to whether Scripture and oral/practical traditions are thereby to be seen simply as parallel or interactive *modes* of transmission, or whether the traditions bring *additional content* beyond the Scriptures. In any case, clear importance is given by Trent to 'the catholic church' as the place and agent, in a 'continuous succession', of the preservation of the gospel and its interpretation (with what will become an increasingly dogmatized status for the magisterium, or teaching office, of the bishops and, at their head, the pope). In line with its strong sense of tradition, Roman Catholic theology long continued as a principal method the commentary on medieval schoolmen whom the Protestants had often viewed as exemplifying the misuse of reason; and in fact the greater confidence which Roman Catholics placed in unaided human reason led them to value what 'natural theology' could achieve before and outside the light brought by a gospel revelation received in faith. Roman Catholic theologians treated Christian experience with suspicion in so far as it bore an individualistic cast that appeared to characterize Protestantism.

The classic Anglican theologian Richard Hooker (1554–1600) sought to bind Scripture, tradition and reason together while subjecting them all to the 'laws' which God had ordained for creation. England, however, became a birthplace and home of several tendencies that privileged above all the place of reason in theology. While Cambridge Platonism still harboured a mystical streak, Isaac Newton's mechanistic account of the universe and John Locke's advocacy of empiricism as a general method influenced theologians towards a naturalistic and rationalistic approach that sought to match the standards and prestige of the rising sciences. In its British and continental forms alike, the Enlightenment questioned or rejected the claim to a special revelation to which the Scriptures had borne witness. According to G.E. Lessing, the 'necessary truths of reason' could not possibly depend on any 'accidental truths of history'; and the critical mind in Germany devoted itself to removing from canonical status those features of the Scriptural story whose apparently miraculous character offended the new science. The historico-critical method was extended also to the development of Christian doctrine in ways which, by showing the contingency of dogmatic formulations, reckoned to challenge their substantive content as traditionally perceived.

Meanwhile, the Cartesian strand of rationalism had, by its focus on the individual subject, ironically prepared the way for the elevation of subjective experience in a sense that denied the sufficiency of reason. While, after the initial Reformation, Reformed and Lutheran orthodoxies had applied a rediscovered Aristotelian syllogistic logic to theology in a synthetic and deductive methodology, an inevitable reaction against such scholasticism gave rise in the seventeenth and eighteenth centuries to a pietism that favoured a 'living faith'. The Scriptures were now searched less for the sake of founding theological systems than for their testimony to experiential patterns of salvation. Hermeneutical intelligence was put, in the typical case of John Wesley, to the service of evangelistic preaching, spiritual renewal and moral growth. Not that pietism was intrinsically opposed to reasonably and ecclesiastically ordered theology. While the religious self-consciousness, for the pietistically formed Friedrich Schleiermacher, consisted experientially in the 'feeling of total dependence', its instantiation as faith in the redeeming God of Jesus Christ inevitably bore a communal or ecclesial character, and 'dogmatic theology is the science which systematizes the doctrine prevalent in a Christian church at a given time' (*The Christian Faith*, revised edition 1830–1, §19).

Reason and experience continued to set the parameters for much of nineteenth-century theology, particularly in the Protestant faculties of German universities, which, while themselves coming to terms in one way or another with Kant's location of religion in the sphere of 'practical reason', largely set the intellectual pace for academic theologians in the English-speaking world also (see KANTIANISM). The rational and empirical approach manifested itself most radically in a positivistic or scientist historicism exercised upon the Scriptures and tradition in ways that inevitably challenged their authority, for they were not amenable to a 'methodological atheism' that had 'the death of God' as its covert presupposition or final result. On the more romantic side, however, a renewed interest in history provided a cultural stimulus to the recovery of vital tradition as a theological force in the Catholic Tübingen school (J.A. Möhler and others) (see ROMANTICISM), in John Henry Newman, and on into some streams of the Thomistic revival of the late nineteenth and early twentieth centuries. In Anglicanism, it was the more traditionally oriented biblical and patristic scholars of the period who kept open for theology rather wider horizons than modern reductionism would have allowed (the Oxford of

the *Lux Mundi* theologians benefited from ecclesial communion with the Cambridge of Westcott and Lightfoot).

In the twentieth century, the chief continuators of the 'anthropological turn' marked by the preference given to reason and experience have been those 'philosophical theologians' who have sensed Feuerbach looking over their shoulder even while seeking to halt, if not reverse, his reduction of theology to anthropology. Characteristic, on the Protestant side, was Paul Tillich, whose 'method of correlation' presented divine revelation as the given but to-be-discovered answer to the questions posed by human existence (*Systematic Theology*, 1951–63). On the Roman Catholic side, Karl Rahner's theology sought to follow the mystery of human self-transcendence as it proceeded towards the encompassing and enabling horizon of divine self-communicating grace (*Foundations of Christian Faith*, 1976, trans. 1978).

From the viewpoint of historic Christianity, however, the most significant feature of the middle third of the twentieth century was the reassertion, in both doctrinal substance and theological method, of the Scriptures and (especially the patristic) tradition. As 'modern civilization', with the connivance of 'liberal Christianity', had led to a world war (and would then lead to another), Karl Barth's commentary on *The Letter to the Romans* of 1922 (the decisive revised edition) brought the strange and powerful vision of a biblical eschatology into dominance within theology, and although the stark dialectics of judgement and salvation came to be slightly moderated in Barth's massive *Church Dogmatics* of 1932–68, this life-work of the most prominent theologian of his time continued to expound Scriptural themes with the support of the patristic and Reformation traditions. His approach meshed with a two-generation flourishing of biblical theology, in which Scripture scholars framed their detailed exegesis within a salvation-historical account of Christianity (*Heilsgeschichte*) that virtually brought them into the realm of dogmatic theology (G. von Rad, W. Eichrodt, G. E. Wright, C.H. Dodd, V. Taylor, O. Cullmann, E. Käsemann and many others). They were gradually joined by Roman Catholic scholars, who brought about a renewal in the biblical aspect of theology in their church (L.

Cerfaux, F.X. Durrwell, R. Schnackenburg and others). Roman Catholics contributed strongly to the recovery of patristic tradition (Y. Congar, J. Daniélou). The ecumenical convergence on the common ground of early tradition owed much also to the work of Eastern Orthodox theologians who had migrated to the west (G. Florovsky, V. Lossky, P. Evdokimov, A. Schmemann, J. Meyendorf). The early 1960s probably marked the high point of a broad consensus in the substance, method and style of theology on the basis of Scripture and the classical tradition.

In the mid- to late 1960s God again briefly died, and in the bereft world theologians attempted to recast the Christian faith in a non-transcendental way: 'the secular city' (H. Cox) was offered 'the secular meaning of the gospel' (P. Van Buren). The last three decades have, however, witnessed a remarkable recovery on the part of theologians and of their principal subject. The recent and contemporary scene is confused but vital, with claims being staked for all four of the principal sources of theology: Scripture, tradition, reason and experience.

The historico-critical study of the Scriptures served well to recall the concreteness of an incarnational religion, but the limits of a positivistic approach have become increasingly apparent; and among the new methods now being tried, it is those broadly describable as literary which appear to have the most to offer theology. In particular, the understanding of Scripture as a narrative or story that renders the divine character, and indeed presence, and invites participation, has achieved influence through the work of H.W. Frei (*The Eclipse of Biblical Narrative*, 1974; *The Identity of Jesus Christ*, 1975). It stands behind the 'cultural-linguistic' approach to theology of G.A. Lindbeck (*The Nature of Doctrine*, 1984): 'A Scriptural world is able to absorb the universe. It supplies the interpretive framework within which believers seek to live their lives and understand reality.' If the potential for this Scriptural infusion into systematic theology has not yet been fully realized, the reason may partly reside in the suspicion with which some of its advocates (such as N. Lash) themselves view 'system'. The 'story' of the Exodus, and of the new exodus enacted in Jesus' ministry, death and resurrection, has, however, been taken up by liberation theologians with their interest in concrete praxis.

Tradition finds its access into current Protestant and Anglican theology by way of the interest in hermeneutics. The philosophical midwives have been H.-G. Gadamer and P. Ricoeur, with their stress on an interpretative community that is both synchronic and diachronic. Texts are traced in the history of their effects (*Wirkungsgeschichte*) and G. Ebeling can see 'church history as the history of the interpretation of Holy Scripture' (*Wort Gottes und Tradition*, 1964). An Anglican example is provided by A. Louth and his advocacy of a 'return to allegory' as a method of reading Scripture (*Discerning the Mystery*, 1983), and a Methodist example by G. Wainwright, who considers the liturgy as a transmissive and hermeneutical continuum for the Christian story or vision (*Doxology*, 1980).

Reason is used reductively by some. In his *Remaking of Christian Doctrine* of 1974, M.F. Wiles stresses the need for economy in substance and argument, but too sweeping a use of Ockham's razor risks shaving off the very beard of Aaron down which the oil of divine bounty flows. Some theologians have taken to heart A. MacIntyre's warning, in *Whose Justice? Which Rationality?* of 1988, that reasoning is conditioned by cultural traditions, and notably in modernity by deleterious effects of the Enlightenment. But post-modern irrational-isms have been countered, on the basis of at least an implicit Logos doctrine and perhaps the redemptive effect of Christian faith on the cognitive capacities, by vigorous assertions of the place of a properly exercised reason. In the Roman Catholic tradition, B. Lonergan applies to theological method the fourfold structure of all knowing: the experience of data, the under-standing of their meaning, the assessment of their value, and finally an evaluative decision (*Method in Theology*, 1971). A critical realism also marks the Reformed T.F. Torrance's insistence on the scientific character of theol-ogy as a discipline governed by its object, with the human knower participating in the given structures of being (*Theological Science*, 1969; *Reality and Scientific Theology*, 1985). The Lutheran W. Pannenberg grounds the scientif-ic character of theology in the status it gives as working hypothesis – to be finally confirmed or falsified – to 'God as the all–determining reality' (*Theology and the Philosophy of Science*, 1973, trans. 1976). The revival in French Catholic theology in the 1970s and 1980s has been largely fuelled by the attention given to the human sciences, and especially semiotics (as in the five-volume collaborative enterprise, *Initiation à la pratique de la théologie* of 1982–3).

Human experience, broadly understood, plays a strongly formative part in much contemporary theology. For E. Schillebeeckx it is the experience of suffering and grace as illumined by the story of Jesus Christ (*Jesus*, 1974, trans. 1979; *Christ: The Experience of Jesus as Lord*, 1977, trans. 1980). The political edge is sharpened – by oppression, conflict and hope for liberation – in much of the theological writing issuing from Latin America and parts of Africa and Asia (the seminal and paradigmatic work was G. Gutiérrez's *A Theology of Liberation*, 1971, trans. 1973). In her systematic *Sexism and God-Talk* of 1983, the North American feminist Rosemary Radford Ruether takes 'whatever promotes the full humanity of women' as the criterion for taking or leaving Scriptural material and looks to supply from 'pagan resources' what is otherwise lacking.

The great diversity of method, style and substance on the current theological scene reflects, and is compounded by the self-conscious attention given to, the diversity of theologians in their own social locations, the publics they seek to address, and the purposes for which they write. Ecumenism at all levels, and in both the synchronic and diachronic senses, is a necessity if further fragmentation is to be avoided (see ECUMENISM).

See also AUTHORITY; BIBLICAL CRITICISM AND INTERPRETATION (1: OLD TESTAMENT and 2: NEW TESTAMENT); TRADITION.

Bibliography

Avis, P. 1986: *The Methods of Modern Theology*. Basingstoke: Marshall Morgan and Scott.

Berkhof, H. [1985] 1989: *Two Hundred Years of Theology: Report of a Personal Journey*, trans. J. Vriend. Grand Rapids: Eerdmans.

Evans, G.R., McGrath, A.E., and Galloway, A.D. 1986: *The Science of Theology*. Basingstoke: Marshall Morgan and Scott; Grand Rapids: Eerdmans.

Fiorenza, F.S. 1991: Systematic theology: task and methods. In *Systematic Theology: Roman Catholic Perspectives*, 2 vols, ed. F.S. Fiorenza and J.P. Galvin. Minneapolis: Fortress, vol. 1, pp. 1–87.

Heron, A.I.C. 1980: *A Century of Protestant Theology*. Philadelphia: Westminster; Guildford: Lutterworth.

Kelsey, D. 1975: *The Uses of Scripture in Recent Theology*. Philadelphia: Fortress; London: SCM Press.

Milbank, J. 1990: *Theology and Social Theory: Beyond Secular Reason*. Oxford: Blackwell.

Nichols, A. 1991: *The Shape of Catholic Theology: An Introduction to its Sources, Principles and History*. Collegeville: Liturgical Press.

Pinnock, C. 1990: *Tracking the Maze: Finding our Way through Modern Theology from an Evangelical Perspective*. San Francisco: Harper and Row.

Placher, W.C. 1989: *Unapologetic Theology: A Christian Voice in Plurastic Conversation*. Louisville: Westminster/John Knox.

Ritschl, D. [1984] 1986: *The Logic of Theology*, trans. J. Bowden. London: SCM Press; Philadelphia: Fortress.

Tracy, D. 1981: *The Analogical Imagination: Christian Theology and the Culture of Pluralism*. New York: Crossroad; London: SCM Press.

Wainwright, G. 1988: *Keeping the Faith: Essays to Mark the Centenary of 'Lux Mundi'*. Philadelphia: Fortress; London: SPCK.

GEOFFREY WAINWRIGHT

Methodism Methodism, which today numbers about sixty million adherents in Methodist and related churches throughout the world, began in the eighteenth century as a movement of evangelistic, moral, sacramental and social revival within the Church of England. It sprang chiefly from the work of the Wesley brothers, John (1703–1791) and Charles (1707–1788). Having in their Oxford days committed themselves to serious Christian practice as members of the 'Holy Club', both brothers underwent in London under Moravian influence at Pentecost 1738 an 'evangelical conversion' in which, as John describes it, 'I felt my heart strangely warmed. I felt I did trust in Christ, Christ alone for salvation; and an assurance was given me that He had taken away *my* sins, even *mine*, and saved *me* from the law of sin and death' (Baker/Heitzenrater 1975–, vol. 18, p. 250). In April 1739, at the insistence of George Whitefield, John 'submitted to be more vile, and proclaimed in the highways the glad tidings of salvation' (Baker/Heitzenrater 1975–, vol. 19, p. 46); and from these beginnings near Bristol there progressed a fifty-year career of open-air preaching which brought converts into the fellowship of tightly structured Methodist 'societies' and 'classes' and encouraged them to seek communion at their parish churches. Both Wesleys were preachers, John the itinerant and Charles the more stable. John was the great organizer and presided at the annual conferences of preachers; Charles was the principal hymn-writer (see MUSIC AND CHRISTIANITY). The Methodist movement spread from England to Ireland and North America, and thence by overseas missions to most parts of the world.

Although some relatively minor shifts can be detected in John Wesley's thought in the last fifty years of his life, and although different nuances can be found between John and Charles (the younger brother remained the more consistently opposed to separation from the Church of England), together they stamped on Methodism a characteristic pattern of thinking and experience. Methodist doctrines are officially expressed in John Wesley's 'Standard Sermons', in his *Explanatory Notes upon the New Testament*, in the Minutes of the Methodist Conferences, and in the abridged version of the Anglican Articles of Religion which Wesley prepared for America. Particularly formative of spirituality, especially in the parts of Methodism remaining under British influence, have been the Wesleyan hymns derived from the *Collection of Hymns for the Use of the People called Methodists* of 1780 (see SPIRITUALITY, CHRISTIAN).

Wesley (by which Methodists mean John, unless otherwise specified) considered himself a classic Christian in the Anglican tradition. In calling himself 'a man of one book' he was indicating that the Scriptures constituted not so much the limits of his reading as the norm of his thinking. He valued the patristic theologians, particularly from the early centuries before the worldly corruption of the church. In his irenic *Letter to a Roman Catholic* of 1749 he set out 'the faith of a true Protestant' in the form of an expansion upon the Nicene–Constantinopolitan creed (Jackson, [1829–31] 1984, vol. 10, pp. 80–6). His writings frequently echo the Book of Common Prayer and the Homilies of the Church of England. In the fifty volumes of his 'Christian Library' he anthologized a wide variety of spiritual authors. Twentieth-century American Methodism has spoken of 'a marrow of Christian truth', a 'living core' that 'stands revealed in Scripture, illumined by tradition, vivified in personal experience, and confirmed by reason' (United Methodist *Discipline* of 1972).

Against deists, Arians and Socinians Wesley held to the doctrines of original sin, the atoning work of Christ and the enabling work of the Holy Spirit, and the 'Three–One God'. These were the objective ground and counterparts to the subjective appropriation of salvation, on which Wesley placed so much practical emphasis that he would characteristically state the 'main doctrines' of Methodism to be 'repentance, faith, and holiness' (for example Jackson [1829–31] 1984, vol. 8, p. 472). Justification was 'by faith alone', with good works as the testimony and test of faith and therefore a condition of *final* salvation. It was 'the regular privilege of believers' to receive an assurance of their present favour with God through the witness of the Holy Spirit with their spirit that they were children of God (cf. Rom. 8: 15f.). New birth through the Holy Spirit was the beginning of sanctification, which was to be brought to a 'Christian perfection' of entire love towards God and neighbour, a moral and spiritual restoration to the Christologically defined 'imago Dei' – even though the errors and frailties of fallen human nature would not finally be overcome this side of death. In twentieth-century British Methodism, the characteristic Wesleyan teachings have been summed up thus: 'All need to be saved; all can be saved; all can know they are saved; all can be saved to the uttermost' (Turner, 1985, p. 45).

Wesley's insistence on the universal sufficiency and scope of Christ's atoning work was accompanied by a rather active view of the faith by which salvation was appropriated: by virtue of Christ's work every man has a measure of free will restored to him, which allows him to accept the gospel and do its works. These traits brought Wesley into conflict with Calvinistic tendencies in the Church of England. He was prepared to come to 'the very edge of Calvinism, 1. in ascribing all good to the free grace of God; 2. in denying all natural free will and all power antecedent to grace; and 3. in excluding all merit from man, even for what he has or does by the grace of God' (Methodist Conference of 1745; see Wainwright, 1987). Yet in his *Predestination Calmly Considered* of 1752 (Jackson, [1829–31] 1984, vol. 10, pp. 204–59) Wesley resolutely argued the case against predestination and an infallible perseverance of the saints, holding that God's promises are both offered to all and conditional upon free acceptance in faith; he liked to quote the Augustinian dictum that 'he who made us without ourselves will not save us without ourselves.' In facing up to the Wesleyan–Calvinist controversy, twentieth-century international conversations between Methodists and Reformed speak rather of 'the fundamental mystery of God's saving grace witnessed to in Scripture' and avow that 'both traditions have gone wrong when they have claimed to know too much about this mystery of God's electing grace and of human responses' (*Together in God's Grace*, 1987).

Christians in the traditions of the magisterial Reformation have in fact suspected Methodism of Pelagian tendencies. That these suspicions are not quite groundless is shown by the 'theological transition' which has been detected in American Methodism. What were secondary poles in a Wesleyan ellipse may take over the dominant position and thus distort the shape of Wesley's vision, with a shift of emphasis 'from revelation to reason', 'from sinful man to moral man', 'from free grace to free will' (Chiles, [1965] 1983).

Wesley's principle of 'we think and let think' has been abused in favour of sentimental ecumenism or even religious indifferentism when it is forgotten that his magnanimity was limited to 'opinions that do not strike at the root of Christianity' (Jackson, [1829–31] 1984, vol. 8, p. 340). In his generous sermon on a 'Catholic Spirit' of 1750, in which he reached out to Baptists and Roman Catholics (to name only those) in a plea for mutual respect and love, Wesley declared that 'a man of truly catholic spirit is fixed as the sun in his judgement concerning the main branches of Christian doctrine' and supposed that the practitioners of a catholic spirit have in common at least 'the first elements of the gospel of Christ' (Baker/Heitzenrater, 1975–, vol. 2, pp. 79–95). He did not consider matters of ecclesiastical government to be church-dividing.

Since the precise distribution of particular items between essential 'doctrine' and variable 'opinion' is itself open to debate, Methodists have shown considerable flexibility in their relations with other churches. They have been sympathetic to the modern ecumenical motto, that Christians 'may all be one, in order that the world may believe.' Methodists, usually of British derivation, have entered into organic unions with other denominations in Canada (1925), South India (1947), North India (1971), Australia (1977) and other places, and in 1969 and 1972 approved plans for unity with the Church of England that were finally blocked by a spoiling Anglican minority. Methodists of American derivation have usually preferred a model of 'reconciled diversity' without 'organizational' union (so in West Germany in 1987, East Germany in 1990, and Austria in 1991).

While Methodists have participated strongly in the multilateral ecumenism represented by the World Council of Churches (and particularly Faith and Order), their most serious theological efforts have more recently been directed towards the bilateral dialogues in which they are represented each time through the World Methodist Council. The dialogue with the Roman Catholic church began in 1967, and after the rather general reports of Denver 1971 and Dublin 1976 a more fixed focus was set on pneumatology ('Towards an Agreed Statement on the Holy Spirit', Honolulu 1981) and ecclesiology ('Towards an Agreed Statement on the Church', Nairobi 1986; 'The Apostolic Tradition', Singapore 1991). Dialogues with the Lutheran World Federation and the World Alliance of Reformed Churches produced, respectively, 'The Church: Community of Grace' (1984) and 'Together in God's Grace' (1987). In 1990 preliminary steps were taken towards dialogues with the Anglican Consultative Council and, through the ecumenical Patriarchate, with the Orthodox churches.

See also ANGLICANISM; ECUMENISM; PROTESTANT THEOLOGY: BRITAIN.

Bibliography

Baker, F., ed. 1975–87, and Heitzenrater, R.P., ed. 1988–: *The Works of John Wesley*, 34 volumes in process. Oxford: Clarendon Press, 1975–83; Nashville: Abingdon, 1984–.

Campbell, T. 1991: *John Wesley and Christian Antiquity*. Nashville: Abingdon.

Chiles, R.E. [1965] 1983: *Theological Transition in American Methodism 1790–1935*. Lanham (Maryland): University Press of America.

Davies, R.E. [1963] 1976: *Methodism*. London: Epworth.

Davies, R.E., George, A.R., and Rupp, E.G., eds 1965–88: *A History of the Methodist Church in Great Britain*, 4 vols. London: Epworth.

Heitzenrater, R.P. 1984: *The Elusive Mr Wesley*, 2 vols. Nashville: Abingdon.

Jackson, T., ed. [1829–31] 1984: *The Works of the Rev. John Wesley, AM*, 14 vols. Grand Rapids: Baker.

Langford, T.A. 1983: *Practical Divinity: Theology in the Wesleyan Tradition*. Nashville: Abingdon.

Meeks, M.D., ed. 1985: *The Future of the Methodist Theological Traditions*. Nashville: Abingdon.

Meeks, M.D., ed. 1990: *What Should Methodists Teach? Wesleyan Tradition and Modern Diversity*. Nashville: Abingdon.

Newton, J.A. 1972: The ecumenical Wesley, *The Ecumenical Review* 24, pp. 160–75.

Norwood, F.A. 1974: *The Story of American Methodism*. Nashville: Abingdon.

Oden, T.C. 1988: *Doctrinal Standards in the Wesleyan Tradition*. Grand Rapids: Zondervan.

Outler, A.C. 1964: *John Wesley*. New York: Oxford University Press.

Rack, H.D. 1989: *Reasonable Enthusiast: John Wesley and the Rise of Methodism*. London: Epworth.

Turner, J.M. 1985: *Conflict and Reconciliation: Studies in Methodism and Ecumenism in England 1740–1982*. London: Epworth.

Wainwright, G. 1983: Methodism's ecclesial location and ecumenical vocation, *One in Christ* 19, pp. 104–34.

Wainwright, G. 1987: *On Wesley and Calvin: Sources for Theology, Liturgy and Spirituality*. Melbourne: Uniting Church Press.

Williams, C.W. 1960: *John Wesley's Theology Today*. Nashville: Abingdon.

GEOFFREY WAINWRIGHT

Míguez Bonino, José (b. 1924) The best-known systematic theologian from Latin American Protestantism. Míguez Bonino was born in Rosario, Argentina, and began his theological formation in 1943 at the Facultad Evangélica de Teología (Union Seminary) of Buenos Aires. Ordained as a Methodist minister in 1948, he took several pastorates and in 1953 started his long career as theological educator, in his alma mater. He edited the quarterly *Testimonium* of the Student Christian Movement and became Superintendent in the Buenos Aires District of the Methodist church. He completed graduate studies in theology at Emory University in Georgia (USA) and doctoral studies at Union Theological Seminary, New York. He was rector of the Facultad Evangélica de Teología from 1960 to 1969 and then director of the postgraduate school known as the Evangelical Institute of Advanced Theological Studies (ISEDET). A lucid interpreter of the classical theology of the Reformation and of contemporary Catholic and Protestant thought, Míguez Bonino was the only Latin American Protestant observer at the Second Vatican Council. His book interpreting this event (*Concilio abierto*, 1968) is one of many works he wrote in Spanish about issues in ecumenism. He has been active in inter-church relations in Latin America and other parts of the world, and participated in the movement for human rights in Argentina. Elected in 1975 as a member of the Presidium of the World Council of Churches, he has written for *The Ecumenical Review*, *The International Review of Mission* and *Concilium*. His writings explore the relationship between the life of the church and the structures of social life, and also the theology of history. Among them are included his classical introduction to liberation theologies, *Doing Theology in a Revolutionary Situation* (1975), his comparative study *Christians and Marxists* (1976), *Room To Be People: An Interpretation of the Message of the Bible for Today's World* (1979) and *Toward a Christian Political Ethics* (1983).

See also LIBERATION THEOLOGY.

Bibliography

ISEDET 1985: *Fe, compromiso y teología: homenaje a José Míguez Bonino*. Buenos Aires: Asociación Interconfesional de Instituciones Teológicas.

minjung theology See KOREAN CHRISTIAN THOUGHT.

mission, theology of Before examining the theologies of mission which underlie current practice, we need to establish the nature, role and validity of theologies of mission.

First, mission has often been identified with overseas mission and been thought of in isolation from the mission of the church in its 'home' environment. For example, the Reformation churches never spawned a missionary movement in the era of the Reformation to foreign countries. They are therefore thought to have been deficient in their mission understanding. However, they did have a clear 'mission' with relation to the cultures, churches and states in which they were set. But that process is seldom studied as 'mission'. Again, mission in the nineteenth century is understood as 'the overseas missionary movement'. The extensive work of city missions in London has been almost completely neglected as an area of mission.

Second, as a result of the eighteenth century Enlightenment movement in Europe, mission and mission theology in the western church was sidelined in the life of the church. The Enlightenment made a distinction between facts and values, neutrality and commitment. It argued that the documents and history of the Christian faith could be studied objectively by nonbelievers, and could be best studied without commitment to the Christian faith. Mission theology, inasmuch as it represented commitment, was considered to be a branch of practical theology, beyond the concern of pure theology which was the technical scholarly enterprise of the objective observer analysing the documents and doctrines of the Christian tradition. This view encapsulated the Enlightenment doctrine of the incompatibility of objectivity and commitment. Those who engaged in mission were identified as committed and therefore incapable of the required neutrality.

It is therefore particularly noticeable that during the great expansion of world mission in the nineteenth and early twentieth centuries, none of the questions raised by such mission for Christian theology ever formed the subject matter of theological reflection in the sending churches – for example the issues of ancestor worship, the world of the spirits, poverty and hunger or even other faiths.

However, the challenge of LIBERATION THEOLOGY and other theologies from 'the periphery' has been that such 'pure theology' was not neutral, but was in fact generated by the particular questions of wealthy European Enlightenment culture. Theology is the product of the interface of the questions of obedience to the Scripture with relevance to the context; to bring the questions from the context of mission to the Scriptures and to address the questions of Scripture to the context. The challenge from mission is to develop a theology forged in the midst of obedient action for the sake of the gospel so as to bring together the apostolic faith and the suffering of the oppressed, the personal and the social, the private and the public, justification by faith and the struggle for peace with justice, and commitment to Christian action empowered by the Holy Spirit in the midst of crises facing the modern world.

Why mission theology?

Why have a theology of mission? Is it not enough to have a Christian theology founded on the Scriptures, and then teach God's people his truth? Such a view itself expresses a theology of mission, an understanding of the way we can and need to share the gospel with others.

A theology of mission answers the question why we share the gospel with others: it is God's will, people are lost without Christ; God's kingdom has arrived and is still to come; God's purpose is to bring all things into harmony with Christ as head; his purpose is to reconcile people to himself, one another and all creation. A theology of mission seeks to relate these together and assign priority between them, if any.

Who? A theology of mission answers the question to whom we address the gospel. Are people all the same as far as the gospel goes, all sinners, rich and poor, black and white, needing to trust Christ? Are they to be perceived as individuals, totally on their own before God? Or is their location in society relevant? Will the good news to a South African black in Soweto contain exactly the same emphases as the good news to a London whizzkid dealing in the stock exchange? In Africa people speak of whole communities turning to Christ. Can people trust Christ as a group? Is the focus on the individual in western churches biblical or cultural? A theology of mission will include a theology of humanity.

Are those who already have a religious commitment, to Islam for instance, to be addressed in the same terms as atheist undergraduates? How is their understanding of God to be evaluated? And how is 'folk religion' in Britain to be evaluated? Is it a bridgehead or a barrier to Christian faith? A theology of mission will include a theology of religions.

What? What is the good news that we are to share? In the New Testament it is defined as good news to the poor. Are the poor the physically poor, or all people who are spiritually far from God? Some argue that what the good news means to people who are physically poor is what it means for everyone.

This raises the question of the categories in which the good news is to be presented. Is the good news the basis on which people qualify for heaven after death? Is the good news first of all to be presented as bad news to people's arrogance and self-sufficient pride? Does the good news for everyone begin with the news that they are guilty sinners, or is it appropriate for those who are powerless, oppressed and demeaned by others to hear first that God loves them and calls them to be his sons and daughters?

Where does the good news challenge or affirm aspects of people's culture and commitments? In some situations the good news may first bring comfort to people in bereavement, or healing in time of sickness, or indictment for injustice, or companionship in loneliness. In his ministry Jesus addressed the sick in different terms to those in which he addressed the Pharisees. What implications does this have for the presentation of the good news?

How? How is the good news shared and how should it be shared? Is the main focus the gospel service on Sunday evening to which members invite their friends? Is preaching the prime means of sharing the good news? How does Christian witness in social responsibility relate to sharing the good news? Some suggest that in the New Testament we see a combination of events and explanations: the church and apostles precipitated events such as healings in the name of Jesus, or freeing people from exploitation, which they then had to explain.

What strategies should be employed to share the good news? For some this is the first and often the only question of mission. But the above should show that the questions of strategy depend on prior theological assumptions. There are those who urge that people are happiest to share the good news with and receive the good

news from those of their own social group. Others urge that the church by its very nature should be a cross-cultural group. If we are to share the gospel with a community of people, what strategies should we employ?

How do we evalute the role of non-Christians in God's mission? If God's purpose includes reconciliation, harmony and peace, the relief of poverty and of injustice, how do we evaluate the work of non-Christians in this area? Do we affirm all work for justice and peace, as long as it is Christians who do it? Or do we see all work which affirms the values of Christ as redemptive in purpose, and pointing towards the necessity of personal allegiance to Jesus?

Where? What role has the context to play in sharing the gospel? What effect does it have on those who express what the gospel means and on the interpreters of the gospel? What effect on their understanding of the gospel have their social position, their experience of society and their commitments? What effect does the context have on those who hear the gospel? Does living among the impersonal filing cabinets and tower blocks that are our city centres produce an impersonal existence which influences both the interpreters and receivers of the gospel? Do we believe the gospel can be communicated most effectively by mass and impersonal means, via print, video or advertising? Or should Christians be seeking together to build community and good human relationships which can become a context and channel for people to receive the love and word of God?

Theologies of mission

A variety of answers to the above questions over decades have produced a variety of theologies of mission which underlie current mission practice. These come out of a long historical tradition.

The debt to Africa The nineteenth century was the apex of mission of national churches beyond their own borders. This movement was the first occasion in history when the propagation of the Christian faith was from a position of overwhelming power. This fact has led to the accusation that this missionary movement was the religious facade and the 'running dog' of capitalism in its colonial phase. Attempts to refute this charge by citing the missionaries' altruistic work and their opposition to capitalism and colonialism miss the point that in the nineteenth century, the European civilizations were in an expansionist phase, of which the missionary movement was at the same time a cause, an expression and a result.

Most mainline churches in these civilizations came out of the Constantinian heritage, which assumed the responsibility of the church for the social and political order. This meant that there was a disposition for the mission dimension of the church to see the political order as a means of extending the rule of God. This inevitably meant that the church was involved with aspects of colonial rule.

The missionary movement was itself one cause of overseas expansion in the country which by 1910 provided the largest number of overseas missionaries – Great Britain. The abolition of the slave trade arose out of the fusion of Christian compassion with eighteenth-century notions of the 'rights of man'. The prohibition of slavery by the British Parliament precipitated a movement to repay the debt to Africa incurred through decades of slavery. So the missionary movement was born out of deep social concern. It was only later in the early twentieth century that a dichotomy occurred restricting mission in some cases to limited ecclesiastical activities.

Repaying the debt to Africa led to missionaries encouraging trade and employment for Africans in the hinterland areas from where the slave traders had drawn their cargoes. The British government became increasingly involved as on occasion the missionaries specifically asked it to intervene politically for the benefit of the local populace.

In India, the initial expression of mission from the British church had been limited to the East India Company providing chaplains for maintaining the Christian religion among their employees. These chaplains were very respectful towards the religions of India. When the East India Company was given its charter in 1813 by the British Parliament, the British Dominions in India were declared to be open to the work of European missionaries. After the 'Indian Mutiny' of 1857, the British government took over the political responsibilities of the East India Company and there was more interference in the affairs of Indians. Missionaries cooperated with British officials and Indians of good will to abolish such customs as 'widow-burning' (suttee). Outcaste groups responded in large numbers because the Christian faith offered them equality. The Hindu faiths developed a social dimension in the Hindu Renaissance. A particular result was the emergence of Gandhi.

This increasing self-confidence sometimes expressed itself as racism. Early mission leaders such as Henry Venn of the Church Missionary Society encouraged indigenous leadership in the new churches. The most outstanding example was Bishop Samuel Crowther of Nigeria. However, Claudius Buchanan and others introduced notions of western superiority into the mission enterprise which undermined this approach. Not until the decolonizing movement after the Second World War did the churches again develop indigenous leadership, in order to retain credibility in nations newly independent from foreign colonial rule.

Mission activity tended to focus on welfare, education, medical missions and building ecclesiastical institutions. There was no focus on developing people in business, industry or trade.

Eschatology Various views on eschatology tended to underlie approaches to mission. Some approaches were highly optimistic about change. This optimism was often linked to views that everything would inevitably improve until the earth was perfect enough for Christ to return to inherit. Such views were replaced by pessimistic views which stressed that nothing would change until Christ returned. This view, reinforced by the Enlightenment suspicion of any claims about the activity of God in history, held that the only expression of the work of God was in the changed inner life of individuals.

The pessimistic view was further strengthened by the experience of the First World War. The Africans saw two European nations (Britain and Germany) whose missionaries had come to preach peace to their warring tribes themselves go to war and enlist their African disciples on each side. This led to great disillusion with the claims of the missionary movement, both in Africa and in their home bases. In Europe the war quashed evolutionary optimism and gave birth to the neo-orthodox movement, which stressed total discontinuity between the work of God and the religious experience of humanity.

The effect of these processes led to a separation of mission from social involvement. Mission tended to be equated with and judged by change in the inner life of individuals through 'churchy' activities. This engendered dependency among lay people on the clergy who performed the key tasks in mission, and undermined the secular callings of people in mission.

Contextualization This total separation of Christian mission from the religious experience of humanity expressed by Karl Barth and the earlier writings of Hendrik Kraemer had the effect of diminishing the possibility of syncretism in mission churches. But it was also experienced as a very demeaning judgement on the religious experience and cultures of host nations. To be Christian one had to cease to be, for example, an Indonesian. Indonesian Christians were called 'black Dutch'.

The demeaning effect of such Protestant neo-orthodoxy has not been the experience of churches founded by Roman Catholic missions. The Roman Catholic understanding of NATURAL LAW paved the way for a greater acceptance of local religious expression. The result has been that in many areas, especially in Latin America, Roman Catholicism is in effect a fusion of Catholicism and folk religion. An example is the elaborate ceremonies in connection with All Saints Day.

The nineteenth-century Protestant mission thinkers expected the triumph of Christianity over other religions through the internal collapse of other religions under the weight of their own contradictions in the face of western rationalism. But other processes were at work, also triggered off by the missionary movement. The spread of education in English was promoted as a method of mission. In India, this introduced a new language with concepts of individual choice and freedom. This led to the birth of the Indian nationalist movement and to Indian independence. In Africa, the mission schools nurtured those who would become the first political leaders of the newly independent nations. The growth of national identity under the colonial yoke was paralleled by a resurgence of national cultures and religions such as Islam and Hinduism, often as a badge of national identity. In such contexts the Christian church

had rapidly to make its leadership, worship and theology credible.

A major shift occurred whereby theologies formulated in the European homelands were increasingly questioned in the light of new challenges from the religious, social and political questions of the mission contexts. Just as mission theology had been an expression of the expansionist culture of nineteenth-century Europe, so it became an expression of the newly independent countries of the post-Second World War period.

Very few of these mission questions and theologies had ever percolated back to the European or North American home bases of the 'sending' churches. We noted above the imperviousness of western theology to mission theology or the questions raised by mission. The direction of theology was always 'from the west to the rest'. This direction still continues today in the context of mission through technological and economic power emanating from North America and the Asiatic tigers of Singapore, Korea and Taiwan. Just as the nineteenth-century theologies of Britain never addressed issues of ancestor worship or famine, so the theologies of mission from North America today concentrate on strategies and counting numbers, with little critical reflection on the formulation of the gospel being shared.

One example of 'one-way missiology' is the mission theology of church growth. This focuses on a saved people who plant churches, gather believers together and plant a witness among people. This model assumes that proclamation of the gospel by word is a priority, and that it results in planting a church which will become independent. The needs and welfare of the surrounding community will then be taken care of automatically. This process assumes and perpetuates a dualism between spirit and matter which gives a priority to the spiritual. A difficulty with the approach is that it tends to ignore the historical aspect of people's lives. It does not take their actual context or situation very seriously. It tends to neglect social change.

However, churches in the two-thirds world have perceived that their identity as churches able to play their role in the worldwide body of Christ depends on their making their own theological contribution (as distinct from being examples and case studies to prove the validity of 'one-way missiology' from the west).

So the movement for contextualization has arisen, which insists that the meaning of God's Word for today for any context is only known in the process of bringing the questions of the context to the text and the questions of the text to the context in a hermeneutical spiral. This differs from 'indigenization', which clothes a gospel message or theology already formulated in a western context in indigenous language and formulae. All theologies are contextual theologies. Contextual theology includes both liberation theology and individualistic theology emanating from the west.

Current theologies of mission This process emerged in the evangelical mission movement, which regarded itself as heir to the nineteenth-century mission movement, and in its slogan of 'evangelization of the world in this generation' in the Lausanne Covenant of 1974.

At Lausanne the movement agreed that both evangelism and social concern were part of the mission of the church, and recovered the original purpose of the movement in repaying a debt to Africa. In paragraph 5, the Lausanne Covenant said:

> We affirm that God is both Creator and Judge of all men. We therefore should share his concern for justice and reconciliation throughout human society and the liberation of men from every kind of oppression . . . Although reconciliation with man is not reconciliation with God, nor is social action evangelism, nor is political liberation salvation, nevertheless we affirm that evangelism and socio-political involvement are both part of our Christian duty . . . When people receive Christ they are born again into his kingdom and must seek not only to exhibit but also to spread its righteousness in the midst of an unrighteous world.

This covenant released large numbers of people in the evangelical mission movement to take part in relief and development organizations. Over the next ten years, these people developed a theology of mission which insisted that mission was the mission of the kingdom of God to transform the whole of life in its religious, social, economic and political dimensions.

Theologies of mission differ in the weight they give to aspects of this mission concern. Some claim that the gospel is about certain beliefs about Jesus Christ and the need to believe in him in order to experience eternal life, which consists in the forgiveness of sins and the assurance of resurrection life after death with him. These can only be experienced by the individual. Converted individuals will as a matter of witness and obedience show love to their neighbours but such love is not constitutive of the gospel. That would be to substitute works for faith.

Others claim that while the gospel includes forgiveness and everlasting life, the focus of the gospel is not on benefits to individuals but on the Lordship of Christ. This Lordship is expressed through his current rule (the kingdom of God) which embraces all of life. This rule brings new relationships with God whereby people are forgiven by God and receive a new status as sons and daughters of God; people are brought into new relationships with each other of mutual forgiveness; and new relationships with the natural order over which they were appointed to have dominion and to steward. The fulfilment of this rule in the new heavens and new earth at the return of Christ will include transformation of all these relationships.

Underlying the differences, and sometimes tensions, between these views, are presuppositions about the nature of humanity and the fall. Is humanity in relation to God essentially constituted of individuals or is it constituted of persons in community? Was the fall therefore fundamentally a sundering only of the relationships between people and God which sundered other relationships as a consequence, or was it a sundering of relationship with God, with the sundering of other relationships as an expression or a dimension of that sundering?

The different answers to these questions produce different theologies and practices of mission. Answers which stress the individual and eternal dimensions of mission can tend to make a priority of verbal evangelism as the expression of Christian mission and to be culturally bound in western culture. They tend to undervalue the contribution that people's own culture and history can bring to their expression of the Christian faith because they are blind to the extent to which western culture (especially individualism) shapes this understanding. They can tend to be tolerant of unjust regimes which allow freedom to preach this sort of gospel, and forget that such regimes promote it because it precludes any judgement of the regime by Christian canons.

Answers which stress the corporate nature of humanity and the Lordship of Christ over all of life are open to the tendency to neglect the need for personal transformation and the impact of the transcendent on life. They can then reduce their understanding and practice of mission to social involvement of a particular sort.

It is therefore always necessary that Christians with different expressions and understandings of mission remain open to what other Christians are saying, which may more faithfully reflect the meaning and intent of the Word of God.

For example in recent years there has been a concern to understand the meaning of mission as good news to the poor. The World Council of Churches tends to have a view that interprets this to mean that the poor are bearers of mission by virtue of the fact that they are poor. Others argue that what the good news of the kingdom of God in the Bible means to those who are poor who respond to it, defines the meaning of the good news for everyone else.

This represents an important shift from the theological dominance of mission by the west in the nineteenth century to a theological leadership among the churches of the poor in the late twentieth. Further expressions of this shift are the concern to rewrite mission history from the point of view of the objects of mission in the two-thirds world, to explore the role in mission of Christian business through entrepreneurial loan schemes in communities of the poor, and to develop equal partnership in giving and receiving between churches in economically powerful and powerless contexts. All four expressions of the shift represent an alternative to 'one-way missiology'.

Interlocutors

It is important to discern the interlocutor of theologies of mission. Much theology of mission has been framed in defensive response to two recent challenges.

One challenge has been that mission has subverted the integrity of indigenous cultures. This view was in fact based on a secular rationalism which insisted that an objective neutrality should be observed by outside groups relating to indigenous cultures. This in fact projected on to such cultures the Enlightenment view of autonomy as the highest expression of humanity, which was an expression of cultural imperialism.

In response to this challenge, much missiology, especially from the USA, has been based on a functional anthropology which has ignored social, economic and political issues.

The second critique was that in the context of religious pluralism, was impossible to insist that any one religion possesses the ultimate authoritative truth about God. With the collapse of western superiority around the world, it is argued that the ideology underlying the uniqueness of Christ as the religious justification of western superiority has been removed. This also represented the imperialistic hegemony of the Enlightenment. For this challenge insisted that the truth about God is beyond any one historical expression. The question is begged about the grounds on which this assertion is made.

The challenge also ignored the witness and experience of Christian converts of non-western races who had maintained the uniqueness of Christ from the position of a minority and powerless community. The particular nature of this challenge is therefore seen to come from a context where the hegemony of the Christian faith in a nation has ended, and where those who profess the faith want to keep a justification for Christian leadership in the national life without accepting the minority position of the Christian faith.

The challenge of religious pluralism in western Europe also demonstrated the way mission thinking in and from the west had bypassed the issue of religion. It had been assumed that religion meant the Christian religion.

A theological basis for mission

The theological basis for mission has been rooted in a number of themes: the themes of God's purpose for creation, that all people are enabled to be stewards and managers of creation in partnership with himself, other people and the created order; that this purpose will be fulfilled in the final kingdom of God in a new heaven and earth to be brought at the return of Jesus, but inaugurated and modelled in his incarnation and ministry, victorious over evil in his cross and resurrection and present now through his Spirit; that in entering this kingdom now, people receive a new identity and status as daughters and sons of God, replacing the false status they have in the world either of 'nobodies' or falsely exalted somebodies; and that the rule of this kingdom is especially welcome to the poor.

See also CULTURE AND THEOLOGY; EVAN-GELICALISM; INDIAN/JAPANESE/KOREAN CHRISTIAN THOUGHT; OTHER FAITHS AND CHRISTIANITY.

Bibliography

Beeching, Jack 1979: *An Open Path*. London: Hutchinson.
Bosch, David 1991: *Transforming Mission*. New York: Orbis.
Houghton, Graham 1983: *The Impoverishment of Dependency*. Madras: Christian Literature Service.
Moorhouse, Geoffrey 1973: *The Missionaries*. London: Eyre Methuen.
Morris, James 1973. *Heaven's Command*. Harmondsworth: Penguin.
Nazir Ali, Michael 1991: *From Everywhere to Everywhere*. London: Collins.
Pettifer, Julian 1990: *Missionaries*. London: BBC.
Samuel, Vinay, and Sugden, Chris 1986: *Sharing Jesus in the Two Thirds World*. Grand Rapids: Eerdmans.
Stanley, Brian 1990: *The Bible and the Flag*. Leicester: Apollos.

CHRISTOPHER SUGDEN

models See LANGUAGE, RELIGIOUS.

modernism The term 'modernist' was first used to refer to a school of Roman Catholic theologians operating towards the end of the nineteenth century, which adopted a critical and sceptical attitude towards traditional Christian dogmas, fostered a positive attitude towards radical biblical criticism, and stressed the ethical, rather than the more theological, dimensions of faith. In many ways, modernism may be seen as an attempt by writers within the Roman Catholic church to come to terms with the outlook of the ENLIGHTENMENT, which had, until that point, largely been ignored by that church.

'Modernism' is, however, a loose term, which should not be understood to imply the existence of a distinctive school of thought, committed to certain common methods or indebted to common teachers. It is certainly true that most modernist writers were concerned to integrate Christian thought with the spirit of the Enlightenment, especially the new understandings of history and the natural sciences which were then gaining the ascendency. Equally, some modernist writers drew inspiration from writers such as Maurice Blondel (1861–1949), who argued that the supernatural was intrinsic to human existence, or Henri Bergson (1859–1941), who stressed the importance of intuition over intellect. Yet there is not sufficient commonality between the French, British and American modernists, nor between Roman Catholic and Protestant modernism, to allow the term to be understood as designating a rigorous and well-defined school.

Among Roman Catholic modernist writers, particular attention should be paid to Alfred Loisy (1857–1940) and George Tyrrell (1861–1909). During the 1890s, Loisy established himself as a critic of traditional views of the biblical accounts of creation, and argued that a real development of doctrine could be discerned within Scripture. His most significant publication, *L'Evangile et l'église* ('The Gospel and the Church'), appeared in 1902. This important work was a direct response to the views of Adolf von Harnack, published two years earlier as *Das Wesen des Christentums*, on the origins and nature of Christianity. Loisy rejected Harnack's suggestion that there was a radical discontinuity between Jesus and the church; however, he made significant concessions to Harnack's liberal Protestant account of Christian origins, including an acceptance of the role and validity of biblical criticism in interpreting the Gospels. As a result, the work was placed upon the *Index* of prohibited books in 1903.

The British Jesuit writer George Tyrrell followed Loisy in his radical criticism of traditional Catholic dogma. In common with Loisy, he criticized Harnack's account of Christian origins in *Christianity at the Cross-*

roads of 1909, dismissing Harnack's historical reconstruction of Jesus as 'the reflection of a Liberal Protestant face, seen at the bottom of a deep well'. The work also included a defence of Loisy's *L'Evangile et l'église*, arguing that the official Roman Catholic 'hostility to the book and its author have created a general impression that it is a defence of Liberal Protestant against Roman Catholic positions, and that "Modernism" is simply a protestantizing and rationalizing movement.'

In part, this perception may be due to the growing influence of modernist attitudes within the mainstream Protestant denominations. In England, the Churchmen's Union was founded in 1898 for the advancement of liberal religious thought; in 1928, it altered its name to the Modern Churchmen's Union. Among those especially associated with this group may be noted Kirsopp Lake (1872–1946), E.W. Barnes (1874–1953), Hastings Rashdall (1858–1924), H.D.A. Major (1871–1961), and William R. Inge (1860–1954). The journal *Modern Churchman*, founded in 1911 by Major, served as an organ for the views of the group.

Rashdall's *Idea of Atonement in Christian Theology* of 1919 illustrates the general tenor of English modernism. Drawing somewhat uncritically upon the earlier writings of A.B. Ritschl, Rashdall argued that the theory of the atonement (see SOTERIOLOGY) associated with Peter Abelard was more acceptable to modern thought forms than traditional theories which made an appeal to the notion of a substitutionary sacrifice. This strongly moral or exemplarist theory of the atonement, which interpreted Christ's death virtually exclusively as a demonstration of the love of God, made a considerable impact upon English, and especially Anglican, thought in the 1920s and 1930s. Nevertheless, the events of the Great War (1914–18), and the subsequent rise of fascism in Europe in the 1930s, undermined the credibility of the movement. It was not until the 1960s that a renewed modernism or radicalism became a significant feature of British Christianity.

The rise of modernism in the USA follows a similar pattern. The growth of liberal Protestantism in the late nineteenth and early twentieth centuries was widely perceived as a direct challenge to more conservative evangelical standpoints. Newman Smyth's *Passing*

Protestantism and Coming Catholicism of 1908 argued that Roman Catholic modernism could serve as a mentor to American Protestantism in several ways, not least in its critique of dogma and its historical understanding of the development of doctrine. The situation became increasingly polarized through the rise of FUNDAMENTALISM in response to modernist attitudes. The Great War ushered in a period of self-questioning within American modernism, which was intensified through the radical social realism of writers such as H.R. Niebuhr. By the mid-1930s, modernism appeared to have lost its way. In an influential article in *Christian Century*, dated 4 December 1935, Harry Emerson Fosdick declared the need 'to go beyond modernism'. In his *Realistic Theology* of 1934, Walter Marshall Horton spoke of the rout of liberal forces in American theology. However, the movement gained new confidence in the post-war period, and arguably reached its zenith during the period of the Vietnam War.

See also LIBERALISM (BRITAIN and USA); ROMAN CATHOLIC THEOLOGY; TRADITION.

Bibliography

Hutchison, William R. 1982: *The Modernist Impulse in American Protestantism*. New York: Oxford University Press.

Ratté, John 1967: *Three Modernists: Alfred Loisy, George Tyrrell, William L. Sullivan*. New York: Sheed and Ward.

Reardon, B.M.G. 1970: *Roman Catholic Modernism*. Stanford, CA: Stanford University Press.

Stephenson, A.M.G. 1984: *The Rise and Decline of English Modernism*. London: SPCK.

Vidler, A.R. 1934: *The Modernist Movement in the Roman Church*. Cambridge: Cambridge University Press.

ALISTER E. MCGRATH

Möhler, Johann Adam (1796–1838) German Roman Catholic theologian and church historian. Educated at Tübingen and ordained in 1819, he was professor of church history first at Tübingen, and from 1835 at Munich. Regarded by some conservatives as unorthodox, he attempted to address the challenge posed to traditional Catholicism by Hegelian philosophy and by the theology of the Protestant modernists such as F.D.E. Schleiermacher; he remains a major influence on Roman

Catholic modernist theologians. A precursor of the modern ecumenical movement, he sought to reconcile the historic theological differences between the Protestant and Roman Catholic churches in *Die Einheit der Kirche* (1825) and *Symbolik* (1832, trans. *Symbolism, or the Exposition of Doctrinal Differences*, 1843).

Bibliography

Fitzer, J. 1974: *Möhler and Baur in Controversy*. Tallahassee, Fl.

Franklin, R.W. 1987: *Nineteenth Century Churches: The History of a New Catholicism in Württemberg, England and France*. New York.

Nienaltowski, R.H. 1959: *Johann Adam Möhler's Theory of Doctrinal Development*. Washington, DC.

Moltmann, Jürgen (b. 1926) One of the most influential of contemporary German Protestant theologians. Since 1967 Moltmann has been professor of systematic theology at the university of Tübingen.

His major works comprise two series. In the first place, there is the trilogy: *Theology of Hope* ([1964] 1967), *The Crucified God* ([1972] 1974) and *The Church in the Power of the Spirit* ([1975] 1977). These represent three complementary perspectives on Christian theology. *Theology of Hope* is not a study of eschatology as such, but of the eschatological orientation of the whole of theology. *The Crucified God* is not only one of the most important modern studies of the cross, but also an attempt to see the crucified Christ as the criterion of truly Christian theology. *The Church in the Power of the Spirit* adds the perspective of the role of the Spirit in the world. The three volumes provide three angles on a single theological vision. Moltmann now sees this trilogy as preparation for the second series of major works, which is still in progress. These are studies of particular Christian doctrines, which together will form a dogmatics. Four volumes have so far appeared: on the doctrines of the Trinity (*The Trinity and the Kingdom of God*, [1980] 1981), creation (*God in Creation*, 1985), Christology (*The Way of Jesus Christ*, [1989] 1990) and the Spirit (*The Spirit of Life*, [1991] 1992). Further volumes on eschatology and theological method are planned. As well as these two series of major works, Moltmann has written many other works, many of which develop what he sees as an essential aspect of the theological task: the implications of his theology for Christian praxis (often with an emphasis on political praxis, in the broadest sense). The following outline of Moltmann's theology deals with topics in the chronological order in which they became major themes in his work.

The dialectic of cross and resurrection This principle is at the heart of Moltmann's early work. It takes the cross and the resurrection of Jesus as in total contradiction: death and life, the absence of God and the presence of God. Yet the crucified and risen Jesus is the same Jesus in this contradiction. By raising Jesus to new life, God created continuity in radical discontinuity. Furthermore, the contradiction between cross and resurrection corresponds to the contradiction between what reality is now and what God promises to make it. In his cross Jesus was identified with the world as it is in its subjection to sin, suffering and death. But since the same Jesus was raised, his resurrection constitutes God's promise of new creation for the whole of the reality with which the crucified Jesus was identified. This fundamental concept is developed in *Theology of Hope* with an emphasis on the *resurrection* of the crucified Christ, as the basis for the hope of new creation, and in *The Crucified God* with an emphasis on the *cross* of the risen Christ, as God's loving identification with the godless and the godforsaken. *The Church in the Power of the Spirit* completes the scheme, in that the Spirit's role is to move reality towards the eschatological resolution of the dialectic.

Eschatology One of Moltmann's most important achievements has been to rehabilitate future eschatology. Along with some other German theologians in the 1960s, he found the future dimension of biblical eschatology – its hope for the real temporal future of the world – to be not, as recent theology had tended to assume, a difficulty for modern Christianity, but the perspective from which Christian faith could prove credible and relevant in the modern world. It is the perspective from which the church can encounter the typically modern experience of history as radical change in the direction of a new future, engage with possibilities for change, assess them in the light of the coming kingdom of God, and promote change in the direction of the kingdom.

In *Theology of Hope* Moltmann understands Christian hope as thoroughly Christological, in that it arises from the resurrection of Jesus, understood as the definitive event of divine promise for the future. Because the resurrection *contradicts* the cross it gives rise to a *dialectical* eschatology, in which God's promise for the future of reality contradicts its present condition. It promises life for the dead, righteousness for the unrighteous, a new creation for a world subject to evil and death. But the *identity* of the one Jesus, crucified and risen, means that the promise is not for some other world to replace this, but for the new creation of this world, in all its material and worldly reality, with which Jesus on the cross was identified.

Christian eschatology is therefore the hope that the world will be different. Only through God's action at the end of history, when God will finally rescue his creation from all evil, suffering and death, and indwell it with the glory of his presence, will the promise given in Jesus' resurrection be fully fulfilled. But the promise is certainly not without effect in the present. The promise reveals the world to be transformable in the direction of its promised future, and so it arouses active hope which seeks out possibilities of change and creates anticipations of the future kingdom of God. This hopeful activity is the church's task in the world.

Theodicy From the beginning Moltmann's theology was concerned with the question of God's righteousness in the face of the suffering and evil of the world. *Theology of Hope* offers an eschatological theodicy. God's promise given in the resurrection of Jesus does not explain suffering, but it does provide hope for God's final triumph over evil, and it thereby also provides an initiative for Christian praxis in overcoming suffering now. In *The Crucified God* this theodicy is deepened by the additional theme of God's loving solidarity with the world in its suffering. Moltmann sees Jesus, in his godforsakenness on the cross, sharing the plight not only of sinners who suffer their own turning away from God, but also of the innocent victims of meaningless suffering, who experience their suffering as abandonment by God. God's love, enacted in the event of the cross, is love which suffers in solidarity with those who suffer. This is a dialectical understanding of God's love,

corresponding to the dialectical understanding of divine promise in *Theology of Hope*. God deals with the world which, in its godlessness and godforsakenness, contradicts him, not only by promising, in the resurrection of Jesus, its new creation in righteousness and glory, but also by entering and embracing and suffering this contradiction in the event of Jesus' death. In this way God's love reaches the godless and the godforsaken and overcomes the contradiction. The cross does not solve the problem of suffering, but by constituting God's loving fellow suffering with those who suffer and his loving protest against their suffering, it changes the problem. Essential to this dialectical understanding of the divine love is Moltmann's rejection of the traditional dogma of the divine impassibility (inability to suffer). God's love is not only active benevolence, but also love which willingly incurs suffering (see SUFFERING, DIVINE).

Doctrine of God It was from his interpretation of the cross in *The Crucified God* that Moltmann's distinctive development of the doctrine of God began. Moltmann understands the cross as an event between the Father and the Son, in which, out of their common love for the world, the Father abandoned the Son to death and the Son willingly suffered abandonment by his Father. In the pain of separation, Father and Son both suffer, though differently. This had three major implications for the doctrine of God. First, it required Trinitarian language of a kind which emphasizes the intersubjective relationship between the divine persons. (At this stage, the Spirit seems less clearly personal than the Father and the Son, but soon emerges, in Moltmann's subsequent work, as the third divine subject.) Second, it required a doctrine of divine passibility, not only in the narrow sense that God can suffer pain, but in the broader sense that God can be affected by his creation. Moreover, because the cross is an event between the Father and the Son, it is in God's own Trinitarian relationships that he is affected by his experience of the world. Therefore, third, Moltmann abandons the traditional distinction between the immanent and economic Trinities, between what God is in himself and how he acts outside himself in the world. The cross is internal to the divine Trinitarian experience. It makes a difference to the Trinity as well as to the world. As Moltmann extends his understanding of God's Trinitarian relationship with the world from the cross to the rest of God's history with the world, from creation to the eschaton, the doctrine of the Trinity becomes a narrative of God's changing Trinitarian relationships.

Moltmann's mature doctrine of the Trinity hinges on a concept of dynamic relationality, which is applied both to God's self-relationships as Trinity and to God's relations with the world. Moltmann adopts a 'social Trinitarian' model of God as three divine subjects in mutual loving relationship, and integrates into this understanding of the Trinity a model of God's relationship with the world as a reciprocal one in which God in his love for his creation both affects and is affected by it. It is as Trinity that God relates to the world, including the world within his own Trinitarian relationships. Therefore the history of God's relationship with the world is a real history for God as well as for the world. All this Moltmann takes to be the meaning of the claim that God is love.

In Moltmann's work after *The Crucified God* the central principle of his early work, the dialectic of cross and resurrection, is subsumed within this broader concept of God's Trinitarian history with the world, which becomes the overarching principle of his later work. With it the notion of dynamic mutual relationality becomes an axiom for understanding God, God's relationship with creation, and all relationships within creation.

The church Moltmann's understanding of the church situates it within God's Trinitarian history with the world, specifically within the missions of the Son and the Spirit on their way to the eschatological kingdom. By participating in these missions, the church has the messianic role of being a provisional anticipation of the coming universal kingdom of God. In Moltmann's view, this vocation can only be adequately fulfilled if the church becomes a 'messianic fellowship' of committed disciples, participating responsibly in the church's mission to the world, a free society of equals, relating to each other and to others in relationships of 'open friendship', and identified with the marginalized and the most needy in society. *Creation* Moltmann's development of this doctrine, in *God in Creation*, is in the context of the

ecological crisis, which requires, in his view, a renewed theological understanding of nature and human beings as God's creation and of God's relationship to the world as his creation. The kind of human relationship to nature which has created the crisis is one of exploitative domination. In its place Moltmann advocates relationships of mutuality between human beings and nature, within a community of creation which, since it is *creation*, is not anthropocentric but theocentric. In order to ground theologically this emphasis on mutual relationships, Moltmann appeals to his doctrine of God, whose own Trinitarian community provides the model for the life of his creation as a community of reciprocal relationships. Moreover, the mutual indwelling which constitutes the relationships between the divine persons Moltmann sees as also characterizing the relationship between God and creation. By emphasizing the role of the Spirit as God's immanent presence indwelling his creation, Moltmann is able to take the nonhuman creation into his narrative of the Trinitarian history of God in reciprocal relationship with the world, and to re-emphasize, in relation to the nonhuman creation, the eschatological goal of participation in God's glory which his theology has always envisaged for the whole of creation.

Christology Ecological concerns remain a dominant context for Moltmann's return to issues of Christology in *The Way of Jesus Christ*. This book is a sustained attempt to relate a hermeneutic of the biblical origins of Christology to a hermeneutic of Christology's modern context. The former reveals a Jesus who is 'on his way' to the eschatological goal of his messianic mission, and whose identity is inseparable from his relationships – both the Trinitarian relationships (so that Moltmann here develops a Spirit-Christology, stressing Jesus' relation to the Spirit as well as to the Father) and his relationships to other people and the whole cosmos. The hermeneutic of the modern context stresses the threat of annihilation which threatens all living beings, and it requires a Christology whose soteriological relevance extends to the healing of the whole creation. The result is a Christology which innovatively combines a discipleship ethic of nonviolence, based on the teaching and praxis of the historical Jesus, with an eschatologically oriented doctrine of the cosmic Christ, in whom all created things will be rescued from transience and annihilation.

See also PROTESTANT THEOLOGY: GERMANY.

Bibliography

Writings

[1964] 1967: *Theology of Hope*, trans. J.W. Leitch. London: SCM Press.

[1972] 1974: *The Crucified God*, trans. R.A. Wilson and J. Bowden. London: SCM Press.

[1975] 1977: *The Church in the Power of the Spirit*, trans. M. Kohl. London: SCM Press.

[1980] 1981: *The Trinity and the Kingdom of God*, trans. M. Kohl. London: SCM Press.

1985: *God in Creation*, trans. M. Kohl. London: SCM Press.

[1989] 1990: *The Way of Jesus Christ*, trans. M. Kohl. London: SCM Press.

[1991] 1992: *The Spirit of Life*, trans. M. Kohl. London: SCM Press.

Critical works

Bauckham, R. 1987: *Moltmann: Messianic Theology in the Making*. Basingstoke: Marshall Pickering.

Conyers, A.J. 1988: *God, Hope, and History: Jürgen Moltmann and the Christian Concept of History*. Macon, Georgia: Mercer University Press.

Gibellini, R. 1975: *La Teologia di Jürgen Moltmann*. Brescia: Queriniana.

Ising, D. 1987: *Bibliographic Jürgen Moltmann*. Munich: kaisre (complete bibliography of Moltmann's works up to 1987).

Meeks, M.D. 1974: *Origins of the Theology of Hope*. Philadelphia: Fortress.

RICHARD BAUCKHAM

music and Christianity Christian thinking with regard to music over the past three hundred years has been dominated by a series of basic, antithetical questions. Is music an artistic expression that is fundamental to the celebration of worship? Or is it a functional ornamentation not absolutely essential within Christian worship? Is the purpose of music in worship to preserve tradition or to celebrate contemporary experience? Are there specifically sacred styles for worship music that are quite different from the secular? Or can secular forms of music be employed as vehicles of praise, proclamation and prayer? Is there, indeed, some kind of correlation or synthesis that can unify all these polarities?

At the beginning of the eighteenth century, views on music were largely inherited from the Reformation era, which generated a number of different understandings of the nature and purpose of music within a Christian context. These disparate approaches were the product of differing theologies of biblical authority. The Reformed tradition, following Zwingli and Calvin, basically held to a restrictive view, that only what Scripture commands can be normative for Christian life and action. With such a premise music was either limited to unaccompanied congregational psalmody (Calvin), or eliminated altogether (Zwingli). Luther, on the other hand, adopted the more open-ended conviction that what Scripture forbids must be obeyed, but everything else is permissible providing Scriptural principles are neither denied nor undermined. The Lutheran tradition, therefore, developed a diversity in liturgical music in which congregational, choral and instrumental music were integrally intertwined, both functionally and artistically, within worship. The Lutheran tradition also developed a theological understanding of the role and function of music. Until about the middle of the eighteenth century it was customary for Lutheran theologians to study music and for church musicians to study theology. Thus in many books of music theory published in Germany in the later seventeenth and early eighteenth centuries, it was argued that theology and music required one another. Specific theological premises undergirded music theory. It was argued, for example, that as the doctrine of the Trinity was fundamental to orthodox Christian theology, so the basic C-major triad, a symbol of the Trinity, was fundamental to an understanding of music theory.

In the wake of medieval excesses of unrestrained polyphony, often based on distinctly secular melodies, and in response to the concerns of the Protestant Reformation, the Council of Trent advocated a chaste, restrained, and unaccompanied style (as exemplified by traditional plainsong and the compositions of Palestrina) as the only appropriate music for the liturgical rites, especially the Mass, of the Roman Catholic church. Such worship music had to serve a primary liturgical function, and be ecclesiastically pure and free from secular influence.

Music within Anglicanism shared both Catholic and Protestant elements. Instead of one integrated tradition, such as the Lutheran model, two alternative solutions developed within Anglicanism: the cathedral tradition with its artistic choral music, and the parish church tradition with its functional congregational psalmody and hymnody.

In the English-speaking world the Reformed practice of metrical psalmody predominated. Musical and poetic matters were superseded by overriding functional and didactic concerns. The 'pure' Word of God, as found in the psalms, was put into metrical form in order to be sung to tunes that would imprint it in the memory and on the heart. The first complete psalter of Sternhold and Hopkins, issued in 1562, had included in its title the phrase 'conferred with the Hebrew', meaning that the psalms were faithful to the biblical originals. The Bay Psalm Book of 1640, prepared by New England Puritans as a replacement for the psalter of Sternhold and Hopkins, announced in its preface:

> God's altar needs not our polishings . . . for we have respected rather a plain translation than to smooth our verses with the sweetness of any paraphrase, and so have attended to conscience rather than to elegance, fidelity rather than poetry, in translating the Hebrew words into English language . . . so we may sing . . . the Lord's songs of praise according to his own will.

At the beginning of the eighteenth century the Independent minister Isaac Watts effectively adopted a new hermeneutic with regard to psalmody. In prefaces to his hymns and psalms, issued in 1707 and 1719 respectively, he argued that it was theologically inconsistent for only Old Covenant songs to be sung in New Covenant worship, therefore the psalms of the Old Testament must be interpreted by the theology of the New Testament. Watts was charged with displacing the divinely inspired psalms of David with hymns of 'human composure'. It was a theological revolution

with regard to the substance of congregational song, but there were also far-reaching musical consequences. Watts contended that the then current practice of 'lining out' the psalms – that is, the congregation singing through a psalm line by line, after the precentor or clerk had read or sung each one – often made both verbal and musical nonsense. Watts, and others, therefore advocated that psalms and hymns should be sung stanza by stanza ('Regular Singing') rather than line by line ('Usual Singing'). In many Independent congregations in both England and New England heated debates ensued. Advocates of Usual Singing charged that with Regular Singing the contaminating seeds of popery would be introduced into Protestant worship. But when Usual Singers were outvoted and seceded to Anglican churches, in which the practice of lining-out continued, the Regular Singers accused them of apostasy! This revolution in congregational song, set in motion by the new hermeneutic of Watts's psalms and hymns, was securely set within the framework of Calvinist theology. But at the same time as it influenced the Calvinist worship of succeeding generations of Presbyterians and Congregationalists, it also prepared the way for the Arminian hymnody of METHODISM, by introducing the possibility of the stanza-by-stanza singing of strophic hymns.

Throughout the eighteenth century, secular influences, especially from opera, increasingly impinged upon the practice of church music. Detractors argued that it undermined the sacred integrity of traditional liturgical music by introducing the secular associations of entertainment. Supporters insisted that the worship of God deserved tasteful music in the 'modern' style.

Around 1700 under the influence of leading theologians, notably Erdmann Neumeister of Hamburg, the operatic recitative and aria were specifically imported into the Lutheran church cantata. In the compositions of Johann Sebastian Bach and his contemporaries, the cantata became a highly developed art form, a kind of musical preaching, rich in theological content, specifically written for its liturgical context.

In England operatic influences can be found in the enthusiastic hymnody of emerging Methodism. Here the theological justification was evangelical rather than liturgical. Driven by their Arminian theology, the Wesley brothers, John and Charles, were concerned to use 'popular' music of the day to reach people with the gospel. Charles Wesley, for example, parodied Dryden's 'Fairest isle, all isles excelling', from *King Arthur*, in his 'Love divine, all loves excelling', so that it could be sung to Henry Purcell's 'operatic' melody, originally written for Dryden's text. One of the earliest composers to introduce new music for Methodist hymnody was J.F. Lampe, a member of the orchestra at Covent Garden opera house in London. Lampe composed a number of tunes for texts by Charles Wesley, *Hymns on the Great Festivals*, issued in 1746, which exemplify the Handelian operatic norms of the day.

In theory, Tridentine principles were adhered to in Roman Catholicism, but in practice operatic elements were frequently imported into the Mass. In Austria, especially in Vienna and Salzburg, operatic Masses, with soloists, chorus and full orchestra, were commonly heard. These were the compositions of Mozart, Haydn and others.

Towards the end of the eighteenth century two very different movements began to exert an influence on the theory and practice of church music: Pietism and the Enlightenment.

Pietism had its roots in English Puritan writings of the seventeenth century. In Germany it grew into a powerful movement within Lutheranism and engendered bitter hostility between its proponents on the one hand, and Lutheran orthodox theologians on the other. German Pietism was largely an ecclesiological phenomenon which, under the successive leadership of Philipp Jakob Spener and August Hermann Francke, sought to complete what was thought to be incomplete in Luther's Reformation. All remnants of Catholicism were to be eliminated and a simple biblical spirituality was to replace what was considered to be an excess of external formalism in Lutheran worship. The movement was fostered by informal *collegia pietatis*, small groups, *ecclesiola in ecclesia*, that met for Bible study and prayer. Part of the Pietists' agenda was the elimination of all remaining elements of the Catholic Mass from the Lutheran liturgy, the eradication of elaborate music, and the virtual replacement of the objective Lutheran chorale by a subjective form of congregational song.

The Enlightenment promoted rationalism as the Christian ideal; anything that was redolent of a superstitious past was to be abolished. In practice the proponents of the Enlightenment followed a similar agenda to that of the Pietists, that is, the elimination of the old liturgical forms and the abandonment of ornate music; but instead of the new Pietist hymnody they promoted their own rationalist hymnody, together with drastically revised versions of the old Lutheran hymns. By the end of the eighteenth century the combined influence of the Enlightenment and Pietist movements in Protestant Germany had reduced the service of worship to little more than a lengthy sermon, a few prayers, and one or two congregational hymns with organ accompaniment.

The nineteenth century was to a large degree a period of reaction and reform. Initial reforms in Germany took place in Berlin in around 1830, when a new hymnal and liturgical order were published. Among the Berlin reformers were Friedrich Schleiermacher, an opponent of the Enlightenment, and G.K.B. Ritschl (the father of Albrecht Ritschl, who later strenuously attacked Pietism). The aim of these leaders was to purge the hymnal of rationalist redaction, promote the old chorale melodies, restore liturgical forms and reintroduce the concept and practice of a choral liturgy. This restoration of Lutheran theology, liturgical practice and church music continued throughout the century and did not entirely come to fruition until the early years of this century.

The Anglican Oxford, or Tractarian, movement of the mid-nineteenth century, and the Anglo-Catholicism (see ANGLICANISM) that followed it, not only had an important impact on the musical aspects of the worship of the Church of England, but also, ultimately, created far-reaching changes across many denominational divides in the English-speaking world and beyond. The movement began with the aim of restoring seventeenth-century high church perspectives, but soon moved in the direction of the medieval church as the ideal for ecclesiastical life, worship and theology. At first, largely through the influence of John Mason Neale and the publications of the Cambridge Camden Society, a primary concern was with architecture, but quickly the preoccupation expanded to include musical matters, especially the recovery of plainchant for the worship of the English church. However, the ideal of congregations singing unaccompanied Gregorian chant was out of step with the spirit of the age and the use of organs was eventually promoted. By the end of the century very few parish churches were untouched by these reforms. Gone were the gallery singers and players at the back of the church; instead the singing was led by a surpliced choir in the chancel, with an adjacent organ to one side at the front of the church; and prose psalms, which hitherto had been communally read in parish churches, were now invariably sung to Anglican chant. Further, the role of the parish choir in singing within the liturgy approximated to some degree to the older tradition of cathedral music.

In Europe there were also similar reforms in the first half of the nineteenth century designed to eradicate the influences of the Enlightenment and secular and operatic elements from Catholic worship. These culminated in the formation of the Caecilian Society in Bamberg, Bavaria, in 1868. Originally the society had the aim of reform in German-speaking areas, but, following papal recognition in 1870, its basic agenda – promoting ancient polyphony, new *a cappella* choral music, vernacular hymnody and the recovery of Gregorian chant – soon spread throughout Europe, North America and elsewhere in the world. Functional liturgical music was the Caecilian ideal, a noble goal, but in the quest artistic concerns were marginalized and national musical characteristics were effectively proscribed. In many respects the culmination of the Caecilian movement was the *motu proprio* of Pope Pius X, dated 22 November (St Caecilia's day) 1903. This pronouncement declared that in the music of the Catholic church Gregorian chant was accorded the primary place. Ancient polyphonic music, especially the liturgical compositions of Palestrina, was second only to the ancient chant. New music for the liturgy was also to be encouraged, but, in contrast with the limitations of Caecilianism, it could be written in a variety of stylistic forms. However, the proviso was added that such new music had to be liturgically appropriate and avoid the 'theatrical' and the 'unseemly'.

While these somewhat backward-looking reforms by Lutherans, Anglicans and Catholics were occurring throughout the nineteenth century, others, instead of eliminating secular influences, deliberately developed them. Among them were the Methodists and other evangelicals who inherited the spirited hymnody of the evangelical revival of the later eighteenth century. Revivalism continued in the early years of the nineteenth century, particularly in North America, where the camp meeting became an established part of the religious scene. At these camp meetings an evangelistic hymnody developed, with extended refrains and repetitions and sung to melodies derived from secular styles. The music functioned as a vehicle to meet people where they were with the message of the gospel. Later in the century, as camp meetings gave way to the organized evangelism of Dwight L. Moody, William Booth, founder of the Salvation Army, and others, the gospel hymn developed as an overt evangelistic tool. Here the undisguised secular style of the music hall song or the Victorian parlour ballad provided the model. Again, the purpose was functional rather than artistic.

At another level there were people like William Gardiner in England and Lowell Mason in the USA who, early in the century, adapted the secular music of Haydn, Mozart, Beethoven and others into hymn tunes and other religious music. Their motivation was to produce the finest music of the day for the worship of their churches. But the popular music of the Victorian period proved to be irresistible. Even the influential *Hymns Ancient and Modern*, which first appeared in 1861 as a self-conscious product of the Oxford movement, in its later editions absorbed the somewhat sentimental style. Barnby, Stainer, Sullivan and others could and did write some stirring hymn tunes that survive in modern hymnals, but they also wrote much in that maudlin style that typifies the period.

During the first half of the twentieth century there was a consolidation of the concerns of the previous century. This was in large measure due to the two world wars which called in question the idea of humankind's inevitable upward drive of progress. Among the older concerns that received new attention were the role and function of choirs in Protestant denominations. In the USA in 1926 John Finley Williamson founded Westminster Choir School at a Presbyterian church in Dayton, Ohio (now

Westminster Choir College, Princeton, New Jersey); and in the United Kingdom the following year, Sydney Nicholson founded the Anglican School of English Church Music, later known as the Royal School of Church Music, Croydon. Both institutions have subsequently broadened their scope to cover a wide variety of denominational approaches to music, a reflection of the development of the ecumenical movement in the twentieth century.

Following the end of the Second World War, a period of change and experimentation called into question virtually every established practice of church music, together with its *raison d'être*. In the English-speaking world Geoffrey Beaumont's *Twentieth Century Folk Mass*, published in 1957, was catalytic. Congregations in various denominations on both sides of the Atlantic introduced the *Folk Mass* into their Sunday worship in the late 1950s and early 1960s. Beaumont also founded The Twentieth Century Church Light Music Group, which published various collections of *Twentieth Century Hymn Tunes*, mainly written in 1930s Broadway style. The success of the *Folk Mass* and the *Twentieth Century Hymn Tunes* generated a rash of imitators throughout the churches as homegrown popular music was composed and adapted for liturgy and hymnody, strongly influenced by the general interest in folk music of the 1960s.

In reaction to this adaptation of popular secular music, the Dunblane Consultations on Church Music, in which Erik Routley played a primary role, attempted to encourage the composition of contemporary music (and texts) for Christian worship that had an integrity that the compositions of The Twentieth Century Church Light Music Group generally lacked. These Dunblane Consultations provided examples for others to follow and opened up a staggeringly productive period of hymn writing which has become known as the 'hymn explosion', associated with such names as Fred Pratt Green, Brian Wren, Fred Kaan, Cyril Taylor, Peter Cutts, Thomas Troeger, Jeffrey Rowthorne, Carl Daw, Jaraslav Vajda, Calvin Hampton, David Hurd, Carol Doran and many others.

The Second Vatican Council created an entirely new atmosphere with regard to church music and hymnody within the Roman Catholic church as a whole. The *Constitution on the Sacred Liturgy*, promulgated on 4 December 1963, promoted three ideals that were to have far-reaching consequences for the music of the church: (1) a wider use of the vernacular in worship, especially the Mass (section 36); (2) the use of hymns, in addition to traditional Office hymns (section 93); and (3) 'religious singing by the people is to be skilfully fostered so that . . . the voices of the faithful may ring out' (section 118). Although not banned by the Council, Latin was effectively excluded from most parishes by the adoption of the vernacular in worship. The demise of the regular use of Latin also meant that the music closely associated with the Latin liturgy was similarly banished from the sanctuary, that is, Gregorian chant in general, and choral settings of the Latin ordinary of the Mass in particular. Hymnals containing congregational, vernacular hymns, which had hitherto not been permitted in the Mass, were published, and responsorial psalmody, similar to that developed by Father Gelineau in France, flourished. Thus in many Catholic churches liturgical choral music was no longer heard. In theory it should have been replaced by congregational singing; in practice it proved to be a difficult exercise. In the effort to get congregations to sing, simplistic music was introduced – in disposable 'missalettes' rather than hymnals – and the people were led by amplified cantors. In some congregations the practice worked, but in many others the cantors effectively replaced the singing of the people.

These changes in Roman Catholic practices were also mirrored in much of Protestant worship. Indeed, the remarkable ecumenical spirit of the twentieth century has created far-reaching cross-fertilizations in both theory and practice. The general shift in thinking about the role of music in worship over the last thirty years or so has been from the artistic to the functional, from the traditional to the contemporary, and from specifically sacred to overtly secular styles. By and large the primary interest has been with pragmatic evangelism and the need for Christianity to be seen to be relevant in this (paradoxically) post-Christian age. But there are those who have been concerned to establish a particular theological understanding of the role and function of music in a Christian context. Among the most important are the

Lutherans Edmund Schlink (1950) and Oskar Söhngen (1967), the Reformed Adolf Brunner (1968) and Erik Routley ([1959] 1978), and the Roman Catholic Winfried Kurzschenkel (1971), who have sought to establish the theological principles on which the practice of church music should be based.

It is noticeable that German theologians have produced the most substantial contributions. This might be expected, given the traditional connection between theology and music within Lutheranism, except that these German authors are not all Lutherans. Further, it is not only in theological monographs devoted to music but also in general works of theology, written by authors with a German background, that one finds a theological understanding of music. For example, Karl Barth in his *Church Dogmatics* makes significant reference to the music of Mozart, and Paul Tillich in his *Systematic Theology* gives a place to the music of Johann Sebastian Bach. By contrast, English writers on theology and music have generally tended to be musicians rather than theologians. This perhaps explains the general malaise concerning the use of music in worship in the English-speaking world. In contrast with the situation in German-speaking countries, very few theological colleges and seminaries on either side of the Atlantic currently give serious attention to the theological, liturgical and practical aspects of music. Therefore, in the absence of leadership from theologians and clergy, church musicians have attempted to establish a theological understanding of their art and profession.

In contemporary Christianity there are two major polarities with regard to music. On the one hand there are the pragmatists, especially in American neo-evangelicalism, to whom questions of art, tradition and suitable style are irrelevant when compared to the more important matters of evangelism and church growth. Whatever music brings people into the church and keeps them there is all that is important. In practice, overt secular musical styles are those that are thought to achieve this, and specifically sacred styles are dismissed as ineffective and 'elitist'. On the other hand, there are those to whom functionality, while being important, is not enough. Echoing Ralph Vaughan Williams, who declared in the preface to *The English Hyman* of 1906 that good music for worship is a

moral issue, they argue that music for the worship of Almighty God must not be banal or mundane. The true worship of the Creator demands from us the highest fruits of our creativity, not merely anything that 'works'. The eternal gospel cannot be commended with disposable, fashionable music styles, otherwise there is the implication that the gospel itself is somehow disposable and temporary.

There is evidence that some on both sides of the divide are beginning to realize that many of the assumptions with regard to music have been culturally conditioned (see CULTURE AND THEOLOGY). The styles and usage of music within Christian worship have frequently been the product of the culture within which they have taken place – European, American, African, African-American, Asian or whatever. If the old antithetical questions continue to be asked within narrow cultural boundaries, current antipathies and conflicts over music styles and content are likely to continue. If a synthesis is possible, then it will only be developed from such primary theological concepts as *kerygma*, *koinonia*, *leitourgia* (Pass, 1989) and *eucharistia* (yet to be given the attention it deserves in this context), or such fundamental theological categories as Christology, ecclesiology and eschatology (Leaver, 1989), which transcend cultural confines.

See also LITURGY AND DOCTRINE; PREACHING, THEOLOGY OF; SPIRITUALITY.

Bibliography

Benson, L.F. [1915] 1962: *The English Hymn: Its Development and Use in Worship*, 2nd edn. Richmond, Virginia: John Knox Press.

Blume, F. [1965] 1974: *Protestant Church Music: A History*, trans. with additional material. New York: Norton.

Brunner, A. [1960] 1968: *Musik in Gottesdienst: Wesen, Funktion und Ort der Musik in Gottesdienst*, 2nd edn. Zurich: Zwingli Verlag.

Ellinwood, L. 1953: *The History of American Church Music*. New York: Morehouse-Gorham.

Fellerer, K.G. [1949] 1961: *The History of Catholic Church Music*, trans. F.A. Brunner. Baltimore, Maryland: Helicon.

Gelineau, J. [1962] 1964: *Voices and Instruments in Christian Worship*, trans. C. Howell. Collegeville, Minnesota: Liturgical Press.

Glover, R., ed. 1990–3: *The Hymnal 1982 Companion*, 3 vols. New York: Church Hymnal Corporation.

Harper, J. forthcoming: *Music of the English Church*.

Hayburn, R.F. 1979: *Papal Legislation on Sacred Music 95 AD to 1977 AD*. Collegeville: Liturgical Press.

Kurzschenkel, W. 1971: *Die theologische Bestimmung der Musik*. Trier: Paulinus-Verlag.

Leaver, R.A. 1989: *The Theological Character of Music in Worship*. St Louis: Concordia.

Pass, D.B. 1989: *Music and the Church: A Theology of Church Music*. Nashville, Tenn.: Broadman Press.

Routley, E. [1959] 1978: *Church Music and the Christian Faith*, 2nd edn. Carol Stream: Agape. (1st edn: *Church Music and Theology*)

Schalk, K., ed. 1978: *Key Words in Church Music*. St Louis: Concordia.

Schlink, E. 1950: *Zum theologischen Problem der Musik*. Tübingen: Möhr.

Söhngen, O. 1967: *Theologie der Musik*. Kassel: Bärenreiter Verlag.

ROBIN A. LEAVER

N

narrative theology 'Narrative theology' is a term that has been applied to a variety of views that draw, in one way or another, on theories of literature and/or literary genres for theological reflection. Even so, it is not clear that these views necessarily ought to be identified as part of one enterprise called 'narrative theology'. Further, not all of those who have been identified as proponents of 'narrative theology' accept such an appellation. As such, there is not so much a distinct position known as 'narrative theology' as there is a variety of ways in which theologians have argued for the significance of narrative for theological reflection.

The very notion of 'narrative theology' derives from developments in the twentieth century. The pivotal figures in its development, though neither uses the term 'narrative theology', are Karl Barth and H. Richard Niebuhr. Both Barth and Niebuhr were dissatisfied with the Enlightenment's emphasis on isolated, objective facts which seemed to privilege science and marginalize theology. They turned to the significance of narrative as a way of explicating theological convictions.

Even so, their own substantive proposals were considerably different from each other. For his part, Barth was primarily concerned to understand Scripture in its witness to God. He did not propose a method for reading Scripture as a narrative. Rather, he displayed such a reading in his theological treatment of various doctrines, arguing that central Christian teachings are best understood in narrative terms. That is, Barth understood the Bible to be an overarching narrative that tells the story of the God of Jesus Christ.

Conversely, H. Richard Niebuhr was primarily concerned to understand how Scripture's witness to God illumines our own self-understanding. While Niebuhr was in some ways close to Barth's views in that both thought that revelation takes the form of a narrative, the crucial difference can be seen in the title of a chapter in Niebuhr's *The Meaning of Revelation* (1941): 'The Story of Our Life'. For Niebuhr, the story of God's action intersects with the stories of particular individuals and communities. Barth would always insist that narrative is significant in telling the story not, or at least not primarily, of *our* life but of God.

More recent discussions of narrative theology have tended to follow the trajectories of either Barth or Niebuhr. For example, Hans Frei not only helped shape the perception of Barth as a theologian who emphasized the narrativity of Scripture, he also extended Barth's proposals in two ways. First, Frei's reading of the history of modern biblical interpretation was an attempt, at least in part, to vindicate Barth's reading of Scripture as a 'realistic narrative' as opposed to an excessive reliance on historical-critical methods of interpretation in general, and the HISTORY OF RELIGIONS SCHOOL of interpretation in particular. Second, Frei's reading of the identity of Jesus Christ in the Gospels was designed to establish the central narrative sequence in Scripture. Even so, Frei was dubious of any general interest in anything that might be identified as 'narrative theology'. Indeed, he was particularly suspicious of attempts to make generalized claims about narrative beyond those claims specific to biblical hermeneutics.

Other theologians such as Eberhard Jüngel and Robert Jenson, similarly influenced by Barth, have also turned to narrative in explicating central Christian doctrines such as the

Trinity. Such a narrative construal of the doctrine of God, at least in their proposals, does not obviate metaphysical questions. Metaphysical questions and issues are raised by the narratives, but those questions and issues must not be presumed to be isolated from the narratives themselves.

On the other hand, there has also been interest in establishing the significance of narrative for understanding human life along the trajectory established by Niebuhr. For example, Stephen Crites has utilized phenomenological philosophy to argue that there is a fundamentally 'narrative quality of experience'. Further, though he is not directly indebted to Niebuhr, Paul Ricoeur's phenomenological hermeneutics has emphasized the narrative quality of experience in articulating a more generalized approach to narrative interpretation whose range of applications includes, but is not limited to, biblical hermeneutics.

The two trajectories established by Barth and Niebuhr are sufficiently different, and even perhaps opposed, that scholars attempting to characterize 'narrative theology' have too often presumed and/or argued that these are the *only* two relevant options for doing narrative theology. At times, this has been specified with reference to the 'Frei–Ricoeur' debate, which was never so much a debate as it was a way of identifying differences in each person's approach to narrative, specifically the importance of narrative for biblical and theological hermeneutics.

Unfortunately, however, this way of positioning the issues has oversimplified both developments in, and the range of options identified by, theological appeals to narrative. There have been developments within the realm of biblical hermeneutics that have made it difficult to assume that the fundamental options are represented by either of the two trajectories. That is, the proposals of such figures as Barth, Niebuhr, Frei, and Ricoeur need to be situated in relation to other strategies. For example, there has been a widespread interest among biblical scholars in narrative theory, both for the reading of specific passages and for the analysis of entire books of the Bible. This reflects its own wide range of interests, competencies, and proposals, ranging from the arguments of Eric Auerbach and Robert Alter through Northrop Frye to the more recent work of Jacques Derrida and Fredric Jameson.

Further, some theologians have focused less on narrative theory than on probing particular kinds of narratives. For example, Sallie McFague (in a book originally published under the name Sallie M. TeSelle) and John Dominic Crossan have, in different ways, used the prominence of parables in Scripture as a context for suggesting that the parabolic structure of certain stories is fundamental for how people learn to perceive reality.

There has also been a strong interest in narrative's significance for a construal of theological ethics, particularly when ethics is understood in the light of Aristotle's emphasis on character. James W. McClendon has argued that biography is important for theology precisely because narrative is crucial to the display of character. He has stressed the importance of narrative not only for character but for the communities of which such characters are a part. More recently, McClendon has developed these arguments in the service of a Christian systematic theology.

Similarly, Stanley Hauerwas develops an account of narrative's significance for Christian life that is both influenced by, and an influence on, the thought of philosophers such as Alasdair MacIntyre. He has also been influenced by theologians such as Barth, Niebuhr, Frei and Crites. Hauerwas contends that narrative is crucial for the display and development of character. Further, the character of Christians is most adequately displayed and developed by being inducted into communities which are themselves shaped by the biblical narrative. Hence Hauerwas's work poses a challenge to any attempt to see narrative theology simply in terms of either of the two trajectories of Barth and Niebuhr.

McClendon's and Hauerwas's emphasis on the narratives of particular communities has also been emphasized by various theologies of liberation, an approach not often associated with narrative theology. Yet in the work of such figures as James Cone, Gustavo Gutiérrez and Johannes Baptist Metz, there is an important linkage between the narratives of particular people or communities and the narratives of Scripture. For example, Cone has drawn on the narratives of African-American people and communities as a context for constructing a theology of liberation. Gutiérrez has similarly drawn on the narratives of Latin American people and communities. Metz has gone even further in explicitly identifying the epistemological and theological significance of narrative for political theologies of liberation. Hence from a variety of perspectives, theologians of liberation have turned to narrative as a way of explicating the relationship between particular social contexts and Scripture.

Narrative theology has been a movement within Christian theology. Even so, it has not been confined to Christians. For example, the Jewish theologian Michael Goldberg has examined the ways in which Jews and Christians have conflicting Scriptural narratives, and conflicting ways of reading those narratives. Such conflicts, Goldberg argues, lead to divergent renderings of both specific doctrines and patterns of life. Hence he suggests that, if Scripture is to be understood as an overarching narrative that provides an identity description of God and the shape of doctrines, then the fact that Jews and Christians have different Scriptures will undoubtedly also lead to different understandings of both the biblical narrative(s) and the narrative(s) of human life.

In addition, the term 'narrative theology' has also been applied to a wide range of interests in the significance of stories and myths for religious understanding. Such a perspective can be found, for example, in the diverse proposals of Robert Detweiler, John Dunne, Sam Keen, and Wesley Kort. These views tend to be more about 'religion' in general rather than specifically theological argument and reflection. Further, they tend to refer more to 'story' and 'stories' than to 'narrative' *per se*.

For many people, 'story' and 'narrative' are essentially interchangeable terms. But the terms also tend, particularly within theology, to point to divergent commitments on issues of knowledge and truth. That is, people who propose to understand 'religion as story' typically understand religion, and hence also story, as a means to understanding people's subjectivity, to illumining particular values, and to giving meaning to people's lives. From this perspective, both religion and story provide a counterbalance to modernity's excessive preoccupation with objectivity and scientific facts. Such views

are typically uninterested in questions of the truth of stories; it is enough that they provide sufficient meaning for people.

From this perspective, religion is significant in reminding people of the value of stories for human life. It helps people understand their own subjectivity, gives their lives meaning, and thus serves as a therapy for overcoming the obsessions of rationalism. Even so, *if* this is the primary meaning somebody has in mind when referring to 'narrative theology', then the movement is not likely to have much long-term impact.

This is because such positions tend to leave in place modernity's bifurcations of object and subject, fact and value, public and private. While it might be good to be reminded of the impact of stories on the latter half of each pair, such a view leaves the former untouched.

Hence the more promising direction for narrative in Christian theology is as an epistemological challenge to those bifurcations. The nature of this challenge has taken several forms. One way, particularly focused in the work of Barth and Frei but also apparent in the interest in 'literary criticism' in biblical studies, is to attack the primacy of modernity's conception of 'historical facts' while acknowledging that narrative is not unrelated to history. Frei does this by using the development of the 'realistic novel' to suggest how Scripture can be 'history-like' without necessarily being 'factual' history.

Even though this attack in general, and Frei's view in particular, have been influential in Christian theology, there is no clear consensus either among historians or theologians on the relationship between narrative and history. This issue is further complicated by the question of truth (see TRUTH, CONCEPTS OF). Does a narrative, say the Gospel of Mark, make a claim to truth independent of any relation to history (for example, because it is 'true to life')? Or does the particular story that is being told, that of Jesus of Nazareth, require stronger commitments to historical contexts? Such questions remain controversial among scholars.

This challenge also sometimes issues in a broader conception of the significance of narrative for theology. Some theologians, such as John Milbank, argue that objects and subjects only exist through the complex relations of a narrative. Hence action, personal identity and even what we claim to know are mediated by particular narratives. The arguments of Alasdair MacIntyre as well as 'postmodern' literary critics have, in diverse and conflicting ways, been influential in the development of this view.

Thus 'narrative theology' is a term that has been applied to views that focus on, among other topics: biblical hermeneutics and literary criticism, human subjectivity, the development of doctrine through the rendering of personal identity, the importance of people's particular biographies, the life of particular communities, and even the linkage of stories to ideas about myth. As such a list indicates, there is at best a family resemblance among such views. Perhaps more probably, there is not so much a family resemblance as a diverse set of often conflicting theological and epistemological judgements which share little more than a common and potentially misleading terminology of 'story' and 'narrative'.

Indeed in this light it is a mistake to ask how 'narrative theology' relates to other 'types' of theology. 'Narrative theology' is neither a coherent movement nor even a distinctive 'type' of theology. Even so, it has been significant in identifying the increasing recognition among theologians that, whatever else their commitments are, 'narrative' is a notion which points to crucial epistemological and theological issues. The importance of narrative for theology is likely to remain. Beyond this point, however, the power and influence of particular proposals for narrative's place in theological reflection is going to depend more on the distinctiveness of those views and less on being identified as part of a distinctive 'type' of, or 'movement' in, Christian theology.

See also BIBLICAL CRITICISM AND INTERPRE-TATION (1: OLD TESTAMENT and 2: NEW TESTA-MENT); LITERATURE AND THEOLOGY; POSTLIBERALISM.

Bibliography

Dunne, J.S. 1973: *Time and Myth*. Garden City, NY: Doubleday.

Ford, D. 1985: *Barth and God's Story*. Frankfurt: Verlag Peter Lang.

Frei, H. 1974: *The Eclipse of Biblical Narrative*. New Haven, CT: Yale University Press.

Goldberg, M. 1985: *Jews and Christians, Getting Our Stories Straight*. Nashville, TN: Abingdon.

Green, G., ed. 1986: *Scriptural Authority and Narrative Interpretation*. Philadelphia, PA: Fortress.

Hauerwas, S. 1983: *The Peaceable Kingdom*. Notre Dame, IN: University of Notre Dame Press.

Hauerwas, S., and Jones, L.G., eds 1989: *Why Narrative?* Grand Rapids, MI: Eerdmans.

Jüngel, E. [1977] 1983: *God as the Mystery of the World*, trans. D.I. Guder. Grand Rapids, MI: Eerdmans.

McClendon, J.W. [1974] 1990: *Biography as Theology*, 2nd edn. Philadelphia, PA: Trinity Press International.

Metz, J.B. [1977] 1980: *Faith in History and Society*, trans. D. Smith. New York: Crossroad.

Milbank, J. 1990: *Theology and Social Theory*. Oxford: Basil Blackwell.

Nelson, P. 1987: *Narrative and Morality*. University Park, PA: Pennsylvania State University Press.

Niebuhr, H.R. 1941: *The Meaning of Revelation*. New York: Macmillan.

Ricoeur, P. [1983] 1984–8: *Time and Narrative*, trans. K. McLaughlin and D. Pellauer. Chicago: University of Chicago Press.

TeSelle, S.M. 1975: *Speaking in Parables*. Philadelphia, PA: Fortress.

L. GREGORY JONES

natural law Natural law theories of various sorts endeavour to explicate and/or apply the notion that (1) there exists an intelligible order that is not an artefact of human practical reason, and that (2) this order is a source of moral directives for human conduct. It is one thing, however, to speak of natural standards for human acts, but it is quite another thing to use the term 'law' in connection with nature. Although there were Stoic antecedents to the formulation of natural standards in terms of law, the fully fledged meaning of a natural law emerged during the medieval period, when it came to denote the way God governs human action through secondary causality. Aquinas held that the natural law is the first way by which human agents participate in the eternal law (Aquinas 1966 I–II, q. 91, a. 2). This participationist view of natural law relied upon a set of contrasts. Natural law was distinguished from the more directly promulgated *lex divina*, first in the Decalogue of the *lex vetus*, and then in the gospel ordinances of the *lex nova*. These in turn were variously contrasted with the *lex* *humana* and human custom. Moreover, Aquinas's scheme of laws served a more general interest in distinguishing between the natural and supernatural determinants of human action en route to beatitude. Medieval scholastics deployed natural law theory to clarify the common ground of ecclesiastical and civil positive laws, and in the fourteenth century adumbrated the modern notion of a natural law of subject right. But it is doubtful that they viewed either natural law or natural rights independently of the theological terms and contrasts.

At the outset of the eighteenth century, the relation between 'law' and 'nature' was appropriated by the new sciences. Whereas Aquinas argued that the term 'law' is predicated of inanimate bodies only *per similitudinem* – by a kind of metaphorical analogy (Aquinas, 1966, I–II, q. 91, a. 2 and 3) – N. Copernicus, R. Descartes, J. Kepler, and I. Newton recast the meaning of natural laws, such that they denoted intelligible, measurable, and predictable regularities in inanimate bodies. Theological and humane meanings of what is law-like about nature gradually appeared derivative and metaphorical in comparison to the properly scientific point of view in which nature is simply 'the way things are apart from human intervention' (Weinreb, 1987, p. 129). In modern thought, the so-called naturalistic fallacy and the is–ought dilemma are believed to be telling reasons against the notion that prescriptive injunctions can be inferred from merely descriptive matters of fact. These problems are due in part to the ambiguity and equivocations which have beset the terms 'nature' and 'law' since the rise of the new sciences.

In so far as the new science of inanimate bodies emphasized a mechanistic view of nature, it became difficult to reassert either philosophical or theological doctrines of intrinsic teleology in human action. While modern theorists retained a conception of extrinsic teleology (design in nature), and at least rhetorically the notion of a divine providence that stands over both the inanimate and humane orders, natural law theory gradually ceased to be a tool for explicating how human action is directed to an ultimate end, whether temporal or supernatural. Cambridge Platonism represents the last systematic effort to interrelate the scientific, humane, and theological themes of natural law. Samuel Clarke, John Locke, and other Enlightenment theorists, including Immanuel Kant, worked to develop moral accounts of reason's relation to nature, but they did so by conceding the ground won by the new science. Attention was turned to the problem of how to retain an objective ground for freedom and moral duty despite the causal, physicalist meanings of natural laws.

Natural law theorists in the seventeenth and eighteenth centuries also faced a new set of political and legal problems. The issues of capital importance were the legitimacy of state power in relation to the individual, and the creation of a rule of law fit to govern a religiously pluralistic citizenry. There can be no question but that, in modernity, natural law theory received a new lease of life by virtue of the need to resolve these questions. And there can be no doubt that its prestige was won, first, during the eighteenth-century revolutionary period, when natural rights were asserted as the ground and origin of legitimate political power; and, second, in the period after the revolutions, when it became necessary to vindicate individual rights against the power of the political majorities unleashed by the democratic revolutions. Since then, the vocabulary of natural or fundamental human rights has become embedded in the political, legal, and moral institutions of western culture.

If the new science placed limitations upon what could be claimed about teleological laws of nature, the issues which became magnetized around the problem of rights required theorists to claim only what are the necessary, self-evident, or indisputable grounds for political consensus about the rule of law. As Hugo Grotius asserted, '[w]hat we have been saying would have a degree of validity even if we should concede that which cannot be conceded without the utmost wickedness, that there is no God, or that the affairs of men are of no concern to Him' (Grotius, [1625] 1925; Prolegomena, #11). Grotius's dictum was hypothetical, and should not be construed to indicate the complete detachment of natural law from religious convictions. The potentially radical thrust of his position is seen more clearly in his remark that 'just as mathematicians treat their figures as abstracted from bodies, so in treating law I have withdrawn my mind from every particular fact' (Prolegomena, #58). With Grotius, and later Samuel Pufendorf, natural law theory became the instrument of legal and academic professionals whose theories represented a quasi-scientific effort to organize the moral foundations of law independent of local knowledges, historical contingencies and those convictions (religious or otherwise) which bespeak merely private judgement. Accordingly, the theological ground of natural law and natural rights, though once again not rhetorically eliminated, was increasingly consigned to private judgement.

These two developments, then, continue in the contemporary period to set the terms of discussion about natural law. The sciences limit natural law theorists to non-metaphysical and non-teleological claims about human nature, while the political requirements limit theorists to articulating only those relatively noncontroversial moral principles which are apt to win consensus about rights. Generally, perfectionistic claims about the human good are subordinated to standards about rights, or what is right in the sense of JUSTICE as fairness. Contemporary liberal theories emphasize basic goods which are needed and claimed by human agents – goods which can easily be contrasted to values which depend upon mere subjective preference or the idiosyncratic lifeplans of particular individuals. Such goods (both substantive and procedural) are the grounds of fundamental rights, constituting the reasons for positive law and constraints on government; and particularly in the context of American constitutional law, they provide grounds for winning legal arguments against the police power of the state.

Protestant churches have had a more complicated relationship with these developments than the Roman church. Protestant legal and intellectual cultures embraced both the scientific and minimalist political conceptions of natural law theory. Calvinism, in particular, became the soil for modern debates about natural law. This was due, on one hand, to the fact that although Calvin criticized the notion of an autonomous natural law, his doctrine was sufficiently ambiguous to permit any number of theories and applications (Hancock, 1989). On the other hand, Calvin's theology was perceived as so amplifying the power of the civil state that

Calvinism became, in effect, the dialectical foil against which the more rationalistic theories of natural rights were developed. Throughout the seventeenth and eighteenth centuries, the subject of natural law became the occasion for, and frequently a symptom of, intra-ecclesial debate within various denominations over the sufficiency and role of reason in matters of doctrine and discipline, natural religion, and the problem of religious toleration. The problem of natural law, then, became diffused, hiding behind other issues and debates.

In *The Social Teaching of the Christian Churches* of 1912 Ernst Troeltsch argued that natural law is best understood in terms of the church–world problematic rather than the older systematic themes of reason–revelation or nature–grace. According to Troeltsch's typology, the church and sect types of ecclesial organization reflect different views of natural law, which are to be understood descriptively and functionally in terms of their respective conceptions of the social mission. His historical and sociological organization of the problem of natural law represents perhaps the clearest and most analytically powerful Protestant contribution to the discussion. Troeltsch's work in this area remained, however, descriptive rather than normative. In this century, Reinhold Niebuhr picked up and developed the church–world perspective, contending that natural law represents the persistent effort to posit a sinless morality that is, at once, too high and pretentious for civil life, and too far short of the agapic ethic unique to Christianity. Stanley Hauerwas has more recently developed this theme, in terms of a sharp contrast between the virtue-ethic unique to Christianity and the effort to advocate a universalistic ethic based upon natural law. While neither Niebuhr nor Hauerwas reject the existence of a natural law, they do displace it either as a primary tool for the churches' witness to the world or as a way to speak of what must be presupposed by a constructive moral theology. Of the major Protestant theologians of this century, Karl Barth, most directly denied any value to, if not the existence of, a natural moral law – even in a strictly theological setting. Natural law, for Barth, is inextricably dependent upon the *analogia entis*, which of course he unequivocally rejected (Barth, [1940] 1957, #36). Thus,

Barth's criticism moved the discussion back more closely to the metaphysical and theological issues which shaped Aquinas's formulation of the natural law.

Catholic philosophers and theologians have retained a more explicit commitment to natural law (see ROMAN CATHOLIC THEOLOGY.) Well into this century, Catholic scholasticism remained stubbornly resistant to the changes wrought both by the new science and by the modern preoccupation with natural rights. Modern papal encyclicals, beginning with *Rerum Novarum* (1891), have articulated the church's moral understanding of the social, economic and political orders in terms of both natural law and natural rights. In *Rerum Novarum*, Pope Leo XIII spoke of a natural right to possess property. The encyclical tradition has for the most part used natural law in addressing questions of social justice; but encyclicals such as *Humanae Vitae* (1968) have also used the concept to tackle matters of individual moral conduct like contraception. Although some theologians have argued that encyclicals and post-conciliar developments have displaced natural law in favour of a new emphasis upon personalism, the mushrooming of rights lan guage in magisterial documents has made the connection between natural law and natural rights all the more pressing. It is noteworthy that Pope John Paul II's one-hundred-year overview of the encyclical tradition in *Centesimus Annus* (1991) makes frequent mention of natural rights, but not of natural law. Both the systematic and semantic connections between natural law and natural rights have increasingly become more postulatory and implicit in the papal social teachings, and one of the chief issues facing the Roman Communion is how to articulate the relationship.

Jacques Maritain, for example, argued that it is necessary to distinguish between common moral principles reached by practical agreement and the theoretical justifications for these principles (Maritain, 1951, ch. 4). It is possible, he suggested, for Catholicism to embrace the modern issue of rights without either abandoning, or winning theoretical agreement about, its traditional view of natural law. That international bodies can agree on natural rights simply indicates pervasive convictions about the ontological order, rather than

philosophical consensus about the epistemological facets of the problem. John Courtney Murray also insisted that the Catholic view of natural law could practically accommodate modern, constitutional understandings of natural rights, so long as the natural law is viewed as a 'skeleton law' indicating only the minimal morality needed for social order (Murray, 1960, p. 316). The most impressive and systematic effort to interrelate natural law and natural rights has been done by John Finnis. Relying upon a new interpretation of Aquinas by Germain Grisez, Finnis has developed a theory of natural law that seeks to show how the moral, political and legal facets of the issue are interrelated according to practical reason's grasp and direction of basic human goods. His account, however, is best described as an effort to secure the objective moral grounds for practical reason, as well as to defend the tradition of exceptionless moral precepts against consequentialism. Finnis's theory has only a very weak connection to the traditional scholastic notions of nature, teleology and theology.

Other contemporary Catholic theorists remain cautious about the rehabilitation of natural law theory, not only with respect to the modern notion of subjective rights (Villey, 1983; Bastit, 1990), but also with regard to its place in moral theology. Henri de Lubac and Hans Urs von Balthasar have pointed out that Aquinas rejected the doctrine of a pure state of human nature. Both held that the tradition, properly interpreted, does not provide an isolatable natural law ethic independent of grace. The nature–grace controversy surrounding the encyclical *Humani Generis* (1950) brought this position into sharp focus. Since the Second Vatican Council, considerable attention has been given to Aquinas's theory of virtue. Vernon Bourke, for example, has argued that Aquinas ought not to be viewed as a natural law ethicist, because his moral philosophy relies upon a notion of right reason according to the virtues rather than anything resembling what modern philosophers mean by law (Bourke, 1974). Elizabeth Anscombe and Alasdair MacIntyre have likewise emphasized the importance of virtue ethics in contrast to law-based accounts of the moral life. It remains to be seen whether this interest in virtue is able to recover and reconnect itself to the theme of natural law. Among Catholic scholars there has yet to emerge a substitute for the scholastic organization of the issues, and as the matter now stands there is no unifying or commonly accepted focus for the various themes of nature, law and practical reason. However, the continued authority of Aquinas (notwithstanding the demise of scholasticism), the belief in a law of nature (as an element in the common theological tradition), as well as the practical implications of the encyclical tradition (despite the skirmishes over the relation between natural law and rights), keep the issue not far from the surface of Catholic moral theology.

See also ETHICS; RELATIVISM, CULTURAL.

Bibliography

Anscombe, Elizabeth 1958: Modern moral philosophy, *Philosophy* 33, pp. 1–19.

Aquinas, Thomas 1966: *Summa Theologiae*, 60 vols. Vol. 28, *Law and Political Theory*, trans. Thomas Gilby, OP. New York: McGraw-Hill.

Balthasar, Hans Urs von 1986: Nine propositions on Christian ethics, trans. Graham Harrison. In J. Ratzinger, H. Schurmann, H.U. von Balthasar: *Principles of Christian Morality*. San Francisco: Ignatius Press.

Barth, Karl [1940] 1957: *Church Dogmatics*, vol. II/1, trans. P.H.L. Parker. Edinburgh: T & T Clark.

Bastit, Michel 1990: *Naissance de la loi moderne*. Paris: Presses Universitaires Francaises.

Bourke, Vernon 1974: Is Thomas Aquinas a natural law ethicist?, *The Monist* 58, pp. 52–66.

Finnis, John 1980: *Natural Law and Natural Rights*. Oxford: Oxford University Press.

Grisez, Germain 1965: The first principle of practical reason, *Natural Law Forum* 10, pp. 168–201.

Grotius, Hugo [1625] 1925: *On the Law of War and Peace*, trans. Francis W. Kelsey. Oxford: Oxford University Press.

Hancock, Ralph C. 1989: *Calvinism and the Foundations of Modern Politics*. Ithaca: Cornell University Press.

Hauerwas, Stanley 1983: *The Peaceable Kingdom*. Notre Dame: University of Notre Dame Press.

Hittinger, Russell 1990: Liberalism and the American natural law tradition, *Wake Forest Law Review* 25, pp. 429–99.

Lubac, Henri de 1946: *Surnaturel*. Paris: Aubier-Montaigne.

MacIntyre, Alasdair 1984: *After Virtue*, 2nd edn. Notre Dame: University of Notre Dame Press.

Maritain, Jacques 1951: *Man and the State*. Chicago: University of Chicago Press.

Murray, John C. 1960: *We Hold These Truths*. New York: Sheed and Ward.

Niebuhr, Reinhold 1964: *The Nature and Destiny of Man*, vol. 1. New York: Charles Scribner.

Tierney, Brian 1988: Villey, Ockham and the origin of individual rights. In *The Weightier Matter of the Law*, ed. John Witte and F.S. Alexander. Atlanta: Scholars Press.

Troeltsch, Ernst [1912] 1931: *The Social Teaching of the Christian Churches*, trans. Olive Wyon. London: George Allen and Unwin.

Villey, Michel 1983: *Le droit et les droits de l'homme*. Paris: University of Paris Press.

Weinreb, Lloyd L. 1987: *Natural Law and Justice*. Cambridge: Harvard University Press.

RUSSELL HITTINGER

natural science and Christian thought See BIOLOGICAL SCIENCE AND CHRISTIAN THOUGHT; PHYSICAL SCIENCE AND CHRISTIAN THOUGHT.

natural theology Natural theology is the knowledge of God (and perhaps also of related topics, such as the immortality of the soul) accessible to all rational human beings without recourse to any special or supposedly supernatural revelation (see REVELATION, CONCEPT OF). As the etymology of the word implies, theology was first studied among the Greeks, for whom God or the gods had become an intellectual problem. The expression 'natural theology' (*theologia naturalis*) seems to have been first used by Augustine with reference to the deepest theological insights of the classical philosophers, insights which in some respects Augustine could acknowledge as anticipating the teaching about God in the '*theologia supernaturalis*' of Christianity (Jaeger, 1947, pp. 1–4). Many other patristic writers had used arguments from pre-Christian philosophers in their theological writings.

The alliance between natural theology and the supernatural, or revealed, theology of Christianity continued through the Middle Ages. In 1077 Anselm in his *Monologion* offered arguments for the existence of God as an alternative to believing on authority, and followed this with his *Proslogion* in which he stated his ontological argument for the existence of God. This famous argument is still debated by philosophers today. It is a purely rational argument, in the sense that it seeks to establish

God's existence from the very concept of God, without any appeal to experience. The place of natural theology in Anselm is also subject to debate. He claims that he believes in order to understand, not that he must understand in order to believe, and this would mean that he is not making his theology depend upon a foundation of natural understanding.

Two hundred years later Thomas Aquinas was using natural theology in a different way. Near the beginning of his great *Summa theologiae*, he explicitly rejects the ontological proof of God's existence and offers instead arguments that are based on what he takes to be universal human experience. He states five such arguments (*Summa theologiae*, Ia, 2, 3) and these constitute the famous 'Five Ways', which many have considered the foundation stone of traditional natural theology. In brief summary, the Five Ways are these:

1   Everything is in process of change, but there must be a first cause of change not itself subject to change.

2   Similarly, everything has a cause, but if we trace back any series of causes, we must come to a first cause which is itself uncaused.

3   The things that we see in the world exist contingently, that is to say, they might not exist. But if everything were merely contingent, there would be nothing at all, so we have to conclude that there is a necessary being dependent for its being on nothing but itself.

4   We are aware of a principle of gradation in the world; some things are higher than others. There must therefore be something which is 'truest, best and most noble' of all, the source of goodness in other things and that which is most fully in being (*maxime ens*).

5   The last argument is from the order and design of nature. Everything in nature is directed to a goal, and this implies an intelligent designer.

The conclusion of each of these arguments is, according to Aquinas, God, as commonly understood. At least, we might say that each argument points to some characteristic that we commonly ascribe to God. So having, as he

believed, established the reality of God, Aquinas goes on to fill out the picture in terms of the Christian revelation.

In Aquinas, natural theology has an auxiliary function, as leading the reader from everyday experience to the specific experience of being addressed by the Christian revelation. When we come to the Renaissance and Enlightenment, with their reaction against authority and tradition, the prestige of natural theology began to increase, at the expense of the theology based on revelation. Lord Herbert of Cherbury, the father of DEISM, set forth in his book *De veritate* of 1624 a natural theology embracing five main points: belief in God as the Supreme Being; the duty to worship God; the identification of such worship with the leading of a virtuous life; the need for repentance; and belief in a future life in which there will be rewards or punishments according to desert. The deists believed that these fundamental beliefs had always been accessible to human reason and constituted the essence of all true religion, including Christianity and other historical religions in which the essential truths had been clothed or even concealed in particular formulations derived from the historical circumstances of the religion concerned. So-called 'revelations' might, through their narrative form, make it easier for the human mind to perceive the essential theological truths, but in principle they are discoverable to reason. The argument from design was especially prized as pointing to God as the author of the laws of nature, while conscience exhibited God as the moral lawgiver. This view found expression in the words of Kant: 'Two things fill the mind with ever new and increasing admiration and awe, the oftener and the more steadily we reflect on them: *the starry heavens above and the moral law within.*'

The later part of the eighteenth century, however, witnessed a hostile critique of natural theology, and perhaps it has never fully recovered from this. A leader in this critique was the Scottish philosopher, David Hume. In his *Dialogues concerning Natural Religion* (published posthumously in 1779) he exposed flaws in the traditional so-called 'proofs' of the existence of God, including the argument from design, which he acknowledged to be the strongest of them. Hume's conclusion punctured the claims that had been made for natural theology. At the most, it might show that the causes of order in the universe 'probably bear some remote analogy' to human intelligence, but this meagre result is said to have no importance for human life. The further point is made that the universe is more like an organism than an artefact, so that its order would be immanent rather than imposed by a transcendent intelligent creator.

Kant's critique of natural theology was more thorough and systematic than Hume's. In his *Critique of Pure Reason* Kant describes natural theology as 'transcendental illusion' and subjects the traditional proofs of God's existence to searching analysis. The ontological argument is rejected on the ground that it makes an illicit transition from idea to reality. The several empirical arguments are rejected on the ground that the categories of understanding which they employ are limited in their application to the phenomena of space and time, and that if we attempt to extend their scope to realities supposedly lying behind these phenomena, then we fall into contradictions. But Kant's attack on natural theology was not motivated by scepticism about religion. His avowed aim was 'to deny knowledge in order to make room for faith'. So seven years after these critical remarks, in 1788, he published his *Critique of Practical Reason*, in which he advances a new argument for the existence of God, the moral argument. For Kant, nothing is more real than man's moral freedom, but morality entails a religious context. Although God, freedom and immortality cannot be proved by the theoretical exercise of reason, they are postulates of the moral life, so that we implicitly accept them in accepting the reality of moral obligation.

While Hume and Kant severely damaged the credibility of natural theology, they certainly did not destroy it, and the controversies which they initiated continued into the nineteenth century and beyond. The battle swayed now one way, now the other. William Paley's *Natural Theology* of 1802 remained very influential for decades, and even today some people remember his famous argument that just as a watch requires a watchmaker to explain its existence, so the apparently purposeful adaptations of living organisms are evidences of an intelligent creator. But eventually this seemingly convincing argument from design was discredited by the superior arguments of Darwin, who accounted for the adaptations in terms of natural selection. The traditional arguments have been again and again criticized, and again and again restated in new forms.

A new attack on traditional natural theology developed in the nineteenth century and reached its peak in the twentieth. This attack came not from sceptical philosophers or scientists, but from theologians who for various reasons believed that attempts to prove God's existence were mistaken. This attitude had already appeared at the Reformation. Calvin, for instance, though not denying that God makes himself known in his works, believed that the sinful human mind cannot rightly perceive him, and distorts the evidences so as to arrive not at God but at its own idolatrous projections. At the beginning of the nineteenth century, Schleiermacher too dismissed the 'proofs' of God's existence, but for a different reason. He believed that human existence itself, in its dependence and finitude, gives an immediate testimony to the reality of God. This could be considered a new kind of natural theology, though it consists not in argument but in a 'feeling' or 'intuition' of a universal presence or revelation of God. In the middle of the century, Kierkegaard too rejected any attempts to prove God's existence, but for the reason that such proofs sow doubt and uncertainty. He taught that before the mystery of God reason 'makes a collision' and at that point we must either turn away from God or make the 'leap of faith' to God as concretely incarnate in Jesus Christ.

The climax of the theological critique of natural theology came in the twentieth century with Karl Barth. His view was much the same as Calvin's. The true knowledge of God is given in the Christian revelation, and the human quest for God, far from supporting revelation, goes against it and leads to idolatry. Barth even saw the attempted Nazification of the German church as a perverted byproduct of natural theology.

Protestant theologians, perhaps due to Barth's great influence, are still suspicious of natural theology. Catholic theology strongly reaffirmed the possibility of a natural knowledge of God at the First Vatican Council of 1870, and one consequence of this was the new openness towards non-Christian religions which found expression at the Second Vatican Council (1962–5). However, theologians of all persuasions would agree that natural theology is abstract and limited in what it can tell us about God. They would deny to it the kind of primacy that was being claimed for it in the Age of Reason.

Those who still practise natural theology would today be more likely to appeal to some general revelation than to the traditional proofs of God's existence, though these are still being restated by some philosophers of religion. The shift from the 'proofs' to general revelation is an acknowledgement that if God is personal, there can be no 'unaided' knowledge of God, but only a knowledge which he grants.

A powerful factor in keeping natural theology alive and in developing new forms of the discipline has been the series of Gifford Lectures, founded by the Scottish judge, Lord Gifford, in 1887.

From what has been said about the controversial character of natural theology and its rejection by some leading philosophers and theologians, it might seem to have become something of a luxury in contemporary religious thought, or even an embarrassment. But this is not so. On the contrary, it is possible that natural theology (though perhaps not in its traditional form) may have an important function in the future. In a secularized society, it provides a bridge from everyday concerns to God-language and the experiences which such language reflects. It will also have a function in the increasingly important dialogue among the religions.

Some theologians have a further suspicion of natural theology because it is virtually absent from the Bible, which dwells on God's saving actions in history. Yet natural theology is not entirely absent, though it does have a very subordinate role. In Christian theology, its role must always be subordinate, though perhaps in an age like the present one, it needs to be given more prominence. The boundary between so-called 'natural' theology and so-called 'supernatural' theology is blurred. Joseph Addison's great hymn, 'The spacious firmament on high' comes straight out of the Enlightenment, but it is a paraphrase of Psalm 19; and Paul's Epistle to the Romans, a kind of summary of the essence of Christianity, does not fail to tell us that 'ever since the creation of the world [God's] invisible nature, namely, his eternal power and deity, has been clearly perceived in the things that he has made' (Rom. 1: 20).

See also EPISTEMOLOGY, RELIGIOUS; EXISTENCE OF GOD, PROOFS OF; PHILOSOPHY OF RELIGION; RELIGION, THEORIES OF.

Bibliography

Baillie, John 1939: *Our Knowledge of God*. Oxford: Oxford University Press.

Cleobury, F.H. 1967: *A Return to Natural Theology*. London: James Clarke.

Farrer, Austin 1943: *Finite and Infinite*. London: Dacre Press.

Jaeger, Werner 1947: *The Theology of the Early Greek Philosophers*. Oxford: Oxford University Press.

Macquarrie, John 1984: *In Search of Deity*. London: SCM Press.

Mascall, E.L. 1966: *He Who Is*. London: Darton, Longman and Todd.

Mascall, E.L. 1971: *The Openness of Being*. London: Darton, Longman and Todd.

Mitchell, Basil 1973: *The Justification of Belief*. London: Macmillan.

Peacocke, Arthur 1979: *Creation and the World of Science*. Oxford: Clarendon Press.

Pringle-Pattison, A.S. 1920: *The Idea of God*. Oxford: Oxford University Press.

Swinburne, R. 1977: *The Coherence of Theism*. Oxford: Oxford University Press.

Swinburne, R. 1979: *The Existence of God*. Oxford: Oxford University Press.

Swinburne, R. 1981: *Faith and Reason*. Oxford: Oxford University Press.

Tennant, F.R. 1928–30: *Philosophical Theology*, 2 vols. Cambridge: Cambridge University Press.

Whitehead, A.N. 1929: *Process and Reality*. Cambridge: Cambridge University Press.

JOHN MACQUARRIE

neo-orthodoxy See BARTH, KARL; PROTESTANT THEOLOGY: GERMANY.

Newman, John Henry (1801–1890) Anglican, later Roman Catholic, theologian and churchman. Newman was born in London, the son of a banker, John Newman, and his wife Jemima, who came from a Huguenot refugee family, the Fourdriniers. In 1816, while at school at Ealing, he fell ill, at the same time that his father's bank failed and the family had to leave their house at Ham and move to Alton in

Hampshire. More significantly, under the influence of an evangelical clergyman on the staff of the Ealing school, Walter Mayers, the young Newman experienced 'a great change of thought'. He 'received into his mind impressions of dogma', became convinced of the two realities of God and himself, and took as mottoes phrases from the evangelical commentator, Thomas Scott: 'holiness rather than peace' and 'growth the only evidence of life'. Mayers nurtured Newman's new evangelical piety and encouraged him to read works by Calvinist divines, with their strong emphasis on the calling and distinctiveness of the elect.

At the end of 1816 he entered Trinity College, Oxford, as an undergraduate, where he won a scholarship; in 1822 he was elected to a fellowship at Oriel College, which partly redeemed his mediocre degree (the result of overwork) two years earlier. At Oriel he found himself in the company of the group of liberal Anglicans known as the Noetics (notably Edward Copleston and Richard Whateley), as well as of the high-church John Keble, and was later joined by other new fellows, Hurrell Froude and Robert Isaac Wilberforce.

Newman's theological mind was formed through exchanges with these men, and he was ordained deacon in 1824 and priest a year later. In 1826 he was appointed as a tutor at Oriel, a position which was eventually to bring him into conflict with the provost, Edward Hawkins, who became critical of the undue influence he thought Newman and his friends were exercising over their pupils. In 1828 he became Vicar of St Mary's, the Oxford university church, where he was to exercise a notable preaching ministry until 1843, many of his sermons subsequently being published in the eight volumes of *Parochial and Plain Sermons*. In 1828 he began to read systematically the Fathers of the church and under their influence moved from his earlier evangelicalism and growing liberalism to a more catholic ecclesiology, in which he was also encouraged by the influence of John Keble and Hurrell Froude as well as by increasing acquaintance with the seventeenth-century Anglican divines.

The constitutional and religious changes signalled by the repeal of the Test and Corporation Acts, Catholic Emancipation and the Reform Bill of 1832 precipitated a concern for the Church of England, particularly amongst Oxford high churchmen. On his return in 1833 from a Mediterranean journey with the Froudes, during which he nearly died of typhoid in Sicily (he interpreted this as a providential deliverance), Newman threw himself into the task of reaffirming the catholic inheritance of the Church of England, playing the leading role in publishing the series of *Tracts for the Times*, which ran until 1841, when Newman's attempt to reconcile the teaching of the Council of Trent with the Anglican formularies provoked sharp reactions from both the bishops and university authorities. Faced with this hostility, and finding his faith in the Church of England growing weaker, Newman withdrew with friends to live a strict semi-monastic life at Littlemore just outside Oxford. In 1843 he resigned the living of St Mary's, and in 1845, coterminous with the writing of his *Essay on the Development of Christian Doctrine*, he was received into the Roman Catholic church.

In 1847 he was ordained priest in Rome, and he returned to England to found the Oratory of St Philip Neri in Birmingham the following year. He remained in Birmingham for the rest of his life, apart from a period in the 1850s when he went to Ireland as rector of the new Catholic University of Ireland. As a Roman Catholic he found himself increasingly uneasy with the authoritarian ultramontanism often identified in England with his fellow convert Henry Manning, who became Cardinal Archbishop of Westminster. When the proposal was mooted to define papal infallibility (which was eventually done at the First Vatican Council in 1870) Newman was among the inopportunists. On the other hand he remained adamantly opposed to 'liberalism', which he saw as reducing revealed religious truth to subjective opinion. An article by Charles Kingsley implying that Newman had demonstrated the equivocation and deceit that Kingsley believed characterized Roman Catholic clergy provided Newman with an opportunity to set out the development of his own religious views in an autobiographical account of his pilgrimage from Anglicanism to the Church of Rome. The *Apologia pro vita sua* ([1864] 1967) is a classic of religious autobiography and did much to assist a Protestant reading public to appreciate Catholicism. *The Dream of Gerontius*, written the following year (1865), likewise enabled a more sympathetic understanding of Catholic eschatology, particularly after the poem was used by Elgar as the basis of an oratorio (in 1900). Having endured suspicion from ultramontanes, Newman found himself accorded full recognition when Leo XIII created him a cardinal in 1879. He died at the Birmingham Oratory in 1890 and is buried at Rednal.

Newman liked to maintain that he was 'not a theologian', by which he meant that he was never trained in the tradition of post-Tridentine neo-scholasticism. His thought was formed by his Oxford classical education, which provided a significant Aristotelian shaping of his epistemology; Joesph Butler's *Analogy of Religion* of 1736; the Scriptures; the Fathers (particularly the Alexandrian Fathers); and the Caroline Divines. His first book, *The Arians of the Fourth Century*, was completed in 1832, just before he set out with the Froudes on his Mediterranean journey. This study of the Arian controversy introduced Newman to the problem of the nature and development of doctrine; the way in which implicit faith becomes explicit; the place of economy and allegory in this process, and the nature and character of creeds, particularly in relation to the doctrine of the Trinity. It is also in this work that Newman introduces the idea of the 'dispensation of paganism', marking the movement of his own thought on the nature and character of revelation. The *Arians* is important both for its historical discussion of the controversy itself and for Newman's methodological reflections on the nature of doctrine. The same balancing of methodology and historical example is evident later in the *Essay on Development*. His edition of Athanasius's anti-Arian writings in the early 1840s testifies to the importance of Athanasius in particular for Newman's Christology.

The question of creeds and the development of doctrine appears in a more ecclesiological context in the *Lectures on the Prophetical Office of the Church* of 1837. In these lectures, developing out of a correspondence with the French Catholic abbé J.-N. Jager, Newman defends the Church of England as a *via media* between Roman Catholicism and popular Protestantism. Against Roman concepts of authority, which Newman believed discounted the authority of Christian antiquity, Newman sets Scripture and the Fathers, interpreted by the Vincentian canon of what has been believed 'always, everywhere, and by all'. Against the Protestant *sola scriptura*, he points to the importance of tradition – both 'prophetic', that is, implicit in liturgies, prayers and the life of the church, and 'episcopal' in the formal pronouncements of bishops and councils. Christianity, he maintains, is corporate and ecclesial, and therefore necessarily involves authority. The individualism of private judgement in Protestantism is fissiparous and leads to rationalism and liberalism. When Newman republished these lectures as a Roman Catholic (*The Via Media of the Anglican church*, [1877] 1990) he added an important preface, portraying the church as reflecting the offices of Christ as prophet, priest and king in its theologically reflective, devotional and political/institutional role, all of which needed to be kept in balance for the church to be true to its own identity. (Ultramontane papalism was an imbalance in relation to the theologically reflective role.)

In the *Lectures on the Doctrine of Justification* of 1838 Newman attempted to find a *via media* between justification by faith and justification by works. His emphasis on sanctification and his suspicion of a merely imputed righteousness was marked by a return to an emphasis on the imparted righteousness of the indwelling Christ. His categories are again patristic rather than scholastic. Although the lectures have proved an important theological resource in twentieth-century ecumenical discussion of justification, there is justice in the criticism that Newman's understanding of Luther's teaching is defective.

The theme of the development of doctrine, adumbrated in the *Arians*, was treated by Newman in the last of his University Sermons, and given more extended treatment in the *Essay on Development* of 1845. The fact of development is not questioned. All churches have developed. But, if Christianity is a revealed religion intended for all time and existing in a world of change, how are true developments to be distinguished from false? Newman suggests a number of 'tests' (later modified to 'notes'): (1) preservation of type or idea; (2) continuity of principles; (3) power of assimilation; (4) early anticipation; (5) logical sequence; (6) preservative additions; (7) chronic continuance. In the second half of the *Essay* he attempts to apply these tests or notes to particular historical instances in the life of the church. But in addition to these 'tests' Newman also argues that there is an antecedent probability that a revealed religion of saving truth such as Christianity must, if it is to be maintained through the flux of history, have an infallible expounder. A living magisterium was necessary; and that was what Rome claimed to possess. By such process of argument Newman became a Roman Catholic. But he remained a reluctant definer of doctrine, for definitions are always in danger of narrowing or distorting the mystery. The sense that the highest state of the church is the pure white light of contemplation while doctrines are the refracted colours of the spectrum never entirely left him.

Newman's theological output as a Roman Catholic included his 1850 *Lectures on Certain Difficulties felt by Anglicans in submitting to the Catholic Church*, his 1851 *Lectures on the Present Position of Catholics in England*, the important article 'On Consulting the Faithful in Matters of Doctrine' (in *The Rambler* of 1859), and his response to Gladstone's criticism of the decrees of the First Vatican Council in *A Letter to the Duke of Norfolk* of 1875. But the two most significant works were *An Essay in Aid of a Grammar of Assent* ([1870] 1985) and *The Idea of a University* ([1873] 1967). *The Grammar of Assent* was Newman's fully worked out defence of the rationality of religious belief, a topic which had occupied him since his Anglican university sermons on the subject and Tract 73, 'On the Introduction of Rationalistic Principles into Religion'. Newman expounds a theory of cumulative arguments and the operation of the 'illative' sense of moral judgement (akin to Aristotle's concept of *phronesis*) to defend the moral propriety and intellectual integrity of faith. (By 'illative', Newman means an ability to reach religious certitude by processes which lie outside the limits of strict logic.) Newman distinguishes between certainty and certitude, and between notional and real assent. It remains one of the most important analyses of religious belief, and is one of the few works which Newman wrote other than as a response to a particular challenge or situation. *The Idea of a University*, which grew out of Newman's attempt to provide an educational and philoso-phical framework for the new Catholic University of Ireland, is likewise a landmark in writing on the nature of university education, and treats in particular the place of theology within such a comprehensive framework.

Newman's influence as a religious thinker was considerable in his own day, but has become increasingly recognized since, particularly within the Roman Catholic church since the Second Vatican Council, described by some as 'Newman's Council'. The demise of neo-scholastic theology has made Newman's more personalist and patristic theology attractive. The publication of his *Letters and Diaries* and a commitment to publish his unpublished Anglican sermons is making even more material available to scholars. Within the Roman Catholic church the papal declaration that Newman was 'Venerable' marks a significant stage in the process of his canonization.

In particular in the areas of ecclesiology and the dialectic of faith and reason Newman's questions and answers have been found to be highly pertinent to contemporary theological discussion.

See also ANGLICANISM; ROMAN CATHOLIC THEOLOGY.

Bibliography

Writings

[1864] 1967: *Apologia pro vita sua*, ed. M.J. Svaglic. Oxford: Clarendon Press.

[1870] 1985: *An Essay in Aid of a Grammar of Assent*, ed. I.T. Ker. Oxford: Clarendon Press.

[1873] 1967: *The Idea of a University*, ed. I.T. Ker. Oxford: Clarendon Press.

[1877] 1990: *The Via Media of the Anglican Church*, ed. H.D. Weidner. Oxford: Clarendon Press.

1961–: *The Letters and Diaries of John Henry Newman*, 31 vols. Oxford: Clarendon Press (vols 1–6); and London: Nelson (vols 11–31).

Ker, Ian, ed. 1989: *The Genius of John Henry Newman: Selections from his Writings*. Oxford: Clarendon Press.

Critical works

Gilley, Sheridan 1990: *Newman and His Age*. London: Darton, Longman and Todd.

Ker, Ian 1988: *John Henry Newman: a Biography*. Oxford: Clarendon Press.

Ker, Ian 1990: *The Achievement of John Henry Newman*. London: Collins.

GEOFFREY ROWELL

Newton, Isaac (1642–1727) English scientist and mathematician. Brought up in Lincolnshire, Newton went up to Trinity College, Cambridge, in 1661. In 1666, after witnessing the famous fall of an apple, he worked out virtually the entire theory of gravity. He was made a professor of mathematics in 1669, and a Fellow of the Royal Society in 1671. He also represented Cambridge University in Parliament in 1689–90 and 1701–2. In 1703 he was made President of the Royal Society, and was knighted in 1705. He was buried in Westminster Abbey. Among his publications are the *Philosophae naturalis principia mathematica* (1687), usually known as the *Principia mathematica*) and the *Optics* (1704).

Newton is justly famed for his extraordinary achievements in science – although this was by no means his only interest, as he also studied alchemy and biblical chronology. He developed the theory of gravity, and discovered in 1666 that white light, passed through a prism, displays a colour spectrum. He also advanced a corpuscular theory of light, which was later disproved. He created the reflective telescope. He also proposed, in contradiction to G.W. Leibniz, the basis of differential calculus. At root, Newton was seeking a few fundamental, generalized laws which would explain the working of the universe, perhaps the quest of science ever since. It is difficult to overestimate his influence on subsequent science and philosophy.

Bibliography
Manuel, F.E. 1968: *A Portrait of Isaac Newton.* Cambridge, Mass. and London.
Newton, I. 1959–77: *Correspondence*, 7 vols, ed. H.W. Turnbull. Cambridge.

Niebuhr, H[elmut] Richard (1894–1962) North American theologian. A brother of Reinhold Niebuhr, he taught at Yale Divinity School from 1938 until his death. Influenced by E. Troeltsch and M. Weber, he analysed Christian denominations as sociological groupings, arguing that doctrinal differences were both a product of and instrumental in shaping social conditions. On the left wing of the American neo-orthodox school, he was critical of the social gospel movement, whose attempts to recover gospel ethics he regarded as unrealistic. Although he stressed the importance of historical revelation, and saw the Christian revelation as offering access to the Absolute, he did not regard Christian understanding as absolute, and therefore saw room for other religious approaches to God, advocating what he called a 'radical monotheism'. His major contribution was the attempt to integrate schematically Christian belief and issues relating to the modern world – social, political, ethical and religious. His works include *The Meaning of Revelation* (1941), *Christ and Culture* (1951) and *Radical Monotheism and Western Civilisation* (1960).

Bibliography
Diefentaler, J. 1986: *H. Richard Niebuhr: A Lifetime of Reflections on the Church and the World.* Macon, Gd.
Fowler, J.W. 1974: *To See the Kingdom: The Theological Vision of H. Richard Niebuhr.* Nashville, Te.
Hoedemaker, L.A. 1970: *The Theology of H. Richard Niebuhr.* Philadelphia.

Niebuhr, Reinhold (1892–1971) North American Presbyterian minister, theologian and political philosopher. The son of an immigrant Lutheran pastor, he studied at Yale and started his ministry in 1915 in Detroit, moving in 1928 to Union Theological Seminary, New York, where he was professor of applied theology until 1960. His thought is influenced by K. Barth and E. Brunner. Disillusion with supposedly progressive modern industrial methods in Detroit led him to abandon the optimistic belief in evolving human goodness that had characterized his earlier liberal theology. He developed a theology of the social and political life grounded in the doctrine of original sin, which he saw in corporate terms: the structure or group is more powerful socially and politically – and therefore more prone to abuse – than the individual; politics rather than ethics is the necessary regulator of human society. He became identified with Marxism, although in later life he sought to distance himself from it, and offered a stringent critique of American social and political institutions. His works include *Does Civilisation Need Religion?* (1927), *Moral Man and Immoral Society* (1932), *The Nature and Destiny of Man* (1941–3) and

Children of Light and Children of Darkness (1945).

Bibliography
Fox, R.W. 1985: *J. Reinhold Niebuhr: A Biography*. New York.
Harries, R., ed. 1986: *Reinhold Niebuhr and the Issues of Our Time*. London.
Kegley, C.W., and Bretall, R.W., eds 1984: *Reinhold Niebuhr: His Religious, Social and Political Thought*. New York.

Nietzsche, Friedrich Wilhelm (1844–1900) German philosopher. A brilliant student, Nietzsche became professor of classical philology at Basle University in 1869. He resigned due to ill health in 1879, and spent the rest of his life in solitude. He became insane in 1889, and died in 1900. Most of his books are in the form of essays or memorable aphorisms. Among his most important works are *The Birth of Tragedy* (1872), *Human, all too Human* (1878), *The Gay Science* (1882), *Thus Spoke Zarathustra* (1883) and *Beyond Good and Evil* (1886).

Nietzsche is renowned for his attack on Christianity, and indeed on theism in general. He argued that the logical result of loss of faith was the corresponding rejection of Christian moral values. These values, Nietzsche claims, induce a 'slave mentality' and elevate the weak at the expense of the strong. For this reason he also rejected democracy, as the device by which the weak masses held power over the strong individual. Nietzsche inverted Christian values, propounding a vision of a race of supermen, creating their own values, driven by a 'will to power' – a concept he derived from Arthur Schopenhauer. He insisted that the only real value is life, and that our ultimate aim must be to say 'Yes' to it.

Early in his philosophical career, Nietzsche was greatly influenced by Richard Wagner: indeed, he dedicated *The Birth of Tragedy* to Wagner. Later, however, he rejected Wagner's work, considering it to be Christian in inspiration. Nietzsche's work has had a significant influence on politics, religion and literature.

See also EXISTENTIALISM

Bibliography
Copleston, F. 1942: *Friedrich Nietzsche: Philosopher of Culture*. London.
Hollingdale, R.J. 1985: *Nietzsche: The Man and his Philosophy*. London.
Nehamas, A. 1985: *Nietzsche: Life as Literature.*. Cambridge, Mass., and London.

Norway See PROTESTANT THEOLOGY: SCANDINAVIA.

Nygren, Anders (1890–1977) Swedish Lutheran bishop, theologian and philosopher of religion. Prominent in the foundation of the World Council of Churches, he was a significant ecumenist and professor of theology at Lund. His theological method, known as 'motif-research', studied Christianity as a social-historical phenomenon by identifying its recurring symbols and comparing them with those of other religions. His major work, *Agape and Eros* (trans. 1932–9), identifies the basic motifs of 'agape' (selfless love) and 'eros' (love seeking self-fulfilment in God), tracing them through the history of the church and discussing their theological implications for Christian ethics and the doctrines of atonement and grace. For him, the Reformation's great contribution was to restore 'agape' to the central position in the church's understanding of salvation, in place of the more Jewish ethos of 'law' and the Greek ethos of 'eros', which, he held, had previously predominated. He was critical of Protestant liberalism. Together with Gustav Aulén's work, Nygren's is comparable to contemporaneous developments in German theology, particularly the dialectical theology of R. Bultmann and K. Barth. Other works include a commentary on Romans (1944), and *Meaning and Method* (trans. 1972).

Bibliography
Hall, T. 1978: *Anders Nygren*. Waco, Te.
Kegley, C.W., ed. 1970: *The Philosophy and Theology of Anders Nygren*. Carbondale, Ill.
Wingren, G. 1958: *Theology in Conflict*. Edinburgh.

O

Orthodoxy, Eastern   See EASTERN ORTHODOX THEOLOGY.

other faiths and Christianity   In the modern world Christians cannot ignore the existence of other religions. Global communications, extensive travel, migration, colonialism, and international trade are all factors that have brought the religions closer to each other in both destructive and creative ways. The religiously plural world in which Christians live consists of ancient traditions, sometimes older than Christianity, with many millions of followers. These include Judaism, Islam, Hinduism and Buddhism. There are also numerically smaller groups with varying degrees of antiquity, such as Jainism, Sikhism, Confucianism and of course African religions. Also, never far from western media attention, there are the new religious movements with complex relations to the more established traditions, such as the Unification church, the International Society for Krishna Consciousness, Rastafarianism, and New Age movements. Religious plurality raises many practical and theological questions for Christians: Should Buddhist meditation groups be allowed the use of church halls? How should religious education be taught? What kind of social and political cooperation or opposition is appropriate with people of other faiths? And how should Christians react to the intolerance within certain faiths – with equal intolerance? There are also fundamental theological issues at stake. If salvation is possible outside Christ/Christianity, is the uniqueness of Christ and the universal mission of the church called into question? Or if salvation is not possible outside Christ/Chris-

tianity, is it credible that a loving God would consign the majority of humankind to perdition, often through no fault of their own? Can Christians learn from other faiths? Can they be enriched rather than diluted or polluted by this encounter?

There have been many different Christian responses to the world religions in the modern age. Equally, there are many different motives behind these attitudes involving theological, political, social and economic factors. For Christians living in the twentieth century there is also the recent history of colonialism and imperialism in which many parts of the non-Christian world have been subjugated by white Christian powers, two world wars, and the destruction of nearly a third of Jewry within a culture deeply nourished by Christianity. This chequered history has caused a crisis in confidence both within Christianity and also in its relation with the world faiths.

No set of categories is adequate to analyse and deal with the complexity of the topic, but it may be helpful to label three types of theological response to other religions for heuristic purposes. There are of course considerable differences between theologians belonging to the same 'camp', and many features of overlap between different approaches. I shall call these three approaches: *pluralism* (that all religions are equal and valid paths to the one divine reality, and Christ is one revelation among many equally important revelations); *exclusivism* (only those who hear the gospel proclaimed and explicitly confess Christ are saved); and *inclusivism* (that Christ is the normative revelation of God, although salvation is possible through religions other than Christianity). Various presuppositions undergird each approach, often revolving around Christology and the doctrine of God. It might be said that the three approaches are derived from the emphasis given to either one or both of two crucial theological axioms: that *salvation is given by God in Christ (solus Christus)* and that *God loves and desires the salvation of all men and women*. Those who emphasize the former move towards exclusivism, and those who emphasize the latter tend towards pluralism. In the following survey, I will outline the main theological considerations of each approach, identify some of its major representatives, and indicate some of the criticisms directed against it. I cite criticisms to indicate the open-ended and vigorous discussion taking place in contemporary theology. In the final section I will outline some major trends running across the three categories, which further enrich the modern debate on Christianity's relation to the world faiths.

Pluralism, exclusivism and inclusivism

Pluralism Pluralist theologies have been developed most forcefully in the modern period, although there are minor traces present in earlier Christian history. There are important differences among pluralists. Some argue that all religions have a common core or essence that can be historically identified, often within the mystical traditions of the world religions. A variation on this argument is that a straightforward historical comparison of the religions will not show this common essence, but rather within the different traditions the 'esoteric' believers who have penetrated in depth their own tradition will discover the non-duality of God and the soul, a unity that transcends all formulations. 'Exoteric' believers, on the other hand, absolutize their symbols and creeds and fail to penetrate to the transcendent unity of religions. To exoteric believers, Christ and/or the church become the only way to salvation (Schuon, 1975). Another form of pluralism begins from a consideration of historical relativity and it is argued that all traditions are relative and cannot claim superiority over other equally limited and relative ways to salvation (Arnold Toynbee and Ernst Troeltsch) (see RELATIVISM, CULTURAL). Yet again, others argue that all religions have important and substantial historical differences and the view of a common

essence is in danger of compromising the integrity of each particular tradition by emphasizing only one aspect of that tradition. The real unity of religions is found not in doctrine or mystical experiences but in the common experience of salvation or liberation (Hick, 1988; Swidler *et al.* 1990). It will be instructive to look in detail at one modern pluralist, John Hick, who combines elements of all the above approaches. It may be added that there are others who argue that the unity of religions lies in their common projection of unfulfilled human potential (Ludwig Feuerbach), or in their common suppression and control of the masses (some forms of Marxism), or as indicating a common psychic origin (Carl Jung), but this entry will concentrate on theological contributions to the debate.

Hick argues that the *solus Christus* assumption (that salvation is only through Christ) held by exclusivists is incompatible with the Christian teaching of a God who desires to save all people. There are many millions who have never heard of Christ through no fault of their own, before and after New Testament times – the invincibly ignorant. It is therefore un-Christian to think that God would have 'ordained that men must be saved in such a way that only a small minority can in fact receive this salvation' (Hick, 1977, p. 122). Hick therefore proposes a *theocentric* revolution away from the *Christocentric* or *ecclesiocentric* positions that have dominated Christian history. Hence, it is God, and not Christianity or Christ, towards whom all religions move, and from whom they gain their salvific efficacy. He argues that the doctrine of the incarnation should be understood mythically – as an expression of devotion and commitment by Christians, not as an ontological claim that here and here alone God has been fully revealed. Hick stresses the doctrine of an all-loving God over that of the *solus Christus* principle.

Hick's arguments are not exclusively theological. He also develops his thesis through an inspection of the history of religions. He discerns a common soteriological structure, whereby the major religions exhibit a turning from 'self-centredness to Reality-centredness', a turning away from a destructive egotism to that of a compassionate, loving and caring attitude towards all creatures (Hick, 1988). Holiness and

OTHER FAITHS AND CHRISTIANITY

goodness are not the exclusive rights of Christianity. This phenomenon reinforces the necessity of a theological paradigm shift from Christocentrism to theocentrism.

A recent development in Hick's position has come in response to the criticism that his theological revolution is still theocentric and thereby excludes non-theistic religions. This development in his position indicates the kind of issues and problems encountered by a full-blown pluralism. Hick (1988) makes a Kantian-type distinction in order to allow for non-theistic religions and overcome his theistic bias. He distinguishes between a divine noumenal reality 'that exists independently and outside man's perception of it' which he calls the 'Eternal One', and the phenomenal world, 'which is that world as it appears to our human consciousness'. The various human responses to the Eternal One are seen as both theistic and non-theistic (for example, God, Allah, Nirvana or Brahman). In this way Hick tries to overcome an underlying theistic essentialism.

The above arguments cumulatively suggest that Christians can fruitfully view the history of religions as a history of God's/the Eternal One's activity without making any special claims for Christianity. Christian attitudes to other religions need not be characterized by a desire to convert or claims to superiority, but can show a will to learn and grow together towards the truth. Mission should be carried out to the secular world by the religions jointly, rather than towards each other. Hick suggests that exclusivism and inclusivism cannot provide such fruitful conditions for inter-religious dialogue.

There have been a number of objections to Hick's thesis, some of which indicate problems with pluralism more generally. First, there are objections to the way in which the centrality of Christ within Christianity seems to be bypassed. It is argued that Hick's initial theocentric revolution is based on a shaky premise. He rejects the *solus Christus* for he thinks it leads to the a priori damnation of non-Christians. Theologically this is not necessarily the case, as we shall see below. Furthermore, when Hick proposes a theocentric revolution away from a Christocentrism he is in danger of severing Christology from ontology and introducing a free-floating God divorced from any particular revelation. The theistic religions, including Christianity, centre on revelatory paradigms for their discourse and practice. Hick's theocentrism pays little attention to the importance of historical particularity. In fact, the theological basis of his proposals (that of an all-loving God) is undermined if Hick cannot give normative ontological status to the revelatory events upon which this axiom is grounded – (originally for Hick) that of the revelation of God in Christ. Christology is important precisely because it is *through Jesus* that Christians claim that God has revealed himself in a unique (although not necessarily exclusive) manner. A theocentrism without a Christocentrism is in danger of leading towards an abstract common denominator and thereby to a reductionist 'God'. Pluralist approaches are in danger of relativizing or denigrating particularity, so central to the historical religions.

Another objection to pluralist theologies concerns the doctrine of God. In Hick's context, this relates to his attempt to overcome his initial theistic bias. If the meaning of 'God' lacked specificity in Hick's theocentrism, it seems further relativized in his more recent works, for 'God' is seen as one aspect of the 'Eternal One' that apparently can also be characterized with opposite predicates. Finally all such predicates are from the human side and are thereby not applicable to 'God'. Hence, God cannot be said to be personal or loving in a proper ontological sense. The Kantian noumenon encounters a similar problem in not providing for a correspondence between phenomena and things-in-themselves. Hick seems to be close to a transcendental agnosticism (that is, affirming a transcendence without any qualities). Despite his stress on soteriocentrism, the liberated lifestyle, can he properly address the question of the nature of the God/the Eternal One who actually saves and liberates people, or is his doctrine of 'God' in danger of avoiding all particularities so as to accommodate every particularity? Clearly, the outcome of such difficulties remains unresolved, but these questions highlight the theological centrality of Christology and the doctrine of God in the discussion about other faiths.

Exclusivism Exclusivism has a more ancient pedigree than that of pluralism, and many modern-day exclusivists tend to be more biblically oriented than do pluralists. Again there are substantial variations within this type of approach, but mainline exclusivists tend to share two basic premises. The first concerns the fallen nature of men and women. All forms of religion are idolatrous, ultimately representing the quest to grasp God in ways that are inevitably characterized by sin and error. Indeed, these religious formulations may often represent the heights of creative genius and imagination, but may equally reflect the depths of depravity and self-deception. Basically, human beings do not have the power to save themselves despite their very best efforts. Second, gratuitously and through no merit of men and women, God has disclosed himself in the person of Jesus Christ and it is through Christ alone that a person can come to God, a God who is both loving and merciful and also a God of judgement. The astounding event here is not that God chose this particular way to reveal himself, but that he has revealed himself at all to those unworthy of him. The scandal of particularity, so scandalous to pluralists, is also the miracle of grace in a fallen world. Many from the Reformed, Lutheran and Calvinist traditions share such a theological outlook.

The working out of these theological considerations, where clearly the *solus Christus* principle is central, tends towards an exclusivist direction. Most boldly stated, it leads to a position in which all non-Christians are damned even if they did not have the chance to hear the gospel. (Clearly, many nominal Christians share the same fate without faith.) Such is the proclamation of the Congress on World Mission at Chicago in 1960: 'In the years since the war, more than one billion souls have passed into eternity and more than half of these went to the torment of hell fire without even hearing of Jesus Christ, who He was, or why He died on the cross of Calvary' (Percy, 1961, p. 9). Although the internal logic of this position is coherent, it has been criticized on two basic grounds. Biblically, there is evidence that God has made himself known in creation and through history before the time of Christ. The former point has often led to a natural theology that allows for a rational ability to discern God. The latter has often led to a theology of revelation that allows for God's self-disclosure outside Christ. Second, such a position has also

been criticized on the ground that theologically the doctrine of God here reveals a capricious and unworthy God, for this God allows the damnation of people who have never even had the chance to hear the gospel preached. (This was Hick's criticism, as seen above.)

Others have developed from the same theological starting point but gone on to qualify the status of the non-Christian regarding damnation, as well as the status of the non-Christian religions regarding revelation. Concerning damnation, many argue that the non-Christian will not simply be consigned to hell fire through no fault of their own, but rather the Christian can trust that God's power and victory over darkness will be triumphant, in ways not known to us at present (Hendrik Kraemer, Carl Braaten). While not always stated explicitly, the logic of this position requires some sort of post-mortem confrontation with Christ (George Lindbeck, Origen Jathanna). Criticism of this strategy, clearly developed to retain the coherence of the *solus Christus* principle, centres on two apparent weaknesses. First, it fails to take seriously the historical and social nature of men and women and projects their destiny into a moment's decision after death. Second, it still does not face the question of the possibility of God's self-revelation outside Christianity, despite the apparently grace-filled lives of many non-Christians who respond to what they perceive as revelation within their own religious traditions.

In respect of this last problem, some theologians have allowed for the possibility of God's light shining within the religions of the world, but argue that this is also clouded and distorted in the context of sinfulness and error. Hendrik Kraemer (1938), the Dutch missionary theologian, was keen to emphasize this dialectical judgement on all religions. They are both the result of a response to God's promptings as well as, and far more significantly, a method of self-justification. Similarly, Emil Brunner can write appreciatively of the religions of grace such as Bhakti Hinduism and Amida Buddhism, but finally finds them religions of 'cheap grace' for neglecting the reality of sin and the need for forgiveness. Abandoning oneself to God's love is only a partial truth and not salvific; acceptance in faith of Christ's redemptive work is central to such theologies. Here the criticisms of such positions centre around the reality of the faith of Israel before Christ. Is not the 'Old' Testament valid grounds on which to recognize a valid and salvific faith before an explicit confrontation with Christ? Furthermore, is not the history of Israel evidence of a religious tradition grappling, often successfully, with God? Finally, can such a priori theological principles be applied to the multiplicity and complexity of religions without proper knowledge of each one in its particularity?

It is clear that the lines between exclusivism and pluralism are clearly drawn in regard to Christology and the doctrine of God, and although 'religion' is often theologically criticized (following Karl Barth), the place of the Christian community has varying degrees of importance among exclusivists. The place of mission is also obviously very differently construed. For most pluralists, mission is to be directed towards secular and materialist traditions, and in relation to the world religions should take the form of social cooperation and aid. Dialogue, sharing and mutual discovery are the key note. Not all exclusivists advocate the latter and some are deeply suspicious of such goals displacing the preaching of the gospel. The emphasis within exclusivist groups would be on worldwide evangelism, which would often include forms of social and political action, the latter overlapping with projects supported by pluralists. Despite many deep lines of division, one may, ironically, notice some overlap in the universalist theologies of exclusivists influenced by Karl Barth and pluralists such as John Hick. It will also be clear below that some exclusivists have much in common with inclusivists.

Inclusivism Inclusivism also has a venerable pedigree in the Christian tradition. Quite a number of Roman Catholics share this approach, with variations. The main concern of inclusivists is to balance the two central axioms in this debate: *solus Christus* and the universal salvific will of God. Many maintain that while Christ brings salvation into the world, God's grace is not absent in his creation and in history. However, the various intimations of God's grace find their source and completion in grace made flesh: Jesus Christ. Hence, inclusivism has often been related to theologies of fulfilment, drawing on the ancient tradition of *a preparatio evangelica*. (Fulfilment theologies are not intrinsic to inclusivism.) Most inclusivists therefore positively affirm the light that is to be found in the world religions, while still retaining the importance of mission and the unique role of Christ. One of the most influential is probably Karl Rahner, whose form of inclusivism is shaped by his theological anthropology. He argues that the precondition of finite (categorial) knowledge is an unconditional openness to being *(Vorgriff)*, which is an unthematic, pre-reflective awareness of God – who is infinite being. Our transcendental openness to being constitutes the hiddenness of grace. Men and women therefore search through history for a categorial disclosure of this hidden grace. In Jesus' total abandonment to God, his total 'Yes' through his life, death and resurrection, he is established as the culmination and prime mediator of grace. Therefore Christian revelation is the explicit expression of grace which men and women experience implicitly in the depths of their being when, for example, they reach out through the power of grace in trusting love and self-sacrifice, or in acts of hope and charity.

Rahner ([1954–84] 1961–; [1976] 1978) attempts to balance the *solus Christus* principle with that regarding the universal salvific will of God, so as to maintain that Christ is the sole cause of salvation in the world but that this salvific grace may be mediated within history without an explicit confrontation with Christ. Such is the case in the history of Israel. If with Israel, may it not in principle be the case with other religions of the world? Rahner's Roman Catholicism demands that Christology and the doctrine of God are not prised apart from the church, so that it is important for Rahner to maintain that Christ is historically mediated through the church. This means that Rahner must reconcile membership of the church as the means of salvation and the possibility that salvific grace is mediated outside the historically tangible borders of the church. He does this along the lines of the traditional Catholic teachings regarding the *votum ecclesiae* (a wish to belong to the church), and the related notion of implicit desire. His application however is novel.

Rahner argues that if salvific grace exists outside the visible church, as he believes it does in the history of Israel, in creation and in conscience, then this grace is causally related to both Christ (always and everywhere – as prime mediator) and his church. Furthermore, given the sociohistorical nature of men and women, grace must be mediated historically and socially. The incarnation is paradigmatic in suggesting this. Hence, if and when non-Christians respond to grace, then this grace must be mediated *through* their religion, however imperfectly. Rahner thus coins the term 'anonymous Christian' and 'anonymous Christianity'. The first refers to the source of saving grace that is responded to and the second refers to its dynamic orientation towards its definitive historical and social expression in the church.

Because God has already been active within the non-Christian partner (*a preparatio evangelica*), the Christian can be open to learning about God through the non-Christian religions. Furthermore, the Christian is also free to engage in active social and political cooperation when appropriate. Hence, the inclusivist has a firm theological basis for fruitful dialogue. Given Rahner's notion that grace seeks to objectivize itself, mission is clearly important.

Rahner and various other proponents of inclusivism have been criticized by both pluralists and exclusivists. Many have found Rahner's notion of the 'anonymous Christian' imperialist and offensive to non-Christians. From the exclusivist wing, it is argued that Rahner's and other forms of inclusivism compromise the *solus Christus* principle in a fundamental manner. Salvation is made possible without surrender to Christ, thereby rendering Christ unnecessary in the economy of salvation. Does Rahner sever grace from Christ, fitting Jesus as the best and other figures in history as less good expressions of an a priori notion of grace? Furthermore, an ecclesiological criticism is that Rahner's invisible church is unbiblical and also detracts from the importance of explicit confession as a criterion for membership. Pluralist critics have charged Rahner with tortured logic: trying to argue the necessity of Christ and the church for salvation, while clearly acknowledging that those who have not known Christ or the church can be saved. Such is the criticism made by Hick.

It is clear that pluralism, exclusivism and inclusivism all have strengths and weaknesses.

While I have tried to present all three positions as fairly as possible, I am obliged to state my preference for an open-ended form of Trinitarian inclusivism. The doctrine of the Trinity has not been decisive in shaping this debate, although I believe it should and can be. The Trinity is important, for it lies at the heart of Christian faith and safeguards both the particularity and universality of Christianity. It affirms the decisiveness and uniqueness of Christ as being the revelation of God, thereby maintaining the importance of the particular and historical. At the same time, through Trinitarian thought, Christians can affirm the universal activity of the Holy Spirit in history – and can explain the relationship of the Spirit to Christ in a non-triumphalist manner. As the Holy Spirit deepens and enriches the Christian faith in Christ, as promised in John 14, it is thereby intrinsic to Christianity to be attentive to the Holy Spirit within the world religions. This open-ended inclusivism need not pass any a priori judgement, negative or positive, in relation to the world religions but can be open to critical, constructive and committed encounter with people from other faiths (D'Costa 1986, 1990).

In the discussion above, various aspects of the debate on Christianity's relation to other faiths have been left untouched. I will now turn to some of these issues.

Methodology and indigenization

It has been argued that a general theology of religions, such as has been discussed above, neglects to take the contingencies of history and the variety of religions and their individual dynamics seriously enough. This type of criticism has various directions in which it can be developed. It is argued by some that religions are like languages, requiring that an adherent work at learning them before competence and understanding are achieved. Similarly, the concepts within each tradition are not perspicacious to the outsider; therefore positive or negative judgements are not appropriate, and neither are easy comparisons of similarities and differences. Hence in this respect 'there is no damnation – just as there is no salvation – outside the church. One must, in other words, learn the language of faith before one can know enough about its message knowingly to reject it and thus be lost' (Lindbeck, 1984, p. 59). This view, while rightly stressing the difficulties of cross-religious understanding, is in danger of overplaying the incommensurability of the different traditions. Another type of argument, again revolving around the definition of religion, is the questioning of the very term 'religion' as designating intelligible largescale entities such as Hinduism or Buddhism. These traditions have varied so profoundly according to historical circumstances that it is not appropriate to pass any sort of judgements on these entities as 'religions'. One only has people with their individual faith (Smith, 1978). Both these approaches alert us to the difficulties raised according to the definition of religion being employed.

Another sort of criticism of a general theology of religions is that the relationship between Christianity and Judaism, Christianity and Buddhism and so on, is unique in each instance, with its own specific dynamics. For example, the Roman Catholic document, resulting from the Second Vatican Council, concerning the world religions (*Nostra Aetate: Declaration on the Relation of the Church to Non-Christian Religions* of 1965) makes it clear that the relationship of the Church to Judaism is very special for unique historical and theological reasons. Judaism, after all, is the root of the cultivated olive tree on which the wild olive branches of the Gentiles have been grafted (see Rom. 11: 17–24). It is the tradition out of which Jesus comes, and its Scriptures are shared with Christianity: the Hebrew Bible/the 'Old' Testament. The relationship with Islam, again, is unique in its shared monotheism and shared descent from Abraham.

Many would want to push this case further and more radically. Some argue that the relationship with Judaism is totally unique and incomparable to that with other religious traditions, for Christ came to bring the Jewish covenant to the Gentiles, not to negate the Jewish covenant. It is sometimes argued that traditional Christology is intrinsically anti-Semitic, for in claiming Jesus to be the intended Messiah, all those who did not accept him as such have forfeited their covenant relationship with God. The 'Jews' have failed to recognize their Messiah and have also killed him (the charge of deicide). Rosemary Radford

Ruether has argued that it is this anti-Jewish Christology, so central to mainstream Christian tradition, that led eventually to the camps of Treblinka and Auschwitz (Ruether, 1974). Ruether and others argue that Christianity must rid itself of such claims. Hence, both Christianity and Judaism are valid covenants with God, one for the Gentiles and one for the Jews (see also James Parkes and Paul van Buren). It is since the Holocaust that Jewish–Christian relations have moved towards this development, although there is certainly no consensus on these questions. It should also be noted that while some theologians see this as a *sui generis* relationship, others, like Radford Ruether, extend the principle to challenge Christian superiority and self-assertion and develop a theology of religions on pluralist lines.

There are also important developments in theology which have inevitably affected the debate in the theology of religions. Two such examples are FEMINIST THEOLOGY and LIBERATION THEOLOGY. Feminist theologians often approach inter-faith questions with a very different agenda from that so far examined. The primary focus is often the oppression and marginalization of women within the religions, thereby raising questions of canonicity (Elizabeth Schüssler Fiorenza), patriarchal structures (Radford Ruether and Ursula King) and so on. The focus thereby changes so that the meeting and uniting of women between the different traditions takes priority. The liberation theologians, increasingly from the old traditional mission fields and ex-colonial outposts, have caused two sorts of shift in the theology of religions. Paul Knitter, for instance, has developed a pluralist outlook taking as his starting point the oppression and injustice within society and the way in which religions critically respond to this challenge. Hence 'the framework for a Christian theology of religions is not church, Christ, or God but *soteria* or the kingdom of God' (Swidler *et al.*, 1990, p. 37; Knitter, 1985). Such an approach has been criticized for trying to avoid questions concerning truth claims and the intrinsic relationship of theory to practice. Theology cannot be transposed into politics. Other theologians have utilized the insights of liberation theology while marrying them to their own situation of dialogue. Hence M.M. Thomas (1987) in India has argued that Christ is central to the transformation of Indian society socially and politically. In this respect Christians may be involved in a fundamental questioning of some aspects of Hinduism. Christianity's major contribution to a pluralist world is in dismantling the structures of oppression. Aloysius Pieris (1989) has developed an Asian theology of liberation, in which a theology of religions is married to liberation theology and Asian spirituality. Pieris is concerned that Christians in dialogue and solidarity with people from other religions help to release the liberating potential implicit within the soteriologies of the great world religions. The age of religious imperialism should also be dismantled with the structures of political and cultural imperialism that have characterized western Christianity's relationship to eastern countries.

A major aspect of the relationship between Christianity and other faiths is the question of indigenization or inculturation. The question concerns the manner in which Christianity is transformed as it moves into different environments and the rules regarding the legitimacy of such changes. There are analogies here to the debate about the relationship of Christianity to secularism. To utilize and employ terms and concepts from an alien world view runs close to assimilating that world view and in the long run losing one's uniqueness and distinctiveness – or so it has been argued. Early Christianity was itself a transformation of Judaism, and in its entry into the Greek philosophical world, it began to employ Greek metaphysics to articulate Christian truth. There was heated debate then, as there is now over similar issues. Problems have arisen, for example, as Christians living within a Hindu environment have sought to incorporate the thought world of Śankara and Rāmānuja (major Hindu philosophers) in the way that Aquinas utilized Aristotle and Averroes, to present Christian thought intellectually. Or more radically, some have tried to incorporate readings from Hindu religious books such as the *Vedas* and *Upanishads* within the liturgy. Do such developments enrich Christianity in incorporating and transforming what is noble and wise, or is this another form of imperialist 'borrowing', syncretistic muddle and dilution of the gospel? Some third world Christians argue that this

kind of indigenous theology is in danger of marginalizing the at least equally important question of liberation from sociopolitical oppression. Such theologians often prefer to speak of a 'theology of incarnation' which is concerned with the cultural, religious and political aspects of Christianity understood within the horizons of that particular country. Indigenization still smacks of a western kernel dressed in oriental clothing.

There are many other aspects of the question that remain undiscussed in this article. There is the question of the historical relationship between the actual religions and Christianity (see JUDAISM AND CHRISTIANITY; ISLAM AND CHRISTIANITY), the question of mission (see MISSION, THEOLOGY OF), the relationship of the theology of religions to systematic theology, the relationship between a theology of religion to a theology of culture (see CULTURE AND THEOLOGY), the question of conflicting truth claims (see TRUTH, CONCEPTS OF), and the allied areas of natural theology, nature and grace, and revelation. However, it is hoped that the reader has gained a sense of the complexity and excitement in this field of theology.

See also RELIGION, THEORIES OF.

Bibliography

Camps, A. 1983: *Partners in Dialogue: Christianity and Other World Religions*. New York: Orbis.

D'Costa, G. 1986: *Theology and Religious Pluralism*. Oxford and New York: Blackwell.

D'Costa, G., ed. 1990: *Christian Uniqueness Reconsidered: The Myth of a Pluralistic Theology of Religions*. New York: Orbis.

Hick, J. 1977: *God and the Universe of Faiths*. London: Fount.

Hick, J. 1988: *An Interpretation of Religion*. London: Macmillan.

Knitter, P. 1985: *No Other Name? A Critical Study of Christian Attitudes Towards the World Religions*. London: SCM Press.

Kraemer, H. 1938: *The Christian Message in a Non-Christian World*. London: Edinburgh House Press.

Lindbeck, G. 1984: *The Nature of Doctrine: Religion and Theology in a Post Liberal Age*. London: SPCK.

Percy, J., ed. 1961: *Facing the Unfinished Task: Messages Delivered at the Congress on World Mission*. Grand Rapids: Eerdmans.

Pieris, A. 1989: *An Asian Theology of Liberation*. New York: Orbis.

Rahner, K. [1954–84] 1961– : Christianity and the non-Christian religions. In *Theological Investiga-*

tions, vol. 5. London: Darton, Longman and Todd.

Rahner, K. [1976] 1978: *Foundations of Christian Faith*. London: Darton, Longman and Todd.

Ruether, R. 1974: *Faith and Fratricide: The Theological Roots of Anti-Semitism*. New York: Seabury.

Ruether, R. and McLaughlin, E., eds 1979: *Women of the Spirit. Female Leadership in Jewish and Christian Traditions*. New York: Simon and Schuster.

Schuon, F. 1975: *The Transcendent Unity of Religions*. New York: Harper and Row.

Smith, W.C. 1978: *The Meaning and End of Religion: A New Approach to the Religious Traditions of Mankind*. London: Sheldon.

Swidler, L., Cobb, J.B., Knitter, P.F., Hellwig, M.K. 1990: *Death or Dialogue?* London: SCM Press.

Thomas, M.M. 1987: *Risking Christ for Christ's Sake*. Geneva: World Council of Churches.

GAVIN D'COSTA

Otto, Rudolf (1869–1937)   German Lutheran theologian; professor of systematic theology at Breslau (1914–17) and at Marburg (1917–29). His thought had much in common with that of F.D.E. Schleiermacher, and he was interested in Kantian philosophy. His main work is *The Idea of the Holy* (1917), a study of religion which rejects the idea that religion can be reduced to a purely sociological/historical phenomenon, and focuses on the essential, supra-rational experience of God common to all religions. This he called the experience of the 'holy', but the moral overtones of the term led him to adopt the term 'numinous' (from the Latin 'divinity', 'spirit'), with which he became associated. Though he emphasized the place of the mysterious and the subjective, he upheld the importance of the rational, objective mind in building a structure of practical belief on the foundation of the numinous. He was a student of Eastern religions, making a comparative analysis of the nature of mysticism in *Mysticism East and West* (trans. 1970); but he held that the Christian religion offered the most advanced representation of the numinous.

Bibliography

Almond, P.C. 1984: *Rudolf Otto: An Introduction to his Philosophical Theology*. Chapel Hill, NC.

Crosby, D.A. 1981: *Interpretive Theories of Religion*. Berlin, NY.

Davidson, R.F. 1947: *Rudolf Otto's Interpretation of Religion*. Princeton.

P

Pannenberg, Wolfhart (b. 1928) German theologian. Wolfhart Pannenberg was born in Stettin (then part of Germany; now included in Poland), and began theological studies after the Second World War at the University of Berlin. His early theological studies were subsequently based at Göttingen and Basle, where he completed his doctoral thesis on the doctrine of predestination of the noted scholastic theologian John Duns Scotus (published in 1954). His *Habilitationsschrift*, a treatise on the role of analogy, led to his securing a teaching appointment at Heidelberg, where he remained until called to a chair of systematic theology at the *Kirchliche Hochschule* at Wuppertal in 1958 as a colleague of Jürgen Moltmann. After a period at the University of Mainz (1961–8), he moved to the University of Munich, where he has remained.

The most distinctive feature of Pannenberg's theological programme, as it emerged during the 1960s, is the appeal to universal history. Such views are developed and justified in the 1961 volume *Offenbarung als Geschichte* ('Revelation as History') edited by Pannenberg, in which these ideas are explored at some length. This volume established Pannenberg as a leading young theologian of the period. Pannenberg's essay 'Dogmatic Theses on the Doctrine of Revelation' opens with a powerful appeal to universal history:

> History is the most comprehensive horizon of Christian theology. All theological questions and answers have meaning only within the framework of the history which God has with humanity, and through humanity with the whole creation, directed towards a future which

is hidden to the world, but which has already been revealed in Jesus Christ.

These crucially important opening sentences sum up the distinctive features of Pannenberg's theological programme at this stage in his career. They immediately distinguish him from the ahistorical theology of Rudolf Bultmann and his school on the one hand, and the suprahistorical approach of Martin Kähler on the other. Christian theology is based upon an analysis of universal and publicly accessible history. For Pannenberg, revelation is essentially a public and universal historical event which is recognized and *interpreted* as an 'act of God'. To his critics, this seemed to reduce faith to insight, and deny any role to the Holy Spirit in the event of revelation.

Pannenberg's argument takes the following form. History, in all its totality, can only be understood when it is viewed from its end point. This point alone provides the perspective from which the historical process can be seen in its totality, and thus be properly understood. However, where Marx argued that the social sciences, by predicting the goal of history to be the hegemony of socialism, provided the key to the interpretation of history, Pannenberg declared that this was provided only in Jesus Christ. The end of history is disclosed proleptically in the history of Jesus Christ. In other words, the end of history, which has yet to take place, has been disclosed in advance of the event in the person and work of Christ.

This idea of a 'proleptic disclosure of the end of history' is grounded in the apocalyptic world view, which Pannenberg argues provides the key to understanding the New Testament interpretation of the significance and function of Jesus. Whereas Bultmann chose to demythologize the apocalyptic elements of the New Testament, Pannenberg treats them as a hermeneutical grid or framework by which the life, death and resurrection of Christ may be interpreted (see CHRISTOLOGY).

Perhaps the most distinctive, and certainly the most commented upon, aspect of this work is Pannenberg's insistence that the resurrection of Jesus is an objective historical event, witnessed by all who had access to the evidence. Whereas Bultmann treated the resurrection as an event within the experiential world of the disciples, Pannenberg declares that it belongs to the world of universal public history.

This immediately raises the question of the historicity of the resurrection. A group of Enlightenment writers, including David Hume and G.E. Lessing, had argued that our only knowledge of the alleged resurrection of Jesus was contained in the New Testament. In that there were no contemporary analogues for such a resurrection, the credibility of those reports had to be seriously questioned. In a similar vein, Ernst Troeltsch had argued for the homogeneity of history; in that the resurrection of Jesus appeared to disrupt that homogeneity radically, it was to be regarded as of dubious historicity. Pannenberg responded to these difficulties initially in an essay on 'Redemptive Event and History', and subsequently in *Jesus – God and Man* ([1964] 1968). His basic argument against this position can be set out as follows. Troeltsch has a narrow view of history, which rules out certain events in advance, on the basis of a set of provisional judgements which have improperly come to have the status of absolute laws. Troeltsch's unwarranted 'constriction of historico-critical enquiry' was 'biased' and 'anthropocentric'. It presupposed that the human viewpoint is the only acceptable and normative standpoint within history. Analogies, Pannenberg stresses, are always analogies *viewed from the standpoint of the human observer*; that standpoint is radically restricted in its scope, and cannot be allowed to function as the absolutely certain basis of critical enquiry. Pannenberg is too good a historian to suggest that the principle of analogy should be abandoned; it is, after all, a proven and useful tool of historical research. Yet, Pannenberg

insists, that is all that it is: it is a working tool, and cannot be allowed to define a fixed view of reality.

If the historian sets out to investigate the New Testament already precommitted to the belief 'dead people do not rise again', that conclusion will merely be read back into the New Testament material. The judgement 'Jesus did not rise from the dead' will be the presupposition, not the conclusion, of such an investigation. Pannenberg's discussion of this question represents an impassioned and impressive plea for a neutral approach to the resurrection. The historical evidence pointing to the resurrection of Jesus must be investigated without the prior dogmatic presupposition that such a resurrection could not have happened.

Having argued for the historicity of the resurrection, Pannenberg turns to deal with its interpretation within the context of the apocalyptic framework of meaning. The end of history has proleptically taken place in the resurrection of Jesus from the dead. This maxim dominates Pannenberg's interpretation of the event. The resurrection of Jesus anticipates the general resurrection at the end of time, and brings forward into history both that resurrection and the full and final revelation of God. The resurrection of Jesus is thus organically linked with the self-revelation of God in Christ and establishes Jesus' identity with God, and allows this identity with God to be read back into his pre-Easter ministry.

Pannenberg's Christology has been the subject of excitement and criticism in about equal measure. The idea of establishing the gospel on the basis of universal history seemed a daring and creative gesture, allowing theology to reclaim the intellectual high ground that many had thought had long been forfeited to Marxism. The idea of a Christology 'from below' seemed to offer new possibilities to Christian apologetics. In particular, it seemed to bypass the trap laid by Ludwig Feuerbach, who had argued that the Schleiermachian type of Christology from below (beginning from human experience) was little more than a Christology constructed through the objectification of human feelings and their projection onto the figure of Jesus. Pannenberg, by his appeal to history, is able to avoid the line of thought which leads to Feuerbach's impasse by insisting that Christology arises out of history, not out of human feelings of redemption or the presence of God. The recognition of an objective historical criterion prevents a degeneration into a vulnerable Jesuology of personal experience.

Although centring on the issue of universal history and its implications for Christian theology, Pannenberg has made significant contributions in other areas. He has made noted contributions to anthropology, such as *What is Man?* ([1962] 1970) and *Anthropology in Theological Perspective* of 1983. In these works, Pannenberg explores the relationship between anthropology and Christian truth-claims. Sensitive to the modern secular situation in western culture, Pannenberg indicates that anthropology is a – perhaps *the* – central area of conflict between atheism and faith. Christian theology's claims to universality (closely linked to Pannenberg's appeal to universal history) must therefore be justified with reference to anthropology. In his *Theology and the Philosophy of Science* ([1973] 1976), Pannenberg explored the nature of theological statements, and their grounding and justification in the light of the biblical tradition and critical reflection.

Most recently, Pannenberg has published a three-volume *Systematic Theology* ([1988] 1991), in which his methodological explorations (such as those found in *Jesus – God and Man*) are allowed to find full-blown systematic expression. The basic structure of these volumes (surveyed by Grenz, 1990) suggests that Pannenberg's programme is likely to remain of considerable interest for some time to come.

See also PROTESTANT THEOLOGY: GERMANY.

Bibliography

Writings
[1962] 1970: *What is Man?*, trans. Philadelphia: Westminster Press.
[1964] 1968: *Jesus – God and Man*, trans. London: SCM Press.
[1967–71] 1970–3: *Basic Questions in Theology*, 3 vols, trans. London: SCM Press.
[1973] 1976: *Theology and the Philosophy of Science*, trans. London: Darton, Longman and Todd.
[1988] 1991: *Systematic Theology*, vol. 1, trans. Grand Rapids: Eerdmans.

Critical works
Grenz, Stanley J. 1990: *Reason for Hope: The Systematic Theology of Wolfhart Pannenberg*. New York: Oxford University Press.
Schwöbel, Christoph 1989: Wolfhart Pannenberg. In *The Modern Theologians*, 2 vols, ed. David F. Ford. Oxford: Blackwell, vol. 1, pp. 257–92.

ALISTER E. MCGRATH

Pascal, Blaise (1623–1662) French mathematician, philosopher and religious writer. He was educated privately by his father, and showed considerable ability in the field of the natural sciences, in which he retained an interest in later life. His 'first conversion' took place in 1646 following contact with the Jansenists (then suspected of Protestant leanings by many Catholic writers). In 1654, his 'definitive conversion' took place, characterized by his discovery of the 'God of Abraham, the God of Isaac, the God of Jacob, and not of philosophers and scientists'. Pascal subsequently engaged in a vigorous defence of the basic idea of Jansenism, which was published as *The Provincial Letters* in the period 1656–7.

Important though Pascal was as a defender of the ideas of Jansenism, his chief contribution to the development of modern Christian theology lay in his APOLOGETICS. Setting to one side the traditional rational proofs of the existence of God, Pascal chose to begin from the inexplicable phenomenon of human nature, and the tensions which it demonstrates. For Pascal, human nature is characterized by its corruption and selfishness, yet possesses the ability to realize its condition. Christianity, according to Pascal, is able to explain this tension better than any other philosophy. Pascal's famous 'wager' reflects his conviction of the explanatory power and internal coherence of the Christian faith. This approach, developed in the *Pensées*, is generally regarded as one of the most significant contributions to apologetics in a period increasingly dominated by rationalism, on the part of both Christianity's defenders and detractors.

Bibliography

Broome, J.H. 1965: *Pascal*. London.
Kraishaimer, A. 1980: *Pascal*. London.
Pascal, B. [1656–7] 1967: *The Provincial Letters*. Harmondsworth.
Pascal, B. [1670] 1966: *Pensées*. Harmondsworth.

pastoral care, theories of Christian pastoral care is that activity within the ministry of the church which is centrally concerned with promoting the well-being of individuals and of communities. The ultimate aim of pastoral care is that of ministry as a whole, that is, to increase love between people and between people and God. Its specific functions are healing, sustaining, reconciling, guiding and nurturing.

Although pastoral care has been a feature of the Christian church since the earliest times, a substantial body of theories did not form around it before the present century. There has been a tendency towards atheoretical pastoral pragmatism which concentrates on what is functional in particular situations. This article briefly summarizes some main trends in the recent history of pastoral care theories. It then goes on to look at some important contemporary developments in this area. Its scope is limited to developments in the English-speaking world, particularly in the USA and the United Kingdom. Throughout, it should be borne in mind that pastoral care is a pluriform, variegated activity whose practice and theoretical formulation varies widely according to historical, geographical, sociological, traditional and confessional factors. This brief survey must therefore necessarily be selective and at a high level of generalization.

Historical considerations
Although many important theological works and insights have emerged from essentially practical pastoral situations (for example some of the theological works of St Augustine), historically, the practice of pastoral care has not elicited sophisticated theory from the best minds of the church. From the earliest times, it was high doctrinal theological activity which mostly engaged ecclesiastical intellectuals, not the everyday activities of ministry. Today there continues to be an inverse relationship between the amount of pastoral work undertaken by Christians (a great deal) and the amount of theory formulated in relation to it (very little).

As recently as the nineteenth century, training for the practical work of pastoral care in the Protestant tradition appears to have consisted of a mixture of apparently common-sense advice together with an imitative apprenticeship with an experienced pastor after ordination. Within the Roman Catholic tradition, pastoral care continued to focus on the due administration of the sacraments together with the application of moral theology. Pastoral care was firmly practical and clerical, consisting of hints and tips about practice and the acquisition of certain techniques to the exclusion of enlightening or enlivening theory, which was confined to the academically more significant areas of theology.

The theorization of contemporary pastoral care, such as it is, derived its impetus and direction not from theology, but from the advent of psychological and psychoanalytic theories and practices which were taken up by liberal Protestant denominations in America from about 1900 onwards (see LIBERALISM (BRITAIN and USA); PSYCHOLOGICAL SCIENCE AND CHRISTIAN THOUGHT). A kind of 'therapeutic revolution' in pastoral care, focused around the use of talking cures, gathered momentum throughout this century. By the 1960s a highly professionalized pastoral care movement had emerged in North America. Taking individual counselling as its main paradigm of action, the movement was much influenced by the techniques and theories of humanistic psychologists such as Sigmund Freud, Abraham Maslow, Carl Rogers, Erich Fromm, Eric Berne and Fritz Perls.

An important byproduct of this particular model of professionalized care was the production of research and theoretical literature which, while focusing on pastoral practice, began to be undergirded by theological interest and theorizing from thinkers like Seward Hiltner. A climate of theological interest and debate was fostered in the 1950s and 1960s by the prevalence of Tillichian theories of critical correlation, the importance of the person's existential experience, and the significance of concepts such as *Angst*. These were highly congruent with humanistic psychological concerns. It must, however, be emphasized that theology was very much the weaker and junior partner to the various techniques of counselling and psychotherapy which had attained dominance in the practice of pastoral care.

Britain and western Europe generally were not to feel the effects of the therapeutic revolution in pastoral care theory and practice until after the Second World War. Early pioneers of psychologically informed pastoral care included the prominent Methodist Leslie Weatherhead, the Congregationalist psychotherapist Harry Guntrip and the Anglican R.S. Lee. Later on, Frank Lake evolved his 'clinical theology' (psychodynamic theology related to pastoral issues), which was widely disseminated throughout Britain in seminars for parochial clergy. The continuing existence of organizations such as the Westminster Pastoral Foundation and the Association for Pastoral Care and Counselling bears witness to the colonization of British pastoral care by enthusiastic converts to American ways. A significant literature, chiefly embodied in the SPCK 'New Library of Pastoral Care' (1982–), reveals the extent and indigenization of mainly psychodynamic ideas within a certain sector of British pastoral practice. It is important to recognize, however, that much contemporary British pastoral care theory and practice is not psychodynamically oriented. Indeed, much pastoral care is not illuminated by any theory at all, other than a kind of utilitarian pragmatism.

The size and dynamism of the American pastoral care movement has moved outwards from liberal Protestant denominations to include post-Second Vatican Council Roman Catholics and evangelical Protestants. However, with its maturing since the 1970s, the movement has become more diverse and self-critical. It is to some of the diverse contemporary critical theoretical trends in pastoral care that we now turn.

Contemporary critical theories of pastoral care
Counselling provides a clear, practical, coherent and useful paradigm for professional pastoral care. But it also has substantial limitations. It tends towards individualism, professionalization, cultural narrowness, crisis-centredness and a focus on technique. More particularly, the paradigm of non-judgemental individual counselling appears to have little space for specifically religious concerns and perceptions. It is in reaction to this myopic world view in pastoral care that new, implicitly or explicitly critical theories have begun to emerge. Much of this critical theory is to be found exemplified in the twelve volumes of the American Fortress Press series 'Theology and Pastoral Care'

(1983–7), to which the reader is referred. These theories are now briefly considered.

Recovering the religious and theological tradition
One of the most apparent effects of pursuing the secular counselling paradigm as *the* model for pastoral care was, as we have seen, a loss of contact with theology and the specifically religious tradition. This tendency has been most vigorously highlighted by the American theologian Thomas Oden. Having experimented with and written about many of the contemporary therapies popular within the American pastoral care movement in the 1960s and 1970s, Oden became aware of the way in which the historical wisdom of the specifically religious tradition in Christianity had become completely marginalized in pastoral care. The psychoanalysts appeared to have supplemented the doctors and spiritual teachers of the church and Christian identity had been lost. Turning his back on contemporary therapies, Oden has subsequently devoted the last decade to rehabilitating traditional Christian wisdom, for example the pastoral teaching of the sixth-century pope Gregory the Great, and establishing its relevance to contemporary pastoral needs. Although Oden has been criticized for pursuing the past to the exclusion of the present, thus sacrificing some of the hard-won knowledge and technique derived from contemporary therapeutic methods, his constructive and systematic project on classic pastoral care, begun with his book, *Pastoral Theology* (1983), forms a valuable corrective to the inadvertent marginalization of theology and tradition by pastors preoccupied with counselling methods.

Rediscovering the Bible and the use of hermeneutic methods Alongside the rehabilitation of the Christian pastoral tradition, there is new interest in the use of the Bible in pastoral care. While recognizing the problems of cultural difference and interpretation inherent in the pastoral use of the Bible, Donald Capps argues that it can still have a prominent place in pastoral care. He suggests that the use of the Bible should be guided by the particular needs and circumstances of the person in need, that it should reflect pastoral sensitivity to the person's physical and psychological limitations, that it should be used in a way consistent with good counselling principles (for example, it should not be used moralistically) and that it should be related to the emotional dynamics of the caring encounter. Used in this way, the Bible can have a powerful and beneficial disclosive effect in pastoral care. Capps believes that the Bible, used with awareness of the different genres it contains, can help to structure pastoral encounters (for example, the Psalms of lament in the Old Testament can help to structure pastoral care with bereaved people). A similar approach is adopted by Oglesby (1980), who argues that there are some central underlying themes in the Bible, such as initiative and freedom, fear and faith. These can be identified and then used to inform pastoral care. A further extension of the use of the Bible in pastoral care theory is to be found in Alastair Campbell's *Rediscovering Pastoral Care* (1986), where biblical images of the courageous shepherd, the wounded healer and the wise fool are used to expand and interpret the role of pastors today. Finally, it should be noted that the hermeneutic methods used initially to understand classic texts such as the Bible are now being used by writers such as Capps to understand actual pastoral situations themselves. (See BIBLICAL CRITICISM AND INTERPRETATION (1: OLD TESTAMENT and 2: NEW TESTAMENT).

Recognizing the corporate, communal and socio-political dimensions of pastoral care Using counselling as a paradigm for pastoral care has torn that activity away from its context within the ecclesiastical and wider community and colluded with a sense of apolitical individualism. This balance has started to be redressed, particularly by British thinkers who have been able to retain a greater sense of corporate awareness and responsibility in their thought. R.A. Lambourne was an early critic of the counselling-dominated professionalized pastoral care movement. He theorized about pastoral care from the perspective of one who believed that pastoral care should be lay, voluntary, and diffuse in the community, motivated as much by a struggle for corporate excellence as a struggle against individual defects. More recently, Peter Selby has argued that personal care must be situated within a struggle for a just society if the hurts of today are not to be institutionalized and perpetuated into the future. While some awareness of the connections between wider

society and the troubled individual has been evident in North America, it seems largely true that, in Lambourne's words, the theory and art of loving has become separated from the theory and art of justice in the modern pastoral care movement there (Wilson, 1983).

Re-siting pastoral care within the horizon of values and ethics Although one of the main features of Christianity from an outsider's point of view might be its emphasis on values and morals, these aspects were largely ignored in the pastoral care movement until Don Browning began critical and constructive work in this area. Browning has pointed up the values implicit in all human activity, and the dangers of uncritically accepting the values of secular counselling into pastoral care, which should have its own self-conscious value system based in the church, itself a community of moral discourse. He has outlined a revised correlational approach whereby positive critical practical theologies of care can be evolved by correlating interpretations of the central Christian tradition with questions and answers implicit in various interpretations of contemporary human experience arising from, for example, the social sciences.

Escaping from crisis and pathology The counselling paradigm has tended to concentrate on the needs of people when they are in crisis. An important countervailing trend in recent pastoral care theory has been an emphasis on working holistically with people in the normal circumstances of their everyday lives and communities to maximize their well being. In this connection, some recent theorists have explored the importance of the standard human life cycle and the specific tasks and challenges it throws up for faith and functioning. Others have tried to create normative practical theologies for dealing with the ordinary situations of life such as the family or ageing. The significance of worship and spirituality and the ways in which these activities interact with human growth and flourishing are also being investigated in creative and useful ways.

Extending the scope and boundaries of pastoral care Modern pastoral care theories were originally formulated in white-, male- and clerically-dominated liberal Protestant denominations in North America. Gradually, the moorings to these origins are being slipped and pastoral care is becoming more inclusive. Pastoral care theorizing is now an interdenominational activity. Since the Second Vatican Council with its emphasis on the humanizing role of the church and the importance of the lay apostolate, Roman Catholics in particular have begun to contribute a great deal. Feminist perspectives and the pastoral care of and by women are beginning to assume a major role (see FEMINIST THEOLOGY). Lay people are recognized as making an important contribution to the theory and practice of pastoral care. The intercultural nature of appropriate pastoral care theory is being explored. The distinctive needs and contributions of, for example, black people in pastoral care are being recognized. The tensions and opportunities afforded by an international dimension in the pastoral care movement are becoming apparent. There is starting to be an inter-religious dimension to pastoral care, represented strongly in the USA by increasing interest in the subject amongst liberal Jewish rabbis.

Conclusion

Pastoral care theories have multiplied in the present century. Escaping from a simple counselling paradigm, they have become more critical, pluriform and diverse. As an activity, pastoral care is still substantially focused upon the acquisition of usable techniques and unsupported by good critical theory (this is particularly true in Britain where there are very few pastoral theologians). It remains relatively isolated from main currents in contemporary theology, and effective dialogue needs to be enhanced in this area for the mutual benefit of both activities. Some main currents in contemporary critical pastoral care theories have been described in this article. A fuller appreciation of the interests, scope, diversity, coherence and fragmentation of this subject can best be assayed by consulting the two recently published dictionaries of pastoral care cited in the bibliography below. These act as authoritative landmarks in the evolution of a very confusing field.

See also PASTORAL THEOLOGY.

Bibliography

Browning, D.S. 1983: *Religious Ethics and Pastoral Care*. Philadelphia: Fortress Press.

Campbell, A.V. 1986: *Rediscovering Pastoral Care*. London: Darton, Longman and Todd.

Campbell, A.V., ed. 1987: *A Dictionary of Pastoral Care*. London: SPCK.

Capps, D. 1981: *Biblical Approaches to Pastoral Counselling*. Philadelphia: Westminster Press.

Capps, D. 1984: *Pastoral Care and Hermeneutics*. Philadelphia: Fortress Press.

Glaz, M., and Moessner, J.S., eds 1991: *Women in Travail and Transition*. Minneapolis: Fortress Press.

Hiltner, S. 1958: *Preface to Pastoral Theology*. Nashville: Abingdon.

Hunter, R.J., ed. 1990: *Dictionary of Pastoral Care and Counselling*. Nashville: Abingdon.

Oden, T.C. 1983: *Pastoral Theology*. San Francisco: Harper and Row.

Oglesby, W.B. 1980: *Biblical Themes for Pastoral Care*. Nashville: Abingdon.

Pattison, S. 1988: *A Critique of Pastoral Care*. London: SCM Press.

Ramshaw, E. 1987: *Ritual and Pastoral Care*. Philadelphia: Fortress Press.

Selby, P. 1983: *Liberating God*. London: SPCK.

Wilson, M., ed. 1983: *Explorations in Health and Salvation*. Birmingham: Institute for the Study of Worship and Religious Architecture, University of Birmingham.

STEPHEN PATTISON

pastoral theology Christian pastoral theology is that aspect of the theological task which informs and reflects on pastoral ministry within the Christian community. In the broad sense, pastoral ministry covers, for example, preaching, teaching, healing, counselling and spiritual direction, all of which are sometimes – but by no means exclusively – the work of the clergy. 'Pastoral theology' in this broad sense thus brings together homiletics, catechesis, poimenics, paraklesis and ascetical theology, each overlapping with systematic, historical and moral theology.

Although the term 'pastoral theology' does not seem to have been used until about 1750, theologians throughout the history of the church have developed pastoral theology in this broad sense. (See, for example, J.T. McNeil, *A History of the Cure of Souls*; W.A. Clebsch and C. Jaekle, *Pastoral Care in Historical Perspective*; K.E. Kirk, *The Vision of God*; M. Thornton, *English Spirituality*; D.Tidball, *Skilful Shepherds*.)

By the mid-eighteenth century a narrower focus was developing, however, and this was furthered by F.D.E. Schleiermacher's work on 'practical theology', which he understood to be a reflective theology of the practice of the church. Within reflective practical theology, 'pastoral theology' focused on the care of souls, which was often related entirely to the homiletic and sacramental functions of the priesthood. This reflective and integrated, though narrow, approach contrasted with another trend, which understood pastoral theology only as the application of dogmatics to practical issues, sometimes in terms of moral guidance, sometimes related to the confessional and the practice of penance.

Since the Second World War a number of trends may be discerned. In the USA, Seward Hiltner, inspired by the work of Anton Boisen, developed an academic approach to pastoral theology (*Preface to Pastoral Theology of* 1958), which came out of enquiry from a 'shepherding perspective' on the operations and functions of the church and the ministry, and sought to draw theological conclusions from such enquiry. He saw pastoral theology as requiring an 'operation-centred' rather than a 'logic-centred' method, and his reflective-practitioner model had a significant impact on pastoral training in the USA. Many have shared the view that pastoral theology must take the form of theological reflection on praxis (some drawing on the model of LIBERATION THEOLOGY). On the other hand, Hiltner's fellow countryman Thomas Oden, having written widely on the dialogue between systematic theology and psychology, has more recently (1983) produced a major *Pastoral Theology*, which is focused largely on the work of the clergy, and which seeks to apply the insights of the classical Christian tradition to ministerial function. On the continent, Eduard Thurneysen in 1962 provided a *Theology of Pastoral Care* from a Barthian perspective, in which pastoral ministry was understood exclusively as a form of preaching the Word of God, though the human sciences were helpful as auxiliary disciplines in that task. In Britain Frank Lake's massive *Clinical Theology* of 1966 offered a theologico-psychological basis for pastoral care derived from a Christocentric model of spiritual development and the post-Freudian object relations theories of Melanie Klein and W.R.D. Fairbairn, while Robert Lambourne (*Community, Church and Healing*

of 1963) argued theologically for the significance of the role of the community in illness and health.

It is clear that the term 'pastoral theology' is currently used in a variety of ways, some of which betray different approaches to theological method, some of which differ as to the appropriate content of the discipline. There is much to be said for recovering the earlier broad sense of the term (though some would here prefer 'practical theology'), understanding 'pastoral theology' as an umbrella discipline working at the interfaces of theological tasks which inform and reflect on the various aspects of pastoral care, PREACHING and spirituality (see SPIRITUALITY, CHRISTIAN).

To be involved in Christian pastoral ministry is to be caught up into the ministry of Christ to the Father in the Spirit for the sake of the world. The ministry of Christ includes prophetic proclamation, teaching and parakletic counsel, as well as diakonic service. The goal of pastoral ministry is to 'proclaim Christ, warning every man and teaching every man in all wisdom, that we may present every man mature in Christ' (Col. 1: 28).

Pastoral theology includes, therefore, a theology of preaching, rooted in the gospel of the kingdom of Christ and open to the activity of the Holy Spirit in accommodating the Word of God to human need. It includes a theology of healing (and of suffering), related to the preaching of the kingdom of Christ and giving visible expression to the gospel. It includes a theology of counselling, modelled on the parakletic ministry of the Holy Spirit, comforting, guiding, warning and exhorting. It includes an ascetical theology, exploring the dynamics of the spiritual life and the processes of growth to spiritual maturity through prayer and sacrament. All will be set within a theology of the created yet fallen world which is being redeemed in Christ, and being drawn towards its fulfilment in the purposes of God.

In all this, there are several levels to the pastoral theological task (see Browning, 1983). There is, for example, the level of fundamental dogmatic assumptions, our basic metaphors for God, which govern our theological framework and method. There is the level of moral values, explicated by ethical theory and traditions of Christian moral reasoning, which set boundaries to and guidance in pastoral ministry. There is the level of sociological, cultural and political determinants, which affect the understanding of and approaches to the pastoral task. There is the level of personal pastoral application, where in particular the insights of the human sciences need to be brought into dialogue with dogmatic theology.

The task of pastoral theology essentially has the nature of a conversation. On one side of the dialogue are the traditions of Christian historical, systematic, moral and ascetical theology. On the other are the personal and social demands of the pastoral situation. This conversation is two-way. It is for the pastoral theologian to bring the resources of the tradition to bear on the particular pastoral event, illuminating and guiding, at each of the above levels. It is also necessary for the pastoral event to be allowed to confront the tradition and contribute to the ongoing theological task.

See also PASTORAL CARE, THEORIES OF.

Bibliography

Anderson, R.S., ed. 1979: *Theological Foundations For Ministry*. Edinburgh: T & T Clark; Grand Rapids: Eerdmans.

Browning, D.S. 1983: *Religious Ethics and Pastoral Care*. Philadelphia: Fortress Press.

Hiltner, S. 1958: *Preface to Pastoral Theology*. Nashville: Abingdon Press.

Oden, T.C. 1983: *Pastoral Theology*. San Francisco: Harper and Row.

Oglesby, W.B., Jr, ed. 1969: *The New Shape of Pastoral Theology*. Nashville: Abingdon Press.

Tidball, D.J. 1986: *Skilful Shepherds*. Leicester: IVP.

DAVID J. ATKINSON

Pentecostalism and charismatic Christianity Pentecostalist and charismatic (or neo-Pentecostal) Christianity manifests religious phenomena which, so its adherents believe, reproduce or reintroduce the miraculous charismata of the New Testament. To begin phenomenologically is helpful because despite wide differences in organization, style, social class and doctrine between charismatic Christians, the experiential dimension of the many Pentecostalist movements appears remarkably constant. 'Happy clapping', tambourine banging, snake handling and leg lengthening are just some of the many subcultural and epiphenom-

enal variations in Pentecostal practice, but essentially it is the conviction that modern Christians can be infused with the power of the Holy Spirit in ways similar to the disciples of the New Testament that is the distinctive flavour of charismatic Christianity. In this respect, whether we are looking at the classical Pentecostal denominations at the beginning of the century, or the so-called Renewal movement within the mainline denominations, or again at the many maverick or independent charismatic movements, the experiential hallmarks are much the same.

It is a fascinating fact, though it is impossible to be certain as to why this should be so, that Pentecostalism and its mutational offshoots are essentially a twentieth-century phenomenon. It is true that glossolalia was a minor feature of the early Shakers in England during the eighteenth century, and tongues stuttered briefly in North America among the early Mormons in the 1820s and the Millerites in the 1840s. But only the Catholic Apostolic Church which grew up in the shadow of Edward Irving's ministry (1792–1834) in London can be said to be a genuine precursor of modern twentieth-century Pentecostalism. And even this fact needs the caveat that Irving was a high church Calvinist and the Catholic Apostolic Church was in many ways closer to Tractarianism than evangelicalism.

Classical origins of Pentecostalism

Charles Fox Parham (1873–1929) can claim to be the father of the modern Pentecostal movement. He was deeply influenced by the holiness teachings of Protestant evangelicalism and late nineteenth-century adventism. In 1901 at Topeka, Kansas, during a Holy Spirit outpouring highlighted by 'speaking in tongues', he formulated what were to become the tenets of classical Pentecostalism, including the 'Baptism of the Holy Spirit' as a second blessing subsequent to conversion. By 1905 he also saw the phenomenon of speaking in tongues as the initial evidence of the new experience. However, Parham believed that the outbreak of tongues was evidence of a 'latter reign' revival which would herald the second coming of Christ. For him the charismata of tongues was essentially a miracle of grace, whereby Christians could supernaturally evangelize in the mother tongues of the different nations of the world.

It is not unfair to say that he confused the *xenolalia* (speaking in foreign languages) of the Day of Pentecost, as recorded in Acts 2, with the ecstatic or unintelligible 'language' of *glossolalia* mentioned by St Paul in 1 Corinthians 12. This confusion is not unimportant because the dominant features of Pentecostal religion have been glossolalia, divine healing, and 'sing-along' hymns and choruses, with speaking in foreign languages a marginal and little recorded activity. This confusion carried over into the burgeoning revivals of the early twentieth century so that in effect the word 'Pentecostal' as the title of the new enthusiasm is a misnomer. Nevertheless this exegetical mistake had an important consequence for classical Pentecostalism: it was fervently evangelistic, for it believed that the new tongues not only heralded the end-time but would overcome the language barriers created by the debacle of Babel. (Although most present-day Pentecostals no longer see tongues as a major evangelistic tool, and the exegetical mistake is now widely acknowledged, they remain evangelistic in an expansionist way, which is still not a normative feature of Renewalist charismatics.)

If Parham can claim to be the father of Pentecostalism, it was one of his followers who really put the new enthusiasm on the map. This man, Joseph William Seymour (1870–1922), was a son of African American slaves. As a leader of the Parham-inspired Apostolic Faith Mission, he was pastor of the Azusa Street Mission in Los Angeles, California, where in 1906–8 there was an outbreak of Pentecostal revival – with its tongues, healings, miracles and lively singing. The revival was clearly evangelical, adventist and deeply under the influence of holiness teaching and the tenets of Parham's own theology. Ironically Parham, who was racist, was rejected by the Azusa Street elders in 1906; and after public charges of sodomy in Texas in 1907, he never really recovered his leadership of the nascent Pentecostal movement.

The Azusa Street revival was more than a symbol of Pentecostal origins, and more important than providing the raw data of Pentecostalist history and hagiography. It was a recapitulation of the abolitionist and integrationist hopes of the Great Awakening of eighteenth-century American enthusiasm. For a short while black and white worked together across the colour bar; as one of the early leaders put it, 'the colour line has been washed away by the blood.' Tragically Pentecostalism was soon to develop along segregationist lines and numerous accounts of Pentecostal history have not paid due regard either to the inter-racial characteristics of the Azusa Street Mission or to the separate and somewhat earlier beginnings of black American Pentecostalism (see MacRobert, 1988).

But if Azusa failed, like the first Great Awakening, to keep black and white together in harmony, it can certainly be claimed as the origin of many a twentieth-century Pentecostal denomination. The Apostolic Faith Church of God (Franklin, Virginia) can trace a direct line to Azusa Street, and both the Pentecostal Assemblies of the World (Los Angeles) and the Assemblies of God (America's largest classical Pentecostal church) claim their origins in part from Azusa. Furthermore, existing denominations became Pentecostal as a result of Azusa Street and its subsequent missions (the Church of God in Christ and the Church of God, Cleveland, Tennessee, would be the most obvious examples).

But the influence of Azusa reached beyond the boundaries of the USA and there is strong empirical evidence of a rare anthropological and sociological phenomenon – a genuine diffusionism. Azusa was visited by missionaries and curious clergymen from around the world who took back with them both the experience of the 'baptism' and the somewhat loose theology of the revivals. In particular one of the famous 'Cambridge seven', Cecil Polhill (1860–1938), and Thomas Ball Barratt (1862–1940) from Norway took the Pentecostal message back to Europe. It was the revival in Norway under Barratt that encouraged the Anglican vicar, Alexander Alfred Boddy (1854–1930), to encounter the new revival at first hand and it was at his church at Monkwearmouth in Sunderland, England, that an interdenominational Pentecostal centre began in 1908.

The involvement of these men from the upper classes gives the lie to the simplistic view that Pentecostalism was a religion exclusively of the disinherited (see Anderson, 1980). In

Britain, however, revivalism soon developed along sectarian and working-class lines and, following the American experience, denominations emerged in opposition to each other. By the mid-1920s Britain could claim three significant Pentecostal denominations, The Elim Foursquare Gospel Church which was Presbyterian in structure, the Assemblies of God which was Congregationalist, and the much smaller Apostolic Church which, like the earlier Catholic Apostolic Church, could claim to be led by a charismatic apostolate. Other Pentecostal denominations throughout the world (notably the black-led Church of God in Christ) have been episcopalian along the more traditional lines of the United Methodist Church in North America. In this respect classical Pentecostalism mirrors the ecclesiastical shape of the Reformation churches of the sixteenth and seventeenth centuries.

Classical Pentecostals may have been the pioneers of twentieth-century charismatic religion, but it would be a mistake to see them as a spent force. Not only do the global figures run into over a hundred million (see Barrett, 1989), but relatively small groups such as the Elim movement in Britain (with some 30,000 to 40,000 members) and the Assemblies of God (with perhaps a further 10,000 adherents) show a stable though slow growth. New indigenous Pentecostalist sects are springing up in South America at a truly amazing rate (see Martin, 1990). It also holds true that much of the growth of charismatic activity in eastern Europe, Asia and Africa can really be understood as an extension of classical Pentecostalism *per se*, and not only as part of the more recent charismatic Renewal.

The charismatic Renewal movement

Classical Pentecostalism became intertwined with the fundamentalist movement (see FUNDAMENTALISM) of the early twentieth century (See marsden, 1980). Consequently there was a separatist, anti-intellectual and anti-ecumenical air about Pentecostalism. The British Assemblies of God pastor, Donald Gee (1891–1966), was one of the few who believed that Pentecostals should be active in the World Council of Churches, but it was a South African-born naturalized American pastor of the Assemblies of God, David Du Plessis

(1905–1987), 'Mr Pentecost' as he was called, who can claim to have done more than any other individual to encourage dialogue between Pentecostalists and mainline churches.

Like the founding leader of the Elim church, Principal George Jeffreys (1889–1962), Du Plessis had always dreamed of a worldwide Pentecostal revival, and from the mid-1960s to the present day it could be claimed that in some respects such a dream has come true. Unlike classical Pentecostalism, it is doubtful whether the same sort of diffusionism marks the beginnings of this 'second wave', or phase, of charismatic activity. In fact throughout the 1950s the somewhat maverick and marginal characters of classical Pentecostalism, such as William Branham (1909–1965) and Oral Roberts (b. 1918), had already influenced mainline Christians. Perhaps the declaration in 1959 that the Episcopalian priest of St Mark's, Van Nuys, California, Dennis Bennett (b. 1917), had received the baptism in the Holy Spirit and spoken in tongues could be said to be one of the triggers of neo-Pentecostalism. But it was only one of many and soon, remarkably, charismata were being reported in every mainline denomination in the world from Southern Baptist to Roman Catholic.

There was no doubt that itinerants such as Du Plessis played a major role in spreading the word, but the 1960s had an anarchic and spontaneous air about them, and the Renewal, as it was increasingly being called, was in no sense orchestrated or manipulated by a single or central organization. No doubt the declaration of support in the early 1970s from such eminent Catholics as Cardinal Suenens (b. 1904) gave the movement some respectability. In particular, the Roman Catholics lent a certain amount of doctrinal weight to the somewhat unsystematic and anecdotal method of Pentecostal theology (see Gelpi, 1971; McDonnell, 1978). The Catholics, and many Anglicans, were happy to accept the experiential side of the Renewal but rejected the two-stage, or first and second blessing, theology of classical Pentecostalism. The very presence of the historic churches in Pentecostal territory led to a hands-off stance from many classical Pentecostals who had been led to believe that the older churches were apostate and incapable of genuine spiritual renewal (see Richards, 1971).

From 1970 to 1980, however, it seemed that nothing could stop the bandwagon effect of the Renewal. It became increasingly commonplace to see priests dancing in full vestments, praising God in tongues, and shouting out 'thank you, Jesus'. In many ways the decade of 1970 to 1980 was the golden era (to date) of the Renewal movement, and perhaps the Kansas City Conference of 1977 remains the Woodstock of ecumenical charismatic experience. Some leading evangelical figures (see Packer, 1980) attempted some serious theological critique of the movement, but even they were jollied along by the upbeat Renewal even if they were less than sanguine about the charismata *per se*. Without any doubt the songs of the Renewal, like the choruses of Pentecostalism before them and the sounds of the house churches after them, were sung at missions, conventions and churches that were not overtly charismatic.

No one can say with certainty how many people were caught up in the new Pentecost, though participants at the World Council of Churches' consultation on the Renewal at Bossey in Switzerland in 1980 thought that some three to four million people had been affected (though it must be said that the consultation did not always distinguish clearly whether the spectacular growth of the charismatic movement in the third world was neo-Pentecostalism or old-style sectarianism; recent evidence suggests that it is likely to be a hybrid of both (see Martin, 1990)).

Clearly the charismatic Renewal in the first world has been a gentrified or middle-class version of Pentecostalism. Like its classical cousin, it has majored in tongues, healings, new songs and intense excitement. Unlike Pentecostalism, and much to the amazement of sociologists (see Walker, 1983), the Renewal has not only been middle-class (though not exclusively) but it has also appeared to contradict the rules of sociological evidence: charismatics have not automatically become sectarian or separatist; on the contrary, the majority of Renewalists remained in their churches (though it might be argued that this amounts to a sectarian implant). In Britain there was a committed ecumenism throughout the 1970s and 1980s which has remained to this day. No one represents this stream of the Renewal better than Canon Michael Harper (b. 1931), who

from his days as curate at All Souls, Langham Place, London (until 1964) to the World Conference of Charismatics held in Brighton (in June 1991) has sought to bring together Christians from every denomination.

Independents and mavericks

It was Harper, however, who first alerted the British charismatics to the fact that all was not well in the charismatic camp (Harper, 1980), for in the mid 1970s, beginning in North America and spreading to Europe, a movement known as 'shepherding' or 'discipling' split the charismatic movement down the middle. In part this split was precipitated by a desire for the charismatic movement to 'come of age' and move on to a more committed discipleship.

In the event this split did not slow down charismatic movements, but it did herald a greater fragmentation of charismatic activity. Henceforth both classical Pentecostalism and neo-Pentecostalism were both bled and fed by numerous independent, and often extremely controversial, movements. It needs to be recognized, however, that the independent maverick is not a new phenomenon in Pentecostalism. Since the days of the Azusa Street Mission there have been men and women who have been either totally independent of or marginally related to denominations.

The roll call is long and each figure has been involved in some form of scandalous accusation. The so-called 'televangelists', for example, follow in a long line of 'charismatic stars' who have always rested uneasily within the denominational structures. In this respect Jimmy Swaggert (b. 1935), Jim and Tammy Bakker (b. 1940 and 1942) and Oral Roberts (b. 1918) are the heirs of Aimee Semple McPherson (1890–1944), William Branham (1909–1965), A.A. Allen (1911–1970), and T.L. Osborne (b. 1923). Kenneth Hagin (b. 1917) and Kenneth Copeland (b. 1937) continue in this tradition. (Pat Robertson (b. 1930) is a more educated and urbane charismatic but can be said to be in the same mould.)

In some respects most of these independents can be understood to be 'bible-belters' who have influenced Christians beyond the normal boundaries of classical Pentecostalism. But the Renewal has also produced its own controversial leaders. One remembers the flamboyant Kathryn Kuhlman (1907–1976), and today the former Dominican priest Francis McNutt (b. 1925) and the Californian charismatic John Wimber (b. 1934) have in their different ways had considerable impact on both mainline denominations and independent churches. Britain's most well-known charismatic itinerant – from the Renewal sector at least – is probably Colin Urquhart (b. 1940).

But the split to which Harper was alluding in the mid-1970s was more than an issue of new independent personalities supplanting the old ones; it was part of the growth of what has become a virtual 'third wave' of Pentecostal activity. The so-called shepherding ministry, particularly through the instigation of the 'Fort Lauderdale five' of Christian Growth Ministries, has had repercussions throughout America, the Antipodes, Africa, Asia and Europe.

In Britain, for example, under the influence (amongst others) of two of the Lauderdale five, Ern Baxter (b. 1914) and Bob Mumford (b. 1930), a loose-knit movement composed of 'streams' of independent networks combined discipleship teaching with a commitment to the five-fold ministry of Ephesians 4. This ministry was understood in terms of a charismatic apostolate, and throughout the 1980s these 'Restorationist' fellowships (see Walker, 1989) were the fastest growing Christian movement in Britain. Under the leadership of such men as Bryn Jones (b. 1940), this movement has seen the emergence of at least two 10,000-strong formations which begin to have the same denominational solidity as do Wimber's Vineyard churches, as they become firmly established in North America and England.

Strictly speaking the shepherding movement *per se* seems to be a spent force, though the continued growth of independent networks influenced by the five-fold ministries grows apace. The Restorationists in Britain, for example, may now be divided into quite distinct networks but they have been augmented (and to a certain extent have been overtaken) by a mushrooming of independent charismatic churches who can be said to be 'fellow travellers'. One such group, the Ichthus house church, may have no more than two thousand people in its South London network, but their influence is considerable within the English Evangelical Alliance (founded in 1846) and

throughout charismatic circles generally. In this respect they perform a similar function to an earlier 'house church movement' in the 1960s and early 1970s, in Chard in Somerset.

Many of the Restorationist networks, independent charismatic fellowships, Ichthus, and others outside the mainline Renewal movement and the classical Pentecostal denominations, are increasingly being linked together under the nebulous but popular title, 'the new churches'.

In North America too, although the 'shepherding' group involved in the Christian Growth Ministries no longer operates and despite the fact that the 'Fort Lauderdale five' have been disbanded, their influence is still considerable. Charles Simpson (b. 1937), for example, one of the leaders of this group, now heads up the Fellowship of Covenant Ministers and Conferences with over 350 church affiliations. A much smaller network, with informal links with Bryn Jones in Britain, is that led by Larry Tomczak and C.J. Mahaney from their Covenant Life Church in Gaithersburg, Maryland. The largest affiliation of independent charismatic churches is the 350–400 churches of the National Leadership Council founded in 1979, with its strength along the panhandle of Florida and in the southern American states.

A fourth stage?
Strictly speaking the notion of a 'third wave' of Pentecostalism was coined by the missiologist Peter Wagner (b. 1930) to denote a Pentecostalism that was inclusive, irenic and harmonious. In practice, it could be argued, the third wave has been an eclectic mixture of independent mavericks, Renewalists and indigenous Pentecostalism, whose sociological formation may yet end in sectarian denominations if not new religious movements. Be that as it may, there is strong evidence that the 1990s are witnessing an amalgam of all three stages – or waves – of Pentecostalism.

This is particularly true in Britain. The independent growth of the Spring Harvest festivals, which can now boast some 80,000 residents during the spring holiday, is infused with Renewalists, some classical Pentecostals, new church members, and evangelicals who have no particular charismatic brief. Furthermore John Wimber, whose influence is perhaps greater in Britain than North America, has performed the remarkable feat of being acceptable to both Renewalists and Restorationists as well as to other independent groups. The 'Make Way' marches for Jesus which since 1989 have annually put some 200,000 people on the city streets have primarily been a new church initiative with support from many Pentecostalists, Renewalists and non-charismatic evangelicals.

As longstanding a Pentecostal denomination as Elim has invited to its Bognor Bible Week an 'apostle' from Restorationism and a South African evangelist who preaches a similar 'health and wealth' gospel to Hagin of Oklahoma. Nothing could be more strange, however, than to see John Wimber (at least temporarily) caught up with some of the prophets of Kansas who are a throwback to the earlier Pentecostal Holiness movements and the circle of followers connected with Pentecost's most controversial figure, William Branham. Paul Cain, the most widely known of these prophets, has had considerable impact on Anglican charismatics and was invited to be the main speaker at Spring Harvest in 1992.

Historical research shows (Hocken, 1986) that Pentecostal religion cannot be neatly dissected into three, or four, stages even though this is a useful analytic distinction. Charismatic religion is essentially pragmatic: the crowds follow the action, and the 'stars' – regardless of theological or denominational affiliation – often call the tune. Nevertheless it is a remarkable fact that although there have been numerous cults of the personality and clear heretical elements in Pentecostal religion, on the whole Pentecostalism has remained within the bounds of historic orthodoxy in the same sense that we can say Montanism – despite its wildness and messianic pretension – remained Christian in the early Christian centuries. (Baptizing in the name of Jesus only is perhaps the most perennial charge of heresy against Pentecostals. It crops up in the Nestorian and modalistic 'Oneness theology' of classical days, and again with William Branham in the 1940s and in Chard in Britain in the 1960s and 1970s. More recently charges of gnosticism and 'new thought' metaphysics against Hagin and Copeland have been made (see McConnell, 1990).)

It remains to be seen over the next decades whether the separatist trends of charismatic religion will undercut its new-found ecumenism. In Britain it is already the case that the new church/Wimber alliance is somewhat alienated from a significant section of Catholic charismatics as well as some Anglican and house church groups. Just as the 1970s witnessed a 'showdown' between the ecumenical renewal and the discipling movement, so the mid-1990s may see a division between those who stand by an apostolic/prophetic model of Ephesians 4, and those who do not. A truly fourth wave would be a long-term alliance of all charismatic groups, for if the third wave provided a new impetus it did not lead in itself to charismatic integration.

Pentecostalism could, of course, go full circle and begin the twenty-first century as it began the twentieth: with schism and dispersion. There will, however, be one fundamental difference. Charismatic Christianity began as a minority religion of the disinherited, but it has now arguably come into its inheritance and become one of the largest and most potent forces in world Christianity. It has perhaps somewhat recaptured the racial integrationist hopes of Azusa Street (though both African Americans and Afro Caribbeans feel their separate organizations are necessary in the light of the incipient racism of many white churches). Certainly it has demonstrated that its energy and mutational power is greater than any historian or social scientist could have foreseen when the Apostolic Faith Mission visited Los Angeles in 1906.

See also DISPENSATIONALISM; EVANGELICALISM (BRITAIN and USA); PNEUMATOLOGY.

Bibliography

Anderson, R.M. 1980: *Vision of the Disinherited: The Making of American Pentecostalism*. Oxford: Oxford University Press.

Barrett, 1989: Statistics global: table 1, column 4. In Burgess and McGee, 1989, p. 812.

Burgess, M., and McGee, G.B., eds 1989: *Dictionary of Pentecostal and Charismatic Movements*. Grand Rapids: Regency, Zondervan.

Farah, C. 1987: America's Pentecostals: what they believe, *Christianity Today*, October 16.

Gelpi, D.L. 1971: *Pentecostalism: A Theological Viewpoint*. New York: Paulist Press.

Harper, M. 1980: *Charismatic Crisis, the Charismatic Renewal, Past, Present and Future*. Hounslow: Hounslow Printing Company.

Hocken, P. 1986: *Streams of Renewal: Origins and Early Development of the Charismatic Movement in Great Britain*. Exeter: Paternoster Press.

Hollenweger, W. 1972: *The Pentecostals*. London: SCM Press.

McConnell, D.R. 1990: *The Promise of Health and Wealth: A Biblical and Historical Analysis of the Faith Movement*. London: Hodder and Stoughton/C.S. Lewis Centre.

McDonnell, K. 1978: *The Charismatic Renewal and Ecumenism*. New York: Paulist Press.

MacRobert, I. 1988: *The Black Roots and White Racism of Early Pentecostalism in the USA*. London: Macmillan Press.

Marsden, G. 1980: *Fundamentalism and American Culture*. Oxford: Oxford University Press.

Martin, D. 1990: *Tongues of Fire: The Explosion of Protestantism in Latin America*. Cambridge, MA: Blackwell.

Packer, J. 1980: Theological reflections on the charismatic movement, *Churchman* 94, 1-2.

Richards, W.T.H. 1971: *Pentecost is Dynamite*. Lakeland: Cox and Wyman.

Sullivan, E. 1971: *Can the Pentecostal Movement Renew the Churches?* London: BCC.

Walker, A. 1983: Pentecostal power: charismatic movements and the politics of Pentecostal experience. In E. Barker, ed., *Of Gods and Men: New Religious Movements*. Mercer: University Press.

Walker, A. 1989: *Restoring the Kingdom: The Radical Christianity of the House Church Movement*, revised edition. London: Hodder and Stoughton.

Walker, A. 1990: Charismatics on the march, *Religion Today* 6, 2.

Wimber, J. 1985: *Power Evangelism*. London: Hodder and Stoughton.

ANDREW WALKER

philosophical theology Though the two terms PHILOSOPHY OF RELIGION and 'philosophical theology' are sometimes used interchangeably, more commonly 'philosophical theology' is taken to mean the use of philosophy within theology, as distinct from when it functions as a preparatory justification for it, and that is how the term will be understood in what follows.

Eighteenth-century philosophy threw up a number of challenges which continue to occupy theology to this day, for instance David Hume's attack on proofs of God's existence, G.E. Lessing's stress on the contingent character of all historical evidence and, most notably of all, Immanuel Kant's insistence on the limits of human knowledge. No eighteenth-century attempt to respond to these challenges has survived the test of time. So it is only really with the nineteenth century that we find major lasting attempts to write theology from a particular philosophical perspective, the two most important continental figures being Friedrich Schleiermacher and Søren Kierkegaard. In saying this it is perhaps significant that both could equally well be described as philosopher or theologian.

The reason why Schleiermacher (1768–1834) is so often called the father of modern theology is because he gave to theology that experiential turn that has characterized much theological writing up to the present day. It was his solution to the Kantian critique of the transcendental illusion, the claim that through reason we can get beyond the limits imposed by this empirical world to knowledge of a transcendent divinity not so confined. Schleiermacher accepts the Kantian restraints but insists that knowledge of God is already given to us with our knowledge of the world, in that it is given as part of our experience. In appealing thus to experience he can be seen as part of the romantic reaction to the ENLIGHTENMENT (see ROMANTICISM), the substitution of experience and feeling for the formal categories of reason which had characterized the earlier movement. Indeed his *On Religion: Speeches to its Cultured Despisers* of 1799 was specifically written to persuade friends within that tradition, like Friedrich Schlegel, how religion might fit naturally into such a picture. In this he was considerably helped by the upsurge of interest in pantheism at the time, created in part by J. Jacobi's disclosure of Lessing's dying declaration of pantheism. The result is the highly complimentary terms in which B. Spinoza is mentioned. By the time he came to write *The Christian Faith* (1821–2) the pantheism is less obvious, but the experiential aspect remains just as pronounced, prompting the question whether his Christology involves anything more than a difference in degree rather than kind between Jesus and ourselves. Jesus' experience of the divine is, unlike ours, uninterrupted, but there seems no obvious ontological difference.

Kierkegaard (1813–1855) studied under the most distinguished exponent of G.W.F. Hegel in the Denmark of his time, H.L. Martensen. He showed more initial sympathy for Hegel's contemporary, Friedrich von Schelling, though attendance at his lectures in Berlin quickly led him to change his mind. He came to see both philosophers as attempting to do the impossible: erect metaphysical systems in a post-Kantian world. However, in marked contrast to Schleiermacher, this did not lead him to stress the immanent character of our experience of the divine. Instead he urges us to consider whether, though we cannot break through the empirical limits of our knowledge, the transcendent God may in fact have done so. It is this possibility which makes him so excited by the doctrine of the incarnation and by its paradoxical character in particular. For, if the infinite and transcendent (what is by Kantian definition beyond the possibility of our knowledge) has become finite and immanent, then, that language should be struggling to describe this, as in paradox, would seem inevitable. But he insists that no proof is possible that this has indeed happened (any such claim would be to challenge the Kantian limits). Instead all one can do is present the individual with the issue, and leave the individual to decide for himself or herself. It is for this reason that he is seen as the principal precursor of existentialism: one has to make a 'leap of faith', and all that may be assessed is the quality of that commitment, because there are no objective criteria upon which it can be based. It is also for this reason that Kierkegaard adopts his peculiar style, with competing voices in a work and it often being far from clear which is really the author's: he too must stand back to let the readers decide for themselves. If it is to be a free choice, the only help he may give is indirect: presenting the reader with a number of alternative pictures of reality, often in the form of story. In proceeding in this way Kierkegaard believes himself to be following the example of Jesus, since he regards it as no accident that Jesus also normally adopted an indirect method of teaching, that is, the parable.

But it was Schleiermacher whose influence was to be dominant in nineteenth-century German theology, and indeed that influence continues to be felt today in writers apparently as diverse as Paul Tillich and Karl Rahner. Even Karl Barth, who was responsible for attempting to move theology in a very different direction, acknowledged him as a force to be reckoned with. Barth's rejection of natural theology might

be taken to imply that he could have no place (except negatively) in the story of philosophical theology, but even he finds himself influenced by the underlying philosophical assumptions of Kierkegaard. Thus there are several positive endorsements of Kierkegaard in *The Epistle to the Romans* of 1919, the work which marks Barth's decisive rejection of Schleiermacher's approach.

In this outline surprise may be felt at the omission so far of any reference to G.W.F. Hegel (1770–1831). This has been for two reasons. First, although he had studied theology at Tübingen, unlike Schleiermacher and Kierkegaard one cannot really describe him as a theologian in his own right. His writings even when on religion are essentially philosophical. Second, though he did exercise considerable influence on theology in the nineteenth century, it is only really in the twentieth that one finds major writers in systematics utilizing his ideas. At the time his influence was most felt in two rather different directions, on biblical scholars like F.C. Baur and D.F. Strauss and in the development of left-wing Hegelianism towards atheism, as in the writings of Ludwig Feuerbach and Karl Marx. The result is that nineteenth century adaptations fail to come to terms with Hegel's doctrine of God. Instead we observe the borrowing of less central features of his thought, such as the dialectical character of history and the subordination of religious imagery to philosophical concepts. Strauss well illustrates the latter and Baur and former, though the most famous example of all is Marx's inversion of the theory as dialectical materialism. An unexpected development at this stage was his influence on the Roman Catholic theologian, J.A. Möhler, in his *Symbolik* of 1832.

Meanwhile in nineteenth-century England a rather different pattern was emerging. Schleiermacher's *Speeches* were not translated into English until 1893 and *The Christian Faith* had to wait even longer, until 1928. Likewise the influence of Hegel did not begin to be felt until Sterling's *The Secret of Hegel* of 1865.

S.T. Coleridge (1772–1834) is thus a rather untypical English theologian of the nineteenth century in that he made strenuous efforts to acquaint himself with German thought. He was well acquainted with the writings of both Kant and Schelling, and in fact spent almost a year studying in Germany. In assessing his use of Kant it is important to observe that when Kant's three Critiques are taken together they offer a very much more positive view of religion than when the first, the *Critique of Pure Reason* of 1781, is read in isolation. Even so, though the terminology is Kantian (*Vernunft* and *Verstand*), it cannot be said that Coleridge's use of the distinction between reason and understanding in his *Aids to Reflection* of 1825 is a legitimate development of what Kant had in mind. Understanding is correctly treated as the faculty of sensory awareness, but reason seems to be given independent powers of intuitive awareness that has more in common with Plato than Kant. His borrowings from Schelling were such as sometimes to lead to justified accusations of plagiarism. What he seems to have particularly admired in him was Schelling's attempts to secure a view of God that avoided supernaturalism and made him the ground of all that is, and as with Schelling this led to accusations of pantheism.

J.H. Newman (1801–1890) by contrast is much more a typical English figure of the nineteenth century. His education at Oxford had been very much in the Aristotelian tradition (Plato was not introduced to the curriculum until the reforms of B. Jowett later in the century), and the most studied Christian author, Joseph Butler (whom Newman described as the greatest name in the Anglican church) was similarly imbued. Admittedly, with his study of the church Fathers came a more Platonic influence, and this is well reflected in the motto which he asked to be inscribed on his tomb: from shades and images into truth. None the less the Aristotelian stamp remained marked, particularly in his approach to the justification of religious belief. Thus in *The Grammar of Assent* of 1870 it is significantly to Aristotle that he appeals to justify the use of more informal patterns of reasoning, while *The Idea of a University* of 1873 contains a famous encomium on the 'great Master'.

In the case of the third major name in English nineteenth-century theology, F.D. Maurice (1805–1872), the influence is more straightforwardly Platonic (in part because of his education at Trinity College, Cambridge, under J.C. Hare). What he particularly liked about Plato was his insistence that all earthly things point to,

and participate in, a greater, unseen reality. This led to charges that he was an emanationist and did not really believe in the creation.

But the influence of classical philosophy continued well into the twentieth century, whether one takes the Platonism of Charles Gore or the Aristotelian Thomism of Eric Mascall as representative. This is no doubt in part to be explained by the fact that until at least the Second World War the ideal pattern of Anglican clerical education included the study of classics as an essential prerequisite to that of theology. Indeed, Gore may be used to provide a fascinating contrast to attitudes in Germany. For, while Adolf von Harnack (1851–1930) argued at length in his *History of Dogma* and more briefly in *What is Christianity?* (of 1900) that Greek influence on theology had been a disaster, his English contemporary, Charles Gore (1853–1932), culminated his life's writings in his Gifford Lectures, *The Philosophy of the Good Life* of 1930, by insisting that it was divine providence which had ensured the uniting of Hebraism and Hellenism in the patristic period.

However, this is not to say that non-classical influences were unknown within Anglicanism. In fact by the end of the nineteenth century interest in Hegel had become considerable, the best example of this perhaps being the writings of J.R. Illingworth (1848–1915). But for the most profound engagement with continental philosophy one must really look to theologians outside the Church of England. John Oman (1860–1939), through works like *Grace and Personality* of 1917 and *The Natural and the Supernatural* of 1931, succeeded in naturalizing to English soil the experiential approach of Schleiermacher.

From the time that Rudolf Bultmann and Paul Tillich became colleagues of Martin Heidegger at the University of Marburg (1921 and 1924 respectively) until their deaths (1966 and 1965), existentialism was to be the dominating philosophical influence on German theology. Indeed, Karl Rahner, who studied under Heidegger at Freiburg from 1934 to 1936, ensured that that influence continued until his own death in 1984.

EXISTENTIALISM was in many ways a natural vehicle through which Christian theology could be reformulated, because unlike traditional metaphysics it specifically addressed questions that seemed to be the obvious secular equivalents to faith, sin and salvation. It also demanded decision and offered assessment of rival styles of life. Even so, the alliance was not a wholly natural one. For, despite his Catholic upbringing and great admiration for Luther, Heidegger always refused any religious allegiance. Indeed part of the argument of his most important work, *Being and Time* of 1927, is that Kant had shown the impossibility of our asking any questions about what is beyond the world. Instead we must accept our subjective world as the given, and the only proper questions concern our experienced relation to it – *Dasein*, 'being there', rather than Being in itself (*Sein*), except in so far as the latter refers to the ground of *experienced* reality. But the fact that the work opens with the 'Question of Being' and ends with talk of this having been disclosed in a preliminary, non-conceptual way inevitably meant that the work could be seen as raising religious questions. The various complimentary references to Kierkegaard as a precursor must also have helped, although in one of them he astonishingly accused Kierkegaard of still being too much under the influence of Hegel.

Heidegger draws a major contrast between authentic and inauthentic existence. He suggests that most of us are inclined to retreat from anxiety in the face of our responsibilities into a situation of impersonal conformity, what he calls *das Man* (the neuter article giving additional weight to the characterization). Authentic existence, by contrast, involves us living in explicit relation to the most obvious fact of human existence, the inevitability of death. *Dasein* thus becomes a matter of us accepting our limitations as well as our freedom, and seeing what we can achieve in the here and now. Bultmann adopts a very similar picture in his contrast between the life of sin and that of faith. So in his *Essays: Philosophical and Theological* ([1952] 1955, p. 81) he writes: 'What is the real crux of sin? What is it, if sin is unresponsiveness to the future? It is dread – the dread of the man who is unwilling to surrender to what is a mystery to him.' That reference to dread (*Angst*) also recalls Kierkegaard's analysis of original sin in his *Concept of Anxiety*, and in fact one finds the reduction of sin to psychological tension in

the face of freedom a recurring theme in a number of theologians at this time who are influenced by existentialism, among them also Tillich and Reinhold Niebuhr.

Bultmann in many ways represents the purest use of existentialism by a theologian. He was of course primarily a biblical scholar, but his philosophical position meant that he thought that historical and 'life' questions could not easily be disentangled. Heidegger had drawn a contrast between *existentiell* and *existential*, meaning roughly by the former one's personal 'existential' standing in relation to the future and by the latter the more general question of the use of 'existentialist' categories. When Bultmann came under Heidegger's influence, he seems initially to have concluded that it was the task of the exegete solely to evoke the first, whereas in his later writings he allows a greater degree of objectivity to emerge by insisting that he was concerned with both. Demythologization is thus concerned both with identifying the underlying existentialist objectives of the New Testament writers and with the way in which they might be made existentially alive to us today.

It is sometimes suggested that Bultmann's philosophical position is unintelligible without also taking into account the influence of Marburg's earlier neo-Kantian school, in particular through his teacher Wilhelm Herrmann. Certainly his attack on 'objectifying' God represents one of their concerns, but the attack is also fully intelligible within the existentialism of Heidegger. For since on his view access to entities beyond experienced reality is in principle impossible, God must either be identified through the whole of that reality or not at all. Bultmann's hostility to miracle is thus not just a matter of his belief that the world is a closed causal system, it is also a matter of underlying philosophical conviction.

With Tillich, however, there is no doubt that besides existentialism we must also reckon with the influence of Schelling. Thus, while *The Courage To Be* of 1962 or the second volume of his *Systematic Theology* of 1957 display obvious signs of leading existentialist ideas, parts of the first volume with its account of the nature of God reveal the continuing influence of the philosopher upon whom he wrote his doctorate. In explaining Tillich's interest in Schelling one may point to two main factors. First, there is the fact that of all nineteenth-century philosophers it was Schelling who took the notion of myth and symbol most seriously, particularly in his later writings. But second, and perhaps even more importantly, it was Schelling even more than Hegel who conceived of God as the reconciliation of all opposites. So it is to Schelling that we should look when we find Tillich using his method of correlation to argue that God is not merely beyond the polarities of freedom and destiny, individualization and participation, and form and dynamics (what I am and what I might become), but beyond even the contrast between essence and existence. The result is that it becomes inappropriate even to speak of God's existence. Not only that, God must be beyond even the polarity between being and non-being and so in some sense beyond good and evil.

In Rahner's case the principal additional influence to bear in mind is that of transcendental Thomism. This takes its inspiration from the writings of the Belgian Jesuit Joseph Maréchal, in particular his *Le point de départ de la metaphysique*, begun in 1922. His objective was to offer a Kantian reading of St Thomas Aquinas. This is not as absurd as it may initially sound, given the lapse of so many intervening centuries. Aquinas had assigned a key role in his epistemology to what he calls the active or agent intellect, and this might be taken to bear some analogy to Kant's insistence that we are not purely passive in perception but actively structure our experience by imposing upon it certain basic notions such as space, time and cause. These he identifies as the 'synthetic a priori' because they must be known in advance of our experience if we are to make sense of it. Maréchal's contribution is to question whether the concept of God might not itself be a further such transcendental condition. The point is that to impose structure implies an awareness of bounds and limits, but to impose a limit is already to stand outside or transcend that limit. So it looks as though every act of knowledge on the Kantian scheme has as the transcendental condition of its possibility the transcending of a limit, and thus knowledge as a whole the transcending of all limits. But, Maréchal observes, this is very much what we mean by God. This kind of argument finds itself

reflected most explicitly in Rahner's most philosophical work, *Spirit in the World* of 1939, but it is repeated at a more popular level throughout his writings. He argues that in all our experience we are being challenged to go beyond it, for instance in an unconditional commitment of love to another, or, to give a very different example, in the irritation we sometimes feel at the incompleteness of some present experience. Again and again we are being summoned by God as 'the infinite horizon' to transcend present patterns, and it is this fact which enables Rahner to describe as 'anonymous Christians' those nonbelievers who respond to such challenges.

The influence of existentialism appears to have declined because it was regarded as too individualistic and too subjective; some would say too neurotic. Currently in German Protestant theology undoubtedly Hegel has the greatest influence (see HEGELIANISM). This can easily be seen in the writings of J. Moltmann and E. Jüngel and, to a lesser degree, in W. Pannenberg. It would be tempting to detect continuity with his impact upon the nineteenth century, but the stress is in fact quite different. Though the nature of history continues to be a point of focus, the dialectical character of history in general is not. Rather, what interests all three contemporary theologians is Hegel's doctrine of the Trinity, and history only becomes relevant in so far as it fulfils a crucial role in Hegel's version of this doctrine. According to Hegel in what is perhaps the most famous passage of his philosophy ('Lordship and Bondage' in *Phenomenology of Spirit*), personality cannot exist in isolation but is forged through projection into something other than oneself and only achieves equilibrium when a reconciliation has been effected between the first two elements. It is this understanding of personhood which Hegel applies to his understanding of the Trinity in his *Lectures on the Philosophy of Religion* of 1827 and elsewhere. The obvious advantage it has for theology is that, if true, the Trinity would cease to be a strange exception to the nature of personal existence but in fact definitive of what grounds all personal existence.

Of the three, Eberhard Jüngel (b. 1934) stands nearest to Barth. Thus in *God as the Mystery of the World* of 1977 he continues

Barth's attack on NATURAL THEOLOGY, and indeed blames it for the rise of atheism in the modern world. Though an earlier work was devoted to Barth's doctrine of the Trinity, its very title (*God's Being is in Becoming*) indicated the future Hegelian direction of his thought, and this emerges with full force in the 1977 book. In essence the argument is that the only way to avoid the self-justification implicit in all natural theology is to recognize that we must start from the cross as God's justification of us, of his maximum disclosure of him entering in love into something other than himself, in particular suffering and death. This, he holds, legitimates Hegel's talk of the death of God and even speaking of divine 'perishability'. Indeed, he argues, it is perishability which makes room for possibilities and so for the bringing of what is truly positive out of the negative. He thus stands at an enormous distance from traditional (Aristotelian) metaphysics, which would describe God as *actus purus*, as without any unrealized possibilities.

Jüngel's erudition, combined with his insistence on pressing paradox to its limits, means that he is not an easy writer to understand. His colleague at Tübingen, Jürgen Moltmann (b. 1926), though sharing Jüngel's concentration on the cross as the revelation of the Trinity, expresses his Hegelian perspective in ways which show much more continuity with the existing Hegelian tradition. This is in large part due to the fact that his encounter with Hegel has been more indirect, in particular through Marxist writers in the Frankfurt school and Ernst Bloch, whose *Principle of Hope* of 1959 was an important influence on Moltmann's first major work, *Theology of Hope* of 1965. The result has been a willingness in his most famous work, *The Crucified God* of 1973, to speak freely of 'the history of God'. The Trinity is seen as 'an event in history' whereby God enters into the maximum degree of alienation from himself (bearing the condemnation of sin on the cross) so that he might thereby open up 'the future of history as the Spirit'. His position requires such a sharp differentiation between the persons of the Trinity that he has been accused by some of tritheism and by others of interpreting biblical language too literally.

Of the three it is undoubtedly Wolfhart Pannenberg (b. 1928) who is philosophically the best informed, and indeed his early research interests were on the two medieval philosophers, Aquinas and Scotus. His influential defence of the doctrine of the incarnation in *Jesus: God and Man* of 1964, with its claim that Jesus' divinity is vindicated by the way in which his resurrection anticipates the end of history, depends crucially for its plausibility on assuming a directional character to history of a kind which Hegel would have endorsed. But as a matter of fact it is to biblical apocalyptic that Pannenberg finally appeals. Yet his more recent writings have disclosed underlying Hegelian presuppositions, though of a very different kind from Jüngel and Moltmann. In *Metaphysics and the Idea of God* of 1988 he argues that time is only fully intelligible in relation to its completion, because the story of time can only be seen to have a meaning when it is pulled out of time and told timelessly; so the timeless, he holds, is the foundation of the temporal and the latter unintelligible without it. This is only a small part of a larger argument towards the notion of God as the Absolute which recalls the neo-Platonic foundations of Hegel's thought, though quite alien to the way in which he is used by Jüngel and Moltmann.

One major reason why both of them became excited by Hegel was his willingness to speak of divine suffering. It is likewise problems of theodicy which have ensured the continuing popularity of PROCESS THEOLOGY in the USA. This owes its origins to the English philosopher A.N. Whitehead (1861–1947), who while in Cambridge participated with Bertrand Russell in writing *Principia Mathematica*. But by the time *Process and Reality* came to be published in 1929 he was already a professor of philosophy at Harvard. Here Charles Hartshorne was one of his research students, and it was he who was responsible for moving Whitehead's thought in a more explicitly Christian direction. The origin of the name lies in the substitution of process for substance as the main philosophical category, the argument being that with Newton modern science has shown motion to be the natural category, not rest as Aristotle had believed. Accordingly, the argument continues, all things should be seen as in a state of motion or self-creation, God included, since God should be seen not as an exception to universal metaphysical principles but as their chief exemplification. Building on this basis, the problem of suffering is given a twofold answer. First, it is thus possible to distinguish an aspect of the divine nature which is affected by suffering in the world, his 'consequent' as distinct from his 'primordial' nature. In fact, Whitehead feels free to speak of 'the great companion – the fellow-sufferer who understands'. But, second, there is also an element of tragedy built into the world, because, though God seeks to 'persuade' natures within it to move in certain directions, there is no guarantee that this will happen since they retain entirely the power of self-direction.

The two theologians within this movement who currently exercise most influence are John Cobb (b. 1925) and Schubert Ogden (b. 1928). The former has now abandoned the more technical process vocabulary which characterized his early *A Christian Natural Theology* of 1965, but his governing theme of creative transformation through novelty remains very much in keeping with the school. Ogden in *The Reality of God* of 1967 makes much of the image of the world as God's body. This is useful in highlighting the panentheistic character of such theology, in which, though God is not identical with the world, he is profoundly affected by it. As illustrative of a very different strand in current American theology, one might note the use of Wittgenstein in George Lindbeck's account of *The Nature of Doctrine* of 1984.

In England Maurice Wiles exhibits the continuing influence of the empiricist tradition (though with very different results from its impact on Newman), while John MacQuarrie is Britain's most distinguished representative of the existentialist form of philosophical theology, perhaps not surprisingly in one who himself translated Heidegger's *Being and Time*. The impact of more recent developments in continental philosophy is on the whole quite small (H.-G. Gadamer being a possible exception), but Don Cupitt has used the deconstructionism of Jacques Derrida to bolster his version of non–objective (atheistic?) Christianity.

See also PROTESTANT THEOLOGY (BRITAIN; GERMANY; USA); ROMAN CATHOLIC THEOLOGY.

Bibliography

Brandt, R.B. 1941: *The Philosophy of Schleiermacher*. Westport: Greenwood Press.

Bultmann, R. [1952] 1955: *Essays: Philosophical and Theological*, trans. J.C.G.Greig. London: SCM Press.

Fackenheim, E.L. 1967: *The Religious Dimension in Hegel's Thought*. Chicago: University of Chicago Press.

Küng, H. [1970] 1987: *The Incarnation of God: An Introduction to Hegel's Theological Thought*, trans. J.R. Stephenson. Edinburgh: T & T Clark.

McFarland, T. 1969: *Coleridge and the Pantheist Tradition*. Oxford: Clarendon Press.

MacQuarrie, J. 1963: *Twentieth Century Religious Thought*. London: SCM Press.

MacQuarrie, J. 1973: *An Existentialist Theology: A Comparison of Heidegger and Bultmann*. Harmondsworth: Penguin.

Newsome, D. 1974: *Two Classes of Men: Platonism and English Romantic Thought*. London: John Murray.

Pojman, L.P. 1984: *The Logic of Subjectivity: Kierkegaard's Philosophy of Religion*. Alabama: University of Alabama Press.

Sheehan, T. 1987: *Karl Rahner: The Philosophical Foundations*. Athens: Ohio University Press.

Tillich, P. 1989: *Philosophical Writings*; vol. 1 of *Main Works*. Berlin: De Gruyter/Evangelisches Verlagswerk.

Toews, J.E. 1980: *Hegelianism: The Path towards Dialectical Humanism, 1805–41*. Cambridge: Cambridge University Press.

DAVID BROWN

philosophy of religion Though in the past the two terms have sometimes been used interchangeably, nowadays PHILOSOPHICAL THEOLOGY is normally taken to mean those aspects of theology which raise philosophical questions, whereas 'philosophy of religion' is concerned with whether theology is possible at all in the light of the issues it raises.

These may be grouped under a number of headings:

1 Is the concept of God logically self-consistent? For if the combination of attributes is internally incoherent, then God can no more exist than can a square circle.

2 Even supposing the language self-consistent, what reason have we to suppose it to be meaningful, if it is the application of words learnt for use in this world to a Being of a radically different kind? It is at this point that the question of analogy raises itself.

3   But even supposing the language consistent and meaningful, its use may be pointless if there is a conclusive proof that God does not exist. Here the fact of evil has often been taken to provide just such a proof.

4   Assuming the failure of such negative proofs, have we any positive reasons for belief in the existence of God? What proofs can be offered of his existence?

5   Even granted his existence, is it intelligible to speak of such a very different sort of Being 'acting' in this material world? It is at this point that the question of divine 'intervention ' raises itself with respect to, for example, revelation, miracles and life after death.

Question 1 has only really assumed prominence in recent years. The classical concept of God (that he is omniscient, timeless, immutable, impassible and so on) has come under attack from two very different quarters. To theologians (such as J. Moltmann), this has seemed incompatible with the biblical picture of God, while philosophers (such as A. Kenny, R. Swinburne) have questioned its coherence: Does the notion of a timeless Being who is none the less related to the temporal world make sense? If God has given human beings a contra-causal freedom (required by the most popular way of answering the problem of evil), might it not be the case that even God could not know what human beings will freely choose?

Question 2 is a more traditional issue. Variants of Aquinas's theory of analogy, itself based on Aristotle, continue to be the most popular approach. An influential re-expression is that of Ian Ramsey, in terms of models and qualifiers. Karl Barth rejected the entire approach, preferring to speak of an *analogia fidei* rather than of Aquinas's *analogia entis*. By this he meant that a term like 'father' gains its proper sense from the revelatory context (that is, the context of faith) rather than, as Aquinas argued, that we initially learn what words mean through the natural order and it is only by virtue of a shared order of being that they can then be suitably modified to apply to God. The challenge of verification, once so prominent in philosophical discussion, has now receded. Here the issue had been whether a statement could be meaningful unless one was able in principle to verify its truth. The challenge was popularized in A.J. Ayer's *Language, Truth and Logic* of 1936, but, as he himself admitted, the principle of verification would itself be meaningless on this criterion of meaning. (See LANGUAGE, RELIGIOUS; LOGICAL POSITIVISM.)

Question 3 is likewise a traditional issue. It is an area of philosophical discussion which has generated much hostility from theologians, largely because of misunderstanding of what is meant by talk of a 'solution'. There is a formal inconsistency between the three propositions, that God is omnipotent, that he is all good and that evil exists in the world, which could be used to generate a formal proof that he does not exist. What therefore philosophers are attempting to achieve is not to explain away evil or reduce its significance but simply to show that the incompatibility is more apparent than real. In order to demonstrate this, they must identify some good objective which even God's omnipotence could not achieve except by permitting the existence of evil. The two most favoured candidates are human freedom (the so-called free will defence) and the existence of certain virtues. Thus in the former case it is argued that even God could not guarantee a world in which human beings would always freely choose the good, while in the latter case it is observed that certain virtues are only intelligible given the presence of evil in the world: thus courage makes no sense unless there is something nasty to be feared; while compassion, generosity and so forth are all contingent upon the existence of unpleasant aspects of the world which need remedying. In the eighteenth century G.W. Leibniz claimed that this was the best of all possible worlds, a view which in the light of the Lisbon earthquake Voltaire ridiculed in his novel *Candide*. Today it is commonly contended that it makes no sense to talk of a maximally perfect world, since one can always conceive of something further to be added which would make it that little bit better. Again, some philosophers claim that it makes no sense to discuss the quantity of evil in the world; a notable exception is Richard Swinburne, who in his 'argument from knowledge' maintains that it is only by the consequences of the operation of natural law being serious that the growth of human knowledge becomes possible. (See EVIL, PROBLEM OF.)

Regarding question 4, positive proofs of God's existence have had a complex history (see EXISTENCE OF GOD, PROOFS OF). Here I want to note simply the three main types of general approach which prevail in contemporary English-speaking philosophy of religion. First, among those who continue to accept the need for proofs, while there are occasional writers who continue to maintain the validity of the traditional deductive proofs, the more common pattern is to present them as an inductive, cumulative case for theism. That is to say, they are no longer regarded as conclusive but as offering a probabilistic case. This is the position of both Basil Mitchell and Richard Swinburne. The second major strand stems from the influence of the USA's leading philosopher of religion, Alvin Plantinga. His contention is that the demand for proof is based on the mistaken acceptance of Cartesian foundationalism. According to Descartes, all our knowledge must be built up from secure foundations which are either incorrigible or self-evident, and knowledge of God is neither: so it cannot be a basic belief in a person's overall conceptual system. But, Plantinga objects, even ignoring questions of religion, the whole theory is riddled with difficulties. So, following Calvin, he advocates what he calls a 'Reformed epistemology', according to which religious belief can in fact legitimately function as a basic belief for the Christian. However, he is insistent that this is not irrationalism; for, though there is nothing more basic upon which the Christian bases his belief, there are none the less supporting or confirming factors to which he would wish to point. The third type of approach rejects the question of evidence entirely, whether as logically prior justification or as subsequent confirmation. This position is commonly labelled 'fideism'. Søren Kierkegaard is taken as the most obvious historical precedent, while among twentieth-century philosophers Ludwig Wittgenstein is regarded as the most significant. In Britain D.Z. Phillips is its best-known exponent. The claim is that it is a misunderstanding of the nature of faith to require reasons for it. Kierkegaard is used to illustrate the way in which faith is more a trusting into the unknown than a purely intellectual assent, as in his illustration in *Fear and Trembling* of Abraham's decision to sacrifice his son Isaac.

In the case of Wittgenstein, his notion of 'language games' is used to argue that faith is an entirely distinct human activity bound only by its own internal rules, and that to ask for a justification of that activity is as silly as asking for the justification of football as distinct from an account of the rules of play.

Under question 5, the issue of miracles is the one most frequently discussed, simply because historically justification of belief in the Christian revelation had been based on two grounds, prophecy and miracles. David Hume's challenge in his famous 'Essay on Miracles' of 1748 still sets the terms for the discussion: whether there could ever be sufficient evidence for a miracle to justify allowing this to outweigh the overwhelming evidence for the existence of the particular natural law which has allegedly been violated. The two most common elements noted in response are: first, that the fact that the miracle is a non-repeatable action of a personal agent means that no revision of the natural law is required; second, that the evidential challenge could be met by observing that numerous instances of the law are being weighed against equally numerous instances of the reliability of that particular personal witness.

In the eighteenth century many came to the conviction that it was inappropriate to think of God as intervening in the world at all. This movement, known as DEISM, received its classic refutation in Bishop Joseph Butler's *Analogy of Religion*. This debate continues today, but in a very different form, which explains why the issue is now more discussed among theologians than philosophers. In the eighteenth century the deist objection was that a wholly rational and good God could have no need to intervene in the world since it would already be ordered for the best, whereas the modern debate centres on whether or not we live in a scientifically or historically closed system. Austin Farrer offered a distinctive theory of his own with his notion of double agency.

Among philosophers, apart from miracle the two main other areas of divine action which have received most attention are the idea of response to petitionary prayer and the conceivability of life after death. It is important to observe that in the latter case the philosophical issue is not evidence for existence after death but whether the notion is intelligible, even assuming that God might wish to make it possible. If one accepts the dualism of Descartes, with the soul as a distinct substance, as do some notable modern philosophers such as H.H. Price, H.D. Lewis and R. Swinburne, then immortality of the soul continues to be conceivable. But philosophical thinking has overwhelmingly moved away from this position to various versions of psychosomatic identity. On such an account resurrection of the body becomes the only conceivable way of defending life after death. So on this issue at least philosophers have of late been moving closer to the biblical view.

Recent years have witnessed a considerable revival of interest in philosophy of religion, particularly in philosophy departments in the USA. This interest has also extended to examining the logical coherence of specific Christian doctrines. Current trends are well illustrated by the journal *Faith and Philosophy* (founded 1984).

See also ATHEISM; EPISTEMOLOGY, RELIGIOUS; FAITH AND REASON; NATURAL THEOLOGY.

Bibliography

Abraham, W.J. 1985: *Introduction to the Philosophy of Religion*. Englewood Cliffs, NJ: Prentice-Hall.

Adams, M.M., and Adams, R.M., eds 1990: *The Problem of Evil*. Oxford: Oxford University Press.

Brown, D. 1990: *A Selective Bibliography of the Philosophy of Religion*. Oxford: Sub-Faculty of Philosophy.

Ferré, F. 1970: *Language, Logic and God*. London: Collins.

Hick, J. [1963] 1990: *Philosophy of Religion*, 4th edn. Englewood Cliffs, NJ: Prentice-Hall.

Phillips, D.Z. 1976: *Religion without Explanation*. Oxford: Basil Blackwell.

Plantinga, A., and Wolterstorff, N., eds 1983: *Faith and Rationality*. Indiana: University of Notre Dame Press.

Pojman, L.P., ed. 1987: *Philosophy of Religion: An Anthology*. Belmont, Ca.: Wadsworth.

Rowe, W.L., and Wainwright, W., eds 1989: *Philosophy of Religion: Selected Readings*, 2nd edn. New York: Harcourt Brace Jovanovich.

Swinburne, R. 1977: *The Coherence of Theism*. Oxford: Clarendon Press.

DAVID BROWN

physical science and Christian thought

Over the centuries, theology's relationship with physical science has been more mutually harmonious and fruitful than has been the case with biology. Historians have suggested that the rise of modern science, culminating in the great discoveries in physics in the seventeenth century, was encouraged by the Christian doctrine of creation, which saw the world as both rational and contingent, possessing a divinely ordained order which could only be discovered by looking to see what God had actually chosen to do (Jaki, 1978; Russell, 1985). Although Galileo had his difficulties with ecclesiastical authority, he seems to have been a man of genuine religious belief. Isaac Newton and many of the other founding Fellows of the Royal Society were deeply concerned with theological questions. The great figures of British nineteenth-century physics (Michael Faraday, Clerk Maxwell, William Kelvin, George Stokes) were men of a firm Christian faith which was unshaken by the evolutionary controversies of the day. Among contemporary writers on science and religion it is most commonly the physicists who wish to argue for an intelligence behind the workings of the world, though they do not necessarily do so within conventional theism (Davies, 1983) and some find greater consonance with the dissolving-yet-unified view of Eastern religion than with the sternly realist Judaeo-Christian tradition (Capra, 1976).

Intelligibility

Mathematics is the natural language of physical science. It has been the repeated experience of fundamental physics that its successful theories are characterized by those qualities of economy and elegance which express the property of mathematical beauty. This congruence between the way we think (internal reason) and the structure of the physical world (external reason) has profoundly impressed many physicists. Eugene Wigner called it 'the unreasonable effectiveness of mathematics' and Albert Einstein once said that the only incomprehensible thing about the universe is that it is comprehensible. It does not seem that this fact would be explained in terms of an evolutionary necessity for survival, for the latter could only refer to everyday thought and experience, whilst the rational transparency of the physical world

443

involves counter-intuitive regimes (such as the quantum world) and very abstract mathematics, far removed from the deliverances of common sense.

The instinct of scientists is to seek thorough explanation. The intelligibility and rational beauty of the physical world raises a metaquestion of why the universe should be so, a question going beyond science itself since it is part of the latter's founding faith to assume the possibility of success in its rational enquiry. Theology offers the understanding that the consonance of internal and external reason arises from their common origin in the rationality of the Creator. Herein lies part of the basis of a revived natural theology, offering, not proof, but more comprehensive insight (Polkinghorne, 1988, chapters 1 and 2). In summary, the intelligibility of the physical world speaks of a universe shot through with signs of mind, and theology asserts that it is the Mind of God.

Cosmology

Modern cosmology sees the origin of the physical world as we know it in the fiery explosion of the Big Bang, some fifteen billion years ago. The alternative theory of an ever-lasting 'steady state' universe was discredited by the discovery in 1965 of the cosmic background radiation, a kind of re-echoing whisper from a time about half a million years after the Big Bang, when the cooling brought about by the universe's expansion allowed the first atoms to form. Since the doctrine of creation is concerned with ontological origin (why is there something rather than nothing?) rather than temporal origin (how did things begin?), Big Bang cosmology is of no great fundamental significance for theology. Equally, if the speculations of Stephen Hawking and others that the fuzzing effects of quantum theory in the very earliest instants of cosmic history abolish a dateable 'moment of creation' (Hawking, 1988, chapter 8), that is of concern for physics but not theology. Creation is God's continual sustaining of the cosmos in being, not his mere initiation of its history.

The peculiar properties of the vacuum in quantum theory (it is not the case that when nothing is there, nothing is happening),

combined with a speculative theory called inflation (a kind of early boiling of space), have led some to assert that science can now explain what was previously the preserve of theology, creation *ex nihilo*. The notion is that the universe is a grotesquely swollen fluctuation in a pre-existing vacuum (Davies, 1983, chapter 16). Even if the speculation proved correct, it is an abuse of language to describe this process as creation out of 'nothing'. A quantum vacuum is a highly structured entity whose properties depend upon the physical laws with which it is endowed. It is much more a plenum than a vacuum in the classical sense.

One of the reasons why the cosmologists can speak with such boldness about the very early universe is that it was then very simple, an almost uniform ball of energy. Through its evolving fifteen-billion-year history it has become very diverse and differentiated. The fruitfulness of that process, as much at the physical level through the coming-to-be of galaxies and stars as at the biological level of evolving terrestrial life, has been characterized by an interplay of chance (happenstance – such as the fluctuation of matter distribution which begins the condensation of a galaxy) and necessity (the law of gravity which enhances the fluctuation). One need not view the role of chance as being destructive of meaning, but rather one can conceive chance and necessity as being pale reflections of the twin gifts of freedom and reliability given to his creation by a God who is both loving and faithful (Peacocke, 1979, chapter 3; Polkinghorne, 1988, chapters 3 and 4). Such a view would permit one to construct a 'free-process defence' in relation to physical evil which would parallel the free-will defence in relation to moral evil (Polkinghorne, 1989, chapter 5).

It is a comparatively recent insight of physical science that the fruitfulness of cosmic history depends upon a very delicate set of balances present in the given fundamental physical laws (Barrow and Tipler, 1986; Leslie, 1989). It is not 'any old world' which is capable of evolving men and women (or structures of a comparable complexity, presumably necessary to sustain any form of self-conscious life). This insight is called the 'Anthropic Principle'.

If carbon-based life is to be possible, one needs:

1 the right *kinds* of laws (such as quantum mechanical, to give the right sort of chemistry);

2 the right *constants of nature* (specifying the intrinsic strengths of fundamental forces, such as gravity and electromagnetism);

3 the right *circumstances* (for example, the universe must be big enough to last long enough for life to evolve within it).

Particularly striking are the considerations relating to the second point. They concern all stages of cosmic history: (1) the very early universe (for example, to ensure an acceptable balance of hydrogen and helium after the 'first three minutes' of cosmic nuclear reactions); (2) star formation: to ensure that steadily burning main-sequence stars are possible, that their nuclear reactions produce all the necessary heavier elements which are not made in the first three minutes (every atom of carbon in our bodies was once inside a star), and that some first-generation stars will explode as supernovae and so make those elements available as part of the chemical environment of second-generation planets; (3) properties such as the special chemistry of carbon and the remarkable behaviour of water, which seem indispensable to the evolution of complex physical systems. Often several different considerations constrain the same set of constants. These constraints prove compatible with each other and together they place very narrow limits on what can constitute a world of anthropic fruitfulness.

The significance of that conclusion might be modified in a number of ways by suggestions whose force must be assessed by disputable judgement. It has been urged that many, perhaps all, of the fruitful coincidences might be found to be entailed by a yet undiscovered deeper physical theory. That might be so to some extent, but many anthropic specifications, including such general requirements as quantum theory and gravity, do not appear to be necessary features of every possible world. It has also been urged that reliance on carbon-based life shows a lack of imagination. Might not other universes be made fruitful by 'thinking plasmas' or the like? Those who make such claims are drawing large intellectual blank cheques.

Setting such arguments aside, there remains scope for varying assessments of the significance of the Anthropic Principle, ranging from dismissal as a mere tautology to strong claims that there is a necessity for the universe to be capable of evolving observers within it. The present writer would espouse the mediate view that our attention has been drawn to an interesting fact about the universe which seems to call for some sort of explanation.

One such explanation offered is the proposal that there are many different universes, with many different sets of law and circumstance. If that were the case, it would not be surprising if by chance one of them possessed the right anthropic specification, and that, of course, is the one we inhabit, because we could not appear on the scene anywhere else. Although this idea is sometimes presented as having a scientific basis (for example, by illegitimate appeal to 'many worlds' quantum theory), careful analysis shows that it is really metascientific, going beyond that for which we have adequate experimental warrant. An alternative metaphysical hypothesis, of equal coherence and greater economy, would be that there is only one universe, which is not 'any old world' in its delicate balance of law and circumstance, but a creation endowed by its Creator with the properties necessary for its fruitful potentiality. Here would be a second insight of a revised NATURAL THEOLOGY, pointing to a revived argument from design which appeals, not to the unacceptable intervention of a God of the gaps within physical process, but to the foundational laws which are the ground of the possibility of any such process (Davies, 1983, chapter 12; Polkinghorne, 1988, chapter 2).

Cosmologists not only peer into the past; they can attempt to descry the future. Cosmic history on the grandest scale is a tug-of-war between two opposing tendencies: the impetus of the Big Bang, thrusting matter apart; the relentless force of gravity, pulling it together. They are evenly balanced and we do not know enough to say which will win. If expansion prevails, the galaxies now flying apart will continue to do so for ever. Within themselves they will decay into low-grade radiation – the modern version of a universal heat death. If gravity wins, the present expansion will one day be halted and reversed. What began with the Big Bang will end in the Big Crunch, as the universe falls back into a cosmic melting pot. Both scenarios extend billions of years into the future, but eventually either reduces the outcome of cosmic history to futility. Physics does not encourage a simple evolutionary optimism within the process of the present world, and theology must take account of this in its discussion of hope and eschatology.

Relativity

The physics of the twentieth century has been characterized by two revolutionary developments. The first of these was Albert Einstein's theory of special relativity, which led to the unexpected conclusion that the simultaneity of events is not an absolute property but depends upon the state of motion of the observer. In consequence, Newtonian absolute time was abolished and it became necessary to speak of spacetime as an integrated whole. (The later theory of general relativity would lead to further integration, bringing together matter and spacetime structure.) It is important, however, to emphasize that Einstein's theory is as much concerned with absolutes as with relatives. All observers agree on a quantity called 'interval' and the causal relationships between events are perceived identically by them. Time has not been spatialized and whether the future is open or not is not determined by relativity theory but by the causal properties of the dynamics incorporated into it.

Quantum theory

Much the more significant of the twin twentieth-century revolutions in physics was that which led to quantum theory. The reliable objective world of the everyday was found to be cloudy and fitful at its subatomic roots. Werner Heisenberg tells us that if we know where an electron is, we can't know what it's doing, and vice versa (the uncertainty principle). The quantum world is an unpicturable world.

Sixty-five years of the exploitation of quantum mechanics have shown it to be a highly successful predictive theory. Yet there are unresolved questions of how the theory is to be interpreted. Most physicists believe that the uncertainty principle expresses an ontological indeterminism in the subatomic world (individual quantum events are sometimes said to be 'uncaused'), but David Bohm (1980) constructed an alternative account, of equal empirical adequacy, where all events are

determined, but by partly indiscernible causes ('hidden variables'), so that uncertainty in that case is due to ignorance.

The central perplexity in interpreting quantum theory is to understand how measurement takes place, how it is that the fitful quantum world always yields a definite answer on any occasion of experimental investigation. No wholly satisfactory account of measurement in quantum theory has yet been given. Most physicists subscribe to the idea that it results from the intervention of large 'classical' measuring instruments. This was the basis of the so-called 'Copenhagen interpretation', hammered out by Niels Bohr and his colleagues in the early days of the subject. Yet that account insufficiently acknowledged the problem of how such measuring instruments could arise in a world where all the constituents of matter are quantum mechanical in their behaviour. An entirely different proposal is the so-called 'many universes' interpretation. This asserts that all the possible results of a quantum measurement actually occur, but in a continually proliferating portfolio of universes (which accounts for our perspective-view that in this universe only one result happens). Such prodigality does not appeal to many physicists, except for the cosmologists. Those who wish to apply quantum theory to the whole universe (a not necessarily feasible aim) cannot afford to rely on a role for external measuring apparatus! Until the measurement problem is fully solved, it is not possible to say precisely what degree of coupling between observer and observed is implied by quantum mechanics. All interpretations (other than Bohm's) imply some degree of observer influence, but it would not be justified to concur with the more extreme claims for 'observer-created reality'.

Three aspects of quantum theory are likely to be of particular interest to theology (Polkinghorne, 1991, chapter 7):

1 The counter-intuitive quantum world reminds us of the limited effectiveness of common sense. The theory permits electrons to behave sometimes like waves and sometimes like particles. Such an everyday impossibility is made intelligible through an understanding of what Niels Bohr called 'complementarity' (the use of apparently conflicting models in mutually exclusive domains of experience). He believed

this principle would also find applicability outside physics. Of course, it is not a mere slogan permitting the paradoxical embrace of any fancied pair of incompatibles, but it may afford analogical help when such apparent contradictions are enforced by experience. There have been attempts to use the idea in Christology.

2 Einstein, Boris Podolsky and Nathan Rosen identified a curious feature of quantum theory (the EPR effect). Subsequent analysis by John Bell, and experimental investigation by Alain Aspect, have revealed it as the presence of a totally unexpected togetherness-in-separation (non-locality). Once two quantum entities have interacted with each other, they retain a counter-intuitive power to affect each other, however far apart they may subsequently separate. Paradoxically, the subatomic world is not one which can be described atomistically. Here is a powerful analogical resource for holism, much better than that of a field, which has appealed to some theologians (Wolfhart Pannenberg, Thomas Torrance). Fields are spread out physical entities, but their separate parts behave independently – not so for elementary particles.

3 The elusive quantum world is clearly not naively objective. Yet most physicists have resisted suggestions that it should be regarded in a positivist sense as just a useful manner of speaking. They believe in electrons. Ultimately the defence of electrons' reality must rest on an appeal to intelligibility as its ground. Physicists believe in the unpicturable electron because, at least partially, they understand it and can use it to understand many other phenomena. This must surely be of interest to theology as it seeks to speak of the Unpicturable Reality of God.

Chaos theory

Some physicists believe that a further revolution is occurring in our thought about the physical world. It is the dynamical theory of chaos (Gleick, 1988). It arises from the recognition that even in Newtonian physics, systems of any degree of complexity are often so exquisitely sensitive to circumstance as to be intrinsically unpredictable. This is sometimes called 'the butterfly effect': that a butterfly stirring the air with its wings in Beijing today can affect the storm systems over New York in a fortnight's time.

Unpredictability is concerned with epistemology, what we can know. Scientists are realists, so that for them what we can know and what is the case are thought to be closely associated. It is, therefore, a natural (but not logically forced) option to move on from unpredictability to speak of the ontological notion of openness, to take chaos theory as intimating a picture of physical process containing genuine novelty. In that case, the future is not a mere rearrangement of the past; instead we live in a world of true becoming. This would have the attractive consequence of physics' beginning to speak of a world of which we could conceive ourselves as inhabitants.

Chaotic systems face a variety of future possibilities of development, not discriminated from each other by differences of energy but by something more like information input ('this way'). This envelope of possibility offers scope for the 'downward causality' of human intentionality. In a primitive way we begin to conceive how we might act in the world (Polkinghorne, 1991, chapter 3).

Open physical process is not confined to the complexities of the human brain. There seems scope to consider how there might be divine action also through information input, necessarily hidden within the unpredictability of flexible development (Polkinghorne, 1989). Certainly a merely mechanical view of the physical world is dead; science does not enforce a deistic account of God's relationship to his creation.

One consequence of a world of true becoming is that it puts in question the coherence of a Boethian view in which God sees all of cosmic history 'at once'. Time assumes an inescapable significance, which encourages a bipolar (eternity/time) account of the divine nature, quite independently of any appeal to Whitehead's metaphysics (see PROCESS THEOLOGY). To say that God did not know the future would not be to attribute imperfection to him, if the future is not yet there to be known.

Methodology

Biology contraverts any imperialistic claim by physics to reduce the former to the latter, by asserting the autonomy of the new level of organization that living beings represent, and the novelty of the concepts required for its adequate discussion. One should note that physics itself is a many-layered subject. The discussion of the behaviour of condensed matter requires many concepts (such as energy gaps) not simply reducible to elementary particle physics. If largescale systems really do act as the determinants of quantum measurement, then that too represents an emergent pattern of behaviour within physics (Polkinghorne, 1986, chapter 6). This might be connected with another emergent property, irreversibility. The basic laws of physics are reversible; they do not discriminate between past and future. It is generally believed that our macroscopic experience of the irreversibility of the 'arrow of time', pointing from past to future, is connected with the second law of thermodynamics (the increase of entropy, or disorder, for large isolated systems) but the matter is not well understood.

Many writers relating physics and theology have wished to emphasize a degree of kinship between the two forms of rational enquiry (Barbour, 1974; Peacocke, 1984; Polkinghorne, 1991). The basis would lie in a critical realist account of both disciplines. Realism implies that both are exploring and understanding the way things are. The qualifier 'critical' is necessary because neither deals with an unproblematic objectivity. Both also require acts of judgement, involving the exercise of tacit skills in reaching their conclusions. M. Polanyi (1958) emphasized the role of such judgements in science, making it a form of 'personal knowledge' which could never be delegated to a computer ('we know more than we can tell'), though pursued in a convivial community and with universal intent. Of course, physics and theology differ greatly in their subject matter; the one concerned with the physical world which we transcend and can put to the experimental test, the other concerned with the encounter with God where testing must give way to trusting.

See also BIOLOGICAL SCIENCE/PSYCHOLOGICAL SCIENCE/SOCIAL SCIENCE AND CHRISTIAN THOUGHT; CREATION, DOCTRINE OF; EPISTEMOLOGY, RELIGIOUS.

Bibliography
Barbour, I.G. 1966: *Issues in Science and Religion*. London: SCM Press.
Barbour, I.G. 1974: *Myths, Models and Paradigms*. London: SCM Press.
Barbour, I.G. 1990: *Religion in an Age of Science*. San Francisco: Harper and Row.
Barrow, J.D., and Tipler, F.J. 1986: *The Anthropic Cosmological Principle*. Oxford: Clarendon Press.
Bohm, D. 1980: *Wholeness and the Implicate Order*. London: Routledge and Kegan Paul.
Capra, F. 1976: *The Tao of Physics*. London: Collins.
Davies, P.C.W. 1983: *God and the New Physics*. London: Dent.
Gleick, J. 1988: *Chaos*. London: Heinemann.
Hawking, S.W. 1988: *A Brief History of Time*. London: Bantam Press.
Jaki, S.L. 1978: *The Road of Science and the Ways to God*. Edinburgh: Scottish Academic Press.
Leslie, J. 1989: *Universes*. London: Routledge.
Peacocke, A.R. 1979: *Creation and the World of Science*. Oxford: Clarendon Press.
Peacocke, A.R. 1984: *Intimations of Reality*. Notre Dame: University of Notre Dame Press.
Polyani, M. 1958: *Personal Knowledge*. London: Routledge and Kegan Paul.
Polkinghorne, J.C. 1986: *One World*. London: SPCK.
Polkinghorne, J.C. 1988: *Science and Creation*. London: SPCK.
Polkinghorne, J.C. 1989: *Science and Providence*. London: SPCK.
Polkinghorne, J.C. 1991: *Reason and Reality*. London: SPCK.
Rolston, H. 1987: *Science and Religion*. Philadelphia: Temple Press.
Russell, C.A. 1985: *Cross-Currents*. Leicester: Inter-Varsity Press.

JOHN POLKINGHORNE

pneumatology Language about Spirit is found in many religions and cultures and derives from reflection on two natural phenomena. First, the power and unpredictability of the *wind* provides a metaphor to explain how people in all sorts of circumstances are able to transcend their natural capacity. This phenomenon is ascribed to a transcendent origin, and the word for wind acquires a transferred sense. It becomes a way of talking about God active in the world and in our experience enabling, re-creating and redeeming. Second, that *breath* is a sign of life leads to its use as a metaphor for the essential reality of a person. The words for breath and spirit are always close and thus Spirit language can also be used to speak of the identifying characteristics of a person or group. In this second sense 'Spirit' can have a purely anthropological reference, but one which suggests an intimate connection with God, since 'breath' signifies the mystery of life and of our origin (see ANTHROPOLOGY, CHRISTIAN).

In the languages which ground Christian tradition, Hebrew *ruach* signifies at root 'air in motion', thus energy or power. Of the 378 uses in the Old Testament, more than a third refer simply to wind (for example Gen. 8: 1; Amos 4: 13; Isa. 40: 7). A further thirty-nine refer to the life principle of men and animals (for example Judg. 15: 19; Ezek. 37: 8, 10). Seventy-four times it is used in connection with strong emotions such as anger, grief, sadness, bitterness and longing (for example Gen. 26: 35; Num. 5: 14; Judg. 8: 3). In the later tradition it is a synonym for God (for example Hag. 2: 5; Zech. 4: 6).

The Greek root *pneu* has the same connotation, movement of air relating to both wind and breath. From Homer onwards it was used in connection with the inspiration of poetry. Of the Greek philosophical systems it was most important for Stoicism, which saw it as a world principle manifested at different levels in all reality from God to inanimate objects. As such it was the fifth element ('quintessence') in addition to earth, air, water and fire. This view was important for some of the church Fathers (such as Tertullian).

Old Testament
We can analyse the Old Testament material either thematically or historically, and both approaches are important.

Thematically we can point first to a connection between Spirit and *creation* and, relatedly, *creativity*. Thus, for the priestly writer, it is the *ruach Elohim* which hovers over the primeval chaos (Gen. 1: 2). The implication is that the Spirit is what brings order and form. Relatedly, in the Yahwist account of creation, God breathes (*neshamah*) the breath of life into the creature he has formed (Gen. 2: 7). The Psalmist sees the whole of the natural world as dependent on God's Spirit, which creates and 'renews the face of the ground' (Ps. 104: 30). Extension to new creation is a natural move (Isa. 40: 3), as is the tracing of human creativity to God's Spirit (Exod. 31: 3). Later writings systematize the connection with creation (Wisd. 1: 7; 12: 1).

A second theme is the connection between Spirit and *ecstatic phenomena*. The inspiration of the Judges is often regarded in this way, though the story of Saul's prophesying is probably a better example (1 Sam. 10: 10). This particular story also shows the ground for the later connection between Spirit and *prophecy*. Micah traces his ability to denounce the sin of Israel to the Spirit (Mic. 3: 8). Amos asserts that God reveals his secrets to the prophets and that when the Lord has spoken there is no choice but to prophesy (Amos 3: 7f.). Ezekiel traces his prophecy to the Spirit (Ezek. 2: 2; 3: 24), and after the exile this was generalized into the idea of prophetic inspiration (Neh. 9: 30; 2 Chr. 15: 1).

A third theme emerges in the connection between Spirit and wisdom, made explicitly in Wisdom of Solomon 9: 17 and implied by the shared functions of the two. This means that Spirit is also to be discerned in *rationality* and not simply in irrational or ecstatic behaviour. It is vital, for instance, for the government of the community, as the story in Numbers 11 makes clear.

A fourth theme is the contrast between divine and human spirit, signified in the term 'Holy' spirit (Isa. 63: 10f.), since holiness is what fundamentally distinguishes God and human beings (Hos. 11: 9). The story in Genesis 6: 1f. gives this narrative expression. Human and divine spirit are also fundamentally contrasted in terms of power (Isa. 31: 3).

If we approach this material historically, following as far as possible the chronology of the various biblical documents, a somewhat different picture emerges. We find, for instance, that Spirit language is not used at all consistently but is grouped rather in two great bands – one from before the monarchy, and one afterwards. Thus Spirit language is especially dense in the Book of Judges, where the Spirit inspires men and women to liberate Israel and to give the land peace. Under the monarchy the language almost disappears. The fact that some of the great prophets use the word ironically, to mean 'empty words' (Jer. 5: 12f.), might indicate that the language was devalued by the court prophets, who claimed divine inspiration for oracles which simply underwrote the royal ideology (1 Kgs 22). When the word is used it is to dream of a different kind of ruler, who will fulfil all the hopes vested in the Davidic monarchy (Isa. 11: 2f.). This vision of a new future could be extended to the whole of creation (Isa. 32: 14f.). 'Spirit' thus comes to have a messianic dimension. The second great band of Spirit language, however, is found in the exile, where it becomes one of the main vehicles to express the hope that God will renew Israel, and bring the exiles back to Palestine to live in peace. This is especially the burden of Ezekiel's vision of the dry bones (Ezek. 37) and, importantly, Spirit is seen to inspire the servant (Israel?)'s vocation to 'bring forth justice' to the nations (Isa. 42: 1f.; Isa. 61: 1f.). From this perspective Spirit language is a form of political discourse. It speaks of the creation of a society in accordance with what God wants for human beings on the one hand, and represents a critique of unjust societies on the other.

New Testament

If we take the Christian Bible as a whole then we have to speak of a third band of Spirit language. Whilst the word 'Spirit' is hardly found in the synoptic Gospels, it is central to Paul, John and Acts. The story of Pentecost gives narrative expression to why this is the case (Acts 2).

In the synoptics Spirit is associated above all with Jesus' baptism, where the Spirit descends on Jesus and then 'drives him out' into the wilderness (Mark 1: 8f. and par). In addition Luke represents Jesus as beginning his ministry by referring to Isaiah 61 (Luke 4: 18f.) and Matthew too interprets Jesus through the figure of the servant (Matt. 12: 18=Isa. 42: 1). Both Matthew and Luke refer to Spirit in the birth stories, where Spirit is a way of talking of the creative intervention of God in human history in the person of Jesus. In an important saying Jesus warns against blasphemy against the Spirit (Mark 3: 29), which appears to mean calling good evil. This represents a disposition which closes itself off from God and therefore cannot be forgiven.

The reality behind the Pentecost story (which may or may not have a historical kernel) is discerned in the writings of Paul, who uses the word 103 times, excluding Ephesians. Behind this dense usage is a very intense fact of experience, reflected equally in John's Gospel and Acts, that the early church felt itself in the grip of a new force, which they could only call

'Spirit'. As with the Old Testament, this material is usually treated thematically – when we can speak of the Spirit as creating, sanctifying and giving us unity, but this abstraction should be resisted. The heart of Paul's gospel was that in Christ God had acted to bring a new humanity into being, breaking down all the most fundamental barriers of society, between men and women, races and classes (Gal. 3: 28). The driving force behind this movement is the Spirit of Christ (1 Cor. 12: 13; 12: 3). Spirit language speaks, therefore, about God creating a new world, a world of freedom as opposed to the bondage of the old order from which we are now liberated (2 Cor. 3: 17). In the experience of the new world that we have we are ourselves the first fruits of the whole created order which the Spirit is working to renew (Rom. 8: 12–27). The Spirit is therefore a spirit of hope for this new order (Rom. 15: 13), and here and now it brings forth fruits of the kingdom (Gal. 5: 22) which are opposed to the ordering of the present world of the 'flesh'.

Paul interprets spiritual things to those who have the Spirit (1 Cor. 2: 13), which means expounding the paradoxical power and wisdom of a crucified Messiah. In the same way John understands the giving of the Spirit to follow from Jesus' crucifixion, which he refers to as 'glorification' (John 7: 39). The Spirit is the 'Paraclete' ('exhorter' or 'consoler') who convicts the world in respect to sin, righteousness and judgement (John 16: 8), guides the disciples into the truth about Jesus (John 14: 25), and thus gives them a peace which is 'not as the world gives', not the peace of compromise, religious opiate, or turning a blind eye to evil (John 14: 27). To become a disciple, to follow the crucified Jesus, a person must be reborn 'of the Spirit' (John 3: 3) – here again John resembles Paul in tracing the realization of the new world to what God is doing among us.

Essentially the same point is made by Luke's linking of Spirit, prayer and kingdom language. God guides the course of history through prayer, and the main response to prayer is the gift of the Spirit (Luke 11: 13) which realizes the kingdom in the new community (see KINGDOM OF GOD: NEW TESTAMENT). The Pentecost story makes exactly Paul's point about the breaking down of barriers, and leads directly to that situation where the community had 'all things in common' (Acts 2: 44). In what sense is the Spirit bestowed in baptism? Luke gives no clear answer. Sometimes baptism comes first (Acts 2: 38), but Spirit baptism can come first (Acts 10: 44f.). The texts cannot be read legalistically but point us to the dialectic of God's address and human response.

If we ask about the overall meaning of Spirit language in the biblical writings we can say first that it is that *history cannot be reduced to human history without remainder*. God is at work both in creation and history, and it is the function of Spirit language to say that. Secondly, this means that there is a *directedness* about human history: it is not aimless but moves towards 'the kingdom'. There are concrete realizations of this which we ascribe to God, again using Spirit language. Thirdly, we must talk about the *openness* of history, because God works against all situations which imprison or limit human beings and because, in God, there is always hope for a better future.

When we turn to the post-biblical period two lines of interpretation are open to us, both of which must be followed. There is a history of the *doctrine* of the Spirit, but there is also a history of *Spirit-inspired movements*. These two are related but not identical.

The history of the doctrine in the church
Reference to Spirit in the early creeds is extremely terse. Most creeds probably added simply, 'And we believe in the Holy Spirit.' The doctrine came into prominence towards the end of the fourth century when, in the wake of Arianism, a group arose contesting the divinity of the Spirit. These were vigorously contested by the Cappadocians, one of whom, Gregory Nazianzus, enunciated the important principle of progressive revelation, maintaining that recognition of the full divinity of the Spirit had had to wait until exactly this moment (Oration 31). The debate culminated in the creed of the Council of Constantinople of 381, which recognized that the Spirit was equal with God. Though the Nicene creed may not have been drawn up by this Council it is from this period that we have the classic expression of the doctrine of the Spirit as 'The Lord and giver of life, Who proceeds from the Father and the Son . . . Who spoke by the prophets'.

Controversy attaches to the phrase 'and the Son', which was not part of the original creed. It may have been interpolated in the sixth century but was in any case commonly used in the west by the tenth century. Official acceptance in Rome led to the schism of 1054, which is still unresolved. The fear is that two 'origins' would destroy God's unity and nullify the distinction between Father and Son. Following suggestions of the Russian theologian B. Bolotov, it has recently been proposed that the formula 'from the Father of the Son' might be a way of resolving this ancient dispute.

The phrases which follow mention of the Spirit in the creed have led to the 'appropriation' to the Spirit of creativity (as opposed to origination), sanctification and inspiration. To reflect on the possibility of new life for people ('conversion'), or on the role of Scripture, church or sacraments, is in some sense to do pneumatology. The fact that wherever God works he produces what is new also links doctrine of the Spirit to eschatology. Because Spirit speaks of God entirely immanent in our experience, and therefore in the processes of inspiration, the life of the church, and in human experience in general, discernment is a key issue. How do we decide when God is at work and when a 'lying spirit' (1 Kgs 22: 23)? The question of discernment was immensely sharpened by the Reformation, and especially by John Calvin's teaching about the 'inner testimony of the Holy Spirit' which convinced the believer of the truth of Scripture. The effect of this was to leave each reader to interpret the Bible for him- or herself. Unsurprisingly the Council of Trent formulated a counter-movement which in effect made unwritten tradition the authentic commentary on Scripture. The question who is to interpret tradition prompted an ever narrowing point of reference until the First Vatican Council asserted that when the pope speaks *ex cathedra* on faith or morals he does so infallibly in virtue of the divine assistance of the Spirit. Both sides finally presuppose the 'inspiration' of Scripture. This must not be understood mantically but, in the first instance, simply as a recognition of how Scripture actually functions in the church, because 'church' is that community whose identity is constituted by these documents. It is the community's assent to the claim that God was active in the lives of the biblical actors and their communities, and truly discerned by them. The idea of infallibility, however, whether of Scripture or of the pope, does not reckon sufficiently with God's refusal to overrule us. If ideology is, as Karl Marx said, reason corrupted by self-interest, then there is no theology which is not partly ideology. The ongoing discussion of the whole church is always a question of sorting out the two. The history of this discernment is the history of Spirit. It is a 'hermeneutic labour' (R. Jenson).

After the Reformation the most important developments in the doctrine of Spirit were those of F.D.E. Schleiermacher and G.W.F. Hegel. For Schleiermacher the Spirit was the 'common spirit' of the church, understood on the analogy of a national community. This was not reductionist because for Schleiermacher the foundation of every individual consciousness was the sense of dependence which was 'truly an existence of God' in the believer. Hegel, on the other hand, understood the whole of evolution, and in particular the whole course of human history, as 'the self-realization of absolute Spirit'. Cultural and political development in particular could be understood as the work of the Spirit, a view which fed in to the evolutionary optimism of the later nineteenth century. Complex forms of reaction to these thinkers led to the displacement of the centrality of Spirit discourse until after the Second World War, when the growing importance of Pentecostalism made it once more imperative. The most important developments in pneumatology have been in the theology of mission, especially that of J.V. Taylor, ecclesiology, where the contribution of J. Moltmann is outstanding, and the doctrine of the Trinity, where Moltmann again and R. Jenson have played leading roles (see GOD). Another question of real importance is that of the femininity of the Spirit, which bases itself on an appeal to the feminine gender of Hebrew *ruach*. The appeal, closely linked to wisdom theology (E. Fiorenza) or Mariology (L. Boff) raises complex issues. Insistence on feminine as well as masculine predicates for God can seem to imply that Deity itself is gendered, a suggestion most wish to resist. The association of maternal language with Spirit trades on gender stereotypes begotten by patriarchy. If gender is an ultimate distinction, it is claimed, the Holy Spirit needs to have become incarnate in Mary, in addition to the male incarnation Jesus, a suggestion which owes much to C.G. Jung. The question of how we use analogy to talk about God is crucial in this discussion.

The history of Spirit movements

In critical independence of the history of the doctrine runs the history of movements which appeal to the Spirit. The earliest church was clearly a 'Spirit movement'; but within the canon of the New Testament, by the time of the pastoral epistles, we can see a fading of this enthusiasm and a greater emphasis on order and institution. This situation has always provoked reaction and the first well-known Spirit movement after the New Testament period is Montanism, named after Montanus, who prophesied in the second half of the second century. The movement was apocalyptic and ascetic, castigating the contemporary church for laxity. Montanus foretold an imminent outpouring of the Spirit and Tertullian, in his Montanist period, contrasted lax Christians with those who were 'Spirit filled'.

It is probable that monasticism should also be understood as a form of Spirit movement, but the next absolutely clear movements of this kind are found in the medieval period. In the eleventh century Catharist or Albigensian movements appear in different parts of Europe. These movements were rigorist and distinguished between the perfect, who had received baptism of the Spirit by laying on of hands, and those who had not. A Crusade was mounted against them in 1208, and they were a prime target of the Dominican Inquisition.

Towards the end of the twelfth century the Cistercian abbot Joachim of Fiore wrote his Book of Concords, which looked forward to a new age of the Spirit which would be inaugurated shortly. His works were published in 1254 by one of the Franciscans who opposed the remodelling of the Order, the so-called 'Spirituals', and had an immense influence both on spirituality and on views of the church. His threefold periodization of history was picked up by G.E. Lessing and then appropriated by Hegel.

In the thirteenth century, but with roots far earlier, we find groups professing the 'Free

Spirit'. They were found amongst both intellectuals and simple people. A group in Paris known as the Amaurians expected the Spirit to take on flesh in themselves, and for the movement to spread until everyone would be able to say 'I am the Holy Spirit.' Movements of this kind were often antinomian, and frequently abandoned all sexual restraint. They are found in every century up to the Ranters of the seventeenth-century English Revolution. Dissatisfaction with the established church, mysticism, an emphasis on poverty, and frequent antinomianism, as well as appeal to the Spirit, are characteristic of all of them.

Spirit movements free of moral anarchy are also found, and the constant emergence of new religious orders from the time of Benedict (525) to the present day can probably be regarded in this light. Within Protestantism the Quakers, pietists and Methodists all share an emphasis both on intense personal religious experience, usually in terms of an appeal to the Spirit, and in varying degrees on moral rigorism. In the case of Quakers and Methodists the beginnings of the movement involved a special appeal to the poor.

Twentieth-century Pentecostalism is thus the latest of a long, and perhaps unbroken, series of movements (see PENTECOSTALISM AND CHARISMATIC CHRISTIANITY). Many Pentecostal churches, especially black churches, fulfil the same function as many of the earlier Spirit movements in allowing those who have no power to find a voice. The same forms of ethical rigorism and belief in Spirit baptism frequently crop up. In recent years, the movement has spread widely amongst the middle class, where its function is different and where ideological questions are most important.

To say 'Spirit' is to say 'God at work in the world'. Biblical traditions, church doctrines and Spirit movements all represent the human response to this work. For this reason pneumatology is always essentially unfinished.

Bibliography

Barrett, C.K. 1947: *The Holy Spirit and the Gospel Tradition*. London: SPCK.

Berkhof, H. 1964: *The Doctrine of the Holy Spirit*. London: Epworth.

Brown, C., ed. 1975–8: *New International Dictionary of New Testament Theology*. Exeter: Paternoster Press.

Cohn, N. 1957: *The Pursuit of the Millennium*. London: Secker and Warburg.

Dunn, J.D.G. 1975: *Jesus and the Spirit*. London: SCM Press.

Eichrodt, W. 1961: *Old Testament Theology*. London: SCM Press, chapter 13.

Hollenweger, W. 1972: *The Pentecostals*. London: SCM Press.

Lampe, G. 1977: *God as Spirit*. Oxford: Oxford University Press.

Moltmann, J. [1975] 1977: *The Church in the Power of the Spirit*. London: SCM Press.

Rowland, C. 1988: *Radical Christianity*. Cambridge: Polity Press.

Schweizer, E. 1981: *The Holy Spirit*, trans. R.H. and I. Fuller. Philadelphia: Fortress Press.

Snaith, N. 1948: *The Distinctive Ideas of the Old Testament*. London: Epworth.

Swete, H.B. 1912: *The Holy Spirit in the Ancient Church*. Oxford: Oxford University Press.

Taylor, J.V. 1972: *The Go Between God*. London: SCM Press.

Wheeler Robinson, H. 1962: *The Christian Experience of the Holy Spirit*. London: Fontana.

TIMOTHY GORRINGE

political issues, Christian responses to See CAPITALISM; CHRISTIAN SOCIALISM; KINGDOM OF GOD: POLITICAL AND SOCIAL THEOLOGY; MARXISM; SOCIAL QUESTIONS.

postliberalism 'Postliberalism' designates a recent American theological movement primarily associated with Yale Divinity School and Duke Divinity School. Its central architect has been George A. Lindbeck of Yale. Other exponents of this perspective include Stanley Hauerwas, Ronald Thiemann and Will Willimon, as well as a new generation of theologians and ethicists such as William C. Placher, William Werpehowski and Kathryn Tanner. The movement is both related and indebted to the narrative approach developed in theology by Hans Frei and in philosophy by Alasdair MacIntyre, and to social scientific perspectives that emphasize the importance of culture and language for all experience and thought (see CULTURE AND THEOLOGY; LANGUAGE, RELIGIOUS; NARRATIVE THEOLOGY).

The central tenets of postliberalism are most fully stated by George A. Lindbeck in *The Nature of Doctrine: Religion and Theology in a*

Postliberal Age (1984). Lindbeck sets forth his cultural-linguistic interpretation of religion, which is the guiding presupposition of post-liberalism, by juxtapositioning it to two other historical and contemporary conceptions of religion. The first position Lindbeck calls the cognitivist interpretation of religion. This model, premodern in character although held by some thinkers today, understands religious doctrines as propositional claims about reality with defensible cognitive viability. Such a view, for Lindbeck, is untenable because the grounds upon which it is based, especially the correspondence theory of truth and the assumption that objective, universally valid knowledge is possible, have been eroded.

The second view Lindbeck rejects is termed the experiential-expressivist or, he says, the liberal model. This approach, according to Lindbeck, is the dominant one in theology today. Its historical roots are in Friedrich Schleiermacher's nineteenth-century interpretation of religion as grounded in a pre-linguistic and unmediated form of experience. In this perspective experience is primary, and religious doctrines, symbols, myths and rituals are secondary expressions of this foundational inward state. Moreover, while these secondary expressions are always historically particular and culturally specific, the prior religious experience is both a universal reality and has everywhere a common character. In this view, religions and their doctrines are assessed not in terms of their cognitive status but by virtue of how effectively they bring to expression this basal experience.

For Lindbeck, the experiential-expressivist approach, with its appeal to a universal, common experience, is fundamentally flawed. It takes account inadequately of real diversity and plurality and it fails to recognize the historical, mediated character of all thought and experience. Over and against this way of construing religion, as well as that of the cognitivist model, Lindbeck proposes a cultural-linguistic interpretation of religion.

In this cultural-linguistic or postliberal approach, there is no non-linguistic, unmediated, or universal experience. Human beings are thoroughly social and cultural beings who depend upon cultural and, especially, linguistic resources to make experience possible at all. In the place of the cognitivist's universal reason and the experiential-expressivist's common basal experience, Lindbeck posits an interpretation of humans dependent upon and shaped by their historical and cultural contexts. Moveover, Lindbeck argues that humans not only require specific cultural resources, but most importantly they live in and through overarching interpretative schemas that function to organize experience and establish individual identity in the context of particular communities. These interpretative traditions or religions are historical in nature, arising in specific locations and times and developing through the contingencies of particular histories.

Out of this view, Lindbeck concludes that to be religious is not to have a particular experience or to hold certain beliefs, but rather to interiorize and live through a specific tradition and its fundamental portrayal of life and its meaning. The task of becoming religious is that of learning the interpretative story, the language of faith, and becoming a skilful practitioner of the tradition's way of life.

Doctrines and theological claims in this view are neither primarily cognitive assertions to be proved or falsified, nor the linguistic expression of prior non-linguistic experience. They are the 'rules' or 'communally authoritative teachings' that organize life within a particular tradition, indicate its most fundamental claims, and thereby structure life and identity. Religious traditions designate their 'rules' in different ways, but within the Christian tradition such regulative doctrines are located primarily in the biblical narrative. Hence, for Lindbeck and postliberals, to be Christian is to live out of the vision of reality narrated in the biblical story of God's relationship to the world as it is focused and given content in and through Jesus Christ.

Given these assumptions, a distinctive post-liberal understanding of Christian theology emerges. The task of theology is to describe the central, normative features of the Christian story, to articulate the axial beliefs of the tradition and their relation to one another, and to reflect upon how they have been and should be instantiated in the practices of the community. The primary purpose of theological reflection is to aid the community's appropriation and interiorization of these Christian beliefs and practices and thereby sustain and enhance Christian life and identity.

If theology's task is primarily a descriptive one, the central criterion for assessing theological views is that of faithfulness to the normative foundations of the tradition as these are articulated in the biblical narrative. The theological questions are how well contemporary assertions cohere and fit within the basic framework of the Christian tradition, and how efficacious they are in nurturing Christian identity and practice. 'Truth', for many postliberals, consists in faithfulness to the doctrinal core that gives Christianity its distinctive nature. Since theology is primarily intrasystemic, its validity is measured in terms of its own internal standards, not in relation to some supposedly universal or publicly agreed-upon criteria.

Within this approach, morality is also shaped centrally by tradition. Stanley Hauerwas has most fully articulated the ethical implications of a postliberal position. Eschewing claims of universal moral principles or rules, Hauerwas has argued that morality has to do primarily with the shaping of character and the development of virtue and that these are also intrasystemic affairs in which the moral vision of a community is inculcated in its members. Thus, to be moral is to interiorize the particular vision of a unique historical community and to become a skilful practitioner of the moral precepts of that tradition (Hauerwas, 1981).

Three characteristics can be seen to typify postliberalism. First, it is anti-foundationalist, rejecting all assertions of ahistorical, universal foundations, be they found in reason or experience. Second, it posits a thoroughly social and communitarian vision of human life, thereby repudiating the individualism endemic to modern life and thought. Human experience is mediated through the language and practices of particular communities, and individuals only have identity within those communal contexts. The autonomous, self-subsisting individual does not exist, morally, religiously or intellectually. Third, postliberalism is particularistic and historicist. Humans are not historical or social in general. They receive their identity and experience reality within communities that live out of inherited understandings of life. Their overarching interpretations or world views are not interchangeable or reducible to one another

and neither is the experience that occurs within them.

Increasingly, a new generation of postliberal thinkers are working through the implications of these assumptions in relation to new issues and criticisms. One important issue concerns the reality of pluralism and the question of how traditions should relate to one another (Placher, 1989). On the one hand, postliberalism's theory of distinctive historical traditions provides a basis for acknowledging the particular local character of each tradition and resists the reduction of traditions to some ahistorical sameness. On the other, postliberalism's emphasis upon the intrasystemic nature of theology and ethics seems to provide no basis for conversation among traditions. In response to this concern, postliberal theologians, in particular William Werpehowski and William C. Placher, have extended Hans Frei's notion of an *ad hoc* apologetics in which Christians engage participants of other traditions around specific shared concerns, each bringing to the conversation the distinctive voice of their tradition (Werpehowski, 1986; Placher, 1989).

A closely related issue is that of how Christian theology can and should contribute to the public sphere and the creation of public policy within a radically pluralistic society. A central response of postliberals, especially Stanley Hauerwas, has been to insist that the major way Christians influence the public sphere is through practices that reflect the fundamental commitments of their tradition. Through the witness of the community the broader societal fabric is affected (Hauerwas, 1985). However, this way of contributing to the public arena cannot mean, according to postliberals, accepting the claim that there are universal public standards shared by everyone. Critics of postliberalism, however, have averred that such a response offers little help in adjudicating the conflicts in a pluralistic society that are the result of different traditions simply living faithfully out of beliefs that conflict with one another.

A final, central issue confronting postliberalism, along with other contemporary perspectives, concerns the 'truth' question (see TRUTH, CONCEPTS OF). Most postliberals have spoken of truth primarily in terms of faithfulness to the core claims of a tradition and efficaciousness in the creation of character and identity. Yet this approach appears to many thinkers, postliberal and otherwise, to be a form of radical relativism emptying the notion of truth of any public content. Increasingly, postliberal theologians such as William C. Placher have identified this issue as a significant one that requires further reflection, in a manner that acknowledges the historical nature of truth claims but also recognizes that persons and traditions hold their positions because they believe them to be the case.

Postliberalism is a contemporary theological movement that distinguishes itself from both the projects of the Enlightenment and Schleier-machian liberalism with its assumptions of an unmediated religious experience common to all humans. In their stead, postliberals advocate a return to religious tradition and to the task of interiorizing the values of particular communities. To postliberals, this approach flows from the historical and traditioned nature of life. To postliberalism's critics, this represents a retreat into fideistic isolation, an arbitrary absolutizing of the past and a concomitant failure to recognize the dynamic and innovative nature of traditions. For them, moreover, it embodies a blindness to the multi-traditioned character of contemporary life and a refusal to seek common, public criteria in terms of which pluralistic communities might live.

See also OTHER FAITHS AND CHRISTIANITY.

Bibliography

Frei, Hans W. 1974: *The Eclipse of Biblical Narrative*. New Haven: Yale University Press.
Hauerwas, Stanley 1981: *A Community of Character: Toward a Constructive Christian Social Ethics*. Notre Dame, Ind.: University of Notre Dame Press.
Hauerwas, Stanley 1985: *Against the Nations*. Minneapolis: Winston Press.
Hauerwas, Stanley, and Willimon, William 1985: Embarrassed by God's presence, *The Christian Century* 102, pp. 98–100.
Lindbeck, George A. 1984: *The Nature of Doctrine: Religion and Theology in a Postliberal Age*. Philadelphia: Westminster Press.
MacIntyre, Alasdair 1984: *After Virtue*, 2nd edn. Notre Dame, Ind.: University of Notre Dame Press.
MacIntyre, Alasdair 1988: *Whose Justice? Which Rationality?* London: Gerald Duckworth and Co.
Placher, William C. 1989: *Unapologetic Theology: Christian Voice in a Pluralistic Conversation*. Louisville, Kentucky: Westminster/John Knox Press.
Tanner, Kathryn E. 1988: *God and Creation in Christian Theology: Tyranny or Empowerment*. Oxford and New York: Blackwell.
Thiemann, Ronald E. 1985: *Revelation and Theology: The Gospel as Narrated Promise*. Notre Dame, Ind.: University of Notre Dame Press.
Werpehowski, William 1986: Ad hoc apologetics, *Journal of Religion* 66, pp. 282–301.

SHEILA GREEVE DAVANEY AND DELWIN BROWN

postmodernism As the prefix suggests, the term 'postmodernism' designates the era in western culture following modernism, which period began with the Enlightenment in the seventeenth century and extended through two-thirds of the twentieth century. Modernism is said to describe an initial reliance on the power of reason, objective thinking, the empirical-scientific method and a faith in progress, followed by a disenchantment with these and a replacement of them by a sense of cultural fragmentation, alienation and disintegration of the self – such negativity generated by two shattering world wars, the threat of destruction from nuclear power and the persisting memories of Holocaust horrors. Postmodernism, beginning in the early 1960s, recognizes the traumatic, estranged, and atomized nature of human existence but attempts to render it bearable and even affirmative by adopting attitudes and strategies such as irony, parody, anti-foundationalism and play. Whereas some critics such as Ihab Hassan and Linda Hutcheon view postmodernism as a recuperative way of using the past and charting the future, others such as Charles Newman and Gerald Graff see it as merely a fashionable, misguided posture that avoids facing the crisis of global survival.

Arnold Toynbee (Calinescu, 1987, p. 267) used the term in 1946 to label the present – and possibly last – period of human history following what he called 'Western III (Modernism)'; yet it first gained currency in the fields of architecture and art history. In architectural design, the functional and 'pure' steel and glass perpendicular oblongs of 'high' modernism, conceived by Mies van der Rohe and others and representing earlier twentieth-century Bauhaus ideology, are relieved by the decorative, asymmetrical creations of the later Philip

Johnson, Michael Graves, James Stirling and others. These articulate the language of modernist design but simultaneously subvert it by imposing, in playful and parodic ways, elements that recall the earlier conventions of, for example, classicism and art nouveau (Taylor, 1987, p. 42). Such 'double-coding', as Charles Jencks has called it (1982, p. 111), with its ludic exploitation of the past, is a central feature of postmodernism in all of its manifestations. The Lloyds 'exoskeletal' high-rise building in the City of London is an example of what Jencks (Calinescu, 1987, p. 286) labels 'late-modern', as is the Pompidou Centre in Paris; the Clore Gallery for the Turner Collection, now part of the Tate Gallery in London, is an example of postmodern architecture.

In 1968 the art historian Leo Steinberg used the term 'postmodernism' (Taylor, 1987, p. 40) to characterize the work of artists such as Andy Warhol and Robert Rauschenberg, who challenged the western tradition of visual representation (on which even schools such as abstract expressionism are based) by producing pictures that are images of images rather than of nature (Warhol) and by creating collages in which the objects utilized are relativized and serve as a record of feedback loop overload, of artists' inability to sift and focus the myriad influences bombarding them (Rauschenberg) (Taylor, 1987, p. 65). One sees here how 'problematizing' rather than representation guides postmodern artistic creation. Both the artists' subjects and their methods of execution communicate primarily the difficulty of exercising a conventional discrimination that would permit a 'natural' depiction of our world.

This altered world is conceived, in semiotic terms, as one in which the signifier has replaced the signified as the focus of orientation and value, and in the structural linguistics of the 1950s and 1960s a multidisciplinary theory of the sign emerged that provided an intellectual context (it would be misleading to say, a grounding) for postmodernism. In the structural linguistics propounded early in the century by Ferdinand de Saussure, then later by Roman Jakobson and others, the arbitrariness of the linguistic sign and its interdependence with other signs mark the end of the possibility of fixed, absolute meaning – indeed, for some even the end of the possibility of belief in an

Absolute. Meaning in this view derives from the collusion of sign clusters whose signification changes as the clusters interact with each other, and this infinite interplay disguises the absence of meaning outside the language system or the so-called linguistic universe.

The work of the structural anthropologist Claude Lévi-Strauss and the literary critic Roland Barthes on myth offered the hope that such signifying systems could be mapped, even in their great number and global variety, to disclose overarching linguistic laws that would replace the Judaic/Christian metaphysical constants. In this context structuralism could be understood as a transitional phenomenon between modernism and postmodernism, witnessing to the capacity of the human mind for creating ultimate order while granting the need for a new ordering paradigm. But postmodern and poststructural thinkers such as Jacques Derrida and Michel Foucault, then Jean-François Lyotard and Jean Baudrillard, seriously damaged this epistemological optimism by asserting the underlying capriciousness of language and of the institutions that exploit it, the totalizing eclecticism of the signifying process that frustrates logic, and the emergence of a simulacra technology in which 'natural' representation is replaced by the imitations and replications of electronic, computerized design.

To comprehend the importance of these assertions for postmodernism, one must understand first the tradition of continental idealist philosophy. Immanuel Kant redirected the study of philosophy from metaphysics to epistemology, arguing that one cannot know the nature of reality because all experience of it is conditioned by the a prioris of the human mind (mainly our senses of time and space). Such a prioris may reveal more about the mind itself than about its objects of reflection. This initial uncertainty would evolve into the radical doubt of various modern thinkers after Kant. For Søren Kierkegaard it took the form of ironic commentary that sought to expose the crucial elements forgotten by such dedicated systematizers as Georg Wilhelm Friedrich Hegel and the Lutheran theologians of Copenhagen. For Friedrich Nietzsche such doubt necessitated a total denial of western culture, metaphorized in his announcement of the death of God and leading to his declaration that the will to power is fundamental to the mastery of life to be attained by the 'overman'. In Martin Heidegger it inspired a relentless *Zurückfragen*, an interrogation back to the essence of being that shows itself at last to be a vestige of the outmoded metaphysical tradition it challenges and that needs to be replaced by poetic thinking – an attempt to recover and invent *Grundsprache*, fundamental language that shapes reality.

Even if Heidegger was the first postmodernist, as he has been called, it remained for the poststructuralists since the 1960s to carry through the consequences of Heidegger's (and his above-named predecessors') rejection of both modernist metaphysics and epistemology. Jacques Derrida, above all, in his philosophy of foundational difference (a form of which had animated Jakobson's structural linguistics) countered the assumptions of an original, all-legitimating presence at the heart of western 'logocentric' thought and of the feasibility of totalizing systems. For them he substituted the notions of originary absence, of a trace which precedes its fugitive object, and of undecidability as a way of responding to the rationalist demand for unequivocal answers. Hardly less pivotal has been Michel Foucault, who applied something of the same strategy to historical investigations of institutions and phenomena such as asylums, prisons and sexuality to argue that society's relation to these is always – and always destructively – inadequate, for in establishing and perpetuating them, those in power suppress and victimize those who are not. Here the will to power emerges as far more sinister than Nietzsche had anticipated.

Jean-François Lyotard claims that the *grands récits*, the meta-narratives of western culture, all in one way or another perpetuate secular versions of the Judaic/Christian models and thus serve to legitimize the dominant ideologies they spawned; yet these *récits* are breaking up into a plethora of 'little narratives', mutually contradictory and competitive, that reflect the 'paralogical' and (in Derrida's terminology) differential and undecidable nature of things. Jean Baudrillard's neo-apocalyptic vision intensifies Heidegger's critique of technology and views our age as not only lacking a transcendental absolute but as trapped in an endless network of artificial sign systems – those manufactured by an electronic, computer-driven technology and accepted as simulacra of the real (like Warhol's images of images) for the fulfilment of desire by a society of rampant consumers.

Jürgen Habermas among others denies that the work of the French poststructuralists is an authentic radical thinking that marks the end of modernism. He sees it as part of a reactionary reflex that has prematurely abandoned the modernist rationality and drive towards order, unwilling to help guide it through to its fulfilment. Fredric Jameson sees both a conservative and a liberating postmodernism exerting influence, sometimes in the same phenomena, while Terry Eagleton accuses the poststructuralists, especially Lyotard, of isolating the search for truth from a concern for justice and thus selling out to capitalist (im)morality. The self-described anti-representational pragmatist Richard Rorty, in his insistence that philosophy be conducted through literary interpretation and as a 'conversation of mankind', displays a strain of postmodern provocation, yet his reliance on Dewey and Wittgenstein places him at the same time in the modernist tradition.

The obsession with a universe of language that characterizes postmodernism is most evident in its literary versions. Tactics such as the foregrounding of the text's artifice to destroy the illusion of the work's representational reality, the author's intrusion into the text, the use of multiple plot developments and endings and the parodic exploitation of the literary tradition typify postmodern narrative fiction, poetry and drama, and some literary critics such as Ihab Hassan and Roland Barthes indulge a postmodern playfulness with text and reader in their interpretations. T.S. Eliot is considered the literary modernist father figure against whose portentous (and sometimes pretentious) symbolic artistry the postmodernists react. James Joyce and Robert Musil are recognized as modernist writers whose innovative styles anticipate postmodernism. Samuel Beckett, Jorge Luis Borges, and Vladimir Nabokov are considered transitional figures by some literary-cultural historians and outright postmodernists by others.

Examples of postmodern prose fiction are Robert Coover's short story 'The Babysitter' (multiple interlocking plots that remain unresolved), J.M. Coetzee's *Foe* (Defoe's *Robinson Crusoe* retold in altered form by a female narrator), Italo Calvino's *If On a Winter's Night a Traveller* (author's intrusion, many plots begun and interwoven but none completed, narration as feedback loop), Christine Brooke-Rose's *Thru* (intentional confusion of narrative kinds and levels, parodies of literary criticism), John Fowles's *The French Lieutenant's Woman* (anachronistic imitation of the Victorian novel, multiple endings), and Maggie Gee's *Dying, In Other Words* (the murdered writer's manuscript merges with the novel as a narrative of her life and death). John Ashbery is a representative postmodern poet. Illustrations of postmodern drama are Edward Albee's *Tiny Alice* and Sam Shepard's *A Lie of the Mind*.

Especially in literary studies, women writing on postmodernism have exerted a strong influence, among them Hélène Cixous, Elrud Ibsch, and Patricia Waugh. Linda Hutcheon argues that the postmodern attention to marginalized voices has prompted women to challenge patriarchal biases from the vantage point of postmodernism. Julia Kristeva, Luce Irigaray, and Jane Flax are among those who criticize Freudian and post-Freudian psychoanalytic theory (as in the work of Jacques Lacan) from a feminist perspective, focusing on typically postmodern questions such as the nature and status of subjectivity and the relationship of power and desire.

A number of postmodern novels, such as Umberto Eco's *The Name of the Rose* and Milan Kundera's *The Unbearable Lightness of Being*, have been produced as films, but postmodernism has had an impact on cinematic theory and praxis apart from these appropriations from literature. Traits of it appear in films of directors such as Woody Allen (for example *The Purple Rose of Cairo*) and Terry Gilliam (*Brazil*), and cinematic theory in relation to postmodernism is treated by critics such as Teresa de Lauretis, Christian Metz, and Kaja Silverman.

The principles of postmodernism may seem incompatible with religious faith. Parodic treatments of sacred individuals and creeds, for example (of Jesus in A.J. Langguth's *Jesus Christs* and in the Monty Python film *The Life of Brian*, of Muhammad in Salman Rushdie's *The Satanic Verses* and of Christian fundament-

alism in Margaret Atwood's *The Handmaid's Tale*), are offensive to many believers and suggest that postmodernism is hostile to religious traditions. Yet it is exerting increasing influence in the fields of theology, religious studies and biblical studies, and one could argue that two highly influential theologians of the first half of the twentieth century projected postmodern concepts. The neo-orthodox thinker Karl Barth's insistence that God is the Wholly Other, on whom humans must wait for grace, looks ahead – surely unwittingly – to Derrida's stress on difference (including its emphasis on deferring), while the liberal Paul Tillich's 'God beyond God' suggests the Derridean trace: evidence of an originary absence that is 'present-ed' in our metaphorical recreations of it.

These impulses may anticipate postmodernism mainly as it comes to incorporate poststructuralism, but as early as the 1960s, in the postliberal theology of George Lindbeck, one sees a postmodern accent on language employed to refute the modernist denigration of religious faith. In Lindbeck's view, the newly recognized linguistic universe makes profound faith possible – allows the sacred word to be flexed at last in power. Thus the modernist search after secular substitutes for an 'outmoded' religious belief can now be comprehended as a mistaken yielding to the falsely legitimizing myth of secularism (see SECULARIZATION).

Among the prominent postmodern theologians are Thomas J.J. Altizer, Mark C. Taylor and Robert Scharlemann. Altizer's death of God theology, which owes much to Nietzsche and Tillich, has matured since the 1960s into a radical rethinking of Christian apocalyptic, an effort vigorously postmodern in its investing of highly-charged traditional terms such as incarnation, crucifixion and resurrection with metaphoric-dialectical meaning. Scharlemann, strongly influenced by Heidegger's and Tillich's phenomenology and existentialism, interrogates the nature of theological reflection in contrast to ontological thinking. He shows via a version of Tillich's method of correlation that theological thinking involves a receptive, answering mode that recalls the text in its basic metaphoricity, 'overturns' the existential questions, and urges a realization of meaning as an agreement between the text's imaginative concreteness and the reader's situation. Taylor, who in good measure shares Derrida's preoccupation with Hegel, espouses a profoundly playful anti-systematic theology. Guided by the metaphor of erring, he applies Derrida's rhetorical strategies to wander into the impasses of idealism, deconstruct them on site, and offer in their place multi-allusive varieties of interpretation whose disorderly richness constitutes the 'divine milieu'. Kevin Hart more lucidly than any of the American theologians just mentioned assesses the impact of Derrida's thought on philosophy and theology and insists that the unsystematic mystical tradition offers a possibility for a contemporary negative theology that retains a necessary measure of rational knowledge yet avoids the pitfalls of metaphysics. Seen in this fashion, Derrida's deconstruction can assist a postmodern recovery of a venerable alternative path of faith.

Structuralist biblical exegesis, mainly in the 1970s and 1980s, was an enterprising approach that comprised the first serious challenge to the hegemony of the historical paradigm, especially in its form-critical and redaction-critical expressions that had dominated biblical hermeneutics since the nineteenth century. It was also structuralism that prepared the way for the far more daring postulations of biblical poststructuralism. From the perspective of biblical structuralism, at least, one could argue that structuralism was a late-modernist strategy projecting confidence in the hope that its applied linguistic formulas could produce definitive interpretations to bolster those of a historicism now showing the ravages of age. Poststructuralist biblical exegesis, however, is postmodern in its openness to questions addressed to the text from the contexts of Foucault (what is the power relationship of interpreter and community?), Derrida (how does one interpret a biblical text differently to create purposefully a host of conflicting readings?), and Lyotard (how can biblical texts be anything other than conveyors of an illusory meta-narrative of western capitalism?).

Part of the impetus for the creation of this hermeneutical *laissez faire* comes from the incursions, beginning mostly in the 1980s, of literary critics such as Harold Bloom, Gabriel Josipovici and Frank Kermode into the discipline of biblical studies. One of the most astute of these has been Mieke Bal, whose interpretations of the Hebrew Bible in terms of a network of codes that include narratology and feminism have introduced a remarkable freshness into the field. But scholars within the biblical exegetical 'guild' have been hardly less intrepid. John Dominic Crossan in his poststructuralist phase is an incisive, wide-ranging interpreter of texts such as the New Testament apocrypha and Gospel parables from a deconstructive perspective that seeks to demonstrate, for example, Jesus' own reliance on the paradoxical, playful nature of language to confront the force of institutionally legitimized and hence repressive Scripture interpretation. Werner Kelber's studies of the Gospels utilize Derrida's critique of logocentrism but also argue – as has Walter Ong – that Derrida's near-exclusive focus on writing has caused him to underestimate the potential of orality as embodied in the New Testament stress on the spoken word. Stephen Moore is representative of a younger generation of biblical scholar 'insiders' who, in discussing Hebrew Bible and New Testament texts from perspectives of feminism, reader response, narratology, deconstruction, corporeality, and ecological responsibility combine a judicious adaptation of traditional exegetical methods with a willingness to take postmodern hermeneutical risks.

Finally, postmodernism might be understood as an influential dynamic resulting from the convergence of the *mise-en-abyme* and the feedback loop. The *mise-en-abyme* (named by André Gide) is a literary-artistic device whereby an object (a text, painting, building) interiorizes a model of itself and thus sets off a chain of infinite embodiment, since that model has to contain *its* model and so on (an example is the model of Bourton-on-the-Water at one end of that village (in England), which includes models of the model until these become too small for reproduction). In a feedback loop, part of the information a system generates is devoted to a scrutiny of the system itself, so that its flaws can be detected, corrected, and the system made more efficient. Such self-modelling and self-correction are joined in postmodernism to effect situations in which so much self-reflective information is interiorized by the system that its self-correcting capacities are overwhelmed. Lyotard [1979] 1984, pp. 58–60) sees this as a moment in which the paralogy of postmodern science changes the nature of scientific enquiry into the proliferation of indeterminacies. Yet the relatively new science of chaos and fractal geometry suggest that even this ultimate differentiality is somehow orderly. The unpredictabilities of chaos can be teased into revealing patterns, and the endlessly diversifying shapes of fracta (accessible only as computer-generated images of images) can be made to resemble natural forms. These insights affirm what the postmodern humanities have imagined: the universe as a field of infinite interplay in which humans, never in control, can nonetheless learn how to join in some of its games.

See also BIBLICAL CRITICISM AND INTERPRETATION (1: OLD TESTAMENT and 2: NEW TESTAMENT); LANGUAGE, RELIGIOUS; LITERATURE AND THEOLOGY; POSTLIBERALISM.

Bibliography

Altizer, Thomas J.J. 1990: *Genesis and Apocalypse: A Theological Voyage Toward Authentic Christianity*. Louisville: Westminster/John Knox Press.

Calinescu, Matei 1987: *Five Faces of Modernity: Modernism, Avant-Garde, Decadence, Kitsch, Postmodernism*. Durham: Duke University Press.

Derrida, Jacques 1989: How to avoid speaking: denials. In Sanford Budick and Wolfgang Iser, eds, *Languages of the Unsayable: The Play of Negativity in Literature and Literary Theory*. New York: Columbia University Press.

Eagleton, Terry 1990: *The Ideology of the Aesthetic*. Oxford: Blackwell.

Harvey, David 1989: *The Condition of Postmodernity: An Enquiry into the Origins of Cultural Change*. Oxford: Blackwell.

Hutcheon, Linda 1988: *A Poetics of Postmodernism: History, Theory, Fiction*. New York and London: Routledge.

Jencks, Charles 1982: *Current Architecture*. London: Academy Editions.

Kelber, Werner H. 1991: *The Eclipse of Presence: Transparency and Opacity in the Fourth Gospel*. Madison: University of Wisconsin Press.

Lindbeck, George 1984: *The Nature of Doctrine: Religion and Theology in a Postliberal Age*. Philadelphia: Westminster Press.

Lyotard, Jean-François [1979] 1984: *The Postmodern Condition: A Report on Knowledge*. Minneapolis: University of Minnesota Press.

Moore, Stephen D. 1989: *Literary Criticism and the Gospels: The Theoretical Challenge*. New Haven and London: Yale University Press.

Phillips, Gary A., ed. 1990: *Poststructural Criticism and the Bible: Text/History/Discourse (Semeia 51)*. Atlanta: Scholars Press.

Rorty, Richard 1982: *Consequences of Pragmatism*. Minneapolis: University of Minnesota Press.

Scharlemann, Robert 1982: *The Being of God and the Experience of Truth*. New York: Seabury Press.

Taylor, Brandon 1987: *Modernism, Post-Modernism, Realism: A Critical Perspective on Art*. Winchester: Winchester School of Art Press.

Taylor, Mark C. 1984: *Erring: A Postmodern A/ Theology*. Chicago and London: University of Chicago Press.

R. DETWEILER

preaching, theology of When we trace the stream of Christian preaching to its source, we do not find there a theological system, a philosophical idea or an ethical insight. We find, instead, a cry of surprise and wonder: 'The Lord has risen indeed . . . !' (Luke 24: 34). This startled announcement of the resurrection of Jesus, spoken by astonished people who were only just beginning to believe it themselves, forms the chronological and theological starting point of all Christian preaching. Up to this moment, the disciples had proclaimed the gospel of the kingdom of God by spreading the words *of* Jesus; now their proclamation embraced a new word, a word *about* Jesus. In their deepest sense, all Christian sermons are attempts to repeat this resurrection claim anew, to connect it to the larger story of God's redemptive activity, and to discern its implications for the lives of those who hear.

A theology of Christian preaching, simply put, attempts to understand what is happening when members of the Christian community preach this gospel. It wants to know, at every possible level, what is happening when Christian preachers announce, in public speech, in their own words, and connected to the immediate circumstances of their hearers, the good news of the resurrection of Jesus Christ. For example, we are told in Acts that Paul preached in Athens to the philosophical debating society, and his sermon, after appealing to the experience of his Athenian audience and quoting the religious thoughts of a few of their favourite poets, headed for its theological home: 'God has fixed a day in which he will have the world judged in righteousness by a man whom he has appointed, and of this he has given assurance to all by raising him from the dead' (Acts 17: 31). This announcement of the resurrection was the central and critical point of the sermon, and it reportedly prompted a mixture of scorn, curiosity and belief (Acts 17: 32–4). A theology of preaching wants to ask many questions of such an event. For instance, what is the theological significance of this sermon's reported structure – its move from the immediate experience of the hearers to proclamation of the resurrection? Or what of the content of the sermon – its weaving together the Christian claim with quotations from 'non-Christian' sources? And what about the varied responses of the hearers? Again, why did some come to faith, while others merely scoffed? Was this due to the skill of the preacher, the nature of the message, the disposition of the listeners, the activity of the Holy Spirit or to some combination of these factors?

To express these concerns in a more finely tuned way, a comprehensive theology of preaching seeks to understand preaching as one of the forms of the church's post-resurrection speech, and to do so it attempts to accomplish two main tasks. First, it wants to describe the church's *practice* of preaching. The early church did not construct a self-conscious theology of preaching and then develop a practice to conform to it; it happened the other way around. The apostles, in response to what they had experienced, immediately started to preach, and only later began to ponder such questions as 'What does it mean that we preach?', 'What is the nature of the authority by which we preach?' and 'Are there styles of speaking more suited to the gospel than others?'. The practice of preaching, in other words, was prior to a formal theology of preaching, and a theology of preaching begins, not with a pure theory, but with the concrete activity. A theology of preaching is, therefore, initially a practical theology because it tries to discern the theological meanings inherent in an ongoing practice of the church.

In the second place, though, a theology of preaching wants to step back from the more immediate activity of the church and to enquire, in wider scope, about preaching as an activity of *God*. Is the sermon simply an act of human speaking, or is there any sense in which it is divine speech as well? What, if anything, is God doing through the human words of a sermon? In what way is preaching a present form of the 'Word of God', itself a means of grace and part of the continuing redemptive activity of God in the world? The answers to these and similar questions cannot be fully derived from an analysis of experience and must be sought from other sources. In this light, a theology of preaching is not only practical theology; it is also dogmatic theology.

The church's practice of preaching

The exclamation 'The Lord is risen indeed . . . !' is not yet a formal sermon, but this amazed cry of the earliest church is the seed from which the church's practice of preaching grew, and it contains embryonically the basic elements of a practical theology of preaching, as follows.

The disclosure of God's action First, the church's proclamation is seen to be a response to and an announcement of the prior action of God. Basically, Christian preaching is not religious wisdom, moral persuasion or theological speculation (though Christian sermons may, in a secondary sense, include all of these forms of discourse, and others). Preaching is essentially the disclosure of what God has done, is doing and will do in and for the world. 'The hermeneutic of Christian preaching,' maintains David Buttrick, 'is astonishment of being-saved in the world' (Buttrick, 1987, p. 16).

The act of preaching is not invented by preachers; it is invoked by the redemptive action of God in history. Preaching does not well up from human religious aspirations; it bears witness to what it has seen and heard. 'It all begins,' wrote H.H. Farmer, 'in an Event, or rather The Event, God's Event . . . An event can only establish itself – by happening, by being given. And it can only become generally known by being borne witness to, by being proclaimed' (Farmer, 1942, p. 8). This is why Christian sermons have historically and theologically been derived from and bound to biblical texts, 'for the Bible is the original and authentic witness, and the biblical canon is the context in which the church decided the witness must be known and understood' (Leith, 1988, p. 31).

The language of preaching Preaching occurs, on the one hand, in ordinary human words, words bound by historical circumstance and customary usage, and yet, on the other hand, preaching involves imaginative use of language, shaped by the new realities to which it points. 'Faith comes,' writes Paul, 'through what is heard, and what is heard comes through the word of Christ' (Rom. 10: 17). The word 'Lord', employed by the earliest witnesses to the resurrection, is a title borrowed from the social world of the first century and freighted with political implications. Applied to Jesus, however, and to the event of the resurrection, the title takes on new metaphorical power. This lordship is unlike any lordship the world has known before. 'The task and possibility of preaching,' claims Walter Brueggemann, 'is to open out the good news of the gospel with alternative modes of speech . . . The poetic speech of text and of sermon is a prophetic construal of a world beyond the one taken for granted' (Brueggemann, 1989, pp. 3–4).

The centrality of the resurrection All Christian preaching derives from the resurrection of Jesus, but Christian sermons are not the mere repetition of that claim. The nature of the resurrection as the central truth of Christianity causes preaching to move simultaneously in two directions: towards the telling of the whole biblical story and towards the relating of that story to the present circumstances of the hearers.

Moving in the first direction, the cry 'The Lord has risen indeed . . .' intrinsically demands that more be said, that more of the biblical account be expressed. The preacher must go on to name Jesus as 'the Lord', to recount the narratives by which this Jesus is known, and to place them into the larger story of God's involvement with the world. As Charles Wood has observed, 'The confession "Jesus is Lord" only makes sense within a story. Its value as a confession or reminder of Christian witness depends upon its users' and hearers' acquaintance with some account of who Jesus is and what it means (or how it happens) that he is Lord' (Wood, 1981, p. 103). The Christian preacher will also engage the whole range of literary genres in the canon – psalms,

doctrinal instruction, wisdom, apocalyptic and so on – because these forms constitute rhetorical pathways, means of access, into the overarching story of God-in-Christ.

Moreover, because the resurrection is the validation by God of the ministry of Jesus, the church must continue that ministry by proclaiming the word about the kingdom that Jesus himself preached. In the words of David Buttrick, 'The community was commissioned to continue Christ's preaching, now unquestionably validated by his resurrection. The kingdom *was*, the new age *had begun*, because, though judged, condemned, and crucified, Christ had risen' (Buttrick, 1987, p. 450).

Moving in the other direction, the claim that Jesus is Lord implies an always evolving connection of the gospel to the present world of the listener; preaching announces that Jesus is Lord for you, for us, for our world, and in certain specific ways. The first witnesses to the resurrection did not stop with the announcement that Jesus had risen. They went on to connect this claim to the persons and to the present life of the community by saying that he had 'appeared to Simon' (Luke 24: 34) and that he was made known to them in the 'breaking of the bread' (Luke 24: 35). Christian preaching is not simply the recapitulation of the biblical story; it is also risky interpretation of how that story connects to the world at hand. 'Such interpretation,' says Brueggemann, 'is the work of preaching. The preacher is not simply to announce the old solutions. The faith question before the congregation is fresh and requires new interpretation.'

The central Christian claim of the resurrection of Jesus necessitates that the whole story of God's action in and for the world be told and that the implications of this story be spelled out in concrete terms for the hearers. This means that a particular Christian sermon may not directly mention the resurrection at all. Sermons are fashioned to multiple needs in the Christian community. They may treat a story from the Old Testament, reflect upon some theological or ethical challenge facing the hearers, explore the implications of the gospel for the institutional life of the church, or attend to some other task. The resurrection is, however, the sun around which the solar system of Christian preaching moves. Even when it is not directly visible, the resurrection gives energy to every Christian sermon and maintains its true orbit.

Preaching as one form of proclamation Preaching, though a specialized activity involving the proclamation of the gospel to the world in missionary settings and the building up of the community faith in a liturgical setting, is not separated from other speech acts in and by the church. This can be seen in Luke 24: 35 by virtue of the connection of the Easter announcement to the ongoing conversation of the community ('then they told what had happened on the road') and to the eucharistic worship of the community (the 'breaking of bread'). The theological continuity between preaching, as the central and 'official' form of proclamation, and all the other ways in which the Christian community proclaims its message through speech, dance, song, conversation and art has been a particular emphasis of contemporary feminist theology. Rebecca Chopp, writing from a feminist perspective, affirms that preaching is but one form of the larger category of proclamation: '[Proclamation] loosens its confinement in the preached word, becoming now the fullness of discourse: the images, stories, voices, symbols, interpretations, and aesthetic productions that Christianity offers in solidarity with a world so desperately seeking to speak of freedom in new ways' (Chopp, 1989, p. 4).

The restoration of peace between God and humanity The overriding purpose of preaching is congruent with the primary aim of the gospel itself: the restoration of peace between God and estranged humanity. Luke tells us the consequence of the Easter affirmation: 'While they were talking about this, Jesus himself stood among them and said to them, "Peace be with you"' (Luke 24: 36). Preaching that seeks peace between God and humanity gives voice to the double hermeneutic implied in the resurrection itself, a refutation of the powers of sin and death, which hold sway over human history, and an affirmation of life offered by God through Christ, a saying 'no to the practices of history in the midst of God's yes to the possibilities of the world' (Chopp, 1989, p. 102).

The expectation of faith Preaching, then, hopes for and expects the response of faith and obedience. 'Christ ought to be preached,' said

Luther, 'to the end that faith in him may be established, that he may not only be Christ, but Christ for you and me.' Through preaching God recreates the church as a community of people who believe the good news that they are forgiven and restored and offer their lives in response to it. 'Every Christian proclamation,' states Jürgen Moltmann, 'is an expression in one way or another of "I absolve thee". Redemption is properly only expressed in language that sets free . . . (that) makes new life possible and allows frontiers to be crossed' (Moltmann, [1975] 1977, pp. 223–4).

The sermon as the Word of God

Recent theologies of preaching, especially Protestant varieties, have been deeply concerned with the relationship between the human word and the divine Word in preaching. They have seen in preaching not only an activity of the church, an expression of human religious discourse, but also an act of God. Christian preaching is not simply *about* the Christian event; it is a *continuation* of the Christian event. Preaching is more than merely 'telling the story', saying words about Christ; in preaching, Christ is genuinely present. Some theologians have even applied the term 'sacrament', and along with it the theology of the real presence of Christ, to the activity of preaching (see Farmer, 1942, p. 15). The risen Christ is both the subject and the object of proclamation.

'The preaching of the Word of God is the Word of God', boldly stated the Second Helvetic Confession. Embodied in this claim is a paradox, and it was Karl Barth who most graphically described its poles: 'As ministers we ought to speak of God. We are human, however, and so cannot speak of God. We ought therefore to recognize our obligation and our inability, and by that very recognition give God the glory' (Barth, [1925] 1928, p. 186).

If it was true, as Barth claimed, that speaking of God was not only an obligation but also an impossibility, then how could preaching, which inescapably involves human speech, in any sense be called the Word of God? Barth's answer was that God freely and graciously chooses to speak through the words of the preacher, but in a way not at all dependent upon the capacities or powers of the human instrument. 'Proclamation,' Barth claimed, 'is human language in and through which God speaks, like a king through the mouth of his herald . . .' (Barth, [1932] 1936, p. 57).

When another Swiss theologian, Emil Brunner, objected that Barth had stated the separation too sharply between the divine and human spirit and proposed that even in fallen humanity there remained some formal 'capacity for revelation' or 'point of contact' for the proclamation of the gospel, Barth responded with a thundering '*Nein!*'. 'If . . . there is an encounter and community between God and humanity,' Barth insisted, 'then God, himself, must have created for it conditions which are not in the least supplied (not even "somehow," not even "to some extent"!) by the existence of the formal [possibility of being addressed]' (Barth, [1934] 1946, p. 85).

Barth, with his vigorous emphasis upon preaching as the unilateral act of God towards humanity, and Brunner, with his affirmation of some prior readiness in humanity to hear the gospel, articulated well the opposing ends of the kerygmatic (or Word of God) theology of preaching, and most contemporary theologies of preaching have either taken up some aspect of their relative positions or attempted to forge a middle way between them. The liberal tradition in Protestant thought, most clearly exemplified by the 'project' or 'life situation' approach to preaching of the American Harry Emerson Fosdick and to some extent by the theology of Paul Tillich, and most Roman Catholic understandings of preaching, clearly stand closer to Brunner's side of the debate, by virtue of its claim that the human situation poses questions, that is to say, general religious needs, to which the gospel supplies responses. There is, in other words, something already present in human experience that prepares humanity for the hearing of the gospel.

Bultmann, on the other hand, stood closer to Barth. 'The word of preaching,' he states, 'confronts us as the word of God. It is not for us to question its credentials. It is we who are questioned . . .' (Bultmann, [1948] 1961, p. 41). Bultmann moved a bit towards the middle, however, by connecting faith in the word of preaching to human self-understanding. 'Faith and belief,' he said, 'are never blind, arbitrary decisions. They offer us the alternative between accepting or rejecting that which alone can illuminate our understanding of ourselves' (pp. 41–2).

However, there are at least two serious problems with the positions of Barth and Brunner and their heirs. First, largely missing is any coherent and highly developed doctrine of the church. Most of the neo-orthodox kerygmatic theologies are basically individualistic, assuming that preaching is a transaction between God (or the gospel) and individuals through the intermediate term of the preacher (though Barth's later work shows modification right on this point). Second, it is difficult, especially working from the Barthian end of the spectrum, to create a meaningful practical theology. When preaching is so strongly described as the work of God alone, it is difficult to provide meaningful descriptions of the roles and responsibilities of the preacher, the sermon and the listeners, save some vague assertions about the call to be obedient. How, for example, does one develop a theological analysis of sermon structure or of the rhetoric of preaching when one has, in advance, declared the human capacities in the preaching moment to be theologically out of bounds?

One of the more promising recent developments has been a renewed emphasis upon ecclesiology as the starting point for developing a theology of preaching. Rather than beginning with an abstract concept of 'the Word of God' as an event transcending all context, an ecclesiological approach to the theology of preaching takes seriously the claim, expressed in the following way by Moltmann, that 'the proclamation of the gospel always belongs within a community, for every language lives in a community or creates one' (Moltmann, [1975] 1977, p. 224).

The ecclesiological approach neither needs to discover some universal capacity in individuals for hearing the gospel (as in Brunner), nor is it required on methodological grounds to deny such (as in Barth). It starts rather with the phenomenon of the church, a fellowship gathered around the gospel story and possessing the conviction that as it retells, celebrates and lives out that story in worship and mission, it is, through the Holy Spirit, in the presence of the living Christ.

This approach offers the possibility of harmony between the dogmatic and practical approaches to the theology of preaching. It sees the action of God, the real presence of Christ, embedded in all that the church is and does. People do not hear the word of preaching apart from the network of relationships and commitments that make up the social texture of their lives. People are not so much compelled to belief and obedience by isolated sermons as they are by participation in a fellowship of faith that is nurtured by preaching. Christ is present to the church not simply in the discontinuous moment of preaching, but in the whole of the church's life, including preaching.

This means that the preacher can be understood not primarily as the herald, one who arrives from the outside, but as a witness, one who is commissioned by the church to encounter the biblical story on behalf of the church and then to tell the truth about what has been heard and experienced there (see Long, 1989, pp. 19–47). Preaching, therefore, assumes a variety of voices – announcing news, singing doxologies, providing instruction, pondering moral and institutional dilemmas – as the gospel works its way into the life of the church.

See also LITURGY AND DOCTRINE; PASTORAL THEOLOGY; SPIRITUALITY, CHRISTIAN.

Bibliography

Barth, Karl [1925] 1928: The word of God and the task of the ministry. In *The Word of God and the Word of Man*, trans. D. Horton. New York: Pilgrim Press, pp. 183–217.

Barth, Karl [1932] 1936: *Church Dogmatics* I/1: *The Doctrine of the Word of God*, trans. Edinburgh: T & T Clark.

Barth, Karl [1934] 1946: No! answer to Emil Brunner. In E. Brunner, *Natural Theology*, trans. Peter Fraenkel. London: Centenary Press, pp. 67–134.

Brueggemann, Walter 1989: *Finally Comes the Poet: Daring Speech for Proclamation*. Minneapolis: Fortress Press.

Bultmann, Rudolph [1948] 1961: New testament and mythology. In *Kerygma and Myth: Rudolph Bultmann and Five Critics*, ed. Hans Werner Bartsch, trans. New York: Harper and Row, pp. 1–44.

Buttrick, David 1987: *Homiletic: Moves and Structures*. Philadelphia: Fortress Press.

Buttrick, David 1988: *Preaching Jesus Christ: An Exercise in Homiletic Theology*. Philadelphia: Fortress Press.

Chopp, Rebecca S. 1989: *The Power to Speak: Feminism, Language, God*. New York: Crossroad.

Duke, Robert W. 1980: *The Sermon as God's Word: Theologies for Preaching*. Nashville: Abingdon Press.

Farmer, H.H. 1942: *The Servant of the Word*. Philadelphia: Fortress Press.

Fichtner, Joseph, OSC 1981: *To Stand and Speak for Christ: A Theology of Preaching*. New York: Alba House.

Forsyth, P.T. 1964: *Positive Preaching and the Modern Mind*. Grand Rapids: Eerdmans.

Leith, John H. 1988: *The Reformed Imperative: What the Church Has to Say That No One Else Can Say*. Philadelphia: Westminster Press.

Lischer, Richard 1981: *A Theology of Preaching*. Nashville: Abingdon Press.

Long, Thomas G. 1989: *The Witness of Preaching*. Louisville, Ky: Westminster Press.

Moltmann, Jürgen [1975] 1977: *The Church in the Power of the Spirit*, trans. New York: Harper and Row.

Stuempfle, Herman G., Jr 1978: *Preaching Law and Gospel*. Philadelphia: Fortress Press.

Wood, Charles M. 1981: *The Formation of Christian Understanding: An Essay in Theological Hermeneutics*. Philadelphia: Westminster Press.

THOMAS G. LONG

Presbyterianism In its broadest context Presbyterianism is defined first of all in ecclesiastical terms as being one of the three main forms of church government (the other two being episcopal and congregational), in which the church is governed by presbyters (that is, elders, from the Greek (*presbuteros*); and second in doctrinal terms as sharing in the theological agenda of John Calvin (1509–1564) and his followers. Furthermore, as part of the worldwide church, Presbyterianism is identified as being both Protestant and Reformed. Thus, the roots of Presbyterian identity derive from two primary sources; first from the New Testament witness to the development of the early, apostolic church, and second from the development of the Protestant Reformation in the sixteenth century under the direction of Calvin and his successors. It is from these biblical and historical roots that the contemporary Presbyterian church has developed. Thus, while its biblical identity derives from the New Testament witness concerning the early apostolic church, the identity of modern Presbyterianism is primarily bound to its theological and ecclesiastical beginnings in sixteenth-century Europe and their subsequent developments throughout the world.

Presbyterianism in the British Isles
The roots of modern Presbyterianism in the British Isles may be traced back to John Knox (1514–1571) and to the historical developments throughout England, Scotland and Ireland during the late sixteenth and the entire seventeenth centuries. The ecclesiastical, political, social and cultural conflicts of this period led to the outbreak of Civil War (1642), which involved those in England and Scotland who were supportive of and/or committed to Presbyterianism. In an attempt to end the Civil War, parliament sought the support of the Scots, and to that end the Solemn League and Covenant (an agreement between the English and the Scots which stated that in return for Scottish military assistance the English agreed to a programme of Presbyterian reform in the English, Scottish and Irish churches) was approved (1643). The first act of parliament was to abolish the episcopal system and the calling of the Westminster Assembly (1647). Along with the Scots Confession of 1560, the Westminster Confession of Faith and its catechisms became the essential foundation of modern Presbyterianism in England, Scotland and Ireland, as well as in the USA.

The restoration of the monarchy in England (1660) and the passing of the Act of Uniformity (1662) by the new parliament ended any hopes for the implementation of Presbyterian reforms. Through much of the late seventeenth and early eighteenth centuries Presbyterianism in England suffered heavy losses. However, in northern England many congregations maintained their Presbyterian loyalties, mainly due to their close relationships with fellow Presbyterians in Scotland and Ireland, where the Revolution Settlement (1688–9) provided for the subsequent establishment of the Church of Scotland.
Scotland To a great extent, from this point on Presbyterianism became most closely associated with developments within the Church of Scotland, which increasingly and affectionately was referred to as 'Mother Kirk' (mother church). Over the centuries there have been many changes and developments in the Church of Scotland, as well as a proliferation of

dissenting Presbyterian churches, usually grounded in either theological disputes or political allegiances.

One of the most contentious issues during this period was 'lay patronage', whereby wealthy laypeople were granted the right of appointing ministers for the congregations in their region. This caused many divisions among Presbyterians in Scotland, the worst being in 1843 when Thomas Chalmers led a third of the ministers and elders and almost all of the missionaries out of the Church of Scotland and called itself the Free Church of Scotland. However in 1874 lay patronage was abolished and each congregation was given the right to elect its own ministers. In 1900 the Free Presbyterian Church and the United Presbyterian Church of Scotland merged into the United Free Presbyterian Church of Scotland. While many other smaller Presbyterian churches and bodies continued to exist, the two largest bodies of Presbyterians (the Church of Scotland and the United Free Church of Scotland) merged in 1929 to form the present-day Church of Scotland. The membership of this body currently stands at over two million and is the largest body of Presbyterians in the United Kingdom.

Since its humble beginnings in 1560 when Presbyterianism in Scotland numbered six ministers and thirty-five elders, the Church of Scotland's General Assembly now numbers over twelve hundred commissioners. The synods of the Church of Scotland are becoming less and less a factor, while presbyteries and kirk sessions continue to be active in the overall life and ministry of the church. However, there are three tendencies in the Church of Scotland that are important: (1) the increasing centralization of the Church of Scotland, evidenced by the growing number of General Assembly committees and offices being established and staffed in Edinburgh; (2) the pattern of decreasing membership of the Church of Scotland over the past few decades, which shows little sign of reversal; (3) the relationship of the Church of Scotland to the growing independence movement, which seeks Scottish independence from Great Britain.

The Church of Scotland has been very influential in the historical and theological development of Christianity generally and of Presbyterianism specifically. This is true for

467

several reasons. First, it has been deeply committed to the theological enterprise. Some of the greatest theological institutions and scholars are associated with the Church of Scotland: institutions such as Edinburgh, Aberdeen, St Andrews and Glasgow, and scholars such as Donald and John Baillie, Thomas and James Torrance and others. Second: the Church of Scotland has been deeply involved in both the missionary enterprise (especially in China and India) and the ecumenical movement of the twentieth century. In both cases it has been at the forefront. Third, and closely related to the previous point, the Church of Scotland has been instrumental in the 'planting' of Presbyterianism in other lands, especially in Ireland and subsequently in the USA and Canada.

Ireland The Presbyterian church in Ireland dates from the Plantation of Ulster in the seventeenth century, when the English parliament as well as adverse social conditions encouraged many Scots to settle in the north of Ireland. Again, the influence of the Church of Scotland in the establishment of Presbyterianism cannot be underestimated, as it sought to provide ministry to those migrating to Ireland. The first presbytery was established in 1642, and by 1659 there were five. However, the Scots-Irish began to experience political, economic and religious conflicts in the late seventeenth and early eighteenth centuries, due primarily to decisions taken by the English parliament in relation to the Irish, as well as to severe drought and starvation. This subsequently led to mass migration from Ireland (and Scotland) to America, where the Scots-Irish exerted a significant influence on life in the early colonies, on the revolutionary ferment which led to the colonies' Revolutionary War with England, and on the establishment of the USA (see below).

One of the largest controversies to beset the Irish Presbyterian church occurred during the eighteenth century, when an internal conflict arose between conservatives ('Old Lights') and liberal radicals ('New Lights'). Central to the debate was the question of subscription to the Westminster Confession of Faith. The 'New Lights' and non-subscribers in the Synod of Ulster prevailed, but the conflict led to the formation of several congregations and presbyt-

eries of Seceders who adhered to subscription to the Westminster Confession of Faith (the Presbyterian Synod of Ireland-Seceders).

Throughout the late eighteenth and the early nineteenth centuries both synods were deeply affected by the evangelical-revivalist movement that was sweeping the British Isles. The effect was that the ethos of the Synod of Ulster (the New Light Presbyterians) became more orthodox and evangelical, mainly as the result of another internal conflict during the 1820s which ended in the practice of subscription to the Westminster Confession of Faith being restored in 1835. This led to a new spirit of cooperation between the two synods, particularly in relation to world missions and the task of evangelizing the Irish people, who were in the midst of significant population growth due to industrialization and urbanization. By 1840 the Synod of Ulster had 292 congregations and the Synod of Ireland (Seceders) had 141 congregations. Throughout the 1830s various discussions and proposals were made for the union of the two synods, and this process was completed when in June 1840 the two synods reunited in Belfast as the reconstituted Presbyterian Church in Ireland.

In 1921 the partition between Northern Ireland and the Republic of Ireland was established. The Presbyterian Church in Ireland continued to play a significant role, especially in Northern Ireland. However, the Presbyterian Church in Ireland, particularly since the current 'troubles' began in the late 1960s, continues to struggle for its identity both internally and externally. Several recent General Assemblies have focused upon doctrinal disputes, ecumenical relations (especially with Roman Catholics and membership of the World Council of Churches) and the role of the church in a divided society (especially with regard to political and cultural aspirations).

England Following the union of the English and Scottish parliaments (1707), there was a marked renewal in Presbyterianism in England as the Scots began to settle in the major cities of England and establish independent Presbyterian churches. These churches then sought recognition as a synod of the Church of Scotland. However the General Assembly rejected such overtures and encouraged them to organize as the Presbyterian Church in England. This process began in 1836 and was completed in 1842, when several independent Presbyterian congregations joined with congregations in the Presbytery of Northumberland which had been established as early as 1783. There was a further organization of several other associations of Presbyterian churches in England (in 1847 and 1863) calling itself an English Synod of the United Presbyterian Church. In 1876 these two branches of Presbyterianism in England united as the Presbyterian Church of England, consisting of 260 congregations, ten presbyteries and around 50,000 members.

During the late nineteenth century and into the twentieth century the Presbyterian Church of England grew to over 350 congregations with over 60,000 members. Many of its ministers were called from the Church of Scotland and the Presbyterian Church in Ireland, but increasingly the Presbyterian Church of England began to train its own ministers at what became known as Westminster College (originally founded in London in 1844), located in Cambridge since 1899. Among the church's more notable theologians can be mentioned John Oman, H.H. Farmer and Colin Gunton. The church was also deeply involved in global missions (particularly in China and India) and in the ecumenical movement.

In 1972 the Presbyterian Church of England united with the Congregational Church to form the United Reformed Church (the URC). While affirming the essential doctrines of the Reformed tradition, the URC continues to manifest a revised form of Presbyterian government wherein ministers and elders are members of the various councils of the URC. There are twelve provincial moderators who give general oversight to the congregations under the guidance and direction of the General Assembly. In very recent times there has been an ongoing dialogue between the United Reformed Church and the Methodist Church in England concerning possible unification. Oddly enough the Church of Scotland continues to have a presbytery in England consisting of nine congregations, and the Presbyterian Church of Wales has over fifty congregations in England, most of which are Welsh-speaking churches.

The future of Presbyterianism in England is a point of continuing debate as its numbers continue to decrease. Two issues are at the forefront of this discussion; first, there is the question concerning the role of nonconforming churches in relation to the Church of England, and second, directly related to the first issue, is the nature of Presbyterian identity in possible further unifications between the URC and other Christian denominations (such as the Methodists).

Presbyterianism in the USA

The roots of Presbyterianism in the USA may be traced primarily back to English and Scots-Irish immigration into the North American continent. The earliest settlers to the American colonies were the English Puritans who settled in New England. Having left England in 1641 just before the Civil War, the Puritans were those who had sought to 'purify' the Church of England of Roman Catholic influences and of government control through the English monarchy. The Puritans came to America with a vision of establishing a community founded upon the law and purposes of God that would be a Christian witness to the whole world. Therefore they were committed to a strictly disciplined lifestyle based upon their definitions of orthodoxy in both faith and practice, which in turn had specific implications for both the church and society. Their settlement concentrated in what became known as New England.

The second major influence upon early Presbyterianism in America was the immigration of the Scots-Irish. There were two main waves of Scots-Irish immigration: the first during the late seventeenth century to the mid-eighteenth century, and the second during the middle of the nineteenth century to the early twentieth century. While the Scots-Irish did settle in New England, they also moved further south and west and settled in what became New Jersey, Pennsylvania, Delaware and Maryland, and later in Ohio and the Carolinas (North and South). Together, the Puritans and the Scots-Irish Presbyterians provided the essential ideological, cultural and political framework for early America.

With the formulation of the Presbytery of Philadelphia in 1706, Presbyterianism in America became more defined in its form and content. Concerned for the orthodoxy of the church, the Synod of Philadelphia adopted the Westminster

Confession of Faith as the doctrinal standard of American Presbyterianism in 1729. It was during this period that controversy arose within Presbyterianism, primarily focusing upon issues related to the vitality of spiritual piety among clergy and laity alike. Led by Gilbert Tennent, there was a call for a 'conversion' of the Presbyterian ministry; for ministers who would be both orthodox in their theological doctrine and passionate in their Christian piety.

In the early 1740s there was a major division between the 'revivalists' or 'New Side' Presbyterians (including Gilbert Tennent, George Whitefield and Jonathan Edwards) and the 'Old Side' Presbyterians, who were primarily committed to doctrinal orthodoxy as the mark of true Christianity. The New Side prevailed, and revivalist preaching began to bear fruit as new churches were established, younger clergy were trained and societal institutions were founded by those associated with the New Side. The New Side appeared to demonstrate a better awareness of the spiritual needs of those coming to the New World from the Old World. From henceforth this New Side emphasis upon a strong commitment to personal piety and religious experience became an essential element of mainstream Presbyterianism in America.

Leading up to the American Revolutionary War, Presbyterians were divided between loyalty to the English monarch and the revolutionary spirit which sought independence from the English monarchy. However, when the Declaration of Independence was issued (1776) and the Revolutionary War broke out, Presbyterians were almost unanimously supportive of the war. John Witherspoon, a prominent Presbyterian minister and academic, signed the Declaration of Independence and many Presbyterians were involved in the writing of the United States Constitution. The Presbyterian church was also supportive of Thomas Jefferson's attempts to disestablish the Church of England in the colonies before the war. Following the Revolutionary War and the adoption of the United States Constitution, in 1787 the Presbyterian church adopted a declaration of religious freedom which not only expressed the Presbyterian position concerning the relationship between church and state, but also became an expression of the religious ethos of the newly founded United States of America. It basically affirmed that God alone is Lord of the conscience and that all people are free to exercise their conscience as an expression of their right to private judgement in all religious matters of faith and practice.

As Presbyterianism grew in the American colonies before, during and after the Revolutionary War, its organizational structure changed to accommodate such growth, even to the point that in 1788 the General Assembly of the Presbyterian Church in America was established and was able to meet for the first time in July 1789.

As America grew and moved westward during the early part of the nineteenth century, the Presbyterian church linked with the Congregationalists in a cooperative plan (Plan of Union in 1801) for the establishment of new churches on the American frontiers. During this period, many developments were taking place in the training of Presbyterian ministers. Harvard College abandoned all commitment to any standard of doctrinal definition and later became a centre of unitarianism. Presbyterian evangelicals established Andover Seminary (1808) with the aim of training 'orthodox' ministers who would adhere to the essential doctrines of the Reformed and Presbyterian tradition. However, out of their suspicions of the Plan of Union (believing that it would lead to the erosion of orthodoxy and piety) and their perceptions of negative developments within many traditional strongholds of education (such as Harvard), another internal conflict arose among Presbyterians which divided between the 'Old School' (critics of the Plan of Union) and the 'New School' (supporters of the Plan of Union) in 1837. The 'New School' was behind the founding of Union Theological Seminary in New York City (1836), while the 'Old School' continued to support Princeton Seminary, which had been established in 1812 after separating itself from Princeton College and becoming an autonomous institution for the education of the clergy.

The role of Princeton Seminary in the history of Presbyterianism in the USA cannot be underestimated. Arguably, Princeton has been the centre of the only true American school of theology, known simply as 'Princeton theology'. Theologians associated with the Princeton school of theology during the nineteenth and early twentieth centuries include Archibald Alexander (1772–1851); Charles Hodge (1797-1878); Archibald Alexander Hodge (1823–1886); Benjamin Warfield (1851–1921) and of course J. Gresham Machen (1881–1937). In more recent times Princeton Seminary has had such notable scholars as John Mackay, James McCord and Bruce Metzger, to name a few.

The division between Old School and New School Presbyterianism continued throughout the nineteenth century. Two ecclesiastical divisions occurred in 1810 when the Presbytery of Cumberland, Kentucky, broke away from the General Assembly, along with the formulation of the Christian Church (Disciples of Christ), many of whom were Presbyterians.

The slavery issue exposed the divisions even more greatly. The Old School and New School had reached an 'agreement' whereby the northern Old School leaders agreed not to condemn slavery in exchange for the support of the Presbyterian churches in the south. However, increasingly the New School in the north began to support the movement towards the abolishment of slavery more actively.

With the withdrawal of the Confederate States of the south came the establishment of the Presbyterian Church in the United States ('southern Presbyterians') after 1865; an attempt to reunite the division of 1837 was successful and the Presbyterian Church in the United States of America was re-established in 1870.

Throughout the nineteenth century and into the early twentieth century many Presbyterians in New England and elsewhere identified themselves with unitarianism and/or the New School, thereby continuing the theological and doctrinal controversies, particularly over the issues of biblical authority, the use of the historical-critical method of biblical interpretation and the affirmation of the essential tenets of the Presbyterian traditions.

These controversies led to more division, this time between the 'fundamentalists' (led by J. Gresham Machen of Princeton Seminary) and the 'modernists'. In 1936 Machen, having already established an Independent Board of Foreign Missions, organized the Orthodox Presbyterian Church, a church that was intended to be more faithful to the theology of John Calvin and the Westminster Confession of Faith.

While these controversies continued throughout the 1920s and 1930s the Presbyterian Church in the United States of America continued to grow. However, there were obvious signs that the Old School–New School division within the Presbyterian church remained, particularly in relation to how the church should relate to modern developments in American society. Immediately after the Second World War Presbyterianism experienced another period of significant growth, and was encouraged by developments in the Sunday school movement, in the task of worldwide evangelism and in its involvement in the ecumenical movement after the first meeting of the World Council of Churches in Amsterdam in 1948.

However since the period of the 1960s mainline Presbyterianism has suffered tremendous loss in membership. Continuing debates on social and political issues have remained fierce and manifested a politicization of the church between conservatives and liberals, particularly on issues as diverse as war and peace, abortion, sexual lifestyles, race relations, wealth and poverty, women's rights, inter-religious dialogue and ecumenical relations.

There has also been a consolidation of theological identity within the Presbyterian Church in the United States of America as its book of creeds and confessions has grown to eleven creeds, confessions, catechisms and declarations, most of which date back to the period from the early church through to the Protestant Reformation, yet including the Barmen Declaration from Germany (1934) as well as the Confession of 1967 and the Brief Statement of Faith of 1991.

There are at present nine different denominations in the USA that call themselves Presbyterian. Essentially, they may be categorized in the following way:

1 Presbyterian churches which have strong European roots;
2 Presbyterian churches which have been the result of various mergers and unions through the centuries;

3 Presbyterian churches which are the result of doctrinal, ecclesiological or political divisions.

The vast majority of Presbyterians in the USA are those in the Presbyterian Church in the United States of America (PCUSA), which exists by virtue of a merger in 1983 between the mostly southern United Presbyterian Church in the United States of America (UPCUSA) and the mostly northern Presbyterian Church in the United States (PCUS). The membership of the PCUSA numbers approximately three million. The other major Presbyterian churches in the United States include the Orthodox Presbyterian Church (OPC), the Presbyterian Church in America (PCA) and the Evangelical Presbyterian Church (EPC).

The future of Presbyterianism is coloured by the continued loss of membership among mainline Presbyterians. This parallels the losses by other mainline churches in the USA (especially the Methodists and the Episcopals). The focal points of the future appear to be in the moves of the ecumenical movement towards Christian unity and its development of a Christian approach to religious pluralism, as well as in the role of the church in America generally.

In 1988 the PCUSA moved its denominational headquarters from New York City to Louisville, Kentucky. In the move there was a great deal of denominational reorganization, streamlining and decentralization. This has demonstrated the real impact of diminishing membership and influence of the PCUSA. Facing the Presbyterian church is the question of how it may be relevant to the needs of a changing America and a changing world. Will the church meet the widespread need and desire for spiritual direction and renewal in an age of increased secularity? Will the church maintain continuity with its historical and theological roots? Will the church continue to be more concerned with social and political concerns to the neglect of the spiritual and theological issues of modern America?

Whatever the future holds for Presbyterianism in the USA, it is clear that the current state of Presbyterianism in America may largely be traced to the fact that the perpetual conflict between the Old Side/School and the New Side/School is still unresolved. Throughout its history over the past two centuries this debate has continued, with each side prevailing at different times, in different places and under different leadership. It has also led to further divisions among Presbyterians in America. The main question therefore must be asked: in the light of the continuing membership losses in the PCUSA and the continuing division among Presbyterians in America, will there be a demise of influence of the New School which has prevailed in recent decades, and will a return of the Old School revive the Presbyterian church in the USA in such a way that it may have both a powerful spiritual and social witness?

See also EVANGELICALISM: USA; FUNDAMENTALISM; PROTESTANT THEOLOGY (BRITAIN and USA).

Bibliography

Loetscher, Lefferts A. 1983: *A Brief History of the Presbyterians*. Philadelphia: Westminster Press.

Longfield, Bradley 1990: *The Presbyterian Controversy*. Oxford: Oxford University Press.

McKim, Donald, ed. 1992: *Encyclopedia of the Reformed Faith*. Louisville: Westminster/John Knox Press.

Rogers, Jack 1991: *Presbyterian Creeds*. Louisville: Westminster/John Knox Press.

BRYAN BURTON

process theology Process theology conceives the world to be a social organism, an interdependent and interrelated whole, growing towards its satisfaction through a network of mutual influences among which are the persuasive aims of God; in this process, God is affected by the world as well as affecting it. The theology is based upon process philosophy as formulated by Alfred North Whitehead, especially in his systematic treatment *Process and Reality* ([1929] 1967), and as developed by Whitehead's pupil Charles Hartshorne. Modern influences upon process thought can be traced in G.W.F. Hegel, William James, H. Bergson and C.S. Pierce.

In contrast to traditional metaphysics based on substance and essence, reality according to process philosophy is characterized by becoming, change and event. The basic building blocks of reality at a subatomic level are understood as events of extremely brief duration, which reach a peak of satisfaction and then perish, to be succeeded in the stream of life by other entities. These droplets of becoming, or 'actual entities', can also be called 'actual occasions' or occasions of experience, and they all enjoy some kind of feeling appropriate to their level of existence. Change happens against a background of permanence, which is the organizing principle of growth itself. All entities have some freedom to create themselves, growing towards a feeling of satisfaction through a process of 'concrescence' during which they 'prehend' (i.e. grasp) data of experience from a number of sources. They receive influence in this way from previous entities and from God, who is thus the ground of both order and novelty. Growth is possible because each entity is dipolar (the term 'bipolar' is also sometimes used), having a mental and physical aspect to its being. Through its physical pole it prehends past entities in its environment as well as God, and thereby grows to satisfaction; through its mental pole it can grasp ideals and values, called 'eternal objects'.

It is a key principle of process thought, then, that causation is a matter of influence and persuasion, not coercion. Entities influence others by presenting themselves to be objectified within another's experience (in an external relationship), and so entities are influenced by others when they themselves freely grasp hold of others (in an internal relationship); when an entity has reached satisfaction and has perished, it ceases to be a subject and becomes an object to be prehended by others in a process of 'transition'. Thus entities build up into 'societies', which are the large-scale objects in the world that we normally perceive – stones, chairs, people. If there is a build-up of the mental pole in the process of transition, then entities of a high degree of mentality are formed which finally emerge as consciousness, whereas inanimate objects are formed through a build-up of physical stability. Process thought, conceiving the world as an organic whole moving in a purposeful way towards the gaining of values, thus takes the human experience of being mind and body and possessing creativity as a clue to the whole nature of reality.

God's action is, like that of the actual entities, persuasive and not coercive. God 'keeps the rules' of the process, and so he is also dipolar, though this is envisaged in a rather different way by Whitehead and Hartshorne. Whitehead regards God as an actual entity, though unlike all other actual entities he does not perish. His mental pole is a 'primordial nature' which is immutable and in which he envisages all the possibilities there are for the world ('a vision of eternal objects'); these he sorts into values, graded by their relevance to any particular situations whatever, and from them he presents each actual entity with an 'initial aim' as it sets forth on its path of growth towards satisfaction. In its forming of its own 'subjective aim' or sense of purpose, however, the entity is free to aim for intensity of feeling in ways that may accept, modify or reject the divine influence. While God's primordial nature is independent of the world (and even unconscious of it), he also has a 'consequent nature' corresponding to a physical aspect, by which he himself prehends the world and is thus affected and 'caused' by it. Here he absorbs the effects of worldly action and decision into himself, and is the 'fellow-sufferer who understands' (Whitehead, [1929] 1967, p. 532). Indeed, all entities have a kind of eternal life in God, an 'objective immortality' in that the values they have achieved are preserved within the divine consequent being.

Hartshorne, however, understands the dipolarity of God by analogy not with an actual entity but with a human person, that is as a 'society' of entities. He names God's world-independent aspect as his 'abstract essence' and his world-dependent aspect as his 'concrete aspect', these corresponding to the enduring character of a person or his 'bare, individual existence' and the many actual states of his experience. Associated with this shift of perspective is Hartshorne's disagreement with Whitehead that God can envisage all possibilities for the world in his primordial nature; this seems to him to restrict the freedom of actual entities, as values must be able to emerge newly from the creative advance rather than being entirely offered by God. So the abstract essence of God does not contain a vision of detailed possibilities, but is the ground of possibility for his concrete aspect which is a kind of receptacle for all worldly experience and achievement, and by which God is supremely related to the world. The aim which God offers to entities is therefore not specific, but a general setting of limits for their decisions, mitigating the risk and maximizing the promise of freedom.

God's persuasive causation is thus of two kinds, stemming both from his vision of possibility and from his experience of actuality. In his dipolar nature he persuades both by his aims and by his sufferings as he offers himself to be prehended by the world. First he offers an aim, understood either as specific possibilities that will make for maximum satisfaction and beauty (Whitehead) or as a general purposefulness that sets boundaries for healthy choices (Hartshorne). Second, all entities are influenced as they feel the effects of their decisions and actions upon God, and as they feel his evaluation and harmonizing of these effects within the 'creative synthesis' of his consequent or concrete aspect. Divine causation *necessarily* takes this form of being conditioned by creaturely freedom because it is so demanded by creativity, which is the ultimate principle of reality rather than God himself.

Process theology thus concentrates attention on the nature of God's activity, redefining omnipotence in terms of persuasion. Correspondingly, omniscience is understood as God's perfect knowledge of both possibility and actuality, without equating the two. While perfect in his total relation to all past and present actuality, God continually 'surpasses himself' as he embraces newly emergent actuality that could not be foreknown in detail. Divine love, it is stressed, must mean being affected and changed by those who are loved (Hartshorne, 1967, p. 75). Critics, however, have questioned whether the two aspects of God's being – the necessary and the contingent, the immutable and the mutable, the unrelated and the related – are properly integrated with each other in process thought. In reply, some process theologians in the tradition of Whitehead have proposed that God forms the initial aims in his primordial nature through drawing upon experience of the world within his consequent nature; so through 'propositional feelings' he imagines what it would be like for an entity to realize the particular values he envisages (for example Cobb, 1966, p. 156). Hartshorne aims at a wholeness between the abstract and concrete aspects of God through his analogy with a person, though it should be observed that the analogy is not exact as the 'enduring character' of *human* persons is not totally unaffected by experience and relationships, and indeed it seems desirable for the sake of personality that it should not be.

In the application of process principles to other Christian doctrines, attempts have been made to interpret a dipolar concept of God in terms of the triune symbol. There are different versions corresponding to the two main strands of process thought; for example, in the tradition of Whitehead, Bracken (1985) argues for a divine society of primordial, consequent and (so-called) 'superjective' natures; in the tradition of Hartshorne, Ogden (1980) finds the Father to be the whole abstract essence, the Son to be the aspect in God externally related to the world (loved by all) and the Spirit the aspect internally related to the world (loving all). The relational and social view of reality, its interpretation of substance in terms of event, and the way that subjects are constituted by their 'presence' in each other seem to make process thought an apt partner for Trinitarian theology. However, while process thought certainly presents a unity and plurality within God's relationship to the world, it is difficult to find anything like inner mutual relationships between the different dimensions of God's own being.

Any process Christology must underline the free human response of Christ to the divine purpose or Logos as a way of understanding the nature of incarnation. However, theologians who follow Whitehead's account of God's vision of particular possibilities can envisage his giving an aim to Jesus which had a unique content (for example Griffin, 1973, p. 218), whereas those following Hartshorne's view of God's aim as setting general limits for human choices will find the specialness of Jesus inhering only in his responsive prehension of God (for example, Ogden, 1982, pp. 79–85). Overall, process accounts of the inclusion and eternalizing of human experience within God offer useful insights into the way that the particular historic event of Jesus can have a transforming effect upon life today.

Process theology has a distinctive contribution to make to theodicy, as it can extend the 'free-will defence' of the existence of evil and suffering beyond what is usually called the 'moral evil' of human decisions (see EVIL, PROBLEM OF). Because nature at every level is creative, it can fail to respond to the divine lure to move beyond triviality, or can fail to cooperate with the divine aim of healing the discord that accompanies greater complexity of experience (Griffin, 1976, pp. 280–3). God can only persuade his creation, not coerce it. However, it has been an often repeated criticism of process thought that while it removes responsibility for evil from God, it leaves God powerless to overcome it. An answer may be offered along several lines. First, while the effects of all past actions are present in God's world-related nature, he 'transmutes' them rather than gathering them indifferently into himself, saving what is worth preserving; thus the possible tragedy to which he opens himself is not the eternal presence of evil within his being, but the absence of some good that the world might have produced, a 'tragedy of unfulfilled desire' (Hartshorne, [1941] 1964, p. 294). Second, process theology at least provides support for hope that the persuasive love of God *will* lure creation on to the greatest possibilities of satisfaction and so to the state Whitehead called 'peace'.

Further, some process thinkers have attempted to produce a process eschatology in the sense of a conscious eternity for finite beings in whom evil has been overcome in divine harmony. Griffin (1976) has maintained that the conscious survival of human souls is not inconsistent with Whitehead's views on prehension, and, rather differently, Marjorie Suchocki (1988) has recently argued for a 'subjective immortality' of all actual entities in the consequent nature of God; she argues, in a modification of Whitehead, that at the point when actual occasions have completed concrescence and are enjoying satisfaction, God can prehend their subjective immediacy, and they can in turn subjectively experience their transformation in God.

In a theology of social affairs, process thought has an evident strength in supplying a metaphysical basis for ecology; its vision of a cosmic society challenges homocentrism and affirms the emergence of value in every part of the natural world, while recognizing differences in levels of value. Process contributions to political theology (such as Cobb, 1982) and

economic theory (such as Cobb and Daly, 1989) have thus tended to urge an ecological dimension to these areas, while taking a politically 'liberal' approach based on the primacy of persuasion.

Process thought has been of widespread influence in modern theology, even beyond the confines of those who accept the whole system of dipolar theism. Proposals such as the persuasive nature of God's activity, God's suffering with the world, and a responsiveness to divine influence at all levels of creation, have also commended themselves to theologians who prefer to root these themes in the self-limitation of the Creator rather than in the primacy of creativity.

See also GOD; PHILOSOPHICAL THEOLOGY; PROTESTANT THEOLOGY: USA; SUFFERING, DIVINE.

Bibliography

Bracken, J.A. 1985: *The Triune Symbol: Persons, Process and Community*. New York and London: University Press of America.

Cobb, J.B. 1966: *A Christian Natural Theology: Based on the Thought of Alfred North Whitehead*. London: Lutterworth Press.

Cobb, J.B. 1982: *Process Theology as Political Theology*. Manchester: Manchester University Press, Philadelphia: The Westminster Press.

Cobb, J.B., and Daly, H. 1989: *For the Common Good: Redirecting the Economy Towards Community, The Environment, and a Sustainable Future*. Boston: Beacon Press.

Cobb, J.B., and Griffin, D.R. 1976: *Process Theology: An Introductory Exposition*. Belfast: Christian Journals.

Ford, L.S. 1978: *The Lure of God: A Biblical Background for Process Theism*. Philadelphia: Fortress Press.

Griffin, D.R. 1973: *A Process Christology*. Philadelphia: The Westminster Press.

Griffin, D.R. 1976: *God, Power and Evil: A Process Theodicy*. Philadelphia: The Westminster Press.

Hartshorne, C. [1941] 1964: *Man's Vision of God, and the Logic of Theism*. Hamden: Archon Books.

Hartshorne, C. [1948] 1976: *The Divine Relativity: A Social Conception of God*. New Haven: Yale University Press.

Hartshorne, C. 1967: *A Natural Theology for our Time*. Illinois: Open Court.

Ogden, S.M. 1980: On the Trinity, *Theology* 83, pp. 97–102.

Ogden, S.M. 1982: *The Point of Christology*. London: SCM Press.

Suchocki, M.H. 1988: *The End of Evil: Process*

Eschatology in Historical Context. Albany: State University of New York Press.

Whitehead, A.N. [1929] 1967: *Process and Reality: An Essay in Cosmology*, 2nd edn. New York: Macmillan.

PAUL S. FIDDES

Protestant theology Protestantism designates the understanding of Christian beliefs and practices which arose as a result of the sixteenth-century Reformation. The term 'Protestant' came into being in the aftermath of the Second Diet of Speyer (1529), to refer to those who objected to the Diet's intolerance towards evangelical attitudes within Germany. Protestantism has generally been understood to embrace those western European and North American churches which chose to distinguish themselves from Roman Catholicism and maintain their religious independence.

Protestant thought has always been characterized by a certain spirit of restlessness, a reluctance to accept ideas on the basis of external authority, and a love for independence of thought. The Enlightenment, which made an appeal to precisely these qualities, thus had a deep impact upon Protestantism, whereas its influence upon Roman Catholicism and Eastern Orthodoxy was much less marked. 'The Renaissance was a Catholic, the Enlightenment a Protestant phenomenon' (Hugh Trevor-Roper). Protestant theology has thus been much more sensitive to intellectual and cultural developments in the secular world, especially in the universities, than – until very recently – its Roman Catholic and Orthodox equivalents. In particular, there have been strong regional variations, reflecting the different social and cultural worlds to which Protestant theology has been obliged to relate and respond during the course of its development since the eighteenth century. The opportunities for creativity are enormous, and are reflected in the complex developments of the period. Simple generalizations concerning the development of 'Protestant thought' are thus of little value, given the diversity that has emerged within global Protestantism since the Enlightenment.

Given the importance of Protestant thought to this volume, it was decided at an early stage that the only manner of approaching the subject which was capable of doing justice to its complex regional variations was to survey the subject by region, with articles on Protestant theology in Australia, Britain, Canada, Germany, the Netherlands, Scandinavia, South Africa and the USA, all following this introduction to the topic. This panoramic survey will allow an appreciation of the diversity, linked with patterns of commonality, which exists within global Protestantism at the end of the twentieth century. Each article has been written by a scholar resident in the region with a first-hand knowledge of the local situation. Also of interest will be the articles on CHINESE/INDIAN/JAPANESE/KOREAN CHRISTIAN THOUGHT.

Different traditions of Protestantism are discussed under ANGLICANISM; BAPTIST THOUGHT; DISPENSATIONALISM; EVANGELICALISM; FUNDAMENTALISM; LUTHERANISM; METHODISM; PENTECOSTALISM AND CHARISMATIC CHRISTIANITY; PRESBYTERIANISM; QUAKERISM.

See also CHRISTOLOGY; ECCLESIOLOGY; ECUMENISM; ENLIGHTENMENT; ETHICS.

Protestant theology: Australia Australia is a federation of states, each dominated by a capital. Geographical isolation and distinctive histories have resulted in each city having a particular theological tinge. There has thus come about a range of Australian Protestant theologies, in part due to the various currents of European (especially British) thought, in part due to local factors.

Until the 1920s, most theological work was restricted to preparation for denominational ministries, in isolation from the universities, since these were constituted upon secularist foundations (especially Sydney and Melbourne Universities). Only since the 1970s have local undergraduate degrees in theology been available, and Australian approaches to theology begun. In that time, however, a rapid increase in theological activity has come about, with accredited undergraduate and postgraduate programmes available in all capital cities, growing relationships with some universities, development of Aboriginal theological education and a wide range of less formal adult theological education.

The universities and theology

As with theological perspectives, so it is with university relationships: each capital has a distinctive pattern. Sydney and Queensland Universities offer (postgraduate) BD degrees, taught largely by theological college staff, but they have not attracted a great deal of support. Sydney has recently established a School of Religious Studies, as has Latrobe (Melbourne), while Macquarie (Sydney) and the Australian National University (Canberra) have history of ideas units, but none of these are used for theological education. Flinders (Adelaide) and Murdoch (Perth) offer undergraduate degrees in theology in co-operation with local colleges: this has been possible in part because these universities were founded in the last twenty years. Since 1992 joint arts/theology degrees have been offered at Monash and Melbourne (the theology components being taught by Melbourne College of Divinity institutions, however, not the universities). Most Australian tertiary institutions have no religious or theological faculties, and those that do exist are small.

Individual scholars have made their mark in university contexts. Edwin Judge and Richard Horsburgh (Macquarie) have led for some years a significant project in early Christian documents. Barbara Thiering (Sydney) specializes in Christian origins, and Qumran. Ken Cable (Sydney), Robert Withycombe (Canberra) and Stuart Piggin (Wollongong and now Macquarie) have done much work in Australian church history, as have Bruce Kaye in ethics (University of New South Wales), John Painter in New Testament (Latrobe), and John Thompson in Old Testament (now retired from Melbourne). Hans Mol and David Hickman (Australian National University) and Gary Bouma (Monash) have set forward sociological reflection on Australian religion. Education has been well served by William Andersen and Anna Hogg (Sydney) and Brian Hill (Murdoch). There are many Roman Catholic scholars active in this way as well, especially in philosophy.

Strands of Protestant theology in Australia

At least four major strands of Protestant theology are represented in contemporary Australia: conservative, ecumenical, lay-oriented, and Aboriginal.

The conservative spectrum The conservative spectrum is numerically strongest in the (Keswick) Conventions, and the Bible colleges. There is at least one of the latter in each state, ranging from small bodies to substantial degree-granting institutions. They focus on students gaining biblical knowledge, with some specializing in theology for crosscultural mission. Some denominational colleges are conservative, including those sponsored by the Lutheran church (in South Australia), the Reformed church (Geelong, Victoria), the Presbyterian church (Sydney, Brisbane and Melbourne), some Churches of Christ (Queensland and New South Wales), some Baptist Unions (Queensland, NSW, and South Australia) and the Seventh-Day Adventists (rural NSW). Anglican colleges in the conservative strand include Moore College, sponsored by the strongly evangelical diocese of Sydney, and Ridley College, Melbourne, an independent evangelical institution. Numerically the student bodies at these colleges represent by far the largest proportion of Protestant theological students in Australia.

Moore and Ridley Colleges form the major base for scholarly conservative Protestant theology. Moore's Reformed ethos was particularly shaped by the work of principals Nathaniel Jones (1897–1911), T.C. Hammond (1936–53), David Broughton Knox (1959–85) and vice-principal D.W.B. Robinson (later Archbishop of Sydney). A distinctive ecclesiology has developed around this school, centred in a distinctive eschatology, along with stress on the sovereignty of God and the rational character of divine revelation. Other scholars whose major work has been done at Moore include William Dumbrell (Old Testament), William Lawton (Australiana), Alan Cole and Peter O'Brien (New Testament). Ridley College developed a broader evangelical theology under principals Stuart Barton Babbage (1947–63), Leon Morris (1964–79) and Maurice Betteridge (1979–92). Babbage became a major statesman in theological education, especially as registrar of the Australian College of Theology (1972–91), the national Anglican examining and accrediting body. Morris is the most prolific Protestant Australian theological author, stressing the centrality of the redemptive love of God in the cross of Christ. Others associated with Ridley have included Keith Cole (church history and missions), David Williams, John Pryor and Colin Kruse (New Testament) and Charles Sherlock (liturgy and theology).

In recent years responses to the charismatic movement and feminism have seen much constructive conservative theological work in the area of biblical hermeneutics. The work of Geoffrey Bingham (New Creation Ministries, Adelaide) has also been influential in more conservative circles.

Ecumenical approaches Ecumenical approaches include the range of mainstream European Protestant theology, but with a generally conservative tone (see ECUMENISM). Its impetus has centred in the gradual coming together of Methodist, Congregational and many Presbyterian churches, which climaxed in 1977 with the formation of the Uniting Church of Australia. (Presbyterians who did not enter the union established separate theological colleges.) Melbourne is the city where ecumenical approaches are most prominent, evidenced in the cooperation between Methodist, Presbyterian, Congregational and Anglican churches there in the Melbourne College of Divinity (founded 1910). This has grown from being an external examining body into a college of teaching institutions, especially under the leadership of John Henley (dean 1975–90).

Melbourne has also been the centre of ecumenical liturgical work. Harold Leatherland, a Congregationalist with a strong liturgical interest, was a significant figure in the middle of the twentieth century: his work, together with that of the Methodist Austin James, led to the formation of the Ecumenical Liturgical Centre in 1964. Recently in this area the Uniting Church scholars D'Arcy Wood (Adelaide, now Canberra) and Robert Gribben (Melbourne) have been prominent. Roman Catholics and Protestants (of both evangelical and ecumenical orientation) now work together closely in many areas of theology and church life in Melbourne, especially through the Victorian Council of Churches.

The Methodist, Presbyterian and Congregational colleges in Melbourne joined to form the United Faculty in 1969, then moved in 1972 to join with Trinity (Anglican) and the Jesuits to form a unique integrated teaching body. Trinity

is an Anglican college of liberal catholic tradition, and has had several scholars linked with it over many years: Barry Marshall (spirituality), James Grant (church history), Max Thomas, John Gaden and Richard McKinney (theology), and John Wright (Old Testament). Protestant scholars closely associated with the work of the United Faculty of Theology include Harry Wardlaw (theology and philosophy), Davis McCaughey and Nigel Watson (New Testament), Ian Breward (church history), John Bodycomb and Graeme Griffin (pastoral theology) and Norman Young (theology). Similar cooperation between the Victorian Baptist Union (which sponsored Whitley College), and the Victorian Conference of the Churches of Christ (College of the Bible), led to the formation of the Evangelical Theological Association in 1974. ETA scholars include William Tabbernee (church history, now teaching in the USA), Ken Manley (church history) and Athol Gill (New Testament).

In Adelaide, the Anglican, Uniting and other colleges formed the Adelaide College of Divinity in association with Flinders University in the early 1980s. (A similar pattern has emerged in Perth with Murdoch University, and recently in Queensland with Griffith University.) Adelaide is the centre of Lutheran church life, and distinctive contributions have been made by Lutheran theologians, including the redoubtable Herman Sasse (theology) and more recently Norman Habel (Old Testament). Gabriel Herbert and Gilbert Sinden (Society of the Sacred Mission in Crafers) were influential Anglican liturgists. Perth scholars have included William Loader, Michael Owen, Noel Vose and Colin Honey. The Anglican Archbishop, Peter Carnley, formerly of Brisbane, is a scholar in philosophical theology.

The Sydney College of Divinity formed in the early 1980s, including St Patrick's College (Catholic), Leigh College (Uniting) and later St Mark's Canberra (Anglican), but not Moore College (Anglican) or Morling (Baptist). The SCD differs from other local ecumenical bodies in that it does not have a university link or ecumenical teaching body, but is a federation of colleges. Sydney's theological history includes the famous heresy trial of Samuel Angus, which influenced developments in the non-Anglican Protestant tradition considerably. Prominent

Uniting Church theologians based in Sydney include Gordon Dicker, Alan Loy and Graeme Ferguson (theology), Graham Hughes (theology and liturgy), Howard Wallace (Old Testament) and John Brown (mission). New South Wales has also had some Anglican bishop theologians, notably Bishops Ernest Burgmann (social ethics), Charles Pilcher (theology), Arthur Garnsey (liturgy), Marcus Loane (church history), Donald Cameron (ecumenics), Donald Robinson (New Testament and liturgy), Paul Barnett (New Testament) and Bruce Wilson (sociology).

Brisbane has two cooperative theological consortia, both of recent formation. The Brisbane College of Divinity brings together St Pius XII (Roman Catholic), Trinity (Uniting) and St Francis (Anglican) colleges, with an ecumenical flavour. Links are emerging between the BCD and Griffith University. Kenmore (Churches of Christ), the Baptist College, and Queensland Bible College are of conservative evangelical orientation, and accredited with the (Anglican) Australian College of Theology. (David Parker (QBC) has done considerable work on the history of fundamentalism in Australia.) Both groups have contact, however, as seen in their joint organizing of the 1990 conference of the Australian and New Zealand Association of Theological Schools.

'Lay' and feminist theology Canberra was the venue of the Zadok Centre for the Study of Australian Christianity. Sponsored by evangelical Protestant bodies, it works cooperatively with St Mark's Library, an Anglican institution: together they serve a wide constituency, including many parliamentarians. Its directors have included David Millikan (theology and the arts), Peter Marshall (ethics) and John Harris (Aboriginal studies). Robert Banks developed in Canberra the 'theology of everyday life', a theme taken up in some depth by Zadok (he is now Professor of the Ministry of the Laity at Fuller Seminary, USA). Such emphases on reflection upon 'lay' Christianity have become widespread, not only through particular institutions such as Zadok, and the Uniting Church-based Education for Lay Ministry Centre in Sydney, but also in some theological colleges (especially Whitley and Ridley in Melbourne). Publishers catering for such 'lay' perspectives have emerged, notably Albatross, ANZEA and Lancer (Sydney) and Acorn (Melbourne).

Since the mid-1970s a growing number of women have studied theology formally, or begun to do theology themselves. Women have been ordained in the Uniting Church (and its predecessors) since its inception. The struggle over the ordination of women in the Anglican church has focused much feminist theological work, but its influence is far wider. A small number of women now teach in theological colleges, and women form large minorities, or in some cases majorities, in their student bodies. But many more women are actively involved in theological work beyond church structures. Muriel Porter, Janet Nelson, Peta Sherlock and Linda Walter are writers of influence from Melbourne, as are Pat Brennan, Marie Tulip and Erin White in Sydney, but much of this ferment is coming about in group or colloquium work. Men who have contributed significantly in this area include Kevin Giles (Adelaide) and John Gaden (Melbourne and Adelaide).

Aboriginal theology The fourth – and most distinctive – strand is Aboriginal theology, now focused at Nungalinya College, Darwin, and its related centres all over northern and central Australia. Its work involves community development, along with theological education for both women and men in ministry. A growing number of Koori (Aboriginal) theologians are coming to the fore, especially in the areas of art and (largely oral) history, community leadership and the transmission of traditional languages. Scholarship concerning indigenous peoples was dominated by anthropological studies until recently, secular, Catholic and Protestant. More theological work is now under way, by both Aborigines (such as Anne Pattel and Djiniyini Gondarra (Nungalinya)) and others (such as John Harris and Robert Bos). (See CULTURE AND THEOLOGY.)

The Australian and New Zealand Association of Theological Schools (ANZATS) Whatever their place on the theological spectrum, nearly all theological colleges (including Roman Catholic and Greek Orthodox as well as Protestant schools) belong to ANZATS. Together with the Australian and New Zealand Association of Theological Scholars, it forms an effective meeting place for theologians of all traditions. Specialist societies have formed in recent years, including the Australian Academy of Liturgy, the Australian Association of Religious Educators, the Evangelical History Society, and the Australian Association for the Study of Religion. A number of scholarly journals (many crossing the theological traditions) are now well established, including *Colloquium*, the *Australian Biblical Review*, the *Reformed Journal of Theology*, the *Australian Journal of Liturgy*, the *Journal of Christian Education*, the *Journal of Religious History*, *Interchange*, *Pacifica* and *Lucas*. Some local publishers are putting out high-standard theological work, notably Collins Dove, David Lovell (Melbourne), Lutheran (Adelaide) and St Mark's (Canberra), as well as a number of Roman Catholic presses.

The Australian context
In each of these areas, a growing concern with theology in and for Australian contexts has begun to emerge since the 1970s. It has its roots in the reawakening of Australian self-consciousness since the 1972 election of a Labour government, and has been especially furthered by feminist and indigenous theology. Yet it has wider roots in theological perception. Themes such as the land, fate, success and failure, and the desert are typical recent theological concerns, reflecting Australian geography and history. They are being explored with regard to church tradition in what Tony Kelly (a Melbourne-based Roman Catholic) has called 'a framework of collaborative creativity'.

The Christian Research Association (Melbourne) has undertaken sociological studies of Australian religious ideas and practice, closely linked with the work of Peter and Sue Kaldor in Sydney and the longer-standing National Catholic Research Centre. Various church commissions are making substantial submissions to government at all levels over issues of social concern. These go far beyond the traditional Australian churches' concern with alcohol, Sunday observance and gambling laws, although these need ongoing comment. Theologians (notably Chris Budden, Clive Harcourt-Norton, Alan Nichols and Keith Suter) and church social policy commissions have contributed in some depth to issues such as immigration policy and multiculturalism, the economics of welfare and tax structures, defence arrange-

ments, housing, education, abortion and genetic engineering.

Protestant theology in Australia is many-faceted. It has lacked much of the sophistication of the European and North American university traditions, and only in the last twenty years has grown beyond largely sectional, geographical and denominational interests. Nevertheless, the present scene is full of promise, with growing relationships with the universities, a more cooperative spirit emerging in most places, and exploration of the Australian context deepening.

See also the other articles on PROTESTANT THEOLOGY.

Bibliography
Black, A.W., ed. 1991: *Religion in Australia*. Sydney: Allen and Unwin.
Bodycomb, J. 1978: *The Naked Churchman*. Melbourne: JBCE.
Breward, I. 1988: *Australia: 'The Most Godless Place Under Heaven?'* Adelaide: Lutheran.
Cable, K., and Judd, S. 1987: *Sydney Anglicans*. Sydney: AIO.
Ellem, E.W., ed. 1990: *The Church Made Whole*. Melbourne: David Lovell.
Harris, D., Hynd, D., and Millikan, D. eds 1982: *The Shape of Belief: Christianity in Australia Today*. Sydney: Lancer.
Hayes, V.C., ed. 1979: *Towards Theology in an Australian Context*. Adelaide: AASR.
Lawton, W.J. 1988: *Being Christian, Being Australian*. Sydney: Lancer.
Lawton, W.J. 1990: *The Better Time to Be*. Sydney: UNSW.
Millikan, D. 1981: *The Sunburnt Soul*. Sydney: ANZEA.
Mol, J.J. (Hans) 1969: *Christianity in Chains*. Melbourne: Nelson.
Mol, J.J. (Hans) 1971: *Religion in Australia*. Melbourne: Nelson.
Nelson, J., and Walter, L. 1989: *Women of Spirit*. Canberra: St Mark's.
Porter, M. 1989: *Women in the Church*. Melbourne: Penguin.
Porter, M. 1990: *Land of the Spirit?* Geneva: WCC.

CHARLES SHERLOCK

Protestant theology: Britain A survey of three hundred years of British Protestant theology, including ANGLICANISM, can best take its start from the Act of Uniformity and promulgation of the Book of Common Prayer in 1662. This established the Church of

England as an episcopalian church and provoked the departure into nonconformity of dissenting Presbyterians and Independents (Congregationalists), together with Baptists and Quakers (see BAPTIST THOUGHT; PRESBYTERIANISM; QUAKERISM). In Scotland, Presbyterianism, long dominant, was finally established in 1690, ensuring the lasting influence of Calvinism.

By the end of the seventeenth century, ecclesiastical oppression and dogmatic authority generally were yielding to toleration. The influence of René Descartes (1596–1650) and of scientific advances, especially the work of Isaac Newton (1642–1727), elevated reason as arbiter of truth in religion and morality, effecting revolutionary changes of attitude, which John Locke (1632–1704) articulated and powerfully reinforced, thus setting the stage for the eighteenth-century ENLIGHTENMENT.

The shift from external revelatory authority to the thinking moral person was welcomed by the seventeenth-century moderate theologians known as 'latitudinarians'. Like the Cambridge Platonists, with whom they were associated, they believed that the natural world reflected and therefore revealed the glory of the Creator. The deists after them (see DEISM), influenced by Locke and the earlier work of Lord Herbert of Cherbury (1583–1648), confronted traditional authority with greater hostility, determined to maintain the freedom of Enlightenment thought, banish speculation and restrict religion within limits permitted by reason and common sense. God remained little more than the skilful creator of the Newtonian world-machine, and Jesus a teacher of moral virtue. Opposing such views, William Law emphasized Christ's indwelling in the soul.

The deists' early use of critical methods to undermine biblical authority provoked lasting hostility to biblical criticism amongst conservative Christians. Opposition to deism also came from Bishop J. Butler (1692–1752), whose respect for reason was matched by his recognition of its limits – the 'book of nature' was as 'full of dark mystery' as the Bible. Despite affirming mystery and conscience, Butler was far removed in spirit from the Methodists, John Wesley (1703–1791) and George Whitefield (1714–1770), with whom he clashed (see METHODISM). They diverged towards Arminianism and Calvinism respectively, yet the emotional enthusiasm and personal religion they espoused (so influential in nineteenth-century evangelicalism) further exposed the limitations of deism and rationalism.

Though Wesley (influenced by Law) called believers away from evidences to 'the light shining in their hearts', the appeal to 'Evidences of Christianity' (see EXISTENCE OF GOD, PROOFS OF) reappeared with William Paley (1743–1805). He argued from the design of the world (like a watch) to a supreme Designer; but religion of the heart soon found renewed expression in the protest of ROMANTICISM against arid, impersonal religion with its utilitarian ethic.

'Evidences of Christianity! I am weary of the word. Make a man feel the want of it . . . and you may safely trust to its own evidence' wrote S.T. Coleridge (1772–1834). He combined unusual familiarity with German philosophy and theology with a searching spirit and originality to become the most seminal theological thinker of the nineteenth century. With natural as well as revealed theology under attack, Coleridge, like F.D.E. Schleiermacher (1768–1834) in Germany, turned to religious experience for knowledge of God, thus making room for imagination and poetry in theology, and for critical reflection that resisted exclusive claims to truth, allowing free enquiry in living, personal communion with God.

Though Coleridge influenced the Tractarians, or high church party of the Anglican church, in their espousal of personal religion, they turned from religious experience as the basis of theology to the church seen as divine institution, linking the objectively real incarnation to believers in every age.

Coleridge's influence was more directly felt in the broad church, with its tolerant breadth of mind exemplified by Thomas Arnold (1795–1842) and Dean Stanley (1815–1881). For those even less able to accept the tenets of orthodoxy, unitarianism provided space for free enquiry, later to bear fruit in the work of F.D. Maurice (1805–1872) and also Charles Darwin (1809–1882), though both were to become Anglicans.

Maurice was deeply influenced by Coleridge, and profoundly influential in turn. He sought unity grounded in the Trinitarian God whose incarnate Word became the immanent life principle of a new humanity, embracing every

481

person, not just the rescued few. Grace, not sin (as for evangelicals) was the starting point of theology. His conviction that salvation was from sin, not punishment, echoed the views of Thomas Erskine (himself influenced by Law) and his fellow Scotsman, J. McLeod Campbell (1800–1872). With his Platonic sense of an existing transcendental reality and conviction that the truth in every Christian viewpoint is Christ, Maurice resisted all exclusivist claims. Yet he took differences seriously. For his view of eternal life as qualitative, not temporal, and consequent denial of endless torment in hell, he lost his professorial chair.

The dispute over eschatology was the symptom of a deeper crisis. Opposition to ideas of eternal punishment had roots in eighteenth-century optimism and unitarian universalism, which, together with Arminianism, contributed to the erosion of Calvinism. Its seemingly mechanistic doctrines of predestination, penal substitution and eternal torment of the wicked were yielding to a more optimistic faith in progress, emphasis on personal religion and reformatory rather than retributive views of punishment. Such ideas challenged not only the infallibility of Scripture and traditional doctrine, but the very possibility of certainty in faith.

The crisis was heightened by the publication in 1860 of *Essays and Reviews*. With the appearance of this collection of essays by a group of Anglican clergy (and one layman), the challenge of biblical criticism had to be faced at last. It threatened not only conservative views, but those of Maurice's opponent, H.L. Mansel (1820–1871), whose search for 'regulative principles' for thought about God and for moral action (echoing Kant) depended on miraculously inspired Scripture rather than inner experience.

A creative response to the challenge came from Maurice's former Cambridge students – B.F. Westcott (1825–1901), F.J.A. Hort (1828–1892) and J.B. Lightfoot (1828–1889) – who advanced the critical study of the New Testament in a religious spirit and without the philosophical presuppositions that weighed upon early critical work in Germany and provoked such alarm.

Yet secular ideas were spreading. Darwin's *Origin of Species* of 1861 seemingly undermined not only humanity's unique status as created in the image of God, but even more disturbingly, the doctrine of the fall and original sin, and hence the significance of Christ's saving work. The supposed incompatibility of science with the supernaturalism implied in traditional doctrines of God, Christ and the world threatened to isolate theology in intellectual backwaters. A way back into the mainstream came with various forms of immanentist theology – immanentalism, mysticism, and incarnationalism.

'Immanentalism' had roots in latitudinarianism, the broad church, and the liberalism (see LIBERALISM: BRITAIN) of such men as Benjamin Jowett (1817–1893) and Matthew Arnold (1822–1888). Henry Drummond (1851–1897) of the Scottish Free Church popularized ideas of evolution in the spiritual as well as the natural world. In the early twentieth century, a liberal 'new theology', owing much to philosophical idealism and the theology of A. von Harnack (1851–1930), opposed dualism and viewed the cosmic process as the 'incarnation and uprising of the being of God from itself to itself'. It set reason over tradition, dispensed with miracles, and saw Jesus as a purely human moral inspiration for rising humanity, not healing fallen humanity. Sin was a blundering search for God; the 'kingdom of God' the goal of social justice on earth.

Such ideas were reflected in *Foundations* in 1912, published by a group of Anglican idealist theologians in Oxford, and in the work of the Congregationalist A.M. Fairbairn (1838–1912). Their optimism could perhaps only convince in an age confident in human achievement.

Theological liberalism had been consolidated in 1898 when The Modern Churchmen's Union was founded. A prominent supporter, Hastings Rashdall (1858–1924) propounded an exemplarist view of the atonement and held that God's indwelling in Christ was only intelligible if he indwelt humanity as a whole; only Christ's perfect moral conscience made him revealer of God. As late as the controversial Girton conference in 1921, the failure of such as H.D.A. Major to distinguish between Creator and creature provoked the formation of the Commission on Doctrine, which reported belatedly in 1938.

Mysticism and religious experience offered the neo-Platonist Dean Inge (1860–1954) an intellectual basis for his religious faith. Opposed to idealism and its idea of progress, he sought to realize 'in thought and feeling the immanence of the temporal in the eternal and of the eternal in the temporal'.

Incarnationalism was represented in *Lux Mundi* (Gore, 1889). The Oxford contributors in the Anglo-Catholic tradition, influenced by Westcott and the idealist philosopher T.H. Green (1836–1882), believed that the patristic doctrine of the Logos at work in the world as well as in the incarnation offered a synthesis between tradition and criticism. Thus even evolutionary theory could be harnessed to the idea of the incarnation as the culmination of a long, saving process.

Charles Gore (1853–1932), the editor, resolved the clash between Jesus' supposed omniscience and the conclusions of critical study (for example over Davidic authorship of the Psalms), by suggesting that 'the Incarnation was a self-emptying of God to reveal himself under conditions of human nature and from the human point of view' (Gore, 1889, p. 359).

Gore later developed this idea in his kenotic Christology, which attempted to accommodate classical Christological dogmas to recognition of a genuinely human historical Jesus. It appealed not only to a new generation of Anglo-Catholics, such as Frank Weston (1871–1924) and O.C. Quick (1885–1944), but to non-Anglican liberal theologians such as Fairbairn and H.R. Mackintosh (1870–1936), and also to P.T. Forsyth (1848–1921). Criticism arose particularly over the issues of Jesus' personality and apparent change in the Logos.

The incarnationalists pre-empted many of the moral and intellectual objections to Christian orthodoxy, without having to surrender the divine status of Christ. R.C. Moberley (1845–1903) avoided the 'offence' of transactional atonement theories on the model of reconciliation in a Victorian family. Though echoing the Wesleyan Methodist J. Scott Lidgett (1854–1953), the direct debt he acknowledged was to J. McLeod Campbell, who had argued that divine punishment was rendered unnecessary by Christ's perfect awareness of sin and perfect contrition. Moberley added that atonement was assured only if accomplished by someone fully identified with God and with humanity. Hence he emphasized not only the unity of God as personal but that Christ was inclusively human.

Lux Mundi had dismayed older Anglo-Catholics, such as H.P. Liddon (1829–1890), but encouraged the emergence of a less rigid liberal Catholicism, able to resist the extremes of theological liberalism (and also the lure of neo-orthodoxy when liberalism lost its plausibility). Yet in moving from Latin theology of sin and atonement to Greek Logos theology, incarnationalism could be charged with devaluing the cross and obscuring divine judgement by the sense of the inevitability of progress seemingly implicit in the concept of the immanent Logos.

The Congregationalist R.W. Dale (1829–1895) also emphasized the 'living Christ within' and the importance of the church – reflecting the growing free church interest in ecclesiology. He also struggled to maintain the centrality of the atonement in mediatorial terms, avoiding morally offensive substitutionary or inadequate exemplary views.

Resistance to immanentalism and moral optimism came from James Denney (1856–1917) of the Scottish Free Church, and the Baptist Calvinist, C.H. Spurgeon (1834–1892), who both defended substitutionary atonement theories. However, the strongest challenge came from another Congregationalist. An erstwhile liberal, P.T. Forsyth anticipated Karl Barth (1886–1968) in proclaiming the centrality of grace, but a confident prewar generation was not yet ready for the message.

Much nonconformist scholarship in this period was, however, biblical rather than doctrinal. W. Robertson Smith (1846–1894), in particular, pioneered the introduction into Britain of German critical views, besides advancing the study of comparative religion. Ecumenism was encouraged by missionary experience and by the search for new foundations of faith in the face of secularism, and of the changing conceptions of God, the church and revelation.

The trauma of the First World War did not shatter the confidence of liberal theology in Britain as quickly or completely as in Germany. Nevertheless, the idealist philosophy underlying liberalism was to come under increasing strain, not only from the growing pressure of neo-orthodoxy, but from the challenge of logical positivism. More immediately, the seeds sown by Karl Marx, Emile Durkheim, and Sigmund Freud were bearing fruit in the work of novelists, philosophers, and social scientists. A confident agnosticism could interpret human life without God.

In response, theologians in the idealist tradition continued their quest for God immanent in the unfolding evolutionary and historical structures of life, but with greater awareness of the risk of losing the otherness of God in the spirit of the world, and of surrendering the uniqueness of the historic person Jesus to the all-pervasive divine immanence.

William Temple (1881–1944), drawing on the *Lux Mundi* tradition as well as on idealism (through his teacher, E. Caird, 1835–1908), distinguished four distinct levels emerging in the world process – matter, life, intelligence, spirit – the higher depending on the lower, but controlling it rather than controlled by it. The emergence of spirit in humanity pointed to God as the unifying creative spirit of the sacramental whole. Natural theology found its completion in the incarnation. His emphasis on the reality of God in Christ brought Temple close to affirming suffering in God (a theme boldly explored during the agonies of war by the army chaplain, G.A. Studdart-Kennedy (1883–1929), and pursued most recently by the Baptist P.S. Fiddes (b. 1947).

A different account of emergent process was offered by the liberal Anglo-Catholic, L.S. Thornton (1884–1960), who drew on the philosophy of A.N. Whitehead (1861–1947), but emphasized the transcendent order revealed in the creative and redemptive work of Christ. F.R. Tennant (1866–1957) defended natural theology on the lines of Paley, arguing from scientific phenomena to its meaning in ethical theism, while A.E. Taylor (1869–1945) placed more stress on humanity's moral experience as grounds for belief in God.

A renewed emphasis on God discovered in personal encounter – owing much to E. Brunner (1889–1966) and M. Buber (1878–1965) – helped secure the middle ground for those open to Barthian influence but less inclined to abandon all the insights of the immanentist tradition, such as the brothers John and Donald Baillie (1886–1960; 1887–1954) in Scotland. The former held revelation to be given by

God uniquely in Christ but not exclusively to Christians, while the latter offered his classic portrayal of the incarnation in terms of the paradox of grace in *God was in Christ* of 1948.

The 'chastened liberal' Presbyterian, John Oman (1860–1939), also returned to the doctrine of grace, believing that the tension between grace and free will could be overcome when grace was understood as personal encounter. H.H. Farmer (1882–1981) likewise developed a personalist theology, describing God as 'unconditional demand and final succour', whose presence was mediated through persons and the natural world. Christians could claim a special but not exclusive knowledge of God.

The 'unrepentant liberal' theologian and natural historian, Charles Raven (1885–1964), accepted Oman's emphasis on personality as the highest category in evolution, but dwelt more on the unity of all things – nature, history, experience and God – in one evolutionary process. Ironically, his call for a 'new reformation' to bridge the gulf between religion and science virtually coincided with the publication in English in 1933 of Barth's Commentary on Romans by Edwyn Hoskyns (1884–1937), with its radical challenge to liberalism and natural theology.

The Barthian defence of faith could acknowledge, even relish, the godlessness of the age as foil to its proclamation of God as 'wholly other', cutting through all human creations in judgement and mercy. In contrast to immanentism, its problem would be to avoid devaluing the world and almost totally excluding God from it, except in the Christian revelation.

Hoskyns (like A.E. Taylor) had earlier contributed to the important publication, *Essays Catholic and Critical* of 1926 (edited by E.G. Selwyn). His chapter on 'The Christ of the Synoptic Gospels' launched an attack, taken up by the Welsh Congregationalist and New Testament scholar C.H. Dodd (1884–1973), against the monistic view of reality and futuristic evolving kingdom-of-God-on-earth eschatology, which in extreme modernist terms was barely distinguishable from a humanly created utopia. Against the darkening background of European totalitarianism, they proclaimed a 'realized eschatology' – the catastrophic breaking in of God's kingdom through

Christ, transforming humanity. Dodd emphasized that the history of salvation, *Heilsgeschichte*, was the proclamation of God's mighty acts, not mere moral instruction.

Such ideas were developed theologically by the former liberal, Nathaniel Micklem (1885–1976), and other Congregationalists – J.S. Whale (b. 1896), Bernard Manning (1892–1941) and J. Marsh (b. 1904) – who led the 'Genevan revival' against extreme liberalism and naturalistic understandings of the church, sacraments and religion. On a wider front, they participated with scholars from all denominations (including the Anglican A.M. Ramsey (1904–1988), Methodist V. Taylor (1887–1968) and Baptist H. Wheeler Robinson (1872–1945)) in the resurgence of biblical theology.

Anglo-Catholicism also gained strength in the 1930s, attracting famous converts such as T.S. Eliot (1888–1965), W.H. Auden (1907–1973) and C.S. Lewis (1898–1963), whose writings exercised a profound religious influence. E.L. Mascall (1905–1993) and Austin Farrer (1904–1968) drew on Thomism to provide a more strictly theological defence of Christian metaphysics and natural theology, against the alternative of process theology and the contrasting attacks of logical positivism and Barthian revelatory positivism.

In the prewar period, ecumenism had been encouraged by Temple and the nonconformist J. Oldham (1874–1969), and also by Evelyn Underhill (1875–1941) with her sympathetic comparative study of worship in 1936. The impetus was sustained after 1945 as theology became increasingly ecumenical and international. As in prewar years, much scholarly effort in Britain was devoted to biblical and patristic studies, in the belief that the original message and witness of the Bible and early church, freed from prejudices and presuppositions read into them, would still speak to and challenge the contemporary situation. Such studies were also less exposed to the assault of logical positivism with its dismissal of all God-talk as meaningless, while the alternative challenge of R. Bultmann's (1884–1976) call for demythologization of the New Testament in terms of existentialism only came to be felt gradually.

The relative calm of the late 1940s and 1950s proved to be only the lull before the theological storm broke in the 1960s. Once again in response to the challenges of modern thought, theologians themselves, in Cambridge especially, posed radical questions over the possibility of theology and concerning the nature of God and Christ. Then in 1963 *Honest to God* by Bishop John Robinson (1919–1983) brought theological questions before an unexpectedly wide public. Drawing on P. Tillich (1886–1965), D. Bonhoeffer (1906–1945) and Bultmann, Robinson spoke of 'man come of age' and of God as the 'ground of Being' – not 'up there' or just visiting the earth in his Son. To see Jesus, the 'man for others', was to see God.

Despite the anxieties aroused by *Honest to God* in clergy and laity, including, initially, Archbishop A.M. Ramsey, the outcome paradoxically was a recovery of theological confidence, a process assisted by L. Wittgenstein's later philosophy and critique of positivism. The understanding of religious language in terms of 'models' proposed by the philosopher and bishop, Ian Ramsey (1915–1972), helped further to re-establish the possibility of serious theological discussion.

At the same time, the immanentist tradition remained influential through the work of John Macquarrie (b. 1919), who drew on Tillich and Bultmann to develop his own systematic theology. His recognition, following Tillich, of the symbolic character of religious language allowed him, in contrast to Barthian exclusivism, to acknowledge the universality of genuine religious experience through existential encounter with Holy Being, while still emphasizing Christ's cross as the focus and spearhead of the universal reconciling work of God.

Recognition that 'God talk' was symbolic could lead to the more radical conclusion that the God who could not be known perfectly by any, could be known or experienced spiritually equally well by all, with Jesus regarded as one mediator of the divine among others. At the price of undermining traditional Christological and Trinitarian doctrine, ecumenism could be extended from Christianity to other religions, as urged by John Hick (b. 1922) with his call for a Copernican revolution in the evaluation of religions. At the very least the emphasis shifted from beliefs in clearly formulated doctrines towards a disposition of adventurous believing, as advocated by Maurice Wiles (b. 1923).

At the extreme, Don Cupitt (b. 1934) could argue that the word 'God' did not correspond to anything objectively real – God being a construct of the human mind, and Christ simply the embodiment of disinterested love.

At the opposite extreme, the Scottish Presbyterian Thomas Torrance (b. 1913), himself well versed in the natural sciences as well as in Barth and Calvin, affirmed an objectively real Trinitarian God, who could not indeed be found by human beings but who had chosen to reveal himself through his Word. Revelation in Christ was thus the object of theological science, just as the world is the object of natural science. The human role and way to personhood is to respond to what God gives.

On similar lines, but emphasizing the metaphorical character of language in his assault on rationalist assumptions stemming from the Enlightenment, the Reformed theologian Colin Gunton (b. 1941) argues that Christ uniquely reveals not only the triune God but the Trinitarian structure of all reality.

Between these revivals of orthodoxy and the extremes of projectionism stand the challenges to traditional Christian understanding of God and biblical interpretation posed by liberation theology and, more immediately in Britain, by FEMINIST THEOLOGY, witnessing in themselves to a theological pluralism international in scope and creativity.

The fundamental questions facing theology today concerning the reality of God, the status of Christ and the availability of salvation are for the most part not new, but they arise out of new perspectives and a new context of religious and cultural pluralism, resurgent fundamentalisms, and the increasing pressure of secularization. Theology is faced with the danger of once again being driven out of the mainstream of intellectual life into a private cultic world, or of yielding to such radical reconstruction that continuity with its past is lost. Such challenges will in future be faced on an ecumenical and international scale, with Roman Catholic, Orthodox and Protestant theology in its various forms interacting with each other. In its response, British Protestantism would be true to its tradition in expecting the inspiration of the Holy Spirit and denying any exclusive claim to its authority.

See also ECCLESIOLOGY; EVANGELICALISM: BRITAIN; and the other articles on PROTESTANT THEOLOGY.

Bibliography

Cragg, G.R. 1960: *The Church and the Age of Reason 1648–1789*. London: Penguin.

Davies, H. 1961–5: *Worship and Theology in England*, vols 3–5. Princeton: Princeton University Press.

Davies, R.E., and Rupp, E.G., eds 1965–88: *A History of the Methodist Church in Great Britain*, 4 vols. London: Epworth.

Elliott-Binns, L. 1956: *English Thought 1860–1900: The Theological Aspect*. London: Longmans, Green and Co.

Gore, C., ed. 1889: *Lux Mundi: A Series of Studies in the Religion of the Incarnation*. London: John Murray.

Hastings, A. 1991: *A History of English Christianity 1920–1990*, 2nd edn. London: SCM Press; Philadelphia: Trinity Press International.

Hinchliff, P. 1992: *God and History: Aspects of British Theology 1875–1914*. Oxford: Oxford University Press.

Jones, R.T. 1962: *Congregationalism in England 1662–1962*. London: Independent Press.

Ramsey, A.M. 1960: *From Gore to Temple: The Development of Anglican Theology Between Lux Mundi and the Second World War, 1889–1939*. London: Longmans, Green and Co.; New York: Charles Scribner's Sons.

Rupp, G. 1986: *Religion in England 1688–1791*. Oxford: Oxford University Press.

Stephen, Sir L. [1877] 1902: *English Thought in the Eighteenth Century*, 2 vols. London: Smith, Elder and Co.

Stephenson, A.M.G. 1984: *The Rise and Decline of English Modernism*. London: SPCK.

Storr, V.F. 1913: *The Development of English Theology in the Nineteenth Century*. London: Longmans, Green and Co.

Tulloch, J. [1885] 1971: *Movements of Religious Thought in Britain during the Nineteenth Century*. Leicester: Leicester University Press.

Welch, C. 1972 and 1985: *Protestant Thought in the Nineteenth Century*, vol. 1, 1799–1870, and vol. 2, 1870–1914. Newhaven and London: Yale University Press.

Worrall, B.G. 1988: *The Making of the Modern Church: Christianity in England since 1800*. London: SPCK.

TREVOR WILLIAMS

Protestant theology: Canada Protestantism did not gain a foothold in Canada until the British conquest of New France in 1759, and so Canadian Protestant theology spans only a little more than two centuries. Like the Protestant settlers themselves, their stock of ideas came mainly from Britain, Europe and the USA.

The first English theological works to appear in British North America, *Two Mites on . . . Divinity* of 1781 and *The Anti-Traditionalist* of 1783, were written by a Congregationalist revivalist preacher, Henry Alline (1748–1784). Alline drew on the mystical piety of William Law and through him of Jakob Böhme. He taught that the world is an emanation, or 'Outbirth', from God and that salvation consists in the turning of the inmost soul to God. Alline is credited with having produced the first 'Canadian metaphysics' (Armstrong, 1948, p. 103). His theology was criticized by Jonathan Scott (1744–1819), a Congregationalist, who put the case for Calvinist orthodoxy in *A Brief View of . . . Two Mites* of 1784 and by John Wesley, who stated in a letter to William Black that Alline wrote of matters 'too high for him, far above his comprehension . . .' (Wesley, J. quoted by Armstrong, 1948, p. 104). The first Protestant theological college, King's, was established by Anglicans at Windsor, Nova Scotia, in 1789. Its founder Charles Inglis (1734–1816), an Irishman, moved as a United Empire Loyalist from New York to Canada and became the first Anglican bishop of Nova Scotia in 1787.

In the first part of the nineteenth century the main figure was Thomas McCulloch (1776–1843), a Scottish Secessionist missionary who came to Pictou in 1803. He founded Pictou Academy in 1816 and a theological college in 1822. In 1838 he became the first president of Dalhousie College. McCulloch's first theological works were polemical. At the request of Bishop Charles Inglis he responded to the Roman Catholic bishop, Edmund Burke, with a full-scale treatise, *Popery Condemned by Scripture and the Fathers* of 1808, and two years later with *Popery Again Condemned*. His major work, *Calvinism, the Doctrine of the Scriptures*, was published posthumously in 1848. In it he set forth the major themes of Calvinism: the scriptural principle, covenant theology and the doctrine of election, as against its Arminian critics. McCulloch is best known for his

Mephibosheth Stepsure Letters, which according to Northrop Frye establish him as 'the founder of genuine Canadian humour' (Frye, 1960, p. ix).

With the founding of universities and theological colleges under Protestant auspices, philosophy and theology were taught as part of the curriculum by teachers of British origin, mainly Scots. Scottish realism, the characteristic flowering of the Scottish Enlightenment, became the dominant philosophical influence on Anglicans, Baptists, Methodists and Presbyterians. This was complemented by the English deistic approach, as for example in James Beaven of King's College, Toronto, who published *Elements of Natural Theology* in 1850. Earlier he had published *An Account of the Life and Writings of Irenaeus* (in 1841). The main figures in this period were: George Paxton Young (1818–1889), who published *Miscellaneous Discourses . . .* in 1854, and taught philosophy at Knox College and later at the University of Toronto; William Lyall (1811–1890), who taught at the Free Church College in Halifax and later at Dalhousie as professor of logic and psychology; and John Clarke Murray (1836–1917), who taught philosophy at Queen's and later at McGill. All three were Presbyterian ministers.

The leading intellectual figure among the Methodists was A. Egerton Ryerson (1803–1882), founder and editor of the *Christian Guardian*, and founder and principal of Victoria College (1841). He wrote *Scriptural Rights of the Members of Christ's Visible Church* in 1854 and *Canadian Methodism* in 1882. Baptist theologians such as E.A. Crawley (1799–1888) of Acadia University wrote on baptism (*Treatise on Baptism*, 1835), and J.M. Cramp (1796–1881), president of Acadia, wrote *A Textbook on Popery* in 1831, a monumental *Baptist History* in 1868 and *Lamb of God* in 1871.

By the 1870s German idealist philosophy had replaced Scottish realism. The major figure was John Watson (1847–1939), a student of Edward Caird, who went to Queen's, Kingston, Ontario in 1872 and taught there for the next fifty years. He regarded Christianity as an ideal of conduct rather than a historical creed, an approach which he developed in *Christianity and Idealism* of 1897 and *The Interpretation of Religious*

Experience, his Gifford Lectures in 1910–12. Along with other émigrés from Scotland, he sought to combine the new critical ideas with Christianity by drawing on German idealist philosophy to provide the basis for a new understanding of the Christian faith that would be compatible with evolution and biblical criticism and would be less vulnerable than conventional theology to materialist and agnostic attacks (see LIBERALISM: USA). Less liberal than Watson yet open to modern thought, George M. Grant (1835–1902), principal of Queen's University, advocated the 'historical theology' taught by Robert Flint at Edinburgh University. In 1894 Grant published *The Religions of the World*, which showed a tolerant attitude to non-Christian beliefs but maintained that 'non-Christian nations have to assume the methods and instruments of Christian civilization in order to succeed.' Agnes M. Machar, a Presbyterian feminist author, defended a liberal version of Christianity against its critics. She wrote a novel *Roland Graeme: Knight* in 1892, in which she argued the need for a socially oriented faith.

The introduction of the critical approach to Scripture proved controversial. George C. Workman (1848–1936), a Methodist, was dismissed from his position at Victoria University for his views that Old Testament prophecies were not conscious predictions of the coming of Christ. John Campbell, professor of Old Testament at Presbyterian College, Montreal, almost suffered the same fate for a lecture on 'The Perfect Book or the Perfect Father'. 'Higher criticism' was defended by J.E. McFadyen (1870–1933) at Knox College, Toronto, in his *Old Testament Criticism and the Christian Church* of 1903, by Robert A. Falconer (1867–1943) of Presbyterian College, Halifax, in *The Truth of the Apostolic Gospel* of 1904, and by W.G. Jordan (1852–1939) of Queen's, Kingston, in *Biblical Criticism and Modern Thought* of 1909. The most formidable opponent of biblical criticism was Sir William Dawson (1820–1899), principal of McGill and a leading anti-Darwinian who set forth his views in *Nature and the Bible* of 1875 and *The Origin of the World* of 1877. Canadian Protestant churches were also affected by the American fundamentalist/ modernist controversy (see FUNDAMENT-ALISM) – particularly the Baptists, who suf-

fered a small rupture caused by T.T. Shields, a vigorous opponent of 'modernism and Romanism'.

There was considerable interest in social action during the early part of the twentieth century. J.S. Woodsworth (1874–1942), a Methodist clergyman, later the leader of the socialist Commonwealth Co-operative Federation Party, wrote *My Neighbor* in 1911, and another able exponent of the social gospel, Salem G. Bland (1859–1950), wrote *The New Christianity; or, The Religion of a New Age* in 1920. Another important work on economic and social reform, a kind of manifesto for Christian socialism, was *Towards the Christian Revolution* of 1936, edited by R.B.Y. Scott and Gregory Vlastos.

In 1924 the *Canadian Journal of Religious Thought* was founded as a forum for Canadian religious writers. Methodists, Congregationalists and two-thirds of the Presbyterians formed the United Church of Canada in 1925. The church union produced a considerable body of literature both before and after the event, but this focused mainly on organizational rather than on theological issues.

The theology of Karl Barth gained its foothold in Canada through the advocacy of W.W. Bryden (1883–1952) of Knox College, Toronto, who in *The Christian's Knowledge of God* of 1940 criticized liberal theology for its neglect of the Word of God. John Line (1885–1970) of the United Church's Emmanuel College also supported the neo-orthodox emphasis. He wrote *Doctrine of the Christian Ministry* of 1959. This circle included Arthur C. Cochrane, who wrote *The Church's Confession under Hitler* of 1962, and James D. Smart (1906–1982), author of such works as *What a Man Can Believe* of 1944, *The Divided Mind of Modern Theology: Karl Barth and Rudolf Bultmann* of 1967, and *The Teaching Ministry of the Church* of 1954.

One of the most significant theological works to appear in this period was written not by a theologian but by a professor of classics at Trinity College, Toronto, C.N. Cochrane (1889–1945). In his *Christianity and Classical Culture* of 1940, Cochrane traced the transition from pagan to Christian culture in the first few centuries AD and drew the important lesson that the church may contribute more to the world by maintaining its Christian identity than by seeking to harmonize it with the values of the surrounding culture.

Canadian Protestant scholars have made significant contributions to biblical studies. J.F. McCurdy (1847–1935) of the University of Toronto is generally recognized as the father of biblical studies in Canada. He wrote a three-volume work, *History, Prophecy and the Monuments* of 1896–1911. One of his students, Theophile J. Meek (1881–1966) published an authoritative work on *Hebrew Origins* in 1936. Both E.F. Scott and William Manson taught for several years in Canada. Other noteworthy biblical scholars include F.W. Beare, R.B.Y. Scott, G.B. Caird, George Johnston, J.D. Smart, S.M. Gilmour, John Wevers, R.C. Culley, Peter Richardson and John Hurd.

Protestant theology in Canada, as elsewhere, has been motivated by the need to affirm, reinterpret and even to revise the tradition it has received. Since the 1960s the need to revise has been dominant. Contemporary movements such as liberation, feminist and process theologies have been influential, but Canadian theology tends on the whole, like Canadians themselves, to be moderate, cautious and always in search of a *via media*. Two significant Protestant thinkers, both at McGill University, Montreal, deserve mention. J.C. McLelland has concentrated on the philosophy of religion and theology but more recently has turned his attention to the issue of religious pluralism and proposed what he terms a 'modal' approach to signify the step from categories analysing human experience to those responsive to possibilities on a cosmic scale. Douglas J. Hall has argued the need for contextuality and identified significant crises (pluralism, Auschwitz, Marxism, apocalyptic consciousness) that define the context. In the first volume of his projected three-volume work, *Thinking the Faith*, Professor Hall has sought to make a case for an indigenous Christian theology in a North American context.

See also the other articles on PROTESTANT THEOLOGY.

Bibliography

Armour, L. and Trott E. 1984: *The Faces of Reason*. Waterloo: Waterloo University Press.

Armstrong, M.W. 1948: *The Great Awakening in Nova Scotia 1776–1809*. Hartford: American Society of Church History.

Bryden, W.W. 1940: *The Christian's Knowledge of God*. Toronto: Thorn Press.

Cochrane, C.N. 1944: *Christianity and Classical Culture*. London: Oxford University Press.

Cook, R. 1985: *The Regenerators*. Toronto: University of Toronto Press.

Frye, H. Northrop 1960: Introduction. In McCulloch, Thomas, *The Stepsure Letters*. Toronto: McLelland and Stewart.

Gauvreau, M. 1991: *The Evangelical Century*. Montreal: McGill-Queen's.

Grant, J.W. 1976: Religious and theological writing to 1960. In *Literary History of Canada*, ed. C.F. Klinck, 2nd edn, vol. 2. Toronto: University of Toronto Press.

Hall, D.J. 1989: *Thinking the Faith*. Minneapolis: Augsburg.

McKillop, A.B. 1979: *A Disciplined Intelligence*. Montreal: McGill-Queen's.

McLelland, J.C. 1989: *Prometheus Rebound*. Waterloo: Wilfred Laurier Press.

Moir, J.S. 1982: *A History of Biblical Studies in Canada*. Chico, California: Scholars Press.

Thomson, J.S. 1965: Literature of religion and theology. In *Literary History of Canada*, ed. C.F. Klinck. Toronto: University of Toronto Press.

WILLIAM KLEMPA

Protestant theology: Germany Protestant theology in Germany originated with the Reformers of the sixteenth century. Of diverse intellectual and theological origins, it was from the beginning an academic discipline taught at the universities of the Protestant states of Germany. The rich variety and often controversial pluralism which it developed in the course of its history had theological, but also political, origins. It derived from the state-based reorganization of church life and public education according to the principle *cuius regio, eius religio* whose impact on the complex development of Protestant theology in Germany can hardly be overestimated.

Typically, Protestant theology is predominantly soteriological in orientation. It reflects a Christ-centred Trinitarian faith in God (*solus Christus*) and hence accepts the Word of God as testified by Scripture as the supreme arbiter in all matters of faith (*sola scriptura*). Its formative period was the seventeenth century, when Lutheran and Reformed divines worked out their doctrinal systems of scholastic orthodoxy in response to post-Tridentine Roman Catholicism and in confessional and political opposition to each other. It moved into its self-reflective phase in the eighteenth century when the internal criticism of pietism and the external rise of enlightened reason forced it to define its distinctly Protestant (as opposed to merely confessional Lutheran or Calvinist) position beyond its rejection of the Roman papacy and its claims to authority in more positive theological terms. Philosophically generalized by German idealism, its ethos had a formative impact on the intellectual and cultural formation of German society in the nineteenth century. It suffered a major setback through the disestablishment of the Protestant churches after 1918 and the collaboration of many Protestants with the Nazi regime, from which it never wholly recovered. It still holds a privileged position by being taught at state universities by state-paid professors of theology. But although it has produced many fine theologians and important contributions to the study of theology in this century, its influence on society at large and on church life in particular has been continuously diminishing.

The term 'Protestant'

Originally the term 'Protestant' referred to the legal protest made by six princes and fourteen south German cities at the Diet of Speyer in 1529. This protest was directed not against Rome but against the rescinding of the unanimous declaration of the earlier Diet of Speyer in 1526 that until a General Council met every prince should be free to introduce religious changes. The religious import of this legal protestation was that in questions of religion and faith the only authority to be obeyed was the Word of God, not a political body or a majority vote. It was in the light of this that Lutherans, and soon all Reformation movements opposed to Rome, were called 'Protestant' by their critics, while they themselves preferred to describe their position as 'evangelical'. But the separation from the more radical enthusiast and Anabaptist movements after 1525, the breach between Martin Luther and Ulrich Zwingli in 1529 and the Peace of Augsburg in 1555 made it quite clear that mainstream 'evangelical' Protestantism remained firmly in the traditions of western Christianity and that the opposition between

Lutherans and Calvinists was as great as their common opposition to Rome. It was not before the seventeenth century and the bitter experiences of the wars of religion that both Lutherans and Calvinists adopted – via England and western Europe – the neutral (political) description of Protestants as their common name. By this time it was clear that the Protestant break with Rome was permanent; that the religious unity of the empire could not be restored by force; that western Christianity was definitely dissolved into a variety of confessional traditions, churches and religious movements; and that this plurality of conflicting religious convictions could only coexist peacefully if the common affairs of human life were based on natural law and principles of reasonableness established independently of religious commitments. So the eighteenth century saw European culture well on the way from a pluri-religious to an increasingly secular society.

Protestant self-understanding

For Protestant theology to come to grips with this, it had to work out its self-understanding in changing contexts and with differing emphases. While there is a clear continuity of theological orientation due to the confessional self-determination of the Lutheran and Reformed churches in the sixteenth and seventeenth centuries, German Protestant theology has produced different types of theology in different periods since the Reformation. In the sixteenth and seventeenth centuries it defined itself primarily vis-à-vis Roman Catholicism and the more radical spiritualist and (Ana)Baptist traditions in Lutheran or Reformed (Calvinist) terms. The rejection of obedience to the Roman papacy (Bossuet, [1688] 1841), the self-demarcation against Baptist, spiritualist and anti-Trinitarian movements, and the opposition between Lutheran and Calvinist orientations have since been fundamental traits of Protestant theology.

In the eighteenth century the primary points of reference were the dissenting and nonconformist pietist traditions, the enlightened synthesis of humanist and Renaissance traditions with the new spirit of empirical and mathematical science, rational philosophy and Confucian ethics, and the growing ENLIGHTENMENT secularism. This led to an even greater internal diversification of Protestant theology and to the disintegration of confessional orthodoxy by rationalism and supranaturalism, neologism and a growing historical consciousness. The self-conscious engagement with rationalist and idealist philosophies and the wholehearted commitment to critical historical scholarship have left their mark on German Protestant theology.

In the nineteenth century it had to come to grips with the rise of nationalism, industrialism and the social problems in its wake, but also with the progress of the natural sciences, technology and historical scholarship. This led, on the one hand, to the resurgence of a confessionalism based on the national churches, with a strong commitment to missionary, charitable and social activities. On the other it also prompted unionist attempts to overcome the old Protestant antagonisms and paved the way to neo-Protestant liberalism, preoccupation with the historical sciences, identification with the culture and religous system of the day, and the loss of eschatological outlook. Protestant social ethics, which had always been torn between honouring the authorities in power as ordained of God (especially in the Lutheran traditions) and prophetically denouncing the world in the light of the reign of Christ and the coming kingdom of God (in the more Calvinist traditions), now became closely wedded to the bourgeois values of national German society.

The twentieth century not only saw the disestablishment of the Protestant churches after 1918, the collapse of Protestant liberalism and conservative confessionalism before and during the Nazi regime, and the failure of many churches and individuals to resist the lure of nationalism and to find their place in a democratic society. It was also characterized by the rediscovery of an eschatological orientation, the opposition of dialectical theology to religious liberalism, conservative traditionalism and pietist subjectivism, the experiences of church struggle, Holocaust and the political disasters of the Second World War, the rise of religious pluralism and indifferentism, the ecumenical movement and the overcoming of the old divide between Lutheran and Reformed churches, and the economic, social and political developments that led to European unity and the collapse of the Marxist regimes in eastern Europe towards the end of the century.

Protestant theology in this period became more international and ecumenical in outlook and less prone to confessional demarcations against other Christian churches both within and outside the Protestant camp. It became hermeneutically sensitive to the difference between the Word of God and the Bible, opposed to Enlightenment theism and its metaphysical consequences, and increasingly Trinitarian in orientation. But it also became aware of the haunting legacy of Christian anti-Judaism, the depreciation of women in the church, the issues of theological feminism, and the need to develop new forms of political theology. It grappled with the manifold moral and social problems of a secular industrial society, its materialism and religious indifferentism, the erosion of commitment to the Christian churches and their progressive marginalization in German society. So in the latter part of the century German Protestant theology was more open to theological developments outside the German-speaking world than at any time since the sixteenth century.

Central problems of Protestant thought
It follows from what has been said that the central problems of German Protestant theology were characteristically different at different times in its history. In the sixteenth and seventeenth centuries its major tasks were to clarify the stand of evangelical Protestantism *vis-à-vis* both Roman Catholicism and radical ('enthusiast') religious movements such as the Anabaptists and anti-Trinitarians, and to sort out the doctrinal differences between Lutheran and Calvinist convictions within the Protestant camp. In the seventeenth and eighteenth centuries the emphasis shifted to the internal differences between theological orthodoxy and pietism and to the external differences between, on the one hand, the claims of revealed religion and, on the other, Enlightenment rationalism (reason) and empirical science (nature). In many respects the complex movement of the Enlightenment constituted the most significant development in the intellectual history of German Protestant thought since the Reformation and before the ecumenical reorientation in our century. The rise of historical-critical thought during the later Enlightenment replaced the predominantly metaphysical understanding of

491

reality inherited from antiquity by an essentially historical view of the world. So from the end of the eighteenth century Protestant theology was dominated by the question of history, concentrating particularly on the relationship between revelation and history and between Christianity and other religions, on the impact of modern science on the Christian faith, and on its role in modern society.

In the twentieth century the disestablishment of the churches after the First World War, the breakdown of Protestant identification with the culture of bourgeois Germany, and the rediscovery of eschatological orientation (dialectical theology) and the Reformation heritage (Luther renaissance) led to a new concentration on the problems of faith and God, law and gospel, church and state, Christology and justification. The church struggle in the Nazi period, Barmen, and the ambivalent experience of the confessional church furthered the ecumenical orientation of German Protestant theology and paved the way towards greater unity among the Protestant churches. Thus the Leuenberg Concord between the Lutheran, Reformed and United churches in 1973 in fact ended the centuries-old doctrinal divisions that had characterized German Protestantism since the Reformation. And the last decade of the century saw a growing unity among Protestants in Europe, including not only the great national Protestant churches but also Baptist and Methodist free churches and the heirs to the more radical Reformation movements such as Hussite, Waldensian and Mennonite churches. After the Second World War the experience of the 'death of the God of theistic metaphysics' resulted in a renewed interest in biblical tradition, exegetical (demythologizing) and hermeneutical questions. This led to a renaissance of Trinitarian thought in academic theology and to a self-conscious engagement with present-day religious, social and political issues in the ecumenical and practice-oriented theological reflections of church bodies and synods. In particular the unsolved problems in the relationship between Christianity and Judaism, the ecumenical relations with Roman Catholicism after the Second Vatican Council, the active but controversial participation in the ecumenical process of the World Council of Churches, the issues of theological feminism,

and the need for the Christian churches to define their role in an increasingly multinational and pluri-religious culture in German society were central to Protestant thought in the latter part of the century.

Different needs and problems have thus occasioned German Protestantism to develop, through adaptation and resistance, a variety of theologies through the centuries, always trying to recover and redetermine what it took to be essential in new situations and changing contexts. But for all this diversity, there is also a remarkable continuity, due mainly to two factors: the continuing existence of the territorial churches of the Reformation, and the continual reflection of academic theology on the peculiar character of Protestant theology in contrast to Roman Catholicism, required by the historical fact that theological faculties at German universities must by law be either Protestant or Roman Catholic. Through the years this has led to a series of self-referential meta-reflections on the 'essence' of Protestantism which are characteristic of German Protestant theology since the Enlightenment.

The common core of Protestant theology
The common core of Protestant theology before 1700 consisted in the rejection of papal authority and the authoritarian clericalism of Roman Catholicism, as well as of the more radical spiritualist, Anabaptist and unitarian movements, and in the insistence that God's grace is mediated only through his Word in law and gospel so that the Bible is the ultimately binding Word of God and the individual consciousness enlightened by the Spirit is the ultimate arbiter in matters of religion and salvation. Accordingly theological reflection concentrated on four major issues: the understanding of salvific grace as worked out in the doctrine of justification by faith alone (*sola fide*); the mediation of grace through Christ and the Spirit in word and sacrament (*solus Christus, solo verbo*); the Bible as the only source of the church's proclamation of justifying faith in Christ and as the ultimate norm of all Christian teaching, creeds, confessions and forms of polity (*sola scriptura*); and the question of authority in the church as answered by the doctrine of the priesthood of all believers, that is, the conviction that all believers are priests who can intercede

for one another, not only the ordained clergy, and that nobody can be forced against conscience, Scripture and reason in matters of faith for the sake of authority.

It was this latter aspect which became prominent when, in the wake of the Enlightenment, Protestant thinkers sought to determine the 'essence' or 'principle(s)' of Protestantism more explicitly. The sixteenth and seventeenth centuries saw numerous attempts to mediate between the religious parties by stating what is common, central and essential to all Christian life and faith. According to Martin Bucer, for example, the 'substance of the Christian faith' (*substantia Christianismi*) is not any doctrine or article of faith but the wholehearted and total trust in God and Christ. In the orthodox period and early Enlightenment a number of thinkers (A. Hunnius, G. Calixt, C. Crusius, G.W. Leibniz) tried to overcome the confessional divisions by distinguishing fundamental articles of faith which are shared by all Christians from non-fundamental ones on which believers may differ without loss of salvation. This concentration on what is central and necessary to the Christian faith was generalized by the quest of the 'essence of Christianity' in the Enlightenment. Some (especially deists) answered it by identifying it with the permanent truths of natural theology. Others, more aware of the problem of history, used the dialectics of internal essence and external form to relativize all actual forms of Christianity to be only historical manifestations (appearances) of an underlying principle (essence). While this was never fully realized by any of its contingent historical manifestations, it was only accessible through the whole historical process of its realizations (see H. Wagenhammer, *Das Wesen des Christentums* of 1973).

The same dialectics of form and content, appearance and essence, fact and principle were applied to Protestantism in numerous attempts from the mid-eighteenth century to determine its 'essence' or 'principle(s)'. They can be grouped into four characteristic approaches. The first understands Protestantism as the religious manifestation of a non-religious (or not merely religious) principle which is not, and need not be, realized only in religious forms of life. The second sees Protestantism governed by a principle which necessarily leads to specific forms of religious life. The third denies that Protestantism is historically and theologically coherent enough to be explained by one underlying principle at all. And the fourth seeks to combine these approaches by identifying the principle of Protestantism as the critical standard by which all religious and non-religious historical forms of Protestantism should be judged. These four approaches are now described in more detail.

First approach Immanuel Kant described the inexplicable fact of freedom as the transcendental principle of autonomous moral self-determination and of all truly human life and was, for this reason, called the 'philosopher of Protestantism' by F. Paulsen (1899) and others; but it was above all G.W.F. Hegel who worked out this idea in philosophical detail. For him the willingness 'to accept nothing among one's convictions that has not been justified by thought' is the 'peculiar principle of Protestantism' (*Grundlinien der Philosophie des Rechts*, 1821). It grounds the freedom of the individual in both its private and public dimensions. For freedom is the ultimate ground not only of private morality, uncoerced by external authorities of whatever sort and guided only by the insights of reason and consciousness, but also of public law and political institutions, the objective historical 'realm of realized freedom'. The Protestant principle of the Reformation ('Here I stand!') is the 'principle of the independent and in itself infinite personality of the individual, of subjective freedom'. As such it is of more than mere local or passing historical significance. It marks the beginning of the full religious, social and political realization of freedom and autonomy in the modern state which has transformed the world.

In the nineteenth century this understanding of the Protestant principle of freedom as the beginning of modernity and the foundation of the modern state inspired both the more liberal Protestant ethos of R. Rothe and the national conservatism of F.J. Stahl. Both contributed in their different ways to the formation of the culture-Protestantism which dominated Germany in the latter part of the nineteenth century. For if Protestantism is grounded on the principle of subjective freedom which is most adequately realized in the modern state, then the distinction between church and state is bound progressively to disappear. With the Reformation, Christianity has moved into its secular phase in which the point of the Christian religion is realized not only for the few in the church but for all in the constitutional state.

The same conviction of the progressive realization of the Protestant principle of subjective freedom also guided F.C. Baur in his work on the history of dogma. For him the Reformation was the decisive turning point in the history of Christianity. The Protestant critique of Roman Catholicism was fundamentally the protest of autonomous subjectivity against the heteronomous authority of the church. This autonomy was not realized once and for all by the Reformation but is 'a principle capable of infinite development' (*Lehrbuch der christlichen Dogmengeschichte*, 1867). It is also to be upheld *vis-à-vis* the Bible, which Protestants treat critically just because they accept it as authority. And it cannot fully be understood without taking the whole, and still developing, history of Protestantism into account. It follows that if we want to understand any Christian doctrine we must trace its historical development, and it comes as no surprise that most of the major Protestant theologians in the nineteenth century have at the same time been historians or actively engaged in historical research.

Second approach Baur was not simply applying Hegelian ideas to the study of doctrine. As a young man he was deeply impressed by F.D.E. Schleiermacher's *The Christian Faith* of 1821–2, which he rightly regarded as inaugurating a new post-Enlightenment phase in Protestant theology. With this book Schleiermacher sought to justify the union between Lutheran and Reformed churches in Prussia after 1817 by describing their doctrinal positions as two equally valid forms of Protestantism, and Protestantism and Catholicism as two equally legitimate forms of Christianity. The latter difference is, as he succinctly stated in §24 of his *Christian Faith*, that 'the former makes the individual's relation to the Church dependent on his relation to Christ, while the latter contrariwise makes the individual's relation to Christ dependent on his relation to the Church.' This identified, in an admirably clear way, ecclesiology and the role of the church in the Christian life of faith as the central point at issue

between Protestantism and Roman Catholicism; and this has been borne out by the theological and dogmatic developments in the nineteenth and twentieth centuries.

Schleiermacher's insight was not immediately grasped by his contemporaries. A. Twesten, his pupil and successor in Berlin, coined the phrase, the 'two principles of Protestantism', that is, the 'formal principle' of Scripture and the 'material principle' of justification by faith alone. And it became a widely held conviction, influentially stated by A. Ritschl, that only the two principles together defined the distinctive character of Protestantism. A special status is assigned to the Bible in Protestant life and thought as the normative witness to God's revelation. But the seventeenth-century theories of the infallible and inerrant inspiration of the biblical texts in all details of content or even verbal expression were widely dismissed as making an idol of the Bible. The biblical texts are historical documents and must be treated according to the general principles of historical criticism and interpretation; the biblical canon is not closed but theoretically open; and although the Bible has ultimate authority in all matters of faith and salvation, theology is not slavishly tied to it but is required to exercise the freedom of critical judgement and reflective reason in interpreting the biblical texts, as much as with any other text. Some, like R. Hagenbach, have therefore concluded that 'the principle of free enquiry' is 'the true principle of Protestantism'; and even in our century it was held by G. Ebeling (1950) that the historical–critical method bears a special affinity to the Protestant spirit.

This was also the conviction of A. Harnack at the turn of the century. In his widely read *The Essence of Christianity* of 1900 he analyses the differences between Protestantism and Catholicism in terms of reformation or 'critical reduction' and revolution or evangelical criticism of church dogma and canon law. Protestantism reduced the essence of Christianity to the Word of God and the inner experience of faith which corresponds to it. And it objected in principle to all attempts to place the church, its dogma or its laws above the gospel. It is the historical task of Protestantism to safeguard this freedom of true evangelical Christianity against all attempts at religious and moral heteronomy.

Third approach The Schleiermacher–Ritschl–Harnack tradition of understanding Protestantism in terms of a (never fully realized) principle or set of principles by which it is clearly marked off from Roman Catholicism came to an end with E. Troeltsch ([1906] 1966). He took Protestantism seriously as a complex historical phenomenon, too diverse to be understood as the successive historical manifestation of one and the same underlying principle, and properly accessible only in terms of the canons of historical-critical method. In his profound historical analysis of Protestantism he identified not the Reformation, but the Enlightenment as the decisive turning point in the intellectual history of the West. The Reformation and its aftermath still belonged to the religious culture of the middle ages without any direct impact on the modern world. Protestantism, accordingly, is not explicable as a single and coherent historical phenomenon. Rather we must distinguish between, on the one hand, the premodern 'old Protestantism' of the orthodox period in the sixteenth and seventeeth centuries which continued the uniform religious culture of the middle ages, accepted supernatural revelation and the dogmatic method in theology, and marked itself off against humanism, spiritualism and the more radical Baptist movements, and, on the other, the post-Enlightenment 'neo-Protestantism' which embraces the liberal ideas of freedom, autonomous subjectivity, religious and political tolerance, free scientific enquiry and historical method with its principles of criticism, analogy and correlation. In neither sense, however – and here Troeltsch most clearly departs from Hegelian accounts – can Protestantism be seen as a source of the modern world: old Protestantism is still medieval and premodern, while neo-Protestantism is already part of modernity.

It is here that M. Weber's sociological account of Protestantism ([1904–5] 1930) differs from Troeltsch's historical analysis, which otherwise he parallels in many ways. He focuses on the causal connection between Protestant, especially Calvinist, ethics and the rise of capitalism, and he diagnoses the impact of this 'ascetic Protestantism' on western society as a process of 'disenchantment' which prepared and reinforced the means–end rationality that characterizes the modern sociocultural system of the west.

Fourth approach Troeltsch's and Harnack's versions of liberal Protestantism and their close involvement with the bourgeois culture of Germany were sharply criticized by K. Barth and the other proponents of dialectical theology after the First World War. For them 'Protestantism' was a term theologically compromised by neo-Protestantism. They preferred to call their own position 'evangelical', not only because this was closer to the original Reformation usage but because – as especially Barth made clear in both his *Christian Dogmatics* and *Church Dogmatics* – their theology was meant to explicate not the self-understanding of a particular (Protestant) church, tradition or religious party, but the Word of God by which all forms of Christianity, including Protestant ones, must be judged. P. Tillich agreed with this but formulated his programme precisely in terms of the Protestant principle to which he gave a new and important twist. He distinguished between the historically contingent formations (*Gestalten*) of Protestantism and the universally valid principle of Protestantism which he found expressed in the Reformation doctrine of justification by grace alone (Tillich, 1950). This principle is the permanent protest against, and criticism of, our human temptations to confound the conditional and the unconditional, to elevate finite religious or profane powers to the status of infinite or absolute power. All historical forms of Protestantism are necessarily conditioned and concrete forms of life. They are true only if, as finite and specific formations (*Gestalten*) of grace, they include both a specific form and the protest against this form, a concrete historical realization and its negation. This intrinsic dialectics safeguards Protestantism in its assigning of absolute value or permanent validity to any doctrines, forms of life or institutions, and it explains its inner dynamics to be *semper reformanda*, always on the move to better and more adequate *Gestaltungen* in our profane reality.

Protestant thought and theology

Protestant thought and theology has been pluralist from the beginning. Its sense of identity was not based on the unchanging character of church doctrine or the continuity of ecclesial institutions and traditions but on the permanent proclamation of God's Word as law and gospel, that is, the justification of the sinner by faith alone as testified by Scripture. Scripture, not church doctrine, was accepted as the fundamental norm and source of Christian life and theological reflection, and the confessions and catechisms of the sixteenth century as adequate restatements of the central tenets of biblical teaching in those historical circumstances. Whereas the Lutheran churches subscribed to the *Augsburg Confession* (1530) as their authoritative confession, the Reformed tradition always knew a variety of confessions and catechisms. After many failures, attempts to overcome the Protestant divide only succeeded in this century in the wake of the Barmen Declaration (1934) with the Leuenberg Concord (1973), which proved to be of more than merely passing or regional importance. The Leuenberg Concord especially has established itself as a paradigm of Protestant ecumenical theology that overcomes old divisions without swerving from the fundamental Protestant tenets of *solus Christus*, *sola scriptura*, *sola gratia*, and *sola fide*. *Scripture* The assertion of the Bible as the *norma normans* of all Christian life and thought has led Protestant theology since M. Chemnitz, M. Flacius, J. Gerhard and A. Hunnius to develop and defend a doctrine of the authority of the Bible. While Luther insisted on the *viva vox evangelii* as the Word of God, theologians in the orthodox period identified the (written) Word of God with the canon of the Old and New Testaments which they claimed to be not only inspired but inerrant and infallible. Some even went so far as to hold theories of dictation which made not only the content but the wording of the biblical texts part of God's revelation. On the other hand, the canon never became officially closed in Protestantism, and this openness of the canon served as a constant reminder that the Bible is not to be turned into an icon or idol. It is the authoritative witness to the grace of God in Jesus Christ. Hence the biblical texts were to be made available to every individual. But this *verbum externum* cannot be understood as the Word of God without the working of the Spirit in the heart of the reader or listener. Hence the orthodox doctrine of the inspiration of Scripture requires the parallel doctrine of the inner testimony of the Holy Spirit: only together do they justify the conviction that the biblical texts are the normative Word of God. Although this was clear in theory, orthodox theologians in practice used biblical texts as inspired premises for dogmatic conclusions or claimed, as pietism did, a specific *hermeneutica sacra* for them.

For this reason, the rise of historical criticism in the Enlightenment constituted a major challenge to both Protestant orthodox and pietist theologies. While pietist theologians reacted to this by postulating a *theologia regenitorum* open only to those who are reborn, academic theology distinguished between history and dogma, biblical exegesis and dogmatic and moral doctrine and, since the beginning of the nineteenth century, widely accepted the post-Enlightenment views of biblical criticism. Biblical texts have to be treated as any other ancient literary text. This inspired a formidable and exemplary study of the biblical texts, their ancient settings and historical and literary developments in German Protestant theology during the past two hundred years. But it also produced a growing divide between academic theology and the life of the church. For by concentrating on the biblical texts as such it tended to overlook the fact that these texts must be placed in the context of the life of faith, the proclamation of the church and the working of the Spirit in order to become accessible as the Word of God. So in a sense the history of the Protestant study of the Bible since the Reformation can be described as a series of attempts to determine the proper context in which these texts have to be studied. While the Reformers insisted that not Scripture but the use of Scripture to provoke faith in Christ (*usus scripturae*) is what theology has to study if it wants to understand the Word of God as law and gospel, orthodox theologians theoretically restated, and thereby changed, this by claiming the perspective of law and gospel to be the decisive dogmatic framework for studying the biblical texts. Instead of concentrating on the faith-provoking use of Scripture, they dogmatically placed the biblical texts in a doctrinal context. This was too theoretical for pietism, and not theoretical enough for the Enlightenment. Thus whereas pietists claimed not doctrine but the life of the believer to be the proper context for studying the biblical texts, the Enlightenment insisted on the context of reason and experience as the only adequate way to make sense of them.

The study of the Bible has since become torn between the ills of private subjectivity and the dangers of objectifying generalizations or historical descriptions devoid of individual commitment. In the nineteenth century history, other religions, the natural sciences and modern culture became the predominant contexts in which biblical texts were placed, studied and interpreted. The outcome was an immensely increased knowledge of the historical development, cultural immersion, literary refinement and religious richness of the biblical texts, but at the same time a growing awareness of their at best relative difference from other religious texts, traditions and experiences. Instead of demonstrating its uniqueness, the comparative and historical approaches to the Bible proved its cultural dependence and religious relativity. This made it increasingly difficult for theology to use it as the authoritative norm and source of Christian faith. In the light of the rediscovery of the eschatological nature of the Christian faith by J. Weiss, F. Overbeck and C. and J.C. Blumhardt, theologians like R. Bultmann reacted to the theological breakdown of these historifying and relativizing approaches after A. Schweitzer and Troeltsch by insisting on the existential structures of human life as the key to a proper understanding of the biblical texts and the universal validity of their kerygmatic message. And from the middle of the twentieth century methods of literary criticism and critical hermeneutics became increasingly used to correct the shortcomings of a merely historical-critical, sociological or psychological study of Scripture.

However, none of these methods helped to recover the theological import of Scripture. For the decisive question is not the method but the object of biblical study: as long as theologians study merely the texts rather than the faith-provoking *use* of these texts, their study of the Bible is ultimately a-theological. Biblical exegesis which concentrates on the biblical texts in their various historical/sociological/psychological contexts is a merely historical/sociological/psychological discipline. Dogmatic theology must move beyond this by considering the faith-provoking use of these texts in the life of the church if it is to arrive at theological conclusions for today. (See also BIBLICAL CRITICISM AND INTERPRETATION (1: OLD TESTAMENT and 2: NEW TESTAMENT.)

Theological method The distinction between historical and dogmatic theology is itself a result of Protestant self-reflection on theological method (see METHOD IN THEOLOGY). Since the seventeenth century it has distinguished different branches and disciplines of theology no longer in terms of their subject matter (biblical, moral and dogmatic theology) but in terms of the methods used for studying them (*theologia positiva, theologia scholastica*). In 1787 J.P. Gabler defined biblical theology as a historical discipline distinct from dogmatics, whose task is to restate the Christian faith in a way 'adequate to our time'. Theology's external relationships with other disciplines are thus mirrored in the internal differentiation of theological disciplines according to the tasks pursued and methods used.

This found classical expression in Schleiermacher's *Brief Outline of the Study of Theology* of 1811, which defined the basic pattern of the study of Protestant theology in Germany for the nineteenth and twentieth centuries. For him theology is a positive, that is, non-speculative or non-foundationalist, science. Just as in the case of medicine and law, both its place in the university and its internal organization are determined by its practical task, the furthering of Christian life in modern society. This leads to its differentiation into three major disciplines. As philosophical theology it relates to the realm of knowledge and science, as practical theology to the realm of life in general and Christian life in particular, but in its central part which comprises both exegetical and dogmatic theology it is fundamentally a historical discipline. This balanced conception and practical grounding of theology avoided both the speculative foundationalism of the idealist tradition and the reduction of theology to a merely historical and comparative study of religion(s), which has endangered the existence of independent theological faculties at German universities from J.G. Fichte, Paul de Lagarde and Overbeck to the present day.

Barth accepted this practical and church-related orientation of theology but criticized Schleiermacher for placing human religion and piety rather than the authoritative Word of God at its centre. And W. Pannenberg tried to move beyond both Barth and Schleiermacher in his *Theology and the Philosophy of Science* of 1973 by returning to the traditional definition of theology as the science of God. The differentiated unity of theology is to be understood not in terms of method but in terms of the unity of its subject matter: God, the all-determining reality. This reality cannot be directly experienced in the world but becomes only indirectly accessible in the subjective anticipations of the totality of meaning which is presupposed in all particular experiences. This turns theology into a systematic super-science that seeks to detect the indirect co-givenness of God in all areas of human experience and science. And since the experience of reality as a whole finds symbolic expression primarily in the historic religions, a theory of the history of religions is fundamental for theology. Thus whereas Schleiermacher outlined theology as a fundamentally practical enterprise based on the reality of organized religion or church life, and Barth conceived it as a fundamentally critical enterprise based on God's revelation in Jesus Christ, Pannenberg returned to a pre-modern understanding of theology as a theoretical super-science of the totality of reality.

Doctrine of God Developments in theological method have manifest implications for the doctrine of GOD. Protestant theology has always insisted on a close relationship between *cognitio dei* and *cognitio hominis*, God and faith, theology and anthropology, and it largely followed Luther, who defined the proper subject matter of theology as *homo reus et perditus et deus iustificans vel salvator*. But this soteriological emphasis in the doctrine of God was worked out in different ways in the history of Protestant theology.

1 The first Lutheran dogmatics, Philipp Melanchthon's *Loci communes* of 1520, did not contain a separate tract *De Deo* but insisted that to know Christ, and hence God, is to know his benefits towards us. Thus the very Melanchthon who inaugurated the reception of Aristotelian metaphysics into Protestant theology provided the decisive argument for neo-Protestant criticism of all metaphysical theology. In the aftermath of Kant the *pro nobis* was taken not merely in a soteriological but in an epistemological sense. We cannot know what God is in himself, as W. Herrmann put it, but only what he does in and for us. By fundamentally distinguishing between objectified and existential reality, Bultmann interpreted this to mean that the essential relatedness of God and human being does not allow theology to talk about either God or human existence in objectifying terms. Instead we have to interpret all statements about God as statements about human existence in both a soteriological and epistemological sense. This concurred with Schleiermacher's attempt to move beyond the objectifying talk of God in religion, theology and philosophy by showing that all objectifications of God are contingent determinations of our God-consciousness and as such are manifestations of an underlying indeterminate structure of God-consciousness which is the pre-reflective capacity, common to all rational beings, for awareness of an existential relation to that to which we owe our existence, whereas it owes its existence neither to us nor to anything else. Hence 'God' does not name a (supernatural) being but 'the Whence of the feeling of utter dependence'. Accordingly 'all attributes that we ascribe to God are not to be taken as denoting something special in God, but only something special in the way in which the feeling of utter dependence is related to him' (*The Christian Faith*, §50).

2 The Protestant emphasis on the non-objectification of God is an attempt to safeguard the fundamental difference between God and created being in the tradition of Exodus 20: 4 without completely denying the knowability of God. Hegel, who took the principle of subjectivity to be the principle of Protestantism, identified Kant's and Fichte's transcendental philosophies as explications of this principle. Kant's critique of Enlightenment theism and its proofs of the existence of God can be seen as a philosophical reworking of the Protestant insistence on a close correlation of God and faith, in that he combines a denial of all theoretical knowledge of God with the postulate of his existence based on the requirements of practical reason. Protestant theology of the nineteenth and twentieth centuries would be unthinkable without his 'I had to abolish knowledge to make room for faith' (*Critique of Pure Reason*). Fichte went even further by

applying this principle to the notion of God itself, that is, to the application of any concepts, in particular the concept of person or personality, to God. For him, whatever is conceptualized cannot be God. It is against this background that Protestant theology, while clinging to the soteriological emphasis of the doctrine of God, developed an increasingly critical attitude towards all sorts of metaphysical theism. Elaborating Blaise Pascal's distinction between the God of the philosophers and the God of Abraham, Isaac and Jacob, it took an explicitly anti-metaphysical and anti-theistic turn, which characterizes such different positions as Schleiermacher's criticism of natural theology, Ritschl's rejection of all metaphysics in theology, Harnack's view of the corruption of the original gospel by Hellenist thought, K. Barth's and D. Bonhoeffer's critique of the traditional understanding of divine omnipotence, impassibility and transcendence, J. Moltmann's and E. Jüngel's insistence on a Trinitarian anti-theism and D. Soelle's paradoxical postulate of atheist belief in God.

3 But it was L. Feuerbach who in his *Essence of Christianity* of 1841 took this anti-theistic attitude to its atheistic extreme. Claiming to explicate Luther's soteriological correlation of God and faith he held that 'consciousness of God is man's self-consciousness; knowledge of God is man's self-knowledge'. For him God is the self-objectification and self-externalization of man's self-knowledge as species being. This made theology an epiphenomenon of anthropology, and it forced Protestant theologians from then on explicitly to mark off their own soteriological accounts of God from this anthropological atheism which made religion the creation of human imagination. Four types of approach to coming to grips with Feuerbach have become particularly prominent.

The first is to place the theological project in the context of a (broadly understood) religious or natural account of God. Thus W. Pannenberg claims, against all tendencies to dissolve or eliminate the concept of God in Protestant theology, that we need a general notion of God that fixes minimal conditions for coherent talk of God if we want to make sense of the gospel and come to grips with Feuerbach's verdict on theology. The Protestant distrust of metaphysics must thus be corrected by transcendentalist (T. Rendtorff, E. Herms) or anthropological (Pannenberg) foundations of Christian talk of God, by recourse to 'original revelation' (P. Althaus) or by placing it in the context of an account of the history of religions as the history of the appearance of the unity of God (Pannenberg).

This is set against the second approach, Barth's attempt to interpret the impossibility of objectifying knowledge of God as manifestation of his sovereign freedom to make himself accessible only in and through his self-revelation. Starting from the insight that God can only be known through God as revealed in Jesus Christ, Barth embraced Feuerbach's view of anthropology as the mystery of theology and turned it into a verdict on the whole neo-Protestant tradition since Schleiermacher. Theology must start from the (eschatological) fact of God's self-revelation, not from epistemological considerations of its possibility or assumptions about a fundamental structure of utter dependence or religious a priori of human existence. The fact of God's self-revelation as Lord (*Church Dogmatics* I/1 §8) manifests God's being as the one who loves freely (*Church Dogmatics* II/1 §28); and this in turn requires a Trinitarian account of God who reveals himself as love by freely identifying with Jesus Christ on the cross. Thus the mystery of God is his humanity, and his divinity his self-humiliation until death for us. But then Feuerbach's thesis has to be put on its head: theological statements are not anthropological statements in disguise, but all anthropological statements have to be understood as being derivative from Christology (*Church Dogmatics* II/1) and hence in the last resort from the doctrine of the Trinity.

Barth's comprehensive reworking of the doctrine of God in Christological and Trinitarian terms reflects insights which were first worked out in Hegel's speculative philosophy. The contents of the Christian or absolute religion can be philosophically reconstructed, justified and appropriated in a dialectical process outlined in the *Science of Logic* of 1812. And just as the truth of religion is preserved in philosophy, so the truth of the doctrine of the Trinity is preserved and completed in the speculative theory of the internally differentiated Absolute. Theological

Hegelianism was very influential in the nineteenth century (K. Daub, P. Marheineke, R. Rothe). It has recently been rigorously renewed by F. Wagner, who claims that the only consistent way to oppose the charge of Feuerbach is to base theology not on the consciousness, language or facts of religion but on the self-unfolding process of the self-determining self-determination that is the Absolute.

A fourth attempt takes a vigorously Trinitarian approach. Thus E. Jüngel opposes both traditional theism and atheism with a Trinitarian account of the God who has revealed himself through the cross of Christ as redeeming love. God is the mystery of the world, but we are unable to discern that mystery unless we place our experience of the world in the light of God's self-revelation in Christ, that is, re-experience all our experience in faith. Thus faith is not the projection of ideal humanity into the idea of God but a second-order experience of the world in which we discern it as (fallen) creation in the light of the love of God disclosed in Christ. God has appropriated death on the cross of Christ, and we cannot adequately talk of God unless we take this into account. Hence in so far as atheism is the negation of theism, it critically belongs to every truly Trinitarian account of God.

The four reactions to Feuerbach all concur in that they rediscover and restate the doctrine of God in Trinitarian terms. After the prevailing theism of the nineteenth century this is one of the most distinctive developments of German Protestant theology in the (second half of the) twentieth century.

The Trinity The Protestant renewal of Trinitarian theology in the twentieth century starts with Barth, who reacted to the widespread neglect of the doctrine of the Trinity in western theology in his time. Few denied that it was one of the principal mysteries of faith. But it was of little practical significance to the life of faith. Since Augustine and scholastic Augustinianism, Trinitarian thought had come to wear an abstract air, and the western inclination towards a unitarian formulation of the doctrine of God was even further increased by the Enlightenment. Where the doctrine of the Trinity was not held on merely traditionalist grounds, it was discarded altogether or it took on a speculative life of its own.

According to K. Rahner, the first decisive move in the isolation and subsequent sterilization of the doctrine of the Trinity was the separation of the discussion of 'the one God' from the discussion of 'the triune God'. The doctrine of the Trinity became a doctrine alongside others rather than the frame of reference or the grammar of all the others. The Reformation did not achieve a restoration of Trinitarian thought; and at the beginning of the nineteenth century Schleiermacher rightly observed that to achieve this was still one of the unfulfilled tasks of Protestant theology. It remained so for another century. Since the Enlightenment, discussions of the Trinity have become subordinated to a preoccupation with the unitary being of God. Philosophical theism – the belief in the existence of a supreme and beneficent Being – was widely taken over by Christian theologians. Nineteenth-century attempts to defend Trinitarian thought against these developments led to its absorption into the discussion of the being of God as Absolute, where it took on a speculative life of its own. But this estranged it even further from the life of the church. It left the figurative language of faith without adequate conceptual form. And it opened up a gap between the life of faith and the intellectual engagement with the problem of God.

Philosophers were first to react against these developments. With Feuerbach, K. Marx, S. Freud and F. Nietzsche the speculative movement and its attempted rescue of Trinitarian thought came under vigorous attack. Yet since its close association with the Christian tradition had made its vulnerability the vulnerability of Christian theology as well, the criticism of these thinkers was largely unacceptable to (liberal) theology. Only when, in the twentieth century, theology gradually began to divorce itself from Enlightenment theism and its aftermath, could it come to grips with both the speculative tradition and its critics by taking a vigorously Trinitarian and explicitly anti-theistic approach.

Anti-theism, that is, the rejection of Enlightenment theism, its consequences and its antithesis (atheism), has thus been one of the major motives for Trinitarian theology today. It is the common denominator of such different theologies as those of Moltmann, Jüngel, Pannenberg and Wagner. They all agree that

Christian theology, in order to move beyond the barren alternatives of theism and atheism, must be Trinitarian in character. But they differ widely and even irreconcilably in the ways in which they ground their Trinitarian positions.

For E. Jüngel, as for Barth in his later years, the doctrine of the Trinity is Christologically grounded (Jüngel, *Entsprechungen: Gott–Wahrheit–Mensch*). Originally Barth's doctrine of the Trinity was 'bound up with the concept of revelation, in the strict sense of God's self-revelation which is grounded in God's Trinitarian self-unfolding' (Pannenberg, *Basic Questions in Theology*, 1967–71). This invited the criticism that Barth's doctrine, by working out the structure and implication of the *Deus dixit*, 'is fashioned out of the logic of God as absolute subject' (J.B. Webster, *Eberhard Jüngel*, 1986) and that his 'construal of the Trinity as the self-unfolding of a divine subject inevitably does damage to the co-eternity of the divine persons, diminishing their plurality to mere modes of being subordinate to the divine subject' (Pannenberg). But as the *Church Dogmatics* evolved, the emphasis shifted away from the inner structure of revelation towards the history of Jesus and, in particular, the cross. And in stressing the 'displacement' between Father and Son on the cross, Barth increasingly intensified the divine plurality.

Jüngel criticizes Barth for not taking that process far enough. His own work on the Trinity starts from God's self-identification with the crucified on the cross, and he conceives its function in working out the identity of God's being-for-himself and his being-for-us in the person of Jesus Christ. If God has identified himself with the crucified one, we must 'distinguish God from God' (Jüngel, *Unterwegs zur Sache*, 1972). But the unsurpassable contrast between Father and Son on the cross is not a 'contradiction within God' (Jüngel, *God as the Mystery of the World*, 1977). God – as Spirit – remains at the same time related to himself in this contrast. This is why we must give not merely a binitarian, but a Trinitarian account of God. Jüngel follows a long tradition of western thought when he describes the Spirit as the reassertion of unity after difference. But he has difficulty in articulating, with any clarity, the personal agency of the Spirit. So instead of pressing

from the event of the cross towards an account of the Trinity as an irreducible plural society, he turns to working out the *unity* of the self-differentiated God in terms of the concept of love: because God is love, he is essentially related, both in himself and in the sense of being open to what is different from him. In God 'to be' and 'to be related' are one and the same; and the character of the ontological relationality of God is love, that is, in Jüngel's definition, 'the unity of life [self-relation] and death [self-loss] in favour of life'. Hence even in his self-abasement on the cross, God is not foreign to himself but eminently true to himself: 'in giving himself away, he does not lose but becomes himself' (Webster) because, as God, he does not simply *act lovingly* but ontologically *is* love. Hence there is no need to posit 'an essence of God behind his loving *pro nobis*, for his aseity takes form as loving self-renunciation'.

Jüngel uses the concepts of 'love' and 'relation' to retain the coherence and unity of the divine being without sacrificing the sense of 'displacement' which is introduced into the being of God by the cross. J. Moltmann starts from the same Barthian legacy but moves in a different direction. His case for the necessity of Trinitarian discourse is developed from asserting God's real relation to human pain and suffering, supremely exemplified by the cross. On the cross, he says, God was abandoned by God. He not merely holds, as Jüngel does, that the cross occasions the distinction between God and God, but understands the separation of Father from Son in the dereliction of the cross in a full mythological sense. He is able to do this because for him the divine self-separation on the cross is grounded in the priority of persons over relations and the repudiation of any reduction of the three persons to the absolute subject as substance. For him, the primordial reality is the plurality of the persons, and '*the unity of God is only actual in that plurality*' (Pannenberg, *Basic Questions in Theology*). So he develops a pluralist account of a social Trinity of Father, Son and Spirit linked together only by what he calls the Trinitarian history of God. That is to say, the Trinity itself is seen in terms of God's involvement in historical becoming, and although Moltmann goes so far as to deny a definite *taxis* between the persons 'in favour of a trinity that can be taken "in any order", he nevertheless relates it to our progressive ordering towards a free, creative, relationship of "friendship" to God in the Holy Spirit' (J. Milbank). However, while this ensures that God is not seen as a closed monad, but as a community of loving interaction open to a reality beyond itself, Moltmann so much stresses the personal agency of Father, Son and Spirit, that it becomes difficult to see how it can still be said to be one and the same God. Moreover, in his account of the separation of Father and Son on the cross he does not succeed in doing justice to the agency of the Spirit *vis-à-vis* Father and Son. He has attempted to remedy this by developing an account not only of the kenosis of the Son but also of the kenosis of the Spirit. But this in fact increases his difficulty in distinguishing clearly between the agency of the Son and that of the Spirit, and virtually bars him from ascribing to the Spirit not merely the function of demonstrating the openness of the triune community but also of establishing its unity by overcoming the difference between Father and Son.

Moltmann's difficulties with the unity of God are one reason for W. Pannenberg to look for a different solution. He agrees with Jüngel and Moltmann that Barth's earlier attempt to develop the doctrine of the Trinity from the formal notion of revelation as expressed in the statement 'God reveals himself as the Lord' is unsatisfactory. Instead of starting from the formal notion of revelation, we must start from the content of God's revelation in Christ. But for Pannenberg this is not so much the cross and the relationship between Father, Son and Spirit in terms of which the cross can be understood as a salvific and revelatory event. Rather it is the particular relationship of the historical Jesus to God and, in particular, the fact that Jesus distinguished himself clearly from the God he called Father and, in renouncing himself completely, made room for the action of the Father and the coming of his kingdom. If this is interpreted, as Pannenberg interprets it, as the self-revelation of God, the way in which Jesus distinguishes himself from the Father discloses that there is an eternal relationship of Father and Son in God. Jesus' self-distinction from God manifests the eternal self-differentiation of the Son from the Father, which corresponds to the self-differentiation of the Father from the Son; and this, for Pannenberg, is the key for a correct interpretation of the cross of Christ (Pannenberg, *Systematic Theology*, 1988).

However, even if we accept this move from the historical fact of Jesus' obedient attitude to the God he called Father to the eternal mutuality of self-differentiation between Father and Son, we are still left with a binitarian rather than Trinitarian account of God. Only when we move from the cross to the resurrection do we get an adequate understanding of the third person, for the resurrection, not the cross, 'depicts the dependence of the Father and the Son on the Spirit as the medium of their community' (Schwöbel, 1990, p. 276). Accordingly Pannenberg describes the three persons as three mutually dependent centres of activity and not as three modes of being in one subject.

This conception of the Trinity has a number of important consequences: it dissolves the traditional western distinction between immanent and economic relations in so far as 'the mutual self-differentiation of Father, Son and Spirit in the divine economy must be seen as the concrete form of the immanent Trinitarian relations' (Schwöbel, 1990, p. 275). Moreover, the 'mutuality of their active relationships implies for Pannenberg . . . that the *monarchia* of the Father has to be understood as the result of the cooperation of all three persons' (p. 276) in the divine economy. 'From this perspective the world as a whole can be seen as the history in which it will be finally demonstrated that the Trinitarian God is the only true God' (ibid.).

However, this claim about the eschatological vindication of the Trinity leaves Pannenberg with a problem which he fails to solve. If the full realization of the *monarchia* of the Father is the kingdom, and if this is brought about only as the final result of the cooperation of all three persons in history, the divine unity of these three centres of activity is hidden and obscure in the course of history. Pannenberg emphasizes the 'eschatological resolution of the tension between the persons of Father, Son and Spirit in revelation and the hiddenness of the unity of God in the world' (Schwöbel, 1990, p. 277). But 'the question is how the three persons of the Trinity can be understood as presenting one divine essence without reducing them to moments or aspects of the one essential Godhead and without positing the divine essence as a fourth subject lurking behind the persons of Father, Son, and Spirit' (p. 277). It is here that Pannenberg's account fails most conspicuously. He does not succeed in offering a Trinitarian solution to the problem of the unity of God which is more than an eschatological postponement. Rather he gets stuck in a dualist cul-de-sac: on the one hand he develops the difference of Father, Son and Spirit from his account of revelation in terms of Jesus' self-distinction from the God he calls Father; on the other hand he grounds the unity of God in a metaphysical concept of God's essence prior to and independent of revelation: the concept of God as Infinite. This concept of God, at which we can arrive independently of revelation, as Pannenberg is at pains to show (in *Systematic Theology*), is normative and regulates all our thinking and speaking of God, including our accounts of the Trinity. For whatever we want to say about Father, Son and Spirit on the basis of revelation, it must accord with the fundamental idea of God as the Infinite.

It is here that F. Wagner criticizes Pannenberg for not going far enough. He hopes to remedy the revelationist leftovers which he detects in Pannenberg by basing his account of the Trinity on a theory of the Absolute in the tradition of Hegel and W. Cramer. For him, a convincing and tenable account of God must start from the idea of the Absolute and not from any particular event or understanding of God in history, tradition or religious consciousness. For unless what we say about God is grounded in a theory of the Absolute, which gives content to the idea of God without recourse to religious consciousness and its varying conceptions of God, we shall not be able to distinguish our account of God from superstitious and irrational belief or escape the charge of Feuerbach. On the other hand, the theory of the Absolute must be such that it allows us to explain or make sense of the actual ways in which religious consciousness conceives God. Wagner hopes to achieve this by describing God as the process of absolute self-determination, that is, as the self-determination which determines itself to determine itself. This presupposes an internal differentiation of God into that which determines itself, that which can be determined by itself and that which is the self-determination of the self-determinable by the self-determinator. And he understands this threefold distinction as a conceptual reworking of the difference between Father, Son and Spirit. Hence he claims to have shown that before we turn to analysing revelation or any other event or fact of religion, we can, in purely rational or conceptual terms, arrive at a theory of the Absolute which is intrinsically Trinitarian in structure and character: the Trinity may be a mystery of faith, but it is rationally transparent to philosophical reason.

It is obvious that some very hard questions must be asked as to Wagner's understanding of reason, rationality, conceptual construction and, in particular, his view of the working of language and the translatability of the figurative language of faith into the conceptuality of a theory of the Absolute. All this invites a number of well-known Wittgensteinian criticisms. Nevertheless, the problem that he seeks to tackle is a real one: the doctrine of the Trinity is only an adequate doctrine of God if it is more than a mere expression and manifestation of Christian tribalism. It must be construed to provide an account of *God* – not of a Christian God (whatever that may be) or of some particular beliefs about Father, Son and Spirit which Christians (but not Jews or Muslims) happen to hold over and above their common belief in God. The God of Christian faith is not a particular Christian God but God as experienced and worshipped by Christians. And a doctrine of the Trinity will be inadequate if it fails to make this clear.

That *anti-theism* is a common motive of Protestant Trinitarian theology today was already noted. As its second major characteristic has now emerged its *Christological orientation*, that is, its focus on the history of Jesus and, in particular, the nature of the involvement of God with the death of Jesus upon the cross. This is even true of Wagner, who seeks to show that what Christians confess about God in the light of the death and resurrection of Jesus Christ is a universal truth about God, accessible not only to faith but also to reason. So present-day Protestant Trinitarianism clearly reflects its traditional soteriological concern and Christ-centred faith.

Christology The question of the significance of Jesus Christ lies at the heart of Protestant theology, and in CHRISTOLOGY it has made the most important contributions to Christian theology since the Enlightenment (McGrath, 1986). The Reformers appropriated classical Chalcedonian Christology (see the third chapter of the *Augsburg Confession* of 1530) but reworked it soteriologically. Theologians in the orthodox period systematically distinguished between the person and the work or office of Jesus Christ in terms of an ontology of nature, person and act. To bring this ontological account of Christ into line with the biblical story, and in particular with Philippians 2: 5ff., the basic text for Lutheran Christology, they developed the doctrine of the two stages of Christ's life, the *status exinanitionis* and *status exaltationis*. But with the Enlightenment and the rise of historical consciousness, the problem of history and the question of the relationship between dogma and history became too pressing to be left to such a doctrinal appendix. It permeated the whole Christology and theology of Protestantism and caused its most profound reorientation since the Reformation. It kept its soteriological emphasis, and hence the categorial distinction between person and work of Christ. But it now restated it in terms of the 'historical Jesus' and his 'meaning for us'.

In 1774–8 G.E. Lessing published the Wolfenbüttel Fragments of H.S. Reimarus's *Schutzschrift für die vernünftigen Verehrer Gottes* which inaugurated over a century's QUEST OF THE HISTORICAL JESUS. For the Enlightenment, the ultimate arbiter of knowledge and truth in religion and theology as well as in all other areas was neither Scripture nor tradition, but reason and experience. It thus challenged the metaphysical Christologies of orthodoxy on epistemological, rationalist and moralist grounds. The rationally unacceptable two natures doctrine was replaced by more reasonable moral or aesthetic interpretations of Christ's significance. The doctrine of the uniqueness of the God-Man was restated in terms of Jesus as a morally perfect man, a teacher of truth in his lifetime and a supreme example of self-giving in his death. And the reliability of the biblical accounts of Christ on which the doctrinal claims concerning his unique status were based was questioned with increasing scepticism. Lessing interpreted the contrast between the authority of the 'written tradition' and its 'inner truth' in terms of the difference between 'accidental truths of history' and 'necessary truths of reason'; and he confessed to being personally unable to cross 'the ugly great ditch' between history and reason, between the particularity of historical fact and the generality of rational truth, which did not allow the deduction of the doctrinal accounts of Christ from the biblical accounts of Jesus (*Über den Beweis des Geistes und der Kraft*, 1777). Likewise, Kant regarded it as impossible for any individual historical being to be the full revelation of eternal truth. Kant believed that the 'ideal of a humanity well pleasing to God' was indeed encapsulated in the idea of a man like Jesus Christ. But the practical belief in such a son of God does not require 'any example from experience' but is based on the requirements of practical reason alone. This ideal or archetype is self-authenticating even if there was never a human being exemplifying it (*Religion within the Limits of Reason Alone*, 1793).

Protestant theology did not follow Kant's proposal, which went beyond the Enlightenment accounts of Jesus as moral teacher and example of moral perfection. But throughout the nineteenth century and beyond, it accepted Kant's close correlation of Christology and the idea of the kingdom of God. This is as true of Schleiermacher and Hegel as it is of Ritschl and Barth. Schleiermacher developed his Christology in *The Christian Faith* by arguing back from 'the state of the Christian, inasmuch as he is conscious of divine grace' (§§91–112) to its sufficient cause, the redeeming influence of Jesus on the collective life of the Christian community. The collective life of the Christian community owes its existence to the archetypal potency and perfection of Jesus' God-consciousness, mediated historically and socially through normal causal channels. He is redeemer in that he, and he alone, is the archetype of the final perfection of God-consciousness, and at the same time the one in which it was historically manifested. As such he exerts an assimilative power capable of bringing about an increasing perfection of God-consciousness in us, by drawing us not by supernatural magic or as moral model of perfect humanity but through the normal channels of communicating the gospel into the Christian community that is dominated by his perfect God-consciousness.

This novel starting point allowed Schleiermacher to reconstruct and appropriate both the orthodox Christological dogma and the Enlightenment criticism of it. By transcending the supernaturalism of orthodoxy as well as the rationalism and naturalism of the Enlightenment, he inaugurated a new area of Christological thought. This was partly due to his new understanding of nature and history and, in particular, to his (romantic) conception of the *individual universal* that went beyond the Enlightenment contrast of particularity with generality in distinguishing history and nature. History is the realm of human action and to be studied by ethics; nature and realm of events governed by causal laws and to be studied by physics; religion mediates between the two by combining the individuality of autonomous action with the universality of natural law. A. Ritschl restated this from neo-Kantian premises as the dichotomy between fact and value, and argued that Christological statements are not metaphysical statements of supernatural facts about Christ's nature but value-judgements about his 'value for us'. Jesus' calling (*Beruf*) was 'the establishment of the universal ethical fellowship of mankind' (*The Christian Doctrine of Justification and Reconciliation*, 1870-4). Those who believe in him as Christ participate in the kingdom of God as mediated through the community of faith. And they are reconciled to God in that they thereby participate in the same qualitative relationship to God as Jesus, the founder of their religion. Thus Jesus' uniqueness is understood not ontologically or metaphysically but historically: he is the unique founder of the Christian church. This rejection of metaphysics and of the metaphysically interpreted classical Christology was typical of liberal theology towards the end of the nineteenth century. It was brought to its logical conclusion by A. Harnack, who insisted that dogma was the Hellenistic corruption of the original simple gospel which was rediscovered in the Reformation. The irreducible element of the gospel concerns man's relationship with God the Father and the infinite value of the human soul, whereas 'Jesus does not belong to the gospel as one of its elements, but was the personal realization and power of the gospel, and we still perceive him as such' (*The Essence of Christianity*). Through the Christian community

we are linked to him historically, not theologically, in that to have faith in Jesus Christ is to have faith in God the Father, like Jesus Christ, rather than to believe any dogma about Christ. Christological problems are thus turned either into particular problems of history or universal problems of human personality, and the Christian faith is interpreted historically as a religiously founded culture of humanity and the infinite value of personality.

The conflict between universal validity and historical uniqueness had already governed Hegel's critique of Schleiermacher. For him, the identification of archetypal God-consciousness with the historical Jesus is unfounded as long as it is only inferred as sufficient cause from the religious consciousness of grace. Instead we must argue from God to religious consciousness, not the other way round. The incarnation must be the starting point, not the reinterpreted conclusion, of Christological reflection, for the ideal unity of God and man is demonstrated through the appearance of God in history in the person of Jesus Christ. But upon what grounds can we justify the identification of the speculative principle of the incarnation with the historical individual Jesus Christ? This was D.F. Strauss's, and in a sense also S. Kierkegaard's, question addressed to both Hegel's and Schleiermacher's Christologies. But whereas Strauss took the speculative horn of the dilemma, Kierkegaard took the historical one. Thus Strauss argued that the speculative idea of divine-human unity cannot be historically embodied in one specific individual but only in the whole history of the human species – an idea that was effectively taken up by Feuerbach's anthropotheism. For Strauss, the historical Jesus has at best only an accidental connection with the archetypal Christ. Hence the tasks of historical criticism and doctrinal theology must not only be distinguished but must clearly drift apart. Attempts to base a life of Jesus on the Gospel accounts are doomed to failure, as he showed in his *The Life of Jesus* of 1835–6 in that they are heavily impregnated with mythical expressions of religious imagination, that is, they report not only facts of Jesus' life but, in the form of factual discourse, the way the significance of his life was perceived and experienced by the early Christian community. Doctrinal theology that is concerned with truth cannot start from a reinterpretation of these imaginative myths, but only from the speculative idea of divine–human unity. And this, as he proved by his own monistic pantheism, may be done in a way that has little, if any, connection with the historical figure of Jesus of Nazareth. Kierkegaard, on the other hand, sought to solve the dilemma between historical uniqueness and universal validity by concentrating not on the speculative idea of divine–human unity but on the 'absolute paradox' of becoming contemporary to the incarnate son of God in faith. But by interpreting faith as ahistorical contemporaneity with Jesus, he, just as Strauss, dissolved the theological significance of the historical Jesus: the life of Jesus, beyond the mere fact of his existence, is without religious significance. Both Strauss and Kierkegaard thus paved the way for R. Bultmann's programme of demythologizing in the twentieth century.

Not only Strauss and Kierkegaard reacted critically to the quest for the historical Jesus that dominated Christology following Schleiermacher's *Life of Jesus* published posthumously in 1864. In the second half of the century a number of fundamental criticisms emerged from various theological quarters: (1) the kenotic critique of G. Thomasius; (2) the dogmatic critique of M. Kähler; (3) the apocalyptic critique of J. Weiss and A. Schweitzer; and (4) the historical critique of E. Troeltsch.

1 Confessional Lutherans like E. Sartorius, E. König, C. Hofmann and Thomasius who sought to retain traditional Christological orthodoxy in the face of historical criticism and the life of Jesus movement, turned to Philippians 2: 7 and its idea of a self-emptying of the divine in the incarnation as well as to the Lutheran doctrine of the *communicatio idiomatum* to accommodate incarnational Christology to the full historical humanity of Jesus. Operating within the circle of the two natures doctrine they interpreted the incarnation not as the assumption of humanity but as the self-emptying, or laying aside, of divinity. But if the kenosis is taken to mean a self-limitation of the divine in the sense that the eternal Son actually changed himself into a man and allowed his eternal self-consciousness to be completely extinguished (W.F. Gess), then we are not only faced with the problem of distinguishing

the kenosis from the annihilation of the Son of God, but also of accommodating the idea of divine self-limitation to that of divine unchangeability and impassibility. The latter problem Thomasius sought to solve by distinguishing between immanent and relative attributes of God, for example between absolute power and omnipotence, or absolute truth and omniscience. The kenosis is an expression of the divine rather than a denial of it, in that it is the Son's voluntary renunciation of those divine attributes that were incompatible with a genuinely human existence without thereby also divesting himself of those immanent attributes that define his divinity as his free capacity to limit himself. Self-limitation here becomes not only compatible with, but supremely characteristic of, God's divinity. And although this was sharply criticized by J. Dorner for dissolving the fundamental postulate of divine unchangeability, it was taken up in modified ways in the Trinitarian Christologies of the later Barth, Moltmann and Jüngel.

2 In quite a different way Kähler in *The So-Called Historical Jesus and the Historic, Biblical Christ* of 1892 criticized the Jesus of the 'Life-of-Jesus' movement as an invention of the modern historical mind which was no better than the dogmatic Christ of traditional Christology that it sought to replace. For him, 'the real Christ is the preached Christ' whose saving significance is encapsulated in the New Testament portrait of Christ as saviour. Hence the 'biblical, historical (*geschichtliche*) Christ', not the 'historical (*historische*) Jesus' of the pseudo-historical theology of liberal Protestantism is the proper starting point for Christology.

3 Although Kähler was severely criticized by W. Herrmann, O. Ritschl and others for misrepresenting the value of historical-critical method and ignoring the problem of whether the 'historical Christ' of the Bible was not merely a product of faith rather than a fact of history, the general thrust of his criticism was borne out by Schweitzer's *Quest of the Historical Jesus* of 1906. He saw the whole life-of-Jesus approach as operating within fundamental alternatives, of which he thought we must always accept the first and reject the second: either purely historical or purely supernatural; either synoptic or Johannine; either eschatological or non-eschatological. For him, the

rediscovery of the apocalyptic character and strongly eschatological bias of Jesus' proclamation of the kingdom of God by J. Weiss had called Ritschl's essentially Kantian interpretation of the kingdom of God as the exercise of the moral life in society into question, and made Jesus a strange figure from an alien first-century apocalyptic milieu without similarity to the Christ of the doctrinal Christology of the church.

4 From a different angle Troeltsch and the HISTORY OF RELIGIONS SCHOOL also radically undermined the foundations of constructive theology by historical research. For Troeltsch, the quest for the historical Jesus was not historical enough. Historical method consistently applied according to the principles of criticism, analogy and correlation must study Christianity as any other religion. It also bars any way from historical accounts of Jesus to dogmatic conclusions as an unfounded *metabasis*. The centrality of Christ within the Christian community is to be explained sociologically and psychologically, not religiously or theologically. Whereas theologians from Schleiermacher to Harnack saw the significance of Jesus in his formative influence on the creation of the Christian community, which still allowed for some sort of doctrinal expression, Troeltsch analysed Christianity in general social terms, without recourse to a specific influence of Jesus beyond the sociopsychological requirements of the Christian community to ground its cult in historical fact.

This radical dissolution of dogmatics into historicism has been strongly counteracted since the First World War. The Either–Or way in which liberal Protestantism posed the Christological problem, as well as the historical and humanist approach by which it sought to solve it, was radically rejected by (1) the dialectical Christologies of K. Barth and E. Brunner; (2) the kerygmatic Christology of Bultmann; (3) the hermeneutical theologies from Fuchs to Ebeling; and (4) the Trinitarian Christologies of Moltmann and Jüngel.

1 For Barth it was the risen Christ rather then the historical Jesus who is central to Christology. Hence its fundamental framework is eschatology, not history and morality. Just as Schleiermacher argued from the historical fact of the Christian consciousness of grace to Jesus'

perfect God-consciousness as its sufficient cause within the paradigm of history, so Barth argued from the eschatological reality of the risen Christ to a Trinitarian account of God as its sufficient cause within the paradigm of eschatology. For him, Christology starts from a specific divine activity, not from historical facts and their (private or cultural) meaning or significance; and its task is to explain this divine activity not in terms of an *analogia entis* and doctrine of analogical predication but in terms of an *analogia fidei*, by showing it to be grounded in the free and loving being of the triune God. Thus a Christ-centred eschatological realism of divine activity rather than a Jesus-centred historicism or person-centred existentialism is his answer to the Christological developments of the nineteenth century. And this is worked out in detail in the monumental Christology of his *Church Dogmatics*.

2 While Bultmann agreed that historical research can never lead to any conclusion that can serve as the basis of faith, he differs from Barth in that he interprets the eschaton, not realistically as an act of God in time and history, but existentially as the moment of existential crisis in which we are confronted by the divine kerygma addressed to us. The kerygma is not mere information about God, but conveys insights concerning our human existence. It does not only inform us about authentic existence but occasions a crisis and demands an existential decision on our part. Since the kerygmatic character of the New Testament message is buried under man-made myth, Bultmann propagates the existential demythologization of the New Testament. Its proclamation of the way of life inaugurated by the Christ-event can and must be restated in contemporary existential terms because it is a present possibility for us and may be appropriated as our own. The kerygma goes beyond history in that it compresses the existential significance of the history of Jesus into an eschatological demand. But there is no way to go beyond the eschatological kerygma to more basic historical foundations without dissolving it: the fact of Jesus' existence, not any details of his actual life, is all that is necessary for the kerygma to effect the existential transition from inauthentic to authentic existence. Hence Christology which

explicates the kerygma knows Jesus only as the one who is proclaimed as Christ. The quest for the historical Jesus is not only impossible (as the form-critical approach to the Gospels made clear) but theologically unnecessary and illegitimate. For the historical Jesus and his message as such have no decisive significance for the Christian faith.

3 Many, like E. Käsemann, G. Bornkamm, E. Fuchs, G. Ebeling or W. Pannenberg, did not agree. For them, it is of vital importance that faith in Christ has its roots in the person and proclamation of Jesus. For the kerygma-based Christology of the church would be an imaginative illusion if it were a misinterpretation of the life and message of the historical Jesus. Thus the new quest of the historical Jesus is not another attempt to reconstruct a life of Jesus from the gospels, but to demonstrate that the kerygma arises with Jesus himself rather than with the primitive Christian community. His life and message were implicitly what his proclamation as Christ has made explicit, as Fuchs seeks to demonstrate from the total correspondence between Jesus' life and message, Pannenberg from Jesus' filial relationship to the God he called Father, and Ebeling from the way the event of the cross has become the word of the cross. The relationship between the Jesus of history and the Christ of faith, and hence between history and dogma, is thus focused on the eschatological relationship between cross and resurrection.

4 By restating this in terms of the relation between the death of Jesus and the life of God, J. Moltmann and E. Jüngel have argued that because of God's creative identification with the crucified Jesus as disclosed in the resurrection, the theological problem of the crucified Jesus is the problem of the crucified God, which can only be solved in Trinitarian terms. Explicating the eschatological relation between cross and resurrection, Christology is thus once again emphatically grounded in Trinitarian theology and the Christian doctrine of God in the cross of Christ.

Ecclesiology One of Schleiermacher's important legacies to Protestant theology is that every Christology implies an ECCLESIOLOGY, and vice versa. Just as they did not want to depart from traditional Christological doctrine, the Reformers did not want to found a new church but

renew the old one. Yet the political, social and religious situation soon forced them to create state-based territorial churches independent of Rome. These Lutheran, Reformed and (later) united churches were organized according to the principle *cuius regio, eius religio*; existed in a close symbiosis with state and society until 1918; and before the Enlightenment, made it difficult if not impossible for other religious and minority groups to practise their own faith. The controversies between Lutheran and Reformed churches in the orthodox period, the rise of pietist reform movements in the seventeenth and eighteenth centuries, the confessionalist awakening and growing secularism in the nineteenth century, the restructuring of the churches after 1918 and the questioning and partial overcoming of traditional confessional divisions in the ecumenical endeavours of the twentieth century have all left their stamp on German Protestant ecclesiology.

The Protestant revolt against authoritarian clericalism is clearly reflected in the Lutheran and Reformed confessions of the sixteenth century. The church is a *creatura verbi divini* and church government a matter of all Christians, not just the clergy. For while the public proclamation of the gospel through word and sacrament requires an ordained ministry, those ordained are only functionally, not sacramentally, set apart from other Christians. That is to say, neither the distinction between clergy and laity nor that between ministry and episcopacy are of any deeper theological significance: they only mark differences of tasks and functions within the Christian community that in principle are open to, and the duty of, every Christian.

This devaluation of church hierarchy and the corresponding revaluation of the equal rights and duties of every Christian in the church has had numerous practical and theoretical effects on German Protestant ecclesiology. It is reflected in the fact that church government in Lutheran and Reformed churches was never left to the ordained ministry alone. It inspired the pietist reform movement in forming *ecclesiolas in ecclesia* (P.J. Spener). And it shows in the Lutheran doctrine of the two regiments of God that explains the relationship between church and society not in institutional terms but by stating the different rights and duties of every

Christian to engage in both ecclesial and political activities without confusing or merging them. However, the Protestant view of the church is not monolithic. Even within the Lutheran or Reformed traditions it has allowed for widely differing ecclesiological visions and developments since the Enlightenment. At the one extreme the church is seen to achieve its end only by dissolving into society, thereby transforming it into a culture dominated by the values of humanity, personality and mutual love. Thus by distinguishing between church and religion in the tradition of Kant and Hegel, the church is understood as a means for more general religious ends which, as in particular R. Rothe argued, can only be realized by a transition of Christianity from its church-based form into the secular form of the modern state. This view lies at the bottom of the cultural Protestantism of the nineteenth century and also governs the 'Christianity outside the church' movement of the twentieth century. At the other extreme there is the neo-Lutheran confessionalism of C. Harms, W. Loehe and A.F.C. Vilmar in the nineteenth or W. Elert in the twentieth centuries, which insists in the light of the Augsburg Confession, chapter 7, and the doctrine of the two regiments on the irreducible existence of the church in, and its permanent contrast to, society. However, the church is not a *civitas platonica*, as Melanchthon had pointed out, since its constitutive activities, the proclamation of the gospel by word and sacrament through which God the Spirit works faith and salvation, are public events in time and history. The church is a complex reality both hidden (not invisible!) in society as God's activity and at the same time visible and part of society as human activity. Orthodox theology concentrated more on the first aspect, neo-Protestant ecclesiology on the second. Since the activities of the church are part of the general fabric of actions and institutions that make up society, as Schleiermacher and Hegel have shown in their different ways, ecclesiology cannot proceed in merely doctrinal terms. Instead any theologically viable account must include external perspectives on the church such as are provided by social philosophy (Schleiermacher), the social sciences (Troeltsch), the philosophy of culture (Tillich), philosophical (Bonhoeffer) and empirical sociology or the sociology of organizations (E. Herms; N. Luhmann).

This need to combine doctrinal and extra-doctrinal considerations in theological accounts of the church is most obvious in the case of church law. At the turn of the century R. Sohm claimed that there exists a fundamental contradiction between church law and the essence of the church as *ecclesia invisibilis*, whereas Harnack insisted that the development of church law in the early centuries was both adequate and indispensable for the Christian church as a visible historical institution. The problem posed itself again in the crisis of German Protestantism marked by the Barmen Declaration (1934), which claimed that the church has to pay witness to Jesus Christ not only by its gospel message but also by its institutional order and regulations. Bonhoeffer was one of the first to see this clearly and to take the sociological form of the church as a dogmatic problem (*Sanctorum Communio*, 1927). His understanding of the church as 'Christ existing as community' and his (later) views of the church as essentially a 'church for others' have deeply influenced Protestant public opinion and ecclesiology after 1945. In the German Democratic Republic they inspired the programme of a 'church in socialism', and in both East and West Germany they contributed considerably to the ecumenical reorientation of Protestant theology in the second half of the twentieth century.

In the twentieth century Protestant theology has moved into its ecumenical phase (see ECUMENISM). But the problem of the unity of the Christian churches has been part of its history from the beginning. In the Reformation period it showed in the Protestant demand for a general ecumenical council; in the seventeenth century in the attempts to base a union on the '*consensus quinquesaecularis*' (G. Calixt) or on 'fundamental articles' acceptable to all Christians; in the eighteenth century in the pietist attempt (A.H. Francke, N. Zinzendorf) to give priority to Christian life and experience over confessional orthodoxy; in the nineteenth century in the external and internal mission and *diakonia* irrespective of confessional or religious ties; and in the twentieth century in the ecumenical movement, which was started and dominated by Protestant churches for half a century. German Protestant theology actively participated in this process. It achieved remarkable results, such as the Leuenberg Concord (1973) and numerous bilateral and multilateral agreements with other churches and confessional traditions. But it also reproduced its differences concerning the task of the church and its relation to society and politics at an international level, and introduced its own divisions between liberal and conservative or evangelical positions on church, mission, political theology and social engagement of the churches into the ecumenical movement. It has influenced the ecumenical movement and was influenced by it, and its future is now indissolubly tied up with the future of the worldwide Christian movement. Within this new context German Protestant theology is still very much alive today; it has a rich legacy to convey to a world that is increasingly pluralist and diversified, secular and ahistorical; and it knows that it can only be true to its past if it faces up to the problems of today and tomorrow.

See also LUTHERANISM; PHILOSOPHICAL THEOLOGY; and the other articles on PROTESTANT THEOLOGY.

Bibliography

Barth, K. 1973: *Protestant Theology in the Nineteenth Century: Its Background and History*. Valley Forge: Judson Press.

Birkner, H.-J. 1971: *Protestantismus im Wandel. Aspekte – Deutungen – Aussichten*. Munich: Claudius.

Bossuet, J.-B. [1688] 1841: *Histoire des variations des Eglises protestantes, Oeuvres*, vol. 4. Paris: Didot Frères.

Dorner, J.A. 1867: *Geschichte der protestantischen Theologie, besonders in Deutschland*. Munich: Cotta.

Ebeling, G. 1950: Die Bedeutung der historisch-kritischen Methode für die protestantische Theologie und Kirche, *Zeitschrift für Theologie und Kirche* 47, pp. 1–46.

Frank, G. 1862–1905: *Geschichte der protestantischen Theologie*, 4 vols. Leipzig: Breitkopf und Härtel.

Frey, C. 1989: *Die Ethik des Protestantismus von der Reformation bis zur Gegenwart*. Gütersloh: Gütersloher Verlagshaus G. Mohn.

Graf, F.W., ed. 1990: *Profile des neuzeitlichen Protestantismus*, vol. 1, Gütersloh: Gütersloher Verlagshaus G. Mohn.

Greschat, M., ed. 1978: *Theologen des Protestantismus im 19. und 20. Jahrhundert*, 2 vols. Stuttgart: Kohlhammer.

Groh, J.E. 1982: *Nineteenth Century German Protestantism: The Church as Social Model*. Washington DC: University Press of America.

Härle, W., and Herms, E. 1982–3: Deutschsprachige protestantische Dogmatik nach 1945, *Verkündigung und Forschung* 27, pp. 2–100; 28, pp. 1–91.

Heim, K. 1963: *The Nature of Protestantism*. Philadelphia: Fortress Press.

Heron, A. 1980: *A Century of Protestant Theology*. Philadelphia: Westminster Press.

Hirsch, E. [1946] 1968: *Geschichte der neueren evangelischen Theologie im Zusammenhang mit den allgemeinen Bewegungen des europäischen Denkens*. Gütersloh: Gütersloher Verlagshaus G. Mohn.

Huber, W. 1987: *Protestantismus und Protest. Zum Verhältnis von Ethik und Politik*. Reinbek bei Hamburg: Rowohlt.

Kähler, M. 1989: *Geschichte der protestantischen Dogmatik im 19. Jahrhundert*, ed. E. Kähler. Wuppertal/Zurich: Brockhaus.

Lohff, W. 1985: *Die Konkordie reformatorischer Kirchen in Europa: Leuenberger Konkordie*. Frankfurt am Main: Lembeck.

McGrath, A.E. 1986: *The Making of Modern German Christology: From the Enlightenment to Pannenberg*. Oxford: Blackwell.

Marty, M.E. 1972: *Protestantism*. New York: Holt, Reinhart and Winston.

Mildenberger, F. 1981: *Geschichte der deutschen evangelischen Theologie im 19. und 20. Jahrhundert*. Stuttgart: Kohlhammer.

Moltmann, J., ed. 1990: *Religion der Freiheit: Protestantismus in der Moderne*. Munich: Kaiser.

Müller, H.M. 1991: *Kulturprotestantismus: Beiträge zu einer Gestalt des modernen Christentums*. Gütersloh: Gütersloher Verlagshaus G. Mohn.

Paulsen, F. 1899: *Kant der Philosoph des Protestantismus*. Berlin: Reuther und Reichard.

Ritschl, O. 1908–27: *Dogmengeschichte des Protestantismus*, 4 vols. Leipzig: J.C. Hinrichs'sche Buchhandlung; vols 3–4. Göttingen: Vandenhoeck und Ruprecht.

Rupp, G. 1977: *Culture-Protestantism: German Liberal Theology at the Turn of the Twentieth Century*. Missoula: Scholars Press.

Schütte, H. 1966: *Protestantismus. Sein Selbstverständnis und sein Ursprung gemäss der deutschsprachigen Theologie der Gegenwart und eine kurze katholische Besinnung*, Essen-Werden: Fredebeul und Koenen.

Schwöbel, C. 1990: Wolfhart Pannenberg. In *The Modern Theologians: An Introduction to Christian Theology in the Twentieth Century*, vol. 1, ed. D.F. Ford. Oxford: Oxford University Press, pp. 257–92.

Tillich, P. 1948: *The Protestant Era*. Chicago: University of Chicago Press.

Tillich, P. 1950: *Der Protestantismus: Prinzip und Wirklichkeit*. Stuttgart: Steingrüben.

Troeltsch, E. [1906] 1966: *Protestantism and Progress: A Historical Study of the Relation of Protestantism to the Modern World*, trans. Boston: Beacon Press.

Weber, M. [1904–5] 1930: *The Protestant Ethic and the Spirit of Capitalism*, trans. T. Parsons, ed. R.H. Tawney. London: Allen and Unwin.

Welch, C. 1972–85: *Protestant Thought in the Nineteenth Century*, 2 vols. New Haven: Yale University Press.

MICHAEL MOXTER AND INGOLF U. DALFERTH

Protestant theology: the Netherlands   The eighteenth century witnessed major developments in the approaches to Christian theology in the Netherlands. Three universities continued to dominate the nation at this juncture: Leiden, Franeker and Utrecht, with the last-mentioned playing a significant role in the life of the national church.

At the beginning of the eighteenth century, systematic theology in the Netherlands was still dominated by Reformed scholastic theology: Johannes à Marck's compendium *Christianae theologiae medulla didactico-elencticae* of 1690 dominated systematic teaching during almost the entire eighteenth century. This dogmatic work is classic and learned, balanced in argumentation and biblical in content. His pupil and successor in the University of Leiden, Bernhardinus de Moor (1709–1780), cherished the legacy of his spiritual father and of Voetius and set down the treasures of scholastic scholarship in his monumental life's work of seven volumes (De Moor, 1761–1778). It has been called 'the tomb of Reformed dogmatics', but it still embodies the theoretical power of the broad scholastic tradition. A Marck had also been an impressive interpreter of the Old Testament, and published commentaries on books such as Nahum (1700), the Song of Songs (1703) and the Pentateuch (1713). However great this style of theology might be, it seems to belong to the past. In this same tradition the master of biblical theology was Campegius Vitringa (1659–1722). His work and influence were the missing link between the classic systematics of the past and the linguistic and historical theology of the future; his monumental *Commentarius in librum prophetiarum Iesaiae* of 1714–20 is still noteworthy.

On the other hand we meet the famous names of linguistic theology in the Schultens dynasty: Albert Schultens (1686–1750) with his son Jan Jacob Schultens (1716–1778) and his grandson Hendrik Albert Schultens (1749–1793), and Joan Alberti (1698–1762), Albert Schultens's friend and colleague in Leiden. Their work was rooted in the revolutionary work done in the study of Greek at the university of Franeker by Lambert Bos (1670–1717), whose work matured in the new-style Greek scholarship of Tiberius Hemsterhuis, Franciscus Hemsterhuis's father (1685–1776). The Netherlands schools of Franeker and Leiden, led by Albert Schultens, inaugurated a modern philological approach in Semitic language studies as developed in Indo-Germanic linguistics on the basis of the scholastic construction of a grammar and syntax for Latin. Schultens's Hebrew grammar, *Institutiones ad fundamenta linguae Hebraeae* of 1737, taught generations of scholars, until it was replaced by Gesenius's immortal grammar which went through many editions after 1818. Schultens's Copernican revolution in the study of Semitic languages consists in the thesis that Arabic, Hebrew and other Semitic languages (which he termed 'dialects') are sister languages, so that Hebrew is no longer considered to be the sacred mother language. He also published rich and original commentaries on Job (*Liber Jobi* of 1737) and Proverbs (*Proverbia Salomonis* of 1748).

Alberti and Wetstein did much to promote Greek lexicography and the research of parallelisms in Greek in order to elucidate difficult expressions in the New Testament and the Fathers, and in the twentieth century Van Unnik and his colleagues would pursue this line of research for the *Corpus Hellenisticum* of 1958.

In the eighteenth century there was a delicate balance between solid systematical scholarship and the new creative linguistic approach which effected a shift of concentration to the languages, just as the transition of many (natural) philosophers to the natural sciences caused a shift from analytical thought to experimental work. In the meantime, the scientific revolution resulted in the emergence of physico-theology, and in the course of the century the traditional divisions between Voetians and Coccejans, and even between Cartesians and anti-Cartesians, became obsolete. A new field of force came into existence in a specific Protestant Enlightenment.

However optimistic the opening of the eighteenth century may have been, its closing years were tinged by deep pessimism, not least on account of the social and academic consequences of the French Revolution. The next century of theology in the Netherlands would see the development of a hitherto unparalleled tension between theological liberalism (see LIBERALISM (BRITAIN and USA)) (called 'modern theology') and orthodoxy, which tore asunder the old national Reformed church. In this change two professors of philosophy in the University of Utrecht played a decisive role: Philip W. van Heusde (1778–1839) and Cornelis W. Opzoomer (1821–1892).

Franciscus Hemsterhuis's combination of a new type of Platonism with the common-sense philosophy within the Reformed tradition bore fruit in the inspiration which came from Van Heusde. Van Heusde was mainly influential in theological circles and was the father of the mildly liberal Groninger movement. In the middle of the century Opzoomer introduced critical empiricism (J.S. Mill) and made a major contribution to Reformed theology by forcing his young idealistic colleague Joannes Henricus Scholten (1811–1885) of Leiden University into an extremely radicalized liberalism. During the 1840s Scholten evolved into a new-style modern theologian: theology is the science of religion on the foundation of the sciences in general. His views on rationality and theology entail a necessitarian world view, based on the central concept of God's absolute sovereignty. Therefore he could see himself as a strict Calvinist. Thus we meet the strange fact that both Calvin's doctrine of God and extremely liberal 'Calvinism' of the nineteenth century share the same deterministic core which excludes free will. He was very influential in the world of Dutch ministers and expressed his theological, anthropological and biblical views in great works such as *De Leer der Hervormde Kerk* (1848–50), *De vrije wil* (of 1859) and *Das Evangelium nach Johannes* (of 1867). The later opponents within Reformed theology, Abraham Kuyper (1837–1920) and Herman Bavinck (1854–1921), were also pupils of his.

However, his movement did not excel as much in systematics or New Testament scholarship as in Old Testament scholarship and the history of religion. The master of Old Testament scholarship is Abraham Kuenen (1828–1891). Already in his *Historico-critical Inquiry into the Origin and Composition of the Hexateuch* of 1861–5 (French trans. 1866–79, English 1886, German 1887–94) he laid the foundation of the theory which would later on become famous as the Graf-Wellhausen hypothesis.

Still more important are the contributions to the 'scientific' study of religions. Cornelis Petrus Tiele (1830–1902), a Remonstrant theologian and minister, taught history of religions in the seminary of his church from 1873 and was appointed to the new chair in history of religion of the theological faculty of Leiden University in 1877. (P.D. Chantepie de la Saussaye was appointed to such a chair in Amsterdam in 1878, and Paris followed in 1879.) Tiele was a pioneer of the new 'scientific' historical approach, as La Saussaye was in the phenomenology of religion. His monograph on the religion of Zarathustra dates from 1864. Tiele, who was familiar with Avestan, Akkadian and Egyptian, was one of the first historical theologians to offer a survey of a number of religions based on a philological study of original sources, in his *Outline of the History of Religion, to the Spread of the Universal Religions* of 1876 (trans. 1877), the sixth edition of which was Tiele-Söderblom's Compendium of 1931. He acted as Gifford Lecturer in 1896 and 1898.

The second Dutch founder of the 'science' of religion was the much younger Pierre Daniël Chantepie de la Saussaye (1848–1920). His *Manual of the Science of Religion* ([1887–9] 1891) is one of the discipline's first, and still great, documents. It consists of introductory, phenomenological, ethnographical and historical parts. Philosophy of religion studies the essence of religion; history of religion (as an empirical discipline) its manifestations. Phenomenology mediates between both. Its task is to collect and classify the various religious phenomena and to establish their meanings (objects of worship, religious actions and communities, sacred persons and scriptures, myth and doctrine). The message of comparative religion is a theological one, because in the end everything depends on the objective aspect of God speaking in nature, life and faith.

In Leiden his most congenial pupil was Gerardus van der Leeuw (1890–1950). He also influenced liberal students and ministers, however, the so-called *malcontenten* and later *Rechtsvrijzinnigen* who made a substantial contribution to the new theological climate of the twentieth century, in sharp contrast to the stark intellectualism of the liberals of the first two generations: B.D. Eerdmans, K.H. Roessingh, G.J. Heering, H.T. de Graaf and H. de Vos. Van der Leeuw took up the thread of La Saussaye's phenomenology, adding a psychological perspective. His *Religion in Essence and Manifestation* ([1933] 1938) is a classic, and provides an overall treatment of the objects of religious experience in terms of ideal types. After Tiele and La Saussaye much of the field of phenomenology of religion has been dominated by the Dutch tradition, as in the work of W.B. Kristensen, H. Kraemer and C.J. Bleeker, for example, besides Van der Leeuw. Van der Leeuw's theology is sacramental in inspiration: the basic sacrament is the incarnate, crucified and risen Lord as Christ, who is the foundation of re-creation. The core of his ontology is that reality is open to this deepest sacrament.

Basically Van der Leeuw's and La Saussaye's theology is that of Pierre Daniël's father (Daniel Chantepie de La Saussaye), who led the theological opposition to Scholten's explosive modern theology in the 1850s alongside the reaction of the Reveil movement. Himself gripped by this movement, La Saussaye the elder added a philosophical approach to faith and spirituality. Utterly sensitive to the rationalism of both liberalism and conservatism, he eschewed naturalism and supernaturalism. He revived an Augustinian type of theology on the foundation of Calvin and traditional Reformed doctrine by acknowledging the Israelite character of biblical revelation (Isaäc da Costa) and by absorbing the new philosophies and Friedrich Schleiermacher's and Alexandre Vinet's works in particular. His *Beoordeling van het werk van J.H. Scholten* of 1859 is a masterpiece of fair, incisive and creative criticism. He saw the whole of reality in the light of the ontic Christ in a Johannine fashion. So not only theology, but the whole of sciences and humanities, has to become Christological.

Together with his friend and colleague Johannes Hermanus Gunning Jr (1828–1905) and Nicolaas Beets (1814–1903), Daniël Chantepie de la Saussaye restored the confidence of the orthodox ministers between the liberal left and Calvinist right wings, with the result that Pierre Daniël, J.J.P. Valeton (author of the splendid *De Psalmen*), and I. van Dijk formed the centre of the second generation of 'ethical theologians' who exercised a major influence for four generations.

However, these 'ethical theologians' were unable to satisfy the disappointments of the strictly Calvinistic 'kleine luiden' (ordinary people). Their piety was made vocal theologically in a new articulation of the traditional Reformed doctrine. The great leaders were A. Kuyper and H. Bavinck, F.L. Rutgers and P.J. Hoedemaker, although Hoedemaker left the coalition in 1886 and went his lonely theocratic way in the old national church.

The liberal and 'ethical' theologians excelled in the history and phenomenology of religions and in biblical scholarship; systematic theology, however, remained in the hands of the strictly Reformed thinkers. Their work was deeply rooted in popular Reformed religion and their theoretical contributions formed the outcome of an enormous process of division and renewal of Reformed life and thought that marked and marred the Dutch Protestant world for more than a hundred years. The main theological centres became the theological faculty of the Free University at Amsterdam (from 1880) and the already existing Theological Seminary (at present Theological University) at Kampen, besides smaller institutes in Apeldoorn and Kampen.

The most powerful leader was Kuyper: founder of the first political party of the country and an extremely influential journalist with his own newspaper, founder of the Free University and the uncrowned spokesman of the Reformed churches (since the *Doleantie* in 1886), which numbered in their heyday almost one million members. He was also a creative thinker. As the theoretical architect of this renewed Calvinism, he created an overall theological theory of knowledge and science in the three massive volumes of his *Encyclopaedie der heilige godgeleerdheid* (1894). He sees the history of systematic theology crowned by his own movement: the future form of world theology will be a Calvinist theology, spreading from western Europe to the USA. These ideas were eloquently expressed in his original *De gemeene gratie* of 1902–4, on the large scale of a theology of culture and history.

In 1901 he became prime minister, and his successor in the Amsterdam chair of systematic theology was Herman Bavinck from Kampen, a solid thinker of quite unusual learning. He further explored in depth the new theoretical possibilities and dilemmas of Reformed dogmatics in order to rebuild it within a broad framework of a philosophy of revelation *(The Philosophy of Revelation* of 1908, trans. 1953), which also had to result in a theological psychology and theory of education. His main contribution consists in the four massive volumes *Gereformeerde Dogmatiek* (Reformed Dogmatics) in two editions, of 1895–1911. His indirect successor in Kampen was Klaas Schilder (1890–1952), a learned, critical and poetic dogmatician (see *Wat is de hemel?* of 1935), who criticized constructively Kuyper's theological legacy and negatively Karl Barth's new challenge. Humanity and the church exist in a definite context of salvation history, judged by the ursurmountable holiness of God which historically expresses itself in his wrath in an ontological priority over love.

Bavinck's second successor in Amsterdam was the constructive and open-minded Gerrit Cornelis Berkouwer (b. 1903). His main achievement is his impressive series *Dogmatische Studiën* in eighteen volumes of 1947–70 (most of them translated as *Studies in Dogmatics*). His basic idea is that of the correlation of faith and revelation, which is God's coming in Christ in order to save. All his works are extremely informative and spiritually inspiring, but there is a certain lack of analysis and systematization. In his biblical orientation he profits from the start of a new exegetical tradition after Kuyper and Bavinck (J. Ridderbos, G.C. Aalders, F.W. Grosheide, N.H. Ridderbos).

However, since the 1920s the main factor has been the influence of Karl Barth. He is *par excellence* the twentieth-century theologian of Dutch theologians. Nowhere were his volumes more avidly read than in Dutch vicarages. First Catholic and Calvinist opposition was bitter;

then the 'ethical' (K.H. Miskotte) and confessional (T.L. Haitjema) theologians succumbed to his inspiration and in the end he was embraced by almost everyone.

All important theologians after the Second World War played a vital role in the renewal process of the Netherlands Reformed church during the 1940s under the dynamic guidance of the missionary and ecumenical strategist Hendrik Kraemer (1888–1965). By then the grand old man of theology was already Dr Oepke Noordmans (1871–1956), who embodied the very best of the entire Protestant tradition in a very personal way, welcomed Barth and gave a new impetus to pneumatology in his often poetical *Gestalte en Geest* of 1955. He viewed the work of the Spirit as a comforting balance of fragments in which God secures continuity despite human discontinuity. There is only creation as re-creation (*Herschepping*, of 1933). Humanity only shines through in the light around the cross.

Miskotte's influence was much more formative and his friends and disciples dominated the scene up to the present, although the Barth orientation has very much weakened by now. In Amsterdam the Miskottian inspiration blended with several strands of that rich cultural centre into the Amsterdam school, which concentrates hermeneutically on the text of the Old Testament in the historical context of the Exile. In Utrecht it blended with the Van Ruler line and the conspicuous result was E.J. Beker's (Amsterdam) and J.M. Hasselaar's *Wegen en kruispunten in de dogmatiek* of 1978–90, in five volumes. In Kampen the preference for Calvin and Luther is still vital, with much interest in Noordmans and Miskotte, but the greatest international influence is now exerted by the internationally oriented but still typically Dutch *Christian Faith* by Hendrikus Berkhof ([1973] 1986), which is sympathetic and critical of tradition, and based on a thorough biblical and historical foundation.

Since the 1950s, Dutch theology has gone through a period of post-Barthian reaction, fuelled by the writings of the brilliant Utrecht dogmatician Arnold van Ruler (1908–1970), whose theocratic theology of culture is a unique blend of Calvin, Reformed scholasticism and Troeltschian liberalism. The close relationship which he postulates between creation and the eschaton leads to the Christ-event being seen as little more than an intermezzo. The period has also seen the continued development of biblical scholarship of distinction, represented by writers such as T.C. Vriezen (Old Testament) and W.C. van Unnik (New Testament). Other theological thinkers have flourished outside the realm of academic theology, such as B. Nieuwentydt, G. Groen van Prinsterer, P. Kohnstamm, H. Dooyeweerd, and A.E. Loen (1896–1991), whose *De vaste ground* of 1945 stands in the front rank of works of theological philosophy.

The cultural revolution of the 1960s caused new developments in modern Dutch culture, with largely negative implications for the church and Christian theology. Nevertheless, the past greatness of Dutch theology allows the future to be viewed with hope, despite the difficulties of the present.

See also BIBLICAL CRITICISM AND INTERPRE-TATION (1: OLD TESTAMENT and 2: NEW TESTA-MENT); and the other articles on PROTESTANT THEOLOGY.

Bibliography

Alberti, J. 1746: *Hesychii Lexicon cum notis doctorum virorum*, 2 vols. Leiden. S. and J. Luchtmans.

Bavinck, H. [1908] 1955: *The Doctrine of God*, trans. H. Bavinck. Grand Rapids: Eerdmans (vol. 2 of *Gereformeerde Dogmatiek*).

Berkhof, H. [1973] 1986: *Christian Faith: An Introduction to the Study of the Faith*, trans. and ed. S. Woudstra. Grand Rapids: Eerdmans.

Berkhof, H. [1985] 1989: *Two Hundred Years of Theology. Report of a Personal Journey*, trans. H. Berkhof. Grand Rapids: Eerdmans.

Berkouwer, G.C. [1974] 1977: *A Half Century of Theology*, trans. and ed. L.B. Smedes. Grand Rapids: Eerdmans.

Chantepie de La Saussaye, P.D. [1887–9] 1891: *Manual of the Science of Religion*. London and New York: Longmans, Green and Co.

Jong, O.J. de 1985: *Nederlandse kerkgeschiedenis* (Dutch church history). Nijkerk: G.F. Callenbach.

Kraemer, H. 1938: *The Christian Message in a Non-Christian World*. London: Edinburgh House Press.

Kuenen, A. [1861–5] 1886: *An Historico-critical Inquiry into the Origin and Composition of the Hexateuch*, trans. Ph. Nicksteed. London: Macmillan.

Kuyper, A. 1894: *Encyclopaedie der heilige godgeleendheid*, 3 vols. Amsterdam. Trans. of vol. 1, 1953 and vol. 2, A. Kuyper, 1954: *Principles of Sacred Theology*. Grand Rapids: Eerdmans.

Leeuw, G. van der [1933] 1938: *Religion in Essence and Manifestation: A Study in Phenomenology*. London: G. Allen and Unwin.

Loen, A.E. 1965: *Säkularisation*. München: C. Kaiser.

Miskotte, K.H. 1963: *Wenn die Götter schweigen*. München: C. Kaiser.

Moor, B. de 1761–78: *Commentarius perpetuus in Johannis Marckii Compendium theologiae christianae didactico-elencticum*, 7 vols. Leiden: J. Hasebroek and J.H. van Damme.

Nauta, D. and Groot, A. de 1978–88: *Biografisch lexicon voor de geschiedenis van het Nederlandse protestantisme* (Biographical lexicon for the history of Dutch Protestantism), 3 vols. Kampen: J.H. Kok.

Noordmans, O. 1960: *Das Evangelium des Geistes*. Zürich: Evangelischer Verlag.

Rasker, A.J. 1986: *De Nederlandse Hervormde Kerk sinds 1795* (The Netherlands Reformed church since 1795). Kampen: J.H. Kok.

Ruler, A.A. van 1947: *De Vervulling van de Wet* (The fulfilment of the law). Nijkerk: G.F. Callenbach.

Scholten, J.H. 1848–50: *De Leer der Hervormde Kerk in hare grondbeginselen uit de bronnen voorgesteld en beoordeeld* (The doctrine of the Reformed church in its basic principles presented and evaluated from the sources), 2 vols. Leiden: P. Engels.

Tiele, C.P. 1897–9: *Elements of the Science of Religion*, 2 vols, trans. C.P. Tiele. Edinburgh and London: W. Blackwood and Sons.

ANTONIE VOS JACZN

Protestant theology: Scandinavia The Lutheran Reformation has shaped both Scandinavian theology and church life. Each of the Scandinavian Lutheran churches has been, and to some extent still remains, a state church, with theological studies and research occurring at state universities responsible for the education of the clergy (see LUTHERANISM).

The strong position of the university professor as a civil servant has encouraged free research and liberal thinking (see LIBERALISM (BRITAIN and USA)), sometimes leading academic theology into conflict with church authorities. Nevertheless, it has also been a tradition that many bishops and church leaders come from among academic theologians. In such cases the professor-bishop manifests the close bonds between church and state in his own person.

From the eighteenth century traditional Lutheran theology has been continuously challenged by pietistic movements, their influence being quite strong in all the Scandinavian countries. However, the majority of these pietistic and neo-pietistic revival movements have remained within the structures of the state churches. The Scandinavian 'pietists' have often understood themselves as the true followers of Luther, so that according to their view it is their task to renew the church and theology from within.

The Nazi Occupation of Denmark and Norway in the Second World War made the church–state relationship more complicated, as the theological problems of conformity to the state became evident. The active participation of Nordic churches in the ecumenical movement has also strengthened the critical attitude towards the academic theology sponsored by the state (see ECUMENISM). But nevertheless the old university traditions continue to exist and grow, the traditional Nordic faculties of theology including Uppsala (faculty founded 1477), Copenhagen (1479), Helsinki (1640), Lund (1666) and Oslo (1811). The theological institutions and faculties at Aarhus, Reykjavik, Oslo/Menighetsfakulteten, Stavanger and Turku/Åbo were founded during the twentieth century.

Traditionally, the influence of German Protestant theology has been strong. In recent times, however, the orientation towards Britain and the USA has grown rapidly, partially due to the popularity of Anglo-Saxon analytical philosophy in Scandinavian universities.

Sweden

After the Reformation Swedish theology was dominated by Lutheran orthodoxy. Throughout the eighteenth century pietistic influence came mostly from Germany. The writings of Henric Schartau (1757–1825) are essential to the theological evaluation of pietism within the Lutheran state church. A pastor in the university city of Lund and a leader of a moderate revival movement, Schartau rejected the pietistic stress on personal experience and held that God does not command anything contrary to either Scripture or reason. Schartau's biblicism led him to criticize lay theology and separatist movements. In his view, clarity in doctrine and faithfulness to the historic church

are essential for growth in godliness (Arden, 1965, p. 2307). Schartau's theology provided a model for the peaceful coexistence of revival movements and the official church body.

A more enthusiastic theology was proclaimed by the great evangelical leader Carl Olof Rosenius (1816–1868), a city missionary in Stockholm, who held close contacts with the Protestant missionary associations of Britain and America. His influential writings stress the importance of the spiritual struggle and sanctification. However, Rosenius was convinced that any renewal of Swedish church life must take place within the established church.

Swedish academic theology has flourished throughout the twentieth century. Einar Billing's dissertation *Luthers lära om staten* (Luther's Teaching concerning the State, 1900), marks the beginning of the Swedish 'Luther renaissance' and the emergence of so-called 'motif research'. Another epochal study was Nathan Söderblom's *Uppenbarelsereligion* (Revealed Religion, 1903), in which the author sought to focus his attention upon the psychology behind the explicit theology of Luther (Arden, 1965, pp. 2307–9).

The importance of Luther for Swedish theology is no coincidence, but should be understood against its Scandinavian historical background. Most Scandinavian theologians try to identify themselves with Luther, the result being a rich variety of portraits of the Reformer. For instance, in 'motif research' Luther's thought often stands for the most profound biblical motif against which all other theological motifs are measured.

The most prominent representatives of motif research, or 'Lundensian Theology', are Anders Nygren and Gustaf Aulén. However, the methodological foundation of the Lundensian school was already laid by Billing and Söderblom. The notion of 'motif' is directed towards discerning the fundamental meaning behind the historical text. With the aid of this notion Lundensian methodology claims to achieve a philosophically valid foundation for systematic theology (Lindström, 1960, p. 1161). Thus motif research has some similarity to the neo-Kantian and Troeltschian approaches to religion.

Nathan Söderblom (1866–1931) was perhaps the most eminent Scandinavian theologian of the twentieth century. As Archbishop of Sweden (1914–1931), Söderblom played an important role in the formation of the ecumenical movement, his extensive academic work concentrating on the comparative study of religions as well as on systematic theology. Even before Rudolf Otto, he emphasized the importance of the notion of 'holiness'. He also investigated the complex notions of revelation and natural theology in the history of religions. His 1931 Gifford Lectures, published as *The Living God* ([1932] 1962) give an overview of his theology.

Another influential Lundensian was Ragnar Bring (1895–1988), who together with Nygren and Gustaf Wingren contributed to the emergence of the philosophical orientation now so common in Scandinavian systematic theology. In Bring's theology, systematic problems arise from confrontation with the fundamental principles of Luther's thought.

In biblical research the Scandinavian traditio-historical school at Uppsala (I. Engnell, H.S. Nyberg, H. Riesenfeld, B. Gerhardsson) has provoked much discussion. It stresses the importance of oral tradition and cult as the fixed forms of biblical message, thus bearing much resemblance to the British myth and ritual school (S.H. Hooke). Other interests of Swedish biblical scholarship include the history of near-eastern religions (for example H. Ringgren) and New Testament theology (K. Stendahl).

In contemporary Swedish systematic theology the Lundensian orientation has to some extent been replaced by an analytical and philosophical approach. During the 1980s there has been an ongoing methodological debate between the older and newer approaches to theology, with, however, Luther research still prominent (for example B. Hägglund).

Typical of current Swedish theology is the programmatic book *Människan och Gud* (Man and God, 1982), in which Jarl Hemberg, Ragnar Holte and Anders Jeffner outline a modern, rational approach to the study of dogmatics. Their aim is to avoid the shortcomings of both materialism and positivist philosophy, while nevertheless proceeding from rational premises. The authors take the fact of religious experience and certain aspects of Karl Heim's philosophy of religion as their point of departure, proceeding to argue that it is possible at least to some extent to advance reasons for the relevance of Christian faith today.

Denmark

As in Sweden, both Lutheran orthodoxy and eighteenth-century pietism had their periods of strong impact in Denmark. Later, Danish theology was shaped by two important figures of the nineteenth century: Søren Kierkegaard and N.F.S. Grundtvig (1783–1872). Grundtvig succeeded in creating a fruitful theological synthesis which managed to avoid the shortcomings of both a subjective pietism and a latitudinarian state church. He stressed the importance of the two Lutheran sacraments, baptism and Eucharist, for the entire life of the church. However, he did not emphasize the ordained ministry but held that Jesus Christ himself is immediately present and active in the church. The universal priesthood of all believers was one of his essential ideas, Luther being his favourite theologian.

Grundtvig's extensive writings on Nordic mythology reveal his theoretical interest in history and language. He desired to educate the Danish people not only in religion, but also in the cultural heritage of their country. A pedagogical talent, Grundtvig was successful in bringing about a network of so-called 'folk high schools', adult education institutes, which in the course of time have extended their influence to all of Scandinavia.

One of Grundtvig's opponents was Hans Lassen Martensen (1808–1884), professor of systematic theology and later Bishop of Seeland. Martensen represents the mid-stream of Danish Lutheranism, rejecting both Kierkegaardian and pietistic individualism in his support of a Lutheran theology integrating religion with cultural life.

The impact of Kierkegaard and Grundtvig also dominates twentieth-century Danish theology, with German influences, especially Barthianism and existential theology (see EXISTENTIALISM), playing a more important role than in Sweden. K.E. Løgstrup (1905–1981) compared Kierkegaard's and Heidegger's philosophies, contributing to the Grundtvigian line of cultural and natural theology, combining ethical and even aesthetic themes with theology. Another prominent Kierkegaardian existential theologian is Johannes Sløk (b. 1916).

The extensive Danish Luther scholarship can also be traced back to Grundtvig's influence. Sometimes Lutheran theology has come into conflict with Barthianism (R. Prenter). Today, the historical approach to Reformation theology has produced significant results (L. Grane).

In biblical studies, the emergence of liberal theology and historical criticism created many tensions during the nineteenth century (Grane *et al.*, 1980, pp. 442–8). The influence of Julius Wellhausen's historical school was considerable in academic theology. In the early twentieth century Danish exegetical studies (J. Pedersen, V. Grønbech) contributed to the formation of the British myth and ritual school. Vilhelm Grønbech (1873–1948) especially, professor of the history of religions and an expert in Germanic religion and early Christianity, was active in the Danish theological debate.

In recent times the emergence of the analytical philosophy of religion is visible, partly due in all Scandinavian countries to the dominance of the English language. Ecumenical, spiritual and contextual issues have also gained importance (for example A.M. Aagard). The intensive study of medieval philosophy (for example J. Pinborg) has revealed many theologically interesting themes.

Ole Jensen's influential monograph *Theologie zwischen Illusion und Restriktion* (1975) demonstrates how cultural and existential ideas still shape modern Danish systematic theology. Jensen criticizes the German neo-Protestants Wilhelm Herrmann and Rudolf Bultmann for separating 'nature' from 'spirit' and thus converting the material world into an inferior reality usable as the means to a higher end. He further argues that modern environmental problems are partly due to the neo-Protestant contempt of the natural world. Jensen's work has stimulated recent discussion of the Protestant contribution to environmental ethics.

Norway

From 1536 to 1814 Norway was a province of Denmark, and from that time until 1905 in union with Sweden. As in Sweden, the pietistic movements have traditionally been strong, but so have the liberalist trends too. At the end of the nineteenth century conservative theologians criticized not only progressive authors of fiction (B. Bjørnson, G. Brandes), but also the advocates of the historical interpretation of the Bible.

These schisms led to the foundation of the so-called 'free faculty' of theology (Menighetsfakulteten) in Oslo in 1908. Since that time, Norwegian pastors have been educated both in the liberal university faculty of Oslo and in the 'free faculty'. However, both faculties have employed prominent scholars, and in more recent years cooperation between the faculties has become significant.

The first remarkable theological achievements were made by biblical scholars. Carl Paul Caspari (1814–1892), a German Jew by birth, had a high reputation as an Old Testament scholar. Sigmund Mowinckel's (1884–1965) studies on the Psalms have become classics. A pupil and discussion partner of Hermann Gunkel, he interpreted the Psalms as cultic poetry, reconstructing an annual enthronement festival at the heart of Israel's religion. New Testament research has also flourished within the university faculty (N.A. Dahl, J. Jervell).

In systematic theology Johannes Ording (1869–1929) was a radical Ritschlian, in the spirit of Ritschl and Julius Kaftan applying neo-Kantian epistemology to the problems of religious language. Although he was often considered as a destructive liberalist, his final goal was, nevertheless, apologetical, aimed at indicating the unquestionable subjective validity of religious propositions.

The leading personality in the conservative free faculty was Ole Hallesby (1879–1961), a representative of a rigorous Lutheran pietism. Hallesby considered theology to be a science in the service of the church. His biblicist viewpoint was critical towards many of the achievements of academic theology, his influence extending to all Scandinavian countries.

More recently, Luther research has occupied a significant place in academic theology (for example I. Asheim, I. Lønning, O. Modalsli). The fundamental problems of modern systematic and ecumenical theology have been extensively discussed in the works of Per Lønning, professor and bishop. His magnum opus, *Der begreiflich Unergreifbare* (1986), is a Lutheran synthesis of twentieth-century theology. According to Lønning, the Lutheran idea of 'Deus absconditus' becomes a key notion in solving the hermeneutical and philosophical problems of modern theology.

Finland

A province of Sweden until 1809 and an autonomous part of the Russian empire until 1917, Finland has been influenced by both western and eastern Christendom. However, the great majority (more than ninety per cent) of the population have traditionally been Lutherans, and the Lutheran state church flourished even throughout the period of Russian rule.

In theology, Swedish and German impact has been considerable, the Swedish language dominating university studies until the late nineteenth century. The pietistic and neo-pietistic revival movements have been even stronger than in Sweden. Among the pietistic lay leaders, Paavo Ruotsalainen (1777–1852) especially has shaped the mentality of Finnish Lutheranism. His importance is not due to theological writings, but to his original understanding of Christian spirituality as opposed to all types of self-righteousness and hierarchical structures.

The collision of liberal theology with pietistical biblicism has been in many ways similar to in Norway. In Finland, however, it has not led to the formation of a 'free faculty', but to a coexistence of different theological strains of thought within the faculty of theology at the University of Helsinki.

During the late nineteenth and early twentieth centuries the biblicist approach to dogmatic issues was dominant, owing to the considerable influence of the conservative German theologians J.T. Beck and Karl Heim. Osmo Tiililä (1904–1972) was the last representative of this tradition.

The new generation begins with Seppo Teinonen (b. 1924), who introduced the modern ecumenical, particularly Roman Catholic, approach to Finnish theology. Mikko Juva, President of the Lutheran World Federation 1970–7 and Finnish Archbishop 1978–82, contributed to the formation of today's internationally active Finnish Lutheranism. In contemporary academic theology, too, ecumenical issues play an important role. The intensive negotiations between the Finnish Evangelical-Lutheran church and the Russian Orthodox church have especially revealed theologically interesting convergences.

However, the international contributions of Finnish theologians have mostly been limited to specialist issues, including the Septuagint (I. Soisalon-Soininen), deuteronomistic literature (T. Veijola) and, quite naturally, Luther research (L. Pinomaa, T. Mannermaa).

In today's Finnish theology, the New Testament scholar Heikki Räisänen is a prominent advocate of liberal biblical criticism. His *Beyond New Testament Theology* (1990) is an attempt to evaluate modern research and to sketch guidelines for a radical historical understanding of the New Testament. Räisänen emphasizes the fundamental difference between 'historical' and 'theological' understanding, his own model of the historical interpretation of the New Testament concentrating upon the dialectic between tradition, experience and interpretation.

Iceland

Earlier, close bonds with Danish cultural life dominated Iceland's theology and church life. As in other Scandinavian countries, both pietism and the liberal theology had their periods of strong influence.

A peculiar Icelandic phenomenon is the impact of spiritism and theosophy on theology and church. Especially in the theology of Haraldur Nielssen (d. 1928), an advocate of liberal theology, a curious combination of neo-Protestantism and spiritism is visible. Nielssen considered that spiritism can be a modern alternative to materialist ideologies (Einarsson, 1987, p. 366).

Today, the spiritist tradition, once strong within the Icelandic clergy, has largely lost its influence. The faculty of theology at the University of Reykjavik educates most of the theologians for the ministry in the Lutheran state church.

Today's Scandinavian context

The Nordic theological faculties have established positions within their universities, with dissertations written in English, German and

Nordic languages. Although there remain many contacts with Germany, there is hardly any systematic theology inspired by Barthianism. Barth's theology is studied widely, but mostly from a critical Lutheran viewpoint.

The philosophy of religion is popular. Philosophical tools are mostly those of the analytical, Anglo-Saxon tradition, but also Kantian and neo-Kantian themes continue to be current.

Traditio-historical exegetics still has some influence in Sweden, but not, for example, in Finland. In biblical studies, a plurality of methodological approaches can be found, historical-critical research being dominant in the universities, but with conservative and even fundamentalist attitudes prevailing in pietistic circles.

Traditional pietistic movements endure strongly, especially in Norway and Finland, often with some cooperation with English-speaking evangelical organizations. Due to their close connection with Scandinavian missionary societies, many pietistic theologians are active in the field of missiological studies.

The active ecumenical participation of Scandinavian churches has actualized the need for contextual theologies. Some themes of liberation and feminist theology are being discussed, but the academic study of these topics is only beginning.

See also the other articles on PROTESTANT THEOLOGY, especially in GERMANY.

Bibliography

Arden, G.E. 1965: Swedish theology. In *The Encyclopedia of the Lutheran Church, vol. 3.* Minneapolis: Augsburg Publishing House, pp. 2305–11.

Billing, E. [1900] 1971: *Luthers lära om staten*, 2nd edn. Karlskrona: Verbum.

Einarsson, S. 1987: Island. In *Theologische Realenzyklopädie 16*, Berlin and New York: Walter de Gruyter, pp. 358–68.

Grane, L., Andersen, N.K., Banning, K., and Glebe-Møller, J. 1980: *Kobenhavns Universitet 1479–1979. Bind V: Det teologiske Fakultet.* Kobenhavn: Gads forlag.

Hall, T. 1970: *A Framework for Faith: Lundensian Theological Methodology in the Thought of Ragnar Bring.* Leiden: Brill.

Hemberg, J., Holte, R. and Jeffner, A. 1982: *Människan och Gud. En kristen teologi.* Malmö: Liber.

Jensen, O. 1975: *Theologie zwischen Illusion und Restriktion: Analyse und Kritik der existenz-kritizistischen Theologie bei dem jungen Wilhelm Herrmann und bei Rudolf Bultmann.* München: Kaiser.

Knight, D.A. 1973: *Rediscovering the Traditions of Israel. The Development of the Traditio-Historical Research of the Old Testament with Special Consideration of Scandinavian Contributions.* Missoula: Society of Biblical Literature.

Lindhardt, P.G. 1982: *Skandinavische Kirchengeschichte seit dem 16. Jahrhundert.* Die Kirche in ihrer Geschichte, vol. 3 M3. Göttingen: Vandenhoeck.

Lindström, V. 1960: Motivforschung. In *Die Religion in Geschichte und Gegenwart*, vol. 4. Tübingen: Mohr, pp. 1160–3.

Lønning, P. 1986: *Der begreiflich Unergreifbare: 'Sein Gottes' und modern-theologische Denkstrukturen.* Göttingen: Vandenhoeck.

Molland, E. et al. 1955: *Nordisk teologi. Idéer och män. Festskrift till Ragnar Bring.* Lund: Gleerup.

Molland, E. 1988: *Norges kirkehistorie i det 19. århundre*, 2 vols. Oslo: Gyldendal.

Murtorinne, E. 1988: *The History of Finnish Theology 1828–1918.* Helsinki: Societas Scientiarum Fennica.

Pentikäinen, J. and Krug, B. 1983: Finnland. In *Theologische Realenzyklopädie 11.* Berlin and New York: Walter de Gruyter, pp. 178–92.

Radler, A. 1989: Der Einfluss des theologischen Werkes von Karl Barth auf die skandinavische Theologie. In *Luther und Barth*, ed. J. Heubach. Erlangen: Martin Luther Verlag, pp. 53–84.

Räisänen, H. 1990: *Beyond New Testament Theology: A Story and a Programme.* London: SCM Press.

Schwarz Lausten, M. 1981: Dänemark, I. Kirchengeschichtlich. In *Theologische Realenzyklopädie 8*, Berlin and New York: Walter de Gruyter, pp. 300–17.

Sundkler, B. 1968: *Nathan Söderblom. His Life and Work.* Lund: Gleerup.

Söderblom, N. [1903] 1930: *Uppenbarelsereligion*, 2nd edn. Stockholm: Diakonistyrelse.

Söderblom, N. [1932] 1962: *The Living God.* Boston: Beacon.

Søe, N.H. 1965: *Dansk teologi siden 1900.* København: Gads.

Thorkildsen, D. 1984: *Johannes Ording, Religionsfilosof og apologet.* Oslo: Universitetsforlaget.

1952–7: *Nordisk teologisk uppslagsbok*, 3 vols. Lund: Gleerup.

RISTO SAARINEN

Protestant theology: South Africa South African Christian thought exists at the interface of western and the emerging third world theologies and may be subdivided into theology whose principal interlocutor is western thought and that which has primarily debated with apartheid. The former represents the legacy of European missionary endeavour and continues to engage with the western debate. The latter has emerged in the context of ecclesiastical and popular struggle with apartheid within South Africa itself and represents South Africa's distinctive contribution to wider Christian thought. Hence the bulk of this article will focus upon the latter.

Theology in dialogue with western tradition

Within the Afrikaans-speaking community continental Reformed theology has traditionally been the primary interlocutor, reflecting the former's Dutch heritage. Until the mid-nineteenth century such Christian thought was generated only at the ecclesiastical level. However the foundation in 1859 of the first Dutch Reformed theology seminary at Stellenbosch enabled academic theology to develop. Whilst a number of Afrikaans-speaking theologians have been identified with 'apartheid theology', many have and continue to be actively engaged in the broader western debates. Among the more senior systematic theologians presently engaged in this way are J.J.F. Durand, J. Heyns, J.W.V. van Huyssteen, W. Jonker and A. König, whilst J. Kinghorn, J.N.J. Kritzinger and D.J. Smit represent some of the more prominent younger theologians.

A similar focus is reflected in the English-language tradition. Likewise originally expressed through church structures, the foundation in 1947 of the first English-medium divinity faculty at Rhodes' University, Grahamstown, represented the birth of a more academic approach. Among notable systematic theologians presently working in dialogue with western theology are B. Gaybba (Catholic) and K. Nürnberger (Lutheran).

Contextual theologies

A considerable amount of contextual thought has been generated in South Africa over the past two hundred years, which can be classified as either promoting or in conflict with racial separatism. 'Apartheid theology' represents the former, whilst John de Gruchy has labelled the latter 'theologies of resistance and transformation', which he distinguishes as 'Confessing theology', 'black theology', 'African theology', 'feminist theology' and 'prophetic theology' (de Gruchy, 1991: pp. 217–22). Each of the latter regards theology as a practical discipline rather than a speculative one, and adopts an interdisciplinary methodology, emphasizing the importance of correct socioeconomic and political analysis as a foundation from which to practise theology.

Apartheid theology

Apartheid theology represents that peculiar expression of Calvinist thought unique to South Africa, sometimes called 'Afrikaner Calvinism'. Its distinctive characteristic is its anthropology of ethnic (*volk*) separatism, which developed in response to the socioeconomic threats facing the settlers, combined with a literalist reading of Scripture (see FUNDAMENTALISM). Initially an informal and popularist theology, by the early twentieth century it came to be married with a peculiar interpretation of the doctrine of creation of the Dutch Calvinist, A. Kuyper, together with contemporary nationalist theories. Combined, these rooted the separation of peoples in the creative design of God and suggested a unique role for the Afrikaner *volk* in the purposes of God. In addition, the influence of A. Murray's Scottish evangelicalism and Justus du Plessis's Pentecostalism contributed a pietistic dimension to Afrikaner Calvinism, particularly to its ecclesiology. This enabled dominant voices within the Afrikaans-speaking churches, supported by theologians such as A.B. du Preez, F.J.M. Potgieter and E.P. Groenewald, to supply the theological rationale for segregation throughout both society and the church, by arguing that the unity of the church was a mystical, invisible and eschatological unity which did not conflict with the inviolable and segregated structures of creation.

Whilst apartheid theology has been prominent, it has, nevertheless, been opposed from within the Afrikaans-speaking community. During the course of the twentieth century figures such as B.B. Keet, B. Marais, J.

Lombard, J.A. van Wyk, B. Naudé, F.P.D. Möller and N. Smith have spearheaded this opposition, whilst over the last twenty years ecclesiastical documents of the largest Afrikaans-speaking white church, the Nederduitse Gereformeerde Kerk (NGK), the Dutch Reformed church, have witnessed a gradual critique of apartheid anthropology culminating in 1982 with the signing by 123 Dutch Reformed church (DRC) ministers of an *Open Letter*. A parallel process also emerged within the smaller Gereformeerde Kerk (GK) and is reflected in the *Koinonia Declaration* of 1977.

Among contemporary Afrikaans-speaking theologians, J.J.F. Durand, D. Bosch, A. Boesak, H.W. Rossouw, J. Kinghorn, J.N.J. Kritzinger and D.J. Smit have been especially vocal in their opposition to apartheid theology, and the recent *Rustenberg Declaration* (1990) exposes the influence of their contribution at the ecclesiological level.

Confessing theology

South African Confessing theology has derived much of its inspiration from the 'Confessing Church' of Nazi Germany, in particular from the Barmen Declaration of 1934 and the theology of both D. Bonhoeffer and K. Barth. Initiated under the auspices of the Christian Institute of South Africa led by Beyers Naudé, it was a reaction both to the failure of the Cottesloe Consultation of 1960 to convert the protagonists of apartheid theology, and to the effects of the Sharpeville massacre of that year. It sought to create a theology to counter that dominant in the white DRC, using its journal *Pro Veritate* as a mouthpiece. Its influence can be seen in the anti-apartheid theological document, *The Message to the People of South Africa* (1968), published by the South African Council of Churches (SACC). More recently this theological approach has been significant in the establishment of the non-racial 'Belydendekring' (Confessing circle) of Reformed Christians. It also influenced the drafting of the *Belhar Confession* (1982), which itself contributed to the decision of the 1982 meeting of the World Alliance of Reformed Churches (WARC) to declare as a *status confessionis* the belief that apartheid is a heresy. According to de Gruchy (1991, p. 219) Confessing theology is characterized by its Christological and ecclesiological foci and has recently begun a programme to reappropriate classical Christian thought. Prominent contemporary 'Confessing' theologians are B. Naudé, A. Boesak, W. Kistner, D. Bax, S. Govender, J. de Gruchy, and C. Villa-Vicencio.

Black theology

Black theology in South Africa is an indigenous theology, albeit influenced by its North American cousin (see BLACK THEOLOGY) and, latterly, by Latin American liberation theology (see LIBERATION THEOLOGY). Emerging in the 1960s, in tandem with the black consciousness movement associated with Steve Biko, it has attempted to reinterpret the Christian tradition from the perspective of the black experience in South Africa. Although black theology sees its roots in the black nationalists of the late nineteenth century, such as N. Tile and J. Dwane, the major expression of South African black theology came with the publication of a series of essays entitled: *Black Theology: The South African Voice* in 1970. Despite the book's banning by the government, its protagonists continued the debate and, in 1986, an anthology of essays under the title of *The Unquestionable Right to be Free* was published (Mosala and Thlagale, 1986).

Over the past twenty years, the term 'black' has been transformed from a racial category into a symbol for the oppressed and their allies in South Africa. However, much of the theology continues to be somewhat occasional, occupied with methodological questions and bound to a western epistemology.

Given its context, South African black theology regards itself as a liberation theology, sharing similar themes with those of Latin America, though identifying the biblical category 'the poor' with the term 'black' and having particular concern for a proper articulation of Christian anthropology. Prominent among South Africa's black theologians are M. Buthelezi, D. Tutu, A. Boesak, S. Dwane, F. Chikane, B. Goba, S. Gqubule, M. Motlhabi, B. Thlagale and E. Mosothoane, as well as those currently engaged at university level, such as S. Maimela, T. Mofokeng, and I.J. Mosala. A useful summary of South African black theology can be found in L. Kretzschmar's *The Voice of Black Theology in South Africa* (1986).

Christian African theology

Christian African theology has tended to be overshadowed by black theology in the South African context, although latterly there has been a *rapprochement* between the two disciplines. The principal focus of Christian African theology has been the relationship of traditional African religion and culture to Christianity, with the aim of liberating African Christian thought from the cultural bondage of colonialism and giving space for indigenous expressions of the faith (see CULTURE AND THEOLOGY). Inspired by the Xhosa prophets Ntsikana and Nxcle and the informal theology of the African Independent churches, African theology's most prominent academic representative has been G. Setiloane, though a number of those classified as 'black theologians', such as S. Dwane and D. Tutu, span both theological approaches.

In its early stages, Christian African theology tended to be ethnographic, seeking to reconstruct an ideal and rustic African past, independent of the scourge of colonialism. However, this employed a rather static and archaic view of culture. Latterly African Christian thought has adopted a more anthropological approach aiming to relate the Christian faith to the experience of contemporary Africans, increasing numbers of whom are predominantly urban dwellers. Creating a theology to cope with issues such as survival, political instability, migratory labour and socio-economic oppression, as well as with the theology of God, ancestor veneration, traditional rites of passage and the issue of 'humanness', therefore, occupies the current agenda of African Christian theology.

Christian African theologians have generally seen traditional African religion and theology as a *preparatio Christi*, though debate continues concerning the extent of their compatibility with existing Christianity. As with black theology, most of the literature still deals with methodological questions, together with the nature of culture, rather than with constructive theology, and there is also a parallel discussion concerning an indigenous, theological epistemology.

Prophetic theology

Prophetic theology in South Africa has gained prominence through the publication in 1986 by the Institute for Contextual Theology of *The Kairos Document*. The product of extensive 'grass roots' consultations during the political crises of 1984–5, it sought to expose those theological perspectives which explicitly (state theology) or effectively (church theology) supported apartheid, whilst suggesting an alternative (prophetic) theology which could challenge it. The distinctive contribution of prophetic theology lay in its reading of the 'signs of the times' and in its assertion that 'kairos' moments – that is, moments of opportunity and possibility – could thereby be discerned, with consequent demands upon Christians to ally themselves with the structural interests of the poor. Basing their theological analysis upon insights from both sociological and economic theory, the kairos theologians further asserted that much South African Christian thought was nothing more than idolatry, using theological language and imagery to legitimize the vested interests of those benefiting from an oppressive status quo. At present promoted by the Institute for Contextual Theology, prophetic theology has among its protagonists A. Nolan, whose book *God in South Africa* (1988) is the only systematic theology written by a South African contextual theologian. Other important figures are M. Motlhabi, F. Chikane and J. Cochrane, although prophetic theology prefers to be known as a democratic or 'people's theology', rather than one characterized by individual theologians. This is evident in the broad range of Christians who signed the sequel to *The Kairos Document, The Road to Damascus: Kairos and Conversion* of 1989. A further effect of prophetic theology has been to stimulate the development of a more indigenous evangelical theology (see EVANGELICALISM), as seen in the document *The Evangelical Witness in South Africa* of 1988.

Feminist theology

FEMINIST THEOLOGY in South Africa is still in its infancy. Influenced by its western counterpart, it addresses the question of female oppression in South Africa, especially since black women, in particular, represent the most oppressed category of people in the country. Despite this, feminist issues have been regarded as secondary to the demands of black theology as a whole. In part, this has been due to ambiguity surrounding the participation of white women in the creation of an indigenous feminist theology. More pertinently, it reflects the dominance of men in the South African theological debate. Nevertheless, articles in recent editions of the *Journal of Theology for Southern Africa*, together with essays in *The Unquestionable Right to be Free* (Mosala and Thlagale, 1986), reveal the increasing contribution of feminist theology to the South African scene in its struggle to articulate new, inclusive theological symbols and structures. Foremost among contemporary feminist theologians are D. Ackermann, M.H. Keane and L. Kretzschmar.

See also the other articles on PROTESTANT THEOLOGY.

Bibliography

Boesak, A. 1976: *Farewell to Innocence*. New York: Orbis.

Borchardt, C.F.A., and Vorster, W.S., eds 1980–88: *South African Theological Bibliography*, vols 1–3. Pretoria: University of South Africa.

de Gruchy, J.W. 1986: *The Church Struggle in South Africa*, 2nd edn. Grand Rapids: Eerdmans.

de Gruchy, J.W. 1990: *Liberating Reformed theology*. Grand Rapids: Eerdmans; London: Geoffrey Chapman.

de Gruchy, J.W. 1991: South African theology comes of age, *Religious Studies Review* 17, no. 3.

Institute for Contextual Theology 1986: *The Kairos Document: Challenge to the Church*. Johannesburg: Skotaville.

Kretzschmar, L. 1986: *The Voice of Black Theology in South Africa*. Johannesburg: Ravan.

Moore, B., ed. [1970] 1973: *Black Theology: The South African Voice*. London: C. Hurst and Co.

Mosala, I.J. 1989: *Biblical Hermeneutics and Black Theology in South Africa*. Grand Rapids: Eerdmans.

Mosala, I.J. and Thlagale, B. 1986: *The Unquestionable Right to be Free*. Johannesburg: Skotaville.

Nolan, A. 1988: *God in South Africa*. Cape Town: David Philip.

Setiloane, G. 1986: *African Theology: An Introduction*. Johannesburg: Skotaville.

Villa-Vicencio, C. 1988: *Trapped in Apartheid*. New York: Orbis.

JOHN B. THOMSON

Protestant theology: USA Because most of the enduring American settlements were made by Protestant Europeans (though they were neither the earliest European arrivals nor the original Americans), America's theology may mistakenly be considered simply an extension of Europe's and especially England's. Certainly from the beginning European texts were studied and European rallying cries (*sola gratia, sola scriptura, sola fide*) repeated. Yet the Atlantic crossing produced sea changes, and shortly American theological debates and religious convictions took shapes more suited to the new circumstances than the old. While some have interpreted these facts in a way that denies any real theology to this New World, it is better simply to recognize that here as in the old, context mattered. If we take account of this as well as of traditional and biblical elements in the formation of American Protestant thought, we gain a better idea of it and can more fairly compare American with other thought.

Three contextual elements are inescapable: the spaciousness of the American continent, a rich, sparsely inhabited wilderness before the first lasting English settlement appeared (Jamestown, Virginia, 1607); the slow, inexorable appearance of liberty (especially religious liberty) with its attendant pluralism in forms unknown in the (European) past; and the sweet, even cloying, context of success – economic, political, cultural and institutional – as the new settlers and their churches flourished. *Spaciousness* meant the challenge of geographical discovery and the accompanying sense that God had more light, more truth, yet to break forth from Scripture (John Robinson's Leyden farewell to the American 'Pilgrims'). *Liberty* (to be sharply distinguished from mere tolerance) grew partly from this spaciousness: a sect persecuted in one place had only to seek another; yet by the 1830s all the American states had disestablished their churches, and *de facto* freedom became enshrined in law as well. *Success* meant that the gospel had to be discovered all over again; in America the gospel was neither an anodyne for oppressed masses nor a prop for oligarchy, but the truth for people making it on their own who nonetheless yearned for nature's God or sought Jesus' friendship. (Exceptions to success were the victims of colonization and of black slavery and the experience of the south in the Civil War;

each of these with its aftermath had theological consequences.) These three colour the American development throughout.

Beginnings to 1800

While contextual themes framed American theology, they did not determine it. Protestantism, H.R. Niebuhr believed, must be understood from its beginning as a rediscovery of the present sovereignty of God: for the Catholic *visio Dei* Protestantism substituted *regnum Dei*. This applied not only to Calvin but to Luther as well, and Niebuhr might have added Anabaptists and pietists also. Two further Christian motifs, the grace of Christ and the hope for God's promised future, are entailed in that present sovereignty (Niebuhr, [1937] 1959, chapter 1). So Protestant theological beginnings in America, as in Europe, present a spectrum of positions, as now one and now another thinker or movement differently assigned priorities of conviction upon encountering the American context.

Thus John Cotton (1584–1652), the most prominent early New England Puritan theologian, preaching justification by faith alone, elicited many conversions in his Boston congregation. This emphasis upon grace was repeated by his disciple Anne Hutchinson (1591–1643), America's first woman theologian, who privately taught Cotton's biblical interpretations to prominent Bostonians. Diminishing the importance of good works led to her subsequent trial and banishment for 'antinomianism'. She found refuge in Rhode Island, a new colony led by Roger Williams (c.1603–1683), who had himself been banished from Massachusetts Bay (1635). While Williams had shared Cotton's 'by faith alone' Puritanism and his intense spirituality, he had believed even more strongly in the underlying Protestant principle, God's immediate sovereignty. This doctrine had radical ethical consequences for Williams: he denied the King's right (and hence Boston's right) to pre-empt Indian lands, or to enforce religious conformity upon settlers, who must rather respond directly to God. Williams thus based religious liberty upon divine sovereignty. Such freedom struck a political note that would reverberate in the later, Federal period (Bill of Rights, 1791), though largely upon pragmatic rather than Williams's theo-

logical grounds. If we consider the popularity among success-oriented Boston business folk of Hutchinson's (and Cotton's) 'antinomianism', or note Cotton's belief that Williams's banishment, given America's spaciousness, was 'not counted so much a confinement, as an enlargement' (cited in Mead, 1963, p. 13), we glimpse factors that were shaping American theology – and see as well the severe tension they produced. To H.R. Niebuhr as historian, the persistent dilemma of Protestantism in Europe and America was how to enjoy the freedom entailed by present divine sovereignty without producing oppression or anarchy. Thus American theology from the beginning was shaped by immediate ethical concerns, not because (as in later reductionisms) these Protestants denied the transcendence or immanence of God, but because their sense of the divine in human life made a present, challenging difference to faith on earth.

These motifs come together afresh in the thought and life of Jonathan Edwards (1703–1758), America's foremost theologian until the twentieth century (and perhaps beyond). A fourth-generation American, Edwards was nonetheless alert to British developments, cutting his teeth on John Locke's sensationalist epistemology and developing to match it an idealist metaphysic rather like Berkeley's. Yet his chief contribution was theological: challenged in his pastoral ministry by Enlightenment deism and the Arminianism he regarded as its pawn, Edwards sought a firm basis for a theology of grace in Scriptural, historical and personal narrative. Thus at least in intention he foreshadowed NARRATIVE THEOLOGY, projecting before his untimely death 'a great work, which I call a "History of the Work of Redemption", a body of divinity . . . thrown into the form of a history' (letter to the Princeton Trustees, 1757, quoted in Faust and Johnson, 1962, p. 411), though of this only a sermonic skeleton appeared. Yet his intentions were not wholly thwarted. When a revival had broken out in Edwards's Northampton (Congregational) parish and across the colonies (the Great Awakening of the early 1740s), Enlightenment critics and rigid Calvinists had alike disparaged it. But in a series of pamphlets culminating in a *Treatise concerning Religious Affections* of 1746 Edwards showed how in narrative context 'truly gracious religious affections' could be distinguished from false or misleading signs of divine grace. This analysis permitted him to steer clear of antinomianism as well – for authentic religious affections challenged sharp business practices and the greed bred of success. Nor were the notes of present divine sovereignty and imminent eschatology lacking. Firm in the Reformed tradition, Edwards combined predestination with human responsibility (*Freedom of the Will* of 1754; *Nature of True Virtue* of 1755), and eschatological vision with belief in present progress ('Notes on the Apocalypse', Edwards, 1957– , vol. 5): America's spaces were shortly to be filled with true Christians. His dismissal from his Northampton pulpit was apparently engineered by merchant-class members who understood all too well this radical challenge. Thus Edwards brought together active divine sovereignty, the grace of Christ and millennial hope in a tense construction.

From 1800 to 1917

When nineteenth-century European intellectual currents (Kant, Schleiermacher, Hegel, Marx) flowed into America, they, too, were changed in passage, and their influence mingled with new contextual elements (the western frontier, the struggle over slavery, the industrial revolution – space, liberty, and success again). There were also new developments in the churches: revival, denominational self-awareness, and the drive to social reform. For faith it was a dynamic century. The number of creative and influential theologians multiplied geometrically, so that not all can usefully be mentioned here.

Edwards's successors fell into rival schools (New Divinity men versus Old Calvinists); each seized elements of his heritage but not the whole, and their dominance diminished. A central Old Calvinist figure was Nathaniel W. Taylor (1785–1858), a Yale Congregationalist. Determined to make Protestant orthodoxy palatable in evangelistic settings, Taylor rejected inherited depravity ('sin is in the sinning'), and sought to justify the ways of a Calvinist God to self-sufficient Americans, thus pressing close to the Arminianism Edwards had feared. As decades passed, the New England theologies declined into mere piety or moralism (Haroutounian, 1932), ceasing to meet the challenges of the century. Much of New England opted for unitarianism, a complex if compact movement that attracted some of America's best minds. While the earliest unitarians here were Anglicans (King's Chapel, Boston, 1785), soon many Congregationalists turned to its biblicist, rational, and socially conservative themes (rejecting the Trinity as an unbiblical, unsettling doctrine). Unitarianism evolved, however, in the hands of Boston pastor William Ellery Channing (1780–1842) into a wide-ranging doctrine of human spiritual growth and perfectibility. Unitarianism interacted (from the 1830s) with transcendentalism, a philosophical-literary movement that profoundly influenced American life, especially via Ralph Waldo Emerson (1803–1882) and Henry David Thoreau (1817–1862). But Emerson moved outside every church, there joining Thoreau ('I am my own church'), so that Americans understood the writings of these two as philosophy or literature, not theology. In that role their religious influence was pervasive, through, for example, Emerson's 'Self-Reliance' of 1841 (in Emerson, 1983) and Thoreau's *Walden* of 1854 (in Thoreau, 1985).

These diverse trends all converged in their encounter with the modern critical challenge to the Bible as theological source book (*sola scriptura*). Considering two explicitly churchly theologians will reinforce this impression. The Congregationalist Horace Bushnell (1802–1876) addressed the problem of biblical authority from the standpoint of a long pastorate. Himself deeply influenced by romanticism (F.D.E. Schleiermacher, S.T. Coleridge, Emerson), he preached to practical Hartford, Connecticut, business folk who thought they knew what the Bible said but found that hard to believe. To them Bushnell preached a 'progressive orthodoxy' that retained the old doctrinal labels (Providence, election, atonement, salvation, grace, faith), but he gave these a new (or rediscovered) organic setting in the life of family, church and nation. An important tool for Bushnell was a theory of language that distinguished in all speech two 'departments' or modes: one the physical, using words to refer to objects in the physical world; the other the intellectual, using the terms of the first in another sense to refer to 'thought and spirit'. The latter department was necessarily imprecise, necessarily false as well as true, and yet perfectly suited to what lay beyond the senses. Thus the two worlds that language described were not earth and heaven, but nature and the supernatural, the latter being the realm of intellect and spirit here and now (see his 'Dissertation on . . . Language', of 1849). In this mode he addressed the major controversies of his day, revivalism (*Christian Nurture* of 1847), Christology (*God in Christ* of 1849), atonement (*The Vicarious Sacrifice* of 1866), treating each in a mediating fashion that staked out between Calvinist orthodoxy and unitarianism a claim for evangelical liberalism (see Bushnell, 1964).

Consider now the Presbyterian Charles Hodge (1797–1878), chief architect of the Princeton theology that persisted among evangelicals far into the twentieth century. Where Bushnell intentionally met the demands of the age with revision and reconception, loving the old yet determined to match it with the new, Hodge rather gloried in the belief that at least at confessional Princeton everything remained the same: the seminary had never 'originated a new idea'. Yet his performance may have exceeded his intentions. Believing the Reformed faith to be simply the Bible correctly understood and logically interpreted, his purpose was to prove its trustworthiness (employing Scottish common-sense philosophy) and then to interpret it in support of the Reformed position. For the latter, he looked over the head of Edwards to the seventeenth century (Westminster symbols, Synod of Dort, and especially the conservative Swiss Calvinist Francois Turretin). Hodge conceived his task as a strictly scientific one: as he supposed, the inductive gathering of 'facts' (in this case, from Scripture) followed by 'deductions' from those facts (Hodge, 1871–3, vol. 1). Yet this procedure reveals his unsought originality; by treating the Bible as a book of science-like 'facts', he obscured its narrative form, making of it only a quarry for his searches. His method dominates his treatment of biological evolution: while as a construal of facts evolution was permissible, the Darwinian version was impossible, since it denied the direct creation of man and denied the presence of design (that is, purpose) in nature – thus twice scorning biblical teaching (see Welch, 1972–85, vol. 2, chapter 6). On evolution, as on biblical infallibility, Hodge typified one side of a growing bifurcation in Protestant thought, as Bushnell did the other. If, as has been argued (E.R. Sandeen), American fundamentalism sank one of its roots into the soil of the Princeton theology, Hodge is not totally without responsibility.

In this period American Christianity struggled with problems unconceived a century earlier. The Civil War (1861–5) revealed a capacity for largescale human evil previously unknown in modernity. Moreover, the war did not so much solve the slavery issue as mutate it into a new sort of racism, virulent in north and south alike. Massive immigration from southern Europe and Asia produced working conditions previously unknown in America; these spelled success for some while creating disaster for many. Beneath the surface there lurked as well the unexplored issue of gender in society. To address these problems in theological perspective there arose the social gospel movement (Handy, 1966), foreshadowed in the post Civil War holiness revivals and peaking in the labours of Walter Rauschenbusch (1861–1918), Baptist pastor and seminary professor at Rochester, New York. Well educated, warmly converted, as a child of immigrants sensitive to outsider Americans, Rauschenbusch melded the theme of organic human solidarity and the human plight (cf. Bushnell) with insights drawn from the Bible, social studies, and Marxist thought into a rich polyphony. His earliest book, *The Righteousness of the Kingdom*, published only posthumously (1968), sounded the key: Jesus had come preaching that righteousness and summoning all to a new way of life, but an oppressive ecclesial Christianity had forgotten him. Now, however, a new light was dawning: it was time for institutions, not just individuals, to be converted and enter the kingdom. In *A Theology for the Social Gospel* ([1917] 1978) Rauschenbusch defended the assumptions behind this summons: these included a searching view of sin as part of a 'kingdom of evil', of Jesus as the initiator of the kingdom, and of baptism and the Lord's supper as acts of allegiance to the kingdom. Though as a movement the social gospel vanished, all these themes would recur in the century to follow.

From 1918 to the present

Because theology is a self-involving discipline (the convictions it explores are those whose adoption or rejection makes of us the people and communities that we are) it is even more true here than in most disciplines that as we approach our own times our judgements are necessarily subjective. This section cannot reliably select the American theologies that will endure; at best it can call attention to those that have created great interest at the time. Of these the most striking is Protestant FUNDAMENTALISM. Born of a convergence of various religious concerns and movements, it was united by its opposition to the liberal movement (see LIBERALISM: USA) (to such as Bushnell, Rauschenbusch, and their successors) and to the modernist movement (described below). Yet more than a backlash from liberalism and modernism in theology, fundamentalism independently expressed a deep cultural disquiet, a 'no' not only to biological evolution and cultural pluralism, but to modernity in its entirety. This negation would have been more profound had it found a satisfying basis for theological reconstruction. Its own basis (biblical inerrancy, Christ's virgin birth, blood atonement, physical resurrection, and imminent return, in one summary) afforded no enduring platform, and fundamentalism has so far produced no major theologian (though J. Gresham Machen (1881–1937) is often suggested), while its dearly captured institutions, schools, seminaries and denominations repeatedly slid away into a milder EVANGELICALISM (as at Fuller Theological Seminary in California, where philosopher Edward J. Carnell (1919–1967) presided over the change – see Marsden, 1987) or (as with Jehovah's Witnesses) migrated to the fringe of American Christianity.

Even less capable of dominating the stage was the modernist movement of the early twentieth century (see MODERNISM). An intellectual centre here was the Divinity School of the University of Chicago, which more than any American institution shaping theology focused upon critical historiography, social-scientific study of religion, and current philosophies such as pragmatism and process thought. On this basis, the Chicago school formed the nucleus of some significant developments in American theology. Henry Nelson Wieman (1884–1975)

believed we can discover empirically the creative source of human good, which he labelled 'God'; with Charles Hartshorne (b. 1897), Bernard Meland (b. 1899) and Bernard Loomer (1912–1985), he adopted and adapted the process philosophy of Alfred North Whitehead (1861–1947) to produce a theological naturalism, more empiricist in the others and rationalist in Hartshorne, that they believed fit for the demands of modernity (see PROCESS THEOLOGY). For example, evolution, anathema to their theological opponents, suited the Chicago school perfectly. While its earlier representatives concentrated upon philosophical prolegomena to theology, their student John Cobb (b. 1925), later professor at Claremont, California, ranged over the topics of theology from a process perspective. As the Chicago movement waned, it was cross-fertilized by newcomers such as the existentialist Langdon Gilkey (b. 1919), the Roman Catholic David W. Tracy (b. 1939) and the French Protestant Paul Ricoeur (b. 1913).

If modernism as such had vanished, this was hardly due to fundamentalism – these two rarely conversed, though they often covered the same ground, and though they shared strikingly similar American features such as concern for the faith of the laity and for pragmatic effectiveness. Yet both were rivalled at mid-century by a third movement, neo-orthodoxy, that made its way without evident regard for either method – or either movement. Reinhold Niebuhr (1892–1971) was the elder son of a German-born pastor father who baptized his children into what became the Evangelical and Reformed church, eventually the United Church of Christ. After theological studies in his denomination's schools and at Yale, Reinhold became pastor of a small church in Detroit, Michigan, and in due course professor at Union Theological Seminary (1928–60). At first his enormous energies were absorbed by social criticism, undertaken from a Marxist-Christian standpoint, but his politics, while remaining critical of western pretensions, gradually shifted to a New Deal liberalism, and he forsook his earlier pacifism to encourage entry into the Second World War. Underwriting this shift, Reinhold developed a theology informed by his Calvinist and (especially) Lutheran heritage, and more broadly by the Augustinian tradition. At Union he was especially stimulated by a refugee from Nazi Germany, Paul Tillich (1886–1965), whose 'method of correlation' later unfolded in a *Systematic Theology* (1951–63) that transposed neo-orthodoxy into idealist and existentialist categories. In his Gifford Lectures, *The Nature and Destiny of Man* (1941–3), Reinhold provided his own mature theology. Against the optimism he felt had guided the social gospel, humanity here appeared precariously balanced between sensuality and spiritual pride, and sure to fall repeatedly into one or the other – and sinfully to deny it had fallen. Only Jesus takes the way of self-denial; for ourselves to take that way is to become irrelevant to history; thus we 'inevitably' (though 'not of necessity') sin. Redemption comes in the form of grace, assured at the cross, but finally available only 'beyond history', so that our species lives by hope if it lives at all. The 'impossible ideal' of love is nevertheless not irrelevant, since it forms the criticism of that proximate justice which in this life is the best we can, but what we must, attain. Life in these tense paradoxes had a grandeur that the nominally Christian mid-century American public, still successful but no longer conscious of limitless space and freedom, often found awesome and fascinating.

If Reinhold was a public theologian, his younger brother Helmut Richard Niebuhr (1894–1962) was a theologian's theologian. Intensely introspective, teaching his students at Yale Divinity School, writing books and articles in carefully crafted English, H. Richard was less well-known than his brother, but not less significant. Again his focus was ethics, broadly construed as social and cultural interpretation. And he shared the general neo-orthodox orientation to revelation as the key to faith's knowledge. Liberalism was flayed as a faith in which a 'God without wrath brought men without sin into a kingdom without judgement through the ministrations of a Christ without a cross.' That was written ([1937] 1959, p. 193) of Edward Bellamy's romantic socialism, yet it was understood as a wider neo-orthodox rejection of America's recent theological past. However, Richard Niebuhr's relation to liberalism was more complex. He was a disciple of Troeltsch, and Troeltsch's theological problems, the problem

of religious knowledge in a relativistic world and the status of Christian faith in the light of that relativism, could not simply be dismissed by the appeal to revelation. Thus in *The Meaning of Revelation* (1941) he identified several related meanings: revelation was the content of faith that has come to us from the past; it was also that event in history that illuminates and provides meaning to all other history; thus finally it was God disclosing himself to us in our history so as to judge, transform and remake us: 'When we find out that we are no longer thinking him, but that he first thought us, that is revelation' (p. 153). Thus H. Richard pressed through the liberal preoccupation with subjectivity and criticism to discover – God. Yet this required both recourse to narrative in order to make sense of experience ('The Story of Our Lives') and return to an Edwardsean (and Reformed) sense of the greatness of God ('The Deity of God'). Niebuhr looked backwards and forwards in establishing his own standpoint.

Neo-orthodoxy did not survive the 1960s; its principal labourers retired, and its implied affirmation of the spaciousness, liberty and success of the American story seemed less appealing in the era of Vietnam. In its place, no single successor arose. Older forms of Christian thought continued to produce literature, train ministers and shape liturgy and life. Most conspicuous among Protestants was evangelicalism, but this was a vague term that could embrace revivalism, evangelical liberalism, chastened fundamentalism, charismatics, and the heritage of Anabaptism (Baptists, Disciples, Mennonites, Pentecostals and so on) alongside some mainline Protestants, so that it had no single meaning. In the absence of suitable theological leadership, it cohered through shared programmes, institutions and intuitions (Marsden, 1987).

A striking if short-lived 'movement' was the 'death of God' theology of the 1960s: again a mere convergence, in this case of scholars rather than institutions, it brought together the Hegelian culture history of Thomas J.J. Altizer (b. 1927), a logical positivist (mis)reading of the later Wittgenstein by Paul M. van Buren (b. 1924), and still other questionings of the received Christian doctrine. Inconclusive though it was, the death of God movement, rather like fundamentalism, touched a deep disquiet in the American religious intellect.

American Protestant theologians played an important role in the worldwide ecumenical movement: Paul Sevier Minear (b. 1906) linked the mid-century's 'biblical theology' to ecumenism; Albert Cook Outler (1908–1989) related his confessional Methodism to classic and modern Catholicism; the Lutheran George Lindbeck (b. 1923) provided a sophisticated analysis of Christian doctrinal disagreements. Others, such as Franklin H. Littell (b. 1917) and Paul van Buren, reached beyond Christianity to embrace post-Holocaust Judaism theologically. And still others, including John Cobb and Wilfred Cantwell Smith (b. 1916) explored the relationship of Christian doctrine to other religions in and beyond America.

Narrative motifs, mentioned above, were self-consciously addressed by theologians in this period, often in the wake of H. Richard Niebuhr and his junior colleague Hans W. Frei (1922–1988), whose *Eclipse of Biblical Narrative* (1974) triggered a number of attempts to recover the missing narrative element in biblical faith.

Other theological tendencies were closely allied to social movements: in the wake of Martin Luther King, Jr (1929–1968), though at some distance from the racial reconciliation he stressed (King, 1986), a BLACK THEOLOGY appeared; its standard bearer was James Hal Cone (b. 1938). A feminist movement (see FEMINIST THEOLOGY), renascent in the 1970s, addressed the neglected gender issues of a century or more earlier; Protestant theological approaches to this were made by Letty M. Russell (b. 1929), Marjorie Suchocki (b. 1933) and others. Recognizing the note of *liberty* in these and still other causes, one may call them collectively North American liberation theologies. In this connection appears Robert McAfee Brown (b. 1920), who engaged ecumenical and political themes.

Finally, one may note a recovery in this period of theologies stemming from the Radical Reformation. These lifted up such themes as discipleship, nonviolent political action, Christocentrism, and the voluntary or believers' church: significant names include Franklin Littell (b. 1917), James Wm McClendon, Jr (b. 1924), John Howard Yoder (b. 1927) and Stanley Hauerwas (b. 1940).

In retrospect, it appears that while Protestant theology in the USA has responded to Enlightenment themes such as the flight from authority, and to the new western awareness of a plural context, it has also been affected by its own setting (space, liberty, success and their limits) and by its lively inner history. Despite promising beginnings, so far no American theology seems adequate to the possibilities thus uncovered.

See also DISPENSATONALISM; ECUMENISM; PENTECOSTALISM AND CHARISMATIC CHRISTIANITY; POSTLIBERALISM; POSTMODERNISM; and the other articles on PROTESTANT THEOLOGY.

Bibliography

Ahlstrom, Sydney, ed. 1967: *Theology in America: The Major Voices.* New York: Bobbs-Merrill.

Ahlstrom, Sydney 1972: *A Religious History of the American People.* New Haven: Yale University Press.

Bushnell, Horace 1964: *Horace Bushnell*, ed. H. Shelton Smith. Library of Protestant Thought. New York: Oxford University Press.

Clebsch, William A. 1973: *American Religious Thought: A History.* Chicago: University of Chicago Press.

Edwards, Jonathan 1957– : *The Works of Jonathan Edwards.* New Haven: Yale University Press.

Emerson, Ralph Waldo 1983: *Essays and Lectures*, ed. Joel Porte. Library of America. New York: Viking Press.

Faust, Clarence H. and Johnson, Thomas H., eds 1962: *Jonathan Edwards: Representative Selections*, revised edn. New York: Hill and Wang.

Frei, Hans W. 1974: *The Eclipse of Biblical Narrative.* New Haven: Yale University Press.

Handy, Robert T., ed. 1966: *The Social Gospel.* A Library of Protestant Thought. New York: Oxford University Press.

Haroutounian, Joseph 1932: *Piety Versus Moralism: The Passing of the New England Theology.* New York: Holt and Co.

Hodge, Charles 1871–3: *Systematic Theology*, 3 vols. New York: Charles Scribner and Co.

King, Martin Luther 1986: *A Testament of Hope: The Essential Writings . . .* , ed. James M. Washington. San Francisco: Harper and Row.

Marsden, George M. 1980: *Fundamentalism and American Culture.* New York: Oxford University Press.

Marsden, George M. 1987: *Reforming Fundamentalism: Fuller Seminary and the New Evangelicalism.* Grand Rapids: Eerdmans.

Mead, Sidney 1963: *The Lively Experiment: The*

Shaping of Christianity in America. New York: Harper and Row.

Niebuhr, H. Richard [1937] 1959: *The Kingdom of God in America*. New York: Harper and Row.

Niebuhr, H. Richard 1941: *The Meaning of Revelation*. New York: Macmillan.

Niebuhr, Reinhold 1941–3: *The Nature and Destiny of Man: A Christian Interpretation*. Gifford Lectures. New York: Charles Scribner's Sons.

Rauschenbusch, Walter [1917] 1978: *A Theology for the Social Gospel*. Nashville: Abingdon Press.

Rauschenbusch, Walter 1968: *The Righteousness of the Kingdom*. Nashville: Abingdon Press.

Reid, Daniel G., Linder, Robert D., Shelley, Bruce I., and Stout, Harry S., eds 1990: *Dictionary of Christianity in America*. Downers Grove, Illinois: InterVarsity Press.

Sandeen, Ernest R. 1970: *The Roots of Fundamentalism*. Chicago: University of Chicago Press.

Smith, H. Shelton, Handy, Robert and Loetscher, Lefferts A. 1960: *American Christianity: An Historical Interpretation with Representative Documents*, 2 vols. New York: Scribner's.

Thoreau, Henry David 1985: *A Week on the Concord and Merrimack Rivers*; *Walden*; *The Maine Woods*; *Cape Cod*; ed. Robert F. Sayre. Library of America. New York: Viking Press.

Tillich, Paul 1951–63: *Systematic Theology*. Chicago: University of Chicago Press.

Welch, Claude 1972–85: *Protestant Thought in the Nineteenth Century*, vol. 1, 1799–1870, and vol. 2, 1870–1914. New Haven: Yale University Press.

JAMES WM MCCLENDON, JR

psychological science and Christian thought Psychology emerged as an independent field of systematic enquiry only in the latter part of the nineteenth century. Before that, contributions to psychology were to be found largely within philosophy or theology. Modern psychology has attempted to be 'systematic', both in its mode of making observations (often quantitative, but not necessarily so), and its style of theorizing (as precise as possible, so it is easier to detect when a theory is wrong). Psychoanalysis sits somewhat uneasily within modern psychology because of its different epistemological basis. However, it is with the psychological ideas of Freud and Jung that much work on the interface of theology and psychology has been concerned.

Simultaneously with the development of psychology as an independent discipline, 'religion' has also become a field of study. The concept of 'religion' – and even more tellingly of 'religions' – is a more recent one than is often realized. It incorporates the implicit assumption that different religions have common features about which it is possible to generalize, and that these are open to systematic, objective study (see RELIGION, THEORIES OF). Psychology is of course only one of the disciplines that have studied 'religion'; anthropology and sociology have also made important contributions.

This article will begin with a brief survey of the 'psychology of religion', though later it will also consider the scope for interdisciplinary work between psychology and theology. There are two pioneering figures in the psychology of religion, whose influence cannot be exaggerated. These are William James and Sigmund Freud. The issues they raised are still highly topical, and they are the best place to begin.

William James

James's *Varieties of Religious Experience* (1902) was first delivered in Edinburgh as the Gifford Lectures. The title conveys the essence of James's approach; the focus was to be on religious *experience*. His emphasis on experience in matters of religion was not novel. Schleiermacher, at the beginning of the nineteenth century, believed that he had found in religious experience, especially in the feeling of 'absolute dependence', a new and more secure foundation for theology. However, James approached the description of religious experience in a more systematic and empirical way than had Schleiermacher.

Characteristic of the *Varieties* is James's identification of the primary features of mysticism as (1) defying verbal expression but (2) being 'noetic' (i.e. seeming to be a state of knowledge). James seemed to regard religious experience as having a pure, immediate, authoritative 'core' that might then be interpreted and elaborated in social and linguistic forms. This raises issues about the relation between experience and language in religion (see LANGUAGE, RELIGIOUS), and about the authority of experience in religion.

The selection of personal experience as the primary focus of psychological study may appear to neglect the role of language and social life. Elsewhere, James had shown himself well aware of social influences on experience, for example that people see only what they have been taught to see. However, in his work on religious experience, James either lost sight of this point, or at least did not emphasize it as explicitly as one might wish. Linked to James's relative neglect of social influences on religious experience is his tendency to accept the authority of religious experience too uncritically. He is, of course, correct to point out that people who have religious experiences often accept them as being authoritative, but he does not see sufficiently clearly that it is quite another issue whether they are justified in doing so.

There are good contemporary discussions of the issues raised by James's approach to religion, by Proudfoot (1985) from the standpoint of philosophy of religion, and by Lash (1988) from the standpoint of theology. Though James's *Varieties* should not be read uncritically, it still represents a carefully observed, vividly described, systematic description of religious experience. As such it remains unsurpassed in the psychology of religion.

Sigmund Freud

While James had been sympathetic to religion, Freud was critical of it. Indeed, it is largely to Freud that we owe the widely held view that there is an intrinsic antipathy or rivalry between psychology and religion. We will focus here primarily on Freud's monograph, *The Future of an Illusion* ([1927] 1928). His other books on religion are more anthropological in focus.

The heart of Freud's thesis is that religion represents an immature way of coping with unpleasant reality. In developing this thesis Freud took over Feuerbach's view that 'God' is not an objective reality but a projection of the human mind. However, Freud elaborated the functional value of this illusion in coping with psychic threat, and also postulated its origins in phases of psychic development ('anal', 'Oedipal' and so on). Freud saw the development of belief in God as (in the words of Ricoeur, 1970, p. 248) 'successive displacements of the father figure onto the totem, then onto spirits and demons, then onto the Gods, and finally onto the God of Abraham, Isaac and Jacob and the God of Jesus Christ . . .'.

Freud's critique of religion is not as devastating as might at first appear. His psychological theories, and the adequacy of his methodology, remain matters of keen debate. Even Freud's admirers would admit that his essentially clinical methodology was stretched in dealing with a cultural phenomenon such as religion. Also, though Freud called religion an 'illusion', he admitted that this did not necessarily mean it was wrong. 'Illusion' for Freud was a technical term that he distinguished from '*de*lusion'. To call religion an illusion in his technical sense is not necessarily any more derogatory than when modern theologians talk about it as 'myth'.

For all the apparent hostility of Freud to religion, recent scholarly work has tended to emphasize that a Freudian perspective in theology is not necessarily as unhelpful as might at first appear. W.W. Meissner (1984) is one of a group of recent psychoanalytic writers, influenced by D.W. Winnicott, who have emphasized that religion, like art and play, can be adaptive and creative (see Watts and Williams, 1988, pp. 33–7). P. Homans (1970) has emphasized the value to theology of the point that concepts of God frequently are human projections, being distorted and inadequate. He draws out the relationship between the attempt by writers such as Paul Tillich to transcend inadequate forms of theological theism, and Freud's exposure of the inadequacy of human concepts of God. Freud's point that concepts of God often arise through projection does not necessarily imply that they *always* do so, or that there can be no reality of God that transcends human misconceptions of him. What psychoanalysis has called 'projective' concepts of God are no more to be defended than what theology has called 'idolatrous' concepts of God.

Contemporary empirical psychology of religion

Contemporary empirical studies of religion have eschewed both James's attempt to shield religion from criticism (on the basis of the 'noetic' quality of religious experience) and Freud's apparently unsympathetic critique of religion as 'illusion'. In contrast, they have sought a neutral, objective stance, relying much more heavily on quantitative data. It will be considered by some, especially those familiar with the 'hermeneutic' perspective of continental philosophy, that there is something simplistic in the way such quantitative studies of religion seek to achieve objectivity by using detached, impersonal methods of observation and measurement. I would prefer to formulate this point in terms of how far such 'objective' methods of enquiry limit the range of psychological questions about religion that can be addressed. However, I think it is clear that the empirical approach to religion has by now amassed considerable information that is both interesting and dependable. It should not be ignored. Brown (1988) has provided an admirable brief review of such work, and Spilka *et al.* (1985) a fuller survey.

The majority of empirical work on religion has focused on beliefs and practices, though religious experience, religious knowledge and the effects of religion have also been considered. Particularly fruitful has been the study of individual differences, that is, the beliefs and practices of different kinds of people. For example, how does the emotional adjustment of religious people compare with the rest of the population? It has turned out that the answer to this question depends on the level of religious commitment of the person concerned. Highly committed religious people are better adjusted than the average member of the population. In contrast, those with a more nominal adherence to religion are *less* well adjusted than average.

Another important line of work has been on the development of religious understanding in children. Of course it has to be recognized that this does not proceed in exactly the same way, and at the same rate, in all children. However, the basic pattern that emerges is that up to the age of nine children tend to see God in concrete, anthropomorphic terms. There then follows a period in which God begins to be seen in supernatural rather than superhuman terms, and in which a gulf begins to open up between scientific and theological explanations of events. From thirteen onwards, there is an increasing tendency to see God in symbolic, spiritual terms, with anthropomorphic concepts being largely abandoned.

There are many other topics on which the psychology of religion has yielded interesting findings, as can be illustrated with a few brief examples. It has been found that *conversion* of the sudden type is most likely to appear in adolescence, but is frequently not permanent. *Glossolalia*, or 'speaking in tongues' has been shown by psycholinguistic studies to be different in form and structure from known languages. Powerful, personal *religious experiences* of a serene presence beyond oneself are remarkably common, though most people keep the experience to themselves, assuming that no one would understand.

It is impossible within the brief space available here to do more than indicate something of the scope of such empirical studies of religion. There is much information here that has important implications for those planning church activities and mission.

Jungian theology

The work of C.G. Jung on religion represents not merely an approach to the psychological study of religion, but an interdisciplinary enterprise involving psychology, theology and many other disciplines. Jung, like Freud, took as his empirical base his analytical work with patients. However, to help him interpret this, he turned to relevant historical and cultural sources such as alchemy. The two kinds of material were then used to interpret each other. For example, he saw his clinical material as enabling him to understand the psychological significance of alchemy; equally, alchemy enabled him to understand the symbolic themes he encountered in his patients' dreams. It was in this context that Jung approached religion, though his views changed considerably during the forty years over which he wrote about religion. The best single exposition is probably the 'Introduction to the Religious and Psychological Problems of Alchemy' in *Psychology and Alchemy* ([1944] 1953). There are many popular books on Jungian psychology and religion, but a dearth of more scholarly and critical secondary sources. Important exceptions are J.W. Heisig's *Imago Dei* (1979) and H. Chapman's *Jung's Three Theories of Religious Experience* (1987).

Jung did not disagree with Freud's view that God was a projection from the unconscious. However, he increasingly emphasized the *collective* unconscious as a source of the image of God. The status of the collective unconscious is always a little unclear, though increasingly Jung seemed to see it as a kind of supra-material shared consciousness. Jung talks about the image of God in the psyche, but it is unclear whether God actually exists independently of this image. Jung insisted this was not a question for him as a psychologist. Sometimes he writes as though it would be absurd to suppose the existence of a 'metaphysical' God outside the psyche; at other times he writes as though he personally assumed the existence of such a God.

Jung also differed from Freud in being more interested in the function of religion, and in taking a positive view of its contribution to human life. (This functional approach is something he shares with modern psychoanalytic writers on religion like W.W. Meissner.) Jung increasingly saw the *Self* (vs. the *ego*) as an image of Christ in the psyche, and as a pointer towards a state of wholeness or individuation. The *Self* is, for Jung, the centre of the whole personality, whereas the *ego* is the centre of consciousness of the person's current state of development. Much that theology would wish to say about God and the transcendent, Jung says within the psychological domain about the *Self*. For example, the *ego* cannot work out its own salvation (or 'individuation'). Rather, it must recognize the need to concentrate on something beyond itself, whether this is formulated as the *Self*, or as God.

The theological fruitfulness of Jung's ideas is well illustrated by the topic of evil (Philp, 1958). Jung saw evil, like God, as having both personal and collective origins. He emphasized the reality of evil as something to be contended with, criticizing the *privatio boni* doctrine which he believed denied this (though as Philp has argued, he may have misunderstood the doctrine). Jung also stressed the interrelatedness of good and evil, finding a place for both in his somewhat heterodox 'quaternity'. Theological reflections on the dark aspects of the modern world, such as the nuclear threat, have been much enriched by Jung's ideas on evil. For example, Jungian religious thought has enabled Garrison (1982) to return, in a modern way, to an understanding of the wrath of God as inherent to his nature.

Though Jung's work has been influential within theology he is far from being a representative psychological voice. There is also doubt about the adequacy of his methodology for the issues he addresses. Despite the richness of his work, he frequently seems to be both unclear and uncritical. It will be argued

that Jung's work does not represent the only possible approach to interdisciplinary collaboration between theology and psychology.

Prospects for the interface between theology and psychology

Theological writings undoubtedly display an extreme wariness of psychology; the term 'psychological' is most often used in the pejorative sense. This stems, not only from hostile critiques of religion such as Freud's, but from a concern that sympathetic *rapprochements* between psychology and theology (whether from psychologists like Jung or theologians like Tillich) result in theology sliding away into psychology.

There are several concerns intertwined here. Recent theology has emphasized the collective, not merely private, nature of the Christian religion. Psychology, in contrast, has been thought to deal with the merely private. Because of this, theology is currently more open to interdisciplinary work with sociology than with psychology. However, all human disciplines need a balanced concern with both the individual and the collective, and psychology retains a handhold on the collective through 'social psychology'; it is not restricted to the private and the individual.

Next, there are fears about 'reductionism', that is, that psychology will explain away the content of theology without remainder (just as physiology has sometimes aspired to explain away psychology without remainder). Increasingly, however, it is recognized that reductionism is an untenable enterprise, and that each domain of systematic discourse says things that cannot be said in any other domain. Related to this is the concern to safeguard theological objectivity against what may be seen as the 'subjectivity' of psychology. This is a large issue, but suffice it to say that there are many trends in twentieth-century thought towards regarding the distinction between the objective and the subjective as an obsolete one.

The increasing acceptance of such points should clear the ground for more fruitful interdisciplinary work between theology and psychology, removing both any aspirations by psychologists to devour theology and fears by theologians that an encounter with psychology can only result in the demise of theology.

Rather, the most fruitful form of interdisciplinary work will be to map one domain of discourse onto the other, without expecting that this can be done exhaustively or without remainder. Such an approach will clearly be different both from a reductionist psychological critique of religion, and also from the ostensibly 'neutral' study of religion by contemporary empirical psychology. It is to be hoped that it will draw on core areas of modern psychology, not just on 'fringe' figures like Jung, however talented and distinguished. *Cognitive* psychology and the psychology of *personality* seem potentially fruitful areas.

An example would be the understanding of prayer in terms of attributional processes (see Watts and Williams, 1988, chapter 8). All people (including the non-religious) face constant implicit questions about the causal explanation for events in their lives. (Are these to be attributed to themselves, to other people, to chance, to temporary or permanent factors, and so on?) How events are attributed has far-reaching consequences, and the study of them has been a central topic in recent, mainstream psychology. For the religious person, attributions to God are important. Much prayer, thanksgiving and confession, for example, seems to be a reflection on how events should be attributed.

The functional significance of attributions to God is only just beginning to be studied, but they seem to function as a hybrid between attributions to oneself and to others. The effects of attributions to God are to be distinguished from the position of helplessness that arises if everything is seen as a matter of luck or chance; equally they can be distinguished from the pride and shame that result if everything is attributed to oneself. Further, the emotional impact of attributions to God will depend on the kind of relationship people feel they have with God. Some religious people seem to identify so closely with God that an attribution to him comes too close to being an internal attribution. Others see God as so remote that attributions to him are too external. Both can, in different ways, be dysfunctional.

Much work remains to be done on this topic.

It is presented as an example of the non-reductionist mapping between topics in theological and psychological discourse, to the enrichment of both. There now seem to be good prospects for fruitful, non-reductionist collaboration between theology and mainstream, contemporary psychology.

See also BIOLOGICAL SCIENCE/PHYSICAL SCIENCE/SOCIAL SCIENCE AND CHRISTIAN THOUGHT; PASTORAL CARE, THEORIES OF.

Bibliography

Brown, L. 1988: *The Psychology of Religion: An Introduction.* London: SPCK.

Chapman, H. 1987: *Jung's Three Theories of Religious Experience.* Newark: E. Mellen.

Freud, S. [1927] 1928: *The Future of an Illusion,* trans. W.D. Robson-Scott. London: Hogarth Press.

Garrison, J. 1982: *The Darkness of God: Theology After Hiroshima.* London: SCM Press.

Heisig, J.W. 1979: *Imago Dei: A Study in C.G. Jung's Psychology of Religion.* London: Associated Universities Press.

Homans, P. 1970: *Theology After Freud: An Interpretative Inquiry.* Indianapolis: Bobbs-Merrill.

James, W. 1902: *Varieties of Religious Experience.* New York: Longmans, Green.

Jung, C.G. [1944] 1953: Psychology and alchemy. In *Collected Works of C.G. Jung,* vol. 12, ed. H. Read, M. Fordham and G. Adler. London: Routledge and Kegan Paul.

Lash, N. 1988: *Easter is Ordinary: Reflections on Human Experience and the Knowledge of God.* London: SCM Press.

Meissner, W.W. 1984: *Psychoanalysis and Religious Experience.* New Haven: Yale University Press.

Philp, H. 1958: *Jung and the Problem of Evil.* London: Rockliff.

Proudfoot, W. 1985: *Religious Experience.* Berkeley: University of California Press.

Ricoeur, P. 1970: *Freud and Philosophy: An Essay on Interpretation.* New Haven: Yale University Press.

Spilka, B., Hood, R.W., and Gorsuch, R.L. 1985: *The Psychology of Religion: An Empirical Approach.* Englewood Cliffs, NJ: Prentice-Hall.

Watts, F., and Williams, M. 1988: *The Psychology of Religious Knowing.* Cambridge: Cambridge University Press.

FRASER N. WATTS

Q

Quakerism Quakerism is the faith, practice and church polity of the Religious Society of Friends, a Christian denomination which originated in England in the 1650s, quickly spreading to North America. The world Quaker population is now about 250,000, the largest centres being the USA and Kenya. There are two main theological groupings. Evangelicals are numerous outside Britain, and generally call pastors to serve their congregations. Liberals, to whose ranks British Quakers belong, preserve the traditional silent worship, having no paid or trained ministry. Their assemblies are called as 'meetings', following the generic seventeenth-century term for dissenters' places of worship. The differences arise from historical and theological controversies in the nineteenth century over what the original faith meant in greatly changed circumstances.

Early Quaker doctrine can be found in the works of George Fox (1624–1691), Isaac Penington (1616–1679), William Penn (1644–1718) and Robert Barclay (1648–1690). It is systematic in nature, though seldom portrayed as such, and each of its main elements sooner or later involves the rest. Friends often portrayed their historical significance as the completion of the Reformation, employing the conception of the apostasy of the historic church from the new covenant of apostolic times (2 Tim. 3: 1), and themselves as signs of a new gathering of the true church. They preached an inward spiritual millenarianism. The new covenant was considered as a purely inward phenomenon, pointed to by such prophecies as Jeremiah 31: 33. Thus the outward signs of ecclesiastical order like episcopacy and ordination were rejected, and women were given spiritual equality in the church (Acts 2). Creeds were not considered confessions of personal covenantal faith, but outward tests of orthodoxy imposed during the apostasy, and were, and are, avoided.

These doctrines amounted to a metaphysical dualism which helped to create much that is distinctive and valuable in Quakerism, but also facilitated division when the peculiar circumstances which gave rise to Quakerism fell away. The strength of the distinction between 'inward' and 'outward' knowledge of God meant the development of the silent meeting for worship, which might have spoken contributions of prayer, preaching, testimony or praise, but no leader, congregational singing or set prayers. Dependence on the direct guidance of God meant that no votes were taken at meetings for church affairs. The same distinction underlay the disuse of outward symbols and therefore sacramental practice, where Friends would assert they had the substance but rejected the form. Contemporary Quakers of both branches reject the necessity for outward ceremonies of baptism and communion and accept the same basic principles of worship and church order.

The other main features of traditional Quakerism flowed from this, having their origins in the covenantal experience and their confirmation in Scripture. Life is a testimony to the truth, so requires constant witness in small as well as large things. Conventional titles and terms of address were, and still are, not used, and Friends refused to pay tithes for the upkeep of what they saw as an apostate church. They therefore made provision for education and for their own poor, and developed a strong internal discipline. This life was marked out by the 'plain dress' of grey or brown, with use of the familiar form of address to all comers. As is well-known, they have always maintained a strong pacifism, believing that all war is inconsistent with the spirit and teaching of Christ.

The central Quaker doctrine is that of the 'inward Light'. It derives from such New Testament passages as John 3: 19, 9: 5; 2 Corinthians 4: 6; Ephesians 5: 8–14. The emphasis here is Christological, incarnational, soteriological and moral. At the same time, however, the covenantal doctrine required that access to Christ through the Light should be logically independent of knowledge of the Scriptures, though no disharmony between the two was envisaged. John 1: 9 was understood to imply that the Light is universal and available to those with no outward, formal knowledge of the historic Christ. Scripture was held to be perfectly harmonious with the Light, and was one of the checks by which one could discern if one was rightly guided. In traditional Quakerism, therefore, Scripture is highly, but not ultimately, authoritative.

This is possibly the root of the historical divisions within the denomination. Early Quakerism seems to have a fairly strong affinity to earlier continental Anabaptism. Churches of this type have a theological need to justify their special status as a right rather than a concession, and to claim toleration thereby. In seventeenth-century England the theological need was to deny the claims of Calvinistic Puritanism. The Quakers used the doctrine of the universal Light to overcome the rigours of the doctrine of predestination, and the conception of an inward covenant to elevate the spiritual and moral dimensions of Scripture above the doctrinal.

Underlying this was an attempt to find a firmer basis for authority than a text which was the occasion of bitter controversy and was used to justify severe persecutions. But what resulted was a loss of the original balance as EVANGELICALISM and liberalism (see LIBERALISM (BRITAIN and USA)) each claimed half of the inheritance. Evangelicals placed greater emphasis on an infallible text, liberals felt less constrained by it in the face of the historical-critical method, seeing reason as one of the functions of the Light. Both of these positions can be seen as responses to the problems raised by the Enlightenment.

By the beginning of the nineteenth century, evangelicalism was well entrenched in the Society of Friends. Quakerism was more assimilated to the mainstream of religious culture and had lost its original sense of apostasy and renewal. Its principles came to be expressed as true interpretations of an infallible text and less as an experience of the new covenant. The religious and ethical testimonies seen to be fundamental to its unique form of Christianity now came to be seen as its 'peculiarities' – that which Quakers profess over and above what they share with other evangelicals. In England, Ireland and in America, those of evangelical persuasion sought to use the structures of the Society to enforce conformity with this interpretation of Quakerism. In the British Isles they were largely successful.

In the USA and Canada, however, a series of separations occurred between 1827 and 1854. Both parties preserved the whole range of traditional testimonies, practices and values. But for some, evangelicalism had supplanted the traditional Quaker theology. It had been able to do this for various reasons. Quakerism has no historical event of national significance from which to date its origin and therefore its identity; there is no historical statement of belief round which controversy is obliged to circle; Friends have always been suspicious of theological learning and have neglected it; the loose structure by which the Quaker world is divided into 'yearly meetings' – the equivalent of synods (some overlapping in territory) – means that there has never been a central and undisputed authority.

The non-evangelical branch in these controversies formed the matrix from which emerged liberal Quakerism, which in due course supplanted evangelicalism in Britain relatively easily. Its roots lie in traditional practices and values, nineteenth-century rational religion and the straightforward liberalism of mainline Protestantism.

Because liberal Quakerism preserves the traditional doctrine that access to Christ is available independent of Scripture, it has been greatly influenced by the opinion of Rufus Jones (1863–1948) that Quakerism is essentially a type of mystical religion. This has encouraged the appearance of the view that Quakerism is not necessarily Christian at all. Liberal publications show a sympathy with New Age ideas, feminist theology, a strong concern for the use of psychological insights in nourishing religious faith, and an interest in all forms of radical religion, theist and non-theist. There is a movement towards 'universalism', which in Quaker terms connotes a range of views which assert a basic unity in all religions. At the same time, traditionalist types of Quakerism survive strongly.

Across the theological divisions, the Quaker testimonies to simplicity, truth and peace retain a vital motivating force. The conception that the Light is in all has created the powerful conviction that no human contrivance can ultimately prevail against the leadings of God, and that therefore no human being is dispensable or inferior to any other, and all are entitled to equal respect. This is often summarized in the statement that Friends believe there is 'that of God in every one', the phrase going back to the founder, George Fox. This leads to mission and service work, often of a pioneering kind. Quakers were at the heart of the anti-slavery movement, and have traditionally been concerned with pacifism and prison reform. The value of simplicity draws increasing numbers of Friends into the environmental movement.

There is a clear assumption in Quakerism that politics and religion cannot be separated, and this idea has roots in each of its main historical influences – Anabaptist, evangelical and liberal. There is a Quaker United Nations Office working as a recognized non-governmental organization at the United Nations in both New York and Geneva. European Friends have an Office for European Affairs in Brussels, and the Friends Committee on National Legislation was the first registered religious lobby on Capitol Hill in Washington. Quaker Peace and Service of London Yearly Meeting and the American Friends Service Committee are active in relief and development in most parts of the world, in 1947 corporately receiving the Nobel peace prize.

See also PROTESTANT THEOLOGY (BRITAIN and USA); SACRAMENTAL THEOLOGY.

Bibliography

Barbour, H. and Frost, J.W. 1988: *The Quakers*. Westport, Conn.: Greenwood Press.

Barclay, Robert 1678: *Apology for the True Christian Divinity*. London.

Creasey, Maurice 1962: *'Inward' and 'Outward': A Study in Early Quaker Language*. London: Friends Historical Society.

Fox, George 1694: *Journal*. London: Northcott.

Greenwood, J. Ormerod 1975–8: *Quaker Encounters*, 3 vols. York: Sessions.

Gurney, J.J. 1827: *Observations on the Religious Peculiarities of the Religious Society of Friends*. London: J. and A. Arch.

Hamm, Thomas, D. 1989: *The Transformation of American Quakerism – Orthodox Friends 1800–1907*. Bloomington: Indiana University Press.

Ingle, Larry H. 1986: *Quakers in Conflict: The Hicksite Reformation*. Knoxville: University of Tennessee.

Jones, Rufus M. 1927: *The Faith and Practice of the Quakers*. London: Methuen.

Penington, Isaac 1681: *Works*. London: Clark.

Penn, William 1694: *A Brief Account of the Rise and Progress of the People called Quakers*. London: T. Sowle.

Scott, Janet 1980: *What Canst Thou Say? Towards a Quaker Theology*. London: Quaker Home Service.

JOHN PUNSHON

R

Radford Ruether, Rosemary (b. 1936) North American feminist theologian. She was professor of historical theology at Howard University's School of Religion from 1967 to 1972, has taught at the divinity schools of Harvard and Yale and in Scandinavia, and is currently professor of applied theology at the Garrett Evangelical Theological Seminary in Evanston, Illinois. She has been influential in the formation of 'liturgical communities' which seek by their reformulation of the language and ideas of traditional Christianity to effect a 'liberation of humanity from patriarchy' and a healing of 'the splits between "masculine" and "feminine", between mind and body, between males and females as gender groups'. *Women-Church* of 1986 offers liturgies for the use of such communities which mark life experiences formally unacknowledged by the traditional church, including rites for lesbian partnerships, and the healing of rape. For the time being, these 'autonomous bases' are to exist apart from and alongside the traditional church, both as a challenge to ecclesiastical patriarchy and as a nurture base for women seeking 'rebirth into a new community of being and living'. Ambivalent towards the biblical origins of Christianity which are, she maintains, largely patriarchal in character, she nevertheless regards Jesus as the embodiment of the reversal of patriarchy, who can be encountered 'in the form of our sister' in the community of faith which bears his identity. Religious symbol and symbolic action are important in her thought, as are political and social issues, and a revival of the idea of the sacredness of nature. She is a prolific writer, whose major works include *Sexism and God-Talk* (1983) and *Womanguides* (1985).

See also FEMINIST THEOLOGY.

Rahner, Karl (1904–1984) German theologian. Karl Rahner was born on 5 March 1904 in Freiburg. He entered the Society of Jesus in 1922. Recognizing his gifts, the Society directed him towards the study of philosophy; his period of study included work at Freiburg under Martin Heidegger. Rahner's doctoral dissertation on Thomas Aquinas was published in 1939 as *Spirit in the World*, to considerable critical acclaim, yet to the disquiet of some of his mentors, who regarded it as excessively influenced by existentialism. From 1937 to 1964 Rahner was a teaching member of the faculty of theology of the University of Innsbruck, Austria. This was followed by positions at the universities of Munich and Münster, until his retirement in 1971. By the time of his death in 1984, Rahner was firmly established as one of the leading dogmaticians of his day, with a reputation which transcended national and denominational boundaries.

Rahner published relatively few books. Indeed, two of his three most significant books were published at an early stage in his career: *Spirit in the World* in 1939 and *Hearers of the Word* in 1941. These works represent significant explorations in philosophical theology, reflecting the renewed interest in neo-Thomism typical of much Roman Catholic theology in the interwar period, although drawing on such diverse sources as the existentialism of Martin Heidegger and the broadly Kantian reading of Aquinas found in the writings of Pierre Rousselot and Joseph Maréchal. His later volume *Foundations of Christian Faith* ([1976] 1978) represents an important exploration of the rational foundations of central themes of Christian theology.

Yet these systematic treatments of central themes of Christian theology must not be allowed to create the impression that Rahner develops a theological system. His modest reference to himself as 'an amateur theologian' perhaps reflects this point. Rahner is probably best regarded as a theologian concerned to explore the full range of Christian thought, unfettered by the limitations and rigidities of a fixed system, and free to explore a given topic in whatever manner seemed appropriate in its specific case. This theological programme is reflected in the literary form with which Rahner is especially associated: the essay.

One of Rahner's most significant achievements is the rehabilitation of the essay as a tool of theological construction. The most significant source for Rahner's thought is not a substantial work of dogmatic theology, but a relatively loose and unstructured collection of essays published over the period 1954–84, known in English as *Theological Investigations*. These essays, which extend over sixteen volumes in the original German (*Schriften zur Theologie*), and twenty volumes in the still incomplete English edition, bring out the manner in which a relatively unsystematic approach to theology can nevertheless give rise to a coherent theological programme.

The transcendental method
Rahner's general approach to theology can be seen as exemplifying the agenda characteristic of the 1930s: a Christian response to the secular loss of the transcendence of God. Whereas earlier generations attempted to meet this challenge through accommodationist strategies such as liberalism and modernism, Rahner and his circle argued that the recovery of a sense of the transcendent could only be achieved through a reappropriation of the classical sources of Christian theology, especially Augustine and Thomas Aquinas. Rahner's particular approach involves the fusion of Thomism with central aspects of German idealism and existentialism. This allowed him to avoid the unimaginative and somewhat sterile neo-scholasticism of his day, which contented itself with little more than a derivative reiteration of Thomist positions and failed to interact with the intellectual environment of modernity.

Rahner was convinced that the polarity between 'transcendence' and 'immanence' was false, and had been imposed upon Christianity by secular world views. He argues that ordinary human experience is unintelligible unless it is interpreted in the light of the transcendent mystery of God. The term 'transcendental reflection' is used to refer to this principle of reflection upon human experience in the light of the mystery of God. Given the undeniable existence of certain things (such as the human experience of subjectivity), Rahner argues that these things point towards a transcendent horizon, without which they are ultimately unintelligible. This forces the question: 'What is the *a priori* transcendental condition for the possibility of [human] subjectivity?' Humans transcend themselves in every act of questioning and thinking, by which they demonstrate themselves to be both part of the natural world and yet simultaneously oriented towards the mysterious horizon of being that Christians know as God. Humans are able to reach out beyond themselves and their finite world towards an infinite horizon of hope and love. For this reason, Rahner can declare that 'the dilemma of the "immanence" or "transcendence" of God must be overcome without sacrificing one or the other.' Humans possess a unique ability to discern the transcendent element of their situation. There is thus an implicit, unthematic and unreflective knowledge of God latent within humanity, which it is the function of transcendental reflection to identify.

Having established that humans are by nature open to the revelation of God, Rahner proceeds to explore the nature and limits of that revelation. 'Transcendental revelation' conveys to us a sense of relation to God; it requires supplementation, in that this natural sense of being 'open to God' is in itself inadequate. A natural knowledge of God needs to be complemented by a supernatural (in the sense of something which goes beyond nature) knowledge of God – which, for Rahner, is 'categorical revelation'. 'Categorical revelation'

is not simply given with the spiritual being of man as transcendence, but rather has the character of an event. It is dialogical, and in it God speaks to man, and makes known to him something which cannot be known always and everywhere in the world simply through the necessary relation of all reality in the world to God in man's transcendence.

Yet this latter revelation does not contradict nature; at every point, Rahner is concerned to emphasize the continuity between the human order and the purposes and activities of God. For Rahner, this revelation reaches its climax and fulfilment in Jesus Christ, who 'is the historical presence of this final and unsurpassable word of God's self-disclosure: this is his claim and he is vindicated in this claim by the resurrection.'

Christianity and other religions: an inclusivist approach

Rahner is widely regarded as the most significant advocate of an 'inclusivist' model of the relationship of Christianity to other religions. This approach rests largely upon the transcendental method itself, which allows us to distinguish a 'natural' knowledge of God (which may take a non-categorical and unreflective form), and a specifically Christian knowledge for God ('categorical revelation'), which extends and develops this natural knowledge of God by making known 'something which cannot be known always and everywhere in the world'. This dialectical relationship between these two styles of revelation constitutes the framework for Rahner's discussion of the relationship between Christianity and non-Christian religions.

In the fifth volume of his *Theological Investigations* Rahner develops four theses, setting out the view not merely that individual non-Christians may be saved but that the non-Christian religious traditions in general may have access to the saving grace of God in Christ:

1   Christianity is the absolute religion, founded on the unique event of the self-revelation of God in Christ. But this revelation took place at a specific point in history. Those who lived before this point, or who have yet to hear about this event, would thus seem to be excluded from salvation – which is contrary to the saving will of God.

2   For this reason, despite their errors and shortcomings, non-Christian religious traditions

are valid and capable of mediating the saving grace of God, until the gospel is made known to their members. After the gospel has been proclaimed to the adherents of such non-Christian religious traditions, they are no longer legitimate, from the standpoint of Christian theology.

3   The faithful adherent of a non-Christian religious tradition is thus to be regarded as an 'anonymous Christian'.

4   Other religious traditions will not be displaced by Christianity. Religious pluralism will continue to be a feature of human existence.

We may explore the first three theses in more detail. It will be clear that Rahner strongly affirms the principle that salvation may only be had through Christ, as he is interpreted by the Christian tradition. 'Christianity understands itself as the absolute religion, intended for all people, which cannot recognize any other religion beside itself as of equal right.' Yet Rahner supplements this with an emphasis upon the universal saving will of God: God wishes that all shall be saved, even though not all know Christ. 'Somehow all people must be able to be members of the church.'

For this reason, Rahner argues that saving grace must be available outside the bounds of the church – and hence in other religious traditions. He vigorously opposes those who adopt too-neat solutions, insisting that either a religious tradition comes from God or that it is an inauthentic and purely human invention. Where writers committed to a more 'exclusivist' approach, such as Hendrik Kraemer, argue that non-Christian religious traditions were little more than self-justifying human constructions, Rahner argues that such traditions may well include elements of truth.

Rahner justifies this suggestion by considering the relation between the Old and New Testaments. Although the Old Testament, strictly speaking, represents the outlook of a non-Christian religion (Judaism), Christians are able to read it and discern within it elements which continue to be valid. The Old Testament is evaluated in the light of the New, and as a result certain practices (such as food laws) are discarded as unacceptable while others are retained (such as the moral law). The same approach can and should, Rahner argues, be adopted in the case of other religions.

The saving grace of God is thus available through non-Christian religious traditions, despite their shortcomings. Many of their adherents, Rahner argues, have thus accepted that grace without being fully aware of what it is. It is for this reason that Rahner introduces the term 'anonymous Christians' to refer to those who have experienced divine grace without necessarily knowing it. This term has been heavily criticized, particularly by those committed to a pluralist approach to the religious traditions of humanity. For example, John Hick has suggested that it is paternalist, offering 'honorary status granted unilaterally to people who have not expressed any desire for it'. Nevertheless, Rahner's intention is to allow for the real effects of divine grace in the lives of those who belong to non-Christian traditions. Full access to truth about God (as it is understood within the Christian tradition) is not a necessary precondition for access to the saving grace of God.

Rahner does not allow that Christianity and other religious traditions may be treated as equal, or that they are particular instances of a common encounter with God. For Rahner, Christianity and Christ have an exclusive status, denied to other religious traditions. The question is: can other religious traditions give access to the same saving grace as that offered by Christianity? Rahner's approach allows him to suggest that the beliefs of non-Christian religious traditions are not necessarily true, while allowing that they may, nevertheless, mediate the grace of God by the lifestyles which they evoke – such as a selfless love of one's neighbour.

See also CHRISTOLOGY; OTHER FAITHS AND CHRISTIANITY; ROMAN CATHOLIC THEOLOGY.

Bibliography

Writings

[1954–84] 1961– : *Theological Investigations*, 20 vols, trans. London: Darton, Longman and Todd.
[1976] 1978: *Foundations of Christian Faith*, trans. New York: Seabury.

Critical works

Marshall, Bruce 1987: *Christology in Conflict: The Identity of a Saviour in Rahner and Barth*. Oxford: Blackwell.
O'Donovan, Leo, ed. 1980: *A World of Grace: An Introduction to the Themes and Foundations of Karl Rahner's Theology*. New York: Seabury.
Pedley, C.J. 1984: An English bibliographical aid to Karl Rahner, *Heythrop Journal* 24, pp. 319–65.
Vorgrimler, Herbert 1986: *Understanding Karl Rahner*. New York: Crossroad.

ALISTER E. MCGRATH

Rauschenbusch, Walter (1861–1918)   North American theologian and leader of the social gospel movement. Born into a German pastor's family in Rochester, NY, and educated at the University of Rochester and in Germany, he became a pastor of a German Baptist church in New York in 1886. From 1897 until his death he was a professor first of New Testament and then of church history at Rochester Theological Seminary. His first-hand experience in New York of the deprivation of the inner city influenced the development of his thought, and he aligned himself with the Christian socialists. With the publication of *Christianity and the Social Crisis* in 1907 he became a recognized leader of the social gospel movement; in it he expounded the Old Testament prophets as a model for a contemporary Christian response to the developing social and economic institutions in America. Influenced by, among others, F.D. Maurice, the concepts of the kingdom of God and the incarnation were crucial in his thought. The kingdom of God was for all people, and its reality in the world is progressively revealed as humanity moves towards its goal of perfection. In *Christianity and the Social Order* of 1912, he sets out this optimistic vision of progressive Christianization, which would be achieved by human solidarity and by forswearing the abuse of power inherent in competition and excessive profit. Other works include *The Social Principles of Jesus* (1916), which achieved wide popularity by being distributed by the YMCA, and *A Theology for the Social Gospel* (1917).

Bibliography

Handy, R.T., ed. 1966: *The Social Gospel in America, 1870–1920*. New York.
Hopkins, C.H. 1967: *The Rise of The Social Gospel in American Protestantism*. New Haven, Conn.
Hudson, W.S., ed. 1984: *Walter Rauschenbusch, Selected Writings*. Mahwah, NJ.

reason See APOLOGETICS; EPISTEMOLOGY, RELIGIOUS; EXISTENCE OF GOD, PROOFS OF; FAITH AND REASON; PHILOSOPHY OF RELIGION.

relativism, cultural The term 'cultural relativism' (sometimes 'historical relativism') is used to refer to the perception that ideas, values and practices can only be properly understood in the context of the cultural or historical setting in which they are found. Though still by no means part of everyone's intuitive awareness, perception of this kind has recently become a great deal more common. Celebrity shades into notoriety and widening circulation induces unclarity; so the term has come to be applied to a wide range of matters, sometimes rigorously but often loosely. The notion is found liberating, perplexing, alarming or repellent. Many think and act relativistically in happy innocence of doing any such thing. For any theology that is accustomed to thinking in terms of timeless truth, static orthodoxy and rock-like identity, the implications of such an approach are of great importance; and as traditional Christian theology has been characterized by conceptions of fixity of one kind or another, relativistic awareness creates problems and has given rise to considerable discussion.

A brief historical survey illuminates what is involved. Roughly down to the later Middle Ages, there was little sense of the differences (of manners, dress, architecture and so on) between present and past, and between various periods of the past; little capacity to 'place' the past in imagined and distinguishable sequence. This is not to deny that there was often a tenacious sense of tradition (for example, in relation to property possession or ecclesiastical privilege). Nevertheless, all but the recent past was viewed hazily, and dissolved easily into fragments of information and sheer legend.

First in Italy, and then more generally, the early Renaissance saw a capacity to appeal to a reconstructed, imagined past; but this was still done so as to justify and encourage present tendencies and often present novelties (for example, Italian cities modelled their claims against traditional lordship on ancient Roman republican institutions, and English Parliament men in the 1640s appealed to supposed Anglo-Saxon liberties against the pretensions of the Stuart monarchy). There was now a lengthening of perspective and a dawning sense of historical period: the civilization of ancient Greece could be 'felt' as in contrast to the alleged barbarism of the medieval period.

The development of a genuine sense of 'the pastness of the past' and of its endless and profound diversity can be traced to the thought, initially ignored, of Giambattista Vico (1668–1744). He it was who saw human history as a series of discrete but interconnected cultures, each of which had its own values, characteristics and self-understanding. They were not to be seen as ranged in order of value (such as from more to less primitive) or as working towards some desirable goal (such as the unhindered operation of human reason), but as having each its own validity and structure of meaning. In so far as other cultures were independent and self-contained, they were opaque to the outside observer. Nevertheless, provided the observer recognized their otherness and resisted the tendency to domesticate them to familiar modes of life, it was possible to 'enter into' other cultures by the painstaking exercise of imagination (*fantasia*). After all, however great their differences, human beings have much in common by way of aspirations and characteristics.

In Vico's thought, the essence of the idea and of the perplexity of cultural relativism is already sketched out. Partly taken up by J.G. Herder and others, this approach to history and knowledge, now with more specific reference to Christianity, is associated pre-eminently with the work of Ernst Troeltsch, particularly in the latter part of his life (1865–1923). His sense of historical relativism (*Historismus*, historicism) rests on the belief that a thoroughly historical mode of perception is now inevitable, and 'the historical and the relative are identical.' Christianity is seen to have been extraordinarily diverse in its manifestations, even in the mainstream, and its different forms of life and belief are intelligible in relation to the cultural settings in which they took their rise.

Such relativism comes up against four chief antagonists (and Troeltsch himself was far from immune to their force). First, the traditional picture of Christianity. From the second century Christian belief had lived with a picture of itself which placed great emphasis on identity in terms of fixity and of unchanging orthodoxy over against the buffeting of variegated heresy. It is summed up in the fifth-century Vincentian Canon, which defined true faith as consisting of 'what is believed everywhere, always, and by all'. Developing historical knowledge in the nineteenth century made it impossible to square this ambitious criterion with the facts, and relief was sought, notably by J.H. Newman, in terms of a concept of development: doctrine had developed, but not simply randomly and at the behest of shifting cultural patterns. Within its own sufficiently enclosed tradition and by its own providential momentum, it had grown from its origins to greater fullness and explicitness. Thus 'new' beliefs were elucidated, drawn out of the past, not invented in response to a transient present. It was possible to continue to see the heart of Christian identity in the constant 'faith once delivered to the saints'.

Second, the notion (owing much to G.W.F. Hegel, prominent in nineteenth-century German Protestantism, and not wholly dissimilar to theories of development) that Christianity embodies an 'idea' which gradually unfolds itself in history and works towards full disclosure. This principle of uniform historical continuity does not fit well with a sense of intelligible but independent cultural patterns within which beliefs are to be understood.

Third, the appeal to Christian origins and the historical Jesus as normative. Though this appeal is always vulnerable to the paucity of evidence for these distant events and though it is all too evident that they have been interpreted in innumerable different and often conflicting ways, it seems inescapable that Christian identity must always seek to transcend these limitations and reckon to do so sufficiently for its own coherence.

Fourth, the appeal to reason. In this respect, like the traditional picture of Christianity, this involves an absolute criterion, essentially unchanging even if rarely achieved, by which ideas from various settings may be measured and assessed. Like the other three antagonists, reason resists the fluidity which a sense of cultural relativism engenders and interposes a norm against which historical phenomena can be judged.

By the very candour and apparent indifference with which relativism accepts the diversity of cultural manifestations of (in this instance) Christian belief as 'the bottom line', it naturally provokes not only bewilderment but a determination to find modes of stability which weaken its effect. For many, the matter is all the more acute when the same considerations are applied to ethics, where various theories of NATURAL LAW seek to reduce and to dam the apparently essential amorality of any strongly relativistic approach. If cultural relativism leads to an inability to judge and evaluate the beliefs and practices of the past and, presumably, of the present of which one is part, and if it warrants only a shoulder-shrugging acceptance of whatever complex of ideas and institutions is found to exist, then it seems to be an agent of irresponsibility towards any kind of moral or religious commitment – or at least to make such commitment arbitrary, transiently valid or frankly fideistic.

These 'antagonists' may be viewed in a more beneficent light: as indicating strategies by which the devastating effects of relentless relativism may be mitigated – not just because it is so alarming for faith but because of weaknesses inherent in relativism itself. Thus, it is evident that while standards and modes of reasonableness vary from one period to another and one culture to another, these are not wholly opaque to each other, nor is it impossible for patient discussion to bring about increased understanding. Again, while styles of statement of Christian belief vary, it is not meaningless to seek (though often hard to achieve agreement about) ways in which one form of belief, belonging to one cultural setting, has at least a measure of equivalence to another form, belonging to another setting, making allowance for the particularities of both cases. Persistence with such attempts has clear practical importance not only in arriving at an understanding of the past, but in modern ecumenical discussions between the heirs of disparate Christian traditions, not to mention inter-faith dialogue where similar factors are in play.

Finally, there is room for negotiation and accommodation between, on the one hand, theories of development as a way of looking at Christian diversity through history and, on the other, the viewing of the past as a series of sheerly different cultural 'moments' or complexes ('totalities', Troeltsch). Both sides of that divide are ready to ascribe value and some kind of validity to the past, and many relativists are keen to escape from the trap of being so resolute in their 'time-boundness' that they are deprived of a standing-ground from which to judge various forms of belief and of any confidence with which to assert their own convictions. The relativity of the relativizers has proved the most damaging (as well as the easiest) of considerations to level against them. All the same, Christian theology is not without longstanding resources with which to respond to such charges. The assertion of Christian belief in the shape of rock-like, unchanging orthodoxy is only one element in the theological tradition, and is balanced by a sense of diffidence about the possibility of human speech and conceptualizing of the divine. The sense of the inadequacy, provisionality and limitedness of discourse about God found in the ancient apophatic tradition and in mystical writers throughout Christian history has something of a counterpart, appropriate to a historically sensitized culture, in the modesty of the claims for religious truth made from the standpoint of cultural relativism. Both manifest what may be regarded as a commendable diffidence. It is perhaps not surprising that there was a strong mystical tendency and a strong sense of the value of the tradition of worship in the Christian community in the life of Ernst Troeltsch.

Much of this account has taken cultural relativism as a rather general style of awareness found in some educated circles in the modern world, especially among those with a developed sense of history. In so far as that awareness centres on the astonishing diversity of other cultures (in past or present) and on their considerable impenetrability unless effort is devoted to the task, it has almost become a commonplace. Much of what is involved is obvious once it is pointed out. Both conservative and liberal elements in Christian thought are agreed about the essence of the phenomenon, though they may disagree about its extent or about the problems it undoubtedly raises when it comes to Christian statement and practice. Moreover, brash indeed is the trained Christian evangelist of today who is unaware of the need to understand the cultural setting of

the work and of the subtle problems of the adaptation of the (British version of the?) gospel to other cultural contexts (see MISSION THEOLOGY OF). All this is true, despite the many instances (for example in over-direct use of the Bible or in easy appeal to Christian tradition in relation to modern Christian decision-making) in which awareness of this kind seems wholly lacking.

Nevertheless, it is apparent that the subject can profit from a good deal more careful analysis than it has tended to receive. A number of distinct concepts have been grouped together under the umbrella of cultural relativism, and sometimes the sense of the distinctiveness of different 'belief-contexts' has been taken up with such enthusiasm that it has been made to perform a number of very different tasks. Sarah Coakley (1979 and 1988) has contributed notably to the elucidation of these matters.

In the first place, it is evident that sometimes the expression 'cultural *relativism*' is used where some looser category would be more accurate, such as (her suggestion) 'relationism'. There may be discussion whether there is advantage in keeping the former term, thus holding together related aspects of a single identifiable brand of sensibility, as well as in making distinctions for the sake of philosophical clarity. Preference is likely to depend on context: whether the interest is primarily in a phenomenon of our culture or in conceptual accuracy. But undoubtedly relativism is often used to refer to matters that are unproblematic truisms: for example, that (as already discussed) successive statements of Christian beliefs may be related by way of increased clarification, as when an earlier period has simply lacked the conceptual and linguistic resources to bring out truths that have been, as it were, 'lurking' from the start; or there are platitudes, such as those dependent on the fact that of course truths always exist in some context or other.

Relativism is more strictly involved where claims to truth are seen as valid for a given cultural framework, and not for others. Except for missionaries or educationists from outside a given culture, this may often give rise to little difficulty. The outsider will be content (for example as an anthropologist) simply to observe the beliefs-in-context of a particular culture, whether in the past or the present. Their appropriateness and coherence will be noted in terms of the total picture or pattern in which they are placed. There will be argument about how far the outsider can *understand* the alien beliefs. It may be held that true understanding is possible only for insiders, those for whom they are part of an absorbed and 'lived' pattern. But there may be the contrary contention that, with effort of empathy, the outsider may have the privilege of *both* imagining what it is like to hold those beliefs *and* bringing detached judgement to bear on them. It may, however, be held that, at least as far as truth is concerned, such assessment is no part of the observer's role (at any rate if it is that of the professional sociologist or anthropologist). But evidently, for certain purposes such self-denial is an unnecessary impoverishment.

Once the light has dawned (or the relevant aspect of innocence has been lost), the phenomena addressed by the ideas summed up in the term 'cultural relativism' cannot be gainsaid. Difficulty centres on the following matters.

1 Given that Christian belief has expressed itself in many different ways and that these are illuminated (and often explained) by a knowledge of their cultural context, how is the diversity to be understood? Is it really a matter of gradual elucidation of an original and sufficient seed of faith until some goal of perfect understanding is reached (at the End? in heaven?), and we shall know even as we are known? Is the Christian tradition such that each generation builds upon all its predecessors, somehow absorbing and developing all that has gone before? Or is it much more a matter of selectivity and (subjectively useful) adoption in relation to the past? Are we to think of a providential ordering which makes the best of our capacities, in diverse cultural and personal contexts, to relate to God and to form ideas about him; which works not in terms of progress from one period to another (any more than from one individual to another), but rather by way of different styles of appropriateness? In other words, the question raised at the start of this paragraph is not our worry!

2 Is there any escape (should it be desirable) from the entrapment of us all in the limitations – and opportunities – of our cultures? Is it sufficient that we should exercise

modesty about the claims we make for our own perceptions of Christian belief, recognizing their transience? For a faith which has a missionary task, is this reticence a weakness (as at first sight it undoubtedly appears) or a strength – for only by adaptability and by recognition of the role of the subjective can it be communicated to new people and settings? But if so, is there some non-negotiable 'essence' of Christianity which must simply use various cultural forms as clothing or instruments? Is there any hope of agreeing even on that, without risking the cacophony of the past breaking out afresh? For traditional cultural relativism was often postulated on the supposition that cultures (usually envisaged as in the west) succeed each other through history. In the modern world, they are as likely to live cheek by jowl in the same street; and those that supposedly belong to some past era retain their vigorous devotees, living waxworks!

3 Focusing on the matter of Christian identity, to what extent are the 'worlds' of the Bible accessible to us (Nineham, 1976)? In so far as they are opaque, how are we to view our appropriation of it, and indeed of past phases of Christian doctrine, notably the classic formulations of the patristic period? To what extent is Christian belief, including the interpretation of the Bible, to be seen as 'free-wheeling' through history – whether because it can do no other, as such is the real character of human development, or because intelligibility in the present culture is impossible apart from such apparently disorderly freedom?

See also CULTURE AND THEOLOGY; LIBERALISM (BRITAIN and USA); OTHER FAITHS AND CHRISTIANITY; POSTLIBERALISM; SOCIAL SCIENCE AND CHRISTIAN THOUGHT; TRADITION.

Bibliography

Abraham, W.J. 1982: *Divine Revelation and the Limits of Historical Criticism*. Oxford: Clarendon Press.

Barton, J. 1979: Reflections on cultural relativism, parts I and II, *Theology* 82, pp. 103–9, 191–9.

Coakley, S. 1979: Theology and cultural relativism: what is the problem?, *Neue Zeitschrift für systematische Theologie und Religionsphilosophie* 21, pp. 223–43.

Coakley, S. 1988: *Christ without Absolutes*. Oxford: Clarendon Press.

Dewart, L. 1967: *The Future of Belief*. London: Burns and Oates.

Drescher, Hans-Georg 1992: *Ernst Troeltsch: His Life and Work*. London: SCM Press.

Küng, H., and Tracy, D., eds 1989: *Paradigm Change in Theology*. Edinburgh: T & T Clark.

Lukes, S. 1974: Relativism: cognitive and moral, *Proceedings of the Aristotelian Society* supplement 48, pp. 165–89.

McGrath, A.E. 1990: *The Genesis of Doctrine*. Oxford: Blackwell.

MacIntyre, A. 1981: *After Virtue*. London: Duckworth.

Nineham, D.E. 1976: *The Use and Abuse of the Bible*. London: Macmillan.

Pailin, D.A. 1990: *The Anthropological Character of Theology*. Cambridge: Cambridge University Press.

Runzo, J. 1986: *Reason, Relativism and God*. London: Macmillan.

Shorter, A. 1988: *Towards a Theology of Inculturation*. London: Chapman.

Trigg, R. 1973: *Reason and Commitment*. Cambridge: Cambridge University Press.

Troeltsch, E. [1902] 1972: *The Absoluteness of Christianity*. London: SCM Press.

Williams, B.A.O. 1974–5: The truth in relativism, *Proceedings of the Aristotelian Society* 75, pp. 215–28.

Winch, P. 1958: *The Idea of a Social Science*. London: Routledge and Kegan Paul.

LESLIE HOULDEN

religion, philosophy of See PHILOSOPHY OF RELIGION.

religion, theories of There are many different theories of religion both within Christian thought and outside it. The very use of the word 'religion' implies a theory of religion, and we can see this by looking at two theorists who have cast doubts upon the word religion from different viewpoints. For Karl Barth religion is a human being's upward search for God which is discontinuous with revelation, which is God's downward revealing of himself to human beings; therefore religion has negative connotations amounting to unbelief. For Wilfred Cantwell Smith the word religion also has negative vibrations because it has been used in many conflicting ways, most of which depersonalize religion, which he considers to be basically personal piety (in the sense of having a warm religion or a cold religion). He goes so far as to claim that three theories of religion should be dropped: the view that religion is an overt system of beliefs, practices and values seen as an ideal, as in 'true Christianity'; the view that religion is an overt system of beliefs, practices and values seen as a sociological and historical phenomenon, as in the 'Christianity of history'; and the view that religion is a 'generic summation' distinct from other spheres of life such as politics and economics. Indeed he claims that the word religion should be abandoned, at least in all but the first personalist sense, because 'the term "religion" is confusing, unnecessary and distorting' (Smith, 1964, p. 48). Smith wishes to replace the terms 'religion' and 'religions' by his own terms 'faith' and 'traditions'. Although both Barth and Smith have had some influence, neither of their negative theories of religion have been widely accepted. But they serve to illustrate the fact that there are widely divergent theories and definitions of religion, which we will look at in this article.

Barth and Smith also illustrate two different approaches to theories of religion, the approach from within Christian theology and the approach from within religious studies. Within Christendom there was one religious option – that of Christianity. Islam and Judaism were seen not as options in their own right but as heretical forms of Christianity. The main structures of Christian theology came into being in this monolithic situation. When the Christian tradition escaped its European captivity at the end of the fifteenth century and began to discover other religious traditions and religious forms, it theorized about them on the basis of the notion of Christendom; it is only recently that Christendom has disappeared and the theological world view that went with it. Thus Christian theological theories of religion, even if they were not judgemental, saw religion and other religions mainly from the standpoint of Christian faith, from the standpoint of theological concepts and from the standpoint of *theos* or God. Religious studies, on the other hand, theorizes about religion on the basis that there are many religious traditions which are to be viewed as objectively as possible, that many methods and approaches are relevant in the study of religion, and that the focus of religion is not God but the believer's approach to God or whatever is considered to be transcendent reality. These two varied approaches, though they occasionally overlap, usually lead to different theories of religion, as we will analyse now.

Theories from Christian theology

In modern Christian thought there can be identified seven possible theological theories that Christian theology could exercise in relation to religion and religions, and they each imply a theory of religion. The first is absolute exclusivism: the notion that other religions are misguided, that they have no access to God or true spirituality, that no compromise is possible with them, and that they must be seen in terms of truth over against falsehood. This can take two main forms: the notion that religion is to be found in exclusive doctrinal propositions – as found for example in the 'fundamentals' of the inerrancy of the Bible, the supernatural acts of God, the virgin birth, the miracles, the resurrection, the deity and infallible power of Christ, his sacrificial atonement and penal substitution, and the final judgement at the Second Coming of Christ – and the notion that religion is to be found in exclusive institutions and sacraments, as found in the Roman Catholic statement *extra ecclesiam nulla salus*, 'outside the church there is no salvation'. The implication is that true religion has to do with correct belief in God, or worship in the correct sacramental institution.

The second theory is that mentioned above, associated with Barth and also H. Kraemer, that there is a discontinuity between revelation, which is God's seeking out human beings through the Word of God revealed in Christ, and religion, which is the human attempt to seek out God. Although, in this theory, 'religion' may include Christianity as well as other religions, it is seen negatively as human groping and ultimately human unbelief in the face of God's self-disclosure.

The third theory, well defined in A. van Leeuwen's *Christianity in World History* (1964), stresses the liberating effect of religion in alliance with the forces of science, technology and SECULARIZATION. It was the Jewish and Christian traditions with their stress upon creation, consummation, prophecy, incarnation, history, matter, the body and this world that provided the framework within which modern science and secularization could arise

with their promise of justice and freedom over against the other 'ontocratic' religions with their traditional world views. True religion here is that which opens up humane possibilities of justice, freedom and development, in contrast to ontocratic religion which does not.

The fourth theory is that of fulfilment: that all religious traditions have partial access to truth, to spirituality and to transcendence, but Christianity has access to them in their fullness. This theory can take three forms. The first form asserts that there is an essence of religion that is common to all religions, but that the Christian tradition contains it more fully than the others. This notion that there is a basic element in religion that is essential to it is a significant theory of religion quite apart from its theological implications. Thinkers have differed in their estimate of what this basic element is that is contained in all religions. For Lord Herbert of Cherbury and deists such as John Locke, John Toland and Matthew Tindal it was a rational natural religion (see NATURAL THEOLOGY) centred on the existence of God, the need for worship and morality, and the idea of reward and punishment in a future life; for Immanuel Kant it was the practice of the moral imperative; for Friedrich Schleiermacher the essence of religion lay beyond the rationalism of the deists or the ethics of Kant in the feeling of absolute dependence from which the concept of God derives; for Rudolf Otto it lay in a numinous sense of the holy; and more recently in the thought of H.H. Farmer it rested in personal encounter with God. (Quite separate from fulfilment theology, and the particular theories of the essence of religion (rational with the deists, ethical with Kant, feeling with Schleiermacher, numinous with Otto, personal with Farmer), is the notion that there is such a thing as an essence of religion in general, or indeed an essence of a particular religion such as Christianity. Historians among others have problems with this.) The second form of fulfilment theology asserts that Christianity fulfils other traditions, for example the law of Israel or the philosophy of Greece, or other religious types. R.C. Zaehner is an interesting example of a thinker who combined fulfilment theology with a theory of religious types. He claimed that there were two types or poles of religious life, the prophetic pole centred upon

Israel and the mystical pole centred upon India. There is thus not one essence of religion, there are two main types of religion, roughly corresponding to monotheistic and eastern religion, both of which are fulfilled by Christianity. The third form of fulfilment theology is more dynamic, and it thinks in terms of the fulfilment of process. Thus G.W.F. Hegel's Christianity fulfils a dialectical process of development; there are echoes of Hegel's ideas in the process theology of thinkers such as A.N. Whitehead and Charles Hartshorne; and for Pierre Teilhard de Chardin we are in the throes of a process of creative evolution whereby the whole cosmos, including religion and religions, is moving in the direction of the Omega Point and the Cosmic Christ. At this point religion is no longer a static essence or a static set of types, it is in dynamic process.

The fifth theory is that of universalization theology, the attempt to universalize Christian views of religion to include other religions within their orbit. Thus according to Raimundo Panikkar salvation by faith is present in all religions. God uses them as the normal channels whereby their followers attain salvation; and Christ, the Lord, the Word has not been confined to the human Jesus but has been more widely at work. Although it applies Christian vocabulary to other religions in phrases such as Panikkar's 'unknown Christ of Hinduism', this theory is basically irenic.

The sixth theory, centred upon the notion of dialogue, is also irenic. This acknowledges that religious traditions are not the same but holds that they need to understand each other, to discuss with each other, to pass over into each other and see the universe through each other's eyes. The theory of religion built into dialogue is that religions are historically different yet they are changing and they can learn from each other, and that they may share a common responsibility for helping to build a new world of peace and harmony. They do not share a common essence or a common language but they do share an open concern for the world that will develop in the next millennium.

The seventh theory is that of relativism, and this was exemplified in Ernst Troeltsch's thought after 1915. According to this viewpoint religions are relative to the culture in which they are found, for example Islam is the main religion of the Middle East; religious truth is relative to the person who holds it, for example Krishna may be religious truth for one person and Christ for another; and religions are moving along different paths to the same ultimate goal. Thus religions are not superior or inferior to one another, they are just different. (See RELATIVISM, CULTURAL; TRUTH, CONCEPTS OF.)

Before we leave theology let us look at the theory of religion developed by John Hick and Wilfred Cantwell Smith in their notion of theology of religion. Essentially it is a strikingly sophisticated extension of Troeltsch's relativistic view outlined above, taken in a direction that has implicitly set up a new religious endeavour that we may call the theology of religion. They claim that we should stop thinking in terms of religions as mutually exclusive groups. The point of 'religion', if we are to use that word in spite of Smith's strictures, lies not in religious traditions in their own right. They are means to the end of enabling human beings to move from self-centredness to Reality-centredness, whether that Reality be seen in terms of a personal God or an impersonal Absolute. This opens up the possibility of erecting universal theological categories that are relevant and applicable not just to one religion but to all religions.

Theories from religious studies

By contrast with the theologically tinged theories of religion mentioned above, in religious studies the notions of transcendence, faith, dialogue, theology, beliefs and religious truth have not figured largely, especially on the social sciences side of religious studies. Peter Berger, although himself a Christian, has talked about methodological atheism in the sociology of religion, and Ninian Smart has talked about methodological agnosticism in the phenomenology of religion. Moreover the need for religious studies to establish itself independently of theology increased the probability that its theories of religion would distance themselves from theological concerns. In practice theories have often been associated with particular disciplines. Thus anthropological theories emerged from the interest of anthropologists in smallscale societies in primal regions, psychological theories arose out of the concern of psychologists for the religious experience of the modern individual, and sociological theories resulted from the investigations of sociologists into religious communities and communities in general. It it as well to make a distinction between theories of religion that arose naturally out of the methods of the three social sciences mentioned above and overarching theories of religion that transcended the scientific approach and amounted, in the theory of a Marx and a Freud, to a metaphysic, to a secular world view that provided an alternative to religion. The theories of the early anthropologists at the end of the nineteenth and the beginning of the twentieth centuries were dominated by the leitmotif of evolution, which they accepted wholeheartedly by contrast with the theologians, and by the search for the origins of religion. A succession of anthropologists and others theorized about how religion began and about the stages of its evolution from its beginnings up to the modern period. For Charles de Brosses religion originated in fetishism, for Max Müller in nature myths, for Herbert Spencer in the belief in ghosts, for E.B. Tylor in animism, for J.G. Frazer in magic, for R.R. Marett in pre-animism, for A. Lang and W. Schmidt in original monotheism, for E. Durkheim in totemism. For most of these thinkers religion evolved from its original simplest form, whatever they conceived that to be, usually through polytheism up to its present stage of monotheism. They looked upon primal tribes as being 'survivals' from earlier periods in whom we could see what our own religion used to be like. In contrast to this, from about 1890 the psychology of religion offered theories which assumed that religion had mainly to do with religious experience, above all the religious experience of individuals as they underwent conversion, prayer, mystical sensations and abnormal states of mind. In his classic, *The Varieties of Religious Experience*, William James defined religion as 'the feelings, acts and experiences of individual men in their solitude, so far as they apprehend themselves to stand in relation to whatever they consider the divine' (James, 1902, p. 31). The point lay not in the divine but in the individual's religious experience, whether it be one of healthy-mindedness or a more traumatic and transforming one associated with being a 'sick soul'. Shortly afterwards Emile Durkheim, the father

of modern sociology, reacted with a diametrically opposed sociological theory. He defined religion as 'a unified system of beliefs and practices relative to sacred things, that is to say, things set apart and forbidden – beliefs and practices which unite into one single moral community called a church, all those who adhere to them' (Durkheim, [1912] 1976, p. 47). For him religion was primarily a social fact and it could be treated only in terms of its social function, for the forces before which the believer bowed down were social forces.

The anthropology, psychology and sociology of religion have developed and grown since the time of the early anthropologists James and Durkheim, and have produced newer and in the main less startling theories of religion. However, we see in Durkheim a tendency towards a reductionistic theory of religion that is present also in Karl Marx and Sigmund Freud. For Durkheim God is virtually equated with society, and religion is virtually reduced to sociology. Freud did not concur with James's conscious view of religious experience and opened up the unconscious side of human nature in his depth psychology. His theory of religion is contained in an allegorical story about early males devouring their dominant father who kept to himself the females they desired, and then out of remorse identifying with the father who was also God. This fits into Freud's notions of the Oedipus and Electra complexes, and he claims that the dependence humans feel in relation to human fathers becomes projected, idealized and sublimated in the father figure of God. Thus religion is an illusion objectively but feels real subjectively. For Freud God is virtually equated with the projected father, and religion is virtually reduced to depth psychology. Marx too, following Ludwig Feuerbach, saw God as a projection of human desires and ideals. But it was not enough to show people that in religion they were objectifying their own nature, it was necessary to remove the social and economic conditions that made religion necessary, and when this happened it would naturally wither away. Thus for Marx God is virtually equated with an alienation in human consciousness, and religion is virtually reduced to an expression of human distress and a way of veiling its true causes. The question is raised in regard to Marxism, Freudian depth psychology, civil religion (which together with nationalism is in part indebted to Durkheim's theories), and other secular alternatives to religion such as secular humanism, scientific positivism, and utilitarianism as to whether they are not in some sense themselves 'religions'. If a substantive theory and definition of religion is given, such as belief in God or (as Tylor put it) belief in spiritual beings, then clearly, as they themselves claim, they are not religions. However if a functional definition of religion is given such as J.M. Yinger's 'a system of beliefs and practices by means of which a group of people struggles with the ultimate problems of human life' (Yinger, 1970, p. 190f.) then they are, as Ninian Smart puts it, world views that are functionally equivalent to religions. Moreover in this wider sense it can be claimed that all human beings have implicit beliefs and practices by means of which they struggle with the ultimate problems of human life, and therefore in this sense the capacity for religion is part of human nature, human beings are 'religious animals', and implicit religion is present in everyone.

To return to religious studies, two of the crucial elements within that enterprise have been the history of religion and the phenomenology of religion. A large part of their work has involved the patient investigation of texts and of historical contexts and of religious phenomena. Many documents or oral traditions in many religious traditions, even if they have been discovered, have yet to be studied in depth. It is usually when this has been done, and much has been done, that classifications can be made and theories built up. In the history of religion the theory has recently arisen that it is possible to attempt to work out the global history of religion, not just as the separate histories of separate religions, but as an overlapping and interlocking history of the global sweep of religion from beginnings to the present day. This is now possible because of the amount of work that has been done in particular histories of religion and also because of the human sense of living in a global world wherein different cultures and religious traditions are 'in it together' ecologically, humanely and spiritually, as never before. The phenomenology of religion has arisen during this century, in the work of scholars such as W.B. Kristensen, G.

van der Leeuw, M. Eliade, Smart and J. Waardenburg on the basis of two theories of religion. In the first place it was a reaction against theories of religion that implicitly or explicitly reduced it to something other than itself, to theology, to anthropology, to psychology to sociology, and to history in the history of religions school, and were unable or unwilling to look at religion in its own right. To counter this the phenomenologists used the notions of *epoché* and *Einfühlung*: putting into brackets one's own presuppositions in order to understand religious phenomena as they are and the world view of others, and empathizing warmly and imaginatively with the thought and action world of humans in all religious traditions. This assumes that it is possible to detach oneself sufficiently to be unaffected by one's religious – or agnostic or atheistic – prejudices, and at the same time to be able to use personal qualities, attitudes and self-knowledge in order to walk a couple of miles in the moccasins of others. The theory that such an enterprise is possible and desirable is at the heart of religious studies.

Another theory in the phenomenology of religion and in religious studies generally concerns the art and necessity of comparison, and we will end by looking at the theories of religion built into different ways of comparing religion. The starting point lies in the famous phrase of Max Müller, 'he who knows one religion knows no religion' (Sharpe, 1975, p. 27). However, granted that comparison is important, the question is: how do we compare, what do we compare, what is the motive of comparison, and what are the theories lying behind it? It is possible to identify six ways of comparing religion, each with their underlying theory.

The first way of comparison is the way of evaluation – to look out from within one religious tradition in the direction of the others and to ask: how are we truer, more divine, fuller, better, or the same as they are? We looked at this approach in our analysis of the Christian theological attitudes to other religions, and it is well to remember that all religions can apply similar approaches to all other religions on the basis of evaluating other religions in comparison with themselves.

The second, negative, way is to compare religions in order to find that they cannot be compared. They are *sui generis*; they are not better or worse, or true or false; they are radically different; they are not giving different answers to the same questions, they are asking different questions; they swivel around their own unique axes: God through Christ, Allah through the Koran, Yahweh through the Torah, Brahman through a Hindu God, Nirvana through the Buddha.

The first two ways of comparing religion assume the theory that religion is centred upon religions as distinct entities that are different. The third way goes in the opposite direction and uses comparison to show the similarity between religious traditions, on the basis that there is a transcendent unity of all religions and at core they are the same. The Bahā'īs are a new religious tradition claiming that God has manifested himself on earth in successive manifestations such as Krishna, Abraham, Zoroaster, Moses, the Buddha, Jesus, Muhammad, the Bāb and Bahā'ullāh. Although Bahā'ullāh may attract more attention than his forerunners, in principle they are equal partners in a series and there is an underlying unity in the story of human religiousness. Another approach stressing the basic unity of religions is that of the perennial philosophy school, *philosophia perennis*. Its theory is that at the outward level of scriptures, doctrines, laws, communities and rituals religions are clearly different, but that they converge inwardly and spiritually upon the perennial philosophy that lies at the heart of all religious traditions. Its assumption is that the heart of religion lies in metaphysical spirituality and at that core religions are one whereas in secondary matters they are different.

The fourth way of comparison focuses upon themes rather than religious traditions and argues that religion has to do with basic typologies, patterns, themes and elements rather than religions as separate symbol systems. Phenomenologists of religion have placed particular emphasis upon typologies as basic systems and patterns that reveal the sacred in structured ways. Mircea Eliade, for example, in his *Patterns in Comparative Religion* brings together many comparative examples of typologies and symbols to do with the sky, the sun, the moon, water, stones, the earth, vegetation and farming, sacred time, sacred place and

myth, and he shows how these (and other) symbols form 'autonomous systems' (Eliade, [1949] 1958, p. 449). Thus, for example, in the typology of pilgrimage many examples of pilgrimage can be brought together from a gamut of world religions and analysed within the structure of pilgrimage. The stress is upon typologies rather than the historical contexts from which they come, but this way of comparison is able to lay bare some basic structures of religious life around the world. A similar sort of comparison is found in the work of Carl Gustav Jung and his followers, who compare various myths, symbols, archetypes and spiritual principles that have been present in religious traditions with resemblances across time and space because they are 'symptoms of the unconscious'. Similarly at the level of primal religion the anthropologist Claude Lévi-Strauss has stressed the centrality of myth as having a structure of its own.

The fifth way of comparison is to compare by excluding transcendence, even Eliade's notion of the sacred or Otto's notion of the holy, and this is common in the social sciences. The sociologist of religion Joachim Wach was able to compare five kinds of religious groups – groups that are part of society such as family or kinship groups, groups that are specifically religious such as churches, sects and cults, religious groups based on occupation such as warriors, merchants and peasants, religious groups in their relation to the state, and religious groups based on charismatic leadership – without becoming involved in the question of transcendent Reality. The issue is whether transcendence is ignored because it is irrelevant to the social scientist's task or whether it is not supposed to exist at all. Ninian Smart has brought out the notion of the transcendent-as-experienced and suggested that the scholar has to take seriously the believer's experience of transcendence but remain aloof from the question as to whether it is 'true'.

A final way of comparison is through the use of models of religion. If a framework of what a religion is can be worked out in depth and detail, the model can be used as a means of comparison. An influential recent model is that of Ninian Smart. He claims that a religion is 'a six-dimensional organism, typically containing doctrines, myths, ethical teachings, rituals, and social institutions, and animated by religious experiences of various kinds' (Smart, 1969, pp. 16–17). He has recently added a seventh, aesthetic, dimension to the other six, and he suggests that each religion can be understood in terms of the interrelatedness of its seven parts, and that different religions can be compared by means of this seven-dimensional model. It has been suggested that a variant on this model might be helpful, containing eight interlinked elements: religious community, ritual, ethics, social/political involvement, scripture/myth, doctrine, aesthetics and spirituality. It is also suggested that at the beginning of the model there be an indication of the notion of transcendence in the religion concerned, together with the mediating symbol by means of which transcendence is made available to human beings on earth (God in Christ, Allah in the Koran, Yahweh in the Torah, Brahman in a Hindu deity or the Atman, and Nirvana in the Buddha or the Dharma), and at the end of the model there be the ingredient of intention or faith by means of which the model becomes integrated and whole and real to religious persons (Whaling, 1986, pp. 37–47). In this way theories of religion derived from theology in the widest sense and religious studies can be combined.

The debate about theories of religion within Christian theology, within religious studies, and between theology and religious studies continues to be wide-ranging. It is important that it should be as comprehensive as possible and as complementary as possible because although it is an academic debate it has consequences for the religious life of human beings.

See also OTHER FAITHS AND CHRISTIANITY; PHILOSOPHY OF RELIGION; SOCIAL SCIENCE AND CHRISTIAN THOUGHT.

Bibliography

Durkheim, Emile [1912] 1976: *The Elementary Forms of the Religious Life*, trans. London: Allen and Unwin.

Eliade, Mircea [1949] 1958: *Patterns in Comparative Religion*, trans. London and New York: Sheed and Ward.

Evans-Pritchard, E.E. 1965: *Theories of Primitive Religion*. Oxford: Oxford University Press.

Hick, John 1989: *An Interpretation of Religion*. London: Macmillan.

James, William 1902: *The Varieties of Religious Experience*. New York: Longmans Green.

Leeuw, G. van der [1933] 1938: *Religion in Manifestation and Essence: A Study in Phenomenology*, trans. London: Allen and Unwin.

Leeuwen, Arend T. van 1964: *Christianity in World History*. New York: Scribner.

Sharpe, Eric 1975: *Comparative Religion: A History*. London: Duckworth.

Smart, Ninian 1969: *The Religious Experience of Mankind*. New York: Scribner.

Smith, Wilfred Cantwell 1964: *The Meaning and End of Religion*. New York: Mentor.

Thomas, Owen C. 1969: *Attitudes Towards Other Religions: Some Christian Interpretations*. New York: Harper and Row.

Waardenburg, Jacques 1973: *Classical Approaches to the Study of Religion*, 2 vols. The Hague: Mouton.

Whaling, Frank 1984–5: *Contemporary Approaches to the Study of Religion*, vols 1 and 2. Berlin, New York, Amsterdam: Mouton.

Whaling, Frank 1986: *Christian Theology and World Religions: A Global Approach*. Basingstoke: Marshall Pickering.

Yinger, J.M. 1970: *The Scientific Study of Religion*. New York: Macmillan; London: Collier-Macmillan.

FRANK WHALING

religions, school of history of See HISTORY OF RELIGIONS SCHOOL.

resurrection The ENLIGHTENMENT debates about the resurrection of Jesus concerned its factuality and, subsequently, its very meaning. For many decades apologists for orthodox faith (see APOLOGETICS) remained largely content to argue for the credibility of the resurrection. After the First World War its significance for revelation, faith, hope and redemption gradually caught the attention of more western theologians. In Eastern Orthodox Christianity and in very many Christian communities of the west, belief in Jesus' resurrection long remained in untroubled possession, untouched by the Enlightenment controversies.

The Enlightenment

During the eighteenth century the deists (see DEISM) often challenged the factuality of Jesus' resurrection by raising even larger questions: about God's action in the world and the very nature of Christianity. While accepting a personal Creator of the universe, they generally denied that God intervenes in the natural order of things – a position that rules out the possibility of the resurrection and miracles. They argued that in religious matters reason was a sufficient guide, without any necessary help from some special divine revelation through which God would have added some new truth, in principle unknowable by the light of human reason. This meant that salvation was not and could not necessarily be tied to a particular historical revelation, communicated progressively through the history of the Jewish people and culminating in Christ's incarnation, life, death, resurrection and the sending of the Holy Spirit. In his *Christianity as Old as the Creation* of 1730, a work that quickly became known as 'the Bible of the deists', Matthew Tindal drew a conclusion that fairly naturally followed from doubting or denying the distinctive revelation and salvation confessed by Christians: religion was only the practice of morality in obedience to the divine will. The Christian religion was not centred on the resurrection of the crucified Jesus as the climax of God's special revelation and salvific intervention in human history.

Two points should be noted about this global, 'dogmatic' challenge to Christ's resurrection. First, it drove a wedge between the world of ideas and truths, on the one hand, and the world of facts and events (to which the resurrection belongs), on the other. G.E. Lessing declared: 'Accidental truths of history can never become the proof of necessary truths of reason' (Chadwick, 1957, p. 53). This classical dictum would be echoed in their own way by Immanuel Kant ('the historical can serve only for illustration, not for demonstration'), Johann Gottlieb Fichte ('only the metaphysical can save, never the historical') and other Enlightenment philosophers. At the very least this meant reducing the resurrection to an accidental truth of history, a mere illustration and something historical that cannot save human beings. At the most, as we shall see, some deists expressly denied the factual truth of the resurrection. Second, when eighteenth-century rationalism challenged a distinctive revelation and salvation coming through Christ, it often spoke of his incarnation, life and death. In *Emile* Jean Jacques Rousseau typified this silence about the resurrection: 'You preach to me

God, born and dying, two thousand years ago, at the other end of the world, in some small town, I know not where; and you tell me that all who have not believed this mystery are damned' (Rousseau, [1762] 1974, p. 269). It is not that the champions of orthodoxy necessarily had more to say about Christ's resurrection as such. In his classic refutation of deism, *The Analogy of Religion* of 1736, Joseph Butler argued for the inherent credibility of Christian revelation but did so with hardly a reference to Jesus' resurrection.

Besides its general 'dogmatic' opposition to the resurrection as involving unacceptable claims to a special revelation and a specifically historical salvation, eighteenth-century rationalism also rejected the evidence for their religion to which Christian apologists typically pointed: prophecies and miracles. At the end of the seventeenth century John Locke still agreed that (1) miracles provided the primary (external) evidence for the truth of revelation, and (2) the fulfilment of prophecy, albeit to a lesser degree, also counted as evidence. In the 1720s Thomas Woolston attacked the evidential value of Christ's miracles, and what was considered the greatest of all miracles, the resurrection. This came under fire also from Peter Annet in his *The Resurrection of Jesus Christ Considered* of 1744. For some the closed system of Newtonian physics seemed to rule out the miraculous. For others, the problem was rather establishing the factuality of miracles, without which they could have no evidential value. In *Emile* Rousseau put this latter difficulty: 'Who will venture to tell me how many eyewitnesses are required to make a miracle credible? What use are your miracles, performed in proof of your doctrine, if they themselves require so much proof?' (ibid., p. 263).

Against the deists, such writers as Thomas Sherlock in 1729, Gilbert West in 1747, John Leland in 1754–6 and Luke Hooke in 1763 normally aimed to establish the (historical) truth of the resurrection as the supreme proof of Christ's claim to be the Son of God. In doing so, they faced objections raised by Annet, Woolston and others, some of which go back as far as Celsus in the second century and Porphyry in the third: the differences between the Easter accounts in the Gospels, the failure of the risen Christ to show himself to the general public and the suspicion of deliberate fraud on the part of the disciples. The apologists for the resurrection usually took Matthew to be the oldest Gospel (which meant paying considerable attention to his guard story), tried to harmonize the Easter accounts, and (like Origen, St Athanasius, St Augustine and many others before and after them) argued that remarkable effects in the origin and history of Christianity required an adequate cause, the resurrection of Jesus.

The climax of eighteenth-century challenges to the resurrection came with David Hume and Hermann Reimarus. In his *Enquiry Concerning Human Understanding* of 1748, Hume rejected belief in miracles as unreasonable and wrote off as incredible any claims about a resurrection from the dead, no matter what the testimony supporting these claims. By denying any necessary causal connections between our sense impressions, he also called into question universally valid laws of nature. Thus Hume excluded natural laws and their necessary inferences, as well as possible exceptions to such laws (in particular, miracles and the resurrection).

The inconsistencies and contradictions he found in the resurrection narratives and the absence of any Easter appearance to the Jewish people at large led Reimarus to revive the hypothesis of apostolic fraud (Matt. 28: 11–15). The disciple came to Jesus' tomb at night, stole the body and then fabricated the story of his resurrection.

William Paley, in his *View of the Evidences of Christianity* of 1794, represented features of the standard response to Reimarus and Hume. Like Origen against Celsus in the third century, Paley argued that the heroic sincerity and sufferings of the disciples ruled out the hypothesis that they had fraudulently invented the story of Jesus' resurrection. Against Hume, Paley claimed that belief in God and the possibility of divine revelation lend credibility to miracles and, specifically, that of the resurrection. Primarily it is not the weight of human testimony but the power of God that can make the resurrection believable.

During the nineteenth and into the twentieth century, among both their supporters and their opponents, F.D.E. Schleiermacher, David Friedrich Strauss and the HISTORY OF RELIGIONS SCHOOL affected much thinking and writing about Christ's resurrection – at least in the western world.

In *The Christian Faith* of 1821–2 Schleiermacher maintains that the disciples recognized in Jesus the Son of God without any premonition of his resurrection from the dead. What was true then of his redeeming efficacy remains true now. Christ communicates this God-consciousness to believers, without their faith needing the support of the resurrection. Relying on John's Gospel (which he takes to be wholly written by an eyewitness), Schleiermacher in his *Life of Jesus* (published posthumously in 1864) accepts the historicity of Jesus' resurrection, which he interprets very realistically as the revivification of a corpse. If at times his language suggests a merely apparent death, he rejects that hypothesis, which has been entertained by Annet, H.E.G. Paulus and a procession of non-scholarly authors down to the present. But it is Jesus' inner life and his perfect God-consciousness, rather than his resurrection, that remain deeply significant for Schleiermacher's influential view of Christian faith and theology.

Rejecting rationalist attempts to explain away historically the empty tomb, Strauss reduces the resurrection to a purely 'inner' event in the life of the disciples. Incapable of thinking of Jesus as dead, they were deluded into thinking that he had risen and appeared to them. In various forms this view, which denies that the resurrection was an event for Jesus, has continued down to the present. Some go beyond Strauss. Instead of arguing for the merely subjective experience of hallucinated disciples, they assert that the 'resurrection' message itself did not proclaim some new fact about the crucified Jesus but merely an eternal, mythical truth that can be verified over and over again in the lives of his followers. Thus talk about Jesus' resurrection expressed and expresses not so much a purely subjective *experience* as a purely subjective *claim* on the part of the disciples. The difficulty with this line of interpretation, however, remains something that Paley pointed out long ago. The primary assertion of the New Testament witnesses is that Jesus himself had risen from the dead. One can reject their assertion, but their primary claim is clearly about something that happened to the crucified Jesus himself.

The history of religions school, somewhat like Celsus in the second century, argued that the stories about Jesus' resurrection were not unique. The Christian claims about Jesus were only another version of stories about dying and rising gods and heroes. However, serious parallels and historical connections between such legends (and their attendant cults) and the origins of the message about Jesus' resurrection have been discounted by most scholars, even if the hypothesis lingers on in the popular mind.

Right through the Enlightenment and beyond, Christian hymns, liturgy, creeds, poetry, painting and sculpture peacefully professed and celebrated faith in Jesus' resurrection. Apologists for this faith, at times lacking a sharp sense of the historical problems, continued to put their case for Christ's resurrection. Together with his miracles and prophecies, it demonstrated the truth of his claims to a divine identity and mission. After thus serving as an apologetic foundation, the resurrection was often forgotten and a theology was developed on the basis of the INCARNATION.

The twentieth century

In the twentieth century many western theologians rediscovered the theological significance of the resurrection. In both his dialectical (1914–31) and definitive (1931–68) periods, Karl Barth expounded the paschal mystery in terms of eschatological revelation and reconciliation. Barth came to maintain ever more strongly that (1) Christ's death and resurrection have in themselves changed the world, and (2) that the resurrection is an objective event in itself. For the existential interpretation of Rudolf Bultmann, the message of the resurrection discloses the eschatological, salvific meaning of the cross. Meeting Christ in the church's preaching, through faith we can come to a new self-understanding and existence. Despite his stronger concern for the historical evidence, Barth agreed with Bultmann that by itself such evidence cannot ground Easter faith.

Ecumenical dialogue, increased contacts with Eastern Orthodox Christianity, the liturgical revival (led by Benedictine scholars) and the biblical movement made Roman Catholic thinking more resurrection-centred. Where the First Vatican Council (1869–70) never mentioned it, in *Dei Verbum* (its Constitution on Divine Revelation) the Second Vatican Council (1962–5) acknowledged the paschal mystery as the definitive climax of God's self-communication in salvation history. *Gaudium et Spes* ('Joy and Hope'), the Council's long 'Constitution on the Church in the Modern World', understood the contemporary human condition in the light of the risen Christ. That document coincided with the emergence of Jürgen Moltmann's theology of hope, which interpreted the resurrection as the eschatological divine promise grounding our Christian hope. The 1970s saw the publication of numerous Christological studies. Many of these Christologies took the resurrection of the crucified Jesus as their centre and leitmotif.

Some difficulties that dogged the Enlightenment debates about the resurrection have been classified and dealt with by modern biblical criticism. The earliest Christian writer, St Paul, incorporated in his letters kerygmatic and liturgical traditions about Jesus' resurrection and exaltation that reach back to the first years of Christianity. In studying the Gospel material on the resurrection, Markan priority is widely accepted, as well as the need to use redaction and form criticism in examining the Easter narratives of all four Gospels (see BIBLICAL CRITICISM AND INTERPRETATION 2: NEW TESTAMENT).

Most exegetes agree that the appearance and empty tomb traditions originated in relative independence. The appearances of the risen Christ have been interpreted as mystical, pneumatological, ecstatic, revelatory and conversion experiences. The nature and function of these appearances call for further examination and reflection, along with the nature of the risen body and the theological significance (and not merely the historicity) of the empty tomb.

Current debates in resurrection theology include epistemological and ontological issues. Does the approach of Karl Rahner to the paschal mystery and the structure of Easter faith offer some middle ground between Wolfhart Pannenberg's attempt to validate the resurrection historically and the 'fideist' option represented by Willi Marxsen? Finally, belief in Christ's resurrection claims an extraordinary divine intervention in human history. The ontological, deist questions about God's action in the world are still very much with us. What sense can we make of such special divine causality?

See also CHRISTOLOGY; DOCTRINE AND DOGMA; EPISTEMOLOGY, RELIGIOUS; ESCHATOLOGY; HISTORICAL JESUS, QUEST OF; PREACHING, THEOLOGY OF; REVELATION, CONCEPT OF.

Bibliography

Carnley, P. 1987: *The Structure of Resurrection Belief.* Oxford: Clarendon Press; New York: Oxford University Press.

Chadwick, H., ed. and trans. 1957: *Lessing's Theological Writings.* Stanford: Stanford University Press.

Craig, W.L. 1985: *The Historical Argument for the Resurrection of Jesus during the Deist Controversy.* Lampeter: Mellen House; Lewiston, NY: Edwin Mellen Press.

Fuller, R.H. 1971: *The Formation of Resurrection Narratives.* London: Collier Macmillan; New York: Macmillan.

Leland, J. 1754–6: *A View of the Principal Deistical Writers That Have Appeared in England in the Last and Present Century*, 3 vols. London: B. Dod at the Bible and Key.

Marxsen, W. [1968] 1970: *The Resurrection of Jesus of Nazareth*, trans. M. Kohl. London: SCM Press; Philadelphia: Fortress Press.

O'Collins, G. 1987: *Jesus Risen.* Mahwah, NJ: Paulist Press; London: Darton, Longman and Todd.

O'Collins, G. 1988: *Interpreting the Resurrection.* Mahwah, NJ: Paulist Press.

Perkins, P. 1984: *Resurrection: New Testament Witness and Contemporary Reflection.* London: Geoffrey Chapman; New York: Doubleday.

Rahner, K. [1976] 1978: *Foundations of Christian Faith*, trans. W. Dych. London: Darton, Longman and Todd; New York: Seabury Press.

Rousseau, J.J. [1762] 1974: *Emile*, trans. B. Foxley. London: Dent.

GERALD O'COLLINS

revelation, concept of In much classical Christian usage, revelation refers both to the act of God's self-disclosure to humanity and to the knowledge of God which results from such divine action. Since the Enlightenment the concept of revelation has been a major target in the criticism of Christian theology, and it remains a primary issue in attempts to reconstruct a coherent account of the nature and grounds of Christian belief in God.

For most of the history of Christian theology before the modern era, the concept of revelation (whether explicitly articulated, or, more often, merely implied in usage and patterns of argument) has its place as part of a larger framework of convictions about God and God's relation to human persons. Although the concept is often associated with ideas of 'veil-lifting', it is primarily concerned not with the communication of esoteric information but with the disclosure by God of God's character, purposes for and requirements of humanity. So construed, the notion of revelation thus implies that knowledge of the being and ways of God is God's own gift, and not the fruit of human creativity or searching. Because it is revealed, knowledge of God is the gift of divine grace, and a participation in God's self-knowledge. Further, in characterizing God as the giver of knowledge of God, the concept of revelation thereby also characterizes human persons as recipients (rather than producers) of such knowledge. Accordingly, revelation and FAITH are closely correlated: faith is the anthropological counterpart of revelation. 'Faith' is here understood not as mental assent but as trustful, receptive disposition of the self towards the self-disclosure of an agent beyond the self. The loci of such self-disclosure are variously identified as, for example, inner illumination, Holy Scripture heard as God's Word, or the authoritative tradition of church teaching. All such loci are, however, conceived as relative to God's supreme self-disclosure in and as Jesus Christ, and to the activity of God the Holy Spirit in enabling perception of and response to God's gracious gift of knowledge of God. Understood in this way, the concept of revelation, classically conceived, is more than an epistemological category, furnishing a foundation for subsequent Christian belief. Revelation does not just answer the question of how claims to knowledge of God can be authorized, but is a consequence of prior convictions about the prevenience of God in all God's relations with humanity.

With the rise of fundamental theology and philosophical prolegomena to theology in the early modern period, this coinherence of the concept of revelation with grace, Spirit and faith began to disintegrate. The Enlightenment critique of revelation was prepared in some measure by Christian theology itself, when natural philosophy was granted the task of establishing on non-theological grounds the possibility and necessity of revelation. The effect of this development was to extract the concept of revelation from its home in the dogmatic structure of Christian theology by assigning it a place in apologetics or foundations. This 'shift from assumption to argument' (Thiemann, 1985, p. 11) is also associated in some measure with the rise of scholastic styles of theological systematization in both Protestant and Roman Catholic circles. More particularly, increasing reliance on Aristotelian methods of argumentation, and the quasi-Cartesian search for indubitable certainty in theology did much to undermine the correlation of revelation and faith. In effect, revelation shifts from being an implication of Christian conviction to furnishing the grounds from which Christian conviction can be deduced.

The ENLIGHTENMENT saw the rise of a number of severe objections to the concept of revelation which have largely conditioned the history of the concept to the present day. First, the Enlightenment treated with severe scepticism any claims about divine intervention, thereby calling into question a major component of the understanding of God's relation to the world which undergirded the classical understanding of revelation as divine activity upon human agents. Second, the Enlightenment principle of the sufficiency of human reason as the final arbiter in claims to knowledge called into question the concept of revealed knowledge of God. Part of the cogency of this principle rested in its anti-authoritarian emphasis and its attempt to liberate thought from the traditions, customs and unexamined assumptions of confessional religious communities. Moreover, the principle inverted the terms in questions concerning knowledge of the divine: it was no longer (as in the classical tradition) revelation which offers the framework within which reality is interpreted, but rather human reason which furnishes the context within which claims to knowledge of God have to be justified. Further, both deists in England and Neologians in Germany argued that the notion of revelation is superfluous, since natural religion, understood in moral terms, contains all that is of value in supposed supernatural revelation.

Third, the Enlightenment marked the beginnings of history as a critical science, a development whose destructive effect on traditional understandings of revelation can hardly be overstressed. In effect, the rise of critical history established the historicity, and therefore the relativity, of all human projects, including religion. Within such a sense of history, Christian faith found it increasingly difficult to articulate its claim to offer an overarching interpretation of the whole process of human history (as is found in Augustine's *City of God*, for example). Its traditional claim to possess an external standpoint, afforded by revelation, from which to survey human history in its entirety, was subverted by growing awareness that the Christian religion is itself within the historical process. The difficulties for the Christian understanding of revelation can be seen on two fronts. (1) The rise of critical history introduced an element of idealism in thinking about Christian faith, in the sense that the Christian religion comes to be regarded as a historical product, and therefore as incapable of offering direct access to transcendent reality. Christian knowledge of God is constructed rather than immediately received from divine revelation, and shares in the contingency and limitation of all human activities. Accordingly, it cannot pretend to absoluteness. (2) This means, therefore, that Christian claims to knowledge, and the loci of supposed Christian revelation, are relative. The most obvious effect of this principle can be seen in its application to the study of the Bible. In the hands of seventeenth-century Protestant divines, the Bible became the locus of divine revelation, offering a secure repository of revealed truth out of which Christian claims could be warranted. As historical study was applied to the Bible in the latter part of the eighteenth and the nineteenth centuries, however, the status of the Bible shifted. As it is placed within human history, it no longer furnishes a canonical narrative which circumscribes and interprets the general history of humanity, but rather is subsumed within a historical scheme constructed upon a different basis. Thereby once again – as an entire tradition from G.E. Lessing to Ernst Troeltsch and beyond emphasized – the absoluteness of Christianity came to be problematic. This was felt with particular acuteness as critical study of the New Testament in the nineteenth century began to erode the historical reliability of its accounts not only of the history of the early church but also of the career of Jesus himself, thereby seeming to sap the foundations of God's self-revelation in Christ (see BIBLICAL CRITICISM AND INTERPRETATION 2: NEW TESTAMENT).

One frequent response by Christian theology to these problems took the form of apologetic attempts to defend the legitimacy of Christian claims to revelation on historical grounds. A particularly telling example of this development was the use of the resurrection of Jesus as proof for the possibility and reality of divine revelation. In both the Roman school of fundamental theology (classically expressed in the documents of the First Vatican Council) and some styles of Protestant Christology, historical demonstration of the empty tomb and the resurrection appearances of Jesus came to carry the burden of furnishing indubitable warrants for Christian belief (on the Roman Catholic tradition, see Fiorenza, 1985). The RESURRECTION of Jesus was thereby transformed into a rationally established ground for belief in divine revelation, rather than being envisaged as part of the content of God's self-disclosure to be received by faith.

A rather different response to the Enlightenment's restrictions upon Christian claims to revelation was undertaken by the liberal Protestant tradition which stemmed from the work of Friedrich Schleiermacher. Accepting the Enlightenment's critique of the metaphysical and theological structure of Christian theology in its classic formulations, this tradition sought to re-ground Christian beliefs about revelation by identifying human religious experience as the locus of God's indirect self-disclosure. Revelation is thus not a matter of direct divine intervention or communication, but is more concerned with the givenness of the Christian community's religious experience, most of all its experience of redemption, which defies purely natural explanation. Such experience mediates knowledge of the divine origin of religious awareness, and so offers the grounds for language, albeit indirect language, about the activity of God. In effect, the liberal Protestant tradition sought to reconstruct the notion of revelation in a way which took serious account of the limits imposed by the Enlightenment, yet doing so without falling into the positivism of fundamental theology and apologetics. Its reintegration of revelation with the phenomenon of human faith has proved deeply influential on much constructive Christian theology to the present day. Nevertheless, its difference from the classical tradition rests in its reticence in appealing to the notion of divine prevenience, a reticence which in the judgement of some later critics (notably Karl Barth) exposed what was considered the anthropocentric character of the liberal theological enterprise, and its tendency to absolutize ecclesial experience.

Reaction to the liberal Protestant reconstruction of the concept of revelation is usually associated with the work of Barth and other 'dialectical' or 'neo-orthodox' theologians such as Emil Brunner and (in certain respects) Rudolf Bultmann. Barth's work, both in its earlier, predominantly critical, phase and in its mature constructive expression in the *Church Dogmatics*, constitutes the most ambitious attempt in the present century to rework the affirmations of the classical Christian tradition concerning God's self-disclosure. Barth's understanding of revelation, formally expounded in the opening volumes of the *Dogmatics* but implied throughout the argument of his massive work, is best understood as an attempt to recover the axiomatic character of the being and activity of God in matters of theological knowledge. Barth identifies revelation neither as information concerning God (as in the Protestant scholastic tradition), nor as the whence of religious experience (as in the liberal tradition from which he turned decisively in the early part of his career), but in terms of the self-manifestation of God as Father, Son and Spirit. Revelation is thus God's own being in its movement towards humanity in covenant love, above all in God's taking flesh in the person of Jesus Christ. In this movement, God posits himself, and makes human persons into knowers of God, evoking faith by the activity of the Holy Spirit. Much of the cogency of Barth's understanding of revelation is contained not simply in its formal statement but in the confidence with which it imbues Barth's descriptive exposition of the objects of Christian doctrine. Moreover, whilst the doctrine of revelation formally functions as the epistemological basis for

Barth's theology, it does so only as part of a primary conviction that God is both ontologically and noetically prior to all other realities: 'God reveals himself as Lord.' This move by Barth is in part an attempt to respond to the Enlightenment's repudiation of revelation, not by apologetic defence but by refusing the terms of the critique. Barth is consistently hostile to allowing terms such as 'reason' or 'history' to exercise authority over theological reflection, since to accord them the kind of status given them by the Enlightenment is in effect a covert denial of the non-derivative, absolute character of God's self-manifestation. Thus for Barth, discussion of the possibility or warrantability of God's self-revelation already exceeds the limits of the subordinate status which he ascribes to questions about the external conditions for revelation. Many of the critiques of Barth's understanding and use of revelation hinge on this assertion of the axiomatic status of God. For some, this leads to what Dietrich Bonhoeffer called 'positivism of revelation': an isolation of the grounds of Christian faith from the contingencies of historical existence, and thus a protection of Christian theology from serious exposure to critique. For others, Barth's doctrine is rooted in an irrational commitment to a particular claim to revelation which ought properly to be subject to rational appraisal.

In a quite contrary direction to Barth, many twentieth-century theologians, both Catholic and Protestant, have rooted an understanding of revelation in aspects of the phenomenology of human existence. Rudolf Bultmann, originally associated with Barth in his earlier work, shared Barth's critique of the immanentist aspects of the liberal tradition. However, under the influence both of neo-Kantian and existentialist philosophy and of aspects of the Lutheran tradition, Bultmann laid particular stress not on the objectivity of divine revelation so much as on the existential situation of the believer who, brought into crisis by revelation, is called to a new mode of existence. Theologies of correlation (above all in the work of Paul Tillich, but also in a number of North American theologians influenced by him, notably Langdon Gilkey) move in something of the same direction as Bultmann, by articulating a phenomenology of human existence which functions as an anthropological grounding of the possibility of revelation. Thus aspects of human historical experience (such as finitude or contingency) raise the question of humanity's dependence upon a source external to itself. Such theological schemes are insistent that revelation not be considered as a body of information derived from sources other than that of historical experience, but as an interpretation of the human condition, in particular of those aspects of human experience which signal a gratuitous divine reality independent of human projection. In the transcendental Thomist tradition which has enjoyed considerable prestige in twentieth-century Roman Catholic theology, many of the same moves are undertaken. The account of divine revelation undertaken by Karl Rahner, for example, begins from an elaboration of an anthropology in which human selfhood is constituted through openness to the transcendent. Analysis of human existence in its self-transcendence within history thus functions as a basis for establishing the possibility of revelation.

A third strand of contemporary reflection on revelation has attempted to reintegrate revelation and history. H. Richard Niebuhr's mid-century classic *The Meaning of Revelation*, straddling both Protestant liberal and Barthian positions, argued that the concept of revelation is best understood in the context of the inner (rather than merely external, factual) history of selves in community: in Christian usage, revelation refers to 'that special occasion which provides us with an image by means of which all the occasions of personal and common life become intelligible' (Niebuhr, 1941, p. 109). Niebuhr's work has proved deeply influential upon recent developments in narrative theology, which have sought to correlate theological concepts with issues of personal identity formation. More recently, Pannenberg has developed a theological scheme in which revelation is understood in terms of an eschatological manifestation of the meaning of the whole of history, anticipated in the resurrection of Jesus Christ.

The variety of responses to the Enlightenment's challenge to classical formulations of the concept of revelation have, then, bequeathed to current theology a highly diverse agenda of issues. At one level, the concept requires for its elaboration some coherent notion of divine agency – although the criteria for coherence in this case are themselves matters of very considerable dispute (see Abraham, 1982 for an attempt to elaborate such criteria). At another, it requires clarification of the relation of God's self-disclosure to history. In part, this means continued stocktaking of the implications of the historical (and thus socioeconomic and political) determinants upon all human knowledge, and a careful separation of Christian thought about revelation from both historical positivism or naturalism on the one hand, and dogmatic, ahistorical positivism on the other. It also means that developing a concept of revelation will involve steering a path through a number of hermeneutical problems concerning the relation of the givenness of revelation (whether in events in the past or in inherited documents) with its reception and appropriation in forms of corporate life very different from those surrounding its original occurrence. A further emerging issue is the need to distinguish claims to revelation from a triumphalist or oppressive *use* of revelation as a heteronomous concept, warranting and maintaining the assured knowledge and power of certain interest groups (see Ricoeur, 1980). Finally, the absoluteness and exclusiveness which have classically formed part of the Christian revelation claim have become increasingly difficult to support, not simply in the light of historical relativity but also in view of the religious pluralism of the global community.

To this agenda of issues, at least two approaches can be discerned in contemporary debate. One approach puts the notion of revelation on hold, seeking first to elaborate the grounds (anthropological, phenomenological, philosophical) of its possibility and only then making use of it in constructive theology. A different approach suggests that the persuasiveness of the notion rests not in the skilful defence of its possibility so much as on its use as part of a set of convictions about God, the contingency of history and the essential receptivity of persons. This second approach proposes that the grammar of the concept of revelation becomes intelligible in the context of forms of Christian religious life within which such convictions flourish, and that the association of revelation with the apologetic enterprise

in the past spelled the end of its capacity to operate with conviction.

See also EPISTEMOLOGY, RELIGIOUS; FAITH AND HISTORY; FAITH AND REASON.

Bibliography
Abraham, W.J. 1982: *Divine Revelation and the Limits of Historical Criticism*. Oxford: Oxford University Press.
Baillie, J. 1956: *The Idea of Revelation in Recent Thought*. Oxford: Oxford University Press.
Barth, K. [1932] 1975: *Church Dogmatics* I/1. Edinburgh: T & T Clark.
Brunner, E. [1941] 1947: *Revelation and Reason: The Christian Doctrine of Faith and Knowledge*. London: SCM Press.
Bultmann, R. [1929] 1961: The concept of revelation in the New Testament. In *Existence and Faith*. London: Collins, pp. 67–106.
Downing, F.G. 1964: *Has Christianity a Revelation?* London: SCM Press.
Dulles, A. 1970: *Revelation Theology: A History*. London: Burns and Oates.
Fiorenza, F.S. 1985: *Foundational Theology*. New York: Crossroad.
Gilkey, L. 1969: *Naming the Whirlwind: The Renewal of God-Language*. Indianapolis: Bobbs-Merrill.
Hart, R.L. 1968: *Unfinished Man and the Imagination: Toward an Ontology and a Rhetoric of Revelation*. New York: Herder and Herder.
MacDonald, H.D. 1959: *Ideas of Revelation. An Historical Study AD 1700 to AD 1860*. London: Macmillan.
MacDonald, H.D. 1963: *Theories of Revelation: An Historical Study 1860–1960*. London: George Allen and Unwin.
Niebuhr, H.R. 1941: *The Meaning of Revelation*. New York: Macmillan.
Pannenberg, W., ed. [1961] 1968: *Revelation as History*. London: Sheed and Ward.
Rahner, K. [1941] 1969: *Hearers of the Word*. New York: Herder and Herder.
Ricoeur, P. 1980: Toward a hermeneutic of the idea of revelation. In *Essays on Biblical Interpretation*. Philadephia: Fortress Press, pp. 73–118.
Thiemann, R.F. 1985: *Revelation and Theology: The Gospel as Narrated Promise*. Notre Dame: University of Notre Dame Press.
Tillich, P. 1951: *Systematic Theology*, 3 vols. Vol. 1, *Reason and Revelation, Being and God*. Chicago: University of Chicago Press, pp. 71–159.

JOHN B. WEBSTER

rights, human See ETHICS; JUSTICE; NATURAL LAW; SOCIAL QUESTIONS.

561

Ritschl, Albrecht (1822–1889) German Protestant theologian. Originally of the Tübingen school, and professor of theology at Bonn (1851–64) and Göttingen (1864–89), his thinking exercised considerable influence on liberal theologians of the late nineteenth and early twentieth centuries, including Adolf von Harnack and Ernst Troeltsch. Suspicious of mystical and individualistic religion, Ritschl stressed the importance of the community of believers – the church – as the vehicle of salvation. He argued against 'absolutists' from the early church Fathers onwards, whose claims for, for instance, the eternal, pre-existent nature of Jesus he traced back to philosophical hellenizations of the original gospel of the historical Jesus. God had worked in history, but since no empirical proofs could be made about this, all theological statements were 'value judgements'. His theology was moralistic in emphasis: Jesus was divine in the sense that he was fully and perfectly human. His main works were *Die christliche Lehre von der Rechtfertigung und Versöhnung* (1870–4) and *Die Geschichte des Pietismus* (1880–6).

Bibliography
Barth, K. 1959: *From Rousseau to Ritschl*. London.
Mueller, D.L. 1969: *An Introduction to the Theology of Albert Ritschl*. Philadelphia.
Richmond, J. 1978: *Ritschl: A Reappraisal*. London.

Roman Catholic theology With the beginning of the eighteenth century Roman Catholic theology showed no sign of vigour. In Protestant countries Roman Catholics were too preoccupied with consolidating their position in a still hostile environment to have much time for theology, apart from polemics, outside the seminaries. On the European continent Jansenism remained a powerful force, and its rigoristic morality, if not its dogmatic system, exerted a wider influence in English-speaking countries too. St Alphonsus Liguori's *Moral Theology* of 1753–5 presented a middle position between Jansenistic rigorism and what was regarded as the laxer Jesuit probabilism; his theory of 'equiprobabilism' taught that a person was free to choose between lines of conduct which enjoyed equal support from approved church authorities. As the century progressed the agenda was set by the need for the church to make out a case against the Enlightenment, such as the romantic poet Chateaubriand's *Génie du christianisme*, which expounded a Christian apologetic based on an appeal to the feelings.

Beginning with the French Revolution and continuing with Bismarck's *Kulturkampf* in Germany, the church in Europe suffered frequent persecution. The eighteenth and nineteenth centuries were a period when the papacy especially felt itself under attack from many sides. It had been humiliated from without under Napoleon. From within its teaching authority was threatened by the Catholic writers G. Hermes (1775–1831) and A. Günther (1783–1863), who tried to produce a synthesis of Catholic thought with Kantianism and idealism which would diminish the need for revelation. Gallicanism in France, Febronianism in Germany and Josephinism in Austria attempted to abolish the pope's temporal, and to limit his spiritual, power. It was in reaction to such tendencies that Pius IX's Syllabus of Errors was published in 1864, summarizing the teaching of his encyclicals and addresses against various manifestations of liberalism (see LIBERALISM: BRITAIN). In the same spirit the First Vatican Council (Vatican I, 1869–70) promulgated its decrees on reason, revelation and faith (*Dei Filius*), and papal primacy and infallibility (*Pastor Aeternus*). Though most of the minority group of bishops who opposed the infallibility decree (in most cases because they regarded it as inopportune rather than erroneous) eventually made their submission, the German historian J.J.I. Döllinger opposed the substance of the decree, which he saw as the product of papal absolutism, and was excommunicated. His associate Lord Acton, by contrast, the leading member of a group of liberal Catholic thinkers in England, was equally opposed to the decree and to the Roman Catholic tendency to centralize authority, but remained a member of the Roman church to the end of his life.

The nineteenth century was still not a period of great creativity. The privileged status which Pope Leo XIII accorded to the philosophical and theological system of Thomas Aquinas did not encourage the development of fresh thought. This was the period of the development of the national colleges in Rome, in which the best of the future priests from all over the world were formed in the mould of *Romanità*. Most theological writing was in the form of manuals for seminary students inspired by a neo-Thomist scholasticism. Some of the most important work of this type was produced in Rome by G. Perrone (who helped J.H. Newman to find his feet in Roman Catholic theology after his conversion), and J.B. Franzelin (who played an important part at the First Vatican Council) and L. Billot. Nevertheless the period did witness the emergence of several highly original figures, some of whom have had an enduring influence on Roman Catholic thought. The first great evidence of vitality came from the Catholic Faculty at Tübingen, where J.S. Drey and J.A. Möhler worked out the beginnings of a theory of doctrinal development and an understanding of the church as a community of believers (see TRADITION); at the same time – long before the beginning of the modern ecumenical movement in the Roman Catholic church – they accepted the emphasis placed on religious experience by such Protestant theologians as F.D.E. Schleiermacher. It was at Tübingen too that J.E. Kühn produced his dogmatic studies, and the historian K.J. Hefele (1809–1893) wrote his monumental history of the councils; the latter was among the last to accept Vatican I's infallibility decree. Karl Adam (1876–1966), W. Kasper and J. Ratzinger have continued the Tübingen tradition in the present century. At Cologne M.J. Scheeben (1835–1888) wrote several works exploring the doctrine of the supernatural as well as an influential *Handbuch der katholischen Dogmatik* of 1873–82, which combined a scholastic treatment with material taken from the Fathers and modern theologians.

The towering figure of nineteenth-century theology was John Henry Newman, though his leading ideas were formed while he was still an Anglican and his influence among Roman Catholics has been greater in the twentieth century than in his own. From him came four great ideas which, after being subjected to initial suspicion, have gained an established place in Catholic thinking: the development of doctrine; the sovereignty of conscience ('the aboriginal Vicar of Christ, a prophet in its informations, a monarch in its peremptoriness'); the authority of the instinct of faith (*sensus fidei*) possessed by all members of the church, among whom the laity play a full part; and the recognition that religious conviction is based not on logically irrefragable proof but on the convergence of probabilities on the basis of which the 'illative sense' arrives at moral certainty. The entry of so significant a figure into the Roman Catholic church in 1845 (only sixteen years after the Catholic Emancipation Act was passed by the British Parliament) greatly increased the self-confidence of the Roman Catholics in Britain. After he had left Anglicanism his writings continued to attract wide attention in the country at large, not least *The Idea of a University*, the lectures on the aims of Christian higher education which he delivered in 1852 in the Catholic University he had founded in Dublin at the request of the Irish bishops. Newman's views however encountered opposition in the USA from another convert, O. Brownson (1803–1876), himself a powerful apologist for Roman Catholic values in his own country.

Another original figure of the nineteenth century, A. Rosmini-Serbati (1797–1855), the founder of the Rosminian congregation or Institute of Charity, did not fare so fortunately as Newman. His theory that all knowledge took place within the contemplation of universal being was misunderstood and condemned by the Roman Holy Office as a version of N. Malebranche's ontologism, according to which the basis of knowledge was the immediate experience of God. His analysis of 1848 of the shortcomings of the church, entitled *Of the Five Wounds of the Holy Church*, also incurred ecclesiastical censure.

The social movement
From the 1830s industrialization in countries with sizeable Catholic populations, such as France and Germany, led to the growth of a 'Catholic social movement', whose experience and ideas prepared the way for the long line of papal encyclicals which have been the main means through which Catholic social teaching has developed. The series began in 1891 with Leo XIII's *Rerum Novarum*, which championed the right to private property, even when unequally distributed, provided the good things of life 'abound for (all) on a reasonable basis'. It defended both the wage system and the right of workers to form associations; class

warfare however it condemned. Pius XI's *Quadragesimo Anno* commemorated the fortieth anniversary of *Rerum Novarum* in 1931, clarifying and developing the teaching of that document, and giving guidance on the Christian response to the problems of mature capitalism. The principle of subsidiarity, always implicit in Catholic social philosophy, was here formally identified; its relevance in this context was the necessity for the smaller organization to retain its autonomy unless the common good requires a larger to replace it. John XXIII published two important social encyclicals. *Mater et Magistra* (1961) put forward the ideal of a state of property-owning, interdependent citizens; the welfare state is needed for social provision, private property for the guarantee of freedom and responsibility. *Pacem in Terris* (1963) is important among other things for its treatment of human rights. Continuing the thought of these encyclicals, the Second Vatican Council (1965) in its Pastoral Constitution on the Church in the Modern World (*Gaudium et Spes*) affirmed the church's duty to be involved in 'the joys and hopes, the griefs and the anxieties' of the present age (n. 1); it also promulgated a Declaration on Religious Freedom. The series of social encyclicals has continued under Paul VI with *Populorum Progressio* (1967) on development and the solidarity of the human race; and under John Paul II with *Laborem Exercens* (1981) on the dignity of work, and *Sollicitudo Rei Socialis* (1987), resuming the subject of development. Celebrating the centenary of *Rerum Novarum* in *Centesimus Annus* (1991), the same pope considered the needs of the third world and the former communist countries of eastern Europe, and recommended a capitalism 'at the service of human freedom in its totality . . . the core of which is ethical and religious'. (See also SOCIAL QUESTIONS.)

There have been many imaginative attempts to put the ideas of these encyclicals into practice. The formation of the Christian Democrat parties in Europe and their development after the Second World War was largely inspired by their teaching. One influence in the study and implementation of Roman Catholic social teaching has been the Young Christian Workers' movement, founded by Abbé (later Cardinal) Joseph Cardijn (1882–1967). During the Second World War the priest-worker movement had sprung up in France as a means of recovering the working class for the church, and the initiative of Cardinal E.C. Suhard (1874–1949) led to the establishment of the *Mission de Paris* in 1943; the priest-worker experiment was, however, suppressed by Rome in 1953 after their social involvement had led some of the priests to renounce their orders. In Britain the Catholic Social Guild promoted the study of the church's social ethics; in the USA a leading figure was Dorothy Day (1897–1980), who founded the influential journal *The Catholic Worker*.

Modernism

The modernist crisis at the end of the nineteenth century and the beginning of the twentieth was the cause of new restrictions placed on Catholic thinking. The term 'modernism' refers to various manifestations of a tendency to accept 'modern' religious ideas which had first appeared among Protestants. With regard to Scripture this showed itself as the acceptance of critical, even sceptical, biblical scholarship (in this respect J.E. Renan (1823–1892) could be regarded as a forerunner of the movement); with regard to doctrine, as the belief that dogmas were no more than symbolic expressions of an experience of God immanent within the soul. Pius X's encyclical *Pascendi*, which condemned the movement, gave it a more systematic articulation than its own exponents had done. A. Loisy in France and G. Tyrrell in England were both excommunicated for their refusal to submit to the church's ruling, while the works of L. Laberthonnière (1860–1932) were placed on the Index; M. Blondel (1861–1949), however, and F. von Hügel succeeded in adhering to many modernist insights without ceasing to be members of the church. (See MODERNISM.)

Another progressive tendency to which the Vatican gave a more definite form than it actually possessed was the so-called 'Americanism'. This was a name which opponents gave to ideas attributed to Isaac Hecker (1819–1888), the founder of the Paulists, and to those like the Archbishop of St Paul, John Ireland, who wrote about him; these American writers taught that the church should adjust to the democratic values of society current in the USA. In 1899

Leo XIII condemned five alleged theses of Americanism in a letter *Testem Benevolentiae*; Cardinal James Gibbons of Baltimore tried to prevent the condemnation, but subsequently denied that anyone held the censured opinions.

Biblical scholarship

The suppression of the modernist movement led to the stifling of biblical scholarship among Roman Catholics for decades; a series of Responses published by the Pontifical Biblical Commission gave detailed rulings against many of the critical and historical conclusions which had become commonplace outside the church, insisting, for example, that Isaiah was the work of a single author. Other decisions on doctrinal and moral matters were given by the Holy Office and other Vatican bodies. Pius XII's encyclical *Humani Generis* (1950) rejected other modern theological speculations. The Index of Prohibited Books, first issued in 1557, was one of the principal means for controlling the publication of new ideas. Although the Index was abolished in 1966, the Holy Office (since renamed the Congregation for the Doctrine of the Faith) has continued to exercise a tight rein over the writing and lecturing of priests whose writings have been judged unorthodox.

Although the Second Vatican Council gave explicit approval to the use of critical biblical research and modern philosophy in theological investigation, greater freedom was already entering Roman Catholic Scriptural scholarship even before the Council. M.-J. Lagrange had founded the Ecole Biblique in Jerusalem in 1890, though his own Old Testament writings incurred the suspicion of Rome. Pius XII's encyclical *Divino Afflante Spiritu* (1943) encouraged critical and historical biblical research, emphasizing the need to interpret the text according to the literary *genre* employed by the author. Roman Catholic scholars have long played a full part in cooperative ventures with other experts, such as the deciphering and interpreting of the Dead Sea Scrolls and the production of translations of the Bible. The *Jerome Biblical Commentary* under the Roman Catholic editorship of R. Brown, J. Fitzmyer and R. Murphy has attained a position of authority outside as well as inside their own church. Roman Catholics have played a prominent part in biblical archaeology; the

work of R. de Vaux on the Dead Sea Scrolls deserves special mention. Much consideration has been given to the understanding of biblical inspiration. As early as the first half of the nineteenth century the Tübingen school propagated the view that the divine authorship of Scripture did not involve verbal dictation or obviate the need for creativity on the part of the human author. J.B. Franzelin (d. 1886) proposed that God communicates the ideas to the writer, whose contribution is to express them in words. Lagrange saw that the process of inspiration includes the historical and social processes which contribute to the formation of the writer's mind. P. Benoit distinguished between inspiration and inerrancy; the truth which God intends to reveal is not contained in every sentence but emerges from the whole.

Theology pre-1962

Some of the most fruitful Roman Catholic theological work has been written according to a historical method; the theological truth has been allowed to emerge from the historical study of particular patristic or medieval sources. Two writers who have pursued this method most successfully have been the Frenchmen H. de Lubac and Y. Congar. De Lubac first emerged as a writer on ecclesiology. His influential book *Catholicism* ([1938] 1950), which he described as 'a study of dogma in relation to the corporate destiny of mankind', showed the link between the doctrines of the church and the Eucharist: 'the Eucharist makes the church and the church makes the Eucharist.' In 1946 he published *Surnaturel*, arguing against the neo-Thomist hypothesis of a 'state of pure nature' (i.e. without grace) in which man could live in purely natural happiness without reference to a supernatural end. De Lubac maintained that the true interpretation of Aquinas's doctrine was that man was created with a natural dynamism towards the supernatural, so that pure nature could never exist. This work was suppressed by Rome; Pius XII's encyclical *Humani Generis* was generally assumed to include an attack on de Lubac's position, though at the end of his life the Frenchman maintained that it was not his views which were the encyclical's target. Indeed after Vatican II, at which he participated as a consultant (*peritus*), de Lubac was able to republish his ideas in *The Mystery of the*

Supernatural (1965; trans. 1967) and *Augustinianism and Modern Theology*, 1965, trans. 1969). Congar also, after being silenced by Rome, was vindicated and played an influential part at the Council. He was a pioneer among Roman Catholics of church unity (see ECUMENISM), and in such works as *Jalons pour une théologie du laicat* of 1953 explored the vocation of the layperson in the church.

In the first half of the twentieth century the lead in Roman Catholic theology was given by the French. A series of great multi-volume encyclopedias, the *Dictionnaire de théologie catholique* (1903 onwards), the *Dictionnaire d'archéologie chrétienne et de liturgie* (1907 onwards), and the *Dictionnaire de spiritualité* (1932 onwards), helped to place theology on a sound scholarly basis. The Maurists, the monks of the Benedictine Abbey of St-Maur, had devoted a corporate effort to the production of reliable editions of the Fathers since the late seventeenth century; in the nineteenth the French Abbé J.-P. Migne made these and other patristic texts available to a wider public in his Latin and Greek Patrologies. French patristic scholarship spread the influence of the Greek Fathers in the west and produced the handy and originally (no longer alas) inexpensive *Sources chrétiennes* series of texts. The Frenchman P. Teilhard de Chardin (1881–1955), already distinguished in the scientific field for his work in palaeontology, produced in *The Phenomenon of Man* (1955, trans. 1959) a synthesis of scientific evolutionary theory with St Paul's understanding of a cosmic Christ as the dynamic principle of the creative process. These theological ideas, which he was forbidden to publish during his lifetime, though they were circulated privately, made an immediate impact when they were published after his death. His spirituality, based on an understanding of the world as the 'divine *milieu*', the field of divine action and Christian response, has withstood criticism better than his writings on the theology of science.

The greatest creativity in the pastoral performance of the liturgy has likewise been evident in France and Belgium. The standard for plainsong was set by the French abbey of Solesmes under the inspiration of Prosper Guéranger (1805–1875); the credit for originating the pastoral liturgical movement has been given to the Belgian monk Lambert Beauduin. The translations and music of J. Gelineau have given a popular impetus to psalm singing in the vernacular (see MUSIC AND CHRISTIANITY). By contrast, the historical liturgical research of the Abbey of Maria Laach, the home of such scholars as Ildefons Herwegen (1874–1946) and O. Casel (1886–1948), and the studies of J. Jungmann on the history of the Mass were carried on in German-speaking lands. This vigorous liturgical movement had already produced significant results before Vatican II, and prepared the way for the more sweeping changes which the Council was to make (see also LITURGY AND DOCTRINE). In America and Britain Mary Douglas and Victor Turner contributed to the understanding of liturgy with their anthropological studies of ritual; another anthropologist E. Evans-Pritchard (1902–1973) carried out fieldwork among primitive tribes which became a model for future workers.

The first half of the twentieth century saw a growing self-confidence among English-speaking Roman Catholics, as their numbers increased and they came to play an increasing role in public life. In England H. Belloc (1870–1973) and G.K. Chesterton (1874–1936) were effective apologists for Christian values; between the wars it became almost fashionable to be converted to Roman Catholicism. There was evident among such writers a nostalgia for the Middle Ages when Aquinas was the model for rational thought and, in Belloc's phrase, Europe was the faith – a tendency continued by the Jesuit M.C. D'Arcy and the Dominican Vincent McNabb. In the USA a growing number of Catholic universities, of which the first was founded at Georgetown in 1791, contributed to the developing influence of the church; the President of Notre Dame, T. Hesberg, has been an adviser on education for more than one president of the USA. The searchings of the American convert poet turned Trappist, Thomas Merton, for a contemporary spirituality, beginning with *The Seven Storey Mountain* (1948), attracted a following far beyond the boundaries of his own church and country.

The Second Vatican Council

The Second Vatican Council (1962–5) was a watershed in the evolution of Roman Catholic thought. Pope John XXIII conceived and initiated it; Paul VI carried it through to its conclusion. Unlike Vatican I, it had as its aim not the definition of new dogma but the *aggiornamento* of the church (i.e. its adaptation to the needs of the day). Much debate has centred on Pope John's apparent advocacy of a developing and even pluriform doctrine in his opening speech, in which he put forward the deceptively simple distinction between the unchanging truths of the faith and the way in which they are formulated.

Nevertheless the Council's ideas did not spring forth without preparation; many of its most fruitful insights had been first put forward by theologians like Congar and de Lubac, who, now fully rehabilitated, were present at the council as consultants (*periti*). It promulgated sixteen documents: on the liturgy, social communication, the church, the church in the modern world, ecumenism, non-Christian religions, religious liberty, the eastern Catholic churches, the office of bishops, the renewal of religious life, the ministry and life of priests, the training of priests, the lay apostolate, missionary activity, Christian education and revelation. Among its most innovative features were its commitment to freedom of conscience and ecumenism, its vision of a church which shared the fears and aspirations of the modern world, its placing of the papacy within the shared responsibility (collegiality) of all the bishops, its rejection of the view that the Jews of today were in any way guilty of Christ's death, its understanding of the vocation and spirituality of the laity, and its vision of Christian life 'accommodated to the genius and the dispositions of each culture' (Decree on Missions, *Ad Gentes*, 22). Missionary institutes were established to promote this process of 'inculturation'.

It was the Council's liturgical reforms which made the most immediate impact on the church, especially the permission it gave for the use of vernacular languages in place of Latin. All sacramental rites were revised so as to clarify their meaning, to remove accretions which obscured their purpose, to increase the participation of the people, and to give a more prominent place to the proclamation of Scripture (see SACRAMENTAL THEOLOGY). The most striking changes occurred in the sacraments of initiation (baptism, confirmation and first communion). The new *Rite for the Christian Initiation of Adults* (1972) introduced an adult catechumenate modelled on the practice of the fourth-century church. The liturgy for the Easter Vigil had already been revised as early as 1951, when it was transferred to its proper place on Holy Saturday night instead of being anticipated on the Saturday morning. The process of liturgical revision was aided by works of biblical theology such as F.X. Durrwell's *The Resurrection* ([1950] 1960), with its renewed emphasis on the place of Christ's resurrection in the process of redemption.

At the time of the Council the church was said to be divided between conservatives and progressives: some of the decrees indeed, such as the decree on revelation, *Dei Verbum*, contain old and new ideas placed side by side in unresolved tension. The most strenuous opponents of the reforms gathered under the leadership of Archbishop Marcel Lefebvre. They were best known for their refusal to accept either the changes in the Mass or its vernacular form; but at the heart of the movement lay an authoritarian, right-wing ideology in the spirit of Action Française, which could not accept the Vatican teaching on religious liberty and episcopal collegiality. Lefebvre eventually took his followers into schism when he illicitly consecrated four bishops, a schism which continued after his death in 1991. In the other direction, however, many expressed disappointment at the slow rate at which the Council's decisions have been implemented. Symptomatic of the intellectual polarization which followed Vatican II was the founding of two rival periodicals, the 'progressive' *Concilium* and the 'conservative' *Communio*.

It is undeniable that in some respects the results of Vatican II went far beyond the expectations of the participating bishops. The charismatic movement, for example, spread rapidly (see PENTECOSTALISM AND CHARISMATIC CHRISTIANITY). The Council's new understanding of the responsibilities of the laity encouraged a new interest in the spirituality of laypeople and the development of lay ministries in the church, with laywomen as well as laymen often serving as auxiliary eucharistic ministers. The importance the Council placed on the duty to follow one's conscience may have contributed to the widespread refusal to accept the papal

567

condemnation of contraception as final (see below). In some areas, such as the Netherlands, a tradition of staunch traditionalism was replaced almost overnight by uninhibited experimentation which matched the national mood of the young. In reaction Pope John Paul II, having successfully thrown his influence behind the resistance of many eastern European countries to communist hegemony, urged the western world to imitate the uncompromising Christian values of the east. During his pontificate a number of movements flourished which aimed at the spiritual renewal of the Roman Catholic church by the defence of firm doctrinal and moral standards; prominent among them are the Neo-catechumenate and the Opus Dei Association (now a 'personal prelature') founded in 1928 by J.M. Escrivà de Balaguer; controversy surrounded the pope's decision to beatify him in 1992.

Philosophy
In the field of philosophy, for most of the twentieth century neo-Thomism continued to be the dominant school. Two of its most distinguished exponents were the French laymen Jacques Maritain (1882–1973) and Etienne Gilson (1884–1978). Both devoted many years of their lives to the Pontifical Institute for Medieval Studies which was founded in Toronto in 1929. But Roman Catholics have also been active in other areas. F.C. Copleston's many-volume *History of Philosophy* (1946–75) has been a mainstay for generations of students. Others, such as M. Dummett, G.E.M. Anscombe and P. Geach, have achieved distinction in linguistic philosophy. Others again, such as G. Marcel (1889–1973) and M. de Unamuno (1864–1936), have been among those associated with existentialist thought. Another existentialist, Martin Heidegger, acted as a catalyst for the development of Karl Rahner. Max Scheler (1874–1928) was associated with phenomenology – though he eventually renounced his Catholicism – as was Edith Stein (1891–1942), who was to die in Auschwitz as a Carmelite nun; the movement's characteristic emphasis on the human person has had an influence on the writings, and even the official declarations, of Pope John Paul II, who as a young priest had chosen Scheler as his subject for an academic dissertation.

Rahner was the most famous exponent of a school of thought known as 'transcendental Thomism'. At the beginning of this movement stood two Jesuits: the Frenchman P. Rousselot (d. 1915) and the Belgian Joseph Maréchal (d. 1944), whose *Le point de départ de la métaphysique* (1922–6) was an attempt to show that the consequence of the Kantian transcendental critique was not the impossibility of knowledge of objective realities, as Kant himself maintained, but the awareness of an objectively existing God at the heart of human experience. Combining this theory with the epistemology of Thomas Aquinas, Rahner attempted to show that God was the horizon towards which all human striving moved. This horizon is first perceived indirectly without verbal or conceptual formulation, and is the necessary precondition of all activity of the intellect and the will. Consequently unbelievers who affirm values of truth and goodness are, without realising it, affirming the existence of God and of Jesus Christ who is the embodiment of those values; accordingly they can be described as 'anonymous Christians'. This positive evaluation of non-believers involves a radical reinterpretation of the principle accepted since the time of St Cyprian in the third century that 'outside the church there is no salvation'. Vatican II appeared to confirm the main drift of this theory of Rahner's when it stated that the church is 'the universal sacrament of salvation', and that salvation is open to those who 'through no fault of their own have not yet attained to the express recognition of God yet who strive, not without grace, to lead an upright life' (Decree on Church, nn. 48, 16). Rahner applied his principles to a variety of theological questions in a large number of articles which were collected in his multi-volume work *Theological Investigations* ([1954–] 1961–). B. Lonergan in his work *Insight* of 1957 put forward a different form of transcendental Thomism which owed no debt to existentialism; in the light of this he set out in his work *Method in Theology* of 1972 a programme systematizing the methods and subject matter of the whole theological enterprise.

Systematic theology
The twentieth century has seen a new proliferation of works of systematic theology

which have broken free from the constraints of the manuals and the traditional scholastic treatises. P. Schoonenberg, E. Schillebeeckx and H. Küng are among the most influential writers in this field. Schoonenberg has written in Dutch on a wide range of dogmatic subjects, but the majority of his work remains untranslated into English; best known to English-speaking readers is his work on original sin. Schillebeeckx's writings by contrast are well known outside his own country. After a number of works on sacramental theology and the Virgin Mary, he turned his attention to Christology with two volumes, *Jesus* of 1975 and *Christ* of 1977. He made also a radical reassessment of ordained ministry in his book *The Church with a Human Face* (1985). The range of Küng's work includes *Justification* (1957, trans. 1964), an irenic dialogue with Barth's thought; works of apologetic and fundamental theology, such as *Does God Exist?* (1978, trans. 1980); and a number of ecclesiological works, some of them, such as *Infallible?* (1970, trans. 1971), radical criticisms of traditional Roman Catholic positions. They led to the loss of his canonical status as a professor of Catholic theology, so that he turned his attention to the study of non Christian religions. The only systematic theologian to show an originality to match that of Rahner has been Hans Urs von Balthasar, whose monumental trilogy *Herrlichkeit* of 1961–9, *Theodramatik* of 1973–83 and *Theologik* of 1985 seems likely to have a growing influence in years to come. The hidden God, he believed, is to be known not so much through categories derived from philosophy as through symbols which unfold God's nature through their beauty and dramatic power as well as their truth; hence the subtitle of *Herrlichkeit*, 'A Theological Aesthetics'. An interpreter of the thought of Karl Barth, he produced his own version of a theology of the cross.

The church and its doctrines

Both before and after the Council much attention has been paid to the theology of the church. In the aftermath of Vatican I, theological reflection on the nature of the church tended to concentrate on its visible organization, especially the papacy and the magisterium, or office of teaching. Pius XII's encyclical *Mystici Corporis* (1943) considered the church as the body of Christ, identifying it with the Roman Catholic church in communion with the pope. However the historical researches of scholars such as Congar and the impetus of ecumenism led to the recognition that papal primacy and infallibility were exercised in cooperation with the bishops and within the instinct of faith and the shared responsibility of the whole church. At the same time there have appeared a series of investigations by O. Semmelroth, K. Rahner and E. Schillebeeckx of the sacramental nature of the church. (See also ECCLESIOLOGY.)

The extreme Marian piety of writers like St Grignion de Montfort (1673–1716), which would ascribe to the Blessed Virgin an autonomous position in the distribution of the grace won by her Son, gave place in the Council to an ecclesially based theology of Mary, which sees her as the model of discipleship and of the church. For this reason the bishops at Vatican II rejected the proposal that a document should be devoted exclusively to Mary, and instead treated of her in the course of the document on the church. At the same time, however, great attention has been paid to a succession of apparitions of the Blessed Virgin, from Lourdes in the nineteenth century to Medjugorje in the late twentieth, generally to young people, and with a recurrent message calling the church to prayer and penance; some of the places of the appearances have become popular centres of pilgrimage. Pope John Paul II's own devotion to the Blessed Virgin has given a strong confirmation to the Marian movement.

Much creative work has also been done on the central doctrines. K. Rahner represented the persons of the Trinity as three modes of being rather than a society of three distinct personalities. Though the three persons exercise a single, undivided operation in the world, the mutual relations of their inner life are reflected in the contribution of each to the common causality. 'The economic Trinity is the immanent trinity.' Rahner's Christology is also distinctive, and follows from his ontology: in Jesus Christ the dynamism towards God in human nature reaches its fullest expression, as does God's creative movement towards his creatures (see CHRISTOLOGY).

An article which Rahner wrote for the fifteenth centenary of the Council of Chalcedon has been identified as a turning point in

Roman Catholic Christology. According to Rahner the Council's dogma that Christ possessed both divine and human nature in one person did not rule out further investigation, indeed was a basis for it. A. Grillmeier took up this challenge in his studies of the early history of the doctrine; H. Urs von Balthasar and W. Kasper are among the many who have sought to cast light on its meaning. Much interest has been shown in Christ's psychology, especially on the question whether his human mind had access to the self-awareness and the infinite knowledge of the divine mind. Rahner, Lonergan and J. Galot are among those who have tried to answer this question, as was J. Maritain before them.

Moral theology

In the post-conciliar period a revolution took place in the study of moral theology, though again it must be said that the decisive ideas had emerged before the Council. The study of the subject in the seminaries had formerly been regarded primarily as a training of priests for the hearing of confession; instruction took place largely by means of the analysis of hypothetical 'cases of conscience', for the solution of which great reliance was placed on the opinions of approved authorities. In the place of this traditional method emphasis shifted to the consideration of the biblical and doctrinal principles in the light of which particular cases were to be judged. According to G. Gilleman and B. Häring all morality was derived from the two great evangelical commandments to love God and love one's neighbour.

Traditionally moral theology presupposed a doctrine of immutable NATURAL LAW, so that a distinction was drawn between moral principles which are true in so far as they are in accordance with rational human nature, and moral obligations which derive from the positive law of the church. Much reliance was placed on the principle of double effect, according to which a good end may never be sought by evil means, though unintended evil consequences may sometimes be tolerated in pursuit of a greater good. A new understanding of morality now sprang up which went by the name of 'consequentialism' or 'proportionalism'; exponents of this view such as C. Curran and the Jesuits J. Fuchs and R.A. McCormick main-

tained that the morality of an action was determined not by moral absolutes but by the balance of consequences. The most articulate opposition to this new moral theology has come from a group of English-speaking laymen among whom are G. Grisez, J. Finnis, W. May and J. Boyle.

Another innovation in modern moral theology has been the interpretation, proposed by L. Monden and others, of mortal sin in terms of a 'fundamental option' away from God, made with complete clarity and personal commitment, in contrast with the fundamental option for God which is the habitual free orientation of the person in a state of grace.

At the same time much study has been devoted to the doctrine of original sin. P. Schoonenberg and, once more, Rahner have been in the forefront of the discussion. For them there is no need for Christians to try to defend the scientifically indefensible theory that the whole human race descended from a single couple, nor the morally indefensible theory that because of the sin of this couple their descendants incurred an inherited moral guilt. Original sin, it is suggested, is a social reality, a sinful situation and an absence of grace into which all human beings are born; it conflicts with the image of God impressed on their nature and the supernatural destiny for which they were created. At the same time other writers have investigated the connection between the doctrine of sin and the experience of guilt.

The issue which has done most to make Roman Catholics, not least the laity, re-examine traditional moral teaching has been that of marriage and SEXUAL ETHICS, especially contraception. The pre-1983 Code of Canon Law declared that the primary end of marriage was the procreation and education of children, while the secondary end was the mutual help of the partners and a 'remedy for concupiscence'. Following this tradition, Pius XI in his encyclical *Casti Connubii* (1930) declared that to prevent the conjugal act attaining its natural result is an unnatural act which is 'intrinisically immoral'. However a feeling was growing within the church that contraception, especially by means of 'the pill', could in certain circumstances be justified because the marriage act would still be able to fulfil its function as an expression of love between the partners. The majority of a commission which Paul VI set up to study the question favoured permitting contraception under certain conditions. The Pope, however, concurring with the judgement of the minority, in his encyclical *Humanae Vitae* (1968) declared that, since the unitive and procreative ends of marriage must not be separated, every use of the marriage act must be open to the transmission of human life. Many devout Roman Catholic couples judged themselves entitled to follow their own consciences in rejecting this teaching, either on principle or in its application to their particular circumstances. The result has been that the authority of the church's magisterium has been reduced in the eyes of many, while, probably because of this issue, the number of people making use of sacramental confession has seriously declined in many countries. (See also ETHICS.)

Political theology
In the twentieth century there has been much interest in political theology. In France and Belgium Action Française under the leadership of C. Maurras attracted many Roman Catholics with its combination of royalism and religious conservatism; though condemned by Rome in 1914 and 1926, it continued in existence until the defeat of Germany in the Second World War. Charles Péguy (1873–1914) on the other hand appealed to medieval history in his advocacy of a form of CHRISTIAN SOCIALISM. The work of C. Dawson, who showed that religion merited consideration as a factor in the development of nations, was influential in English-speaking countries in the 1930s. In Italy G. Gentile (1875–1944), an associate of B. Croce, applied his idealist philosophy to political and educational theory, and found it provided an intellectual foundation for fascism; he served as a minister in one of Mussolini's early administrations. The American John Courtney Murray was the architect of the Declaration on Religious Liberty of Vatican II. Since the Council J.B. Metz has propounded a political theology understood as a critical reflection on society in the light of Jesus' eschatological message.

Towards the end of the twentieth century the most influential form of political theology has been the LIBERATION THEOLOGY promoted by G. Gutiérrez, L. Boff, J. Sobrino and others in Latin America. Many of their insights were endorsed by the bishops of the subcontinent at Medellín (1968) and Peubla (1979). According to this school of thought God's saving activity includes liberation from social and economic oppression, so that the church is obliged to help the underprivileged not only by succouring them in their needs but by political action to correct the unjust social structures. Much use is made of the Exodus from Egypt, in which God's saving work included the freeing of the Israelites from slavery as well as the spiritual benefits involved in the Covenant. The Magnificat is quoted to show that God is on the side of the poor; the church too must make a 'preferential option for the poor'. Pastorally, parishes are often divided into small 'base communities' in which Scripture is studied and applied to local social needs. The Vatican Congregation for the Doctrine of the Faith issued two Instructions on the subject in 1984 and 1986 which, while criticizing certain 'dangers', such as the use of Marxist concepts (especially that of class struggle), the willingness to advocate the use of violent means, and what the Vatican saw as a reductionist interpretation of Scripture and the central dogmas of the church, propounded its own understanding of liberation and reaffirmed the church's commitment to the poor. Liberation theologians insist that their theology grew out of the needs of their own subcontinent, and cannot be transplanted into other regions; each area must reflect on its own needs and produce a theology to meet them. A theology of liberation designed for Asian lands where Christians are in a minority has been worked out by A. Pieris.

The feminist movement
Roman Catholics (or former members of that church), such as Mary Daly, Rosemary Radford Ruether and Elizabeth Schüssler Fiorenza, have played a prominent part in the feminist movement, which aims to correct what is seen as a 'patriarchal' tradition in society (see FEMINIST THEOLOGY). This has contributed to a new concern to identify the psychological differences between the sexes and to reassess the gender roles in society. In English-speaking countries, especially the USA, considerable efforts have been made for the use of

'inclusive' language in worship and biblical translations with regard both to human beings and to God. (It seems likely that the structural peculiarities of the English language have influenced this movement.) There has been a mounting pressure for the ordination of women, with the American church again to the fore. In 1976 the Vatican Congregation for the Doctrine of the Faith in a document entitled *Inter Insigniores* set out its reasons for judging that the Roman Catholic church 'in fidelity to the example of the Lord, does not consider herself authorized to admit women to priestly ordination.' In 1988 Pope John Paul II devoted an encyclical *Mulieris Dignitatem* to the role of women in the church and society, in the course of which he confirmed the CDF's judgement.

Other develpments

The post-conciliar period has seen the church recognizing increasingly the need to adapt to a pluralistic society. In traditionally Catholic countries like Ireland there has been mounting pressure on the church to refrain from opposing legislation, for example on divorce, which is contrary to Roman Catholic ethics but in accordance with the moral values of wider society and increasingly advocated by more liberal Catholics; in Italy the church's opposition did not prevent the legalization of divorce. On the other hand, where Catholicism is a minority religion, its adherents have been gradually discarding what has been called their 'ghetto mentality' and become more aware of the moral leadership they can exercise in public life. In such regions serious efforts have been devoted to ecumenism with separated Christians and the 'wider ecumenism' with non-Christian faiths. The former challenge has been most keenly felt, but perhaps too timidly met, in Northern Ireland, where religious differences have led to economic oppression of the Catholic minority and to sectarian violence.

Throughout this period Roman Catholics have been prominent in scientific research. Besides Teilhard de Chardin one can cite R.G. Boscovich (1711–1787) of Dubrovnik, whose study of atomic physics and astronomy continued a long Jesuit tradition of scientific work, the Augustinian geneticist of Brno G.J. Mendel (1822–1884), L. Pasteur (1822–1895) and M. Curie (1867–1934). Roman Catholics were not among the pioneers of psychology, though recently members of the church like A. Godin and K. O'Connor have produced significant work in the psychology of religion. Some of the most significant Roman Catholic thought has been expressed in the form of novels, such as those of François Mauriac, Graham Greene, Georges Bernanos, Henri Daniel-Rops and Flannery O'Connor and the fantasies of J.R.R. Tolkien; in plays, such as those of Paul Claudel; in architecture, such as the Gothic revival churches of A.W.N. Pugin (1812–1852); in art, such as the work of G. Rouault (1887–1958), Eric Gill and David Jones; in poems, such as those of R.M. Rilke (1875–1926), G.M. Hopkins and Francis Thompson and *The Dream of Gerontius* by J.H. Newman; and even in the music of composers such as F. Poulenc, O. Messiaen, and – as Karl Barth would say, supremely – W.A. Mozart.

See also Authority; Romanticism.

Bibliography

Bugnini, A. [1983] 1990: *The Reform of the Liturgy 1948–1975*, trans. M.J. O'Connell. Collegeville: Liturgical Press.

Burtchaell, J.T. 1969: *Catholic Theories of Biblical Inspiration since 1810*. Cambridge: Cambridge University Press.

Carlen, C. 1990: *The Papal Encyclicals 1740–1981*, 5 vols. Ann Arbor: Pierian Press.

Copleston, F.C. 1946–75: *A History of Philosophy*, 9 vols. London: Burns, Oates and Washbourne/ Search Press.

Daly, G. 1980: *Transcendence and Immanence: A Study in Catholic Modernism and Integralism*. Oxford: Clarendon Press.

Dawson, C. 1929: *Progress and Religion: An Historical Enquiry*. London and New York: Longmans.

Dorr, D. 1985: *Option for the Poor: One Hundred Years of Catholic Social Teaching*. Maryknoll, NY: Orbis.

Durrwell, F.X. [1950] 1960: *The Resurrection*, trans. R. Sheed. London: Sheed and Ward.

Ellis, J.T. 1965: *American Catholicism*. New York: Image Books.

Fink, P.E., ed. 1990: *A New Dictionary of Sacramental Worship*. Collegeville: Liturgical Press.

Gilleman, G. 1952: *Le primat de la charité en théologie morale*. Paris: Desclée de Brouwer.

Grisez, G. 1983: *The Way of the Lord Jesus*, vol. 1: *Christian Moral Principles*. Chicago: Franciscan Herald Press.

Häring, B. [1954] 1963–7: *The Law of Christ*, trans.

E.G. Kaiser. Cork: Mercier Press.

Jedin, H., ed. [1962–] 1965– : *Handbook of Church History*, trans. and ed. H. Jedin and J.P. Dolan. London: Burns and Oates.

Lubac, H. de [1938] 1950: *Catholicism*, trans. L.C. Sheppard. London: Burns, Oates and Washbourne.

Lubac, H. de 1946: *Surnaturel*. Paris: Aubier.

McCormick, R.A. 1989: Moral theology 1940–1989: an overview, *Theological Studies* 50, pp. 3–24.

Maréchal, J. 1922–6: *Le point de départ de la métaphysique*. Paris: Alcan.

Merton, T. 1948: *The Seven Storey Mountain*. New York: Harcourt and Brace.

Monden, L. [1965] 1966: *Sin, Liberty and Law*, trans. J. Donceel. London: G. Chapman.

Rahner, K. [1954–] 1961– : *Theological Investigations*, trans. C. Ernst *et al*. London: Darton, Longman and Todd; Baltimore: Helicon; New York: Seabury.

Rahner, K. 1967: Der dreifaltige Gott . . . In *Mysterium Salutis*, ed. J. Feiner and M. Löhrer. Einsiedeln: Benziger, vol. 2, pp. 317–401. Trans. J. Donceel, 1970: *The Trinity*. London: Burns and Oates.

Rousselot, P. [1908] 1935: *The Intellectualism of St Thomas Aquinas*, trans. J.E. O'Mahony. London: Sheed and Ward.

Schillebeeckx, E. 1985: *The Church with a Human Face: A New and Expanded Theology of Ministry*, trans. J. Bowden. London: SCM Press.

Schoonenberg, P. [1962] 1965: *Man and Sin*, trans. J. Donceel. London: Sheed and Ward.

Uleyn, A. [1966] 1969: *The Recognition of Guilt*, trans. M. Ilford. Dublin: Gill and Macmillan.

Vorgrimler, H. 1967–9: *The Second Vatican Council*, 5 vols, trans. L. Adolphus *et al*. London: Burns and Oates; New York: Herder and Herder.

EDWARD YARNOLD

romanticism Although this term may be used in the broad sense of a certain attitude of mind not confined to any one age or cultural tradition, it usually refers to a movement or tendency of thought and sensibility which characterized European literature, art and philosophy during the first half of the nineteenth century. It was to some extent anticipated by intellectual developments back in the eighteenth century (such as in the writings of J.J. Rousseau), but the movement as a whole acquired its identifying features – diverse indeed as these were – in reaction to the ideals of the ENLIGHTENMENT, against which, in some important respects, it sharply protested. But although romanticism may be seen on a number of counts as the negation of classicism it is conspicuous for what it affirmed rather than for anything it may have been concerned to deny. For the period in question, in its manifold achievements, must be reckoned as one of the most remarkably creative in modern European history.

The romantic movement

What, then, were its overall aims, and wherein did its unity lie? One has only to pose these questions to perceive a basic problem. For although the movement's objectives can be specified fairly easily, their consistency has been doubted. Thus an erudite and discerning critic, A.O. Lovejoy ([1924] 1948), could descry only 'a plurality of romanticisms', without unitary perspective. It is a view, however, which must be challenged. Romanticism may be impossible to define in a few words, but its expression is not difficult to identify. The romantic spirit, whether in letters, or in the arts (music especially), or in philosophy, or even in religion, is almost immediately recognizable when met with. Lovejoy himself, however, later (in 1960) declared that romanticism 'more than any other one (*sic*) thing has distinguished, both for better or worse, the prevailing assumptions of the mind of the nineteenth century'. For what, fundamentally, we encounter in romanticism is a temper or disposition of thought which colours all it touches. Even where the romantic viewpoint may seem at odds with itself unity is evinced in an underlying mood or pervasive ethos.

To understand the movement's aims and positive achievements its polemical attitude towards the standards of the Enlightenment has to be appreciated. Primarily, it set itself, in J.S. Mill's words, 'against the narrowness of the eighteenth century'. It deplored the latter's merely critical and analytical concept of reason as opposed to its own, which by contrast it saw as intuitive and synthetic. Although its stress was upon the particular or individual more than the universal or general, it held that truth is to be discovered in the apprehension of the whole rather than in abstraction of the parts. Or if it did fasten on the part, the detail, it was for the meaning which this embodied as symbolical of the whole. Thus the finite becomes the vehicle of the infinite. As William Blake put it: 'To see the world in a grain of Sand,/And a heaven in a Wild Flower,/Hold Infinity in the palm of your hand,/And Eternity in an hour.' Alike in romantic art and romantic philosophy there is a persistent conviction that the finite is not self-explanatory and self-justifying, but relates necessarily to an infinite 'beyond' as at once its ground and informing purpose. So August Wilhelm Schlegel (1767–1853), when distinguishing romantic art from classical, found that whereas the latter was doubtless 'simpler, cleaner, more like nature in the independent perfection of its works', the former, despite its fragmentary presentation, was somehow 'nearer to the mystery of the universe'.

But although the romantics turned against the 'mechanistic philosophy' of the Newtonian physics and deprecated what Thomas Carlyle called 'a half-world distorted into looking like a whole' – he had the French *encyclopédistes* in mind – they did in fact accept, tacitly if not always explicitly, much of the Enlightenment way of thinking. For while abjuring its abstractly critical procedures, the romantics by no means rejected the scientific method as such. Knowledge of the phenomenal world, once gained, could not be dismissed or ignored. Nevertheless science needed to be framed by wisdom, or what Samuel Taylor Coleridge (1772–1834) described as 'the knowledge of the laws of the whole considered as one'. The task facing the new age was to create a new *style* in philosophy, in accordance with a more transcendental view of reason itself as 'the source and substance of truths above sense'.

This account of reason as intuitive and creative is closely linked in romantic thought with the idea of nature. Man and nature are not dualistically contrasted, as in CARTESIANISM. The natural world is to be conceived not as a mechanical construct but as a living organism embodying a 'spirit' with which man communes through his reason as 'the organ of the supersensuous'. William Wordsworth (1770–1850) in *The Prelude* (1805 version) – that prime textbook of romantic nature-mysticism – relates how when he was a boy 'every natural form, rock, fruit or flower' – nay, even the 'loose stones' on the highway – assumed for him 'a moral life': ' . . . the great mass/Lay bedded in the quickening soul, and all/That I

beheld, respired with meaning.' It is this feeling for the oneness of man and nature that gives to much romantic philosophy its anthropomorphic slant, which in the metaphysical systems of the great German idealists receives powerful, if at times – as in F.W.J. von Schelling (1775–1854) – all too darkling expression. As they see it, finitude in nature and in human existence becomes, when properly understood, a manifestation of the one infinite Life. F.D.E. Schleiermacher (1768–1834), in his early *Reden über die Religion* of 1799, will have nothing of a duality of worlds, the natural and the supernatural, the here and the hereafter, the realm of man and the realm of God. The divine is not, as in Enlightenment thinking, an *inference* from the being and order of phenomena. It is reality as apprehended in its totality, as 'the Universal', 'the One and the Whole', 'the Divine life and action of the All'. Accordingly religion for Schleiermacher is, in much-quoted words of his, 'to have sense and taste for the Infinite, to be in the bosom of the Universe and feel its boundless life and creative power within your own'. The note of pantheism here is evident, though not all the romantics, even those who were not orthodox Christians, found God in nature quite so readily. The poet Alfred de Vigny did not; its cold indifference to suffering appalled him. Nor, in fact, did that eccentric religionist William Blake; nor did Lord Byron, whose intellectual outlook remained that of the Augustans. But in the main the romantics knew no frontiers between the natural and the supernatural: Carlyle's 'natural supernaturalism' aptly designates their view. The natural was to be raised to the supernatural, the spiritual made visible. Essentially the same insight would seem to be communicated in the paintings of D.C. Friedrich.

It is sometimes said that the romantic movement was intrinsically German, even though it had strong repercussions elsewhere, especially in France. The truth or otherwise of this claim cannot be argued here. But the iteration of the mere names of J.G. Herder, J.W. Goethe (in his earlier phase at least) and Friedrich Schiller, of J.G. Fichte and Friedrich Schelling, of Novalis, Friedrich Hölderlin and the Schlegels (Friedrich in particular), of Heinrich von Kleist and Ludwig Tieck and Wilhelm Wackenroder – not to mention the efflorescence of romanticism in music – is enough to testify to the vitality of the movement in the German-speaking world. But in France during the same period we have F.-R. de Chateaubriand, Mme de Staël, Benjamin Constant, Alphonse de Lamartine and Alfred de Musset, albeit that the 'official' commencement of the movement is wont to be dated from 1830, with Victor Hugo as at once its herald and leading exemplar. In England romanticism is of course associated with Wordsworth and Coleridge (both as poet and thinker), Byron – the archetypal romantic, as a man if not always distinctively so as a writer – Percy Bysshe Shelley and John Keats, even though Shelley's own outlook preserved many of the traits and prejudices of the Enlightenment. In Italy Giacomo Leopardi was unquestionably a romantic, as was Nikolaus Lenau in Austria, José de Espronceda in Spain, Adam Mickiewicz in Poland and Mikhail Lermontov in Russia. As regards religion some were freethinkers; others were Catholics born or, like Friedrich Schlegel, converted. The Protestant Schleiermacher was the movement's theologian *par excellence*.

German speculative philosophy

The romanticist idea of the unity of finite and infinite – that the infinite is the *totum* of the finite – is bound to raise the question of connections between the romantic movement and German metaphysical idealism. To describe the latter simply as the philosophy of romanticism, as has sometimes been done, would be exaggerative and misleading. In the first place, metaphysical idealism was not merely a product of romanticist intellectualism; on the contrary, speculative thought of this type, particularly as elaborated in the systems of Fichte and Schelling – behind which of course is that of Immanuel Kant (see KANTIANISM) – was itself a potent influence on the romantics. Coleridge's philosophical musings, for example, contain a large admixture of Schelling. Secondly, the philosophers reflected romanticist attitudes only in varying degree. The affinity is clearest with Schelling, most notably in his early *Naturphilosophie* of 1799. Nature he here calls *das werdende Ich* – the Ego in the making – since in nature the implicitly spiritual strives towards ever fuller self-awareness. In J.G. Fichte (1762–1814), who began as an ardent disciple of Kant,

an almost aggressively ethical concern is at first present; but in his later thought it is the notion rather of the one infinite divine Life that is uppermost, and with it his preoccupation becomes increasingly religious. With G.W.F. Hegel (1770–1831), however, the concept of Reason, the Idea, is all-dominant. His assertion that the real is the rational and the rational the real may be taken as the motto of his entire system. Moreover, he derided what he saw as the excesses of romantic sentiment and spoke slightingly in this regard of Schleiermacher, then his eminent colleague at Berlin. Yet Hegel also had his romanticist leanings, evident in his philosophy of history, probably the most significant and durable part of his teaching. Even his use of the word Reason (*Vernunft*) carries romanticist overtones.

Schelling's critique of Fichte centres on what he took to be the latter's inadequate view of nature. For nature is not merely the non-ego; it is wholly independent of the finite self and exists in its own right, so that a true philosophy of mind will include nature itself in an intelligible scheme, demonstrating its essential oneness with personal consciousness, which is the *telos* of the universal process. The drift of Schelling's earlier philosophy is therefore pantheistic. However, in his later work, produced only after many years of torpid inactivity – thus disappointing the brilliant promise of his youth – he outlines a philosophy which he describes as 'positive', distinguishing it from the 'negative' theorizing which preceded it. Indeed he goes on to affirm the personal being of God and the fallenness of man, to the point where he approaches orthodox Christianity. The notion of a Fichtean 'moral order' or a Hegelian 'Absolute Idea' will not, he contends, meet the needs of a troubled soul.

The religious concern of all the idealist philosophers is apparent, and Friedrich Nietzsche's snide comment that they were in fact concealed theologians is not without truth. But a quest of the ultimate springs of religious commitment was an important aspect of romanticist thought generally. The Enlightenment criticism had at one level been effective; before it the old orthodoxy was in retreat. But at another level it was superficial. Religious faith had a deeper foundation than the specious logic of 'arguments' and 'evidences' (see EXISTENCE OF GOD, PROOFS OF); its true cognitive media were feeling and intuition. And if religious belief were necessary for the fullest development of man's spiritual potential, it had to be reconstructed in a manner distancing it from the rational theology which Kant had virtually destroyed. Schleiermacher's *Reden* mark a new era in religious thought. True religion, he declared, 'is an affection, a revelation of the Infinite in the finite.' It is 'to live in the endless nature of the Whole', 'to perceive and divine with quiet reverence' the place assigned to each and all. In Schleiermacher romanticism, idealism and Christian belief converge. His later work, *Der christliche Glaube* (*The Christian Faith*, 1821–2; second edition 1830–1) develops a 'subjective' or experiential theology appropriate, in his view, to the intellectual needs of the time.

The sense of history
Although idealism may then represent a facet (the 'holistic') of the romantic movement, romanticist imagination for the most part inclined to the particular rather than the general, to history rather than abstract thought. In fact nineteenth-century historicism may be said to have had its beginnings in the romanticist sense of the historical past, as so vividly portrayed in, for example, the novels of Sir Walter Scott, by whom Alessandro Manzoni, Alfred de Vigny, Victor Hugo and even Honoré de Balzac were all influenced. The romantics' concern for the historical was something new. The Enlightenment, although it had its eminent historians in such as David Hume and Edward Gibbon, did not greatly appreciate it. Past ages, except for the classical, were redolent of ignorance and superstition. But for the romantic mind the infinite was present not only in every finite entity but in each successive epoch, indeed in every passing moment of time. Hence no age was without its intrinsic significance and typical excellence. Like life itself, man's civilization was felt to be organically continuous. No single phase of the historical process was to be repudiated or disvalued, since the process *as a whole* carries meaning. The genesis of a thing is as essential to an understanding of it as is its final state – a perception heavily underscored by Hegel. 'Is time, then, not ordered as Space is?' asked J.G.

Herder, whose *Ideen zur Philosophie der Geschichte der Menschheit* of 1784–91 places him among the pre-romantics. History was not mere contingency and succession but a sequence of events open to philosophical comprehension. The historical, as the romantics saw it, is all-important for the present life of man and must be taken with all due seriousness, an attitude which goes far to explain how the nineteenth century – and such names as those of Barthold Niebuhr, Leopold von Ranke, Julius Wellhausen and Theodor Mommsen testify to it – gave birth to historiography as a science (cf. E. Cassirer, *The Problem of Knowledge*).

However it was not, at the outset, scientific history which caught the romantics' interest but traditional. Following the destructive violence of the French Revolution a mood of nostalgia for the remoter past invaded the European mind. Tradition now called for respect and even veneration, not derision. For tradition is a vehicle of continuity, an ark of permanence in the flux of time. The medieval world particularly fascinated because of its distance and strangeness. Also it was signally Christian. The very things which eighteenth-century rationalism found repellent captivated romanticist sensibility; not only the picturesqueness of the Catholic middle ages, memorialized in the splendour of the Gothic, appealed to them, but faith, dogmatic religion, hierarchy, unalterable divine law likewise. In the words of Novalis: 'Those were beautiful, brilliant times, when Europe was a Christian country, and a simple Christian faith dwelt in this humanized region of the world.'

Romanticism and Catholic revival
A portent of this changing attitude was the appearance in 1802 of *Le Génie du Christianisme* by F.-R. de Chateaubriand (1768–1848). Its publication coincided with the conclusion by Napoleon Bonaparte, as First Consul, of the Concordat with the Vatican which restored Catholicism as the acknowledged religion of the French people. The book's reception surpassed its author's best hopes. It was sharply criticized as well as warmly praised, but it was everywhere discussed. Intended as apologetic, a vindication of the historic role of Christianity in European civilization, it extolled the Catholic religion as 'the most human, the most favourable to liberty,

to the arts and sciences, of all the religions that have ever existed'. The work's patent defect was that it made practically no use of logical argument. With all the resources of an elegant rhetoric Chateaubriand aimed only at the heart and the imagination. Subtitled 'The Beauties of the Christian Religion', the book dealt only very cursorily with 'Dogmas and Doctrine', a field in which its author had no competence and probably little interest. But if as a serious defence of Christianity his undertaking was without weight, his true purpose – wherein he succeeded – was to create a new cultural atmosphere in which the sense of mystery could again breathe. More, it made traditional faith and piety intellectually fashionable, as Chateaubriand himself noted, with permissible satisfaction.

Of greater substance philosophically was the *Essai sur l'indifférence en matière de religion* of Chateaubriand's fellow Breton, the priest H.-F. de Lamennais (1782–1854), which came out in 1817 after the Bourbon restoration. Here again is an elaborate apology for Catholicism, but one with a fresh approach to the apologetic problem. The traditional method, relying on the 'evidences' of miracle and prophecy, is, Lamennais feels, no longer serviceable. The apologist's first task is to gain the reader's sympathies, which is best done by showing that faith is natural to man. Rationalism fails to take this into account, and its procedures lead, in fact, only to doubt and scepticism. But by what general principle, if not rational persuasion, is belief to be determined? The only possible answer is *authority*, based ultimately on the 'common consent' (*sensus communis*) of mankind. The individual judgement is weak in isolation, but certainty can be built on common experience as such. Hence truth is likely to be found where authority is clearest and most assured, that is, in the Catholic church, and more particularly in the voice of the papacy; Lamennais was indeed among the first exponents of nineteenth-century ultramontanism. But his hopes that the papacy would ally itself with the democratic movement in politics were dashed when the 'liberal Catholic' movement in France, of which he was himself the acknowledged leader, was condemned by Pope Gregory XVI in 1832. Thereafter his ardour for Catholicism cooled, whilst his faith in democ-

racy grew. His revolutionary *Paroles d'un croyant*, published in 1834, brought his ecclesiastical career to an end, and with it also his profession as a Catholic. By the time of his death he had become a deist.

If Chateaubriand's defence of Christianity was overtly aesthetic, his underlying motivation was social: Catholicism should be promoted as the 'ideology' (as we now would say) of a reconstituted society. With Lamennais this social interest is explicit; religion, he holds, is not simply a matter of personal sentiment. Protestantism he scorned. Yet his ideological gods – even democracy – seemed in the end to fail him. At heart he was a romantic individualist.

Apart from the Protestant Schleiermacher, romanticism in Germany had notable representatives in the Catholic faculty at Tübingen university, in the persons of Johann Sebastian Drey (1777–1853) and Johann Adam Möhler (1796–1838), both of whom were influenced by Schelling, as both also favoured the genetic method in theology. Möhler is best remembered for his *Symbolik* of 1832, in which he views the church in historical perspective as essentially the embodiment of a living and therefore *developing* tradition. In England the one theological thinker associated with romanticist attitudes was Coleridge, whom J.S. Mill characterized as 'one of the two great seminal minds of England' of his age; the other being Jeremy Bentham, Coleridge's antithesis. The former's *Aids to Reflection* of 1825 made little public impact at the time, but it had very considerable influence on subsequent Anglican teaching. The apprehension of truth in religion, Coleridge believed, could not be independent of the will. Faith is rooted in man's *moral* experience and mere ratiocination has little or nothing to do with it, spiritual need being the soil whence it springs. At certain points there is an evident resemblance between Coleridge's views and those of J.H. Newman (1801–1890), but to see in Tractarianism a further expression of romanticist feeling is only questionably justifiable. (See ANGLICANISM; PROTESTANT THEOLOGY: BRITAIN).

It is apparent, then, that during the period under review philosophy, theology, history and political theorizing were all areas of intellectual endeavour in which romanticist energizing is detectable. But is this Protean movement – for after even a brief survey of its numerous manifestations one is bound to revert to the problem raised at the outset – sufficiently homogeneous to disclose an essential unity and consistency? The query, as has already been indicated, is not easy to answer conclusively. Lovejoy's response was, as we have seen, negative. But other commentators have tended not to agree with him (cf. R. Wellek, 'The Concept of Romanticism', in *Concepts of Criticism* (1963)). For there would seem to have been a distinctively romanticist 'psychology', or mental stance, conferring upon the multiform cultural achievements of the age a recognizable similarity of tone. One might venture to identify it with an intensified sense of *individuality*, meaning thereby not the bare truism that individuals, each and all, have their own particular being, but that reality, the world of the non-ego, is always in some respect and measure a reproduction of the ego itself, and that dogmatic 'fixities' and 'certainties', in Carlylean language, must be discounted in favour of the relativist standpoint of personal interest and experience. As Friedrich Schlegel put it: 'It is precisely individuality that is the original and eternal thing in man.' Truth itself cannot in the final resort be detached from the individual's subjectivity. Schleiermacher perceives this well enough at the level of moral insight. 'There dawned upon me', he writes in the *Soliloquies* of 1802, 'what is now my highest intuition. I saw clearly that each man is meant to represent humanity in his own way, combining its elements uniquely so that it may reveal itself in every mode, and all that can issue from its womb be made actual in the future of unending time.' Søren Kierkegaard (1813–1855), whose own place in the current of nineteenth-century romanticism is hardly to be contested, carries the paradox of subjectivity even farther when he declares in the *Concluding Unscientific Postscript* of 1846 that 'the highest truth attainable for an existing individual' is 'an objective uncertainty held fast . . . in the most passionate inwardness'; except that for Kierkegaard truth, albeit apprehended individually, is supremely a matter not of self-realization but of divine revelation. In romantic thought generally, however, subjectivity is a mode of human cognition. Thus cultural forms are relative to the particularity of human experience and are not to be judged by those 'objective' canons of unity, balance, harmony and completeness to which classicism made insistent appeal.

It is not surprising therefore that the artist, with his presumed higher sensitivity and powers of expression, should have been regarded by the romantics as the type-figure, the true hero, of the age. Promethean, often misunderstood, rebellious, visionary and striving, he is prophet and man of action in one. Aside from the dazzling example of Napoleon Bonaparte, it was a personality like Byron's which could kindle the ardour of a generation. But Byron might also well be seen as himself Childe Harold or Manfred or Cain, fated and tormented by the consciousness of his own fate. So one meets with yet another nuance of the romantic attitude: its melancholy and pessimism, even its yen for the demonic. Of this romantic disenchantment with life, most poignantly expressed by Giacomo Leopardi, the great philosophical exponent was Arthur Schopenhauer (1788–1860), whose *Die Welt als Wille und Vorstellung* of 1819 (second, enlarged edition 1844; third edition, again augmented, 1859), as is now generally admitted, was a tidemark in the thought of its epoch. Here pessimism is metaphysical, in that it appears as the consequence of the energizing or driving force in and behind all phenomena, a force recognizable in human consciousness as insatiable desire, and hence the root of all suffering. But the pessimistic mood or disposition of mind – *Weltschmerz*, *le mal du siècle*, worldly sorrow – could readily become morbid, lending strength to Goethe's well-known dictum that classicism spells health, romanticism disease. However, the romantic thinker did at any rate begin the serious probe of those 'abysmal deeps of personality' which the age of Enlightenment failed to comprehend or even realize existed. In this he anticipated Freud.

Romanticist influence on religious thought may be said to have stemmed ultimately from the romantics' repeated stress upon inwardness as the way to reality. Religious truth is less an objective datum than a subjective state, articulated in terms of a 'theology of consciousness'. The medium of revelation is the ego, with its individual needs, hopes and imaginings: 'We fabricate reality after our own devising' (Ugo Foscolo); 'The world is my idea' (Schopenhauer). The consistent claim of the romantic poets, formulated systematically by the idealist philosophers, was that the problem of objectivity can be resolved only by identifying both subject and object in an all-encompassing unity.

The idealist religious philosophy itself, at least in Germany, proved to have only a limited survival value, soon giving way to a version of Kantian moralism, in the shape of the Ritschlian theology. Nevertheless that subjectivization of religious belief which characterized the romanticist standpoint marked the beginning of a process of immanentizing religious reality, which as the century moved on became increasingly apparent. The idea of transcendence, in the face of the decline of metaphysics, appeared more and more difficult to define in a manner that a less speculative philosophy could accommodate. Eternal life is to be lived in some sort here and now, eternity itself being understood as a dimension of the temporal order, with the essential Christian values grounded in human experience and the historical Jesus hailed as the man in whom all men may discern their own morally idealized reflection. Thus a crop of liberalisms and modernisms, Protestant or Catholic, grew up, all endeavouring to preserve what was of tried experiential value in religion while at the same time conceding the necessity of squaring it with the irreversible advances of modern science. Of these developments romanticism was unquestionably a progenitor.

See also LITERATURE AND THEOLOGY; PHILOSOPHICAL THEOLOGY.

Bibliography

Barzun, J. 1961: *Classic, Romantic and Modern*. London: Secker and Warburg.

Bowra, M. 1949: *The Romantic Imagination*. London: Oxford University Press.

Charlton, D.G., ed. 1984: *The French Romantics*, 2 vols. Cambridge University Press.

Furst, L.R. 1969: *Romanticism in Perspective*. London: Macmillan.

Halsted, J.B., ed. 1969: *Romanticism*. New York: Harper and Row.

Hartmann, N. 1923: *Die Philosophie des deutschen Idealismus*. Berlin: de Gruyter.

Haym, R. [1870] 1960: *Die romantische Schule*. Tübingen: JCB Mohr.

Jasper, D. 1985: *Coleridge as Poet and Religious Thinker*. London: Macmillan.

Lovejoy, A.O. [1924] 1948: The Discrimination of Romanticisms. In *Essays in the History of Ideas*. Baltimore: Johns Hopkins Press.

Moreau, P. 1932: *Le Romantisme*. Paris: de Gigord.

O'Meara, T.F. 1982: *Romantic Idealism and Roman Catholicism: Schelling and the Theologians*. Indiana: Notre Dame.

Prickett, S. 1976: *Romanticism and Religion: The Tradition of Coleridge and Wordsworth in the Victorian Church*. Cambridge: Cambridge University Press.

Reardon, B.M.G. 1977: *Hegel's Philosophy of Religion*. London: Macmillan.

Reardon, B.M.G. 1985: *Religion in the Age of Romanticism*. Cambridge: Cambridge University Press.

Schenk, H.G. 1966: *The Mind of the European Romantics*. London: Oxford University Press.

Talmon, J.L. 1967: *Romanticism and Revolt: Europe 1815–1848*. London: Thames and Hudson.

Taylor, R.J. 1970: *The Romantic Tradition in Germany*. London: Methuen.

Thorlby, A.K., ed. 1966: *The Romantic Movement*. London: Macmillan.

Wellek, R. 1963: *Concepts of Criticism*. Newhaven: Yale University Press.

Willoughby, L.A. [1930] 1966: *The Romantic Movement in Germany*. New York: Harper and Row.

BERNARD M.G. REARDON

Rousseau, Jean Jacques (1712–1778) French political philosopher and essayist. He became a Roman Catholic in 1728, but converted to Calvinism in 1754. He was a member of the circle of Encyclopaedists, which included Voltaire and Denis Diderot; he also wrote several operas and had an extensive knowledge of Italian music, which he utilized in articles for the *Encyclopaedia*. In 1749 Rousseau won an essay prize at the Academy of Dijon with his essay *Discourse on the Arts and Sciences*, arguing that the arts had corrupting effects on humanity. He lived in Montmorency in France, and for several periods in Geneva, before travelling to England to stay with David Hume in 1766. Later that year, believing that he was being persecuted, he returned to France, where he died in 1778. Among his works are *Discours sur l'origine et les fondements de l'inégalité parmi les hommes* (1754), *Emile* (1762), *The Social Contract* (1762) and, posthumously, his *Confessions* (1781).

Rousseau believed (in contrast to Thomas Hobbes) that human individuals in their natural state, as 'noble savages', were good, equal and free. This freedom and equality, he argued, had been corrupted by institutions. This view is reflected particularly in *Emile*, where he argued for a creative and natural education for children which was uncorrupted by society. However, this romantic approach is not evident in *The Social Contract*. Here Rousseau advocates a society where, forgoing individual rights, the citizen subscribes to a social bond aiming at the general good. It is in this book that the watchwords of the French Revolution – Liberty, Equality and Fraternity – are first found. Rousseau's thought was very influential, in particular on the work of Immanuel Kant and G.W.F. Hegel.

Bibliography
Cobban, A. 1934: *Rousseau and the Modern State*. London.
Dobinson, C.H. 1969: *Jean Jacques Rousseau*. London.
Hendel, C.W. 1934: *Jean Jacques Rousseau, Moralist*, 2 vols. London.
Rousseau, J.J. 1990: *The Collected Writings of Rousseau*, vol. 1, ed, and trans. R.D. Marters and C. Kelly. Hanover and London.

Russian Orthodox theology See EASTERN ORTHODOX THEOLOGY.

S

sacramental theology   Sacramental theology deals with both the general nature and specific characteristics of the central liturgical rites of the church traditionally called sacraments. Since the thirteenth century the Roman Catholic church has understood seven such rites as being sacraments in the full sense of the word: baptism, confirmation, Eucharist, holy orders (ordination to ministry), matrimony, penance and anointing of the sick – formerly known as the last anointing or 'extreme unction'. Although the Orthodox have never formally limited themselves to a specific list of sacraments, they would also subscribe to the sacramentality of these rites (Meyendorf, 1983, p. 192). The churches that issue from the sixteenth-century reform generally limit the term 'sacrament' – if it is employed at all – to the two principal Christian rites: baptism and the Lord's Supper (Eucharist).

Sacramental theology seeks to understand what these rites called sacraments have in common: how they find their common origin in Jesus Christ; how the ritual sign of each sacrament functions and communicates the grace it signifies. This branch of theology also endeavours to clarify the individual characteristics of the sacraments and to describe their particular effects on those who celebrate them.

Since the 1960s sacramental theology and worship in most churches have undergone important developments due to the influence of the ecumenical movement and the Second Vatican Council. Because of the new ecclesial atmosphere, the churches have discovered an amazing degree of convergence in their understanding of sacraments. This convergence is well expressed in *Baptism, Eucharist and Ministry*, the so-called *Lima Document* issued by the Faith and Order Commission of the World Council of Churches in 1982.

It is natural that developments in sacramental theology parallel the changing emphases in the other branches of theology, since sacraments express the way believers understand the fundamental relationships between God, Christ, the church, humanity and creation. The cultural shifts experienced by those societies where Christians find themselves have also had a profound effect on the way various churches look at sacraments. This article will trace in broad strokes the evolution of sacramental theology since the challenge the Enlightenment posed to sacramental worship during the eighteenth century.

Sacramental theology during the Enlightenment (1700–1800)
Much of sacramental theology during the eighteenth century was simply a restatement of the polemical positions taken by the various Christian churches at the time of the Reformation and Counter-Reformation in the sixteenth century. For Catholics, the Council of Trent (1545–63) had largely reiterated traditional scholastic teachings regarding the seven sacraments – especially the aspects of that teaching challenged by the Reformers. Among the general affirmations made by the Council regarding the sacraments was that there are seven sacraments of the New Law and that these sacraments were instituted and entrusted to the church by Christ – some in a direct way, others indirectly. Trent also affirmed the teaching advanced by Thomas Aquinas in the thirteenth century, that sacraments are instrumental causes of grace – they are a privileged way in which God chooses to interact with human subjects,

and these rites confer the grace they signify *ex opere operato* (that is, from the 'doing' of the rite). This means that the grace conferred by the sacrament is independent of the minister's spiritual state, because God has promised to act through these sacramental signs entrusted to the church; this is to ensure that God's grace is not frustrated by the evil life of those ordained to administer the sacraments. An individual receives the sacrament 'fruitfully', that is, receives the grace God offers in the sacrament, provided that no obstacle stands in the way of this grace, such as serious sin or lack of faith (*ex opere operantis*).

Because they were able to find unequivocal biblical warrants substantiating Christ's institution of only two sacraments – baptism and Eucharist – the Reformers rejected the other five as mere human inventions. Roman Catholic teachings regarding the sacraments struck the Reformers as both unscriptural and as promoting a kind of mechanical 'works righteousness' that suggests that human beings need to do something in order to manipulate God into saving them. They also accused Catholics of underestimating the role of personal faith and commitment in the fruitful reception of a sacrament.

Since the first Protestant theologians wished to emphasize the personal response in faith to the sovereign action of God in baptism and the Lord's Supper as the most important element in making a sacrament efficacious, outward ceremonial surrounding the administration of the sacraments was simplified in most churches of the Reform. In some churches of the radical Reformation, the importance of moral assent to the truths of the faith over and above exterior ritual expression led some to insist that only people capable of a mature faith could efficaciously receive a sacrament. This logically led certain groups within the radical Reformation to deny the validity of infant baptism and insist on rebaptizing adult converts to their churches (Anabaptists). In other Christian bodies, all outward ceremony was eliminated from worship (Quakers) or severely moderated in a desire to avoid all suggestions of idolatrous manipulation of God (Puritanism) or to emphasize the personal commitment to God's truth over and above outward show (pietism).

It would be a mistake, however, to suppose that the concerns of the Enlightenment had no effect on the way the different churches interpreted and celebrated the sacraments. The intellectual ferment of this period caused a crisis in the way the traditional Christian faith was understood and expressed in the worship of many churches. The newfound emphasis on human reason promoted a loss of confidence in the teachings of revealed religion preached by the churches. No longer did the church have a monopoly in explaining the world. Rather, the nascent sciences – physics, biology, anatomy, astronomy – had largely discredited many of the traditionally held religious and philosophical tenets regarding the place of humanity in the universe as well as the principles of causality. The exploration of the globe by Europeans who came into contact with new cultures, many with their own sophisticated religious beliefs, also tended to relativize the absolute claims to the truth made by Christianity.

This intellectual ferment also extended into the sacred sciences. Exegetes, employing a new historical-critical method, cast doubts upon Christianity's long-cherished claim that the Gospels contained the very words and intentions of Jesus. Church historians, in uncovering evidence that many practices of the various churches thought to date from the time of the apostles had, in fact, developed quite recently, also cast a shadow on the 'immemorial traditions of the church'. The place of sacramental worship was not only challenged by these developments, but thrown into crisis. One historian of the period comments that 'the objective aspect of the crisis would become visible when the historical critical reading of the New Testament and ancient Christian writers laid open to question the traditional accounts of how the church was established and the sacraments instituted. Any supposition of a 'perpetual tradition of the holy fathers' about church and sacraments . . . was in fundamental jeopardy if New Testament scholarship could show that the formulas of the institution of the Gospels were not authentic and did not reflect the original intention of Jesus (Pelikan, 1989, pp. 23–4).

The traditional Christian claim to truth, of course, is expressed in worship – in the proclamation of the Word and the celebration of the sacraments. By calling into question the reliability of biblical revelation and the interpretation of the Christian tradition offered by the various churches, the Enlightenment tended to reduce the worship of many of the churches to moral exhortations. Religion was considered 'useful' only to the extent that it promoted the common good and helped to order society. The deeply held Christian belief that God is a God of history – immanently active and involved with creation – was increasingly threatened by an image of the deists' God minimally involved with the world. All that could not be explained by reason was suspect, especially claims about the presence of God in Christ, Christ's presence in the sacraments, and their effects on those who receive them.

Although the two sacraments accepted by most of the churches of the Reform (baptism and Eucharist) were still practised because they were based on biblical commands, they were 'celebrated . . . infrequently and with little enthusiasm' (White, 1989, p. 53). Because they involved the manipulation of material elements (water, bread and wine), sacraments tended to be viewed as vestiges of a superstitious and dark past, now no longer necessary in a century illumined by the light of reason. Crichton describes the religious atmosphere well by saying 'the *philosophes* and the Encyclopedists saw in sacramental worship hardly more than the relics of primitive religions which were now becoming known in an elementary way . . . Religion was the non worship of an inoperative Deity combined with tedious moralism and an emphasis on duty. In this atmosphere the sacraments had no place' (Crichton, 1973, p. 2).

The reaction to the challenge to the sacraments posed by rationalism varied from church to church. Many Roman Catholics simply ignored the intellectual trends of the age and retreated into an apologetic fideism that would persist in some quarters until the Second Vatican Council. The Orthodox, on the periphery of these debates, generally took a similar course of action. In Protestantism, the countercurrent 'sacramentalism' of early Methodism can be explained at least in part as a reaction to the excessive rationalism in the Anglican church resulting from the Enlightenment.

The nineteenth century

Sacramental theology in the nineteenth century continued to be affected by the tendency towards rationalism begun during the Enlightenment. However, the strong intellectual and cultural current known as romanticism also influenced the way sacraments were understood. This intellectual movement developed as a direct reaction to the Enlightenment's excessive claims regarding reason. With its predilection for the emotional, exotic and symbolic, the romantic movement served as a catalyst for a renewed interest in sacramental worship in both Roman Catholicism and among some Protestant churches. Its nostalgic view of the European Middle Ages (one only need think of Sir Walter Scott's *Ivanhoe*) was decisive in influencing the religious imagination of the age, that yearned for a simpler, less complicated time.

This renewal began as essentially a restoration of medieval monastic/Benedictine worship by Dom Prosper Guéranger (1805–1875), with his refounding of the monastery of Solesmes, France, in 1833. In reaction to devotional excesses of his day, Guéranger's programme of renewal focused on making the official liturgy of the Roman Rite (the Mass and the Liturgy of the Hours) central to the monastic life of prayer. His classic work *L'Année liturgique (The Liturgical Year)* became a source book for this renewal. Later disseminated by the monasteries founded from or influenced by Solesmes – such as Beuron and Maria Laach in Germany and Maredsous and Mont César in Belgium – this movement did much to create a climate in which sacramental liturgy was viewed as the prayer of the assembly and not merely rubrical directives. While Guéranger's naive medievalism and ultramontanism are viewed by many today as singular flaws in his approach to worship and sacraments, he succeeded in sparking a renewed interest in both liturgical and sacramental theology that went beyond the manualist scholasticism and rubricism of the era.

In a parallel fashion romanticism also provided a catalyst for a restoration of sacramental worship among some Protestants. The Oxford movement within the Church of England, Mercersberg theology in the American Calvinist churches and the efforts of Johann Loehe (1808–1872) in Lutheranism sought to restore sacraments to the place they had enjoyed prior to the triumph of rationalism during the Enlightenment.

In both Roman Catholicism and Protestantism, however, the renewal in sacramental worship during the nineteenth century sometimes developed without a serious theological foundation. Attempts at renewal often appeared as simple rubrical changes which failed to challenge sufficiently the individualistic and sentimental notions of worship and religion that predominated during this period. There were, however, notable exceptions. Several Roman Catholic and Protestant theologians, influenced by the advances in Scripture, patristics and the history of theology, tried to build a more solid theological base for the sacraments. A Roman Catholic author, for example, who would prove to be a lasting influence within the liturgical movement of the twentieth century, was Matthias Scheeben (d. 1888) whose book *Die Mysterien des Christentums (The Mysteries of Christianity)* insisted that the sacraments could be rightly understood only in relationship to the church and therefore should not be considered apart from this context. The Oxford movement in Anglicanism championed by leaders such as E.B. Pusey – by whose name the movement is sometimes identified – combined a renewed eucharist theology with a commitment to the improvement of the social order – especially in the large cities of the European industrial revolution. It would be only in the twentieth century, however, that the ground prepared by such visionaries as Guéranger, Loehe, Scheeben and Pusey would begin to sprout with more substantial advances in both the theology and the celebration of the sacraments in many of the churches.

The twentieth century

It was the maturing liturgical movement that gave the impetus to a renewed understanding of the practice and theology of sacraments during the late nineteenth and early twentieth centuries. Substantiating their claims by citing studies in the fields of Scripture, patristics, and church history, the members of the movement emphasized that liturgy should be considered the public worship of the church – as a communal activity that required the participation of all the faithful, not simply the clerical few. Thus, in the early 1900s Pope Pius X – by encouraging more frequent reception of the Eucharist and the restoration of Gregorian chant to promote popular participation – gave official recognition to the broad aims of the liturgical pioneers.

Perhaps the greatest theological contribution to a renewed understanding of the sacraments during the first part of the twentieth century was made by Odo Casel, a Benedictine monk from the Rhineland Abbey of Maria Laach in Germany, and a scholar of early Christianity. Writing in the period between the two world wars, Casel rediscovered the concept of liturgical memorial as essential for an adequate understanding of both Jewish and Christian worship. He argued that in order to see the sacraments as *actions* of Christ rather than simple 'sacred objects' they had to be studied in their celebrative context – the liturgy of the church. Casel based his approach on studies of the Greco-Roman 'mystery': a rite that, in invoking the past, makes a saving event present and accessible to those participating in the celebration. For Casel the liturgy makes present the unique and unrepeatable mystery of Christ – his suffering, death and resurrection – through the Christian community's calling to mind of these saving events.

Casel's approach introduced a more dynamic view of the sacraments than was permitted by manualist scholastic theology, and one which returned the discussion to patristic sources of sacramental worship. In emphasizing that a sacramental celebration allows the faithful to experience anew the saving mystery and presence of Jesus Christ, he went beyond the rather narrow manualist view of sacraments that saw them primarily in functionalist terms as instrumental causes of grace – grace being understood as a quantifiable 'thing' conveyed to the individual soul through a worthy reception of the sacrament. While some of Casel's theories were criticized for being too reliant on the pagan Greco-Roman religions to explain the Christian mysteries and for his lack of more specific attention to the ecclesial dimension of the sacraments, his work has had a decisive influence on subsequent sacramental and liturgical theologians because it reproposed the liturgy itself as a theological locus. His theory of the *Mysterienlehre* (mystery theology) or *Mysteriengegenwart* (mystical presence of

Christ in the liturgy) would prove seminal for many of the scholars and pastors who prepared the ground for the renewal of the liturgy mandated by *The Constitution on the Sacred Liturgy* of the Second Vatican Council.

Writing just before the council, Edward Schillebeeckx also made contributions that helped balance Casel's *Mysterienlehre* and provide a solid theological foundation for the conciliar teaching on the liturgy. Schillebeeckx took a Christological approach in his important work *De sacramentele Heilseconomie (The Sacramental Economy of Salvation)* of 1952, reworked and simplified in *Christus, Sacrament van de Godsontmoeting (Christ the Sacrament of the Encounter with God* [1960] 1963). His approach, however, also included insights into sacraments made possible by anthropology and phenomenology.

Schillebeeckx built his discussion of all sacraments on the relationship between Christ and the church, which itself is described as a sacramental relationship based on the incarnation. Christ himself is the primordial sacrament (*Ursakrament*) from which all the other sacraments derive. 'The man Jesus, as the personal visible realization of the divine grace of redemption, is *the* sacrament, the primordial sacrament because this man, the Son of God himself, is intended by the Father to be in his humanity the only way to the actuality of redemption' (ibid., p. 15).

Just as the incarnation of Christ allowed humanity the possibility of encountering God in a new, direct way, so the sacraments, as the actions which most constitute the church – that ongoing incarnation of Christ – offer the possibility of a personal, saving encounter with Christ. The seven sacraments are simply specifications and focused manifestations of the presence of Christ to the world. A presence that is both celebrated and called forth in remembering the paschal mystery – a metahistorical event that transcends space and time. The saving power of the paschal mystery is thus continually reproposed in the sacramental worship of the church.

This approach opened up new vistas to sacramental theology. No longer was it necessary to view the sacraments and their effects in extrinsicist, objectivist and functionalist scholastic categories (this rite is performed to obtain this grace). Rather, the very concept of sacramental grace is seen in terms of interpersonal encounter – which offers a more convincing way of understanding sacraments and their effects. In the incarnation, God in Christ addresses us as a human being among human beings, thus making all of human life and every human encounter potentially revelatory of the grace of God.

About the same time, Karl Rahner took the church as his point of departure for sacramental theology. In *Kirche und Sakramente (The Church and the Sacraments* [1961] 1963) Rahner began his discussion by defining the sacraments in their relationship to the church. 'Viewed in relation to Christ, the church is the abiding promulgation of his grace giving presence to the world. Viewed in relation to the sacraments, the Church is the primal and fundamental sacrament' (p. 19). Thus, for Rahner, the church is the foundational sacrament (*Grundsakrament*). The seven sacraments are particular expressions of the one church-sacrament. It is from this perspective that he is able to overcome the difficulty in advancing the dominical institution of the sacraments in the light of modern biblical historical criticism, which has thrown Christ's direct, formal 'institution' of even baptism and the Eucharist into doubt. Given Rahner's understanding of the church as the foundational sacrament, it can be affirmed that sacraments were instituted by Christ in so far as the church, in reflecting on its experience of Christ in the paschal mystery and under the promptings of the Spirit, determined that seven rites are especially revelatory to the faith community of God in Christ and therefore should be termed sacraments.

The liturgical reforms of Vatican II

The Second Vatican Council broached the issue of worship and sacraments in its very first document, *The Constitution on the Sacred Liturgy (Sacrosanctum Concilium* of 1963). This document largely reflects the basic insights of Casel, Schillebeeckx and Rahner: the necessity of understanding sacraments not as discrete ritual mechanisms of grace, but in their relationship to Christ and the church – specifically, in their relationship to a concrete Christian community at prayer. For this reason, in its discussion of the sacraments, the

Constitution makes communal celebration of the sacraments normative – a revolutionary shift in emphasis from the time before the council, when it was normal for the Eucharist to be celebrated by a priest and a server or when it was common for anointing to be administered without others present. On this score, the Council clearly called for reform: 'Whenever rites, according to their specific nature, make provision for communal celebration involving the presence and active participation of the faithful, it is to be stressed that this way of celebrating them is to be preferred, as far as possible, to a celebration that is individual and, so to speak, private.'

The Council also advanced a much more dynamic view of the role that celebrating the sacraments plays in the growth of faith. The importance of the quality of the sacramental celebration for the believer's gradual appropriation and maturation in the faith is expressed in the Constitution's general treatment of the sacraments found in article 59:

[Sacraments] not only presuppose faith, but by words and objects they also nourish, strengthen, and express it; that is why they are called 'sacraments of faith.' They do indeed impart grace, but, in addition, *the very act of celebrating them* disposes the faithful most effectively to receive this grace in a fruitful manner, to worship God rightly, to practice charity. [my emphasis]

It is evident from this article that the Council fathers placed a new emphasis on the old scholastic dictum *sacramenta significando efficiunt gratiam* (sacraments cause grace by signifying). While there is no dispute about sacraments being efficient causes of grace, the documents of Vatican II insist that attention also be paid to how the grace is communicated, the fact that sacraments communicate grace *significando* – by signifying. The reforms in Roman Catholic sacramental worship mandated by the Council were essentially attempts to help the celebration of the sacraments 'signify' or communicate more effectively. For this reason secondary celebrative elements that tended to overshadow the central action of many of the sacraments were eliminated and the language of the rites was changed to the vernacular – all in an effort to help the sacraments 'speak' more clearly of the grace they signify.

Another major gain of the Council that had a profound effect on ecumenical dialogue about sacraments and worship was the recovery of the intrinsic relationship between word and sacrament – both are judged necessary for a complete sacramental celebration because both are ordered to the assembly's encounter of Christ in worship. In emphasizing the importance of the sacred Scripture in the life of the church and by affirming Christ's saving presence in the Word proclaimed in the liturgical assembly, the Council made it possible to develop a truly ecumenical sacramental theology based on a theology of the Word of God (Rahner, 1973, pp. 275–7).

The future of sacramental theology
In the decades following the Second Vatican Council, various approaches have been employed to understanding how sacraments function in the life of the church as well as in the lives of individual believers. Other fields of enquiry, especially the social sciences, have proved fruitful dialogue partners in enhancing appreciation of how sacraments 'work' in a liturgical context. A common characteristic of many of these approaches is their examination of the relationship between the liturgy itself – the ritual context in which the sacraments are celebrated – and the experience of human life as it is lived outside the ritual context. There are various ways to use this approach, depending upon one's point of departure: psychology (Cooke, 1965); sociology (McCauley, 1969); anthropology (Worgul, 1980); political analysis (Segundo, [1971] 1974); narrative theology (Boff, [1975] 1987); systematic theology (Kavanagh, 1984; Kilmartin, 1988); communication and symbol theory (Ganoczy, [1979] 1984; Power, 1984; Lawler, 1987; Chauvet, 1990).

The effort to highlight relationships between Christ, the church, the liturgy, the sacraments and the Christian life has returned sacramental theology to its position as a sub-speciality under the broader area of enquiry known as liturgical theology. It is no longer methodologically tenable to examine the sacramental actions of the church apart from their liturgical context, as if sacraments were abstract ideas that could float free of their celebrative moorings. It should come as a surprise to no one that substantive ecumenical convergence on the sacraments of baptism and the Eucharist has been found through reflecting on the living prayer of the church; an approach which leaves room – in a way that books and learned debates cannot – for the action of the Spirit of Christ that prepares the followers of Christ for that oneness only God can bestow.

See also EASTERN ORTHODOX THEOLOGY; ECCLESIOLOGY; LITURGY AND DOCTRINE; REVELATION, CONCEPT OF.

Bibliography

Boff, Leonardo [1975] 1987: *The Sacraments of Life; The Life of the Sacraments*, trans. John Drury. Washington DC: Pastoral Press.

Casel, Odo [1960] 1962: *The Mystery of Christian Worship and other Writings*, trans. Charles Davis, ed. Burkhard Neunheuser. London: Darton, Longman and Todd.

Chauvet, Louis-Marie 1990: *Symbole et Sacrement*. Paris: Éditions du Cerf.

Cooke, Bernard 1965: *Christian Sacraments and Christian Personality*. New York: Holt, Rinehart and Winston.

Crichton, J.D. 1973: *Christian Celebration: The Sacraments*. London: Geoffrey Chapman Publishers.

Fink, Peter 1990: Sacramental theology after Vatican II. In *The New Dictionary of Sacramental Worship*, ed. P. Fink. Collegeville, MN: Liturgical Press.

Ganoczy, Alexandre [1979] 1984: *An Introduction to Catholic Sacramental Theology*, trans. William Thomas. New York: Paulist Press.

Kavanagh, Aidan 1984: *On Liturgical Theology*. New York: Pueblo Publishing Co.

Kilmartin, Edward 1988: *Christian Liturgy*. Kansas City: Sheed and Ward.

Lawler, Michael 1987: *Symbol and Sacrament: A Contemporary Sacramental Theology*. New York: Paulist Press.

McCauley, G. 1969: *The Sacraments for Secular Man*. New York: Herder and Herder.

Meyendorf, John 1983: *Byzantine Theology: Historical Trends and Doctrinal Themes*. New York: Fordham University Press.

Pelikan, Jaroslav 1989: *The Christian Tradition*, vol. 5: *Christian Doctrine and Modern Culture (since 1700)*. Chicago, Ill.: University of Chicago Press.

Power, David 1984: *Unsearchable Riches*. New York: Pueblo.

Rahner, Karl [1961] 1963: *The Church and the Sacraments*, trans. W.J. O'Hara. New York: Herder and Herder.

Rahner, Karl 1973: What is a Sacrament? *Worship* 47, pp. 274–84.

Schillebeeckx, Edward [1960] 1963: *Christ the Sacrament of the Encounter with God*, trans. Paul Barret. New York: Sheed and Ward.

Schmemann, Alexander 1973: *For the Life of the World: Sacraments and Orthodoxy*. New York: St Vladimir.

Segundo, Juan Luis [1971] 1974: *The Sacraments Today*, trans. John Drury. New York: Orbis.

Thurian, Max, ed. 1983: *Ecumenical Perspectives on Baptism, Eucharist and Ministry*. WCC Faith and Order Paper 116. Geneva: World Council of Churches.

White, James 1989: *Protestant Worship: Traditions in Transition*. Louisville, Kentucky: Westminster/John Knox Press.

Worgul, George 1980: *From Magic to Metaphor: A Validation of the Christian Sacraments*. New York: Paulist Press.

MARK R. FRANCIS

salvation See SOTERIOLOGY.

Sartre, Jean-Paul (1905–1980) French existentialist philosopher, novelist and playwright. He was educated in Paris and Berlin, taught for a period and after war service embarked on a career as a writer, atheist philosopher and Marxist political activist. His atheism was characterized by an awareness of the importance of 'God' to much of humanity, and although uninterested in traditional arguments for the existence of God, much of his work engages with the Christian concept of God, which he learned and rejected in his youth. *Existentialism and Humanism* (1946, trans. 1948) contains echoes of Husserl and the existential theologian Martin Heidegger. *Being and Nothingness* (1943, trans. 1956), presents his philosophy of phenomenological ontology, in which he distinguishes between two modes of being: 'In-Itself' and 'For-Itself'. The fusion of the two modes represents 'God' – but such a fusion is nonexistent and impossible: humanity itself is understood as the For-Itself (the condition of consciousness) seeking fulfilment in the In-Itself, a complete state of pure being described by Sartre as 'never anything but what it is'. Man's 'passion' for this fulfilment is, however, doomed from the outset, and the refusal to accept the authentic 'absurd' is an expression of 'bad faith' which reduces human freedom. These terms find their richest popular expression in his novels and plays, notably *Nausea* (1938, trans. 1949), *The Flies* (1943, trans. 1947), *In Camera* (1944, trans. 1946) and *Dirty Hands* (1948, trans. 1949).

See also EXISTENTIALISM.

Bibliography

Jolivet, R. 1967: *Sartre: The Theology of the Absurd.* Westminster, Md.

King, T.M. 1974: *Sartre and the Sacred.* Chicago, Ill..

Theunissen, M. 1984: *The Other: Studies in the Social Ontology of Husserl, Heidegger, Sartre and Buber.* Cambridge, Mass.

Scandinavia See PROTESTANT THEOLOGY: SCANDINAVIA.

Schaeffer, Francis (1912–1984) North American Protestant evangelical apologist. He studied at Westminster Theological Seminary, Philadelphia, and became a minister of the Bible Presbyterian church, before moving to Switzerland in 1948. Here he established the L'Abri Christian community at Huemoz, a centre attracting thousands of young people, whether Christians seeking to relate their faith to the modern world or non-Christians seeking an alternative to secular humanistic philosophies, especially the prevailing existentialism. His theology was influenced by Calvinism, and he emphasized common grace and the reliability of Scripture; he also studied cultural history, working with Hans Rookmaaker to produce critiques of modern trends in art history. He travelled extensively on lecture tours, and other L'Abri centres were established outside Switzerland; his works, written for laypeople, include *Escape from Reason* (1968), *The God Who is There* (1968), *He is There and He is Not Silent* (1972) and *How should We then Live?* (1980).

Bibliography

Dennis, L.T. 1986: *F. A. Schaeffer: Portraits of the Man and his Work.* Westchester, Ill.

Ruegsegger, R.W., ed. 1986: *Reflections on Francis Schaeffer.* Grand Rapids, Mi.

Schelling, Friedrich von (1775–1854) German idealist philosopher. He was educated at Tübingen and held posts as professor of philosophy at Jena, Würzburg, Erlangen, Munich and Berlin. Originally a disciple of J.G. Fichte, and through him of I. Kant, he differed from them in positing the Ego as the underlying and absolute principle of reality, of which the universe is an expression. This thinking, presented in *Vom Ich als Prinzip der Philosophie* (1795) was developed in *Ideen zu einer Philosophie der Natur* (1797), a work of transcendental philosophy with pantheistic overtones, in which he conceived of nature as being a single organism unconsciously working towards consciousness; human beings were not separate entities but simply at an advanced stage of this process. His idealistic theories are systematically applied to Christianity in later works, such as *Philosophie und Religion* (1804) and *Philosophische Untersuchungen über das Wesen der menschliche Freiheit* (1809). Influenced by G.W.F. Hegel, he applied the dialectical principle to the history of Christianity, notably in his analysis of the dynamic of the Trinity and of the early church. The thought of this late period prefigures twentieth-century existentialist theories, and has influenced the work of Paul Tillich and Gabriel Marcel.

Bibliography

O'Meara, T.F. 1982: *Romantic Idealism and Roman Catholicism: Schelling and the Theologians.* Notre Dame, Ind.

Tillich, P. 1974: *The Construction of the History of Religion in Schelling's Positivist Philosophy.* Lewisburg, Pa.

Schillebeeckx, Edward (b. 1914) Belgian Roman Catholic theologian. A Dominican priest, he studied at Louvain and the Ecole des Hautes Etudes, Paris, and taught at Louvain and, from 1957 to 1983, at the Roman Catholic University of Nijmegen in the Netherlands. He acted as an adviser to the Dutch bishops at the Second Vatican Council, and his progressive thought has been influential on theological reform in the Catholic church; his work has been subject to official investigation, but not condemned. His early study of the contemporary implications of sacramental theology in the patristic era was later developed in *Christ the*

Sacrament of the Encounter with God (1957, trans. 1963), which shows the influence of existentialist and personalist thought, arguing against the mechanistic view of transubstantiation associated with scholastic sacramentalism and for sacrament as encounter. His development of a theological hermeneutic (in *The Understanding of Faith*, trans. 1974) shows the influence of M. Heidegger, French 'nouvelle theologie', Marxist social theory and linguistic philosophy. Stressing the cultural and historical context in which biblical principles were formed, he sees the main task of hermeneutics as being to reinterpret those principles, which are not static and unchangeable, in the light of the contemporary context. His major works of Christology, *Jesus* (1975, trans. 1979) and *Christ* (trans. 1980), relate the early church's understanding of Jesus – which he claimed to be more Jewish and eschatological than previous Christologies had allowed – to that of modern Christians, exploring how Jesus is experienced as 'Lord' in the early and the modern church.

Bibliography

Bowden, J. 1983: *E. Schillebeeckx: Portrait of a Theologian*. New York and London.
Schreiter, R.J. 1988: *The Schillebeeckx Reader*. Edinburgh.
Schreiter, R., and Hilkert, M.C., eds 1989: *The Praxis of Christian Experience: An Orientation towards E. Schillebeeckx*. San Francisco.

Schleiermacher, Friedrich Daniel Ernst (1768–1834) German theologian, often called 'the father of modern theology'. Schleiermacher gave German Protestant thought a distinctive impulse and direction for the nineteenth century, and either influenced or anticipated much in what later came to be called liberal Protestantism, both in Germany and beyond. In identifying the essence of religion as a distinctive 'feeling', and that of Christianity in particular as a special form and intensity of this emotion, he exemplified and considerably shaped the modern emphasis upon the inward, experiential and personalistic nature of faith. Debate and at times controversy still surround Schleiermacher, of such perennial significance are the issues he raised.

Life and work

The son of a Reformed chaplain in the Prussian army, Schleiermacher was educated by the Moravians and from their fervent piety and communal life received his earliest and most formative religious experience. While by his late teens he had intellectually outgrown their narrowness of outlook, he forever found their warm-hearted devotionalism congenial to his own understanding of the core of religion as the 'pious emotions'. After study at Halle and several years of teaching and pastoral work, in 1796 Schleiermacher was appointed preacher at the Charité Hospital, Berlin. For educated society, the last decade of the century represented the climax of the Enlightenment, and the Age of Reason was being both summed up and transcended by the philosophy of Immanuel Kant. But, especially in literary circles, the decade also saw the advance of ROMANTICISM. Schleiermacher was drawn into romantic circles particularly through his friend, the poet Friedrich Schlegel.

This was the context for Schleiermacher's first – and perhaps most widely influential – theological work, *On Religion: Speeches to its Cultured Despisers* ([1799] 1893). A highly original piece of apologetics, the *Speeches* argued that it was only by attacking the wrong targets that the cultured sceptics of the day could dismiss religion. Religion, Schleiermacher argued, was not a philosophy, nor abstract metaphysical thought, nor natural science, nor adherence to dogmatic formulae ('quantity of knowledge is not quantity of piety'), nor aesthetics, nor even morality (though, equally, religion never subsists in isolation but always in conjunction with these human concerns and activities). Rather, religion was a distinct *feeling, sui generis*, the feeling of *dependence*, 'a sense and taste for the infinite'. The book excited younger Protestant thinkers and drew the attention of romantics, even such as Goethe who, however, was also somewhat repelled by Schleiermacher's insistence on the communal element in religion, and hence on the importance of the church.

After a short period as a pastor in Pomerania, in 1804 Schleiermacher was appointed to a chair in theology at Halle. His fertile mind found outlet in lectures ranging widely in theology and philosophy, including the then quite novel subject of hermeneutics, that is, the contemporary understanding and interpretation of historical texts. Schleiermacher's pioneering role here was closely linked to his growing attention to the historical origins of Christianity and the person of Christ, exemplified in his short *Christmas Eve: Dialogue on the Incarnation* ([1806] 1967).

In 1806 Prussia suffered disastrous military defeat by Napoleon, and Halle was excised from Prussian control. The following year Schleiermacher, always vigorously patriotic, now became a vehement advocate of the Prussian cause and returned to Berlin, where Friedrich Wilhelm III was determined to found a new university as the intellectual centre of a new Prussia. Schleiermacher became deeply immersed in the planning and execution of this project, becoming professor of theology and eventually rector of the university. His lecturing became even more prodigious, covering New Testament, systematic, historical, philosophical and practical theology. But theology for Schleiermacher was not just a collection of diverse subjects. His *Brief Outline of the Study of Theology* ([1811] 1966) set out a view of theology as a unified whole in three main divisions: philosophical, historical and practical. Brief maybe, but this agenda helped to generate a vital new sense among Protestant theologians – often in retreat from post-Enlightenment philosophers who dismissed them as hopeless survivors from the dark ages – that they, no less than other scholars, were engaged in a certain kind of science with an integrity, and therefore a proper discipline, of its own. The crowning masterpiece of this second Berlin period, and of his whole life, was the massive *Christian Faith* ([1821–2, revised edition 1830] 1928). Based on his dogmatics lectures, the book constituted the most systematic, largescale treatment of Protestant doctrine since John Calvin's *Institutes* three centuries earlier.

Schleiermacher was deeply involved in contemporary social and political life. His warm-blooded patriotism nerved him for a number of adventures in the movement for Prussian liberation from Napoleonic rule during 1806–13, earning him a somewhat subversive reputation in the eyes of the state. Much of his influence on the contemporary scene was exercised through his notable preaching ministry in the Trinity Church. Among his confirmation candidates was the young Otto von Bismarck, future architect of the Prussian Empire. He became controversially embroiled with Friedrich Wilhelm III over the formation of the United Church of Prussia and its liturgy. He was no cloistered academic, then, and his funeral drew thousands onto the streets of Berlin.

Theology

While Schleiermacher identified the essence of religion as feeling, and warned against confusing piety with intellectuality or dogmatic formulations, his thought is in fact one of the most rigorously disciplined in the history of Protestantism. His theology exhibits a definite structure, crystallized in the tightly argued paragraphs of his *Christian Faith*.

In the *Speeches* the young Schleiermacher stated: 'True religion is *sense and taste for the infinite*' and 'The contemplation of the pious is the *immediate consciousness* of the universal existence of all finite things, in and through the Infinite, and of all temporal things in and through the Eternal.' The 'pious consciousness' is a feeling of *dependence*, more precisely stated in *Christian Faith* as the feeling of *absolute dependence*. Schleiermacher's thought thus has a subjective focus, but it should not on that account be deemed to be sheer 'subjectivism'. Schleiermacher's careful analysis of religious feelings always has in view, at least by implication, the infinite and eternal reality to which these feelings are responses. But it remains true that for Schleiermacher the subject matter of theology is not, directly, the divine reality itself, but always the human, religious consciousness of the divine presence in which all things exist and cohere. The *Speeches* are sometimes held to be pantheist in tone, but Schleiermacher did not identify the world or cosmos with the 'infinite and eternal'. Rather, he held that it is always in and through one's experience of the whole interconnecting realm of the finite that there comes a sense of dependence upon the infinite ground of all things. This sense of dependence, he argued, may not actually be evident in all people, but its realization belongs to essential humanity.

The mature Schleiermacher was greatly preoccupied with the distinctiveness of Christianity as lying in the fact that 'in it everything is related to the redemption accomplished by Jesus of Nazareth.' By redemption Schleiermacher means the inward transformation of the self from the evil state of God-forgetfulness to the state of God-consciousness, that is, the state in which the sense of absolute dependence predominates over all else. The distinctiveness of Jesus lay in his own perfect God-consciousness which was 'a veritable existence of God in him'. Christ's redeeming work consists in the impartation of his God-consciousness to the believer. The suffering of the cross is not as such the means of redemption, but it is the token of the Redeemer's willingness to enter into 'sympathy with misery', and hence is a sign of his willingness to share his blessedness.

The God-consciousness of the believer being the primary reference point for theology, Schleiermacher expounds the whole range of Reformed doctrines as relating to this phenomenon: 'Christian doctrines are accounts of the Christian religious affections set forth in speech.' For example, the concept of divine omnipresence refers to the universality of the possibility of pious consciousness in each circumstance and in every occasion of human experience. Schleiermacher was consequently not afraid to call his theology 'mystical', centred as it was upon the personal communion of the believer with the wholly God-conscious (and in that sense divine) Christ.

Schleiermacher's Christ, however, is no timeless, ahistorical figure. In fact Schleiermacher was a pioneer in recognizing the importance of study of the 'historical Jesus' and quickly identified a problem which was to challenge Christianity down to the present: how absolute significance can be accorded to a figure who, as a genuinely human being, must have been enmeshed in the particular social and cultural context of his time and place. Closely related to this concern was his recognition of theology's need for a science of interpreting documents from the past, whereby they could be read with due respect to the author's intended meaning as capable of being understood in the present. So was born, as a conscious discipline, *hermeneutics*, on which Schleiermacher lectured extensively. Philology and human sensitivity had to combine in order 'to understand the text at first as well as and then even better than its author'.

If Schleiermacher's theology tends to the 'subjective', this does not mean individualism. The believer's experience of God can only be maintained through actual relationship with Christ, who is thus more than a mere model of piety to be copied in one's own strength. Religion demands to be expressed and communicated: 'The religious self-consciousness, like every emotional element in human nature, leads increasingly in its development to fellowship or communion; and communion which, on the one hand, is variable and fluid, and, on the other hand, has definite limits, i.e. is a Church.' For Schleiermacher, religion – and its verbalized refinement in theology – is essentially communal, just as humanity is inherently social.

Significance
Schleiermacher's significance as originator or precursor of much of modern Protestant theology is immense. His location of religion in inward, emotional sensibility signalled a massive transfer of theological interest to the experiential, indeed psychological, flavour of much modern Protestant thought, while his great attempt at dogmatics provided a model for later theologians to emulate, even for such figures so different from Schleiermacher (and from each other) as Karl Barth and Paul Tillich. His centring of Christian theology on the historical Jesus, and on Jesus' own consciousness of God, became almost axiomatic for several generations of Protestantism. His historiographical and hermeneutical insights were taken up and developed by such as Wilhelm Dilthey, while his identification of religion as a universal human phenomenon, of which Christianity was the highest moral and spiritual form, was archetypal for the later study of 'comparative religion'.

In the eyes of twentieth-century neo-orthodox theology, thanks above all to Karl Barth, much of this is tantamount to saying that Schleiermacher led the great defection whereby liberal theology focused on human potentiality and religiosity at the expense of God's own reality, majesty and grace. Schleiermacher's attention to 'religion', says Barth, betrays a self-confinement within the 'anthropological horizon', an error manifest right down to Rudolf Bultmann's preoccupation with 'existence in faith'. Indeed for much of the twentieth century it has been difficult to approach Schleiermacher unprejudiced by the Barthian polemic. Barth himself, however, retained a wistful admiration for Schleiermacher, eventually speculating that 'all might not be lost' with him, especially if we await a theology 'predominantly and decisively of the Holy Spirit'. For the sake of fairness, therefore, it is important to read all that Barth said about Schleiermacher – and even more important to read Schleiermacher himself at first hand.

See also CHRISTOLOGY; GOD; PHILOSOPHICAL THEOLOGY.

Bibliography

Writings

[1799] 1893: *On Religion: Speeches to Its Cultured Despisers*, trans. John Oman. London: Kegan Paul, Trench, Trubner and Co. (also Harper Torchback edn 1958).

[1806] 1967: *Christmas Eve: Dialogue on the Incarnation*, trans. T. Tice. Richmond, Virginia: John Knox Press.

[1811] 1966: *Brief Outline of the Study of Theology*, trans. T. Tice. Richmond, Virginia: John Knox Press.

[1821–2] 1928: *The Christian Faith*, trans. H.R. Mackintosh and J.S. Stewart. Edinburgh: T & T Clark.

1860: *The Life of Schleiermacher as Unfolded in his Autobiography and Letters*, 2 vols, trans. Frederica Rowan. London: Smith, Elder and Co.

[1864] 1975: *The Life of Jesus*, trans. S. Maclean Gilmour, ed. J.C. Verheyden. Philadelphia: Fortress Press.

[1959] 1977: *Hermeneutics: The Handwritten Manuscripts*, trans. J. Duke and J. Forstman. Missoula, Montana: Scholars Press.

Critical works

Barth, K. 1959: Friedrich Schleiermacher (Chapter 8). In Barth, *From Rousseau to Ritschl*. London: SCM Press.

Barth, K. [1978] 1982: *The Theology of Schleiermacher: Lectures at Göttingen 1923–24*. Edinburgh: T and T Clark; Grand Rapids: Eerdmans.

Clements, K.W. 1987: *Friedrich Schleiermacher: Pioneer of Modern Theology*. London: Collins. (Re-issued 1990. Edinburgh: T and T Clark.)

Gerrish, B.A. 1984: *A Prince of the Church: Schleiermacher and the Beginnings of Modern Theology*. Philadelphia: Fortress Press; London: SCM Press.

Niebuhr, R.R. 1965: *Schleiermacher on Christ and Religion*. London: SCM Press.

Reardon, B.M.G. 1985: *Religion in the Age of Romanticism: Studies in Early Nineteenth Century Thought*. Cambridge: Cambridge University Press.

Redeker, M. 1973: *Schleiermacher: Life and Thought*. Philadelphia: Fortress Press.

Sykes, S. 1984: *The Identity of Christianity: Theologians and the Essence of Christianity from Schleiermacher to Barth*. London: SPCK.

KEITH W. CLEMENTS

Schweitzer, Albert (1875–1965) German theologian, physician and musicologist. Academically brilliant, he gained a doctorate in philosophy in the same year as entering the pastorate at Strasburg (1899); the following year he gained a doctorate in theology and in 1901 he published a ground-breaking work, *The Mystery of the Kingdom of God*, and became a lecturer at the University of Strasburg. His next book, *The Quest of the Historical Jesus* (1906, trans. 1910) developed themes of his first. In it he surveyed the history of biblical criticism, and argued that the attempt of contemporary liberals to rediscover the truly 'historical' figure of Jesus was as misplaced as their predecessors' reading of the narrative as literal history: the key to its understanding is not historical but eschatological. Jesus himself was expecting the end of the age, and the radical ethics he preached were meant to herald it. When the end of the age did not follow upon his preaching of the kingdom, he chose self-sacrifice as a way of bringing it about (see HISTORICAL JESUS, QUEST OF). His 1911 book, *Paul and His Interpreters* (trans. 1912), identified the same underlying key to the teaching of Paul. Schweitzer's theology attracted criticism from liberal and conservative theologians alike, but remains influential. In 1911 he took his medical degree, and in 1913 he relinquished his academic career and went with his wife as a missionary doctor to French Equatorial Africa. Here he spent most of his life serving the poor and sick at his hospital at Lambaréné. *On the Edge of the Primeval Forest* (1921, trans. 1922) is his account of life on the mission field; whilst *Philosophy of Civilization* (1923) outlined his humanitarian principles, identifying 'reverence for life' – embracing all life forms, including plants and insects – as a key principle of the teaching of Jesus. He was also a gifted organist and musicologist. He was awarded the Nobel Peace Prize for 1952.

Bibliography

Brabazon, J. 1975: *Albert Schweitzer*. New York.

Ice, J.L. 1971: *Schweitzer: Prophet of Radical Theology*. Philadelphia.

Marshall, G.N., and Poling, D. 1971: *Schweitzer*. New York.

science and Christian thought One of the most important developments in the modern period has been the emergence of the sciences, especially the natural sciences, as important intellectual disciplines. Since their inception, the sciences have raised questions of fundamental importance for Christian thought, as may be seen from the Copernican theory of the solar system, the Darwinian theory of evolution and the Freudian analysis of the psychological origins of belief in God.

For the purposes of this discussion, the sciences have been broken down into four separate articles, each written by a specialist in the appropriate field.

See BIOLOGICAL/PHYSICAL/PSYCHOLOGICAL/SOCIAL SCIENCE AND CHRISTIAN THOUGHT

secularization The word 'secular', originating from the Latin *saeculum*, meaning an age or era, has had a long and complicated history. In medieval times secular clergy lived 'in the world', in contrast to religious clergy who were associated with monasteries or various orders. Later, secularization also implied the state taking away property from the church (Shiner, 1967). The notion that the secular indicates an absence of the religious emerges strongly during the ENLIGHTENMENT, when fundamental religious propositions began to be abandoned. Today, secularization implies a process whereby a society rejects or disregards religious beliefs, practices and symbols. When it has totally rejected such characteristics, a state of secularity may be said to exist. The notion of secularization is only possible in a society where what is religious can be carefully differentiated from what is not. This is difficult in certain pre-literate societies and with a traditional religion, such as Hinduism.

By contrast, secularism refers to a consciously held ideology, where adherents deliberately attempt to bring about a state of secularity. In Britain, the movement began in the nineteenth century and was led by G.D. Holyoake (1817–1906) and C. Bradlaugh (1833–1891). It actively sought the demise of religion and propagated a humanistic ethic. Similar movements appeared in other European countries.

Crudely stated, the level of secularization in a society is inversely proportional to the level of religion. In practical terms, all turns on how religion is defined and how, if at all, it can be measured. The definition of religion has always raised considerable difficulty (see RELIGION, THEORIES OF). For the sociologist, two main approaches have been accepted. It is defined as (1) a system of beliefs and practices related to an ultimate being, beings, or to the supernatural; or (2) as that which is sacred in a society – ultimate beliefs and practices which are inviolate (Aquaviva, 1979). The adoption of one or other of these definitions leads to different positions about the nature of secularization.

Émile Durkheim saw secularization proceeding in two modes. The first, similar to the thinking of Auguste Comte, was that secularization has been in existence from very early times, when man, who lived in an essentially religious society, began to remove religious axioms from science, medicine, philosophy, art, law and so on. By receiving secular autonomy, these activities were no longer subject to religious or ecclesiastical controls. Man's history has thus been the history of his secularization. But, secondly, the process has not been uniform. Since the Renaissance and the Reformation it has been accelerated and covers larger areas of social life.

Secularization today can best be examined in three dimensions.

Political secularization This exists in societies where the state in its constitution or structure makes little or no reference to religion. It may permit the presence of a religion or religions but it neither makes use of religious ideas in its government nor interferes in the internal affairs of a religion. Previous periods of history saw a close relation between religion and the state, as in the case of theocracy or where a religion was established by law. In these examples, the law and its enforcement agencies might be used to strengthen the position of the religion through civil penalties and even persecution. On the other hand, the official religion has usually supported the state to maintain stability and order. Some cases have occurred where the state was seen as the secular arm of a church and therefore in the final analysis was controlled by it.

Political secularization usually means an absence of religion in state institutions, such as education, medicine, hospitals, social work, local government and so on.

In Europe, political secularization has emerged through a series of laws which have repealed sanctions and given freedom to various religions and Christian denominations. Countries allowing freedom of worship have historically tended to be Protestant rather than Catholic. Two countries constitutionally secular today are India and Turkey. The USA, whilst not identified with a particular denomination, and as the earliest leader of religious liberty, retains the notion of God in its constitution, although all its major institutions are secular. Wherever political secularization occurs, religion becomes privatized and socially confined to places of worship. Belonging to a religious group thus means doing so on a voluntary basis, and local churches have become sectarian.

Political secularization has given rise to religious pluralism where all religions in a society have a legally equal status. The result has been viewed as a market place situation in which would-be religious adherents select the 'brand' of religion they want. It is more obvious in societies where many religions and denominations exist, as in the USA, than in countries dominated by one religion, such as Poland. Multiple choice weakens the notion of the ultimate validity or superiority of any one religion. Through relativism all religions are seen to be much the same. Acceptance thus rests on individual subjective plausibility rather than on an awareness of objective truth (see RELATIVISM, CULTURAL).

Intellectual secularization This implies the absence of religious references in cognitive propositions. When Nietzsche said that God was dead, he implied that no one could any longer believe in God. The statement was intended to be both philosophical and one describing the belief of nineteenth-century intellectuals. The rejection of religious ideas and language, especially those of Judaeo-Christian origin, is frequently attributed to the growing acceptance of scientific thought and achievements in discovering the truth of the natural world. God as a person, creator and sustainer of the universe has no place here and religion, it is held, no longer provides truth.

Science sees religion as a natural phenomenon. Sociologists, psychologists, and other intellectuals have offered a scientific explanation of religions and their institutions, as well as of personal experience. *A prima facie* such explanations undermine traditional claims. Higher and lower criticism have similarly challenged the sacred texts with regard to their truth-assertions. Geological findings and evolutionary theories have cast doubt on the cosmogony and cosmology asserted by religions (see Pratt, 1970).

Intellectual secularization primarily refers to the cognitive positions of an elite, who are seen as the intellectual leaders of society – scientists, philosophers, artists, writers and so on.

Personal secularization This occurs where the beliefs and actions of individuals show no regard for the claims or demands of religion. Scientific ideas may grow slowly (and indeed all changes in religion tend to be gradual) but in a simplified form they percolate down to the man in the street, who has come to accept many of them. Traditional concepts about God have thus been eroded. God, where such a belief still exists, has become a god of the gaps, working in areas of life which are not at the present or cannot be satisfactorily explained by science. In this way personal religious faith becomes weaker or is never embraced. Individual religious action may follow a similar path. The 'most religious' action is that of attendance at places of worship; another relates to moral behaviour where it is given a religious base. An examination of the belief and action components of individuals allows the possibility of measurement, which is difficult to establish in other types of secularization. In this way indicators are to hand which might be said to measure the presence or absence of religion objectively. Such indicators lend themselves to statistical analysis and relate to various aspects of belief, church membership, church attendance, financial giving, level of baptisms, marriages and religious burials, etc. Further, such statistics can be related to periods of time, country, region, denomination, class, age, occupation and sexual differentiation.

Generalized findings of surveys suggest that men have been more influenced by personal secularization than women; the young more than the old; the working classes more than the middle classes; urban dwellers more than country people; traditional Protestant countries more than Catholic ones; central-western Europe more than the USA. Covering all denominations, adult church attendance in England today is of the order of 10 per cent for an average Sunday. In many countries in Europe now so great is the level of secularization that variations in levels of religious adherence between social classes, regions, and so on is minimal and of little significance.

The reasons people give for their disenchantment with or withdrawal from institutional religion cover an enormous range, from doctrines about God to the latest pronouncements of the Vatican. The secularization of individuals in western Europe, however, has not given rise to atheism or a hostility towards religion, but rather to a general attitude of indifference in seeing religion as antiquated and irrelevant to their needs. People do not argue against it, they bypass it. Further, many of those who are associated with the churches decide themselves what doctrines and moral teachings they will accept and what they will disregard.

The relation between the three dimensions of secularization is complicated, as various combinations can be seen to occur and where in some societies one component is weak another is strong.

Controversy over secularization has often confused description (and indicators) with causality. The notion that secularization is to be examined in three dimensions implies that it is not necessarily a unified or coherent force, largely because of the complex nature of religion. Most sociologists refer to 'causes' or 'influences' with no consensus in the ranking of their importance.

Rationally inclined thinkers place emphasis on intellectual secularization, which has impinged on nearly every domain of religious life. Since man proceeds from some cognitive assertion, it is argued, his actions are determined by what he knows or believes. To assume scientific truths means that religion has little or nothing to offer. But the fact remains that religion in the west has been a long time dying and people have not totally abandoned religious beliefs and practices, despite the enormous growth and acceptance of scientific ideas. Max Weber, in accounting for what he called the disenchantment of the world, proposed a theory of rationalization in which everyday life has become dominated by technology, bureaucratization and calculated means of achieving goals. Other sociologists also not convinced about the ubiquitous and negative consequences of scientific thought have focused on social influences which might have affected the rate of secularization. They point to the expansion of cities, with the alleged loss of communal life (compared with that of the village), to the workplace, which stands removed from family life, to monotonous factory work, to a prevailing materialist and consumerist outlook, and to geographical and social mobility, which breaks up religious affiliation.

It is impossible to prove that any one particular factor has brought about secularization, or even contributed to it. All that can be shown empirically is a high level of probability between the factor and the phenomenon. Further explication has to be offered which frequently contains questionable presuppositions about the nature of man and how he is socialized, not least religiously.

The root cause of secularization has sometimes been laid at the feet of Judaism and Christianity (Berger, 1967). Strands exist in the Old Testament which emphasize man's humanity, and stress ethics and social justice more than ritual and sacrifice. The theme was taken up by Christ. In recent times the emphasis on man's well-being in this life has come to the fore. By proclaiming the man-centred element of Christianity and the necessity of social justice and the fulfilment of human needs, the transcendental and eschatological components have become weaker.

An older variation of this thesis is that Protestantism has given rise to modern secularization. It broke the authority of the Catholic church, allowed nations to emerge and encouraged individual autonomy, which uncritically allowed the acceptance of science and changes in philosophy. In a simplistic way Protestantism is seen to be its own gravedigger, as indeed is Christianity.

With the use of statistical analysis, much of the early concern for personal secularization came from the European churches, especially in Britain, in realizing that the growth of nineteenth-century cities was accompanied by the religious alienation of the working classes. Churchmen attempted to analyse the causes and to offer remedies, such as the building of more churches, increased pastoral activity, changes in liturgical worship and mission activity (Gray, 1911). But the pouring in of great resources has not reversed the general trend. And now that the churches' reserves have decreased, certainly in terms of political leverage, and they have fewer buildings and clergy, secularization proceeds virtually unchecked. In the 1960s and 1970s some theologians in the English-speaking world incorporated into their thinking secular ideas, such as the death of God, and could be said to have thereby accelerated secularization.

Since the 1960s also a vigorous debate has arisen as to whether or not secularization has actually occurred in modern western society. Some sociologists of religion (such as Martin, 1965) have challenged the very notion of secularization as being inaccurate and ideological. Four issues are crucial. (1) The problem of comparing the level of religion in society today with that of previous decades or centuries. There has been a tendency, it is argued, to inflate or assume past levels of religious belief and practice. (2) There is still a considerable amount of religion or religiosity in allegedly secular societies, for example common or folk religion, which includes ideas about divinity, superstitions and the practice of astrology along with the acceptance of rites of passage, and civil rights movements. (3) Some sociologists would go so far as to assert that everybody is to some degree religious: the only issue is to find its mode of expression (see Luckmann, 1967). They argue that what has been called secularization has been religious change, not the decline of religion. (4) Institutional Christianity flourishes in many parts of the world, such as in the USA, Ireland and Poland, and is growing fast in Africa south of the Sahara. In some parts of the world evangelical and Pentecostal Christians are increasing rapidly. Sects and new religious movements also show no signs of abating. A mounting interest in religion in eastern Europe is reported since the peaceful revolution of 1989.

In the debate about secularization, the case of the USA has in recent times been held up as a negative example to the secularizing trends evident in Europe. As *the* modern society of the world, it is the most prosperous industrialized country known to man. But it has great urban conurbations, high geographical and social mobility, was a pioneer and stalwart upholder of religious pluralism, and is renowned for the multiplicity of churches and sects within its borders. By European standards, here is the recipe for secularization. But no matter the indicator – church membership, church attendance, financial giving, belief in God, general attitudes towards the importance of religion – all statistics and polls show America to be more 'religious' than most European countries. Sociologists prefer to try to account for American religion rather than to analyse the situation in terms of secularization – a term which is generally avoided. Yet the explanations offered have not been convincing.

The USA is virtually secularized at the political level. Religion very seldom enters into philosophy, the arts, or political thinking. The relative absence of secularization is with the individual. There is a high level of personal commitment either to a religious system or to religion in general. For most Americans, dissatisfaction with one church or denomination does not mean giving up religion altogether but embracing one or a series of religious bodies until contentment is achieved. Other factors, negative and positive, have also been suggested in trying to account for a relatively high level of religiosity. For example, in America there has been: (1) no working-class or blue collar alienation from the churches, nor has there been any anticlericalism, and there is no significant correlation between occupation and religious commitment, though this does not apply to particular denominations; (2) an absence of intellectual attacks on religion *per se*; (3) little relation between personal religious life and public life, which might create general hostility. Religion has been excluded from economics, politics and education, although in recent years there is clear evidence that many evangelicals are now concerned with social issues, as in the case of the Moral Majority. In a more positive vein, Americans have placed great store on religious organization, ethnic churches have had a strong appeal to immigrant groups, churches have helped to integrate American society by smoothing over discontent and offering the hope of stability, any guilt arising from a sense of success and world dominance has been assuaged by religious beliefs and practices, and to be American has come to mean being 'religious'. All this gives rise to some form of a civil religion (see Herberg, 1955).

Critics of the American religious scene have pointed to its superficiality, its world-affirming or secular characteristics, and to its aggressive evangelical fundamentalism. Fundamentalism tends to separate totally the private from the social, and projects a religion which completely encloses the individual in the ancient thought-forms of biblical literalism or the ideology of extreme sects. Despite religious commitment, American life is dominated by secular ideals.

Religious affiliation in the USA has shown great fluctuations in the past. The 'lowish' 1930s gave way to the flourishing years after the Second World War, when church membership had a greater increase than the rise in population. Despite the relative growth of Roman Catholicism, America is held to be a Protestant country with an estimated two-thirds of the population seeing themselves as evangelicals. Even prominent statesmen, for example Charles Colson, have been known to become evangelists, and American missionaries are numerous all over the world.

Will the present relatively low level of secularization in America continue? At a much earlier period, de Toqueville observed that America was a very religious country. As some churches decline today, so others grow. Some might argue that a time lag between Europe and America means that one day the various forces of secularization associated with the Enlightenment and modern industrial ideology will make their mark. That American religion is to be seen in social and political terms is confirmed by the example of adjacent Canada. Socially and religiously Canada stands mid-way between the USA and Europe, but in recent times it has been showing signs of increasing secularization.

In general the future is impossible to predict, but all indications suggest that secularization, as here defined, will continue and that all traditional churches, Catholic and Protestant, face severe institutional problems in the years ahead. The focus has been on western societies where secularization itself emerged and where it is relatively easy to describe and analyse. But in many countries outside Europe and the USA into which the package of western ideology, industrialization and consumerism has penetrated, latent secularization in one form or another follows in its wake. In some nonwestern countries a reaction to this is to be seen in the growth of so-called Islamic fundamentalism, but whether the upsurge will persist is open to question.

See also SOCIAL SCIENCE AND CHRISTIANITY.

Bibliography

Aquaviva, S.S. 1979: *The Decline of the Sacred in Industrial Society*. Oxford: Blackwell.

Berger, P.L. 1967: *The Sacred Canopy*. New York: Doubleday.

Chadwick, O. 1975: *The Secularization of the European Mind in the Nineteenth Century*. Cambridge: Cambridge University Press.

Dobbelaere, K. 1981: *Secularization: A Multi-Dimensional Concept*. (*Current Sociology* 29, 2.) London: Sage Publications.

Gilbert, A.D. 1976: *Religion and Society in Industrial England*. London: Longman.

Gray, W.F., ed. 1911: *Non-Church-Going: Its Reasons and Remedies*. London: Oliphant.

Herberg, W. 1955: *Protestant–Catholic–Jew*. New York: Doubleday.

Luckmann, T. 1967: *Invisible Religion*. New York: Macmillan.

McLeod, H. 1981: *Religion and the People of Western Europe 1789–1970*. Oxford: Oxford University Press.

Martin, D. 1965: Towards eliminating the concept of secularization. In *The Penguin Survey of the Social Sciences*, ed. J. Gould. Harmondsworth: Penguin, pp. 169–82.

Martin, D. 1978: *A General Theory of Secularization*. Oxford: Blackwell.

Pickering, W.S.F. 1968: Religion a leisure-time pursuit?. In *A Sociological Yearbook of Religion No. 1*, ed. D. Martin. London: Student Christian Movement Press, pp. 77–93.

Pratt, V. 1970: *Religion and Secularization*. London: Macmillan.

Shiner, L. 1967: The concept of secularization in empirical research, *Journal for the Scientific Study of Religion* 6, pp. 207–20.

Wilson, B.R. 1976: *Contemporary Transformations of Religion*. London: Oxford University Press.

W.S.F. PICKERING

sexual ethics Sexual ethics deals with fundamental questions about the nature of human sexuality and its expressions. It reflects on the morality of the nature, causes and manifestations of sexuality ranging from natural law, fertility and infertility, contraception, masturbation, premarital and extramarital sex, adultery, rape and incest, pornography and promiscuity, heterosexuality, homosexuality and bisexuality, as well as the personal, social and theological aspects of human sexuality.

The west has seen a revolution in sexual mores and attitudes in the last century. The rise of the women's liberation movement and the sexual revolution typified by the 'swinging sixties' and modern forms of contraception like the 'pill' have transformed society's attitude to and acceptance of sexual behaviour. The church has not been immune, and while traditional Christian morality has maintained a biblical and historical account of what is right and wrong in sexual matters, many inside the church have questioned and rejected those values and replaced them with a more liberal outlook. At the heart of that debate lies the issue of how far traditional theological thinking can and ought to be modified by modern sociological, psychological and biological advances in knowledge.

Sexual identity is fundamental to human beings. Sexuality is a biological reality. Our chromosomal make-up is the basis of our masculinity or femininity. As the person develops from childhood to adulthood, sexual organs grow and the bodily changes are matched by hormonal, psychological and behavioural changes. It is also clear that social conditions and factors play an important part in the developing sexual roles. Thus many distinguish between sex, which is usually a biological description, and gender roles, which are usually socially and psychologically defined. This is a variation of the theme of nature versus nurture in terms of human development, and doubtless both have crucial parts to play in the process of sexual development and status.

Sexuality is among the essential, determining features of humanity (see ANTHROPOLOGY, CHRISTIAN). It is a constitutive part of our human nature and finds expression in our psychological make-up and in social and cultural settings, which are marked by moral judgements. It is vital to distinguish sex from sexuality and realize that there is much more to sexuality than genital activity. Sexuality is part of the whole person and it has many varied expressions in relationships.

At the core of our understanding of sexuality is the biological function of reproduction. Sexual characteristics seem to play a key role in attracting a mate with whom to reproduce. The universal form of such mating seems to be marriage, and reproduction creates the family unit. But sexuality may have many other functions and purposes in a society than reproduction.

The key link between the biological account of sexuality and theological thought has been the doctrines of NATURAL LAW. They have focused on the ways in which human bodies were designed and how male and female bodies fit together in a natural way and come together in such a way that procreation occurs. This has led to the valuing of such 'natural' processes as good and right and consequently all deviations from the natural as bad and wrong. In this way, masturbation, contraception and sexual expression of homosexuality have been dismissed as unnatural and wrong. There are, in addition to such natural law arguments, biblical grounds for moral judgements on these issues.

Masturbation has been traditionally regarded as sinful and wrong in its departure from the normal and natural purpose of sexual expression in procreative terms. With the psychoanalytic theories of Freud and the growth of biological and psychological studies of sexual behaviour, masturbation is now often seen as a normal stage of adolescent development where the individual stimulates himself or herself to relieve sexual tension and provide pleasure. While there is little evidence that such activity has any long-term harmful effects, many still regard masturbation as less than ideal in terms of its self-centredness, its concentration on pleasure and its substitution of oneself rather than a relationship with another human being.

The sense of unnatural as wrong has been applied to anything and everything which interferes with the natural process of procreation. Thus coitus interruptus, or the withdrawal method of sexual intercourse, has been morally condemned along with contraception. It is important that we understand that not all contraception is regarded as evil, but only that which artificially intervenes in the natural processes of procreation. Thus the rhythm method of contraception, which depends on the regularity of the woman's monthly menstrual cycle and encourages sexual intercourse only in the so-called 'safe' period, is morally acceptable in Catholic teaching. The other forms of contraception, ranging through mechanical devices, hormonal stimulation and barrier methods, are rejected as unnatural and interfering with the proper purpose of sexual intercourse. To this must be added moral repugnance at any and every use of abortion as a late form of contraception. With the growth of medical technology the line between contraceptives and abortions is not always clear, for many contraceptives act as abortofacients.

The use of what is natural as a moral standard by which to judge the issues of sexual morality is relevant in dealing with the moral questions surrounding infertility. At least one in ten couples who wish to have children are unable so to do. The causes of infertility are both male and female, and various treatments, both surgical and hormonal, may help. But often such treatments may require the collection of sperm for artificial insemination. This requires masturbation, and for many that is in itself sufficient reason to reject it as unnatural. Some Catholic scholars argue that if the husband is the donor of the sperm the masturbation is permissible for it is not merely a selfish or pleasurable act, but it is geared towards procreation and so fulfils the natural test for sexual behaviour.

If the infertility is more serious then donor sperm may be required, and this raises moral questions about whether artificial insemination by donor is a form of adultery. Even though this is clearly the intervention of a third party into the marriage relationship, it is not strictly adultery in the commonly understood sense. But moral issues of parenting, appropriate sexual expression, the limits of technology, and the likely consequences on the child who results and on the marriage must be borne in mind.

Female infertility may be dealt with by egg donation or even by surrogacy, where another woman carries the fertilized egg on behalf of the social mother. Again, intervention of a third party, the separation of sexual intercourse from procreation, the artificiality of the setting and procedure, and the likely consequences of such treatments are all moral issues which are hotly debated. A strict application of natural law would forbid most of these practices. Before examining other areas of sexual ethics, the biblical framework for morality needs to be explored.

A biblical framework

From the very beginning it is clear that human beings are sexual beings. The Genesis account is of man being created and finding that loneliness was too great to bear. So womankind was created because man on his own was inadequate. Provocatively, that suggests that human beings are made in the image of God as male or female. They are meant to live in harmony with each other by complementing and fulfilling each other in mutuality and reciprocity. Sexuality and its expression were natural and innocent. God gave humanity the good gift of sexual expression with the command to be fruitful and multiply (Gen. 1: 27–8). This pattern of complementing each other leaves no room for subordination or superiority. When the two became one flesh they became more than just sexually one. They were uniting their personalities and creating a new unity. This unity was broken in the fall, where the perfect relationship was marred by disobedience. This led directly to a breach in their relationship with each other, where the one blames the other, where they are no longer innocent but embarrassed and aware of their nakedness, where the woman becomes subservient to the male, and where procreation, the fruit of sexual intercourse, becomes painful.

As the Old Testament develops, the God-given pattern of marriage is enunciated as leaving the old ties and relationships of family and blood, cleaving to each other in a mutually exclusive relationship and becoming one flesh. Many will point to the existence of polygamy in the Old Testament, but it is interesting to note that Jacob's polygamy came about as a result of trickery on the part of Laban and Abraham's attempts to take a second woman ended in disaster. In fact it is clear that the taking of wives by the Israelite kings was seen as a departure from God's pattern, an attempt to be like the kings of other nations, and almost uniformly ended with disaster in which the royal wives led the king astray from God and his ways. Sexual love is celebrated in the Scriptures in the Song of Solomon and the picture of marriage is used by Hosea and Ezekiel as a symbol of God's union with his people. This same picture is used in Ephesians to describe the unity of Christ and his church. For many this is the basis of the idea of the indissolubility of marriage. Coupled with the full under-standing of becoming one flesh, with the reality of God's joining of man and woman together so that they become one – a new unity – and with the force of vows taken until death parts, the mystery of the marriage bond seems to be well expressed in terms of what cannot be dissolved or broken, even if the couple lives apart and goes through some kind of legal divorce. In the eyes of God the partners are still married, as far as the indissolubilist is concerned.

This leads to the issue of divorce, which was permitted in the Mosaic law. Christians are divided over the permissibility of divorce, and the debate focuses on passages in Matthew 19 where Jesus, or as some commentators suggest the early church, allows divorce on the basis of porneia – sexual naughtiness. This seems to cover a wider set of sexual wrongdoing than simply adultery. The Pauline privilege in Corinthians likewise seems to allow the possi-bility of divorce if the unbelieving partner no longer wishes to continue the marriage. While opinions are divided over the permissibility of divorce, the heart of the debate seems more to focus on the issue of remarriage, which seems expressly forbidden in Mark's teaching about marriage. To remarry is to commit adultery. What is universally agreed is that Christ taught a high doctrine of marriage, elevated the role of women in that relationship, and stressed the creation pattern which was God's good gift and ultimate intention for lifelong, monogamous commitment. Jesus also reiterated the creation pattern of marriage as leaving, cleaving and one flesh in the context of questions about divorce.

That sexual relationships break down is witnessed to by the fact that the law of the Old Testament forbade adultery and sexual aberrations like homosexual relationships and incest (Lev. 20: 10; Ex. 20: 14; Deut. 5: 18, 22: 13–21; Lev. 19: 29, 18: 22). The seriousness of such sexually immoral acts is shown in the New Testament by Paul's warning that fornicators, the impure, those who engage in genital homosexual acts and adulterers have no inheritance in the kingdom of God (Eph. 5: 5; 1 Cor. 6: 9).

Many see in the very detailed instructions about sexual acts in the Pentateuch the basis not only of moral restraint and ethics but also public health concerns. The increase of sexually transmitted diseases raises moral questions about confidentiality and the protection of those at risk. The tragedy of AIDS means that people are most vulnerable in sexual activity where they or their partner have been unfaithful or exposed to HIV by some other means. The protection of others has become more important morally than defending the individual's right and confidentiality. The sexual ethical norm of traditional, biblical Christianity has therefore been to reject all premarital and extramarital sexual activity as falling short of the proper context of sexual expression which is in marriage. On the same basis, homosexual acts, rape and incest are wrong. It is little surprise then that these have been criminal offences and that law, as well as morality, has condemned them. In recent times, however, there has been a liberalization and change in the law regarding homosexual practice.

The church in England was deeply involved in the decriminalization of homosexual acts and this led a number of theologians to propound a new perspective on sexuality and sexual ethics. This is called 'personalism' and stresses that any moral judgements to be made concerning sexual activity need to ask how such acts help human persons grow and flourish. In a way this still uses a kind of natural law, believing that certain kinds of activities expressed in appropriate settings do lead to human growth and avoid human diminishing. J. Dominian expresses the need for certain factors to be present before such growth can occur. These mean that sexual acts must contribute to the quality of relation-ships between people. No matter how these activities may be seen in themselves and in their own natures, as long as they serve human growth they are morally good. Such growth needs permanence, security and commitment. Those who emphasize personal relationships as the moral measure of sexual acts recognize that adultery and homosexual activity as well as premarital and extramarital sexual activities may be not just permitted but encouraged on this basis, but stress that marriage will continue to be the most likely setting in which such personal growth will be nourished. Personalism joins with traditional sexual morality in condemning rape and incest as being harmful and destructive of the individual. Likewise prostitution, pornography and promiscuity are viewed negatively for the way they depersonalize those who engage in acts of prostitution and those who are exploited by pornography and for the reinforcement of poor relationships between people which lies at the basis of pornography, as well as for the impersonalization of sexuality which is the necessary result of sexual promiscuity.

Homosexuality has been the focus of debate in terms not only of changes in sexual attitudes but as the nub of deciding what is natural. Many claim that homosexual acts are unnatural, but the opponents of such views emphasize that sexual acts committed by homosexual people are also done in the name of sexual love by heterosexuals. By 'natural' may be meant what is statistically normal, what is usual in society or the animal or human species, or what is natural to the individual. If homosexuality is not merely a stage of human development and is genuinely part of the biological and psychological make-up of an individual, then the nature of moral imperatives concerning sexual expression needs careful examination. Traditionalists claim that there must be no false distinction between the rules for homosexual and heterosexual people. God's standards are the same for all. Sexual expression is to take place in the context of marriage. By definition, homosexual people cannot be married to each other, thus they must be chaste in the way that single and unmarried people are called to be chaste. Some regard this as a demand for celibacy. In reality, celibacy is a vocation chosen for the sake of some higher calling. Jesus Christ was chaste and celibate, yet he was fully a man, and this shows

that genital activity is not fundamental to being human. While homosexuals may accept this, they claim that if God has made them to be homosexual people then they ought not to be denied the opportunity for personal fulfilment and growth through sexual activity and satisfaction.

Sexual deviance may be relatively harmless, as in transsexualism, or lead to sexual offences against others. Thus medicine and law have important moral concerns as to treatment and control, recognizing problems over the use of limited medical resources in such cases and the need to protect individuals and the community from abuse. Law and legality is different from morality, and in making moral judgements Christians must distinguish clearly between moral arguments which are based on principles and those which rest on consequences. Both are an important part of Christian moral reflection.

The move in the twentieth century is towards stressing the importance of sexual relationships and expressions in terms of interpersonal relationships. Theologically this means a move away from seeing procreation as the primary role of sexual expression and replacing it with the unitive and supportive role which helps reinforce and develop a relationship and the people in it. It is also a move away from erotic, self-centred love towards a genuine love and care for another which is not simply family love, but is marked by the agapeic love of God which is self-giving and concerned for the well-being and flourishing of the other in the relationship (see LOVE, CHRISTIAN). Non-Christians complain that Christians are obsessed with sexual matters, and it may be true that such a powerful and vulnerable area of life and experience makes many of us uneasy. Clearly people need to understand their own sexuality and the nature of sexuality in itself. They must beware of repressing sexuality in a facile and harmful way, though many testify to being able to sublimate those drives into other areas of life. This will mean rejecting both prudery and exhibitionism and ensuring that sexual behaviour is not merely what is socially or legally permissible, but is both understood and practised in the light of a total grasp of the nature, role and place of sexuality in relation to God and his standards for humanity. Marriage thus will remain the focus and norm for the judgement of sexual behaviour. The church needs to work out carefully how to develop and encourage proper expression of sexuality for all of us, especially for the single, widowed, divorced and celibate. Sexuality is God's good gift and is to be enjoyed and celebrated. It is a wonderful servant, but always in danger of becoming a powerful and destructive master.

See also ETHICS; MEDICAL ETHICS; ROMAN CATHOLIC THEOLOGY; SOCIAL QUESTIONS.

E. DAVID COOK

Bibliography

Catholic Truth Society 1975: Decleration on certain questions concerning sexual ethics. In *Sacred Congregation for the Doctrine of Faith*.

Dominian, J. 1977: *Proposals for a New Sexual Ethic*. London: Darton, Longman and Todd.

Nelson, J.B. 1979: *Embodiment: An Approach to Sexuality and Christian Theology*. Minneapolis: Augsburg Publishing.

Thielicke, H. 1964: *The Ethics of Sex*, trans. J.W. Doberstein. London: Clarke.

situation ethics See ETHICS; LOVE, CHRISTIAN.

social questions Down the ages social questions – meaning primarily issues of social JUSTICE and the right ordering of the political and economic spheres – have played a variety of roles in Christian theology. Theology has usually understood itself as having a responsibility to address such matters, directly or indirectly, and often social issues have acted as triggers or stimuli for theological endeavour. But at times there has been concern that social questions might drive and determine the theological enterprise, so that theology becomes an ideological weapon rather than a serious engagement with public truth.

Medieval theology, within the parameters of Christendom assumptions, developed a highly complex, sophisticated and intellectually rigorous way of treating social questions. This operated at two levels. First, there was discussion and debate about the relation of church and state (with other systems such as the economy being treated as part of, or analogous to, the state). Here the questions at issue concerned the boundaries, functions and competence of each. The details of significant medieval controversies and fundamental disagreements in this area do not concern us here. But it is important to note that hardly anyone suggested that theology did not belong in the public realm, or that it was possible to discuss coherently social, economic and political questions independently of theological considerations. In premodern times there was no such thing as a theologically innocent political theory; even as secular or pagan a thinker as Machiavelli cannot avoid taking up theological positions in his work. Before Grotius it was hardly thought possible to treat social issues *etsi Deus non daretur*.

Second, medieval theology developed patterns of systematic and rigorous discourse in relation to a number of specific social questions among which war, wages and prices were the most important. The underlying assumption here was that in a sinful world human aggression and acquisitiveness need to be curbed and checked. Human beings have an inbuilt tendency to distort ideas of value, justice and goodness to suit their interests. These distortions need to be measured and corrected against objective standards nurtured in the Christian tradition and rooted in Scripture, of which theology is the steward. But the absolute demands of the gospel are possible only for a few. In the public realm these standards need to be tempered and adjusted if they are to be helpful. But despite such compromises the validity of the absolute standards of perfection must never be lost sight of.

Out of this kind of discourse emerged the teaching on the JUST WAR. War, aggression, is for the Christian inherently sinful, but in this broken and imperfect world sometimes inevitable and necessary. Just war theory suggested criteria for judging whether it was legitimate to go to war (*ius ad bellum*) and constraints on the waging of war aimed at minimizing the damage and encouraging a quick cessation of hostilities (*ius in bello*).

The discussion of the just wage and the just price was based on the assumption that market transactions are basically suspect from a Christian point of view because they are motivated by greed and acquisitiveness, not love or justice. Hence the weak and the poor require protection against the strong and the rich. Prices must not be such as to produce an excessive profit for the seller, nor so high that basic goods are denied to the needy. Wages should be such as to keep the worker and the family in a decent and acceptable standard of life.

The details and the problems of medieval social thought do not concern us here. But the seriousness with which medieval theology addressed the issues must be recognized, and its sheer intellectual achievement applauded. Its influence is still powerfully with us.

From the Reformation period both Protestant and Roman Catholic churches continued to address social questions, for a long time doing little more than repeating the positions reached in the late Middle Ages. But new complicating factors emerged which raised major problems for the continuation of this tradition of social teaching. Divided churches were often much less able to enforce discipline, particularly on the powerful. Lutherans and some others increasingly adopted a version of the two kingdoms theory, which in effect handed over the social, economic and political spheres to the unfettered influence of the secular authorities, and regarded economic and political theory as subjects effectively independent of theology (see SECULARIZATION). 'National churches' were often established in such a way that they were deeply beholden to the state and could hardly question it. The growth of pietism, initially on Lutheran soil and encouraged by the romantic movement, reinforced an individualistic understanding of the faith. Such internal pressures to withdraw from engagement with social questions in the public arena meant that for much theology and for many Christians the only appropriate responses to social problems were palliative rather than prophetic, handouts to the deserving poor rather than engagement with the issue of poverty, for example.

There is also much strength in the argument developed particularly forcefully by R.H. Tawney to the effect that the increasing complexity of the economic, social and political systems in early modern times posed new and difficult questions of a quite unprecedented sort, and made it far more difficult to enforce traditional Christian norms or restraints on power. The churches were incapable of rising to this challenge, Tawney argued, and they

simply continued to mouth the slogans and the rhetoric of the medieval period, which became increasingly irrelevant to the new and rapidly changing situation:

> In an age of impersonal finance, world-markets and a capitalist organization of industry, [the Church's] traditional social doctrines had no specific to offer, and were merely repeated, when, in order to be effective, they should have been thought out again from the beginning and formulated in new and living terms . . . Faced with the problems of a wage-earning proletariat, it could do no more than repeat, with meaningless iteration, its traditional lore as to the duties of master to servant and servant to master.
>
> *(Tawney, 1926, pp. 184–5).*

And such responding in traditional vein to the social questions of a few generations back rather than reacting intelligently to those of today is depressingly frequent in the history of Christian social thought.

The Enlightenment strongly encouraged a privatization of theology, and accelerated the decline of Christian social thought. Most Enlightenment social thinking attempts to operate independently of the tradition, as a comparison of Immanuel Kant's tract *Eternal Peace* and the just war theory illustrates. Increasingly social theory developed *etsi Deus non daretur*, and a common assumption emerged that moral and theological considerations have little bearing on political, economic and social affairs. The tendency in the early nineteenth century to treat economics and politics as part of natural theology does not contradict this, for it represents a strange alliance with the classical economics and the new social sciences so that theology's task becomes the discernment of the movements of a benign 'invisible hand' operating mysteriously in structures of society which are God-given and therefore beyond question by the pious. No longer is social theology's primary task the constraint of the powerful and building dykes against sin. Instead of wrestling with systemic evil and the sins of the powerful it is the drunkenness, immorality, improvidence and fecklessness of the weak and of the victims which attract attention. The social, economic and political systems were regarded as parts of the divinely sanctioned order of things.

Roman Catholic social teaching also tended to ossify in the seventeenth and eighteenth centuries, and well into the nineteenth, partly as an instance of the comprehensive Catholic rejection of modernity and romantic wistfulness for medieval Christendom, partly because of an obsession with issues relating to the papal states and Italian politics.

Evangelicals in the same centuries tended to oscillate between individualistic pietism and forms of practical social concern (often labelled 'practical Christianity') such as campaigns against the slave trade, child labour in factories, the state of the prisons and so on. Although people such as Charles Grant, Zachary Macaulay and James Mill from the 'Clapham Sect' had strong views on how Britain as the imperial power should behave in relation to India, in terms both of allowing missionary effort and of opposing practices such as suttee (the burning of widows on their husbands' funeral pyres), they did not undertake a critique of imperialism as such, let alone of the social structure at home or the nature of the links between Britain and India. That was left to a few missionaries who were led to see that if caste was fundamentally incompatible with Christianity class might fare little better, and increasingly found themselves criticizing imperialism and racism on explicitly Christian grounds.

The second half of the nineteenth century was a period when social questions became unavoidable, even for theologians, and began once again to influence the theological agenda quite explicitly. The industrial revolution and the associated urbanization bred a widespread and obvious deprivation, disease and despair which had to be addressed by a theology with any claim to relevance.

The social gospel movement was the most significant nineteenth-century American response to the problems of industrial CAPIT-ALISM. Under the banner of liberal progressive theology, and led by Washington Gladden (1836–1918) and Walter Rauschenbusch (1861–1918), it was influential until the Second World War, when it effectively collapsed under vigorous attack from Reinhold Niebuhr and other 'neo-orthodox' theologians. A mainly Anglican Christian Socialist movement started in England in the mid-nineteenth century, with some contact with the Catholic Socialists in France. Its major theologian and theorist was F.D. Maurice, and it led to the formation at the end of the century of the Christian Social Union, whose leaders included Bishop Westcott (1825–1901), Henry Scott Holland (1847–1918) and Charles Gore (1853–1932) (see CHRISTIAN SOCIALISM).

Very different was the Religious Socialist movement in Switzerland and Germany, which deeply influenced Karl Barth, Paul Tillich and many others. This called for a thoroughgoing break with liberalism and a radical critique of Christianity rather after the style of Søren Kierkegaard's 'Attack on Christendom'. The prophetic figure of Franz Overbeck (1837–1905) with his thoroughgoing, rather Nietzschean, critique lurked in the background, but the main leaders were Christoph Blumhardt the younger (1842–1919), Hermann Kutter (1863–1931) and Leonhard Ragaz (1868–1945). The Religious Socialist movement encouraged Barth and many others to take the social question with profound seriousness in the context of a renewed awareness of the goodness of God and the centrality of the Christian hope. It also propelled Barth into membership of the Social Democratic party and shaped the socialism which F.W. Marquhardt has argued was a determinative element in Barth's theological development throughout his life. But whatever views one may have about Marquhardt's thesis, it is certainly the case that Barth right up until his death devoted considerable attention to the social question and took up positions which were consistently radical.

A very different style of response to 'the social question' is the official social teaching of the Roman Catholic church. This started in the pontificate of Leo XIII with the promulgation of the encyclical *Rerum Novarum* in 1891, and has been continued in a notable series of encyclicals, conciliar documents, statements from the Congregation for the Defence of the Faith, and (most interestingly) in pastoral letters from bishops' conferences, most notably the letters on war and peace and on the economy issued by the US Catholic Bishops' Conference. The most important documents in the series are: *Rerum Novarum* (1891), *Quadragesimo Anno* (Pius

XI – 1931), *Mater et Magistra* (John XXIII – 1961), *Pacem in Terris* (John XIII – 1963), *Gaudium et Spes* (the Second Vatican Council – 1965), *Populorum Progressio* (Paul VI – 1967), *Octogesima Adveniens* (Paul VI – 1971), *Laborem Exercens* (John Paul II – 1981), *Certain Aspects of the Theology of Liberation* (Sacred Congregation for the Defence of the Faith – 1984), *Christian Freedom and Liberation* (SCDF – 1986), *Sollicitudo Rei Socialis* (John Paul II – 1987), and *Centesimus Annus* (John Paul II – 1991). (See ROMAN CATHOLIC THEOLOGY.)

These documents, and particularly those that emanate from the pope himself, claim to present a unified body of authoritative teaching on social issues, even a 'social doctrine'. The degree of authority is by no means clear. The First Vatican Council (1870) declared the infallibility of the pope when speaking *ex cathedra*, that is, 'when he is performing the function of pastor and teacher of all Christians and in accordance with his supreme Apostolic authority defining a teaching about faith or morals to be held by the Universal Church'. But although there have been 'infallible' definitions since that time, and none of the social teaching formally has this status, through the phenomenon of 'creeping infallibility' it has a very high authority indeed for Roman Catholics, as is shown in the documents of the Second Vatican Council:

> This religious submission of will and mind must be shown in a special way to the authentic teaching of the Roman Pontiff, even when he is not speaking *ex cathedra*. That is, it must be shown in such a way that his supreme *magisterium* is acknowledged with reverence, and the judgements made by him sincerely adhered to, according to his manifest mind and will.
>
> *(Lumen Gentium §25).*

Integral to the understanding of papal authority underlying these documents is the pretence that here we have to deal with a tradition of teaching which evolves or develops without contradiction or change of direction. The possibility that the church might have erred in the past cannot be allowed. Thus when a high-powered international advisory commission recommended a change in the traditional

Roman Catholic position on birth control, the pope rejected its advice and proceeded to promulgate *Humanae Vitae* (1951), in which the traditional view is strongly reaffirmed. But in fact there have been quite fundamental, if unacknowledged, changes in the century of teaching with which we are concerned. At its start, the official social teaching of the Roman Catholic church was part of its repudiation of liberalism, modernity and modern industrial society. It was full of nostalgia for Christendom; it attempted to rehabilitate premodern notions such as that of the just wage with the minimum of modification; and it argued in a deductive way from principles embodied in natural law. Accordingly, the teaching was of an apparently timeless and general nature, rarely explicitly addressing specific issues or particular local themes. But with the pontificate of John XXIII and the Second Vatican Council there has been a major, if unacknowledged, methodological shift. The more recent documents are concerned above all with 'discerning the signs of the times', and do this with far more reference to Scripture than to natural law or other abstract principles. One notable instance of this is the remarkable central chapter in *Centesimus Annus* (1991) on the events of 1989.

Catholic social teaching has down the years developed an important and influential critique of various forms of socialism on the one hand, and of capitalism on the other. It has strong and consistent emphases on the need to protect workers and weak groups in society against the powerful, on the importance of fellowship or solidarity, and on the desirability of as many decisions as possible being taken at the local or community level. This last is the so-called principle of 'subsidiarity', which while increasingly neglected in ecclesiastical affairs has commended itself widely in secular social thinking. Indeed it is not too much to say that Catholic social teaching has provided the main ideological underpinning for the immensely influential Christian Democratic movement in Europe, and has had considerable impact elsewhere as well. This accounts for many of the marked differences between Anglo-Saxon neo-conservatism, as represented by Reaganism and Thatcherism, and European Christian democracy. The latter is firmly committed to measures to protect workers and the vulnerable against unbridled market forces because such provisions are enjoined in Catholic social teaching; the former see any 'social provisions' which constrain market forces as harmful to the proper, and beneficial, working of the free market system.

There is, however, a possibility of tension with the Vatican when attempts are made to adapt Catholic social teaching to specific contexts and local situations. These problems have been most obvious in recent years in relation to the two major pastoral letters of the US Catholic bishops, and the growth of Latin American liberation theology. The two US Pastorals, *The Challenge of Peace* of 1983 and *Economic Justice For All* of 1986, differed from the papal encyclicals in two particularly striking ways: they emerged as the result of a prolonged process of public debate and discussion of successive drafts in the course of which the bishops attended to a wide range of criticisms, comments and suggestions from many quarters; and second, the final documents presented themselves not so much as authoritative teaching which should bind the consciences of the faithful but as serious contributions to moral debate and challenges to responsible decision making. This process clearly raised important questions about the nature of the church's teaching office and the ways in which it is to be expressed today. Are bishops simply channels for the communication of papal teaching to the faithful, or are they entrusted with a responsibility to apply, interpret, modify and criticize if necessary the teaching of Rome? The Vatican clearly saw these Pastorals as something of an implicit challenge to the centralization of the teaching office in Rome. And when different hierarchies disagree while both sides claim to be faithfully interpreting papal teaching, as the US bishops differed about nuclear deterrence from the German and French hierarchies, problems about the coherence and clarity of Catholic social teaching arise in an acute form.

In promoting an open process rather than delivering a barrage of pronouncements, in producing statements which make little claim to authority save that which inheres in their arguments and evidence, in declining to constrain the conscience but rather addressing to different categories of people the kind of considerations they should take into account,

the US bishops have in fact been pointing to a very different way of engaging with social questions from that espoused by Rome.

Similar issues have been raised far more sharply by the emergence of LIBERATION THEOLOGY in Latin America. Liberation theology presents itself as a contextualized grassroots theology, but for the most part it has respected the hierarchy and the ecclesiastical institution, and in its turn has found significant support among the bishops. Rome has been concerned not only by liberation theology's differences from traditional teachings in a number of areas and its close liaison with Marxism, but above all by its challenge to centralized hierarchical authority in the church. Liberation theology's approach to social questions is sharply divergent from that of official social teaching. While the Vatican has consistently attempted to tread a middle path between left and right, liberation theology has asserted the need to take sides, and suggested that a preferential option for the poor necessarily involves taking a political stance which is an uncompromising recognition of the reality and unavoidability of class conflict. Liberation theologians sometimes argue that they are operating within the parameters of official social teaching, but they are more frequently sharply critical of what they see as bland moralizing without serious social analysis and an assumption that the church is, and ought to be, above the fray.

On the Protestant side the most interesting responses to social questions in the twentieth century were notable individual projects ignited by one or other of the great global events of the century – the rise of fascism and the resultant Holocaust, the Bolshevik revolution, the long interaction between Christianity and MARXISM and the recent collapse of the communist project in eastern Europe, and the growing awareness of vast structures of oppression and exploitation which continue to cause human poverty, degradation and death on a vast scale as well as the rape of the natural environment. Barth's early association with the Religious Socialists, his ministry as the 'Red pastor of Safenwil' and his response first to the rise of Hitlerism and then to the cold war lend credence to the thesis that a socialist commitment was a constant thread in his life's work. Certainly he emphasizes even in his late writings the need for a preferential option for the poor, the obligation on the theologian *qua* theologian to engage with social questions, and the view that the only possibilities worth considering are the various socialist options on offer. Reinhold Niebuhr, again, was stimulated by his experience in Detroit at the depth of the depression to put the social question at the heart of his theologizing. And there were many, many others.

Did the ecumenical movement develop a social teaching in any way comparable to that emanating from Rome? The answer to this question can only be 'Yes' and 'No'. Life and Work, one of the two branches of the embryonic ecumenical movement (the other being Faith and Order), devoted itself to social, political and economic questions, and these have occupied an increasingly prominent – in some people's view far too prominent place in the work of the World Council of Churches. The belief that 'doctrine divides but service unites' was articulated at the time of the Stockholm Conference (1925) out of which Life and Work emerged. The Oxford Conference on Church, Community and State (1937) was a landmark, laying down standards for rigorous theological consideration of social questions which have seldom been excelled in its preparatory volumes and in its debates. Oxford addressed particularly the implications of mass unemployment and the threat of war consequent on the rise of Nazism and fascism in Europe. This work fed into the development of the notion of 'the responsible society', in which those who exercise power are answerable to God and to the people, and responsibility is nurtured in freedom. The responsible society was the pivotal notion in the new World Council of Churches' social thinking, until it was effectively challenged at the 1966 Geneva Conference on 'Christians in the Technical and Social Revolutions of our Time' and the Uppsala Assembly of 1968. These events marked a more radical stance in the WCC, largely under the influence of the increasing number of representatives from third world churches. The concept of the responsible society was broadened into the notion of 'a just, participatory and sustainable society', which was given pride of place at the Nairobi Assembly (1975). More recently attention has shifted to a 'conciliar process' towards a covenant between the churches for 'justice, peace and the integrity of creation'.

It is not too strong to suggest that the WCC no longer has a consistent, carefully thought through and incremental social teaching expressed in documents which is in any way comparable to the official teaching of the Roman Catholic church. Indeed large parts of its constituency would question whether such a body of teaching is desirable. What the WCC does have is an ability to express the anger, frustration and expectations of victims of injustice, exploitation and oppression, to 'speak for the dumb'. It is not at present so good at using these cries as a resource for serious theology. But there are signs that that may well come. Meanwhile, the 'view from below' is often rather disjointed, tends to see social questions in black and white terms, and sometimes makes rather simplistic connections between belief and action. It is at its best when it encourages a confessional approach building on the precedent of the Barmen Declaration to issues such as apartheid, where the integrity of the gospel is at stake. More controversial is the suggestion that the world economic system is so evil and unjust that it should be denounced and witnessed against (Duchrow, 1987).

The Christian church is one of the few institutions which is capable of, and has a responsibility for, speaking for the dumb. And their voice must surely be an essential ingredient in any serious engagement with social questions. Furthermore, in modern pluralist societies there seems to be a deep uncertainty about fundamental social values and shared goals. Here there is both an opportunity and a responsibility to offer Christian insights in a time of confusion, the sort of confusion that hurts individuals and corrodes community.

See also ECONOMIC ANALYSIS AND ETHICS; ETHICS; KINGDOM OF GOD: POLITICAL AND SOCIAL THEOLOGY; MEDICAL ETHICS; SEXUAL ETHICS; WAR AND PEACE; WORK AND LEISURE.

Bibliography

Baum, G., and Ellsberg, R., eds 1989: *The Logic of Solidarity*. Maryknoll: Orbis.

Coleman, J., ed. 1991: *One Hundred Years of Catholic Social Thought*. Maryknoll: Orbis.

Duchrow, U. 1987: *Global Economy: A Confessional Issue for the Churches?* Geneva: World Council of

Churches.

Duff, E. 1956: *The Social Thought of the World Council of Churches*. London: Longman.

Forrester, D.B. 1988: *Theology and Politics*. Oxford: Blackwell.

Forrester, D.B. 1989: *Beliefs, Values and Policies: Conviction Politics in a Secular Age*. Oxford: Clarendon.

Hennelly, A.T., ed. 1990: *Liberation Theology: A Documentary History*. Maryknoll: Orbis.

John Paul II 1991: *Centesimus Annus*. London: Catholic Truth Society.

Mahoney, J. 1987: *The Making of Moral Theology*. Oxford: Clarendon.

Northcott, M.S., ed. 1991: *Vision and Prophecy: The Tasks of Social Theology Today*. Edinburgh: Centre for Theology and Public Issues.

Novak, M. 1989: *Catholic Social Thought and Liberal Institutions*, 2nd edn. Oxford: Transaction.

Preston, R.H. 1981: *Explorations in Theology – 9*. London: SCM Press.

Preston, R.H. 1983: *Church and Society in the Late Twentieth Century*. London: SCM Press.

Preston, R.H. 1987: *The Future of Christian Ethics*. London: SCM Press.

Tawney, R.H. 1926: *Religion and the Rise of Capitalism*. London: John Murray.

Walsh, M., and Davies, B., eds 1991: *Proclaiming Justice and Peace*. London: CAFOD/Collins.

DUNCAN FORRESTER

social science and Christian thought The relationship between social science and Christian thought is problematic, and its interpretation presents considerable difficulties. 'Social science' is not a simple unity, but a complex of disciplines that have emerged and differentiated themselves in the post-Enlightenment era, above all in the late nineteenth century and the first half of the twentieth. A consideration of the relation between social science and Christian thought during this period would involve a comparative history of both, but this is as yet unwritten. At the level of broad generalization, the social sciences can in the first instance be said to have evolved and expanded at the territorial expense of Christian and religious thought. This ongoing but divergent relationship is itself part of the complex process usually subsumed under the catch-all category of SECULARIZATION (Chadwick, 1975). The historical process of secularization was explained by the distinguished American sociologist Peter Berger as 'the process by which sectors of society and culture are removed from the domination of religious institutions and symbols', which 'affects the totality of cultural life and of ideation, and may be observed in the decline of religious contents in the arts, in philosophy, in literature and, most important of all, in the rise of science as an autonomous, thoroughly secular perspective on the world.' This process of secularization has a subjective aspect in the secularization of consciousness. Berger further argued that 'this means that the modern West has produced an increasing number of individuals who look upon the world and their own lives without the benefit of religious interpretations' (Berger, [1967] 1969). In reality, the situation is far more complex than this over-simple secularization model might imply.

Christian theology as such has tended to retreat into intellectual 'nature reserves' (Ernst Käsemann) or into what Ernst Bloch (in the case of Karl Barth) called the 'safe stronghold of transcendence'. Religious thought in a more general sense has undergone ambiguous displacements and transmutations in what George Steiner has suggestively described as the twentieth-century 'afterlife' of religion. Indeed whilst Berger reflected a substantial body of postwar opinion, the phenomenon of secularization can now been seen to involve not only the loss of the traditional 'sacred', but also its multiplex and ambiguous reconstitutions, a process now overtly re-legitimated in the 'condition of postmodernity' (Harvey, 1989).

The social sciences stand awkwardly between the traditional cultural and human interests of the west and the nascent autonomous forms of knowledge associated with physical science: the object of enquiry is bound up with the former, yet social scientific methods have drawn upon the latter. The result is a constant crisis of identity underlying the professionalized disciplinary specializations that constitute social science as a whole. Sociological reflection conceived on a grand scale, notably by Max Weber, Emile Durkheim, Talcott Parsons, Niklaas Luhmann, Anthony Giddens and Hans Blumenburg, for example, is ambitious and polymathic and lends substance to the claim that, historically speaking, the discipline has deposed and succeeded theology as 'queen of the sciences'. Significantly, Wilhelm Dilthey excluded theology from his reconfiguration of the *Geisteswissenschaften* (Dilthey, 1910–27). The progressive societal marginalization and transformations of religion and religious thought in post-Enlightenment western culture and society thus underly any review of their relation with the social sciences. Such a situation in turn implies an encounter and dialogue between centre and periphery of very considerable complexity. Nevertheless, what Michel Foucault regarded as the interlinked 'deaths' of God and man in the history of the 'human sciences' (*les sciences humaines*) (Foucault, [1966] 1970), makes a renewal of reflection on the origin and nature of the values of humankind a high priority within the social sciences. The axiomatic basis of knowledge of the 'human', the modern *episteme*, is ripe for re-exploration and renewal.

Given the historical divergence of the social sciences and Christian thought, a limiting, yet representative strategy is required. Since the early Enlightenment, the emergent human and social sciences have to a considerable degree grown out of the criticism of religious phenomena and theological discourse. The remarks of the young Karl Marx still remain significant as a commentary upon the history of the formulation of theory in the social sciences: 'For Germany the criticism of religion is in the main complete, and criticism of religion is the premise of all criticism' (Marx, 1959, p. 37).

As noted above, there is as yet no fully informed account of the dissociations and displacements of religious phenomena and theological discourse construed from the standpoint of the history of social science. Two strands in the history of the social sciences do, however, relate directly to religion as such: these are the sociology and the anthropology of religion (see RELIGION THEORIES OF). As distinct subdisciplines, they provide a provisional point of access to the complex and problematic situation outlined above. In this role, the sociology (O'Toole, 1984) and the anthropology (Leach, 1985) of religion have a double relationship with religion (and thus with religious thought). On the one hand, practitioners in the subdisciplines constantly reflect upon the canonical contributions of their 'founding fathers' (whose work in turn often emerged from the critical appraisal of religion);

on the other, present-day researchers address contemporary forms of religion and religiosity. Both sociologists and anthropologists alike, it is important to note, usually investigate the phenomenon of *religion*. 'Religious' and 'Christian' thought are thus most frequently conceived from these socio-scientific standpoints as parts of the raw material of research, and not as dialogue partners, real or potential. This categorical dismissal is unfortunately often reinforced by a formal divorce within the academic study of religion between the uneasy cluster of disciplines known as 'religious studies' and its sometimes methodologically petrified forerunner 'theology'.

The status of religious thought in relation to the socio-scientific enterprise is perhaps best understood when this disjunction is incorporated into the threefold categorization offered by the concepts of 'pre-modernity', 'modernity' and 'postmodernity'. The sciences of man and society have been quintessential expressions of the development of 'modernity' (Habermas, [1985] 1987; Blumenberg, [1966] 1983). Religious thought as a factor in religion appears to much social science as a premodern survival, an anachronism sustained, for example, by the careful conservation of theology as an academic discipline or by the persisting ideological impulses that may inform the religious behaviour and belief systems of both Christianity and non-Christian religions, sects, and the new religious movements. Such a juxtaposition (often over-simple) of scientific modernity and mythological premodernity has been disrupted by the articulation of the 'postmodern condition' (Lyotard, [1979] 1984) (see POSTMODERNISM). In postmodernity, the hegemonic conflict of modernity and premodernity is being displaced by a dynamic pluralism, that is, by a societal 'market' crowded with the competing claims of many possible cultural identities (including religious forms of life). These are refunctionable along with a myriad other sociocultural artefacts in the overall context of a world system (Wallerstein, 1976) which is driven by internationalized market economies towards 'globalization' (Robertson, 1991). In consequence, 'Christian thought' now finds itself in a position to compete (along with other religious identities) for the attention and allegiance of a global audience. Thus the panoptic vision of the great historian and phenomenologist of religion Mircea Eliade (1907–1987) is no imaginative figment but an anticipation of the possible futures awaiting enactment in a New Age:

> For years I have had in mind a short, concise work, which could be read in a few days. For continuous reading reveals above all the fundamental unity of religious phenomena and at the same time the inexhaustible newness of their expressions. The reader of such a book would be given access to the Vedic hymns, the Brahmanas, and the Upanishads a few hours after he had reviewed the ideas and beliefs of the Paleolithics, of Mesopotamia, and of Egypt; he would discover Sankara, Tantrism and Milarepa, Islam, Giochino de Fiore or Paracelsus, the day after he had meditated on Zarathustra, Gautama Buddha, and Taoism, on the Hellenistic Mysteries, the rise of Christianity, Gnosticism, alchemy, or the mythology of the Grail; he would encounter the German illuminists and Romantics, Hegel, Max Müller, Freud, Jung, and Bonhoeffer, soon after discovering Quetzalcoatl and Viracocha, the twelve Alvars and Gregory Palamas, the earliest Cabalists, Avicenna or Eisai.
>
> *(Eliade, [1976] 1978).*

Eliade's all-embracing anticipation of virtually unlimited appropriations of religious identities comprises both extreme relativism and new possibilities for the re-legitimation of religious belief systems which are to coexist in tension (that is, once humankind has fully acknowledged the passing of the 'grand narratives' of both Christian premodernity and an attritive modernity). Eliade's vision of a religiously informed humanism is built upon an extraordinary knowledge of world history and prehistory drawn together in and through an all-comprehensive theory of myth; its conditions of realization are a function, not least, of the distribution and availability of cultural capital (Bourdieu, 1972).

The origins of the socio-scientific study of religion in the nineteenth century are intimately related to the Enlightenment critique of religion and its assertion that the unique prescriptive truths of the Judaeo-Christian world view were both morally oppressive and historically problematic. The Enlightenment sought to locate the origins of religion in human experience, rather than divine revelation. As David Hume wrote in 1757 in *The Natural History of Religion*: 'There is an universal tendency among mankind to conceive all beings like themselves, and to transfer to every object those qualities with which they are familiarly acquainted, and of which they are intimately conscious.' Thus human beings anthropomorphize the physical world and can only correct this 'natural tendency' by 'experience and reflection'. The same tendency which ascribes 'malice or good will to every thing that hurts or pleases us' is, according to Hume, 'not less, while we cast our eyes upwards; and, transferring, as is too usual, human passions and infirmities to the Deity, represent him as jealous and revengeful, capricious and partial, and, in short, a wicked and foolish man in every respect but his superior power and authority' (Hume, [1757] 1969, p. 21). The assumption that religion is of human origin underlies the socio-scientific study of religion; the further assumption that religious thought and theology are largely epiphenomenal and anachronistic has informed much social science.

The contributions of, for example, such figures as (besides Hume) Auguste Comte, J.G. Frazer, E.B. Tylor, Herbert Spencer and W. Robertson Smith were of central importance in the emergence of the socio-scientific study of religion. Out of these diverse efforts to represent the origins of religion in historical, genetic and evolutionary terms, the formal subdiscipline of the anthropology of religion was to grow. Both the anthropology and the sociology of religion have developed around a longstanding problem of definition: if religion was of thoroughly human origin, then what was it? James Frazer confronted this question when he sought to distinguish magic and religion in his classic, eclectic (but problematic) synthesis, *The Golden Bough*, of 1890:

> There is probably no subject in the world about which opinions differ so much as the nature of religion, and to frame a definition of it which would satisfy everyone must obviously be impossible.

All that a writer can do is, first, to say clearly what he means by religion, and afterwards to employ the word consistently in that sense throughout his work. By religion, then, I understand a propitiation or conciliation of powers superior to man which are believed to direct and control the course of nature and of human life. Thus defined, religion consists of two elements, a theoretical and a practical, namely a belief in powers higher than man and an attempt to propitiate or please them.

Bronislav Malinowski (1884–1942), a later pioneer in the anthropological study of religion, worked in the aftermath of the speculative academic anthropology of the nineteenth century. The foundation of his achievement lay in descriptive ethnography, supremely of the Trobiand Islanders with whom he lived as a participant observer from 1914 to 1918. Malinowski stressed the integral nature of primitive societies and their religion. He argued that any individual artefact should be seen playing a role in a culture which should be understood as a whole, that is as a complex and interrelated set of institutions which between them function to satisfy certain primary biological needs of members of the society in question. He concluded (reflecting the influence of the sociologist Emile Durkheim) that:

> religion, by sacralizing and thus standardizing the other set of impulses, bestows on man the gift of mental integrity . . . [in the face of death] religion counteracts the centrifugal forces of fear, dismay, demoralization, and provides the most powerful means of reintegration of the group's shaken solidarity and of the re-establishment of its morale. In short, religion here assures the victory of tradition and culture over the mere negative response of thwarted instinct.
>
> *(Malinowski, 1948, p. 53)*

Whereas the Enlightenment critique of religion was largely directed against Christianity, the development of the anthropological study of religion in the nineteenth century largely focused its attention upon cultural contexts distant from a decreasingly Christian Europe. It was only later, and controversially, that the implications of these investigations were applied to contexts closer to home. The same cannot be said for the foundational thinkers of sociology, for present purposes here limited to Marx, Weber and Durkheim. All three grounded their initial reflection in the European experience and then widened the scope of their attention.

Karl Marx (1818–1883) conceived the reductive interpretation of religion to be the first step in the revolutionary overthrow and demystification of social structures in which religion functioned as the alienated, inverted and thus the epiphenomenal representation of the true nature of a conflictual social reality. In the theory of alienation and the development of the concept of ideology, Marx made major contributions to sociological theory of continuing importance to the sociology of religion. Yet the development of the Marxist critique of religion (which owed much to Ludwig Feuerbach) was disappointing; dangerously, it was the relatively unsophisticated justification of the even cruder diktats of Lenin's ruthless separation of religion and the state. In fuller terms, Marx outlined the first stages in the development of the theory of ideology which has in developed (and disputed) forms exercised immense influence in social science:

> The production of notions, ideas and consciousness is from the beginning directly interwoven with the material activity and the material intercourse of human beings, the language of real life. The production of men's ideas, thinking, their spiritual intercourse, here appear as the direct efflux of their material condition. The same applies to spiritual production as represented in the language of politics, laws, morals, religion, metaphysics, etc., of a people. The producers of men's ideas, notions, etc., are men, but real active men as determined by a definite development of their productive forces and the intercourse corresponding to those productive forces up to its remotest form. Consciousness [*das Bewusstsein*] can never be anything else but conscious being [*das bewusste Sein*], and the being of men is their real

life-process. If in the whole of ideology men and their relations appear upside down as in a camera obscura this is due as much to their historical life-process as the inversion of objects on the retina is due to their immediate physical life-process.

(Marx, 1959)

It is against Marx's immensely influential and reductive account of religion (and the other items in the cultural 'superstructure' or *Überbau*) that Max Weber (1864–1920) may be said in part to have reacted. Whereas Marx proposed an interpretative framework in which religion was understood as a phenomenon of alienation and displacement, Weber's methodology was based initially upon the quantitative accumulation of complex social data, which through the generation of 'ideal types' itself suggested the means for qualitative interpretation. Thus in his sociology of religion Weber avoided the monolithic reductionism of Marx when he maintained that: 'To define "religion", to say what it is, is not possible at the start of a presentation such as this. Definition can be attempted, if at all, only at the conclusion of the study' (Weber, [1922] 1956).

Max Weber has remained a figure of undiminished importance in the human and social sciences. Often seen as a counterpoise to Marx, Weber provided many of the basic concepts of British and North American sociology: 'rationalization', 'ideal type', 'unintended consequences of social action', 'charismatic authority', 'the iron cage of bureaucratic life', 'the Protestant ethic' and so on. Weber disputed the Marxian view of the epiphenomenal status of ideas in relation to socioeconomic reality without relapsing into the opposing 'idealist' view, characteristic all too frequently of post-Enlightenment Christian and religious thinkers. Weber was above all both the prophet and the interpreter of the forms of modernity and instrumental rationality associated with the rise and triumph of industrial capitalism. The consequences of this last for the quality of human life were immeasurable:

No-one knows who will live in this cage in the future, or whether at the end of this tremendous development entirely new prophets will arise, or there will be a great rebirth of old ideas and ideals, or,

if neither, mechanized petrification, embellished with a sort of convulsive self-importance. For of the last stage of this cultural development, it might well truly be said: 'Specialists without spirit, sensualists without heart; this nullity imagines that it has attained a level of civilization never before achieved'.

(Weber, [1904–5] 1930, p. 182).

Weber and his pupil Ernst Troeltsch (1865–1923) were jointly responsible for the initiation and development of theories of institutional typology (the celebrated church–sect distinction) which related the social structure of religious organizations to belief and religious behaviour. The initial dichotomy noted by Weber in *The Protestant Ethic and the Spirit of Capitalism* was applied by Troeltsch in a systematic study of the whole western Christian tradition. H.R. Niebuhr took up the argument and applied it to the growth of denominations. The further refinement and sophistication of this theoretical model has proved particularly fruitful in the study of North American Protestantism, sects (Wilson, 1969) and postwar new religious movements (Beckford, 1985). Most recently the church–sect typology and stratification theory has been applied to the study of the New Testament church (Esler, 1987).

An important and wide-ranging debate concerning the origin, meaning, form and ultimate consequences of the process of social change known as 'secularization' took place after the Second World War. Bryan Wilson, David Martin and Peter L. Berger have been leading contributors in the discussion of a complex phenomenon which strongly affected Christian theology (an influence seen above all in Dietrich Bonhoeffer's 'religionless Christianity'). There has been profound disagreement as to whether a 'general theory of secularization' (Martin, 1978) is possible or even desirable. Fuller sense of this debate can be made when it is related to the major works of the German social theorists Jürgen Habermas, Niklaas Luhmann and Hans Blumenberg.

Emile Durkheim (1858–1917) was the leading figure in the professionalization of sociology as the science of society (as distinct from social philosophy or social psychology), that is, as a recognizable discipline with its own epistemological and methodological foundations. Active during a period of rapid transformation in French society and a social order haunted by the memory of the revolution of 1789 and its rupture with the *ancien régime*, Durkheim sought to provide an enlightened scientific basis for social legislation, indeed for the preservation of social cohesion itself. In works like *The Division of Labour in Society* of 1893, *The Rules of Sociological Method* of 1895 and his study *Suicide* of 1897, Durkheim laid the theoretical basis for his last major works on belief and knowledge, particularly as found in religious systems.

In *The Elementary Forms of Religious Life* of 1912 Durkheim presented religion as an essential feature of collective life; thus ritual practice (religious function) is given priority over formal beliefs in the organization and continuity of religious systems. Belief in God (a feature of only some, and not all, religious systems) is subordinated to a universal separation between the profane and sacred worlds which Durkheim regarded as truly fundamental. Thus he argued that: 'A religion is a unified system of beliefs and practices relative to sacred things, that is to say, things set apart and forbidden – beliefs and practices which unite into one moral community called a Church, all those who adhere to them'. In fuller terms, religion (along with its contemporary analogates) plays an indispensable role in socialization; society needs religion.

Sacred things are those whose representation society itself has fashioned; it includes all sorts of collective states, common traditions and emotions, feelings which have a relationship to objects of general interest, etc.; and all those elements are combined according to the appropriate laws of social mentality. Profane things, conversely, are those which each of us constructs from our own sense data and experience; the ideas we have about them have as their subject matter unadulterated, individual impressions, and that is why they do not have the same prestige in our eyes as the preceding ones. We only put into them and see in them what empirical observa-

tion reveals to us. Now, these two sorts of mental state constitute two kinds of intellectual phenomena, since one type is produced by a single brain and a single mind, the other by a plurality of brains and minds acting and reacting on each other. This duality of the temporal and the spiritual is not an invention without reason and without foundation in reality; it expresses in symbolic language the duality of the individual and the social, of psychology proper and sociology. That is why for a long time the initiation into sacred things was also the operation by which the socialization of the individual was completed. At the same time, as man entered into the religious life, he assumed another nature and became a new man.

(Durkheim, 'Concerning the Definition of Religious Phenomena', in Pickering, 1975, pp. 95–6)

Durkheim's general conclusions, 'that religion is something pre-eminently social', that 'religious representations are collective representations which are the expression of collective realities' and that 'rites are ways of behaving which only come into being at the heart of assembled groups and whose function is to create, maintain and to re-establish certain mental states within these groups' (Pickering, p. 111), have passed entire into the axioms of francophone sociology of religion, a subdiscipline which continues to serve as a means of analysing the capacity of societies to bring about the socialization necessary to the preservation of public order.

In contrast with the functionalist approach pioneered by Emile Durkheim, phenomenologists of religion like Rudolf Otto, Gerhardus van der Leeuw and Mircea Eliade have maintained (albeit in different ways) that the sacred is an irreducible and universal dimension of human existence and that religious experiences lie at the base of culture itself. Eschewing Rudolf Otto's terminologically spectacular but intuitive articulation of the numinous of the '*Mysterium, Tremendum et Fascinans*' (Otto, [1917] 1923), van der Leeuw took up the methodological insights of Edmund Husserl and applied them to religion. Thus:

Phenomenology is the systematic discussion of what appears. Religion, however, is an ultimate experience that evades our observation, a revelation which in its very essence is, and remains, concealed. But how shall I deal with what is thus ever elusive and hidden? How can I refer to 'phenomenology of religion' at all? Here there clearly exists an antinomy that is certainly essential to all religions, but also to all understanding; it is indeed precisely because it holds good for *both*, for religion and understanding alike, that our own science becomes possible. It is unquestionably quite correct to say that faith and intellectual suspense (the *epoche*) do not exclude each other.

(van der Leeuw, [1933] 1938, p. 683)

Making a virtue of epistemological necessity, van der Leeuw made the twentieth-century 'crisis' (Husserl, [1954] 1970) of the European sciences an agnostic starting point for the study of religion. It is, it need scarcely be said, less than satisfactory in the long term to separate off the phenomenological analysis of religious inwardness (and even the artefacts of religion) from the ultimately complementary approaches taken by anthropology towards culture, and sociology towards society, respectively. It is in North America that this lesson has been most thoroughly learned.

Talcott Parsons (1902–1979) was, following his translation of Weber's *The Protestant Ethic*, the chief adapter of German sociology, in particular that of Weber, into American social science. His integration and synthesis of diverse strands of thought into a complex theory of social action has had a powerful influence upon the development of sociology as a widely taught, professionalized discipline. Parsons's pupils, the anthropologist Clifford J. Geertz, and the sociologist of religion Robert N. Bellah, have in turn had a substantial and beneficial influence upon the social-scientific study of religion. In Geertz's 'thick' and 'thin' approaches to the conceptualization and analysis of cultures, and in Bellah's development of 'symbolic interactionism', powerful tools are made available for the multidisciplinary, empathetic and nonreductive procedures that are indispensable to any adequate grasp of the function of religion or its surrogates in advanced capitalist society. Re-

ligion is human and it is integral to the condition of humankind (however dispersed, inverted or even degraded it may have become). In the context of such a recognition, Geertz's methodological refusal to divorce the cultural fabric of meaning from social structure, and thus anthropology from sociology, is profoundly emancipatory. So, he argues:

> Interpretative explanation trains its attention on what institutions, actions, images, utterances, events, customs, all the usual objects of social-scientific interest, mean to those whose institutions, actions, customs, and so on they are. As a result, it issues not in laws like Boyle's, or forces like Volta's, or mechanisms like Darwin's, but in constructions like Burckhardt's, Weber's, or Freud's: systematic unpackings of the conceptual world in which condottieri, Calvinists, or paranoids live. Culture is the fabric of meaning in terms of which human beings interpret their experience and guide their action; social structure is the form that action takes, the actually existing network of social relations.
>
> *(Geertz 1966)*

The relation between social science and specifically Christian (besides religious) thought is fraught with difficulties associated with the dissociation and fragmentation of cultural identities in the growing pluralism of the modern period. Humankind now exists in the extremely complex nexus represented by the conflict between on the one hand an invasive world system that transforms ever more effectively all facets of human life into marketable commodities and, on the other, the resurgence of cultural identities overshadowed by the coming ecological crisis, an 'ecological eschaton'. Market choice, informational integration and global competition have, it is arguable, replaced the struggle of monolithic hegemonies, all the more so since the near-total collapse of Marxist socialism.

For Christian thought confronted by the richness and diversity of the human social sciences the strategic choices are stark. On the one hand it is possible to recapitulate the type of transcendental critique analogous to that of the later thought of Karl Barth (or indeed of the Reformed Dutch neo-Kantian philosopher Hermann Dooyeweerd in *A New Critique of Theoretical Thought* of 1953–8). Thus the English social ethicist John Milbank has reverted (on the basis of monumental learning) to a re-pristinated transcendental Augustinianism (Milbank, 1990). This consists in the reassertion of the absolute truth of God comprised in a Christian 'social theory' that consigns the whole historical evolution of the social sciences as the science of actual societies to the status of perverted, overambitious instrumental reason. The price paid for this is departure from the empirical societal realities it is and always has been the purpose of social science to grasp, represent and interpret. Apparently at the other extreme, in his *Letters and Papers from Prison*, Dietrich Bonhoeffer embraced the ineluctable reality of secularization and sought to consolidate the absolute dichotomy between all-pervasive, penultimate historicism and the radical ultimacy of Christian discourse. Both positions are in reality different faces of the same coin: the reality of secularization. Yet the former waits in Adornian 'hibernation' for the coming catastrophe, whereas the latter accepts the call to active discipleship in the human disorder that is society, despite the apparent departure and absence of God.

Can we in the final analysis accept the terms of this dichotomy? On the one hand we are confronted by transcendental critique that reinstates divine reason above the mish-mash of error and violence that is historical human life; on the other by the uncritical acceptance of a seamless web of modernity desperately challenged by the passionate inwardness of Christian discipleship. Both positions suffer the enslavement of *anamnesis*; it is exclusively to the *past* that both in effect refer. In the postmodern condition it is increasingly the market that rules through choice (both trivial and life-determining). Markets do not thrive on the glories or the failures of the past; they demand proleptic thinking, the pre-conceptualization of strategies that will engage the attention of human agents exercising choice. Relevant here is Ernst Bloch's idea of the horizon of anticipatory consciousness: the recognition that future hope should inform human intentionality (Roberts, 1990) will have to confront the history of the differentiation of the human and social sciences. This approach entails risking the rediscovery of new life-enhancing analogies in the engagement of Christian thought with the human and social sciences – or the possibility of failure.

See also CULTURE AND THEOLOGY; RELATIVISM, CULTURAL; and see BIOLOGICAL SCIENCE/ PHYSICAL SCIENCE/PSYCHOLOGICAL SCIENCE AND CHRISTIAN THOUGHT.

Bibliography

Beckford, J. 1985: *Cult Controversies: The Societal Response to New Religious Movements*. London: Tavistock.

Berger, P.L. [1967] 1969: *The Social Reality of Religion* (American title: *The Sacred Canopy*). London: Faber, esp. chapters 5–7.

Blumenberg, Hans [1966] 1983: *The Legitimacy of the Modern Age*. Cambridge, Mass.: MIT.

Bourdieu, P. 1972: *Outline of a Theory of Practice*. Cambridge: Cambridge University Press.

Chadwick, O. 1975: *The Secularization of the European Mind in the Nineteenth Century*. Cambridge: Cambridge University Press.

Dilthey, W. 1910–27: *Der Aufbau der geschichtlichen Welt in den Geisteswissenschaften*. Leipzig.

Eliade, M. [1976] 1978: *A History of Religious Ideas*, vol. 1. trans. Chicago: Chicago University Press.

Esler, P.F. 1987: *Community and Gospel in Luke–Acts: The Social and Political Implications of Lucan Theology*. Cambridge: Cambridge University Press.

Foucault, M. [1966] 1970: *The Order of Things: An Archaeology of the Human Sciences*, trans. London: Tavistock.

Geertz, C.J. 1966: Religion as cultural system. In *Anthropological Approaches to the Study of Religion*, ed. M. Banton. London: Tavistock, pp. 1–46.

Habermas, J. [1985] 1987: *The Philosophical Discourse of Modernity: Twelve Lectures*, trans. Cambridge: Polity Press.

Harvey, D. 1989: *The Condition of Postmodernity: An Enquiry into the Origins of Social Change*. Oxford: Blackwell.

Hume, D. [1757] 1969: *The Natural History of Religion. In Sociology and Religion: A Book of Readings*, ed. N. Birnbaum and G. Lenzer. Englewood Cliffs, NJ: Prentice Hall.

Husserl, E. [1954] 1970: *The Crisis of European Sciences and Transcendental Phenomenology*, trans. Evanston, Ill.: Northwestern Press.

Leach, Sir Edmund 1985: The anthropology of religion: British and French schools. In *Nineteenth Century Religious Thought in the West*, ed. N. Smart *et al.* Cambridge: Cambridge University Press, pp. 215–62.

Leeuw, G. van der [1933] 1938: *Religion in Essence and Manifestation: A Study in Phenomenology*, trans. London: Allen and Unwin.

Lyotard, J.-F. [1979] 1984: *The Postmodern Condition: A Report on Knowledge*. Manchester: University of Manchester Press.

Malinowski, B. 1948: Primitive man and his religion. In *Magic, Science and Religion*. New York: Doubleday, pp. 17–53.

Martin, D. 1978: *A General Theory of Secularization*. Oxford: Blackwell.

Marx, K. 1959: extracts from *Contribution to the Critique of Hegel's Philosophy of Right – Introduction* and *The German Ideology*. In *Marx and Engels on Religion*, trans. Moscow: Progress Publishers, pp. 37–52; 65–72.

Milbank, A.J. 1990: *A Treatise against Secular Order*. Oxford: Blackwell.

O'Toole, Roger 1984: *Religion: Classic Sociological Approaches*. Toronto: McGraw Hill.

Otto, R. [1917] 1923: *The Idea of the Holy: An Inquiry into the Non-Rational Factor in the Idea of the Divine and its Relation to the Rational*, trans. Oxford: Oxford University Press, pp. 1–41.

Pickering, N.F.S., ed. 1975: *Durkheim on Religion*, containing extracts from Concerning the definition of religious phenomena (pp. 95–6) and *The Elementary Forms of Religious Life* (pp. 102–23). London: Routledge and Kegan Paul.

Roberts, R.H. 1990: *Hope and its Hieroglyph: A Critical Decipherment of Ernst Bloch's 'Principle of Hope'*. Atlanta: Scholars Press.

Robertson, R. 1991: The globalization paradigm: thinking globally. In *Religion and Social Order*, vol. 1, pp. 207–24.

Wallerstein, I. 1976 *The Modern World System*, 3 vols. New York: Academic Press.

Weber, M. [1904–5] 1930: Asceticism and the spirit of capitalism. In *The Protestant Ethic and the Spirit of Capitalism*, trans. Talcott Parsons, ed. R.H. Tawney. London: Allen and Unwin, chapter 5.

Weber, M. [1904–5] 1947: *The Theory of Social and Economic Organization*. London: Collier Macmillan.

Weber, M. [1922] 1956: *The Sociology of Religion*. London: Methuen.

Wilson, B. 1969: A typology of sects. In *Sociology of Religion: Selected Readings*, ed. R. Robinson. Harmondsworth: Penguin, pp. 251–81.

RICHARD H. ROBERTS

socialism, Christian See CHRISTIAN SO-CIALISM.

sociology of religion See SOCIAL SCIENCE AND CHRISTIAN THOUGHT; SECULARIZATION; RELIGION, THEORIES OF.

soteriology The term 'soteriology' (from the Greek *soteria*, 'salvation') is increasingly used to refer to what was traditionally designated 'theories of the atonement' or 'the work of Christ'. Soteriology embraces two broad areas of theology: the question of how salvation is possible and in particular how it relates to the history of Jesus Christ; and the question of how 'salvation' itself is to be understood. These questions have been the subject of intense discussion in the modern period.

The relation between Christology and soteriology
In the great works of systematic theology dating from the periods of high scholasticism and Protestant orthodoxy, a rigorous distinction was made between the 'person of Christ' (see CHRISTOLOGY) and the 'work of Christ'. In the modern period, this distinction has been generally abandoned, on account of an increasing recognition of the inextricable connection of these two areas of theology. Christology and soteriology are increasingly being regarded as the two sides of one and the same coin. A number of considerations have led to this development.

The first is the influence of a Kantian epistemology (see KANTIANISM). Kant argued that we can only know the *Ding-an-sich* in terms of its effect upon us. If this general approach is translated to the cluster of issues centring upon the identity and significance of Jesus Christ, it would seem to follow that the essence or identity of Christ (i.e. Christology) cannot be separated from his effect or impact upon us (i.e. soteriology). This is the approach adopted by Albrecht Ritschl in his *Christian Doctrine of Justification and Reconciliation* of 1874. Ritschl argued that it was improper to separate Christology and soteriology, in that we perceive 'the nature and attributes, that is the determination of being, only in the effect of a thing upon us, and we think of the nature and extent of its effect upon us as its essence.'

The second consideration is the general recognition that, even in the New Testament, there is a strong correlation between the

Christological titles of Jesus and their soterio-logical substructure. 'A separation between Christology and soteriology is not possible, because in general the soteriological interest, the interest in salvation, in the *beneficia Christi*, is what causes us to ask about the figure of Jesus' (Wolfhart Pannenberg).

Despite this consensus, there is continuing disagreement over the emphasis to be given to soteriological considerations in Christology. For example, the approach adopted by Rudolf Bultmann appears to reduce Christology to *das Dass* – the mere fact 'that' a historical figure existed, to whom the kerygma can be traced and attached (see HISTORICAL JESUS, QUEST OF). The primary function of the kerygma is to transmit the soteriological content of the Christ-event. A related approach, found in A.E. Biedermann and Paul Tillich, draws a distinction between the 'Christ principle' and the historical person of Jesus. This has led some writers, most notably Pannenberg, to express anxiety that a Christology might simply be constructed out of soteriological considerations (and thus be vulnerable to the criticisms of Ludwig Feuer-bach), rather than grounded in the history of Jesus himself (see FAITH AND HISTORY).

Interpretations of the work of Christ

Modern discussions of the meaning of the cross and resurrection of Christ are best grouped around four central controlling themes or images. It must be stressed that these are not mutually exclusive, and that it is normal to find writers adopting approaches which incorporate elements drawn from more than one such category. Indeed, it can be argued that the views of most writers on this subject cannot be reduced to or confined within a single category without doing serious violence to their ideas.

Sacrifice The New Testament, drawing on Old Testament imagery and expectations, presents Christ's death upon the cross as a sacrifice. This approach, which is especially associated with the Letter to the Hebrews, presents Christ's sacrificial offering as an effective and perfect sacrifice, which was able to accomplish that which the sacrifices of the Old Testament were only able to intimate, rather than achieve. This idea is developed subsequently within the Christian tradition. For example, in taking over the imagery of sacrifice, Augustine states

that Christ 'was made a sacrifice for sin, offering himself as a whole burnt offering on the cross of his passion.' In order for humanity to be restored to God, the mediator must sacrifice himself; without this sacrifice, such restoration is an impossibility. For Augustine, this sacrifice is commemorated in the Eucharist:

> Before the coming of Christ, the flesh and blood of his sacrifice were foreshadowed in the animals which were killed; in the passion of Christ, these types were fulfilled by the true sacrifice [of Christ on the cross]; after the ascension of Christ, this sacrifice is commemorated in the sacrament.

Similar ideas may be discerned in the theology of the Middle Ages, and into the early modern period.

The sacrificial offering of Christ on the cross came to be linked especially with one aspect of the threefold office of Christ (*munus triplex Christi*). According to this typology, which dates from the middle of the sixteenth century, the work of Christ could be summarized under three 'offices': prophet (by which Christ declares the will of God), priest (by which he makes sacrifice for sin) and king (by which he rules with authority over his people). The general acceptance of this taxonomy within Protestantism in the late sixteenth and seventeenth centuries led to a sacrificial under-standing of Christ's death becoming of central importance within Protestant soteriologies. Thus John Pearson's *Exposition of the Creed* of 1659 insists upon the necessity of the sacrifice of Christ in redemption, and specifically links this with the priestly office of Christ.

> The redemption or salvation which the Messiah was to bring consisteth in the freeing of a sinner from the state of sin and eternal death into a state of right-eousness and eternal life. Now a freedom from sin could not be wrought without a sacrifice propitiatory, and therefore there was a necessity of a priest.

Since the Enlightenment, however, there has been a subtle shift in the meaning of the term. A metaphorical extension of meaning has come to be given priority over the original. Whereas the term originally referred to the ritual offering of slaughtered animals as a specifically *religious* action, the term increasingly came to mean heroic or costly action on the parts of individuals, especially the giving up of one's life, with no transcendent reference or expectation.

This trend may be seen developing in John Locke's *Reasonableness of Christianity* of 1695. Locke argues that the only article of faith required of Christians is that of belief in his Messiahship; the idea of a sacrifice for sin is studiously set to one side. 'The faith required was to believe Jesus to be the Messiah, the anointed, who had been promised by God to the world . . . I do not remember that [Christ] anywhere assumes to himself the title of a priest, or mentions anything relating to his priesthood.'

These arguments are developed further by Thomas Chubb (1679–1747), especially in his *True Gospel of Jesus Christ Vindicated* of 1739. Arguing that the true religion of reason was that of conformity to the eternal rule of right (see DEISM), Chubb argues that the idea of Christ's death as a sacrifice arises from the apologetic concerns of the early Christian writers, which led them to harmonize this religion of reason with the cult of the Jews: 'As the Jews had their temple, their altar, their high priest, their sacrifices and the like, so the apostles, in order to make Christianity bear a resemblance to Judaism, found out something or other in Christianity, which they by a figure of speech called by those names.' Chubb, in common with the emerging Enlightenment tradition, dismissed this as spurious. 'God's disposition to show mercy . . . arises wholly from his own innate goodness or mercifulness, and not from anything external to him, whether it be the sufferings and death of Jesus Christ or otherwise.'

Even Joseph Butler, in attempting to reinstate the notion of sacrifice in his *Analogy of Religion* of 1736, found himself in difficulty, given the strongly rationalist spirit of the age. In upholding the sacrificial nature of Christ's death, he found himself obliged to concede more than he cared to:

> How and in what particular way [the death of Christ] had this efficacy, there

are not wanting persons who have endeavoured to explain; but I do not find that Scripture has explained it. We seem to be very much in the dark concerning the manner in which the ancients understood atonements to be made, i.e., pardon to be obtained by sacrifice.

Horace Bushnell's *Vicarious Sacrifice* of 1866 illustrates this same trend in the Anglo-American theology of the period, but in a more constructive manner. Through his suffering, Christ awakens our sense of guilt. His vicarious sacrifice demonstrates that God suffers on account of evil. In speaking of the 'tender appeals of sacrifice', Bushnell might seem to align himself with purely exemplarist understandings of the death of Christ; however, Bushnell is adamant that there are objective elements to atonement. Christ's death affects God, and expresses God. There are strong anticipations of later theologies of the suffering of God, when Bushnell declares:

> Whatever we may say or hold or believe concerning the vicarious sacrifice of Christ, we are to affirm in the same manner of God. The whole Deity is in it, in it from eternity . . . There is a cross in God before the wood is seen on the hill . . . It is as if there were a cross unseen, standing on its undiscovered hill, far back in the ages.

The use of sacrificial imagery has become noticeably less widespread since 1945, especially in German-language theology. It is highly likely that this relates directly to the rhetorical debasement of the term in secular contexts, especially in situations of national emergency. The secular use of the imagery of sacrifice, often degenerating to little more than slogan-mongering, is widely regarded as having tainted and compromised both the word and the concept. The frequent use of such phrases as 'he sacrificed his life for King and country' in British circles during the First World War, and Adolf Hitler's extensive use of sacrificial imagery in justifying economic hardship and the loss of civil liberties as the price of German national revival in the late 1930s, served to render the term virtually unusable for many in

Christian teaching and preaching, on account of its negative associations. Nevertheless, the idea continues to be of importance in modern Roman Catholic sacramental theology, which continues to regard the Eucharist as a sacrifice, and to find in this image a rich source of theological imagery (see SACRAMENTAL THEOLOGY).

Christus Victor The New Testament and early church laid considerable emphasis upon the victory gained by Christ over sin, death and Satan through his cross and resurrection. This theme of victory, often linked liturgically with the Easter celebrations, was of major importance within the western Christian theological tradition until the Enlightenment. With the advent of the Enlightenment, however, it began to fall out of theological favour, increasingly being regarded as outmoded and unsophisticated. The following factors appear to have contributed to this development.

1   Rational criticism of belief in the resurrection of Christ raised doubts concerning whether one could even begin to speak of a 'victory' over death.
2   The imagery traditionally linked with this approach to the cross – such as the existence of a personal devil in the form of Satan, and the domination of human existence by oppressive or satanic forces of sin and evil – was dismissed as premodern superstition.

The rehabilitation of this approach in the modern period is usually dated to 1931, with the appearance of Gustaf Aulén's *Christus Victor*. This short book, which originally appeared in German as an article in *Zeitschrift für systematische Theologie* (1930), has exercised a major influence over English-language approaches to the subject. Aulén argued that the classic Christian conception of the work of Christ was summed up in the belief that the risen Christ had brought new possibilities of life to humanity through his victory over the powers of evil. In a brief and very compressed account of the history of theories of the atonement, Aulén argued that this highly dramatic 'classic' theory had dominated Christianity until the Middle Ages, when more abstract legal theories began to gain ground. The situation was radically reversed through Martin Luther, who reintroduced the theme. However, the scholastic concerns of Protestant Orthodoxy led to its being relegated once more to the background. Aulén argued that this approach could no longer be allowed to be the victim of historical circumstances; it demanded a full and proper hearing.

Historically, Aulén's case was soon found to be wanting. Its claims to be treated as the 'classic' theory of the atonement had been overstated. It was indeed an important component of the general patristic understanding of the nature and mode of procurance of salvation; nevertheless, if any theory could justly lay claim to the title of 'the classic theory of the atonement', it would be the notion of redemption through unity with Christ.

Nevertheless, Aulén's views were sympathetically received. In part, this reflects growing disenchantment with the Enlightenment world view in general; more fundamentally, perhaps, it represents a growing realization of the reality of evil in the world, fostered by the horrors of the First World War. The insights of Sigmund Freud, drawing attention to the manner in which adults could be spiritually imprisoned by their subconscious, raised serious doubts about the Enlightenment view of the total rationality of human nature, and lent new credibility to the idea that humans are held in bondage to unknown and hidden forces. Aulén's approach seemed to resonate with a growing realization of the darker side of human nature. It had become intellectually respectable to talk about 'forces of evil'.

His approach also offered a *tertium quid*, a third possibility, which mediated between the two alternatives then on offer within mainstream liberal Protestantism – both of which were regarded as flawed. The classic legal theory was regarded as raising difficult theological questions, not least concerning the morality of atonement; the subjective approach, which regarded Christ's death as doing little more than arousing human religious sentiment, seemed to be seriously religiously inadequate. Aulén offered an approach to the meaning of the death of Christ which bypassed the difficulties of legal approaches, yet vigorously defended the objective nature of the atonement. Nevertheless, Aulén's *Christus Victor* approach did raise some serious questions. If offered no rational justification for the manner in which the forces of evil are defeated through the cross of Christ. Why the cross? Why not in some other manner?

Since then, the image of victory has been developed in writings on the cross. Rudolf Bultmann extended his programme of demythologization to the New Testament theme of victory, interpreting it as a victory over inauthentic existence and unbelief. Paul Tillich offers a reworking of Aulén's theory, in which the victory of Christ on the cross is interpreted as a victory over existential forces which threaten to deprive us of authentic existence. Bultmann and Tillich, in adopting such existentialist approaches, thus convert a theory of the atonement which was originally radically objective into a subjective victory within the human consciousness (see EXISTENTIALISM).

In his *Past Event and Present Salvation* (1989), Oxford theologian Paul Fiddes emphasizes that the notion of 'victory' retains a place of significance within Christian thinking about the cross. Christ's death does more than impart some new knowledge to us, or express old ideas in new manners. It makes possible a new mode of existence:

> The victory of Christ actually *creates* victory in us . . . The act of Christ is one of those moments in human history that 'opens up new possibilities of existence'. Once a new possibility has been disclosed, other people can make it their own, repeating and reliving the experience.

Legal approaches A third approach centres on the idea of the death of Christ providing the basis by which God is enabled to forgive sin. This notion is traditionally associated with the eleventh-century writer Anselm of Canterbury, who developed an argument for the necessity of the incarnation on its basis. This model became incorporated into classical Protestant dogmatics during the period of orthodoxy, and finds its expression in many hymns of the eighteenth and nineteenth centuries. Three main models were used to understand the manner in which the forgiveness of human sins is related to the death of Christ.

1 Representation. Christ is here understood to be the covenant representative of humanity. Through faith, believers come to stand within the covenant between God and humanity. All that Christ has achieved through the cross is available on account of the covenant. Just as God entered into a covenant with his people Israel, so he has entered into a covenant with his church. Christ, by his obedience upon the cross, represents his covenant people, winning benefits for them as their representative. By coming to faith, individuals come to stand within the covenant, and thus share in all its benefits, won by Christ through his cross and resurrection – including the full and free forgiveness of our sins.

2 Participation. Through faith, believers participate in the risen Christ. They are 'in Christ', to use Paul's famous phrase. They are caught up in him, and share in his risen life. As a result of this, they share in all the benefits won by Christ, through his obedience upon the cross. One of those benefits is the forgiveness of sins, in which they share through their faith. Participating in Christ thus entails the forgiveness of sins, and sharing in his righteousness.

3 Substitution. Christ is here understood to be a substitute, the one who goes to the cross in our place. Sinners ought to have been crucified, on account of their sins. Christ is crucified in their place. God allows Christ to stand in our place, taking our guilt upon himself, so that his righteousness – won by obedience upon the cross – might become ours.

With the onset of the Enlightenment, this approach to the atonement was subjected to a radical critique. The following major points of criticism were directed against it.

1 It appeared to rest upon a notion of original guilt, which Enlightenment writers found unacceptable. Each human being was responsible for his or her own moral guilt; the very notion of an *inherited* guilt, as it was expressed in the traditional doctrine of original sin, was to be rejected.

2 The Enlightenment insisted upon the rationality, and perhaps above all the *morality*, of every aspect of Christian doctrine. This theory of the atonement appeared to be morally suspect, especially in its notions of transferred guilt or merit. The central idea of 'vicarious satisfaction' was also regarded with acute suspicion: in what sense was it *moral* for one human being to bear the penalties due for another?

These criticisms were given added weight through the development of the discipline of the 'history of dogma' (*Dogmengeschichte*: see DOCTRINE AND DOGMA). The representatives of this movement, from G.S. Steinbart through to Adolf von Harnack, argued that a series of assumptions, each of central importance to the Anselmian doctrine of penal substitution, had become incorporated into Christian theology by what were little more than historical accidents. For example, in his *System der reinen Philosophie* of 1778, Steinbart argued that historical investigation disclosed the intrusion of three 'arbitrary assumptions' into Christian reflection on salvation:

1   the Augustinian doctrine of original sin;
2   the concept of satisfaction;
3   the doctrine of the imputation of the righteousness of Christ.

For such reasons, Steinbart felt able to declare the substructure of orthodox Protestant thinking on the atonement to be a relic of a bygone era.

More recently, the idea of guilt – a central aspect of legal approaches to soteriology – has been the subject of much discussion, especially in the light of Freud's views on the origin of guilt in childhood experiences. For some twentieth-century writers, 'guilt' is simply a psychosocial projection, whose origins lie not in the holiness of God but in the muddleheadedness of human nature. These psychosocial structures are then, it is argued, projected onto some imaginary screen of 'external' reality, and treated as if they are objectively true. While this represents a considerable overstatement of the case, it has the advantage of clarity, and allows us to gain an appreciation of the considerable pressure that this approach to the atonement is currently facing.

Nevertheless, this view continues to find significant representatives. The collapse of the evolutionary moral optimism of liberal Protestantism (see LIBERALISM (BRITAIN and USA)) in the wake of the First World War did much to raise again the question of human guilt, and the need for redemption from outside the human situation. Two significant contributions to this discussion may be regarded as precipitated directly by the credibility crisis faced by liberal Protestantism at this time.

P.T. Forsyth's *Justification of God* (1916), written during the war years, represents an impassioned plea to allow the notion of the 'justice of God' to be rediscovered. Forsyth is less concerned than Anselm about the legal and juridical aspects of the cross; his interest centres on the manner in which the cross is inextricably linked with 'the whole moral fabric and movement of the universe'. The doctrine of the atonement is inseparable from 'the rightness of things'. God acts to restore this 'rightness of things', in that he makes available through the cross a means of moral regeneration – something which the war demonstrated that humanity needed, yet was unable to provide itself.

> The cross is not a theological theme, nor a forensic device, but the crisis of the moral universe on a scale far greater than earthly war. It is the theodicy of the whole God dealing with the whole soul of the whole world in holy love, righteous judgement and redeeming grace.

Through the cross, God aims to restore the rightness of the world through rightful means – a central theme of Anselm's doctrine of atonement, creatively restated.

More significant is the extended discussion of the theme of 'atonement' or 'reconciliation' (the German term *Versöhnung* can bear both meanings) to be found in Karl Barth's *Church Dogmatics*. The central section (IV/1, §59, 2) addressing the issue is entitled – significantly – 'The Judge Judged in Our Place'. The title derives from the *Heidelberg Catechism*, which speaks of Christ as the judge who 'has represented me before the judgement of God, and has taken away all condemnation from me'. The section in question can be regarded as an extended commentary on this classic text of the Reformed tradition, dealing with the manner in which the judgement of God is in the first place made known and enacted; and in the second, is taken upon God himself (a central Anselmian theme, even if Anselm failed to integrate it within a Trinitarian context).

The entire section is steeped in the language and imagery of guilt, judgement and forgiveness. In the cross, we can see God exercising his rightful judgement of sinful humanity (Barth uses the compound term *Sündermensch* to emphasize that 'sin' is not a detachable aspect of human nature). The cross exposes human delusions of self-sufficiency and autonomy of judgement, which Barth sees encapsulated in the story of Genesis 3: 'the human being wants to be his own judge'.

Yet alteration of the situation demands that its inherent wrongness be acknowledged. For Barth, the cross of Christ represents the locus in which the righteous judge makes known his judgement of sinful humanity, and simultaneously takes that judgement upon himself.

> What took place is that the Son of God fulfilled the righteous judgement on us human beings by himself taking our place as a human being, and in our place undergoing the judgement under which we had passed . . . Because God willed to execute his judgement on us in his Son, it all took place in his person, as *his* accusation and condemnation and destruction. He judged, and it was the judge who was judged, who allowed himself to be judged . . . Why did God become a human being? So that God as a human being might do and accomplish and achieve and complete all this for us wrongdoers, in order that in this way there might be brought about by him our reconciliation with him, and our conversion to him.

The strongly substitutionary character of this will be evident. God exercises his righteous judgement by exposing our sin, by taking it upon himself, and thus by neutralizing its power. The cross thus both speaks 'for us' and 'against us'. Unless the cross is allowed to reveal the full extent of our sin, it cannot take that sin from us:

> The 'for us' of his death on the cross included and encloses this terrible 'against us'. Without this terrible 'against us', it would not be the divine and holy and redemptive and effectively helpful 'for us', in which the conversion of humanity and the world to God has become an event.

Exemplarist approaches A central aspect of the New Testament understanding of the meaning of the cross relates to the demonstration of the love of God for humanity. With the rise of the Enlightenment world view, increasingly critical approaches were adopted to theories of the atonement which incorporated transcendent elements – such as the idea of a sacrifice which had some impact upon God, or Christ dying in order to pay some penalty or satisfaction which was due for sin. The increasingly sceptical attitude to the RESURRECTION tended to discourage theologians from incorporating this into their theologies of atonement with anything even approaching the enthusiasm of earlier generations. As a result, the emphasis of theologians sympathetic to the Enlightenment came to focus upon the cross itself. However, many Enlightenment theologians also had difficulties with the 'two natures' doctrine. The form of Christology which perhaps expresses the spirit of the Enlightenment most faithfully is a degree Christology – that is to say, a Christology which recognizes a difference of *degree*, but not of *nature*, between Christ and other human beings. Jesus Christ was recognized as embodying certain qualities which were present, actually or potentially, in all other human beings, the difference lying in the superior extent to which he embodied them.

When such considerations are applied to theories of atonement, a consistent pattern begins to emerge. This can be studied from the writings of G.S. Steinbart, I.G. Töllner, G.F. Seiler and K.G. Bretschneider. Its basic features can be summarized as follows.

1　The cross has no transcendent reference or value; its value relates directly to its impact upon humanity. Thus the cross represents a 'sacrifice' only in that it represents Christ giving up his life.
2　The person who died upon the cross was a human being, and the impact of that death is upon human beings. That impact takes the form of inspiration and encouragement to model ourselves upon the moral example set us in Jesus himself.
3　The most important aspect of the cross is that it demonstrates the love of God towards us.

This approach became enormously influential in rationalist circles throughout nineteenth-century Europe. The mystery and apparent irrationalism of the cross had been neutralized; what remained was a powerful and dramatic plea for the moral improvement of humanity, modelled on the lifestyle and attitudes of Jesus Christ. The model of a martyr, rather than a saviour, describes the attitude increasingly adopted towards Jesus within such circles.

The most significant challenge to this rationalist approach to the cross is due to F.D.E. Schleiermacher, who insisted upon the *religious* value of the death of Christ. Christ did not die to make or endorse a moral system; he came in order that the supremacy of the consciousness of God could be established in humanity. Nevertheless, Schleiermacher was often represented as teaching a view of the atonement as *Lebenserhöhung*, a kind of moral elevation of life (as in the account set forth by Gustaf Aulén). His distinctive ideas proved to be capable of being assimilated to purely exemplarist understandings, rather than posing a coherent challenge to them.

The most significant statement of this approach in England is to be found in the 1915 Bampton Lectures of the noted modernist Hastings Rashdall (see MODERNISM). In these lectures, Rashdall launched a vigorous attack on traditional approaches to the atonement. The only interpretation of the cross which is adequate for the needs of the modern age is that already associated with the medieval writer Peter Abelard:

> The church's early creed, 'There is none other name given among men by which we may be saved', may be translated so as to be something of this kind: 'There is none other ideal given among men by which we may be saved, except the moral ideal which Christ taught us by his words, and illustrated by his life and death of love.'

Other English writers who adopted similar or related approaches include G.W.H. Lampe and John Hick. In his essay 'The Atonement: Law and Love', contributed to the liberal Catholic volume *Soundings*, Lampe launched a fierce attack on legal approaches to his subject, before commending an exemplarist approach based on 'the paradox and miracle of love'.

The position of John Hick is of especial interest, in that it relates to the place of the work of Christ in inter-faith dialogue (see OTHER FAITHS AND CHRISTIANITY). The religious pluralist agenda has certain important theological consequences. Traditional Christian theology does not lend itself particularly well to the homogenizing agenda of religious pluralists. The suggestion that all religions are more or less talking about vaguely the same thing finds itself in difficulty in relation to certain essentially Christian ideas – most notably, the doctrines of the INCARNATION, atonement and the Trinity (see GOD). The suggestion that something unique is made possible or available through the death of Christ is held to belittle non-Christian religions. In response to this pressure, a number of major Christological and theological developments may be noted. Doctrines such as the incarnation, which imply a high profile of identification between Jesus Christ and God, are discarded, in favour of various degree Christologies, which are more amenable to the reductionist programme of liberalism. A sharp distinction is thus drawn between the historical person of Jesus Christ, and the principles which he is alleged to represent. Paul Knitter is but one of a small galaxy of pluralist writers concerned to drive a wedge between the 'Jesus-event' (which is unique to Christianity) and the 'Christ-principle' (accessible to all religious traditions, and expressed in their own distinctive, but equally valid, ways). Viewed in this pluralist light, the cross of Christ is thus understood to make known something which is accessible in other manners, and which is a universal religious possibility. Thus Hick argues that the Christ-event is only 'one of the points at which God has been and still is creatively at work within human life'; his distinctiveness relates solely to his being a 'visible story', and not an 'additional truth'.

The cross: constitutive or illustrative?

In his *Lehre von der Versöhnung* of 1898, Martin Kähler posed the following question concerning theories of the atonement: 'Did Christ just make known some insights concerning an unchangeable situation – or did he establish a new situation?' With this question we come to a central aspect of soteriology. Does the cross of Christ illustrate the saving will of God? Or does it make such a salvation possible in the first place? Is it constitutive or illustrative?

The latter approach has been characteristic of much writing inspired by the Enlightenment, which treats the cross as a historical symbol of a timeless truth. John Macquarrie firmly defends this approach in his *Principles of Christian Theology* of 1977:

> It is not that, at a given moment, God adds the activity of reconciliation to his previous activities, or that we can set a time when his reconciling activity began. Rather, it is the case that at a given time there was a new and decisive interpretation of an activity that had always been going on, an activity that is equiprimordial with creation itself.

A similar approach is associated with Maurice F. Wiles, who argues in his *Remaking of Christian Doctrine* of 1974 that the Christ-event is 'in some way a demonstration of what is true of God's eternal nature'. Brian Hebblethwaite concurs: 'it needs to be stated quite categorically that God's forgiving love does not depend on the death of Christ, but rather is manifested and enacted in it.'

Yet the debate is far from over. In his *Actuality of Atonement* (1988), Colin Gunton suggests that non-constitutive approaches to the atonement run the risk of falling back into exemplarist and subjective doctrines of salvation. Yet it is necessary to say that Christ does not just reveal something of importance to us; he achieves something for us – something without which salvation would not be possible. Raising the question of whether 'the real evil of the world is faced and healed *ontologically* in the life, death and resurrection of Jesus', Gunton argues that there must be a sense in which Christ is a 'substitute' for us: he does for us something that we ourselves cannot do. To deny this is to revert to some form of Pelagianism, or a purely subjective understanding of salvation.

This theme has been taken up in *Atonement and Incarnation* (1991) by Vernon White, who argues for the constitutive nature of the Christ-event on moral grounds. Real reconciliation demands that something must 'happen in response to moral evil'. Reconciliation demands that evil be confronted in history – which can only happen through the Christ-event.

> The only adequate 'undoing' of past disruption involves the attempted recreation of something new . . . [This] is exemplified throughout the incarnate life, and pre-eminently in the cross and resurrection. God overcomes evil and achieves reconciliation, first by experiencing the consequences of it, both in terms of his own temptation to live for self, and in terms of the assault of other people's selfishness on him.

White is thus able to ground the constitutive nature of the cross of Christ through God's encounter with human suffering in history – something which had to 'happen'.

A similar issue underlies the distinction between *objective* and *subjective* approaches to atonement. The former suggests that there is a change in the external situation – that is, that God is in some way affected by the cross of Christ. The latter argues that it is our perception of the situation which is radically altered. It will be clear that the former corresponds broadly to constitutive, and the latter to illustrative, approaches to atonement. The parallel, however, is not exact.

The nature of salvation

What is the salvation that is made known or possible through the death of Christ? 'Salvation' is an enormously complex notion, embracing a number of related and mutually interacting ideas. The following major themes may all be discerned in modern discussions of the subject, and are noted simply to indicate the complexity of the subject, as well as to allow the reader to gain an appreciation of some of the characteristic emphases within modern theology.

It must be stressed that a major theological point underlies the various manners in which salvation is interpreted. The growth of Christianity in recent centuries, chiefly through missionary work, has raised the issue of *contextualization*. How should the vocabulary and conceptual framework of the Christian tradition be adapted or refined to meet the new situations into which the Christian faith has expanded? Harvey M. Conn is one writer to raise the importance of this question, noting that salvation is to be *particularized* in terms of the situation addressed by the gospel at any given moment. Historically, this has meant that notions of salvation have varied from one cultural context to another – a point which lends added weight to Wolfhart Pannenberg's plea that Christologies should not be constructed solely on soteriological foundations, but should engage with and be grounded in the history of Jesus of Nazareth. A brief survey will indicate the considerable diversity of concepts of salvation which have gained influence since 1700.

Deification The motif of deification dominates the soteriology of the early church, as can be seen from the writings of (to note but a few examples) Athanasius and the Cappadocian Fathers. It has remained an integral part of Eastern Orthodox theology in the modern period, and plays a significant role in the theology of modern writers within this tradition such as Vladimir Lossky.

Righteousness before God The notion of righteousness before God (*coram Deo*) played a major part in the development of Luther's doctrine of justification in the sixteenth century. Lutheran orthodoxy, especially during the eighteenth century, retained this emphasis on justification. Both pietist and Enlightenment writers regarded the notion of 'imputed righteousness' with some suspicion, considering it to amount to a legal fiction or moral deception. This led to an increased emphasis upon holiness within the pietist tradition, and upon morality within Enlightenment circles, and an increasing reluctance on the part of mainstream Protestant theologians to make use of the imagery of justification. In part, this is due to the increased use of the imagery of union with Christ within Calvinist theological circles.

Union with Christ The notion of a personal union between the believer and Christ was a significant element of patristic soteriologies. The notion of a union with Christ was developed by both Luther and Calvin at the time of the Reformation; only in the writings of the latter, however, did it assume a major soteriological role. In later Calvinism, the idea comes to be of central importance. Eighteenth-century Calvinist writers in both Europe and America regarded this emphasis upon union with Christ as bypassing the moral difficulties raised by the Lutheran concept of justification. In that believers were genuinely united to Christ, they were entitled to share in his righteousness.

Moral perfection The characteristic view of the Enlightenment was that religion, where it could be approved, was concerned with the moral improvement of humanity. In its typical form, this view argues that Jesus is to be regarded as a teacher of the moral life, which is conformity to the will of God. This will, which can be known equally well through reason as through the teaching of Christ, was distorted by New Testament writers, who sought to add various arbitrary or self-serving doctrines to the simple moral religion of Jesus.

In its more developed form, this approach subsequently drew upon the ideas of Immanuel Kant, especially in his *Religion within the Limits of Reason Alone*. Kant discussed the role of Jesus in relation to the 'ideal of moral perfection', and related this to the notion of the 'kingdom of God', understood as a realm of ethical values. This approach would have considerable influence within liberal Protestantism, especially the Ritschlian school, which regarded Jesus as 'the founder of a universal moral community'.

Consciousness of God F.D.E. Schleiermacher, reacting against purely rational or moral conceptions of Christianity, developed the idea that human salvation was to be discussed in terms of the domination of God-consciousness. This consciousness finds its prototypal expression in Jesus of Nazareth, and is thence made available as a possibility within the community of faith.

Genuine humanity The rise of existentialism in the twentieth century is widely regarded as linked with a sense of dehumanization in contemporary western culture. A number of writers have therefore argued that salvation is to be understood in terms of the rediscovery and restitution of genuine humanity. Significant contributions here were made by Eberhard Grisebach and Friedrich Gogarten, drawing on the personalism of Martin Buber. In his *Gegenwart: Eine kritische Ethik* of 1928, Grisebach analysed the dilemma faced by modern humanity in terms of a quest for authentic human identity. Gogarten argued, especially in his later work *Mensch zwischen Gott und Welt* of 1956, that soteriology concerns the question of how a human can become a person – a genuine 'Thou' in a world which threatens to depersonalize human existence, and reduce it to the level of an 'It'.

Political liberation Latin American LIBERATION THEOLOGY has emphasized the political aspects of the notion of salvation, and may be regarded as a recovery of the social, political and economic aspects of biblical (especially Old Testament) approaches to the theme. This move, which may be regarded as a protest against purely individualist conceptions of salvation (such as those noted immediately above), has met with considerable resistance from those who regard salvation as a privatized matter, divorced from the affairs of this world. Gustavo Gutiérrez's *Theology of Liberation* of 1971 and José Miguel Bonino's *Towards a Christian Political Ethics* of 1983 represent typical accounts of politicized concepts of salvation, drawn from Roman Catholic and evangelical traditions respectively.

Conclusion
This brief survey of the understandings of salvation in modern Christian thought has touched on the main issues of debate. Inevitably, most have been discussed at only a fraction of the length that they merit. It will, however, be clear that discussion of these issues – including the contextualization of salvation – will remain a perennial task of responsible Christian theology.

Bibliography
Aulén, Gustaf 1931: *Christus Victor: An Historical Survey of the Three Main Types of the Idea of the Atonement*. London: SPCK.
Baillie, D.M. 1956: *God was in Christ: An Essay in Incarnation and Atonement*. London: Faber and Faber.
Daly, R.J. 1978: *The Origins of the Christian Doctrine of Sacrifice*. London: Darton, Longman and Todd.
Dillistone, F.W. 1984: *The Christian Understanding of Atonement*. London: SCM Press.
Fiddes, Paul 1989: *Past Event and Present Salvation*. London: Darton, Longman and Todd.
Forsyth, P.T. 1916: *The Justification of God*. London: Duckworth.
Gunton, Colin E. 1988: *The Actuality of Atonement*. Edinburgh: Clark.
McGrath, A.E. 1985: The moral theory of the atonement, *Scottish Journal of Theology* 38, pp. 205–20.
McGrath, A.E. 1986: *Iustitia Dei: A History of the Christian Doctrine of Justification*, 2 vols. Cambridge: Cambridge University Press.
MacKinnon, D.M. 1966: Objective and subjective conceptions of atonement. In *Prospect for Theology*, ed. F.G. Healey. Welwyn: Nisbet.
Morris, Leon 1965: *The Apostolic Preaching of the Cross*. Leicester: Inter-Varsity Press.
Rashdall, Hastings 1919: *The Idea of Atonement in Christian Theology*. London: Macmillan.
Swinburne, Richard 1989: *Responsibility and Atonement*. Oxford: Clarendon Press.
Sykes, S.W. 1991: *Sacrifice and Redemption: Durham Essays in Theology*. Cambridge: Cambridge University Press.
White, Vernon 1991: *Atonement and Incarnation: An Essay in Universalism and Particularity*. Cambridge: Cambridge University Press.
Wiederkehr, Dietrich 1979: *Belief in Redemption: Concepts of Salvation from the New Testament to the Present Time*. London: SPCK.
Yarnold, Edward 1978: *The Second Gift: A Study of Grace*. Slough: St Paul.

ALISTER E. MCGRATH

South Africa See PROTESTANT THEOLOGY: SOUTH AFRICA.

South America See LIBERATION THEOLOGY.

Spirit, Holy See GOD; PNEUMATOLOGY.

spirituality, Christian At the beginning of the eighteenth century the word 'spirituality' in English had not evolved into its modern usage. Indeed this article could be written in terms of its development, largely under French influence, from things pertaining to the clergy to the 'interior' life, the spiritual dispositions which control our relations both with God and the world. At the start of our period it was just beginning, in France, to gain its association with mysticism and prayer, although used pejoratively against the quietists. 'La nouvelle spiritualité de Madame Guyon' was criticized as leading to a Christian life in a spiritual stratosphere remote from material and human reality. In the eighteenth and especially the nineteenth centuries, 'spiritualité' came to refer, without reproach, to the practice of piety and asceticism; and so, gradually, into English parlance today, where it is one of those invaluable words of which the meaning seems obvious until one attempts to define it (Brooks, 1975, p. 205). But we may say that Christian spirituality is the theory and practice of Christian living, believed to be under the inspiration of the Holy Spirit.

It will be best to treat the subject by surveying the various trends and schools in relation to their intellectual and social contexts, bearing in mind that in our world we are all neighbours but not all contemporaries. Some Christians today are innocent of the post-Enlightenment intellectual debates, of the arguments about language and symbolism, about God, about women, about the Bible. It is a mistake to treat the latest notions as the norm for those 'ordinary', obscure and non-intellectual people, some from the ethnic groups whom we are always being told, in the favoured jargon, not to 'marginalize'. Besides which, in spirituality above all, tradition is of the greatest influence. What we learn at our mother's knee shapes our whole lives even if we are trying to escape it, while the past is always being rediscovered in parts. Eighteenth-century English bishops thought Julian of Norwich a demented eccentric, but she has seemed in so many ways to speak to our age, and studies have proliferated even though there is the inveterate danger of making her a modern feminist in the popular mind. Even more significant is the fact that most spirituality is a growth from roots laid down at the beginnings of Christianity and in many instances long before.

The English spiritual teachers of the early eighteenth century drew on vast resources from traditions old and new, but there was, as already instanced, an impoverishing ignorance of and contempt for the Middle Ages.

Anglican rigorists like William Law knew little of the 'discretion' of St Benedict, or the joy in creation of St Francis, while the great Bernardine tradition, with its fine German inheritance through Hildegard of Bingen and the sisters of Helfta, to say nothing of the great Victorines, was little known. There is in fact something faintly off centre, exotic, about the mystic devotees at the beginning of the eighteenth century. They over valued women like Antoinette de Bourignon and Mme Guyon, and saintly ascetics like Gregory Lopez and M. de Renty counted for more with them than St John of the Cross or St Theresa.

(Rupp, 1986, p. 207)

This was also true in France. In 1699 Rome condemned F. Fénelon's *Explication des maximes des saintes sur la vie intérieur* after the bitter and unedifying quarrel with J.B. Bossuet, but Fénelon's personality and teaching had a 'drawing loveliness' and his influence continued throughout the eighteenth century long after his death in 1715 and especially in England. Alexander Knox declared that 'no Catholic was more popular in Protestant countries than Fénelon.' To love without thought of reward, to love even if one's final destiny is hell, is what every lover feels at times in the ardour of devotion and desire. It is the lover's hyperbole, but it may be un-Christianly individualistic, an egoism *à deux* I must wish for others' happiness and the coming of the kingdom of God – and it denies hope.

Jean-Pierre de Caussade (1675–1751) claimed that his teaching on contemplative prayer was not contrary to that of Bossuet or tainted with quietism, which may be roughly defined as a passive waiting on God, dispensing with the outward and corporate professions of the Christian religion and even with philanthropy. The great watchwords of his teaching are 'abandonment to divine providence' and 'the sacrament of the present moment'. The former, though different from the quietists' passivity, in some sense rehabilitates Fénelon in that 'abandon' includes being ready to accept the worst possible outcome in the knowledge that we are never out of the hands of God who is love. The latter has proved of great value in our own time when the danger for so many is to wallow in the failures of the past, or constantly to be living life in the future in hope or dread of things to come.

The early eighteenth century in England saw the triumph of the moralists. The age of reason, the Enlightenment, replaced the passionate devotion, with its acrimonious and sometimes bloody divisions, of the preceding century. The eucharistic spirituality of Lancelot Andrewes, with its patristic inheritance and witty wordplay, and the Puritan scholasticism of election, justification by faith and imputed righteousness were alike supplanted by the teachings of those whom their detractors called latitudinarians, represented by an influential treatise, *The Practice of Christian Graces*, better known by its subtitle, *The Whole Duty of Man*, of 1658. This was written by a Royalist high churchman, Richard Allestree, but its ideal is that of the Prayer Book's 'godly, righteous and sober life'. Holy Communion is one of the Christian's duties, the fulfilment of which leads to holiness which is happiness. There is no teaching on contemplative prayer, which the eighteenth-century Anglicans might well have dismissed with their predecessor Lord Clarendon and the Puritan John Owen as tending to a 'dull and lazy lethargy', a mortified and moping spirit, incapable of 'magnanimous activity'.

The Non-Jurors continued the tradition of Caroline spirituality, often in the form of a more extreme sacramental devotion, though Orthodox not Tridentine. But their most famous representative, William Law, not wholly typical and much engaged in their irate infighting, always characteristic of separatist minorities, has a rigorist strain born out of a deep pessimism about human nature and a revulsion from human life, especially sex. In his denunciation of the stage, his rules about dress and cosmetics, his proscription of the profession of attorney, his distrust of marriage, he is the typical Puritan of caricature, much more than those who, historically, bear that name. Yet his great treatises on *Christian Perfection* and *A Serious Call to a Devout and Holy Life* were of decisive influence on John Wesley, Samuel Johnson, and in the next century John Keble. In later life he was captivated by Jakob Böhme (1575–1624), the German mystic, with his weird creation mythology and pseudo-Dionysian Hellenism interspersed with moving affirmations of the divine love. He became reconciled to the Quakers, who he had earlier opposed, in his condemnation of oath taking and war; and he wrote of the catholic spirit in words similar to those of John Wesley, not in terms of church order and sacramental validity, but as 'a Communion of Saints in the Love of God and all Goodness' far transcending orthodoxy.

Joseph Butler, the greatest of the moralists, cannot be charged with 'enthusiasm' or extravagance. He was a sombre realist, aware that from many aspects this is a poor ruin of a world and that religion comes to us with apparent contradictions, its work half-done, its revelation incomplete. Yet he preached on the love of God in terms which have been called Augustinian (Burnaby, 1938, pp. 294ff.). His influence extended into the next century, to J.H. Newman and William Gladstone, who in 1873 wrote that without him he did not think that he ever would have been right. Butler speaks eloquently of our true happiness being in the love of God, which is not a matter of self-interest. God himself 'may be to us all that we want', our life, our joy, our comfort and our portion forever. His preaching soars at this point and is not without enthusiasm. He anticipates 'all that was deepest and truest in the Methodist appeal to the heart' (Church, 1895, p. 42).

Butler, Law, the French, and the German pietists, with their indebtedness to the English Puritans and their belief in prayer as the great instrument of love against sin, would be united in the Johannine assertion, 'We love him, because he first loved us.' But we must notice a tradition of 'affectionate' spirituality represented in the dissenting heirs of Richard Baxter, the seventeenth-century Puritan, who combined theological eclecticism with deep seriousness, and was of that catholic spirit which Law and Wesley expounded (Nuttall, 1951, *passim*). The leading divines were Isaac Watts (1674–1748) and Philip Doddridge (1702–1751). They averred that there was a place for rapture and emotion in the Christian life, and that preaching might well be with tears both of wonder at the divine love, and sorrow for sinners. Yet they knew the dangers of the rhetoric of affection. Watts wrote on logic and *The Improvement of the Mind*. With a Miltonic confidence in reason, he combined the rational and the evangelical. His *Guide to Prayer* is chiefly concerned with public prayer. It offers a rigorous and full analysis of the parts of prayer. There are wise counsels on the use and abuse of book prayers and on posture. Doddridge, who delighted in prayer and lived often with God, and remained serene and confident amid many sorrows, was engaged in the training of ministers and preachers. He was on good terms with Anglicans and was a protagonist of missions overseas. *On the Rise and Progress of Religion in the Soul* was written at Watts's instigation, has been translated into nine languages including Tamil and Syriac and is a classic of evangelical spirituality, much used in the Church of England until our own time. It traces the development of the Christian life from first conversion to the honouring of God in death. He honours the ordinances, particularly the Lord's Supper, but he writes of the 'absence' of Christ in the sacrament, for 'he is not here; he is risen' and the Supper is not the heavenly feast. Yet it is a table spread with bounties, as his much-loved hymn declares.

Hymns were a characteristic of affectionate spirituality and of pietism, as they had been of Reformed and sectarian Christianity since the Reformation. But now they were an expression of rapture in Doddridge, in Watts – much the greater hymnographer – and, above all, in Charles Wesley. The last wrote hymns on the great Christian doctrines and on the experience and growth in grace of the individual believer, a conspectus of spirituality from conviction of sin, through pardon and then the vicissitudes of the Christian life, to the attainment of perfect love (see METHODISM). In this tradition hymns are both part of liturgy – they interpret and paraphrase Scripture and assist the movement of worship to its climax in Eucharist and offering, whether or not the bread and wine are there – and a means of grace in private devotion. They lift up heart and voice in song, sometimes expressing pathos and penitence as well as praise. They are also to be prayed in private. This is what nonconformists and Methodists have found as well as pietists and Lutherans, converted criminals on the way to the gallows, soldiers on the battlefield, Dietrich Bonhoeffer in prison, and many a believer at the beginning and ending of the day (see MUSIC AND CHRISTIANITY).

Methodist spirituality was a path to perfection. Like the Eastern Orthodox and the pietists, John Wesley took II Peter 1: 4 seriously, the promise that we may be partakers of the divine nature, and Matthew 5: 48, the 'future imperative' that we shall be perfect as our heavenly Father is perfect. This implied the continued working of God's grace and the refusal to set any limits to it; and it meant fulfilling the two great commandments, total love of God and neighbour. This perfection might be attained even in this life, mortal and ignorant as we remain, through the 'means of grace'. Wesley divided these into the instituted – prayer (private, family, public), Scripture (read, meditated, heard), The Lord's Supper, fasting and Christian conference – and the prudential. These last included Wesley's own adaptation of the Societies which had been a feature of later seventeenth-century spirituality both in England and France and were found among the Moravians. The Methodist Societies, Bands and Classes into which converts were divided were intended both for fellowship and mutual spiritual direction. The revolutionary aspect of this is not only that it is 'societary' ('help us to help each other Lord') but that it is lay. The 'directors' are not officials, duly set aside, but ordinary men and women with a knowledge of God.

Wesley's spirituality was, in the words of George Croft Cell, a synthesis of the Protestant ethic of grace and the Catholic ethic of holiness. It has been said that the Wesleyan revival was not only evangelical but sacramental, and this is true in that Wesley believed that the Lord's Supper was not only a 'confirming' but a 'converting' ordinance and in that Methodist celebrations, more frequent than was usual in the parish churches, were thronged with enthusiastic receivers. The *Hymns on the Lord's Supper* of 1744 was a best-seller. It is a paraphrase of the Anglican Daniel Brevint's *The Christian Sacrament and Sacrifice* of 1673, with an affirmation both of the real presence and the eucharistic sacrifice, which seemed to some Anglo-Catholics of the next century to be a harbinger of the Oxford movement. But it is doubtful whether the high doctrines registered with the majority of Wesley's converts, though the belief in the sacrament as of perpetual obligation did.

The Methodist revival was only part of the eighteenth-century evangelical revival (see EVANGELICALISM: BRITAIN), which was largely Calvinist in theology as against Wesley's Arminianism. Selina, Countess of Huntingdon (1707–1791) was one of the few of the nobility who experienced evangelical conversion, as

Ronald Knox wrote, 'not so much a conversion from sin as a conversion from righteousness' (*Enthusiasm*, p. 485). She used her wealth in philanthropy but also to propagate evangelical Christianity, particularly among her peers, in contrast to Wesley's *penchant* for the lower middle classes and the poor. She attracted the great evangelical preacher George Whitefield and many able young clergymen, but she eventually quarrelled with Wesley because she feared that his Arminianism made him flirt dangerously with salvation by works. In the early 1780s she had to separate from the Church of England and form her own 'Connexion', with its own ordained ministers, owing to court action against her building a chapel in Spa Fields, London, which resulted in all her proprietary chapels being regarded as homes of Dissenting congregations. Newman paid her tribute in the next century. He was much moved 'by the sight of a person simply and unconditionally giving up this world for the next . . . She acted as one ought to act who considered this life a pilgrimage, not a home' (Rupp, 1986, p. 471).

The Church of England evangelicals also preferred not to desert the parochial system for Wesley's itinerancy. Their work was done from settled pulpits and, though not all of the nobility like Selina, they were often drawn from the substantial classes. It is not insignificant that one of their greatest preachers and pastors, Charles Simeon (1759–1836), was vicar of Holy Trinity, Cambridge, from 1783 until his death. Their appeal was to those who would become leaders of society, like those interrelated families who would form the Clapham Sect in the early nineteenth century.

Their spirituality was based on preaching (see PREACHING, THEOLOGY OF), to convert, instruct and guide. Hearing the word was all-important, but attendance on public proclamation was accompanied by a regular life of early rising, prayer in private and in household, 'the daily portion' of Scripture studied and interpreted conservatively, and Sabbath observance. The Christian week, from Sunday to Saturday, was more important than the Christian year. The Olney Hymns of John Newton, the converted slave captain, and William Cowper, the 'stricken deer' as he called himself, the poet often plunged into melancholia, were their staple

diet. Prayer meetings were looked on by John Newton 'as the most profitable exercises in which Christians can engage'. They had nothing of that reserve which was so characteristic of the Tractarians. They were much engaged in social works, for instance William Wilberforce and the emancipation of the slaves, and later Lord Shaftesbury (1801–1885) and the Factory Acts; and missions overseas were no less a priority than with Methodists.

Later in the nineteenth century they became more revivalist. The Keswick Convention (1875) led to a holiness movement. Hymns with choruses became popular, not least as a result of the mission of the American evangelists Moody and Sankey in 1882. Sentimentality crept in as it did throughout Victorian life – witness the novels of Charles Dickens – although the fervent expression of emotion is not wholly to be deplored, as when the hymn 'Safe in the arms of Jesus' was played at Lord Shaftesbury's funeral in 1885 by the band of the Costermongers Temperance Association. Choruses have remained a part of evangelical spirituality and have proliferated in the last quarter of the twentieth century, often with mantra-like repetitions. They are usually traditional in language and imagery and without the theological profundity of Watts, Wesley or Cowper.

There has been profound evangelical teaching on prayer, as in Ole Hallesby's book of that title, which has been in print for more than forty years. 'Helplessness united with faith produces prayer' he writes; 'without faith there can be no prayer.' Even so, for prayer to become our native air, the miracle wrought by the Holy Spirit is necessary (cf. Rom. 8: 26). Yet there is a link with the contemplative tradition: 'Prayer is something deeper than words.' 'To pray is nothing more than to lie in the sunshine of God's grace' (Hallesby, [1948] 1976, pp. 22, 13, 12.).

Roman Catholic spirituality continued the sixteenth-century strain of 'holy wordliness'. Richard Challoner's *The Garden of the Soul* of 1740 is indebted to Francois de Sales. After a doctrinal summary, it provides devotions for each part of the day. Alban Butler's *The Lives of the Saints* published between 1756 and 1759 is a sober study presenting the saints as examples of life in the world. The Mass and Mary were central to Roman Catholic devotion. The tabernacle on the altar was the focus of much prayer, both in private visits and in extra-liturgical services like Benediction. Piety was individualist. One prayed at the Mass rather than praying the Mass. There was rather tawdry baroque art and much meditation on the physical sufferings of Christ in his passion, as in F.W. Faber's hymn, 'O come and mourn with me awhile.' Faber is at times over-sentimental, addressing Mary as 'Mamma' for instance, yet movingly proclaiming the infinity of the love of God.

John Henry Newman, convert from Angli-canism, brought his own spiritual genius to the Roman church. His, too, was a spirituality of 'the trivial round, the common task' in the words of his Anglican friend John Keble's poem. Keble reminded him of St Philip Neri, whose Oratorian disciple he became. Newman's counsels were often humdrum: 'go to bed in good time and you will be perfect.' His was a unitive spirituality of the whole person, body and soul. You do not only feel the movement of the heart towards God; you go to church, pass along the aisle to the holy table, receive Christ's body. And it was unitive of clerical and lay, there was no holiness of the one different from the other; and unitive of all Christian people, promoting 'mutual sympathy between estranged communions and alienated hearts'.

Baron von Hügel (1852–1925), the Austrian nobleman who lived in London and wrote in (at times tortuous and teutonic) English, was much influenced by Newman, though he thought him too depressing ever to be canonized. Von Hügel distinguished three elements in religion, the mystical-emotional, the historical-institutional and the intellectual-scientific. Each was neces-sary. He himself was a friend of the Catholic modernists, but survived their condemnation and was a typical Catholic in his devotions, with visits to the Blessed Sacrament and the rest. He wrote an epoch-making book on *The Mystical Element of Religion* (of 1908) and was himself a renowned spiritual guide, turning Evelyn Underhill towards Christocentric religion. His counsels are enshrined in *Letters to a Niece* of 1928 and other writings, which include the wisdom of his own confessor, the Abbé Huvelin.

The Oxford movement, which dates from 1833, sought to recover the catholicity of the English church against its being an arm of the state and a pawn of politicians (see ANGLI-CANISM). In its beginnings it was concerned with spirituality rather than ceremonial. Its leaders saw in the *Book of Common Prayer* a buried catholicism, which it was their mission to revive. They reacted against Methodism and evangelicalism, which, they believed, sought salvation by emotion and excitement and cheapened the divine mystery. Reverence was the first disposition of the Christian mind. E.B. Pusey was their 'doctor mysticus' and there is contemplative rapture and ecstasy as he unfolds the mystery of union with Christ, above all in the Eucharist. Benedicta Ward has recognized '"the huge silence and great quiet" of Nitria, Scetis and the Cells, within the nineteenth-century pages' (Rowell, 1986, p. 222). Yet he translated French Roman Catholic works on confession.

The movement broke free of Oxford and found its mission in the slums, where it borrowed the colour and splendour of the Roman Church and illegally used the Missal and much else. It restored the religious life. It was at its best when it was a Caroline revival rather than a Tridentine importation. In the mid-twentieth century, it produced what has been considered its own 'school', represented by Bede Frost's *The Art of Mental Prayer* of 1931 and especially by F.P. Harton's *The Elements of the Spiritual Life* of 1932, a rigorous account of Christian asceticism in Roman categories. Martin Thornton, in several books, distin-guished an English school of spirituality based *inter alia* on 'the speculative–affective syn-thesis', the liturgy, habitual recollection and spiritual direction. But he ignores Protestantism except in its more modern radical guise. The finest exponent of Anglican Catholic spirituality for the twentieth century is Michael Ramsey, notably in *Sacred and Secular* (of 1967) and *Be Still and Know* (of 1981).

Later twentieth-century spirituality has pro-duced a vast armoury of books of all kinds. Ecumenism has resulted in a free flowing of spiritual life and traditions. Ignatian spirituality has transformed practices of prayer across the denominations, not least among Baptists. Spirituality has run parallel with radicalism, sometimes as a refuge from its icy blasts along the journey, sometimes as its natural partner.

The medieval Meister Eckhart, rightly or wrongly, is seen to teach a holism which frees the adherents of historic religions from 'the scandal of particularity' and the confinement of creeds and finds echoes in those aware both of our kinship with nature and the burning need of social justice. Don Cupitt denies the objective truth of God, yet for him spirituality is central to the Christian life. It must be autonomous. It cannot depend on external circumstances, not even on God. Mysticism, which earlier in the century was given new vogue by Inge, von Hügel and Evelyn Underhill, is in the ascendant. The English mystics have greater circulation than in their own time and there are many fine studies of the Carmelites Teresa and John of the Cross. Mysticism appeals because of suspicions of history, which is uncertain, at the mercy of changing interpretations and new discoveries, and, dirtiest of words, elitist. Mysticism also rests on personal experience.

Those who opposed mysticism as often delusory and leading away from ethical activity, John Oman, Reinhold Niebuhr and Bishop Gore, seem to have few heirs, possibly because, as Owen Chadwick has said, we are aware of the impotence of words. We carry on our dialectic in the dark; before God we are blind. Yet there is an overwhelming conviction of the purpose and the reality of (his) light (Chadwick, 1990, p. 317f.).

There may be discerned a drift away from the Jesus of history in the spirituality of the decades to 1970, in spite of the techniques of Ignatian meditation. The liberal school of the first fifty years of the century taught a meditation which, in the words of John Ruskin, 'sought to be present as if in the body at each recorded event in the life of the Redeemer'. There is now less certainty about the records, the confession by some of a vast ignorance about many of the details of Christ's earthly life. Do we touch more than the outskirts of his ways? Other faiths which cannot be dismissed as heathen errors, and whose techniques, Buddhism, Yoga, Transcendental Meditation for instance, influence many Christians, challenge his finality. Yet he is still seen, though through a glass darkly, as the window into God, and the cry of dereliction is felt to be the word of God for the age of Auschwitz. At the same time, there are new spiritualities of power worldwide, even what some would call Christo-fascism. LIBERATION THEOLOGY among the poor and oppressed, particularly in Latin America, is fearful of the pessimism and morbidity of a Christian emphasis on the tragic. And the charismatic movement (see PENTECOSTALISM AND CHARISMATIC CHRISTIANITY), with its speaking with tongues, has brought freedom and confidence and deliverance from inhibitions for very many. Black spirituality is now experienced in the west and north and has a fervour, a convinced faith and a power of extempore prayer, which some feel shame the agnosticism of sophisticated half-believers. In some places, the longer ending of St Mark's Gospel seems to be fulfilled.

The Eucharist has retained and increased its hold, with new liturgies and a more communal understanding, though less sense of mystery and adoration. Communion at 8 followed by non-communicating High Mass at 11 at which one pondered and adored and which turned the young Michael Ramsey from Congregationalist to Anglo-Catholic has now almost disappeared. But many would agree with John Burnaby that there is in 'the memorial of the precious death and passion of God's dear Son, a safeguard against misunderstanding or misuse of the act of prayer which no defects in verbal expression can remove' (Vidler, 1962, p. 237). Intercession, with all its problems, is for many the part of prayer which seems most real to them, and the Eucharist is its supreme place, even to the extent of some moves to restore it to the canon itself.

Feminism is bound to have an effect on spirituality which cannot as yet wholly be measured. How far will it go? The prominence now given to women spiritual guides of the past, the value of women as teachers and directors, the use of inclusive language, are now established at least officially (see FEMINIST THEOLOGY). But what of our understanding of God and of truth and error? Will this be revolutionized, with old 'heresies' rehabilitated and new images of God, with spiritualities of creation and the womb?

One feature of twentieth-century spirituality, which has seen some decline in the monastic life, has been the creation of communities, mixed and including the married. Iona was the pioneer, but Taizé, where the brothers are celibate, has a far-extending influence. And both – and others – are agents of spirituality, reviving worship and prayer allied to manual work.

The Roman Catholic theologians Karl Rahner and Hans Urs von Balthasar, both influenced by Karl Barth, have written on prayer, not despising petition. Balthasar has produced a theological aesthetics, a sign of the contemporary concern with the spirituality of art and beauty. But the transcendent beauty of God is seen in the kenosis of the cross, and union with God is to share in the eternal sacrifice which is the heart of the Blessed Trinity.

See also LITURGY AND DOCTRINE; LOVE, CHRISTIAN; PASTORAL THEOLOGY; SACRAMENTAL THEOLOGY.

Bibliography

Brooks, Peter N., ed. 1975: *Christian Spirituality*. London: SCM Press.

Burnaby, John 1938: *Amor Dei*. London: Hodder and Stoughton.

Chadwick, Owen 1990: *The Spirit of the Oxford Movement*. Cambridge: Cambridge University Press.

Church, R.W. 1895: *Paschal and Other Sermons*. London: Macmillan

Cupitt, Don 1980: *Turning Away from God*. London: SCM Press.

Elliott, Charles 1985: *Praying the Kingdom*. London: Darton, Longman and Todd.

Flew, R. Newton 1934: *The Idea of Perfection in Christian Theology*. Oxford: Oxford University Press.

Hallesby, O. [1948] 1976: *Prayer*. London: Hodder and Stoughton.

Jay, Elisabeth, ed. 1983: *The Evangelical and Oxford Movements*. Cambridge: Cambridge University Press.

King, Ursula 1989: *Women and Spirituality*. London: Macmillan.

Nuttall, G.F. 1951: *Richard Baxter and Philip Doddridge*. Oxford: Oxford University Press.

Outler, Albert C. ed. 1964: *John Wesley*. New York and Oxford: Oxford University Press.

Rattenbury, J.E. 1948: *The Eucharistic Hymns of John and Charles Wesley*. London: Epworth.

Rivers, Isabel 1991: *Reason, Grace and Sentiment*, vol. 1. Cambridge: Cambridge University Press.

Rowell, Geoffrey, ed. 1986: *Tradition Renewed*. London: Darton, Longman and Todd.

Rupp, Ernest Gordon 1986: *Religion in England 1688–1791*. Oxford: Clarendon Press.

Thornton, Martin 1963: *English Spirituality*. London: SPCK.

Vidler, A.R., ed. 1962: *Soundings*. Cambridge: Cambridge University Press.

GORDON S. WAKEFIELD

Strauss, David Friedrich (1808–1874) German biblical critic and political theorist. He studied theology at Tübingen and Berlin, and was influenced by the thought of F.C. Baur, F.D.E. Schleiermacher and G.W.F. Hegel. He was removed from his teaching post at Tübingen following the controversy provoked by his best-known book, *Das Leben Jesu* (1835–6, trans. *The Life of Jesus* by George Eliot, 1846). In it he subjected the Gospel accounts to a historical-critical re-examination, concluding that the narratives are mythological rather than historical in character: they represent a projection of the messianic expectation of early Christians, focused on the man Jesus, in the period between his death and the writing of the Gospels. He applied Hegelian dialectic to the growth of the early church, and argued for the impossibility of attributing divinity to one human being only; rather, the incarnation takes place in humanity as a whole. The book is a watershed in the history of New Testament criticism, and prefigures the later German liberal Protestant 'quest for the historical Jesus'. Later works developed his political theory, whilst in works such as *Die christliche Glaubenslehre* (1840–1) and *Der alte und der neue Glaube* (1872, trans. 1873), he moved increasingly away from religious orthodoxy, espousing scientific materialism as well as presenting his increasingly strong nationalism.

See also BIBLICAL CRITICISM AND INTERPRETATION 2: NEW TESTAMENT.

Bibliography

Cromwell, R.S. 1974: *D.F. Strauss and his Place in Modern Thought*. Fairlawn, N.J.

Harris, H. 1982: *D.F. Strauss and his Theology*. Edinburgh.

suffering See EVIL, PROBLEM OF; SUFFERING, DIVINE.

suffering, divine The idea that God suffers with his creation has become prominent in modern Christian thought, challenging traditional concepts of an impassible God that were formulated in both the patristic and medieval periods.

Four major motives may be identified for attributing suffering to God, the first being reflection upon the nature of love, drawing insights from modern psychology. While classical theists such as Augustine, Thomas Aquinas and John Calvin were content to define love as an attitude and action of goodwill to another person, and so could affirm that God loves impassibly, much recent thought has insisted that love involves sharing of feelings and sympathy (for example Williams, 1968). For the one who loves, awareness of another's suffering thus means participation within it; as applied to God, this insight has been strengthened by Old Testament studies of the Israelite prophets and their portrayal of God's 'pathos' with and for his people (Fretheim, 1984).

A second reason for affirming divine suffering has been Christological, with particular attention to the presence of God in the cross of Jesus. The traditional view that God suffered 'in the human nature' of Christ effectively isolated suffering within the humanity of Christ, removing it from his divine nature and so from the inner being of God. By contrast, recent theologians have found a witness to divine passibility in God's oneness with the *whole person* of Christ (whether this oneness is understood as a matter of function or being), and others have concluded that the event of the cross reveals that weakness and humility are characteristic of God's triune nature. Third, the belief that God suffers has seemed to be a powerful element in defending the justice of God in a suffering world. It has provided a 'practical theodicy' which assures the sufferer of God's presence; it has entailed a denial, especially among liberation theologians, that God himself inflicts suffering; and it has helped to make credible a free will defence of evil and suffering, since a suffering God also shares the consequences of the risks of freedom. Fourth, the modern world picture has suggested a Creator involved in suffering. If the world is a living organism, a community which is growing and developing in mutual relationship rather than a machine, then it seems that God can only fulfil his purposes for creation by acting and suffering within it rather than remaining invulnerable and detached. While this world view has been stressed by process theology, it has by no means been limited to it.

The modern historical development of the conviction that God suffers has produced themes that remain in most discussion today. Perhaps the greatest initial impulse towards the formulation of divine passibility was provided by Hegel's insistence that Absolute Spirit can only be vital when it goes out beyond itself to face opposition and negation in a movement of self-sacrifice. Horace Bushnell, in his study of atonement, made the influential claim that the cross must reveal something eternally true about the nature of God. Karl Barth found the sovereignty of God to lie in his freedom, including the freedom to choose to be conditioned as well as to be unconditioned by his world. More recently, Eberhard Jüngel has found an answer to the claim that 'God is dead' by speaking of the 'death of the living God' (1968); that is, God is not irrelevant to the world because, like it, he is involved in 'perishability', though in being so he overcomes death and makes it serve him. A key figure among those developing a 'theology of the cross' in modern times has been Jürgen Moltmann, opposing the concept of divine apathy in order to affirm God's solidarity with the poor and oppressed as 'the crucified God' ([1972] 1974). Hans Urs von Balthasar has affirmed the 'immutability' of God in the special sense that God does not need to change in order to suffer; within God's triune relationships, suggests Balthasar (1983), there is eternally a 'separation motivated by love' because of the infinite distinction of persons, and this can be the basis for God's suffering of alienation within a sinful world. Finally, process theology has been influential, portraying God as the 'fellow-sufferer who understands' (A.N. Whitehead), sharing in the conditions of becoming within the world, absorbing into the world-related aspect of his being all its experience and achievement, and harmonizing it within himself to produce an influence upon future states of the process of reality.

Modern advocates of divine passibility have, however, had to develop answers to several substantial problems associated with the idea. In defence of impassibility it has been urged that the only explanation for a changing world could be a God who is immune from change, expressed in the classical terms of having 'necessary being' and 'aseity'. In answer, theologians of divine suffering tend to accuse this view of being a remnant of the 'negative transcendence' of Platonic philosophy, where God as Absolute Being cannot by definition be involved in Becoming; in contrast they argue that only a God who is himself involved in contingency could create a changing world. An affirming of the 'aseity' of God (that he is *a se*, or 'from himself' alone) has traditionally been thought to entail that God is unconditioned in every way, whereas a suffering God must by contrast be involved in change, both in terms of receiving injury from outside himself and having a movement of pathos within. Theologians of divine suffering have distinguished, therefore, between God's aseity understood as being self-existent and as being unconditioned; they have proposed that a self-existent God could freely *choose* or *desire* to limit himself, in a 'kenosis' or self-emptying, for the sake of creating a world in which there are personalities who enjoy their own freedom. The alternative idea (for example, Lee, 1974), that God suffers in the sense of simply changing *himself* rather than being conditioned by external forces, seems to undermine the element of vulnerability in suffering. Process theologians, however, have not thought it appropriate to maintain ideas of ascity and voluntary kenosis at all, understanding God's conditioning by the world and his suffering within it as a necessary part of the process of creativity.

Whichever view be adopted here, it seems that the idea of a God who is affected or conditioned by the world raises further problems of divine temporality and omniscience. To suffer must mean to change from one state to another and so to be involved in some sense in time, and it is also hard to conceive of God's sharing in the real vulnerability of suffering if he were to be simultaneously present in the past, present and future and so to know the outcome of all events in detail. In response to these problems it may be suggested that omniscience be defined as God's knowledge of all actualities *and* all possibilities, rather than his knowing future possibilities *as* actualities already. Correspondingly, a distinction can be made between divine perfection and completion; God is perfectly related to all reality that there is,

while being open to being completed by reality that has not yet come to be. Such ideas thus present God as having a different relationship to time from finite beings, while not being absolutely timeless; this state of being may be grounded either simply in the nature of reality (as in process theology) or in the self-limitation of the Creator (as in, for example, Jürgen Moltmann, [1980] 1981).

Perhaps the strongest objection to the idea of divine passibility is that a suffering God could not inspire worship or provide consolation to a sufferer. If suffering were located in the inner being of God then it would be eternalized, whereas – it is objected – unless the divine bliss were finally undisturbed by suffering, human sufferers could have no hope in the overcoming of evil. Thus the problem of human suffering might be said to be actually increased by the inclusion of God among the victims of the universe. In reply, theologians who affirm divine suffering point out that human views of power are conditioned by our own political and social context; the idea of a God who exhibits his power by keeping himself invulnerable from suffering quickly becomes a God who sanctions a human chain of political and ecclesiastical domination ('political and clerical monotheism', as Moltmann ([1980] 1981) describes it). It is urged that true power is not coercion but persuasive love, and that this is not only worthy of worship but able finally to overcome evil. Some (such as Fiddes, 1988) relate this to a doctrine of atonement, in which the participation of God in suffering has a transforming and creative effect upon human personalities. While, from this viewpoint, some suffering must be eternal in the being of God, his bliss is understood to outweigh suffering without cancelling it out; it is seen as a mark of the humility of God that he is willing to open himself to a tragedy of unfulfilled desire, understood not as the presence of evil within his being but as the absence of good that the world might have produced.

In the light of the problems mentioned above, it has been suggested that it would be better to maintain *both* the impassibility *and* the passibility of God, drawing on a distinction between God's inner being and his activity in the created universe. Pathos would then be ascribed to God's outward relationship with humankind, and not to his essential attributes. It is urged that this has the theological and pastoral advantages of combining the philosophical idea of an unchanging divine principle with the personal, living God of the Hebraic-Christian tradition. Process theologians thus propose a 'dipolar' (or bipolar) theism, where an immutable and necessary aspect of the divine being has a grasp of possibility, and a mutable and contingent aspect embraces all actuality. Other theologians draw upon a distinction between the 'immanent Trinity' and the 'economic Trinity', or even between an impassible Father and a passible Son. This approach, it is suggested, retains more of the mystery of God's being, as well as avoiding the worst dangers of anthropomorphism, such as the capricious and passionate behaviour of the Greek gods scorned and satirized by the Greek philosophers.

Those theologians of divine suffering who find this distinction an invalid one certainly acknowledge the final mystery of God's being, but argue on the basis of God's self-revelation that his external activity must have at least some 'correspondence' or analogy to his essence. In particular, it is urged that if the cross of Jesus does indeed reveal the triune nature of God, then there can be no other 'immanent' Trinity than the one which has a suffering involvement with humanity at its centre. Correspondingly, it is argued that it would be better to distinguish between the divine persons of the Trinity in terms of their different *modes* or *kinds* of participation in suffering. Finally, it seems to some that the problem of human suffering demands that the God who created a universe in which evil and suffering were a real risk of freedom, should himself participate in the consequences of that risk without reserve in his inner being.

Whether or not a theodicy leads the Christian thinker to affirm suffering in the inner being of God in this way, there seems little doubt that the problem of human suffering has been the most powerful motivation in recent years for affirming the suffering of God.

See also EVIL, PROBLEM OF; GOD; HEGE-LIANISM; PROCESS THEOLOGY.

Bibliography

Balthasar, H.U. von [1969] 1990: *Mysterium Paschale: The Mystery of Easter*, trans. A. Nichols. Edinburgh: T & T Clark.

Balthasar, H.U. von 1983: *Theodramatik, IV: Endspiel*. Einsiedeln: Johannes Verlag.

Barth, K. [1940] 1957: *Church Dogmatics* II/1, trans. G.W. Bromiley and T.F. Torrance. Edinburgh: T & T Clark, paragraph 28, 'The Being of God as the One who Loves in Freedom'.

Fiddes, P.S. 1988: *The Creative Suffering of God*. Oxford: Clarendon Press.

Fretheim, T.E. 1984: *The Suffering of God: An Old Testament Perspective*. Philadelphia: Fortress Press.

Jüngel, E. 1968: Vom Tod des lebendigen Gottes. Ein Plakat, *Zeitschrift für Theologie und Kirche* 65, pp. 93–116.

Jüngel, E. [1977] 1983: *God as the Mystery of the World: On the Foundation of the Theology of the Crucified One in the Dispute between Theism and Atheism*, trans. D.L. Guder. Edinburgh: T & T Clark.

Kitamori, K. [1946] 1966: *Theology of the Pain of God*, trans. M.E. Bratcher. London: SCM Press.

Lee, J.Y. 1974: *God suffers for Us: A Systematic Enquiry into the Concept of Divine Passibility*. The Hague: Martinus Nijhoff.

McWilliams, W. 1985: *The Passion of God: Divine Suffering in Contemporary Protestant Theology*. Macon: Mercer Press.

Moltmann, J. [1972] 1974: *The Crucified God: The Cross of Christ as the Foundation and Criticism of Christian Theology*, trans. R.A. Wilson and J. Bowden. London: SCM Press.

Moltmann, J. [1980] 1981: *The Trinity and the Kingdom of God*, trans. M. Kohl. London: SCM Press.

Mozley, J.K. 1926: *The Impassibility of God: A Survey of Christian Thought*. London: Cambridge University Press.

Wheeler Robinson, H. 1940: *Suffering Human and Divine*. London: SCM Press.

Williams, D.D. 1968: *The Spirit and the Forms of Love*. Welwyn: James Nisbet.

PAUL S. FIDDES

Sweden See PROTESTANT THEOLOGY: SCANDINAVIA.

T

Teilhard de Chardin, Pierre (1881–1955) French theologian and scientist. A Jesuit priest and teacher, but forbidden to teach because of unorthodox ideas, he was also an eminent geologist and palaeontologist, working for a period in China, where he contributed to the study of one form of early man. He spent his last years in the USA. As a scientist he wrote more than 170 articles and technical papers, but during his lifetime he was debarred from publishing his theological and philosophical works. Published after his death, they were highly influential in the developing understanding of the relationship between science and religion. In *The Phenomenon of Man* (1955, trans. 1959), he attempted to construct a phenomenology of the universe based on scientific, theological and philosophical ideas. The evolutionary process is one of increasing complexity, involving ever higher levels of consciousness and directed towards the ultimate goal of a supreme centre or 'Omega point' which becomes identified with Christ. For him all matter is sacred, since Christ is the organic centre of the universe; the universe is in the evolutionary process of 'Christification'. Other writings include devotional books, notably *Le Milieu divin* (1957, trans. 1960), and speculative books such as *The Future of Man* (trans. 1964).

Bibliography

Cuénot, C. 1965: *Teilhard de Chardin*. London.
Hanson, A., ed. 1970: *Teilhard Re-Assessed*. London.
Speaight, R. 1967: *Teilhard de Chardin: A Biography*. London.

Temple, William (1881–1944) English bishop and theologian. Himself the son of an archbishop of Canterbury, he was Bishop of Manchester (1921–9), Archbishop of York (1929–42) and Archbishop of Canterbury (1942–4). Activated by a concern for social problems and for the human interface between Christianity and politics and economics, he remains a figurehead for Christians seeking to combine personal religion with social action. Emphasizing the theological importance of the incarnation as a starting point for the dignity and worth of man, he was widely respected as a Christian voice in the sphere of politics, economics and social development, as well as a leader in the church. *Christianity and Social Order* (1942) was influential in the development of the emerging welfare state. He co-produced the significant report of 1938 on doctrine in the Church of England, and his support for ecumenism led him to become a president of the committee for the formation of the World Council of Churches (1938). His writings include works of philosophy and theology, such as *Mens Creatrix* (1917), *Christus Veritas* (1924) and *Nature, Man and God* (Gifford Lectures, 1934), as well as devotional writings such as *Readings in St John's Gospel* (1939–40).

Bibliography

Craig, R. 1963: *Social Concern in the Thought of William Temple*. London.
Padgett, J.F. 1974: *The Christian Philosophy of William Temple*. The Hague.
Suggate, A.M. 1987: *William Temple and Christian Social Ethics Today*. Edinburgh.

theodicy See EVIL, PROBLEM OF.

Thielicke, Helmut (1908–1986) German Lutheran preacher and theologian; a professor at Heidelberg, Tübingen and, from 1954, Hamburg. His powerful preaching was temporarily silenced by the Nazis from 1940, but his emphasis on the preached word as a necessary accompaniment to theological enquiry was influential in postwar Germany. Concerned to contextualize the message of the gospel in the modern world, he attempted to steer a course between accommodation with secularism, and traditionalist caution which would 'repeat Luther's sayings about government unaltered in a democratic age instead of adjusting them to the new situation'. He responded to modern nihilism and secular determinism by emphasizing the sovereignty of God in Christ in history, and highlighting the dual themes of judgement and grace. Much of his study centred on evolving a practical theological approach to the ethical dilemmas of the modern world; by rooting his discussion in orthodox dogma he appealed, if controversially, to evangelicals, whilst understanding and appealing to liberals. His published works, many translated into English, include collections of sermons and systematic theological series, notably *Theological Ethics* (1958–64, trans. 1966), and his work of dogmatics, *The Evangelical Faith* (1968 on, trans. 1974–7).

Bibliography

Bromiley, G. 1984: Helmut Thielicke. In *A Handbook of Christian Theologians*, ed. D.G. Peerman and M.E. Marty. Nashville, Tn.

Higginson, R. 1976: Thielicke: Preacher and Theologian, *The Churchman* 90 (July/September).

Tillich, Paul (1883–1965) German-American theologian, commonly regarded as one of the most significant and influential Protestant theologians of the twentieth century. Paul Tillich was born on 20 August 1886 in Starzeddel in Germany (today Staro Siedle in Poland), the son of a conservative Lutheran pastor. From 1904 to 1909 he studied theology at the universities of Berlin, Tübingen and Halle, and then embarked on his doctorate. During the First World War Tillich served as a military chaplain, but by the end of the war had resumed his academic career and was lecturing at the University of Berlin. After holding academic posts in Marburg and Dresden, he was called to a chair in philosophy at the University of Frankfurt in 1929. His views led him into conflict with the Nazis, and in 1933 he accepted an invitation to become visiting professor at Union Theological Seminary in New York, where he taught until he retired in 1955. He was then appointed University Professor at Harvard, one of the greatest distinctions for any scholar in American academic life. At the time of his death he was probably the most widely known theologian in America.

Unlike Karl Barth, his one-time ally and later opponent, Tillich was from the beginning intent on relating theological thought to non-theological reflection and seemingly non-religious spheres of culture. Tillich's wide-ranging influence outside theology, on psychotherapy, political theory and the interpretation of culture, reflects the fact that Tillich's theology was programmatically developed as *apologetics*, as an attempt to render Christian faith and religion in general intelligible and attractive to the 'cultured among its despisers'. Tillich's view of the whole of theology as apologetic theology, as an 'answering' theology responding to the questions raised by the situation of its time, later conceptualized in the method of correlation between message and situation, has the effect that the majority of Tillich's writings are relatively short books, occasional papers and published lectures addressing specific aspects of the religious situation of the time. His *magnum opus*, the *Systematic Theology*, published in three volumes between 1951 and 1963, is as much a systematic exposition of his thought as the 'meta-theory' of his theological method. It also participates in the dynamic, constantly self-modifying movement of Tillich's theology, where relatively few invariant elements are frequently recombined to accommodate the need for new or reformulated answers occasioned by new questions. If one wants to understand the vital elements of Tillich's thought one therefore cannot simply offer a general analysis of the basic tenets of his system, but one has to follow the correlations he forged between specific questions arising in specific cultural situations and the specific attempts he made to respond to these challenges theologically.

The heritage of idealism (1886–1916)

At Halle Tillich came under the influence of Martin Kähler (1835–1912). Tillich owes to Kähler two formative stimuli for his thought: the interpretation of the concept of justification as the organizing centre of Christian dogmatics and the view that belief in Christ cannot be based on the results of historical research on Jesus of Nazareth. The most decisive influence on his thought, however, came from his extensive engagement with the thought of the idealist philosopher Friedrich Wilhelm von Schelling (1775–1857), whose philosophy is the topic of Tillich's PhD thesis from 1910 and the thesis submitted in 1912 for the licentiate in theology, at that time the equivalent of a theological doctorate. From Schelling Tillich appropriated the general idealist conception of the identity of thinking and being as the principle of truth and some of the most central concepts of his theology: the interpretation of the God–World relationship as one between the unconditioned and the conditioned, the view of God as ground and abyss of being and the notion of the 'God above God', the ultimate reality transcending religious symbolism and philosophical conceptuality. This idealist programme is pursued in Tillich's *Habilitationsschrift* of 1915 (a further thesis required in German universities for recognition as an academic teacher) in which Tillich offered a critique of the concept of the supernatural in theology before F.D.E. Schleiermacher, announcing the later much repeated slogan that theology has to move beyond the alternatives of supranaturalism and naturalism.

The turning point: theology of culture and socialist decision (1916–33)

Tillich experienced the First World War as an absolute catastrophe, the collapse of the bourgeois period of European culture and the end of a theology that could exist in a happy alliance with the bourgeois optimism of progress and stability. After the end of the war Tillich, by then a lecturer at the University of Berlin without a permanent post and dependent on lecture fees from his students, supported all political and cultural movements, from radical socialism to expressionist art, in which this disruptive experience was expressed and radi-

cally new paths for society, culture and theology were explored. The published lecture 'On the Idea of a Theology of Culture' of 1919 offers his programmatic response to this new situation. Historical experience has revealed the disruption of the unity of culture, spheres of culture are disclosed in their radical autonomy, they have liberated themselves from any religious heteronomy. In such a situation religion is marginalized to a separate sphere alongside other spheres of culture engaged in permanent conflict with all forms of autonomous expression. This conflict can only be overcome when religion is interpreted as the experience of the unconditioned, the experience of absolute reality which grows out of the experience of the ultimate nothingness of everything conditioned. The religious content can therefore only be grasped through the autonomy of cultural forms of expression as the unconditioned which breaks through the conditioned forms and creates a new theonomous unity of culture. The radical socialist programme is for Tillich at that time the promise of a new cultural unity which is not based on the ruins of the past, but on the creative transformation of the absolute moment in history, the *kairos*, which he saw in the breakdown of the old order of society. *Religious socialism* keeps this radical element alive in socialism, by confronting each social order with the judgement and promise of the kingdom of God.

Much of the revolutionary enthusiasm of the immediate postwar period is from the mid-1920s slowly transformed into more general theories in which Tillich explores aspects of the initial vision of the new synthesis of religion and culture. While his immediate postwar theology brought him in contact and to a mutual understanding with representatives of the 'theology of crisis' like Karl Barth and Friedrich Gogarten, Tillich increasingly came to occupy a place on the fringes of academic theology. Tillich later described this position as a standpoint 'on the boundary' between theology and philosophy, between the church and secular culture. In this time Tillich developed his interpretation of modern culture in a rich variety of aspects, from expressionist art to modern dance, from science to politics, comprehensively summarized in *Die religiöse Lage der Zeit* (*The Religious Situation of the*

Times) in 1926. Many of Tillich's formative categories for the religious interpretation of culture are for the first time formulated in this time: the question of the *Gestalt* of grace, the expression of ultimate meaning in reality, the Protestant principle, the prophetic criticism of all attempts to cast the reality of grace in objective 'sacramental' forms and, for Tillich perhaps most important of all, the category of the demonic which expresses the event, where destructive powers seem to create their own forms. All this forms the background to the book *The Socialist Decision* of 1933, where Tillich offers a clear-sighted critique of the conservative political romanticism of bourgeois conservatives and the revolutionary political romanticism of national socialism, both grounded in a myth of origin which can only be overcome by the prophetic criticism of socialism. It was this book which led in April 1933 to Tillich's becoming the first Protestant theologian to be suspended from a university post after the Nazis came to power.

Emigration, existentialism and Systematic Theology *(1933–65)*

Tillich first experienced emigration as a 'second death' after the 'first death', the experience of the existential threat of non-existence he had encountered on the battle fields of the First World War. In retrospect it is possible to see this experience of displacement as one of the major motives for Tillich's reformulation of his thought in terms of an ontological existentialism which tries to identify and describe existential states which, although described in personal, even autobiographical, concreteness, in virtue of their ontological character point to a common dimension of depth underlying different cultural-linguistic frameworks of interpretation. During the Second World War Tillich applied his theology of culture to a practical theology of politics, by becoming the president of Self-Help for Emigrés from Central Europe and in 1944 president of the Council for a Democratic Germany. From 1942–4 the Voice of America broadcast a political address by Tillich every Sunday to Europe.

After the end of the war Tillich returned to the development of his theology of culture, but now under the new conditions created by the experiences of the World War which are laid bare in their 'dimension of depth' by existential analysis. The first volume of Tillich's published sermons, *The Shaking of the Foundations* of 1948, later to be followed by *The New Being* of 1955 and *The Eternal Now* of 1963, expresses the common denominator of his analysis of the situation. The same theme is explored in the collection of papers from the same year, *The End of the Protestant Era*, where Tillich argues that the historical and spiritual presuppositions of Protestantism in humanism are no longer capable of overcoming the experience of the spiritual vacuum, the all-pervasive crisis of meaning after the war. The personal dimension of this crisis is explored in *The Courage to Be* of 1952. The ontological anxiety of the void of absolute meaninglessness can, according to Tillich, only be answered by a form of courage which is based on the absolute faith of being unconditionally accepted, totally affirmed, which, in turn, is interpreted as the experience of being grasped by the power of Being itself. This absolute faith is correlated to the God above the God of theism who appears when the God of theism is submerged in the anxiety of doubt and despair. The social dimension of this crisis is analysed in *Love, Power and Justice* of 1955, where Tillich argues that their common ontological foundation and the basis of their unity is God as Being itself who is revealed in the crucified Christ and is concretely experienced in the Spirit Community where the overcoming of the ambiguities of love, power and justice offers fragmentary anticipation of their complete and unambiguous actuality in the kingdom of God. The theological and philosophical foundation of these reflections is offered in *Biblical Religion and the Search for Ultimate Reality* of 1955. Tillich argues (against Pascal) that the God of Abraham, Isaac and Jacob and the God of the philosophers is the same God. The structural identity of biblical religion and ontology is here developed in terms of the correlation between the suprapersonal ground of being and the personal encounter of God and humanity in the God who is both Being itself and personal being itself.

At Harvard Tillich published another book that became a theological bestseller: *The Dynamics of Faith* of 1955. The thesis developed in this book that faith is to be interpreted as the experience of being grasped by that which concerns us ultimately is supplemented by a number of writings on religious symbolism which explain how the unconditioned ground of being can be expressed and addressed in religious acts.

These books, almost all of which were based on series of lectures, accompany the development and publication of the *Systematic Theology*, Tillich's attempt to integrate his reflections into a unified conceptual framework. In the first volume, published in 1951, Tillich also offers a general account of the theological and philosophical method he had applied in so many specific explorations. This procedure, which he dubs the 'method of correlation', is the endeavour in philosophical reflection to discover in our cultural situation and express the existential questions which are answered by the theological interpretation of the symbols of the Christian message. Correlation therefore appears as the unity of dependence and independence between existential questions and theological answers which brackets the divergence and convergence of philosophy and theology. This leads to a polar structure in each of the five parts of the *Systematic Theology*. Part I, 'Reason and Revelation', correlates the human quest for knowledge with the religious concept of revelation. Part II, 'Being and God', relates the analysis of being in its essential structures to the concept of God as Being itself. Part III, 'Existence and the Christ' (published separately in vol. 2 in 1957) develops the situation of existential estrangement, expressed in the power of sin, and the quest for salvation which finds its answer in Jesus the Christ who is the appearance of New Being under the conditions of existential estrangement. Volume 3, published in 1963, presents parts IV and V, 'Life and the Spirit' and 'History and the Kingdom of God', in which the reality of life as it exists factually as a mixture of essential and existential elements and so as ambiguous life is described as the question which finds its answer in the presence of the divine Spirit. In the last part this is applied to the historical dimension of life where the eternal kingdom of God can already be experienced in a fragmentary form and so provides meaning in the vacuum of meaninglessness. The core of the *Systematic Theology* is clearly its Trinitarian structure in parts II-IV, from which Tillich separates for convenience of exposition parts I and V. In true idealist fashion the work culminates in the massive doctrine of the Spirit in the last volume. The *Systematic Theology* is one of the most significant theological works of this century. It offered an integrative framework for Tillich's thought and inaugurated a new period of theological engagement with his theology. It is nevertheless not a closed system, but documents in the subtle modifications and reformulations which Tillich introduces in volumes 2 and 3 the constantly evolving character of his thought.

The future of Tillich's theology
Tillich gave his last lecture under the title 'The Significance of the History of Religions for the Systematic Theologian' on 11 October 1965 in Chicago. After the lecture he suffered a heart attack and died ten days later. This last lecture, in some ways the fruit of his cooperation with Mircea Eliade at the University of Chicago from 1962 and of his increased recognition of the concrete particularity of non-Christian religious traditions since his visit to Japan in 1960, offers the vision of a 'religion of the concrete Spirit' as the *telos* of the history of religions which unifies ecstatic and rational elements in religion and so documents the battle of God against religion (i.e. the demonic distortion of its essential elements) within religion. Here we see the last new modification in Tillich's thought after the completed *summa* of the *Systematic Theology* in which there are indications that he is prepared to overcome some of the metaphysical reconceptualizations of religion for an increased acknowledgement of religion as documented in the concrete particularity of living religious traditions.

Tillich's apologetic theology has variously been criticized for the imposition of an allegedly alien metaphysical framework of interpretation on the concrete reality of the Christian revelation and for developing a philosophical doctrine of God as impersonal Being itself, for ignoring the historical particularity of the incarnation as the foundation of an authentically Christian faith and for taking leave of the personal character of God the Spirit in order to offer a humanist philosophy of Spirit. Much of the criticism converges in the claim that Tillich's emphasis on the *apologetic* task of theology is not sufficiently undergirded by an equally decisive emphasis on its *dogmatic* task, the faithful exposition of the truth claims of authentic Christian faith. The varied, dynamic and constantly self-modifying character of Tillich's theology calls for a specific assessment of each individual criticism. If, however, it is true that faith in the triune God as the ground of all being, meaning and truth is a constitutive and authentic element of the Christian revelation, Tillich's attempts to translate this conviction into a theological interpretation of reality which can engage in dialogue with all cultural forms of expression will remain an inspiration or a challenge for contemporary theologians and a corrective against all attempts to interpret the autonomy of theology as a permanent state of self-isolation.

Bibliography

Writings
1951, 1957, 1963: *Systematic Theology*, vols 1–3. Chicago: University of Chicago Press.
1987– : *Main Works/Hauptwerke*, vols 1–6, ed. Carl Heinz Ratschow. New York/Berlin: de Gruyter.

Critical works
Adams, J.L., Pauck, W., and Shinn, R.L., eds 1985: *The Thought of Paul Tillich*. San Francisco: Harper and Row.
Clayton, J. 1980: *The Concept of Correlation*. New York/Berlin: de Gruyter.
Pauck, W., and Pauck, M. 1976: *Paul Tillich, His Life and Thought*, vol. 1. New York: Harper and Row.
CHRISTOPH SCHWÖBEL

Tolkien, [J]ohn [R]onald [R]euel (1892–1973) English scholar and novelist. He was educated at Merton College, Oxford, and became professor of Anglo-Saxon (1925–45) and then English literature (1945–59) at Oxford. His scholarly publications include an edition of *Sir Gawain and the Green Knight* (1925, with E.V. Gordon) and a critical study of *Beowulf* (1937). He was also a member of The Inklings, the group of Oxford writers which included C.S. Lewis and Charles Williams, and is now best known as the creator of his own mythology, contained in a series of novels peopled by strange creatures with their own history and language. The world of *The Hobbit* (1937) and *Lord of the Rings* (3 vols, 1954–5), evokes an age of rural idyll and innocence which comes under threat from the forces of evil, inspiring courage and self-sacrifice in unlikely heroes. Critics have seen strong Christian overtones in his work, including the themes of divine sovereignty and the problem of evil, and human free will and predestination, although he denied any 'allegorical intentions, general, particular or topical, moral, religious or political'. The serious moral tone of the novels combined with the vivid fantasy of the characters' creation has assured them a cult following. Other novels, notably *The Silmarillion* (1977), were published posthumously.

Bibliography

Fuller, E. *et al.* 1974: *Myth, Allegory and Gospel: An Interpretation of Tolkien, Lewis, Chesterton and Williams*. Bethany Fellowship.
Urang, G. 1971: *Shadows of Heaven: Religion and Fantasy in the Writing of Lewis, Williams and Tolkien*. Boston.

Tolstoy, Leo (1828–1910) Russian novelist and social theorist. Born into an aristocratic family whose estate near Tula he later inherited, he was widely read, and the works of J.J. Rousseau influenced the development of his theories of social reform. He published several early novels, but it is with *War and Peace* (1863–9) that his fame as a novelist was established. *Anna Karenina* followed (1873–7), but after a mystical religious crisis around 1880, which he describes in *Confession* (1879–82), he confined himself mainly to religious and moral works, including *What I Believe* (1883) and *The Kingdom of God is Within You* (1892–3). In them he developed his particular emphasis, derived from his reading of the Sermon on the Mount, on the personal, ethical dimension of Christianity, while rejecting its supernatural aspect. Arguing against the divinity of Christ, and inspired by the simplicity and dignity of the peasant labourers on his estate, he believed in man's innate power to live in love and peace with all men. Increasingly, he renounced property and family life, living a life of radical simplicity and manual labour. His espousal of non-resistance to evil and his rejection of all forms of authority (including that of police, magistrates and governments) has been described as 'Christian anarchism'. His unorthodoxy and criticism of Orthodox church dogma led to the banning of his books in his lifetime, and to his excommunication by the church in 1901.

Bibliography
Craufurd, A.H. 1912: *The Religion and Ethics of Tolstoy*. London.
Maude, A. 1918: *The Life of Tolstoy*, 2 vols. London.
Troyat, H. 1970: *Tolstoy*. Harmondsworth.

Torrance, Thomas (b. 1913) Scottish churchman, theologian and philosopher of science. He studied philosophy, classics and theology at Edinburgh, and at Basle under K. Barth (whose English edition of *Church Dogmatics* he later co-edited). He taught church history and dogmatics at Edinburgh until 1979, and was also a Church of Scotland moderator for 1976. His major contribution is in the study of the relationship between the natural sciences and what he calls the 'science' of theology. Both areas of investigation take an objective 'given' as their starting point: for the natural sciences it is the natural world, for theology it is the 'given' of God's self-revelation in Jesus Christ; furthermore, these two areas of investigation, far from being incompatible, are part of a unified understanding of reality. He traces the development in scientific investigation from a 'dualistic', subject–object method to a more integrative style in which the natural scientist is not detached from the object of his study but is in relationship to it. Similarly, he argues, the Christian theologian is in relationship with the object of his study, Jesus Christ. Torrance's Christocentric theology is influenced by John Calvin (whom he has translated) and Barth, as well as by the early church Fathers, whose credal formulations express the reality of God just as scientific formulations express the reality of the natural world. His work attempts to go beyond these external formulations to the substance of the reality behind them, and to develop a scientific method of doing so. His works include *Theology in Reconstruction* (1965), *Christian Theology and Scientific Culture* (1980) and *Reality and Scientific Theology* (1985).

Bibliography
Heron, A.I.C. 1980: *A Century of Protestant Theology*. Cambridge.
Langford, T.A. 1972: T.F. Torrance's *Theological Science*: a reaction, *Scottish Journal of Theology* 25 pp. 155–70.
Palma, R.J. 1984: T.E. Torrance's Reformed Theology, *Reformed Review* 38, 1.

Tracy, David (b. 1939) North American Roman Catholic theologian. He studied at the Gregorian University in Rome during the Second Vatican Council, and later became professor at Chicago. In 1989 he participated in an important Catholic conference with Hans Küng (proceedings published as *Paradigm Change in Theology: A Symposium*, 1989). He is renowned for his emphasis on pluralism in theology and the possible positive effects of such pluralism. His works include *Blessed Rage for Order* (1975), *The New Pluralism in Theology* (1975) and *The Analogical Imagination* (1988).

Tracy has been extensively concerned with the development of theological method, an interest manifested in his work on fellow theologian Bernard Lonergan, culminating in his book *The Achievement of Bernard Lonergan* of 1965. Tracy's own work has concentrated on the construction of models to act as a basis for theological work in general, and for systematic theology in particular. He suggests that theological reflection should correlate two primary sources: common human language and experience, and the texts of Christianity.

In *The Analogical Imagination* Tracy continued to develop his pluralist theme, arguing that theology must be a public activity, addressing three audiences: the church, the academic world and society in general. Insights which can feed into Christian theology may come from a variety of secular sources, such as art and literature; Christianity must be aware of the plural sources which it can use in constructing theology. This pluralism does not mean that the figure of Christ is no longer central to Tracy's theology; rather, he describes Christ as a cultural 'classic', able to transform human existence. This concept of the religious 'classic' is a particularly significant part of his theology.

tradition Tradition is the process by which the revelation made by Jesus Christ is passed on and interpreted from age to age. The word is also used concretely in reference to the particular beliefs and practices which are handed down in this way.

In recent centuries Christian thinking about tradition has concentrated on two questions. The first concerns the relation between tradition and Scripture: does tradition constitute a second source of revelation which adds to what is contained in Scripture? The second concerns the development of doctrine: does tradition simply reaffirm the original revealed truth, or does it broaden the content of revelation in the process of handing it on?

Scripture and tradition

During the period covered by this encyclopedia, an appeal was frequently made to unwritten tradition in order to explain why some doctrines have little direct justification in Scripture or the beliefs of the early church. Beginning with E. Schelstrate at the end of the seventeenth century, it became common for Roman Catholic polemicists to attribute the lack of Scriptural support for some doctrines to the *disciplina arcani*, the silence which catechumens had to observe concerning certain beliefs and practices (Chadwick, [1957] 1987, pp. 68–9). Some Tractarian writers (such as I. Williams) argued in the same way, appealing to the 'principle of reserve'. More commonly however Anglican writers turned to Vincent of Lérins (d. *c.*450), who advocated fidelity to the tradition held everywhere, continuously and by general consent; *quod ubique, quod semper, quod ab omnibus* (*Commonitorium* 23: 57–9). This formula became known as the 'Vincentian canon', and played a great part in the discussions of the nineteenth century.

The Reformation insistence on Scripture alone meant that tradition cannot be a source of revealed knowledge; Scripture with the aid of the internal light of the Holy Spirit given to the individual was its own interpreter. It did not, however, follow that tradition was unimportant. Most forms of early Protestantism maintained the decisive significance of the *consensus quinquesaecularis*, the faith of the early centuries, as a confirmation of the right interpretation of Scripture, but not as a criterion or a source (Congar, [1960–3] 1966, pp. 139–45). FUNDAMENTALISM, which changes Christianity into a 'religion of the book', was a later development.

Many Protestant writers on tradition, in the spirit of the Centuriators of Magdeburg, took it as axiomatic that the church had suffered a fall which had affected its teaching. F.C. Baur believed that the Catholic corruption of the pure gospel was already evident in the Pastoral Epistles (Pelikan, 1971, pp. 53–4). Gottfried Arnold (d. 1714) saw the true continuity with the early church as a continuity not in dogma or episcopal succession but in 'true mystical theology' (ibid. p. 49). For A. von Harnack the corruption was a process of Hellenization; dogma was 'a work of the Greek spirit on the soil of the gospel' (ibid. pp. 63–4). J.L. von Mosheim (d. 1755) was a pioneer in the 'nonpartisan' study of dogma and heresy.

Later Protestant orthodoxy however, while belittling the authority of the early church, made the doctrinal tradition of the Reformation a norm for the interpretation of Scripture (Ebeling, [1964] 1968, p. 139). Other writers attached supreme importance to the *experience* of God: F.D.E. Schleiermacher to the feeling of 'God-consciousness', R. Bultmann to an existential decision; traditional dogma was of value only in so far as it gave rise to this experience. For all of these writers the history of dogma is an important study, but not as a *source* of revealed knowledge.

Modern biblical scholarship, both Roman Catholic and Protestant, has devoted much attention to the investigation of the primitive kerygma and oral traditions which preceded the formulation of the written Gospels. But it does not follow that for Protestant scholars tradition *continues* to be a source of revelation: according to O. Cullmann, 'by establishing the *principle* of a canon the Church recognized that *from that time* the tradition was no longer a criterion of truth' (1956, p. 90).

All recent Roman Catholic writing about tradition has to take account of the Council of Trent's reply to the *sola scriptura* in its first decree (1546), on 'the sacred books and apostolic traditions'. This decree affirmed that the gospel which Jesus Christ proclaimed and entrusted to the apostles is the 'source of the whole truth of salvation and rule of conduct', and that 'this truth and rule are contained in written books and in unwritten traditions.' Both the Scriptures and 'the traditions concerning both faith and conduct' are to be accepted 'with a like feeling of piety and reverence'. This affirmation was misrepresented by Catholics and Protestants alike as a 'two-source' theory. However, recent Catholic scholars (such as Geiselmann, [1962] 1966; Congar, [1960–3] 1966) have established that Trent expressly rejected a form of words which stated that the 'truth and rule' were contained '*partly* (*partim*) in written books, *partly* in unwritten traditions'; thus the Council chose not to affirm that some revealed truth is contained in tradition but not in Scripture (Congar, [1960–3] 1966, pp. 156–69, 206–7).

The First Vatican Council did little more than quote the Tridentine decree; the Second Vatican Council (Dogmatic Constitution on Divine Revelation, *Dei Verbum*) did the same, though without attempting to reconcile the passage with the affirmation that Scripture and tradition 'flowing from the same divine well-spring . . . merge into a unity' and 'form one sacred deposit of the word of God' (*Dei Verbum*, nn. 9–10). The Vatican II decree, however, introduced a further factor, the magisterium or teaching authority of the church, which 'by God's most wise design' is so closely linked with Scripture and tradition 'that one cannot stand without the others' (ibid. n. 10). In this the Council was reflecting the theories of many post-Tridentine theologians, such as R. Billuart, J.B. Franzelin and L. Billot, according to whom tradition, which is always a *source*, becomes a *rule* of doctrine only when it is endorsed by the authority of the church (Congar, [1960–3] 1966, pp. 182, 196–209). Protestant writers like O. Cullmann, however, believe this Catholic emphasis on the magisterium detracts from the importance of the apostolic tradition (1956, p. 84); some Catholic critics believe more weight should be given to the role of the theologian.

For Y. Congar tradition *is* a separate source of revelation, but one that is secondary to Scripture. All saving truth is contained at least implicitly in Scripture; unwritten tradition is nothing more than the true interpretation of Scripture within the life of the church. Under the guidance of the Holy Spirit the church provides in each age the true interpretation of Scripture, which is not necessarily what the human biblical author intended ([1960–3] 1966, pp. 304–5, 408–9). Among the many strands that go to make up this continuity of faith, the

liturgy plays an important part, according to the saying *lex orandi, lex credendi* or, in the original form of Prosper of Aquitaine's saying, *legem credendi lex statuat supplicandi* (see pp. 354–9, 427–35; Wainwright, 1980, pp. 218–50).

Development

Christians have generally agreed that there has been no new revelation since the apostolic age. St Paul's understanding of tradition seems to leave no room for development: 'stand firm and hold to the traditions which you were taught by us' (2 Thess. 2: 15; cf. 1 Cor. 11: 23; Col. 2: 8; 1 Tim: 6: 20). The Catholic charge against the gnostics was that they had no authority to add to the apostolic rule of faith. However Vincent of Lérins (see above) did believe that doctrines underwent a 'growth' analogous to that of the body, while retaining their 'integrity'. His 'canon' was intended as a test for distinguishing between genuine and false growth. Nevertheless it was not until the nineteenth century that the problem of development received much investigation.

It could of course be conceded that unchanging revelation could be better understood through advances in scholarship (J. Butler, d. 1752), or its logical implications better understood (F. Suarez, d. 1617). But in the first half of the nineteenth century the Catholic Tübingen school, especially J.M. Sailer and J.A. Möhler, saw the need for dogma to develop. Möhler believed, just as the history of a nation is the expression of its 'national spirit', so too the Holy Spirit calls into existence 'a society, which . . . should be the living exposition of the truth'. Diversity is a characteristic of the church, because the Word of God must be 'received by all the energies of the human mind' and 'ever progressively unfolded to our view' ([1832] 1894, pp. 266, 281, 290–2).

Newman referred to Möhler's theory in the *Essay on Development*, but seems to have arrived at his own theory of development independently in answer to the argument he had himself used as an Anglican, that while Rome seemed to have a greater claim to catholicity, the innovations Rome had made in doctrine and discipline gave Canterbury a clearer title to apostolicity. Brought up in the belief that 'growth [is] the only evidence of life' ([1864] 1967, p. 19), he held that 'here below to live is to change, and to be perfect is to have changed often' ([1848] 1878, p. 40). In his first book, *The Arians of the Fourth Century*, Newman had spoken of verbal definitions of doctrine as 'imperfect' representations 'in a foreign medium' of the 'unseen' 'object of religious veneration', 'practical devotion' and 'moral feelings' ([1833] 1897, pp. 158–60). In his *Essay on Development* he took this theory further, speaking of 'ideas' which 'no one term or proposition . . . will serve to define', but which have 'life' and 'grow' when they incorporate other ideas, as people grow morally in the power to understand them ([1848] 1878, pp. 35–9). But not all changes represent authentic growth; Newman therefore proposed a number of tests (such as lasting vigour and power of assimilation) for distinguishing between true growth and false growth or corruption. In addition God has provided the church with an infallible authority for distinguishing true from false developments. Newman later brought into consideration another factor, namely the *consensus fidelium*, the witness of the faithful to the apostolic tradition ([1859] 1961).

Newman's theory was criticized both inside the Roman Catholic church (for example by O. Brownson) and outside that church (for example by J.B. Mozley) for his failure to explain clearly the nature of the seminal 'idea' from which doctrines develop. Sometimes Newman appeals to 'feeling' in terms reminiscent of Schleiermacher. Such expressions have been taken as an anticipation of MODERNISM; G. Tyrrell, for example, regarded interior experience as the basis of revelation, and traditional doctrines as symbols of such feeling. For Newman, however, the revealed 'idea', while it cannot be reduced to propositions, can be given conceptual expression, however inadequate, in propositional form.

In the Roman Catholic church of the twentieth century M. Blondel worked out, in opposition to modernism, a theory of tradition which resembles that of Newman. Tradition is the process by which the church, beginning with the 'initial gift, not entirely formulated or even clearly understood so far', passes from the 'lived implicit' (*l'implicite vécu*) to the 'known explicit' (*l'explicite connu*). It is 'a life which includes . . . feelings, thoughts, beliefs, hopes and actions' (quoted in Congar, [1960–3] 1966,

pp. 360, 363–4). Blondel was, however, as reluctant as Newman to define the 'initial gift', being more concerned with the process of development. Congar did seek to define the ultimate content of tradition; for him it is not particular truths but the 'Christian mystery', 'the covenant relation accomplished in Jesus Christ' (ibid. pp. 389–90).

Liberal Protestants since D.F. Strauss have often formulated one aspect of the problem of a developing tradition as that of the relationship between the Jesus of history and the Christ of faith (see HISTORICAL JESUS, QUEST OF). For K. Barth, on the other hand, as for Congar, the Word of God speaks to the church through Scripture in every age. But Barth in his *Church Dogmatics* saw tradition as the record of the way the Word of God was heard in earlier ages, to be treated with 'love and respect', but not as a source or criterion of truth over or beside Scripture. Revelation, and even the authority of Scripture itself, is not a permanent reality but an event depending at each moment on God's freedom. M. Wiles (1967, p. 172) suggests that the principle linking developing dogmas is a 'continuity of fundamental aims'.

The relation between Scripture and tradition, and the development of doctrine, have been the subject of several recent ecumenical documents. Notable among these are the reports of the Faith and Order Commission of the World Council of Churches:'Tradition and Traditions', (F. and O. Paper 42, 1965), the Anglican–Orthodox Dialogue (Moscow Statement 1976), the USA Lutheran–Catholic Dialogue (*Teaching Authority and Infallibility in the Church*, 1978), the Anglican–Roman Catholic International Commission (ARCIC I, *The Final Report*, 1982; ARCIC II, *Church as Communion*, 1991). This last statement grounds tradition in the gift to the church of the Holy Spirit, who 'reminds' the church of Christ's teaching (see John 14: 26) and guides it in the 'unfolding' of revelation.

See also AUTHORITY; DOCTRINE AND DOGMA; REVELATION, CONCEPT OF.

Bibliography
Campenhausen, H. von [1960] 1968: *Tradition and Life in the Church*, trans. A.V. Littledale. London: Collins.
Chadwick, O. [1957] 1987: *From Bossuet to Newman*. Cambridge: Cambridge University Press.

Congar, Y. M.-J. [1960–3] 1966: *Tradition and Traditions*, trans. M. Naseby and T. Rainborough. London: Burns and Oates.

Cullmann, O. 1956: *The Early Church*, trans. A.J.B. Higgins. London: SCM Press, pp. 55–99, 'The Tradition'.

Ebeling, G. [1964] 1968: *The Word of God and Tradition: Historical Studies Interpreting the Divisions of Christianity*, trans. S.H. Hooke. London: Collins.

Geiselmann, J.R. [1962] 1966: *The Meaning of Tradition*, trans. W.J. O'Hara, Qu. Disp. 15. Freiburg: Herder; London: Burns and Oates.

Möhler, J.A. [1832] 1894: *Symbolism or Exposition of the Doctrinal Differences between Catholics and Protestants as Evidenced by their Symbolical Writings*, trans. J.B. Robertson. London: Gibbings.

Newman, J.H. [1833] 1897: *The Arians of the Fourth Century*. London: Longmans Green.

Newman, J.H. [1848] 1878: *An Essay on the Development of Christian Doctrine*. London: Rivingtons.

Newman, J.H. [1859] 1961: *On Consulting the Faithful in Matters of Doctrine*. London: G. Chapman.

Newman, J.H. [1864] 1967: *Apologia pro vita sua*. Oxford: Oxford University Press.

Nichols, A. 1990: *From Newman to Congar: The Idea of Doctrinal Development from the Victorians to the Second Vatican Council*. Edinburgh: T and T Clark.

Pelikan, J. 1971: *Historical Theology: Continuity and Change in Christian Doctrine*. Theological Resources. New York: Corpus; London: Hutchinson.

Wainwright, G. 1980: *Doxology: A Systematic Theology*. London: Epworth Press.

Wiles, M. 1967: *The Making of Christian Doctrine*. Cambridge: Cambridge University Press.

EDWARD J. YARNOLD

Trinity, doctrine of See GOD.

Troeltsch, Ernst (1865–1923) German theologian and sociologist. After initial periods at the universities of Göttingen and Bonn, Troeltsch settled at Heidelberg for the formative period of his scholarly career, 1895–1915. Strongly influenced by the HISTORY OF RELIGIONS SCHOOL, Troeltsch made major contributions to a number of areas of theology centring upon the relation of Christianity to culture. At the sociological level, he was deeply indebted to the ideas of Max Weber (1864–1920), whose ideas he did much to publicize. His *Absoluteness of Christianity* of 1902 explored the cultural conditioning of religious beliefs, and the impact of this upon Christianity's claims to absolute truth. His *Social Teaching of the Christian Churches* of 1912 dealt with the relation between the cultural situation of the churches and their social ethics. And, in a series of seminal essays in the closing years of the nineteenth century, he examined the impact of historicist ways of thinking on Christian theology, particularly in relation to Christology (see FAITH AND HISTORY).

See also RELATIVISM, CULTURAL.

Bibliography

Clayton, J.P., ed. 1976: *Ernst Troeltsch and the Future of Theology*. Cambridge.

Coakley, S. 1988: *Christ without Absolutes: A Study of the Christology of Ernst Troeltsch*. Oxford.

truth, concepts of The commonsense understanding of truth, traceable as far back as Aristotle, takes it to mean the agreement or correspondence between a proposition and an existing state of affairs, as when someone says, 'It is raining in Glasgow today', and observation or enquiry shows that this is indeed the case. But there are a great many instances where we claim to be speaking the truth that are not simple propositions of this kind and that demand different criteria for judging their truth or falsity. It was a theologian, R.C. Moberly, who wrote: 'Truth is manifold and multiform. There are truths of material fact; truths of abstract statement; truths of historical occurrence; truths of moral experience; truths of spiritual experience; and that truth is deepest and truest, which most includes and unifies them all' (in *Atonement and Personality* of 1901). Not only theologians but the practitioners of many other disciplines would call for the recognition of a plurality of forms of truth. But perhaps few of them would be willing to accept Moberly's final point that there is a truth which can be described as 'deepest and truest' and which 'includes and unifies' all the other truths. Admittedly, the fact that we use the word 'truth' in all these different contexts would suggest that there is something in common to all the different forms of truth. There would seem to be at least a 'family resemblance', in Ludwig

Wittgenstein's phrase. At any rate, it will not be sufficient simply to say that the different disciplines have each a particular concept of truth. Each would have to say why it feels entitled to claim truth, and one would want to ask the theologian whether he has criteria for truth comparable in clarity to those recognized in other disciplines. It must be acknowledged that theologians sometimes appear to evade the question of truth. Doctrines are commended because they unify the believing community rather than because they are claimed to be true. Sometimes recourse is made to the fact that the Hebrew word for 'true' expresses an attitude of trust which is contrasted with the intellectual connotations of the corresponding Greek word. Admittedly, religious belief is something more than intellectual assent to a proposition, but it cannot be separated from the problem of intellectual truth. To believe *in* God has overtones of a personal trust which takes one beyond the bare belief *that* there is a God, but it makes no sense to believe *in* God without believing *that* there is a God, that is, the act of faith in God entails a truth-claim for the proposition that there is a God.

A few examples may now be given to show the variety of truth-claims that will be met in theological writings. Some concern matters of historical fact, and these will be tested in the same way as any other historical assertions. An obvious illustration is the assertion that Jesus was crucified during the time when Pontius Pilate was procurator of Judaea. This is a central event for Christianity, and has been incorporated into both the Apostles' and the Nicene creed. Its truth as a fact of history is very well attested from ancient written testimonies, some dated to about twenty years after the event. But theology is never just the claim that such and such events happened in the past. The events are recalled because they are supposed to have significance for the spiritual life of human beings even today. Concerning the crucifixion of Jesus, Paul says that 'Christ died for our sins' (1 Cor. 15: 3). Certainly this implies the historical statement that Christ died, but it goes much further than asserting the historical fact. Could we say perhaps that here the criterion of truth is to be found in the Christian experience of salvation? Paul and the early Christians and then subsequent generations of

Christians have found in the cross a significance that has given them an experience of forgiveness and renewal which some of them at least have sought to elaborate in various theologies of atonement. The theologies are sometimes far from clear, but those who construct them cannot doubt their own experience of salvation, and since this has arisen from their encounter with the cross of Christ, they are prepared to claim that Christ died for their sins and to claim further that they have convincing evidence of this in their experience. Admittedly, we are dealing here with a case that is more subjective than the relatively straightforward case of the historical proposition that Christ was crucified under Pontius Pilate. But to those who have experienced the cross in a religious sense, the one type of truth-claim is no less convincing than the other. We shall have to take up this question of subjectivism again in a moment. But here we may note that although theological language, as in theories of atonement, may be indirect, analogical or metaphorical, as compared with the literal language in which we speak of matters of objective fact, this theological language makes its own truth-claims and ways can be devised for testing them (see LANGUAGE, RELIGIOUS).

From the theological point of view, even what we call 'mythology' may be a vehicle of truth. For many centuries, the stories of creation and the fall, contained in the first three chapters of Genesis, were regarded by many people as literally true, that is to say, accounts of observable happenings which we could have perceived if we had been there. Few people would still think of the stories in such a way. We call them 'myth', and though this is a term hard to define, we may think of it as covering those stories in which archaic peoples tried to express how they understood their own identity and their relation to the world and to such powers as might govern the world. Unfortunately, the word 'myth' has been devalued in modern usage, and is often understood to mean simply a story with no foundations and no claims to truth. But if we take the idea of myth seriously as standing for a form of discourse which speaks of issues of the highest importance for human life, we see that myths can be true or false. The early myths of Genesis teach several essential truths about the human being:

1 a human being is creaturely and finite, dependent on a reality beyond his or her own;
2 a human being has vast potentialities, because made in the image and likeness of God;
3 human beings are essentially social rather than individual entities, for it was the human couple, male and female together, that was made in the image and likeness of God;
4 we read too, in the story of the fall, that the human being is flawed, has fallen short of its potentiality and is in a state of sin.

These characteristics add up to the essential self-understanding of the everyday man or woman. It is a true understanding of the human being that is conveyed in the mythology if we recognize ourselves in the picture it presents, if reflection on ourselves leads to the same conclusions that we find in the biblical description of the human condition. There is a further point in the Genesis mythology, though perhaps it is not so much a description as a value-judgement. The material world is, so we are told, created by God and even enters into the being of the human race as made out of the dust of the ground. The material world is therefore said to be good. In this respect, biblical religion differs sharply from some eastern religions, in which it is held that matter is inherently evil and not created by God.

In most disciplines, truth is taken to belong to propositions, to assertions made in words. In Christian theology, it is recognized that there is a truth more ultimate than the truths which we express in words. Perhaps that is what Moberly had in mind when he said, 'That truth is deepest and truest, which most includes and unifies [all other truths].' What could this truth be? Could it be the truth of God, which Christians believe is manifested in the truth of Christ, the Word or Logos of God? According to John's Gospel, Jesus Christ claimed, 'I am the way, the truth and the life' (John 14: 6). But what does it mean to say that a person is the truth, rather than a proposition or a doctrine? Some theologians would reply that the basic truth of Christianity is the living, personal truth of Christ, and that the propositions of creeds and theological systems are true only to the extent that they are 'true to' the reality of

Christ, pointing us to it and illuminating it for us. But theologians differ among themselves in the matter of the importance of doctrines compared with the importance of the personal truth of Christ. In patristic times and again in nineteenth-century Catholicism, great importance was attached to the actual verbal formulae. In the twentieth century, first among Protestants and then among Catholics also, there has been a swing away from propositional theology to the originative revelatory event which is the source of Christian truth. To see more clearly what it means to refer truth to a person, we may consider some teaching of Søren Kierkegaard and Martin Heidegger.

Kierkegaard asks, 'What is truth, and in what sense was Christ the truth?' He answers, 'Christ is the truth in such a sense that to be the truth is the only true explanation of what truth is.' Truth 'is not the duplication of being in terms of thought . . . the truth consists not in knowing the truth but in being the truth' (Kierkegaard [1846] 1945, p. 159). Or we might say 'in doing the truth' or 'walking in the truth', both of which are also Johannine expressions. The truth in this sense is inseparable from the way that leads to it and from the life in which it is manifested. Kierkegaard distinguishes between the kind of truth that can be written on a piece of paper and instantly appropriated by anyone who reads it, and the personal truth of Christ which must be inwardly and passionately appropriated. He calls this second kind 'subjective truth', but this does not mean that we can please ourselves about what we take to be true; it means that there are truths which can be understood only by an inward wrestling, truths that are inseparable from the way that leads to them and the life which they form. Perhaps they would be better termed 'existential' rather than 'subjective'.

A somewhat similar understanding of truth is found in Heidegger. He too sees the locus of some truths in existence rather than in propositions. He is never tired of reminding us that in Greek truth is *aletheia*, literally 'unconcealment'. Truth is essentially an *event* which takes place when concealments and distortions are removed and something is exposed as it really is. Heidegger avoids Kierkegaard's word 'subjective', but he agrees that truth is always *for* a person who can be 'in the truth' and appropriate the truth. The self-consciousness of the human being is the locus in the universe (so far as we know) where the opacity of things can come to light. The human being is like a clearing in a forest. In this being occurs overtness, the possibility of standing in the light of truth, though also the possibility of being in untruth when concealment and distortion have taken over.

Do these reflections on truth help us to see more clearly what is meant by the claim that Christ is the truth? What is it that he brings into the light of unconcealment? Could we say that it is the true humanity, and that it is our own conscience, our deepest self-awareness, that attests what we see in Jesus Christ as the truth of our own humanity? But then Christian theology leads us to another step. If the human being is made in the image and likeness of God, and if that image is brought to light in Jesus Christ, then in him we see God, the ultimate creative reality, and we see him in terms of love. In Paul's words, Christ 'is the image of the invisible God' (Col. 1: 15).

So the search for the meaning of truth brings us into Christology. This was clearly recognized by Dietrich Bonhoeffer, who pointed out that if Christ is indeed the Logos, as Christianity has claimed, then Christology is logology. No doubt this is a stupendous claim but it does seem to be the claim that Christian theology must make for Jesus Christ. He is himself the living primary truth that comes before all doctrines and theological propositions.

But this does not make theology superfluous. If the primary truth is to be explored, communicated and appropriated, this can only happen through language. Admittedly, the full reality of Christ (or of personal existence generally) can never be fully transcribed into words. Yet there is a duty to use language towards a fuller understanding of the truth of Christ. The language will never be quite adequate, but it is successful to the extent that it brings us nearer to 'that truth which is deepest and truest', to use again Moberly's phrase.

See also EPISTEMOLOGY, RELIGIOUS; NARRATIVE THEOLOGY; POSTLIBERALISM.

Bibliography

Bradley, F.H. 1914: *Essays on Truth and Reality*. Oxford: Oxford University Press.

Gadamer, Hans-Georg [1960] 1975: *Truth and Method*, trans. London: Sheed and Ward.

Kierkegaard, Søren [1846] 1945: *Concluding Unscientific Postscript*, trans. Oxford: Oxford University Press.

JOHN MACQUARRIE

U/V

Voltaire, pseudonym of François Marie Arouet (1694 1778) French author and philosopher. Born in Paris, Voltaire abandoned a career in law to write. Much of his literary output was considered scandalous, and he spent time in the Bastille. He was exiled to England in 1726, where he became familiar with British philosophy, in particular that of John Locke and Isaac Newton. On his return to France, his *Lettres philosophiques* were burnt in the streets of Paris. In his later writings, he attacked both religious bigotry and atheism. He is frequently regarded as the embodiment of the eighteenth-century Enlightenment in France. His works – seventy volumes in total – include *Oedipe* (1717), a rewriting of the tragedy of Oedipus, *Lettres philosophiques* (1734) and *Candide* (1759).

Voltaire's writing popularized the work of English philosophers such as Newton and Locke in France – indeed, it was his implied criticism of France which led to his unpopularity. He advocated tolerance and freedom of speech, except for Roman Catholics, who he despised, and atheists, who he considered to threaten the order of society. He was himself sceptical of many aspects of religion – *Candide*, for instance, being a satire on G.W. Leibniz's belief that all is for the best in the best of all possible worlds. He contributed articles to Denis Diderot's famous *Encyclopaedia* on various topics including liberty and the soul.

While Voltaire's writing certainly contributed to the atmosphere which led to the French Revolution, he himself would not have expected or incited revolt against the monarchy.

Bibliography
Noyes, A. 1936: *Voltaire* London.
Rowe, C. 1955: *Voltaire and the State*. New York.
Topazio, V.W. 1967: *Voltaire, a Critical Study of his Major Works*.
Voltaire, 1968: *The Complete Works*, ed. T. Bestermann. Geneva.

W

war and peace The tradition common to theologians and lawyers in the sixteenth and early seventeenth centuries, now called the JUST WAR tradition, was based on the idea that the resort to war and its methods of prosecution could be conceived, despite the lack of formal jurisdiction, as an extension of the ordinary acts of coercive judgement performed by governments. This theory was supported by a strong doctrine of NATURAL LAW, on the one hand, and of positive international law, on the other, which was held to have developed out of natural law by traditional practice and was legally as well as morally binding. In the course of the seventeenth century a new line of thought – the self-styled 'modern moral science' – overtook this scholastic tradition, and by 1700 it was in eclipse.

The basic change was in the concept of natural law, formerly understood as the reflection of divine law within the human mind. Reconstructed now from below, it was given a new derivation in the interest of individuals in self-preservation; political association was interpreted correspondingly as a conventional construction to protect these 'natural rights'. The effect was to draw a sharp line between civil society and the 'state of nature' which lay before it and beyond it. This undermined the belief that international relations, lying outside the sphere of civil order, were mapped out by unwritten principles of law comparable to the statute-law which held sway within it. With this belief collapsed the conception of war as a judicial act. Questions about war were now subordinated to these new concerns with the constitution of states and their rights in relation to one another. Together with this shift in philosophical direction occurred the disappear-

ance of direct theological involvement in international theory. Although many of the political and legal philosophers who carried thinking forward in the later seventeenth and eighteenth centuries were Christians, and argued explicitly as such, it was not until the twentieth century that those whose intellectual concerns lay primarily with theology claimed a major interest in these debates again.

The eighteenth-century discussion can be divided into two phases, naturalist and constitutionalist, which differed in their understanding of the state of nature which was supposed to obtain between independent civil societies. The first phase, represented by John Locke, Christian Wolff and Emmerich de Vattel, conceived it as essentially a peaceful condition, governed by the natural rights of civil communities which imposed the obligation to mutual cooperativeness and the right to peaceful enjoyment of liberty. War, on these terms, was justified on broadly self-defensive grounds, as the nation's pursuit of its own right. Its scope was limited; there was no title of government deriving from conquest, since political theory attributed to each civil society a moral personality which could not be dissolved except by the free act of the citizens who constituted it. There was some difference of emphasis on how this applied to war against uncivilized peoples.

The second phase, arising from more sceptical philosophical sources and finding fullest expression in the political thought of Immanuel Kant, conceived the state of nature as a state of war, and as such outside any principles of justice. Since our moral nature abhors such a vacuum of principle, our primary duty in international affairs is to construct legal and constitutional bonds between peoples – by voluntary federation, if possible, though forcibly imposed relations (but not conquest or enslavement) were also valid. The pursuit of 'perpetual peace' depended on constitutional construction. If the concept of international law had tended to recede in the first phase to a concept of negative rights and obligations, its importance was reasserted in the second phase, but on a purely constitutional basis. Kant thought that the right to make war in self-defence was almost indefinitely permissive, and so morally insignificant. Neither natural law nor the traditional law of nations could impose moral restraints upon the resort to war apart from formal conventions. Nor did Kant recognize moral limits to the means of conducting war, apart from those imposed by the moral personality of the agent and the goal of federal relations. Spying was wrong because it demeaned the spy, and made future trust between nations more difficult.

The discussion was transformed in the nineteenth century by a combination of new philosophical questions and military developments. The philosophical interest in history encouraged the view that there was a hidden purpose in events, a cunning of providence, whereby even war could be seen to serve the goal of perpetual peace. The military developments were the turn towards what Karl von Clausewitz called 'absolute war' – the mobilization of whole nations to wage war with the utmost ferocity. This, too, was widely accepted as a providential device: it made wars more costly and more solemn; it discouraged trivial and frequent resort to war; it was 'the preparation for a state of international law, the means . . . to make the need for it more keenly felt' (F.D.E. Schleiermacher). Hand in hand with the logistical totalization of war went its ideologization. *Raison d'état* was replaced by war for great causes: the divine purpose for the development of civilization, or the sanctity of the moral personality of a nation. A sense that war might be necessitated by religious conviction – absent in practice since the mid-seventeenth century and in theory for longer than that – began to be evidenced again, most notably in justifications of the American civil war, as in the famous 'Battle Hymn of the Republic' by J.W. Howe. The reaction to these high claims was a revived pacifism which took its stand explicitly on the character of primitive Christianity and the ethical teaching of Jesus. Tolstoy's writings of the 1880s and 1890s were especially influential in promoting a portrait of Jesus as an opponent of all forcible resistance, not only between states but within civil government itself.

The beginning of the twentieth century saw an attempt to formalize the legacy of the just war and natural rights theories in a series of international treaties, the Hague Conventions of 1907. This implied a renewed interest in the principles of conducting war justly (*ius in bello*), and especially in the principle of noncombatant immunity. This emphasis was, however, immediately threatened by technical advances: the development of the military aeroplane gave birth to the idea of 'strategic air war' against centres of population, which, it was hoped, would end any war almost as soon as it was begun. The positive assessment which the nineteenth-century strategists had made of absolute war lay behind this aspiration, which achieved its fullest expression, later in the twentieth century, in the conception of stable deterrence by mutually assured destruction. Not until after the Second World War did the initiative in international law gain pace again with the Geneva Conventions of 1949 and Protocols of 1977, the latter concerned especially with updating *ius in bello* principles for the missile age. While formally avoiding locking horns with strategic doctrine on the subject of nuclear weapons, the tendency of legal developments was to tighten the requirements for protection of noncombatants and to demand increased precision and caution in aerial and missile attack.

Theologians, meanwhile, affected by a strong reaction from historicist idealism in the wake of the First World War, found themselves divided between a Tolstoyan pacifism (which found an echo in the Lambeth Conference of 1930) and a 'realism' typified by the American Protestant Reinhold Niebuhr. Basing itself on a reading of Augustine which gave a central emphasis to the idea of original sin, this realism urged the inevitability of conflict arising from self-interest in social groups and states, while unmasking the pretensions both of religious and ideological justifications for it and of otherworldly pacifist programmes for avoiding it. The experience of strategic bombing campaigns in the Second World War then turned theologians' attention to the *ius in bello* question of noncombatant immunity, and encouraged a rediscovery of the just war tradition, led by Roman Catholic thinkers (notably J.C. Ford), who were followed, as the cold war nuclear confrontation deepened, by Protestants in search of a non-pacifist critique of the strategy of counter-population warfare, among whom P. Ramsey was the most prominent. This just war revival made a significant impression on the Second Vatican Council's document on 'The Church in the Modern World' of 1965.

The foundation of the United Nations Organization in 1948 gave an important focus to some traditional theological reservations about the nation-state system, and encouraged the hope for a world peace held in place by a single international authority. This was reflected especially in the increasingly restrictive interpretations advanced by the popes of traditional just war permissions, apparently confining the right to resort to force to national self-defence in situations of immediate danger. The protection this appeared to afford to entrenched regimes of oppression was a contributory irritant to provoke the reaction of LIBERATION THEOLOGY, which, though not usually explicit about its doctrine of justified force, inclined to sympathize with movements of popular resistance.

Each phase in the modern period, then, has had its own way of organizing the questions of war and peace; but there have been some recurrent discussions, of which we may identify a few leading ones.

One concern, emerging for the first time in the modern period in Kant but with deep roots in traditional eschatology, has been to connect decisions made in an imperfect, strife-torn world with the future hope of God's kingdom. 'Philosophy too', urged Kant, 'may have its chiliastic expectations.' Among them is perpetual peace, an idea which cannot be realized, yet entitles us, he argued, to act *as though* it were a reality. Against the idealist 'as though' was pitted the realist 'not yet' – the element of political realism which has best claim to ancestry in a dictum of Augustine: 'we ought not before the appointed time to desire to live with those alone who are holy and righteous.' Reinhold

Niebuhr's concession that the idealist and realist strands, 'illusion' and 'reason', must coexist in civilization if progress is to be made, offers a generous interpretation of history, but apparently no way forward with the deliberative question: Shall we, then, cling to our illusions? It is difficult to maintain a course of action as ethically required that appears to embrace unreality; it is equally difficult to recommend a course of action as Christian that appears to ignore the reign of God. A strategy for justifying war, or refusing to justify it, had better claim its posture as the only appropriate response to the realities that exist – not excluding the divine purposes.

It makes a difference if we think we can discern God's purposes not only 'behind' the present realities, controlling and mastering them, but 'within' them, shaping them transparently towards the realization of eschatological peace. In that case certain postures with regard to war appear to 'go with' or 'run counter to' the grain of history. Kant represented the inherent purposes of history as impersonal ones – 'Nature' working out her plan in despite of human intentions. For a theologian such as P.T. Forsyth, writing at the end of the idealist period in 1916, God would only work through human will and moral judgement and through the transforming presence of the church within the world. In both these accounts war plays a positive part in the historical process – if it did not, the claim to discern purposes *within* history would be empty – and both accounts conclude that international institutions are a goal to which the nations should be striving. But the conscientious thinker in Kant's account can simply step aside from the necessity of war and observe it; while Forsyth's Christian believer has to identify himself with the working of God's judgement and become 'the whip in Christ's hand'. Both ways of reading the purpose of history were, of course, to prove controversial. In the mid-twentieth century 'historicism' was often decried as the seedbed of fanatic ideology. After the First World War theologians experienced a dramatic loss of certainty about the progress of civilization. The revival of just war doctrine was due in part to its appeal to a conception of secular justice which begged no questions about God's designs in world history.

At the same time, however, as thinkers were growing sceptical of the historical necessity that was to produce them, international institutions became a reality – not for the first time, but for the first time in the modern period – and were no longer a gleam in an idealist philsopher's eye. Their character had to be the subject of some reflection. On the one hand, there was a long tradition of sympathy for the idea of a unified political realm which would reflect on earth the universal rule of God; on the other, the biblical critique of empire would not permit theologians to deny the importance of national pluralism within the concept of world order. The success of the idea of international law was due to its encompassing both poles, unitary and pluralist, in its imagination of a legal order to which sovereigns could be bound without loss of their autonomy.

If, now, to this legal order there is added an actual jurisdiction, can the balance be maintained? Or will centripetal pressures open the way to imperial dominion? J. Maritain was especially prominent in arguing, in the years after the Second World War, that true pluralism was consistent with unitary world government. Yet anxieties remained, and were focused on the United Nations Organization. Conflicting aspirations were cherished for this body and reflected in its Charter. Some of its supporters hoped to see it claim a monopoly of armed force to punish and remedy infractions of international justice. Others hoped to see it prove the superior authority of reasoned discourse over force. When its jurisdiction has been exercised in a purely declarative manner, it has been criticized for impotence; when it has been sanctioned by force, as most notably in the Gulf War of 1991, it has been criticized as a tool of imperial ambition. What the experiment makes clear is that the existence of an international jurisdiction is not, in fact, the same thing as perpetual peace. It is not the sovereign nation-state alone that occasions war, but the fact that human beings live and act in communities, however structured. The question of how, and whether, force may justly be deployed to restrain unjust force still arises. The benefit is simply that the use of reactive force is subject to the disciplines of worldwide deliberation and international law.

Finally, there is a cluster of questions about the relation of political morality to the broader moral principles that surround and underpin it. Of these we can isolate three.

First, JUSTICE may be harsh, and that before we broach the question of killing. How is it accommodated in an ethic where all commands are summed up in the twin command of love to God and neighbour? Not everyone agrees that it is accommodated. Some Christian voices have urged 'willingness to sacrifice, in the interests of non-resistant love, all other forms of human solidarity' (J.H. Yoder). Others, especially of Lutheran provenance, have argued that the state, as an order of creation, is not required to express love. More commonly, however, theologians have justified the claims of justice as derived from love, perhaps by some such formula as P. Ramsey's 'justice is love distributed', that is, responding to the rival claims of two or more competing neighbours. Yet not every application of justice is equally an expression of love. It has been a commonplace of western thought that justice is a formal notion to be filled with variable content. Some acts of justice are more generous than others. The tendency of Christian thought in the modern period has been to press notions of justice outwards, to accommodate a wider observation of realities that bear upon a given case, aspiring to, but not replicating, the perfect harmony of justice and mercy in the atonement. Hence the need to complement the idea of 'distributed love' with one expressed in another Ramseyan formula: 'love-transformed justice'.

Second, is killing a moral evil which we are bound at all costs to avoid? The distinction between a moral and a non-moral evil can be rendered in terms of what is evil *as action* and what is evil *as suffering*. Not every action that involves the suffering of evil is an evil action. The non-pacifist tradition has represented the justified belligerent as suffering the evil of necessity, but not as doing evil. The alternative view finds evil in the action itself, as 'the manifestation of our hatred of God' (S. Hauerwas). The curious hybrid notions of 'sin within the realm of necessity' (J. Ellul) and 'responsible assumption of guilt' (H. Thielicke) capture dramatically the subjective moral tension which belongs to a decision of such gravity, but they leave the deliberative question in paradox and so seem to have more rhetorical than conceptual persuasiveness.

The idea that killing in war is evil, but not evil action, is sometimes supported by appeal to the 'principle of double effect': killing in war, it is said, intends directly only the disablement of the aggressor, not his death. This is open to the rebuttal that the disablement envisaged by conventional military attack requires that soldiers should be killed for the force to be disabled; their deaths are not incidental to the pursuit of the goal. It is better to grasp the nettle, and to say: if acts of war are sometimes justified, some acts of intentional killing are justified. The question then is, which?

Here we see the potential importance of a judicial conception of war, distinguishing it from acts of self-defence, apparently disallowed in Jesus' teaching, to which the natural rights tradition tended to reduce it. From this concept there follows the need for a distinction equivalent to that between the guilty and the innocent: the relevant distinction in the conduct of war is traditionally understood to be that between combatant and noncombatant. Another, more persuasive, appeal to double effect is commonly made within the just war tradition to excuse the killing of noncombatants where it is genuinely unintended, that is, extrinsic to the practical logic of the attack. Thus aerial bombardment of civilian populations is regarded as a sin and a crime, but distinguished from bombardment of military installations in which civilian lives are incidentally put at risk.

Third, perhaps the most effective arguments deployed for Christian pacifism have been those appealing to the conduct and teaching of Jesus and to the practice of the ante-Nicene church. Much purely historical debate has surrounded the latter, and the picture remains confused, not only by the variety of early Christian practice but by the unclarity of the moral stance behind ecclesiastical disapproval of military service. The pacifist portrait of Jesus himself has fallen out of scholarly favour, to the extent that Jesus has sometimes (for instance by S.G.F. Brandon) been represented as a revolutionary, though this reaction has been generally thought too extreme.

Most Christian thinkers have been ready to agree that the church must represent the uncoercive harmony of God's reign, must demonstrate the willingness to suffer rather than retaliate, and must be free to minister to both sides in any conflict, fostering reconciliation wherever possible. The question is, to what extent this demands detachment from the coercive tasks of government. Here the question of war merges with other questions: imprisonment, acts of force to defend civil order, monetary fines and other punishments, even certain forms of economic control, are also put in doubt. For the Christian individual the question means: can he or she participate in any or all of these tasks? For the church as a whole it means: can it recognize equally the validity of either decision on the individual's part, to the extent of offering pastoral support and counsel for the pursuit of either, thereby treating the matter as one of individual vocation? Or must it encourage one decision in preference to the other, treating those who disagree at best as weaker consciences? (This in general terms; particular circumstances may prompt a non-pacifist church to discourage participation for special reasons, for instance in a war perceived as aggressive or unjust.)

Whether pacifists can accept a purely vocational account of their profession has divided opinion in the traditional peace churches. It secures a place for their witness, certainly, but abandons the attempt to recruit the church for the moral abhorrence of each and every act of war. Support of peace, like the justification of war, is a movement of various philosophical convictions and diverse opinions. It is sometimes surprising how much convergence there may be between the one movement and the other.

See also ETHICS; SOCIAL QUESTIONS.

Bibliography

Ellul, J. 1969: *Violence*, trans. C.G. Kings. New York: Seabury.

Forsyth, P.T. 1917: *The Christian Ethic of War*. London: Longmans Green.

Hornus, J.-M. 1960: *Evangile et Labarum*. Geneva: Labor et Fides.

John XXIII 1963: *Encyclical: Pacem in Terris*.

Johnson, J.T. 1981: *Just War Tradition and the Restraint of War*. Princeton: Princeton University Press.

Kant, I. 1970: Idea for a universal history with a cosmopolitan purpose (1784), Perpetual peace (1795) and The metaphysical elements of right

(1797). In *Political Writings*, ed. H. Reiss, trans. H.B. Nisbet. Cambridge: Cambridge University Press.

Niebuhr, R. 1932: *Moral Man and Immoral Society*. New York: Scribners.

Ramsey, P. 1961: *War and the Christian Conscience*. Durham, NC: Duke University Press.

Roberts, A., and Guelff, R., eds 1989: *Documents on the Laws of War*, 2nd edn. Oxford: Oxford University Press.

Tolstoy, L. [1893] 1894: *The Kingdom of God is Within You*, trans. C. Garnett. New York and London: Cassell.

OLIVER O'DONOVAN

Warfield, Benjamin Breckinridge (1851–1921) North American Presbyterian theologian. A professor of theology at Princeton Theological Seminary, New Jersey, he was, like his predecessor Charles Hodge, a scholar of Calvinism and a conservative defender of Reformed theology against growing American liberalism. His views on the divine inspiration and inerrancy of Scripture are set out in the essay 'Inspiration' (1881) which he wrote with A.A. Hodge; Scripture was, he held, self-authenticating, and its truthfulness had been demonstrated throughout church history. Historical study of the Bible should approach the text as inspired, and not of purely human origin. Though not widely accepted, his views continue to influence some forms of evangelicalism to this day. He opposed the subjectivism of much contemporary revivalism and of romantic liberalism, which, he held, overestimated the nature of man and underestimated the objective work of God in history. His many writings include articles, reviews, pamphlets and hymns, and are brought together in the ten-volume *The Works of Benjamin B. Warfield* (1927–32, reprinted 1981).

Bibliography

Gerstner, J.H. 1974: Warfield's case for biblical inerrancy. In *God's Inerrant Word*, ed. J. Warwick Montgomery. Minneapolis, Mn.

Meeter, J.E., and Nicole, R. 1974: *A Bibliography of Benjamin Breckinridge Warfield 1851–1921*. Nutley, NJ.

Wells, D.F., ed. 1985: *Reformed Theology in America*, article on Warfield by W.A. Hoffecker. Grand Rapids, Mi.

Weber, Max (1864–1920) German sociologist. A professor at Freiburg (1894–6), Heidelberg (1896–7) and Munich (1918–20), he is, with Emile Durkheim, the founder of modern sociology. His analysis of the modern social structures of economy and law, his comparative studies of cultures and his development of a methodology of sociology were complemented by his interest in the psychological and spiritual needs and aspirations of humanity. His best-known work on religion and society, *The Protestant Ethic and the Spirit of Capitalism* (1904–5, trans. 1930), traces the role of Protestant doctrine – particularly predestination and sanctification – in the development of modern capitalist societies. A believer in human self-determination, he rejected what he saw as the determinism both of Protestant dogma and of Marxist economic and social theory. In *The Sociology of Religion* of 1922 he extended the range of his investigation to ancient Judaism and eastern religions, examining the impact of different religious systems on political and social structures. The book's ground-breaking work to establish sociological categories of religious leaders and their followers was developed by his friend and colleague Ernst Troeltsch.

Bibliography

Bendix, R. 1966: *Max Weber*. London.

Budd, S. 1973: *Sociologists and Religion*. London.

Freund, J. 1968: *The Sociology of Max Weber*. London.

Käsler, D. 1988: *Max Weber: An Introduction to his Life and Work*. Cambridge.

Wesley, John (1703–1791) English evangelist and founder of METHODISM. He was educated at Christ Church, Oxford, and in 1725 was ordained deacon. Whilst a fellow at Lincoln College, Oxford, he led a Christian group called 'the Methodists', which included his brother Charles and George Whitefield, who practised a methodical system of religious observance. After a period as his father's curate, he went to Georgia as a missionary, where he encountered Moravian Christians who stressed the doctrines of justification by faith alone and the assurance of salvation. Returning to London, he attended a meeting of Moravian Christians in Aldersgate, London, on 24 May 1738, when, on hearing

Luther's Preface to Romans read, he had an experience of evangelical conversion which proved life-changing. Largely disowned by the established church, he conducted preaching tours, often in the open air, throughout the British Isles, becoming a major figure, with Whitefield, in the evangelical revival which brought Christianity to the industrial working class of the eighteenth century. He ordained preachers to extend the work in America; although he had wished to remain part of the established church, Methodism eventually grew into an independent movement. His theology stressed the personal relationship of faith with Jesus Christ, the grace of God, the work of the Spirit to bring about moral change in the believer and good works.

Bibliography

Green, V.H. 1964: *John Wesley*. London.
Schmidt, M. 1962–73: *John Wesley: A Theological Biography*. London and Nashville, Tn.
Tuttle, R.G. 1978: *John Wesley: His Life and Theology*. Grand Rapids, Mi.

Wingren, Gustaf Fredrik (b. 1910)   Swedish theologian. His name is associated with Anders Nygren, whom he succeeded as professor of systematic theology at Lund, and also indirectly with the other major modern Swedish theologian, Gustaf Aulén, and with Karl Barth. Wingren has sought to integrate the doctrines of creation and redemption, studying the nature and status of man outside Christian redemption. Modifying the emphasis on 'agape' of Nygren's motif theology, he sees creation and moral law as the foundational theological principles. His works include *Theology in Conflict* (trans. 1958), *Man and Incarnation* (trans. 1959), *Creation and Law* (trans. 1961) and *Gospel and Church* (trans. 1964).

Bibliography

Erling, B. 1960–1: Swedish theology from Nygren to Wingren, *Religion in Life* 30.
Schilling, S.P. 1966: *Contemporary Continental Theologians*. London.

Wittgenstein, Ludwig Josef Johann (1889–1951)   Austrian philosopher. Born in Vienna, and baptized a Roman Catholic, Wittgenstein studied engineering at Berlin and Manchester from 1908 to 1911. His interest in mathematics brought him to Cambridge, where he worked under, and later alongside, Bertrand Russell from 1912. Taken prisoner in Italy during the First World War, he completed his most famous philosophical work, the only work published in his lifetime, *Tractatus Logico-Philosophicus* of 1921. As a result of his conclusions, Wittgenstein temporarily eschewed philosophy, but later became a fellow of Trinity College, Cambridge (1930–6), and subsequently professor. After his death, his influential book *Philosophical Investigations* was published in 1953.

Wittgenstein's primary concern was language and its limitations. In his *Tractatus*, he considered the way in which language mirrors fact. For a sentence to have sense, it must reflect the structure of the world; only language which states facts is meaningful. Religion and ethics, as non-factual, cannot be spoken about; hence his famous saying 'whereof one cannot speak, thereof one must be silent.' In his later work, however, Wittgenstein criticized many of the conclusions of his *Tractatus*. He developed the concept of 'language games', rejecting the idea that words must stand for objects. Meanings of words are given by their use; words are used differently in different contextual situations, or language games. What is important is knowing the rules of the language games in which one is participating.

Some of Wittgenstein's ideas about language games have been taken up in modern theology, most notably in G.A. Lindbeck's *The Nature of Doctrine* of 1984.

See also LANGUAGE, RELIGIOUS; LOGICAL POSITIVISM.

Bibliography

Gellner, E. 1959: *Words and Things*. London.
Hanfling, O. 1989: *Wittgenstein's Later Philosophy*. London.
Hudson, W.D. 1975: *Wittgenstein and Religious Belief*. London.

work and leisure   It is impossible to trace the history of attitudes towards work and leisure during the past three centuries without pushing that history back two centuries earlier to the Reformation. Christian and secular thinking about work in the post-Reformation era is rooted in the revolution that the Reformation effected in the workplace.

The original Protestant ethic

Today we approach the concept of 'the Protestant ethic' through a cloud of contradictory eulogies and denunciations. The confusion is exacerbated by the way in which the meaning of the label has changed, with today's use of the phrase meaning virtually the opposite of what it originally meant. The so-called Weber thesis that equated Protestantism with capitalism has clouded the issue still further. Yet what the Reformers taught about work is easily reconstructed from primary sources (for surveys and bibliographic references, see Hill, 1964, pp. 124–218; Ryken, 1986, pp. 23–36; Ryken, 1987, pp. 87–115). Four major themes may be distinguished.

First, the Reformers affirmed the value of work and the virtue of being industrious. This was one of the most common themes from the pulpit and in Puritan treatises for more than a century. The example of Adam and Eve's work in the Garden of Eden before the fall was buttressed by other biblical data to prove that work is an important part of God's intended purpose for human life.

Corresponding to this praise of work was the Puritan critique of idleness. Few topics elicited such a continuous stream of scorn from the Reformers as idleness (not having a useful occupation) and sloth (lack of diligence in work).

Second, the original Protestant ethic asserted the sanctity of all legitimate types of work. In doing so, it rejected a centuries-old Catholic dichotomy between sacred and secular activities. For the Reformers, all of life was God's. Applied to the subject of work, this attitude produced the doctrine of calling – a belief that God issued every person a general call to the Christian life and a particular call to a specific occupation (livelihood) and specific tasks.

Luther, more than anyone else, helped to establish this viewpoint. 'Seemingly secular works,' he wrote, 'are a worship of God and an obedience well pleasing to God.' The effect of such thinking was to sanctify common work. It made every task consequential by claiming it as the arena for glorifying God. The worker, in this view, is a steward of God, serving God not only *in* his or her work but actually *through* the work itself.

Third, the original Protestant ethic was clear about the spiritual and moral ends of work. The Reformers presented a united chorus that the primary purpose of work is to glorify God and benefit society. Denunciations of people who pursued work and wealth to satisfy personal interests were incessant. The idea of the 'self-made person' did not appeal to the Reformers. Protestantism proclaimed an ethic of grace, and on the subject of work it decisively separated success from human merit. Luther sounded the keynote when he wrote that riches 'are purely blessings of God, blessings that at times come to us through our labours and at times without our labours, but never because of our labours; for God always gives them because of His undeserved mercy.'

A final theme in the original Protestant ethic was the ideal of moderation in work. While denouncing idleness, the Reformers nevertheless set limits to work and the acquisition of money. One of the enforced limits was a strict sabbatarianism, which was perhaps the only way for 'the industrious sort' to protect themselves and their employees from themselves. But beyond this external control on work, Puritan preachers regularly warned against excessive devotion to one's worldly calling. At the heart of their view of work was a great paradox, which Cotton Mather defined as 'diligence in worldly business and yet deadness to the world'.

How did leisure and recreation fare in such a robust work ethic? Not very well, though not as badly as most people think (for surveys and references to primary sources, see Wagner, 1982; Ryken, 1987, pp. 100–10). The early Protestants affirmed leisure in principle, and they enjoyed a wide range of recreations. But their play ethic was essentially an extension of their work ethic (leisure improved one's ability to work), and their extreme devotion to work led to an anaemic leisure ethic in practice.

The original Protestant ethic was the assumed framework in Protestant countries (especially England and America) during the sixteenth and seventeenth centuries. No one seriously questioned it, and conscientious Christians embodied its assumptions in daily living. Once the Protestant ethic became this firmly entrenched, Christian thinkers for nearly three centuries afterwards took it for granted and felt no need to tamper with it. The history of attitudes towards work after the Reformation era is mainly a story of secular forces that modified the Protestant ethic.

Until we come to the middle of the twentieth century, then, Christian defences of work such as were common in the Reformation era were nearly nonexistent. The original Protestant ethic became so much a part of western culture that it was an invisible safety net that was assumed to be the correct Christian response to changing attitudes towards work. Christians did not feel a need to forge a Christian work ethic because they lived by what the Reformers had said. Since the Reformers had based their work ethic on the Bible, moreover, their doctrine of work seemed the natural one for Christians to pursue in daily living and to fall back on when challenged by rival attitudes.

The afterlife of the Protestant ethic

The first thing that happened to the original Protestant work ethic is that it became secularized (Michaelsen, 1953). The praise of work remained, but the spiritual and social purposes of work were lost. Work itself ceased to be viewed as a calling from God, the ideal of moderation gave way to an ambitious pursuit of wealth, and self-reliance replaced a sense of stewardship.

The new attitude is fully evident in Benjamin Franklin's *Poor Richard* proverbs, which asserted, for example, that 'God helps them that help themselves' and that 'early to bed, and early to rise, makes a man healthy, wealthy, and wise.' Adam Smith built his edifice of a market system of supply and demand on the premise that in the economic sphere people appeal 'not to [each other's] humanity but to their self-love'. Similarly, John Locke propounded a view that made work valuable because it was useful as the means of acquiring property.

This view of work as the beginning of wealth was forged by people who had grown up in a Protestant milieu. They retained the emphasis of the Protestant ethic on the virtue of working but discarded the theological framework of calling, stewardship and service to humanity. Perhaps because of this mixture of old and new,

the record of a Christian response to the new outlook is impossible to document.

The Enlightenment work ethic based on economic self-interest produced its inevitable results in the next century with the industrial revolution. The specialization of labour produced the alienation of the worker and accompanying ills (monotony of tasks, loss of trained skills, inability to see a total purpose in one's isolated task, depersonalization, and loss of pride in one's work). The nineteenth century saw two major answers to these problems, but Christian thinkers did not contribute significantly to the dialogue.

The dominant answer was MARXISM. Marxism sought to free the worker from the curse of a system that viewed work as an economic commodity that is bought and sold, with its accompanying exploitation of the worker. Recoiling from the estrangement of the worker under capitalism, Marx asserted a high view of work, which for him was 'the very touchstone for man's self-realization' and the thing 'which should make him happy'. The proposed solution, a collectivist plan for a working class that would redeem society, was too institutionalized to accord well with Christianity, though the Marxist diagnosis of the crisis of work in an industrial society is congenial to Christianity in principle.

A second response to the industrial revolution was a romanticist idealizing of work. Sensing that industrial work was dehumanizing, the romanticists urged a return to something more natural. The foremost spokespersons for this tradition were John Ruskin and Thomas Carlyle. They exalted the work of one's hands as the Puritans had done, but without the surrounding theological framework. The Victorian Carlyle wrote (in language reminiscent of the Reformers) 'There is a perennial nobleness, and even sacredness, in Work . . . The latest Gospel in this world is, Know thy work and do it.' This Victorian praise of work sometimes goes by the name of 'Puritanism', but it is a misnomer. Writers such as Ruskin and Carlyle valued work in itself, not as service to God and society. They also differed from the original Puritans by pinning their hope for reform on the external conditions of work instead of the inner attitude of the worker.

One can only guess how Christians responded to the nineteenth-century crosswinds. They would have found much with which to agree in the protest against work in an industrial society and in the affirmation of work itself. Whether they recognized how much of the theological and moral framework of the Protestant ethic had been lost is a moot question.

Similar silence surrounds Christian attitudes towards leisure. The industrial society produced the triumph of utilitarianism. Benjamin Franklin's outlook had been that 'leisure is time for doing something useful.' Later Jeremy Bentham equated pleasure with profit, his stock question being, 'What is the use of it?' The industrial society, meanwhile, made people less the owner of their time and created a distinct cleavage between work and leisure by separating them in space and time. Again we look in vain for a record of Christian responses to these developments in society at large, but the utilitarian spirit had always been strong in the Protestant ethic, and there is little reason to suspect that Christians objected any more strongly to what was happening than did their secular neighbours.

Christian attitudes towards work in the twentieth century

The second half of the twentieth century has produced a steady stream of writing by Christians about work and leisure. This body of writing has been a response to the cultural crisis in both work and leisure, and it has rooted itself in the Bible and (to a lesser extent) in the Reformation legacy.

The crisis in work is perceived in terms of overwork, dissatisfaction in work, unemployment or underemployment (work that does not utilize a person's abilities), and lack of incentive in the workplace. In the later decades of the century there has also been a growing consensus on what constitutes the leisure problem: a shrinking amount of leisure, poor quality of leisure in a mass society, inability to value leisure apart from work, and (for a minority) the idolizing of leisure. Books and workshops by Christians on these very problems have become important among Christian intellectuals and laypeople.

The evangelical Protestant tradition has dominated discussions of work (Forrester, 1953; Minear, 1954; Boggs, 1962), and appeals to Reformation roots have been common (Wingren, 1957; Ryken, 1987). Books and workshops on career counselling have also entered the discussion (Clark, 1981; Moran, 1984). In this movement we can discern both a theology of work and an ethics of work.

The Book of Genesis provides the starting point for a Christian theology of work. God is pictured there as a worker who made people in his image and entrusted to them the task of cultivating the Garden of Eden. The doctrine of the fall balances this picture of work as human fulfilment by introducing the competing idea of work as a curse. Christian thinking about work has operated within this tension, striving to uphold work as inherently meaningful while acknowledging its abuse.

Twentieth-century Christian attempts to reclaim work in a fallen world begin where the Protestant ethic had begun – by declaring the sanctity of all legitimate types of work. The dignity of common work, accompanied by a disparagement of the perennial tendency to elevate clerical or church work, has been a common theme of recent workshops. The idea that God calls people to ordinary vocations and that people can serve God through those tasks has likewise loomed large in contemporary Christian thought about work.

The worker as steward, with the service of God and society as the goal of work, is another cornerstone of a Christian theology of work. In contrast to prevailing theories that make the worker, the employer or the society the owner of work, the Christian idea of stewardship makes God the owner, with work viewed as something that is offered back to God.

Christian thought on work has built an ethical programme on this theological foundation, again amply supported with biblical data. Work has been viewed as a moral duty laid on the human race by God. Its purposes include the provision for human needs, self-fulfilment and the glory of God.

Christian discussions have also placed work into various relationships. When related to the worker, work is viewed in terms of satisfaction, joy and reward for toil. When viewed in relation to society, work becomes a means of providing for one's own needs so as to avoid being a burden, of providing for the needs of others, and of promoting the functioning of society. In relation to God, work is the means by which one demonstrates obedience, gratitude and stewardship. Christian thinkers have also looked at the relationship of the worker with his or her work, in terms of a responsibility to excellence, to doing work with zest and to the avoidance of making work an idol.

Behind all of the Christian discussions of work lurks a desire to avoid common tendencies on the secular scene. In place of the undervaluing of work, Christian apologists offer an endorsement of work as inherently good and meaningful. In place of the overvaluing of work, they advocate an ideal of moderation in work. Against a prevailing individualism in the workplace, they offer a social vision of work as promoting the common welfare and a theological vision of work as service to God. And as a counterpoint to collectivist and industrialist trends that minimize the individuality of the worker, they offer the possibility of work as affording legitimate self-fulfilment and personal reward.

Christian responses to leisure in the twentieth century

Contemporary Christian defences of leisure have run a parallel course to discussions of work. They have been prompted by a perceived need to respond to the leisure problem as it is defined by the secular world and experienced within the Christian community. Protestant apologists for leisure have drawn upon biblical themes and contemporary leisure theory (Lehman, 1974; Johnston, 1983; Ryken, 1987), while Catholic theorists have been able to tap a long contemplative tradition (Pieper, 1952).

A Christian theology of leisure takes its cues from a Christian view of work. It notes, for example, that rest from work is just as much a creation ordinance as is work. If the God of Genesis is the one who works, he is also the one who rests. The example of Jesus underscores the same rhythm of work and leisure. Christian defences of leisure have also highlighted the ideas of sabbath (rest from labour) and worship as providing both a model and mandate for leisure.

A belief that God values the non-utilitarian has fed Christian defences of leisure. So have biblical affirmations of pleasure and enjoyment. The endorsement of celebration and festivity in the Bible, especially as seen in the Old Testament religious festivals, has also been prominent in Christian discussions. In contrast to the aversion that early centuries of Christianity displayed towards culture and entertainment, the effects of the fall on leisure have not attracted much discussion from contemporary Christian theorists, probably because they see their main task as awakening an interest in leisure in a work-oriented society.

While modern Christian discussions of work are oriented towards abuses in society at large, the defences of leisure seem largely addressed to the Christian community. At every stage in the history of Christian thought, writing on work has vastly exceeded that on leisure. Leisure has always been a topic of neglect in the Christian church. The hidden agenda of Christian writers on leisure has thus been the desire to convince Christians that leisure is a necessary part of the Christian life.

Summary

The best Christian thinking on work and leisure has combined these two topics. Doing so accords with both contemporary social theory and the rhythm of life laid down in the early Old Testament and followed by Jesus. Daily life itself shows the interrelatedness of work and leisure.

But Christianity adds a theological dimension to this commonplace by showing the common theology and morality of both work and leisure (Johnston, 1983; Ryken, 1987). Both work and leisure are rooted in the doctrine of creation, since God created both work and leisure and also engaged in both activities. Work and leisure both call for moral choice and stewardship, both share the ideal of enjoyment and self-fulfilment, both have been infected by sin, both require moderation, and both are part of Christian worship broadly defined.

Twentieth-century Christian thinking about work and leisure stands as a contrast to secular thinking. While it has generally agreed with secular sources on the nature of the contemporary crisis in work and leisure, it has provided answers in terms of a theological and moral context that is absent from other discussions. The most prominent features of that context have been an acceptance of the Bible as the primary authority, respect for what the Christian tradition has said about work and leisure, and belief in a doctrinal matrix that includes the ideas of creation, fall, stewardship, service and worship.

See also CAPITALISM ; CHRISTIAN SOCIALISM; ECONOMIC ANALYSIS AND ETHICS.

Bibliography

Boggs, Wade 1962: *All Ye Who Labor*. Richmond: John Knox.

Clark, Martin E. 1981: *Choosing Your Career*. Phillipsburg, NJ: Presbyterian and Reformed.

Forrester, W.R. 1953: *Christian Vocation*. New York: Charles Scribner's Sons.

Hill, Christopher 1964: *Society and Puritanism in Pre-Revolutionary England*. New York: Schocken.

Johnston, Robert K. 1983: *The Christian at Play*. Grand Rapids: Eerdmans.

Lehman, Harold D. 1974: *In Praise of Leisure*. Scottdale, PA: Herald Press.

Michaelsen, Robert S. 1953: Changes in the Puritan concept of calling or vocation, *New England Quarterly* 26, pp. 315–36.

Minear, Paul S. 1954: Work and vocation in Scripture. In *Work and Vocation: A Christian Discussion*, ed. John Oliver Nelson. New York: Harper, pp. 32–81.

Moran, Pamela 1984: *The Christian Job Hunter*. Ann Arbor: Servant.

Pieper, Josef 1952: *Leisure the Basis of Culture*, trans. Alexander Dru. New York: Pantheon.

Richardson, Alan 1952: *The Biblical Doctrine of Work*. London: SCM Press.

Ryken, Leland 1986: *Worldly Saints: The Puritans as They Really Were*. Grand Rapids: Zondervan.

Ryken, Leland 1987: *Work and Leisure in Christian Perspective*. Portland: Multnomah.

Wagner, Hans-Peter 1982: *Puritan Attitudes Towards Recreation in Early Seventeenth-Century America*. Frankfurt: Verlag Peter Lang.

Wingren, Gustaf 1957: *Luther on Vocation*, trans. Carl C. Rasmussen. Philadelphia: Muhlenberg.

LELAND RYKEN

worship and theology See LITURGY AND DOCTRINE.

A Glossary of Theological Terms

analogy of being (*analogia entis*) The theory, especially associated with Thomas Aquinas, that there exists a correspondence or analogy between the created order and God, as a result of the divine creatorship. The idea gives theoretical justification to the practice of drawing conclusions concerning God from the known objects and relationships of the natural order.

analogy of faith (*analogia fidei*) The theory, especially associated with Karl Barth, which holds that any correspondence between the created order and God is only established on the basis of the self-revelation of God.

anthropomorphism The tendency to ascribe human features (such as hands or arms) or other human characteristics to God.

apophatic A term used to refer to a particular style of theology, which stresses that God cannot be known in terms of human categories. 'Apophatic' (which derives from the Greek *apophasis*, 'negation' or 'denial') approaches to theology are especially associated with the monastic tradition of the Eastern Orthodox church.

Calvinism An ambiguous term, used with two quite distinct meanings. First, it refers to the religious ideas of religious bodies (such as the Reformed church) and individuals (such as Theodore Beza) who were profoundly influenced by John Calvin, or by documents written by him. Second, it refers to the religious ideas of John Calvin himself. Although the first sense is by far the more common, there is a growing recognition that the term is misleading. The term 'Reformed' is used increasingly in its place.

charism, charismatic A set of terms especially associated with the gifts of the Holy Spirit. In Roman Catholic theology, the term 'charism' is used to designate a spiritual gift, conferred upon individuals by the grace of God. Since the early twentieth century, the term 'charismatic' has come to refer to styles of theology and worship which place particular emphasis upon the immediate presence and experience of the Holy Spirit.

consubstantiation A term used to refer to the theory of the real presence, especially associated with Martin Luther, which holds that the substance of the eucharistic bread and wine are given together with the substance of the body and blood of Christ.

demythologization An approach to theology especially associated with the German theologian Rudolf Bultmann and his followers, which rests upon the belief that the New Testament world view is 'mythological'. In order for it to be understood within, or applied to, the modern situation, it is necessary that the mythological elements should be eliminated.

dialectical theology A term used to refer to the early views of the Swiss theologian Karl Barth, which emphasized the 'dialectic' between God and humanity.

Donatism A movement, centring upon Roman North Africa in the fourth century, which developed a rigorist view of the church and sacraments.

Ebionitism An early Christological heresy, which treated Jesus Christ as a purely human figure, although recognizing that he was endowed with particular charismatic gifts which distinguished him from other humans.

eschaton A term, deriving from the Greek word for 'the last thing', which is used to refer to the Christian expectation of the final end of history.

exemplarism A particular approach to the atonement, which stresses the moral or religious example set to believers by Jesus Christ.

Five Ways, the A standard term for the five 'arguments for the existence of God', especially associated with Thomas Aquinas.

fourth Gospel A term used to refer to the Gospel according to John. The term highlights the distinctive literary and theological character of this gospel, which sets it apart from the common structures of the first three gospels, usually known as the 'synoptic Gospels'.

homoousion A Greek term, literally meaning 'of the same substance', which came to be used extensively during the fourth century to designate the mainline Christological belief that Jesus Christ was 'of the same substance as God'. The term was polemical, being directed against the Arian view that Christ was 'of similar substance (*homoiousion*)' to God.

hypostatic union The doctrine of the union of divine and human natures in Jesus Christ, without confusion of their respective substances.

incarnation A term used to refer to the assumption of human nature by God, in the person of Jesus Christ. The term 'incarnationalism' is often used to refer to theological approaches (such as those of late nineteenth-century Anglicanism) which lay especial emphasis upon the social and political consequences of God's becoming human.

kenoticism A form of Christology which lays emphasis upon Christ's 'laying aside' of certain divine attributes in the incarnation, or his 'emptying himself' of at least some divine attributes, especially omniscience or omnipotence.

kerygma A term used, especially by Rudolf Bultmann and his followers, to refer to the essential message or proclamation of the New Testament concerning the significance of Jesus Christ.

limited atonement An approach to the doctrine of the atonement, especially associated with Calvinist writers, which holds that Christ's death is only effective for those who have been elected to salvation.

liturgy The written text of public services, especially of the Eucharist.

modalism A Trinitarian heresy, which treats the three persons of the Trinity as different 'modes' of the Godhead. A typical modalist approach is to regard God as active as Father in creation, as Son in redemption, and as Spirit in sanctification.

neo-orthodoxy A term used to designate the general position of Karl Barth, especially the manner in which he drew upon the theological concerns of the period of Reformed orthodoxy.

ontological argument A form of argument for the existence of God especially associated with the eleventh-century scholastic theologian Anselm of Canterbury.

orthodoxy A term used in a number of senses, of which the following are the most important: orthodoxy in the sense of 'right belief', as opposed to heresy; and orthodoxy in the sense of a movement within Protestantism, especially in the late sixteenth and early seventeenth centuries, which laid emphasis upon need for doctrinal definition.

parousia A Greek term, which literally means 'coming' or 'arrival', used to refer to the second coming of Christ. The notion of the parousia is an important aspect of Christian understandings of the 'last things'.

patripassianism A heresy which arose during the third century, associated with writers such as Noetus, Praxeas and Sabellius. It centred on the belief that the Father suffered as the Son; that is, that the suffering of Christ on the cross is also to be regarded as the suffering of the Father. According to these writers, the only distinction which existed within the Godhead was a succession of modes or operations. In other words, Father, Son and Spirit were just different modes of being, or expressions, of the same basic divine entity. Modern discussions of the 'suffering of God' have avoided this modalist approach, by stressing that the suffering of the Son differs from that of the Father.

patristic An adjective used to refer to the first centuries in the history of the church, following the writing of the New Testament (the 'patristic period'), or to thinkers writing during this period (the 'patristic writers'). For many writers, the period thus designated seems to be *c*. 100–451 (in other words, the period between the completion of the last of the New Testament writings and the Council of Chalcedon).

Pelagianism An understanding of how humans are able to merit their salvation, which is diametrically opposed to that of Augustine of Hippo, placing considerable emphasis upon the role of human works and playing down the idea of divine grace.

perichoresis A term relating to the doctrine of the Trinity, often also referred to by the Latin term *circumincessio*. The basic notion is that all three persons of the Trinity mutually share in the life of the others, so that none is isolated or detached from the actions of the others.

pietism An approach to Christianity, especially associated with German writers in the seventeenth century, which places an emphasis upon the personal appropriation of faith and the need for holiness in Christian living. The movement is perhaps best known within the English-language world in the form of Methodism.

radical Reformation A term used with increasing frequency to refer to the Anabaptist movement – in other words, the wing of the Reformation which went beyond what Martin Luther and Ulrich Zwingli envisaged.

Reformed A term used to refer to a tradition of theology which draws inspiration from the writings of John Calvin and his successors. The term is now generally used in preference to 'Calvinist'.

schism A deliberate break with the unity of the church, condemned vigorously by influential writers of the early church, such as Cyprian and Augustine.

scholasticism A particular approach to Christian theology, associated especially with the Middle Ages, which lays emphasis upon the rational justification and systematic presentation of Christian theology.

Scripture principle The theory, especially associated with Reformed theologians, that the practices and beliefs of the church should be grounded in Scripture. Nothing that could not be demonstrated to be grounded in Scripture could be regarded as binding upon the believer. The phrase *sola scriptura*, 'by Scripture alone', summarizes this principle.

Septuagint   The Greek translation of the Old Testament, dating from the third century BC. The abbreviation LXX is generally used to refer to this text.

Sermon on the Mount   The standard way of referring to Christ's moral and pastoral teaching in the specific form which it takes in chapters 5–7 of Matthew's Gospel.

sola fide   A term meaning 'by faith alone', which gives expression to the belief, emphasized by Martin Luther, that the justification of sinners takes place on the basis of faith alone, as opposed to human works or achievements. (The faith in question is understood as a work of God, rather than a human achievement.)

sola gratia   A term, meaning 'by grace alone', referring to the principle, especially associated with the sixteenth-century Reformation, that human salvation is totally a work of divine grace.

sola scriptura   See Scripture principle.

solus Christus   A slogan, meaning 'Christ alone', which expresses the strongly Christocentric style of certain types of Protestant theology, especially those associated with John Calvin and his later followers, such as Karl Barth.

synoptic Gospels   A term used to refer to the first three Gospels (Matthew, Mark and Luke). The term (derived from the Greek word *synopsis*, 'summary') refers to the way in which the three Gospels can be seen as providing similar 'summaries' of the life, death and resurrection of Jesus Christ.

synoptic problem   The scholarly question of how the three synoptic Gospels relate to each other. Perhaps the most common approach to the relation of the three synoptic Gospels is the 'two source' theory, which claims that Matthew and Luke used Mark as a source, while also drawing upon a second source (usually known as 'Q'). Other possibilities exist: for example, the Griesbach hypothesis, which treats Matthew as having been written first, followed by Luke and then Mark.

theodicy   A term coined by G.W. Leibniz to refer to a theoretical justification of the goodness of God in the face of the presence of evil in the world.

transubstantiation   The medieval doctrine according to which the bread and the wine are transformed into the body and blood of Christ in the Eucharist, while retaining their outward appearance.

two natures, doctrine of   A term generally used to refer to the doctrine of the two natures, human and divine, of Jesus Christ. Related terms include 'Chalcedonian definition' and 'hypostatic union'.

Zwinglianism   A term used generally to refer to the thought of Ulrich Zwingli, but often to refer specifically to his views on the sacraments, especially on the 'real presence' (which for Zwingli was more of a 'real absence').

Index

Note: Page references in **bold** type indicate chief discussion of major topics and persons; those in *italics* indicate the Glossary. Where names of contributors to the *Encyclopedia* are indexed, the references are to citations in articles other than their own articles.

Compiled by MEG DAVIES